W9-COZ-517

"Duranti has brought together a stellar collection of original essays that will surely become a foundational resource in linguistic anthropology."

Deborah Tannen, *Georgetown University*

"Duranti … has done more than anyone else in the past generation to establish linguistic anthropology as a scholarly field.... Designed to be user-friendly … *A Companion to Linguistic Anthropology* … is an impressive achievement, and will be of great value to its field and neighboring fields, for a long time to come. This *Companion* may be a culmination of Duranti's considerable work to establish linguistic anthropology."

Dell Hymes, in *Journal of Sociolinguistics*

"This hefty, immaculate volume inaugurates the innovative series of *Blackwell Companions to Anthropology*, and does so with academic panache … Intelligible for readers with no previous knowledge of the field ... A resource of genuine utility in academic libraries with any interest in linguistics or anthropology."

Reference Reviews

"A valuable contribution to linguistic anthropology, this book comprises the best articles by some of the best authors. In it, Duranti celebrates the rich diversity of linguistic anthropology by integrating new advances in sociolinguistics, discourse and conversation analysis, gender and ethnic studies, and other sister cross-disciplines. Moving well beyond early studies of varieties of language and folklore, this book offers insights into the cultural dimensions of power, social inequality, identity, and many other dimensions of talk and text in their sociocultural contexts. This will serve as a true companion for many students and scholars in many disciplines."

Teun A. van Dijk, *Universitat Pompeu Fabra*

"With this *Companion*, Duranti continues his creative role in giving shape to linguistic anthropology as a field. The chapters will be valuable not only for students, but also for colleagues. They bring together a considerable range of those active in the field, and of important foci of research. To mention just two: it is hard to imagine greater clarity than that brought to linguistic diversity by Mithun, for example, or to the nature of language ideologies by Kroskrity."

Dell Hymes, *University of Virginia*

Alessandro Duranti is Professor of Anthropology and Director of the Center for Language, Interaction and Culture at UCLA. His books include *From Grammar to Politics: Linguistic Anthropology in a Western Samoan Village* (1994), *Linguistic Anthropology* (1997), *Key Terms in Language and Culture* (2001), and *Linguistic Anthropology: A Reader* (editor, 2001). In 1999 he received a John Simon Guggenheim Fellowship and the UCLA Alumni Distinguished Teaching Award. He is a former president of the Society for Linguistic Anthropology and former editor of the *Journal of Linguistic Anthropology*. In 2001 Duranti received the American Anthropological Association/Mayfield Award for Excellence in Undergraduate Teaching.

Blackwell Companions to Anthropology

The Blackwell Companions to Anthropology offer a series of comprehensive syntheses of the traditional subdisciplines, primary subjects, and geographic areas of inquiry for the field. Taken together, the series represents both a contemporary survey of anthropology and a cutting edge guide to the emerging research and intellectual trends in the field as a whole.

Forthcoming

A Companion
to Linguistic
Anthropology

Edited by Alessandro Duranti

Blackwell
Publishing

© 2004, 2006 by Blackwell Publishing Ltd

BLACKWELL PUBLISHING
350 Main Street, Malden, MA 02148-5020, USA
9600 Garsington Road, Oxford OX4 2DQ, UK
550 Swanston Street, Carlton, Victoria 3053, Australia

The right of Alessandro Duranti to be identified as the Author of the Editorial
Material in this Work has been asserted in accordance with the UK Copyright,
Designs, and Patents Act 1988.

All rights reserved. No part of this publication may be reproduced, stored in a
retrieval system, or transmitted, in any form or by any means, electronic,
mechanical, photocopying, recording or otherwise, except as permitted by the
UK Copyright, Designs, and Patents Act 1988, without the prior permission of
the publisher.

First published 2004 by Blackwell Publishing Ltd
First published in paperback 2006 by Blackwell Publishing Ltd

1 2006

Library of Congress Cataloging-in-Publication Data

A companion to linguistic anthropology / edited by Alessandro Duranti.
    p. cm. – (Blackwell companions to anthropology; 1)
    Includes bibliographical references and index.
    ISBN 0-631-22352-5 (alk. paper)
    1. Language and culture. I. Duranti, Alessandro. II. Series.

    P35.C59 2003
    306.44–dc21

                                                        2003056026

ISBN-13: 978-0-631-22352-8 (alk. paper)
ISBN-13: 978-1-4051-4430-8 (paperback)
ISBN-10: 1-4051-4430-0 (paperback)

A catalogue record for this title is available from the British Library.

Set in 10/12.5pt Galliard
by Kolam Information Services Pvt. Ltd, Pondicherry, India
Printed and bound in the United Kingdom
by TJ International, Padstow, Cornwall

The publisher's policy is to use permanent paper from mills that operate a
sustainable forestry policy, and which has been manufactured from pulp
processed using acid-free and elementary chlorine-free practices. Furthermore,
the publisher ensures that the text paper and cover board used have met
acceptable environmental accreditation standards.

For further information on
Blackwell Publishing, visit our website:
www.blackwellpublishing.com

Contents

Synopsis of Contents

Part I: Speech Communities, Contact, and Variation

1 Speech Community
Marcyliena Morgan

A critical examination of the notion of speech community is crucial for the discipline of linguistic anthropology, a field devoted to the study of what speakers can and cannot do with words in the context of their everyday life. This chapter starts from a sociopolitical view of the speech community as a group that can define speakers' identity, citizenship, and belonging. Only through the integration of local knowledge and communicative competence in discursive activities can members identify insiders from outsiders, those passing as members, and those living in contact zones and borderlands.

2 Registers of Language
Asif Agha

This is the first comparative framework for the study of registers, defined as linguistic repertoires stereotypically associated with particular social practices or persons who engage in such practices. After outlining methods for their identification and study, the author discusses several aspects of registers in social life: their institutional dissemination in society; their tropic uses in interaction; their ideological character; factors influencing the growth or decline of registers; and the extension of register models from linguistic to non-linguistic signs. The chapter illustrates these phenomena with examples from several languages and societies.

3 Language Contact and Contact Languages
Paul B. Garrett

Language contact gives rise to a wide variety of outcomes, including bilingualism, codeswitching, pidginization, creolization, language shift, and language "death."

These diverse outcomes are contingent upon multiple intersecting factors, linguistic as well as social, historical, demographic, politico-economic, and ideological. Language contact must therefore be regarded as a socially situated, culturally mediated phenomenon – one that gives rise to particular types of communicative practices and, in some but not all cases, to distinct new codes and identities.

4 Codeswitching
Kathryn A. Woolard

Codeswitching is a speaker's use of two or more language varieties in a single speech event. In response to earlier views of codeswitching as unsystematic and indicative of inadequate linguistic control, a view of such practice as skilled, systematic, and socially meaningful has become established. Debates remain over how best to characterize this systematicity, and competing approaches propose varying social motivations or functions of codeswitching. These debates in turn bring researchers to question the discreteness of codes and the role of strategy and intentionality in codeswitching practices. This chapter responds critically to these newer questions and suggests that they can best be resolved by placing the phenomenon of codeswitching within more general theoretical frames and by drawing on generalizable constructs such as voicing and indexicality.

5 Diversity, Hierarchy, and Modernity in Pacific Island Communities
Niko Besnier

The Pacific Islands are linguistically one of the most diverse regions of the world. This diversity is directly linked to sociocultural dynamics at play in many communities in the area, which attribute prestige to multilingualism and encourages linguistic differentiation over time, despite the language attrition that has taken place in the twentieth century. Linguistic anthropologists have found in Pacific Island societies fruitful grounds for the investigation of the way in which language, social structures, and cultural dynamics are interwined.

6 The Value of Linguistic Diversity: Viewing Other Worlds through North American Indian Languages
Marianne Mithun

The birth of linguistic anthropology is linked to the gradual discovery by Europeans of the profound differences among North American languages. For some, such differences seem accidental, arbitrary, and inconsequential, while for others, they reflect deep intellectual, cultural, and social differences. Samples of the nature of the diversity are presented, then the communicative forces that create and refine them are discussed, along with the cultural and social purposes they may serve.

7 Variation in Sign Languages
Barbara LeMaster and Leila Monaghan

Contrary to popular belief, deaf sign languages are not universal. Different groups have their own distinctive ways of signing. This variation is a resource for communicating a complex range of information within shifting interactional contexts. The authors discuss a number of approaches to the study of sign variation, including how sign languages vary according to nation, region, ethnicity, gender, Deaf cultural identity, and language contact.

Part II: The Performing of Language

8   Conversation as a Cultural Activity
Elizabeth Keating and Maria Egbert

Conversation is a vital resource for anthropologists in their goal to understand societies from the local perspective, and yet the systematic study of conversation from an anthropological perspective is quite recent. Looking at conversation as an activity, this chapter examines its role in a wide range of social practices, including language socialization, the constitution of identity and the establishment of authority, and the discursive organization of experience that characterizes narratives and institutional talk.

9   Gesture
John B. Haviland

Gesture is a pervasive resource in human communication, sometimes complementing speech, at other times substituting for it. And yet, gestures have often been studied separately from languages. Breaking with this tradition, this chapter links gesture to the expressive inflections of language, showing that gestures exhibit the formal properties of other linguistic signs, participating in communicative action, and engendering cultural ideologies involving standards of behavior and theories of language and mind.

10   Participation
Charles Goodwin and Marjorie Harness Goodwin

Helped by the use of new audio-visual technologies, researchers studying the details of face-to-face interaction have felt the need to develop new frameworks for the understanding of how meaning is communicated across speakers and contexts. The notion of *participation* has replaced *conversation* and the speaker–hearer dyad of earlier research. This chapter starts from a critical examination of Erving Goffman's influential notion of "footing" to provide a comprehensive framework for the notion of participation that includes not only the speaker and her talk, but also the forms of embodiment and social organization through which multiple parties build action together while both attending to, and helping to construct, relevant action and context.

11   Literacy Practices across Learning Contexts
Patricia Baquedano-López

In its broadest sense, literacy refers to the competent use of knowledge and interpretive skills in culturally defined activities. This chapter provides a brief theoretical

overview of the study of literacy and emphasizes the importance of investigating literacy development in its cultural and historical context, that is, as
practices that are contingent on the moment, but which also encode a historical
trajectory. The chapter also includes illustrative examples of the role of language in
literacy practices and development across learning contexts, both in and out of
schools.

12   Narrative Lessons
Elinor Ochs

Narratives imbue unexpected life events with a sense of temporal and causal orderliness. They bring the remembered past into present and projected possible realities,
enhancing continuity of selves in the world. In construing life events, competent
narrators alternatively construct a coherent logic of experience or probe the authenticity of narrated experience. These two narrative practices vary in scope of (co-)
tellership, tellability of recounted events, embeddedness in surrounding discourse,
linearity, and moral certainty.

13   Poetry
Giorgio Banti and Francesco Giannattasio

After distinguishing poetic procedures from poetry in a strict sense, some formal
features of poetically organized discourse (POD) are described, such as its links with
music, metric typology, and aspects of poetic languages. Poetry proper is seen as a
cultural choice by listeners or readers who regard a text as poetic. The authors discuss
kinds of POD not regarded as poetry and intermediate forms with prose and plain
discourse. The chapter closes with a discussion of how and when poetry proper is
produced and circulated.

14   Vocal Anthropology: From the Music of Language to the Language of Song
Steven Feld, Aaron A. Fox, Thomas Porcello, and David Samuels

This chapter takes up the intellectual background to, and contemporary practice
of research into the intertwining of language and music. It combines an overview
of the key historical issues concerning language–music intersections, and three ethnographic case studies, one focusing on the linguistic mediation of musical and especially timbral discourse, and the others focusing on connections between the singing
voice and place, class, ethnicity, agency, difference, and social identity.

Part III: Achieving Subjectivities and Intersubjectivities through Language

15   Language Socialization
Don Kulick and Bambi B. Schieffelin

Since its inception as a methodological and theoretical paradigm in the 1980s,
language socialization has been applied to a variety of contexts and cultures. In this

chapter the authors examine its potential for understanding not only culturally predictable outcomes, but also culturally elusive subjectivities. By looking closely at the relationship between language and the socialization of desire and fear, they show how the study of language socialization can be extended into domains that have traditionally appeared problematic or unapproachable for anthropologists and linguists.

16   Language and Identity
Mary Bucholtz and Kira Hall

In the last few decades, identity has become a key notion within the social sciences, anthropology included. This chapter offers one model of identity as the outcome of semiotic processes, especially language. Readers are first introduced to four well-researched processes of how identity is formed (practice, indexicality, ideology, and performance). Then the discussion turns to less explored and yet fundamental issues regarding the sorts of identity relations that are formed through these semiotic processes: sameness/difference, authenticity/inauthenticity, and authority/delegitimacy.

17   Misunderstanding
Benjamin Bailey

After discussing the impossibility of complete intersubjectivity, the chapter moves on to review communicative practices through which a degree of intersubjective understanding is constituted. Two contrasting research perspectives on misunderstandings in inter-cultural and inter-gender communication are reviewed, one of which views misunderstandings as a cause of poor inter-group relations, the other as a result of pre-existing social conflicts. It is argued that misunderstandings are not so much about decoding utterances, but about negotiating sociocultural worlds.

18   Language and Madness
James M. Wilce

Madness includes linguistic (particularly pragmatic) deviance. Two troubling stances are found in popular and scholarly discourse: (1) blaming the mad for breakdowns in interactions central to human experience dehumanizes them; (2) treating diagnostic labels and institutional interactions as forms of psychiatric power constitutive of madness overly politicizes madness. A synthesis is proposed: if madness problematizes interaction yet reflects social environments as much as neurons, linguistic anthropologists can offer new ways to analyze speech environments that help or exacerbate madness.

19   Language and Religion
Webb Keane

"Religious language" refers here to ways of using language that seem to the users themselves to be linguistically unusual and to involve non-ordinary kinds of action or identity. Often these marked forms of language occur when language users face some kind of presumed ontological difference. Religious practices commonly involve manipulations, often strong and highly self-conscious, of ubiquitous formal and pragmatic features of language. They can therefore provide analysts with comparative insights into local intuitions and ideologies about relations among linguistic form, discursive practices, and different modes of agency.

Part IV: The Power in Language

20   Agency in Language
Alessandro Duranti

Agency is a recurrent theme in contemporary social theory and yet it is difficult to find a precise definition of it. This chapter breaks with this tradition by providing a working definition of agency that becomes the basis for a distinction between two dimensions of agency in language: performance and encoding. Close attention to the performance of language suggests that even before constituting specific speech acts, the use of language affirms the speaker as a potential agent. From a cross-linguistic comparison of the encoding of agency, we learn that all historical-natural languages (1) have ways of representing agency, (2) display a variety of grammatical devices for doing it, and (3) have strategies for agency mitigation.

21   Language and Social Inequality
Susan U. Philips

In every society and social context, some forms of talk and the speakers associated with them are valued more than others. This relative valuing of language forms plays a major role in the constitution of social inequalities. This chapter analyzes how linguistic anthropologists have examined such inequalities in bureaucratic settings, in gender relations, in political economic relations, and in European colonial encounters.

22   Language Ideologies
Paul V. Kroskrity

Launching from a definition of language ideologies which combines criteria regarding speakers' awareness of their linguistic and discursive resources and their political-economic position in socioeconomic systems, the chapter provides a brief historical account of why this theoretical movement occurs relatively late in twentieth-century linguistic anthropology. This provides relevant background for understanding current research which exemplifies five important features of language ideologies including awareness, multiplicity, and involvement in identity construction.

Preface

Over the last one hundred and plus years, linguistic anthropology has grown to cover almost any aspect of language structure and language use. From a discipline that was at first conceived to provide the tools for the documentation of endangered languages, especially in North America, it has become an intellectual shelter and a cultural amplifier for the richness of human communication in social life that is only selectively recognized in other communication-oriented fields such as linguistics or psychology. At any gathering of linguistic anthropologists, it is not uncommon to find experts on a wide range of linguistic and other cultural phenomena, including bilingualism, narrative, poetry, music, sign languages, literacy, socialization, gender, speechmaking, conflict, religion, identity, cognition, pidgins and creole languages, register, and oratory. Some of these scholars can be thought of as "linguists" in the narrow sense because of their training or because of their knowledge of the grammatical patterns of specific languages or language families. Others belong to linguistic anthropology not because of their expertise in grammars and language families, but because they identify with the methods or concerns of the field, find inspiration in its literature, and want to contribute to it by further expanding the study of language use as a cultural activity. In spite of being the smallest of the four subfields of anthropology as conceived in the USA at the end of the nineteenth century – the other three being archaeological, biological (formerly "physical"), and sociocultural anthropology – linguistic anthropology has produced a rich body of contributions, many of which may not be known to students and scholars in other fields within the humanities and the social sciences. The essays in this *Companion* are an attempt to remedy this situation by providing detailed discussions of some of the most important foci of study within contemporary linguistic anthropology. Each chapter is intended to present a topic, with a related set of issues and generalizations, that will help readers understand the intricacies of a particular tradition of inquiry and acquire a sense of where it is heading in the near future. No previous knowledge of the field is assumed by the authors of the chapters and considerable care has been taken in defining key concepts specific to each area of study without sacrificing the flow of the presentation.

Those readers who might find some of the terminology still daunting are invited to make use of one or more of the existing introductions to linguistic anthropology (e.g. William Foley's *Anthropological Linguistics: An Introduction*, William Hanks' *Language and Communicative Practices*, or my *Linguistic Anthropology*) and the collective lexicon of linguistic topics that I edited for the *Journal of Linguistic Anthropology* (vol. 9, republished by Blackwell under the title *Key Terms in Language and Culture*), with seventy-five mini-essays on a corresponding number of themes in the study of language from an anthropological perspective.

What distinguishes this *Companion* from textbooks, dictionaries, encyclopedias, and other collections of essays in linguistic anthropology is that the contributors to this collection had sufficient space to simultaneously provide an introduction to their area of study, a detailed discussion of its most innovative and challenging dimensions, and a set of illustrative examples. They have created state-of-the-art reports that also constitute important contributions in their own right. It is for this reason that the essays collected here should be of interest to both novices and experts. This collection offers an unprecedented look at language from an interdisciplinary and yet fundamentally anthropological perspective.

The overall organization of this *Companion* partly resembles the organization of my *Linguistic Anthropology: A Reader* and partly moves toward new themes and intellectual connections. As can be gathered from the Synopsis of Contents (which contains brief abstracts for all chapters), this collection is particularly rich, on the one hand, in the treatment of linguistic diversity and creativity and, on the other, in the crucial role performed by language in understanding as well as constituting subjective and intersubjective worlds. It covers established areas in linguistic anthropology such as language socialization, literacy, and register, and more recently established areas such as language ideology, pragmatic deviance, and vocal anthropology. A number of authors also revisit domains of study – everyday narratives, conversations, and sign languages – which were first established in disciplines outside of anthropology. Finally, the General Bibliography at the end includes additional references for readers who want to further explore some of the themes found in the chapters. As I look at the result of this collective effort, I feel confident that the chapters in this *Companion* offer a set of original and intriguing contributions that look at the past while setting the tone for future research on language as a cultural product and cultural resource.

Alessandro Duranti
Summer 2003

Acknowledgments

I thank the contributors for their willingness to be part of this collective endeavor and for their patience in revising their first drafts in the light of my views as to the goals of this volume. I am also grateful to Parker Shipton for asking me to conceptualize this Companion in the first place and to my wonderful editor at Blackwell, Jane Huber, always accessible, supportive, and interested in new ideas. The preparation of the General Bibliography at the end of the volume was made possible by the additional efforts of a number of contributors who sent extra references and by the editorial and computer skills of Steven P. Black. Finally, I wish to thank Justin Richland for his careful work on the index; and Margaret Aherne, champion desk editor, who makes us all look better, at least in print.

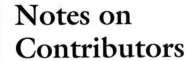

Notes on Contributors

Asif Agha is Associate Professor of Anthropology, Linguistics, Folklore and South Asian Studies at the University of Pennsylvania. He is the author of *Structural Form and Utterance Context in Lhasa Tibetan* and a number of articles including "Schema and Superposition in Spatial Deixis" and "Concept and Communication in Evolutionary Terms."

Benjamin Bailey is Assistant Professor in the Department of Communication at the University of Massachusetts, Amherst. He is the author of *Language, Race, and Negotiation of Identity: A Study of Dominican Americans*. His research interests center on ethnic and racial identities in face-to-face interaction in urban, United States, immigrant contexts.

Giorgio Banti is Professor of Historical Linguistics at the University "L'Orientale," in Naples. He is the author of "Arabic Script for Languages other than Arabic around the Mediterranean," "Notes on Somali Camel Terminology," and other publications on Afro-Asiatic and Indo-European languages and cultures. He also wrote "Music and Metre in Somali Poetry" (with Francesco Giannattasio).

Patricia Baquedano-López is Assistant Professor in Language and Literacy, Society and Culture at the Graduate School of Education, University of California, Berkeley. Her research investigates the literacy development and language socialization of culturally diverse children in and out of schools. She is the author of a number of articles, including "Creating Social Identities through *Doctrina* Narratives" and (with Paul Garrett) "Language Socialization: Reproduction and Continuity, Transformation and Change."

Niko Besnier currently teaches in the Department of Sociology and Anthropology at the University of Amsterdam. His books include *Literacy, Emotion, and Authority:*

Reading and Writing on a Polynesian Atoll and *Tuvaluan: A Polynesian Language of the Central Pacific*.

Mary Bucholtz is Assistant Professor in the Department of Linguistics at the University of California, Santa Barbara. She is co-editor of *Gender Articulated* (with Kira Hall) and *Reinventing Identities* (with A. C. Liang and Laurel Sutton). Her research interests include language and gender, language and youth, and African American English.

Alessandro Duranti is Professor of Anthropology at the University of California, Los Angeles. His books include *From Grammar to Politics: Linguistic Anthropology in a Western Samoan Village* and *Linguistic Anthropology*. He has also edited *Rethinking Context: Language as an Interactive Phenomenon* (with Charles Goodwin), *Key Terms in Language and Culture*, and *Linguistic Anthropology: A Reader*.

Maria Egbert is Wissenschaftliche Oberassistentin at the Institute of Education and Communication in Migration Processes at the University of Oldenburg, Germany. She is the author of *Der Reparatur-Mechanismus in deutschen und interkulturellen Gesprächen*. Her research interests include conversational practices of affiliation and disaffiliation, native/non-native speaker interaction, and the interface of interaction with syntax and lexis.

Steven Feld is Professor of Anthropology and Music at the University of New Mexico. His books include *Sound and Sentiment*; *Music Grooves* (with Charles Keil), *Senses of Place* (with Keith Basso), and *Bosavi–Tok Pisin–English Dictionary* (with Bambi B. Schieffelin). His CDs include *Voices of the Rainforest*; *Bosavi: Rainforest Music from Papua New Guinea*; and *Bells and Winter Festivals of Greek Macedonia*.

Aaron Fox is Assistant Professor of Music at Columbia University. He is the author of *Real Country*, an ethnography of Texas country musical culture. His research interests include working-class musical culture, computer-aided sound analysis, and poetics.

Paul B. Garrett is Assistant Professor of Anthropology at Temple University. His areas of interest include language socialization, the Caribbean region, and language contact. His most recent publication (with Patricia Baquedano-López) is "Language Socialization: Reproduction and Continuity, Transformation and Change."

Francesco Giannattasio is Professor of Ethnomusicology at the University of Rome "La Sapienza." His research interests range from Somali music to traditional Italian folk music. His publications include *Il concetto di musica* and *Sul verso cantato* (co-edited with Maurizio Agamennone).

Charles Goodwin is Professor of Applied Linguistics at the University of California, Los Angeles. He is the author of *Conversational Organization: Interaction between Speakers and Hearers* and editor of *Conversation and Brain Damage*. Research interests include video analysis of talk-in-interaction; grammar in context; gesture, gaze, and embodiment as interactively organized social practices; aphasia in discourse; cognition in the workplace; courtroom discourse; language in the professions; and the ethnography of science.

Marjorie Harness Goodwin is Professor of Anthropology at the University of California, Los Angeles. She is the author of *He-Said-She-Said: Talk as Social Organization among Black Children*, and articles on language in children's peer groups, with particular emphasis on how the social worlds of preadolescent girls are constructed through language.

Kira Hall is Assistant Professor in the Departments of Linguistics and Anthropology at the University of Colorado, Boulder. Her publications include the edited collections *Gender Articulated* (with Mary Bucholtz) and *Queerly Phrased* (with Anna Livia). She is currently completing a book on the linguistic and cultural practices of Hindi-speaking hijras in India.

John B. Haviland is Professor of Anthropology and Linguistics at Reed College and Investigador/Profesor at CIESAS (Mexico). His research concentrates on Chiapas, Mexico, and Queensland, Australia. His books include *Gossip, Reputation, and Knowledge in Zinacantán* and *Old Man Fog and the Last Aborigines of Barrow Point*.

Webb Keane is Associate Professor of Anthropology at the University of Michigan. He is author of *Signs of Recognition: Powers and Hazards of Representation in an Indonesian Society*, and articles on cultural and semiotic theory, missionaries, modernity, voice and agency, national and local languages, and language ideologies.

Elizabeth Keating is Associate Professor of Anthropology at the University of Texas, Austin. She is the author of *Power Sharing: Language, Rank, Gender, and Social Space in Pohnpei, Micronesia*. Her research includes work on relationships between new technology and language practices, specifically with American Sign Language in videotelephonic communication.

Paul V. Kroskrity is Professor of Anthropology at the University of California, Los Angeles. His books include *Language, History, and Identity: Ethnolinguistic Studies of the Arizona Tewa*; *Regimes of Language: Ideologies, Polities and Identities*; and *Language Ideologies: Practice and Theory* (co-edited with Kathryn Woolard and Bambi B. Schieffelin). He also co-authored (with Jennifer F. Reynolds) the CD-ROM *Taitaduhaan: Western Mono Ways of Speaking*.

Don Kulick is Professor of Anthropology at New York University. His published works include *Language Shift and Cultural Reproduction: Socialization, Self, and Syncretism in a Papua New Guinean Village*; *Travesti: Sex, Gender, and Culture among Brazilian Transgendered Prostitutes*, and *Taboo: Sex, Identity, and Erotic Subjectivity in Anthropological Fieldwork* (co-edited with Margaret Willson). His most recent book is *Language and Sexuality* (with Deborah Cameron).

Barbara LeMaster is Professor in the Departments of Anthropology and Linguistics at California State University in Long Beach. Her research interests include Deaf sign languages, language socialization, and identity formation. She is the author of a number of articles, including "What Difference Does Difference Make? Negotiating Gender and Generation in Irish Sign Language," and (with Mary Hernandez-Katapodis) "Learning to Play School: The Role of Topic in Gendered Discourse Roles among Preschoolers."

Marianne Mithun is Professor of Linguistics at the University of California, Santa Barbara. She is author of *The Languages of Native North America* and numerous other works on language structure, its development, and use. She has worked with a dozen Native communities on language documentation and revitalization.

Leila Monaghan is a linguistic anthropologist who teaches in the Department of Communication and Culture at Indiana University. She has co-edited the book *Many Ways to be Deaf* (with Constanze Schmaling, Karen Nakamura, and Graham Turner) and with Richard Senghas has written on Deaf communities for the *Annual Review of Anthropology*. She also does research on the interrelationship between language and literacy.

Marcyliena Morgan is Associate Professor of Communication at Stanford University. Her books include *Language and the Social Construction of Identity in Creole Situations* and *Language, Discourse, and Power in African American Culture*. Her research interests include African American English, language ideology, identity, and gender and youth in the African Diaspora.

Elinor Ochs is Professor of Anthropology and Applied Linguistics at the University of California, Los Angeles. Her books include *Culture and Language Development: Language Acquisition and Language Socialization in a Samoan Village*; *Interaction and Grammar* (co-edited with Emanuel Schegloff and Sandra A. Thompson), *Developmental Pragmatics* (co-edited with Bambi B. Schieffelin), and *Constructing Panic: The Discourse of Agoraphobia* and *Living Narrative: Creating Lives in Everyday Storytelling* (both co-authored with Lisa Capps).

Susan U. Philips is Professor of Anthropology at the University of Arizona. She is the author of *The Invisible Culture: Communication in Classroom and Community on the Warm Springs Indian Reservation*, and *Ideology in the Language of Judges: How Judges Practice Law, Politics and Courtroom Control*. Her current research interests include language and ideological diversity in Tongan legal discourse and Tongan talk about women and men.

Thomas Porcello is Assistant Professor of Anthropology at Vassar College. He is co-editor (with Paul D. Greene) of *Wired for Sound: Engineering and Technology in Sonic Cultures* and is the author of articles on discursive and technological practices of music production, sound engineering and technological change, and music and local identity.

David Samuels is Assistant Professor of Anthropology at the University of Massachusetts, Amherst. His articles on contemporary Western Apache language, music, popular culture, and identity include "Indeterminacy and History in Britton Goode's Western Apache Placenames: Ambiguous Identity on the San Carlos Apache Reservation" and "The Whole and the Sum of the Parts, Or, How Cookie and the Cupcakes Told the Story of Apache History in San Carlos."

Bambi B. Schieffelin is Professor of Anthropology at New York University. She is the author of *The Give and Take of Everyday Life: Language Socialization of Kaluli Children* and co-editor (with Kathryn Woolard and Paul V. Kroskrity) of *Language Ideologies: Practice and Theory*. Her recent publications on language change and Christian missionization include "Introducing Kaluli Literacy: A Chronology of Influences" and "Marking Time: The Dichotomizing Discourse of Multiple Temporalities."

James M. Wilce is Professor of Anthropology at Northern Arizona University. He is the author of *Eloquence in Trouble: The Poetics and Politics of Complaint in Rural Bangladesh* and the editor of *Social and Cultural Lives of Immune Systems*. He is currently working on a new book, *Crying Shame: Metaculture, Modernity and Lament*. His research interests include semiotics, representations, and issues surrounding language and globalization.

Kathryn Woolard is Professor of Anthropology at the University of California, San Diego. Her publications include *Double Talk: Bilingualism and the Politics of Ethnicity in Catalonia*; *Language Ideologies: Practice and Theory* (co-edited with Bambi B. Schieffelin and Paul V. Kroskrity), and *Languages and Publics: The Making of Authority* (co-edited with Susan Gal).

PART **I** Speech Communities, Contact, and Variation

CHAPTER 1

Speech Community

Marcyliena Morgan

1 INTRODUCTION

This chapter focuses on how the concept *speech community* has become integral to the interpretation and representation of societies and situations marked by change, diversity, and increasing technology as well as those situations previously treated as conventional. The study of the speech community is central to the understanding of human language and meaning-making because it is the product of prolonged interaction among those who operate within shared belief and value systems regarding their own culture, society, and history as well as their communication with others. These interactions constitute the fundamental nature of human contact and the importance of language, discourse, and verbal styles in the representation and negotiation of the relationships that ensue. Thus the concept of speech community does not simply focus on groups that speak the same language. Rather, the concept takes as fact that language represents, embodies, constructs, and constitutes meaningful participation in a society and culture. It also assumes that a mutually intelligible symbolic and ideological communicative system must be at play among those who share knowledge and practices about how one is meaningful across social contexts.[1] Thus it is within the speech community that identity, ideology, and agency (see Bucholtz and Hall, Kroskrity, and Duranti, this volume) are actualized in society.

While there are many social and political forms a speech community may take – from nation-states to chat rooms dedicated to pet psychology – speech communities are recognized as distinctive in relation to other speech communities. That is, they come into collective consciousness when there is a crisis of some sort, often triggered when hegemonic powers consider them a problem or researchers highlight them and rely on them as a unit of study.[2] Thus, while speech community is a fundamental concept, it is also the object of unremitting critique. In fact, it has been blamed for poor literary skills, epidemics, unemployment, increases in crime, and so on.[3]

Many of the critical arguments surrounding speech communities concern two contrasting perspectives on how to define language and discourse. The first focuses on the analysis and description of linguistic, semantic, and conversational features that are gathered from a group and are in turn deemed to be stable indicators of that speech community. The second perspective refers to the notion of language and discourse as a way of representing (Hall 1996; Foucault 1972). In this case the focus is on how language is used to construct relationships, identity, and so on. Though these perspectives can be complementary, they are often in contention with each other. The choice of perspective can have far-reaching implications for the speech community in question as well as for the concept in general.

Members of speech communities often recognize that these two perspectives coexist, though the linguistic analysis, absent of speakers' beliefs, politics, and social reality, is often considered to be the "objective" and accurate description of speech community from the perspective of the dominant culture. Thus a national language can be proclaimed, even if it is only spoken by an elite few, and one dialect can be declared the prestige variety. At the same time, members of speech communities may also recognize that the cultural hegemony that is sustained, enforced, and reproduced can also be incorporated and acted on discursively and literally to highlight representation of others who reside outside its boundaries (cf. Gramsci 1971; Bourdieu 1991). That is to say, membership in a speech community includes local knowledge of the way language choice, variation, and discourse represents generation, occupation, politics, social relationships, identity, and more.

Throughout the social sciences, there has been a growing awareness of the importance of the nature of discourse in the representation of local knowledge, culture, identity, and politics. This is especially true in the works of cultural anthropologists whose ethnographies are situated within communities whose members are aware of social and cultural differences and where transmigration, social identity, and memory of imagined and experienced notions of *home* are part of the cultural fabric. For example, the power of discourse in the representation of the lives of Asian Americans is found in the work of Dorinne Kondo (1997), who explores how Asian American playwrights' and actors' performance of identity is in part a manifestation of their community norm of mediating multiple language ideologies and heteroglossia (Bahktin 1981).[4] The work of Marta Savigliano (1995) is also provocative as she demonstrates how Argentinians, through dancing and singing tango, use language and symbols associated with African Diasporan speech communities as a mediator and symbol for critiques of modern discourse, politics, and injustice. It is also integral to Kesha Fikes' (2000) work on Cape Verdeans in Cape Verde and Portugal. Fikes explores how transnationals rely on African language usage and referents to frame membership in multiple speech communities that represent both resistance to and inclusion of an African Diasporan speech community, and how they use these same referents to index the Portuguese metropole in contrast to rural Cape Verde as well. In this sense the study of creole languages, more than any other area of linguistics, provides invaluable insight into the nature of diasporic migration, ethnicity, nationalism, identity, and language loyalty (see Garrett, this volume).

As the previous cases suggest, describing speech community is no simple matter. It cannot be defined by static physical location since membership can be experienced as part of a nation-state, neighborhood, village, club, compound, on-line chat room, religious institution, and so on. What's more, adults often experience multiple communities, and one's initial socialization into a speech community may occur within a culture with communicative values that differ from those of other cultures and communities one encounters later in life. In this chapter, I argue that the concept of speech community often incorporates shifts in attitudes and usage and that the notion of language that binds it is constructed around several major theories regarding language as a social construct. They include: language and representation, language and diversity, attitudes toward language use, and language and power. The speech community is recognizable by the circulation of discourse and repetition of activity and beliefs and values about these topics, which are constantly discussed, evaluated, corroborated, mediated, and reconstituted by its members. One's awareness of these issues is determined by whether and to what degree speech communities are in crisis. For some, awareness is ingrained in the cultural fabric and thus represents unmarked usage that encompasses the community's historicity, politics, ideology, representation, and so on. Though these values are agreed upon, that does not necessarily mean that there is complete consensus about the implementation of these principles. Rather, what is at stake is knowledge of the symbolic, market, and exchange value of varieties and styles within and across speech communities.

2   RECOVERING THE SPEECH COMMUNITY

Linguists have used many strategies to analyze how people throughout cultures and societies of the world build, seek, find, and thrive in their communities – every day. In some cases, the speech community concept itself has come to signify a particular way of looking at peoples and cultures so that it has been viewed as focusing too much on difference and not on the complexities of difference and power.[5] Kathryn Woolard (1985) explores the relationship between difference and power in her analysis of how communities discursively mediate hegemony.[6] Woolard's analysis of language loyalty in Catalan explores how Catalonians overwhelmingly choose the Catalan language over Castilian as a sign of status, even though they know it is stigmatized by the larger society. Woolard suggests that the Gramscian notion of cultural hegemony and Bourdieu's concept of cultural capital not only explain but also anticipate that social actors consider language to be a part of their social action. Both Gramsci (1971) and Bourdieu (1991) analyze dominant culture's ability to impose its interpretation of others, and especially non-elites, on entire populations and speech communities. Those in power present their own perspective as *the way* to understand the world so effectively that those who are subordinated and marginalized also accept this view as "common sense," reasonable and "natural." In spite of this, because discourse is dialogic and representational, speakers have opportunities to interrogate hegemony as well. What is shared among its members is language ideology, beliefs about language, identity, and membership, and attitude toward language use. As Woolard explains, "The two aspects of linguistic authority or hegemony, then, are knowledge or control of a standard, and acknowledgement or recognition of it: to translate into empirical sociolinguistic terms, behavioral proficiency and attitudes" (Woolard 1985: 741).

While it is true that members of speech communities can shape their discursive practices to represent their beliefs and values, it is also true that the current state of technological communication, globalization, and transmigration continues to test its viability as a useful concept. Yet this represents a challenge to the analyst, who must work in a shrinking and more visible cultural and social world, rather than to the concept itself. This challenge is illustrated in the words and images of the US hiphop artist Guru and the French hiphop artist MC Solaar. In the prelude to their music video "Le Bien, Le Mal – The Good, The Bad," MC Solaar telephones Guru to arrange a meeting. Each man is filmed in separate outdoor locations while talking to the other on their cell phones. MC Solaar is in Paris and speaks to Guru in French using *verlan* – urban French vernacular that incorporates movement of syllables and deletion of consonants.[7] Guru is in New York and uses hiphop terminology and African American English (AAE) as he talks to MC Solaar.

Paris

MC Solaar: C'est longtemps depuis qu'on a vu Guru Gangstarr.[8]
                (It's been a long time since we've seen Guru from Gangstarr.)
                C'est pas cool, s'il venait a Paris?
                (It will be fly [very cool] if he comes to Paris.)
Friend: Ouais.
                (Yeah)
MC Solaar: On essait de l'appler
                (Let's give him a call.)

New York

Guru *(on phone)*:   Hello – Who dis? Solaar! What up Man? Yeah!
                     No I'm comin' man. I know I'm late Yo! Hold up for me
                     al(r)ight. Baby! I'm on my way now al(r)ight! Peace!

At the end of the conversation, Guru leaves to meet MC Solaar and descends stairs into a New York subway. When he ascends the subway, he is in Paris! Then the two begin their song about the contradictions of life in respective cities and shared speech community.[9]

In "Le Bien, Le Mal – The Good, The Bad," MC Solaar and Guru present a speech community in which they share the same style of speaking, method of grammatical innovation, lexical creativity, and more – but not the same linguistic system. In the case of these hiphop artists, the speech community is not linguistically and physically located but is bound by politics, culture, social condition, and norms, values, and attitudes about language use. The types of speech communities described above – which are partially constructed through transnationalism, technology, music, and politically and socially marginalized youth – were treated as subordinate in earlier descriptions of speech community if they were considered at all. In fact, an analysis of these earlier theories about speech community provides important insight into the nature of some of the issues that still remain today.

2.1   Early definitions of speech community

Reservations and questions regarding the utility of the speech community concept have existed at least since 1933 when Leonard Bloomfield wrote: "A group of people who use the same set of speech signals is a *speech-community*" (1933: 29). This definition reflects a common belief of the time, that monolingualism – one language, one nation-state – is the canonical example of speech community (e.g. Anderson 1983). In this case, a community is considered to be a "social group of any size who reside in a specific locality, share government, and have a common cultural and historical heritage" (Random House Dictionary). At this particular time linguistic anthropology was mainly concerned with historical relationships of language families (Lyons 1981; Hudson 1980) and language was viewed as the result of history and politics but not as integral and entangled in it – and therefore not as an aspect of historicity and the context of politics and social life.[10] Within the confines of descriptive and structural linguistics, the speech community reflected the linguist's definition of language described above and thus it was a product and result of what was simply called *contact*.

Of course, discovering the history of and describing the world's languages is a very important business, and in many respects early definitions corresponded to Western arrogance and its responsibility to "represent the world correctly" – and with itself as the reference point (Said 1978). From this perspective, it is not surprising that while Bloomfield considered the speech community to be the most important kind of social group, his evaluation of contact situations did not assume that various sectors of society interacted with each other in a complementary way.[11] Instead, communities that arose out of European aggression and cultural hegemony were relegated to supplemental status. Unfortunately, the notion that viable speech communities could not exist under such circumstances suggests that the great cultural and social restructuring and reconstitution accomplished by colonized and conquered people were inconsequential in light of the enormity of the catastrophic events that they endured. This perspective also greatly influenced earlier works of language and contact and pidgin and creole studies, where African languages were thought to have marginal influence and where creoles were often treated as not quite a language at all (see below).

Bloomfield's conception of the homogeneous speech community represented the canon in linguistic anthropology until Noam Chomsky (1965) began to challenge the concept's utility. Chomsky's work critiqued descriptive and structural analyses of language and introduced a theoretical approach that explored the human capacity to produce language rather than language as a social construct. In *Aspects of the Theory of Syntax*, Chomsky (1965) introduced the distinction between competence and performance and abandoned the model that incorporated the speech community as the basis of linguistic analysis. The possibility of discovering human linguistic capacity was found in the cognitive, psychological self that develops irrespective of where performance of that knowledge resided – the speech community. Instead of resolving the conflict between whether the speech community constitutes language and discourse or is constituted through linguistic descriptions, Chomsky insistently argued that the essence of language resides in discovering the mechanism and theory behind the human ability to produce language. By regulating people's actual use of language to descriptions of linguistic problems (e.g. false starts, errors, etc.) the speech community suddenly was at risk of becoming the garbage dump for linguistic debris – what remains after theoretical analysis is complete.

As Chomsky's theories began to attack the concept's foundations, new generations of linguistic anthropologists began to offer more evidence of its importance for both members of speech communities and theorists who sought to develop analyses of language and discourse in groups. However, the most difficult tasks remained. Those were to determine: the role of cultural hegemony; the construction and reconstruction of values, norms, and standards in speech community representation; and why group differences do not destroy speech communities.

2.2   Retrieving the speech community

The work of John Gumperz (1968, 1972a, b) revived the concept of the speech community by considering it a social construct. Instead of focusing on the single language model he defined it as "any human aggregate characterized by regular and frequent interaction by means of a shared body of verbal signs and set off from similar aggregates by significant differences in language usage" (1972b: 219).[12] Gumperz focused on interface communication and determined that the notion of consistent, repetitive, and predictable interactions and contact is necessary for a speech community to exist. He argued that regardless of the linguistic similarities and differences, "the speech varieties employed within a speech community form a system because they are related to a shared set of social norms" (1972b: 220). This formulation could incorporate the sociolinguistic research that was occurring in cities at the time (see below) and reconstituted the notion of speech community to include more than languages and language boundaries, but also values, attitudes, and ideologies about language. Thus, while the concept speech community initially focused on language systems, relationships, and boundaries, it expanded to include the notion of social representation and norms in the form of attitudes, values, beliefs, and practices – and the notion that members of speech communities work their languages as social and cultural products.

Many direct and indirect efforts to reclaim the integrity of speech community that complemented Gumperz's interpretation emerged. In particular, Dell Hymes described the speech community as a "fundamental concept for the relation between language, speech, and social structure" (1964: 385). He considered the question of boundaries essential in order to recognize that communities are not by definition fixed units. In fact, Hymes' model of ethnographies of communication/speaking argued for the importance of communicative competence – the knowledge a speaker must have to function as a member of a social group. Communicative competence is based on language use and socialization within cultures and one becomes knowledgeable of both grammar and appropriateness across speech acts and events that are evaluated and corroborated by others. Hymes' argument that competence was "the interrelationship of language with the other codes of communicative conduct" (1972: 277–8) replaced the notion that a language constitutes a speech community with a code of beliefs and behaviors about language and discourse and knowledge of how to use them.

Yet the discussion of dialect and notions of standards as well as rigid and overlapping borders between communities did not incorporate an analysis of the social and political conditions that these communities reflected, and thus the nature of what contact means in terms of power and representation remained peripheral to analyses of speech community.

2.3   Sociolinguists and social actors

One of the greatest challenges to the reformulated concept of speech community described above actually came from the field of sociolinguisties and creole language studies. This is not surprising since sociolinguistics is the study of language variation and the identification of features that systematically differ from other varieties. Similarly, creole language studies must shift through contact language systems in order to determine whether one is distinct enough from all other languages present to be called a language in and of itself.[13] Thus both areas focus on the differences among and within speech communities that resulted from discrimination in terms of class, gender, race, and colonial conquest. In a field notorious for proclaiming that the difference between a language and a dialect is who controls the army, one could predict that the social, cultural, and political parameters of speech communities would encroach on sociolinguistic methodologies that are often apolitical.

William Labov's (1972) definition of speech community addressed the question of methodological strategies and focused on the relationship of such sociological categories as race, class, and gender to variation in language use. Labov contrasted speech community attitudes toward linguistic variables and corroborated Hymes' depiction when he wrote, "The speech community is not defined by any marked agreement in the use of language elements, so much as by participation in a set of shared norms" (1972: 120–1). Moreover, he found that though these norms were often at odds with prestige standards, it did not mean that speakers within and outside of speech communities did not use them. Instead, it is necessary to consider their value within social contexts. As Gregory Guy explains,

> One reason that shared norms form part of the definition of the speech community is that they are required to account for one of the principal sociolinguistic findings regarding variation by class and style, namely that the same linguistic variables are involved in the differentiation of social classes and speech styles. (1988: 50).

In contrast, Milroy and Milroy (1992), who conducted research in Belfast and Philadelphia, believe that contrasts in attitudes toward varieties within and between speech communities were embedded in social class methodology rather than in social stratification of speech communities themselves. They argued that in Labov's notion of sociolinguistic speech community the shared norms of evaluation were also the very linguistic norms that symbolize the divisions between them. Rather than reflecting a shared belief, they assert that Labov's findings "are more readily interpretable as evidence of conflict and sharp divisions in society than as evidence of consensus" (1992: 3).

But speech communities can indeed have consensus about divisions and use the same symbols to reflect their opinion about divisions and bring about consensus. That is, it is possible to represent views about variable choice through some form of consensus, and variables can have different values depending on the social and cultural context without representing conflict. For example, the African American speech community considers it ludicrous to think that a professional would use vernacular AAE in formal settings unless it was done intentionally to make a point.[14] Moreover, conversations among middle-class members often include imitations of speakers using AAE in formal settings to signify that listeners outside of the African American speech community are bigoted. Zentella (1997) makes a similar argument for Spanish and English codeswitching in New York: "Relationships among language, setting and meaning are not fixed. Switching into Spanish in public or into English at home does not necessarily communicate intimacy or distance, respectively" (1997: 3).

Labov interpreted speech community values that recognize social differentiation within and between communities by contrasting dominant and overt norms with what he calls covert norms (1972: 249). While he described covert norms as a preference for the social dialect irrespective of the role of standard varieties, the question of how these norms function and whether they are, in fact, covert in the same way to members of the speech community still remains.[15] Yet, while members of speech communities value many language varieties, speakers and theorists sometimes have different agendas about how to view these varieties. Theorists are concerned with variation as it relates to norms and linguistic patterns while members of speech communities are concerned with variation as a form of representation that is not fixed but fluid within multiple interactions.[16] As Eckert explains: "The claim that the social unit that defines one's sociolinguistic sample constitutes a speech community, then, is above all a way of placing the study itself rather than the speakers" (2000: 33).

For the most part, sociolinguistic training focuses on the identification and analysis of linguistic variation compared to sociological variables such as ethnicity, class, age, and gender. The difficulty is in incorporating attitudes about language and the notion of shared and corroborated beliefs into the analysis of linguistic practices. If speech community members are not aware of these forms, linguists often argue that they are not aware of what constitutes their speech community. But John Rickford (1985) argues that sociolinguistics must also pay attention to what speakers actually believe about how their language practices reflect their social lives. He investigated ethnicity as a sociolinguistic boundary by comparing linguistic variation between a black and a white speaker on the South Carolina Sea Islands. While he found that social differentiation between speakers was marked at the morphosyntactic level, he argued that Sea Islanders were well aware of the function of the norms of their speech community, in spite of the contrasts.[17]

In this case the definition of community and social context creates a dichotomy between the knowledge developed by theorists versus the abstract communicative and linguistic knowledge of speakers involved in everyday interactions. In fact, one of the more persistent challenges in creole language studies and sociolinguistics in general is to determine the extent and ways in which information or linguistic facts gathered from a particular speech community can, in some way, benefit that community (Labov 1980, 1982). In creole language studies, this challenge often comes in the form of questions about power and hegemony when discussing historical linguistics and European colonization. Modern creole language situations have arisen mainly from European conceived and controlled plantation systems that brought together people of different nations, cultures, and languages to serve as either indentured workers or slaves (Garrett, this volume). While the situations from which creole languages have emerged can be described merely as examples of language contact, that denotation is hardly sufficient if one considers the complex ways in which these communities of speakers currently use language to mediate and substantiate multiple realities that constitute their world. These situations also provide an opportunity to illuminate the sites of contention in which creole language speakers and descendants negotiate and seek power. How linguists address these questions is as important to the speech community under study as the linguistic information that has been assembled.

3   REPRESENTATION AND DISCOURSE ABOUT LANGUAGE SYSTEM

While proficiency in a common language is a significant component of many speech communities, this knowledge need not be in relation to a standard dialect or norm or even a single language (Romaine 2000; Wodak et al. 1999). Irrespective of whether the speech community is based on a common activity and practice, is marginalized, incorporates dominant ideology, or is in resistance to it, its members must have communicative competence in relation to discourse about how language and/or language variety function in specific contexts and constitute the speech community. Consequently, discourse may focus on linguistic practices that are indicative of the variety or language, in contrast to and dialogic with other dialects and languages. Zentella (1997) explores the necessity and expectation that speech community members share knowledge in her description of the New York Puerto Rican (NYPR) speech community where:

> interactions rely on shared linguistic and cultural knowledge of standard and non-standard Puerto Rican Spanish, Puerto Rican English, African American Vernacular English, Hispanized English, and standard NYC English, among other dialects. Speakers understand the overt and covert messages of fellow community members because they can follow varied linguistic moves and fill in the gaps for other speakers or translate for themselves. In the process they ratify each other's membership in the community and contribute to the re-shaping of NYPR identity. (1997:3)

Discourse about which linguistic features represent the speech community may come from linguistic study and from the communities themselves. For example, in Morgan (1994, 2001), I argue that while sociolinguistic descriptions of the African American speech community have yielded tremendous insight into the dialect, these analyses have also prompted educators, social scientists, and some linguists to argue that it is the main cause of educational and economic inequities. In fact, the African American speech community operates according to an elaborate integration of language norms and values associated with the symbolic and practical functions of African American English (AAE) and General English (GE).[18] One outcome is what I have called *reading dialect* (Morgan 2002), a code-shifting practice that occurs "when members of the African American community contrast or otherwise highlight what they consider to be obvious contrasting features of AAE and GE in an unsubtle and unambiguous manner to make a point" (2002: 74). This produces an environment where both varieties symbolize ideologies regarding African American cultural practices. In terms of language choice, GE is the only variety that one can *choose* to speak since it is often learned in formal settings outside of the home and from those who are not members of the speech community. On the other hand, AAE is a variety that one may choose *not* to speak since it is the language through which one is socialized into the speech community. That is, in the African American speech community, both AAE and GE function as the language of home, community, history, and culture. For families that use both varieties, one is not necessarily valued over the other though one may be considered more contextually appropriate. Within this system AAE is not only what one may hear and speak at home and in the community, but also it is the variety that delivers formal and informal knowledge as well as local knowledge and wisdom. It is the language of both the profound and the profane.

On the other hand GE, rather than AAE, has a context-free exchange value outside of the speech community.[19] Within the dominant cultural system, GE usage represents hegemony, is considered "normal" and indexes intelligence, compliance, and so on. Although speakers may not be aware of all grammatical relationships and systems in their repertoire, by the time they are adults they know that AAE usage may be stigmatized within dominant cultural systems and may be considered deviant and index ignorance. They know the politics of language use and attempt to adjust accordingly. In this way theories about AAE and GE linguistic structure and usage are part of everyday philosophizing in the speech community and these "philosophies of language" regarding social reality are radically different from those of linguists in many ways.[20] Poet Bruce George demonstrates this in an excerpt from his poem "Bone Bristle" (2002).

> While their house is a house
> That Black built
> Brick by brick.
> Their synergistics are antagonistic
> Towards our linguistics.
> But our rhyme has reason
> And our syllogisms are valid enough.
> Enough to make non-sequiturs follow logic
> Without putting a stop to cultural reasoning.
> (Bruce George, 2002: "Bone Bristle Def Poetry Jam")

Through standard usage, George demonstrates educated or "high" knowledge to critique what he perceives as society's antagonism toward a black speech that represents black speakers. He continues:

> We have plenty of gray matter to withstand
> Your mental jousting
> We have plenty of gray matter to overstand
> Your subterfuge

George *reads* the exclusive standard speech community by introducing the word 'overstand' in place of 'understand'.[21] The use of 'overstand' signifies that George, as part of the African American speech community, fully understands the attitudes, injustices, and so on associated with dominant discourse and practices around his speech community.

Though speech communities may take any and all of these forms and more, it is not an infinitely malleable concept, changing shape, form, and meaning according to scholarly need or any new gathering of people. Rather speech communities reflect what people do and know when they interact with one another. It assumes that when people come together through discursive practices, they intend to behave as though they operate within a shared set of norms, local knowledge, beliefs, and values. It means that they are aware of these things and capable of knowing when they are being adhered to and when the values of the community are being ignored.[22]

4 DIVERSITY, INTERACTION, STYLE, AND USAGE

Even when members are aware of the values, attitudes, and norms of discourse of a speech community, their positive standing is not always guaranteed, especially when regular travel and transmigration are the norm. Instead, membership in and across speech communities requires the negotiation of languages, dialects, discourse styles, and symbolic systems as part of normal practice. The following passage from my field notes about an incident which took place in Jamaica portrays a fair sense of the levels of mediation necessary to function successfully across speech communities and – to paraphrase Clifford Geertz – how "extraordinarily 'thick' it is" (1973: 9):[23]

> While walking in the hills of a section of Jamaica populated by members of her extended family, Myrna and I discussed the details of a complicated misunderstanding that had occurred the night before. We were a group of four mutual friends in our mid-thirties enjoying the hospitality of Myrna's mother, Mrs. Hightower. The group included Myrna, who was born in Jamaica and lived in London for 20 years and had returned to Jamaica to live; Krystal, who was born and raised in London; Carol, who spent most of her life in Jamaica and finally me, from Chicago. As we walked up the hill into the countryside – and away from Mrs. Hightower's house – Myrna and I talked about the fine points of the previous night's conversation and what went wrong. We were going over the details of how we had somehow managed to offend Myrna's mother Mrs. Hightower.
>
> The night before, one of us made a sarcastic comment that Mrs. Hightower thought was intended for her but was actually a response to earlier activities and interactions we had had in town that day. At first, we naively laughed upon realizing that Mrs. High-tower thought we were talking about her. Our laughter was not out of disrespect but because we never considered that she would think we would insult her directly or indirectly. Unfortunately, laughing was one of the worse things we could have done. Mrs. Hightower simply didn't believe us and refused to accept our apology or explanation of how we could not have possibly been referring to her. She then glared at her daughter and mumbled something in Jamaican creole – which prompted Krystal to try to offer a more detailed explanation. I suppose it may have seemed comical as we all panicked and yelled to Krystal to stop talking so that she would not try to convince Mrs. Hightower of our innocence. We knew that further explanation could be interpreted as a sign that we were trying to talk our way out of the offense rather than clarify our intentions. Krystal either didn't understand or couldn't stop explaining and ploughed ahead with her clarification. Mrs. Hightower then said something under her breath and I could only hear the words "renk" and "rass".[24]

It was at that point in our conversation in the mountains that Myrna and I came across the goat.[25] We were immediately alarmed and understood that someone was near who might have heard our conversation about the night's mix-up. Sure enough, things went from bad to worse when a wiry old man suddenly appeared holding a machete. He looked through us with deep, disapproving eyes and a stern facial expression. He was obviously a cousin of Myrna and Mrs. Hightower and though we greeted him, he said nothing in return, and led the goat away.[26] He disappeared as quickly as he had appeared and we rushed back to tell Mrs. Hightower that her cousin may have misunderstood our conversation about her, but it was too late. Somehow she had been informed before we arrived that we had been discussing her, though I'm convinced we beat her cousin down that hill. The entire weekend was then spent making deeper mistakes and trying to make amends.

As our Jamaican vacation began we considered ourselves members of a shared speech community – confident in our ability to recognize the subtleties of Caribbean interactions and mediate any misunderstanding that might arise. Yet, only Carol and Mrs. Hightower were fully socialized as a member of this speech community – as a child, adolescent, young adult, and adult. As our secure world began to unravel, it did so around persistent beliefs – held by each of us – that we knew the rules and were competent. Krystal lived in a heavily Jamaican community in London and I've conducted ethnographies throughout Jamaica. We both knew that one cannot defend oneself with this kind of misunderstanding. Once the defense and apology are stated, one must simply wait out the situation – but that was not what Krystal did that fateful evening. Myrna had spent much of her childhood in Jamaica, and we both were aware that her family lived in the surrounding area and often listened to conversations of those walking in their hills. Yet we behaved as though we had privacy. In fact, anyone could have heard us and reported back to Mrs. Hightower at any time during our "private" walk. Later Carol, the only one to emerge with her social face intact (and the only one to whom we all continued to speak), summed it up this way: "Too much London, too much America, and not enough Jamaica."

While the consequences of my interactions in that Jamaican vacation may be particular to the situation, they are not unique. It demonstrates how integration and knowledge of different norms of communication and the negotiation and mediation of power and identity that accompany this integration are often also a part of everyday discourse in speech communities. In this respect, Mrs. Hightower was well within her right to invoke an exclusive Jamaican interpretation on our interaction. And Krystal was well within hers as she pleaded for a more British interpretation of the situation.[27] This type of negotiation is an aspect of social life in speech communities and not part of a social imaginary – though it may be a product of it. Moreover, this type of interaction is especially common for those from cultures whose secondary socialization may have included voluntary and involuntary changes in education, in class and status, in geographical locations and regions through migration and transmigration, and who may have experienced a change in occupation and even method of contact which in turn introduced a way of speaking and communicating (e.g. the Internet).

5 PRACTICING SPEECH COMMUNITIES

Some speech communities exist in relation to specific practices, activities, and social relationships (Lave and Wenger 1991). These communities are constructed as unique and different from others, often fulfilling a specific need or purpose. Because of this, members are most likely aware of their role and relationship to other speech communities as part of normal functioning. Communities of practice range from total institutions such as prisons and mental institutions (Goffman 1961) to situations with more relaxed rules that range from schools to drama groups. For example, Michael Halliday (1978) reported on identity and the construction of underground speech communities in institutions and urban areas. His research on antilanguages in prisons provided insight into the construction of embedded speech communities that utilized dominant linguistic and discourse styles within a contrasting interpretive framework so that prisoners could effectively talk with agency using discourse associated with acceptance of their incarceration. Thus the speech community can be a symbolic entity that both creates and indexes its existence as a hidden product of society and the institutional structure.

While members of non-dominant speech communities often acknowledge and incorporate the standard, they do not control it or the knowledge associated with it. Perhaps one of the contexts where this is most evident is within the institution of education, especially in the USA. These institutions typically expose the tyranny of the standard, especially as it socializes children to the norms of cultural and communicative hegemony (cf. Briggs 1986). Educational institutions convey not only specific and specialized knowledge, but also the presumption that the prestige variety is more valuable than that acquired in conversations in the homes of those who do not characterize the dominant language (e.g. Bourdieu and Passeron 1977; Woolard 1985). In fact, Bourdieu writes: "Integration into a single 'linguistic community', which is a product of the political domination that is endlessly reproduced by institutions capable of imposing universal recognition of the dominant language, is the condition for the establishment of relations of linguistic domination" (1991: 46). Thus antilanguage is more than resistance to hegemony. It is the simultaneous recognition of an oppositional discourse.

The speech community has had a complicated role in education as some educational psychologists and sociolinguists have assumed that only the middle class share the school speech community ideal. In fact, there have been many studies that reveal contrasts between home values toward literacy skills (e.g. Ward 1971; Heath 1983; Baquedano-López, this volume). These studies reveal that black and working-class children have not had practice in school prestige models. Yet the school is aware of the home speech community and its version of cultural capital, and it is designed to replace the home speech community with its own ideology rather than introduce another speech community. The result is that the school language is variously described as representing "the elitist traditions of education" (Adger 1998: 151) where there is only one acceptable variety. In contrast, the home acknowledges and at times incorporates both, and only chooses to abandon dominant discourse at times of civil unrest – or when representation and identity are called into question. Thus the wider speech community learns the value of both discourses and the value of their representations. Unsurprisingly, there are many possible scenarios reported in the literature of how students might respond to this situation. One is that the school speech community is unsuccessful in convincing students that exchange has equivalent value and students introduce innovations in creating new values for these models. This is the case reported by Woolard regarding Catalan. She writes:

> we cannot read hegemony – saturation of consciousness – directly from the institutional domination of language variety. Just as nonstandard practices may accompany standard consciousness, so it is logically possible that standard linguistic practices may accompany or conceal resistant consciousness, as a form of accommodation to coercion rather than the complicity essential to the notion of cultural hegemony. (1985: 741)

In an effort to address poor performance of African American and Spanish-dominant children in the US educational system, some educators and linguists have suggested that there exists a conflict between home language and school language. This is also the case for youth who engage in hiphop culture and who have it in mind to expose the hegemonic ideology represented by the standard by employing African American and bilingual linguistic norms. Yet the conflict is not between the two – they are a part of each other and rely on each other for existence. Rather, conflict occurs with the education system and its attempt to assert hegemony.

6   CONCLUSION: POWER AND IDENTITY

Throughout this chapter I have attempted to demonstrate ways in which speech community represents the location of a group in society and its relationship to power. This relationship is important to understand how social actors move within and between their speech communities. Speech communities may be marginal and contested, some are part of dominant culture and others a part of practice that may encompass all of the above. I have introduced some of the involvedness inherent in each example of speech community to demonstrate that members actively engage these complexities of language and representation. Yet, three questions remain. How do speech communities manage to incorporate hegemonic norms and how do they also produce norms, values, and attitudes that do not incorporate hegemony and are in opposition to the dominant discourse? Finally, what is the role of researchers and theorists in the construction of this crisis?

In her work *Gender Trouble* (1990), Judith Butler discusses the inherent problems in the development of language of representation to reflect feminist theory. She writes: "The domains of political and linguistic 'representation' set out in advance the criteria by which subjects themselves are formed, with the result that representation is extended only to what can be acknowledged as a subject. In other words, the qualification for being a subject must first be met before representation can be extended" (1990: 2–3). Butler is concerned that the very language we use to refer to our speech communities and call them into recognition actually reinscribes the symbolic system of dominant culture. Yet, the discourse that introduces cultural difference both highlights the speech community and alters dominant discourse as well. As Homi Bhabha explains, "It is in the emergence of the interstices – the overlap and displacement of domains of difference – that the intersubjective and collective experiences of *nationness*, community interest, or cultural value are negotiated" (1994: 2).

Perhaps one of the most persuasive examples of this is the development of the hiphop speech community. This community was conceived on the streets of New York's brown and black boroughs and bred according to African American counterlanguage practices (Morgan 2002). The hiphop nation is constructed around an ideology that representations and references (signs and symbols) are indexical and create institutional practices. While its originators hailed from the Caribbean, Latin America, and New York and New Jersey's black communities, they coalesced within African American cultural practices where norms and values are communicated through symbols and specific and often ritualized practices rather than through explicit institutions. These practices are simply referred to as the WORD – so that any culture that adopts hiphop must incorporate African American language ideology. This does not mean that youth belong to one world-wide speech community. But it does mean that like Guru and MC Solaar described earlier, their identity is tied to the power derived from a shared discourse and system of representation. With modernity, the accessibility of what were previously national and cultural boundaries has resulted in people from outside these cultures appropriating the language of speech communities with which they have no social or cultural relationship. In fact cultural conflict can arise when those who are familiar with communities where they may not share membership use a language or jargon for emphasis, play, or to align with an "outside" identity within the boundaries of their own communities. In this case the style of speaking may be readily identified as belonging to a particular community, but the value norms and expectations of the source community do not accompany it. What's more, the words and expressions may be used out of context and in ways considered inappropriate and offensive.

Researchers of speech communities have an especially difficult task because their job is often to contrast communities of speakers rather than identify the workings of the speech community. To paraphrase Edward Said, researchers must avoid promoting communities of interpretation as they market themselves as experts at the expense of recognizing the complexities within speech communities that may compromise their particular objectives (1978: 337, 345). This challenge will only increase as communities increase in access to each other and subsequently increase in complexity. It is therefore essential that researchers recognize speech communities on their own terms and be explicit about their methodologies, relationships, and interests to them.

Speech community is not a concept that unravels with conflict, complex situations, and shifts in identity. As Hall (1996) states: "Discourse is about the production of knowledge through language. But it is itself produced by a practice: 'discursive practice' – the practice of producing meaning. Since all social practices entail meaning, all practices have a discursive aspect. So discourse enters into the influences of all social practices" (201–2). Instead of problematizing the notion of speech community, conflicts highlight its efficacy in exploring the relationship between linguistics and identity, politics and society – in producing meaning.

The concept of speech community binds the importance of local knowledge and communicative competence in discursive activities so that members can identify insiders from outsiders, those passing as members, and those living in contact zones and borderlands. In a recent seminar, Homi Bhabha suggested that the main issue of modernity is no longer identity but citizenship. This statement is of particular significance to the study of speech communities because it immediately calls into question both the notion of standard language as representation and "proof" of citizenship as well as the ideological, political, and social forces at work that cause us all to claim or refuse membership. That is, the notion of the isolated and unconnected autonomous speech community can only exist within the most rigid confines of a linguistic science of the past.

The linguistic science of the future is indebted to speakers whose existence ties them to others in ways that validate their social lives at every turn. It is because of this that our explorations into speech communities and our proclamations of their existence must direct attention to the importance of identity, citizenship, and belonging. The concept of speech communities immediately introduces old and new political arguments, theories, and ideologies. This emergence brings changes within the speech community as implicit knowledge becomes engaged in active discourse and the speech community and its subjects are in turn changed by it.

NOTES

1 Of course concepts like mutual intelligibility and meaning are complex in and of themselves. The point here is that speech communities are also political and historical sites where social meaning is intrinsic in talk.

2 See Bucholtz and Hall (this volume) and Mercer (1994) for discussion of identity coming into question when it is in crisis.

3 This is true for the 1997 "Ebonics" case in the USA, as well as arguments among sociologists that participation in the speech community leads to unemployment (e.g. Wilson 1987, 1996; Massey and Denton 1993).

4 In speech communities where there is multiple contact across social class, status, and sometimes national origin, local ideologies of language often reflect heteroglossia (Bakhtin 1981), the shifting of styles or linguistic codes that exist within and often among communities.

5 Rampton (1998) argues that the comparison of speech communities limits the overall analysis of specific communities. Similarly, Irvine and Gal (2000) argue that complexities are missed because power within is not examined.

6 Also see Morgan (2002), Wodak et al. (1999), Zentella (1997), Heller (1995).

7 For example, 'blouson', the French word for jacket, would be 'zomblou'. Verlan is used widely in the suburbs of Paris and also incorporates Arabic slang as well.

8 Of course Solaar not only speaks French slang, but is an innovator.

9 "Le Bien, Le Mal," 1993. Guru with MC Solaar. Jazzmatazz. Chrysalis Records (EMI), New York.

10 This omission comes back to haunt the term since sociolinguists' notion of context began to differ greatly from that of anthropology (see below).

11 Of course I do not mean to suggest that Bloomfield was at fault here. Until as late as the 1960s, many linguists assumed that the contact situation that resulted from the Atlantic slave trade meant there was no mutual intelligibility among captives.

12 This is reprinted from 1968 "The Speech Community"' in *International Encyclopedia of the Social Sciences* (Macmillan), pp. 381–6.

13 This is to say nothing of the complex arguments necessary to assign pidgin, creole, semi-creole, or dialect designations for languages that arose from plantation contact situations.

14 Comedian Chris Rock's 1996 HBO television special, "Bring the Pain," includes a hilariously angry routine regarding non-African Americans' repeated mention that Colin Powell, a black army general and later attorney general of the USA, spoke clearly.

15 They could also index an ideology that actually devalues dominant language norms.

16 Labov's (1972) first basic principle of social judgments is: "social attitudes toward language are extremely uniform throughout a speech community" (p. 248). He includes the footnote: "In fact it seems plausible to define a speech community as a group of speakers who share a set of social attitudes towards language" (fn. 40, p. 248). The argument here is that this is probable within the scope of the linguistic study. As I have argued elsewhere (Morgan 1994), varying attitudes may be a norm in some speech communities though a particular methodology may not capture it.

17 Rickford's respondents were a black woman and a white male. He argues that gender differences were not as important as race in this case.

18 The distinction here is similar to Labov's (1998) comparison of African American and General English components. Here, AAE includes usage across social class and other interactions and discourses where speakers use both dialects. GE refers to prestige and not white working-class usage unless otherwise indicated.

19 American advertising uses AAE linguistic and verbal expressions to represent urban sophistication as well as all social classes.

20 Smitherman (1991) provides a very useful discussion of this notion in her article on the significance of the name "African American." Of course Berger and Luckman (1966) in their text on language as a construction of social reality discuss language as representing subjective and intersubjective worlds.

21 Pollard (1983) describes this as a Category II word "in which words bear the weight of their phonological implications" (p. 49).

22 Though Grice has explored some of these notions, his theory does not focus on multiple and contradictory interpretations of what is meant as a shared norm.

23 This incident took place as I was conducting fieldwork that included two of the women's families. All names have been changed as well as some details that might identify those involved. Of course, the outcome of this interaction would have an effect on the rest of my field experience.

24 Both terms are rude terms that refer to forms of rudeness.

25 During fieldwork in Jamaica I was warned that I should always assume that any goat I saw was closely watched by someone and belonged to somebody, whether I saw the person or not.

26 People in the hills assumed they were related since they shared the same last name and histories. This was, of course, a common occurrence at the end of plantation slavery where surnames were assigned irrespective of biological kinship.

27 Though in this case, one would normally acquiesce to Mrs. Hightower's interpretation because of her age.

REFERENCES

Adger, C. T. (1998). Register Shifting and Dialect Resources in Instructional Discourse. In S. Hoyle and C. T. Adger (eds.), *Kids Talk: Strategic Language Use in Later Childhood* (pp. 151–169). Oxford: Oxford University Press.

Anderson, B. (1983). *Imagined Communities*. London: Verso.

Bakhtin, M. (1981). *The Dialogic Imagination: Four Essays* (trans. C. Emerson and M. Holquist; ed. M. Holquist). Austin: University of Texas Press.

Berger, P., and Luckman, T. (1966). *The Social Construction of Reality*. Harmondsworth: Penguin Books.

Bhabha, H. (1994). *The Location of Culture*. London: Routledge.

Bloomfield, L. (1933). *Language*. New York: Holt, Rinehart & Winston.

Bourdieu, P. (1991). *Language and Symbolic Power*. Cambridge, MA: Harvard University Press.

Bourdieu, P., and Passeron, J.-C. (1977). *Reproduction in Education, Society, and Culture*. London: Sage.

Briggs, C. (1986). *Learning How to Ask: A Sociolinguistic Appraisal of the Role of the Interview in Social Science Research*. Cambridge: Cambridge University Press.

Butler, J. (1990). *Gender Trouble: Feminism and the Subversion of Identity*. London and New York: Routledge.

Chomsky, N. (1965). *Aspects of the Theory of Syntax*. Cambridge, MA: MIT Press.

Eckert, P. (2000). *Linguistic Variation as Social Practice*. Cambridge, MA: Blackwell.

Fikes, K. (2000). Santiaguense Cape Verdean Women in Portugal: Labor Rights, Citizenship and Diasporic Transformation. Manuscript. Department of Anthropology, University of California, Los Angeles.

Foucault, M. (1972). *The Archaeology of Knowledge & The Discourse on Language*. New York: Pantheon Books.

Geertz, C. (1973). *The Interpretation of Cultures*. New York: Basic Books.

Goffman, E. (1961). *Asylums: Essays on the Social Situation of Mental Patients and Other Inmates*. New York: Anchor Books.

Gramsci, A. (1971). *Selections from the Prison Notebooks*. New York: International Press.

Gumperz, J. (1968). The Speech Community. In P. P. Giglioli (ed.), *Language and Social Context*. Harmondsworth: Penguin.

Gumperz, J. J. (1972a). Introduction. In J. J. Gumperz and D. Hymes (eds.), *Directions in Sociolinguistics: The Ethnography of Communication* (pp. 1–25). New York: Holt, Rinehart and Winston.

Gumperz, J. J. (1972b). The Speech Community. In P. P. Giglioli (ed.), *Language and Social Context* (pp. 219–231). Harmondsworth: Penguin.

Guy, G. (1988). Language and Social Class. In F. J. Newmeyer (ed.), *Linguistics: The Cambridge Survey – IV. Language: The Socio-cultural Context* (pp. 37–63). Cambridge: Cambridge University Press.

Hall, S. (1996). The West and the Rest: Discourse and Power. In S. Hall, D. Held, D. Hubert, and K. Thompson (eds.), *Modernity: An Introduction to Modern Societies* (pp. 118–227). Oxford: Blackwell.

Halliday, M. A. K. (1978). *Language as Social Semiotic: The Social Interaction of Language and Meaning*. London: Edward Arnold.

Heath, S. B. (1983). *Ways with Words: Language, Life and Work in Communities and Class-rooms*. Cambridge: Cambridge University Press.

Heller, M. (1995). Code-switching and the Politics of Language. In L. Milroy and P. Muysken (eds.), *One Speaker, Two Languages: Cross-linguistic Perspectives on Code-Switching* (pp. 158–174). Cambridge: Cambridge University Press.

Hudson, R. A. (1980). *Sociolinguistics*. Cambridge: Cambridge University Press.

Hymes, D. (ed.) (1964). *Language in Culture and Society: A Reader in Linguistics and Anthropology*. New York: Harper and Row.

Hymes, D. (1972). On Communicative Competence. In J. B. Pride and J. Holmes (eds.), *Sociolinguistics* (pp. 269–293). Harmondsworth: Penguin.

Irvine, J., and Gal, S. (2000). Language Ideology and Linguistic Differentiation. In P. Kroskrity (ed.), *Regimes of Language* (pp. 35–84). Sante Fe, NM: School of American Research Press.

Kondo, D. (1997). *About Face: Performing Race in Fashion and Theater.* New York: Routledge.

Labov, W. (1972). *Sociolinguistic Patterns.* Philadelphia: University of Pennsylvania Press.

Labov, W. (1980). Is There a Creole Speech Community? In A. Valdman and A. Highfield (eds.), *Theoretical Orientations in Creole Study* (pp. 369–388). New York: Academic Press.

Labov, W. (1982). Objectivity and Commitment in Linguistic Science: The Case of the Black English Trial in Ann Arbor. *Language in Society* 11: 165–202.

Labov, W. (1998). Co-existent Systems in African-American Vernacular English. In S. S. Mufwene, J. R. Rickford, G. Bailey, and J. Baugh (eds.), *African-American English: Structure, History and Use* (pp. 110–153). London and New York: Routledge.

Lave, J., and Wenger, E. (1991). *Situated Learning: Legitimate Peripheral Participation.* Cambridge: Cambridge University Press.

Lyons, J. (1981). *Language and Linguistics: An Introduction.* Cambridge: Cambridge University Press.

Massey, D. S., and Denton, N. A. (1993). *American Apartheid: Segregation and the Making of the Underclass.* Cambridge, MA and London: Harvard University Press.

Mercer, K. (1994). *Welcome to the Jungle: New Positions in Black Cultural Studies.* New York and London: Routledge.

Milroy, L., and Milroy, J. (1992). Social Network and Social Class: Toward an Integrated Sociolinguistic Model. *Language in Society* 21: 1–26.

Morgan, M. (1994). The African-American Speech Community: Reality and Sociolinguistics. In M. Morgan (ed.), *Language and the Social Construction of Identity in Creole Situations,* (pp. 121–148). Berkeley: Center for African-American Studies.

Morgan, M. (2001). "Ain't Nothin' But A G Thang": Grammar, Variation and Language Ideology in Hip Hop Identity. In S. Lanehart (ed.), *African American Vernacular English* (pp. 185–207). Amsterdam and Philadelphia: John Benjamins.

Morgan, M. (2002). *Language, Discourse and Power in African American Culture.* Cambridge: Cambridge University Press.

Pollard, V. (1983). The Social History of Dread Talk. In L. Carrington (ed.), *Studies in Caribbean Language* (pp. 46–62). St. Augustine, Trinidad: Society for Caribbean Linguistics.

Rampton, B. (1998). Speech Community. In J. O. Verschueren, J. Blommaert, and C. Bulcaen (eds.), *Handbook of Pragmatics.* Amsterdam: John Benjamins.

Rickford, J. (1985). Ethnicity as a Sociolinguistic Boundary. *American Speech* 60: 99–125.

Romaine, S. (2000). *Language in Society: An Introduction to Sociolinguistics.* Oxford: Oxford University Press.

Said, E. (1978). *Orientalism.* New York: Pantheon.

Savigliano, M. (1995). *Tango and the Political Economy of Passion.* Boulder, CO: Westview Press.

Smitherman, G. (1991). What Is Africa to Me? Language, Ideology and African American. *American Speech* 66: 115–132.

Ward, M. C. (1971). *Them Children.* New York: Holt, Rinehart and Winston.

Wilson, W. J. (1987). *The Truly Disadvantaged.* Chicago: University of Chicago Press.

Wilson, W. J. (1996). *When Work Disappears: The World of the New Urban Poor.* New York: Knopf.

Wodak, R., de Cillia, R., Reisigl, M., and Liebhart, K. (1999). *The Discursive Construction of National Identity.* Edinburgh: Edinburgh University Press.

Woolard, K. A. (1985). Language Variation and Cultural Hegemony: Toward an Integration of Sociolinguistic and Social Theory. *American Ethnologist* 12: 738–749.

Zentella, A. C. (1997). *Growing Up Bilingual: Puerto Rican Children in New York.* Malden, MA: Blackwell.

CHAPTER 2

Registers of Language

Asif Agha

1 INTRODUCTION

Language users often employ labels like "polite language," "informal speech," "upper-class speech," "women's speech," "literary usage," "scientific term," "religious language," "slang," and others, to describe differences among speech forms. Metalinguistic labels of this kind link speech repertoires to enactable pragmatic effects, including images of the person speaking (woman, upper-class person), the relationship of speaker to interlocutor (formality, politeness), the conduct of social practices (religious, literary, or scientific activity); they hint at the existence of cultural models of speech – a metapragmatic classification of discourse types – linking speech repertoires to typifications of actor, relationship, and conduct. This is the space of register variation conceived in intuitive terms.

Writers on language – linguists, anthropologists, literary critics – have long been interested in cultural models of this kind simply because they are of common concern to language users. Speakers of any language can intuitively assign speech differences to a space of classifications of the above kind and, correspondingly, can respond to others' speech in ways sensitive to such distinctions. Competence in such models is an indispensable resource in social interaction. Yet many features of such models – their socially distributed existence, their ideological character, the way in which they motivate tropes of personhood and identity – have tended to puzzle writers on the subject of registers. I will be arguing below that a clarification of these issues – indeed the very study of registers – requires attention to *reflexive social processes* whereby such models are formulated and disseminated in social life and become available for use in interaction by individuals. Let me first introduce some of the relevant issues in a preliminary way.

Individuals become acquainted with registers through processes of socialization that continue throughout the life span (see Kulick and Schieffelin, this volume); hence every member of a language community cannot identify all of its registers with equal ease, let alone use them with equal fluency. Such differences depend on the particular life-course and trajectory of socialization of the individual speaker; for example, uneducated speakers tend to be unfamiliar with literary registers, older speakers don't know current youth slang, and scientific and technical terminologies often require years of specialized training to master. An individual's *register range* – the variety of registers with which he or she is acquainted – equips a person with portable emblems of identity, sometimes permitting distinctive modes of access to particular zones of social life. In complex societies, where no fluent speaker of the language fully commands more than a few of its registers, the register range of a person may influence the range of social activities in which that person is entitled to participate; in some professions, especially technical professions, a display of register competence is a criterion of employment. Differences of register competence are thus often linked to asymmetries of power, socioeconomic class, position within hierarchies, and the like.

A variety of registers in English and other languages have been studied and documented in recent years (see references). Some of these are known only to specialized communities of speakers, others are more widely known. Some lack official names, others have their own dictionaries. Some are highly valued in society; others (such as varieties of slang) are derogated by prescriptive institutions but positively valued by their users. Some are widely recognized as the habits of particular groups. Others – such as Standard English – are promoted by institutions of such widespread hegemony that they are not ordinarily recognized as distinct registers at all. In a common ideological view, Standard English is just "the language," the baseline against which all other facts of register differentiation are measured. Yet from the standpoint of usage Standard English is just one register among many, highly appropriate to certain public/official settings, but employed by many speakers in alternation with other varieties – such as registers of business and bureaucracy (Nash 1993), journalism and advertising (Ghadessy 1988), technical and scientific registers (Halliday 1988), varieties of slang (Eble 1996; Gordon 1983), criminal argots (Maurer 1955; Mehrotra 1977) – in distinct venues of social life.

The above discussion lays out – in a rather impressionistic fashion – several issues that pertain to the existence and use of registers in social life. Let me now offer a more precise characterization of registers, focusing on three main issues.

2   THREE ASPECTS OF REGISTERS

A register is a linguistic *repertoire* that is associated, culture-internally, with particular social practices and with persons who engage in such practices. The repertoires of a register are generally linked to systems of speech style of which they are the most easily reportable fragments. From the standpoint of language structure, registers differ in the type of repertoire involved, e.g., lexemes, prosody, sentence collocations, and many registers involve repertoires of more than one kind; from the standpoint of function, distinct registers are associated with social practices of every kind, e.g., law, medicine, prayer, science, magic, prophecy, commerce, military strategy, the observance of respect and etiquette, the expression of civility, status, ethnicity, gender. Given this range, a repertoire-based view of registers remains incomplete in certain essential respects. Such a view cannot explain how particular repertoires become differentiable from the rest of the language, or how they come to be associated with social practices at all. These features are identified by appeal to *metapragmatic models of speech*, that is, culture-internal models of actor (role), activity (conduct), and interactant relationship (social relations) associated with speech differences. I discuss this issue in section 3.

Like other cultural models, registers are *historical formations* caught up in group-relative processes of valorization and countervalorization, exhibiting change in both form and value over time. For instance, when prestige registers used by upper-class/caste speakers are imitated by other groups, the group whose speech is the sought-after variety often innovates in its own speech habits, seeking to renew or transform the emblem of distinction (see, e.g., Honey 1989; Errington 1998). Competing models of register value sometimes exist within societies as well (Hill 1998; Irvine and Gal 2000) and contribute to historical changes in register systems. At any given phase, or historical stage, a register formation involves a *social domain* of persons (e.g., a demographic group) that is acquainted with the model of speech at issue; the boundaries of this social domain may change over time or remain relatively constant, depending on the kinds of institutions that facilitate register competence in society (see sections 4 and 8 below).

The *utterance* or use of a register's forms formulates a sketch of the social occasion of language use, indexing contextual features such as interlocutors' roles, relationships, and the type of social practice in which they are engaged. If the current scenario of use is already recognizable as an instance of the social practice the utterance appears appropriate to that occasion; conversely, switching to the register may itself reconfigure the sense of occasion, indexically entailing or creating the perception that the social practice is now under way. A register's tokens are never experienced in isolation during discourse; they are encountered under conditions of *textuality* (cooccurrence) with other signs – both linguistic and non-linguistic signs – that form a significant context, or *co-text*, for the construal of the token uttered. The effects of cooccurring signs may be consistent with the effects of the sign at issue, augmenting its force; or, the sign's co-text may yield partially contrary effects, leading to various types of partial cancellation, defeasibility, hybridity, or ironic play. I discuss these issues in section 6.

Each of the above paragraphs lays out a distinct perspective on register formations that I discuss in more detail below: a repertoire perspective, a sociohistorical perspective, and an utterance perspective. All three are necessary, of course, since registers are repertoires used in utterances by particular sociohistorical populations.

But let us first consider a more basic issue. How are registers identified by linguists?

3   METAPRAGMATIC STEREOTYPES OF USE

In order to find samples of a register the linguist requires a set of directions for locating instances of language use where tokens of the register occur and a criterion for differentiating these from other types of speech that occur in the same stretch of discourse. Here the linguist must turn to the competence of language users. Traditional discussions of registers have long relied on the assumption that language users make "value judgments" (Halliday 1964) about language form, that they are able to express "evaluative attitudes towards variant forms" (Ferguson 1994: 18). All empirical studies of registers rely on the metalinguistic ability of native speakers to discriminate between linguistic forms, to make evaluative judgments about variants.

The study of such evaluative behaviors allows linguists to distinguish a register's repertoires from the rest of the language and to reconstruct metapragmatic models of speech associated with them by language users. In the special case where a linguist studies a register of his or her native language, such evaluations are available in the form of introspectable intuitions. In general, however, linguists rely on native evaluations which are overtly expressed in publicly observable semiotic behavior. Such behavior may consist of language use: e.g., linguistic utterances which explicitly describe a register's forms and associated values; or, utterances which implicitly evaluate the indexical effects of cooccurring forms (as "next turn" responses to them, for example) without describing what they evaluate; such behavior may include non-linguistic semiotic activity as well, such as gestures, or the extended patterning of kinesic and bodily movements characteristic of ritual responses to the use of many registers. All such behaviors are metalinguistic in nature since they tell us something about the properties of linguistic forms whether by decontextualizing the forms and describing their properties or by evaluating their effects while the forms are still in play. Such evaluations tell us something, in particular, about the pragmatics of language – that is, the capacity of linguistic forms to index culturally recognizable activities, categories of actors, etc., as elements of the context of language use – thus constituting the class of metapragmatic evaluations of language.

Although such metapragmatic data are necessarily *overt* – in the sense of palpable, perceivable – they may or may not be linguistically expressed; and, if linguistic in character, such behaviors may or may not be denotationally *explicit* with respect to the properties ascribed to the register's forms. In their most explicit form, such evaluations consist of metapragmatic discourse, i.e. accounts which *describe* the pragmatics of speech forms. Several genres of metapragmatic discourse occur naturally in all language communities, for example, verbal reports and glosses of language use; names for registers and associated speech genres; accounts of typical or exemplary speakers; proscriptions on usage; standards of appropriate use; positive or negative assessments of the social worth of the register. In some cases such accounts are institutionalized in normative traditions of lexicography and grammatology; these play a different kind of role in establishing the register as a social formation and in maintaining or expanding the social domain of its users.

A register is a social regularity: a single individual's metapragmatic activity does not suffice to establish the social existence of a register unless confirmed in some way by the evaluative activities of others. Thus in identifying registers linguists observe not only that certain kinds of metapragmatic typifications *occur* in the evaluative behavior of language users but, more specifically, that certain patterns of typifications *recur* in the evaluative behaviors of many speakers. But in talking of recurrent typifications we have moved beyond individual acts of typification to the order of stereotypes of discourse.

To speak of *metapragmatic stereotypes* is to say that social regularities of metapragmatic typification can be observed and documented as data. The simplest kind of social regularity takes the following form: many persons typify criterial speech forms in the same way, for example, assigning the same metalinguistic predicates (e.g. "is slang," "is polite," "is used by older persons," etc.) to the forms at issue. But this is a very special case. In the more general case the scheme of valorization may exhibit various forms of *sociological fractionation* – including cases where one group resists the scheme of values upheld by another (countervalorization), or misrecognizes, or ideologically distorts, such values in fashioning norms for itself (see sections 5 and 9). The assumption that a register's forms and values are modelled symmetrically by all speakers (i.e., are "uniformly shared") is often a default assumption in many works in the literature. But the extent and degree of sharedness is an empirical question that requires systematic study in each case. The very possibility of such study lies in the fact that register distinctions are evidenced in overtly perceivable metapragmatic activity. Indeed, from an empirical standpoint, metapragmatic stereotypes are not ideas in the head. The main evidence for their existence lies in overt (publicly perceivable) evaluative behavior of the kinds described above, i.e., behavior embodied in sensorially palpable signs such as utterances, texts, gestures.

This aspect of metapragmatic activity – that it is expressible in publicly perceivable signs – is not just a matter of convenience to the analyst. It is *a necessary condition on the social existence of registers*. Let us consider why this is so.

4   STEREOTYPES AND SOCIALIZATION

Since the collection of individuals that we call a society is constantly changing in demographic composition (due to births, deaths, and migrations, for example) *the continuous historical existence* of a register depends upon mechanisms for the replication of its forms and values over changing populations (e.g., from generation to generation). The group of "users" of a register continuously changes and renews itself; hence the differentiable existence of the register, an awareness of its distinctive forms and values, must be communicable to new members of the group in order for the register to persist in some relatively constant way over time.

A minimal condition on such processes is that the typifications of speech through which register values are communicated to others, and hence circulated through society, be embodied in sensorially perceivable signs. Such processes depend upon interaction between people mediated by artifacts made by people – whether directly, as in the case of conversation (here the artifact, or thing made, is an utterance), or more indirectly through the production and use of more perduring artifacts (books, electronic media, other semiotically "readable" objects) that link persons to each other in communicative behavior across larger spans of space and time (Sapir 1949). In linking persons to each other such semiotic artifacts also link persons to a common set of representations of speech, both explicit and implicit ones, thus making possible the large-scale replication of register stereotypes across social populations.

4.1   Institutions of replication

To speak of the socialization of individuals to registers and of the replication of registers across populations is to look at the same issue from two different points of view. The latter large-scale perspective, focusing as it does on social practices and institutions, helps explain demographic regularities of individual competence. The spread of register competence in society is linked to metalinguistic institutions of diverse types, both formal and informal ones. These differ in the principles of recruitment whereby individuals come to be exposed to the process of socialization, and hence in the regions of social (demographic) space to which individuals competent in the register typically belong. Let us consider some examples.

Prescriptive socialization within the family plays a critical role in the early acquisition of many registers. In the case of honorific registers – registers associated with decorum, etiquette, and deference (see Agha 2002) – metapragmatic activity that prescribes appropriate use occurs commonly in most societies (see, e.g., Morford 1997; Smith-Hefner 1988). In the most transparent cases such acts are formulated as denotationally explicit injunctions to the child as addressee; but other, more implicitly prescriptive activity – such as jocular accounts of defective speech (Agha 1998), the implicit "modeling" of speech for bystanders (Errington 1998) – occurs as well. By communicating register distinctions to children such metapragmatic activity expands the social domain of register competence from one generation to the next within the family unit.

Processes of register socialization continue throughout adult life as well. One cannot become a doctor or a lawyer, for example, without acquiring the forms of speech appropriate to the practices of medicine or law, or without an understanding of the values – both cognitive and interactional – linked to their use. In these cases the process of language socialization typically involves extended affiliation with educational institutions, such as law school or medical school, through which individuals acquire proficiency in the use of profession-specific registers of the language. Overt prescription plays a role here but other types of more implicit metalinguistic activity occur routinely as well (Mertz 1998). Once acquired, proficiency in the register functions as a tacit emblem of group membership throughout adult life and, in cases such as law or medicine, may be treated as an index of achieved professional identity.

In societies with written scripts and mass literacy a variety of normative public institutions – such as educational institutions, traditions of lexicography and grammatology, school boards and national academies – serve as loci of public sphere legitimation and replication of register stereotypes over segments of the population. The effect is particularly marked for prestige registers such as the Standard Language. When effective, such methods may result in the growth or rise of a register formation in society by extending a more or less uniform competence in a prestige register over relatively large segments of the population. Yet processes of register dissemination and replication are inevitably constrained by principles that limit the participatory access of individuals to criterial institutions (e.g., mechanisms of gatekeeping in elite schools). Hence, in practice, register stereotypes and standards are never replicated perfectly over a population of speakers.

4.2   Social asymmetries

All speakers of a language do not acquire competence in all of its registers during the normal course of language socialization. In the case of registers of respect and etiquette, only individuals born into privileged circumstances tend to acquire competence over the most elaborate locutions. In the case of registers of scientific discourse competence over technical terminologies typically requires years of specialized schooling. In the case of registers associated with particular venues of commercial activity (the stock exchange, the publishing house, the advertising firm) proficiency in specialized terms is usually attained through socialization in the workplace. In many societies, certain lexical registers function as "secret languages" (thieves' argots, the registers of religious ritual, magical incantation, etc.) since their use is restricted to specialized groups by metapragmatic proscriptions against teaching the forms to outsiders.

Thus, two members of a language community may both be acquainted with a linguistic register, but not have the same degree of competence in its use. Many speakers can recognize certain registers of their language but cannot fully use or interpret them. The existence of registers therefore results in the creation of social boundaries within society, partitioning off language users into groups distinguished by differential access to particular registers, and to the social practices which they mediate; and through the creation and maintenance of asymmetries of power, privilege, and rank, as effects dependent on the above processes.

5   Stereotypes and Ideology

I observed earlier that registers often have an ideological – hence "distorting" – character. How does the "ideological" aspect of registers relate to the notion of stereotype discussed above? Now, to say that stereotypes of register form and value exist is merely to say that socially regular patterns of metapragmatic typification can be observed and documented as data. Such models are not "false" or "incorrect" in any definitional sense. The question of whether a system of stereotypes is ideological – in the sense of "distorting" – is empirically undecidable if an order of internally consistent stereotypes is viewed in isolation from all other observable facts. Yet register systems are typically found to be ideological formations – in several senses – when subjected to further kinds of empirical analysis. Why should this be so?

I observed earlier (section 3) that the activity of formulating hypotheses about register stereotypes employs many diverse kinds of data. *There is no necessity that the results of these data should be wholly consistent with each other for all speakers.* Indeed the logical basis of the claim that some order of stereotypes is ideological is that two sets of metapragmatic data imply the existence of distinct models. I now describe a few varieties of ideological distortion that are very common in languages of the world. I turn to ethnographic examples in the next section.

The first type of case involves the ideological character of *competing valorizations.* In so far as register systems vary society-internally particular socially positioned models may contrast with each other as alternative systems of normativity. Each is ideological from the perspective of the other in so far as it gets the (normative) facts incorrect. Why do competing models of normativity coexist in societies? Two kinds of reasons are very common. The first is merely a result of the asymmetries of replication noted above: individuals differ in their access to institutions through which register competence is reproduced over historical populations (e.g., some are born in elite families, attend elite schools; others lack these opportunities). Another reason is that systems of normative value invariably serve the interests of some speakers, not others; they are therefore subject to manipulation, differential allegiance, and society-internal competition. These factors often play a critical role in the sociohistorical transformation of register systems.

2/ A second ideological aspect of registers derives from the open-ended possibilities of *functional reanalysis*. Registers are open cultural systems in the sense that once a distinct register is culturally recognized as existing within a language, its repertoires are susceptible to further reanalysis and change. For example, when prestige registers spoken by privileged groups are emulated by others they are often perceived as "devalued" by speakers of that privileged group; the group frequently innovates in its speech, creating hyperlectal distinctions within prestige forms. In the case of repertoires of youth slang, which change very rapidly, forms that were once "cool" soon become passé and are replaced by new emblems of in-group identity; in this case, competence over "current" repertoires is frequently reanalyzed as a system of inter-generational positioning. Every such reanalysis is a "distortion" of a prior stage of the register that now constitutes a new system of enactable values. When the products of such reanalyses coexist synchronically within societies they contribute to systems of competing valorization – alternative models of normativity – in the sense noted above.

3/ A third reason that stereotypes have an ideological character is that stereotype judgments typically underdifferentiate the semiotic orders of *lexeme* and *text*. Native judgments about registers are often formulated as models of the pragmatic values of isolable words and expressions (e.g., that some words are inherently polite, some not). But since lexemes are never experienced in isolation from other signs in interaction, the effects of co-textual signs (i.e., signs cooccurring with the lexeme) may on a given occasion of use either be congruent with or, by degrees, may cancel the stereotypic effects of the lexeme in question. Register distinctions can thus be manipulated interactionally to achieve effects which – though dependent on the stereotypic values of particular lexemes – are, at the level of text, significantly at odds with such values. Common examples of this are cases such as the use of female speech by males, the use of honorific language to enact veiled aggression, the use of technical terminologies not to do technical work but to tell jokes about their users. In all of these cases the stereotypic values of a register's lexemes are implemented in discourse – they make certain personae recognizable through speech – but the devices in question are contextualized by other framing devices so that the overall effect of entextualized usage departs significantly from the stereotypic effect of the lexemes troped upon.

I now turn to a range of examples that illustrate the issues discussed above.

6   ENTEXTUALIZED TROPES

One sense in which registers are ideological constructs is that the range of effects that can be implemented through the contextualized use of a register is always much larger than the range of effects reported in explicit stereotypes of use. The reason is simple. When we speak of contextualized use we are no longer speaking of effects implemented by the register's tokens; we are concerned rather with the effects of an array of cooccurring signs of which the register token is a fragment. This larger – often multi-modal – array of signs itself implements semiotic effects that *may or may not be consistent* with the stereotypic values of the text-fragments that we recognize as the register's forms. Let us consider some examples.

6.1 Gender indexicals

In many languages differences of speech are enregistered as indexicals of speaker gender. The fact that the structure of these repertoires varies enormously from language to language is entirely unsurprising once we see that the unity of the register phenomenon derives not from aspects of language structure but from a metapragmatic model of language use.

Table 2.1 illustrates a phonolexical register of gender indexicals. In the Native American language Koasati, a phonolexical alternation between forms of -*s* and its absence distinguishes stereotypically male and female speech in indicative and imperative forms of the verb. Haas (1964) observed that language users readily formulate metapragmatic accounts linking form contrasts to speaker gender and employ such accounts in socializing children to the register: "parents were formerly accustomed to correct the speech of children of either sex, since each child was trained to use forms appropriate to his or her sex" (1964: 230). When fully socialized, however, adults are entirely aware that the register comprises a model of performable persona, one that can be manipulated in various ways: "Members of each sex are quite familiar with both types of speech and can use either as occasion demands." I return to this point below.

Table 2.2 illustrates a register of gender indexicals in Lakhota, whose formal repertoires are rather different. In this case the metapragmatic typifications offered by native speakers are highly comparable to the Koasati case (viz., "male" vs. "female" speech); but the *object repertoires* of the register (the forms that are objects of native typification) involve contrasts of sentence-final clitics rather than contrasts of verb stem.

Table 2.1 Phonolexical registers of speaker gender in Koasati

Gloss	A	B	Phonological alternations
(a) Repertoire contrasts			
1 'I lifted it'	lakawwilí	lakawwilí	—
2 'you are lifting it'	lakáwč	lakáwč	—
3 'he will lift it'	lakawwā̆ˇ	lakawwáˇs	-ā̆ˇ ~ -áˇs
4 'I am lifting it'	lakawwîl	lakawwís	-îl ~ -ís
5 'don't lift it'	lakawčîn	lakawčiˇs	-în ~ -îˇs
6 'he is lifting it'	lakáw	lakáws	-áw ~ -áws
	↓	↓	
(b) Metapragmatic stereotypes	"female"	"male"	

(*Source:* Haas 1964)

Table 2.2 Lexical registers of speaker gender in Lakhota

Illocutionary force	A	B
(a) Repertoire contrasts		
Formal questions	hųwe	hųwo
Command	ye	yo
Familiar command	nitʰo	yetʰo
Opinion/emphasis	yele, ye	yelo
Emphatic statement	kʃto	kʃt
Entreaty	na	ye
Surprise/opinion	yemą	yewą
	↓	↓
(b) Metapragmatic stereotypes	"female"	"male"

(*Source*: Trechter 1995)

In both cases – indeed, in all cases of the enregisterment of gender – the unity of the phenomenon derives not from a particular feature of grammatical structure but from a model of expected or appropriate conduct; and, in all cases, actual behavior may or may not conform to the model. But how is behavior that is contrary-to-stereotype construed by interlocutors?

Whereas folk models of language use typically link isolable pieces of language to variables of context, the actual use of a register's forms – its textual implementation – connects tokens of the register to other cooccurring signs by relations of contiguity or copresence; such surrounding material, both linguistic and non-linguistic in expression, forms a semiotic co-text that is itself construable. The construal of contrary-to-stereotype usage is mediated by features of co-text. The most transparently intelligible case of men uttering women's speech (or vice versa) occurs when the register is framed co-textually by a reported speech construction. Such constructions denotationally distinguish the utterer from the character reported, thus allowing men to utter women's speech, and vice versa, without taking on the characterological attributes of the other gender: "Thus if a man is telling a tale he will use women's forms when quoting a female character; similarly, if a woman is telling a tale she will use men's forms when quoting a male character" (Haas 1964: 229–30).

There are cases, however, of much more implicit framing by co-textual signs that give contrary-to-stereotype behavior a tropic significance; here the co-textual frame of the register token allows the usage to be construed as implying a metaphoric persona for the speaker. In the following Lakhota case, the utterance is produced by a man who unexpectedly sees his two-year-old nephew at his house one evening. The man uses male speech in the initial exclamation of surprise but switches to female speech in the segment in which he calls out to the child:

(1) Gender tropes in Lakhota (Trechter 1995: 10)

wąlewą	hiyu	wele:	'Look who's come!'
male: interjection: surprise	he: came	female: assertion	

The man's use of female speech is tantamount to an interactional trope, the performance of an affective, caring persona stereotypically associated with women speaking to young children. The usage is partly inappropriate (i.e., inappropriate to stereotypes of male speech) but construable in co-textual terms as conveying warmth, affection, and care toward the child. The construal of the utterance as a meaningful trope by someone – as involving speaker's warmth, affection, or other maternal qualities, for example – requires more than knowing facts of cultural enregisterment (viz., that *wele* is a female form); it requires access also to features of a participation framework (viz., that a man was speaking to a two-year-old; that the little child has turned up unexpectedly) that are readable from the semiotic co-text of utterance at the moment of speaking. Under such conditions, the usage, though contrary-to-stereotype along the dimension of speaker indexicality, is both meaningful and effective vis-à-vis its interactional frame.

6.2   Professional registers

Many register contrasts are stereotypically associated with forms of professional conduct, such as the law, medicine, and so on. Although the official rationale for the use of the register may have little to do with the performance of particular roles and relationships, the mere fact of register differentiation in language – that distinct registers are associated with distinct practices – generates paradigms of social identity linked to speech forms. Hence for audiences familiar with the register a competent display of its forms makes palpable a recognizable persona of the speaker and a typifiable mode of interpersonal engagement with interlocutors.

A classic early study of such a case is Ferguson's 1983 account of "sports announcer talk," a variety of speech used by sportscasters in radio and television broadcasts. The commercially routinized use of the variety involves a particular kind of electronically mediated setting in which the sportscaster has direct visual access to a sporting event, which unfolds concurrently with the broadcast, and the audience is a large, spatially distributed collectivity that may number in the millions. The dissemination of sports talk through the electronic media is a form of institutional replication that can expand awareness of the register as well. An avid sports fan has more than a passing acquaintance with this variety of talk. Moreover, anyone who is acquainted with the register – not necessarily a sportscaster – can employ the register in acts of strategic manipulation of roles and identities in a variety of ways.

The following illustrates the use of the register by two eight- and nine-year-old boys who employ sports announcer talk as a way of reframing their own game-playing activities. During the course of games like ping-pong and basketball the boys switch to the register of sports announcer talk in a spontaneous manner. In the excerpt the two boys, Ben and Josh, indexically depersonalize their current play activity by using last names in describing each other's actions; they also employ many of the devices noted in table 2.3 to inhabit the persona and mantle of a sports announcer. In this turn-by-turn engagement the players use the register competitively, as part of "the game."

(2) Tropes of speaker identity or persona in English (Hoyle 1993)

Josh: So eleven eight, Hoyle's lead.
        Hoyle serves it!

Ben Green cannot get it ... over the net
and it's twelve eight Hoyle's lead now.
Ben: Hoyle takes the lead by four.
Josh: [fast] Green serving.
        [fast] Hoyle returns it.
        THEY'RE HITTING IT BACK AND FORTH!
Ben: Ach-boo:m!
Josh: And Ben Green hits it over the table!
        And it i:s thirteen eight.
        Hoyle's lead.

Table 2.3   Some features of 'sports announcer talk'

- Omission of sentence-initial deictics (e.g., anaphors, determiners) and present-tense copula:
  e.g., *[It's a] pitch to uh Winfield. [It's a] strike. [It's] one and one*
- Preposed location and motion predicates:
  e.g., <u>*Over at third*</u> *is Murphy.* <u>*Coming left again*</u> *is Diamond*
- Preponderance of result expressions:
  e.g., *He throws <u>for</u> the out.*
- Epithets and heavy modifiers:
  e.g., <u>*left-handed throwing*</u> *Steve Howe* ...; *Larry Milburn,* <u>*3 for 4 yesterday*</u>, *did not face* ...
- Use of the simple present to describe contemporaneous activities:
  e.g., *Burt ready,* <u>*comes*</u> *to Winfield and it'<u>s</u> lined to left but Baker'<u>s</u> there and <u>backhands</u> a sinker then <u>throws</u> it to Lopez*

(*Source*: Ferguson 1983)

In the stretches of talk where the sports announcer register is used there is clearly a second-order game going on – quite distinct from the ping-pong itself! – a game which is played entirely through talk, and whose object is to control representations of the first-order game in a persona more authoritative than the boys' own. When problems arise within the ping-pong game itself (e.g., scorekeeping disputes, arguments about the rules, external events that interfere with the game) the boys switch back to everyday speech, thus abandoning the sportscaster persona in favor of the now more pressing concerns of the first-order game (see Hoyle 1993 for further details). Hence the switching back and forth between sportscasting and everyday registers corresponds to a switching between imaginary and real identities keyed to specific interpersonal ends within this complex bout of "play."

7   FRAGMENTARY CIRCULATION

The young boys who employ the register of sports announcer talk in the above example do not do so consistently or with a full command of its niceties. Indeed the fragmentary nature of their usage – particularly the switching back and forth between everyday and sportscasting registers – constitutes the particular kind of multi-leveled play in which these two individuals are engaged. Yet when registers are used in a fragmentary way in public sphere discourses such fragmentary usage can have broader sociological consequences too.

When a register that is regularly employed in one social practice is deployed in a partial or fragmentary way in another, such a usage may confer some legitimacy – a peppering of prestige – upon its speaker/author, particularly when the target audience is unfamiliar with authentic uses of the source register. The use of statistics by insurance salesmen, or of terms from psychology in popular "self help" books, has something of this character. But such fragmentary use may also have consequences for the competence of the hearer or reader. Thus watching courtroom dramas or war movies on television does equip the audience with a smattering of legal and military terminology – enough perhaps to recognize some terms and expressions, to engage in language play and jokes – though not usually enough to write a legal brief or, thankfully, to mount a military campaign.

Systematic access to register distinctions requires much more careful methods. The data of military terminology in table 2.4 were gathered through a study of military documents (Lutz 1990). How was the analyst able to find the corpus? By employing native metapragmatic classifications, including terms for speech varieties and their users, as a set of directions for finding published samples of military discourse – Pentagon manuals, defense department contracts, course catalogs at military academies, and the like – where elaborate uses of this written register occur. For most English speakers only a fragmentary exposure occurs – mostly through forms of popular media, fiction, and the like – that may acquaint ordinary speakers with the existence of the register, and even a passing familiarity with some of its forms; e.g., *surgical strike* and *collateral damage* are now widely known, especially given media coverage of recent wars. Yet most of the forms in table 2.4 are unfamiliar and perhaps ludicrous to the Standard ear.

Hence even to speak of "competence" in a register requires a distinction between *types* of competence. I said earlier that no speaker of a language fully commands more than a few of its registers; we may now observe that most speakers of a language are aware of the existence of many more registers than they fully command, that is, they can passively recognize a much larger range of registers than they can actively (fluently) employ in their own speech. Hence, for many registers, the *competence to recognize* the register's forms has a wider social distribution (i.e., is an ability possessed by many more persons) than *the competence to use* its forms. Such asymmetries of competence may even function as principles of value maintenance under certain

Table 2.4 American military register

Pentagon lexicon ("Militarese")	Standard English
aerodynamic personnel decelerator	parachute
frame-supported tension structure	tent
personal preservation flotation device	life jacket
interlocking slide fastener	zipper
wood interdental stimulator	toothpick
vertically deployed anti-personnel device	bomb
portable handheld communications inscriber	pencil
pre-dawn vertical insertion	a night-time parachute drop
manually powered fastener-driving impact device	hammer

(*Source*: Lutz 1990)

conditions. In the case of certain prestige registers (e.g., forms of upper-caste/class speech) the register is widely recognized in society, but spoken fluently by very few persons. The fact that it is positively valued by a group larger than its fluent speakers may create conditions where the register, now a scarce good, becomes a sought-after commodity – even one that can be purchased for a price, through schooling, elocution lessons, and the like (Honey 1989).

8   REFLEXIVE PROCESSES: STATIC VERSUS DYNAMIC MODELS

In a review of the early literature on registers Douglas Biber observes that "most register studies have been atheoretical" (1994: 36), tending to employ static taxonomic and descriptive schemes rather than principled definitions. Recent work has focused more on reflexive semiotic processes and institutions (Silverstein 1996; Agha 1998, 2002; Irvine and Gal 2000) through which register distinctions are effectively maintained and transformed in social life. Let me now comment on the way in which the reflexive approach to registers advocated here improves upon and moves beyond the limitations of earlier, more static approaches.

The term "register" was first coined by T. B. W. Reid in the course of a discussion of functionally significant differences in language use. Reid proposed that differences of utterance-form involve differences of "register" whenever distinct forms are viewed as appropriate to "different social situations" by users (Reid 1956). Although the intention behind the definition was to illuminate forms of action – e.g., Reid speaks of "systems of linguistic activity" as his larger space of concern – Reid's formulation remained incomplete in several respects: it lacked a theory of how speech was linked to "social situations" in the first place, how such links were identified by the analyst, and how register use could meaningfully extend beyond the special case of "appropriate use." I have observed above that the link between speech and situation involves a metapragmatic model of action (section 2); that its recovery by analysts is based on the study of socially situated evaluative data (3); and that the significance of utterances is inevitably a matter of patterns of entextualization, some among which trope upon the model itself (6).

Some of the early difficulties – particularly anxieties about "the discreteness of registers and the validity of register boundaries" (Ferguson 1982: 55) – derive from Reid's choice of terminology itself. The term "register" is a pluralizable count noun of English that formulates a suggestion about the social phenomenon that it denotes – a default Whorfian projection, or implication about denotatum (see Silverstein 1979; Lee 1997) – that is fraught with difficulties: the pluralizability of the term implies that register-s are collections of objects – like button-s and pebble-s – that can be identified and enumerated in an unproblematic way. Yet unlike collections of pebbles the registers of a language have a differentiable existence only in so far as – and as long as – they are treated by language users as functionally recognized partitions within the total inventory of its expressive means. The countable-and-pluralizable view of registers has other misleading implications, for example, that each register is a closed set of forms, that each member of the set is endowed with "inherent" pragmatic values, and so on.

Now every register does involve a repertoire of forms. But the boundaries of the register depend on the social-semiotic processes described earlier. A register exists as a bounded object only to a degree set by sociohistorical processes of *enregisterment*, processes by which the forms and values of a register become differentiable from the rest of the language (i.e., recognizable as distinct, linked to typifiable social personae or practices) for a given population of speakers. From the processual perspective sketched above it should be clear that worries about the discreteness of register boundaries are fruitless and misplaced since there exist in every society social-semiotic processes through which various kinds of boundaries and limits associated with registers can be reset in regular ways. Relative to such processes, every register exhibits various kinds of growth and decline, expansion or narrowing, change or stabilization. Three dimensions of register change are particularly noteworthy, as indicated in table 2.5.

The repertoire characteristics of a register, dimension A, include features such as repertoire size, grammatical range, and semiotic range (see section 10). As registers become centered in formal metadiscursive institutions – such as national academies, schooling, traditions of lexicography, the work of corporations – the repertoire of the register may grow over time, such elaboration resulting in part from processes of institutional codification.

Changes in pragmatic value, dimension B, are cases where the stereotypic effects of usage undergo a degree of functional reanalysis and change. When Standard Languages arise out of regional dialects – such as Parisian French or London English, to take familiar European cases – the derived national Standard no longer effectively marks speaker's locale but comes to index the non-specificity of speaker's place of origin. In most societies, and for the majority of speakers, regional dialects are acquired first through socialization in the family, and the national Standard acquired later through formal institutions such as schooling. Hence competence in the Standard language commonly becomes emblematic of additional attributes, such as speaker's class or level of education; such attributes sometimes function as status entitlements – facilitating access, for example, to select social circles, higher-wage employment, upper echelons of government service, and other privileges (see Honey

Table 2.5 Some dimensions of register organization and change

A. **Repertoire characteristics**
- Repertoire size: number of forms
- Grammatical range: number of form-classes in which register forms occur
- Semiotic range: types of linguistic and non-linguistic signs associated with the register's use (lexical, prosodic, kinesic)

B. Range of **pragmatic values**
- Stereotypes of user, usage, setting of use
- Positive or negative values associated with the register

C. **Social domain(s)** of the register
- Categories of persons that can recognize (at least some of) the register's forms
- Categories of persons fully competent in the use of the register

1989) – that are less accessible to those speaking non-Standard varieties of the language.

These changes are often linked to changes in the social domain of the register, namely dimension C in table 2.5. Formal institutions often play an official role in expanding competence over prestige registers of a language – through programs that expand literacy, primary education, or specialized training for particular professions; however, other more informal and seemingly disinterested types of institutional mechanisms invariably play a role as well. Specific genres of public media (including entertainment genres) serve as carriers for many kinds of popular registers, serving to expand their social domains over particular populations. In the case of Anglo-American teenage slang, genres such as pop music, the movies, teen lifestyle magazines, and the like have, since the 1950s, made possible the creation of national teenage slangs which have forms that are common to youth populations in many different geographic locales (Hudson 1983).

Thus although dimensions such as A–C can in principle be characterized for any register, any such account is merely a sociohistorical snapshot of a phase of enregisterment of linguistic features for particular users. Changes along these dimensions are often linked to one another. Indeed, as the social domain of the register (C) changes – e.g., as in the social expansion of scientific registers of chemistry or medicine in recent times, or through the disappearance of once firmly institutionalized forms of discourse, such as alchemy – both the repertoires and the stereotypic effects of their use are inevitably transformed.

9   Sociological Fractionation

The above considerations should make clear that registers are social formations, but not necessarily *sociologically homogenous* formations. To say that they are social formations is to observe that metapragmatic stereotypes of speech that are criterial in the identification of registers *have a social domain*, that is, are replicable across some population of evaluators. But register stereotypes rarely have a maximal distribution (i.e., are rarely invariant for *all* speakers of the language). In many of the most interesting cases competing models of aspects of a register coexist within the same society, each potentially ideological or distorting from the perspective of the other.

The simplest type of such case is when two different stereotypes associated with the same form have different social domains. In the case of honorific registers, for instance, it is commonly observed that two speakers will identify the same form as honorific but will specify different conditions for its appropriate use. Now, both kind of evaluations – that a form "is honorific" and that it "is used under such-and-such conditions" – are metapragmatic typifications of the form's pragmatic values. The point at issue now is that both may be socially regular – may function as stereotypes – but for *different* social domains of evaluators.

Let us consider an example. Speakers of French readily agree that the second-person pronoun *vous* is polite in pragmatic effect (and that *tu* is not specifically polite); this, then, is a metapragmatic stereotype about the lexeme *vous*, one having a wide social domain. The persons who assent to the lexeme stereotype can be divided into sub-groups with respect to various standards of appropriate usage. Janet Morford shows that a particular pattern of *vous* usage – "having your children say *vous* to you" – is held to be unacceptable by lower-class speakers; it is described as snobbish, a way of putting on airs (Morford 1997). In contrast, upper-class speakers view this pattern of usage as a sign of the family's refinement and class position. In this case, stereotypes of lexeme value are the same for the two groups: both agree that the lexeme *vous* is polite. But stereotypes of appropriate use by children diverge by social class; these differences are reanalyzed as emblems of contrastive family status.

Such a reanalysis of variation-in-use into emblems of group status frequently reveals something of the larger social processes that connect groups to each other. The case of Egyptian Arabic, as reported by Alrabaa (1985), is particularly instructive in this regard. Alrabaa's study is a questionnaire-based investigation of stereotypes of use associated with the informal and solidary pronouns *inta / inti* 'you (m./f.)' and the more formal pronouns *ḥaḍritak/ḥaḍritik* 'you (m./f.); polite'. At the level of stereotypes of speaker persona, upper-class and lower-class youths offer different models of usage that are, moreover, mirror images of each other. Upper-class youths claim to use the solidary/informal forms, which they believe lower-class speakers to use; and lower-class speakers lay claim to more polite/formal lexemes, which they perceive as upper/middle-class usage. A comparison of stereotypes of self and other usage thus reveals that each social group ideologically formulates a self-positioning modeled on perceptions of the other. Upper-class youths are motivated by an ideology of egalitarianism to adopt what they perceive as "the system of 'the people' (*al-sha'b*)." Lower-class users are motivated by a more stratificational ideology, an emulation of "what they presume to be the middle-class values" (Alrabaa 1985: 649).

A particularly important source of such folk stereotypes in modern societies is the circulation of representations of speech and speakers in genres of public sphere discourses, including the mass media. Alrabaa gives us a glimpse of the processes relevant to the Egyptian case: "In off-the-record comments during our interviews, both older and younger upper-class informants did often express a conviction that lower-class informants would be 'looser,' less formal, etc. This upper-class belief is also reflected in many movies and television comedies, which frequently present a stereotype of the bawdy, raucous lower-class character who addresses all listeners as *inta / inti* = [German] *Du*, [French] *tu*" (p. 648).

An awareness of the fact that stereotypes of usage differ society-internally often motivates tropes of identity that play upon such stereotypes. Thus in the French case

Table 2.6 Egyptian Arabic: positional stereotypes of self and other

	Group₁: Upper-class youths	Group₂: Lower-class youths
Stereotype of self-report	claim to use solidary *inta/inti* forms	claim greater use of the formal *ḥaḍritak/ḥaḍritik* pronouns
Stereotype of others' usage	say that lower-class speakers use the *inta/inti* forms	say that upper/middle-class speakers use the *ḥaḍritak/ḥaḍritik* forms
Ideological positioning	egalitarian (self-lowering)	stratificational (self-raising)

(*Source*: Alrabaa 1985)

above – where the pattern of interactional text "using *vous* for one's parents" is stereotypically viewed as an emblem of upper-class families – Morford reports the case of an upper-class individual who, when seeking to enter politics, asked his children to switch from *vous* to *tu* in addressing him in public; the goal here is strategic, an effort to perform a more demotic image of his own class origins in the electoral process (Morford 1997).

A parallel case – now involving age and generation, rather than class – is reported in Swedish by Paulston (1976). In the period in which the study was conducted (*ca.* 1970), the use of the polite pronoun *ni* was already undergoing reanalysis and replacement by the use of informal *du* in many social situations. In address among strangers, the use of *ni* still remained the norm for older, upper-class speakers; the use of *du* in this setting was expanding but associated largely with younger speakers. Awareness of the stereotype allowed a range of interactional tropes, such as the following: "Even some 70-year-old upper-class ladies find it agreeable to be ad-dressed as *du* in the street; they say it makes them feel younger" (1976: 367). The capacity of the usage to make someone "feel younger" is a direct consequence of the existence of a culture-internal stereotype associating *du* usage with young people. The stereotype provides a framework for evaluating the unexpected usage and yields the trope of perceived identity as a performed effect.

10 SEMIOTIC RANGE

My final remarks concern the semiotic range – the range of semiotic devices that exist as elements – of a register's repertoires. Linguists have long been interested in the linguistic signs that belong to a register's repertoires. Yet since registers involve cultural models of speech pragmatics (e.g., that a particular speech repertoire is appropriate to a type of conduct) such models are easily extended to accompanying non-linguistic signs. Hence a register's linguistic repertoires often comprise only a part of its semiotic range, the range of devices deployed routinely and appropriately in its use.

Registers of oral discourse differ from written registers in the kind of semiotic range possible. In written registers of scientific prose, for example, various forms of non-linguistic (pictorial, diagrammatic) display cooccur with the use of specialized terminologies, a feature of scientific discourse that influences its lexico-syntactic conventions as well. A variety of non-linguistic devices – photographs, typography, specialized uses of color, serial arrangement, other visual signs – cooccur routinely with distinctive linguistic repertoires in many other written registers, such as those of commercial advertisement (Toolan 1988), "compressed English" (Sinclair 1988), newspaper headlines (Carter 1988), invoices and service contracts (Bex 1996), and others.

The semiotic range of *spoken* registers is typically linked to the kinds of displays that are possible in face-to-face interaction. In the case of registers of honorific speech (Agha 2002) the utterance of honorific expressions in many languages is felt to be most appropriate when accompanied by particular forms of physical and material display, such as prosodic and kinesic activity, bodily comportment, dress, arti-factual display, seating arrangement, order of rising and sitting down, and the like

(Duranti 1992). Part of the reason that stereotypes of use (including norms of appropriate use) that are associated with linguistic signs are often extended to non-linguistic signs is that metapragmatic terms used by language users to formulate specifically metalinguistic accounts may also be used to formulate more broadly metasemiotic accounts. Thus when we look across languages we find that terms such as "politeness," "refinement," or "respectability" are often used to articulate and prescribe norms of utterance; but these terms are used for non-linguistic activities as well, such as lowering the head, bowing, putting palms together, dressing appropriately, and so on. For example, the Thai term *mâi suphâap* 'impolite' is predicable of utterances and kinesic activity but also of physical objects: "casual sandals and revealing or immodest women's clothes ... are called *mâi suphâap* 'impolite' and symbolize a lack of concern and respect for authority" (Simpson 1997: 42).

Such classifications generate likenesses between otherwise disparate signs – clothing, gesture, speech, etc. – by linking all of them to norms of politeness. All of these signs can, moreover, cooccur with each other in social interaction. The fact that sign repertoires in different channels receive a unified (or at least overlapping) metasemiotic treatment has the consequence that certain kinds of socially valued language are felt to be used most felicitously and appropriately when accompanied by certain kinds of non-linguistic displays. Consider the following example from Javanese:

> A complicated etiquette dictates the way a person sits, stands, directs his eyes, holds his hands, points, greets people, laughs, walks, dresses, and so on. There is a close association between the rigor with which the etiquette of movement is observed and the degree of refinement in speech. The more polite a person's language, the more elaborate are his other behavioral patterns; the more informal his speech, the more relaxed and simplified his gestures. (Poedjosoedarmo 1968: 54)

Cases of this kind involve a type of *cross-modal iconism* whereby forms of polite speech are treated as resembling signs of other kinds – paralanguage, gesture, body comportment, artifactual accompaniment – in interpersonal significance. Such likenesses do not exist naturally or inertly, of course; they are actively motivated by metasemiotic discourses and practices of various kinds.

In the Javanese case the ethnometapragmatic terms *alus* 'refined, polite' and *kasar* 'coarse' are central to such norms of deference and demeanor. The term *kasar* 'coarse' is used to describe semiotic behaviors of many kinds, including a register of lexemes (table 2.7) and one involving prosodic patterns (table 2.8).

The forms of the *kasar* lexical register are grasped by native speakers in terms of highly negative stereotypes of use and user: "*Kasar* words are always considered vulgar. They are not usually used by the upper class. Even lower class people usually use them only in anger" (1968: 64). The contrasts are therefore conceptualized – particularly by upper-class persons – as differentiating a system of speaker-focal demeanor indexicals, i.e., as forms that make palpable characterological attributes of speaker. The term *kasar* is also associated with prosodic contrasts that index similar speaker attributes (see table 2.8); specific values of a range of prosodic features, including speech tempo, volume, and dynamic range, are treated as instances of

Table 2.7 Javanese *kasar* 'coarse' vocabularies

	Gloss	Ngoko *'ordinary'*	Kasar *'coarse'*
Nouns:	eye	*mripat*	*mata*
	mouth	*tjangkem*	*tjatjat*
	stomach	*weteng*	*wadhoq*
Adjectives:	dead	*mati*	*modar*
	pregnant	*meteng*	*mblendheng, busong*
	stupid	*bodho*	*gablag*
Verbs:	eat	*mangan*	*mbadhag*
	copulate	*saresmi*	*laki*

(*Source*: Poedjosoedarmo 1968)

Table 2.8 Javanese *kasar* 'coarse' prosody

	Alus 'refined'	*Kasar* 'coarse'
Tempo:	slower	more rapid
Volume:	softer	louder
Dynamic range:	more monotonous intonation	greater extremes of intonation

(*Source*: Poedjosoedarmo 1968: 55)

kasar 'coarse' behavior, and gradiently opposed values along each dimension of contrast as *alus* 'refined'.

Hence from the standpoint of this cultural scheme *kasar* 'crude, coarse' demeanor is exhibited by *both* lexemes (table 2.7) and prosodic patterns (table 2.8). The term *kasar* is now a metasemiotic construct used to typify otherwise disparate phenomenal behaviors. Such behaviors are now likened to each other – grouped together – under a metasemiotic classification, one which brings diverse object-signs, such as prosodic and lexical forms, under characterological rubrics, such as coarseness, that are indirectly associated with caste and class distinctions (see also Irvine 1990).

11 CONCLUSION

I have been arguing that the phenomenon of register inevitably involves models of enactable behavior linked to performable signs of various kinds. Although my main concern has been with registers of language I have argued that such models are easily extendable to non-linguistic signs by the same general processes through which they come to be linked to language in the first place. Whether the object-signs are linguistic or non-linguistic, or both, the metasemiotic processes through which awareness of register classifications is formulated and disseminated invariably involve language use as part of the total process.

I have observed also that registers are historically changing systems that are shaped by processes linking groups to each other in social space. In some cases the social domain of persons acquainted with the register is tightly delimited by institutional processes; other registers have a more amorphous social distribution. Thus to understand the social existence of a register requires some clarity not only about the metapragmatic models that typify its forms and values but an understanding also of the social processes through which such models are institutionally disseminated across social populations.

Finally, the actual use of a register may fully conform to the metapragmatic model associated with its repertoires (e.g., when a legal register is used appropriately within a court of law) or it may not. In the latter case a range of tropes of personhood, enacted conduct, relationship to interlocutor, and the like, are mediated by the model itself and can be played upon – even manipulated – through contextualization by accompanying signs. This type of flexibility in use is one of the most interesting features of register systems and hence a point that I have illustrated with numerous examples in the discussion above.

REFERENCES

Agha, A. (1998). Stereotypes and Registers of Honorific Language. *Language in Society* 27(2): 151–194.

Agha, A. (2002). Honorific Registers. In K. Kataoka and S. Ide (eds.), *Culture, Interaction and Language* (pp. 21–63). Tokyo: Hituzisyobo.

Alrabaa, S. (1985). The Use of Address Pronouns by Egyptian Adults. *Journal of Pragmatics* 9: 645–657.

Bex, T. (1996). Cohesion, Coherence and Register. In T. Bex, *Variety in Written English*, ch. 5 (pp. 90–112). London: Routledge.

Biber, D. (1994). An Analytic Framework for Register Studies. In D. Biber and E. Finegan (eds.), *Sociolinguistic Perspectives on Register* (pp. 31–56). New York: Oxford University Press.

Carter, R. (1988). Front Pages: Lexis, Style and Newspaper Reports. In M. Ghadessy (ed.), *Registers of Written English* (pp. 8–16). London: Pinter.

Duranti, A. (1992). Language and Bodies in Social Space: Samoan Ceremonial Greetings. *American Anthropologist* 94: 657–691.

Eble, C. (1996). *Slang and Sociability: In-group Language among College Students.* Chapel Hill: University of North Carolina Press.

Errington, J. J. (1998). *Shifting Languages: Interaction and Identity in Javanese Indonesia.* New York: Cambridge University Press.

Ferguson, C. A. (1982). Simplified Registers and Linguistic Theory. In L. K. Obler and L. Menn (eds.), *Exceptional Language and Linguistics* (pp. 49–66). New York: Academic Press.

Ferguson, C. A. (1983). Sports Announcer Talk: Syntactic Aspects of Register Variation. *Language in Society* 12: 153–172.

Ferguson, C. A. (1994). Dialect, Register and Genre: Working Assumptions about Conventionalization. In D. Biber and E. Finegan (eds.), *Sociolinguistic Perspectives on Register* (pp. 15–30). New York: Oxford University Press.

Ghadessy, M. (ed.) (1988). *Registers of Written English: Situational Factors and Linguistic Features.* London: Pinter.

Gordon, D. P. (1983). Hospital Slang for Patients: Crocks, Gomers, Gorks and Others. *Language in Society* 13: 173–185.

Haas, M. (1964). Men's and Women's Speech in Koasati. In D. Hymes (ed), *Language in Culture and Society* (pp. 228–233). New York: Harper and Row.

Halliday, M. A. K. (1964). The Users and Uses of Language. In M. A. K. Halliday, A. Macintosh, and P. Strevens (eds.), *The Linguistic Sciences and Language Teaching* (pp. 75–110). Bloomington: Indiana University Press.

Halliday, M. A. K. (1988). On the Language of Physical Science. In M. Ghadessy (ed.), *Registers of Written English* (pp. 162–178). London: Pinter.

Hill, J. H. (1998). "Today There Is no Respect": Nostalgia, "Respect," and Oppositional Discourse in Mexicano (Nahuatl) Language Ideology. In B. B. Schieffelin, K. A. Woolard, and P. V. Kroskrity (eds.), *Language Ideologies: Practice and Theory* (pp. 68–86). New York: Oxford University Press.

Honey, J. (1989). *Does Accent Matter? The Pygmalion Factor.* London: Faber and Faber.

Hoyle, S. M. (1993). Participation Frameworks in Sportscasting Play: Imaginary and Literal Footings. In D. Tannen (ed.), *Framing in Discourse* (pp. 114–145). New York: Oxford University Press.

Hudson, K. (1983). Pop Music as Cultural Carrier. In K. Hudson, *The Language of the Teenage Revolution*, ch. 3 (pp. 36–52). London: Macmillan.

Irvine, J. T. (1990). Registering Affect: Heteroglossia in the Linguistic Expression of Emotion. In C. A. Lutz and L. Abu-Lughod (eds.), *Language and the Politics of Emotion* (pp. 126–161). Cambridge: Cambridge University Press.

Irvine, J. T. and Gal, S. (2000). Language Ideology and Linguistic Differentiation. In P. V. Kroskrity (ed.), *Regimes of Language* (pp. 35–84). Santa Fe, NM: School of American Research Press.

Lee, B. (1997). *Talking Heads: Language, Metalanguage, and the Semiotics of Subjectivity.* Durham, NC: Duke University Press.

Lutz, W. (1990). *Doublespeak.* New York: Harper Collins.

Maurer, D. (1955). *Whiz Mob: A Correlation of the Technical Argot of Pickpockets with Their Behavior Pattern.* Gainesville, FL: American Dialect Society.

Mehrotra, R. R. (1977). *The Sociology of Secret Languages.* Delhi: Indian Institute of Advanced Study.

Mertz, E. (1998). Linguistic Ideology and Praxis in U.S. Law School Classrooms. In B. B. Schieffelin, K. A. Woolard, and P. V. Kroskrity (eds.), *Language Ideologies: Practice and Theory* (pp. 149–162). New York: Oxford University Press.

Morford, J. (1997). Social Indexicality and French Pronominal Address. *Journal of Linguistic Anthropology* 7(1): 3–37.

Nash, W. (1993). *Jargon: Its Uses and Abuses.* Oxford: Blackwell.

Paulston, C. B. (1976). Pronouns of Address in Swedish: Social Class Semantics and a Changing System. *Language in Society* 5: 359–386.

Poedjosoedarmo, S. (1968). Javanese Speech Levels. *Indonesia* 6: 54–81.

Reid, T. B. W. (1956). Linguistics, Structuralism and Philology. *Archivum Linguisticum* 8(1): 28–37.

Sapir, E. (1949). Communication. In D. G. Mandelbaum (ed.), *Selected Writings of Edward Sapir* (pp. 104–110). Berkeley: University of California Press.

Silverstein, M. (1979). Language Structure and Linguistic Ideology. In P. R. Clyne, W. F. Hanks, and C. L. Hofbauer (eds.), *The Elements: A Parasession on Linguistic Units and Levels* (pp. 193–247). Chicago: Chicago Linguistic Society.

Silverstein, M. (1996). Monoglot "Standard" in America: Standardization and Metaphors of Linguistic Hegemony. In D. Brenneis and R. Macaulay (eds.), *The Matrix of Language: Contemporary Linguistic Anthropology* (pp. 284–306). Boulder, CO: Westview Press.

Simpson, R. S. (1997). Metapragmatic Discourse and the Ideology of Impolite Pronouns in Thai. *Journal of Linguistic Anthropology* 7(1): 38–62.

Sinclair, J. (1988). Compressed English. In M. Ghadessy (ed.), *Registers of Written English* (pp. 130–136). London: Pinter.

Smith-Hefner, N. J. (1988). The Linguistic Socialization of Javanese Children in Two Communities. *Anthropological Linguistics* 30(2): 166–198.

Toolan, M. (1988). The Language of Press Advertising. In M. Ghadessy (ed.), *Registers of Written English* (pp. 52–64). London: Pinter.

Trechter, S. (1995). Categorical Gender Myths in Native America: Gender Deictics in Lakhota. Special Issue: Sociolinguistics and Language Minorities, *Issues in Applied Linguistics* 6(1): 5–22.

3 Language Contact and Contact Languages

Paul B. Garrett

1 INTRODUCTION

One of the more intriguing episodes of language contact, and surely one of the best-documented, begins in 1789 in the aftermath of the now legendary mutiny on the *Bounty*. Having put Captain William Bligh and those crewmen who had remained loyal to him into an open boat and cast them adrift, the twenty-five mutineers now faced another concern: avoiding capture by the British navy. Their first destination was the Polynesian island of Tubai (about 300 miles south of Tahiti), but they soon came into conflict with the island's inhabitants; so they set sail once again, this time for Tahiti, where Captain Bligh and the crew had enjoyed an extraordinarily warm reception during a previous visit. Sixteen of the mutineers opted to remain there – and were taken into custody when a British vessel arrived some months later (Shapiro 1968: 27–48).

The other nine mutineers, fearing just such an eventuality, had decided to forgo the known pleasures of Tahiti and to seek a more remote place of refuge. Of these nine, four were English and two Scottish; there was also one American sailor, one from Guernsey, and one (of British heritage) from the Caribbean island of St. Christopher. They took with them six Polynesian men (as "servants") and twelve women ("consorts"), one of whom had a young daughter with her. The group eventually put ashore on the uninhabited South Pacific island of Pitcairn. From the outset, the tiny settlement was fraught with tensions, both inter-ethnic and interpersonal. By 1800, only one of the nine mutineers remained alive (most of the others having died violent deaths), along with ten of the Polynesian women and twenty-three children who had been born on the island (Holm 1989: 546–51; Sebba 1997: 136–40).

The Pitcairn settlement was discovered by the crew of a British navy ship in 1814. They were astonished to find that the children and youth spoke fluently a language unlike any that they had heard before (although it seemed a kind of decidedly "ungrammatical" English). It is now known that this language, a creole now referred to as Pitcairnese – or *Pitkern*, in the language itself – combined elements of Tahitian and the various Englishes spoken by the original nine mutineers. Although the founding adults of the settlement presumably had continued using their native languages with those who shared them, another code had emerged to facilitate communication among those of differing linguistic backgrounds.[1] It was this new code that their children had acquired from birth.

Published data and research on Pitkern are surprisingly scarce. One piece of continuous text, the chorus of a song, is shown below (from Sebba 1997: 138–9):

Ai law yuu mais darlen	I love you my darling
Tek mii lornga yuu	Take me with you
Dem ai f'yoen miek mais haat kepsais	Your eyes make my heart capsize
Yus haan iin main daa tenda	Your hand in mine is so tender
Miek ai fiil guud	It makes me feel good
Yuu d'wan iin mais haat mais darlen	You're the one in my heart my darling
Ai law yuu.	I love you.

Pitkern's lexicon is clearly derived primarily from English; certain words can even be traced to the specific dialects (e.g. Scots) that were spoken by particular mutineers (Holm 1989: 550). There is phonological influence from Tahitian, which contributed various lexical items itself; these in turn were influenced phonologically by the mutineers' Englishes. But Pitkern is not just a haphazard mix of Tahitian and English, and some of its grammatical features are not clearly attributable to either of its two source languages. Significantly, however, among these are features that Pitkern has in common with numerous creole languages around the world.

Much less is known about the circumstances under which most other contact languages have taken form. In the vast majority of cases, the populations involved have been much larger, and the relevant historical records are both far more complex and far less complete. Like Pitkern, however, most of these languages are of quite recent origin, having arisen no more than three to four centuries ago in contexts associated with European exploration and colonialism. The tantalizing possibility of reconstructing their developmental trajectories from available evidence and accounting for differing degrees of influence from different sources has made these languages intriguing to investigators in several disciplines. According to McWhorter (1997: 175–6), the following brief sentence in Saramaccan (a creole language of Suriname) contains lexical and structural elements traceable to English, Portuguese, and Dutch as well as the African languages Kikongo, Igbo, and Gbe:

Hεn wε wan dáka, dí mujέε-miíi táki dεεn tatá táa un kέ pindá
'So one day the girl told her father that you wanted peanuts'

Saramaccan is more than just an amalgam of these several languages, however: it is the outcome of a complex intersection of linguistic, historical, and social processes, "a language spoken fluently every day by people, many monolingual, of a distinct and established culture." As this suggests, the ongoing developmental trajectories of contact languages also demand attention, for like all languages they continue to change over time. Pitkern, although still spoken today by descendants of the original twenty-eight settlers, is reported to be going into decline (Sebba 1997: 138). Haitian Creole and Papua New Guinea's Tok Pisin, in contrast, are each spoken by millions of people and have been standardized and officialized as languages of formal instruction, literacy, and government. Meanwhile new contact languages are taking shape around the world, such as "Town Bemba" in urban Zambia since the 1950s (Spitulnik 1998), *Gastarbeiterdeutsch* ("guest-worker German") in German cities since the early 1980s (Blackshire-Belay 1993), and *Idioma de Señas Nicaragüense* ('Nicaraguan Sign Language') within a newly constituted Deaf community in Nicaragua since 1980 (Kegl, Senghas, and Coppola 1999; Senghas 2003).

2 DEFINITIONS AND APPROACHES

Contact languages will be defined here as those languages and language varieties, of varying degrees of stability and historical depth, that are known historically to have emerged from situations of social contact, of varying durations and degrees of intensity, among speakers of two or more previously existing languages. Typically (as seen above), similarities between a given contact language and one or more of its source languages can readily be identified – in the lexicon or in particular grammatical subsystems, for example. The contact language is not fully mutually intelligible with any of these pre-existing languages, however, and is used within some community of speakers (broadly conceived) in which an autonomous set or subset of norms for its use has also emerged. The contact language is thus sufficiently distinct from its source languages to be regarded more or less unproblematically – on structural, historical, and ethnographic grounds, if not necessarily on political and ideological grounds – as a discrete code.[2]

The emergence of a contact language is one possible outcome of language contact, but it is not a necessary outcome, nor even a particularly common one. *Language contact* occurs whenever and wherever two or more human groups with different languages – and in most cases, different cultures and worldviews as well – encounter one another and attempt to engage in linguistic communication.[3] These encounters may be intended or unintended; fleeting or enduring; relatively egalitarian or marked by significant asymmetries of power (Philips, this volume); peaceful and mutually beneficial or coercive, exploitative, and otherwise detrimental to one or more of the groups involved. Such broadly defined variables as these are clearly important considerations in any approach to language contact, since such encounters always occur within contexts that are shaped in part by historical and macrosociological factors that impinge (if in different ways) on all of the groups involved. But as Sahlins (1985) observes in setting forth his notion of the "structure of the conjuncture," any instance of intercultural contact should also be analyzed in microsociological terms as an interaction, within a specific historical context, between "historic agents" who enact disparate symbolic systems and bring to bear differing interests and cultural categories; this yields differing interpretations of any given event, including the initial encounter itself (pp. xiv, 153–4). With specific regard to language, it must be borne in mind that speakers, both as members of social groups (of varying sizes and compositions) and as individual agents, can and do use language creatively to express and negotiate their complex, shifting identities (Bucholtz and Hall, this volume), to assert and advance their interests, and to pursue specific ends (Duranti, this volume); furthermore, they use language in ways that, while partially constrained by social convention and locally constituted systems of cultural meaning, are at the same time situated and contingent, and hence fundamentally indeterminate (Bailey, this volume).

As these considerations suggest, any given instance of language contact can have a wide range of potential outcomes, ranging from stable bilingualism or multilingualism to the "death" of one or more – sometimes all but one – of the languages involved (along with their speakers, in some cases).[4] The sheer variety of possible outcomes presents challenges for linguistic, sociolinguistic, and linguistic anthropological approaches alike. The languages traditionally referred to as pidgins and creoles are the best-known examples of contact languages, but they constitute a remarkably diverse group themselves; those who study them disagree over such fundamental matters as how the terms *pidgin* and *creole* should be defined, how creoles differ from pidgins, and whether or not pidgins and/or creoles collectively constitute a "special" type of language that can meaningfully be distinguished from the rest of the world's languages. Meanwhile other types of contact languages that defy categorization as either pidgins or creoles – variously referred to as "semi-creoles," "creoloids," "mixed languages," "intertwined languages," "bilingual mixtures," and "indigenized varieties" – have also attracted the attention of researchers, and have introduced new complexities into the aforementioned controversies. Finally, other outcomes of language contact are too dynamic to be reified as codes at all and must be conceptualized as processes or practices, such as codeswitching (Woolard, this volume), "crossing" (Rampton 1995), language shift (Gal 1979; Kulick 1992), and language obsolescence and "death" (Dorian 1989; Crystal 2000).

Formally oriented linguists have been both fascinated and perplexed by this diversity of outcomes, but they have also been able to discern certain cross-linguistic commonalities – in the tense-mood-aspect systems of creole languages with quite different source languages, for example – that may provide important insights into the mechanisms of historical language change (Thomason and Kaufman 1988) and the nature of the human language faculty (DeGraff 1999). Sociolinguists have sought to account for (and bring order to) this same diversity by investigating the relationships among language structure, patterns of variation in language usage, and specific characteristics (demographic, social, historical, etc.) of the communities in which contact languages have emerged and continue to develop (e.g. Chaudenson 2001; Le Page and Tabouret-Keller 1985; Mufwene 1996; Rickford 1987; Silva-Corvalán 1994; Singler 1996). Linguistic anthropologists, meanwhile, have generally been less concerned with the development of typologies and other broad classificatory schemata, or with theoretical debates about the genesis of contact languages and their relationship to the rest of the world's languages; they have instead focused on the ways in which speakers in specific situations of contact use the languages available to them as a cultural resource in situated social interaction and in the construction of self and community (e.g. Errington 1998b; Gal 1979; Hill and Hill 1986; Irvine and Gal 2000; Kulick 1992; Rampton 1995; Schieffelin 1996; Spitulnik 1998; Tsitsipis 1998; Urciuoli 1996; Woolard 1998; Zentella 1997). Linguistic anthropologists are thus generally less interested in contact languages *qua* specific codes exhibiting particular formal characteristics than in language contact *qua* a socially situated, culturally mediated phenomenon that gives rise to particular kinds of communicative practices, some but not all of which may result in the emergence of distinct new codes.

Anthropological approaches to language contact demand attention to the fact that *languages* do not actually come into contact in any meaningful sense. Rather, *speakers* of languages come into contact, and they do so under a wide range of historical and social circumstances. These range from relatively fleeting, highly domain-specific encounters, such as souvenir sales transactions between tourists and locals, to enduring, centuries-long episodes of coexistence (mutually consensual or not, peaceful or not) between large populations with disparate histories and cultures, such as have resulted from European colonialism and, more recently, from other forms of "globalization" (Appadurai 1996; Hannerz 1996). All such episodes of contact occur in what Pratt (1992: 6–7) conceptualizes as "the contact zone": a kind of "social space" in which human groups previously separated by geography and/or history "come into contact with each other and establish ongoing relations, usually involving conditions of coercion, radical inequality, and intractable conflict." Pratt notes explicitly that she borrows her notion of contact from linguistics (particularly pidgin and creole linguistics), but it is intended "to foreground the interactive, improvisational dimensions" of such encounters and to "emphasiz[e] how subjects are constituted in and by their relations to each other." As will be seen in the sections that follow, these are central issues in contemporary linguistic anthropological approaches to language contact.

3   A Case Study: Language Contact in St. Lucia, Past and Present

In the Caribbean island of St. Lucia, the present-day official language is English – a legacy of the island's former status, for a century and a half (1814–1979), as a British colony. But in St. Lucians' everyday interactions, one commonly hears utterances such as the following (rendered here phonemically,[5] followed by a rendering in standard English orthography and a gloss):

> *muuv in do reen*
> *(Move in the rain)*
> 'Get out of the rain'

> *hii sending stoon biihain piipl*
> *(He sending stone behind people)*
> 'He is throwing stones at people'

> *ai bai bred in hiz han*
> *(I buy bread in his hand)*
> 'I bought bread from him'

> *maisef skraching mii*
> *(Myself scratching me)*
> 'I itch'/'I feel itchy'

To a native speaker of North American or British English who has recently arrived in St. Lucia (as a tourist, for example), these utterances would probably sound quite odd; depending on the context in which they occur, they might seem to make no sense at all, or might easily be misconstrued. Yet each word spoken can readily be identified as an "English" word. What, then (our hypothetical visitor might wonder), is going on here?

With sufficient time and attention, what the visitor would eventually come to understand is that the English language in St. Lucia has been strongly influenced by several decades of sustained contact with St. Lucia's other language: an Afro-French creole known as Kwéyòl or Patwa. Kwéyòl is itself a contact language with European and African roots; it became established during a French colonial period, 1642–1814, that preceded the aforementioned British colonial period in the island's history. Kwéyòl is commonly called a "French creole," but a French visitor to St. Lucia would find it quite impossible to follow, much less participate in, a Kwéyòl conversation; indeed, he or she would be considerably worse off than the American or British tourist encountering St. Lucia's non-standard English vernacular for the first time. The following examples give some idea of the extent to which Kwéyòl differs from contemporary metropolitan French:[6]

> *Mwen méte'y asou tab-la*
> *Je l'ai mis sur la table*
> 'I put it on the table'

> *Lapli té ka tonbé*
> *Il pleuvait*
> 'It was raining'

> *I pli ho pasé ou*
> *Il est plus grand que toi/vous*
> 'He is taller than you'

> *Bonm-la pòkò plenn*
> *Le seau n'est pas encore plein*
> 'The bucket is not yet full'

As these few examples suggest, Kwéyòl's lexical relationship to French is readily discernible. In the first sample sentence shown, for example, it is apparent that Kwéyòl *mwen* derives from the French first-person singular pronominal form *moi*, that the Kwéyòl verb *méte* derives from *mettre* (probably via the second-person plural inflected form *mettez*), and the noun *tab* from *table*. In the second sentence matters are less transparent, but even here one can readily and reasonably surmise that the Kwéyòl noun *lapli* represents a reanalysis of the French noun phrase *la pluie* 'the rain', and the verb *tonbé* is clearly a reflex of French *tomber* 'to fall'; thus we see that Kwéyòl does not have a unitary verb meaning 'to rain' such as exists in French (*pleuvoir*), but instead uses a more semantically transparent (if also more periphrastic) noun + verb construction: 'rain' + 'to fall', literally 'rain falls', in the present tense. Our sample sentence is not in the present tense, however, and far less obvious is the derivation and grammatical function of the particles *té* and *ka* which precede the verb in fixed order, modifying it for tense (anterior) and aspect (nonpunctual) respectively, while the verb – quite unlike in French – remains morphologically invariant.

To what can these preverbal particles and their grammatical functions be attributed? To a regional dialect of French that figured prominently in Kwéyòl's early development? To one or more of the African languages that likewise played a role? To certain universals of linguistic structure, or universal principles of adult second-language acquisition? To some mutually reinforcing combination of these factors? The tense-mood-aspect systems of creole languages, which show remarkable consistencies across time and space but also certain areas of difference, have been one of the most heavily studied and intensely debated areas in creole linguistics; the question posed here thus has potential to be a controversial one, and in any case it has no simple answer. Furthermore, all of the factors mentioned above must be considered with due regard to the sociocultural and ideological circumstances in which they have operated. As in many cases of language contact, St. Lucia's contemporary sociolinguistic situation reflects a social history in which speakers of different languages have come together under a variety of circumstances, including plantation slavery, formal schooling, and (most recently) international tourism. Each episode of contact has left its mark on the language varieties currently spoken, which continue to undergo contact-induced changes.

Once the sole language of most of the population, Kwéyòl continues to be spoken by a majority of St. Lucians; most now also speak some variety of local English, however, and there are numerous indications that a process of language shift is now underway (Garrett 2000). Meanwhile, one significant result of this secondary, contemporary case of language contact is that the vernacular variety of English spoken by most St. Lucians – which will be referred to here as VESL, an acronym for "Vernacular English of St. Lucia" – owes at least as much to Kwéyòl as it does to the English of the former British colonial administration (Garrett 2003). Returning to the set of VESL examples presented previously, various contact-induced processes can be seen to be at work. Consider

> *hii sending stoon biihain piipl*

When this sentence is juxtaposed to its Kwéyòl equivalent, it becomes clear that there are direct lexicosemantic and syntactic correspondences:

> *hii sending stoon biihain piipl*
> *I ka voyé woch dèyè moun*
> 3SG NONPUNC send/throw rock(s) behind/at people
> 'He is throwing stones at people'

Apart from the omission of the auxiliary verb (*is*) and the plural suffix (*-s*) in the VESL utterance – features commonly found in pidgins and creoles as well as in various vernacular Englishes and English as a second language – the sentence's decidedly non-standard quality is attributable to the literal translation of the Kwéyòl words *voyé* and *dèyè* as *send* and *biihain* ('behind') respectively. Similarly, in the next example it is clear that the VESL utterance is a calque, or literal translation, of its Kwéyòl equivalent:

ai bai bred in hiz han
Mwen achté pen an lenmen'y
1SG buy bread in hand 3SG POSS
'I bought bread from him'

The prepositional phrase *in hiz han* is clearly patterned on *an lenmen'y*, the corresponding construction in Kwéyòl. Note also that although the VESL verb *bai* is in the past tense here, this is not indicated morphologically (as it is in Standard English *bought*); zero-marking of non-stative verbs indicates the simple past in VESL, as it does in Kwéyòl and other creoles.

As the St. Lucian case suggests, language contact is a dynamic, ongoing process that unfolds on multiple levels simultaneously. Examples of contact-induced change such as the preceding can be identified and described in formal terms (as has been done here to a minimal extent), but this is only part of the story. One must also ask why these particular processes have occurred in this particular case of contact, resulting (for the time being, at least) in this particular outcome. The sections that follow outline the varied results of language contact and some of the factors (particularly social factors) that tend to give rise to them.

4 BILINGUALISM AND MULTILINGUALISM

As noted previously, language contact does not always give rise to a new contact language; such an outcome is in fact rather exceptional. Today as in the past, *bilingualism* and *multilingualism* are probably the most common outcomes of language contact; indeed, it is safe to assume that most of the world's population is at least bilingual. Bilingual/multilingual situations vary considerably, however, in terms of intensity (i.e., the number of languages involved and the extent to which speakers draw on them in the course of everyday life) as well as stability. At one extreme are cases such as Jackson (1983) encountered in an intensely multilingual (but sociocultturally homogenous) area of Amazonia in which every individual belongs to one of at least twenty exogamous "father-language" groups. One of the languages, Tukano, is shared by all as a lingua franca; nevertheless, because multilingualism is highly valued and the maintenance of code boundaries is a key aspect of local social organization, all adults speak at least three languages, and some as many as ten. At the other extreme are cases of language shift and death, to be examined in a later section. Language shift is not always preceded by widespread bilingualism, but even where this is the case it may give way abruptly and surprisingly rapidly to monolingualism.

In dealing with the wide range of bilingual/multilingual phenomena, researchers have found it useful to make certain broad analytic distinctions, such as between societal bilingualism and individual bilingualism, dominant languages and subordinate languages; such notions as "semi-speaker" (referring to an individual speaker who has limited, perhaps only "passive" or receptive, competence in a second language) have also been suggested (Dorian 1982). The concept of *diglossia*, first proposed by Ferguson (1959), has been a particularly influential one; it refers to a type of societal bilingualism that is relatively stable and involves two codes that are historically related but hierarchically differentiated by domain and function. Ferguson's four illustrative cases were French and Haitian Creole in Haiti; classical and demotic (colloquial) Greek in Greece; classical and colloquial Arabic in many Middle Eastern societies; and High German and Swiss German in Switzerland. In each case a "High" variety and a "Low" variety coexist within the community as a whole and within the repertoires of many individual speakers, but are kept sharply differentiated. The Low variety is the vernacular, used in informal conversation with peers and intimates, in giving instructions to servants, and in soap operas and political cartoons. The "High" variety, in contrast, is "highly codified (often grammatically more complex)" and is "the vehicle of a large and respected body of written literature"; it is "learned largely by formal education and is used for most written and formal spoken purposes but is not used by any sector of the community for ordinary conversation" (1959: 336).

Ferguson's concept was taken up by numerous other researchers (Hudson 1992), many of whom modified it (almost always broadening its scope) so as to make it applicable to other relatively stable situations characterized by functional differentiation and social compartmentalization of two or more codes.[7] In following years a few researchers went so far as to propose such terms as *triglossia, multiglossia,* and *polyglossia* (see various references in Hudson 1991), while others retained *diglossia* but extended it (usually with significant modifications) to situations such as the coexistence of English and approximately four hundred indigenous languages in Nigeria (Akinnaso 1989) – surely a far more intensely multilingual situation than Ferguson had in mind when he coined the term. Others re-examined Ferguson's four "classic" examples, revealing that these situations are more complex than Ferguson (1959) had suggested.[8]

Controversy and some confusion resulted, ultimately prompting Ferguson (1991) to "revisit" his original concept and to reaffirm his primary intent in formulating it: to help establish a general typology of sociolinguistic situations, which in turn would serve as a foundation upon which to build sociolinguistic theory. Although there is still disagreement over how the term *diglossia* should be defined, how narrowly or broadly it should be applied, and what specific cases best exemplify it (Hudson 1992: 618), the concept has been an enduringly influential one and continues to serve as an important point of reference for research in bilingual/multilingual settings. Taken as Ferguson intended – as a model or ideal type that is approximated to a greater or lesser extent by real-world situations – it remains valuable.

The literature on bilingualism and multilingualism now spans several disciplines including linguistics and sociolinguistics, psychology, sociology, anthropology, and education (Appel and Muysken 1987, and Romaine 1995 provide useful overviews). Recent work by linguistic anthropologists emphasizes the "fuzziness" or fluidity of code boundaries and the ways in which speakers actively and creatively exploit that fluidity as they construct, negotiate, and challenge the discourses and social boundaries that particular codes index. Urciuoli (1996) finds that for Puerto Ricans in New York City, the subjective experience of being bilingual involves a shifting sense of the boundary between Spanish and English. Within an "inner sphere," that is, with family, friends, and neighbors, the two codes seem to work together seamlessly and fluidly. In contrast, interactions in the "outer sphere" with strangers and persons in positions of authority cause code boundaries to be thrown into sharp relief; here there is much concern with "order," with keeping the two codes separate and distinct. Failure to do so is to leave oneself vulnerable to racializing hegemonic forces which seize upon any trace of "disorder." Zentella's (1997) long-term work in a New York City Puerto Rican community reveals not just two codes, but a "bilingual/ multidialectal repertoire" or "spectrum of linguistic codes" that encompasses contact varieties such as "English-dominant Spanish" and "Hispanized English" in addition to "standard Puerto Rican Spanish," "standard New York City English," and African American Vernacular English. Zentella's analysis centers on the situated deployment of these varieties as speakers move in and out of various domains and interactional contexts, with attention to the social (and ultimately political) consequences of acquiring and using each. As Woolard (this volume) notes, other recent work has focused attention on hybrid, syncretic, heteroglossic, and dialogical phenomena that tended to be abstracted away (or purposely ignored) in earlier bilingualism research paradigms. Notions of simultaneity and bivalency (Woolard 1998), inspired in large part by postmodernist and Bakhtinian theory, suggest that a given form need not be confined to one code; it can participate fully in two (or potentially more) linguistic systems in contact, and can index simultaneous identities and discourses.

5   CONTACT-INDUCED CHANGE WITHOUT EMERGENCE OF DISCRETE NEW CODES

Only in rare cases do bilingualism and multilingualism approximate the "ideal" type conceptualized in the pioneering work of Weinreich (1953) – in which the individual speaker keeps his or her languages entirely separate, thereby avoiding "interference." Far more common are those cases of language contact in which the languages involved influence each other to varying degrees but without giving rise to distinct new codes.[9] Contact can give rise to change in any of a language's subsystems (Sankoff 2002); research has generally revealed that the lexicon is most susceptible to contact-induced influence, followed by phonology, syntax, and morphology, in that order. Thomason (2001: 70–1ff), for example, presents a "borrowing scale" indicating that "nonbasic vocabulary items are the easiest to borrow," while "inflectional morphology is hardest to borrow."

A close examination of Kwéyòl as currently spoken in St. Lucia, particularly among young people, suggests that it has been influenced on all of these levels through its sustained contact with English. Numerous English words have entered Kwéyòl's lexicon; many, not surprisingly, are nouns referring to recent technologies and social phenomena (e.g. *konpyouta* 'computer'), but others are verbs (e.g. *try, mean, hope*), adverbials (*just, really, still*), and function words (*because, about, so*) for which Kwéyòl equivalents have always existed. Yet many St. Lucians today never use the attested Kwéyòl equivalents and cannot produce them if asked to do so (though they may recognize and understand them if they hear them used). Meanwhile the assimilation of English-origin lexemes (shown here in Kwéyòl orthography) such as *djrayv* 'to drive', *tjray* 'to try', and *fridj* 'refrigerator' has effectively resulted in the introduction of a new phoneme, /r/, into Kwéyòl's phonemic inventory (Allen 1994). At the level of syntax, as Kwéyòl is increasingly being used in broadcasting, public speaking, and other domains that were once the exclusive preserve of English (Garrett 2000), passive and anticausative constructions (evidently patterned on English constructions) have become prevalent, particularly among speakers who are fully bilingual in Kwéyòl and Standard English.[10] Meanwhile certain characteristically creole syntactic processes have become conspicuously absent, such as reduplication (for emphasis of adjectives) and predicate clefting (for emphasis of verbs). Like most creoles, Kwéyòl has little in the way of morphological processes, but even here English influence can be detected, as when bilingual speakers attach the suffix -é onto a Kwéyòl noun in order to create an adjective, apparently on the English pattern of adding the suffix -y to a noun (as in *rock* + -y → *rocky*). Formerly in Kwéyòl, one who is fortunate would have been said to 'have luck' (*ni chans*), as in *Ou ni chans* 'You are lucky' (literally 'You have luck'). But it is now becoming commonplace to say *Ou chansé* (*chans* + -é → *chansé* 'lucky'), suggesting that [noun + -é] may be on its way to becoming a productive process in Kwéyòl comparable to [noun + -y] in English.

Over time, the accretion of changes such as these can result in *language convergence*, in which two or more languages come to resemble each other structurally while retaining their distinct lexicons and, typically, continuing to be regarded as distinct languages by their speakers.[11] Gumperz and Wilson (1971) describe a case in which Marathi, Urdu, and Kannada as spoken in the multilingual Indian village of Kupwar have become structurally congruent to a remarkable degree, despite the significant typological differences that originally existed among them. The Balkan *Sprachbund* ('language area', or more literally, 'language union'), comprising Romanian, Bulgarian, Serbo-Croatian, Macedonian, Albanian, and Greek, presents another exemplary case (McMahon 1994: 218–20; Thomason 2001: 105–9; see also Irvine and Gal 2000: 60–72), as do the Native American languages of the Pacific Northwest (Thomason and Kaufman 1988). A driving force in language convergence is the need for maximal second (or third, or *n*th) language learnability: convergence tends to occur in multilingual situations in which language functions as a salient marker of ethnic or other group identity (e.g. caste identity in Kupwar), but in which intergroup communication is necessary and/or desirable. Persons living in such communities commonly speak at least two (often more) of the languages involved, though they may consider only one to be the language of their own group. In such a situation, language learnability is greatly facilitated by direct, transparent grammatical correspondences between the codes involved. (Lexicons, in contrast, tend to remain sharply distinct since maintenance of lexical differences typically does much of the semiotic work of differentiation among codes, and among those who speak them.) Over time, as generations of speakers acquire the various codes (one as first language, another as second language, etc.), the results of "transfer" phenomena associated with second language acquisition may accrue to the extent that all of the languages involved, whatever their original typological differences, come to share what is essentially a single grammar. In addition to facilitating the acquisition by individuals of multiple codes, convergence also maximizes intertranslatability by making direct morpheme-by-morpheme translation a viable communicative strategy.

Far more common than full-blown language convergence are cases in which contact-induced influences are largely unidirectional, typically affecting a "minority" or otherwise non-dominant language. Silva-Corvalán's (1994) work on Spanish–English bilingualism among Mexican Americans demonstrates that Spanish in Los

Angeles has been influenced through multiple contact-related processes; these have resulted in an overall simplification of the Spanish verb system and some structural convergence with English.[12] As Thomason (2001), Sankoff (2002), and others stress, linguistic structure always conditions the effects of language contact to some degree, but structural factors come into play only through social contact between speakers. Thus processes of contact-induced change are shaped in large part by the social contexts in which they occur. Thomason and Kaufman (1988: 4) remark, "We certainly do not deny the importance of purely linguistic factors such as pattern pressure and markedness considerations for a theory of language change, but the evidence from language contact shows that they are easily overridden when social factors push in another direction."

Indeed, in some contact situations social factors can be shown to operate quite independently of linguistic structure to produce language change. A case in point is described by Schieffelin (1996, 2000) in her work on the introduction of literacy among the Kaluli of Papua New Guinea by Christian missionaries. Missionization has involved some degree of contact between Kaluli and two languages introduced by the missionaries, Tok Pisin and English; but even more consequential has been exposure to a new way of using (and thinking about) language that is associated with these two languages, namely literacy practices (Baquedano-López, this volume). The missionaries' introduction of written materials in Kaluli introduced not merely a new technology, but also a new form of evidence – something with which the Kaluli are very much concerned culturally as well as linguistically. The Kaluli language provides its speakers with a broad range of evidentials – lexical and morphological means of indicating the source or the nature of the evidence upon which an utterance is based. To some extent the use of evidentials in Kaluli is grammatically obligatory, and even where not obligatory it is a crucial aspect of culturally meaningful language use. The Kaluli therefore faced a dilemma when confronted with written materials concerning religion, health, and other momentous matters – in effect, new sources of knowledge, authority, and truth. Schieffelin demonstrates that their response has included the creation of innovative evidential forms as well as novel ways of using those that already existed. Her work thus shows that languages may be as pervasively affected by sustained contact between disparate worldviews and ideologies of language as by contact between the languages themselves.

6   Pidgins and Creoles

In the 1960s, at about the same time that sociolinguistics was taking form, the field of pidgin and creole linguistics was beginning to take shape as scholars from North America, Europe, and the Caribbean came together to exchange data and ideas (Holm 1988: 42–6). This was a momentous development, for these languages were generally held in low esteem even by their own speakers; at worst they were regarded as mere "gibberish," at best as "corrupted" or "bastardized" versions of the European languages to which most were clearly related. As Holm (1988: 3) notes, even linguistic scholars had generally regarded them as "freakish exceptions that were irrelevant to any theory of 'normal' language"; and as Thomason and Kaufman (1988: 1–2) note, some went so far as to deny the possibility that "mixed languages" (i.e., languages descended from more than one "parent" or "mother" language) could possibly exist.[13]

As pidgin and creole linguistics became a distinct area of inquiry in subsequent years, many of the scholars involved were as much concerned with the social and historical conditions of these languages' origins as with their structural characteristics. This preoccupation with the genesis of pidgins and creoles is largely attributable to the fact that these languages were known to have arisen relatively recently. The majority had originated in the tropical zones, typically on islands and along coasts, where contact had occurred between Europeans (especially Portuguese, Spanish, French, British, and Dutch), the indigenous inhabitants of these areas, and later the enslaved and indentured inhabitants of still other territories (mainly West Africa, but also other parts of Africa and South and East Asia). These were among the territories that Europeans variously "discovered," explored, conquered, missionized, plundered, exploited, ruled, administered, and settled, mostly between the early sixteenth and late nineteenth centuries. The "classic" setting for the emergence of a creole language is the colonial plantation society, but pidgins and creoles have also emerged through various other types of contact such as trade and work cooperation between groups of comparable power and social status (e.g. Russenorsk, along the Arctic coast of Norway in the eighteenth and nineteenth centuries), military recruitment and conscription (e.g. Juba Arabic, in the southern Sudan in the mid to late nineteenth century), and labor migration (e.g. Fanakalo in southern African mining areas, also in the mid to late nineteenth century).[14]

A *pidgin* generally emerges from extended or repeated (yet limited) social contact between members of two or more groups that have no language in common. Numerous pidgins have arisen through trade, for example – a situation in which some means of rudimentary communication is needed, but in which no group learns the language of any of the other groups involved due to factors such as mutual distrust and lack of social contact outside the trading context. Like trade itself, a pidgin is typically a matter of negotiation and compromise; the language of a particular powerful (or prestigious, or otherwise dominant) group may provide the bulk of the lexicon, but the meanings of words and the ways in which they are used in the pidgin may be strongly influenced by the languages of less powerful groups. A pidgin is in many respects reduced or simplified in that it lacks features that are found in its source languages but are not essential for communication (e.g. inflectional morphology, gender, and case). Pidgins also tend to have simplified phonological structures (e.g. consonant clusters are reduced) and limited vocabularies. In all of these respects, pidgin-speakers make maximal use of minimal linguistic resources, for example by using a single word for several different functions. An example from Tok Pisin centers on the noun *gras*, derived from English *grass* but pressed into service to yield a much broader range of meanings: *gras nogut* 'weed', *gras bilong pisin* 'feather', *gras bilong dog* 'dog fur', *gras bilong fes* 'beard', *gras antap long ai* 'eyebrow', etc. (Romaine 1994: 183). Because pidgin-speakers have their native languages to fall back on within their own communities, a pidgin is not the primary language of any community of speakers; it is an auxiliary language, and is generally restricted to particular domains and contexts of interaction (perhaps only those in which it originated).

The term *creole* is somewhat more difficult to define, but it is useful to begin by considering how a creole differs from a pidgin (itself a contentious issue). Unlike a pidgin, a creole is a fully elaborated language – lexically, grammatically, stylistically, and otherwise – that serves the full range of its speakers' communicative needs. It is the primary language of a community of speakers, for whom it is typically the language of ethnic identity; and in most cases it is acquired as a first or native language by children. Until the 1980s, it was widely accepted that "nativization" was the main distinguishing factor between a pidgin and a creole; nativization was thought to engender the regularization, stabilization, expansion, and structural elaboration that transformed a pidgin into a full-fledged language (i.e. a creole).

The role of nativization in creolization came under intense debate after Bickerton's (1981, 1984) "language bioprogram" hypothesis galvanized the field of pidgin and creole linguistics. Prior to this, theories of creole genesis had largely been concerned with the roles of substrate and superstrate languages. The substrate languages (e.g. African languages, in the case of the Atlantic creoles) were thought collectively to have provided much of the grammatical structure of the nascent creole, while the superstrate language (the socially dominant language, generally a European language) contributed the bulk of the lexicon; with few exceptions, researchers attributed greater influence to the former, assuming that European languages had been the "target" of language acquisition but that access to the target had been severely limited by social and demographic factors.[15] Bickerton, however, proposed that creolization occurs when children, born into an environment in which their linguistic input is rudimentary, unstable, and generally "chaotic" (such as in a plantation society in its early formative stages), fall back on an innate "blueprint" for language that allows them (obligates them, in fact) to construct a fully elaborated language despite the availability of only severely limited linguistic input. An implication of Bickerton's hypothesis was that creole languages, as recent creations, should reflect this language bioprogram (i.e., the genetically endowed, universal human language faculty) much more directly and transparently than older languages do; the hypothesis also offered an explanation for structural similarities among diverse creole languages, particularly in their tense-mood-aspect systems.

Bickerton's hypothesis generated controversy in part because it was a direct attack on what he characterized as "substratophile" theories of creole genesis, which at the time were widely accepted. Bickerton's universalist hypothesis attracted a following, but many other creolists responded by pointing out important shortcomings, including its lack of attention to the social and historical circumstances of creole genesis. Singler (1992) argued, for example, that children could not have played the crucial role in creolization that Bickerton suggests since there were relatively few women present in early plantation societies and even fewer children (due to low fertility rates and high rates of abortion and infant mortality attributable to the inhumane conditions of plantation slavery). Others pointed out that the nature of the linguistic input available to children in such societies would not have been what Bickerton claims, arguing that there is little reason to suppose that adults would have spoken a nascent pidgin with children to the exclusion of their own native languages or that the break in linguistic transmission from one generation to the next would have been so sharp as to preclude significant adult (i.e. substratal) influence on the emergent creole.

Although researchers before and after Bickerton's controversial proposal had often disagreed about the mechanisms by which pidgins become transformed into creoles, a linear, unidirectional "life-cycle" model (first proposed as such in Hall (1962), but prefigured in earlier work) was widely accepted. The life-cycle was conceptualized as a matter of progressive stabilization and expansion of the pidgin, in its structure (phonology, lexicon, grammar, etc.) as well as in its expressive and social functions:

Jargon (the incipient pidgin, rudimentary and unstable)
↓
Stabilized pidgin
↓
Expanded pidgin
↓
Creole

In later years the life-cycle model was generally understood to include the possibility of *decreolization*, a process whereby ongoing contact between a creole and its super-strate (lexifier language) gives rise to a "continuum" of lects ranging from basilectal (the "deepest" creole varieties) to acrolectal (those most closely approximating the standard language). Linking the basilectal and acrolectal poles in an uninterrupted cline is an array of intermediate or mesolectal varieties. The continuum model, sometimes called the "post-creole continuum," was used to conceptualize diachronic change (as presupposed by the life-cycle model) as well as to describe the considerable synchronic variation encountered in many creole settings. Alleyne (1985: 169) reports that all of the following forms meaning 'I was going' were recorded in the casual conversation of two Jamaican men as they painted a room:

I was goin (g)   (acrolectal)
me did goin   (mesolectal)
mi was a go   (mesolectal)
mi en a go   (basilectal)

Another case to which the continuum model has often been applied is that of Guyanese Creole; O'Donnell and Todd (1980) report no fewer than eighteen distinct forms for the phrase 'I gave him'.[16]

The assumption that every creole had started out as a pidgin and could be located at some point in the "life-cycle" seemed relatively unproblematic with respect to the Atlantic creoles, which for years had been the primary focus of research. As research-ers learned more about Pacific pidgins and creoles, however, it became increasingly clear that some of these languages had developed along quite different trajectories and that multiple pidginization and creolization scenarios were in fact possible. Tok Pisin and related Melanesian pidgins had become stabilized and elaborated to a greater extent than had previously been thought possible for a pidgin; furthermore, they had done so without becoming nativized and had persisted in this non-nativized state for a surprisingly long period of time (more than a century in some cases). In some communities researchers actually found that they were able to document the nativization process as it was occurring – something that had never been possible in research on the Atlantic creoles. This revealed, among other things, that nativization (and the stabilization and structural elaboration that had previously been associated with it) need not be the defining feature of creolization. Rather, the crucial distinction between pidgin and creole now appeared to have more to do with a language's role in the social life of a community and in the communicative practice of those who speak it: a pidgin is a secondary language, while a creole – whether or not it has become nativized – serves as the primary language of a community (Jourdan 1991: 192–4).

Concern with social factors is clearly manifested in "gradualist" explanations of creole genesis that have been put forth by Chaudenson (1992, 2001), Mufwene (1996, 2000), and Singler (1996), among others. Previously, approaches to creole genesis espoused by Bickerton as well as many of those who argued most vociferously against his universalist approach (e.g. "substratophiles," or substratists) had been in general agreement on at least one thing: that creoles are the products of what Thomason and Kaufman (1988) characterize as "non-genetic development" or "abrupt" creolization – that is, they result from a break in "normal transmission" of language. Gradualist approaches suggest that creolization, particularly in plantation settings in which there may never have been a stable pidgin stage, may actually have been an extended process that occurred over multiple generations. Gradualists make extensive use of demographic, historical, and even economic data in order to piece together the social circumstances under which speakers of different languages would have come together and what might have motivated various aspects of their language use. Gradualists differ among themselves on various points, however. Chaudenson takes a strongly superstratist approach to the origins of French-lexified creoles, minimizing the input of African languages; he assumes that French was the target language of slaves, and that the creole diverged from metropolitan French as successive waves of newly arrived Africans acquired increasingly disparate "approximations" of French (due to limited access to the target and imperfect learning). Singler, in contrast, focusing on the Haitian case, attributes significant influence to particular African substrate languages that came to be heavily represented within the sharply increasing slave population during the "sugar boom" years.

Increasingly since the early 1980s, researchers have made the social circumstances under which creoles have developed historically and/or exist currently their primary focus.[17] Sankoff's aptly titled volume *The Social Life of Language* (1980) set an important precedent and firm foundation for this trend. As Jourdan (1991) and various others have since suggested, it may well be that sociohistorical considerations, particularly those concerning the relatively recent timeframe within which creoles have developed, are ultimately the best criteria for distinguishing them from the rest of the world's languages.

7   NEITHER PIDGINS NOR CREOLES: OTHER CONTACT LANGUAGES

The notoriously polysemous term *creole* has proven as difficult to define as ever in recent years as linguists and others have revisited the fundamental question of whether or not creoles as a group differ (structurally, sociohistorically, or otherwise) from the rest of the world's languages – and if so, precisely how (see e.g. Mufwene

1986; Thomason and Kaufman 1988; Thomason 1997b; McWhorter 1997, 1998; DeGraff 1999). Some recent statements concerning the nature of creole languages and their relationship to other languages, such as Mufwene (1997), go so far as to propose that there is in fact no structural basis for classifying particular languages as creoles. Mufwene provides an insightful discussion of *creole* and other terms that have commonly been used in referring to contact-induced language varieties, pointing out that they have been applied to a sociohistorically particular set of languages in ways that have not been (and indeed cannot be) rigorously based on structural criteria.[18] Ultimately Mufwene, like Jourdan, Singler, and others, calls for greater attention to the specific social and historical contexts in which all contact languages, broadly conceived, have emerged.

Debate on these points has been fueled by increasing interest in contact languages that are not easily classifiable as either pidgins or creoles. Thomason (1997a: 1) characterizes these non-pidgin, non-creole varieties as "a third type of contact language – bilingual mixtures that (unlike pidgins and creoles) must have been created by bilinguals." Examples include the varieties characterized by Bakker and Mous (1994) and Bakker and Muysken (1995) as "mixed" or "intertwined" languages – a particular type of contact language in which the inflectional morphology and grammar of one language combines with the lexicon of a second. Sebba (1997: 16) defines language mixing or intertwining as "two languages combining in such a way that (usually) the grammar of one language is 'grafted on' to the vocabulary of another – or vice versa." An early reference to such a language is Goodman's (1971) description of Mbugu or Ma'a (combining Bantu grammar and Cushitic vocabulary), which was later examined by Mous (1994); other examples are Anglo-Romani and Media Lengua (described below). Yet another group of languages that have proved problematic for classification purposes are "indigenized" varieties such as Indian English (Kachru 1983) and "Singlish" or Singapore English (Kuiper and Tan Gek Lin 1989), to take but two well-documented examples from the "anglophone" world.[19]

Many such contact languages (like most if not all creoles) function as salient markers of ethnic or other group identity. As this suggests, contact languages must always be considered in terms of what they mean to, and how they are used by, those who create and speak them. These are particularly important considerations in cases where speakers apparently have made deliberate decisions to manipulate their languages in certain ways. The most extreme cases in terms of linguistic outcome may be the most telling in other regards as well. Take for example Anglo-Romani, spoken by Roma living in Britain. A very large portion of its original Romani vocabulary has been replaced by English, and virtually nothing is left of Romani's original Indic structure; some vocabulary is thus all that remains of the language that originally came into contact with English. Based on these facts alone, a complete shift to English and the imminent "death" of Anglo-Romani might well be the expected outcome. Crucially, however, the relatively small set of Romani lexical items that remains suffices for Anglo-Romani to serve its speakers as an in-group or "secret" code (Hancock 1984; Thomason 2001: 200–18). Anglo-Romani seems to have stabilized around these few remnants of Romani lexicon, and presumably it will remain stable as long as "Gypsies" remain a stigmatized minority that actively resists assimilation. Another interesting case is Media Lengua (literally 'Half Language' or 'Halfway Language'), which has a vocabulary that is almost entirely Spanish but a grammar that is almost entirely

Quechua. Media Lengua is the language of ethnic identification for a central Ecuadorian community of several hundred speakers that regards itself as culturally neither "Spanish" nor "Quechua," but situates itself Janus-like between these two salient ethnolinguistic categories in Ecuadorian society. (Most if not all Media Lengua-speakers also speak Spanish and/or Quechua, and interact regularly with speakers of these languages.) Although not regarded as a "secret" language like Anglo-Romani, Media Lengua is not used with outsiders and serves as an important marker of a self-consciously separate group identity (Muysken 1981, 1997).

8   LANGUAGE SHIFT AND OBSOLESCENCE

Language shift refers to a situation in which a community of speakers effectively abandons one language by "shifting" to another (not necessarily by conscious choice). Until fairly recently, approaches to language shift tended to attribute it to macrosociological factors such as "modernization" and "development," with all of the associated phenomena that these typically entail (e.g. industrialization, urbanization, migration). The first to problematize this orientation was Gal (1978, 1979), who pointed out that the crucial thing that a study of language shift must accomplish is to explain how such macrosociological processes come to be interpreted by individual speakers in ways that have direct bearing on everyday language use. Taking an ethnographic approach to an ongoing case of language shift in a bilingual (German–Hungarian) Austrian community near the Hungarian border, Gal investigates individual speakers' understandings of how language use articulates with other sociocultural categories such as gender, ethnicity, and occupation. These subjective understandings play a crucial role in language shift as speakers reconceptualize and re-evaluate their own (and others') personal relationships to the identities and values that are integrally (but differentially) bound up with, and mediated by, the languages of their community. Gal thus shifts the emphasis from broadly (and often vaguely) defined social phenomena to individual agency and practice.

Taking Gal's insight to heart – and using Sahlins's (1985) notion of "structure of the conjuncture" to put a new twist on it – Kulick (1992: 9) asks, "Why and how do people come to interpret their lives in such a way that they abandon one of their languages?" Kulick's study of rapid language shift in Gapun, an isolated village in Papua New Guinea, is based in the language socialization paradigm; it was the first language socialization study to be carried out in a multilingual setting, and the first to examine language shift in progress from this perspective. (See Garrett and Baquedano-López 2002 for a discussion of recent language socialization studies carried out in language contact settings.) Kulick vividly demonstrates how everyday practices and ways of thinking can give rise to language shift and influence its progression. Focusing on local ideologies of language, self, and modernity and the ways in which these intermeshing belief systems inform language socialization practices, he explains how and why this process escapes the comprehension and control of those involved.

Perhaps the greatest value of approaches such as those of Gal and Kulick is their effectiveness in linking multiple levels of analysis, as more recent studies have continued to do. Errington (1998a, b) shows that the study of language shift in

Indonesia must take into account the influence of semi-authoritarian state institutions, organs of a state intent on bringing about the "modernization" and "development" of a large, ethnically and linguistically diverse postcolonial nation-state (and on setting in place certain mechanisms of social control). Similarly in some respects, Tsitsipis (1998) examines the emergence of a Greek national consciousness and the increasing integration of Arvanítika–Greek bilingual communities into the modern Greek nation-state as a central factor in the shift away from Arvanítika. Although they are concerned with the state and other institutions as sites in the production and exercise of ideology and power, Errington and Tsitsipis, like Gal and Kulick, also take microethnographic approaches to situated language use and explore the resulting tension between micro and macro perspectives. Focusing on how and why language shift is occurring at the level of small communities and through the everyday usage of individual speakers in face-to-face interaction, both also consider how ideologies of language are contested and challenged at local levels, thus treating language shift as "the study of a people's conceptions of themselves in relation to one another and to their changing social world, and of how those conceptions are encoded by and mediated through language" (Kulick 1992: 9).[20]

Language shift often, though not always, entails *language obsolescence* – the attrition or decline of the language away from which speakers are shifting, in some cases resulting in language "death" (Dorian 1989). Like language shift, language obsolescence most often occurs in situations where a "minority" language (i.e., a language with relatively few speakers, a state of affairs which in many cases also entails non-literacy, non-standardization, lack of institutional backing, etc.) is in sustained contact with a "dominant" language. Language obsolescence may occur gradually over the course of many generations or there may be a sudden "tip" (Dorian 1981; Mertz 1989) followed by precipitous decline. Dorian (1982) shows that in the former case the presence of "semi-speakers" of varying levels of proficiency may complicate efforts to define the community of speakers as well as to assess the relative vitality of the language within that community. The fate of a language and the rate at which it is progressing toward that fate at a given point in time are in any case difficult to predict; both are subject to multiple simultaneous influences from a constellation of densely interrelated factors.

A central concern in studies of language obsolescence is the non-reproduction of the obsolescent language, that is, the non-transmission of the language from adults to children – a phenomenon that has sometimes been characterized as language "suicide" (Denison 1977; McMahon 1994).[21] Kulick (1992), however, shows that in at least some cases "suicide" is an inappropriate metaphor. By attributing a particular type of agency to their children, by linguistically accommodating them and respecting their personal autonomy (which are traditional ideals), and by ignoring or criticizing children's use of Taiap (the traditional vernacular), adults in Gapun create a situation in which "there is no demand on children to speak Taiap, nor is there any reward for speaking it" (p. 222). Adults do not perceive this state of affairs, however, nor their own role in creating it. In exasperation, they instead blame their children for willfully refusing to learn and use Taiap. Schmidt (1985) describes a similar phenomenon in an aboriginal Australian community: adults' language purism, and their frequent corrections and criticisms, effectively inhibit younger speakers from using the language.

Recent research on language socialization in contact settings (Garrett and Baque-dano-López 2002) suggests that ideologies of language (Kroskrity, this volume) and the everyday communicative practices that are conditioned by them play a significant role in determining whether or not a case of language obsolescence will ultimately end in language death. Ideology of language is a crucial consideration in the decline of Kwéyòl in St. Lucia. Many children are not acquiring it as their home and community vernacular due in large part to adults' determination that they learn "English" – a local metalinguistic category that is broad enough to include VESL, which is in fact what many children are now acquiring as their first and only language. In St. Lucians' ideology of language, English and Kwéyòl are considered qualitatively different: for example, it is believed that English, unlike Kwéyòl, needs to be taught explicitly, and that Kwéyòl has deleterious contaminating effects on children's de-veloping "English" (but not vice versa). Some local intellectuals and cultural activists have made concerted efforts to elevate Kwéyòl's status and have made it the focus of "preservation" efforts, particularly since St. Lucia's independence in 1979. They have had considerable success in changing public sentiments toward Kwéyòl, which is now widely regarded as a *sine qua non* of St. Lucia's cultural heritage and post-independence national identity. But they have not challenged the underlying ideology of language that continues to guide everyday communicative practices, including language socialization practices in which a deeply Kwéyòl-influenced "English" (VESL) is privileged over Kwéyòl itself by adults who believe themselves to be acting in the best interests of their children (Garrett 2000). Thus the process of language shift continues largely unabated.

9   CONCLUSION

As the various cases examined above make clear, the consequences of any particular case of language contact are contingent upon multiple factors – structural, historical, demographic, politico-economic, social, cultural, ideological – and they remain con-tingent (and hence subject to change) over time. Understanding the nature of this contingency is one of the major challenges for linguistic anthropological research on language contact. Many recent studies have in common a concern with the workings of power in and through language – a crucial consideration in any approach to language contact since, as Pratt (1992) emphasizes, language contact more often than not is characterized by significant asymmetries of power. In some cases the struggles that this entails, generally between speakers of a "dominated" language and agents of a "dominant" language and the hegemonic forces behind it, are more or less explicit (e.g. Hill and Hill 1986; Jaffe 1999; Urla 1988). Historically, this was certainly true in colonial contact settings, where symbolic domination was backed up by vigorously applied physical force. But as Hill (1998) shows in her analysis of "Mock Spanish" in the United States, the workings of power in contemporary contact settings – in this case through racist discourses that marginalize and derogate Spanish-speaking ethnic groups – may be much more subtle, at times even ambiguous or indeterminate (in expression if not in ultimate effects). Hanks's (2000) work on the encounter between Spanish and Maya in colonial Yucatán suggests productive ways of approaching the issue of languages or codes in contact by treating discourses, genres, and texts as sites of negotiation and contestation over the terms on which groups in contact relate to one another.

By treating language contact as a dynamic process or phenomenon, linguistic anthropological research emphasizes communicative practice – what speakers do with codes, rather than the codes themselves. In some contact situations the "codes" involved are in fact rather difficult to pin down, reminding us that any code is ultimately a reification, an abstraction from communicative practice. Spitulnik's (1998: 50) work on Town Bemba shows it to be fluid, heteroglossic, and thus far relatively diffuse, a "moving target" for the investigator (if not for its speakers); she suggests that it be regarded not as a distinct code, but rather as "a cover term for a set of Bemba-based multilingual practices, which are iconic, indexical, and symbolic of 'urbanity' and 'modernity' in Zambia." Analytically and metalinguistically elusive varieties such as this hold considerable interest, particularly for what they can reveal about the cultural and ideological contexts within which they are embedded. The St. Lucian contact variety that has been referred to here as "VESL" is of course not labeled as such by its speakers, who refer to it simply as "English"; despite its decidedly non-standard features, VESL in St. Lucia is rarely talked about in ethno-metalinguistic terms as being anything other than "English" (quite unlike the English-lexified creoles spoken in Jamaica, Barbados, and other "anglophone" Caribbean territories). From an analytic perspective, this erasure (in Irvine and Gal's (2000) sense) of VESL is an oversimplification of matters, but a culturally and ideologically significant one that plays a role in ongoing processes of contact-induced language change and its social consequences. Kwéyòl is going into decline even as it is gaining unprecedented status as a "real" language: a national language, a language that can be held to standards of "grammaticality" and "purity," a language of literacy and official communication, and so on. Ironically, as Kwéyòl is entering into such new domains, it is being used less and less in some of its old vernacular domains (including, crucially, the socialization of children), where its functions are being taken over by VESL. But in those contexts where Standard English is preferred if not required – e.g. in schools and other institutional settings – VESL and its speakers are held in low regard, or at best are seen as presenting a problem. Thus the relationship of inequality that formerly obtained between English and Kwéyòl has been "recursively" reproduced (Irvine and Gal 2000) such that it now obtains between (Standard) English and VESL.

As all of these cases suggest, the study of language contact and contact languages calls for theories and methods that can cope with variability and indeterminacy of specific forms as well as heterogeneity and dynamism in higher-level linguistic and cultural systems. These being perennial challenges for the study of language and culture more generally, advances in the study of language contact and contact languages should prove to be advances for linguistic anthropology as a whole.

NOTES

For their helpful comments, I thank Alessandro Duranti, Christine Jourdan, and Peter Snow. I alone am responsible for any and all shortcomings.

1 This is not to suggest that the code emerged solely for this reason, which would surely be an oversimplification of matters. It is well worth considering, for example, what part the code played in the emergence of a Pitcairnese identity – particularly in light of the fact that the community continued to exist as such, and that its members continued to speak Pitkern among themselves, for years after being discovered and subsequently relocated (in 1856) to Norfolk Island, where they lived in sustained contact with English-speaking "mainlanders" (Holm 1989: 547–9).

2 *Code* is used here as a maximally value-neutral cover term that comprises languages as well as language varieties, dialects, registers, etc. But like all such terms, it can quickly become problematic. Alvarez-Cáccamo (1999) provides a concise overview of its utility as a working concept as well as some of its potential shortcomings; see also Woolard (this volume).

3 In most cases the languages involved are spoken, but they may be signed, as when members of different Deaf communities come into contact (LeMaster and Monaghan, this volume; Senghas 2003) or when a signed language is in contact with a spoken language (Lucas and Valli 1992). The term "speaker" as used herein should be understood to include signers.

4 Also well worthy of mention here are those cases in which contact results in a heightened sense of distinctive group identity which is symbolically maintained – sometimes cultivated and elaborated – through linguistic difference. Such situations also tend to be characterized by widespread multilingualism and strongly positive evaluation thereof, however. See, e.g., Jackson (1983), Laycock (1982), Sankoff (1980), Irvine and Gal (2000).

5 The system of phonemic transcription used here is that used by Rickford (1987) for Guyanese (an English-lexified creole); Rickford's system, in turn, is based on that devised by Cassidy (1961) for Jamaican.

6 The orthographic system used for representing Kwéyòl is the now widely accepted system set forth in Louisy and Turmel-John (1983).

7 Fishman (1967) was especially influential in this respect.

8 Part of what subsequent research revealed is that social and political changes had significantly altered the relationships between "High" and "Low" varieties in the years since 1959, particularly in Haiti and Greece.

9 Weinreich devotes several paragraphs to the topic "Crystallization of New Languages from Contact" (1953: 69–70, 104–6), but otherwise regards language contact as primarily a phenomenon of individual bilingualism (and as a potential threat to the integrity of discrete language systems).

10 See Duranti (this volume) on the use of such constructions as a means of "mitigating" agency.

11 Similar in many respects, but yielding a different outcome, is the process known as koinéization, which gives rise to a language variety called a *koiné* (Siegel 1985). Koinéization occurs when sustained contact among a number of dialects (or closely related languages) – through a process of convergence that is usually referred to as "dialect-leveling" – results in a single language variety that typically shows some simplification (i.e. particular features present in particular contributing varieties, but not others, are dropped), but retains most if not all of those features that the contributing varieties have in common. The term *koiné* originally referred to the variety of Greek that emerged in this manner and rose to prominence in the Hellenistic period.

12 Mendoza-Denton (1999) provides a review of recent literature focusing on Spanish–English language contact in the USA.

13 This denial reflected the strength of commitment in historical linguistics since the mid-nineteenth century to the Comparative Method (which involves, among other things, the reconstruction of unattested proto-languages as the forebears of contemporary languages)

and to the *Stammbaum* ('family tree') model of genetic relationship, in which each language descends, through gradual divergence, from a single pre-existing language. Processes of language change were thought to be gradual, regular, and accretional, and were assumed to be driven primarily (if not exclusively) by internal, intrasystemic causes. The first to break decisively from this orthodoxy and to study contact languages systematically was German linguist Hugo Schuchardt (1842–1927), but the significance of his work went largely unrecognized until the latter half of the twentieth century.

14 Holm (1989) provides profiles of these and virtually every other known contact language.
15 See Baker (1990) for a critique of the notion of "target" language in pidgin and creole linguistics.
16 The continuum model has been much debated; see Rickford (1987) for a sophisticated application of the model to the Guyanese case that considers its strengths but also acknowledges some of its shortcomings. Le Page and Tabouret-Keller (1985) provide a critique of the continuum and a proposal for an alternative "multidimensional" model.
17 Also of interest in this regard is anthropological work that considers creolization as a cultural (as opposed to linguistic) phenomenon, e.g. Drummond (1980) and Hannerz (1987, 1996).
18 McWhorter (1998) provides a recent argument for the feasibility of identifying a "creole prototype" and for regarding creoles as a distinct class of languages based on common structural features.
19 See Smith and Forman (1997) and the journal *English World-Wide* as representative of the rapidly growing literature on "indigenized" Englishes.
20 As Peter Snow (p.c.) points out, language *maintenance* in contact settings is rarely problematized and treated as a phenomenon worthy of study in its own right. Dorian (1998: 17) observes, "Currently we understand the motivating factors in language shift far better than we understand the psychosocial underpinnings of long-sustained language maintenance." See Paulston (1994) for a comparison of several cases of language maintenance in multilingual situations, and Kroskrity (1993) for an ethnographic study of language maintenance among the Arizona Tewa.
21 See also Constantinidou (1994) in this regard, and on the real and perceived role of women in bringing about language shift and obsolescence.

REFERENCES

Akinnaso, F. N. (1989). One Nation, Four Hundred Languages: Unity and Diversity in Nigeria's Language Policy. *Language Problems and Language Planning* 13: 133–146.
Allen, J. (1994). Can English Loanwords Create New Phonemes in St. Lucian French Creole? Paper presented at the Workshop on Developmental Issues in Creole Languages and Linguistics, University of Westminster, London.
Alleyne, M. C. (1985). A Linguistic Perspective on the Caribbean. In *Caribbean Contours*, ed. S. W. Mintz and S. Price (pp. 155–179). Baltimore: Johns Hopkins University Press.
Alvarez-Cáccamo, C. (1999). Codes. *Journal of Linguistic Anthropology* 9(1–2): 28–31.
Appadurai, A. (1996). *Modernity at Large: Cultural Dimensions of Globalization*. Minneapolis: University of Minnesota Press.
Appel, R., and Muysken, P. (1987). *Language Contact and Bilingualism*. London: Edward Arnold.
Baker, P. (1990). Off Target? *Journal of Pidgin and Creole Languages* 5(1): 107–120.
Bakker, P., and Mous, M. (eds.) (1994). *Mixed Languages*. Amsterdam: Institute for Functional Research into Language and Language Use [IFOTT].

Bakker, P., and Muysken, P. (1995). Mixed Languages and Language Intertwining. In *Pidgins and Creoles: An Introduction*, ed. J. Arends, P. Muysken, and N. Smith (pp. 41–52). Amsterdam: John Benjamins.

Bickerton, D. (1981). *Roots of Language*. Ann Arbor: Karoma.

Bickerton, D. (1984). The Language Bioprogram Hypothesis. *The Behavioral and Brain Sciences* 7: 173–221.

Blackshire-Belay, C. (1993). Foreign Workers' German: Is It a Pidgin? In *Atlantic Meets Pacific: A Global View of Pidginization and Creolization*, ed. F. Byrne and J. Holm (pp. 431–440). Amsterdam: John Benjamins.

Cassidy, F.G. (1961). *Jamaica Talk: Three Hundred Years of the English Language in Jamaica*. London: Macmillan.

Chaudenson, R. (1992). *Des Iles, des Hommes, des Langues*. Paris: l'Harmattan.

Chaudenson, R. (2001). *Creolization of Language and Culture*. New York: Routledge.

Constantinidou, E. (1994). The "Death" of East Sutherland Gaelic: Death by Women? In *Bilingual Women: Anthropological Approaches to Second Language Use*, ed. P. Burton, K. Kushari-Dyson, and S. Ardener (pp. 111–127). Oxford: Berg Publishers.

Crystal, D. (2000). *Language Death*. Cambridge: Cambridge University Press.

DeGraff, M. (ed.) (1999). *Language Creation and Language Change: Creolization, Diachrony and Development*. Cambridge, MA: MIT Press.

Denison, N. (1977). Language Death or Language Suicide? *International Journal of the Sociology of Language* 12: 13–22.

Dorian, N. C. (1981). *Language Death: The Life Cycle of a Scottish Gaelic Dialect*. Philadelphia: University of Pennsylvania Press.

Dorian, N. C. (1982). Defining the Speech Community to Include its Working Margins. In *Sociolinguistic Variation in Speech Communities*, ed. S. Romaine (pp. 25–33). London: Edward Arnold.

Dorian, N. C. (ed.) (1989). *Investigating Obsolescence: Studies in Language Contraction and Death*. Cambridge: Cambridge University Press.

Dorian, N. C. (1998). Western Language Ideologies and Small-Language Prospects. In *Endangered Languages: Language Loss and Community Response*, ed. L. A. Grenoble and L. J. Whaley (pp. 3–21). Cambridge: Cambridge University Press.

Drummond, L. (1980). The Cultural Continuum: A Theory of Intersystems. *Man (n.s.)* 15: 352–374.

Errington, J. J. (1998a). Indonesian('s) Development: On the State of a Language of State. In *Language Ideologies: Practice and Theory*, ed. B. B. Schieffelin, K. A. Woolard, and P. V. Kroskrity (pp. 271–284). New York: Oxford University Press.

Errington, J. J. (1998b). *Shifting Languages: Interaction and Identity in Javanese Indonesia*. New York: Cambridge University Press.

Ferguson, C. (1959). Diglossia. *Word* 15: 325–340.

Ferguson, C. (1991). Diglossia Revisited. *Southwest Journal of Linguistics* 10(1): 214–234.

Fishman, J. (1967). Bilingualism with and without Diglossia; Diglossia with and without Bilingualism. *Journal of Social Issues* 23(2): 29–38.

Gal, S. (1978). Peasant Men Can't Get Wives: Language Change and Sex Roles in a Bilingual Community. *Language in Society* 7: 1–16.

Gal, S. (1979): *Language Shift: Social Determinants of Linguistic Change in Bilingual Austria*. New York: Academic Press.

Garrett, P. B. (2000). "High" Kwéyòl: The Emergence of a Formal Creole Register in St. Lucia. In *Language Change and Language Contact in Pidgins and Creoles*, ed. J. H. McWhorter (pp. 63–101). Amsterdam: John Benjamins.

Garrett, P. B. (2003). An "English creole" That Isn't: On the Sociohistorical Origins and Linguistic Classification of the Vernacular English of St. Lucia. In *Contact Englishes of the*

Eastern Caribbean, ed. M. Aceto and J. Williams (pp. 155–210). Amsterdam: John Benjamins.

Garrett, P. B., and Baquedano-López, P. (2002). Language Socialization: Reproduction and Continuity, Transformation and Change. *Annual Review of Anthropology* 31: 339–361.

Goodman, M. F. (1971). The Strange Case of Mbugu. In *Pidginization and Creolization of Languages*, ed. D. Hymes (pp. 243–254). Cambridge: Cambridge University Press.

Gumperz, J. J., and Wilson, R. (1971). Convergence and Creolization: A Case from the Indo-Aryan/Dravidian Border. In *Pidginization and Creolization of Languages*, ed. D. Hymes (pp. 151–167). Cambridge: Cambridge University Press.

Hall, R. A. Jr. (1962). The Life Cycle of Pidgin Languages. *Lingua* 11: 151–156.

Hancock, I. (1984). Romani and Anglo-Romani. In *Language in the British Isles*, ed. P. Trudgill (pp. 367–383). Cambridge: Cambridge University Press.

Hanks, W. F. (2000). *Intertexts: Writings on Language, Utterance, and Context*. Lanham, MD: Rowman & Littlefield.

Hannerz, U. (1987). The World in Creolisation. *Africa* 57(4): 546–559.

Hannerz, U. (1996). *Transnational Connections: Culture, People, Places*. London: Routledge.

Hill, J. H. (1998). Language, Race, and White Public Space. *American Anthropologist* 100(3): 680–689.

Hill, J. H., and Hill, K. C. (1986). *Speaking Mexicano: Dynamics of Syncretic Language in Central Mexico*. Tucson: University of Arizona Press.

Holm, J. A. (1988). *Pidgins and Creoles*, vol. I: *Theory and Structure*. New York: Cambridge University Press.

Holm, J. A. (1989). *Pidgins and Creoles*, vol. II: *Reference Survey*. New York: Cambridge University Press.

Hudson, A. (ed.) (1991). *Studies in Diglossia*. Special Theme Issue, *Southwest Journal of Linguistics* 10(1).

Hudson, A. (1992). Diglossia: A Bibliographic Review. *Language in Society* 21: 611–674.

Irvine, J. T., and Gal, S. (2000). Language Ideology and Linguistic Differentiation. In *Regimes of Language: Ideologies, Polities, and Identities*, ed. P. V. Kroskrity (pp. 35–83). Santa Fe, NM: School of American Research Press.

Jackson, J. (1983). *The Fish People: Linguistic Exogamy and Tukanoan Identity in Northwest Amazonia*. Cambridge: Cambridge University Press.

Jaffe, A. (1999). *Ideologies in Action: Language Politics on Corsica*. Berlin: Mouton de Gruyter.

Jourdan, C. (1991). Pidgins and Creoles: The Blurring of Categories. *Annual Review of Anthropology* 20: 187–209.

Kachru, B. B. (1983). *The Indianization of English: The English Language in India*. Oxford: Oxford University Press.

Kegl, J., Senghas, A., and Coppola, M. (1999). Creation through Contact: Sign Language Emergence and Sign Language Change in Nicaragua. In *Language Creation and Language Change: Creolization, Diachrony, and Development*, ed. M. DeGraff (pp. 179–237). Cambridge, MA: MIT Press.

Kroskrity, P. V. (1993). *Language, History, and Identity: Ethnolinguistic Studies of the Arizona Tewa*. Tucson: University of Arizona Press.

Kuiper, K., and Tan Gek Lin, D. (1989). Cultural Congruence and Conflict in the Acquisition of Formulae in a Second Language. In *English across Cultures, Cultures across English: A Reader in Cross-cultural Communication*, ed. O. García and R. Otheguy (pp. 281–304). Berlin: Mouton de Gruyter.

Kulick, D. (1992). *Language Shift and Cultural Reproduction: Socialization, Self, and Syncretism in a Papua New Guinean Village*. New York: Cambridge University Press.

Laycock, D. (1982). Melanesian Linguistic Diversity: A Melanesian Choice? In *Melanesia: Beyond Diversity* (vol. 1), ed. R. May and H. Nelson (pp. 33–38). Canberra: Australian National University Press.

Le Page, R. B., and Tabouret-Keller, A. (1985). *Acts of Identity: Creole-based Approaches to Language and Ethnicity.* Cambridge: Cambridge University Press.

Louisy, P., and Turmel-John, P. (1983). *A Handbook for Writing Creole.* Castries: Research St. Lucia Publications.

Lucas, C., and Valli, C. (1992). *Language Contact in the American Deaf Community.* New York: Academic Press.

McMahon, A. M. S. (1994). *Understanding Language Change.* Cambridge: Cambridge University Press.

McWhorter, J. H. (1997). *Towards a New Model of Creole Genesis.* New York: Peter Lang.

McWhorter, J. H. (1998). Identifying the Creole Prototype: Vindicating a Typological Class. *Language* 74(4): 788–818.

Mendoza-Denton, N. (1999). Sociolinguistics and Linguistic Anthropology of U.S. Latinos. *Annual Review of Anthropology* 28: 375–395.

Mertz, E. (1989). Sociolinguistic Creativity: Cape Breton Gaelic's Linguistic "Tip". In *Investigating Obsolescence: Studies in Language Contraction and Death*, ed. N. C. Dorian (pp. 103–116). Cambridge: Cambridge University Press.

Mous, M. (1994). Ma'a or Mbugu. In *Mixed Languages*, ed. P. Bakker and M. Mous (pp. 175–200). Amsterdam: Institute for Functional Research into Language and Language Use [IFOTT], University of Amsterdam.

Mufwene, S. S. (1986). Les langues créoles peuvent-elles être définies sans allusion à leur histoire? *Etudes Créoles* 9(1): 135–150.

Mufwene, S. S. (1996). The Founder Principle in Creole Genesis. *Diachronica* 13: 83–124.

Mufwene, S. S. (1997). Jargons, Pidgins, Creoles, and Koinés: What Are They? In *The Structure and Status of Pidgins and Creoles*, ed. A. K. Spears and D. Winford (pp. 35–70). Amsterdam: John Benjamins.

Mufwene, S. S. (2000). Creolization Is a Social, not a Structural, Process. In *Degrees of Restructuring in Creole Languages*, ed. I. Neumann-Holzschuh and E. W. Schneider (pp. 65–84). Amsterdam: John Benjamins.

Muysken, P. (1981). Halfway between Quechua and Spanish: The Case for Relexification. In *Historicity and Variation in Creole Studies*, ed. A. Highfield and A. Valdman (pp. 52–78). Ann Arbor: Karoma.

Muysken, P. (1997). Media Lengua. In *Contact Languages: A Wider Perspective*, ed. S. G. Thomason (pp. 365–426). Amsterdam: John Benjamins.

O'Donnell, W. R., and Todd, L. (1980). *Variety in Contemporary English.* London: Allen & Unwin.

Paulston, C. B. (1994). *Linguistic Minorities in Multilingual Settings: Implications for Language Policies.* Amsterdam: John Benjamins.

Pratt, M. L. (1992). *Imperial Eyes: Travel Writing and Transculturation.* New York: Routledge.

Rampton, B. (1995). *Crossing: Language and Ethnicity among Adolescents.* London: Longman.

Rickford, J. R. (1987). *Dimensions of a Creole Continuum: History, Texts, and Linguistic Analysis of Guyanese Creole.* Stanford: Stanford University Press.

Romaine, S. (1994). *Language in Society: An Introduction to Sociolinguistics.* Oxford: Oxford University Press (2nd edn. 2000).

Romaine, S. (1995). *Bilingualism.* Oxford: Blackwell.

Sahlins, M. (1985). *Islands of History.* Chicago: University of Chicago Press.

Sankoff, G. (1980). *The Social Life of Language.* Philadelphia: University of Pennsylvania Press.

Sankoff, G. (2002). Linguistic Outcomes of Language Contact. In *The Handbook of Language Variation and Change*, ed. J. K. Chambers, P. Trudgill, and N. Schilling-Estes (pp. 638–668). Oxford: Blackwell.

Schieffelin, B. B. (1996). Creating Evidence: Making Sense of Written Words in Bosavi. In *Interaction and Grammar*, ed. E. Ochs, E. A. Schegloff, and S. A. Thompson (pp. 435–460). New York: Cambridge University Press.

Schieffelin, B. B. (2000). Introducing Kaluli Literacy: A Chronology of Influences. In *Regimes of Language: Ideologies, Polities, and Identities*, ed. P. V. Kroskrity (pp. 293–327). (Santa Fe, NM: School of American Research Press.

Schmidt, A. (1985). *Young People's Dyirbal: An Example of Language Death from Australia*. Cambridge: Cambridge University Press.

Sebba, M. (1997). *Contact Languages: Pidgins and Creoles*. New York: St. Martin's Press.

Senghas, R. J. (2003). New Ways to be Deaf in Nicaragua: Changes in Language, Personhood, and Community. In *Many Ways to be Deaf*, ed. L. Monaghan et al. (pp. 260–282). Washington, DC: Gallaudet University Press.

Shapiro, H. L. (1968 [1936]). *The Pitcairn Islanders*, formerly *The Heritage of the Bounty*. New York: Simon & Schuster.

Siegel, J. (1985). Koinés and Koinéization. *Language in Society* 14: 357–378.

Silva-Corvalán, C. (1994). *Language Contact and Change: Spanish in Los Angeles*. Oxford: Oxford University Press.

Singler, J. V. (1992). Nativization and Pidgin/Creole Genesis: A Reply to Bickerton. *Journal of Pidgin and Creole Languages* 7(2): 319–333.

Singler, J. V. (1996). Theories of Creole Genesis, Sociohistorical Considerations, and the Evaluation of Evidence: The Case of Haitian Creole and the Relexification Hypothesis. *Journal of Pidgin and Creole Languages* 11: 185–230.

Smith, L. E., and Forman, M. L. (eds.) (1997). *World Englishes 2000*. Honolulu: University of Hawai'i Press.

Spitulnik, D. (1998). The Language of the City: Town Bemba as Urban Hybridity. *Journal of Linguistic Anthropology* 8(1): 30–59.

Thomason, S. G. (ed.) (1997a). *Contact Languages: A Wider Perspective*. Amsterdam: John Benjamins.

Thomason, S. G. (1997b). A Typology of Contact Languages. In *The Structure and Status of Pidgins and Creoles*, ed. A. K. Spears and D. Winford (pp. 71–88). Amsterdam: John Benjamins.

Thomason, S. G. (2001). *Language Contact: An Introduction*. Washington, DC: Georgetown University Press.

Thomason, S. G., and Kaufman, T. (1988). *Language Contact, Creolization, and Genetic Linguistics*. Berkeley: University of California Press.

Tsitsipis, L. D. (1998). *A Linguistic Anthropology of Praxis and Language Shift: Arvanítika (Albanian) and Greek in Contact*. Oxford: Clarendon Press.

Urciuoli, B. (1996). *Exposing Prejudice: Puerto Rican Experiences of Language, Race, and Class*. Boulder, CO: Westview Press.

Urla, J. (1988). Ethnic Protest and Social Planning: A Look at Basque Language Revival. *Cultural Anthropology* 3: 379–394.

Weinreich, U. (1953). *Languages in Contact: Findings and Problems*. The Hague: Mouton.

Woolard, K. A. (1998). Simultaneity and Bivalency as Strategies in Bilingualism. *Journal of Linguistic Anthropology* 8(1): 3–29.

Zentella, A. C. (1997). *Growing Up Bilingual: Puerto Rican Children in New York*. Malden, MA: Blackwell.

<table>
<tr><td>CHAPTER 4</td><td># Codeswitching</td></tr>
</table>

Codeswitching

CHAPTER **4**

Kathryn A. Woolard

1 INTRODUCTION

A significant segment of sociolinguistic research since the mid-twentieth century has been devoted to understanding how bilingual and multilingual communities organize their multiple linguistic resources. Such research generally falls under the rubrics of *language choice* or *code alternation*. Different principles of language choice have been found to predominate in different bilingual communities.[1] Some attend to the linguistic or social identity of the addressee, others to the setting in which an interaction takes place or the topic under discussion; most depend on some combination of these factors.

Communities also vary in the degree to which they mix their languages together or, in contrast, keep them strictly compartmentalized (as in *diglossia*; see Garrett, this volume). Theoretical debates continue about the power of any possible inventory of principles to account adequately for actual language choice. These debates are most acute when it comes to language mixing within the same conversation and even within a single sentence, as in the following examples of Catalan–*Spanish* (example 1) and English–*German* (2) bilingualism:

(1) Ara, em va sapiguer greu, *porque la verdad, eh*, i ara t'ho dic una altra vegada, Toni: *Hay que ver, Toni, cómo te has envejecido, eh?* (Now, I felt bad, *because the truth is, eh*, and now I'm going to tell you again, Toni: *You ought to see, Toni, how old you've gotten, eh?*) (Woolard 1995: 236)

(2) Go and get my coat *aus dem Schrank da* (out of the closet there). (Gumperz 1982: 60)

Such intimate language mixing is referred to as *conversational codeswitching* or more commonly simply as *codeswitching* (often abbreviated as *CS* in the research literature), and it is the focus of this chapter. Codeswitching can be defined as an individual's use of two or more language varieties in the same speech event or exchange.[2] Although I have introduced this phenomenon in the context of bilingualism, I deliberately use the broad term "language varieties" in this definition. The topic of codeswitching is relevant to all speech communities that have linguistic repertoires comprising more than one "way of speaking" (i.e., all, as far as we know). Codeswitching can occur between forms recognized as distinct languages, or between dialects, registers, "levels" such as politeness in Javanese, or styles of a single language.[3] Some of the most enduringly influential work on codeswitching does not address bilingualism but rather standard–vernacular dialect alternation, such as the case of Norwegian villagers discussed by Blom and Gumperz (1972).

Codeswitching has nonetheless most often been investigated in bilingual and multilingual settings, and such a focus has not necessarily been mistaken. The more distinct the varieties between which speakers switch, the more available for inspection and reflection codeswitching may be, to both analysts and speakers.[4] Work on such salient cases can then facilitate our recognition of related but less apparent phenomena. However, as with many aspects of research associated with minority-language communities, codeswitching has often been viewed as irrelevant to those who don't work in bilingual societies or who choose not to focus on the bilingualism in the societies they do study. Such an exclusive identification of codeswitching with bilingualism is counterproductive. Not only is the extent of the phenomenon overlooked, but also the analysis of codeswitching is too often marginalized from broader theoretical enterprises that should both inform and be informed by such work. (Some notable exceptions to this problem will be discussed below.)

Linguists (mostly sociolinguists and psycholinguists) as well as linguistic anthropologists have studied codeswitching, and different research questions dominate in the different disciplines. Linguistic inquiry is most concerned with establishing the grammatical constraints on codeswitching and understanding how its grammar should be characterized in relation to those of the bilingual's distinct languages.[5] Linguistic anthropologists, in contrast, have been most concerned with the question of its "social meaning": not constraints that work against but rather motivations for and functions of codeswitching. This chapter will focus on this second set of questions. I will consider three of the most influential social approaches to explaining codeswitching and then turn to ongoing debates over them. In the final sections of this chapter, I will discuss the need to encompass codeswitching analysis within more general sociolinguistic theory and consider some of the most promising frames for this.

2   CODESWITCHING AS SYSTEMATIC AND MEANINGFUL

Since the early 1970s, linguistic anthropologists have accepted the view that codeswitching is systematic, skilled, and socially meaningful. This is something of a defensive stance, responding to (earlier) beliefs that the use of more than one linguistic variety in an exchange is neither grammatical nor meaningful, but rather is indicative of a speaker's incomplete control of the language(s). Codeswitches were generally seen from that perspective as lapses of language ability, memory, effort, or attention. Even the sociolinguists most responsible for stimulating research on bilingualism held the opinion that extensive language switching was somehow defective. For example,

Uriel Weinreich wrote in his foundational work on language contact (see Garrett, this volume) that "The ideal bilingual switches from one language to the other according to appropriate changes in the speech situation ..., but not in an unchanged speech situation, and certainly not within a single sentence" (Weinreich 1953: 73).

In response to such judgments, linguists have been at pains to demonstrate that even codeswitching within a single sentence (*intrasentential codeswitching*) is orderly and grammatical. Linguistic anthropologists have in turn tried to show that it is resourcefully deployed to create systematic communicative effects. Where disorder, ineptness, and laxity were once seen, researchers celebrate not only virtuosity but even virtue: codeswitching is taken to enrich communicative potential. "What the outsider sees as almost unpredictable variation becomes a communicative resource for members" (Gumperz 1982: 69).

Despite the positive value that linguistic anthropologists typically attribute to codeswitching, the more negative dominant view has framed the research field in an important way. The fundamental question underlying most anthropologically oriented research on codeswitching is "Why do they do that?" Such a question seems inescapably to derive from the profoundly monoglot and largely referentialist outlook of modern language ideologies, despite linguistic anthropology's overt rejection of such views. It is when only one code is believed necessary to get the communication job done (a job understood as denotational) that the use of more than one needs explanation. Even bilingual defenders of minority languages can hold such biases. As a Catalan activist in Barcelona put it, "a language is an instrument of communication, and with one, enough" (Woolard 1998: 4). In a related approach, codeswitches are sometimes attributed to "lexical gaps" in the primary language or the availability of *le mot juste* in the second. Such explanations stress the referential function of language, its use to talk about, rather than to act in, the world. They privilege the need for exchange of information as driving momentary recourse to a second language. From a different vantage point, we might as easily ask why people who have multiple "ways of speaking" would restrict themselves to a subset of them. It would be at least as sensible to ask what constrains the deployment of the full range of linguistic skills as it is to ask what motivates the use of more than one segment of that range.[6]

2.1 Gumperz: Situational and metaphorical codeswitching

The work of John Gumperz has had not only seminal but enduring influence on the accepted anthropological view of codeswitching. In their study of switching between standard and local dialect in the Norwegian village of Hemnesberget, Blom and Gumperz (1972) showed the systematic communication of specific social information through codeswitches. They also proposed a functional distinction between *situational* and *metaphorical* codeswitching that is still a point of departure for most researchers.[7]

In situational switching, a change of language signals a change in the definition of the speech event, involving "clear changes in the participants' definition of each other's rights and obligation" (Blom and Gumperz 1972: 424). A teacher in a Barcelona high school, for example, chatted with her students before and after class in Catalan but lectured in Spanish. (Situational codeswitching is not necessarily epiphenomenal to some other perceivable contextual changes. A situational code-switch may not simply be triggered by a changed context, but may actually in itself contribute to creating that changed context. So, students fall silent and pick up their pencils when they hear the change in language.) Gumperz (1982: 60–1) later associated this kind of clear, well-established code alternation with Joshua Fishman's version of *diglossia*, in which codes are quite strictly compartmentalized. Situational codeswitching is more likely to be *intersentential* (between sentences) than *intrasentential* (within sentences). Correspondingly, researchers are likely to discuss this as *code selection* or *language choice* rather than as switching, which has come to be identified with less stability in the medium of communication.

Metaphorical switching (which Gumperz (1982: 61) later encompassed under the label of *conversational codeswitching*) is a change in language that does not signal a change in the definition of the fundamental speech event. Interactants do not alter the basic definition of the rights and obligations in operation, but only allude to different relationships that they also hold (Blom and Gumperz 1972: 425). Such allusion is achieved through transient use of a language that serves as a "metaphor" for another social relationship regularly associated with it. This "semantic" effect of metaphorical switching, as Blom and Gumperz called it (or what we might prefer to call its social indexical effect), depends on and exploits speakers' consciousness of typical associations of the language that are more predictably displayed in situational switching. In the following example, a Spanish-speaking mother's switch to English is heard as a warning or mild threat to her disobedient child, because of the authoritative connotations of English for many minority-language speakers in the USA:

(3) *Ven acá. Ven acá.* (Come here. Come here.) Come here, you. (Gumperz 1982: 92)

Gumperz later characterized situational and metaphorical codeswitching as two points on a continuum rather than two contrasting types of codeswitching (see also Bailey 1999). In any case, most later analyses and debates have focused on the more subtle kind of conversational switching that Blom and Gumperz first captured under the label "metaphorical."

2.2   Codeswitching and identity: We/They?

Gumperz proposed that a bilingual's two languages typically signal the contrasting cultural standards of the minority community and the larger society with which they are associated. In his model, bilinguals would tend to regard the ethnically specific minority language as an in-group or *we code* associated with familiarity, solidarity, etc., and the majority language as a *they code* associated with "the more formal, stiffer, and less personal out-group relations" (1982: 66). A classic metaphorical switch occurs when minority-language speakers switch momentarily to the majority language to win or "top" an argument, as when a Hungarian-speaking woman in Austria uses German (*italics*) to retort to her husband:

(4) Husband: Nekem ňem hozu fe, magadnag akko nem szabad inna.
     (If you don't bring it up for me, then you can't drink it yourself.)
Wife: In akkor iszok mikor in akarok. *Deis vird niks kbrak. Das vird niks kbrakt.*
           (I drink when I want to. *I don't even want it. I don't even want it.*) (Gal
           1979: 116)

In such instances, the dominant language metaphorically bestows greater authority
on the speaker, who nonetheless still operates in her role as spouse (or parent in
example (3) above). The specific rhetorical or interactional effect (e.g., authority,
anger, or distancing on the one hand, or softening, a joking tone, or intimacy on the
other) depends on the specific interactional circumstances, but for Gumperz all of
these are achieved by processing through the basic "we" vs. "they" dimension
of contrast.

Not all researchers agree that codeswitching always signals such a macrosocially
informed contrast in identities. Gumperz's model takes the minority ethnic group in a
complex stratified society as the prototype of bilingual communities. However, the
minority-within-majority is only one version of the bilingual community, and does
not fit well with societies such as Papua New Guinea or Indonesia. Researchers
working in those areas have accordingly questioned the we/they contrast as the
foundation of meaning in codeswitching (Stroud 1992; Errington 1998).

Some critics have interpreted Gumperz's we/they contrast as referring to distinct,
on-the-ground groups (Errington 1998), but it is best understood as a trope for a
speaker's variable social positioning rather than a literal reference to enumerable
social entities. This is not simply a postmodern reinterpretation; Gumperz has always
treated identity as multifaceted and shiftable. Since bilingual speakers themselves use
the so-called "they" code metaphorically within in-group conversation, it is always
the case that "they is us," as the comic-strip character Pogo put it (see also Errington
(1998: 11) for a different view of this issue). Gumperz's we/they contrast is a way of
capturing the fact that speakers can shift their own perspective from experience-near
("we" or first-person) to experience-distant ("they" or third-person) vantage points,
as seen in the following example:

(5) I don't quit I . . . I just stopped. I mean it wasn't an effort that I made *que voy a dejar
    de fumar por que me hace daño o* (that I'm going to stop smoking because it's
    harmful to me or) this or that uh-uh. It's just that I used to pull butts out of the
    waste paper basket yeah. I used to go look in the . . . *se me acababan los cigarros en la
    noche* (my cigarettes would run out on me at night). I'd get desperate *y ahi voy al
    basarero a buscar, a sacar* (and there I go to the wastebasket to look for some, to get
    some), you know. (Gumperz 1982: 81)

Perhaps the subject–object pair of "we/us" would work better than does the first–
third person contrast of "we/they" to capture the metaphorical values of the codes as
this speaker shifts between "objective" commentary on and "subjective" acting out
of her own experience of quitting smoking.

Even where researchers do agree that distinct we/they, in-group vs. out-group
values are indexed by linguistic codes, they have cautioned against *a priori* assumptions about which code is the "we code" that speakers identify with most intimately.

This can change across generations, lifespans, or contexts. For example, adolescents may identify with the majority code while their immigrant parents' in-group is identified by the minority code (Sebba and Wootton 1998). Role-playing and performance strategies can affect the code identification that speakers want to display to different audiences (Singh 1983). So can shifts in the ethnic or racial contrasts that are relevant, for example when Spanish-speaking Dominicans in the USA variably stress that they are non-white or not African American (Bailey 2000). Moreover, any code may be "re-functionalized," as Jane Hill (1985) has shown in contemporary Mexico. Among speakers of modern Nahuatl (called Mexicano), elements of Spanish, seemingly the "out-group language," are integrated into an in-group "power code" and bent to in-group purposes.

Finally, not all codeswitching is an ethnic in-group practice. Ben Rampton has proposed the term *crossing* for inter-group codeswitching, switches into a second language associated with a (minority) group of which the speakers are not accepted members. Such speakers recruit linguistic resources not generally thought to belong to them, and thus make linguistic moves that seem to challenge social or ethnic boundaries (Rampton 1995: 280; see also Hill 1993). For example, South Asian and white youths in England "cross" into Caribbean-origin creole to sound hip, and similar crossing has since been identified as a strategy of youth cultures in several societies.[8]

Most anthropological analysts agree with Gumperz that codeswitching is skilled communicative behavior that can be socially meaningful and can help accomplish interactional functions or goals. Where they differ is on the questions of how such meaning is produced and processed, whether explanation must be culture-specific or involve universal principles, the relative explanatory weight of social structure and individual agency, and the extent to which such meaning is fully determined by any set of factors. Although there are many different approaches, two main alternatives to Gumperz's pioneering work have been most influential. They will be discussed in the next sections as "discourse-related" codeswitching and the "markedness model."

2.3   Discourse-related codeswitching

We can see codeswitching as interactionally meaningful without holding that every codeswitch necessarily achieves its meaning as a metaphor of distinct social worlds. As Peter Auer writes, "There is a certain danger for the pendulum to swing too far . . . i.e., to treat each and every instance of language alternation as meaningful in the same 'semantic' way" (Auer 1984b: 105).[9] For Auer, Gumperz's approach, although interpretive and interactional, is too macrosociological, since it assumes that an ethnic contrast created by social structural arrangements is always relevant to speakers and invoked in conversational codeswitching. Closely following the sociological school of *conversation analysis* (see Keating and Egbert, this volume), Auer insists on the *local production* of meaning. That is, only when participants can be seen to be making structurally given social identities overtly relevant in the sequentially unfolding interaction are they considered to be relevant to analysis.[10] Other researchers who don't adhere so closely as Auer to the assumptions of conversation analysis also find interactional functions of codeswitching that are not based in social metaphor.

Rather than always working as a metaphor for juxtaposed social worlds, a change of codes as a speech exchange unfolds can in and of itself create interactional and rhetorical effects, just as contrasts in loudness, pace, and pitch do (Woolard 1988; Zentella 1997). Auer has dubbed this *discourse-related codeswitching* (Auer 1984a; Auer 1998a). So, for example, a switch in codes might signal that one topic of conversation is ending and a new one proposed, mark off a side comment from the main topic, or indicate a change in interactional frame (e.g., from single to multiple addressees). Such discourse functions could be signalled by a language switch in either direction, without invoking associations to different social worlds or relationships, as shown in these two Catalan–*Spanish* switches by a Catalan radio comedian in Barcelona (the linguistic affiliation of the underlined elements is ambiguous):

(6) *Creo que con las crónicas taurinas lo hará mucho mejor, digo yo, vamos, porque si no;*
Bueno! Allavorens moltissimes gràcies a tota la gent maca …
(*I think he'll do much better with the bullfight reports, that's what I say, anyway, because if not,* Well*! So then, many thanks to all the beautiful people …*)

(7) Perquè ahir m'ho va contar, aquest tio té torre, eh. Ai! *Me explico yo por qué ligas tú tanto, eh!*
(Because yesterday he told me, this guy has a house, eh? Hey! *I understand how you pick up so many [women], eh*!) (Woolard 1995: 234–5).

Codeswitching might also be used for discourse functions such as flagging a punchline or indicating that a narrative will shift from the narrator's voice to a direct representation of a character's speech. Each and every particular switched phrase is not necessarily best understood by direct reference to different social worlds associated with the two languages, even when these associations may be crucial in understanding the overarching social significance of the use of two languages in a given speech event (Sankoff 1980: chap. 2; Woolard 1988; see also Myers-Scotton 1993: 117).

2.4   The markedness model

For Carol Myers-Scotton, in contrast to Auer, Gumperz's approach is not generalizing enough. Her *markedness model*, while much in sympathy with Gumperz's interpretations, is intended as a more systematic and universal account. Myers-Scotton (1993: 60) criticizes the view (in fact more directly associated with Auer than Gumperz) that the particular social meanings of specific codeswitches are locally negotiated, the product of the individual interaction in which they occur. For Myers-Scotton, what individuals always negotiate when they codeswitch are "positions in rights-and-obligations balances" (ibid.; also dubbed "RO sets"). Thus, her analysis resembles Gumperz's situational switching, but not his metaphorical switching.

The formal markedness model consists of four main principles:

1 The "negotiation principle": "Choose the form of your conversation contribution such that it indexes the set of rights and obligations which you wish to be in force between speaker and addressee for the current exchange" (ibid.: 113).

2 The "unmarked-choice maxim": "Make your code choice the unmarked index of the unmarked RO set in talk exchanges when you wish to establish or affirm that RO set" (ibid.: 114).

3 The "marked-choice maxim": "Make a marked code choice which is not the unmarked index of the unmarked RO set in an interaction when you wish to establish a new RO set as unmarked for the current exchange" (ibid.: 131).

4 The "exploratory-choice maxim": "When an unmarked choice is not clear, use CS to make alternate exploratory choices as candidates for an unmarked choice and thereby as an index of an RO set which you favour" (ibid.: 142).

The idea of "marked" vs. "unmarked" forms was introduced into structural linguistics as a phonological concept by the Prague School linguists N. S. Trubetzkoy and Roman Jakobson (see Jakobson 1990: 134–40). Although the concept of markedness is now extremely complex and broadly applied to all kinds of linguistic and cultural phenomena, "the general meaning of the marked is characterized by the conveyance of more precise, specific, and additional information than the unmarked term provides" (ibid.: 138).

The proliferation of tokens of the term "unmarked" in the markedness model (e.g., in the unmarked-choice maxim) hints that it does not derive from the Prague School concept. Instead, following common sociolinguistic practice, Myers-Scotton defines the unmarked code as the "expected medium" in a particular type of conventionalized exchange (1993: 89–90). It is expected because it has been used most frequently in such contexts. The markedness model thus reduces markedness directly to *frequency*.[11]

Other interpretations such as Joseph Greenberg's (1966) have also treated frequency as central in the concept of markedness, but there is an important difference. For Greenberg, certain linguistic forms will be more frequent because they are unmarked; frequency is an effect, rather than a cause. The markedness model reverses this order: a linguistic variety is unmarked because it is frequent. Myers-Scotton certainly is not alone in this usage; many sociolinguists and some linguists invoke similar understandings of this multivocal term (see discussions in Andrews 1990; Battistella 1990, 1996). However, this reversal leaves markedness itself no autonomous status and strips the markedness model of any theoretical purchase, since it is fundamentally circular.[12] A linguistic variety is defined as unmarked because it is more frequently chosen, and Myers-Scotton predicts that it will be more frequently chosen by speakers because it is unmarked. For example, "That speakers generally will choose to accept or negotiate the (new) unmarked RO set is predicted by the model" (1993: 115). This is not a prediction but rather a tautological restatement of the definition, reducible to a claim that "speakers will generally choose the RO set that is most frequently chosen."

As applied to codeswitching (unlike phonology), markedness seems most useful when treated as an activity of interactants – that is, an act of marking – rather than as a property of a code. This is the sense in which several contributions to the groundbreaking Gumperz and Hymes (1972) collection invoked the term. In doing so, they were influenced by a dynamic, information-processing version of "marking" and "marking rules" developed by William Geoghegan, one that had only loose ties to the Prague School concept (Geoghegan 1969, 1970, 1971). For Susan Ervin-Tripp, speakers "add optional marking" in order "to add nuances to meaning" (Ervin-Tripp 1976: 61). Use of a single code in an interaction might be unmarked, for example, in that it is neither polite nor impolite, but simply doesn't register on the dimension of politeness. A switch to a second code is a form of marking that can activate a contrast on the politeness dimension, conveying more social meaning and sounding "markedly" rude. Such a conceptualization of markedness flickers in and out of Myers-Scotton's discussions, but it disappears in her explicit formulations. Formally in the markedness model, the "unmarked" variety is as informative as the marked variety, always and equally indexing a specific claim to an RO set, and usually to affective stances such as respect as well (see also Gross 2000 on use of Spanish in the USA).

The theoretical concept that the markedness model clearly and usefully mobilizes is not actually markedness but rather *indexicality*. For Myers-Scotton, linguistic varieties are always socially indexical. That is, through the accumulation of use in particular kinds of social relations, they come to index or invoke those relations, taking on an air of natural association with them (1993: 85). Eliminating the term "markedness" and focusing on indexicality in the markedness model can help clarify the maxims themselves as well as the contribution that the overall argument makes. It also suggests that a fuller theory of indexicality might enhance our understanding of codeswitching, a point I will take up in a later section of the chapter. To be sure, marking as an active process may intersect with an established socially indexical meaning of a code, exploiting, undercutting, or amplifying it. Rather than abandoning the idea of marking entirely, I believe this intersection poses the most interesting remaining problems for codeswitching studies. An important step is to disentangle marking and social indexicality, as the research on discourse-related codeswitching discussed earlier has in essence advocated.

3   REVISING CODESWITCHING THEORY

Since the early 1990s, linguistic anthropologists have questioned assumptions that seem to be shared by all of these explanatory approaches. In this section, I will address three of these questions: the nature of explanation, the discreteness of codes, and the strategic nature of codeswitching.

3.1   What counts as explanation?

Whichever of these explanatory models seems most persuasive, is it enough to explain what codeswitching means where it does occur? Does a full explanation not also need to account for why it does not occur in seemingly similar circumstances? While some bilingual communities may allow intimate mixing of languages, other communities such as the Arizona Tewa (Kroskrity 1998) maintain a strict compartmentalization of codes (Gal 1987: 639). How can we account for this difference, if social psychological motives and interactional functions are presumably universal? These lead us to predict codeswitching in bilingual communities or sectors of communities where it does not in fact occur. *Ad hoc* provisos then need to be added to explanations in order to constrain their predictions. Meeuwis and Blommaert (1994) have criticized the markedness model in particular on this point, but other explanatory approaches are equally susceptible, as Gal (1987) pointed out.

Accounting for where codeswitching does not occur as well as where it does necessitates a turn beyond microsocial principles of interaction to macrosocial structures (Gal 1988; Meeuwis and Blommaert 1994). Cross-cultural or diachronic differences in the permissibility and patterning of codeswitching invite us to consider differences in the way communities are situated within political and economic systems. So, for example, in contrast to the typical pattern identified for ethnic minorities elsewhere, conversational codeswitching has traditionally been rare among Catalans in Spain and German speakers in Romania. Correspondingly, both groups traditionally enjoyed economic superiority in their larger societies, unlike most minority groups (Woolard 1988; Gal 1987). Rather than arising as an automatic response to social structural factors, however, the practice of codeswitching is mediated by speakers' own understanding of their position in that structure (Gal 1987). It is ultimately not any objective positioning or value of a language, but rather speakers' ideological interpretation of and response to that value, that are mobilized in codeswitching. Because of this, codeswitching and related translingual phenomena can provide a window on social and political consciousness, as both Hill (1985) and Gal (1987) have argued.

3.2   How discrete are the codes of codeswitching?

Despite the important differences among them, in all of the prevailing social analyses, codeswitching bilinguals have shed their earlier image as incompetent monolinguals. They have come to look like linguistic Fred Astaires, tapping out multiple codes on flashing footings, dancing circles around monolinguals. Penelope Gardner-Chloros (1995) argues that researchers replaced the old orthodoxy of monolingual norms with a new and equally myth-based orthodoxy of codeswitching.

This orthodoxy is so secure that sympathetic skepticism has finally arisen from within the field. Researchers who do not doubt the competence of their speaking subjects suggest there is greater ambiguity and indeterminacy, less strategy, and perhaps even less meaning and less skill in some forms of codeswitching than have so often been attributed. They bring this skepticism to all of the dominant analyses. This leads to questioning the very category of codeswitching itself: perhaps speakers are not switching between two distinct and clearly bounded varieties after all?

It has always been difficult for analysts to distinguish codeswitching from other language contact or translinguistic phenomena. Where to draw the line between codeswitching and *borrowing, interference,* and/or emerging new *contact varieties* has long been the subject of discussion (see Garrett, this volume; see also contributions to Milroy and Muysken 1995; Auer 1998b). Now, from both anthropology and linguistics have come new acknowledgments of the fuzziness of language systems involved in codeswitching and bilingualism. The most recent work is characterized by more fluid visions of the linguistic structures themselves and of their social significance as they are mobilized by bilingual speakers.

From several directions, researchers have turned toward the phenomenon of simultaneity in bilingual speech. That is, we can think of the two language systems as sometimes being simultaneously rather than sequentially activated in linguistic, cognitive, and/or social senses. Particular linguistic forms are more often seen now not as belonging necessarily to either one code or another, but as fully participating in more than one linguistic system, as "syncretic," "neutral," or "bivalent" (Hill and Hill 1986; Alvarez-Cáccamo 1990; Giacalone Ramat 1995; Hill 1999; Woolard 1999; Muysken 2000; Swigart 2000). Studying what looks like frequent intrasentential codeswitching, several analysts have taken "a monolectal view," seeing not switching between two distinct varieties but a single code of mixed origins (Meeuwis and Blommaert 1998). Swigart, for example, characterizes the following as an example of "Urban Wolof" in Senegal rather than purposive French–Wolof codeswitching:

(8) Parce que *man*, je vois mal qu'une école *boo xamante ne...naka lañu mene seetaan* élève *yi ba nū am* BFEM?

Because *myself*, I don't see how a school *that...how can they supervise the* students *till they get the* BFEM? (Swigart 2000: 113)

The monolectal view may be correct for many such situations, but it is by no means a universal replacement for the category of codeswitching. Contact varieties do not displace switching between distinct linguistic varieties everywhere. In many settings such as Catalonia, even where precise boundaries may be in question, the contrast between language systems is psychologically real and ideologically meaningful to speakers, and remains a resource they can mobilize in interaction.

3.3   Is codeswitching strategic?

Another standard assertion now subject to revision is that codeswitching is an interactional "strategy." I believe that contention over this question is rooted as much in different understandings of strategy as in different views of codeswitching. At issue is whether the term "strategic" presupposes and privileges a speaker's *intentions*, and if so, whether intention implies conscious control. I will try to show this by examining the thoughtful argument of just one principal critic of strategic analysis, Christopher Stroud (1992).

Stroud characterizes all the major analytic approaches as based in speakers' intentions, and as assuming that speakers intend a single specific meaning of a codeswitch to be perceived by their listeners. He argues that such a view derives from a Western language ideology that privileges intentionality, and that such a view misrepresents the dynamics of codeswitching in non-Western societies that do not share such an ideology.

As Duranti explains (this volume), intentionality has different meanings. If by intentionality we mean being directed-toward or being "about" something, then indeed the major analysts argue that codeswitching is intentional. If by intentionality we mean conscious planning, then no, the principal analysts hold that it is not.[13]

Both Gumperz and Myers-Scotton take clear positions on the issue of conscious intention. Gumperz states that "metaphorical switching occurs demonstrably below the level of consciousness. You no more plan a metaphorical switch than you do your choice of tense or mood in speaking." He points out that "people are often not even aware of what they do" (Gumperz 1984: 110). Interactional *functions* rather than speaker *motivations* are the locus of strategies in Gumperz's analysis, and these should not be thought of as simply interchangeable.

The markedness model, in contrast, does make speakers' intentions the key to explanation. Nonetheless, a recent article clarifies that the rational calculation posited in the model as underlying codeswitching is not necessarily conscious (Myers-Scotton and Bolonyai 2001: 16). The authors compare aspects of the process to the rapid recognition and application of well-known, integrated strategies that have been described for emergency workers such as firefighters. This resembles the routine monitoring of actions that Garfinkel says differs from the level of analytical rationalization that is necessary when we are asked to provide an account of those actions (see Duranti, this volume). "Did I switch languages then? I don't know why, I just did" is a common enough reply from codeswitchers that neither Gumperz nor Myers-Scotton would necessarily view as counterevidence to their analyses.

Stroud uses the vocabulary of strategy and intent to analyze a codeswitching performance in Gapun, Papua New Guinea, as "an attempt to draw attention" involving "careful use of indirection," "conversational ploys," "veiled requests," and the "manipulation" of speech (Stroud 1992: 134–7). Ultimately, however, Stroud rejects his own detailed analysis because he cannot know if the participants in the dialogue draw the same conclusion that he would. Any "one instance of codeswitching could be performing one or a manifold of different functions simultaneously" (ibid.: 145). Such possible ambiguity is not, however, a fatal challenge to received models of codeswitching.

If, in codeswitching, Gapun villagers present themselves ambiguously from a number of points of view that listeners can pick up or ignore (ibid.: 148), this means that villagers indeed *are* aware of the rhetorical and pragmatic possibilities of such switching – precisely the point for Gumperz, Myers-Scotton, Gal, Hill, and others. That these possibilities are multiple makes them no less plausible or significant. The fact that Gapuners continually contest the intentions and meanings of such speech (ibid.) is evidence of their importance to participants (and therefore an argument for analysts to go to work).

Ambiguity and multivocality may well be of the essence in codeswitching in Gapun, as Stroud asserts, but this is true of other places where it is used, even in the Western world (Heller 1988). For example, the inherent social and political ambiguity of codeswitching is what recommends it as a tool of humor for radio performers in Catalonia who have a diverse audience (Woolard 1995, 1998). Ambiguity is always characteristic of pragmatic strategies that are not explicitly on-record, unless/until they become thoroughly conventionalized. It is exactly their relative deniability that gives them their social utility. The strategy Gapuners use, like much negative politeness in Brown and Levinson's schema (1978), leaves the interactional commitment to a potential face-threat delicate and open.

The critics of strategy may themselves be most prone to impose Western notions of intentionality on the analysis of speech. It is Stroud who suggests researchers should confirm their interpretation with "the speaker's own thoughts on what he was attempting to achieve with his switch" (1992: 151), thus stepping into the trap identified by Jakobson: "Instead of asking the question, What is the function of the given element in the system of which it is a part? they ask, To what extent is this element accessible to the consciousness of the speakers?" (1990: 106–7).

Most functional analyses of codeswitching eschew recourse to speakers' discursive consciousness of language, but methodological disagreements remain. Conversation analysts like Auer attempt to set strict constraints on evidence, relying only on (what they see as) interactional displays of how an utterance has been taken. Such enactments would be the kind of social accomplishment of meaning that Stroud looks for. (Whether these are themselves partial or misleading performances, and whether relevant interactional displays might be iterated well beyond the initial interaction, would still be in question.) Other functional analyses take as evidence a combination of formal characteristics, structural and sequential placement, characteristics of delivery, and interactants' responses in further exchange (see Hill 1985 for an account of evidence). None of these approaches is the same as one based in speaker-centered motivations and intentions.

The remaining methodological challenges to codeswitching analysis are indeed quite serious. Stroud is right to call into question our preference for tidy accounts over ambiguity, to ask that we provide warrants for interpretations, and to highlight the perennial problem of falsifiability. But these problems are only as insurmountable for codeswitching as for all other topics that concern the interpersonal import of human activity and the conclusions that people draw about the actions of those around them, that is, the stuff of anthropology.

4 Generalizability to Other Linguistic Phenomena

I suggested earlier that codeswitching research needs to overcome its marginalization from broader theoretical enterprises. The markedness model is one such attempt, but I have argued that its fit with markedness theories is more apparent than real. There are other generalizing accounts that allow researchers to approach codeswitching as an instance of a larger phenomenon and bring it to bear on our understanding of language processes, the interaction order, and the macrosocial order. In this section, I will sketch some of the most promising approaches that have been offered.

Gumperz has himself encompassed codeswitching within his more general theory of *conversational inference*. In this view, codeswitching is just one rhetorical resource speakers use to signal how they define the interaction they are in, and how they intend their utterances to be interpreted. All conversationalists, not just codeswitchers, "rely on indirect inferences that build on background assumptions about context, interactive goals, and interpersonal relations to derive frames in terms of which they can interpret what is going on" (1982: 2). Interactants who share backgrounds use "contextualization cues" to signal and infer such interactional frames, allowing them to interpret particular utterances. Codeswitching is one of the many possible cues that speakers rely on; prosody is another principal resource that Gumperz identifies.

5   GOFFMAN: FOOTING

Erving Goffman proposed the general concept of "footing" to account for the "changes in alignment we take up to ourselves and others," among which he included the stances that Gumperz had found to be expressed through codeswitching (1981: 128). Footing is a relationship of speakers to the act of speaking, and we often shift from one foot to another in interaction. Such changes of footing can be signaled in various ways. According to Goffman, switching between language varieties is only one such signaling device, and he identifies "code-switching like behavior that doesn't involve a code switch at all" (ibid.: 127).[14] Just as Gumperz looks to prosodic cues, Goffman sees that bodily orientation and tone of voice can similarly be used to signal significant shifts in alignment of speaker to hearers. Not only is there a broad spectrum of formal techniques for establishing and shifting footing, there is also a continuum of interactional footings. These range from gross changes in the social capacities in which the persons present claim to be active (e.g., in the shift from liminal friendly chat to a proper business exchange) to the most subtle shifts in tone (ibid.: 128).

Goffman characterizes much codeswitching as involving "changing hats," i.e., rapidly altering the social role in which a speaker is active, even though her/his capacity as animator and author remains constant (ibid.: 145). This observation coincides closely with Myers-Scotton's view that RO sets are always at issue in codeswitching, and fits Gumperz's early definitions of situational codeswitching. But Goffman astutely observes that this "sober, sociological" view misses the "free-wheeling, self-referential character of speech" – the essential fancifulness of talk and its fluidities (ibid.: 146–7). Goffman further deconstructs interactional roles in order to capture this fluidity, finding multiple embeddings of different footings. In a single utterance such as "I think that I said that I had once lived there," each "I" represents a slightly different incarnation and alignment of the Self. Recognition of these infinite nuances of footing enriches the possible meanings of codeswitching beyond those identified in the models discussed earlier.

6   BAKHTIN: VOICING

The Russian literary theorist Mikhail Bakhtin provided an interpretive framework and the concepts of *heteroglossia, polyphony,* and *voicing* that have proved very productive for codeswitching studies. For Bakhtin, all societies are linguistically diverse ("heteroglossic"). Language is never really unitary in even the most monolingual settings, but is always stratified by the distinct social experiences of its speakers. "Each word tastes of the . . . contexts in which it has lived its socially charged life" (Bakhtin 1981: 293). Each utterance is thus "filled with echoes and reverberations of other utterances" to which it is related (Bakhtin 1986: 91). Language styles are not only a matter of form but are a fusion of form and circumstances of use. In this way they come to encode the social relations and identities of particular social groups and activities (Pujolar 2001: 31). Language, then, is not only heteroglot but also indexical from top to bottom. Similarities to both Gumperz's and Myers-Scotton's view of the indexicality of codeswitching are apparent here, but its pragmatic effect is tied to an infinite array of voices rather than simply to discrete languages.

The *voice* is the social intention with which a given echoic linguistic form-in-use, or "word," is infused. We receive all our linguistic forms through others' uses, and thus each carries other voices. Most American English speakers can identify, for example, the teacherly voice in an admonition like "Now children, play nicely." Even while the original voice of such an utterance is recognizable, it can be reaccentuated by another speaker, infused with a new social intention. A single utterance can combine a variety of voices, in *polyphony* or dialogue, as when an adult jokingly invokes the teacherly phrase to call colleagues to order.

In the various kinds of *double-voiced word*, the speaker's utterance and intentions enter into dialogue, and sometimes struggle, with the voice and social intentions of others who (might) have uttered the same forms. A double-voiced word may endorse and amplify the intentions of earlier uses, or it may challenge it in irony or parody. For example Jane Hill (1993) argues that when Anglo-Americans use Mock Spanish like the movie tagline "*Hasta la vista*, baby," they are appropriating and subverting a warm Spanish voice for pejorative purposes. When a Barcelona radio comedian switches from Catalan to a *Spanish* advertising voice in the following example, he ironizes his own self-promotion even as he recruits the hyperbolic power of the familiar commercial voice:

(9) Molta atenció, *público habitual . . . eh eh, centenares de miles de personas que habitual-mente nos siguen en todos nuestros desplazamientos*
(Your full attention, *customary audience . . . uh, uh, hundreds of thousands of people who habitually follow us in all our travels*) (Woolard 1995: 243)

Bakhtin's approach offers many advantages in the study of codeswitching. First, like Gumperz's and Goffman's, it enlarges the scope of codeswitching analyses, bringing them into clear relation with phenomena found throughout monolingual as well as multilingual societies. Secondly, like Goffman, Bakhtin allows more multiple social positionings and nuances of meaning to be captured than do dichotomous models. Third, Bakhtin allows these interactional positionings and nuances to be anchored in larger social structures, where Goffman's footings ultimately are anchored in individuals and leave the interaction order disconnected from the social order. Bakhtin's approach better enables codeswitching analysts to articulate the linkages of linguistic form, social context, macrosocial identity, and consciousness of all of these. Fourth, Bakhtin's concept of voicing captures the dynamic side of meaning-making, allowing continuity but also variability, ambiguity, and change in meaning for any given linguistic form or element. For Bakhtin, meaning is not finalized, but rather is always open to re-accentuation through revoicing (Pujolar 2001: 31–2). Fifth, the concept of double-voicing allows the extension of the ideas behind metaphorical codeswitching beyond solidary speech communities to the kind of crossing studied by Rampton.

Finally, Bakhtin allows us a fresh approach to the question of intentionality, a way around the impasse posed by the debate over individual vs. collective agency. In Bakhtin's view, social intentionalities circulate through communities rather than being vested only in the individual. Speakers never are sole owners of their own words, in this view, and so they are unlikely to be sole authors of the intentionality the words communicate. Moreover, voices are evoked by circumstances, and can speak through people at the same time as people speak through them. This more social, less individually agentive view of the ownership of language fits better the communication of social meaning in codeswitching that analysts have been trying to express. "Metaphorical switching," "footing," and "voice" are alternative tropes for this, and it may be that voice is the most flexible and therefore useful.

Bakhtin himself analyzed codeswitching in literary forms, and his schema has been fruitfully applied to conversational codeswitching by a number of researchers (Hill 1985; Rampton 1995, 1998; Woolard 1995, 1998; Tsitsipis 1998; Pujolar 2001). Although Bakhtin allows us to capture nuance, variability, change, and most valuably, the linkage of form to social relations and ideology, there are difficulties in applying his system. Automatic readings of fixed intentionality from linguistic form are tempting, but for Bakhtin, it is intentions, not linguistic markers, that constitute distinct voices. External linguistic markers such as codeswitching are just the deposits of that intentional process, and can only be understood by examining the specific conceptualization they have been given by an intention (1981: 292). Although in theory one can posit a voice behind a particular usage, it is often very difficult to identify this voice or social intention in practice (ibid.: 76).

7 INDEXICALITY

Bakhtin's framework allows us to see that the social indexical value (voicing) of a linguistic form can change, but it does not so easily show us how such change is accomplished. How do we come to infuse or hear different voices in a given form? The social indexicality that is mobilized in codeswitching is not simply a matter of brute statistical correspondence of linguistic and social forms. Rather, a relationship of association must be noticed and interpreted in order to signify. The processes through which indexical meanings are constituted – as opposed to simply deployed – by codeswitching communities are not yet well analyzed. As William Hanks has written, "indexes require instructions" (Hanks 1996: 47).

Michael Silverstein's (1996) development of C. S. Peirce's conception of indexicality can be brought to bear to capture the dynamism that critics have found missing in existing models of codeswitching. Silverstein shows us indexicality not just as a given fact but as a dialectical process of extrapolation of meaning from use and use from meaning. If a specific form presupposes a certain social context, then use of that form may create the perception of such a context where it did not exist before. For example, if a certain linguistic variety is associated with the authority of the classroom or court, it may come to be heard as authoritative language. Its use in a different context can then itself signify authority, in a creative form of indexicality.

The indexical value of a linguistic form can be transferred ideologically not just from context to context, but from context to speaker, or vice versa, and can be transformed in the process. Individuals who use the kind of language now perceived as authoritative can project themselves as authoritative kinds of people. The projected relationship could be partial, false, misrecognized, misconstrued, distorted, etc., but in this kind of creative projection, it comes to be "real" in the way that all performative language can be real (ibid.: 267). Unanticipated turns are often taken in such semiotic spirals. Participants can partition the social world differently, reanalyzing that same variety of language in the same context of use not as authoritative but as the language of anger, effeminacy, or obscenity, to give just some examples documented ethnographically. Those who use the language variety in the hopes of signaling their authority may instead establish their own identity as overbearing, effeminate, or vulgar. For example, many working-class youths in Barcelona use a stylized Andalusian accent to signal their direct, unvarnished access to "simple truth," while others use the same stylized accent to parody aggressive machismo (Pujolar 2001). White youths in the USA and England who use African American Vernacular English or Creole because they see the language as indexing knowledge of popular culture may be heard – and rejected – as trying to appropriate black identity. Over time, with sufficient ideological "oomph" as Silverstein says, later meanings can blend with or even supplant the first one (1996: 267).

Analyses of codeswitching allow only a single order of indexicality when they treat the macrosocial order as inertly embodied in fixed "RO sets" or in-group/out-group dichotomies. Such a structural view gives us only partial insight into speakers' practices. Auer expressed a similar concern when he argued that not only situational but also metaphorical codeswitches need to be seen as models on which speakers base subsequent interactions and interpretation of code choices (Auer 1984b). Silverstein's spiraling play of potentially infinite orders of indexical meaning, one built systematically on another, can help capture "the semiotic plenitude" of codeswitching behavior (Silverstein 1996: 293).

The recurring semiotic processes of iconization, fractal recursivity, and erasure that Irvine and Gal (2000) have identified in linguistic ideology can also be useful tools for thinking about how codeswitching comes to signify socially (see Kroskrity, this volume). In iconization, a linguistic system or feature is interpreted as an image of the essence of a social group (Irvine and Gal 2000: 37). Thus, the aspirated "s" (as in *ehte* for *este*, 'this') of the stylized Andalusian accent in Barcelona is heard as rough, masculine, and authentic, the essence of working-class southern Spanish masculinity (Pujolar 2001). Such an icon is exploited in codeswitching practices.

Metaphorical codeswitching can be thought of as an instance of *fractal recursivity*. In recursivity, an established ideological opposition between two social categories is projected onto some other level of social relations (for example, the contrast between adults and children is projected within individuals, who can "get in touch with their inner child"). Eckert (1980) shows this recursive process at work in Gascon language shift, as the power of a dominant French-speaking world outside the local community is reproduced within that community and even within individuals who strive to use the French language to project empowering images of themselves. This kind of recursive projection would seem to entail a logical contradiction that undermines the persuasiveness of the distinction between child and adult or between majority and minority. But it does not necessarily do so, because such contradictions can be rendered toothless by *erasure*. Erasure renders inconvenient facts – like the use of the powerful linguistic code by the minority community – invisible. Such oversight means that the fact of a metaphorical codeswitch does not necessarily undermine the indexical relationship on which it builds, but rather can actually reinforce and amplify it.

We have a lot of research that shows that social indexicality is brought into play by bilingual speakers through codeswitching. What is needed is more work that shows just how and when indexicality emerges, and when it is reaffirmed, amplified, reformulated, or even dissipated. In some cases, recursive application through codeswitching fortifies a distinction in the value of language varieties, but in others it seems to weaken it. Frequent intrasentential codeswitching arguably can lose its punch, become regularized, and cease to signify socially. Auer (1998a) likens this process to the semantic bleaching of lexical items as they lose their literal meaning and become grammaticalized. The endpoint of such a bleaching process would be the formation of a monolectal code of mixed origins, as discussed earlier. A clearer understanding of the workings of indexicality may resolve not only issues of strategy and social meaning in codeswitching, but also questions about its representation in grammar.

8 CONCLUSION

Since the mid-twentieth century, linguistic anthropology and sociolinguistics have changed the dominant characterization of conversational codeswitching from one of linguistic deviance, corruption, and incompetence to that of systematicity, meaning, and skill. The establishment of this latter view has given rise to debates over how best to represent such systematicity and meaningfulness. These debates have now brought the view of codeswitching nearly full circle, to open questioning by experts of received wisdom about the skill, strategy, and linguistic boundaries involved. If it doesn't become a reflexive undoing of the insights we have already gained, such skepticism will bring new health and vitality to codeswitching studies. These current questions can best be addressed by looking to powerful theoretical constructs – of contextualization, footing, voicing, and indexicality – available to us beyond the confines of research on language choice and codeswitching.

NOTES

1 Throughout this chapter, I will use "bilingual" as a shorthand to refer to bilingual and multilingual communities or speakers.
2 Definitions of codeswitching vary. This definition encompasses research by ethnographers of speaking, whose unit of analysis is the "speech event," as well as interaction and conversation analysts, who start with a speech "exchange." It is not meant to exclude the possibility of codeswitching in written and printed texts. The term is often written as "code-switching" and sometimes as "code switching," but no semantic distinction can be drawn among the different conventions. To the extent that "code" connotes differing encryptions of an independently existing message, *codeswitching* may seem to participate in a discredited "Conduit Metaphor" (Reddy 1979; see Alvarez-Cáccamo (1998, 1999) for the history of the term as well as this criticism). However, as shorthand for a noncommittal idea of "language variety," code is a workable term, since it is widely accepted without any theoretical encumbrances of this kind.
3 Anthropologically, these different kinds of cases can be accounted for by similar principles. Linguistically, however, there is disagreement on whether the grammatical account of codeswitching between languages should be the same as for "shifting" along a style continuum within a language.

4   To be sure, varieties receive the label of distinct "languages" because of history and politics as much as because of linguistic distance. Nonetheless, distinct languages will often – though not always – show more structural distance than other varieties.

5   There are other important linguistic questions about codeswitching that are beyond the scope of this chapter. One concerns language change: is there a causal relation between codeswitching and structural change in language, or between codeswitching and language shift over time? (See, e.g., Gal 1979; Woolard 1989; Muysken 2000).

6   It could be argued that linguists, with their focus on constraints against rather than motivations for codeswitching, do ask this alternative question.

7   There are numerous taxonomies of codeswitching, both formal and functional. These will not be discussed here for lack of space, but are well reviewed elsewhere (Auer 1984a; Jacobson 1998; Muysken 2000).

8   Michael Silverstein observes that such linguistic crossing is a group-bounding device through which young people define their age set, using multilingual access to differentiate it from the older folk, who are more stereotypically characterized as monolingual (or incompetently bilingual) ethnics. The operative ideology is one of "fluid mobility rather than rigid social partition." The trope of crossing restores agency to youth as though they can choose their own identities – "touching, really, for those in truly hemmed-in minority populations, ideologies of mobility notwithstanding, where a certain solidarity develops across demographic divides" (personal communication).

9   As Auer's quotation marks remind us, it is, in our technical vocabulary, "pragmatic" rather than "semantic" meaning that language alternation conveys in Gumperz's model.

10   What is "overtly relevant" of necessity depends on interpretive conventions. Linguistic anthropology has long criticized conversation analysts for not recognizing the culturally based interpretive assumptions smuggled in at the base of this positivist empiricism.

11   In asserting that frequency is the basis of Myers-Scotton's unmarked code, I am following the ideas developed in the 1993 book: "A continuum of relative frequencies of occurrence exists so that one linguistic variety can be identified as the most unmarked index of a specific RO set in a specific interaction type" (p. 89); " . . . in the most conventionalized exchanges, an unmarked code is apparent. It is the expected medium, the index of the unmarked RO set. And it is expected just because it has already appeared often in the community in concert with this RO set" (p. 90). In a helpful and detailed personal communication, Myers-Scotton rejects frequency as defining unmarked choices; rather, she only uses it to identify them (an accepted operational strategy of markedness theory as used by Greenberg and a number of other commentators). Myers-Scotton instead defines unmarked choices as "conforming to prevailing community views for an appropriate RO set" (given specific conditions). But it is not yet clear to me what these community views are based on, if not the rates of occurrence invoked in the passages I cite from the 1993 work.

12   Meeuwis and Blommaert (1994: 398) concluded for other reasons that at the level of theory, markedness as the explanation of codeswitching is "an empty shell."

13   Errington draws a similar distinction when he proposes to discriminate between codeswitching that is strongly intentful/strategic versus weakly intentful/strategic (1998: 193–4).

14   Such an observation has led Alvarez-Cáccamo (1998) to suggest that "codeswitching" should not be defined by a change in language variety at all, but by social meanings. Conflating form and function definitionally seems likely to stymy rather than enhance methodical inquiry.

REFERENCES

Alvarez-Cáccamo, C. (1990). Rethinking Conversational Code-switching. *Proceedings of the Berkeley Linguistics Society* 16: 3–16.

Alvarez-Cáccamo, C. (1998). From "Switching Code" to "Codeswitching": Toward a Reconceptualization of Communicative Codes. In P. Auer (ed.), *Code-switching in Conversation: Language, Interaction and Identity* (pp. 29–50). London: Routledge.

Alvarez-Cáccamo, C. (1999). Codes. *Journal of Linguistic Anthropology* 9(1–2): 28–31.

Andrews, E. (1990). *Markedness Theory: The Union of Asymmetry and Semiosis in Language.* Durham, NC: Duke University Press.

Auer, J. C. P. (1984a). *Bilingual Conversation.* Amsterdam: John Benjamins.

Auer, J. C. P. (1984b). On the Meaning of Conversational Code-switching. In J. C. P. Auer and A. di Luzio (eds.), *Interpretive Sociolinguistics* (pp. 87–108). Tübingen: Gunter Narr Verlag.

Auer, (J. C.) P. (1998a). Introduction: *Bilingual Conversation* Revisited. In J. C. P. Auer (ed.), *Code-switching in Conversation* (pp. 1–24). London: Routledge.

Auer, (J. C.) P. (ed.) (1998b). *Code-switching in Conversation: Language, Interaction and Identity.* London: Routledge.

Bailey, B. (1999). Switching. *Journal of Linguistic Anthropology* 9(1–2): 241–243.

Bailey, B. (2000). The Language of Multiple Identities among Dominican Americans. *Journal of Linguistic Anthropology* 10(2): 190–223.

Bakhtin, M. (1981). *The Dialogic Imagination* (trans. C. Emerson and M. Holquist). Austin: University of Texas Press.

Bakhtin, M. (1986). *Speech Genres and Other Late Essays.* Austin: University of Texas Press.

Battistella, E. L. (1990). *Markedness: The Evaluative Superstructure of Language.* Albany: State University of New York Press.

Battistella, E. L. (1996). *The Logic of Markedness.* New York: Oxford University Press.

Blom, J.-P., and Gumperz, J. J. (1972). Social Meaning in Linguistic Structures: Code-switching in Norway. In J. J. Gumperz and D. Hymes (eds.), *Directions in Sociolinguistics* (pp. 407–434). New York: Holt, Rinehart and Winston.

Brown, P., and Levinson, S. (1978). Universals of Language Usage: Politeness Phenomena. In E. Goody (ed.), *Questions and Politeness* (pp. 56–289). Cambridge: Cambridge University Press.

Eckert, P. (1980). Diglossia: Separate and Unequal. *Linguistics* 18: 1053–1064.

Errington, J. J. (1998). *Shifting Languages: Interaction and Identity in Javanese Indonesia.* Cambridge: Cambridge University Press.

Ervin-Tripp, S. (1976). Is Sybil There? The Structure of Some American English Directives. *Language in Society* 5: 25–66.

Gal, S. (1979). *Language Shift.* New York: Academic Press.

Gal, S. (1987). Codeswitching and Consciousness in the European Periphery. *American Ethnologist* 14(4): 637–653.

Gal, S. (1988). The Political Economy of Code Choice. In M. Heller (ed.), *Codeswitching* (pp. 245–265). Berlin: Mouton de Gruyter.

Gardner-Chloros, P. (1995). Code-switching in Community, Regional and National Repertoires: The Myth of the Discreteness of Linguistic Systems. In L. Milroy and P. Muysken (eds.), *One Speaker, Two Languages* (pp. 68–89). Cambridge: Cambridge University Press.

Geoghegan, W. H. (1969). The Use of Marking Rules in Semantic Systems. *Language Behavior Research Laboratory Working Paper* 26. Berkeley: University of California.

Geoghegan, W. H. (1970). A Theory of Marking Rules. *Language Behavior Research Laboratory Working Paper* 37. Berkeley: University of California.

Geoghegan, W. H. (1971). Information Processing Systems in Culture. In P. Kay (ed.), *Explorations in Mathematical Anthropology*. Cambridge, MA: MIT Press.

Giacalone Ramat, A. (1995). Code-switching in the Context of Dialect/Standard Language Relations. In L. Milroy and P. Muysken (eds.), *One Speaker, Two Languages* (pp. 45–67). Cambridge: Cambridge University Press.

Goffman, E. (1981). Footing. In *Forms of Talk* (pp. 124–159). Philadelphia: University of Pennsylvania.

Greenberg, J. (1966). *Language Universals: With Special Reference to Feature Hierarchies*. The Hague: Mouton.

Gross, S. (2000). Intentionality and the Markedness Model in Literary Codeswitching. *Journal of Pragmatics* 32: 1283–1303.

Gumperz, J. J. (1982). *Discourse Strategies*. Cambridge: Cambridge University Press.

Gumperz, J. J. (1984). Comments. In J. C. P. Auer and A. di Luzio (eds.), *Interpretive Sociolinguistics* (pp. 108–112). Tübingen: Gunter Narr Verlag.

Gumperz, J. J., and Hymes, D. (eds.) (1972). *Directions in Sociolinguistics: The Ethnography of Communication*. New York: Holt, Rinehart and Winston.

Hanks, W. F. (1996). *Language and Communicative Practices*. Boulder, CO: Westview Press.

Heller, M. (1988). Strategic Ambiguity: Codeswitching in the Management of Conflict. In M. Heller (ed.), *Codeswitching* (pp. 77–96). Berlin: Mouton de Gruyter.

Hill, J. H. (1985). The Grammar of Consciousness and the Consciousness of Grammar. *American Ethnologist* 12(4): 725–737.

Hill, J. H. (1993). Hasta la Vista, Baby: Anglo Spanish in the American Southwest. *Critique of Anthropology* (13): 145–176.

Hill, J. H. (1999). Syncretism. *Journal of Linguistic Anthropology* 9(1–2): 244–246.

Hill, J. H., and Hill, K. C. (1986). *Speaking Mexicano: Dynamics of a Syncretic Language in Central Mexico*. Tucson: University of Arizona Press.

Irvine, J. T., and Gal, S. (2000). Language Ideology and Linguistic Differentiation. In P. V. Kroskrity (ed.), *Regimes of Language* (pp. 35–84). Santa Fe, NM: School of American Research Press.

Jacobson, R. (ed.) (1998). *Codeswitching Worldwide*. Berlin: Mouton de Gruyter.

Jakobson, R. (1990). *On Language/Roman Jakobson* (ed. Linda R. Waugh and Monique Monville-Burston). Cambridge, MA: Harvard University Press.

Kroskrity, P. (1988). Arizona Tewa Kiva Speech as a Manifestation of a Dominant Language Ideology. In B. B. Schieffelin, K. A. Woolard, and P. V. Kroskrity (eds.), *Language Ideologies: Practice and Theory* (pp. 103–122). New York: Oxford University Press.

Meeuwis, M., and Blommaert, J. (1994). The "Markedness Model" and the Absence of Society: Remarks on Codeswitching. *Multilingua* 13(4): 387–423.

Meeuwis, M., and Blommaert, J. (1998). A Monolectal View of Code-switching: Layered Code-switching among Zairians in Belgium. In P. Auer (ed.), *Code-switching in Conversation* (pp. 76–98). London: Routledge.

Milroy, L., and Muysken, P. (eds.) (1995). *One Speaker, Two Languages: Cross-disciplinary Perspectives on Code-switching*. Cambridge: Cambridge University Press.

Muysken, P. (2000). *Bilingual Speech: A Typology of Code-mixing*. Cambridge: Cambridge University Press.

Myers-Scotton, C. (1993). *Social Motivations for Codeswitching: Evidence from Africa*. Oxford: Oxford University Press.

Myers-Scotton, C., and Bolonyai, A. (2001). Calculating Speakers: Codeswitching in a Rational Choice Model. *Language in Society* 30(1): 1–28.

Pujolar, J. (2001). *Gender, Heteroglossia and Power: A Sociolinguistic Study of Youth Culture*. Berlin: Mouton de Gruyter.

Rampton, B. (1995). *Crossing: Language and Ethnicity among Adolescents*. London: Longman.

Rampton, B. (1998). Language Crossing and the Redefinition of Reality. In P. Auer (ed.), *Code-switching in Conversation* (pp. 290–317). London: Routledge.

Reddy, M. J. (1979). The Conduit Metaphor: A Case of Frame Conflict in Our Language about Language. In A. Ortony (ed.), *Metaphor and Thought* (pp. 284–324). New York: Cambridge University Press.

Sankoff, G. (1980). *The Social Life of Language*. Philadelphia: University of Pennsylvania Press.

Sebba, M., and Wootton, T. (1998). We, They and Identity: Sequential vs. Identity-related Explanation in Codeswitching. In P. Auer (ed.), *Code-switching in Conversation* (pp. 262–286). London: Routledge.

Silverstein, M. (1996). Indexical Order and the Dialectics of Sociolinguistic Life. In R. Ide, R. Parker, and Y. Sunaoshi (eds.), *Third Annual Symposium About Language and Society, Austin* (pp. 266–295). Austin: University of Texas, Dept. of Linguistics.

Singh, R. (1983). We, They, and Us: A Note on Code-switching and Stratification in North India. *Language in Society* 12: 71–73.

Stroud, C. (1992). The Problem of Intention and Meaning in Code-switching. *Text* 12: 127–155.

Swigart, L. (2000). The Limits of Legitimacy: Language Ideology and Shift in Contemporary Senegal. *Journal of Linguistic Anthropology* 10(1): 90–130.

Tsitsipis, L. D. (1998). *A Linguistic Anthropology of Praxis and Language Shift*. Oxford: Clarendon Press.

Weinreich, U. (1953). *Languages in Contact: Findings and Problems*. The Hague: Mouton.

Woolard, K. A. (1988). Codeswitching and Comedy in Catalonia. In M. Heller (ed.), *Code-switching* (pp. 53–76). Berlin: Mouton de Gruyter.

Woolard, K. A. (1989). Language Change and Language Death as Social Processes. In N. Dorian (ed.), *Investigating Obsolescence: Studies in Language Contraction and Death* (pp. 355–367). Cambridge: Cambridge University Press.

Woolard, K. A. (1995). Changing Forms of Codeswitching in Catalan Comedy. *Catalan Review* 9(2): 223–252.

Woolard, K. A. (1998). Simultaneity and Bivalency as Strategies in Bilingualism. *Journal of Linguistic Anthropology* 8(1): 3–29.

Zentella, A. C. (1997). *Growing Up Bilingual: Puerto Rican Children in New York*. Oxford: Blackwell.

CHAPTER **5**

Diversity, Hierarchy, and Modernity in Pacific Island Communities

Niko Besnier

1 INTRODUCTION

The Pacific Islands are inhabited by some of the most diverse and dynamic human groupings in the world. It is in part thanks to this diversity and dynamicity that sociocultural anthropologists and linguistic anthropologists, since they began conducting fieldwork among Pacific Island peoples, have made important contributions to our general understanding of the complex interaction among language, society, and culture. For example, sociocultural and linguistic diversity has enabled scholars to explore the motivations underlying the efflorescence of lifeways and communicative resources, as well as its limitations and consequences. Similarly, the dynamic nature of social formations, languages, and structures of language use in Pacific Island communities has provided fascinating materials with which we have sought to understand ways in which sociocultural change and linguistic change interface with one another. Research on language, communication, and sociocultural dynamics in the Pacific Islands has thus enabled linguistic and sociocultural anthropologists to explore one of the most fundamental questions of the discipline, namely the internal structure and outer limits of human diversity.

Sociocultural anthropologists never tire of showing that society and culture are inherently changeable, constantly adapted to new situations, absorbing elements from all directions, and transforming themselves in the course of history. As a constitutive element of society and culture, language reflects as well as enacts change, and the Pacific Islands provide fascinating examples of the way in which the relationship among language, society, and culture can at once be stubbornly resilient and constantly in flux. This chapter provides examples of areas of research in which linguistic anthropologists working in the Pacific Islands have contributed to our understanding of the role that language plays in reflecting and contributing to the dynamic character of society and culture.

1.1   Regions and Histories

The Pacific Islands conjure images of extremes and paradoxes. Consisting of a large number of small islands scattered over the largest ocean of the planet, the region presents some of the most extreme patterns of social, cultural, and linguistic diversity anywhere in the world. Diversity, for example, characterizes the range of kinship structures, political organizations, and economic practices found among Pacific Island societies. Cosmologies, ritual practices, and modes of thought all exhibit remarkable variation, particularly since the advent of colonialism and the concomitant importation of new forms of thinking, believing, and feeling. The inhabitants of the Pacific Islands speak numerous and diverse languages. While numbers are very diffi-cult to advance conclusively, about a fifth of the world's languages are spoken in the Pacific, a particularly dramatic figure considering that the region is inhabited by a tiny fraction of the world's population and represents less than 1 percent of the earth's land area.

Deciding what to include under the term "Pacific Islands" is somewhat arbitrary. For the purpose of this chapter, it is expedient and historically logical to use the term to refer to all islands in a region bounded to the west by New Guinea, to the northwest by the Mariana Islands, to the north by Hawai'i, to the extreme southeast by Rapanui (Easter Island), and to the south by New Zealand. The area therefore excludes the Aboriginal societies of Australia, which form a radically divergent cul-tural complex: descendent of populations that migrated into the then joint Australia–New Guinea continent around 40,000 BP, Aborigines conserved a social, cultural, and linguistic homogeneity over the centuries that bears no known relation to the sociocultural forms and languages of the Insular Pacific, and that contrasts sharply with the diversifying sociocultural efflorescence that characterized the Pacific Islands over the centuries.

The regional boundary between the Pacific Islands and the world that lies to the east of the region, namely South America, is easy to draw, in that there are no verified social, cultural, or linguistic commonalities between the two areas, and no evidence of sustained prehistoric contact. In contrast, the regions lying west of New Guinea, i.e., the Indonesian and Philippine archipelagos, display continuities of many different kinds with the Insular Pacific. For example, many languages of Indonesia and the Philippines are related to languages spoken in the Pacific Islands (as well as further afield, in Madagascar, Taiwan, and small pockets in the Southeast Asian mainland). Patterns of social organization and cultural life found in many parts of Indonesia and the Philippines bear resemblances to dynamics prevalent among Pacific Island soci-eties. Where the societies of Indonesia, Malaysia, and the Philippines differ from Pacific Island societies is in terms of their size, history, and contemporary socio-political situation. Not only do Indonesia, Malaysia, and the Philippines have consid-erably larger overall populations than any Pacific Island nation, but most societies and speech communities of Indonesia and the Philippines are also considerably larger than most Pacific Island societies and speech communities. Furthermore, Indonesia, Malaysia, and the Philippines have maintained social and cultural ties with continental Asia much more continuously than the Pacific Islands; as a result, Insular Southeast Asian societies and cultures bear similarities to societies and cultures of the Asian continent that are not found in the Pacific Islands, as a result, for example, of the successive influence of Hinduism, Buddhism, and Islam. These divergent characteristics do lend some support to the identification of a Pacific Island region as separate from Insular Southeast Asia, as long as one bears in mind that important patterns of sociocultural continuity still straddle the boundary between the two regions.

The Pacific Islands are commonly divided into three regions: Polynesia (etymologically, "many islands"), Melanesia ("black islands"), and Micronesia ("small islands"), as illustrated in map 5.1. Polynesia is often described as a "triangle," with as its apexes Hawai'i, Rapanui (Easter Island), and New Zealand, with the addition of the Polynesian Outliers, small communities geographically embedded in Melanesia and Micronesia but that bear cultural, historical, and linguistic affinities to Polynesia. Micronesia inscribes a large arc across the northern and central Pacific, from the tiny island of Tobi, halfway between Palau and the westernmost tip of New Guinea, to Kiribati (Gilbert Islands). Melanesia comprises generally larger islands and island groups than the other two: New Guinea, the Solomon Islands, Vanuatu, New Caledonia, and Fiji. But it is important to bear in mind that these labels are historically contingent, as the product of Europeans' early intellectual and colonial interests in the region. Charles de Brosses, a French sea captain, coined the name "Polynesia" in 1756, but for a century or so it referred to all the Pacific Islands. The tripartite division that we use today was proposed in 1832 by Jules Dumont d'Urville, another French ship captain, but it was already conceptually present in the racialist and evolutionary distinctions that Europeans had been drawing in the Pacific since the Enlightenment. Eighteenth-century writers, for example, viewed the light-complexioned, hierarchically organized, and technologically sophisticated Polynesians as more advanced on a putative universal scale of human development than the more darkly pigmented, politically more fragmented, and less technologically endowed Melanesians (Micronesia did not occupy a prominent place in the European representational preoccupations of the time). Polynesians, particularly Tahitians, came to embody for Europeans of the time the mostly positive image of the morally pure "noble savage," while Melanesians were viewed as examples of animalistic, uncivilized, and dangerous savagery. Directly and indirectly, these complex and often contradictory images of the inhabitants of the various islands would fuel imaginations back in the European world, and for the centuries to come would inform colonial designs and political policies (see Smith 1985 for a masterful discussion of the way in which the artistic production of the times reflects these images). Despite their morally dubious historical associations, the terms "Polynesia," "Melanesia," and "Micronesia" do serve a useful purpose today, not only as convenient geographical labels, but also as strategic self-identificational symbols that some Pacific Islanders use for a variety of political and cultural purposes, particularly where the politics of postcolonial indigeneity are tense (e.g., Hawai'i, New Zealand, New Caledonia).

However, the tripartite division of the Pacific Islands does not reflect the complex prehistory of the human settlement of the region. Archaeological records indicate

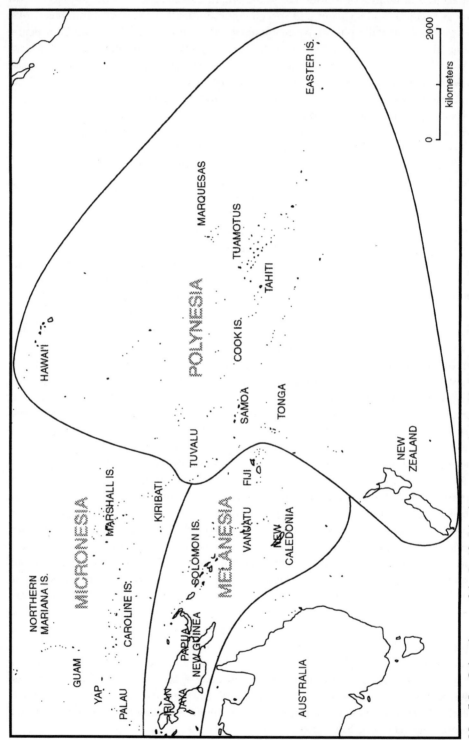

Map 5.1   Cultural areas of the Pacific Islands as commonly identified in the early twenty-first century

that the process through which humans came to inhabit the Pacific Islands was long and complex. Humans appear to have begun settling New Guinea and surrounding islands around 40,000 BP. The most likely origin of these settlers is Southeast Asia, and their relationship to the people who settled Australia around the same time is unknown. They began engaging in plant domestication around 10,000 BP. Several millennia later, new waves of settlers began joining these earlier settlers. Probably originating from the coastal areas of East and Southeast Asia, migrating via Insular Southeast Asia, these intrepid travelers as well as seasoned agriculturalists began descending on the Pacific Islands by sea around 5,000 BP, settling parts of Melanesia and Western Micronesia first, then moving east towards Polynesia and the rest of Micronesia. In Melanesia and Western Polynesia, they are identifiable in archaeological records through remains of an unremarkable but specific style of decorated pottery, which archaeologists call Lapita. Lapita remains have been found in coastal areas throughout Melanesia, all the way to Samoa and Tonga in Western Polynesia (and indeed blurring the boundary between Melanesia and Polynesia), and have been dated from about 3,300 BP until 2,500 BP, when the manufacture and use of pottery seems to have been abandoned for a variety of reasons. These remains bear witness to the first stages in the gradual exploration and settlement of the islands of the region over the course of the centuries, which ended when the descendants of Lapita pottery users settled New Zealand and Hawai'i shortly before 1,000 CE.

The most consequential period in the history of the Pacific Islands since first settlement is arguably the last few centuries, during which time contact between Pacific Islanders and European and European-derived populations intensified. This contact began slowly in the sixteenth century, and until the second half of the eighteenth century was mostly confined to Western Micronesia, where Iberian navigators claimed for the Spanish crown islands that were strategically placed on the trade route between South America and the Philippines, a move that was followed by the virtual decimation, through violence and disease, of the inhabitants of Guam and the Mariana Islands. The rest of the Pacific Islands had no sustained contact with Europeans until the 1770s, when European navigators, James Cook being the most famous among them, began expanding their traveling horizons into Polynesia, Melanesia, and the rest of Micronesia. Following closely on their heels, a host of newcomers soon began reaching the shores of the Pacific Islands, including Christian missionaries, adventurers, small-scale traders, ambitious colonial entrepreneurs, whalers, and of course government agents in charge of furthering the colonial interests of various powerful nations. The increasingly intrusive presence of these various groups, of diverse nationalities (at various times and in various parts of the region, Dutch, British, French, German, Japanese, and North American) and driven by often divergent agendas, had many implications for the social, cultural, and political constitution of the Pacific Islands, as well as for local languages, as I will discuss presently.

The colonial era greatly complicated the composition of the population in several locations. The example of New Zealand serves as a useful illustration of these postcolonial complexities. Voyagers from Eastern Polynesia (e.g., Tahiti, Marquesas, Cook Islands) were the first to settle New Zealand more than a millennium ago, developed into what we know today as Māori society and culture, and remained the sole inhabitants of the two islands until 1840, when settlers from Britain began colonizing New Zealand, competing for land and resources with the Māori, and often appropriating them with little regard to prior ownership. Within a few decades, the Māori had become a disenfranchised, embattled, and numerically insignificant minority in their own land, and their numbers were steadily decreasing due to such factors as a high rate of tuberculosis, aggravated by poverty and marginalization. It was not until after the Second World War that population decline was reversed, and today people who identify themselves as Māori comprise 15 percent of the country's population (3.7 million). The 1960s experienced a Māori cultural renaissance, aspects of which I will describe later in this chapter, and the beginning of a politics of indigenous activism, focused on land claims and demands for political participation. Comparable historical trajectories in colonial and postcolonial times have characterized other Pacific Islands, including Hawai'i, Guam, and New Caledonia. In some cases, colonial-era immigrants to the Pacific and their descendants are people of non-European descent, as is the case of the Japanese, Filipino, and Chinese inhabitants of Hawai'i, Filipinos in Guam, and Indians in Fiji.

While colonialism in its most blatant forms is largely a thing of the past, its impact is still felt in consequential ways in the Pacific Islands. One of the most dramatic aspects of the postcolonial Pacific is the diasporic nature of many societies of the region. For example, numerous Tongans and Samoans today live in New Zealand, Australia, and the United States, and there are more Tokelauans, Cook Islanders, and Niueans living in New Zealand than in Tokelau, the Cook Islands, and Niuē respectively. Some groups have moved from their islands of origin to another island of the Pacific: many Caroline Islanders have settled on Guam, and Wallisians and Futunans are more numerous in New Caledonia than in Wallis and Futuna. The migrations that have given rise to these diasporic communities are often recent, and are fueled by many different motivations, including the search for better economic opportunities. Yet we must also remember that the desire to travel and settle elsewhere is hardly new, since it was fundamental to the aboriginal settlement of the Pacific Islands itself. Diasporic Pacific Island communities generally maintain a strong attachment to their islands of origin, but second- and third-generation Pacific Islanders born in industrial societies of the Pacific Rim often come to understand their identity differently from their parents or grandparents, in response to the different allegiances that they must negotiate.

2   Languages

The numerous languages indigenous to the Pacific Islands form several families of genetically related languages. In other words, they fall into groups containing languages that all derive from an ancestral language, which we surmise to have been spoken at some time in the course of history (see also Mithun, this volume). These linguistic families are very disparate in size, composition, and geographical spread. On the one hand, languages indigenous to all of Polynesia and Micronesia, most of insular Melanesia outside of New Guinea, and some of the coastal areas of New Guinea, constitute a large and widely dispersed family of related languages. Usually referred to as the Austronesian language family, it spans a third of the globe's circumference, from Madagascar to Easter Island. Since it includes a fifth of the world's languages, it is possibly the largest or second largest in the world in terms of the number of distinct but related languages it comprises. The remaining languages of the region are dispersed across the island of New Guinea, in small pockets in the Bismarck Archipelago, Bougainville, the Solomon Islands, and the Santa Cruz Islands, as well as on several islands of the Sunda Archipelago, west of New Guinea. These languages are so diverse from one another that historical linguists have only managed to group them into over a dozen distinct families. These families appear to be unrelated to one another, or at least to have diverged from one another over such a long period of time that historical connections are today undetectable through the ordinary methods of historical linguistics. Linguists refer to these languages as "Papuan languages" or "Non-Austronesian languages," the latter term being particularly useful in that it stresses the fact that these languages do not form a language family but a large assemblage of unrelated linguistic groupings.

The distinct genetic characteristics of Austronesian and Non-Austronesian languages of the Pacific Islands reflect in part the history of human settlement of the region. Although genetic relationships among languages are not necessarily the same as genetic relationships among the speakers of these languages (since communities are known to stop using a language and adopt another, sometimes abruptly, as I will discuss later), the Non-Austronesian languages of New Guinea and adjacent areas are nevertheless associated with human populations that were already present in New Guinea about 40,000 BP. Non-Austronesian languages spoken today are possibly descendants of the ancestral language or languages that these populations spoke. If Non-Austronesian languages did derive from a single proto-language, so much time has elapsed since this ancestral language broke up into various dialects that gradually diverged from one another, that no traces of their genetic affinities remain in their structure as they are spoken today.

In contrast, historical linguists associate the language ancestral to the 500-odd Austronesian languages spoken in the Pacific Islands with the Lapita pottery makers and seafarers who began arriving in the region in 5,000 BP. With the exception of a few dozen languages spoken in western New Guinea and two languages spoken in Western Micronesia (Palauan and Chamorro), these languages form a single distinct branch of the Austronesian family, the Oceanic subgroup (see figure 5.1). This fact, combined with archaeological evidence, the comparison of present-day societies of the region, and what we can reconstruct of the vocabulary of Proto-Oceanic, enables archaeologists to assert that the settlement of the Insular Pacific was accomplished relatively recently by waves of people who shared the same culture, social organization, and language, and were perhaps of the same genetic stock.

Since the advent of colonialism, Pacific Islanders have added to their communicative repertoires a number of extraneous languages. The most visible is English, in standard and localized forms, widely spoken as an auxiliary language in the Pacific Islands that have come under British, Australian, New Zealand, or American colonial rule in the last two centuries. In some regions, such as New Zealand, Guam, and Hawai'i, it is today the dominant language, having replaced local languages, as I will discuss presently. French is the principal international language for the inhabitants of New Caledonia, Tahiti and surrounding island groups, Wallis and Futuna, and, alongside English, Vanuatu. Spanish is the second language of Rapanui (Easter Island), and Bahasa Indonesian, the national language of Indonesia, is the lingua

Map 5.2   Geographical distribution of Pacific Island language families

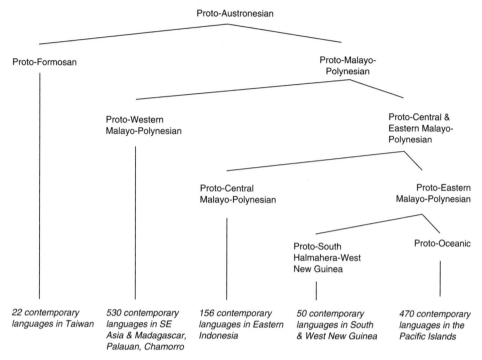

Figure 5.1   Simplified subgrouping of Austronesian languages (after Blust 1995). Most languages spoken in the Pacific Island region are part of the Oceanic subgroup (i.e., descendants of Proto-Oceanic), except for about 50 languages spoken in the South and West of Coastal New Guinea, which form a distinct South Halmahera-West New Guinea subgroup together with a handful of languages of Eastern Indonesia, and Palauan and Chamorro, spoken in Western Micronesia, which fall in the Western Malayo-Polynesian subgroup.

franca of Irian Jaya, the Indonesian-controlled western half of New Guinea. Colonial languages introduced to the Pacific in the past that are no longer used have included German in New Guinea, Samoa, and Micronesia, Spanish and Japanese in Micronesia.

Alongside the languages of colonial powers we also find in the Pacific Islands contact languages that emerged locally in the context of political and economic intrusion from the outside. In the nineteenth century, European colonists recruited Pacific Islander workers to work on plantations in various parts of the Pacific and adjoining areas (Samoa, Papua New Guinea, Northeastern Australia). These workers, principally Melanesians, spoke many different languages, and thus needed a common medium to communicate with their colonial masters and, more importantly, with each other. Thus arose the three English-based creole languages in widespread use in Melanesia: Tok Pisin in Papua New Guinea (historically also referred to as "Neo-Melanesian" or "New Guinea Pidgin"); Solomon Islands Pijin; and Bislama in Vanuatu. All three languages are very similar to one another, are given some form of national-language status in their respective countries, and are very healthy languages in terms of numbers of users, some of whom speak these languages as their mother tongue (a sufficient condition to identify them as examples of creole languages). Other relative newcomers to the Pacific include Fiji Hindi, a creolized form

of Hindi spoken by the descendants of Indian migrants brought to Fiji by the British
to work on sugarcane plantations, as well as Vietnamese and various Chinese dialects,
spoken by small communities in several island groups. Hiri Motu, a simplified form of
the Oceanic language Motu, is used as a lingua franca in parts of Papua New Guinea.

Few absolute statements can be made about the grammatical structures of Non-
Austronesian languages, which are extremely diverse, although some generalizations
can be drawn. These languages tend to have very small inventories of contrasting
phonemes and sometimes have very reduced pronoun systems (e.g., the same form is
sometimes used for both singular and plural or for different persons). The morphology of nouns is generally simple, although some languages exhibit noun classes. In
contrast, the morphological structure of verbs can be extremely complex, often with
patterns of suppletion in verb paradigms. Non-Austronesian languages tend to place
the verb at the end of clauses, and exhibit two unusual features, which are not
exclusive to them but are common among them and uncommon in other languages
of the world. First, verbs are frequently strung together in chains, with the last verb
being the only fully inflected form, and the preceding verbs each describing analytically one aspect of an action or one action in a sequence of actions (verbs are often
inflected to mark whether their referents are sequenced in time or simultaneous).
Pawley (1993: 95) provides a classic example from Kalam, a language spoken in the
Madang Province of Papua New Guinea:

> *b   ak   am mon p-wk   d   ap   ay-a-k.*
> man that go wood hit-break get come put-3RD.SING-PAST
> 'The man fetched some firewood.'

In this example, the Kalam sentence, in which the action is described through a series
of concatenated verbs, is the simplest way of expressing the situation described by the
English translation, where the action is denoted by the single verb "fetch." In such a
system, verbs denote very abstract notions and form a closed class. Complex meanings are expressed analytically by stringing appropriate verbs together. The second
characteristic feature is the marking of switch-reference on verbs, that is, the inflection of verb forms according to whether or not their subject is identical to the subject
of the preceding verb in a verb chain.

The Oceanic languages of the Austronesian family are also very diverse in their
structural characteristics, although they exhibit an air of greater familiarity among
themselves than the Non-Austronesian languages, owing to the fact that they have
been diverging from one another for no longer than three or four millennia. For
example, we find often quite complex pronoun systems in Oceanic languages, as
illustrated in table 5.1, which can mark two or more degrees of plurality and, in
almost all languages, a contrast between inclusive and exclusive forms in the first
person plural ("we including you" vs. "we excluding you"). Possession frequently
distinguishes between different kinds of alienability and other kinds of possession
(e.g., a body part or close kin is marked with a different type of possession from a
mundane object), as illustrated in table 5.2. Noun and verb forms undergo few
morphological derivational changes. Verbs can often be marked with suffixes indicating transitivity, and prefixes indicating a range of semantic functions (e.g., reciprocal,
causative). Verbs are generally clause-initial or clause-medial, and some verb chaining

effects are found, although in much more reduced form than in Non-Austronesian languages.[1]

3   TALK AS COMMODITY IN A MODERNITY-ORIENTED WORLD

The linguistic picture of the Pacific Islands drawn in the last section is one of extraordinary diversity and variety: a multitude of languages, many genetic group-ings, and a vast panoply of structural characteristics. A simple question arises out of this description: how does such a situation of extreme diversity maintain itself over time? In particular, how does linguistic diversity fare in the context of the shrinking and homogenizing tendencies that the world is experiencing at the dawn of the third millennium? The question is not just a linguistic question, but also a sociocultural one: in many parts of the Pacific Islands, particularly Melanesia, the diversity we encounter is not just one of languages but also one of social structures and practices, belief systems, rituals, and cultural ethos. Language, here as elsewhere, offers a strategic window into the dynamics at play.

Anthropologists with an interest in language have long recognized that language in many parts of Melanesia is an important commodity. Several decades ago, social anthropologist Richard Salisbury (1962) conducted fieldwork among the Siane of the New Guinea Highlands, speakers of a Non-Austronesian language numbering about 15,000, who, like other inhabitants of the region, are surrounded by other societies speaking different languages, amongst whom figure the Chuave, about 8,000 strong. The two groups maintain strong links with one another, through frequent intermarriage and exchange, and in active bi- and multilingualism, to the extent that the two languages are used with equal frequency in the border village

Table 5.1   Paradigm of personal pronouns (free-morpheme forms) in Standard Fijian. Paucal pronouns are used in reference to three or more referents up to a small number, plural pronouns for large numbers

Number	Singular	Dual	Paucal	Plural
Person				
first inclusive	—	kedaru	kedatou	keda
exclusive	au	keirau	keitou	keimami
second	iko	kemudrau	kemudou	kemunī
third	koya	irau	iratou	ira

Table 5.2   Paradigm of first-person singular possessive pronouns in Standard Fijian

Form	Used with nouns denoting	Example
-qu	body parts, kinship categories	tama-qu 'my father'
kequ or qau	edibles	kequ madrai 'my bread'
mequ	drinkables	mequ bia 'my beer'
noqu	all other notions	noqu i-lavo 'my money'

where Salisbury conducted fieldwork. On formal occasions, such as ceremonial exchanges, important orators whose native language is Siane are known to speak to other Siane villagers in Chuave, and use a translator, a strategy that contributes desirable prestige to the occasion and to the orator. Songs that his informants dictated to Salisbury were all in Chuave as well as other neighboring languages. Clearly, multilingualism is a high prestige commodity among the Siane, and the multiplicity of languages both enables it to have value and is in turn maintained by the prestige that people assign to it. Diversity is obviously the product of linguistic history, in that languages tend to be numerous when they have been spoken in an area for a long time (Pawley 1981); but linguistic diversity is equally the product of ideological constructs and social action (Irvine and Gal 2000).

The value attached to multilingualism and the linguistic diversity associated with it fits into a broader spectrum of sociocultural dynamics at play in the region. Melanesians have been described as quintessential "modernists" (Robbins 1998), in that they constantly seek out and value the new, different, and exotic, the esoteric potentials of which they exploit fully. This lends a peculiar quality to life in Melanesia that anthropologists working in the region have long striven to capture: "Melanesians have ... been found to be creative, dynamic, episodic, improvisatory people who enact and manage 'flow': people who construct, counterpoise, and interpret what is secret and hidden as opposed to what is revealed and manifest, thereby obviating their own conventional constructions, and thus constituting essentially open, self-transforming, processual societies" (Dalton 2000: 290, cf. Lederman 1998: 440–1). Language use in Melanesia, and the qualities that the region's linguistic situation presents, converges with this general orientation toward the creative, open-endedness, and the processually driven.

It is precisely these qualities that give rise to fascinating forms of linguistic creativity in Melanesia, such as secret codes associated with certain rituals or activities that have religious overtones (Foley 1986: 42–7). Such is the case of the so-called "pandanus languages" that many groups in the Highlands of Papua New Guinea have innovated. The Kalam utilize a special vocabulary in two situations: while gathering the nut of the mountain pandanus, an activity that occupies them for several weeks a year; and while butchering, cooking, and eating cassowaries (Pawley 1992). While neither the pandanus nut nor cassowary meat constitutes a major ingredient of today's Kalam cuisine, both are associated with secrecy and ritual: pandanus nuts, like other forest offerings, are protected by forest spirits who render the nut inedible unless people trick them into thinking that they are not harvesting it; while the cassowary, as humans' cross-cousin, is a ritually potent bird. The phonology of the pandanus vocabulary is the same as that of ordinary Kalam phonology and the syntax of pandanus language is essentially the same as that of ordinary language, but utterances are completely unintelligible to the non-initiated. As illustrated in table 5.3, some pandanus words are borrowed from other languages, others derived creatively from ordinary language, and yet others completely made up. Whatever their derivation, pandanus words and their use result from a conscious effort to conceal meaning in order to fool the forest spirits, at least in the context of pandanus-nut gathering. Kalam pandanus language demonstrates the close kinship between creativity, ritual, and secrecy in the Melanesian symbolic world.

Table 5.3 Examples of pandanus-language word derivations in Kalam (from Pawley 1992: 320)

Ordinary language	Pandanus language	Gloss	Derivation of pandanus form
tw	gaymen	'adze, axe'	borrowed from neighboring language Kobon
kayn	kmn dep	'dog'	OL 'game mammal catcher'
tob	tawep	'foot'	OL '(for) stepping (on)'
mon	su-tk-eb	'tree, wood'	OL 'biting off, gnawing through'
mon	agi-ep	'tree, wood'	OL 'for burning'
kaj	aglams	'pig'	borrowed from neighboring language Kobon
kaj	gney	'pig'	invented
b 'man' bin 'woman' ñ 'boy' pañ 'girl' cp 'dead person'	aduklan	'person'	invented

The value attached to language diversity and creativity in the Melanesian world provide useful insights into the sociocultural dynamics that underlie the remarkable linguistic diversity one encounters in the region. The use of multiple languages in interaction and the manufacture of secret language varieties are motivated by similar attitudes, namely the political, symbolic, and aesthetic value attached to difference-making through language and the over-elaboration of every way of boundary-marking between tiny communities. Sociolinguists such as Sankoff (1980) and Laycock (1982) demonstrate that the same dynamics underlie many other linguistic phenomena in the region, such as grammatical innovations that defy the regular rules of historical linguistics, and can only be attributed to the conscious manipulation of language to emphasize the individuality and distinctness of one's speech community in contrast to its neighbors. Over time, this creativity, agentively induced change, and insistence on difference generates a linguistic picture for the region characterized by extreme fragmentation and diversity.

The Melanesian qualities of open-endedness and creativity encompass not only the world of symbols, but also material conditions of life. And, here as elsewhere, language is not just a symbolic system embedded in cultural worlds, but also a social and political system embedded in social structures and material processes (Gal 1989; Irvine 1989). Why a Siane orator should feel compelled to use the language of a neighboring group to talk to other members of his own village acquires a particular social logic in light of dynamics of power in Melanesian societies, a topic that has preoccupied sociocultural anthropologists for decades. In a typical Melanesian society, persons acquire power not by inheriting it through the bloodline but by convincing others that they are worthy of holding positions of power. In such societies, power is *achieved*, insofar as members of these societies view power as an achievement, and insofar as power is comparatively less predetermined than in other societies of the world. Consequently, power in these societies is inherently precarious and constantly in danger of being undermined by claims to power by other equally worthy competitors. A powerful person is often referred to by the Tok Pisin word *bigman* (in most if not all cases, the holder of overt forms of power in Melanesian societies is male). There are several factors involved in acquiring and maintaining power. One prerequisite is that the person already be recognized as a "great man," i.e., the holder of secret knowledge of ritual and magic, often associated with male initiation cults (Godelier 1986). But not all great men are *bigman*; a *bigman* must be able to mobilize others in accumulating large amounts of wealth for him to redistribute with calculated generosity in spectacular ceremonial gift-giving. Other factors that support the *bigman*'s authority may include his courage in war, reputation as a sorcerer, competence as an agriculturalist, and ability to acquire and support several wives, but the most important are crucially dependent on the *bigman*'s persuasive skills: persuading potential followers that he is indeed the holder of secret knowledge, to contribute materially to gift-exchange ceremonies, to respect him, accept his authority, and support his endeavors.

The intimate relationship between talk and power in Melanesian societies is thus hardly surprising, and astute ethnographers of language have animated the complexity of this connection in specific societies of the region. For example, the Kwanga of the East Sepik Province of Papua New Guinea spend a great deal of time in weekly village meetings with the purpose of discussing rumors about sorcery and other sources of community disharmony (Brison 1992). However, the meetings rarely solve the problems that villagers associate with these rumors. Instead, the meetings allow village men with political aspirations to manipulate public opinion by encouraging others, through allusions, innuendos, and astutely constructed story-telling (what some scholars have termed "veiled speech," e.g., Strathern 1975), to gossip about their intimate knowledge of sorcerers and sorcery, while overtly denying their complicity in bringing about the misfortunes that villagers believe to be the result of sorcery. It is little wonder that, among the Kwanga as well as in many other Melanesian societies (e.g., Goldman 1983; Merlan and Rumsey 1991; Schieffelin 1990; Weiner 1991), talk in its various forms should be given such importance, as they feel entitled to negotiate, inspect, and argue over every event that affects their lives, and do so to a considerably greater extent than members of other societies.

4 PERSONHOOD, CODESWITCHING, AND BODY HABITUS

The secrecy and ambiguity that pervades Kwanga meetings and resulting everyday talk is associated with a way of conceptualizing the person that the Kwanga share with many other societies of Melanesia, which Marilyn Strathern (1988) terms "dividual," i.e., "as a multiple or composite construction, an internal collectivity of identities, for it is this heterogeneity that makes the perception of his or her unitary individuality or singleness not an intrinsic attribute but an achievement comparable to the collective unity of group action" (Strathern 1990: 213). Working with such a construct, people in Melanesia always expect people, as well as their utterances, to be multi-layered. This view of the person, echoed in different forms in various parts of the Pacific (Lutz 1988; Ochs 1988; Ochs and Schieffelin 1984; Shore 1982; White 1991), challenges Western notions of the person that tend to treat it as an internally coherent and externally bounded whole, relatively autonomous of the social relations in which it is embedded.

This expectation is articulated in the linguistic resources that Melanesians invoke in political rhetoric, and linguistic anthropologists who have analyzed such forms of language use can shed light on questions that have preoccupied psychological anthropologists, such as the way in which the particularly Melanesian construction of personhood is articulated in interaction. In the tiny village of Gapun, huddled among swamps and rainforests between the estuaries of the Sepik and Ramu rivers in Papua New Guinea, villagers expect interpersonal communication to be inherently indeterminate, multi-layered, and ambiguous, as one would expect of people working with a dividual conception of the self. It is in this context that Stroud (1992) analyzes the meaning of codeswitching in Gapun oratory between the two languages currently in use in the village: the Non-Austronesian language Taiap, which at the time of Stroud's fieldwork was spoken by a grand total of 89 people; and Tok Pisin, the national lingua franca of Papua New Guinea. A long tradition of sociolinguistic analysis of codeswitching, based mostly on communicative practices in urban industrial societies, has striven to assign it specific social and discourse meanings, such as the expression of solidarity, informality, or emotional involvement. In this tradition of inquiry, indeterminacy of meaning is a problem, which both analysts and interactors must resolve. In contrast, Gapun villagers codeswitch between Tok Pisin and Taiap to *create* ambiguity, and not to resolve it, and thus ambiguity *is* the meaning of codeswitching in Gapun. Gapun villagers view the meaning of talk as polysemic and interactionally constructed: multiple layers of meaning and intentionality can "hide" under the surface of discourse, and the work that audiences must engage in to retrieve hidden layers of meaning is full of potential uncertainty.

What this kind of analysis illustrates is that language use, including the linguistic resources that people utilize in interacting with one another (codeswitching, metaphors, indirectness) are constitutively related to aspects of culture, such as the way in which people construe the self. This point may be paraphrased as follows: linguistic practices provide a locus in which culture is created, confirmed, and perhaps debated, at the same time that they result from social and cultural structures and dynamics (Bauman and Briggs 1990). More specifically, Gapun villagers (as well as many others in the region) organize their interactions so as to articulate a sense of self that is layered and indeterminate. In turn, these cultural meanings are deeply embedded in the world of materiality, of particular ways of understanding and enacting power, and in particular political systems. Language, symbolic structures, and social dynamics are thus interlocked with one another.

However, people in particular societies do not necessarily all agree about how the self is constituted and communicated. Multiple ways of understanding the person coexist in communities and are associated with different and sometimes conflicting ways of using language. The Kwara'ae of the Solomon Islands, for example, have been missionized over the course of the last century by various Christian missionary movements, particularly the Anglican Church and the South Seas Evangelical Church (Watson-Gegeo and Gegeo 1991). The beliefs of members of the two denominations reflect a different orientation toward many issues: Anglicans seek an integration of traditional aspects of Kwara'ae society into modern life, and are culturally conservative, while Evangelicals profess a charismatic and fundamentalist position that seeks to do away with traditional modes of conduct and replace them with modernity-steeped practices, such as an orientation to social change and economic development. Kwara'ae of both denominations encode these different positions in language use: Anglicans use both English and high-rhetoric Kwara'ae as prestige codes, and Solomon Island Pijin and low-rhetoric Kwara'ae as everyday codes, while Evangelicals place English at the top of the prestige hierarchy, followed by Pijin and both forms of Kwara'ae, often claiming that they have "forgotten" the high-rhetoric Kwara'ae associated with traditional oratory. Even in formal contexts, Evangelicals opt for a simple and direct way of talking, sometimes at the risk of sounding, to Anglicans, child-like and inappropriate, while Anglicans opt for features of high rhetorical styles, such as a fluent delivery, a paucity of borrowings from Pijin, and a carefully developed argument structure. The differences between the two groups go further: in partial imitation of the practices of charismatic preachers from industrialized societies, Evangelicals' speech and gestures are loud, flamboyant, and boisterous, and they gesticulate considerably more than Anglicans, whose voice and body habitus are slow, fluid, and measured. So marked are the differences in body habitus between the two groups that Kwara'ae can recognize the church affiliations of people from afar. As Watson-Gegeo and Gegeo (1991) demonstrate, microscopic forms of interaction are constitutive of macrosociological and cultural dynamics, linking the apprehension and presentation of the self, religious practice, and socioeconomic orientation to patterns of language use and body habitus, sometimes in divergent and conflicting ways within the same village or the same society.

5   POWER AND PRACTICE IN HIERARCHICAL POLYNESIA AND MICRONESIA

Just as the languages of the Pacific Islands exhibit formidable diversity, the speakers of these languages also organize their social lives and cultural systems in widely divergent ways from one part of the Pacific to the other. Yet, in the midst of this remarkable diversity, recurring patterns emerge, and it is these patterns of familiarity and systematicity that sociocultural anthropologists have worried about since they began conducting fieldwork among Pacific Islanders.

Contrasting with Melanesia-style governance, in which power is contingent and constantly subject to negotiation, governance in Polynesia typically rests in the hands of a chief, and a great deal of social action, at least at first glance, is designed to maintain the association of power with chieftainship. The chief is generally the eldest son of the previous chief or a male member of a specific chiefly group, who inherits power and, excepting cases of gross personal incompetence, is the object of commoners' respect. This respect is sometimes demonstrated in highly dramatic fashion, as on Tikopia, for example, where commoners crawl up to the chief as a sign of submission and deference, a practice they have maintained to this day despite the momentous changes that Tikopia society has undergone in its encounter with modernity (Firth 1979). In contrast with the achieved nature of power in Melanesia, power in Polynesia is *ascribed*, that is, assigned to particular individuals on the basis of their inherited position in society. In the 1960s and 1970s, anthropologists such as Marshall Sahlins (1963) linked the seemingly fundamentally different patterns of governance in Melanesia and Polynesia with other aspects of the way in which the respective societies are organized. For example, Melanesian societies tend to consist of small autonomous villages, in which kinship is the basis of social organization, since the power of the Melanesian *bigman* depends crucially on his ability to constantly persuade followers to acquiesce to his holding the reins of power, and thus on his ability to come face-to-face with his supporters on a frequent basis. In contrast, Polynesian societies can be much larger entities, since the Polynesian chief's power is largely accepted by all followers, who are expected to believe that the chief is the chief because he is supernaturally anointed (or at least that the system is ordained by God, a common view in the Christianized present), and thus there is no obvious constraint on the number of people that the chief can govern.

The classic distinction between Melanesian and Polynesian systems of governance, remarkable in its conciseness and explanatory power, has been subjected to serious critical scrutiny (e.g., Thomas 1989), and this is where linguistic anthropologists have made important contributions. Indeed, the exercise of power is a notoriously complex affair, and one in which interaction of many different kinds plays an important role. As soon as linguistic anthropologists began to investigate the *practice* of power (as opposed to the more static *structure* of power, which formed the basis of Sahlins' original insights), adding to sociocultural anthropologists' arsenal of ethnographic methods a detailed attention to the analysis of interaction, a more nuanced and complex picture began to emerge.

Samoa is, in many anthropological accounts, a typically hierarchical Polynesian society, dominated by a chiefly system, in support of which non-chiefly people devote a great deal of time and energy. In Falefā, a village on the north shore of 'Upolu, this attention to hierarchy takes the form of constant efforts to maintain a sense of order in everyday life, but a sense of order of a particular type, namely that which elaborates relationships of high vs. low social status, and through which every family and every member of each family is in principle ranked with respect to one another (Duranti 1994). Order of a hierarchical kind is thus over-elaborated in Samoan society, in other words, reinforced on every possible occasion, beyond what is necessary to make the point. So, for example, during village council meetings, or *fono*, in which chiefs of different ranks take part and village matters (e.g., conflicts, bylaws, etc.) are discussed and managed, hierarchy is encoded both spatially and temporally. Spatially speaking, a detailed and well-known pre-set protocol dictates where people sit in the meeting-house, whose two "ends" are for people of highest ranks, while the "front" and the "back" are reserved for people of lower and lowest rank respectively. Hierarchy is temporally elaborated in that the order of mention of participants in the ceremonial recitation that opens the meeting, as well as the order of speakers during the meeting, is ostensibly pre-ordained through a congruent protocol thought to reflect a village-wide hierarchy of roles and kin groups based on a historical charter that harks back to mythological times. These over-elaborated markers of hierarchy, which contrast sharply to the ethos of equality and indeterminacy that permeates formal oratory in Melanesia, are further reinforced by comparable patterns attested outside the meeting-house, in formal and everyday contexts alike.

Yet, while the entire system of hierarchy may at first glance appear immanent and inflexible, the system is in fact much more flexible in practice. For example, the formal part of the *fono* consists in an exchange of *lāuga*, formal speeches, which tend to be lengthy and difficult to interrupt. Most importantly, since protocol dictates the order of speakers, if a low-ranking person speaks, even high-ranking chiefs cannot interrupt him, and this situation opens up the possibility that a lower-ranking person will castigate, uninterrupted, a higher-ranking person. Rank in Falefā thus derives from various sources at once: in the pre-ordained structural ranking of families and their members, as well as in the ceremonial protocol that dictates who speaks before whom at meetings. These different sources can yield potentially conflicting ways of reckoning rank and power.

The over-elaboration of hierarchy in the Samoan village generates a system characterized by extreme competitiveness among villagers: since everyone has to be ranked at all times, and the pre-set ranking order is not necessarily the only way of determining rank, people vie for power in big and small ways at all times. A prototypical relationship that is suffused with competitiveness is that between same-sex siblings, as a cadet can and often does challenge the higher rank bestowed on an older sibling by default because of primogeniture. Such competitiveness, which social anthropologists have called "status rivalry" (Goldman 1970), can be fierce when the stakes are high, such as when two siblings are both candidates to the chiefly title associated with the family to which they both belong. More generally, political practice in Falefā demonstrates that chieftainship, and rank in general, is not a matter of simple absolute power that remains unchanged over generations, but rather is the result of a complex play in which power is negotiated from moment to moment, sometimes resulting in important changes. Village meetings become the prime arena in which this complex play is enacted, and the linguistic resources available to participants (e.g., turn-taking mechanisms) become the tools for the play.

The resulting picture of the practice of power in the highly hierarchical climate of Samoan society is after all not fundamentally different from the practice of power in Melanesian societies that elaborate egalitarianism and treat power as contingent. Like their *bigman* counterparts, who must constantly work to convince fellow villagers to partake in their prestige-accruing endeavors, chiefs in Falefā are vulnerable to the verbal criticisms and perhaps even the withdrawal of support of low-ranking villagers. Society in Polynesia is at once hierarchical and dynamic, and the dynamic nature of society is particularly dramatic in Polynesian societies that lack the pre-ordained foundation of the Samoan village: on Nukulaelae Atoll (Tuvalu), positions of power are by definition precarious, and low social status is an excellent platform from which to undermine those in power. In the play of social ascendance and power erosion in such societies, forms of language use such as gossip, innuendo, and grumbling become tremendously efficacious political tools (Besnier 1993, 1994).

Thus the comparison between Melanesia and Polynesia is as much one of difference as one of similarity. Indeed, just as claims to power in Melanesian societies are predicated on the *bigman* exhibiting the personal, and often inheritable, qualities of a "great man" (e.g., that of being backed by supernatural and mythical forces), Polynesian chieftainship is enshrined in mythology through genealogical descent, and deified in one fashion or another (literally god-like in pre-Christian days, anointed by the Christian God in post-missionization times). And in the same fashion that a Melanesian *bigman* must constantly demonstrate his worthiness as a leader, through persuasive skills, control of rhetorical forms, battle-readiness, and mastery of various prized skills, the Polynesian chief must exude approachability as well as the aloofness associated with high rank, demagogy despite his commanding presence, and readiness to defend his power base despite its apparent stability. Sociocultural anthropologists of Polynesia (Marcus 1989) have captured the dual foundation of Polynesian chief-tainship as having a *kingly side* (ascribed, passive, aloof, protocol-encoded) and a *populist side* (achieved, active, engaged, practice-dependent), and the verbal dynamics at play in the *fono* in a Samoan village articulates precisely the sometimes precarious balance between these two seemingly contradictory expectations. Viewed in this light, the workings of power and rank, and the interactional practices associated with them, display commonalities throughout the Pacific Island region. Whether in the Highlands of Papua New Guinea or in a Samoan village, rank and power are relational: without non-chiefs in Polynesia, there are no chiefs, and without ordinary villagers in Melanesia, there are no *bigman*.

In some Pacific Island societies, rank is elaborated through language in a very overt fashion, in the form of honorifics. Honorifics are special words and sometimes constructions that a speaker employs to denote the hierarchical relationship between, for example, the speaker and the interlocutor or the speaker and the referent of talk. Not surprisingly, honorifics are well suited to languages spoken in societies that vest particular importance in social stratification and where social rank is a determinative aspect of the person. Besides Samoa (Duranti 1992) and Tonga (Philips 1991), we find honorifics in Pohnpei (formerly known as Ponape), an elaborately stratified society of the Caroline Islands of Micronesia (Keating 1998). Pohnpeian society is divided in twenty matrilineal clans, within which each person is ranked with respect to everyone else, according to principles that measure the genealogical distance of the person from the senior matriline of the clan. In both ceremonial and everyday contexts, one of the important ways through which Pohnpeians affirm rank is through the use of vocabulary forms referring to certain restricted semantic domains (e.g., movement, mental states, possession) that either exalt or humble a person partaking in the interaction or being talked about. The honorific forms may be derived from non-honorific forms, or they may be completely unrelated, as illustrated in table 5.4.

Given the nature of Pohnpeian rank, one would expect that the occurrence rules of regular, exaltive, and humiliative to be simple: when speaking to or about a higher-ranking person, use exaltive forms, and when speaking to a lower-ranking person, use humiliative forms. Indeed, native speakers themselves provide a version of this rule when interviewed, stressing its rigidity and predictability. Instead, through a careful analysis of the practice of honorific marking in natural discourse, Keating finds that "the nature of Pohnpeian use of honorific forms is highly fluid and context oriented

Table 5.4   Examples of honorific forms in Pohnpeian (from Keating 1998: 49)

Common word	Honorific word	Translation	Literal meaning of honorific
lingeringer	*engieng*	'angry'	'windy'
pilen mese	*tenihrlap*	'tears'	'big waterfall'
pouk	*malimalih*	'blow'	'typhoon'
tamataman	*ediedinloang*	'remember'	'cloudy sky'
wadek	*doaropwe*	'read'	—

and not as regularized as native speakers imply" (1998: 56). For example, honorific usage depends on the nature of ongoing activities, and does not just reflect a pre-ordained ranking system, but enables interactors to create and negotiate rank. Furthermore, honorifics index more than just social rank: they can also underscore interpersonal solidarity, which, far from being antonymous to hierarchy, is "an important first step in constructing systems of social inequality and resolving contradictions within such systems" (1998: 65). Here again, language offers a rich panoply of tools for constructing social life.

6   Conclusion: Pacific Island Speech Communities in a Sea of Change

I end this overview of the problems and prospects for linguistic anthropology in the Pacific Islands by returning to the topic that I showcased at the beginning of the chapter, namely the extreme diversity and heterogeneity of languages and practices in the Pacific Islands. I already pointed out that this diversity is a product of history as much as it derives from the delights and advantages that some Pacific Islanders find in fostering this diversity. However, to quote an oft-cited cliché, strong forces are afoot today that actively undermine this diversity. The homogenizing forces of globalization run the risk of turning multilingualism into monolingualism in a common colonial language or a lingua franca; encouraging people to forget honorific forms, pandanus languages, and the ceremonial protocol of village meetings; and erasing codeswitching and the distinctions between high and low rhetoric. Where are Pacific Island languages heading at the beginning of the third millennium?

A general point bears stressing at the outset. It is actually very difficult to predict in a general way the particular effect that homogenizing forces will have on languages and communities. For example, some scholars have maintained that the spread of literacy is encouraging monoglotism and the disappearance of local languages in the Pacific (Mühlhäusler 1996). While this may be correct in some cases, literacy ultimately has the effect on languages and social lives that people want it to have. For instance, missionaries introduced literacy to the inhabitants of Nukulaelae Atoll (Tuvalu) 150 years ago, and at the time the only literacy skills that missionaries taught them was reading the Bible. Not only did Nukulaelae Islanders not lose their language as the result of becoming literate (and of being missionized in a foreign language, Samoan), but they also began using their literacy skills, almost immediately, not just to read the Christian Scriptures but also to read and write for a host of purposes, ranging from weaving names and slogans in pandanus mats to communicating with far-away relatives through letters (Besnier 1995).

Indeed, the same dynamics that help maintain diversity and heterogeneity in one setting can help erase it in another. For example, the very dividual self associated with the diversity of languages and ways of speaking in the Papua New Guinea Highlands is deeply implicated in language loss in the tiny village of Gapun (Kulick 1992). Like many other New Guineans, Gapun villagers have an elaborate theory of the self, of which they recognize two principal, dividual components: *hed* (a Tok Pisin word derived from English "head"), associated with stubbornness, selfishness, pride, backwardness, women, and paganism; and *save* (literally "to know" in Tok Pisin), associated with sociability, cooperation, generosity, modernity, men, and Christianity (introduced to Gapun shortly after the Second World War). While these two manifestations of the self are morally polarized, they are both intrinsic to what it means to be human in Gapun ethnopsychology. Crucially, the two principal languages of the community are linked both socially and symbolically with opposite aspects of the self. On the one hand, Tok Pisin is associated with *save*, because it is the language of development, the outside world, and Christianity. On the other hand, the language of *hed* is Taiap, the language of Gapun and of nowhere else.

Gapun children are exposed early to these overarching and complex linkages that tie together different manifestations of the self, languages, attitudes, social contexts, and gender. They also learn from their modernity-oriented seniors that change is desirable, and that change is enacted through Christianity and schooling. Furthermore, and not surprisingly, change speaks one language, namely Tok Pisin, the language of classrooms, catechisms, the state, and white people (as well as heaven). In contrast, Taiap, however valued it may be for its expressiveness and its ties to the land, is ultimately just the language of the ancestors. Thus, while puzzling over and occasionally deploring the fact that their children are no longer learning Taiap, Gapun adults socialize their offspring in a web of meaning that ensures the disappearance of the language. As a result, the number of speakers of Taiap has been steadily decreasing since the 1970s, even though the population of the village has not. At the time of Kulick's fieldwork, no children under 10 used the language in everyday contexts, opting instead for Tok Pisin.

Language loss in Gapun holds several general lessons. One is that a particular theory of the person may have one effect in one context or at a particular historical moment (e.g., encouraging multilingualism) and exactly the opposite effect in another social or historical situation (e.g., fostering the shift to one language). Second, the forces behind language shift are not purely global or macrosociological factors like television, urbanization, or the Internet. What encourages Gapun children not to learn Taiap is the interface between a deeply local ideology of the self in its relation to the world with sociohistorical forces like modernity, conversion to a world religion, and the postcolonial state. The trajectory of a language in the context of competition among different codes is therefore guided by many complex factors, both structural and agentive, although the Gapun case highlights the complexities of agentivity, since one can argue that, ultimately, the villagers (and the world at large) have little to gain from the language shift they are unconsciously implementing.

Perhaps the most distressing situations in the Pacific are those of peoples who have in the course of history experienced serious demographic and sociocultural discontinuities, and have lost not just language but political power, social institutions, and cultural worlds. The classic cases of major colonial disruptions in the Pacific Islands are those of New Zealand and Hawai'i. Through a series of bloody wars resulting from British confiscations of Māori land in New Zealand waged over the course of the nineteenth century, and through political maneuvering culminating in a coup d'état in 1892 that overthrew the century-old Hawai'ian monarchic state, colonists of British and American origins respectively had become, by the end of the nineteenth century, the dominant political force and, in the case of New Zealand, the numerical majority. They subjugated and marginalized the indigenous Māori and Hawai'ian populations in their own homeland, eroding social institutions, cultural structures, as well as languages. In New Zealand, for example, educational authorities variously discouraged, failed to encourage, or forbade the use of Māori in schools as part of the government's politics of ethnic assimilationism between the late nineteenth and mid-twentieth centuries (Simon and Smith 2001: 141–73), a classic situation that has contributed to the attrition of many minority languages around the world, alongside other factors such as urbanization. Today, the Hawai'ian language and the Māori language are spoken by a fraction of the number of speakers of a century ago, although efforts to revitalize their use, in the context of the social and cultural renaissance that the indigenous populations of Hawai'i and New Zealand have brought about since the 1960s, have succeeded in reversing further attrition and preventing the languages from dying out completely. In New Zealand, new cohorts of children are acquiring Māori as their first language again, partly as a result of the establishment, since the early 1980s, of *kohanga reo* 'language nests', preschools where all interactions are conducted in Māori and are focused on Māori activities.

Small, remote, and rural communities are particularly vulnerable to various forms of encroachment from the outside, and to the dramatic consequences that such dynamics can have for local languages and ways of speaking. Yet sometimes language can turn out to be surprisingly resilient, as people can exploit all the potentialities of language to resist encroachment and assert themselves. For example, Fijians from rural northern Viti Levu engage in a form of ceremonial speech-making linked to a prestation ritual called *sevusevu*, which, far from disappearing, is in fact becoming more and more frequent (Brison 2001). While *sevusevu* is grounded in a cosmological logic, villagers have begun to use it as a symbolic representation of certain versions of village lifeways (characterized by consensus, sociality, and tradition), which they pitch against the lifeways of Fijians from more powerful areas of the country, urban Fijians, Fiji Indians, as well as complete outsiders such as tourists. Their local affirmation of a ritualized form of language thus has multiple audiences, some more global than others, and illustrates that outside forces can in fact anchor rather than obliterate local forms of talk.

An even more dramatic case of language resilience and affirmation is that of Rapanui, or Easter Island, which has experienced a dramatic social and cultural history in the last 150 years (Makihara 1998, 2001). One of the most isolated islands of the world, world-famous for its spectacular megalithic remains, Rapanui is today inhabited by about 3,000 people, two-thirds of whom are of Polynesian descent, with the remaining third being migrants of European descent from Chile, the nation-state to which Rapanui is politically annexed. However, at the end of the nineteenth century, Rapanui Islanders were literally on the verge of disappearing. Already weakened by internal conflicts, the Rapanui population was, in the 1860s, targeted by "Blackbirders," or slave raiders roaming the Pacific Islands in search of laborers for guano harvesting fields and country estates in Peru. Survivors who managed to return to the island also brought smallpox, with calamitous consequences. Between 1862 and 1877, the population reduced from over 4,000 to 110, and the islanders endured further hardship during decades of ruthless military rule that Chile imposed on the island from 1888, which lasted well into the mid-twentieth century.

While it is today impossible to reconstruct the exact mechanisms through which Rapanui managed to survive as a language through the catastrophic events of the last century and a half, Makihara's careful collage of historical materials and ethnographic data on language and interaction in contemporary Rapanui society goes to some length in providing clues on the dynamics involved. Today, everyone on the island is bilingual in some form of Rapanui and some form of Spanish. However, the different codes spoken on the island form a continuum, with Standard Chilean Spanish at one end and at the other end Old Rapanui, which no one uses and few understand. In between these extremes are various syncretic ways of speaking, whose structure is a blend of the two languages (e.g., Rapanui phonology and syntax with Spanish morphology and lexicon, with frequent codeswitching), and that are the most widely used codes on the island. These syncretic codes play a crucial function: in the context of the growing sense of ethnic identity among the Rapanui, in opposition to the encroachment of the state and to immigration from the mainland, they serve as an in-group code and a linguistic marker of this identity. Furthermore, the syncretic codes have undermined the functional polarization that characterized the use of Rapanui and Spanish in the past, the former being the language of domesticity and the latter the language of public forums. Today, instead, Rapanui in its various forms permeates all interactional contexts, and thus syncretism, far from undermining the local language, has helped expand its functional range and boosted its vitality.

The success story for sociocultural continuity and language maintenance is perhaps that of Pollap Atoll (formerly Pulap), a small atoll of Chuuk State in the Caroline Islands and one of the least modernized islands of the area. Constructed in reference to other Carolinians and yet not strongly politicized, identity in Pollap, in sharp contrast to Gapun, is suffused with pride for a traditional order and for the maintenance of conservative ways, which pays little heed to the other Carolinians' stereotype of the Pollapese as backward and naive (Flinn 1990). Despite being schooled in another language beyond primary education, despite the fact that their language is not anointed as the symbol of an imagined national community, despite the negative images of them that their neighbors harbor, the Pollapese continue with their lifeways, including their language. It is probably the ties of language to identity in its various forms that will save Pacific Island languages and ways of speaking from disappearing, although these ties alone do not ensure that languages survive.

NOTE

I thank Karen Brison, Alessandro Duranti, Juliana Flinn, Miki Makihara, and Donald Rubinstein for valuable comments on a draft of this chapter.

1   This chapter will say little more about the historical relationships among the languages of the Pacific Islands or their structural characteristics, fascinating topics that others have treated extensively elsewhere: Pawley and Ross (1993; eds., 1994) and Tryon (ed., 1995) for the subgrouping and prehistorical dispersal of Austronesian languages in relation to cultural history; Kirch (2000) for the archaeological history of the Pacific Islands; Foley (1986, 2000) and Lynch, Ross, and Crowley (2001) for linguistic surveys of Papuan and Oceanic languages respectively; Wurm and Hattori (eds., 1981–3) for a linguistic atlas of the region; Wurm, Mühlhäusler, and Tryon (eds., 1996) for an atlas of contact languages in the Pacific.

REFERENCES

Bauman, R., and Briggs, C. L. (1990). Poetics and Performance as Critical Perspectives on Language and Social Life. *Annual Review of Anthropology* 19: 59–88.

Besnier, N. (1993). The Demise of the Man Who Would Be King: Sorcery and Ambition on Nukulaelae Atoll. *Journal of Anthropological Research* 49: 185–215.

Besnier, N. (1994). The Truth and Other Irrelevant Aspects of Nukulaelae Gossip. *Pacific Studies* 17(3): 1–39.

Besnier, N. (1995). *Literacy, Emotion, and Authority: Reading and Writing on a Polynesian Atoll.* Cambridge: Cambridge University Press.

Blust, R. (1995). The Prehistory of the Austronesian-Speaking Peoples: A View from Language. *Journal of World Prehistory* 9: 453–510.

Brison, K. J. (1992). *Just Talk: Gossip, Meetings, and Power in a Papua New Guinea Village.* Berkeley: University of California Press.

Brison, K. J. (2001). Constructing Identity through Ceremonial Language in Rural Fiji. *Ethnology* 40: 309–327.

Dalton, D. (2000). Melanesian Can(n)ons: Paradoxes and Prospects in Melanesian Ethnography. In R. Handler (ed.), *Excluded Ancestors, Inventible Traditions: Essays Toward a More Inclusive History of Anthropology* (pp. 284–305). Madison: University of Wisconsin Press.

Duranti, A. (1992). Language in Context and Language as Context: The Samoan Respect Vocabulary. In A. Duranti and C. Goodwin (eds.), *Rethinking Context: Language as an Interactive Phenomenon* (pp. 77–99). Cambridge: Cambridge University Press.

Duranti, A. (1994). *From Grammar to Politics: Linguistic Anthropology in a Western Samoan Village.* Berkeley: University of California Press.

Firth, R. (1979). The Sacredness of Tikopia Chiefs. In W. A. Shack and P. S. Cohen (eds.), *Politics in Leadership: A Comparative Perspective* (pp. 139–168). Oxford: Clarendon Press.

Flinn, J. (1990). We Still Have Our Customs: Being Pulapese in Truk. In J. Linnekin and L. Poyer (eds.), *Cultural Identity and Ethnicity in the Pacific* (pp. 103–126). Honolulu: University of Hawai'i Press.

Foley, W. A. (1986). *The Papuan Languages of New Guinea.* Cambridge: Cambridge University Press.

Foley, W. A. (2000). The Languages of New Guinea. *Annual Review of Anthropology* 29: 357–404.

Gal, S. (1989). Language and Political Economy. *Annual Review of Anthropology* 18: 345–367.

Godelier, M. (1986). *The Making of Great Men: Male Domination and Power among the New Guinea Baruya* (trans. R. P. Swyer). Cambridge: Cambridge University Press; Paris; Editions de la Maison des Sciences de l'Homme.

Goldman, I. (1970). *Ancient Polynesian Society.* Chicago: University of Chicago Press.

Goldman, L. (1983). *Talk Never Dies: The Language of Huli Disputes.* London: Tavistock.

Irvine, J. T. (1989). When Talk Isn't Cheap: Language and Political Economy. *American Ethnologist* 16: 248–267.

Irvine, J. T., and Gal, S. (2000). Language Ideology and Linguistic Differentiation. In P. V. Kroskrity (ed.), *Regimes of Language: Ideologies, Politics, and Identities* (pp. 35–83). Santa Fe, NM: School of American Research Press.

Keating, E. (1998). *Power Sharing: Language, Rank, Gender, and Social Space in Pohnpei, Micronesia.* New York: Oxford University Press.

Kirch, P. V. (2000). *On the Road of the Winds: An Archaeological History of the Pacific Islands before European Contact.* Berkeley: University of California Press.

Kulick, D. (1992). *Language Shift and Cultural Reproduction: Socialization, Self, and Syncretism in a Papua New Guinean Village.* Cambridge: Cambridge University Press.

Laycock, D. C. (1982). Melanesian Linguistic Diversity: A Melanesian Choice? In R. J. May and H. Nelson (eds.), *Melanesia: Beyond Diversity* (pp. 33–38). Canberra: Australian National University Press.

Lederman, R. (1998). Globalization and the Future of Cultural Areas: Melanesianist Anthropology in Transition. *Annual Review of Anthropology* 27: 427–449.

Lutz, C. A. (1988). *Unnatural Emotions: Everyday Sentiments on a Micronesian Atoll and Their Challenge to Western Theory.* Cambridge: Cambridge University Press.

Lynch, J., Ross, M., and Crowley, T. (2001). *The Oceanic Languages.* London: Curzon Routledge.

Makihara, M. (1998). Rapanui–Spanish Bilingual Language Choice and Code Switching. In C. M. Stevenson (ed.), *Easter Island in Pacific Context, South Seas Symposium: Papers Presented at the Fourth International Conference on Easter Island and the Pacific* (pp. 33–38). Los Osos, CA: Easter Island Foundation.

Makihara, M. (2001). Rapanui–Spanish Bilingualism. *Rongorongo Studies* 11(1): 25–42.

Marcus, G. E. (1989). Chieftainship. In A. Howard and R. Borofsky (eds.), *Developments in Polynesian Ethnology* (pp. 175–209). Honolulu: University of Hawai'i Press.

Merlan, F., and Rumsey, A. (1991). *Ku Waru: Language and Segmentary Politics in the Western Nebilyer Valley, Papua New Guinea.* Cambridge: Cambridge University Press.

Mühlhäusler, P. (1996). *Linguistic Ecology: Language Change and Linguistic Imperialism in the Pacific Region.* London: Routledge.

Ochs, E. (1988). *Culture and Language Development: Language Acquisition and Language Socialization in a Samoan Village.* Cambridge: Cambridge University Press.

Ochs, E., and Schieffelin, B. B. (1984). Language Acquisition and Socialization: Three Developmental Stories. In R. A. Shweder and R. A. LeVine (eds.), *Culture Theory: Essays on Mind, Self, and Emotion* (pp. 276–320). Cambridge: Cambridge University Press.

Pawley, A. (1981). Melanesian Diversity and Polynesian Homogeneity: A Unified Explanation for Language. In K. J. Hollyman and A. Pawley (eds.), *Studies in Pacific Languages and Culture in Honour of Bruce Biggs* (pp. 269–309). Auckland: Linguistic Society of New Zealand.

Pawley, A. (1992). Kalam Pandanus Language: An Old New Guinea Experiment in Language Engineering. In T. Dutton, M. Ross, and D. Tryon (eds.), *The Language Game: Papers in Memory of Donald C. Laycock* (pp. 313–334). Canberra: Pacific Linguistics C-110.

Pawley, A. (1993). A Language Which Defies Description by Ordinary Means. In W. A. Foley (ed.), *The Role of Theory in Language Description* (pp. 87–130). Berlin: Mouton de Gruyter.

Pawley, A., and Ross, M. (1993). Austronesian Historical Linguistics and Culture History. *Annual Review of Anthropology* 22: 425–459.

Pawley, A., and Ross, M. (eds.) (1994). *Austronesian Terminologies: Continuity and Change.* Canberra: Pacific Linguistics C-127.

Philips, S. U. (1991). Tongan Speech Levels: Practice and Talk about Practice in the Cultural Construction of Social Hierarchy. In R. Blust (ed.), *Currents in Pacific Linguistics: Papers on Austronesian Languages and Ethnolinguistics in Honor of George Grace* (pp. 269–382). Canberra: Pacific Linguistics C-117.

Robbins, J. (1998). Between Reproduction and Transformation: Ethnography and Modernity in Melanesia. *Anthropological Quarterly* 71: 89–98.

Sahlins, M. (1963). Poor Man, Rich Man, Big Man, Chief: Political Types in Melanesia and Polynesia. *Comparative Studies in Society and History* 5: 285–303.

Salisbury, R. (1962). Notes on Bilingualism and Language Change in New Guinea. *Anthropological Linguistics* 4(7): 1–13.

Sankoff, G. (1980). Multilingualism in Papua New Guinea. In G. Sankoff, *The Social Life of Language* (pp. 95–132). Philadelphia: University of Pennsylvania Press.

Schieffelin, B. B. (1990). *The Give and Take of Everyday Life: Language Socialization of Kaluli Children*. Cambridge: Cambridge University Press.

Shore, B. (1982). *Sala'ilua: A Samoan Mystery.* New York: Columbia University Press.

Simon, J., and Smith, L. T. (eds.) (2001). *A Civilising Mission? Perceptions and Representations of the New Zealand Native Schools System*. Auckland: Auckland University Press.

Smith, B. (1985 [1969]). *European Vision and the South Pacific*. New Haven: Yale University Press.

Strathern, A. (1975). Veiled Speech in Mount Hagen. In M. Bloch (ed.), *Political Language and Oratory in Traditional Society* (pp. 185–203). London: Academic Press.

Strathern, M. (1988). *The Gender of the Gift: Problems with Women and Problems with Society in Melanesia*. Berkeley: University of California Press.

Strathern, M. (1990). Negative Strategies in Melanesia. In R. Fardon (ed.), *Localizing Strategies: Regional Traditions of Ethnographic Writing* (pp. 204–216). Edinburgh: Scottish Academic Press; Washington, DC: Smithsonian Institution Press.

Stroud, C. (1992). The Problem of Intention and Meaning in Code-switching. *Text* 12: 127–155.

Thomas, N. (1989). The Forces of Ethnology: Origins and Significance of the Melanesia/Polynesia Division. *Current Anthropology* 30: 27–41.

Tryon, D. (ed.) (1995). *Comparative Austronesian Dictionary*, 5 vols. Berlin: Mouton de Gruyter.

Watson-Gegeo, K. A., and Gegeo, D. W. (1991). The Impact of Church Affiliation on Language Use in Kwara'ae (Solomon Islands). *Language in Society* 20: 533–555.

Weiner, J. F. (1991). *The Empty Place: Poetry, Space, and Being among the Foi of Papua New Guinea*. Bloomington: Indiana University Press.

White, G. M. (1991). *Identity through History: Living Stories in a Solomon Island Society.* Cambridge: Cambridge University Press.

Wurm, S. A., and Hattori, S. (eds.) (1981–3). *Language Atlas of the Pacific Area*, 2 vols. Canberra: Pacific Linguistics C-66 and 67.

Wurm, S. A., Mühlhäusler, P., and Tryon, D. (eds.) (1996). *Atlas of Languages of Intercultural Communication in the Pacific, Asia and the Americas*. Berlin: Mouton de Gruyter.

CHAPTER 6

The Value of Linguistic Diversity: Viewing Other Worlds through North American Indian Languages

Marianne Mithun

1 INTRODUCTION

When Europeans first arrived in North America, they found not just new kinds of plants and animals, but also mental worlds they could never have imagined. The languages they knew could not have prepared them to grasp the depth of the linguistic differences to be found in the Americas, nor their import. American languages presented new ways of delineating concepts from the flow of experience, of organizing them, and of combining them into more complex ideas.

The newcomers certainly did not become aware of all of the languages of North America at once. Probably the earliest written record of any North American language is a wordlist recorded from an Iroquoian group living on the St. Lawrence River near present Quebec City. These people, now known as the Laurentians, first met the French explorer Jacques Cartier and his crew in 1534. A word from their language, *Canada* 'village', has now become a place-name recognized throughout the world. Soon afterward, from 1539 to 1543, Hernando de Soto traveled through the Southeast. In 1542 Juan Rodríguez Cabrillo landed on the California coast, and Martin Frobisher arrived on Baffin Island in the Arctic. But the French, Spanish, Dutch, English, Danes, Swedes, and Russians who came to the New World, and their descendants, continued to encounter new peoples in North America for over three centuries. Many California groups were still unknown to outsiders well into the nineteenth century. Nearly 300 distinct, mutually unintelligible languages are now known to have been spoken in North America at the time of first contact, and many more have disappeared with little trace.

The depth of this diversity, the radical and complex ways in which these languages differ from those of Europe and Asia and from each other, came to be appreciated ever more gradually, a process that continues to this day. Many early explorers collected valuable vocabulary lists, but they were in no position to conduct detailed linguistic studies: they were seldom in one place for very long, were untrained for such work, and had other responsibilities and interests. The missionaries who succeeded them typically spent longer periods of time in native communities, and in many cases understood that the success of their endeavors would depend on their ability to communicate in the local language. Their work resulted in records of many languages, particularly translations of liturgical materials and dictionaries, and even some grammars. But as awareness of the linguistic diversity grew, so did the realization that languages were rapidly disappearing and should be documented without delay. In 1787 Thomas Jefferson sent out a call for the collection of vocabularies all over the continent. Lewis and Clarke took his questionnaire on their 1803–1806 expedition through the West. Unfortunately most of the vocabularies commissioned by Jefferson have been lost, but the enterprise continued. Over the eighteenth and nineteenth centuries techniques for collecting material were refined. In 1820 John Pickering, a Boston lawyer, devised a phonetic alphabet so that scribes might be better equipped to cope with unfamiliar sounds in a consistent way. Transcription conventions continued to be polished and were included in questionnaires or "schedules" distributed to fieldworkers by the United States Bureau of Ethnology. The schedules consisted of detailed lists of vocabulary in a variety of domains along with some basic grammatical paradigms and sentences for translation.

The material collected on the schedules proved important for certain purposes, but already by the late nineteenth century it was clear that more needed to be done. The languages were spoken by people with cultures quite unlike those known to Europeans. The central role of language in culture was clearly recognized by those studying both, a fact that was to leave its mark on American scholarship. Franz Boas, probably the most important figure in the shaping of North American anthropology and linguistics, trained his students at Columbia University to focus on the collection of culturally interesting texts, then base their grammars and dictionaries on the speech represented in them. Boas realized, as did his students, particularly Edward Sapir, that many of the most interesting features that differentiate languages emerge only in natural, connected speech, and not in translations of isolated English words and sentences. Translations tend to reveal primarily the kinds of categories, distinctions, and patterns that the researcher is already expecting, particularly those present in the contact language that provides the models for translations. The grammars and grammatical sketches compiled by Boas, Sapir, and their students, in separate volumes and in the *Handbook of American Indian Languages* (Boas 1911, 1922), show the remarkable leaps in insight possible when an understanding of grammatical systems is based on speech in use. As Boas himself noted, capturing natural speech, particularly conversation, at normal speed, with all of its prosodic modulation, is nearly impossible with pen and paper alone. Even so, early researchers left remarkable records. But since the mid-twentieth century, the general availability of tape recorders, video cameras, and computers has greatly expanded the kind of documentation that is possible, and, accordingly, the kinds of questions that can be addressed.

Boas also recognized the fact that all types of speech are not the same. In his introduction to the inaugural issue of the *International Journal of American Linguistics*, he urged the documentation of a variety of genres.

> Up to this time too little attention has been paid to the variety of expression and to the careful preservation of diction. We have rather been interested in the preservation of fundamental forms. Fortunately, many of the recorded texts contain, at least to some extent, stereotyped conversation and other formulas, as well as poetical parts, which give a certain insight into certain stylistic peculiarities, although they can seldom be taken as examples of the spoken language ... On the whole, however, the available material gives a one-sided presentation of linguistic data, because we have hardly any records of daily occurrences, every-day conversation, descriptions of industries, customs, and the like. (1917: 2)

Recognition of the extent and nature of the linguistic diversity in North America has had a significant effect on the development of the disciplines of anthropology, linguistics, and linguistic anthropology. For more than two centuries, scholarly work has been directed at uncovering order in the apparent chaos. One direction of inquiry has been genetic: untangling the origins of the languages and their relations to each other. Another has been typological: investigating whether the languages vary without limit, or fall into major types, perhaps definable in terms of some basic features from which other characteristics follow. A third has been the exploration of relations among language, thought, culture, and society.

2 THE GENETIC PICTURE

Near the end of the eighteenth century it was discovered that the histories of languages could be reconstructed by comparing their modern forms. When words from various languages of Europe and Asia were compared, recurring, systematic correspondences were found (colon indicates lengthened vowel):

English	*thirst*		English	*mother*
Dutch	*dorst*		German	*Mutter*
German	*Durst*		Danish	*mor*
Danish	*tørst*		Old Irish	*máthir*
Gothic	*ɡa-thairsan*		Latin	*ma:ter*
Latin	*torreo:*		Greek	*mé:te:r*
Greek	*térsomai*		Armenian	*mayr*
Armenian	*tʰaramim*		Lithuanian	*mótè*
Sanskrit	*tṛṣyati*		Sanskrit	*ma:tá:*

Similarities among words in these languages are too pervasive and systematic to be due to chance. It was realized that they must be inherited from a common ancestral language. All of the languages that have developed from the same parent language are said to be genetically related and to constitute a language family. The languages above belong to the Indo-European family. By comparing words in such languages, it is possible to reconstruct vocabulary from their common ancestor. The word for 'thirst, dry out' in Proto-Indo-European, the language of the Indo-Europeans, is reconstructed as *ters. As the original Indo-European speech community fragmented, and subgroups went their separate ways, their languages evolved in different directions, yielding the differences we see above.

It was noticed that similarities could also be observed among groups of North American languages. The languages listed below, for example, share numerous resemblances, even though their speakers generally cannot understand one another.

	'five'	'room, house'
Mohawk	wisk	kanónhsa'
Oneida	wisk	kanųhsa'
Onondaga	hwiks	kanǫhsa:yę'
Susquehannock	wisck	onusse
Cayuga	hwis	kanǫhso:t
Seneca	wis	kanǫhso:t
Laurentian	ouyscon	canocha
Huron	ouyche	annonchia
Wyandot	wis	yanǫhša'
Tuscarora	wisk	unę́hseh
Nottoway	whisk	onushag
Cherokee	hi:ski	khanvsulv'i

(Susquehannock, Laurentian, Huron, and Nottoway are no longer spoken. The forms given here were written by explorers and missionaries in earlier times, so the spelling differs more than the actual sounds. In the Laurentian and Huron forms, for example, the French wrote *ouy* to represent *wi*.) The more one compares these languages, the more systematic similarities one finds. All of these languages have developed from a common ancestral language and belong to the same language family, now called Iroquoian.

The collection and comparison of vocabularies culminated in a project undertaken by Major John Wesley Powell to produce an exhaustive genetic classification of the languages of North America. Powell established the Bureau of Ethnology in 1879, which subsequently became the Bureau of American Ethnology. At the Bureau, Powell assembled a team of scholars to collect data, primarily vocabulary, and compare it. The result of the project was the 1891 *Indian Linguistic Families of America North of Mexico*, a classification of the languages into over 50 families, a scheme which stands, with minor revisions, to this day. Scholars continue to refine the classification and search for possible deeper relations among language families. Work also continues on reconstructing the ancestral languages, and on detecting what these reconstructed languages might tell us about the cultures of their speakers.

3   The Vast Linguistic Diversity

Though the basic genetic relations among North American languages are now generally understood, the nature of the differences that distinguish the languages are still being discovered and appreciated. We know that the words of one language seldom correspond perfectly to those of another. In Mohawk, for example, an Iroquoian language now spoken in Quebec, Ontario, and New York State, the word *otsihkwa'* is translated variously as English 'fist', 'knot in a tree', 'doorknob', 'warclub', 'hockey puck', 'button', 'rhutabaga', 'radish', 'turnip', 'carrot', 'sledge hammer', 'push button', 'pudding', 'pool ball', 'lump on the head', and more. In Navajo, an Athabaskan language of the Southwest, the word *ásaa'* is translated 'pot', 'jar', 'bowl', 'bucket', 'kettle', or 'drum'. In Central Alaskan Yup'ik, an Eskimo-Aleut language of Alaska, the word *ella* is translated 'outdoors', 'world', 'universe', 'sense', and 'awareness'. Do these facts mean that Mohawk, Navajo, and Yup'ik speakers are less discerning of detail than English speakers? Or perhaps, alternatively, that they are more capable of generalization?

If we look a bit further we find numerous examples of exactly the reverse: in many cases a single, general term in English has multiple translations in Mohawk, Navajo, or Yup'ik. There is no general term for 'animal' in Mohawk, for example; wild animals are referred to as *kário* and domestic animals as *katshé:nen'* or *-nahskw-*. The 'wild animal' term cannot be possessed, but the 'domestic animal' terms typically are: *akitshé:nen'*, 'my livestock, my pet', *wakenáhskwaien* 'I have an animal, pet'.

Navajo is well known for its elaboration of vocabulary denoting kinds of actions and states. There is no general term for 'toss' in Navajo; for tossing a small, round object such as a stone, ball, loaf of bread, coin, or bottle, a verb based on the stem *-łne'* is used; for tossing something amorphous in texture such as a loose wad of wool or a bunch of hay, the stem *-łjool* is used; for tossing wet, mushy matter like dough or a wet rag, the stem *-łtłéé'*; for tossing a flat, flexible object such as a blanket, tablecloth, bedsheet, towel, or sheet of paper, the stem *-'ah*; for tossing a slender, flexible object such as a string of beads, piece of rope, belt, chain, or paired objects such as socks, gloves, shoes, scissors, or pliers, or a conglomerate such as a set of tools, the unspecified contents of one's pockets, the stem *-łdééL*; for tossing a stiff, slender object such as a match, pencil, cigarette, stick of gum, broom, or rifle, or an animate object such as an animal or a doll, the stem *-łt'e'*; for tossing something bulky, massive, and heavy in the form of a pack or load, such as a quiver of arrows or a medicine pouch, the stem *-yį́*; for tossing something in an open container such as a glass of water, bowl of soup, dish of food, bucket of sand, box of apples, or dirt in a shovel, the stem *-łkaad*; for a conglomeration of objects that can be readily visualized, such as several books, eggs, or boxes, the stem *-nil*. These and additional examples of such richness are described in detail in the 1987 Navajo dictionary by Young and Morgan.

Yup'ik contains no general term for 'boot', but speakers know a large number of words for specific kinds of boots. In his 1984 dictionary, Jacobson lists *nanilnguaraq* 'short skin boot', *amirak* 'fishskin boot', *ayagcuun* 'thigh-high boot with fur on the outside', *catquk* 'dyed sealskin boot', *ciuqalek* 'fancy dyed sealskin boot with dark fur over the shin', *iqertaq* 'sealskin boot with fur inside', *ivrarcuun* 'wading boot', *ivruciq* 'waterproof skin boot', *atallgaq* 'ankle-high skin boot', *kameksak* 'ankle-high skin boot, house slipper', *qaliruaq* 'ankle-high skin boot for dress wear', *piluguk* 'skin boot', and both *cap'akiq* and *sap'akiq* for 'manufactured boot or shoe'. Additional terms are used in individual dialects.

Many words in these languages are neither more general nor more specific than their English counterparts, but simply show different extensions of meaning and use. The Mohawk noun root *-nahskw-* 'domestic animal' mentioned above is also used for 'captive', 'slave', and even, on occasion, 'employee'. The Navajo verb stem *-łne'* for tossing small, compact objects is also used for dropping, pounding, and chopping, all actions causing small objects to move swiftly through the air. The Yup'ik noun *qaliruaq* 'ankle-high skin boot for dress wear' is also used for 'slipper' and 'sock'. Of course the words of a language evoke for their speakers not just logical denotations, but myriad subtle connotations as well, associated meanings that emerge from the contexts in which they have been used and that color future patterns of use.

A word or stem in one language may have no single lexical counterpart in another at all; the only translation might be a multi-word explanation. The Mohawk verb stem *-ont* might be translated 'put something into the oven'. The Navajo verb stem *-tsǫǫz* is translated by Young and Morgan 'for something that has been previously inflated or swollen to become flat and wrinkled upon deflation, as a car tire that loses its air'. The Yup'ik verb stem *mege-* is translated by Jacobson 'to not want to go back to one's undesirable former living situation'.

The discovery of each new language suggests in novel ways that the world is not composed of a single set of inherent concepts, universally observable by all human beings. Certain kinds of terms do recur in language after language, because there are certain circumstances that are universal or nearly universal to the human condition. But even these may hold some surprises. Mohawk does not contain a single, unitary word for 'water'. To refer to drinking water, or water added to soup, Mohawk speakers use the term *ohné:kanos*, a complex expression meaning literally 'cool liquid'. To mention water as a location, as when a stone is in a puddle or river (but not just a cup of water), a different complex word is used: *awèn:ke*. There is, however, a simplex verb root 'be in water': *-o-*.

Sometimes the elaboration of vocabulary in a particular domain correlates in an obvious way with the importance of that domain in the life of speakers. English-speaking carpenters, for example, have special vocabulary referring to their tools, techniques, measurements, qualities of wood, and other aspects of their work. The proliferation of terms for 'boots' in Yup'ik comes as no surprise. Yup'ik also has rich vocabulary for kinds of seals. There are not only distinct words for different species of seals, such as *maklak* 'bearded seal', but also terms for particular species at different times of life, such as *amirkaq* 'young bearded seal', *maklaaq* 'bearded seal in its first year', *maklassuk* 'bearded seal in its second year', and *qalriq* 'large male bearded seal giving its mating call'. There are also terms for seals in different circumstances, such as *ugtaq* 'seal on an ice-floe' and *puga* 'surfaced seal'.

But differences among languages go far deeper than vocabulary. It is often stated that anything that can be expressed in one language can ultimately be expressed in any other. Yet there are differences in what speakers of different languages tend to say and what they choose to say. Languages differ both in what they allow their speakers to express quickly and easily, and what they require their speakers to specify.

Many ideas expressed in a single word in certain North American languages can be expressed only in long phrases or full sentences in languages like English.

(1) Mohawk: Watshenní:ne Sawyer, speaker (p.c.)
   a. *Aetewatena'tarón:ni'*   'I'm worried about it.'
   b. *Tewaka'nikónhrhare'*   'We should make ourselves some cornbread.'

(2) Navajo: Dolly Hermes Soulé, speaker (p.c.)
   a. *Shaajinííyá*   'He had come to visit me.'
   b. *Ałhanéíít'aash*   'We'll get together now and then.'

(3) Central Alaskan Yup'ik: Elena Charles, speaker (p.c.)
   a. *Uitaqaqerciqutenqaa*   'Will you stay for a short while?'
   b. *Atakenritcaaqaat*   'He is not actually their natural father.'

When we see such long words, we know that they are likely to be built up of smaller elements, called *morphemes*, each contributing a meaning of its own. The elements of the words above can be seen below. The first line of each example shows the word essentially as spoken. The second line shows the individual meaningful parts (morphemes). The third line provides a gloss for each morpheme, that is, its approximate meaning or grammatical function. The fourth line provides a literal translation of each morpheme. The fifth line gives a free translation of the word as a whole.

(1) Mohawk (Iroquoian family, Quebec): Watshenní:ne Sawyer, speaker
   a. *Aetewatena'tarón:ni'*
      a-et-wa-ate-na'tar-onni-'
      OPTATIVE-1.INCLUSIVE.AGENT-PLURAL-REFLEXIVE-bread-make-BENE-
      FACTIVE.PERFECTIVE.ASPECT
      should-you.all.and.I-self-bread-make-for
      'We should make ourselves some cornbread.'

   b. *Tewake'nikónhrhare'*
      te-wak-'nikonhr-har-'
      DUPLICATIVE-1.SG.PATIENT-mind-hang-STATIVE
      change-me-mind-hang-ing
      'It is hanging up my mind' = 'I'm worried about it.'

(2) Navajo (Athabaskan family, Arizona): Dolly Hermes Soulé, speaker
   a. *Shaajinííyá*
      sh-aa-ji-níí-yá
      1.SG-to-4.SG.SUBJECT-TERMINATIVE-one.walk.PERFECTIVE.ASPECT
      me-to-he-to.point-went
      'He had come to visit me.'

   b. *Ałhanéíít'aash*
      a-ł-ha-ná-iid-'aash
      RECIPROCAL-with-SERIATIVE-around-1.DUAL.SUBJECT-two.walk.PRO-
      GRESSIVE
      each.other-with-now.and.then-around-we.two-two.walking
      'We'll get together now and then.'

(3) Yup'ik (Eskimo-Aleut family, Alaska): Elena Charles, speaker
   a. *Uitaqaqerciqutenqaa*
      uita-qaqer-ciq-u-ten = qaa
      stay-briefly-FUTURE-INDICATIVE.INTRANSITIVE -2.SG =INTERROGATIVE
      stay-briefly-will-x-you = ?
      'Will you stay for a short while?'

   b. *Atakenritcaaqaat*
      ata-ke-nrite-yaaqe-a-at
      father-have.as.own-NEGATIVE-actually-INDICATIVE.TRANSITIVE-3.PL/3.SG
      father-have.as.own-not-actually-x-they/him
      'He is not actually their natural father.'

One might wonder whether these are actually single words. Several considerations indicate that they are. Most important are the intuitions of speakers. When asked to repeat utterances word-by-word, they pronounce sequences like those above as single units, whether or not they have ever written or read their languages. For the most part, speakers are not conscious of the identity of the individual components of words (unless of course they are trained linguists), because these components, or morphemes, do not occur in isolation. They would not usually be able to isolate the element which means 'mind' in (1b) above, or 'actually' in (3b), though they often do know that these elements of meaning are contained in the word, and manipulate the structures with dazzling skill to create new words.

Structures like the Mohawk *Aetewatena'tarón:ni'* are actually not exact equivalents of English translations like 'We should make ourselves some cornbread'. They offer their speakers choices that are different from those offered by English. In the Mohawk word, the notion 'should' is expressed by the prefix *a-*, a piece of the word that cannot occur by itself. The notion 'we' is expressed by the prefix *-etewa-*, another element that cannot occur by itself and would not even be recognized by speakers in isolation. The bread is expressed in the morpheme *-na'tar-*, again a piece of a word that never occurs by itself. But each of these ideas can also be expressed by full, separate words in Mohawk. For 'should' one can also use the full verb *enwá:ton* 'it is necessary'. There is an independent pronoun *i:'i* that means 'I' or 'we'. The language also contains an independent word for 'bread', *kanà:taro*. Why would languages preserve multiple ways of expressing the same idea? The answer is that these modes of expression are not used in the same way. Speakers choose to express a particular thought in one way or another according to their purpose at the time of speech. Essentially, they select independent words to focus attention on or highlight particularly pertinent information:

   i:'i aetewatena'tarón:ni' '<u>We</u> should make ourselves some bread.'

Of course such differences in patterns of usage emerge fully only when speakers are speaking naturally, and their messages are embedded in larger linguistic and extra-linguistic contexts.

The Mohawk, Navajo, and Yup'ik words above also differ from their English translations in the specific distinctions speakers make. In the Mohawk *Aetewatena'-tarón:ni'* 'We should make ourselves some cornbread', the prefix *-etewa-* does not simply mean 'we'. It specifies that there are three or more of us. If there were only two, a dual pronominal prefix -*eteni*- would have been used instead. Both pronominal prefixes -*etewa*- and -*eteni*- indicate something else not specified in the English 'we'. They are termed *inclusive* pronouns, because they specify that the hearer is included ('you and I'). An *exclusive* pronoun would have been used if the hearer were excluded ('they and I'). The pronominal prefix -*etewa*- makes still another distinction not indicated in the English 'we'. It is a grammatical *agent* pronoun, used to specify that we will be actively instigating and controlling the process. Grammatical *patient* pronouns are used in Mohawk for actions beyond our control, such as shivering or sleeping. The effect of the choice between grammatical agent and patient pronouns can be seen by comparing two verbs built on a compound stem seen earlier, -'*nikonhr-aksen*, literally -mind-be.bad. With an agent pronoun, the verb is *tewa' nikonhráksen* 'we are evil-minded'. With a patient pronoun, it is *ionkhi'nikonhráksen* 'we are sad'. As we can see, then, there is actually no exact Mohawk equivalent to English 'we': Mohawk speakers must make all of the above distinctions in order to speak at all.

In the Navajo example in (2a), *Shaajiniíyá* 'He had come to visit me', the subject 'he' is expressed in a pronominal prefix *ji*-. Unlike its English (or Mohawk) counterpart, the Navajo *ji*- does not specify masculine gender. The same pronoun would be used for a woman. It does show another distinction, however. It means literally 'someone' or 'people'. It was used here by the speaker, Mrs. Soulé, as a token of respect because she was referring to her father. Furthermore, this pronominal prefix did not actually specify that just one person came: Mrs. Soulé would have used the same prefix to refer to both of her parents together. It is still clear from this word that only one person came, however. This is because the verb is built on the root -*yá* 'for one person to go'. An entirely different verb root would be used for two people walking somewhere together: -`*áázh*. Walking alone, walking in pairs, and walking in a larger group, are portrayed in Navajo as different kinds of actions, worthy of different labels.

As can be seen from these examples, different languages allow speakers to specify different things with ease. We can certainly distinguish inclusive from exclusive first person in English if we wish: 'You and I should make ourselves some cornbread' or 'They and I should make ourselves some cornbread'. We can distinguish two from more than two: 'We two will get together now and then' or 'We all will get together now and then.' But we generally do not, because English does not require us to and it is easier not to. Mohawk speakers always do, because they must in order to speak grammatically. Languages may not limit what their speakers can say, but they can differ in what they require, which can ultimately affect what their speakers tend to say, and, in turn, what they tend to hear.

Even where languages do not require their speakers to make certain distinctions, they may facilitate them. If languages are compared only through the ways in which their speakers translate English sentences, many of these more subtle differences do not emerge. In many North American languages, for example, speakers routinely specify the source and reliability of the information they pass on. As George Charles, a Yup'ik speaker, was describing the adventures of two hunters, he made the remark in (4). In English this information might have been rendered 'and they caught a small bird'. The Yup'ik contains a bit more.

(4) Yup'ik: George Charles, speaker (p.c.)
   yaqulcurmek-llu-gguq,
   yaqulek-cuar-mek = llu = gguq
   bird-DIMINUTIVE-ABLATIVE.SG = also = HEARSAY
   and a small bird, they say
   'and, it seems,

pitellinilutek	*taukuk* ...
pi-te-llini-lu-tek	tauku-k
thing-catch-apparently-SUBORDINATIVE-3.DUAL	that.RESTRICTIVE-DUAL
they two apparently caught game	those two
those fellows apparently caught a small bird.'	

Because he was told about this event by someone else, Mr. Charles included the hearsay ending = *gguq* 'they say' after the first word of the clause. Furthermore, since he did not witness the event directly, he qualified the verb 'they caught game' with the suffix *-llini-* 'apparently'. Such attention to the source and certainty of information can be seen in a number of North American communities. Hearsay markers, specifying that the information came from another person, are very common. Many languages contain additional markers, indicating, for example, direct personal witness, auditory evidence, general knowledge, inference, speculation, and more. Such markers are termed *evidentials*.

The brief passage in (4) illustrates another set of distinctions that pervade Yup'ik speech but are barely reflected in English. The demonstrative pronoun *taukuk* 'those' specifies that the hunters were not immediately adjacent to the speaker and that they were two in number (with the dual suffix *-k*); it also indicates that they were stationary, localized in one spot, and visible. The Yup'ik demonstrative system encodes an elaborate set of distinctions, beautifully described by Jacobson (1984: 653–62). Yup'ik terms corresponding to English *this, that, these, those* distinguish not only sets of one, two, and three or more entities, and those that are near the speaker from those further away, but also entities that are up above, upslope, down below, downriver or toward an exit, inside or upriver, outside, over something, or across something. Cross-cutting all of these categories is another distinction among what are termed *restricted, extended,* and *obscured* entities and areas. Restricted demonstratives are used for persons, objects, or areas that are in sight and are restricted in size and range of motion: those that can be viewed fully in a single glance. They are used to pinpoint specific locations: 'right here', 'right there'. Extended demonstratives, by contrast, refer to persons, objects, or areas that are in sight and are longer than they are high or wide, those that cover a broad expanse, or those moving from one place to another: entities that require shifting views to see. They are also used for general, vague areas: 'around here', 'somewhere around there'. Obscured demonstratives refer to entities or areas that are not clearly perceptible.

4 IMPLICATIONS OF THE DIFFERENCES

The differences in vocabulary and grammar we have seen here are only small samples of the kinds of differences to be discovered among languages. Such discoveries have been a continuing source of wonder to anthropologists and linguists, and have raised intriguing questions about potential relationships among language and the thoughts and lives of speakers. For many scholars, these questions have provided the primary stimulus for the study of languages: language is seen as a key to the mind. While we may not be able to observe mental categories and structures directly, it has been hoped that the categories and structures observable in languages might provide some reflection of them, revealing both universal human cognitive structures and areas of possible variation across cultures. Other scholars, concerned with academic rigor, have deemed the investigation of relations among language, thought, and culture inherently unscientific and consequently unworthy of study. Since thought is not directly observable, it is impossible to demonstrate correlations between mental and linguistic structures. Even if correlations could be shown, it would be impossible to establish the directionality of causation. If we find differences among languages, can we conclude that these differences shape the thoughts of their speakers, or that differences in thought and culture have shaped the languages?

These issues remain controversial today, with opinions to some extent a matter of personal taste, to some extent a matter of academic discipline. Some see the primary goal of the study of language as uncovering fundamental, universal principles common to all languages, principles that might help us define the essence of being human. For such scholars, differences among languages are generally viewed as minor and accidental, of little academic interest. For others, the differences are what make the study of languages enlightening and worthwhile. In his introduction to *Linguistic Anthropology: A Reader*, Duranti provides a fine discussion of the kinds of inferences that have been drawn from the differences to be found among languages:

> One possible inference from these observations on linguistic diversity was that languages are arbitrary systems and one cannot predict how they will classify the world (linguistic relativism). Another inference was that languages would develop distinctions and categories that are needed to deal with the reality surrounding the people who speak them (linguistic functionalism). A third inference was that the different conceptual systems represented in different languages would direct their speakers to pay attention to different aspects of reality, hence, language could condition thinking (linguistic relativity). (2001: 11)

These inferences are certainly not incompatible; they are held to varying degrees by substantial proportions of anthropologists, linguists, and especially linguistic anthropologists. As progress has been made in our understanding of the forces that shape the development of languages, it has become possible to examine such issues more productively.

Both vocabulary and grammar can be observed to develop through certain recurring processes. In some cases we can still see the resources used by speakers to create the vocabulary they have needed. The Yup'ik term *amirkaq* 'young bearded seal', for example, was built on the noun *amiq* 'pelt, skin' with the suffix *-kaq* 'raw material for, future', a combination meaning literally 'raw material for a pelt'. The term *qalriq* 'large male bearded seal giving its mating call' was derived from the verb *qalrir-* 'to cry out, shriek'. The term *ugtaq* 'seal on an ice-floe' was derived from the verb *ugte-* 'to climb up onto the top of something'. *Puga* 'surfaced seal' was created from the verb *puge-* 'come to the surface, emerging halfway'. All of these words, *amirkaq, qalriq, ugtaq,* and *puga* now have lives of their own; they are not simply descriptions, but labels in their own right, much like English *screwdriver.* Often, of course, the resources originally used by speakers to create terms are barely discernible after some time has passed. The terms *maklaaq* 'bearded seal in its first year' and *maklassuk* 'bearded seal in its second year' were apparently derived from the noun *maklak* 'bearded seal', but the suffixes are no longer identifiable. The origins of many more words, including the basic *maklak* 'bearded seal', are completely lost in the shadows of time: they are now simply unanalyzable units.

New words can be brought into the language as needed in other ways as well. Some terms are created by extending the original meaning of a word to new uses, often metaphorically or metonymically. The Mohawk verb root *-ont* 'put into the oven' originally meant 'attach at one end', a meaning that it also retains today. At a certain point it came to be used for attaching a pot to a hook or other support over the fire. With repeated use, it took on the added meaning 'put over the fire'. When ovens became a part of daily life, the verb was extended further to refer to putting food into the oven to bake. The Yup'ik noun *teq* is used for both 'anus' and 'sea anemone'. Apparently one took its name from its resemblance to the other. The noun *teru* is used for both 'foot of bed or bedding area' and 'bed partner who sleeps with his body heading in the opposite or perpendicular direction'. The noun *tepa* is used for 'odor', 'aroma', and 'aged fish head'.

Sometimes new words are acquired from other languages. North American communities have varied in their receptiveness to outside influences. In some, there is strong resistance to the adoption of foreign terms, while in others, words from other languages are pervasive. In some areas there was already a long tradition of multilingualism well before Europeans arrived, sometimes associated with extensive intermarriage among small communities, sometimes associated with trade. Yup'ik, for example, contains identifiable words from a number of neighboring languages (Jacobson 1984: 681–9). The Yup'ik *caguyaq* 'conical wooden hat' comes from Aleut *chaxudax* 'visor'; *nuuniq* 'porcupine' comes from Koyukon Athabaskan *noona*; *tupiq'uyaq* 'tent' comes from Inupiaq *tupiq*. Terms for introduced items or concepts are often borrowed from the languages of those who bring the items or concepts. The Mohawk spoken in Quebec contains some nouns from French, such as *timotón* 'sheep' (from *des moutons*), *rasós* 'gravy' (from *la sauce*), and *terentsó* 'quarter' (from *trente sous*). Navajo contains some nouns from Spanish, such as *béégashii* 'cattle' (from *vacas*), *béeso* 'money' (from *peso*), and *damǫ́* 'Sunday' (from *domingo*). Yup'ik contains nouns from Russian, such as *kass'aq* 'Whiteman, priest' (from *kazák* 'Cossack'), *angel* 'angel' (from Russian *ángel*), and *kuuvviaq* 'coffee' (from *kófe*). The borrowed terms in a language can tell us not only who speakers have interacted with, but also something of the nature of their interaction.

The words in a language provide a record of the concepts speakers have considered nameworthy. They can also indicate how speakers have related these concepts logically to others. Mohawk contains many verb stems formed by noun–verb compounding, also called noun incorporation. The verb stem meaning 'to cook', for example, is actually a compound, *-khw-onni*, literally 'meal-make'. The verb 'to sing' is also a compound, *-renn-ot*, literally 'song-stand', that is 'to stand up a song'. A variety of noun stems appear in such compounds, but a substantial number of Mohawk compound verbs contain one of three noun roots: *-'nikonhr-* 'mind', *-ia't-* 'body', or *-rihw-* 'idea'.

Verbs incorporating the noun *-'nikonhr-* 'mind' generally denote events and states that affect people mentally:

(5) Mohawk verbs with incorporated *-'nikonhr-* 'mind'

-'nikonhr-aksen	'mind-be.bad'	=	'be sad'
-'nikonhr-iio	'mind-be.good'	=	'be patient'
-'nikonhr-o'kt	'mind-run.out'	=	'give up'
-'nikonhr-ahnirat	'mind-strengthen'	=	'encourage'
-'nikonhr-otako	'mind-unstand'	=	'tempt'
-'nikonhr-aienta'	'mind-receive'	=	'understand'
-'nikonhr-atsha'ni	'mind-fear'	=	'be brave'
-'nikonhr-atsi'io	'mind-weak'	=	'be cowardly'
-'nikonhr-en'	'mind-fall'	=	'be depressed'

Verbs incorporating the noun *-ia't-* 'body' generally denote events and states that affect animate beings physically:

(6) Mohawk verbs with incorporated *-ia't-* 'body'

-ia't-ata'	'body-put.in'	=	'bury someone'
-ia't-enhawi	'body-carry'	=	'carry someone'
-ia't-ahset	'body-hide'	=	'hide someone'
-ia't-ohseronkw-	'body-caress'	=	'caress someone'
-ia't-ishonhkw	'body-shake'	=	'shiver'
-ia't-aken	'body-see'	=	'be visible'
-ia't-ienen'	'body-fall'	=	'fall down'
-ia't-ionni	'body-extend'	=	'be stretched out'
-ia't-itahkhe'	'body-move'	=	'ride'
-ia't-ahton	'body-disappear'	=	'get lost'

Some verbs that began as descriptions of physical effects of events or states on people have come to be used metaphorically. The verb *-ia't-ahton* 'body-disappear', for example, with middle voice *-at-* 'self', means 'get lost', but the same verb is also used if a person is not following a discussion or becomes confused.

Verbs containing the incorporated noun *-rihw-* 'idea' often denote abstract events:

(7) Mohawk verbs with incorporated *-rihw-* 'idea'

-rihw-ahnirat	'idea-tighten'	=	'prove'
-rihw-isak	'idea-seek'	=	'investigate'
-rihw-atiront	'idea-stretch'	=	'discuss' (with DUPLICATIVE)
-rihw-atihentho	'idea-pull'	=	'recall, remember'
-rihw-isa'	'idea-finish'	=	'decide, promise'
-rihw-aketsko	'idea-raise'	=	'bring up (for discussion)'
-rihw-anonianiht	'idea-overdo'	=	'exaggerate'
-rihw-onni	'matter-make'	=	'cause'
-rihw-atorat	'news-hunt'	=	'gossip'

Like other word-formation processes, incorporation allows speakers to create terms for specific expressive needs. These terms are vocabulary items in their own right, with specific meanings associated with the functions for which they were created and the circumstances in which they are used. The meaning may not be precisely equivalent to those of their parts. This noun *-rihw-* has developed a range of abstract meanings, including not only 'idea' but also 'matter, affair, cause, news, word', and more, depending on the compound in which it occurs. The stem *-rihw-atorat*, literally 'idea-hunt', is used specifically to describe one who is a gossip, that is, always looking for news.

The lists of verbs above constitute only a small sample of the verbs in the language created by incorporating nouns for 'mind', 'body', and 'idea'. This process has left its mark on a significant portion of the vocabulary of the language: it has resulted in an explicit classification of many events and states into those with mental, physical, and abstract effects.

All of these means of developing vocabulary for new concepts, deriving new words, extending old words to new uses, and adopting terminology from other languages, illustrate the fact that languages are adaptable to the needs of their speakers. It is easy to see the cultural foundation of the Yup'ik proliferation of seal and boot terms, and the processes which underlie its development. As we would expect, there is similar richness in terms for kinds of fish and for hunting, trapping, and fishing techniques and equipment. The same processes underlie the development of lexical elaboration in other, more abstract domains. Speakers create vocabulary to name concepts they recognize as nameworthy and want to discuss. The new creations gain a place in the language only through use.

Grammatical distinctions and categories develop in languages through somewhat similar processes. Distinctions expressed the most often by speakers eventually come to be generalized. With repeated use comes abbreviation or erosion of form. We can see such erosion in progress with the English future markers. The originally separate, full verb *will* is now generally reduced in natural speech to just a slight *l* at the end of pronouns and nouns: *I'll go*. The originally separate phrase *be going to*, as in *I am going to eat*, has lost its concrete sense of travelling by foot to another location for a particular activity, to indicate simply an impending situation: *I am going to be hungry*. With the routinization has come erosion of the form: *I'mna eat*. Such processes, sometimes referred to as *grammaticalization*, may take place gradually over centuries, but in some cases we can still see their traces even in North American languages. Among the many grammatical morphemes of Mohawk is an instrumental suffix *-hkw* 'with'. The verb root *-hiaton*, for example, means 'write'. If the instrumental suffix is added to this root, a new verb stem is formed, meaning 'write with':

(8) Mohawk instrumental suffix *-hkw* 'with'
    a. *khiá:tonhs*
       k-hiaton-hs
       1.SG.AGENT-write-IMPERFECTIVE
       'I write (it)'

    b. *khiatónhkhwa'*
       k-hiaton-hkw-ha'
       1.SG.AGENT-write-INSTRUMENTAL-IMPERFECTIVE
       'I write with it.'

The instrumental suffix -*hkw* is pervasive in Mohawk. It is used to form words for objects based on verbal descriptions of their uses:

(9) Mohawk instrumental -*hkw* in use

iehiatónhkhwa'	'one writes with it'	=	'pen, pencil'
iontekhwakon'onhstáhkhwa'	'one makes food tasty with it'	=	'ketchup'
ienonhsohare'táhkhwa'	'one floor-washes with it'	=	'mop'
ienon'tawerontáhkhwa'	'one pours milk with it'	=	'milk pitcher'
ietsi'tsaráhkhwa'	'one puts flowers in with it'	=	'vase'
ionnitskaráhkhwa'	'one fixes a place to lie down with it'	=	'sheets'
iontenawirohare'táhkhwa'	'one tooth-washes with it'	=	'toothbrush'
iontenonhsa'tariha'táhkhwa'	'one heats the house with it'	=	'heater'
iontkahri'táhkhwa'	'one plays with it'	=	'toy'
iontkonhsohare'táhkhwa'	'one face-washes with it'	=	'face cloth'
teiehtharáhkhwa'	'one talks with it'	=	'telephone'
teionrahsi'tahráhkhwa'	'one sets one's feet up with it'	=	'footstool'
iehwistaráhkhwa'	'one inserts money with it'	=	'wallet'
tehatitstenhrotáhkhwa'	'they stand stones with it'	=	'cement'
iakehiahráhkhwa'	'one remembers with it'	=	'souvenir'

The same suffix appears in names of places with identifiable functions, usually preceded by the particle *tsi* 'at, where':

(10a) Mohawk instrumental -*hkw* in names for places

tsi ionterennaientáhkhwa'
'at one lays down prayers/songs with it' =
'the place one prays with'   =   'church'

tsi ieiontskahónhkhwa'
'the place one dines with'   =   'restaurant'

tsi iehwistaientáhkhwa'
'the place one lays money with'   =   'bank'

tsi teionttsihkwa'ekstáhkhwa'
'the place one puck strikes with, one uses to play hockey' =   'arena'

tsi ietsenhaientáhkhwa'
'the place one lays the fire with, holds council'   =   'council office'

tsi iakenheion'taientáhkhwa'
'the place one lays the dead with'   =   'hospital'

tsi iontatia'tahráhkhwa'
'the place one lays bodies with'   =   'funeral home'

We can still discern the origin of the instrumental suffix -*hkw*. It has developed from a verb root meaning 'pick up' which has survived into the modern language. (The duplicative prefix *te-* below marks the change of position of the object lifted.)

(10b) Origin of the Mohawk instrumental suffix *-hkw*
    tekehkhwa'
    te-ke-<u>hkw</u>-ha'
    DUPLICATIVE-1.SG.AGENT-<u>pick.up</u>-IMPERFECTIVE
    'I pick it up, lift it.'

It is easy to see how the verb root evolved into an instrumental suffix. People typically pick up an instrument before using it. Such statements as 'He picked up the knife and cut' are common. From such a statement it is easy to infer that the knife was the instrument of the cutting. In languages with extensive compounding, speakers form compound verbs for such recurring events: 'pick.up-cut', or in the case of Mohawk, 'cut-pick.up'. At an earlier stage in its development, Mohawk allowed compounding of this type. The compounding was the first step in the development of the verbal suffixes.

Navajo has some relatively young verbal prefixes whose origins in full words can still be traced as well. The prefix *'a'ą́-* marks action into a hole or burrow. (The second syllable is automatically lengthened before the final syllable of verbs.)

(11) Navajo prefix *'a'ą́-* 'into a hole'

'a'ą́ą́-tłizh	'I fell <u>into a hole</u>'	(*yitłizh* 'I fell down')
'a'ą́ą́-shna'	'I crawled <u>into a hole</u>'	
'a'ą́ą́-mááz	'I rolled <u>into a hole</u>'	
'a'ą́ą́-lgo'	'I pushed him <u>into a hole</u>'	
'a'ą́ą́-łmááz	'I rolled it <u>into a hole</u>'	
'a'ą́ą́-lwod	'It ran <u>into a hole</u>'	

Young and Morgan trace this prefix to the word *'a'áán* 'hole, burrow', which still survives in the modern language as a noun. Another prefix, *naa-*, indicates that an event or state pertains to war or an enemy. This prefix is traced to the noun *anaa* 'war'. The prefix *łe-* 'into the ashes' is traced to the noun *łeeh* 'dirt, soil'.

In some cases it is still easy to see how the grammar has developed to meet the particular expressive needs of speakers. Yup'ik contains a suffix *-ir-* that can be added to nouns for body parts to create verbs meaning 'have cold X':

(12) Yup'ik suffix *-ir-* 'have cold...'
    a. *ciuta<u>ir</u>tua*
       ciuta-<u>ir</u>-tu-a
       ear-<u>cold</u>-INTRANSITIVE.INDICATIVE-1.SG
       'I have cold ears, my ears are cold.'

    b. *it'ga<u>ir</u>tua*
       it'ga-<u>ir</u>-tu-a
       nose-<u>cold</u>-INTRANSITIVE.INDICATIVE-1.SG
       'I have a cold nose, my nose is cold.'

There is a suffix *-ssur-*, which is added to nouns for game or other food or food-catching equipment, which means 'hunt', 'hunt for', or 'check':

(13) Yup'ik suffix -*ssur*- 'hunt, hunt for, check'

    a. *tuntussurtuq*
       tuntu-ssur-tu-q
       caribou-hunt-INTRANSITIVE.INDICATIVE-1.SG
       'he is caribou-hunting'

    b. *kuvyassurtuq*
       kuvyassur-tu-q
       net-check-INTRANSITIVE.INDICATIVE-1.SG
       'he is fishnet-checking'

Of course most grammatical morphemes are less concrete in meaning and less transparently related to elements of the physical environment. With age, grammatical categories and distinctions tend to become increasingly abstract, as speakers extend them to more contexts and metaphorical uses.

We can see that both vocabulary and grammatical categories emerge out of language use: from the ideas that speakers choose to express the most often, the concepts they choose to name and refer to, the distinctions they choose to note. In this way, thought and culture can be seen to shape language. It is of course important to remember that linguistic categories do not necessarily match the conceptual, cultural, and social categories of speakers at any particular moment. The languages inherited by children are intricate structures that have evolved, piece by piece and step by step, through centuries and even millennia of use. And they continue to evolve at every moment.

The relationship between language on the one hand and thought, culture, and society on the other is by no means unidirectional. One of the most formative cultural experiences is learning language. As children acquire their first language, they learn concepts for which their language provides vocabulary. They learn distinctions they must observe if they are to speak grammatically. They also learn what to say in particular situations (see Kulick and Schieffelin, this volume). Such learning is not necessarily limiting: languages, by their nature, are open-ended, allowing speakers to express things they have never heard, and even to introduce changes to the system.

5   LANGUAGE IN CULTURE AND SOCIETY

Language has other kinds of cultural and social roles as well, and these are of special interest to linguistic anthropologists. Language serves as a powerful tool for creating, maintaining, and celebrating culture and social relationships. An important focus of linguistic anthropology has been the uses to which languages are put by their speakers, both consciously and unconsciously.

Most languages exhibit a variety of speech styles, used in different settings and for different purposes. We are fortunate that there is a wealth of narrative material from North American languages on record. The fact that the study of language and culture in North America developed together for the most part, out of the same scholarly tradition, meant that each was documented as a part of the other, by scholars interested in both. The narrative texts that exist, however, represent only a shadow of the verbal art that was and still is in use. Boas recognized the difficulty of capturing the essence of this art: 'The slowness of dictation that is necessary for recording texts makes it difficult for the narrator to employ that freedom of diction that belongs to the well-told tale, and consequently an unnatural simplicity of syntax prevails in most of the dictated texts' (1917: 1). He was aware of the richness that could not be captured:

> As yet, nobody has attempted a careful analysis of the style of narrative art as practised by the various tribes. The crudeness of most records presents a serious obstacle for this study, which, however, should be taken up seriously. We can study the general structure of the narrative, the style of composition, of motives, their character and sequence; but the formal stylistic devices for obtaining effects are not so easily determined. (1917: 7)

Over the past century, better documentation of verbal art has become possible, and with it has come a fuller appreciation of the powerful and intricate rhetorical skills of gifted narrators. But at the same time, as English has come to replace the traditional languages in many contexts, and evening entertainment has shifted from story-telling to television, such highly developed art and the artists who create it have become scarcer.

A number of North American peoples have magnificent, elaborate traditions of ceremonial oratory. For a variety of reasons, some practical, some out of respect for privacy, there are fewer records of ritual speech than of narrative. In many cases, future generations may consider these among the most important aspects of their heritage. But these traditions can be among the most fragile, since their performance requires exceptional oratorical skill unless they are simply learned by rote. They can disappear well before the language itself. Many communities are currently facing decisions about the most effective and appropriate way to preserve them and pass them on.

Many North American languages contain special speech styles used to or by particular groups of people. Often special vocabulary and even grammar are used in addressing one's elders, particularly in-laws (if they are addressed at all). Special vocabulary and grammar are used with young children and pets, as in many cultures throughout the world, and among some groups, intricate patterns of sound alternations are used as well. Of special interest are distinct styles of speech used by men and women in some communities, or to men and women. In some languages of the Siouan family, the different styles are signaled simply by a syllable or two added to the ends of statements, questions, and commands. In Yana of California, they involve pervasive differences in the sounds of most words. In some languages the men's forms can be seen to be basic and older; in others the women's forms are more basic. In still others, the two styles are simply different. Careful examination of extended speech has revealed, however, that the different forms are rarely simple gender markers. Examining everyday interaction in Lakhota, a Siouan language, Trechter (forthcoming) has found that the forms originally identified as male speech actually signal a kind of authority, and accordingly are used by women in positions of power and avoided by men out of deference. Describing Yana, Sapir (1929) noted that the men's forms were used only by men speaking to men. More recently Luthin (1991) discovered that the two styles were not purely indicators of sex, but rather of level of formality. The men's forms expressed reserve. They were used not only among men but also in formal public speaking and by men speaking to their mothers-in-law.

Issues of language use can have special consequences in multilingual societies. Patterns of language choice were surely important factors in interaction before European contact. In some areas, such as the West, there was a long tradition of relatively stable multilingualism because communities were small and intermarriage was common. People expected to learn their mother's language, their father's language, and the language of their spouse, which might or might not be the same. Issues of language use became more critical with the arrival of Europeans. In some areas, this contact resulted in the sudden decimation or destruction of communities by massacre or epidemic. The deaths of so many speakers resulted in the demise of large numbers of languages, about which little will ever be known. In more recent times, languages have been fading due to language shift, as they are spoken in fewer and fewer contexts and by fewer and fewer speakers. Some shift has been forced, some voluntary. National government and church organizations, in attempts to integrate native people into mainstream society, shipped children off to boarding schools at an early age, where they were punished for speaking their mother tongues. Many returned knowing only English. Those who did remember their first language vowed not to teach it to their children, hoping to spare them the pain they themselves had suffered. Nevertheless, there are still numerous communities with successful bilinguals, individuals skillful in both their traditional language and that of the outside society, speakers who can exploit the vast linguistic resources they control to great effect. A few communities are predominantly bilingual in this way, as in Greenland. Many others contain lively groups of talented bilingual speakers, but children are no longer following in their footsteps. Most contain fewer bilingual speakers every year. In fact the magnificent linguistic diversity and richness of North America is disappearing at an alarming rate, as speakers use their traditional languages in ever fewer contexts, and ever fewer children learn them at all. Ironically, as the languages are disappearing, respect for them and the cultures they represent has become more widespread, both within local communities and outside. Their value as markers of identity has grown, at a time when skill in their use is disappearing.

It is estimated that no more than one or two dozen of the nearly 300 languages spoken in North America 500 years ago will survive another century. The disappearance of these languages, sometimes by force, sometimes by choice, is a tremendous loss. Each represents centuries of development, shaped by patterns of expression of generations of speakers. For the descendants of these speakers, their disappearance means the loss of the center of their intellectual, cultural, and social heritage. For all of us, the disappearance of this magnificent diversity deprives us of opportunities to witness and celebrate alternative creations of the human mind, alternative ways of making sense of experience and passing it on.

REFERENCES

Boas, F. (ed.) (1911). *Handbook of American Indian Languages*, Part 1. Bureau of American Ethnology Bulletin 40. Washington, DC: Government Printing Office.

Boas, F. (1917). Introduction. *International Journal of American Linguistics* 1: 1–8.

Boas, F. (ed.) (1922). *Handbook of American Indian Languages*, Part 2. Bureau of American Ethnology Bulletin 40. Washington, DC: Government Printing Office.

Duranti, A. (2001). Linguistic Anthropology: History, Ideas, and Issues. In A. Duranti (ed.), *Linguistic Anthropology: A Reader* (pp. 1–38). Oxford: Blackwell.

Jacobson, S. A. (1984). *Yup'ik Eskimo Dictionary.* Fairbanks: Alaska Native Language Center.

Luthin, H. (1991). Restoring the Voice in Yanan Traditional Narrative: Prosody, Performance, and Presentational Form. PhD dissertation, University of California, Berkeley.

Powell, J. W. (1891). *Indian Linguistic Families of America North of Mexico.* Bureau of American Ethnology Annual Report 7. Washington, DC: Government Printing Office.

Sapir, E. (1990 [1929]). Male and Female Forms of Speech in Yana. In *The Collected Works of Edward Sapir 5: American Indian Languages* (pp. 335–341). Berlin: Mouton de Gruyter.

Trechter, S. (forthcoming). *The Pragmatic Functions of Gender Deixis in Lakhota.* Lincoln: University of Nebraska Press.

Young, R. and Morgan, W. (1987) *The Navajo Language: A Grammar and Colloquial Dictionary.* Albuquerque: University of New Mexico (revised edn.).

CHAPTER 7

Variation in Sign Languages

Barbara LeMaster and Leila Monaghan

1 INTRODUCTION

The term "sign language" refers to a signed language performed in a three-dimensional space, using hands, face, and body rather than speech, that is understood through vision rather than through hearing. Typically, sign languages emerge among groups of deaf people who need to communicate in a language not dependent on sound. Some hearing groups, however, have also developed sign languages or sign systems of their own such as the signing used by Australian Aboriginal women in mourning (Kendon 1988) or Plains Indian signing (Farnell 1995). Sign languages also differ from the gestures used with most speech (see Haviland, this volume). This chapter will focus on the sign languages of deaf people.

Variation is a key theme throughout this chapter. We begin by outlining the kinds of variations present in sign languages and deal with two common myths about sign languages, first, that there is a universal sign language and, second, that sign language is just spoken language on the hands; then we discuss how sign languages have been influenced by literacy. In sections 2 and 3, we present a more general discussion of how sign languages are related to d/Deaf identity, community, and culture as well as to variations due to region, age, gender, ethnicity, and social setting (with "deaf" referring to audiological and "Deaf" to cultural notions of deafness). In section 4, we consider the work in linguistic anthropology on sign languages and Deaf culture. Key themes include socialization practices in Deaf communities, development of and changes within d/Deaf communities, and sign variation and d/Deaf identities. Finally, we review the kinds of variation possible.

1.1 Myth 1: Sign language is universal

Many people unfamiliar with sign languages believe there is only one way of signing for all deaf people. This is a common misconception. Sign languages are not universal, and they are not universal for the same kinds of reasons that spoken languages are not universal. Geographical, national, political, and social boundaries can separate people by the sign languages they use. Sometimes the differences can be great, as in the differences between whole sign languages, for example, as between Japanese, British, Thai, and American signed languages.[1]

Despite there being no one universal sign language, there are situations in which one can speak of international sign languages. As with the spoken language Esperanto, "Gestuno," or "international signing" (as it is now called), is an invented communication system intended for international use. The World Federation of the Deaf's Unification of Signs Commission accepted the signs of Gestuno. The most recent and extensive dictionary was published in 1975 and has 1,470 signs. Interpreters and officials at international meetings and sporting events most commonly use it. With the unification of Europe, a European lingua franca is developing among European deaf people. Some people are calling this kind of signing "international signing" as well.

Although sign language is not universal, there is something about its nature that enables deaf people to seemingly communicate across language boundaries with other deaf signers more easily than hearing people seem to be able to do with each other. Deaf people improvise, gesture, pantomime, using whatever works, to establish a foundation for communication (Allsop, Woll, and Brauti 1995). Perhaps it is not as much the nature of signing that enables them to do this, but deaf people's practice communicating across language barriers while living in a mostly hearing, non-signing world.

Although not an international language, American Sign Language (ASL), similar to the English language, has had a widespread influence on the world and is often used as a lingua franca elsewhere. There are a number of reasons for this. ASL is the language of the world's largest organized Deaf community, and many Deaf people from throughout the world come to visit the United States. Also, Americans did much of the earliest research on sign languages and deaf communities making information about ASL available worldwide. Furthermore, there has been prolonged and extensive contact among American deaf people and deaf people from many other nations throughout the world. Prolonged and extensive contact with ASL by international deaf people can lead to adoption of ASL as a second language, and familiarity with American Deaf culture by non-American Deaf people. It also can lead to contact varieties of sign languages. ASL has also had a heavy influence on the educational language in many countries outside of the USA through exportation by missionaries and others, or through importation by local educators. For example, some Nigerian deaf schools use ASL in the classroom (Schmaling 2003), and some deaf Thai schools use an ASL-influenced version of their local sign language (Woodward 2003).

1.2   Myth 2: Sign language is signed spoken language

Another myth about sign languages is that they are the same language as the spoken language of their broader community, just done on the hands and face. This is not true. Actual sign languages have grammars that differ markedly from spoken languages in contact with them. In fact, countries which use (essentially) the same spoken language do not necessarily have mutually intelligible sign languages. The sign languages used in the United States, England, and the Republic of Ireland, for example, are quite different from each other. Sign languages do not develop according to the grammatical rules of the spoken languages of their communities. Instead, they have their own complex morphology, phonology, syntax, and semantic rules which sometimes differ markedly from the grammars of spoken languages with which they are in contact.

What complicates recognition of sign languages as wholly different from spoken languages are the kinds of contact signing that emerge as a direct result of the intense contact between signed and spoken languages within a given community. Signers represent a linguistic minority in a sea of spoken language users. Furthermore, the majority of deaf children (90 percent) are born into hearing homes with no history of deafness (Schein and Delk 1974). Therefore, the majority of deaf children are continually surrounded by spoken language from birth, and may not even be exposed to sign language during their period of first language acquisition.

Contact sign languages emerge in many situations where sign languages come into contact with spoken languages, or where two or more signed languages are in close contact with each other. The languages influence each other, producing a contact form of language (see Garrett, this volume).[2]

An example of language contact between English and ASL can be found in the directional ASL sign that encodes the subject and object of the verb, as in the sentences in figure 7.1, "me-GIVE-TO-him/her" and "s/he-GIVE-TO-me." A signer, particularly one for whom English is a first language, may use this directional verb to simply mean "GIVE," without being aware of the ASL grammatical rule which encodes (in these cases) both subjects ("I" and "s/he") and objects ("him/her" and "me") in the movement of this sign. (See figure 7.1.) Since encoding this information by the use of movement and/or handshape is foreign to English grammar, novice contact signers may not know that the subject and object have already been encoded. Instead, they rely on English grammar and make sure they provide a separate sign for each separate English word, "I" "give" "him/her," or, "s/he" "gives" "me." This comes out as the English–ASL contact version, "I me-GIVE-TO-him/her HIM/HER" ["I am giving it to him/her"] or, "S/HE s/he-GIVE-TO-me

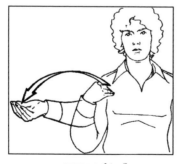 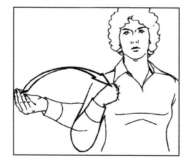

me-GIVE-TO-*him/her*	*s/he*-GIVE-TO-*me*

Figure 7.1   American Sign Language sentences with the directional verb "give", encoding subject and object in the movement of the verb (from Baker and Cokely 1980: 248; reproduced by permission of Dennis Cokely)

ME" ["She/he is giving it to me."]. Inadvertently the subject and object are repeated because English requires the statement of subject and object as separate nouns, while ASL embeds them in the placement of the directional verb. The English–ASL contact version borrows legitimate signs from ASL but adapts them in a peculiar way to suit the foreign grammar of the spoken language, which is English in this case.

The amount of influence spoken languages have on signed languages varies, but because sign languages coexist in the midst of larger spoken language communities, many deaf people's signing shows influence of spoken languages at some point. Contact signing arising from the interaction between ASL and English has features including ASL and ASL-like signs, some English mouthing and occasional spoken words, and reduced ASL and English morphology and syntax. Mouthing is particularly influential in some varieties of sign languages in countries where oral education (where children were expected to learn to lipread or speechread and speak rather than sign) is, or was, prevalent, including Germany, England, New Zealand, and elsewhere.

Given that contact sign languages coexist with existing sign languages, the linguistic boundaries between them may become erased[3] as they often coexist under the name of the existing sign language. For instance, when the term "ASL" is used for sign language classes it is often unclear whether unmixed American Sign Language or some contact form of ASL mixed with English will actually be taught in the class. The mere fact of producing language in a signed form makes it difficult for non-linguists to separate contact forms of sign languages from the sign languages themselves.

In short, the relationship between signed and spoken languages within a given deaf community is essentially twofold. Between the actual languages, there is no inherent relationship. They are generally wholly separate languages with unique grammars, and unique historical origins with respect to one another. On the other hand, within contact forms of signing, the relationship is intertwined. The contact signing represents the often intense relationship between the two languages, and the minority/majority status of sign vis-à-vis spoken language. The result of this is a hybrid communication system similar to pidginization, borrowings, and other contact language processes.

Contact between or among different sign languages also produces contact forms of sign language, although this has received much less attention by sign language scholars than the study of contact between signed and spoken languages. There are many examples of contact among sign languages around the world. For example, British Sign Language (BSL) becomes accessible to Deaf people throughout the British Isles through its portrayal on the BBC (British Broadcasting Corporation) television shows. Many Deaf people in the Republic of Ireland routinely take employment in England when employment is scarce at home, and they interact intensely with the British Deaf community. As a result, many British signs are imported for Irish adaptation and use at home. However, these imported BSL signs are not always recognized as having originated in England, but are sometimes identified as minority Irish variations. For example, in one family of seven Deaf native Irish signers, some BSL signs were mistaken for female forms of ISL signs (LeMaster 2002).

1.3 The relationship between sign languages and written languages

One key aspect of the relationship between signed and spoken languages is that sign languages are by and large not written languages, but are generally in close contact with spoken languages that do have written forms. This has a number of consequences. If deaf people have been introduced to schooling, they will also be familiar with the written forms of spoken languages that are used in all levels of deaf education. These written forms enter sign languages directly via fingerspelling, where words are spelled letter by letter using conventional alphabetic letters rather than signed as entire concepts. Fingerspelling varies in similar ways to other aspects of sign language. Just as there is no universal sign language, there are no universal fingerspelling alphabets; different countries have different systems. The USA and most of Europe and Latin America use one-handed versions of the alphabet, while Britain, Australia, New Zealand, and other former British colonies use a two-handed version. (See Appendix for examples of fingerspelling systems.) Japanese Sign Language uses a syllabic fingerspelling system, similar to written systems for spoken Japanese.

One way fingerspelled letters come into use outside of actual fingerspelled words is through initialization of signs. This is where a signed alphabet letter is used in the sign, usually for part or all of the handshape of the sign (such as using A handshapes for the American sign for ALLOW). Some fingerspelled forms have even gone through simplifying lexicalization processes, tending to delete medial letters. (See figure 7.2 showing how the 'O' in J-O-B is deleted in the fingerspelled loan sign for #JOB, and the 'H' and 'A' are deleted in the fingerspelled loan sign for #WHAT.) The ASL sign WHAT also can be produced with the forefinger and thumb tapping together, and is thought to be the result of fingerspelled W-H-A-T reduced to a simplified final T.

The importance of fingerspelling varies from society to society. It is particularly important in communities that place a high emphasis on literacy in the spoken contact language. Fingerspelling is common, for example, in the United States (see Davis 1989). Other Deaf cultures place less emphasis on fingerspelling. In Thailand, fingerspelling is considered ugly and is discouraged. In places where written

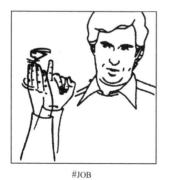

#JOB   #WHAT

Figure 7.2   Fingerspelled loan signs #JOB and #WHAT in American Sign Language (from Baker and Cokely 1980: 117; reproduced by permission of Dennis Cokely)

languages are logographic, such as China and Taiwan,[4] there is also airwriting of entire words, rather than fingerspelling *per se.*

While there is considerable acceptance in at least some parts of the world for fingerspelling, there has been little acceptance within Deaf communities of signed systems formally designed to convey written grammatical forms, such as Seeing Essential English (SEE1) and Signing Exact English (SEE2)[5] in the United States. These forms tend to be even more extreme than the naturally arising contact language forms discussed above. The ASL form I-GIVE-you NOW ["I am giving this to you now"] can become not only the contact form I I-GIVE-YOU YOU NOW but the SEE2 form I AM I-GIVE-you ING YOU NOW.

Systems such as SEE2 were developed, however, to help with the serious problem that deaf children often have in learning to read. Average reading scores for high school graduates in the United States are generally at the third or fourth grade levels,[6] and have been well below the performance of hearing students on standardized tests since 1916. Whether or not these artificial contact sign systems (such as SEE1 and SEE2) help in this process is an empirical question.

More recently, work by Padden and Ramsey (1998, 2000) and others has explored natural sign language oriented strategies of teaching reading to deaf children, including the use of fingerspelling. These approaches seem to be helping this long-term literacy problem in the spoken language of the community.

2   RELATIONSHIPS BETWEEN SIGN LANGUAGE VARIATION AND D/DEAF IDENTITY

Research in the United States has explored the relationships between sign variation and the concepts of pathological deafness, represented by lower-case "d" in "deaf," and sociocultural deafness, represented by upper-case "D" in "Deaf." Pathological deafness refers to deafness resulting from a hearing loss. Sociocultural Deafness refers to cultural, social, and political claims based on an ethnically Deaf identity in opposition to both a pathological view of deafness and to a hearing identity (e.g., Padden and Markowicz 1975[7]). When one refers to the pathological and cultural forms of deafness simultaneously, such as for a deaf person who is also culturally Deaf, the term "d/Deaf" may be used.[8]

There are three levels of social segmentation, which provide a heuristic framework of social diversity within the United States deaf community (LeMaster 1990). They are the "deaf community," the "Deaf culture," and the "Deaf ethnicity." These three terms identify three, sometimes overlapping, groups of people. The most inclusive grouping is the "deaf community." This group is the broadest, including anyone who has an interest in deaf issues. Therefore, it also includes members of the Deaf culture and Deaf ethnicity, among other people who have an interest in deaf issues. The term "deaf community" is taken from Padden's (1980: 92) definition of the American Deaf community and modified to make it even more inclusive:

> A deaf community is a group of people who live in a particular location, share the common goals of its members, and in various ways, work toward achieving these goals. A deaf community may include persons who are not themselves Deaf, but who actively

support the goals of the community and work with Deaf people to achieve them.
(LeMaster 1990: 23)

A wide range of language use including ASL, versions of signed English, oralism, and other forms of communication linguistically marks the US "deaf community," and its membership may include hearing and d/Deaf people. Members of the deaf community do not necessarily also belong to Deaf culture or have Deaf ethnicity.

The second most inclusive group is the Deaf culture, which includes both deaf and hearing people who follow the behavioral rules of the culture and who consider themselves and are considered by other members to be a member of the cultural group. The Deaf culture includes those who learn to behave in appropriate ways, with the most central members being those who are born into a Deaf ethnicity. Linguistically, both the Deaf culture and the Deaf ethnicity are marked by appropriate uses of ASL. An inability to display ASL in appropriate situations leads to the questioning of one's rightful claim to a Deaf cultural or ethnic identity.[9] Those who are culturally Deaf are also members of the deaf community; however, they may or may not be ethnically Deaf.

The third and most exclusive level is Deaf ethnicity. As with all ethnic identities, birthright becomes important. In the case of Deaf ethnic identity, one may lay claim to this identity by birth as a deaf person, or through birth into a Deaf family (as either hearing or deaf themselves) with the use of ASL as a first language (Johnson and Erting 1989; LeMaster 1990).[10] It is essential to a US Deaf ethnic identity that ASL is acquired with first-language fluency. Therefore, some hearing people may claim a Deaf ethnic identity, although they are not deaf themselves. These are hearing children born to Deaf parents, who use ASL as their first language and who are known as CODAs, or **C**hildren **O**f **D**eaf **A**dults. Many CODAs live in Deaf worlds as though they are deaf themselves, and with time, come to realize what it means socioculturally to have hearing in their world. Those who are ethnically Deaf can also participate as central members of Deaf culture (first by birthright, later by choice), and may participate in the deaf community.

How d/Deaf identity plays out in cultures outside of the United States, and even within microcultures within the United States, is only beginning to be investigated.[11] Performing one's identity as a Deaf ethnic identity in a pluralistic United States – a country that emphasizes ethnicity for political, cultural, and financial purposes – can make sense. However, binary distinctions of d/Deaf or Deaf versus hearing, while often used in the United States, may not represent reality. Sometimes what is considered to be a binary "deaf versus hearing" issue is really more an issue about language fluency or cultural awareness and fit.[12] Moreover, culture and language issues within the United States are more aligned along a continuum than segmentable into two binary units. But precisely because deafness is set in opposition to hearing abilities, this binary opposition is used to describe many Deaf culture and language issues around the world. Yet it is important to recognize that these very same binary distinctions in use outside of the United States may not mean the same thing as they do within the United States (Nakamura 2001; LeMaster 2003). We have to keep in mind that the unique histories, cultures, and social sensibilities of each deaf community shape its own language ideologies, uses of language, and sense of community membership. Each community, therefore, requires locally sensitive analysis.

3   Individual and Group Variation in Signed Languages

3.1   Home signs

Although most of the studies discussed above relate to groups of deaf people, the great majority of deaf children are born into homes with no history of deafness and no knowledge of sign language. In these cases where hearing and deaf people coexist without a common language, home signs can emerge.[13] These are signs and a signing style that are invented by a family for their own use. Home signs have been found nearly everywhere, occurring primarily in hearing families with deaf children where there has been no history of signing in the family. Even deaf families that use a natural sign language in the home may, however, invent some signs that are unique to their family, although deaf families are more conservative in their invention and practice of home signs than hearing families.[14]

It is important to underscore that home sign systems developed by isolated families differ significantly from the full-fledged languages that emerge from group situations. This is quite evident in the studies of the emergent Nicaraguan Sign Language[15] and the reports of the signing used by deaf and hearing people on Martha's Vineyard in the late 1800s.[16]

3.2   Variations within specific sign languages according to region, age, sex/gender, and register

Social characteristics, including region, age, gender, and ethnicity, are often represented through variations in sign languages. These variations may be connected to the kind of schooling deaf children receive. Sign language and Deaf culture are more likely to be acquired at school than at home.[17] As we have said, most deaf children (around 90 percent) are born to hearing rather than to deaf parents.[18]

Lucas, Bayley, and Valli (2001) found that region and age in the United States cannot be considered independently of one another, that they function in concert, unlike spoken languages, and that these factors can be connected to the localized nature of residential schools. Schools in the USA tend to serve children from specific states or cities, increasing the likelihood of regional variation. Schools also provide situations where children learn language from their peers, heightening the importance of age variation. Similar residential schools exist in other countries, too, which may also lead to sign language variation among deaf communities surrounding residential schools. For example, regional and age variations linked to schooling practices have been reported in Switzerland, New Zealand, and Thailand.[19] Age by itself is particularly important in Japan, and gender and age relate to gender-segregated schooling in Ireland.[20] School segregation by ethnicity or race also can play an important role in language variation. Differences between African American and white American signing in the USA have been documented, as have differences between various groups in post-apartheid South Africa.[21]

In the USA, regional differences are, at least, both lexical and phonological.[22] Signs for BIRTHDAY provide examples of regional lexical differences, from Philadelphia to

Indiana, from Virginia to a more conventional sign which is used more widely.[23] (See figure 7.3.) Just as with spoken English in the United States, there is a perception of New York ASL signers signing very quickly and Southern ASL signers as signing slowly in comparison to other regions in the United States.[24]

Sign languages (as is true for spoken languages) mark the age of the signer through the choices of signs one uses along with how one performs those signs. Frishberg (1975) documented a number of changes in ASL over time. Notably, many two-handed signs have become one-handed (e.g., in ASL a two-horned cow has become one-horned). Many two-handed non-symmetrical signs have become symmetrical. Many signs occurring outside of the central signing space (normally from the chin to the upper chest area) have moved into that central space. Signs which had blocked the face have moved away from the face. In addition to historical changes in the form of the language, choice of lexical items also can mark one's age.[25] Slang and other terms associated with youthfulness can mark one's age by whether they are used, or used appropriately. For example, some years back the term I-HAVE-REASON was used by younger women to indicate they had their period.[26] It was supposed to be a safe way to talk about their period in front of adults (often in front of teachers who were not supposed to know the sign because of their age group).

However, generational change should not be thought of as a steady march in a specific direction. Sometimes language planning movements, or other influences on a deaf community, can shift sign variation for a given generation, then fall out of fashion, leaving the next generation to take on more "archaic" styles once again.

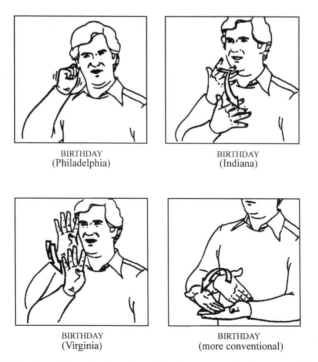

BIRTHDAY
(Philadelphia)

BIRTHDAY
(Indiana)

BIRTHDAY
(Virginia)

BIRTHDAY
(more conventional)

Figure 7.3 Regional variations in American Sign Language for the term "birthday" (from Baker and Cokely 1980: 85; reproduced by permission of Dennis Cokely)

A case in point is the use of the sign DEAF in the United States (discussed in Lucas et al. 2001). The oldest signers (55+ years of age) and the youngest cohorts (under 25) in the study shared the use of the non-citation (non-dictionary) form of the sign. This differed from the middle cohort (signers aged 25 to 54) who preferred a citation, or sign language dictionary, form of the sign for DEAF. The generational differences, where the older and younger cohort shared terms, and the middle cohort differed, may be understood in terms of the perceptions of ASL during these signers' lifetimes. The middle cohort may have found it important to adhere to a dictionary rendition of ASL in order to preserve the language, while both the older and younger cohorts may not have embodied that social prescription. Instead, older signers may have lacked metalinguistic awareness, while for younger signers there is an awareness of ASL as a language that is separate from English.

Variation due to gender or sex also occurs in sign languages. ("Gender" refers to cultural understandings of femininity and masculinity; "sex" refers to associations with one's biological status.) Currently there is little information about this kind of variation in sign languages, compared to research on spoken languages. However, gender distinctions in ASL have been found in the lexicon, in cohesive devices, and in signing space.[27] Gender distinctions in sign languages, as with spoken languages, are probably most prominently found in interactive data, in the performances of sign languages rather than in static lexicons or interpretations of grammars. Therefore, gender distinctions are not as readily apparent in ASL as are other social distinctions involving the lexicon, such as regional or age differences.[28]

The clearest gender distinctions in signed languages come from work on age-graded gendered Irish Sign Language used in the Republic of Ireland (e.g., LeMaster 1990, 2000, 2002[29]). Stemming from sex-segregated deaf school language use, two gender-distinct sign lexicons developed. Signs for common everyday nouns, verbs, and adjectives in the lexicon such as NIGHT, USE, and CRUEL differ by the sex of the signer. Women born before 1930 and men born before 1945 who attended the Dublin deaf schools in Cabra are the most likely to use gendered forms of ISL.[30] (See figures 7.4, 7.5, and 7.6.)

Figure 7.4 Female and male signs for NIGHT in Irish Sign Language (picture copyright Barbara LeMaster)

Figure 7.5   Female and male signs for USE in Irish Sign Language (picture copyright Barbara LeMaster)

Figure 7.6   Female and male signs for CRUEL in Irish Sign Language (picture copyright Barbara LeMaster)

Another type of variation found in ASL, and other sign languages, is by ethnicity or social group. In the case of African American Deaf signing (Aramburo 1989), signing varieties are influenced both by African American Vernacular English used by African American hearing people, and by the separation between white and African American communities more generally. The separation between African American and white people, particularly in Southern communities where, historically, schools were segregated, shows up in signing differences between African American and white signers. African American signers, particularly in the South, have vocabularies that differ from those of white signers living in the same area.[31] (See the black and white examples for

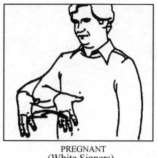

PREGNANT
(Black Southern Signers)

PREGNANT
(White Signers)

Figure 7.7   Black and white Southerners' signs for PREGNANT (from Baker and Cokely 1980: 86; reproduced by permission of Dennis Cokely)

the sign PREGNANT in figure 7.7.) Surely in the pluralistic United States there are other markers of ethnicity in signs, but the research in this area of sign language variation is just beginning.[32]

Just as US Southern segregation left its mark on the signing styles of black and white Americans, South African apartheid deeply affected language forms there. Separate schooling systems and residential segregation have led to many separate forms, particularly lexical forms. A sign language dictionary written during apartheid focused on the many differences between various groups of signers (Penn and Reagan 1994). It has been argued, however, that these signing forms are variations within one larger, mutually intelligible system (Aarons and Reynolds 2003).

Another key factor in language variation is how language reflects and helps create changes in social setting, sometimes discussed as register variation. In early research on the American situation, contact forms of signing and non-contact forms of sign languages were juxtaposed in a diglossic opposition where the contact forms have been referenced as "high" varieties and the non-contact sign language (ASL) as the "low" variety (e.g., Stokoe 1969–70). Later researchers dispute this diglossic characterization of English-influenced versus non-contact ASL. A separate, formal ASL is beginning to be recognized, leading some researchers to argue that both formal and informal forms of ASL are used within the American Deaf community as found in such settings as an academic lecture and a church service (Zimmer 1989; Monaghan 1991).

4   SIGN LANGUAGE VARIATION AND LINGUISTIC ANTHROPOLOGY

Linguistic anthropologists view language as a crucial part of our complex social and cultural world, and as communicating a complex range of information within ever-changing interactional contexts. While a few researchers of American Sign Language concerned themselves with variation early on,[33] linguistic anthropological studies of sign language variation became more frequent starting in the 1980s.

Some linguistic anthropologists have looked at socialization practices within deaf communities, particularly at how explicit and implicit cultural assumptions are passed on to children and adults. Because over 90 percent of deaf children are born into hearing families, there is often a tension between the practices and values of the d/Deaf world and the hearing world. Topics that have been studied in the United States include how deaf children are socialized into deaf residential schools (Erting 1985) and into hearing schools (Keating and Mirus 2001), the issues facing hard-of-hearing people as they negotiate being neither hearing nor deaf (Grushkin 1996), and the problems for a Deaf student in a hearing college classroom caused by the differences between American Sign Language and English (K. Johnson 1991). Studies outside of the United States include how parents, the medical profession, and d/Deaf communities in the USA and Scandinavia differ in their ideas about cochlear implants (Fjord 2001), how new children in Thai schools for the deaf are socialized by older children (Reilly 1995), and of the effects of the church and state on Irish deaf identity in residential schools (LeMaster 1990).

Another major theme of current work in linguistic anthropology is the development of and changes within d/Deaf communities. Since a key socialization strategy world-wide has been oral education systems (where children were expected to learn to speak and to read lips, or "speechread" as it is called today), many studies look at how communities and their associated sign languages developed covertly, away from the eyes of school authorities and parents. One language, Nicaraguan Sign Language, has even been studied since very near its inception. The Nicaraguan government founded the first large-scale schools for the deaf in Nicaragua in the late 1970s. Although the education system was oral, these school children started developing their own sign language, a process that has been documented by a group of researchers since the 1980s. This recognition by researchers has been part of building a strong young adult community (Kegl and McWhorter 1997; A. Senghas 1995; R. Senghas 1997). Similar processes have also been documented later on in the cycle of community development in New Zealand (Monaghan 1996) and Japan (Nakamura 2001), while the historical battles between signing and oral systems have been documented for nineteenth-century Spain (Plann 1997) and the United States (Baynton 1996). Ireland, where the education system was a signing-based one until 1945, provides an interesting counterexample to these studies of communities developing from oral education systems (LeMaster 2000). This process of development has been documented for countries as far spread and different as Austria, Russia, Brazil, and Nigeria (Monaghan, Schmaling, Nakamura, and Turner 2003).[34]

The hallmark of linguistic anthropological studies is attention to the types of sign variation present within a deaf community, and ethnographic descriptions of how language use is tied to d/Deaf identities. Questions about the relative universality of types of signing variation – a national language, a local language, a contact sign/spoken version of sign language, types of social variations, a home language, and so on – and what the local practice of these variations means in terms of defining d/Deaf identities, are questions that are only beginning to be asked by linguistic anthropologists working in the field. The study of signed languages and Deaf communities provides, in some ways, even richer data than studies of spoken language communities. In addition to all the kinds of variations of language found in spoken language communities, analysts must understand the role of disability in the construction of a d/Deaf identity. Linguistic anthropology provides the most comprehensive tools to conduct this research.

5   CONCLUSION

In this chapter, sign languages have been seen as entities unto themselves and as languages used by d/Deaf people. As languages are the reflection of how groups of people communicate, we can also see that when we talk generally about sign languages, we are talking about individual, cultural, and society-level issues.

Although some people still have the misunderstanding that a given sign language is universal, sign languages, like spoken languages, are in fact local phenomena. All groups have their own distinctive ways of using sign language and when groups are cut off from each other, the languages will differ. International sign languages are the function of international communities agreeing on a common system like Gestuno, using a common language like American Sign Language, or developing new ways of communicating face to face despite different national origins and linguistic differences. Sign languages develop wherever there is a group of people who need to communicate by visual means. Not all people with hearing loss, however, use sign languages.

In sociolinguistics, researchers study the effects that social characteristics such as region, age, gender, and social status have on language variation, paying attention to statistically significant or otherwise quantifiable variations of language used within particular populations. In linguistic anthropology, on the other hand, while researchers are also interested in studying the effects of these social characteristics on language variation, their attention is less on small parsings of variation across a wide spectrum of language users, and more on deep descriptions of holistic samplings of variations embedded within a particular culture. Linguistic anthropologists are interested in how languages contribute to the emergence and maintenance, or loss, of cultures. They study language socialization, and the range of linguistic variation within a given population (perhaps within one individual, or one family, or one community). They track developments of culture and language across time. The sections in this chapter on home signing, literacy and deafness, and contact language focus on how deaf people have gained access to the dominant (spoken) language around them.

What the societal and individual ramifications of sign languages have in common is that variation is always a key to understanding developing patterns within deaf communities. Characteristics of sign language users will be reflected in their language and signers will build upon these particularities to create cultures of their own. Variations between individuals and larger societies have profound implications for educational and governmental policies. Although documenting the lives of d/Deaf individuals and d/Deaf communities is just one part of the much larger process of the recognition of the rights of all deaf people, it is a process that allows communities to see where they have come from and where they might like to go.

NOTES

We would like to thank the many people who have helped make this chapter possible, including Alessandro Duranti for inviting us to be a part of this volume and for his comments, and Pamela Bunte, Carol Erting, Paul Garrett, Donald Grushkin, Elizabeth Keating, Misty Jaffe, Kristen Johnson, Ceil Lucas, Laura Miller, Karen Nakamura, Susan Needham, Angela Nonaka, and Richard Senghas for references, comments, and/or suggestions.

We would also like to thank Dennis Cokely for permission to reproduce illustrations here. Thanks also to the Deaf Studies Research Unit, Victoria University of Wellington, New Zealand, for permission to use the New Zealand fingerspelling alphabet.

1 Even signs that are iconic representations of the same object, such as "tree," can differ between languages: see Klima and Bellugi 1979.

2 Some sign language scholars have called this kind of language mixing Pidgin Sign English or PSE, arguing that the mixing between English and ASL is similar to what occurs among pidgins or trade languages where pieces of each language are merged for common use (Fischer 1975, 1978; Woodward 1973a, 1973b). Yet, in the case of language varieties emerging from contact between signed and spoken languages, generally signers employ spoken language grammar while using sign vocabulary often devoid of grammatical markings and conceptually inappropriate. More recently, this kind of language mixing has been called "contact signing" (Lucas and Valli 1992) which is more consistent with current understandings of pidgin and creole languages today.

3 See Irvine and Gal 2000 for the concept of erasure.

4 See Ann 2003 for work on Taiwan.

5 See Ramsey 1989 for a discussion of these systems.

6 See King and Quigley 1985 for a review and Gallaudet Research Institute 1996 for a more recent study; Holt, Traxler, and Allen 1992 for interpreting scores for deaf students.

7 Baker and Battison 1980, Lane, Hoffmeister, and Bahan 1996, Johnson and Erting 1989, Meadow 1972, Padden 1980, Padden and Humphries 1988, Padden and Markowicz 1975, Stokoe 1980, Vernon and Makowsky 1969, Wilcox 1989.

8 This is a convention developed by LeMaster for use in her own work to refer to the situations in which both pathological and social d/Deafness are being referenced simultaneously.

9 See these works for an introduction to this concept: Padden and Markowicz 1975, Stokoe et al. 1976, Woodward 1973c.

10 There is disagreement about whether hearing people can claim Deaf ethnicity. Some scholars argue that they can, based on a birthright in terms of parentage and first language acquisition. Other scholars maintain that the children with this birthright must be deaf, and yet others argue that they can be either deaf or hearing. Most scholars say that they cannot be hearing because they must be physically deaf in order to embody a Deaf ethnic identity.

11 See Erting, Johnson, Smith, and Snider 1994 for Deaf Way I proceedings, and other conference proceedings from the International Symposia on Sign Language Research, the Congresses of the World Federation of the Deaf, the Theoretical Issues on Sign Language Research conferences, and other conference proceedings involving international researchers. Also see newsletters from various deaf organizations from around the world for information on deaf communities and their languages. Also see Ceil Lucas' "Sociolinguistics in Deaf Communities" Series published through Gallaudet University.

12 See both LeMaster 1990 and 1996.

13 Frishberg 1987, Kuschel 1973, Davis and Supalla 1995.

14 Lucas et al. 2001.

15 Kegl and McWhorter 1997, A. Senghas 1995, R. Senghas 1997.

16 Groce 1985.

17 The majority of deaf children (90%) are born into hearing families, while fewer deaf children (10%) are born to deaf parents.

18 Schein and Delk 1974.

19 For discussion on Switzerland see Boyes Braem, Caramore, Hermann, and Hermann 2003. For New Zealand see Collins-Ahlgren 1989, and Thailand see Woodward 2003.

20 See Nakamura 2001 for a discussion on variation by age in Japan, and LeMaster 1990, 1993, 1997, 2000, and 2002 for gender and age variation in Ireland.

21   For the US black/white situation, see Aramburo 1989 and Woodward 1976. See Aarons and Reynolds 2003 for the post-apartheid South African discussion.
22   See Lucas et al. 2001. See also Baker and Cokely 1980, Shroyer and Shroyer 1984.
23   A modified B hand is an open palm, with the thumb crossed over the palm, and the fingers held together tightly.
24   See Woodward 1976.
25   See also Battison 1978, Woodward and Erting 1975.
26   Mel Carter, personal communication.
27   See Baker and Cokely 1980, Lucas et al. 2001, Mansfield 1993, Malloy and Doner 1995.
28   Perhaps this is why Lucas et al. (2001) point out that ASL gender differences are not as important as regional or age differences.
29   See also LeMaster 1997; LeMaster and Dwyer 1991; LeMaster and Foran 1986; Matthews 1996; Ó Baoill and Matthews 2000.
30   See also Burns 1998.
31   See Baker and Cokely 1980, Woodward 1976.
32   Lucas et al. 2001 point out, however, that despite widespread perceptions of quite different signing styles between African American and white signers, their formal interviews revealed only lexical differences, not phonological or syntactic differences.
33   James Woodward has been writing about variation since the 1970s, and has produced an impressive collection of work (Woodward 1973a, 1973b, 1974, 1976, 1980; Woodward and DeSantis 1977). Carol Erting, a linguistic anthropologist, has also been writing about variation and links to Deaf identity since the 1970s (e.g. Erting 1981, 1985). Their joint works include Woodward, Erting, and Oliver 1976 and Erting and Woodward 1979.
34   Space is too limited here for a discussion of general historical works on Deaf cultures, but key works include Gannon 1981, Lane 1984, Van Cleve and Crouch 1989, and Van Cleve 1993.

REFERENCES

Aarons, D., and Reynolds, L. (2003). South African Sign Language: Changing Policies and Practice. In L. Monaghan, C. Schmaling, K. Nakamura, and G. H. Turner (eds.), *Many Ways to be Deaf*. Washington, DC: Gallaudet University Press.
Allsop, L., Woll, B. and Brauti, J. M. (1995). International Sign: The Creation of an International Deaf Community and Sign Language. In H. Bos and G. M. Schermer (eds.), *Sign Language Research 1994* (pp. 171–188). Hamburg: Signum.
Ann, J. (2003). The Chiying School of Taiwan: A Foreigner's Perspective. In L. Monaghan, C. Schmaling, K. Nakamura, and G. H. Turner (eds.), *Many Ways to be Deaf*. Washington, DC: Gallaudet University Press.
Aramburo, A. (1989). Sociolinguistic Aspects of the Black Deaf Community. In C. Lucas (ed.), *The Sociolinguistics of the Deaf Community* (pp. 103–119). San Diego, CA: Academic Press.
Baker, C., and Battison, R. (eds.) (1980). *Sign Language and the Deaf Community: Essays in Honor of William C. Stokoe*. Silver Spring, MD: National Association of the Deaf.
Baker, C., and Cokely, D. (1980). *American Sign Language: A Teacher's Resource Text on Grammar and Culture*. Silver Spring, MD: TJ Publishers.
Battison, R. (1978). *Lexical Borrowing in American Sign Language*. Silver Spring, MD: Linstok Press.
Baynton, D. (1996). *Forbidden Signs: American Culture and the Campaign against Sign Language*. Chicago: University of Chicago Press.
Boyes Braem, P., Caramore, B., Hermann, R., and Hermann, P. S. (2003). Romance and Reality: Sociolinguistic Similarities and Differences Between Swiss German Sign Language

and Rhaeto-Romansh. In L. Monaghan, C. Schmaling, K. Nakamura, and G. H. Turner (eds.), *Many Ways to be Deaf*. Washington, DC: Gallaudet University Press.

Burns, S. E. (1998). Ireland's Second Minority Language. In C. Lucas (eds.), *Pinky Extension and Eye Gaze: Language Use in Deaf Communities* (pp. 233–273). Washington, DC: Gallaudet University Press.

Collins-Ahlgren, M. (1989). Aspects of New Zealand Sign Language. Unpublished PhD dissertation, Victoria University, Wellington, NZ.

Davis, J. (1989). Distinguishing Language Contact Phenomena in ASL Interpretation. In C. Lucas (ed.), *The Sociolinguistics of the Deaf Community*. San Diego, CA: Academic Press.

Davis, J., and Supalla, S. (1995). A Sociolinguistic Description of Sign Language Use in a Navajo Family. In C. Lucas (ed.), *Sociolinguistics in Deaf Communities* (pp. 77–108). Washington, DC: Gallaudet University Press.

Erting, C. (1981). An Anthropological Approach to the Study of the Communicative Competence of Deaf Children. *Sign Language Studies* 32: 221–238.

Erting, C. (1985). Sociocultural Dimensions of Deaf Education: Belief Systems and Communicative Interaction. *Sign Language Studies* 47: 111–126.

Erting, C., Johnson, R., Smith, D., and Snider, B. D. (eds.) (1994). *The Deaf Way: Perspectives from the International Conference on Deaf Cultures*. Washington, DC: Gallaudet University Press.

Erting, C., and Woodward, J. (1979). Sign Language and the Deaf Community: A Sociolinguistic Profile. *Discourse Processes* 2: 283–300.

Farnell, B. (1995). *Do You See What I Mean? Plains Indian Sign Talk and the Embodiment of Action*. Austin: University of Texas Press.

Fischer, S. (1975). Influences on Word Order Change in American Sign Language. In C. N. Li (ed.), *Word Order and Word Order Change* (pp. 1–25). Austin: University of Texas Press.

Fischer, S. (1978). Sign Language and Creoles. In P. Siple (ed.), *Understanding Language through Sign Language Research* (pp. 309–332). New York: Academic Press.

Fjord, L. (2001). Contested Signs: Discursive Disputes in the Geography of Pediatric Cochlear Implants, Language, Kinship, and Embodiment. PhD dissertation, University of Virginia.

Frishberg, N. (1975). Arbitrariness and Iconicity: Historical Change in American Sign Language. *Language* 51: 696–719.

Frishberg, N. (1987). Home Sign. In J. V. Van Cleve (ed.), *Gallaudet Encyclopedia of Deaf People and Deafness*, vol. 3 (pp. 128–131). New York: McGraw-Hill.

Gallaudet Research Institute (1996). Stanford Achievement Test, 9th Edition, Form S, Norms Booklet for Deaf and Hard-of-Hearing Students. (Including Conversions of Raw Score to Scaled Score and Grade Equivalent and Age-based Percentile Ranks for Deaf and Hard-of-Hearing Students.) Washington, DC: Gallaudet University.

Gannon, J. R. (1981). *Deaf Heritage: A Narrative History of Deaf America*. Silver Spring, MD: NAD Publishers.

Groce, N. E. (1985). *Everyone Here Spoke Sign Language: Hereditary Deafness on Martha's Vineyard*. Cambridge, MA: Harvard University Press.

Grushkin, D. A. (1996). Academic, Linguistic, Social and Identity Development in Hard-of-Hearing Adolescents Educated within an ASL/English Bilingual/Bicultural Educational Setting for Deaf and Hard-of-Hearing Students. PhD thesis, University of Arizona, Tucson.

Holt, J. A., Traxler, C. B., and Allen, T. E. (1992). Interpreting the Scores: A User's Guide to the 8th Edition Stanford Achievement Test for Educators of Deaf and Hard of Hearing Students. *GRI Technical Report: 92–1*. Washington, DC: Gallaudet University.

Irvine, J. T. and Gal, S. (2000). Language Ideology and Linguistic Differentiation. In P. V. Kroskrity (ed.), *Regimes of Language: Ideologies, Polities, and Identities* (pp. 35–84). Santa Fe, NM: School of American Research Press.

Johnson, K. (1991). Miscommunicating in Interpreted Classroom Interaction. *Sign Language Studies* 70: 1–34.

Johnson, R., and Erting, C. (1989). Linguistic Socialization in the Context of Emergent Deaf Ethnicity. Wenner-Gren Foundation Working Papers in Anthropology: Ethnicity and Socialization in a Classroom for Deaf Children. In C. Lucas (ed.), *The Sociolinguistics of American Sign Language* (pp. 41–84). New York: Academic Press.

Keating, E., and Mirus, G. (2001). Cross Modal Conversations: Deaf Children and Hearing Peers at School. Department of Applied Linguistics and TESL, UCLA: Crossroads of Language, Interaction, and Culture Conference.

Kegl, J., and McWhorter, J. (1997). Perspectives on an Emerging Language. In E. Clark (ed.), *The Proceedings of the Twenty-eighth Annual Child Language Research Forum* (pp. 15–38). Stanford, CA: CSLI Publications.

Kendon, A. (1988). *Sign Languages of Aboriginal Australia: Cultural, Semiotic, and Communicative.* Cambridge: Cambridge University Press.

Kendon, A. (1997). Gesture. *Annual Review of Anthropology* 26: 109–128.

Kennedy, G., Arnold, R., Dugdale, P., Fahey, S., and Moskovitz, D. (1997). *A Dictionary of New Zealand Sign Language.* Auckland, NZ: Auckland University Press/Bridget Williams Books.

King, C., and Quigley, S. (1985). *Reading and Deafness.* San Diego, CA: College-Hill Press.

Klima, E., and Bellugi, U. (1979). *The Signs of Language.* Cambridge, MA: Harvard University Press.

Kuschel, R. (1973). The Silent Inventor: The Creation of a Sign Language by the Only Deaf-Mute on a Polynesian Island. *Sign Language Studies* 3: 1–28.

Lane, H. (1984). *When the Mind Hears: A History of the Deaf.* New York: Random House.

Lane, H., Hoffmeister, R., and Bahan, B. (1996). *A Journey into the DEAF-WORLD.* San Diego, CA: DawnSign Press.

LeMaster, B. (1990). The Maintenance and Loss of Female and Male Signs in the Dublin Deaf Community. PhD dissertation, University of California, Los Angeles.

LeMaster, B. (1993). When Women and Men Talk Differently: Language and Policy in the Dublin Deaf Community. In T. Wilson, H. Donnan, and C. Curtin (eds.), *Irish Towns and Cities: Anthropological Perspectives on Urban Life.* Belfast: The Queen's University of Belfast, Ireland.

LeMaster, B. (1996). Language and Identity Revisited: Moving from Homogeneous Heterogeneity to Complex Multiplicity. Manuscript from presentation at the 94th Annual Meeting of the American Anthropological Association, November, San Francisco.

LeMaster, B. (1997). Sex Differences in Irish Sign Language. In J. H. Hill, P. J. Mistry, and L. Campbell (eds.), *The Life of Language: Papers in Linguistics in Honor of William Bright* (pp. 67–85). Berlin: Mouton de Gruyter.

LeMaster, B. (2000). Reappropriation of Gendered Irish Sign Language in One Family. *Visual Anthropology Review* 15(2): 1–15.

LeMaster, B. (2002). What Difference Does Difference Make? Negotiating Gender and Generation in Irish Sign Language. In S. Benor, M. Rose, D. Sharma, J. Sweetland, and Q. Zhang (eds.), *Gendered Practices in Language.* Stanford, CA: CSLI Publications.

LeMaster, B. (2003). School Language and Shifts in Irish Deaf Identity. In L. Monaghan, C. Schmaling, K. Nakamura, and G. H. Turner (eds.), *Many Ways to be Deaf.* Washington, DC: Gallaudet University Press.

LeMaster, B., and Dwyer, J. (1991). Knowing and Using Female and Male Signs in Dublin. *Sign Language Studies* 73: 361–396.

LeMaster, B., and Foran, S. (1986). The Irish Sign Language. In *The Gallaudet Encyclopedia of Deaf People and Deafness,* vol. 3 (pp. 82–84). New York: McGraw-Hill.

Lucas, C., Bayley, R., and Valli, C. (in collaboration with M. Rose, A. Wulf, P. Dudis, S. Schatz, and L. Sanheim) (2001). *Sociolinguistic Variation in American Sign Language* (Sociolinguistics in Deaf Communities Series, vol. 7). Washington, DC: Gallaudet University Press.

Lucas, C., and Valli, C. (1989). Language Contact in the American Deaf Community. In C. Lucas (ed.), *The Sociolinguistics of the Deaf Community* (pp. 11–40). San Diego, CA: Academic Press.

Lucas, C., and Valli, C. (1992). *Language Contact in the American Deaf Community.* San Diego, CA: Academic Press.

Malloy, C., and Doner, J. (1995). Variation in ASL Discourse: Gender Differences in the Use of Cohesive Devices. In L. Byers, J. Chaiken, and M. Mueller (eds.) *Communication Forum 1995* (pp. 183–205). Washington, DC: Gallaudet University, Department of ASL, Linguistics, and Interpretation.

Mansfield, D. (1993). Gender Differences in ASL: A Sociolinguistic Study of Sign Choices by Deaf Native Signers. In E. Winston (ed.), *Communication Forum 1993* (pp. 86–98). Washington, DC: Gallaudet University, Department of ASL, Linguistics, and Interpretation.

Matthews, P. (1996). *The Irish Deaf Community,* vol. 1. Dublin: Institiúid Teangeolaíochta Éireann.

Meadow, K. (1972). Sociolinguistics, Sign Language and the Deaf Sub-Culture. In T. O'Rourke (ed.), *Psycholinguistics and Total Communication: The State of the Art* (pp. 19–33). Silver Spring, MD: American Annals of the Deaf.

Metzger, M. (ed.). (2000). *Bilingualism and Identity in Deaf Communities* (Sociolinguistics in Deaf Communities Series, vol. 6). Washington, DC: Gallaudet University Press.

Monaghan, L. (1991). The Founding of Two Deaf Churches: The Interplay of Deaf and Christian Identities. *Sign Language Studies* 73: 431–452.

Monaghan, L. (1996). Signing, Oralism and the Development of the New Zealand Deaf Community: An Ethnography and History of Language Ideologies. PhD thesis, University of California, Los Angeles.

Monaghan, L., Schmaling, C., Nakamura, K., and Turner, G. H. (eds.) (2003). *Many Ways to be Deaf.* Washington, DC: Gallaudet University Press.

Nakamura, K. (2001). Deaf Identities, Sign Language, and Minority Social Movements Politics in Modern Japan (1868–2000). PhD thesis, Yale University.

Ó Baoill, D. P., and Matthews, P. A. (2000). *The Irish Deaf Community, vol. 2: The Structure of Irish Sign Language.* Dublin: Institiúid Teangeolaíochta Éireann.

Padden, C. (1980). The Deaf Community and the Culture of Deaf People. In C. Baker and R. Battison (eds.), *Sign Language and the Deaf Community: Essays in Honor of William C. Stokoe* (pp. 89–103). Silver Spring, MD: National Association of the Deaf.

Padden, C., and Humphries, T. (1988). *Deaf in America: Voices from a Culture.* Cambridge, MA: Harvard University Press.

Padden, C., and Markowicz, H. (1975). Crossing Cultural Group Boundaries into the Deaf Community. Paper presented at the Conference on Culture and Communication, Temple University, Philadelphia, March.

Padden, C., and Ramsey, C. (1998). Reading Ability in Signing Deaf Children. *Topics in Language Disorders* 18: 30–46.

Padden, C., and Ramsey, C. (2000). American Sign Language and Reading Ability in Deaf Children. In C. Chamberlain, J. Morford, and R. Mayberry (eds.), *Language Acquisition by Eye* (pp. 165–189). Mahwah, NJ: Lawrence Erlbaum.

Penn, C., and Reagan, T. (1994). The Properties of South African Sign Language: Lexical Diversity and Syntactic Unity. *Sign Language Studies* 23(85): 319–327.

Plann, S. (1997). *A Silent Minority.* Berkeley: University of California Press.

Ramsey, C. L. (1989). Language Planning in Deaf Education. In C. Lucas (ed.), *The Sociolinguistics of the Deaf Community* (pp. 123–146). San Diego, CA: Academic Press.

Reilly, C. (1995). A Deaf Way of Education: Interaction among Children in a Thai Boarding School. PhD thesis, University of Maryland.

Schein, J., and Delk, M. (1974). *The Deaf Population of the United States*. Silver Spring, MD: National Association of the Deaf.

Schmaling, C. (2003). A for Apple: The Impact of Western Education and ASL on the Deaf Community in Kano State, Northern Nigeria. In L. Monaghan, C. Schmaling, K. Nakamura, and G. H. Turner (eds.), *Many Ways to be Deaf*. Washington, DC: Gallaudet University Press.

Senghas, A. (1995). Children's Contribution to the Birth of Nicaraguan Sign Language. PhD thesis, Massachusetts Institute of Technology.

Senghas, R. (1997). An "Unspeakable, Unwriteable" Language: Deaf Identity, Language and Personhood among the First Cohorts of Nicaraguan Signers. PhD thesis, University of Rochester, New York.

Shroyer, E., and Shroyer, S. (1984). *Signs across America*. Washington, DC: Gallaudet College Press.

Stokoe, W. (1969–70). Linguistic Description of Sign Language. In F. P. Dinneen (ed.), *Monograph Series on Language and Linguistics* (pp. 243–250). Washington, DC: Georgetown University Press.

Stokoe, W. (1980). *Sign and Culture: A Reader for Students of ASL*. Silver Spring, MD: Linstok Press.

Stokoe, W., Casterline, D. and Croneberg, C. (1976 [1965]). *A Dictionary of American Sign Language on Linguistic Principles*. 1st edition, Washington, DC: Gallaudet College Press; 2nd edition, Silver Spring, MD: Linstok Press.

Unification of Signs Commission (1975). *Gestuno: International Sign Language of the Deaf*. Carlisle, UK: British Deaf Association [for] the World Federation of the Deaf.

Van Cleve, J. V. (ed.). (1993). *Deaf History Unveiled: Interpretations from the New Scholarship*. Washington, DC: Gallaudet University Press.

Van Cleve, J. V., and Crouch, B. (1989). *A Place of Their Own: Creating the Deaf Community in America*. Washington, DC: Gallaudet University Press.

Vernon, M., and Makowsky, B. (1969). Deafness and Minority Group Dynamics. *The Deaf American* 21(11): 3–6.

Wilcox, S. (ed.) (1989). *American Deaf Culture: An Anthology*. Silver Spring, MD: Linstok Press.

Woodward, J. (1973a). Some Characteristics of Pidgin Sign English. *Sign Language Studies* 3: 39–46.

Woodward, J. (1973b). Language Continuum, a Different Point of View. *Sign Language Studies* 2: 81–83.

Woodward, J. (1973c). Some Observations on Sociolinguistic Variation and American Sign Language. *Kansas Journal of Sociology* 9(2): 191–200.

Woodward, J. (1974). A Report on Montana-Washington Implicational Research. *Sign Language Studies* 4: 77–101.

Woodward, J. (1976). Black Southern Signing. *Language in Society* 5(2): 211–218.

Woodward, J. (1980). Sociolinguistic Research on American Sign Language: An Historical Perspective. In C. Baker and R. Battison (eds.), *Sign Language and the Deaf Community* (pp. 117–134). Silver Spring, MD: National Association of the Deaf.

Woodward, J. (2003). Sign Languages and Deaf Identities in Thailand and Viet Nam. In L. Monaghan, C. Schmaling, K. Nakamura, and G. H. Turner (eds.), *Many Ways to be Deaf*. Washington, DC: Gallaudet University Press.

Woodward, J., and DeSantis, S. (1977). Negative Incorporation in French and American Sign Languages. *Language in Society* 6(3): 379–388.

Woodward, J., and Erting, C. (1975). Synchronic Variation and Historical Change in American Sign Language. *Language Sciences* 37: 9–12.

Woodward, J., Erting, C., and Oliver, S. (1976). Facing and Handling Variation in ASL Phonology. *Sign Language Studies* 5(10): 43–52.

Zimmer, J. (1989). Toward a Description of Register Variation in American Sign Language. In C. Lucas (ed.), *The Sociolinguistics of the Deaf Community* (pp. 253–272). San Diego, CA: Academic Press.

APPENDIX: FINGERSPELLING SYSTEMS FROM DIFFERENT SIGN LANGUAGES

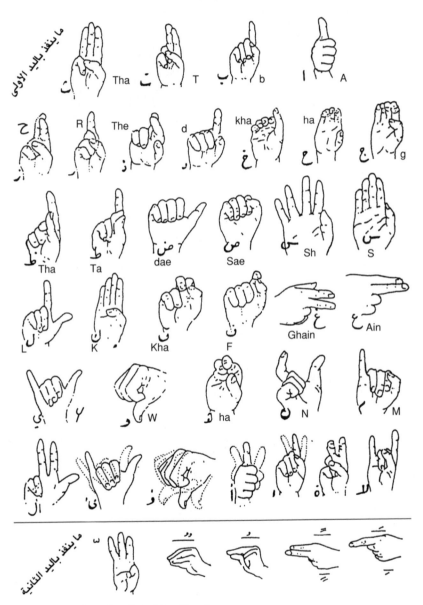

(a) Fingerspelling from Saudi Arabian Sign Language

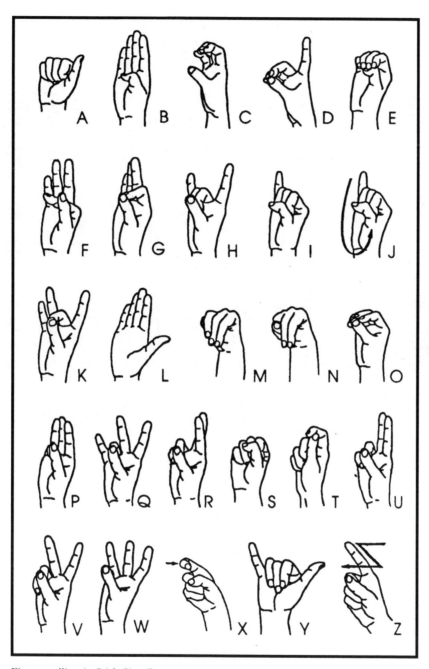

(b)   Fingerspelling in Irish Sign Language

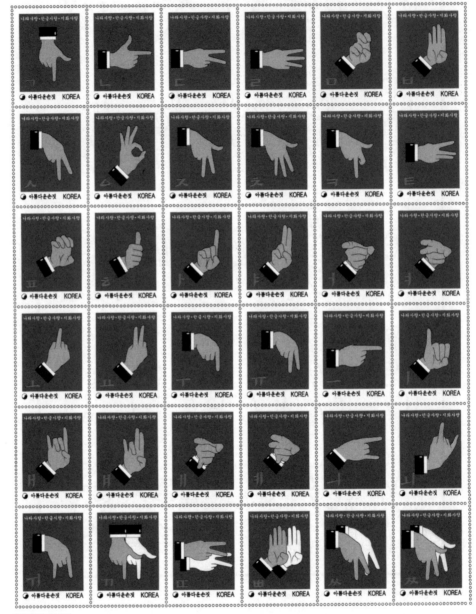

(c)   Fingerspelling in Korean Sign Language

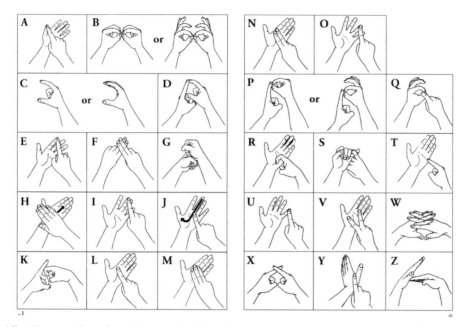

(d) Fingerspelling from New Zealand Sign Language. Reproduced by permission from G. Kennedy, R. Arnold, P. Dugdale, and D. Moskovitz (1998) *A Dictionary of New Zealand Sign Language*. Auckland: Auckland University Press.

PART **II** The Performing of Language

Conversation as a Cultural Activity

Elizabeth Keating and Maria Egbert

1 INTRODUCTION

Conversation plays a vital role in establishing and maintaining cultural habits of individuals and communities – identities, subjectivities, ideas, categories, attitudes, values, and more. Through everyday talk we perform with others a range of important actions and activities: we greet, advise, complain, flatter, argue, tell stories, organize work. We create, maintain, and change meaningful relationships between objects, people, and abstract ideas. We learn how to recognize particular social activities and to speak and act in ways that are appropriate to different contexts. Conversation is a vital resource for anthropologists in their goal to understand a society from the local perspective; what it means to be an ethnographer is to participate in many "ordinary" conversations across multiple contexts and coparticipants, not only while learning the local language but while participating in all kinds of daily activities. Malinowski, who enormously influenced the practice of anthropology, recognized the importance of studying everyday language in order to understand the social function of linguistic forms, which he considered more important than the referential properties of speech (Malinowski 1923: 315). He wrote that words do not merely represent meanings, but rather "they fulfill a social function, and that is their principal aim." He paid attention to the "give and take of utterances which make up ordinary gossip" and saw language "not as an instrument of reflection but as a mode of action" (Malinowski 1923: 315).

However, for almost half a century after Malinowski most anthropologists and linguistic anthropologists who looked at language in context concentrated on analyzing language that occurred in ritual performances. Researchers were motivated in part by the idea that certain institutional sites are "extra" salient in terms of focusing members of a society on key ideas and meanings, and generating and elaborating the kinds of cultural metadiscourses that together make up a coherent system of beliefs. The Durkheimian tradition established ritual as a "site of tremendous ideological power" (Silverstein 1998: 137) with a particular poetics and recurrent sound and visual routines to shape and organize ways of thinking. Conversation itself was not seen as a comparably important ritualized practice. Conversation was also more difficult to accurately record than the formulaic and often repetitive language of ritual and formalized contexts. It was often perceived as chaotic and unstructured and not worth studying (see e.g. Chomsky 1977: 153). However, everyday conversation is now recognized as a complex, highly structured event which conversationalists locally manage, turn-by-turn, moment-by-moment (see e.g. Sacks, Schegloff, and Jefferson 1974; Schegloff 1968), and the analysis of conversation interests scholars in anthropology, sociology, linguistics, ethnology, communication studies, psychology, cognitive science, philosophy, and other fields investigating the emergence of shared meanings. Wittgenstein's ideas about language as a "game" where participants make moves and countermoves within a framework of rules that are flexible in some ways and inflexible in others have been influential. In a conversation, moves that interactants make sequentially and contextually shape other moves in ways that can be carefully studied. Conversation is recognized as the prototypical kind of language use since it is the form children are first exposed to (Levinson 1983: 284), the "primordial site of interaction" (Schegloff 1979).

In this chapter we first discuss some contributions particularly relevant to anthropology of scholars working on conversation, and secondly some approaches to the analysis of conversation as an activity.

2   CONVERSATION AS A CULTURAL PRACTICE

The emergence of conversation itself as an activity worth ethnographic investigation has been the result of the work of pioneering linguistic anthropologists on child language acquisition, on formal educational settings, on the interactive and emergent properties of performance, and on describing language cross-culturally through the ethnography of speaking tradition launched by Gumperz and Hymes (Gumperz and Hymes 1972). Goffman's studies of the orderliness of interaction (1964, 1983), based on his own observations, revealed important ways we could look at how people actively collaborate in the everyday presentation and interpretation of selves and activities, and how interpretations are mediated through conventions learned over multiple, prior contexts and experiences. Garfinkel (1967) discovered a kind of ethics of everyday life where interactants hold each other responsible for behaving in cooperative ways. We can look at "breaches" or where things go wrong to see how members of social groups make explicit what had been implicit, and thus hidden from the ethnographer.

The study of conversation has revealed a number of important aspects of sociality and behavior, including how social actors construct particular contexts and activity types, socialize new members of society, build or resist authority, organize hierarchies, use literacy, produce multiple identities, worship, argue, imagine. Studying speech use across speakers and contexts shows how social distinctions including gender differences emerge in language use, how experience is organized through narrative, how we use gesture, the complexities of indexical relations, and the effects on conversation of cognitive impairments such as aphasia. Speakers use language to create reality by naming and giving meaning to aspects of experience from a particular perspective, as individuals take up particular subject positions and produce themselves through language. Linguists look at language structures as they are evidenced across sequences (Ford, Fox, and Thompson 2002); interactional linguistics, a recent branch within linguistics, is particularly strong in Europe (e.g. Selting and Couper-Kuhlen 2001; Selting 2000). Conversation can be a tool for investigating consciousness and memory. For linguistic anthropologists, goals in studying conversation include a greater understanding of how people manipulate symbolic resources to do a range of activities that can be called "social life" and how these activities might be differently organized across cultures, since talk is shaped for particular contexts and coparticipants (Schegloff 1984; C. Goodwin 1981). Studies of interactions with technological tools (and human–machine interaction) have benefited from techniques of research into conversation. New technological tools can affect the organization of interaction (e.g. Button 1993; Suchman 1987; Keating and Mirus, 2003). Studying conversation has led to a much more accurate understanding of many aspects of language use and meaning-making.

The analysis of conversation rests on an analysis of turns as "acts" or actions produced in interaction. What speakers do, for example describing, greeting, apologizing, requesting, or complimenting, is the focus along with the resources used to accomplish this (see Schegloff 1984 on the many "jobs" questions can do interactionally). The emergence of Austin's speech act theory (Austin 1962) had already directed the attention of linguistic anthropologists to speech as action with socially transforming potential and powers. The idea of language as a powerful social force was not new, however. Many societies believe in the efficacy of language, for example, in the form of incantations that cure illness, curses, and in the ritual words to make an ordinary person into the ruler or chief. The deployment of power through words depends on understanding the distribution of the authority to say particular words, who can say what to whom, and on context or the proper conditions for accomplishment of actions. Local notions of self, strategies of interpretation, speakers' ability to control interpretation, the relevance of "sincerity," intentionality, and the organization of responsibility for interpretation all have implications for the nature of speech activities cross-culturally (Duranti 1988: 222; Hill and Irvine 1993; Rosaldo 1973). Conversations carry sociocultural information including not only speech-act types, but sound and language structure principles, particular vocabularies, and conversation conventions, and ideas about interruptions, overlaps, gaps, and turn length (Schieffelin and Ochs 1986: 3). As Hanks has shown in his study of a Mayan community, looking at conversational forms can add to our understanding of how linguistic forms work to produce meaning in actual interactions and how a linguistic property such as deixis (e.g. the English 'this', 'that', 'here', 'there'), which can be understood only with reference to a particular context, can also only be understood within a particular system of beliefs and practices, for example Mayan agricultural and ritual practices and the way domestic space is organized (Hanks 1990). Talk has a normative structure which members of societies orient to.

"Ordinary" conversation is a collaborative achievement of extraordinary proportions. The intricacies of this activity only become clear when we look analytically at how interactions unfold, and how interactants expertly design turns with often split-second timing to accomplish a range of tasks in specific, unique contexts. Cross-culturally conversationalists have a vast repertoire of devices for constructing

relationships and attitudes, and for organizing activities such as repairing misunderstandings or managing disagreement. The tools of "signifying" and "marking," for
example, are conventional ways to make meaning among African American speakers
as discussed by Mitchell-Kernan (1972), where having a conversation about what to
have for dinner can also be about attitudes and theories of cultural assimilation (1972:
167). An announcement of chitlins[1] in a conversation concerning what a guest will
eat becomes an opportunity for commenting on how eating or not eating customary
African American dishes can indicate attitudes toward the relative value of African
heritage (e.g. soul food) in opposition to adoption of Anglo-American habits, and by
extension values and identity. In example (1), as Mitchell-Kernan describes, "the
manifest topic of Barbara's question was food" but Mary's response indicates that this
is not a conversation about "the relative merits of having one thing or another for
dinner," but rather Barbara is in the "metaphors of the culture," implying that Mary
is an assimilationist:

(1) Attitudes and theories of cultural assimilation (Mitchell-Kernan 1972: 167)
Barbara: What are you going to do Saturday? Will you be over here?
R: I don't know.
Barbara: Well, if you're not going to be doing anything, come by. I'm going to cook
           some chit'lins. [Rather jokingly] Or are you one of those Negroes who don't
           eat chit'lins?
Mary: [Interjecting indignantly] That's all I hear lately – soul food, soul food. If you
           say you don't eat it you get accused of being saditty [affected, considering
           oneself superior].
           [Matter of factly] Well, I ate enough black-eyed peas and neck-bones during
           the depression that I can't get too excited over it. I eat prime rib and T-bone
           because I like to, not because I'm trying to be white.
           [Sincerely] Negroes are constantly trying to find some way to discriminate
           against each other. If they could once get it in their heads that we are all in this
           together maybe we could get somewhere in this battle against the man.
           [Mary leaves.]
Barbara: Well, I wasn't signifying at her, but like I always say, if the shoe fits, wear it.

Different cultures evidence different ideas about the appropriate length of silence
between turn transitions, and this can be one cause of stereotyped ideas about others.
For example, Anglo-Americans typically have a small tolerance for silences between
turns in conversation, whereas Native Americans, such as the Apache studied by Basso
(1979), customarily allow a much longer stretch of silence between turns at talk. To
Native Americans, Anglo-Americans can be perceived as interruptive and dominating,
while at the same time Native Americans can be stereotyped by Anglo-Americans as
taciturn. The different reactions possible to any speaker's utterance are important
aspects of our interpretive habits, and our expectations can powerfully constrain or
form succeeding talk (Schegloff 1992: lvi). Thus the actions of the hearer are
extremely important in interactions since speakers design their language for particular
coparticipants.

An important principle in studying conversation from an ethnographic point of
view is that the inferential consequences which are investigated are not those of the

researcher, but rather those of the participants in the interaction being analyzed. Anthropologists have conceptualized this in terms of emic versus etic perspectives, yet the challenges of achieving a point of view that is based on subjectivities other than the researcher's are well recognized.

We discuss below some specific ways that the investigation of conversation enriches our understanding of aspects of sociality and behavior, including a better understanding of the socialization of new members, the production of identity categories and social relationships, building and resisting authority, the creation and manipulation of imagined worlds, the organization of experience, institutional talk, the use of multiple codes, and the relationship of conversation to aspects of linguistic structure.

2.1 Socialization and conversation

Expert–novice conversations are an excellent site for exploring the articulation of attitudes and practices that become tacit and unremarkable as members of society gain competence. In everyday contexts experts communicate to novices expected ways of thinking, feeling, and acting as well as appropriate language use (Schieffelin and Ochs 1986: 2). Linguistic anthropologists working on language acquisition have shown how children are far from passive learners, but actively organize the sociocultural information that they acquire through participating with others in interactions. Local ideologies about how children learn language differ from one place to another and are embedded in cultural practices and can be themselves a topic of conversation. Some societies rely more than others on conventionalized prompting routines for teaching children sociolinguistic skills (Schieffelin 1986). Literacy-learning events are embedded in conversations, at home and at school (Heath 1986; Cook-Gumperz 1986), and now such literacy events can include the computer. School settings are important arenas for social and cultural reproduction, including what kinds of speech are socially valued, through various interactional performances (Heller 1995).

"Ordinary" family dinner conversations (in North American families) have been an extremely important resource in understanding the socialization of gender and how gendered patterns of authority arise within everyday, multi-generational family settings to be learned by the next generation. Dinnertime conversations in some American families reproduce an Anglo-American paternalistic organization of family structure, not as an individual father's authoritative act, but rather as a collaborative effort initiated by mothers' conversational moves which elevate the authority of fathers (Ochs and Taylor 1995; see also Tannen 2003).

(2) Family dinner (from Ochs and Taylor 1995: 116)
Mom:[2] ((to Jodie)) = oh::You know what? You wanna tell Daddy what happened to
     you today? =
Dad: ((looking up and off)) = Tell me everything that happened from the moment
     you went in- until:
                    [
Jodie: I got a sho:t? =
Dad: = EH ((gasping)) what? ((frowning))

Mothers introduce narratives about themselves and their children that set the fathers up as the primary recipients and as implicit evaluators of the actions, conditions, thoughts, and feelings of the other family members (Ochs and Taylor 1995: 116).

Not every society has a formalized family dinner activity. In Pohnpei, Micronesia, a common setting for evening conversation is the preparation of kava, a Pacific Island drink made from the root of the pepper plant, which is typically shared together by groups of families who live in the same neighborhood. Here, gendered patterns of authority are also modeled, not only through talk but through the order of serving kava. Studying these nightly conversations when a chief or chieftess is present shows the important role lower-status members of the group play in reproducing the very hierarchies which undervalue them (Keating 1998) through choice of language forms. In example (3), a man is directed by another man (Menindei) to take off his shirt and to move to another seating location. Both actions are indicated with a low-status verb, while a few moments later, the action of the chief's speaking is indicated with a high-status verb. The speaker is also low status compared to the chief. Chiefs do not use status-marked speech, rather it is the lower-status members of the community who use these terms and construct hierarchical relationships (Keating 1998: 58).

(3) Pohnpei, Micronesia (from Keating 1998: 58)

Menindei: **patohwansang**   ahmw sehten
take[WITH LOW STATUS].from your   shirt.there
take off your shirt

koh **patohdala**
you move[WITH LOW STATUS].upwards.there
you go up there

(...)   ohlen   nek   **masanihong**uhk
man.that.by.you could tell[WITH HIGH STATUS].to.you
that man ((the chief)) could tell you

dahme pwungen ahmw pahn mwohd
what   right.of your will sit
the correct way for you to sit

2.2   Producing social relationships and categories through conversations

There are no cross-cultural norms about which types of talk produce "female" or "male" gender, but rather the same ways of speaking can in one culture indicate femaleness, in another maleness. For example, in the Malagasy society studied by Keenan (1974), women are direct in their speech, men indirect; women use contemporary speech ways, men use traditional speech ways. This polarity is reversed in many societies. Studying conversational interactions reveals important complexities of the organization of gendered relationships; for example, in Kulick's study of Gapun conflicts in Papua New Guinea, women's kroses (conflict talk) juxtapose female assertiveness and control with men's failures and weaknesses, which undermines the local stereotype of women as antisocial and in need of control (Kulick 1992). Okamoto (1995) investigated feminine speech forms in conversations among Japanese college students and found much more varied speech styles than local ideologies about women's speech would predict. Eckert and McConnell-Ginet (1995) show, in conversations with high school students, important links between gendered behavior and social class, so that performances of female or male gender vary according to whether one belongs to particular social classes. Coates studied the conversations of teenage girls in London and found significant patterns of change in discourse styles over the life course; for example, innovations and agency in discourse declined as the girls grew into adolescence (Coates 1994). Looking closely at playground conversation among second-generation Latina and Asian peers in Los Angeles, M. Goodwin challenges Piaget's work on gender differences in children's games and shows how girls embody multiple forms of argumentation in their play (Goodwin 1998). Using conversations of children talking to their best friends, Tannen describes important gender differences in body alignments and gaze (Tannen 1994).

The production of humorous "moves" in conversation is far from trivial and has important implications and consequences in the work of building relationships and social life. For example, humorous references to the self take different forms in the speech of men and women in mixed and same-gender groups in the USA. Women's humor is seen as "sharing" and "coping" while men's humor is "equalizing" and "defending" in the white groups studied (Ervin-Tripp 1992). While these results will not perhaps surprise readers familiar with some of the aspects of gender differences in some US groups, what is important are the details of how these differences are actually produced across turns at talk, that is, through particular narratives and particular performance qualities. Members of these groups not only tell but *interpret* humorous messages according to gendered categories and practices (Ervin-Tripp and Lampert 1992). Laughter is a choral activity (people don't laugh one at a time) (Jefferson 1984), but different interpretations can be made based on gender and other socially organized categories.

Gender is only one of a number of complex personal identities that are manipulated within embedded contexts in an "ordinary" conversation. One of the early successes in conversation analysis was showing how membership categorization devices and "category-bound activities" work (Sacks 1995: 248; 1964/5; 1972a; 1972b). Sacks showed that identities are achievements produced in the moment rather than *a priori* categories existing apart from particular interactions. He showed how people make relevant certain aspects of membership categories such as "stage of life" categories, link them to particular activities, and provide rules of relevance for selecting such categories, as well as how the categories can be creatively used for other activities such as praising or degrading (1995: 249; see also Egbert, forthcoming; Egbert, Niebecker, and Rezzara, forthcoming). In example (4), Tina engages in membership categorization by indicating that her place of origin is relevant to this part of the interaction:

(4)   German conversation
1 Tina: das is voll zee.
         that is fully viscous.
         it's very tough.

2   ((*brief silence*))

3 Rita: <u>was</u> is das?
           <u>what</u> is that?
           it's <u>what</u>?

4 Tina: das   zieht sich so hin
           that drags itself so PRE
           it's a drag to read

5 Rita: ach so::   <u>zäh</u>.
           oh   i see:: <u>vis</u>cous.
           oh I see:: <u>tough</u>.

           *smiling³
6 →Tina: *ja ich komm aus   ostfriesland
           *yes I   come from east frisia

For anthropologists, the different practices of membership categorization are informative in that they show how the interactants themselves draw cultural lines in particular situations. Particular aspects of social identity are context-sensitive, and a "personal" identity is related to setting and to audience. Interactants display their understanding of the nature of cultural activities such as membership categorization in ordinary conversations, and how something like a "social category" is much more malleable, dynamic, negotiable, as well as more culturally and contextually distinct than we might previously have assumed, or assumed from accounts from conversations *about* such social categories with native speakers.

2.3   Imagining and organizing experience in narrative

Stories emerge within conversations and are active resources for building interpersonal relationships (Mandelbaum 1989) and naturalizing certain ideas about social life. Studying narratives which emerge in everyday settings shows what speakers consider to be reportable as well as aspects of the aesthetics of story-telling and reporting. In some groups creative exaggeration and "lying" play an important role in stories that build identity (Bauman 1996). Stories can be devices for diffusing responsibility for the truth of a particular position (Schiffrin 1990).

Narratives of past events are an important part of what is described as "gossip" which also emerges in everyday conversation. Gossip is a rich resource for anthropologists, since it contains information about others and is a forum for the evaluation of others' behaviors against (at least) prescriptive norms. It is a resource for examining habitual ways speakers in particular societies organize talk about other people (M. Goodwin 1990), and shows us "the kind of behavior most interesting to natives" (Haviland 1977: 182). However, interpretations and discussions about gossip in the anthropological literature often focus on what gossip is about and ignore how gossip is done and the role it plays in the larger sociopolitical aspects of community life (Brenneis 1996: 209), for example, how the contingencies of life restructure rules and even change them in Zinacantan, Mexico, and elsewhere (Haviland 1977: 182). Gossiping in Fiji (and more generally) has been shown to be an activity which builds quite different relationships between the gossipers than between the gossipers and those who are the topics of gossip (Brenneis 1996: 220). In some societies, such as the Pacific Island of Nukulaelae, the identity of those being talked about is routinely withheld and must be elicited by hearers (Besnier 1989).

Looking at conversational differences in how narrative skills are developed at home and school has led to a greater understanding of why children from certain social classes regularly perform better in schools. Many American elementary schools implicitly reproduce narrative activities that are common only to the white middle class, and devalue other ways of organizing experience through narrative (African American, native Hawaiian, or Native North American, for example), which effectively privileges the habits of one group over another (Heath 1986; Boggs 1972), and can lead to false and prejudicial judgments about some American students' abilities and skills (Philips 1974). Literacy practices articulate in interesting ways with other cultural practices (Street 1995; Besnier 1995) and can also be an important site where colonial relationships are mediated and transformed in sometimes surprising ways.

2.4   Building and resisting authority

Whose voice can be heard and which topic can be discussed are locally constituted and show conversational contexts as a "field of power relations" (Lindstrom 1992: 102) where the "truth" of statements is negotiated and linked for legitimacy to local procedures and devices. In conversational interactions in Tanna on the Pacific Island of Vanuatu, truth is a local idea whose opposite is not necessarily falsity (Lindstrom 1992: 117). The local nature and authority of claims made about both normative and interactional identities and relationships varies (Grimshaw 1990: 16), precisely the kind of data anthropologists need in order to understand and compare societies. Anthropologists interested in the cultural organization of "conflict" have looked at the role that everyday conversational contexts play in mediating conflicts, in socializing appropriate management of conflict, and in developing skills in conflict negotiation. Children develop argumentation strategies and knowledge of the valence of particular stances, roles, and strategies for staking out and claiming particular territories in disputes (Corsaro and Rizzo 1990; M. Goodwin 1990). The close analysis of courtroom interactions has revealed how in cross-examination procedures, defendants and witnesses must make their contributions within a particular type of conversational structure that advantages some and disadvantages others in the activity. Certain views of victims and perpetrators are produced and disseminated solely through the sequential control of turns at talk (Drew 1992; see also Jacquemet 1996 for an Italian case). A judge's gavel is a sign of his or her power to control who speaks, when, and for how long. However, in studying such settings we find people quite creative. For example, in a court setting where linguistic output was sanctioned, participants used organized coughing as a means of showing their disagreement and resistance, for example coughing at particular points during a testimony (Alvarez-Cáccamo 1996). It has also been shown that conflict talk can be a cooperative way of speaking as well as a competitive one (Schiffrin 1990).

In some societies age and status differences can affect the rights to turns in a conversation. A classroom teacher is in charge of turn-taking and has the power to prohibit, grant, or limit a pupil's talk. An understanding of turn-taking system(s) and how interactants use such systems provides not only information about power and status but an understanding of the way power and status emerge in interactions and are often related to features of context in ways that are often not acknowledged in discussions of, for example, social stratification and inequality.

2.5   Conversational interaction and language structure

Conversation is a rich resource for linguists investigating grammatical structures in language and examining how culture emerges in grammatical details. Discourse-oriented linguists look at the ways that people use and interpret grammatical tools with each other. Looking at naturally occurring talk has led such linguists to "reexamine long-held views of the nature of language" (Ford, Fox, and Thompson 2002: 9), through looking at patterns across turns. For example, when a speaker adds more talk to their completed turn if a hearer fails to respond, these additions are quite systematic, and function to add more to the prior turn's actions, rather than producing new or different actions (Ford, Fox, and Thompson 2002).

New communicative spaces created by the computer can lead to changes in language and language use. For example, Deaf individuals can now communicate through the Internet across vast distances in space using sign language and this has led to a situation in which signers must change some aspects of communication and develop new ways to communicate. When three-dimensional signs are reproduced in two-dimensional virtual space, signers make adjustments to ensure that all the meaningful features of their signs are visible. New ways to do referential pointing are being developed by signers as they orient to the situation of a non-shared signing space and to how what they are pointing to will be reproduced on their interlocutor's computer screen (Keating and Mirus 2003). In the video frame shown in figure 8.1, two participants sitting side by side, in conversation with another person whose image they can see on their computer screen, simultaneously try different versions of the sentence "who's there with you?" since their interlocutor has not responded. The two signers in the video frame simultaneously produce two different versions of "there" to solve the new problem of how to show "there" in a non-shared, two-

Figure 8.1   Two signers try two different ways to overcome a new problem: how to communicate a specific location ("there") in computer-mediated space (Keating and Mirus 2003)

dimensional signing space. The girl points to her right with her thumb to signify where "there" is, and the boy points straight ahead with his forefinger to signify where "there" is. The "there" they are trying to locate is next to their interlocutor's image on the screen.

(5) experiments with "there" (Keating and Mirus 2003)
Jeff: WHO THAT?
Karen: QUESTION?
Karen: WHO WHO WHO **THERE** (*"there" made with closed fist, thumb pointing to right*)
           [[
Jeff: WHO WHO WHO **THERE** (*"there" made with forefinger pointing straight ahead*)

Signers such as these are in the process of developing new ways to manipulate spatial relations to signify meanings. Other research in computer-mediated discourse shows how power asymmetries from geographic, historical, and economic contexts influence communication practices as well as new interactive features of text production (e.g. Herring 2001).

2.6 Multiple codes

Studying conversation reveals important details about bilingualism and codeswitching. Codeswitching is common in many parts of the world where two or more speech communities come into frequent contact with each other. Codeswitching between languages in the same conversation often adds meanings and these meanings are achieved in ways that are much more systematic than previously believed (Blom and Gumperz 1972). Yet speakers who codeswitch can also defy traditional language conventions and exhibit a high degree of creativity. Such virtuosity can even be a marker of identity (Zentella 1997: 3). Studies of codeswitching show the cultural and linguistic diversity of modern communities, and how aspects of multilingualism and language choice can differ according to gender. Switching languages within a conversation can be a means of realignment for a speaker, or an attempt to control their interlocutor's behavior, or a resource for clarification or emphasis (Zentella 1997: 97). These shifts are not always recognized by conversationalists themselves, showing the importance of studying everyday speech as a research tool. In example (6) Paca says *in English* that she always talks to the researcher (ACZ) in Spanish.

(6) New York City (Zentella 1997: 71)
ACZ to Paca: *¿Qué me hablas a mi?* ("What do you speak to me?")
P to ACZ:To you? In Spanish.
L to P: And in English.
P to L: No, in Spanish.
L to P: You just spoke to her in English!

Lucas and Valli (1992) were surprised to see fluent American Sign Language (ASL) users codeswitch into an English-like sign rather than using the more spatially-dependent grammatical conventions of ASL in conversations in an experimental interview situation (1992: 63). They attributed this to an association in the Deaf community between English-like signing and formality or educational contexts. Using a more English-like sign (with a word order like English and other English-like features) is a common way to signal a register or context shift in the ASL community (see e.g. Stokoe 1969; see also Mather 1991: 138). Choice of what kind of code to use constructs differences in context, just as context can shape the choice of language features (Duranti and Goodwin 1992).

In monolingual settings, differences in code use also exist, but if the differences are not shared, they can be misinterpreted. Significant unrecognized communication problems in conversation can arise between speakers of the same language, who may know only one of several existing sociolinguistic rule systems for the same language. Gumperz shows how speakers of Indian English are misunderstood by speakers of Standard British English because they use different phonological contours for requests. Their prosody can make requests seem like demands to Standard British English speakers and lead to negative stereotyping. Subtle differences in the organization of turns not only in terms of intonation contours, but in terms of lexical choice and the way information is packaged or sequenced, can result in faulty inferences on both sides, which severely disadvantages South Asians seeking to demonstrate their skills to potential employers in job interviews (Gumperz 1992).

Gaze, facial expressions, gesture, posture, body movement, and spatial distance as well as the arrangement of participants and objects in space are important semiotic codes in conversation and influence how we organize and make sense of our activities (see e.g. Kendon 1967, 1990; C. Goodwin 1981; Schegloff 1984; Streeck and Hartge 1992; Hayashi, Mori, and Takagi 2002). Gaze is important in turn-taking and can function to signal when a speaker intends to hand over, or take over the floor, as well as aspects of repair initiation (C. Goodwin 1980; Egbert 1996). Interactants use language, gesture, and visual media to orient each other to particular ways of seeing and interpreting (C. Goodwin 1994). Gestures form an important part of some problem-solving interactions. Sunaoshi, in her work on interactions in a Japanese auto factory situated in the USA, shows how gestures can emerge and be codified when interactants have little or no shared language (Sunaoshi 2000). (Note in example (7), the author's transcription conventions include: vertical lines indicate gesture cooccurring with speech, + + indicates medium length pause, underline means emphasis, xxx indicates something inaudible, < > indicates gestures, = indicates channels simultaneously allocated to two speakers). Note how the gesture "assembly" recurs and pointing is used to identify referents (we have added boldface marking to recurring gestures).

(7) US auto plant (Sunaoshi 2000: 81)

25   I: |he said ++ <u>cannot</u> |assemble ++ today ↓
        <turns to D>| <points to H> |<'**assembly**'>

26   D: (can) we ship tomorrow?

        (Ishige asks Hiki when he will finish fixing the die, and he says it will be Thursday. This part of the interaction occurred in Japanese without gesture)

```
36  D:     oh we need dies (xxx) to | assemble?
                             | <'assembly'>

37  I:                          |no?              |uh =
                     <looks at D, looks down,> | <looks back at D> |<points to H>

38  D:     | = you said    | die's finished
           |<points to I>| <puts hand on die, 'finished'>

           |assembly only?
           |<"assembly">
```

In the auto manufacturing plant, gestures were used to establish and secure mutual understanding at the referential level. They cooccurred with the most fundamental vocabulary and served as a reference point for the main topic being discussed, and gestures were used repetitively to elicit and provide clarification (Sunaoshi 2000: 84).

3   CONSTRUCTING ACTIVITY TYPES AND CONTEXTS: CONVERSATIONS IN INSTITUTIONS

In the development of work on conversation, a distinction has emerged in some research quarters between "everyday" conversation and "institutional" talk (conversations between professionals and between professionals and lay persons, such as in legal, educational, medical, and broadcast media settings; see Drew and Heritage 1992). Acknowledging that it is hard to clearly distinguish institutional talk from other talk, researchers focusing on institutional talk nevertheless note that even when those in institutional interactions are doing "sociable pleasantries" their orientation is to their institutional identities or identities as colleagues (Drew and Sorjonen 1997: 94). Ide's study of the American practice of "small talk" in service encounters shows how Americans chat in a familiar way with complete strangers and display a particular kind of "self" during such transactions at convenience stores (Ide, forthcoming). In institutional encounters it is how the institutional setting shapes or constrains talk and consists of patterns of sequences developed from routinized tasks that is of interest (Drew and Heritage 1992: 19). Patterns include: lexical choice, syntax, prosody, turn design, sequence organization, overall structural organization, and social epistemology and social relations (1992: 29). Some aspects of this work include the study of affiliating or disaffiliating actions, the control of information, asymmetries in turn-taking opportunities, and the design of questions. For example, particular grammatical forms are likely to have certain distributions in given settings (Drew and Sorjonen 1997: 92). Wh-cleft constructions in English (e.g. "what we are attempting to do here") occur much more commonly in institutional settings than in ordinary conversation, and can be a strategy to resume a particular participant framework and re-limit audience participation after a joke or break (Kim 1992). A series of questions prefaced by "and," which are rare in ordinary conversations, can, in institutional activities, construct an agenda-based activity across question and answer sequences (Heritage and Sorjonen 1994). In McElhinny's (1995) study of women police officers, she found that the articulation of the role of police officer with gender role expectations led women police officers to adopt a professional demeanor of emotionless rationality through talk rather than an everyday gendered demeanor, and to withhold sympathy from complainants during domestic violence calls.

The differentiation between ordinary and institutional interactions has been criticized for being analytically unnecessary (Pomerantz and Fehr 1997: 64); however, for an anthropologist, the distinction between the two can elucidate just how conventionalized asymmetries might be routinized as well as actively produced and manipulated through language. We can also study the role of language in formulating what we call "institutions" or institutional contexts and in organizing particular local ideas about them. Problems of defining "institution" are not limited to conversation analysis. Bourdieu gives the following definition: "[a]n institution is not necessarily a particular organization – this or that family or factory, for instance – but is any relatively durable set of social relations which *endows* individuals with power, status and resources of various kinds" (Bourdieu 1991: 8). How such durable sets of relationships are achieved through language across contexts is a question linguistic anthropologists are intensely interested in.

Studying conversation in the medical workplace has shown how patients make important contributions in medical encounters (e.g. Cicourel 1992; Have 1991; Beach 2001) and how notions of illness and the body are locally organized and socialized. Theoretical physicists use ordinary conversation to reorganize and communicate emerging ideas. Studying their conversations shows how they utilize properties of everyday talk to imagine and propose hypothetical relationships between entities (Ochs, Jacoby, and Gonzales 1994).

4 RESEARCH PARADIGMS

The study of conversation has included several different paradigms and perspectives. Within sociology, a field called "conversation analysis" (CA) emerged in the late 1960s, taking as its subject naturally occurring conversations in a range of contexts such as in casual interactions among family and friends and in work-related settings. The so-called Birmingham School emerged from the work of Sinclair and Coulthard, looking at classroom discourse and pedagogic exchange (see Sinclair and Coulthard 1975) with a focus on conversation as an activity for the exchange of information. Analysis of conversation according to Gricean axioms (1975) is still popular with some linguists, although Grice's theories about conversation have been critiqued for the implication that conversations occur between equals in a context of agreement and lack of social differences (Fairclough 1995: 46; Keenan 1974). Discourse analysts study conversation, combining traditions in the study of spoken language and text (e.g. Linell 1998), particularly with regards to issues of power and government (see e.g. Fairclough 1995) and socially produced ideas such as racism (e.g. van Dijk 1991; van Dijk and Wodak 2000), investigating how language is manipulated as a tool for persuasion, and for maintaining particular ideas about social relations. The field of discourse analysis is quite broadly conceived in terms of assumptions, approaches, and methods, but the study of conversation is essential in studies that look at the role of prosody in interpretation and understanding (Couper-Kuhlen 1991), including how speakers strategically deploy prosodic contextualization cues within and across speaking turns. Analysis of discourse markers (Schiffrin 1987) in conversation reveals aspects of the underlying cognitive, expressive, textual, and social organization of discourse (Schiffrin 2001: 66).

Harvey Sacks together with his collaborators was the first to show many of the fine details and the richness and subtleties of conversation and its role in the collaborative "achievement" of social life, how humans organize and interpret their mundane, everyday activities, including everyday or "common sense" theory-building (Heritage 1984; Drew and Wootton 1988). Sacks investigated conversation not initially to explicate the organization of conversation itself, but rather to better describe those activities which are accomplished through language. Sacks, Schegloff, Jefferson, Pomerantz, and other collaborators who developed conversation analysis (CA) focused closely on micro aspects of language use and asked *how* not *why* questions: "how does someone 'properly and reproducibly' come to say such a thing, *this* thing? What is someone doing by saying this thing, and how do they come to be doing it?" (Schegloff 1992: xxix). The study of conversation as it has developed within linguistic anthropology is sociological rather than psychological (Heritage 1984: 241). This does not mean that psychology is left out, but rather that the focus is shifted from the individual to interactive processes that may influence cognition, in line with Vygotsky's (1978) ideas of individual consciousness arising through activities with others. Since it is hard to assert what another might be thinking or experiencing, a focus on the "how" rather than the "why" redirects research away from the focus on the individual versus society to a focus on interaction and the interrelationship of one person's talk to others'. Looking at conversations provides larger units of analysis than the sentence and enables the investigation of meaning as something that is negotiated by at least two interactants rather than controlled by speakers.

4.1 Conversational structures

Although Sacks did not initially have as a goal describing the structures of conversation but rather to investigate the influences of culture on ordinary activities and the way they are accomplished (his main interest was in social interaction), it soon became clear to him and his colleagues that conversation was an "object" (or activity) that could be examined in its own right and its recurring structures described (Schegloff 1992: xvii; Sacks, Schegloff, and Jefferson 1974). That conversation is not only a medium, but an activity itself was recognized by Hymes (1974). Conversation analysts have shown how it is made up of features such as turn-taking, conventionalized sequences, and mechanisms for repair, and with an overall structural organization. In analyzing conversation, one important consideration is the interactional and inferential consequences of speakers' choices between alternative utterances. The different responses possible to an utterance form important aspects of our interpretive habits. Speakers design their talk for particular audiences (this is referred to as "recipient design" in conversation analysis: see e.g. Sacks and Schegloff 1979); hearers provide feedback at key stages in interactions and this cooperation is an important feature of interactional work (Gumperz 1997). Silences can be very meaningful (as in the folk terminology "pregnant pause").

The data segment below from a German dinner conversation shows how people constantly orient to points where the current speaker's utterance is coming to a possible completion and another speaker can take a turn. A report of a child's emergent understanding of gender categories is a relevant next turn at talk when discussing a child's age. (Note that the onset by a new speaker during someone else's turn is marked with a "[".)

(8) German conversation
Klaus: vier jahre is der [schon
            four years is he [already
                              [
Hans: [ja der sagt dass männer also
                             [yes he says that men   you know
Hans: n penis habn und frauen schweißfüße
            have a penis and women sweaty feet

Although there is overlapping talk, the new speaker's starting point is delicately timed at a place in the other speaker's turn where the turn is possibly complete and the remainder of the turn can be anticipated. Turn-constructional units are crucial interactional units by which conversationalists organize turn-taking. In the normal course of making and responding to utterances, participants display to each other their understanding of previous speakers' "acts," evaluating, accepting, and modifying them. Conversational activities are collaborative. For example, an important unit in conversation is an adjacency pair, produced by two people, rather than a single speech act. One example of an adjacency pair is the exchange of greetings (see, for example, Sacks 1987; Schegloff 1968); other examples are question/answer, invitation/acceptance or rejection, request/granting or declining. The two turns of an adjacency pair are produced by two different persons, they follow in a particular order, and they are related to each other by action type (a *good-bye* asks for another *good-bye* and not for *hello* or *nice weather today*). What is important about these is that the production of one, the first pair part, makes the production of the other, the second pair part, relevant and expectable. If a response is not forthcoming, the absence is meaningful as an action with potentially negative implications. Some answers to the first part of an adjacency pair happen quickly and without delay, others are more elaborated and delayed and this can be interpreted by interactants.[4] In an invitation in American English, for example, an acceptance is usually quick, while a rejection is delayed. In American English a certain kind of adjacency pair has an interesting role: to check out the likelihood of whether an invitation or request may be accepted without actually extending an invitation or requesting a favor. This "presequence" is a kind of adjacency pair which regularly precedes particular activities (Terasaki 1996; Schegloff 1988). It gives the recipient hints about what kind of action the speaker is going to do, for example "can I ask you a question?" This resource is often used among American English speakers before an invitation, as in "are you doing anything tonight?" to check out the situation before performing the action. It gives a respondent time to formulate an answer which reduces the chance of having to produce a dispreferred answer, a disaffiliating or a negative response.

Openings and closings of encounters are of great interest to anthropologists because these are typically sites where we can study the establishment of social relations and other social work in the construction of society (Duranti 1992).

There are complex skills required in properly using greetings, when to say them, to whom to say them, and in what manner, since greetings do complex social "jobs," and they reflect and construct complex, multi-faceted relationships. For anyone acquiring a foreign language and approaching a different culture, one of the first items to be learned are greetings. A greeting is a sequence collaboratively built by at least two different speakers.

An opening from a Persian telephone call exemplifies differences beyond dictionary translations of greetings. This conversational opening is different from, say, a Dutch conversation not just in how identification and recognition are achieved, but also in that more social tasks are expected and accomplished by means of a longer sequence (Taleghani-Nikazm, forthcoming). (In example (9), "hhh" signals inbreath; ° signals softer, quieter speech.)

(9) Persian telephone conversation
              ((*ring*))
Sima: alo?
              hello?
Mehdi: alo:?
              hello:?
Sima: bale?
              yes?
Mehdi: salam o aleikom minoo .hhh
              hello minoo .hhh
Sima: salam.
              hello.
Mehdi: man mehdi yoosefzadeh hastam.
              this is mehdi yoosefzadeh.
Sima: salaa:m. hale shom [a:,?
              hello: how are yo   [u:,?
                                              [
Mehdi: [°khoobe(h)° .hhh
                                     [°*I am well(h)°.hh*
Mehdi: [mokhlesim khoob hastin ke shoma?
              [*thank you are you well?*
              [
Sima: [khoob hastin,?
              [*are you well,?*
Sima: kheili mamnoon mersi, mahin khanoom khooban?
              thank you very much thank you, is Mrs. Mahin well?
Mehdi: alhamdolela bad nist.
              praise to God she is not bad.

Due to length restrictions, we cannot show the remainder of the opening but according to Taleghani-Nikazm's study (forthcoming), it is customary in Iran to inquire about the well-being of various family members, minimally the spouse and the children, before moving to the reason for the call. The interactional purpose of how-are-you sequences can give the called person a chance to tell any events out of the ordinary (Schegloff 1979). So when the well-being of a whole list of people is checked, the chances increase that the sequence expands before the caller can approach the reason for the call.

Just as languages have different phrases for greetings, openings of a conversation may also vary in their structure across cultures. Schegloff's analysis of the structure of 500 American telephone conversations (Schegloff 1968, 1979) inspired ensuing comparisons with many other languages, including Dutch (Houtkoop-Steenstra 1991), French (Godard 1977), Greek (Sifianou 1989), Persian (Taleghani-Nikazm, forthcoming), Swedish (Lindström 1994), Taiwanese (Hopper and Chia-Hui Chen 1996), and video-mediated American Sign Language (Keating 2000a).[5]

Anthropologists interested in greetings are likely to analyze face-to-face interaction, where many more behavioral signals beyond speech play a role, such as eye gaze, spatial proximity, and body movements (C. Goodwin 1979, 1981). In some societies the status of the coparticipants relative to each other during greetings is expressed not only through speech but through non-vocal actions (Duranti 1992; Keating 2000b), such as relative body position, bowing, and spatial location of the participants.

When interactants experience trouble producing their turn, or when they have difficulty in hearing or understanding the talk by another speaker, conversational repair mechanisms (Schegloff, Jefferson, and Sacks 1977) are available to them to signal trouble and to restore mutual understanding. There are similarities in repair mechanisms across languages (Schegloff 1987), yet features of the mechanism are sensitive to linguistic and social differences. In American English, the speaker of the repair initiation often tries to be as specific as possible in targeting the trouble source, thus directing the trouble source turn speaker in locating the trouble. In Korean, this principle does not always operate (Kim 1993). When, in an interaction with two speakers of different social status, the lower-status participant has trouble in hearing or understanding a turn by the higher-status participant, the lower-status person uses an unspecified repair initiation even when he or she has partial understanding or can make a good guess about the meaning of the higher-status person's turn. This is explained by native speakers' accounts that an unspecified repair initiation puts less of a constraint on the recipient than a more specific one. This practice allows more options in how the higher-status person may respond to the repair initiation. Similarly, in Western Samoa (Ochs 1988) and among the Kaluli in Papua New Guinea (Schieffelin 1990), "persons are uncomfortable making explicit guesses as to what other persons could be thinking, the thoughts of others that have not been clearly expressed in language or demeanor" (Ochs 1987: 315). Instead of guessing what another person might be meaning or thinking in an utterance unclear to the listener, it is appropriate to ask the other person to repeat part or all of the problematic utterance. Both Samoans (Ochs 1991) and the Inuit in arctic Quebec, studied by Crago (1988), treat trouble in hearing or understanding children's talk by simply ignoring those utterances. A similar result is found in a study of working-class African American families in South Carolina (Heath 1983). In contrast, middle-class white Americans often take up unclear children's utterances and initiate repair. They may also try to express their problem in understanding through facial expressions and gestures or even guess the meaning of the child's utterance.

Repair has been studied for several languages: American English (Schegloff, Jefferson, and Sacks 1977), Thai (Moerman 1977), Quiche (Daden and McClaren in Schegloff

1987), Samoan (Ochs 1988), Tuvalu (Besnier 1989), Ilokano (Streeck 1996), Japanese (Fox, Hayashi, and Jasperson 1996), and German (Uhmann 2001; Selting 2000; Egbert 1996). Recycling as a repair operation has been studied by linguists interested in how far back a speaker "rewinds" an utterance (Fox, Hayashi, and Jasperson 1996; Uhmann 2001). Speakers have been found to orient to specific linguistic units. When in English self-repair is initiated within a prepositional phrase, recycling goes back to the beginning of the prepositional phrase, thus delaying the production of the noun. However, Japanese speakers do not use recycling to delay a noun. Rather, they use a demonstrative pronoun ("that" or "there") and a case particle before producing the noun. Another case particle may follow (Fox, Hayashi, and Jasperson 1996).

Many features of conversational language cannot be found in grammars and dictionaries (see e.g. Schiffrin 1987 on discourse markers). For example, a dictionary of English conversational language could include the item *uh huh* meaning *I'm listening to what you are saying and I realize this is a point where I could take the turn but I want you to continue*, whereas the entry *uhm* would read *I'm in the process of building an utterance and I'm having momentary trouble in speaking*. Aspects of conversational language, including gestural actions, eye gaze, and facial expression, can also be meaningful signals in interaction.

5   CONTEXT: CONTEXTUALIZATION CUES, INFERENCE

A term that has recurred throughout this chapter is "context." Studying spontaneously occurring conversations has enabled a greater understanding of the relationship between talk and the context in which it is used. The term "context" is difficult to precisely define (Duranti and Goodwin 1992: 2), since talk itself forms the context for other talk and is contextualized by other talk (and the term comes from the Latin *contextus*, meaning a "joining together"). Context is socially constituted, interactively sustained, and bounded by time (Duranti and Goodwin 1992: 6). One way to think about how we use context in making meaning in conversation is in terms of foreground and background, or frame. Gumperz shows how conversationalists deploy and rely on "contextualization cues" which guide inference and which can result in serious miscommunication in certain situations where interactants are speaking the same language but without shared inferencing practices (Gumperz 1992).

A critique of the narrow formulation of context in conversation analysis is ongoing (see e.g. Blommaert et al. 2001), particularly the role of historical context. For the questions anthropologists are interested in, the context of a conversation is not enough, but must be supplemented with ethnographic research (see Duranti 1997) and other methodologies for description and interpretation. CA emerged from a discipline (sociology) where, at the time, categories were applied in an *a priori*, pancontextual manner in order to explain aspects of social behavior. A principle of CA that the relevant contexts for interpretation of actions are those contexts created by the participants themselves was a reaction to this. Thus the originators of CA have a particular sociohistorically constituted stand on "context" and "larger social context" that influences the debate about context and the positions taken up within it. Each turn at talk produces a context for the interpretation of the next turn. At the same time, the understanding of a conversational exchange often relies on background that extends beyond the interaction (Cicourel 1992).

6 Recording Conversations

Recording technology has made it possible to collect, transcribe, and analyze complex human interactions which unfold at a rate too rapid to accurately remember or note down. The development of recording technology has made possible a scientific accuracy that overcomes many problems associated with the fact that human interactions are highly complex and people have only a limited awareness of their actual speech behaviors in interaction. There is a disparity well known to ethnographers between what people believe or report they habitually do and what they actually do (Drew and Heritage 1992: 5; Briggs 1986). Intuition, which is often relied on for grammatical judgments about the well-formedness of utterances by native speakers, is unreliable for describing the subtleties of lexical choice in conversation and the way context (including other participants and prior talk) intersects with grammar to produce meanings that are built across speakers and turns. Technology such as video recording enables precise and repeated looks at talk and other communicative or meaningful signals as they emerge in spontaneous ways among people. The hallmark of conversation research is its insistence that the data base consist of audio- or video-taped conversation as it occurs naturally. Of course participants in a conversation to be recorded have to be asked for their consent prior to data collection, so they are aware that they are being taped, yet since they do not know what the particular focus of analysis is, the "observer's paradox" is reduced. Before planning recording, it will be useful to read C. Goodwin's (1993) essay with very practical and helpful suggestions on how to go about it (see also Duranti 1997: chapter 8).

After making audio or video recordings a transcript is made to aid in analysis. As academic disciplines can be characterized by different theoretical underpinnings and research foci, different transcription notations have been developed (see a review in Edwards 2001). No one should begin transcribing without looking at the important paper by Ochs (1979) which demonstrates how decision-making in the process of transcribing may be based on more or less conscious theoretical assumptions and some consequences of these decisions. Decisions on how to transcribe may even lead to a transcriber's stereotyping of a speaker, as Jefferson (1996) demonstrates. A transcript should be treated as a contingent work-in-progress, as it is only a limited representation of an interaction.

7 Conclusions

We have discussed some of the ways conversation is a vital resource for establishing, maintaining, contesting, and analyzing cultural ideas and practices. The study of conversation enables anthropologists to describe and compare a number of aspects of social life and human behavior, as well as to understand aspects of language structure and use. Goals in studying conversation include understanding of how people manipulate symbolic resources to perform a range of activities and how these activities are differently organized across cultures. Features of conversational discourse are culturally organized and convey local conceptions and theories about the world. We have focused here particularly on conversation as it relates to socialization practices, the production of identity and other social relationships, constructions of authority, narrative and the organization of experience, the notion of institutional talk, and the relationship of conversation to aspects of linguistic structure. We have also shown some conversation structures identified by conversation analysts in order to illustrate how conversation can be analyzed as action, and to suggest the level of detail that can be attended to.

NOTES

1 "Chitlins" or "chitterlings" are the intestines of hogs.
2 Left-hand bracket indicates onset of a simultaneous utterance, a colon indicates lengthening of a sound, = indicates there is no interval between speakers, underlining indicates stress, a hyphen following a letter indicates an abrupt cutoff in speaking.
3 In line 6, the asterisk marks the beginning of a non-vocal action, which is described in smaller font and italics in the line above the talk.
4 The work on sequence organization is much too extensive to summarize here. We can only highlight some findings and recommend Schegloff (1990) for an in-depth treatment of this topic.
5 For findings about the structure of closings, see for example Schegloff and Sacks (1973), Button (1987), and Auer (1990).

REFERENCES

Alvarez-Cáccamo, C. (1996). Building Alliances in Political Discourse: Language Institutional Authority and Resistance. In *Folia Linguistica* XXX 3/4, Special Issue on Interactional Sociolinguistics (ed. H. Kotthoff).

Auer, J. C. P. (1990). Rhythm in Telephone Closings. *Human Studies* 13: 361–392.

Austin, J. L. (1962). *How to Do Things with Words*. Oxford: Oxford University Press.

Basso, K. (1979). *Portraits of the Whiteman*. Cambridge: Cambridge University Press.

Bauman, R. (1996). "Any Man Who Keppes More'n One Hound'll Lie to You": A Contextual Study of Expressive Lying. In D. Brenneis and R. Macaulay (eds.), *The Matrix of Language* (pp. 160–181). Boulder, CO: Westview Press.

Beach, W. (2001). Lay Diagnosis. *Text* 21 (1/2).

Besnier, N. (1989). Information Withholding as a Manipulative and Collusive Strategy in Nukulaelae Gossip. *Language in Society* 18: 315–341.

Besnier, N. (1995). *Literacy, Emotion, and Authority: Reading and Writing on a Polynesian Atoll*. Cambridge: Cambridge University Press.

Blom, J.-P., and Gumperz, J. J. (1972). Social Meaning in Linguistic Structures: Code Switching in Norway. In J. J. Gumperz and D. Hymes (eds.), *Directions in Sociolinguistics* (pp. 407–434). New York: Holt.

Blommaert, J., Collins, J., Heller, M., Rampton, B., Slembrouck, S., and Verschueren, J. (2001). Introduction to Discourse and Critique: Part One. *Critique of Anthropology* 21(1): 5–12.

Boggs, S. (1972). The Meaning of Questions and Narratives to Hawaiian Children. In C. Cazden, V. John, and D. Hymes (eds.), *Functions of Language in the Classroom*. Prospect Heights, IL: Waveland Press.

Bourdieu, P. (1991). *Language and Symbolic Power*. Cambridge, MA: Harvard University Press.

Brenneis, D. (1996). Grog and Gossip in Bhatgaon: Style and Substance in Fiji Indian Conversation. In D. Brenneis and R. Macaulay (eds.), *The Matrix of Language* (pp. 209–233). Boulder, CO: Westview Press.

Briggs, C. (1986). *Learning How to Ask: A Sociolinguistic Appraisal of the Role of the Interview in Social Science Research*. Cambridge: Cambridge University Press.

Button, G. (1987). Moving out of Closings. In G. Button and J. R. Lee (eds.), *Talk and Social Organisation* (pp. 101–151). Clevedon and Philadelphia: Multilingual Matters.

Button, G. (ed.) (1993). *Technology in Working Order*. New York: Routledge.

Chomsky, N. (1977). *Language and Responsibility*. Based on Conversations with Mitsou Ronat. New York: Pantheon.

Cicourel, A. V. (1992). The Interpenetration of Communicative Contexts: Examples from Medical Encounters. In A. Duranti and C. Goodwin (eds.), *Rethinking Context: Language as an Interactive Phenomenon* (pp. 291–310). Cambridge: Cambridge University Press.

Coates, J. (1994). Discourse, Gender, and Subjectivity: The Talk of Teenage Girls. In M. Bucholtz, A. C. Liang, L. A. Sutton, and C. Hines (eds.), *Cultural Performances* (pp. 116–132). Berkeley: Berkeley Women and Language Group.

Cook-Gumperz, J. (1986). *The Social Construction of Literacy*. London: Cambridge University Press.

Corsaro, W., and Rizzo, T. (1990). Disputes in the Peer Culture of American and Italian Nursery-School Children. In A. Grimshaw (ed.), *Conflict Talk* (pp. 21–66). New York: Cambridge University Press.

Couper-Kuhlen, E. (1991). A Rhythm-based Metric for Turn-taking. In *Proceedings of the 12th International Congress of Phonetic Sciences, Aix-en-Provence*, vol. 1: 275–278.

Crago, M. (1988). Cultural Context in Communicative Interaction of Inuit Children. Doctoral dissertation, McGill University.

Drew, P. (1992). Contested Evidence in Courtroom Cross-examination: The Case of a Trial for Rape. In P. Drew and J. Heritage (eds.), *Talk at Work: Interaction in Institutional Settings* (pp. 470–520). Cambridge: Cambridge University Press.

Drew, P., and Heritage, J. (1992). Analyzing Talk at Work: An Introduction. In P. Drew and J. Heritage (eds.), *Talk at Work: Interaction in Institutional Settings* (pp. 3–65). Cambridge: Cambridge University Press.

Drew, P., and Sorjonen, M.-L. (1997). Institutional Dialogue. In T. van Dijk (ed.), *Discourse as Social Interaction*. London: Sage.

Drew, P., and Wootton, A. (eds.) (1988). *Erving Goffman*. Cambridge: Polity Press.

Duranti, A. (1988). The Ethnography of Speaking: Toward a Linguistics of the Praxis. In F. J. Newmeyer (ed.), *Linguistics: The Cambridge Survey* (pp. 210–228). Cambridge: Cambridge University Press.

Duranti, A. (1992). Language and Bodies in Social Space: Samoan Ceremonial Greetings. *American Anthropologist* 94: 657–691.

Duranti, A. (1997). *Linguistic Anthropology. Cambridge Textbooks in Linguistics*. Cambridge and New York: Cambridge University Press.

Duranti, A., and Goodwin, C. (eds.) (1992). *Rethinking Context: Language as an Interactive Phenomenon. Studies in the Social and Cultural Foundations of Language* No. 11. Cambridge and New York: Cambridge University Press.

Eckert, P., and McConnell-Ginet, S. (1995). Constructing Meaning, Constructing Selves. In K. Hall and M. Bucholtz (eds.), *Gender Articulated*. New York: Routledge.

Edwards, J. A. (2001). Transcription in Discourse. In D. Schiffrin, D. Tannen, and H. Hamilton (eds.), *The Handbook of Discourse Analysis* (pp. 321–348). Oxford: Blackwell.

Egbert, M. (1996). Context Sensitivity in Conversation Analysis: Eye Gaze and the German Repair Initiator "Bitte". *Language in Society* 25: 587–612.

Egbert, M. (forthcoming). Other-Initiated Repair and Membership Categorization – Some Conversational Events that Trigger Linguistic and Regional Membership Categorization. *Journal of Pragmatics.*

Egbert, M., Niebecker, L., and Rezzara, S. (submitted). Inside First and Second Language Speakers' Trouble in Understanding – Language Strategies Revisited. In R. Gardner and J. Wagner (eds.), *Second Language Talk.*

Ervin-Tripp, S. (1992). Gender Differences in the Construction of Humorous Talk. In K. Hall, M. Bucholtz, and B. Moonwoman (eds.), *Locating Power.* Berkeley: Berkeley Women and Language Group.

Ervin-Tripp, S., and Lampert, M. (1992). Gender Differences in the Construction of Humorous Talk. In Berkeley Women and Language Group (eds.), *Locating Power* (pp. 108–117). Berkeley: Berkeley Women and Language Group, University of California.

Fairclough, N. F. (1995). *Critical Discourse Analysis.* London: Longman.

Ford, C., Fox, B. A., and Thompson, S. A. (eds.) (2002). *The Language of Turn and Sequence.* New York: Oxford University Press.

Fox, B. A., Hayashi, M., and Jasperson, R. (1996). Resources and Repair: A Cross-linguistic Study of Syntax and Repair. In E. Ochs, E. A. Schegloff, and S. A. Thompson (eds.), *Interaction and Grammar* (pp. 185–237). Cambridge: Cambridge University Press.

Garfinkel, H. (1967). *Studies in Ethnomethodology.* Englewood Cliffs, NJ: Prentice-Hall.

Godard, D. (1977). Same Setting, Different Norms: Phone Call Beginnings in France and the United States. *Language in Society* 6: 209–219.

Goffman, E. (1964). The Neglected Situation. *American Anthropologist* 66: 133–135.

Goffman, E. (1983). The Interaction Order. *American Sociological Review* 48: 1–17.

Goodwin, C. (1979). The Interactive Construction of a Sentence in Natural Conversation. In G. Psathas (ed.), *Everyday Language: Studies in Ethnomethodology* (pp. 97–121). New York: Irvington.

Goodwin, C. (1980). Restarts, Pauses, and the Achievement of a State of Mutual Gaze at Turn Beginning. *Sociological Inquiry* 50: 272–302.

Goodwin, C. (1981). *Conversational Organization: Interaction between Speakers and Hearers.* New York: Academic Press.

Goodwin, C. (1993). Recording Human Interaction in Natural Settings. *Pragmatics* 3: 181–209.

Goodwin, C. (1994). Professional Vision. *American Anthropologist* 96: 606–633.

Goodwin, M. H. (1990). *He-Said-She-Said: Talk as Social Organization among Black Children.* Bloomington: Indiana University Press.

Goodwin, M. H. (1998). Games of Stance: Conflict and Footing in Hopscotch. In S. Hoyle and C. T. Adger (eds.), *Kids' Talk: Strategic Language Use in Later Childhood* (pp. 23–46). New York: Oxford University Press.

Grice, H. P. (1975). Logic and Conversation. In P. Cole and J. L. Morgan (eds.), *Syntax and Semantics,* vol. 3: *Speech Acts* (pp. 41–58). New York: Academic Press.

Grimshaw, A. (ed.) (1990). *Conflict Talk.* New York: Cambridge University Press.

Gumperz, J. J. (1992). Contextualization and Understanding. In A. Duranti and C. Goodwin (eds.), *Rethinking Context: Language as an Interactive Phenomenon* (pp. 229–252). New York: Cambridge University Press.

Gumperz, J. J. (1997). On the Interactional Bases of Speech Community Membership. In G. R. Guy, C. Feagin, D. Schiffrin, and J. Baugh (eds.), *Towards a Social Science of Language: Papers in Honor of William Labov,* vol. 2. Philadelphia: John Benjamins.

Gumperz, J., and Hymes, D. (eds.) (1972). *Directions in Sociolinguistics: The Ethnography of Communication*. New York: Blackwell.

Hanks, W. (1990). *Referential Practice*. Chicago: University of Chicago Press.

Have, P. ten (1991). Talk and Institution: A Reconsideration of the "Asymmetry" of Doctor–Patient Interaction. In D. Boden and D. H. Zimmerman (eds.), *Talk and Social Structure* (pp. 138–163). Cambridge: Polity Press.

Haviland, J. (1977). *Gossip, Reputation, and Knowledge in Zinacantan*. Chicago: University of Chicago Press.

Hayashi, M., Mori, J., and Takagi, T. (2002). Contingent Achievement of Co-tellership in a Japanese Conversation: An Analysis of Talk, Gaze, and Gesture. In C. Ford, B. A. Fox, and S. A. Thompson (eds.), *The Language of Turn and Sequence* (pp. 81–122). New York: Oxford University Press.

Heath, S. B. (1983). *Ways with Words: Language, Life and Work in Communities and Classrooms*. Cambridge: Cambridge University Press.

Heath, S. B. (1986). What No Bedtime Story Means: Narrative Skills at Home and School. In B. B. Schieffelin and E. Ochs (eds.), *Language Socialization across Cultures* (pp. 97–126). New York: Cambridge University Press.

Heller, M. F. (1995). *Reading–Writing Connections: From Theory to Practice* (2nd edn.). New York: Longman.

Heritage, J. (1984). *Garfinkel and Ethnomethodology*. Cambridge: Polity Press.

Heritage, J., and Sorjonen, M.-L. (1994). Constituting and Maintaining Activities across Sequences: *and*-prefacing as a Feature of Question Design. *Language in Society* 23: 1–29.

Herring, S. C. (2001). Computer-mediated Discourse. In D. Schiffrin, D. Tannen, and H. Hamilton (eds.), *The Handbook of Discourse Analysis* (pp. 612–634). Oxford: Blackwell.

Hill, J., and Irvine, J. (eds.) (1993). *Responsibility and Evidence in Oral Discourse*. Cambridge: Cambridge University Press.

Hopper, R., and Chen, C-H. (1996). Languages, Cultures, Relationships: Telephone Openings in Taiwan. *Research on Language and Social Interaction* 29(4): 291–313.

Houtkoop-Steenstra, H. (1991). Opening Sequences in Dutch Telephone Conversations. In D. Boden and D. H. Zimmerman (eds.), *Talk and Social Structure* (pp. 232–251). Berkeley and Los Angeles: University of California Press; Cambridge: Polity Press.

Hymes, D. (1974). *Foundations in Sociolinguistics: An Ethnographic Approach*. Philadelphia: University of Pennsylvania Press.

Ide, R. (forthcoming). *Friendly but Strangers: Small Talk and the Creation of Self through Talk in America*. Amsterdam: John Benjamins.

Jacquemet, M. (1996). *Credibility in Court: Communicative Practices in the Camorra Trials*. Cambridge: Cambridge University Press.

Jefferson, G. (1984). On the Organization of Laughter in Talk about Troubles. In J. M. Atkinson and J. Heritage (eds.), *Structures of Social Action: Studies in Conversation Analysis* (pp. 346–369). Cambridge: Cambridge University Press.

Jefferson, G. (1996). A Case of Transcriptional Stereotyping. *Journal of Pragmatics* 26: 159–170.

Keating, E. (1998). *Power Sharing: Language, Rank, Gender, and Social Space in Pohnpei, Micronesia. Oxford Studies in Anthropological Linguistics 23*. New York: Oxford University Press.

Keating, E. (2000a). How Culture and Technology Together Shape New Communicative Practices: Investigating Interactions between Deaf and Hearing Callers with Computer Mediated Videotelephone. *Texas Linguistic Forum: Proceedings of the Seventh Annual Symposium about Language and Society, Austin* (pp. 99–116). Austin: University of Texas.

Keating, E. (2000b). Moments of Hierarchy: Constructing Social Stratification by Means of Language, Food, Space, and the Body in Pohnpei, Micronesia. *American Anthropologist* 102: 303–320.

Keating, E., and Mirus, G. (2003). American Sign Language in Virtual Space: Interactions between Deaf Users of Computer-Mediated Video Communication and the Impact of Technology on Language Practices. *Language in Society* 32: 693–714.

Keenan, E. O. (1974). Norm-Makers, Norm-Breakers: Uses of Speech by Men and Women in a Malagasy Community. In R. Bauman and J. Sherzer (eds.), *Explorations in the Ethnography of Speaking*. New York: Cambridge University Press.

Kendon, A. (1967). Some Functions of Gaze-Direction in Social Interaction. *Acta Psychologica* 26: 22–63.

Kendon, A. (1990). *Conducting Interaction: Patterns of Behavior in Focussed Encounters.* Cambridge: Cambridge University Press.

Kim, K.-H. (1992). Wh-Clefts and Left Dislocation in English Conversation with Reference to Topicality in Korean. Unpublished PhD dissertation, University of California, Los Angeles.

Kim, K.-H. (1993). Other-Initiated Repairs in Korean Conversation as Interactional Resources. In S. Choi (ed.), *Japanese/Korean Linguistics*, vol. 3 (pp. 3–18). Palo Alto, CA: Center for the Study of Language and Information, Stanford University.

Kulick, D. (1992). *Language Shift and Cultural Reproduction: Socialization, Self, and Syncretism in a Papua New Guinean Village*. Cambridge: Cambridge University Press.

Levinson, S. C. (1983). *Pragmatics. Cambridge Textbooks in Linguistics.* Cambridge and New York: Cambridge University Press.

Lindström, A. (1994). Identification and Recognition in Swedish Telephone Conversation Openings. *Language in Society* 23: 231–252.

Lindstrom, L. (1992). Context Contests: Debatable Truth Statements on Tanna (Vanuatu). In A. Duranti and C. Goodwin (eds.), *Rethinking Context*. New York: Cambridge University Press.

Linell, P. (1998). Approaching Dialogue: Talk, Interaction and Contexts in Dialogical Perspectives. *IMPACT: Studies in Language and Society 3.* Amsterdam and Philadelphia: John Benjamins.

Lucas, C., and Valli, C. (1992). *Language Contact in the American Deaf Community.* San Diego, CA: Academic Press.

Malinowski, B. (1923). The Problem of Meaning in Primitive Languages. In C. K. Ogden and I. A. Richards (eds.), *The Meaning of Meaning*. London: Routledge & Kegan Paul.

Mandelbaum, J. (1989). Interpersonal Activities in Conversational Storytelling. *Western Journal of Speech Communication* 53: 114–126.

Mather, S. (1991). The Discourse Marker "Oh" in Typed Telephone Conversations among Deaf Typists. PhD dissertation, Georgetown University.

McElhinny, B. (1995). Challenging Hegemonic Masculinities: Female and Male Police Officers Handling Domestic Violence. In K. Hall and M. Bucholtz (eds.), *Gender Articulated* (pp. 217–244). New York: Routledge.

Mitchell-Kernan, C. (1972). Signifying and Marking: Two Afro-American Speech Acts. In J. J. Gumperz and D. Hymes (eds.), *Directions in Sociolinguistics: The Ethnography of Communication* (pp. 161–179). New York: Blackwell.

Moerman, M. (1977). The Preference for Self-correction in a Tai Conversational Corpus. *Language* 53: 872–882.

Ochs, E. (1979). Transcription as Theory. In E. Ochs and B. B. Schieffelin, *Developmental Pragmatics* (pp. 43–72). New York: Academic Press.

Ochs, E. (1987). Input: A Socio-culture Perspective. In M. Hickmann (ed.), *Social and Functional Approaches to Language and Thought* (pp. 305–319). Orlando, FL: Academic Press.

Ochs, E. (1988). *Culture and Language Development: Language Acquisition and Language Socialization in a Samoan Village. Studies in the Social and Cultural Foundations of Language.* No. 6. Cambridge and New York: Cambridge University Press.

Ochs, E. (1991). Misunderstanding Children. In N. Coupland, H. Giles, and J. M. Wiemann (eds.), *Miscommunication and Problematic Talk* (pp. 44–60). Newbury Park, CA: Sage.

Ochs, E., Jacoby, S., and Gonzales, P. (1994). Interpretive Journeys: How Physicists Talk and Travel through Graphic Space. *Configurations* 2: 151–171.

Ochs, E., and Taylor, C. (1995). The "Father Knows Best" Dynamic in Dinnertime Narratives. In K. Hall and M. Bucholtz (eds.), *Gender Articulated*. New York: Routledge.

Okamoto, S. (1995). "Tasteless" Japanese: Less "Feminine" Speech among Young Japanese Women. In K. Hall and M. Bucholtz (eds.), *Gender Articulated* (pp. 297–328). New York: Routledge.

Philips, S. (1974). Warm Springs "Indian Time": How the Regulation of Participation Affects the Progress of Events. In R. Bauman and J. Sherzer (eds.), *Explorations in the Ethnography of Speaking.* New York: Cambridge University Press.

Pomerantz, A., and Fehr, B. J. (1997). Conversation Analysis: An Approach to the Study of Social Action as Sense Making Practices. In T. van Dijk (ed.), *Discourse as Social Interaction.* London: Sage.

Rosaldo, M. (1973). I Have Nothing to Hide: The Language of Ilongot Oratory. *Language in Society* 2: 193–223.

Sacks, H. (1964/5). Lecture 6: The Mir Membership Categorization Device. In H. Sacks (1995), *Lectures on Conversation*, vol. 1 (ed. G. Jefferson) (pp. 40–48). Oxford: Blackwell.

Sacks, H. (1972a). An Initial Investigation of the Usability of Conversational Data for Doing Sociology. In D. N. Sudnow (ed.), *Studies in Social Interaction.* New York: Free Press.

Sacks, H. (1972b). On the Analyzability of Stories by Children. In J. J. Gumperz and D. Hymes (eds.), *Directions in Sociolinguistics* (pp. 325–345). New York: Holt, Rinehart and Winston.

Sacks, H. (1987). On the Preferences for Agreement and Contiguity in Sequences in Conversation. In G. Button and J. R. Lee (eds.), *Talk and Social Organisation* (pp. 54–69). Clevedon: Multilingual Matters.

Sacks, H. (1995[1992]). *Lectures on Conversation*. Oxford: Blackwell.

Sacks, H., and Schegloff, E. A. (1979). Two Preferences in the Organization of Reference to Persons in Conversation and Their Interaction. In G. Psathas (ed.), *Everyday Language: Studies in Ethnomethodology* (pp. 15–21). New York: Irvington.

Sacks, H., Schegloff, E. A., and Jefferson, G. (1974). A Simplest Systematics for the Organization of Turn-Taking for Conversation. *Language* 50: 696–735.

Schegloff, E. A. (1968). Sequencing in Conversational Openings. *American Anthropologist* 70: 1075–1095.

Schegloff, E. A. (1979). Identification and Recognition in Telephone Conversation Openings. In G. Psathas (ed.), *Everyday Language: Studies in Ethnomethodology* (pp. 23–78). New York: Irvington.

Schegloff, E. A. (1984). On Some Questions and Ambiguities in Conversation. In J. M. Atkinson and J. Heritage (eds.), *Structures of Social Action: Studies in Conversation Analysis* (pp. 28–52). Cambridge: Cambridge University Press.

Schegloff, E. A. (1987). Between Micro and Macro: Contexts and Other Connections. In J. C. Alexander, B. Giesen, R. Munch, and N. J. Smelser (eds.), *The Micro-Macro Link* (pp. 207–233). Berkeley: University of California Press.

Schegloff, E. A. (1988). Presequences and Indirection: Applying Speech Act Theory to Ordinary Conversation. *Journal of Pragmatics* 12: 55–62.

Schegloff, E. A. (1990). On the Organization of Sequences as a Source of Coherence in Talk-in-Interaction. In B. Dorval (ed.), *Conversational Organization and Its Development* (pp. 51–77). Norwood, NJ: Ablex.

Schegloff, E. A. (1992). Introduction. In H. Sacks, *Lectures on Conversation*, vol. 1, pp. ix–lxii; vol. 2, pp. ix–lii. Oxford: Blackwell.

Schegloff, E. A., Jefferson, G., and Sacks, H. (1977). The Preference for Self-correction in the Organization of Repair in Conversation. *Language* 53: 361–382.

Schegloff, E. A., and Sacks, H. (1973). Opening up Closings. *Semiotica* 8: 289–327.

Schieffelin, B. B. (1986). Teasing and Shaming in Kaluli Children's Interactions. In B. B. Schieffelin and E. Ochs (eds.), *Language Socialization across Cultures* (pp. 165–181). New York: Cambridge University Press.

Schieffelin, B. B. (1990). *The Give and Take of Everyday Life*. Cambridge: Cambridge University Press.

Schieffelin, B. B., and Ochs, E. (eds.) (1986). *Language Socialization across Cultures. Studies in the Social and Cultural Foundations of Language* No. 3. Cambridge and New York: Cambridge University Press.

Schiffrin, D. (1987). *Discourse Markers*. New York: Cambridge University Press.

Schriffrin, D. (1990). The Management of a Co-operative Self during Argument: The Role of Opinions and Stories. In A. Grimshaw (ed.), *Conflict Talk* (pp. 241–259). New York: Cambridge University Press.

Schiffrin, D. (2001). Discourse Markers: Language, Meaning, and Context. In D. Schiffrin, D. Tannen, and H. Hamilton (eds.), *The Handbook of Discourse Analysis* (pp. 54–75). Oxford: Blackwell.

Selting, M. (2000). Opening Remarks: Arguments for the Development of an "Interactional Linguistics." Plenary Speech at the Euroconference "Interactional Linguistics", Spa, Belgium, September 16, 2000.

Selting, M., and Couper-Kuhlen, E. (eds.) (2001). *Studies in Interactional Linguistics*. Amsterdam: John Benjamins.

Sifianou, M. (1989). On the Telephone Again! Differences in Telephone Behaviour: England versus Greece. *Language and Society* 18: 527–544.

Silverstein, M. (1998). The Uses and Utility of Ideology: A Commentary. In B. B. Schieffelin, K. A. Woolard, and P. V. Kroskrity (eds.), *Language Ideologies*. New York: Oxford University Press.

Sinclair, J., and Coulthard, R. (1975). *Towards an Analysis of Discourse*. New York: Oxford University Press.

Stokoe, W. (1969). Sign Language Diglossia. *Studies in Linguistics* 21: 27–41.

Streeck, J. (1996). A Little Ilokano Grammar as It Appears in Interaction. *Journal of Pragmatics* 26: 189–213.

Streeck, J., and Hartge, U. (1992). Previews: Gestures at the Transition Place. In J. C. P. Auer and A. di Luzio (eds.), *The Contextualization of Language* (pp. 135–158). Amsterdam: John Benjamins.

Street, B. (1995). *Social Literacies: Critical Approaches to Literacy in Development, Ethnography, and Education*. London: Longman.

Suchman, L. (1987). *Plans and Situated Action: The Problem of Human–machine Communication*. Cambridge: Cambridge University Press.

Sunaoshi, Y. (2000). Gesture as a Situated Communicative Strategy at a Japanese Manufacturing Plant in the US. *Cognitive Studies: Bulletin of the Japanese Cognitive Science Society* 7.

Taleghani-Nikazm, C. (2002). A Conversation Analytical Study of Telephone Conversation Openings between Native and Nonnative Speakers. *Journal of Pragmatics* 34: 1807–1832.

Tannen, D. (1994). *Gender and Discourse*. New York: Oxford University Press.

Tannen, D. (2003). Gender and Family Interaction. In J. Holmes and M. Meyerhoff (eds.), *Handbook of Language and Gender*. Oxford: Blackwell.

Terasaki, A. K. (1996). Pre-Announcement Sequences in Conversation. *Social Sciences Working Paper 99*.

Uhmann, S. (2001). Some Arguments for the Relevance of Syntax to Self-repair in Everyday German Conversation. In M. Selting and E. Couper-Kuhlen (eds.), *Studies in Interactional Linguistics*. Amsterdam: John Benjamins.

van Dijk, T. (1991). *Racism and the Press*. London: Routledge.

van Dijk, T. A., and Wodak, R. (eds.) (2000). *Racism at the Top. Parliamentary Discourses on Ethnic Issues in Six European States*. Klagenfurt: Drava Verlag.

Vygotsky, L. (1978). *Mind in Society*. Cambridge, MA: Harvard University Press.

Zentella, A. C. (1997). *Growing Up Bilingual*. Malden, MA: Blackwell.

CHAPTER 9

Gesture

John B. Haviland

1 INTRODUCTION

People routinely gesture in interaction, and we commonly assume their gestures are meaningful. Interactants themselves may have explicit theories about gesture, which like all cultural productions probably contain grains of both truth and fiction. When and how people gesture seems to reveal something about what they are doing and saying, even though gestures appear to work in multiple ways, some intentional and some inadvertent. Gestures are clearly constructed from repertoires of bodily form derived from both individual idiosyncrasy and cultural tradition. Just as conventional emblematic gestures are undeniably part of communicative repertoires, even the more apparently haphazard, extemporized, and ephemeral movements that routinely accompany speech are often supposed to be significant. In conversation one often cannot avoid reading meaning into gesture, whether or not it seems intentionally produced or directed at someone. Gesture is thus a potential resource for interactants as they negotiate social worlds. It is also a resource that anthropology needs to understand, since no living linguistic tradition has been described in which gesture is absent.

Nonetheless, gesture has a dubious if not downright bad reputation, in common parlance. No matter how "dramatic" someone's occasional *beau geste*, it remains "a mere gesture," and thus suspect as only "token," or worse "empty." The *New Shorter Oxford English Dictionary* cites the following characteristic use: "This was clearly a gesture rather than a seriously intended attempt at suicide." Particular societies may disparage gesture on intellectual, expressive, or class grounds. In linguistic studies, the bodily movements that routinely accompany speech are usually dismissed as irrelevant or, more often, simply pass unremarked.

In Western intellectual history gesture has not always been so readily pushed aside. Perhaps the first systematic treatment of the topic, published in Latin in AD 100 (Quintillian 1924), related oratorical persuasiveness to the effectiveness of the orator's gestural accompaniments (Graf 1992). Classical art of antiquity abounds with symbolic depictions of gesturing bodies: stylized and significant handshapes, postures, facial expressions, and bodily attitudes that show how sensitive artists were to the communicative potential of gesture.

Since the Middle Ages, however, except for grand speculative programs in the eighteenth and nineteenth centuries linking gesture to presumed universals in thought and to the rise of human language – programs that in less ambitious forms continue to the present day – gesture remained unincorporated into Western analytic thought. Furthermore, only with the rise of sound-film and later technologies for iconic recording in the twentieth century did it become possible to afford gesture serious empirical and theoretical attention as part of the human communicative repertoire.

Many authors mention a semiotic complementarity between gesture and its accompanying speech, noting that the four-dimensional, imagistic, embodied channel of gesture has communicative potential inherently different from that of the digital, linearized flow of words. As Kendon (Kendon 2000): 51) puts it, "[s]peakers often employ gesture in such a way as to make something that is being said more precise or complete," sometimes accomplishing this by "provid[ing] the context in terms of which a verbal expression is to be interpreted" (ibid., p. 53). Theorists have also identified other less single-mindedly referential contributions gestures can make to their surrounding discourses, including rhythmic punctuation, signaling of theme and rheme, bracketing metacommentary, changes of perspective, speaker's attitudes, and the like. Central research questions are: what semiotic properties can gestures have? From what do gestural "meanings" derive? How do these meanings coordinate with other aspects of utterances? And what sorts of resources do they thus provide for interactants? This chapter considers these questions by first developing an appropriate anthropological theory of gesture, considering proposed gesture typologies, then locating gesture firmly *within* language in terms of form, practice, and ideology. I draw illustrations from my fieldwork in Chiapas and Australia.

2   GESTURE IN LANGUAGE

When gesture *does* rise to analytical consciousness, the result is too often a "subtract-ive" account: gesture is whatever is left over after other phenomena which fall under more principled descriptions are subtracted. Gesture may be seen as involuntary bodily leakage that "betrays" inner states and attitudes that intentionally communicative channels may be trying to hide. Or gestures may be seen as scattered and only partly conscious bodily accompaniments to spoken language, largely involuntary excrescences of the speaking process itself as imagistic thought struggles to accommodate the digital linearity of language. Gesture is sometimes seen as primitive "attempted" language, grounded in presumed universal iconicity, and thus the first resort of would-be communicators who do not share a linguistic code. Other gesture theorists place an almost diametrically opposite emphasis on *codified* and *culture-specific* gestural substitutes for spoken language: compacted, learned, gestured holo-phrases known as "emblems."

A more appropriate non-subtractive view integrates attitudes and movements of the body, first, into the full repertoire of interactive human communicative resources and, second, into the expressive inflections of language itself. One of the earliest and most eloquent formulations of such a view argues that "speech and gesture are produced together, and that they must therefore be regarded as two aspects of a single process . . . Speakers combine, as if in a single plan of action, both spoken and gestural expression" (Kendon 1997: 110–11).

Part of Kendon's argument for the "single plan" hypothesis derives from robust observations that verbal and gestural performances are mutually synchronized: when a gesture appears to be linked in meaning to a word or phrase (sometimes called the gesture's "lexical affiliate"), the gesture either coincides with or precedes the relevant speech fragment. Some theorists, most notably McNeill (1992; see also McNeill and Duncan 2000) have used such facts to motivate a theory in which both speech and gesture originate in a single conceptual source, whose joint "expression" in the different modalities produces the observed synchronicity between word and movement.

P, a Zinacantec cornfarmer from Chiapas, tells in Tzotzil about leaving a horse sick in a field. When he returned after searching for medicine, he found the horse dead, surrounded by buzzards. As he comes to the punch line, P twice repeats a counter-clockwise circling sweep of his right arm, evidently coinciding in meaning with the Tzotzil word *setel* "circular" (figure 9.1). The crucial detail is where these gestures occur in the temporal unfolding of the overall utterance.

(1) Buzzards circling[1]
k'al lik'ote kere
When I got there – damn!

[right hand circles once][circles again]
   1   2   3   4   5 6
               [downstroke]   [downstroke]
               chamem xa te xa setel   xulem
               dead   already   circular buzzard
  It was already dead; the buzzards were in a circle.

Figure 9.1   "Circling"

Both circling movements are similar: P's right hand turns palm downward, fingers slightly pursed, moves out to the right and circles up; P then makes an abrupt downward stroke, and finishes the circular movement down and back to the right, leaving his hand momentarily at rest. (See figure 9.1.) As can be seen in transcript (1), the first circling motion (positions 1–3) is begun well before P begins to speak his words, and it concludes (position 3) as he says "[it was] dead." He repeats the gesture (slightly higher and closer to the center of the interactional space he shares with his interlocutor) in the subsequent sentence (positions 4–6), producing the downward stroke (position 6) exactly as he says the first stressed syllable of *setel* – evidently the word which the circling gesture "depicts." His hand has returned to rest by the time he finishes the sentence, pronouncing *xulem* 'buzzards', the apparent grammatical subject of the predicate *setel*, with no accompanying gesture. Kendon remarks about a similar example, "[i]t is only by commencing the movements for the gesture in advance of the speech that the synchrony of arm swing and [the associated lexical item] could have been achieved" (1997: 111). Without some sort of expressive "plan," that is, the whole integrated performance could not have been accomplished in its synchronic perfection.

P's circling gestures also do more than "illustrate" his words. In fact, the Tzotzil root *set* has a wide range of meanings, all involving circularity, but in quite different senses; as an adjective, *setel* can apply to the fullness of the moon, the round completeness of a slice of fruit, or a large continuous garden plot, among other things (Laughlin 1975). The exact scene that P wants to conjure – the buzzards arrayed in a circle on the ground around the dead horse – is thus partly conveyed by the form of his gesture: the sweep around some central space (presumably where the horse is meant to be imagined), hand pointing slightly downward to suggest buzzards on the ground and not circling in the air.

3   GESTURE TYPOLOGIES

Modern gesture theorists have been preoccupied with gestural classification, perhaps because ordinary usage conflates under unexamined pre-theoretical labels what seem to be analytically separable phenomena. Returning to the NSOED, the origin of the English word "gesture" is to be found in Latin *gerere* 'bear, carry, carry on, perform' (via medieval Latin *gestura*), and its earliest usage accordingly meant a "manner of carrying the body; carriage, deportment" – a very broad notion which only later comes to be narrowed to "(a) movement of the body or limbs, now only as an expression of thought or feeling; the use of such movements as an expression of feeling or a rhetorical device," and still later to the typical twentieth-century meaning: "[a]n action performed as a courtesy, formality, or symbol to indicate an intention or evoke a response." Recent theoretical treatments question several aspects of these common usages: "manner" (which may imply something stable or established, as opposed to the apparent ephemeral nature of much gesture), "expression of thought or feeling" (which may conflate what might be presumed to be very different cognitive underpinnings), and perhaps most problematic, "intention" with all the attendant difficulties about the nature of the person, the will, and the emergent character of interpersonal interaction.

One influential typology of gesture distinguishes different varieties according to their "language-like" properties on the one hand and their relative integration with or emancipation from speech on the other. At one end of the spectrum are "gesticulations," movements especially of the hands that occur only in coordination with verbalization and are largely meaningless in isolation from speech. (P's circling movement, non-standard and relatively uninterpretable without the word *setel* and the verbal context, is a typical example.) At the other end of the continuum are full-fledged sign languages, in which the gestural channel serves as the vehicle for language itself, and where the movements involved have typical language-like properties: duality of patterning, conventional symbolism, syntax, and so on. Ranging in between are such phenomena as nonce pantomimes (meant to signal on their own, without speech, but non-conventionalized); culture-specific emblems which function as complete "quotable" (Kendon 1992) utterances, independent of or substitutable for speech (giving someone "the finger," for example); or "substitute" sign languages which replace speech in whole or in part under circumstances that require silence.[2]

Unfortunately this typology, too, is essentially subtractive: it gives priority to presumed independent properties of "language" – especially compositionality and conventional meaning – and arrays gesture against them. As a result, important complications in the semiotic modalities, cultural variability, and interactive significance of gesture can be easily overlooked.

Consider the three gestural "types" that have received the most empirical attention in recent literature: (1) conventionalized language-specific emblems, which in most ways are just like words or spoken expressions, except that they are performed in an unspoken modality; (2) gesticulations which "are characterized by an obligatory accompaniment of speech, a lack of language-defining properties, idiosyncratic form–meaning pairings, and a precise synchronization of meaning presentations in gestures with co-expressive speech segments" (McNeill 2000): 1), and of these especially those termed "iconic," that is, whose significations derive from some resemblance between gestural form (signifier) and signified; and (3) "pointing" gestures.

Typical and perhaps unfamiliar emblems from my own field research include the *guya* or "nothing" gesture used by Guugu Yimithirr speakers from Queensland, Australia. The gesturer displays an open, empty palm (figure 9.2), a non-spoken equivalent to the highly functional word *guya* which can mean "nothing, none, all gone" or just "not." In the example, J is describing how he tried to recover the cargo of a boat wrecked during a storm. He found some bananas, but the clothes and salted pork were lost. J presents the "nothing" emblem after talking about how the bananas were strewn around on the beach.

(2) "Guya"
3   mayi-ngay maalbiin-ngay nyulu   maani
    food-PL   banana-PL   3sNOM get+PAST
    He got the food, the bananas.

    . . a . . . .
4   thambarr-in guwaar
    throw-PAST west-R
    It had been thrown up to the west.

..b............ c.....

5   thambarr-in yi:
     throw-PAST here
     thrown all around.

                              R hand up, out to W, circles anticlockwise (fingers pointing S) at a
                              and b, then "*Guya*" hand at c

6   couldn't find the clothes

7   couldn't find the *minha* (meat)

Figure 9.2   *Guya* 'nothing'

A somewhat more lexical emblem in Zinacantec Tzotzil, formed with a curved index
finger approaching but not quite touching a curved thumb, the rest of the fingers
folded into the palm, represents a *copita* (shot glass for liquor). In the following
narrative this gesture provides semantic supplementation, as the corresponding
spoken word, *uch'bajel*, literally signifies any beverage, where what the protagonists
were asking for was *pox*, locally distilled cane liquor.

(3) "Uch'bajel"
17   k'u xak'an xi
      "*What do you want?*" *she said.*

      [..1] [2................ ....]
19   mi oy uch'bajel? o:y . mi mu oyuk
      "*Is there anything to drink?*" "*There is, (do you think) there isn't?*"

                              1. Right hand raised in shot-glass gesture, one stroke at *oy*
                              2. "Copita" hand drops into second stroke at *uch'*, then
                                 down in same handshape to rest

We have already seen an example of typical "iconic" but non-conventionalized
gesticulation in the circling buzzards story. Here is another sequence in Zinacantec
Tzotzil which illustrates first a pointing gesture and then an interestingly interrelated
iconic but non-conventionalized gesture. A man is talking about encountering a
supernatural demon, which he tried to catch. The demon ran off to hide behind
the house cross in the man's yard. First the narrator uses a pointing gesture to his
right to locate his protagonist in a narrated space which he constructs with the

Figure 9.3   *Uch'bajel* 'beverage'

gesture itself (see figure 9.4). He explains that the demon – only the size of a small child – tried to hide *behind* the cross, now using his right hand, its back facing outwards, fingers down, and moving slightly from side to side (see figure 9.5), to portray evidently both the cross and the position of the demon behind it.

(4) "Ijatav"

        ba   j -tzak
        go(AUX) 1E-grab
        I went to grab it.

        1 ..... 2 ....
        i -0   -jatav un
        CP-3A-run_away PT
        It ran away

                1. Turn face to right and sight to spot some distance away, then return to front
                2. Right arm extends out in point to R (SW), then back to rest at knee

Figure 9.4   *Ijatav* 'it ran away'

```
3.....                   4......... ........a....b
te      i -0 -bat        yo`   pat   krus -e
there  CP-3A-go          where back  cross-CL
```
It went there behind the cross.

    3. Look quickly out R again, then back

    4. R arm lifts out R and slightly to front, (a) circles anticlockwise, index finger slightly down, (b) moving all slightly L and held

Figure 9.5 *Yo` pat kruse* 'behind the cross'

4 GESTURE AS LANGUAGE

It is plain from these examples that gesture is "language-like" in several important respects. Emblems are conventional symbols, characteristically self-reflexive, glossable, and quotable (so that both narrator and by extension protagonist can be imagined to be making the *guya* gesture in figure 9.2) much like spoken words or expressions. Moreover, emblems are capable of limited syntax-like construction. That is, they combine with spoken expressions, as logical arguments or predicates. Words provide the subjects – "clothes" and "meat" – for the "predicate" *guya* in J's narrative. Similarly, the *copita* gesture can be understood as parallel syntactic subject (along with the spoken *uch'bajel*) for the existential *oy* 'exist' with which it first cooccurs in line 19 of example (3). Emblems can also combine with other gestures: J's *guya* hand is produced in conjunction with a sweeping, circular motion that can be seen as an iconic rendering of the rolling and tossing of the waves and the direction of the wind which carried the sunken boat's cargo away, suggesting that the loss of food and clothes was a consequence of the depicted movement of wind and waves.

CS Peirce

There is also complete semiotic parallelism between gestures and other linguistic signs in terms of the familiar Peircean trichotomy of icon (e.g., an "hourglass" motion to suggest a particular human body shape, P's circling gesture mimicking the encircling buzzards), index ("pointing toward" or even touching or holding a referent, or in the demon case pointing "as if" toward, and thus indexically creating, a virtual referent), and symbol (a purely conventional "thumbs up" gesture, for example, in addition to other emblems we have seen). The principles on which the signification of gestures and words is based, that is, are exactly the same.

The semiotic parallel between gesture and the rest of language extends to its "arbitrariness" – a degree of non-motivated conventionality – and to its indexical links to contexts of speaking, which display the characteristic range from relatively presupposing – that is, signaling aspects of context already present or taken for granted – to relatively creative (Silverstein 1976) – that is, bringing new aspects of context into relief.

Consider the pointing gesture in figure 9.4. It is easy to forget that the extended index finger pointing hand is pure convention, perhaps because it is such a widespread convention. But conventional it clearly is, as people can point with chin or lips (Sherzer 1972), or with a different finger or fingers, or with quite distinct and significant handshapes (Foster 1948; Poyatos 1983). (And why, as Wittgenstein asked, does one point *toward* a referent as opposed to, say, in exactly the opposite direction, or by placing the hand above the object, etc.?)

Notice the indexical complexity of the pointing gesture. While it may frequently be possible to point at a referent right where it is, when A points to the demon in figure 9.4 there is actually nothing there for him to point at. He creates a virtual location for the narrated demon, a complex layering of both the present space where A sits and the imagined space (his yard with a demon in it) which he invites his interlocutors to create with their minds. His pointing gesture itself "creates" the "referent" at which it points. Having thus established a location, jointly in the imagined narrated space and his immediate physical surround, A can then go on to populate the space further: he places the demon *behind a house cross*, using a representative gesture to show the spatial relation between cross (evidently represented iconically by the extended index finger in figure 9.5) and hiding demon (via a movement of the hand backwards). Indexical gestures are thus susceptible to the typical shifts of deictic center (the perspective from which, for example, direction is to be understood) called "transpositions" by Karl Bühler and characteristic of spoken deictics as well (see Hanks 1990). Transpositions of considerably more complexity are routinely managed in gesture (see Haviland 1996).

Insofar as gestural typologies ignore or minimize such semiotic complexity in the different gestural "types" they isolate, the classificatory impulse seems analytically obfuscating rather than helpful.

Varieties of gesture may instead be aligned against a different tripartite scheme which associates three analytical threads with any linguistic act: form, practice, and ideology (Silverstein (1985). Insofar as they are readily susceptible to such analytical decomposition, gestures again reveal their language-like character. I will concentrate in the next section on formal aspects of gesture, turning at the end of the chapter to practice and ideology.

4.1   Gestural form

First, observe that gesture exhibits highly structured formal articulation. The most influential characterization of the unfolding production of gestures is due to Kendon (1980), who describes three gestural "phases": **preparation**, where the hand or other articulator moves from rest to a position from which the main gesture, or **stroke**, can be produced, followed by a **retraction** to rest. Both preparation and retraction can be omitted, and the stroke may itself be parsed by one or more **holds**.

In the circling buzzards example, P begins with his right hand in his lap. The preparation phase of his gesture involves lifting the hand and moving it out to P's right, at the same time shaping the hand for the circling movement (by extending the index finger and turning the hand palm-inward – see the movement shown as 1 on figure 9.1). The stroke – the first circling gesture – is then performed, punctuated by a brief hold (between movements 3 and 4 on figure 9.1), and then the second circling motion. After the gestural stroke is completed, the hand begins to relax and move back to P's lap in the retraction phase.

Gesture also displays some degree of "morphology" – a systematic association of form with function. Gestural gestalts may often be profitably decomposed into distinct articulations (hand shapes, for example, or certain patterns of movement which are also among the formal primitives of developed sign languages). The typical pointing index finger is one example, and there are also standardized hand forms in emblems – the thumbs up, the "OK" hand and other related families of handshapes, such as that called "the ring", the "hand purse" (Morris 1977: 38; Kendon 1997, 2000), among others.

Conventions of gestural form are of course not limited to fingers and hands. Although the details may vary and the meanings frequently contrast from one cultural context to another, facial expressions (frowns, smiles, eye flashes, winks), gaze (staring and its direction, closed eyes, avoidance or engagement of eye contact), head movements (nods, shakes, tilts), and postures and movements of torso, shoulders, and other body parts may figure in a community's gestural repertoire. Consider the shrug, the haughty nose, the sigh, pointed or pursed lips (see Sherzer 1972), demurely crossed legs, and so on. Even the orientation of the body may have conventional communicative significance, a fact of some importance for recent studies of sign language morphology (see Liddell 2000). Or consider how, in some communicative traditions, one can refer to the time of day by gazing indexically at the zone of the heavens where the sun would appear. An example from a Zinacantec Tzotzil narrative appears in figure 9.6.

In this example, X is describing a fateful truck ride that ended in a crash. He uses his whole torso to illustrate how the truck was so overloaded it swayed ominously from side to side (figure 9.7).

The body itself can also be the indexical space on which gestures are performed. A frequent device in Tzotzil gesture is the use of interactants' own bodies as referents, indicated by pointing, touching, or otherwise rendering prominent certain body parts and bodily attitudes. "*Och i tan ta ssat.* (The ashes entered his eye)," recalls a Zinacantec, talking about a relative who survived a volcanic eruption in 1903. He simultaneously points to his own eye (figure 9.8). Similarly, X describes how another

Figure 9.6 "In the afternoon, about 2 o'clock"

Figure 9.7 "The truck went this way"

Figure 9.8 "Ashes entered his eye"

Zinacantec was hurt in the truck crash. He quotes the injured man and gestures to his own chest, doubly transposing his protagonist onto himself in both word and body. *"Voch'em yàel ko'on,' xi"* ("My chest feels crushed," he said). (Figure 9.9.) In many gestures, a speaker's body provides the vehicle for representing the anatomies of others, protagonists and props alike.

Figure 9.9   " 'My chest feels crushed,' he said"

Nor are speakers limited to their own bodies in gesture. They can also use props. Anthropologists have analyzed the manipulation both of trowels or brushes and of the ground itself together with the associated conceptual artifacts in the didactic gestures of archaeologists (C. Goodwin 1994), or the incorporation of the hopscotch board and stone into gestures about the progress of a children's game (see M. Goodwin 1995). My Zinacantec compadres routinely gesture with the tools in hand: hoes, sticks, and machetes.

In figure 9.10, P demonstrates to his interlocutor which weed to remove from the beanfield by selecting an exemplar and chopping it with his hoe, a kind of mediated "iconic" gesture that also depends obviously on Peircean indexicality.

Aspects of gestural morphology may be systematically deployed to express semantic inflections overlaid on the meaning of a gestalt (Calbris 1990; Kendon 1995). Performing a pointing gesture relatively higher than lower, for example, may system-atically "inflect" the gesture to suggest a relatively more distant referent. In the following extract, J describes walking eastwards one full night to return to his community after the shipwreck. His gesture traces an eastward trajectory (here, east lies behind him), and it rises higher and higher, evidently to emphasize just how far he had to walk, before reaching his destination (shown by a swift final downward point).

Figure 9.10   Pointing out a plant by hoeing it

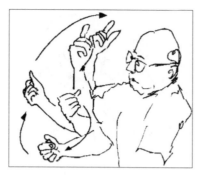

Figure 9.11   "Eastward, eastward..."

(5) Going East to Cape Bedford
```
...... a...... ........... b...... c.......
```
    .. nag aalu nagaalu yi: (.)
    EAST-L   EAST-L   here
    (We kept going) East and East.
    R: up in "bent L," beats downwards at (a), rises to apex above right ear at
        (b) pointing upwards; head bends down and finger sweeps front and
        down to point at ground at (c)

I have examined a further aspect of conventional form in some gestural traditions: the fact that gestures are performed with what might be called the "correct" orientations (Haviland 1993, 2000b). If a narrative protagonist swims north, the gestures illustrating his motion also are performed toward the north, for example. Such highly regimented gestures allow analysts, and presumably interlocutors, to distinguish various "spaces" in which gestures (and their depicted referents) can be performed: those that are intrinsically oriented, and those that are free from such orientational precision, or which respond to different regimenting factors. For example, Guugu Yimithirr speakers such as J tend to orient precisely, in both word and gesture, all events involving directional vectors. However, gestures can also be freed from precise orientation, especially when they are placed in the "interactional" space, either immediate or narrated, between interlocutors.

J describes what he saw when he looked back toward the wrecked boat from the beach: a giant shark fin cutting through the water just where he and his companion had swum to shore. First he represents the shark fin – all three feet of it – in the interactional space between him and his interlocutors (figure 9.12).

(6) Shark fin
```
>............ .... {gesture}......... .........
```
    three feet of.   gagan.gu wanggaar.
    (There were) three feet of fin standing up

When he goes on to describe the direction of the capsized boat, however, he places the fin precisely to the North (figure 9.13), just as it would have been from the vantage point of the beach on which he had been standing at the time.

Figure 9.12   "Three feet of fin"

(6 continued)
　　　　　　　{gesture} . . . .
　　　　　　　thumbuurrgu **gunggaarr** thadaara-y ngali gada-y
　　　　　　　– *going straight north right where we had come.*

That some spaces in which gestures are performed can be precisely oriented in this way provides a further resource for interlocutors: it allows them to transpose, overlay, combine, and laminate various spaces to precise communicational effect. This is what J relies on in the pointing gesture in figure 9.13: his precisely oriented gesture in effect instructs his interlocutors to perform a complex mental calculation, imagining themselves at the narrated spot, and then transposing the current indicated direction onto the narrated shark fin. Here conventionally fixed features of the spaces in which gestures are performed are available for interactive exploitation and interpretation.

　　As a final example of conventionality in gestural form, it is worth mentioning that features of the verbal semantics or morpho-lexical typology of particular languages may be conventionally incorporated into gestural performances. Rather few studies have investigated such phenomena in detail, in part because there are few typological

N

Figure 9.13   "Going straight north right where we had come"

models which provide adequate parameters for comparison in either the spoken or gestural domains. One exception is the typology of motion events proposed by Talmy (1985) and the predicted limited set of possibilities for the lexicalization of motion, a proposal which has inspired multiple cross-linguistic studies of both adult and child language. The gestural performances of speakers of languages which differ in how they lexicalize motion, path, and manner and where such aspects of a narrated event are represented in the clause may be compared (see Müller 1994).

More specifically, Kita (1993) compared Japanese and English descriptions of a scene which involved "spatial information that is difficult to verbalize in Japanese because of the lack of an appropriate lexical item" (Kita 2000: 167) – in this case, an idiosyncratic lexical fact rather than a more general typological pattern. He found an interesting asymmetry, in which English speakers use gestures that evidently correspond to the semantic features of the accompanying lexical item ("swing"), whereas Japanese speakers, lacking any such lexical item, tend to produce pairs of representational gestures, suggesting that different "forces" are at work in their production:

> One force shapes the representational gesture so as to make it as isomorphic as possible with a spatio-motoric model of the stimulus scene. The other shapes the representational gesture so as to make its informational content as compatible as possible with linguistic encoding possibilities. These two forces shape the gestures in the same direction in English utterances, but in Japanese utterances they are in competition. (Kita 2000): 168)

For Kita such phenomena relate to the cognitive processes at work as speakers "retrieve" information to produce linguistic renditions of events, classic "thinking for speaking" (Slobin 1987).

Moreover, languages may exhibit distinct expressive "styles," evidenced in typological patterns of grammar and lexicon. Mesoamerican languages are noted for the lexical hypertrophy surrounding concepts of shape, configuration, and position (Friedrich 1971). My comparative work on three Mayan languages from highland Chiapas suggests that the exuberant use of "positional" roots in spoken Tzotzil, Tseltal, and Ch'ol – part of the local linguistic aesthetic of "speaking well" – has a corresponding gestural expression: iconic gestures tend to cluster around lexical affiliates from the category of positional roots. The circling buzzards example, with which we began, illustrates the general point: the predicate *setel* "in a circle" which P chooses to elaborate in gesture is derived from a positional root *set* which suggests a disc-like shape, a closed arc in a single plane. The root forms the basis for dozens of full lexical forms; these derived words pepper proper Tzotzil speech and seem to attract gestures.

A parallel case from Tseltal offers a useful comparison. Retelling a cartoon episode in circumstances that seemed to constrain him from gesturing at all, a Tseltal speaker, A, makes only five representational gestures in 75 seconds of continuous speech. All five coincide synchronically with motion or positional verbs. Only one such gesture lasts more than a few tenths of a second, and it is illustrated in figure 9.14.

In the original cartoon sequence, an apple tree is shown with a fence in front of it. The cartoon character is unable to reach the apples because of the fence. The narrator's Tseltal phrase appears in example (7).

Figure 9.14   *Makal o joyul* 'closed or surrounded'

(7) "Enclosed tree"
makal   o   joyul   ta- ta mak-teˋ
CLOSED or SURROUNDED by by FENCE
It was enclosed by a fence.

Here both *makal* (from the root *mak* 'close') and *joyul* (from *joy* 'surround') are members of the overall positional class in Tseltal. Although the cartoon image suggests a scene in which the apple tree is behind a straight picket fence running alongside a path, A's version clearly implies that the tree was encircled by a protective fence. He has apparently recoded the geometry – perhaps to coincide with a conventional Tseltal way of enclosing fruit trees – as is shown by his double choice of words, reinforced by the gestured image.

Kendon's (1988) study of the "alternate" sign language of Warlpiri speakers in Australia, where women in mourning forgo speech in favor of signing, sometimes permanently, also suggests semantic and structural links between spoken Warlpiri and the conventionalized sign language that replaces speech. An inverse case is that in which an aphasic person must rely largely on gesture to interact with his interlocutors (Goodwin 2000). The interlocutors, in turn, know that the aphasic person still "has language" – indeed, they knew his former verbal skills well – but has lost the ability to produce it orally. They interpret his gestured communications as homologous to something he *might* have said, or wants to say, that is, against the background of his customary patterns of communication.

5   GESTURE IN ACTION

In its formal properties, then, gesture is language-like. A further hallmark of language is its role in action, its performative character (Austin 1962). How language-like is gesture in this respect?

Emblems clearly involve their own miniature actions. Giving someone "the finger" is as effective an insult as most verbal imprecations, and the gestured pronouncements of the emperor or the umpire carry legislative force: they can order "off with her head" or declare "yer out," and gesturing makes it so. The priest makes the sign of the cross and thereby blesses; the Zinacantec shaman brushes her patient with a pine bough as she prays, and both words and motions are part of removing illness. None of this is surprising, given the fact that emblems are functionally unspoken holophrases, that is, "gesture acts" equivalent to so-called speech acts.

There is an important line of research linking gesture in a more general sense to contexts of action. Much of the work mentioned so far draws conclusions about the *expressive* capacities of gesture from the coincidence of gesticulation and speech in *narrative* or *conversational* contexts: people (re)telling stories, discussing, arguing, reminiscing. However, when people are engaged in other kinds of activities, where the point of the interaction is something other than the talk itself – making things, cultivating gardens, fixing cars, planning and coordinating joint ventures, and the like – the relationships between gesture and word may reveal themselves in different ways. For one thing, the potential emancipation of gesture from talk may be clearer in situations where the hand rather than the mouth is doing the talking.

Consider the simple if controversial example of the common "pointing" gesture with outstretched hand and extended index finger. It has long been suggested that this conventionalized "symbolic" gesture develops out of a child's grasping and reaching motions,[3] and work of Lourdes de León and myself (Haviland 2000a) confirms a developmental sequence among Zinacantec infants beginning with real attempts to grab and ending with clearly symbolic pointing emancipated from real physical manipulation.[4]

Children's early gestural routines are often linked retrospectively with their motoric development and prospectively with their first words. Bates, Bretherton, Shore, and McNew (1983) make the strong claim that "*all* of the child's first words . . . begin as actions or procedures for the child. The infant does not 'have' her first words; she 'does' them" (p. 65). Lock (1993) characterizes some "expressive" or "instrumental" communicative gestures (clapping, for example, or "asking" with an outstretched open palm) as "actions that are 'lifted' from [the child's] direct manipulation of the world" (p. 280).

There is a striking parallel here with the perspective taken by some gesture researchers (see LeBaron and Streeck 2000), that adult representational gestures are linked to non-symbolic, practical, instrumental routines of the hands (and other gesture articulators). Recall P's use of a real hoe and a genuine hoeing motion to signal the sorts of weeds that require hoeing (figure 9.10). Or consider how M, another Zinacantec man, gestures as he describes how people have stolen pine needles from his forest tract, accompanying the highly specific Tzotzil verb *ni`* 'bend down (the flexible end of a longish thing)' with a sequence of motions (figure 9.15) like those one performs in stripping pine needles from a branch.

Teaching situations, playing games, and many other practical activities provide contexts in which one can "explain" or "describe" better by showing or "demonstrating" (Clark and Gerrig 1990) than by saying. Indeed, the teacher's use of diagrams, props, maps, and the blackboard tends to merge into her use of bodily gestures, as demonstrations move off the body and onto the wider stage of the teacher's environment (Ochs, Gonzales, and Jacoby 1996; Roth and Lawless 2002). The field, the court, the archaeological site, and the hopscotch grid become simultaneously field of action and context for demonstration. Moreover, as some authors have demonstrated with great elegance, the origin of many so-called iconic gestures can be directly observed in situations in which interlocutors first directly manipulate objects in the world, and gradually in the course of an interaction

Figure 9.15   "Bend down the tops of the trees"

emancipate their gestures from instrumental action, concurrently often simplifying or stylizing the original manipulative movements as they acquire symbolic properties (LeBaron and Streeck 2000). The natural history here is reminiscent of the initial elaboration and gradual slimming down of complex referring expressions across the course of a collaborative interaction, a process documented semi-experimentally in Clark and Wilkes-Gibbs (1986).

Locating gesture's origins in the conceptual realm of action rather than that of pure symbolization brings us back to another theoretically interesting equivalence between gesture and the rest of language: not only do there exist gesture/speech acts, but the construction of context and the coordination of action (Clark 1997) is achieved in similar ways by both gestures and words. Clark (1997) argues that a family of gestures he calls "placing" – putting an object in a position within an interactive space as a deliberate communication – complements the kinds of indicating we call "pointing." "Placing" one's desired purchase on the clerk's checkout counter is as good if not better a way to signal what one wants as pointing to it on the store shelf. Placing objects, via gesture, is an equally effective way of creating a context – a universe of discourse – within which further interactive communication, by word or gesture, is made possible, a device familiar in sign-language pronouns as well as in situations like the following.

Two Zinacantec neighbors are talking about the seating arrangements at a fiesta in a distant Tzotzil village. First M, the man on the right in figure 9.16, describes how

Figure 9.16   M sets up the scene: women in a circle, incense in the middle

women with ritual obligations are seated in a large circle, incense burning in the middle. He places the women around the space where he sits using both hands, and then he locates the incense with his right hand.

M's interlocutor X, who has witnessed the same ritual on another occasion, elaborates the description, in both word and gesture, building on the spatial scene which M has already initiated and placed onto the local interactive stage. He gives each woman her own incense burner, showing how these too are lined up in a wide circle, with the saint's image located in the center of the circle. (X draws the circle of women and incense burners with his right hand and then "places" the saint image in the middle with his left, partially mirroring M's original performance.)

Finally, X draws the scene once more, emphasizing with an arc traced nearly 360 degrees in the air just how many people are seated in the ritual circle.

Here M's initial gestures "create" a discursive context, and populate it with individual entities (much like the pronouns of American Sign Language). X's continuing description resumes the universe so created and elaborates it both verbally and gesturally. Gesture is action not only by virtue of its direct performativity, but by providing the contextual domain for further action, including the prototypical narrative "action" of reference.

Figure 9.17   X elaborates on the same scene: incense all around, saint in the middle

Figure 9.18   The great ritual circle traced in the air

6   GESTURE AND IDEOLOGY

The third "irreducible" aspect or "level" of a linguistic datum, mediating "the unstable mutual interaction of meaningful sign forms, contextualized to situations of interested human use" in the characterization of Silverstein (1985), is what he calls "the fact of cultural ideology."[5] Gesture – already shown to contextualize "meaningful sign forms" to "situations of use" – further shares with the rest of language a susceptibility to ideological productions. A moment's reflection on what we have already seen shows how deeply ideologized gesture is, and how differential theories about and justifications for (or against) gesture are bound up with its very nature and form. For example, the earliest Western scholarly attention to gesture linked gestural use to purposeful persuasive oratory, on the one hand, and to the "natural" expression of human thought, on the other. At the heart of such approaches to gesture are powerful ideologies about expression, persuasion, appropriate communication, and human nature and its differential expressions. (Moreover, all the theories of gesture espoused in this brief chapter – including my own – are liable to a similar deconstruction.)

One such theory, inspiration both for many popular treatments of gesture and for McNeill's influential research program, is captured in McNeill's opening inscription to *Hand and Mind*, from Napier (1980): "If language was given to men to conceal their thoughts, then gesture's purpose was to disclose them." From pop psychological treatises on how to decipher people's body language to altogether more sinister theories about twitches, ticks, and fidgeting as evidence of culpability (in a criminal trial in which I was once involved as expert witness, a policeman testified that he knew the defendant was guilty because of a pulsating vein in his neck and the shifty way he used his eyes when he talked), there runs a consistent theme that gesture springs involuntarily from the speaker, betraying whatever his or her words may be trying to hide.

Another pervasive ideology of gesture is inherent in the injunction "It's not polite to point." Perhaps because pointing is indiscreet – perceivable, even by the pointee, whether or not the accompanying speech can be heard – or represents untoward attention, poor upbringing, or insufficient self-control, it falls into the clutches of cultural arbiters of value and good taste. (The Cuna "pointed-lip-gesture" has as one of its advantages, according to Sherzer (1972), that it is less obvious a way to point than using the hands.)

Moreover, if Roman orators sought to become more persuasive by choreographing their gestures, it is equally possible that the hyper-expressivity associated with gesture can be a motive for criticism and scorn: gesticulators are over-exuberant, too expressive, probably vulgar. Kendon uses the phrase "communication ecology": a relation between "communicational style – and the role of gesture within this –" and "the ecology of everyday life 'in public' " (Kendon 1997: 117). He notes that "gesturing, like speech, is influenced by cultural values and historical tradition, and its usage is adjusted according to the setting, social circumstance, and micro-organization of any given occasion of interaction" (Kendon 1997: 117). Indeed, Kendon hints at an "ecological" account for the celebrated (or, conversely, notorious) prominence of Neapolitan gestures (Kendon 1995).

There is little doubt that good talkers are often also expert gesturers. Consider the Guugu Yimithirr story-teller J, whom we met in figures 9.2 and 9.12. Here was a man whom everyone in the community knew to be a master story-teller. But what exactly makes a master story-teller? For me, much of J's effectiveness as a raconteur came from his exceptionally skillful gesturing. His gestures were invitations, spare and efficient instructions that elicited interlocutors' active and inferential participation in his narratives. That is, he made his gestures work for him.

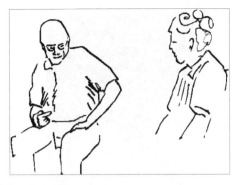

Figure 9.19 "Your father-in-law"

Here is one example. In Australian Aboriginal society in general people try to avoid naming the deceased. In recent Guugu Yimithirr history, some people's names were simply replaced when their bearers died, often erasing quite common words from the permissible lexicon. In one of J's narratives he needs to refer to a long-deceased but powerful old man, who happened to be the father-in-law of his interlocutor R. He accomplishes the reference by uttering an indirect referential noun phrase coupled with a pointing gesture to his interlocutor. The pointing gesture well precedes the spoken characterization that amplifies it, inviting all present – and especially R – to begin to work out for themselves who the intended referent was. The gesture is a discreet, culturally appropriate, and silent alternative to speaking a name that must not be spoken.

(8)   Your old father-in-law
                              {pointing gesture} . . . .
        ngali b   bada gaari gada-y   nhaa-thi   ngaathiina
        1duNOM down not   come-PAST see-PAST father-in-law
        We didn't go down there with –

        = nhanu-mu-gal   nyulu   nguba   ngaliin   gurra-ya
        2sGEN-CAT-ADESS 3sNOM perhaps 1duACC say-PRECAUT
        – with your father-in-law, see, since he was liable to scold us.

Let me end with two final reflections on gestural ideology. First consider how people learn to gesture in the first place – an important topic in its own right that is largely beyond the scope of this chapter.[6] My one-year-old Zinacantec goddaughter Mal, for example, had a large collection of stylized routines, including the deliberately communicative "sleep" gesture shown in figure 9.20. Notable here is the Zinacantec metatheory – that is, ideology – about such communications. Whereas the Western traditions referred to above distinguish between gesture and talk from the beginning, and then try in various ways either to bring the phenomena back together or to distinguish them at a more profound level, Zinacantecs talk about performances like that of Mal simply as speech. The same speech-act verbs used with verbalizations frame descriptions of such little routines: " 'I'm going to sleep,' she says." The same quotative evidential particles are applied to unspoken, or inferred, gestural communications as to words. And the same communicative intentions are attributed to preverbal, gesturing infants as to speaking adults.

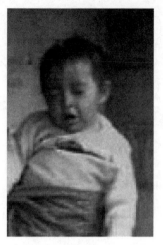

Figure 9.20   Mal's "sleep" gesture

Finally, we may note in passing an entirely different interest in gesture with its own ideological underpinnings: ongoing efforts to make machines more "lifelike" or more "natural" by giving them "gestural" capabilities.[7] Robots, as well as avatars and intelligent agents for computer interfaces, are increasingly equipped to "gesture" in human-like ways, so as to be more effective communicators with human interlocutors. Here is a peculiarly Western notion of naturalness, since the gesturing body could never have been emancipated from the speaking soul except by technological decoupling. Quintillian, the grand ancestor of the whole field of Western gestural studies, lives again after two millennia.

7   CONCLUSION

I began this chapter with questions that grow out of a debate grounded in the sorts of ideologies just considered. Are gestures just involuntary excrescences of the speaking process? Are they inherently linked to language itself? Are they communicative, whether intentionally or despite the speaker's best efforts? What can and do interlocutors make of them?

I argued that gesture is taken as a communicative resource and exploited by interactants, whatever competing psychological theories may argue. Assuming such a position, I considered a range of proposals for classifying gestures and linking them to the rest of language. Working through a parade of examples, I illustrated how word and gesture exhibit complementary meaningfulness; how gesture may be regimented by convention, but also ephemeral, invented, and idiosyncratic; and how gesture shares semiotic modalities with speech. Further to underscore that gesture is part of language, I gave an inventory of the formal properties of gesture – its articulation and morphology – and linked the "meaningful sign forms" thus uncovered to the particularities of specific languages on the one hand, as well as to partially shared techniques of the body and human action, on the other. Finally I turned to cultural ideologies of gesture: linkages between gesture and values, standards of behavior, and theories of language and mind. My conclusion is that gesture is part of language, in its full range of pragmatic functions, and that it is thus as insistently deserving of anthropological attention as spoken words and the deeds they constitute.

NOTES

1 Transcribed examples show the original language, sometimes with a morpheme-by-morpheme gloss, and a free English gloss. Above the speech appear verbal descriptions of synchronized gestures and gesture segments, sometimes labeled to correspond to parts of the accompanying illustrations or to more detailed descriptions following the transcript line.
2 David McNeill has elaborated the typology, breaking it into separate continua with different dimensions, in his seminal book *Hand and Mind* (McNeill 1992) and in McNeill (2000).
3 Vygotsky (1978): 56) calls this process "internalization," as Alessandro Duranti has pointed out to me; see the empirical studies in Carter (1975), McNeill (1985), Hannan (1992).
4 But see Lock, Young, Service, and Chandler (1990).
5 See Kroskrity (this volume).
6 In acquisition, it appears that universally gesture and spoken or other linguistic forms emerge together (whether shared or parallel processes are at work). Gestural routines in which stylized movements play central communicative roles appear before the first recognizable words. Moreover, the so-called "one word stage" is characterized by the production not of "words" alone but of combined gestural and verbalized routines at the earliest stages of language learning. Phenomena such as gestural "babbling" (Petitto and Marentette 1991) or the spontaneous language-like "home sign" systems which arise in contexts where deaf children are not exposed to a pre-existing sign language (Goldin-Meadow 1993) attest to the insistence of manual and other bodily "expressions" in human communication, waiting in the cognitive wings to be summoned on stage by appropriate social and interactive contexts.
7 There is a large relevant literature here beyond my professional expertise. I refer the interested reader to the MIT media lab (http://www.media.mit.edu) and to such volumes as http://www.TechFak.Uni-Bielefeld.DE/ags/wbski/gw2001book for further references.

REFERENCES

Austin, J. L. (1962). *How to Do Things with Words*. Cambridge, MA: Harvard University Press.
Bates, E., Bretherton, I., Shore, C., and McNew, S. (1983). Names, Gestures, and Objects: Symbolization in Infancy and Aphasia. In K. E. Nelson (ed.), *Children's Language*, vol. 4 (pp. 59–123). Hillsdale, NJ: Lawrence Erlbaum.
Calbris, G. (1990). *The Semiotics of French Gesture*. Bloomington: Indiana University Press.
Carter, A. L. (1975). The Transformation of Sensorimotor Morphemes into Words: A Case Study of the Development of "More" and "Mine". *Journal of Child Language* 2: 233–250.
Clark, H. (1997). Indicating and Placing. Paper presented at the workshop "Pointing," Max Planck Institute for Psycholinguistics, Oud Turnhout, Belgium, June 1997.
Clark, H., and Gerrig, R. J. (1990). Quotations as Demonstrations. *Language* 66(4): 764–805.

Clark, H. H., and Wilkes-Gibbs, D. (1986). Referring as a Collaborative Process. *Cognition* 22: 1–39.

Foster, G. M. (1948). *Empire's Children, The People of Tzinzuntzan*. Washington, DC: Smithsonian Institution. Institute of Social Anthropology Publication 6.

Friedrich, P. (1971). *The Tarascan Suffixes of Locative Space: Meaning and Morphotactics*. Bloomington: Indiana University Press.

Goldin-Meadow, S. (1993). When Does Gesture Become Language? A Study of Gesture Used as a Primary Communication System by Deaf Children of Hearing Parents. In K. R. Gibson and T. Ingold (eds.), *Tools, Language, and Cognition in Human Evolution* (pp. 63–85). Cambridge: Cambridge University Press.

Goodwin, C. (1994). Professional Vision. *American Anthropologist* 96(3): 606–633.

Goodwin, C. (2000). Gesture, Aphasia, and Interaction. In D. McNeill (ed.), *Language and Gesture* (pp. 84–98). Cambridge: Cambridge University Press.

Goodwin, M. H. (1995). Co-construction in Girls' Hopscotch. *Research on Language and Social Interaction* 28(3): 261–282.

Graf, F. (1992). Gestures and Conventions: The Gestures of Roman Actors and Orators. In J. Bremmer and H. Roodenburg (eds.), *A Cultural History of Language* (pp. 36–58). Ithaca: Cornell University Press.

Hanks, W. F. (1990). *Referential Practice*. Chicago: University of Chicago Press.

Hannan, Thomas E. (1992). An Examination of Spontaneous Pointing in 20- to 50-month-old Children. *Perceptual and Motor Skills* 74 (April 1992): 651–658.

Haviland, J. B. (1993). Anchoring, Iconicity, and Orientation in Guugu Yimithirr Pointing Gestures. *Journal of Linguistic Anthropology* 3(1): 3–45.

Haviland, J. B. (1996). Projections, Transpositions, and Relativity. In J. J. Gumperz and S. C. Levinson (eds.), *Rethinking Linguistic Relativity* (pp. 271–323). Cambridge: Cambridge University Press.

Haviland, J. B. (2000a). Early Pointing Gestures in Zinacantan. *Journal of Linguistic Anthropology* 8(2): 162–196.

Haviland, J. B. (2000b). Pointing, Gesture Spaces, and Mental Maps. In D. McNeill (ed.), *Language and Gesture* (pp. 13–46). Cambridge: Cambridge University Press.

Kendon, A. (1980). Gesticulation and Speech: Two Aspects of the Process of Utterance. In M. R. Key (ed.), *Relationship between Verbal and Nonverbal Communication* (pp. 207–227). The Hague: Mouton.

Kendon, A. (1988). *Sign Languages of Aboriginal Australia*. Cambridge: Cambridge University Press.

Kendon, A. (1992). Some Recent Work from Italy on *Quotable Gestures (Emblems)*. *Journal of Linguistic Anthropology* 2(1): 92–108.

Kendon, A. (1995). The Open Hand: Observations for a Study of Compositionality in Gesture. Paper presented at the conference "Gesture," Albuquerque, July 1995.

Kendon, A. (1997). Gesture. *Annual Review of Anthropology* 26: 109–128.

Kendon, A. (2000). Language and Gesture: Unity or Duality? In D. McNeill (ed.), *Language and Gesture* (pp. 47–63). Cambridge: Cambridge University Press.

Kita, S. (1993). Language and Thought Interface: A Study of Spontaneous Gestures and Japanese Mimetics. Unpublished PhD dissertation, University of Chicago.

Kita, S. (2000). How Representational Gestures Help Speaking. In D. McNeill (ed.), *Language and Gesture* (pp. 162–185). Cambridge: Cambridge University Press.

Laughlin, R. M. (1975). *The Great Tzotzil Dictionary of San Lorenzo Zinacantan*. Washington, DC: Smithsonian Institution Press.

LeBaron, C., and Streeck, J. (2000). Gestures, Knowledge, and the World. In D. McNeill (ed.), *Language and Gesture* (pp. 118–138). Cambridge: Cambridge University Press.

Liddell, S. K. (2000). Blended Spaces and Deixis in Sign Language Discourse. In D. McNeill (ed.), *Language and Gesture* (pp. 331–357). Cambridge: Cambridge University Press.

Lock, A. J. (1993). Human Language Development and Object Manipulation: Their Relation in Ontogeny and Its Possible Relevance for Phylogenetic Questions. In K. R. Gibson and T. Ingold (eds.), *Tools, Language, and Cognition in Human Evolution* (pp. 279–299). Cambridge: Cambridge University Press.

Lock, A., Young, A., Service, V., and Chandler, P. (1990). Some Observations of the Origins of the Pointing Gesture. In V. Volterra and C. J. Erting (eds.), *From Gesture to Language in Hearing and Deaf Children.* (pp. 42–55). Berlin: Springer Verlag.

McNeill, D. (1985). So You Think Gestures Are Nonverbal? *Psychology Review* 92(3): 350–371.

McNeill, D. (1992). *Hand and Mind: What Gestures Reveal about Thought.* Chicago: University of Chicago Press.

McNeill, D. (ed.) (2000). *Language and Gesture.* Cambridge: Cambridge University Press.

McNeill, D., and Duncan, S. (2000). Growth Points in Thinking for Speaking. In D. McNeill (ed.), *Language and Gesture* (pp. 141–161). Cambridge: Cambridge University Press.

Morris, D. (1977). *Manwatching: A Field Guide to Human Behavior.* New York: Harry N. Abrams.

Müller, C. (1994). Semantic Structure of Motional Gestures and Lexicalization Patterns in Spanish and German Descriptions of Motion-events. *Proceedings of the Chicago Linguistics Society* 30(1): 281–295.

Napier, J. (1980). *Hands.* New York: Pantheon Books.

Ochs, E., Gonzales, P., and Jacoby, S. (1996). "When I Come Down I'm in the Domain State": Grammar and Graphic Representation in the Interpretive Activity of Physicists. In E. Ochs, E. A. Schegloff, and S. A. Thompson (eds.), *Interaction and Grammar* (pp. 328–369). Cambridge: Cambridge University Press.

Petitto, L. A., and Marentette, P. (1991). Babbling in the Manual Mode. *Science* 251: 1483–1496.

Poyatos, F. (1983). *New Perspectives on Nonverbal Communication.* Oxford: Pergamon Press.

Quintillian, M. F. (1924). *Institutio Oratoria.* London: Heinemann.

Roth, W.-M. and Lawless, D. V. (2002). When Up Is Down and Down Is Up: Body Orientation, Proximity, and Gestures as Resources. *Language in Society* 31: 1–28.

Sherzer, J. (1972). Verbal and Nonverbal Deixis: The Pointed Lip Gesture among the San Blas Cuna. *Language and Society* 2(1): 117–131.

Silverstein, M. (1976). Shifters, Linguistic Categories, and Cultural Description. In K. H. Basso and H. A. Selby (eds.), *Meaning in Anthropology* (pp. 11–56). Albuquerque: University of New Mexico Press.

Silverstein, M. (1985). Language and the Culture of Gender: At the Intersection of Structure, Usage, and Ideology. In E. Mertz and R. Parmentier (eds.), *Semiotic Mediation* (pp. 219–260). New York: Academic Press.

Slobin, D. (1987). Thinking for Speaking. In J. Aske, N. Michaelis, and H. Filip (eds.), *Proceedings of the 13th Annual Meeting of the Berkeley Linguistics Society.* Berkeley: Berkeley Linguisitics Society.

Talmy, L. (1985). Lexicalization Patterns: Semantic Structure in Lexical Forms. In T. Shopen (ed.), *Language Typology and Syntactic Description* (pp. 57–149). London: Cambridge University Press.

Vygotsky, L. (1978). *Mind in Society: The Development of Higher Psychological Processes* (M. Cole, ed.). Cambridge, MA: Harvard University Press.

CHAPTER 10

Participation

Charles Goodwin and Marjorie Harness Goodwin

1 INTRODUCTION

In order for human beings to coordinate their behavior with that of their coparticipants, in the midst of talk participants must display to one another what they are doing and how they expect others to align themselves toward the activity of the moment. Language and embodied action provide crucial resources for the achievement of such social order. The term *participation* refers to actions demonstrating forms of involvement performed by parties within evolving structures of talk. Within the scope of this chapter the term is not being used to refer to more general membership in social groups or ritual activities.

When we foreground participation as an analytic concept we focus on the interactive work that hearers as well as speakers engage in. Speakers attend to hearers as active coparticipants and systematically modify their talk as it is emerging so as to take into account what their hearers are doing. Within the scope of a single utterance, speakers can adapt to the kind of engagement or disengagement their hearers display through constant adjustments of their bodies and talk.[1] This is accomplished by speakers through such things as adding new segments to their emerging speech, changing the structure of the sentence and action emerging at the moment, and modulating their stance toward the talk in progress.

Using as a point of departure the analytic framework developed by Goffman (1981) in "Footing," much analysis of participation within linguistic anthropology has focused on the construction of typologies to categorize different types of participants who might be implicated in some way in a speech event. In that speakers can depict, or in Goffman's terms animate, other parties within their talk, phenomena such as reported speech and narrative provide texts that can be mined for rich arrangements of structurally different kinds of participants. However, when this is done participation is largely restricted to phenomena within the stream of speech, and participants other than the speaker are formulated as points on an analytic grid, rather than as actors with a rich cognitive life of their own. In that non-speaking participants are, almost by definition, largely silent, a comprehensive study of participation requires an analytic framework that includes not only the speaker and her talk, but also the forms of embodiment and social organization through which multiple parties build the actions implicated in a strip of talk in concert with each other. From a slightly different perspective a primordial site for the organization of human action, cognition, language, and social organization consists of a situation within which multiple participants are building in concert with each other the actions that define and shape their lifeworld. By lodging participation in situated activities it is possible to investigate how both speakers and hearers as fully embodied actors and the detailed organization of the talk in progress are integrated into a common course of action.

1.1 Goffman's model of participation in footing

We will begin by looking critically at an article that has had enormous influence on the study of participation. In "Footing" Erving Goffman (1981) provided a model of talk that attempted to decompose "global folk categories" such as Speaker and Hearer "into smaller analytically coherent elements" (1981: 129). The rhetorical organization of "Footing," the way in which Goffman presented his argument, had crucial consequences for the strengths and limitations of the model he provided.

First, Goffman calls into question the traditional model of talk as a dyadic exchange between a speaker and hearer (section II of Goffman 1981), and stresses the import-ance of using not isolated utterances, but instead the forms of talk sustained within structured social encounters as the point of departure for analysis (section III). Second, Goffman turns his attention to deconstructing the Hearer into a range of quite different kinds of participants (section IV). These include ratified as opposed to unratified participants, bystanders, eavesdroppers, addressed and unaddressed hearers, and so on. A range of possible forms of participation in talk are also noted, including byplay, crossplay, collusion, innuendo, encounters splitting into separate conversations, and the like. The categories offered by Goffman here were developed through much of his career analyzing human interaction (see for example Goffman 1963, 1971). Finally, Goffman defines Participation Status as the relation between any single participant and his or her utterance when viewed from the point of reference of the larger social gathering. The combined Participation Status of all participants in a gathering at a particular moment constitutes a Participation Frame-work (Goffman 1981: 137). In subsequent sections Goffman calls into question the use of both conversation and states of talk as the analytic point of departure for the study of participation by noting that frequently bits of talk are embedded not in speech events, but in coordinated task activities (for example, the talk that occurs between two mechanics working on a car must take that activity, and not the talk alone, as the primary context for making sense of what the talk is doing).

Once he has decomposed the Hearer into a range of structurally different kinds of participants defined in terms of how they are positioned within an Encounter (which extends beyond the traditional unit of the Speech Event to encompass coordinated action more generally), Goffman turns his attention to the Speaker (sections VII and VIII). He provides a novel and analytically powerful model of a laminated speaker, one who can be decomposed into a range of structurally different kinds of entities.

The categories for types of speaker offered by Goffman include (1) the person actually producing the talk, what he calls an **Animator** (or Sounding Box); (2) the **Author**, or entity responsible for constructing the words and sentences at issue (who can be someone different from the current speaker); (3) the **Principal**, the party who is socially responsible for what is said; and (4), the **Figure**, a character depicted in the Animator's talk. This framework sheds considerable light on the complexity of quoted speech. Consider for example line 44 in figure 10.1 (from M. H. Goodwin 1990: 249). Chopper is telling a story in which he is depicting Tony, with whom he is currently engaged in a dispute, as a coward. Tony is described as running away from a group of boys who confronted him on the street. (An "h" within a parenthesis (h) marks laughter.)

Who is talking in line 44, and how is that question to be answered? The voice being heard belongs to Chopper, who is the *Animator* or Sounding Box in Goffman's framework. However, in line 44 Chopper is quoting the talk of someone else, his protagonist, Tony. Tony is thus a *Figure*. In other contexts (for example, talk by the press secretary for a head of state) one might also want to distinguish the actual *Author* of the words being spoken (a speech writer for example) and the *Principal*, the party who is socially responsible for what is said (the head of state), neither of whom need be the party who is actually speaking. The collection *Animator, Author*, and *Principal* constitute what Goffman calls the *Production Format* of an utterance (a slightly different version of this typology is also introduced in Goffman 1974). The possibility of using expressions such as "he said" or "I said" to embed not only *Figures* but entire scenes with their own production formats and participation frameworks within the current utterance creates enormous possibilities for both speakers and analysts. Thus deictic shifts have to be taken into account (the "I" in line 44 refers not to the party actually speaking the "I", Chopper, the *Animator*, but to the *Figure*, Tony), and by virtue of the laminated structure that emerges through such embedding, speakers can display complicated stances toward the talk they are producing. Thus, one shouldn't put quote marks around line 44, since it contains not only talk to be attributed to Tony, the Figure, but also laughter to be attributed to the Animator as part of the way in which he is evaluating both the talk being quoted and the actions of the party who produced it. Goffman thus offers analytic tools for

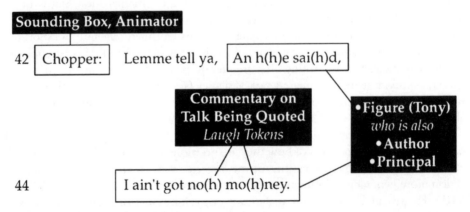

Figure 10.1   Laminated speakers

describing how a single strip of talk can contain an array of structurally different kinds of "speakers" intricately laminated together.

Footing constitutes the analytic point of departure for one important approach to the study of participation. The categories for types of participants offered by Goffman were considerably expanded by Levinson (1988). Hanks (1990) has opposed open-ended category proliferation by noting how a range of different types of speakers and hearers could be logically accounted for as the outcome of more simple and general underlying practices, such as systematic embedding of one participation framework within another (as happens for example in quotation and other forms of reported speech). Irvine (1996) argued that rather than starting from the categories provided by the decomposition of the speaker and audience, one had to focus on the larger processes, including links between participant role and social identity and ties to other encounters, that generate this fragmentation.

There are, however, serious limitations to the analytic approach to participation offered in "Footing." Many of these arise from the way in which speakers are analyzed in one part of the article with one model (the Production Format, and its possibilities for embedding) while all other participants are described in another section with a quite different kind of model (Participation Status and Framework). This has a number of consequences. First, speakers and hearers inhabit separate worlds. Despite noting phenomena such as Mutual Monitoring, no resources are provided for looking at exactly how speakers and hearers might take each other into account as part of the process of building an utterance (C. Goodwin 1981; M. H. Goodwin 1980). Second, the methods offered for investigating participation take the form of a typology, a set of static categories. No resources are offered for investigating how participation might be organized through dynamic, interactively organized practices. Third, there is a marked asymmetry in the analytic frameworks used to describe different kinds of actors. The speaker is endowed with rich cognitive and linguistic capacities, and the ability to take a reflexive stance toward the talk in progress. However, all other participants are left cognitively and linguistically simple. Essentially they are defined as points on an analytic grid (e.g., ratified versus unratified participants, addressed recipients versus bystanders and overhearers, etc.), but without any of the rich structure and intricate practices that make speakers so interesting.

Fourth, this privileges analytically what is occurring in the stream of speech (where grammar is being used to construct intricate laminations and embeddings of different kinds of speakers within a single utterance) over other forms of embodied practice that might also be constitutive of participation in talk, and leads to a subtle but consequential focus on the speaker.

2   Participation as Action

We now want to explore a somewhat different notion of participation, one focused not on the categorical elaboration of different possible kinds of participants, but instead on the description and analysis of the practices through which different kinds of parties build action together by *participating* in structured ways in the events that constitute a state of talk.

2.1   Differentiated participation in courses of action

It was noted above that Goffman's Footing separated speakers from all other participants, and provided one analytic framework for the study of speaker, and a quite different one for everyone else. By lodging participation in situated activities it is possible to investigate how both speakers and hearers as fully embodied actors and the detailed organization of the talk in progress are integrated into a common course of action. The data in figure 10.2 provide an example (see Goodwin and Goodwin 1987 for more extended analysis).

In line 2 Nancy, with "it was *s::so goo:*d," produces an enthusiastic assessment of the pie she has just mentioned. In line 3 with "I love it" Tasha joins in this assessment. One thus finds here multiple parties, both speaker and hearer, collaborating in the production of a single action, an assessment. Moreover, the point where the assessment is produced in their overlapping talk is also marked by a variety of enhanced embodied participation displays including gaze toward each other while enthusiastically nodding. In several different media the collaborative assessment activity reaches a peak or climax here.

Note that Tasha starts to speak before Nancy has actually stated her position, that is, before she has said "*goo:*d." The accomplishment of the simultaneous collaborative assessment requires that Tasha anticipate what is about to happen so that she can perform relevant action at a particular moment by joining in the positive assessment just as it emerges explicitly in the talk. How is this possible? What systematic practices make it possible for her to not just hear what has already been said, but also see what is about to be said? One resource is provided by the emerging syntax of the talk in progress. The intensifier "*s::so:*" occurring in a construction that is clearly about to attribute something to the pie being tied to by "it" projects that an assessment is about to occur. This projection, as well as the experiential character of the assessment, is also made visible through the enhanced prosody (which cannot be adequately captured in the transcript, but which seems to convey both increasing emotional involvement and a "savoring" quality) that starts with the intensifier, and also through aspects of the speaker's body movement (C. Goodwin 2002b). The hearer is thus given a range of systematic resources in language structure, prosody, and the

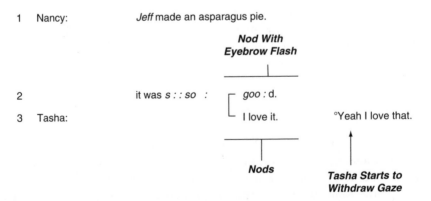

Figure 10.2   Linking speakers to hearers in a common course of action

body for projecting both what is about to be said, and the unfolding structure of the assessment activity as it moves toward a climax.

Several consequences of this for the study of participation will be briefly noted. First, as was seen as well in the last example, a hearer capable of participating in relevant activity in this way must be endowed with an interesting and rich temporally unfolding cognitive life, for example the capacity to use emerging syntax to project future events. Second, the situated activities (here assessment) that participants are constructing through states of talk provide a framework that enables the analyst to investigate as integrated components of a single coherent process a range of phenomena that are typically analyzed quite separately. Speakers and hearers are joined together in a common course of action, one that encompasses not only linguistic structure in the stream of speech, but also prosody, their visible bodies in a range of different ways (e.g., gesture, orientation, and posture), and on occasion structure in the environment. Third, this has methodological considerations. Most simply, many of the phenomena relevant to the study of participation as action will be rendered invisible or lost if analysis focuses exclusively on the talk or texts of speakers.

2.2   The constitution of an actor with aphasia through participation

Privileging rich structure in the stream of speech as a locus for the analysis of both cognition and the complexity of participation in interaction has the effect of denying full status as a participant to someone who lacks complicated speech. We will now look briefly at how a man with severe aphasia is nonetheless able to both function as a competent participant, and display his detailed understanding of the talk in progress, through the way in which he participates in the activities constituted through that talk. Once again the activity we will focus on is assessment.

A stroke in the left hemisphere of his brain left Chil with the ability to say only three words: *Yes* (and its variant *Yeah*), *No*, and *And*. Chil completely lacks the syntax necessary to build the complex utterances through which are constructed the reflexive, intricately laminated speakers that sit at the heart of Footing (and many other frameworks that use Bakhtin's insights into Reported Speech (Voloshinov 1986) as a point of departure for the dialogic organization of culture). The data in figure 10.3, which is analyzed more extensively in Goodwin and Goodwin (2001), provides an example of a simple but pervasive activity, that of assessing or evaluating something (Goodwin and Goodwin 1987). Jere is holding up a calendar with photographs of birds that Pat (Jere's wife and Chil's daughter) has received as a present. Immediately upon seeing the first photograph Pat, with "*hhh *Wow!*" (line 2), produces a vivid appreciation of what she has just seen. This is followed a moment later by a fully formed syntactic phrase ("Those are *great* pictures") which accounts for, and explicates, the speaker's reaction by describing something remarkable in the event being responded to (C. Goodwin 1996).

Despite his limited vocabulary, Chil, the man with aphasia, is also able to participate in the assessment by producing a series of non-lexical syllables – "Dih-dih-dih-dih" (line 1) – which serve to carry an enthusiastic, appreciative prosodic contour. However, his response does not occur until well after Pat's reaction. It might be proposed

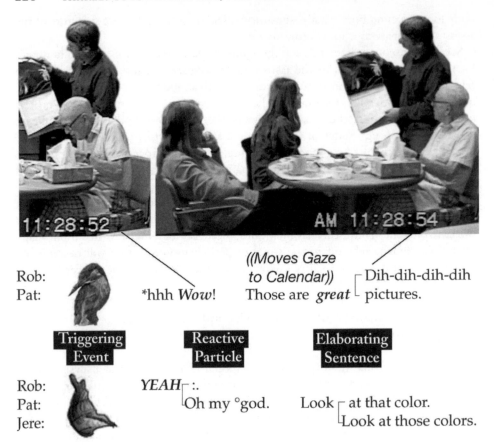

Figure 10.3   Embodied participation in an assessment

that because of his aphasia Chil has cognitive impairments that make it impossible for him to produce action with the rapid, fluent timing characteristic of talk-interaction. This is emphatically not the case. When the videotape is examined, we see that during Pat's "*Wow!*" Chil is looking down at his food. On hearing the "*Wow!*" he immediately starts to raise his gaze. However, he does not move it toward the speaker who produced the "*Wow*," but instead to the calendar that Pat is reacting to. Central to the organization of assessments is a particular kind of experience that requires appropriate access to the event being responded to. It would be quite possible physically for Chil to immediately follow Pat's "*Wow!*" with a congruent reaction of his own, that is to rapidly produce an assessment without waiting to actually see the object being commented on. However, Chil doesn't do this. Instead, by moving his gaze to the calendar he works to put himself in a position where he can independently assess the picture, and only then reacts to it. The very simple lexical and syntactic structure of his response cries masks a more elaborate grammar of practice, one that extends beyond talk to encompass the body visibly acting in a meaningful setting.

As Chil finishes his initial assessment Jere flips the pages of the calendar to reveal a new picture. By changing the form of his assessment to a rich, appreciative "*YEAH:*" Chil displays that he is making a new, different response to this new object, and thus demonstrates that he is closely attending to the changing particulars of the events being assessed.

At the point where Chil moves his gaze to the picture he is positioned as a hearer to Pat's vivid response to the picture, and more generally as a ratified participant in the local encounter. However, despite the way in which such categories constitute the bedrock for one approach to participation, they tell us almost nothing about what Chil is actually doing and even less about what he is thinking. By way of contrast, when the analytic focus shifts to organization of situated activities, such as the assessment occurring here, it becomes possible to recover the cognitive life of the hearer. Through the finely tuned way in which Chil positions his body in terms of what has been made relevant by Pat's talk, he shows his detailed understanding of the events in progress by visibly and appropriately participating in their further development through his gaze shift to the target of the assessment and appreciative talk. Despite his almost complete lack of language others present treat Chil as an alert, cognitively alive, indeed sharp and perceptive participant in their conversation (C. Goodwin 1995, 2002a). An approach to participation that focuses on engagement in multi-party collaborative action provides analytic resources for describing why this might be so.

2.3   Repairing participation between speakers and hearers

Speakers must have systematic methods of determining whether or not someone is positioned as a hearer to their talk. And indeed, rather than simply listening to what is being said, hearers in interaction, though largely silent, have a range of embodied ways of displaying, first, whether or not they are attending to a speaker's talk (for example by gazing toward the speaker (C. Goodwin 1981) or producing brief vocalizations such as continuers (Schegloff 1982)) and second, their stance toward it (through facial displays (M. H. Goodwin 1980) and brief concurrent assessments (C. Goodwin 1986b)). C. Goodwin (1981) finds that speakers who lack the visible orientation of a hearer interrupt their talk. Thus in figure 10.4 the speaker cuts off her

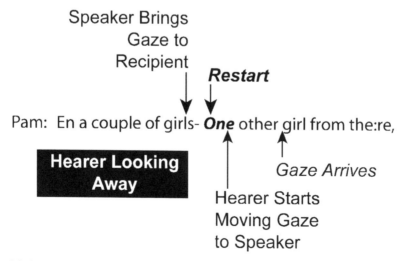

Figure 10.4   Securing the gaze of a hearer

talk in mid-sentence just as she completes the word "girls" and then replaces what she has said so far with a new version of the sentence, thus producing a noticeable restart in her talk. Such restarts function as requests to the hearer who starts to move gaze to the speaker after hearing them. One effect of this is that despite the presence of restarts in the talk the speaker is able to produce a coherent utterance and sentence just when a hearer is visibly positioned to attend to it.

Though "performance errors" such as these restarts provide linguists with their prime examples of how the data provided by actual speech must be ignored by both linguists and language users attempting to discern the grammatical organization of a language, such phenomena in fact provide an in situ analysis of language structure. For example, in figure 10.5 when a hearer looked away over "my son" the speaker drew him back by redoing that phrase as "my oldest son."

Somebody said looking at my:, son my oldest son. he has

Figure 10.5   Repair and the display of language structure

The repair that occurs in figure 10.5 (1) delimits a relevant unit, a noun phrase, in the stream of speech; (2) shows where that unit can itself be subdivided; (3) provides an example of the type of unit, an adjective, that can be added to the noun phrase; and (4) displays that such an addition is optional.

The way in which utterances are shaped by ongoing processes of participation has a range of other consequences as well. For example C. Goodwin (1979, 1981) shows how the structure of an emerging sentence is systematically changed as the speaker moves his gaze from one type of recipient to another. Similarly, speakers add new segments to sentences that have already reached points of possible completion to adapt to changes in the participation status of their hearers. M. H. Goodwin (1980) demonstrates how changing stance-displays by a hearer lead to systematic changes in a speaker's emerging sentence. In sum, the process of creating a participation framework in which speaker and hearer are aligned to each other can shape, and be shaped by, the detailed organization of the talk produced within that participation framework. In light of this it is notable that much of the work on participation that followed "Footing" did not look closely at the detailed organization of actual talk.

There is thus a reflexive relationship between talk and the participation frameworks within which that talk is situated. Consider a speaker who changes in mid-sentence from (1) a report of something that happened for an addressee who hadn't yet heard the news being told, to (2) a request for confirmation as the speaker moves to a new addressee who shared experience of that event with the speaker (C. Goodwin 1979, 1981). As the modification of structure of the talk adapts to changes in the relationship between speaker and hearer it simultaneously formulates that relationship in terms of how it is relevant to the action of the moment. The details of the talk, the action displayed through that talk, and the participation framework, mutually constitute each other. The talk is reflexive in that it refers to itself, but the scope of what counts as "itself" includes not only phenomena in the stream of speech, but also the relevant mutual alignment of speaker, hearer, and action (and frequently also structure in the environment that is attended to as part of the actions of the moment (C. Goodwin 2000)). A model, such as that offered in "Footing," which treats

speakers and hearers in isolation from each other, fails to provide the analytic resources necessary to capture such reflexivity.

3   STORIES AS PARTICIPATION FIELDS

The vision offered in "Footing" of how different kinds of speakers can be laminated
together within a single strip of talk provides powerful tools for the study of narrative
(and indeed this may well be its greatest achievement) (see Ochs, this volume).
Nonetheless, the model it provides is in significant ways incomplete for the investigation of stories. Consider again Chopper's story about Tony acting as a coward, a
section of which was presented in figure 10.1 to demonstrate Goffman's deconstruction of the speaker.

As Goffman himself observed, the characters depicted within the stories told in
everyday conversation are frequently present at the telling. Speakers tell stories about
themselves, their partners, and those they live with on a daily basis. Moreover their
stories are frequently organized as moves within larger social projects. Thus when
Chopper told a story about Tony it was a way of trying to gain advantage over Tony
in their dispute. This contextual frame shaped in detail just how Tony was being
animated (e.g., as a coward whose reported talk was framed by Chopper's laughter at
it). Furthermore Tony was present at the telling not only as a character in Chopper's
talk, but also in the flesh as someone who could and did vigorously contest the way he
was being depicted in the story (see M. H. Goodwin 1990: chapter 10). Finally, a
view of Chopper's laughter, as he reports what Tony said, as simply a display of
footing or alignment, is in important ways inadequate. As Jefferson (1984) has
demonstrated, such laugh tokens can constitute invitations for others to join in the
laughter. Indeed this is just what happened, with the effect that Chopper, through
use of such invocations of participation, was able to create a public multi-party
consensus against his opponent, and thus gain crucial political advantage in their
dispute (M. H. Goodwin 1990: chapter 10). In brief, if analysis focuses only on the
story-world described in the talk we lose how the story is functioning to build action
in the present.

Participation is intrinsically a situated, multi-party accomplishment. For example,
the telling of a story, such as a wife telling friends about a social faux pas her husband
committed over the weekend (C. Goodwin 1984), can create a complex participation
framework that places those present into a range of quite different positions, for
example, speaker, addressed recipient, principal character in the story who is present
at its telling, unaddressed recipient, etc. Some of these positions might seem the same
as those used in "Footing" to describe hearers. However, when they are linked
reflexively to the detailed organization of the talk in progress, a more complex and
dynamic picture emerges. For example, the principal character, e.g., the husband who
did the terrible thing, can expect that he will become the focus of others' attention at
a particular place, the point where what he said is revealed at the climax of the story.
As the story unfolds he can be seen to be using the story's emerging syntax to project
when that will occur and to dynamically rearrange his body as changes in the speaker's
talk modify these projections. When participation is taken into account recipients to a
story are faced not simply with the job of listening to the events being recounted but

also of distinguishing different subcomponents of the talk in terms of the alternative possibilities for action they invoke. Such tasks involve not simply recognition of the type of story component then being produced but also consideration of how the person doing the analysis fits into the activity in progress. Thus the speaker and main character operating on the same subsection of talk, a background segment for example, find that it provides for the relevance of quite different actions for each of them. Those present are engaged in a local, situated analysis not only of the talk in progress, but also of their participation in it, and the multiple products of such analysis provide for the differentiated but coordinated actions that are constitutive of the story as a multi-party social activity (see also Hayashi et al. 2002; Mori 1999).

By virtue of the organization provided by participation an audience to a story is both shaped by the talk it is attending to and can shape what will be made of that talk, and indeed its very structure (Duranti and Brenneis 1986; C. Goodwin 1986a). Prospective indexicals (C. Goodwin 1996) in story prefaces (Sacks 1974, 1995 [1992]), which include initial formulations of what the story will be about (e.g., "The **funniest/most tragic** thing…"), are used by recipients both as interpretive templates to monitor the story as it unfolds, and as resources for locating relevant structure in the story, such as recognition of its climax where shifts in participation by recipients are relevant. These practices, and the interpretive frameworks they generate, can become sites of contestation. Thus a wife can provide a preface that puts her husband in the position of telling a story about a "big fight" that occurred at an auto race (see C. Goodwin 1986a for analysis of this story). However, once he has launched the story, she, in collaboration with other members of the audience, can put into the telling alternative interpretive frameworks (for example that Mike's epic combatants are "all show" and "like little high school kids") that undercut not only Mike's stance toward the events he is describing, but also where crucial features of its structure, such as its climax, will be located. Taking participation into account enables the analyst to move beyond the study of narrative as texts to investigate interpretation, structure, and action as dynamically unfolding, socially organized processes that are open to ongoing contestation.

This perspective on participation sheds new light on both the internal organization of stories and the way in which they can help construct larger social and political processes while linking individual stories into a common course of action that spans multiple encounters with changing participants. An example of this is provided by a gossip dispute activity that the participants, pre-adolescent working-class African American girls who are speakers of African American Vernacular English (AAVE), call He-Said-She-Said (M. H. Goodwin 1990). The focal point of the dispute is a confrontation in which one girl accuses another of having talked about her behind her back. However, the events leading up to the dispute extend far beyond this encounter, and indeed the overall shape of the activity is encapsulated in the distinctive structure of the statements used to build an accusation. As can be seen in figure 10.6 the accuser uses a series of embedded clauses to report a series of encounters in which two girls were talking about a third. In the present, the top stage of the diagram, an accuser confronts a girl who has been talking about her. She states explicitly that she was told this by a third girl, whom we have labeled "I" for Instigator.

He-Said-She-Said confrontations are dramatic and exciting events in the life of the girls' group. While some can be quite playful, others can be used to dramatically

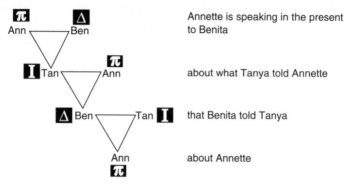

Figure 10.6   He-Said-She-Said accusations

recast the social standing of individual girls in the group. Indeed one family considered moving out of the neighborhood after a He-Said-She-Said confrontation led to their daughter's ostracism. Social scientists have repeatedly described girls' play, disputes, and ability to work with rules as simpler (and thus inferior) to boys' (who are argued to engage in complex games such as football). However, the He-Said-She-Said was far more complex, and extended over a much greater time span than anything found in the neighborhood's boys' peer group. Indeed, with features such as the structure of its accusation statements that systematically provide the grounds for the charge being made, and the way in which it socially sanctions members of the group, the He-Said-She-Said constitutes something like a vernacular legal system. For simplicity the standard symbols used in law courts for plaintiff (π) and defendant (Δ) are used in our diagrams to identify the accuser and defendant in the confrontation.

Within the He-Said-She-Said an actor's current identity is shaped by her history of participation in the process, and indeed this is encapsulated in the structure of the accusation. The three parties cited move through its stages in a regular order. The person being talked to at one stage becomes the speaker at the next, while the person being talked about becomes the hearer in the next stage. A party's identity is constituted by the places she has occupied in the past. Thus, someone is positioned as a defendant in the confrontation because she was the offender at the initial or bottom stage of the process, while being the offended party there – the girl who was being talked about – is what warrants that girl later assuming the identity of accuser. These identities, which shape in detail how an actor participates at different places in the process, emerge from how the act of talking (behind someone's back) is framed by the distinctive structure of the He-Said-She-Said as a situated activity system.

In the confrontation most of the drama focuses on the accuser and defendant. However, an equally crucial player in this process, indeed the one who brings about the confrontation, is the girl who tells the accuser that the defendant has been talking about her behind her back. The girls themselves call this activity *instigating*. An "I" is used to identify the Instigator in our diagrams.

In telling someone that another girl has been talking about her behind her back, an instigator is working to "involve" present participants through eliciting commentary on the absent party's character as well as a public commitment from the "talked about" present party to confront her offender (M. H. Goodwin 1990). However, a party who talks about another runs a particular risk; current recipient might tell the absent party that current speaker is talking about her behind her back. The activity of righteously informing someone of an offense against her can itself be cast as an offense. Implicating her recipient in a similar telling so that both are equally guilty and equally vulnerable leads to a delicate negotiation at the beginning of a story. A speaker brings up the absent party's offenses towards present recipient, requesting the opinion of others without herself stating her own position. For example:

```
 1   Bea:    How- how- h- um, uh h- h- how about me
 2           and Julia, *h and all them um, and
 3           Kerry, *h ⌐and all them-
 4   Julia:         ⌊Isn't Kerry mad at
 5           me or s:omp'm,
 6                       (0.4)
 7   Bea:    I'on' kn ⌐ow.
 8                    ⌊Kerry~always~mad~at somebody.
 9           °I ⌐'on' care.
10   Julia:     ⌊'Cause- 'cause 'cause I wouldn't, 'cau:se she
11           ain't put my name on that paper.
12   Bea:    I know 'cause OH yeah. Oh yeah.
```

Figure 10.7   Co-implication

In lines 4–5 Julia asks a question that describes her relationship to Kerry in a particular way: "Isn't Kerry **mad** at **me** or s:omp'm". Rather than launching into a story and talking negatively about Kerry before Julia has co-implicated herself in a similar position, Bea passes up the opportunity to tell such a story by saying she doesn't know in line 7 ("**I'on'** know"). Subsequently Julia provides an answer to her own question with "'cause-'cause 'cause I wouldn't, 'cau:se she ain't put my name on that **paper**" (lines 10–11). Only then does Bea join in the telling. Similar processes are described by Besnier (1989) with respect to gossip in Nukulaelae. Speakers arrange for their interlocutors to involve themselves in the gossip encounter through use of a particular strategy: withholding information about the most scandalous or otherwise central element of gossip over several turns. When the principal speaker finally provides the withheld item of the gossip (in response to a repair-initiation by an audience member) coparticipants assess the news through interjections and "high affect responses" which implicate them in the co-telling of gossip.

Among the African American working-class girls studied by M. H. Goodwin (1990) once a listener has committed herself to providing a statement that she will avenge the wrong of having been talked about behind her back, the entire group can look forward to the drama of the upcoming confrontation with eager excitement, and talk about it extensively. A girl who fails to carry through with such a commitment is said to "mole out" or back out of a commitment to publicly confront her offender. To secure such a commitment the instigator uses the full participation possibilities of stories described above. This shapes in detail the structure of her stories. For example, the current hearer is always a character in the story, and moreover one who is being talked about by the absent party who is being portrayed as the offender. In multi-party talk a speaker can shift the character structure of the story when one party leaves so that her stories are always addressed to someone who is being portrayed as having been offended against.

Figure 10.8 provides an example of instigator animating in her talk not only her current hearer (the future accuser) and the absent party (future defendant) who disparaged the hearer (by refusing to include her name in a bathroom pass), but also herself opposing the future defendant.

Goffman's deconstruction of the speaker provides relevant and powerful resources for describing analytically the different kinds of speakers (and other actors) animated in this strip of talk. However, a framework that focuses only on the speaker and her talk is seriously inadequate. A participation framework that encompasses both a speaker and a hearer who are reflexively orienting toward each other and the larger events in which they are engaged is absolutely central. The instigator's talk is designed in detail to lead precisely this addressee to perform particular kinds of socially relevant analysis. Thus the speaker not only describes offenses against her addressee, but also how the current speaker strongly opposed that party. Organizing narrative events in this fashion displays a relevant alliance by other group members with the current addressee and against her offender. Moreover the confrontational actions depicted subtly suggest how one can and should act toward the offender, and indeed shortly after this the addressee publicly states that she will confront her offender. The organization of the instigator's story is shaped in detail by the way in which it is embedded in both (1) a local participation framework that includes reflexive mutual orientation between the speaker and a cognitively rich hearer (e.g., one expected to

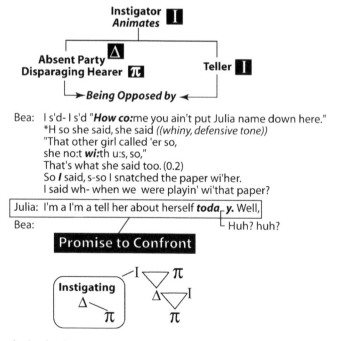

Figure 10.8   An instigating story

perform particular kinds of analysis on the talk in progress that will lead to consequential subsequent action), and (2) structured participation in a course of social and
political action that extends beyond the present encounter, but which is relevant to
how the talk in progress is positioning those present in particular activity-relevant
identities (e.g., offended potential future accuser and instigator).

The larger trajectory of the He-Said-She-Said as it unfolds through time provides
organization for an entire family of linked stories that differ in structure with reference to the specific participation framework within which they emerge. Figure 10.9
depicts a series of linked stories, starting from the bottom where the Instigator tells
the future Accuser that the Defendant has been talking about her behind her back,
and moving to the top, the actual confrontation that follows from this.

At **A** in figure 10.9, as was seen in figure 10.8, the instigator reports past events
that include as main protagonists the current hearer and the party who will eventually
become the defendant. While the stories are set in the past, they are designed to elicit
future action. And indeed, at **B**, when the addressee of these stories promises to
confront her offender, her projections of what will happen there take the form of
stories set in the future with her and the offender as principal protagonists. Because
of space limitations examples of stories at these different stages will not be provided
here (but see M. H. Goodwin 1990). The material inside the box at each stage depicts
schematically relevant features of the stories that occur there.

The instigator moves on to other encounters where she tells others in the group
about the future accuser's promise to confront. The stories through which the
reporting is done here, at **C**, provide a very selective version of the talk and action
that occurred at **A**, the instigating. For example, while the instigator produced most
of the talk at **A**, as she elaborately described the offenses committed against her
addressee, that talk is reduced to a line or two in the report at **C**, which elaborates
instead, with considerable relish, the promise to confront. This both masks the
agency of the instigator in bringing about the confrontation, and constitutes the
upcoming confrontation as a focal dramatic event for the group. The instigator and
the girls she is talking to also construct hypothetical future stories (**D** in figure 10.9)
about what might happen at the confrontation. However, though the protagonists in
these stories are the same as those at **B** (the accuser and defendant) the stories differ
significantly because the participation framework has changed. The girls at **C** are not
animating themselves, and thus assuming a consequential social commitment
through the telling.

Meanwhile the offended party also talks to other girls in the neighborhood. By
telling them what the offender has done to her she harvests second stories (Sacks
1995, vol. II: 3–31) in which others report what the offender did to them (**E** in figure
10.9). When the confrontation actually occurs at **F** the accuser replays these stories as
further evidence for the soiled character of the defendant.

What one finds here is a collection of stories that can be systematically compared
and contrasted in terms of structure and organization (e.g., specific arrangements of
characters and actions). The classical typologies of scholars from Propp (1968) to
Lévi-Strauss (1963) were based upon narratives abstracted from their local circumstances of production. Here, however, differences in the structure of stories that
emerge at alternative positions in this process – including types of characters, relationships between them, temporal organization, precipitating events, and the

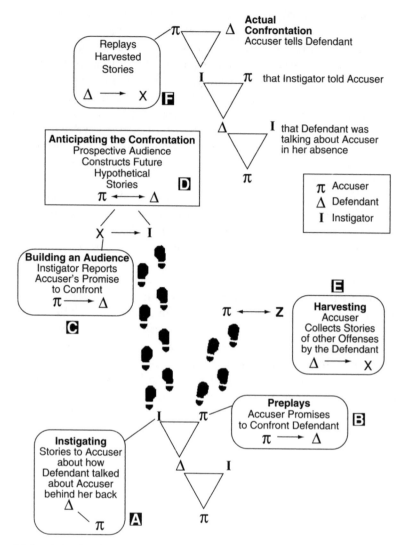

Figure 10.9   A family of stories reflexively embedded within changing participation frameworks

ordering of events into larger sequences – are intimately linked to the ways in which these stories constitute relevant social action by members of a community talking to themselves (not an outside ethnographer) as they participate in consequential courses of action. What one is dealing with is not a text, but cognitively sophisticated actors using language to build the consequential events that make up their lifeworlds.

4   PARTICIPATION IN LINGUISTIC ANTHROPOLOGY

Participation has been one analytic focus within linguistic anthropology since the 1970s. Philips' pioneering and influential study of "participant structures" in American Indian classrooms in Warm Springs (1972) examined how ways of orchestrating student–teacher interaction, allocating turns at talk, and structuring student attention vary across different activities in the classroom. The mismatch between participation in the home, where learning proceeds through observation in community-wide activities, and the school, where individuals are set apart from others, was a major factor contributing to poor school performance (see also Baquedano-López, this volume). Indeed participation has emerged as a major analytic concept for the analysis of schooling. Mehan (1979) and McDermott (1976) analyzed in detail how forms of participation in classroom activities shaped possibilities for learning. Erickson (1979) demonstrated how different norms for interpreting "listening responses" (involving gaze and backchannel cues) of students and counselors can lead to interactional "trouble" in interactions between white teachers and African American students. McDermott and Gospodinoff (1979) use participation to demonstrate how schools are systematically organized for some children to fail. McDermott and his colleagues show how social institutions offer differential access to power, and how this is actualized in conversational sequences. Studies of participation in both classroom activities and the meetings of school bureaucrats (Mehan 1996) have shed important light on how particular kinds of children (for example those classified as Learning Disabled) are marginalized by the school system. Keating and Mirus (2000) use participation to examine multi-modal communication and narrative interactions among Deaf children with hearing peers. Failures in such communication lead to the isolation of Deaf students. Analysis of participant frameworks has been central to the analysis of interaction in a range of institutional settings. Reviewing work on language and power, Philips (this volume) examines how structures of authority constrict turn-taking and rights to speak between bureaucrats and clients in courts, schools, and medical encounters.

The issues raised by attempts to integrate the body and features of the context into the analysis of acts of speaking has shaped a number of important anthropological studies. Duranti (1994, 1997) has analyzed how the placement of bodies in culturally organized space is central to the constitution of a host of events in Samoan society from greetings to political assemblies. Debate in the Samoan Fono, where the community's most important political action occurs, is organized through the interplay between speech, gaze, posture, and material resources (mats, architectural space, etc.) working together to define both actors and action. Keating (1998) shows how hierarchy is constructed in Pohnpei, Micronesia, through body positioning and honorific speech. As Keating (1998: 97) argues, "Honorific verbs status-mark journeys from source areas to goal areas, as well as the areas themselves." Sidnell (1998) demonstrates how the social and interactional construction of space is simultaneously tied to the exercise of social power and argumentation about such social positions in a dispute in an Indo-Guyanese village. Hanks (1996: 198) analyzes the ritual performance of a Mani-Oxkutzcab Yucatec Mayan shaman within the genre reésar. He examines how spirit forces work, and argues that we need to envision a notion of participation that will include a configuration of spaces, objects, genres, and participants (who need not be human) embedded in a wider sociocultural order. Central to the enterprise of shamans, he argues, is the "production and transformation of lived space" including the orientation and movements of actors' bodies within perceptual fields.

Participation has also been central to the analysis of narrative, children's lifeworlds, and language socialization. Analyzing an extensive corpus of dinnertime conversations Ochs and Taylor (1995) investigate asymmetrical forms of turn-taking in the family, specifically a "father knows best" dynamic. Mothers position father as primary audience, judge, and critic of the actions, feelings, thoughts, and conditions of family members, either in the present as a co-teller or in the past as a figure in the story. Further examples of gender asymmetry in family interaction occur in Capps and Ochs' (1995) examination of how the identity of an agoraphobic woman is constructed within narrative interaction. De León (1998) analyzes the emerging participatory competence of Zinacantec (Tzotzil Mayan) infants in their first year of life. She documents the multiple socializing channels within complex participant frameworks within which an infant is embedded. These include polyadic as well as dyadic interactions, and involve eye gaze, posture, and touch. She argues (1998: 152) that traditional middle-class dyadic models of language acquisition are inadequate. In order to study children's socialization into language we need both "native evidence based on local theories of socialization and ethnographic evidence based on a microanalysis of interactions a child is embedded within."

In this article we have not had time to explore in detail how material structure in the environment (rooms, hopscotch grids, Munsell charts, tools, etc.) and technology that links one setting to another expand our notion of human participation in a historically built social and material world (C. Goodwin 2000, 2003; Goodwin and Goodwin 1996; Heath and Luff 1996; Hutchins and Palen 1997; LeBaron and Streeck 2000; Nevile 2001; Ochs et al. 1996). Keating and Mirus (in press) describe how computer-mediated telephone communication among the Deaf leads to new adaptations of sign language and discourse practices developing through this new medium of "techno-social interaction." This technology has radically changed patterns of interaction in the family and friendship groups. The interplay between the semiotic resources provided by language on the one hand, and tools, documents, and artifacts on the other constitutes a most important future direction for the analysis of participation. However, this multi-modal framework should not be seen as something new but instead recognition of the rich contextual configurations created by the availability of multiple semiotic resources which has always characterized human interaction (C. Goodwin 2000).

5   Conclusion

As a set of practices for building relevant social and cultural action talk does not stand alone. Instead, the act of speaking always emerges within complex contextual configurations that can encompass a range of quite diverse phenomena. These include structurally different kinds of actors using the semiotic resources provided by their bodies to construct a range of relevant displays about orientation toward others and the actions in progress, the larger activities that local events are embedded within, past and anticipated encounters, structure in the environment, etc. In so far as such action involves not just language, but rather the interdigitation of different semiotic systems in a variety of media, the question of how such diverse phenomena can be coherently studied emerges. The notion of Participation provides one framework for investigating how multiple parties build action together while both attending to, and helping to construct, relevant action and context.

In this chapter we have contrasted two approaches to the study of participation. One, very well represented in Goffman's "Footing," offers first, the basics of a typology capable of describing many different kinds of participants that could be implicated in the act of speaking, and second, a most important deconstruction of the speaker into a complex, laminated entity capable of not only animating a theater of characters and action, but also rapidly displaying consequential stances toward these characters and the talk in progress. Despite the analytic power of this model, and the way in which it formed the point of departure for a line of important work in linguistic anthropology on participation, it has a number of crucial liabilities. The speaker is analyzed separately from all other participants, and only the speaker is endowed with rich cognitive complexity. The categories provided for other participants essentially locate them as points on an analytic grid. More importantly, because of the way in which the speaker and the hearer(s) inhabit quite separate analytic worlds, study of their reflexive orientation toward each other – the way in which each takes the other into account as they build relevant action together – is lost. The cognitive, reflexive life of the hearer can be recovered by focusing not on the construction of category systems for types of participants, but instead on the practices actors use to participate together in the endogenous courses of action that make up their lifeworlds.

A range of work has been described in which the embodied actions of multiple participants work together to build social action including individual utterances, assessments, stories, families of stories through which political disputes are animated, social institutions such as classrooms and courts, and so on. This framework provides powerful tools for the analysis of embodiment as social practice. It also sheds crucial light on the multi-modal environments within which children become competent linguistic and social actors, and enables us to expand our frameworks for the analysis of agency and morality.

Sitting at the core of almost all theories about human language ability, the moral ability to form social contracts, and social action in general, is what Nussbaum (2001) refers to as "the fiction of competent adulthood," that is an actor, such as the prototypical competent speaker, fully endowed with all the abilities required to engage in the processes under study (e.g., the speaker with the rich linguistic resources that sits at the analytic center of "Footing"). Such assumptions both marginalize the theoretical relevance of any actors who enter the scene with profound disabilities, and reaffirm the basic Western prejudice toward locating theoretically interesting linguistic, cultural, moral phenomena within a framework that has the cognitive life of the individual (albeit one who has internalized social and cultural phenomena) as its primary focus. The man with aphasia who could speak only three words sheds light on such issues. If participation is conceptualized simply as a structural position within a speech event, a point within a typology, then the intricate analysis he is performing of the organization of ongoing activities, his cognitive life as a participant in relevant courses of action, remains inaccessible to study. However, when utterances are analyzed as participation frameworks which invoke a domain of temporally unfolding embodied action through which multiple participants build in concert with each other the events that constitute their lifeworld, then he emerges as a competent actor capable of finely coordinated participation in the activities that make up a state of talk.

Finally, by linking the details of language use to embodiment, culture, social organization, and material structure in the environment, participation provides one framework that can link the work of linguistic anthropologists to that of our colleagues in other fields.

NOTE

1   See for example C. Goodwin (1979, 1981, 1984, 1986a, 1986b, 1987), M. H. Goodwin (1980, 1997) and C. and M. H. Goodwin (1987, 1992).

REFERENCES

Besnier, N. (1989). Information Withholding as a Manipulative and Collusive Strategy in Nukulaelae Gossip. *Language in Society* 18: 315–341.

Capps, L., and Ochs, E. (1995). *Constructing Panic: The Discourse of Agoraphobia*. Cambridge MA: Harvard University Press.

de León, L. (1998). The Emergent Participant: Interactive Patterns in the Socialization of Tzotzil (Mayan) Infants. *Journal of Linguistic Anthropology* 8(2): 131–161.

Duranti, A. (1994). *From Grammar to Politics: Linguistic Anthropology in a Western Samoan Village*. Los Angeles: University of California Press.

Duranti, A. (1997). Polyphonic Discourse: Overlapping in Samoan Ceremonial Greetings. *Text* 17(3): 349–381.

Duranti, A., and Brenneis, D. (eds.) (1986). *The Audience as Co-author*. Special issue of *Text*.

Erickson, F. (1979). Talking Down: Some Cultural Sources of Miscommunication in Inter-racial Interviews. In A. Wolfgang (ed.), *Nonverbal Communication: Applications and Cultural Implications* (pp. 99–126). New York: Academic Press.

Goffman, E. (1963). *Behavior in Public Places: Notes on the Social Organization of Gatherings*. New York: Free Press.

Goffman, E. (1971). *Relations in Public: Microstudies of the Public Order*. New York: Harper and Row.

Goffman, E. (1974). *Frame Analysis: An Essay on the Organization of Experience*. New York: Harper and Row.

Goffman, E. (1981). Footing. In E. Goffman, *Forms of Talk* (pp. 124–159). Philadelphia: University of Pennsylvania Press.

Goodwin, C. (1979). The Interactive Construction of a Sentence in Natural Conversation. In G. Psathas (ed.), *Everyday Language: Studies in Ethnomethodology* (pp. 97–121). New York: Irvington.

Goodwin, C. (1981). *Conversational Organization: Interaction between Speakers and Hearers*. New York: Academic Press.

Goodwin, C. (1984). Notes on Story Structure and the Organization of Participation. In J. M. Atkinson and J. Heritage (eds.), *Structures of Social Action* (pp. 225–246). Cambridge: Cambridge University Press.

Goodwin, C. (1986a). Audience Diversity, Participation and Interpretation. *Text* 6(3): 283–316.

Goodwin, C. (1986b). Between and Within: Alternative Treatments of Continuers and Assessments. *Human Studies* 9: 205–217.

Goodwin, C. (1987). Forgetfulness as an Interactive Resource. *Social Psychology Quarterly* 50(2): 115–130.

Goodwin, C. (1995). Co-constructing Meaning in Conversations with an Aphasic Man. *Research on Language and Social Interaction* 28(3): 233–260.

Goodwin, C. (1996). Transparent Vision. In E. Ochs, E. A. Schegloff, and S. Thompson (eds.), *Interaction and Grammar* (pp. 370–404). Cambridge: Cambridge University Press.

Goodwin, C. (2000). Action and Embodiment within Situated Human Interaction. *Journal of Pragmatics* 32: 1489–1522.

Goodwin, C. (2002a). Conversational Frameworks for the Accomplishment of Meaning in Aphasia. In C. Goodwin (ed.), *Conversation and Brain Damage*. Oxford and New York: Oxford University Press.

Goodwin, C. (2002b). Time in Action. *Current Anthropology* 43: S16–S35.

Goodwin, C. (2003). Pointing as Situated Practice. In S. Kita (ed.), *Pointing: Where Language, Culture and Cognition Meet*. Hillsdale, NJ: Lawrence Erlbaum.

Goodwin, C., and Goodwin, M. H. (1987). Concurrent Operations on Talk: Notes on the Interactive Organization of Assessments. *IPrA Papers in Pragmatics* 1(1): 1–52.

Goodwin, C., and Goodwin, M. H. (1992). Context, Activity and Participation. In P. Auer and A. di Luzio (eds.), *The Contextualization of Language* (pp. 77–99). Amsterdam and Philadelphia: John Benjamins.

Goodwin, C., and Goodwin, M. H. (1996). Seeing as a Situated Activity: Formulating Planes. In Y. Engeström and D. Middleton (eds.), *Cognition and Communication at Work* (pp. 61–95). Cambridge: Cambridge University Press.

Goodwin, M. H. (1980). Processes of Mutual Monitoring Implicated in the Production of Description Sequences. *Sociological Inquiry* 50: 303–317.

Goodwin, M. H. (1990). *He-Said-She-Said: Talk as Social Organization among Black Children*. Bloomington: Indiana University Press.

Goodwin, M. H. (1997). By-Play: Negotiating Evaluation in Story-telling. In G. R. Guy, C. Feagin, D. Schiffrin, and J. Baugh (eds.), *Towards a Social Science of Language: Papers in Honor of William Labov 2: Social Interaction and Discourse Structures* (pp. 77–102). Amsterdam and Philadelphia: John Benjamins.

Goodwin, M. H., and Goodwin, C. (2001). Emotion within Situated Activity. In A. Duranti (ed.), *Linguistic Anthropology: A Reader* (pp. 239–257). Malden, MA and Oxford: Blackwell. (Originally published in *Communication: An Arena of Development*, ed. N. Budwig, I. C. Uzgiris, and J. V. Wertsch. Stamford, CT: Ablex, 2000.)

Hanks, W. F. (1990). *Referential Practice: Language and Lived Space among the Maya*. Chicago: University of Chicago Press.

Hanks, W. F. (1996). Exorcism and the Description of Participant Roles. In M. Silverstein and G. Urban (eds.), *Natural Histories of Discourse* (pp. 160–202). Chicago: University of Chicago Press.

Hayashi, M., Mori, J., and Takagi, T. (2002). Contingent Achievement of Co-tellership in a Japanese Conversation: An Analysis of Talk, Gaze and Gesture. In C. Ford, B. A. Fox, and S. A. Thompson (eds.), *The Language of Turn and Sequence* (pp. 81–122). Oxford: Oxford University Press.

Heath, C., and Luff, P. (1996). Convergent Activities: Line Control and Passenger Information on the London Underground. In Y. Engeström and D. Middleton (eds.), *Cognition and Communication at Work* (pp. 96–129). Cambridge: Cambridge University Press.

Hutchins, E., and Palen, L. (1997). Constructing Meaning from Space, Gesture, and Speech. In L. Resnick, R. Säljö, C. Pontecorvo, and B. Burge (eds.), *Discourse, Tools and Reasoning: Essays on Situated Cognition* (pp. 23–40). Berlin, Heidelberg, and New York: Springer Verlag.

Irvine, J. T. (1996). Shadow Conversations: The Indeterminacy of Participant Roles. In M. Silverstein and G. Urban (eds.), *Natural Histories of Discourse* (pp. 131–159). Chicago: University of Chicago Press.

Jefferson, G. (1984). On the Organization of Laughter in Talk about Troubles. In J. M. Atkinson and J. Heritage (eds.), *Structures of Social Action* (pp. 346–369). Cambridge: Cambridge University Press.

Keating, E. (1998). *Power Sharing: Language, Rank, Gender, and Social Space in Pohnpei, Micronesia.* New York: Oxford University Press.

Keating, E., and Mirus, G. (2000). Cross-Modal Conversations: Deaf Children and Hearing Peers at School. *Crossroads of Language, Interaction, and Culture* 3: 73–90.

Keating, E., and Mirus, G. (in press). American Sign Language in Virtual Space: Interaction between Deaf Users of Computer-Mediated Video Communication and the Impact of Technology on Language Practices. *Language in Society.*

LeBaron, C. D., and Streeck, J. (2000). Gestures, Knowledge, and the World. In D. McNeill (ed.), *Language and Gesture* (pp. 118–138). Cambridge: Cambridge University Press.

Lévi-Strauss, C. (1963). *Structural Anthropology.* New York: Basic Books.

Levinson, S. (1988). Putting Linguistics on a Proper Footing: Explorations in Goffman's Concepts of Participation. In P. Drew and A. Wootton (eds.), *Erving Goffman: Exploring the Interaction Order* (pp. 161–227). Boston: Northeastern University Press.

McDermott, R. P. (1976). Kids Make Sense: An Ethnographic Account of the Interactional Management of Success and Failure of One First-Grade Classroom. Unpublished PhD dissertation, Stanford University.

McDermott, R. P., and Gospodinoff, K. (1979). Social Contexts for Ethnic Borders and School Failure. In A. Wolfgang (ed.), *Nonverbal Behavior: Applications and Cultural Implications* (pp. 175–196). New York: Academic Press.

Mehan, H. (1979). *Learning Lessons.* Cambridge, MA: Harvard University Press.

Mehan, H. (1996). The Construction of an LD Student: A Case Study in the Politics of Representation. In M. Silverstein and G. Urban (eds)., *Natural Histories of Discourse* (pp. 253–276). Chicago: University of Chicago Press.

Mori, J. (1999). *Negotiating Agreement and Disagreement in Japanese: Connective Expressions and Turn Construction.* Amsterdam and Philadelphia: John Benjamins.

Nevile, M. (2001). Beyond the Black Box: Talk-in-Interaction in the Airline Cockpit. PhD dissertation, Department of Linguistics, Australian National University.

Nussbaum, M. (2001). Disabled Lives: Who Cares? *The New York Review of Books* (January 11).

Ochs, E., Gonzales, P., and Jacoby, S. (1996). "When I Come Down I'm in the Domain State": Grammar and Graphic Representation in the Interpretive Activity of Physicists. In E. Ochs, E. A. Schegloff, and S. Thompson (eds.), *Interaction and Grammar* (pp. 328–369). Cambridge: Cambridge University Press.

Ochs, E., and Taylor, C. (1995). The "Father Knows Best" Dynamic in Dinnertime Narratives. In K. Hall and M. Bucholtz (eds.), *Gender Articulated: Language and the Socially Constructed Self* (pp. 97–119). New York: Routledge.

Philips, S. (1972). Participant Structures and Communicative Competence: Warm Springs Children in Community and Classroom. In C. B. Cazden, V. T. John, and D. Hymes (eds.), *Functions of Language in the Classroom* (pp. 370–394). New York: Teachers College Press.

Propp, V. (1968). *The Morphology of the Folktale,* 2nd edn. (trans. T. Scott). Austin: University of Texas Press.

Sacks, H. (1974). An Analysis of the Course of a Joke's Telling in Conversation. In R. Bauman and J. Sherzer (eds.), *Explorations in the Ethnography of Speaking* (pp. 337–353). Cambridge: Cambridge University Press.

Sacks, H. (1995 [1992]). *Lectures on Conversation*, vols. I and II (ed. G. Jefferson, with an Introduction by E. A. Schegloff). Oxford: Blackwell.

Schegloff, E. A. (1982). Discourse as an Interactional Achievement: Some Uses of "Uh huh" and Other Things that Come between Sentences. In D. Tannen (ed.), *Georgetown University Round Table on Languages and Linguistics* (pp. 71–93). Washington, DC: Georgetown University Press.

Sidnell, J. (1998). Collaboration and Contestation in a Dispute about Space in an Indo-Guyanese Village. *Pragmatics* 8(3).

Vološinov, V. N. (1986). *Marxism and the Philosophy of Language*. Cambridge, MA: Harvard University Press.

CHAPTER 11

Literacy Practices across Learning Contexts

Patricia Baquedano-López

1 INTRODUCTION

In recent years we have witnessed a departure from the central concerns that motivated much of the early twentieth-century research on literacy, namely, whether societies were primitive or literate and what cognitive skills could be possibly linked to literacy development. Literacy was then understood, in its more restrictive sense, as the ability to read and write. While at the center of these research concerns was the commitment to modernity and to finding the answers to questions about the diversity of development and learning across societies, a number of consequences ensued from these efforts, some positive, some less benign. Today we continue to build from this foundation and to expand on its scope.

Initially situated in the field of psychology, literacy has become an interdisciplinary subject of study that draws from theoretical and methodological perspectives in linguistics, anthropology, human development, and education, addressing learning as a lifespan process and across a variety of learning contexts (schools, community- and school-based programs, religious institutions, to name but a few). Newer conceptualizations of literacy development, especially those from research carried out in US schools, have sought a more complex understanding of the interplay between local literacy practices (i.e., literacies indigenous to communities) and those of more formal institutional practices (i.e., public education) in an effort to describe the range of literacy practices that individuals experience in their lifetime. This chapter reviews recent approaches to the study of literacy and highlights research addressing the role of language in literacy development, while continuing to make an argument for comprehensive, integrative approaches that consider language (oral and written) as central to the development of literacy in its historical and social context.

2   THE SCOPE OF LITERACY

Central to the main thesis of this chapter is the notion that language (its use, teaching, and learning) works as a mediating, interpretive system in the development of literacy. In this respect, language is considered a tool for learning (Vygotsky 1978; Cole 1985, 1996). Fundamental to this perspective is the recognition that it is through language and through the language practices (the ways participants in interaction employ language forms while engaged in purposeful activity) of particular social or cultural groups that literacy takes place. This necessitates a definition of literacy that accounts for the mediating power of language, a definition that is couched in an understanding of text and context, of what counts as literacy, and the power that social institutions have in shaping what gets to be constructed as literacy.

No longer considered as the ability to read and write, literacy has been increasingly conceived as a process of interpretation. Literacy is part of one's orientation to a lived reality made meaningful through the interpretation of text, that is, to written and oral descriptions and explanations of events that are endowed with sociohistorical value.[1] From this perspective, literacy development entails reformulating existing knowledge and experiences to understand new knowledge (Olson 1985; Langer 1987; Wells 1985; Berthoff 1984). Literacy is thus an interpretive, experiential, and developmental process that is mediated through language. The link between what is already known and what is potential new knowledge takes place through literacy practices that use language as the means to negotiate such connections. Literacy is less a set of acquired skills and more an activity that affords the acquisition and negotiation of new ways of thinking and acting in the world. Literacy is learning to become competent members of a community.

Increasingly, there is a collective sense among literacy theorists to speak of "literacies" or "multi-literacies." A new scholarly endeavor addresses this emergent perspective under the umbrella "New Literacy Studies" of which a prominent international group of researchers called the New London Studies Group[2] has been its most avid proponent. This critical, avant-garde group of intellectuals has proposed a redefinition of literacy that calls for the recognition of the multiplicity of literacies that people develop regardless of their degree of participation in mainstream practices – and even the global economy. Attention to these multiple literacies would account for greater inclusivity in the more institutionalized contexts of literacy instruction in ways that would not privilege only one form of literacy, often at the expense of others.

As with other cultural practices, literacy practices (and the interpretive processes they imply) invoke culturally defined social relations. That is, the process of literacy development is often determined by community and societal structures and ideologies that constrain, give shape to, and transform literacy practices. In this respect, any discussion of literacy implies a discussion of the relations of power that are at play, of the history of particular literacy activities, and of the ways in which that history is encoded in moment-to-moment interaction and is projected in its accumulated trajectory over time (Cole 1996). Literacy then is a product of sociohistorical development and involves a set of practices, which are shaped by political, social, and economic forces. It is embedded in relations of power (Lankshear and McLaren

1993; Luke 1994) where what counts as literacy is never free of sociopolitical consequence.

An example that illustrates this point is found in one educational policy in the state of California. Despite the large number of Spanish-speaking students in public schools and the relative success of bilingual education programs over the span of twenty years (aimed at providing literacy support in the native language), a voter-referendum, Proposition 227, was passed in 1998 eliminating bilingual education in the state. The measure has had a devastating impact on the affective, moral, and cognitive development of students who speak languages other than English and who benefited from such programs. In California alone, Spanish-speakers represent the majority of English limited proficient students (47.9%).[3] In a state where speakers of other languages comprise one quarter of the state's total student population, the elimination of bilingual education reflects ongoing ideologies of the value of other languages *vis-à-vis* the privileged status of English as the language of literacy development and public education.

3   STUDYING LITERACY IN CONTEXT

Since the early 1980s literacy researchers have turned to the writings of Russian psychologist Lev Vygotsky to understand the processes of cognition, thinking, learning, and human development in their sociocultural contexts. Their theoretical approach, most recently termed Cultural-Historical Activity Theory (CHAT) (Cole 1996), offers a more productive perspective for understanding the cultural and historical situatedness of literacy; that is, the development of literacy skills and of literacy practices over time and in particular contexts. It also offers a framework for understanding the social basis of literacy learning, in essence, as a process that takes place through interaction with others and through language as the "tool of tools."[4] Learning and development, from this perspective, are socially mediated through bi-directional, apprentice-like interactions with more expert others and through the use of mediating artifacts or tools, primarily language (grammars, practices) in the construction of meaning (Schieffelin and Ochs 1986; Ochs 1988; Rogoff 1990; Lave and Wenger 1991). This approach to literacy learning is based on a reconceptualization of the relationship between instruction and development where instruction precedes development. In contrast to notions that students or learners (apprentices) must be "ready to learn" before being presented with new material, literacy development from a Vygotskian perspective recognizes the social nature of learning and the bridgeable gap between what needs to be taught and what a student is ready to learn *with assistance*. The act of learning takes place in social interaction through joint, collaborative activity. Learning takes place first at the social level (the inter-personal level) and is later appropriated by the individual (the intra-personal level) (see also Rogoff 1990, 1993). This bridgeable gap is called the zone of proximal development (ZPD) and refers to the cognitive potential of what a learner can do with the assistance of more capable others. This construct has contributed a great deal to our understanding of the relationships and goals of collaborative work in learning contexts and has had its most significant influence in schools. Teaching and learning are not only mutually dependent processes, they are also reflexive and reflective. Thus, from a Vygotskian perspective, teachers (the expert others) are potential learners in any given learning interaction. Learning is a more agential activity and can be best measured as change in participation in activities over time (Rogoff 1993; Gutiérrez and Stone 1997).

The centrality of language in the development of literacy, and more broadly, learning, has also been recognized in recent studies of human development focusing on language socialization. Language socialization studies recognize that language is the medium through which children or novices acquire the knowledge, practices, and other social dispositions that would render them culturally and linguistically competent members of a community. In this respect, language socialization research addresses the ways in which people are socialized *through* the use of language as well as how they are socialized *to* use language (Schieffelin and Ochs 1986). The relevance to literacy development is important. Children and novices are socialized to literacy through the language of literacy activities. These activities reflect the expectations of communities and of the competencies that members learn to display. In this respect the now widely employed notion of "communities of practice" can be a productive way for conceiving activities as contexts where particular schooling practices and competencies are learned, displayed, and valued. At the core of the model of "communities of practice" is the notion that competence develops in social interaction and in collaborative activity (Lave and Wenger 1991; Wenger 1998). In their lifespan, members of society participate in multiple (whether overlapping or disconnected) communities. Moreover, these competencies conform to the expectations of communities of practice in which members participate (e.g., trades and professional groups, and we can also include schools and other institutionalized programs). These competencies can naturally extend to include literacy competencies both in and out of schools, since these are learned in social interaction and collaboration with others and conform to expectations of particular learning communities. One must be careful, however, to avoid thinking of communities of practice as neatly bounded or unproblematic. The inherent heterogeneity of communities affords the possibility of collaboration and for spaces of conflict and tension to occur. As will be discussed later, tension and conflict can in fact be productive strategies for learning.

4   A METHOD FOR STUDYING LITERACY LEARNING IN ITS CULTURAL-HISTORICAL CONTEXT

With the increasing recognition of the linguistic and cultural impetus and constraint on literacy there has been a surge of interdisciplinary efforts to document its development. While cross-fertilization in method is indeed desirable (see Duranti, this volume), the issue of discipline-specific methodology inevitably arises. Disciplines adhere to specific methodologies and researchers look for answers to their research questions from particular theoretical perspectives. Whether one is looking for cognitive, linguistic, cultural, or political explanations of literacy phenomena, research designs will reflect one's disciplinary training and orientation. Moreover, the role of language practices in the study of the development of literacy has not yet become prominent. Finally, a less benign consequence of theoretical and methodological differences in the study of literacy is the production of findings that have negatively influenced policies across social institutions, especially schools. These findings have had a profound impact on the ways we characterize literacy learning processes across cultural groups. More often than not, such investigations have produced monolithic accounts of cultural groups and their literacy practices. These accounts have (sometimes inadvertently) led to deficiency models of learning for non-mainstream groups who are often compared to an American, white, middle-class norm. A case in point is the elimination of bilingual education in California discussed earlier. Arguably, it is not that different methodological and theoretical perspectives may have contributed to this situation, rather it is the lack of a unified research agenda in the study of literacy development that has made it difficult to provide adequate descriptions of literacy practices across and within groups.

Indeed there are many advantages to doing cross-disciplinary work in literacy research. Analyses that take a closer look at grammar and the pragmatics of talk in interaction are invaluable for understanding the cultural practices that construct, maintain, and transform literacy expectations across institutional contexts. Attention to linguistic detail allows for the opportunity to observe emergent literacies *in situ*. Similarly, the study of practices over time in the form of ethnographies helps outline the diachronicity of such practices and to identify recurrent patterns. Drawing from Duranti and Ochs' (1997) study of literacy across two Samoan contexts (an island community and an immigrant community in Southern California), Gutiérrez and Stone (2000) propose a syncretic approach to capture both diachronic and synchronic dimensions of literacy as social practice. According to the authors, "syncretic" means "the principled and strategic use of a combination of theoretical and methodological tools to examine individual actions, as well as the goals and history of those actions" (Gutiérrez and Stone 2000: 150). The value in such a framework lies in its links to cultural-historical activity theory (this is implied in the terms "goals," "history," and "actions") as a productive lens for documenting literacy activities over time. But more importantly, the proposed method acknowledges the constraints of a single method for capturing the complexity of literacy instruction and learning; hence the need for transdisciplinary work. Within a syncretic approach, discourse analytic and ethnographic methodologies are invaluable for situating analyses beyond moment-to-moment interactions to address sociopolitical concerns and ideological stances. The prospects for understanding these relationships in current and future studies look particularly auspicious as we continue to move toward more productive methodological and theoretical ground that will no doubt help render visible the complexity of literacy learning across contexts.

5   ENGAGING LITERACY IN ITS SOCIAL CONTEXT: LEARNING IN AND OUT OF SCHOOL

The engagement of children in literacy is a constant that is organized across social institutions (e.g., in families, schools, day-care centers, after-school programs). A distinction between in-school and out-of-school literacies (or alternatively formal and non-formal learning) is thus useful for assessing the range of practices in which learners participate. A comparison between learning inside schools and learning in out-of-school contexts need not imply a dichotomy. Instead, it is productive to think that each context may employ elements of the other. For example, home literacy practices may resemble school practices during homework activities. Similarly, small group activities in the classroom may look similar to joint activities in home or community settings. Life within and beyond the confines of the average school day is full of opportunities to learn and for novices to become competent members of their communities, employing a range of literacy practices that may or may not always overlap.

A particular example of the study of literacy practices and development across contexts is illustrated in Scribner and Cole's (1981) now classic study of comparative literacies among the Vai of Liberia. The Vai could employ three different languages to engage in three distinct literacy practices across institutional settings: English for Western-style education, Arabic for Qu'ranic instruction, and Vai for local social and economic transactions. While the three literacies (and not all Vai are proficient in these) might lead us to believe that the more literacies, the more "literate" a person is, in the case of the Vai, literacy was highly dependent on the context in which those literacies were employed. The Vai studies highlight the situatedness of literacy practice, its teaching and learning, and the difficulty of making uniform assessments across contexts. Other studies have contributed to our understanding of the role of local literacy practices in ethnic communities and the possible match with academic literacies in schools. Shirley Brice Heath's (1983) description of the literacy practices in the two working-class communities of Roadville and Trackton (described more fully below) suggests that when the practices of the home, the Sunday school, and the public school overlap, children's academic performance increases. Attending to such a continuum of practices underscores the importance of recognizing home and community literacies in curricular development.

5.1   Literacy development inside schools

In her landmark language and literacy study of Roadville and Trackton, two working-class communities in the Piedmont Carolinas, Heath (1983) contends that a formula for academic success might rest in the continuity of certain practices across home and school. In her longitudinal study, the (mostly white) children of Roadville entered schools with a competence that prepared them for tackling school tasks more effectively, while African American children from Trackton developed literacies that did not always match those of the school. A closer look at these two communities' home practices unveils a rich array of language and literacy practices illustrating the ways in which different ethnic communities engage in rich literacy practices with their young as the norm rather than the exception. The fact that the children of Roadville were initially better prepared to use in schools the skills learned at home does not come as a surprise, since historically these practices underlie many schooling traditions, that is, they are based on European, white, middle-class normative values. Yet, the question of what is needed to sustain children's (such as Roadville's) academic success in school continues to drive educational efforts. We continue to question schoolchildren's failure to acquire academic literacies and desperately seek the answers following the match or mismatch model compellingly posited by Heath's study.

In the face of fast-changing demographics in schools, especially in urban centers, literacy reform efforts have also come under pressure to produce effective schools and higher levels of academic literacies. Increasingly, in linguistic and culturally hetero-geneous schooling contexts, what counts as knowledge and how this knowledge is made accessible to students from diverse backgrounds is a question that permeates the educational and political realms, often at the expense of large numbers of non-mainstream students who act as repositories of curricular decisions with little or no opportunities to use home or local repertoires for literacy development.

As noted earlier, literacy learning extends beyond the acquisition of reading and writing skills to the use of more interpretative skills. As an interpretative practice, then, the acquisition of literacy both utilizes prior experience and also creates experiences for learners within and beyond the current activity. This last point has immediate consequences for learners from culturally and linguistically diverse backgrounds, especially in schools. If to utilize prior experience means using the available, local knowledge, how do such learners fare when their prior experience is of little or no relevance to the academic curriculum that they must command? This preoccupation has led to efforts to create alternative pedagogical methods to include students and the local knowledge of their communities in the literacy learning process in schools. Moll's (1992, 2000) and Moll and Gonzalez's (1997) study of "funds of knowledge" has revealed that when teachers learn to identify and use the economic and social relationships that exist in their students' communities they have more opportunities to include this knowledge as a literacy resource. The teachers, who are trained as ethnographers, learn to map out local resources, practices, and literacies that can then be incorporated into the curriculum.

An interesting example of the incorporation of local practices in the curriculum is provided in Lee's (1993) report on the use of African American discourse for teaching high school literature.[5] Through the inclusion of students' own understandings and uses of signifying, indirection, and other cultural and linguistic resources available across many African American communities, Lee (a university professor and researcher who has also taught high school) leads her senior high school students through an analysis of complex literary text and unpacks the intricacies of everyday use of indirection (signifying) in African American discourse.[6]

5.1.1 Bridging literacies: local repertoires in academic language and literacy development

In the excerpt below from Lee (2000), Lee and her students are reviewing the questions they have been answering while trying to interpret the different stances and relationships in Alice Walker's *The Color Purple*. Here the teacher (T) prompts students (S) to consider possible interpretations of the purpose of Celie's (the main character) letters to God and provides links to other characters in Zora Neale Hurston's *Their Eyes Were Watching God* that the students had also read:

T: Because when she writes them her writing is another way of her speaking and expressing herself in things that she can't do. This is an idea to keep in mind because talk does become important in this book, doesn't it? 'Cause does Celie begin to change along the dimensions of talking?

S1: Yes.

T: Where?

S1: She starts signifying. There is a lot of signifying in this book.

T: What is important?

S1: What? The signifying? That depends on where it is at. In some places they were just sitting around jocking. In other places, they were serious, like when they told her, you ugly, you can't cook and all of that, and she came back and crack on him.

T: Does the signifying in that instance have anything to do with the signifying in *Their Eyes Were Watching God*?

S2: Nope.

S3: Yes it do. Because when they were in the store when Jody told Janie that she was ugly and that she was getting old and stuff. That is the same thing he is telling her.

S4: No, he was just trying to front her.

S5: You know how Jody never did want her to say anything. He didn't want her to speak. In a way, Mister was the same way with Celie. She couldn't do nothing but what he told her to say. So in a sense, it's like the same.

S6: I think there is a little bit of similarity to it. They both are trying to front each other.

To those familiar with traditional classroom instruction, dominated by a pattern of initiation–response–evaluation (IRE),[7] the most striking features of this example from this classroom discourse include the amount of talk from students and the number of participants in discussion. Similar to the research on "funds of knowledge," Lee's (1993, 2000) and Heath's (1983) studies illustrate the benefits of knowing and using the students' background knowledge in the development of academic literacies. The excerpt illustrates an engaged exchange among six high school students and their teacher in the interpretation of written dialogue that employs signifying examples. This interpretive classroom practice is precisely what has been illustrated in Heath's (1983) study of Trackton and Roadville students. When local linguistic and cultural repertoires and practices become part of the curriculum, meaning-making and interpretation take on a different dimension – they become a relevant, meaningful, affiliative activity. Local linguistic knowledge becomes a tool for interpretation across different literary texts. Such generative use of local resources for literacy learning underscores the importance of understanding and negotiating local codes, including those in the traditional official (teacher-led) and unofficial (student-generated) discursive spaces of the classroom. It is possible to reorganize even the most traditional classroom instruction to promote literacy development that builds on collaborative interpretive practice.

5.1.2   Learning in the Third Space

A recent body of research in successful urban classrooms examines the possibility of learning in the "Third Space,"[8] a space of negotiation of knowledge, positionality, and competing discourses that can promote literacy development.[9] Rather than dismissing students' talk as potential off-topic disruptions, and much like the data in Mrs. Lee's classroom discussed above, in classrooms where learning is organized in ways that set the conditions for Third Spaces to occur, teachers see students' comments as potential contributions and as the next steps for interpretation and for sustained learning interaction. Indeed, heterogeneous classrooms, where the use of multiple and hybrid[10] linguistic codes and registers are the norm, are also the contexts for the negotiation of competing language practices and the development of potential Third Spaces of learning. Consider the following exchange in a multi-aged Spanish immersion class that included second- and third-graders and their teacher who have been discussing the topic of human reproduction during a six-week lesson on the subject. Previously discussed in Gutiérrez, Baquedano-López, and Tejeda (1999), in this classroom exchange, local knowledge, alternative language registers, non-verbal interpretations, and formal and informal registers contribute to meaning-making. As the teacher writes on the board the questions from a student-generated list on the topic of human development, a student reads out loud: "¿Qué es esperma?" ("what's sperm?"). Jorge, another student in the class, responds to the question on the board:[11]

Official Space	*Third Space*	*Unofficial Space*
S: ¿**Qué es esperma?**		Ss: ((Student rumblings
What is sperm?		and side discussions
T: **Cómo vamos – esa es**		sprouting up))
una buena pregunta. ¿Qué		Jorge: **Es como un** *tadpole*.
es esperma? Ahorita la		It's like a tadpole ((makes
apunto. ¿Cómo crecen lo:s		swimming tadpole motions
esperma?		with his hands))
Since we are – that is a good		
question. What is sperm? I'll		
write it down right now.		
How do the sperm grow?		
((Still writing on the board,		
laughs silently at Jorge's		
description))		
	T: **Jorge, parece como**	
	renacuajos ((turns and faces	
	Jorge smiling)), pero no <u>son</u>	
	renacuajos.	
	Jorge, they look like tadpoles	
	but they are not	
	tadpoles.	
T: ¿**Qué son los espe:rma?**	Anabel: ((Laughs out loud))	
((Writing on the board))		
Muy buena pregunta.		
What are sperms? Very good		
question	Jorge: ((Grins widely))	

In this classroom exchange the potential for the Third Space emerges when the teacher acknowledges Jorge's comments. The teacher's response validates Jorge's knowledge, even though he used English in the context of a Spanish lesson. Moreover, the teacher's translation of "tadpole" into Spanish potentially supplies for the class (and Jorge) the missing lexical reference, in this way expanding their linguistic repertoire. Finally, the positive affective stance of the teacher expressed through her smiling at Jorge's answer and later on when she addresses him directly minimizes laughter as counterscript (as a student practice in opposition to the official space) and incorporates it in the Third Space. Notice too that Anabel laughs out loud and Jorge grins at the teacher's response. During the course of the six-week lesson, there were several instances of the Third Space, partly due to the already hybrid nature of the activity. The lesson had been generated by the students and with parental and school permission it was, in itself, an example of a curricular Third Space.

Whatever the curricular or pedagogical approach, the point that is emphasized through these examples from classroom instruction is clear. Literacy experiences are far more meaningful and productive when local, hybrid repertoires of language and literacy emerge in the learning process; that is, when students' sociocultural backgrounds shape the form and content of the literacy activities of the classroom.

5.2   Out-of-school literacy development

Besides offering a comparison across different learning settings, the study of out-of-school literacy practices opens up a window into the complex nature of community learning settings and of local interpretive practices. As Hull and Schultz (2002) note, many of the studies of literacy out of school have had a significant impact in shaping the field of literacy. Studies on the collaborative nature of computer-mediated activity in after-school programs, for example, illustrate the ways in which language practices influence cognitive activity (Nicolopoulou and Cole 1993; Cole 1996; Stone and Gutiérrez, in press). Educational research in local community institutions, for example, the work of Moss (1994) on African American church sermons, offers insights into the ways in which this genre is a rich literacy event that draws participants affectively and interactionally into community. Farr (1994) and Guerra (1998) have mapped the literacy practices of Mexicano communities in both Chicago and Michoacán, Mexico, charting a continuum of practices that does not stop at geographical or political borders. Together, they have studied the literacy development of an older woman, Josefina, in the form of letters to God as part of a prayer study group. Josefina's writing reveals an interesting blend of genres, letter and prayer, as her personal interpretation of Bible passages and her Christian faith (Guerra and Farr 2002). Duranti, Ochs, and Ta'ase (1995) draw from fieldwork in both (formerly Western) Samoa and a Samoan community in Los Angeles to illustrate the ways in which the same tools for learning afford different literacies and worldviews. For example, reciting a Samoan alphabet tablet with Westernized pictures socializes Sunday school students to American values in Samoa, but in a Samoan church in Los Angeles, the same instrument is a diasporic link to their culture. In what follows I highlight the language practices in two learning contexts, children's Catholic religious instruction at a neighborhood parish and an after-school program for children of elementary school age,[12] to further illustrate learning and literacy development in community settings.

5.2.1   The case of *doctrina* instruction: narrative activity as an interpretive practice

In my study of language and literacy practices at St. Paul's Catholic Church in Los Angeles I investigated the resources that teachers employ to involve students during

Saturday religious instruction that prepares them for First Communion[13] (Baquedano-López 1997, 2000). St. Paul's offers two tracks in its Saturday children's religious instructional program, one in Spanish (called *doctrina*) and the other in English, generally referred to as catechism. While the majority of the population in *doctrina* classes comprised mostly recent Mexican immigrants, there was also a small population of second-generation immigrants who had traveled or lived in Mexico for brief periods of time. The parish also offered catechism classes to a more ethnically diverse student population of European American, Asian, African American, and Latino students, including a few children of Mexican descent (mostly second- and third-generation immigrants). My research in the religious education classrooms centered among other things on narrative as a literacy activity, focusing in particular on one narrative that commemorates the apparition of *Nuestra Señora de Guadalupe* in Mexico in the year 1531. Narrative as an interpretive process is a whole lot more than a recollection of events; indeed, through narrative people make sense of their past as well as their present experiences, in order to influence and project possible outcomes (Ochs and Capps 1996, 2001). In this interpretive dimension, narrative is also a site of literacy.

In the religious narrative of *Nuestra Señora de Guadalupe*, the Virgin Mary is said to have appeared several times to an indigenous craftsman named Juan Diego and instructed him to deliver a message to the local bishop. The Virgin Mary's message was, in essence, a request that the bishop build a shrine in her honor. After several failed attempts to gain an audience before the bishop, Juan Diego finally explained to the Virgin Mary his predicament. He was not a believable messenger, and had even been asked to deliver a sign of the apparition. The Virgin Mary then instructed Juan

Figure 11.1   *Doctrina* children celebrating their First Communion. Photo: Patricia Baquedano-López

Diego to gather roses in his tunic and to take them to the bishop. In the presence of
the bishop, Juan Diego dropped the flowers to the ground and the image of *Nuestra
Señora de Guadalupe* remained imprinted on his tunic.

Through questions posed during the telling of this religious narrative *doctrina*
teachers relate the text of the narrative to the students' present experience. They
explicitly link the children's life experiences to their emerging classroom narrative
version. In the example below, while recounting the setting of the events of 1531, the
teacher, Señora Lala, makes a link between the main character of the narrative, Juan
Diego, and the *doctrina* students in her class:

Lala: **Pero? (pause) Juan Diego**
       But Juan Diego

       no vivía donde vivía el obispo.
       did not live where the bishop lived

       vivía como en un ranchito.
       he lived in a little ranch.

       y como dijo él, había muchos cerros.
       and like he said [referring to a student's previous contribution], there were many
       hills

       entonces, él iba a la doctrina como ustedes.
       then he used to go to doctrina like you.

       iba: (pause) de su ranchito,
       he went from his little ranch

       (pause) hasta dónde estaban? (pause) los sacerdotes.
       to where the priests where

       (pause) a un:: (pause) a una iglesia
       to a church

       que se llama todavía Tlaltelolco.
       that is still called Tlaltelolco

       Allí iba Juan Diego?
       Juan Diego went there

       A?
       To?

       (pause)

       A recibir catecismo.
       to catechism

While teachers often engage in longer elaborations of events, describing in detail the
setting of the apparition or ventriloquizing the voices of the characters of the
narrative, teachers organize narrative tellings expecting the participation of the students. Such participation is built into narrative tellings through the use of intonation
cues which model answers that prompt students to complete the teacher's turn, as
shown by the pauses and question marks in the example above. Such linguistic

features, or contextualization cues (Gumperz 1982), signal to students appropriate ways of interacting, that is, the expected competencies. The content of the narrative is made meaningful to these students by linking a feature of the character of Juan Diego with *doctrina* students' experiences: "*él iba a la doctrina como ustedes*" ("he attended *doctrina* like you"). To involve students and socialize them to the appropriate responses to teachers' questions, teachers model student responses. Lala prompts students in: "*Allí iba Juan Diego? A?*" ("Juan Diego went there, to?"). The answer is subsequently supplied by the teacher in "*a recibir catecismo*" ("to receive catechism instruction"), which restates the link between the students' experiences and Juan Diego's. Both attend catechism (*doctrina*). Figure 11.2 illustrates the ways in which the narrative tellings of *Nuestra Señora de Guadalupe* help construct meaning and interpretation.

Through contextualization cues and other narrative resources teachers and students interactionally achieve a local interpretation of the narrative events. As the seemingly monologic excerpt from a *doctrina* narrative illustrates, the process of interpretation does not necessarily have to include overt talk. An important interpretive link is made in the figure of the past, Juan Diego, who becomes relevant to the students in the present as a *doctrina* student and church goer. As the *doctrina* excerpt illustrates, the narrative activity provides a context for the employment of local literacy resources, which are guided by particular ideological stances as to what constitutes learning. This example of local literacy practice also affords us the opportunity to

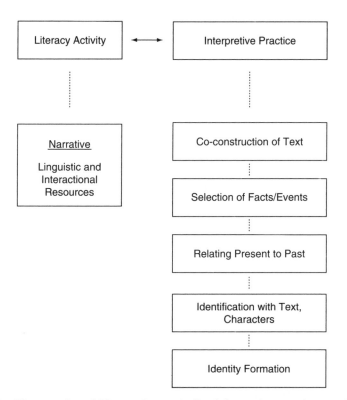

Figure 11.2 The narrative of *Nuestra Señora de Guadalupe* as interpretive practice

appreciate the range of literacy contexts that Latino children experience besides formal schooling, especially when we consider that many children who participate in institutionalized local community instruction (such as *doctrina*) might also attend public schools where they are most likely to engage in literacy practices that may not necessarily utilize their language or knowledge as resources for learning. Such discontinuities may have drastic consequences for failure or success as already suggested in Heath (1983).

5.2.2   The playful world of *Las Redes:* Hybridity as a resource for learning

A foundational notion in the study of human development is the belief that play is conducive to learning. The importance of play in the learning process has been a topic of growing interest across different fields of inquiry and theoretical orientations, and, not surprisingly, pedagogical models of literacy development in which play is fundamental to learning are increasing in number.[14] There is much to learn from the ways in which children organize play activity, particularly since play can promote the development not only of physical skills but also of important linguistic, social, and cognitive competencies.[15] As such, play constitutes an enduring site for understanding children's socialization and learning. Similar to literacy activities, play activities are oriented to future action, where the skills learned and practiced can serve as blueprints for cognitive and cultural ways of interpreting and acting in the world.

The *Las Redes* ("networks")[16] after-school program at an elementary school in Los Angeles is grounded in cultural-historical notions that cognitive development is embedded in social processes and activities, including play. Based on the 5th Dimension model (Cole 1996; Nicolopoulou and Cole 1993; Griffin and Cole 1984), *Las Redes*[17] fosters a culture of collaboration where novices work with more competent others while playing board and computer games, and where the interactions are organized in ways to maximize the inherent material, ideological, linguistic, and ethnic diversity at local urban educational settings. At *Las Redes*, university faculty, postdoctoral fellows, graduate students, and undergraduate students participate playing educational computer and board games with elementary students. Located in a port-of-entry school district, *Las Redes* serves a large population of Latino immigrant (mostly from Mexico and Central America), Tongan, and African American students. At the time when the findings of this study were first reported (1997–2001), English language learners comprised 94 percent of the student population at this school. To understand the dynamicity of linguistic diversity in Los Angeles requires us to recognize its heteroglossia, or its diversity of social voices (Bakhtin 1981), made visible in the exchanges and contact among people of diverse backgrounds. The varieties of Spanish and English spoken at *Las Redes* are a microcosm of the diverse linguistic reality of the city in which it is embedded. This hybridity in language, including the mix of codes and registers, does not only exist within and across communities, it is also inherent in the speech choices of a single individual.

A central component of the interactions at *Las Redes* is a cyber entity called El Maga. Rendered neuter in gender in its Spanish code, "El Maga" responds to email messages from the students at *Las Redes*. As part of the daily activities at the program,

Figure 11.3 Undergraduate and elementary students reading instructions to play computer game at *Las Redes* (Photo: Héctor H. Alvarez)

elementary students write to El Maga about their experiences playing computer or board games. The intent of the exchanges is to problem-solve with El Maga about particular discontinuities with games or with other social interactions. It is also not uncommon for El Maga to respond to queries about her/his/its gender, marital status, and even physical appearance. Overall, the children seem to find El Maga an endearing, all-knowing cyber creature. El Maga is also very knowledgeable about the students' work and participation at the program and has access to such information through the *Las Redes* records and through anonymous direct participation (El Maga's anonymity allows for multiple ways to observe and participate in daily *Las Redes* activities). Because of this novelty element in El Maga, children are initially very engaged with email writing, although interest tends to wane over time. Below I reproduce two examples of correspondence from a database of *Las Redes* email exchanges.[18] These examples help illustrate the extent to which these email exchanges are literacy activities that promote not only learning, but also cultural and linguistic affiliation. Moreover, the email exchange itself is an example of the use of the local hybrid linguistic and cultural repertoire in a learning environment.

Martha and El Maga

A regular participant of *Las Redes*, Martha, a third-grader, emails El Maga about "Reader Rabbit II," a computer game that proves to be problematic for students due to a troublesome bug in the software. The two exchanges reproduced below span a period of a little over a month. In the first exchange, the rather routine nature of Martha's email in English is radically changed by El Maga's response, which includes a key word in Spanish that makes it possible to enter a shared world of interpretation.[19]

Exchange 1
Email from Martha to El Maga:
2/4/97
dear El Maga, are are you? the pond was little bit harder. I couldn't understand the game and Christina helped me figure it out. In the end, I passed the first level and I was surprised. thanks for writing to me.

In this email Martha displays the genre conventions of letter-writing and engages in a narrative description of the game that includes her evaluative reaction to her own performance, which was aided by Christina, an undergraduate student participant of *Las Redes*. This is El Maga's response to Martha's email:

Email from El Maga to Martha:
2/4/97
Dear Martha,
I am doing pretty good, thank you for asking!!! How are you?? I hope you still have that big smile!!! The pond was difficult to figure out, huh? That frog causes many of us problems. It has a mind of its own and sometimes it does not want to do what we program it to do. Que ranita . . .
I am glad that Christina helped you figure out the game. What kinds of things did you both do?? Did the frog do every thing you told it to do???
Write back,
El Maga

El Maga responds by addressing the main problem identified by Martha, that the game was difficult to play. In addressing the problem, El Maga mentions a character of the computer game, the frog, that causes problems to many game players. In the description of the frog, however, El Maga switches to Spanish in the phrase "qué ranita," which humorously translates into "that mischievous frog." The use of Spanish in the description of the unpredictable frog influences the emails that Martha subsequently writes to El Maga. Indeed, the phrase in Spanish restructured the nature of the relationship between Martha and El Maga. In an ensuing response, Martha expresses her surprise at El Maga's being bilingual; in fact, the second message that she writes is entirely in Spanish. El Maga responds also in Spanish, signaling in this way co-membership in a group of Spanish-speaking cyber participants. El Maga's email continues to socialize Martha's involvement and continuing membership in *Las Redes* by focusing on the game activity and following up on the learning task.

The third email exchange, reproduced below, is the most sophisticated response from both parties. Here Martha codeswitches between Spanish and English, addressing a wide range of topics that displays a different kind of agency that expands the email genre convention. In fact, Martha restructures the activity and its goals. Similar to the ways in which *doctrina* teachers appropriate versions of the narrative of *Nuestra Señora de Guadalupe* in addressing their students' experiences, Martha simply appropriates the email exchange as a means to link the activity with her own personal experiences:

Exchange 3
Email from Martha to El Maga:
3/12/97
Dear La maga
don't you like tortillas? Today I played la Corrida de Toros. The game was too easy for me, but in the hard level I was too confused because I didn't read the word list because I was too floja [lazy]. My brother gave me some candy. The candy was so delicious. Quiere probar some candy? [would you want to try some candy?] You could ... buy it in the store! ha ha ha! I make you laugh. I'm funny today because today my boyfriend gave me a kiss. but in a picture! haha hah ... la maga, I decided that you are a girl to me because I am a girl and oscar de la hoya told me el maga is my admirador preferido [my biggest fan] ... se you later alligator, ha, ha, ha. I'm scooby doooooooooo where are you? I'm right here.

In this email Martha still includes the description of the game and her affective reactions to it (being both good at it, but also lazy). She also mentions other figures of her personal life, including her brother who gave her candy – even teasingly offering candy to El Maga. She invokes two characters and personalities that index two different cultural worlds, Scooby Doo the American TV cartoon character, and the Mexican American heavyweight boxing champion Oscar de la Hoya. Even El Maga's identity is changed to a feminine entity "La Maga" as Martha playfully and explicitly informs El Maga that she will be a girl like her. The linguistic and cultural hybridity of this exchange stands in stark contrast to Martha's initial email, and likewise El Maga's response:

Email from El Maga to Martha:
3/12/97
Hi Martha,
Are you kidding – I love tortillas. I make my own. my mom taught me how to make them. do you know how to make tortillas? if you do we must exchange recetas [recipes]. You do make me laugh with your e-mail. keep up the good work and please write me more like you wrote me today. ha ha ha! ai nos vamos, vimos, viendo [we'll see/be seen/ be seeing each other]
El Maga

In this response, El Maga culturally affiliates with Martha by mentioning the fact that tortilla-making is part of El Maga's experiences at home. El Maga also brings to their email correspondence the figure of its/her/his mother. El Maga praises Martha's participation in the computer game and encourages her to continue writing like she did on that day. El Maga ends the email with a popular Spanish playful take on the conjugation of the verb phrase "going to see each other" ("nos vamos, vimos, viendo").

In the hybrid context of the email exchanges between Martha and El Maga, the development of Martha's emails over time move from a report of the game activity[20] (figure 11.4) to a range of activities and characters that incorporates her experiences outside *Las Redes* and which includes her centrally as a developing protagonist (figure 11.5).

Indeed, Martha's email exchanges with El Maga are examples of literacy activities that promote engagement with text by addressing a problem-solving dimension (the report of the computer game interaction) that expands, in the context of interpretive

Figure 11.4   Exchange 1

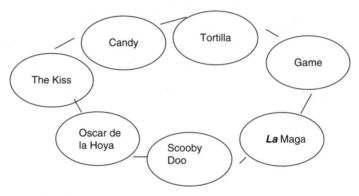

Figure 11.5   Exchange 3

practice, to a more complex web of cultural events. This interpretive practice also includes the elements of selectivity, relatability, affiliation, and identity formation as illustrated in figure 11.6.

Much like Lee's high school lessons on signifying, the Spanish-immersion unit on human reproduction, and the religious education classroom narrative of *doctrina* classes, the email exchanges between Martha and El Maga at *Las Redes* are examples of local ways in which these texts and activities are constructed and interpreted and of how participants make sense of a literacy activity while engaged in it. In all these examples there is an interrelatedness of text, activity, and language (e.g., the use of verbal genres, question–answer sequences, codes, registers, or codeswitching) as mediating tools. Take for example Lee's high school class. The possibility of discussing and affiliating through knowledge and discussion of the shared practice of signifying allows for engaged participation and meaning-making across two literary texts and the students' knowledge of a verbal practice. At *Las Redes*, the email exchanges build on each writer's cultural and linguistic resources as they employ a range of genres from a report to problem-solving to humor, as both Martha and El Maga construct their identities as members of an after-school program and of a larger linguistic and cultural group. The email exchanges in this way signal co-membership beyond the literacy activity and task.

6   Conclusion

The examples of literacy activities described in this chapter collectively illustrate that local cultural and linguistic resources can be used in literacy development and in the organization of learning to allow students opportunities to display what they know

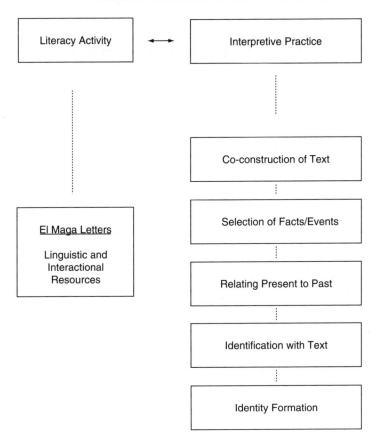

Figure 11.6   Email exchanges as interpretive practice

and to build on it. Finally, the centrality of language in the learning process as exemplified in these excerpts from learning contexts both in and out of school cannot be overemphasized. Understanding language as an interpretive lens can help us to better understand issues in schooling and the complexity of learning. There is still the impending task of documenting how the larger society's ideologies and practices, and the relations of power articulated in what counts as literacy, shape the learning process, especially for linguistically and culturally diverse learner populations. And perhaps this might make us move away from deficit thinking with a focus on the problems of alternative forms of learning. Instead, we might find it more productive to understand how local literacy practices are organized by the participants, how they work for them and can be useful for interpreting new material; in short, how talk and cultural knowledge can create and make possible the imagination of past, present, and possible worlds that promote literacy learning and knowledge for all.

NOTES

1   Giroux (1992) states: "Texts must be decentered and understood as historical and social constructions marked by the weight of a range of inherited and specified readings ... Texts

must also be understood in terms of the principles that structure them. This suggests not only identifying precise ideological interests … understanding how distinctive practices actually frame such texts by looking at the elements that produce them within established circuits of power" (p. 30). See also Wertsch (1997) for a similar argument on the historicity of text.

2   The New London Studies Group 1996.

3   California Department of Education: *English Learner Students and Enrollment in California Public Schools, 1993–2001.*

4   Cf. John Dewey as cited in Vygotsky 1978: 53.

5   Mrs. Lee's class was part of a quasi-experimental design study of underachieving seniors in two urban high schools. The study showed positive correlations between the use of local knowledge (including features of African American Vernacular English) and problem-solving in academic contexts (Lee 1993, 2000).

6   In Lee's words, "To signify within the African-American community means to speak with innuendo and double meanings, to play rhetorically upon the meaning and sounds of words, and to be quick and often witty in one's response" (Lee 2000: 221). See also Gates 1984, 1988; Mitchell-Kernan 1981; Lee 1993; and Morgan 1998.

7   Mehan (1979) and Cazden (1988) provide the first comprehensive analyses of classroom discourse dynamics.

8   The Third Space is a particularly useful concept for capturing the disruption of center–margin, official–unofficial, time–space dichotomies. A productive construct in cultural studies (Bhabha 1994), it is increasingly being used in the study of literacy instruction and learning (see also Wilson 2003).

9   Cf. Gutiérrez, Rymes, and Larson 1995; Gutiérrez, Baquedano-López, and Turner 1997; and Gutiérrez, Baquedano-López, and Tejeda 1999.

10 In this body of work hybridity refers to the coexistence and contradictions that result from employing different linguistic codes and registers.

11 The transcript has been slightly modified. The example is discussed at length in Gutiérrez, Baquedano-López, and Tejeda (1999).

12 This project was part of an ongoing collaborative effort reported in Gutiérrez, Baque-dano-López, and Alvarez, 2001 and in Gutiérrez, Baquedano-López, Alvarez, and Chiu 1999.

13 First Communion is a Catholic sacrament, a rite of passage that signals membership as a more mature member of the congregation.

14 Cf. Nicolopoulou and Cole 1993; Olt and Woodbridge 1993; Griffin and Cole 1984; Vásquez 1994; Cole 1996; Gutiérrez, Baquedano-López, and Alvarez, 2001; Stone and Gutiérrez, in press.

15 Also Baquedano-López and Alvarez (1999) and Baquedano-López, Alvarez, and Gutiér-rez (1998).

16 This was primarily a University of California sponsored project. The P.I. was K. D. Gutiérrez at the University of California, Los Angeles.

17 The program is a response to various political initiatives that threaten the educational channel for ethnic and linguistically diverse students into higher education, most notably the ballot-initiative that passed in 1998 and which banned bilingual education in the State of California (discussed above).

18 These excerpts are discussed at length in Gutiérrez, Baquedano-López, Alvarez, and Chiu (1999) and in Gutiérrez, Baquedano-López, and Alvarez (2001). They are also reviewed in Hull and Schultz (2002).

19 These examples are reproduced as close to the original as possible.

20 Ochs and Taylor (1992) make a useful distinction between a *story* of personal experience and a *report* of personal experience. A *story* is more a problem-centered past-time narrative

that eventually orients tellers (and participants) toward solving some aspect of the narrated events seen as problematic, whereas a *report* does not entail such a problem-centered or problem-solving interaction or treat problematic events as causal events that generate other events. Martha's emails with El Maga illustrate a progression from report to story.

REFERENCES

Bakhtin, M. (1981). *The Dialogic Imagination*. Austin: University of Texas Press.

Baquedano-López, P. (1997). Creating Social Identities through *Doctrina* Narratives. *Issues in Applied Linguistics* 8(1): 27–45.

Baquedano-López, P. (2000). Narrating Community in *Doctrina* Classes. *Narrative Inquiry* 10(2): 429–452.

Baquedano-López, P., and Alvarez, H. (1999). Play, Challenge, and Collaboration at an Urban Elementary After-school Program. American Educational Research Association (AERA), Montreal, Canada, April 23.

Baquedano-López, P., Alvarez, H., and Gutiérrez, K. (1998). Negotiating Fairness at an After-school Club. Paper presented at the 98th annual meeting of the American Anthropological Association, Philadelphia, December 5.

Berthoff, A. (ed.) (1984). *Reclaiming the Imagination: Philosophical Perspectives for Writers and Teachers of Writing*. Montclair, NJ: Boynton Cook.

Bhabha, H. (1994). *The Location of Culture*. London: Routledge.

Biber, D. (1988). *Variation across Speech and Writing*. Cambridge: Cambridge University Press.

California Department of Education (2001). *English Learner Students and Enrollment in California Public Schools, 1993–2001*. http://www.cde.ca.gov/demographics/reports/statewide/lepstpct.htm

Cazden, C. (1988). *Classroom Discourse: The Language of Teaching and Learning*. Portsmouth, NH: Heinemann.

Cole, M. (1985). The Zone of Proximal Development: Where Culture and Cognition Create Each Other. In J. Wertsch (ed.), *Culture, Communication and Cognition: Vygotskian Perspectives* (pp. 146–161). Cambridge: Cambridge University Press.

Cole, M. (1996). *Cultural Psychology: A Once and Future Discipline*. Cambridge, MA: The Belknap Press of Harvard University Press.

Duranti, A., and Ochs, E. (1997). Syncretic Literacy in a Samoan-American Family. In L. B. Resnick, R. Säljö, C. Pontecorvo, and B. Burge (eds.), *Discourse, Tools, and Reasoning* (pp. 169–202). Berlin: Springer.

Duranti, A., Ochs, E., and Ta'ase, E. (1995). Change and Tradition in Literacy Instruction in a Samoan American Community. *Educational Foundations* (Fall): 57–74.

Farr, M. (1994). *En los dos idiomas*: Literacy Practices among Chicago Mexicanos. In B. Moss (ed.), *Literacy across Communities* (pp. 9–47). Cresskill, NJ: Hampton Press.

Gates, H. L. (1984). The Blackness of Blackness: A Critique of the Sign and the Signifying Monkey. In H. L. Gates (ed.), *Black Literature and Literary Theory* (pp. 285–322). New York: Methuen.

Gates, H. L. (1988). *The Signifying Monkey: A Theory of Afro-American Literary Criticism*. New York: Oxford University Press.

Giroux, H. (1992). *Border Crossings: Cultural Workers and the Politics of Education*. New York: Routledge.

Griffin, P., and Cole, M. (1984). Current Activity for the Future: The Zo-ped. In B. Rogoff and J. Wertsch (eds.), *New Directions for Child Development* (pp. 45–63). San Francisco: Jossey-Bass.

Guerra, J. (1998). *Close to Home: Oral and Literate Practices in a Transnational Mexicano Community.* New York: Teachers College Press.

Guerra, J., and Farr, M. (2002). Writing on the Margins: The Spiritual and Autobiographical Discourse of Two Mexicanas in Chicago. In G. Hull and K. Schultz (eds.), *School's Out! Bridging Out-of-School Literacies with Classroom Practice* (pp. 96–123). New York: Teachers College/Columbia University.

Gumperz, J. J. (1982). *Discourse Strategies.* Cambridge: Cambridge University Press.

Gutiérrez, K., Baquedano-López, P., and Alvarez, H. (2001). Literacy as Hybridity: Moving beyond Bilingualism in Urban Classrooms. In M. de la L. Reyes and J. Halcon (eds.), *The Best for Our Children* (pp. 122–141). New York: Teachers College/Columbia University.

Gutiérrez, K., Baquedano-López, P., Alvarez, H., and Chiu, M. (1999). Building a Culture of Collaboration through Hybrid Language Practices. *Theory into Practice* 38(2): 87–93.

Gutiérrez, K., Baquedano-López, P., and Tejeda, C. (1999). Rethinking Diversity: Hybridity and Hybrid Language Practices in the Third Space. *Mind, Culture, and Activity* 6(4): 286–303.

Gutiérrez, K., Baquedano-López, P., and Turner, M. G. (1997). Putting Language Back into the Language Arts: When the Radical Middle Meets the Third Space. *Language Arts* 74(5): 368–378.

Gutiérrez, K., Rymes, B., and Larson, J. (1995). Script, Counterscript, and Underlife in the classroom: James Brown versus Brown vs. Board of Education. *Harvard Educational Review* 65(3): 445–471.

Gutiérrez, K., and Stone, L. (1997). A Cultural-Historical View of Learning and Learning Disabilities: Participating in a Community of Learners. *Learning Disabilities: Research and Practice* 12(2): 123–131.

Gutiérrez, K., and Stone, L. (2000). Synchronic and Diachronic Dimensions of Social Practice: An Emerging Methodology for Cultural-Historical Perspectives on Literacy Learning. In C. Lee and P. Smagorinsky (eds.), *Vygotskian Perspectives on Literacy Research: Constructing Meaning through Collaborative Inquiry* (pp. 150–164). Cambridge: Cambridge University Press.

Heath, S. (1983). *Ways with Words: Language, Life, and Work in Communities and Classrooms.* Cambridge: Cambridge University Press.

Hull, G., and Schultz, K. (2002). Connecting Schools with Out-of-school Worlds: Insights from Research on Literacy in Non-school Settings. In G. Hull and K. Schultz (eds.), *School's Out! Bridging Out-of-School Literacies with Classroom Practice* (pp. 32–57). New York: Teachers College/Columbia University.

Langer, J. (1987). A Sociocognitive Perspective on Literacy. In J. Langer (ed.), *Language, Literacy, and Culture: Issues of Society and Schooling* (pp. 1–20). Norwood, NJ: Ablex.

Lankshear, C., and McLaren, P. (eds.) (1993). *Critical Literacy: Politics, Praxis, and the Postmodern.* Albany, NY: State University of New York Press.

Lave, J., and Wenger, E. (1991). *Situated Learning: Legitimate Peripheral Participation.* Cambridge: Cambridge University Press.

Lee, C. (1993). *Signifying as a Scaffold for Literary Interpretation: The Pedagogical Implications of an African-American Discourse Genre.* Urbana, IL: National Council of Teachers of English.

Lee, C. (2000). Signifying in the Zone of Proximal Development. In C. Lee and P. Smagorinsky (eds.), *Vygotskian Perspectives on Literacy Research: Constructing Meaning through Collaborative Inquiry* (pp. 191–225). Cambridge: Cambridge University Press.

Luke, A. (1994). *The Social Construction of Literacy in the Primary School*. Melbourne, Australia: Macmillan.

Mehan, H. (1979). "What Time Is It, Denise?" Asking Known Information Questions in Classroom Discourse. *Theory into Practice* 18: 285–294.

Mitchell-Kernan, C. (1981). Signifying, Loud-talking, and Marking. In A. Dundes (ed.), *Mother Wit from the Laughing Barrel* (pp. 310–320). Englewood Cliffs, NJ: Prentice-Hall.

Moll, L. (1992). Funds of Knowledge for Teaching: Using a Qualitative Approach to Connect Homes and Classrooms. *Theory into Practice* 31(2): 132–141.

Moll, L. (2000). Inspired by Vygotsky: Ethnographic Experiments in Education. In C. Lee and P. Smagorinsky (eds.), *Vygotskian Perspectives on Literacy Research: Constructing Meaning through Collaborative Inquiry* (pp. 256–268). Cambridge: Cambridge University Press.

Moll, L., and Gonzalez, N. (1997). Teachers as Social Scientists: Learning about Culture from Household Research. In P. M. Hall (ed.), *Race, Ethnicity and Multiculturalism* (pp. 89–114). New York: Garland.

Morgan, M. (1998). More than a Mood or an Attitude: Discourse and Verbal Genres in African-American Culture. In S. Mufwene, J. Rickford, and J. Baugh (eds.), *African-American English: Structure, History and Use* (pp. 251–281). London: Routledge.

Moss, B. (1994). Creating a Community: Literacy Events in African-American Churches. In B. Moss (ed.), *Literacy across Communities* (pp. 147–178). Cresskill, NJ: Hampton Press.

New London Studies Group (1996). A Pedagogy of Multiliteracies: Designing Social Futures. *Harvard Educational Review* 66(1): 60–92.

Nicolopoulou, A., and Cole, M. (1993). Generation and Transmission of Shared Knowledge in the Culture of Collaborative Learning: The Fifth Dimension, Its Play World, and Its Institutional Contexts. In E. A. Forman, N. Minick, and C. A. Stone (eds.), *Contexts for Learning: Sociocultural Dynamics in Children's Development* (pp. 283–313). New York: Oxford University Press.

Ochs, E. (1988). *Culture and Language Development: Language Acquisition and Language Socialization in a Samoan Village*. Cambridge: Cambridge University Press.

Ochs, E., and Capps, L. (1996). Narrating the Self. *Annual Review of Anthropology* 25: 19–43.

Ochs, E., and Capps, L. (2001). *Living Narrative: Creating Lives in Everyday Storytelling*. Cambridge, MA: Harvard University Press.

Ochs, E., and Taylor, C. (1992). Family Narrative as a Political Activity. *Discourse and Society* 3: 301–340.

Olson, D. (1985). Introduction. In D. Olson, N. Torrance, and A. Hildyard (eds.), *Literacy, Language, and Learning: The Nature and Consequences of Reading and Writing* (pp. 1–15). Cambridge: Cambridge University Press.

Olt, A., and Woodbridge, S. (1993). An Assessment of Learning through the Qualitative Analysis of Fieldnotes. Paper presented at the Conference on Assessment and Diversity. University of California, Santa Cruz, Feb. 17–20.

Rogoff, B. (1990). *Apprenticeship in Thinking: Cognitive Development in Social Context*. New York: Oxford University Press.

Rogoff, B. (1993). Children's Guided Participation and Participatory Appropriation in Sociocultural Activity. In R. Wozniak and K. Fischer (eds.), *Development in Context: Acting and Thinking in Specific Environments* (pp. 121–153). Hillsdale, NJ: Lawrence Erlbaum.

Schieffelin, B. B., and Ochs, E. (eds.) (1986). *Language Socialization across Cultures*. Cambridge: Cambridge University Press.

Scribner, S., and Cole, M. (1981). *The Psychology of Literacy*. Cambridge, MA: Harvard University Press.

Stone, L., and Gutiérrez, K. (in press). Problem-finding as Distributed Intelligence: The Role of Changing Participation in Mathematical Problem-solving Activities in an After-school Learning Community. *Mind, Culture, and Activity: An International Journal*.

Vásquez, O. (1994). The Magic of *La Clase Mágica*: Enhancing the Learning Potential of Bilingual Children. *Australian Journal of Language and Literacy* 17(2): 120–128.

Vygotsky, L. (1978). *Mind in Society: The Development of Higher Psychological Processes*. Cambridge, MA: Harvard University Press.

Wells, G. (1985). Pre-school Literacy Related Activities and Success in School. In D. Olson, N. Torrance, and A. Hildyard (eds.), *Literacy, Language and Learning: The Nature and Consequences of Reading and Writing* (pp. 229–255). Cambridge: Cambridge University Press.

Wenger, E. (1998). *Communities of Practice: Learning, Meaning, and Identity*. Cambridge: Cambridge University Press.

Wertsch, J. (1997). *Mind as Action*. Oxford: Oxford University Press.

Wilson, A. (2003). Researching in the Third Space: Locating, Claiming and Valuing the Research Domain. In S. Goodman, T. Lillis, J. Maybin, and N. Mercer (eds.), *Language, Literacy, and Education: A Reader* (pp. 293–307). Stoke on Trent: Trentham Books and The Open University.

12 Narrative Lessons

Elinor Ochs

1 INTRODUCTION

This chapter takes the form of a series of lessons concerning narratives of personal experience. The lessons have been gleaned from analyses of the dynamics of conversational story-telling moments, in which interlocutors turn to friends, family, coworkers, mentors, healers, or others to piece together their experiences. These narratives are central to weaving the fabric of social life in that they forge and sustain social relationships and build shared lifeworlds.

Across the lessons, narratives of personal experience are viewed as a discourse genre, mode of cognition, and social activity. As a culturally stipulated genre, personal narrative exhibits its own internal textual organization, often referred to as plot structure (Aristotle 1982 [4th century BCE]; Propp 1968). The construal of personal experience into narrative entails complex cognitive processes, such as remembering, situating, anticipating, representing, evaluating, and otherwise interrelating life events. As noted by Jerome Bruner (1991: 8–9), "The telling of a story and its comprehension as a story... is a way of processing that, in the main, has been grossly neglected by students of mind raised either in the rationalist or in the empiricist traditions ... But neither of these procedures, right reason or verification, suffice for explicating how a narrative is either put together by a speaker or interpreted by a hearer". As social activity, narratives of personal experience the world over tend to be dialogic, co-told, and even co-authored by those who engaged in the social interaction at hand (Goodwin 1984).

The narrative lessons contained in this chapter propose that personal experience may be rendered either as a coherent narrative with a beginning, a middle and an end or as an enigmatic life episode. The lessons articulate what Ochs and Capps (2001) call a "dimensional approach" (see below) to analyzing these two narrative inclinations, wherein community- and situation-specific discursive, cognitive, and social characteristics of everyday narratives of personal experience are examined as variable realizations of universal narrative dimensions.

2   Ten Narrative Lessons

2.1   Narrative Lesson One: Narratives of personal experience imbue unexpected life events with a temporal and causal orderliness

Narratives may be more or less aesthetically rendered, but they always depict or evoke an *ordered sequence of events*. Consider, for example, a narrative excerpt about a childhood swimming incident (See Appendix for explanation of transcription conventions):

(1a)
Meg: I remember a friend of mine
who was a <u>very</u> (.) ac<u>COM</u>plished swimmer and a diver.
And she took me swimming one time and
(0.4 sec. pause)
She said "Come <u>on</u> let's jump in <u>he:re</u>."
And very trustingly I <u>di:d</u>
and it turned out to be the deep end of the po::ol.
It was unmarked
[it was a-
Lisa: [wow
Meg: The whole <u>pool</u> was deep.
It was a pool for doing laps or something.
It was ALL DEEP
Lisa: Uh huh
Meg: And uh
(0.6 sec. pause)
And I re<u>mem</u>ber just gulping water
and thinking I was going to drown
and being very <u>afRAID</u> swimmer.

Meg recounts a sequence of events in which (1) a friend takes her swimming, (2) the friend invites her to jump together in a particular area of the pool ("Come <u>on</u> let's jump in <u>he:re</u>"), (3) Meg "trustingly" jumps, (4) Meg discovers it is deep, (5) Meg gulps water, thinking "I was going to drown" and feeling "very afraid."

Sequentiality of events is a criterial property of all varieties of narrative and figures centrally in definitions of the genre. Linguist William Labov, for example, establishes narrative as a sequence of (at least) two clauses which are temporally ordered (1972). Similarly, literary philosopher Paul Ricoeur (1981) considers the "chronological dimension" (along with plot configuration) to be a central narrative property. Even a simple sequence of two events across time constitutes a narrative logic, in that the two events are positioned in relation to one another. In strictly temporal sequences, one event is first and the other occurs later as a second event:

Event 1 (Precedes →) Event 2

In many narratives, however, the temporal ordering belies a more complex narrative logic. Why do narrators select these two events to temporally juxtapose and not others? Why, in the above excerpt, does the narrator temporally conjoin the event of jumping into a deep pool with the events of gulping water and fearing for her life? The temporally ordered events are usually not random occurrences but rather are linked in situationally relevant ways. In juxtaposing the events, narrators typically convey that the antecedent event (e.g. jumping into a deep pool) somehow gives rise to or *affords* the possible occurrence of the subsequent event (e.g. gulping water and experiencing fear):

$$\text{Event 1} \quad \left(\begin{array}{c} \text{Precedes} \rightarrow \\ \text{Affords} \rightarrow \end{array} \right) \quad \text{Event 2}$$

That is, even without linguistic markers of origin, possibility, probability, consequence, entailment, and utility, temporally ordered events may implicate some form of derivative or causal relation.

2.2   Narrative Lesson Two: The life events that receive narrative attention tend to be cast as unusual, in that they are unexpected or problematic

The experiences recounted by tellers are often those that disrupt the ordinary business of daily life (Labov 1966). For example, in the above excerpt, Meg focuses on the childhood event of diving into a pool over her head. While some of these reportable events may be anticipated, most are rendered as unexpected ("and it turned out to be the deep end of the po::ol"). In many narratives of personal experience, the events run counter to personal, familial, or community assumptions about how events should unfold and how life should be lived. As Bruner (2002: 31) notes, "Narrative is a recounting of human plans gone off the track, expectations gone awry." Moreover, across speech communities, the narrated events are often problematic from the perspective of the teller or protagonist (Ochs and Capps 2001). The activity of narrating unforeseen, problematic life events raises awareness of expectations and provides a social modality for coping with such experiences.

The unanticipated or problematic character of an event lends a certain *frisson* and a focal point of interest to narration. Such an event often constitutes the pivotal element around which the *plot* is constructed (Burke 1962). The unusual event creates dramatic tension by raising interest in the setting that provoked the unexpected or problematic event in the first place and the events that subsequently transpired. Settings are critical elements of the plot, in that they not only situate but also establish a rationale for the reportable event and/or its aftermath, e.g. depicting relevant times, locations, shared knowledge, prior events, and situational conditions. In the above excerpt, for example, the narrator provides the relevant setting that her friend was "a <u>very</u> (.) acCOMplished swimmer and diver" and that the pool was deep. Prior to this excerpt, the narrator had provided yet another element of the setting central to the import of her experience:

(1b)

Meg: My mother never bothered to give us swimming lessons
      [until I was thirt↑e:en.
Lisa: [Aww
Meg: And so I had a fear of water =
Lisa: = Umhm?
Meg: I liked to <u>swim</u>
      but I would never go in the deep end,
      and I was okay as long as I stayed <u>out</u> of that deep end.

These elements of the setting provide a rationale for why Meg's diving into a pool that turned out to be deep led to her sensation of nearly drowning. Moreover, background statements such as "I would never go in the deep end" and "I was okay as long as I stayed out of that deep end" foreshadow the traumatic pool experience that subsequently transpires. Narrators sometimes withhold such background information until well into the narrative for dramatic effect (e.g. what film theorists call "slow disclosure" (Sharff 1982)), or because they only gradually understand how an experience is grounded in past or present conditions, or because they otherwise have reasons to conceal these points of relevance (Ochs, Smith, and Taylor 1989).

In addition to linking the unexpected or problematic events to settings, narrative plot lines also relate such events to their aftermaths. For example, narrators may build a narrative logic by recounting how an unexpected or problematic event brought about a protagonist's *psychological* or *physiological response*. Meg, for example, recounts how diving into a pool led to her awareness of being in deep water and her fearfulness. Subsequently, she elaborates more enduring psychological outcomes:

(1c)

Meg: and after that thinking of myself as um
      (0.3 sec pause)
      <u>not</u> measuring up when it came to swim↑ming
Lisa: Umhm
Meg: Feeling in<u>FER</u>ior to my friend and embarrassed
      that I'd nearly drowned.

It is also common for tellers to recount subsequent *attempts* of a protagonist to resolve or come to terms with the problematic or unexpected nature of an event. Later in her narrative, for example, Meg recounts how she partly overcame her sense of helplessness:

(1d)

Meg: When I did get instruction at the YMCA
      I proved to be a competent enough swimmer.

Even so her self-confidence never fully returned:

(1e)

Meg: But I <u>still</u> wouldn't uh- (0.3 sec pause) say

I'm a stro::ng swimmer.
I-in fact you know I still fee:l in many ways um (0.4 sec pause) still some fear of the water.

Indeed, these feelings of fear and anxiety mushroomed into panic disorder in Meg's adult life (Capps and Ochs 1995a, b). This eventual outcome is related to another possible aftermath of an unexpected or problematic event, namely changes in the state of a person or object. Thus, narrators recount how, for example, a snowboarding accident led to a debilitating injury, eating a chili pepper resulted in a burnt mouth, an earthquake toppled buildings, and so on (Ochs and Capps 2001).

2.3 Narrative Lesson Three: Narratives of personal experience are organized in terms of human time, wherein the experienced present is tied to a remembered past, an anticipated future, and/or an imagined moment

When tellers recount narratives of human experience, they tend to become enveloped in a temporal frame of reference that resonates with their experience, memory, anticipation, and imagination. Complementary to objectively measured time, a phenomenological sense of time draws upon the philosophical notion that human beings bring memories of their lived pasts and their projected or imagined, yet to be realized, life courses into their consciousness of the present (Augustine 1961[4th century CE]; Husserl 1991; Heidegger 1962; Ricoeur 1984, 1985, 1988). In Heidegger's framework, rememberings of past experience are filtered through one's current cares, through which *Dasein* (Being) is constituted, about mortality and an uncertain future. Certain past experiences may vividly invade our current consciousness (e.g. diving into a deep pool), while others remain at a distance. Alternatively, the recollection of the past may provoke thoughts and actions that orient toward future event horizons.

The future-directedness of a narrative often takes the form of unfolding forward-moving events that are fueled by prior events and circumstances. As noted in Lesson Two, a setting may foreshadow a problematic event, and/or a problematic event may provoke physical changes of state or protagonists' intentions, desires, and actions. While Meg's narrative of her childhood diving experience is characterized by a succession of unintended, uncontrollable misfortunes, temporality in other narratives involves more controlled future-oriented responses, such as preparing or carrying out a plan of action. In excerpt (2a) below, for example, a mother recounts to her son how a burglary at a bank prompted the installation of a protective window for the bank tellers:

(2a)
Mother: And you know what happened today
         when I went to the bank?
Son: What.
Mother: Not that anything happened
         but they had to install a high high

((*raises hand high above head, looking up*))
bullet proof windo:w (.) in front of
where the tellers take your money
(0.2 sec. pause)
because a couple months ago
[there was a burg - there was a armed robber =

Son: [are they ( )
Mother: = that went in there.
            And he <u>hurt</u> some of the tellers
            and said "Give me your money"

This excerpt also illustrates the point that temporality in narrative does not necessarily flow in chronological order. The narrative episode begins with the reporting of a constructive modification of the local bank then moves on to the dangerous incident that motivated this change.

Narratives about a past incident may be linked to future-directed life events beyond the time frame of the past experience recounted. In some cases, the recounting of past events "instigates" a projection into the yet-to-be-realized future (Goodwin 1990). In other cases, speculation about what the future holds may lead interlocutors to return to a relevant past incident. For example, just prior to the bank robbery narrative, family members warn the five-year-old son of the family not to bring a pretend cigarette lighter that he has fashioned out of aluminum foil to school. His mother and older sister speculate that it could be mistaken for an actual lighter:

(2b)
Son: MOM LOOK
                (0.3 sec. pause)
                [MOM a cigarette lighter
                [((*lifts handmade aluminum foil toy "lighter" toward Mother*))
Daughter: I <u>hope</u> not.
Mother: That really looks like one Brian
                [I thought you ha↑d one
Father: [((*looks at Son*))
Son: A little one
Daughter: [Well <u>don't</u> take that to school
                [((*looking at her brother*))
Son: [Why?
                [((*looking at his sister*))
Mother: ((*looks at Daughter*))
Daughter: You could get in bi:g trouble.
                If I took something like that to school?
                ((*looks at Father*))
                And the teacher thought it was a cigarette lighter?
                [She'd- I'd get suspended
                [((*looking at her brother, vertical head nods*))
Father: We ↑ we really know that it's not a cigarette lighter right?
Son: Yeah

Mother: But somebody <u>else</u> might not know it's
Daughter: Yeah

At this point, Mother links possible future trajectories of teachers mistaking a toy cigarette lighter for a real one to bank tellers mistaking a toy gun for the genuine item:

(2c)
Mother: [Kind of like that-
             [(*(looks at Son)*)
Son: [What would the teacher do if I?
             [(*(looks at Mother)*)
Mother: like that toy <u>gun</u> I was telling Billy the other day
             that people have been arre:sted
             [(*(looks at Father and back at Son)*)
Father: [(*(looks at Mother)*)
Mother: for pulling out toy <u>guns</u> in <u>ba:nks</u>
             because sometimes the bank teller thinks
             it's a real robber
             (*(looks at Father)*)
             (0.4 sec. pause)
Father: (*(nods)*)
Daughter: with a real <u>gun</u>

After this confirmation by Father and Daughter of the hazards of toy guns and by implication toy lighters, Mother launches the narrative (see (2a)) of the installation of a bullet-proof window in the bank after a robbery ("And you know what happened today when I went to the bank?").

Excerpts such as this illustrate the intermingling of imaginings and rememberings in narrative activity. Interlocutors may traverse multiple temporal domains in the course of ordering a sequence of events in narrative form. These temporalities are brought into dialogic consciousness through the medium of narrative. In excerpt (2b), Daughter constructs a narrative that depicts a sequence of hypothetical future happenings:

"If I took something like that to school?"
→ "And the teacher thought it was a cigarette lighter?"
→ "She'd- I'd get suspended"

In excerpt (2c) Mother then recounts a past common sequence of events in which people "pulling out toy <u>guns</u> in <u>banks</u>" "have been ar<u>rested</u>" because they were thought to be "a real robber". This scenario in turn draws the Mother and her interlocutors (excerpt (2a)) to recount the frightening bank robbery sequence of events leading to the recent installation of a protective window. In this manner, anxiety thoughts about the future prompt the remembering of past perils.

2.4   Narrative Lesson Four: The transformation of personal experience into a variety of narrative logics is one of the distinguishing accomplishments of the human species

The semiotic renderings of life events by certain other species are highly circumscribed and highly conventionalized, focusing on a single recent or impending occurrence, such as the presence of food or a predator (Deacon 1997; Gould and Gould 1988; Sugiyama 1996; von Frisch 1967). Human narrators, alternatively, have the luxury of a rich repertoire of symbolic forms and historically informed genres (e.g. gossip, testimonials, confessions, eye-witness reports, diaries, memoirs, dream performances) as well as stylistic strategies to nuance their renderings of personal experience. And the events rendered in narrative form extend as far as the interface of culture and the human mind allows through the workings of memory, anticipation, and imagination.

The drive to impose a logic on life experience is ubiquitous, cutting across languages and social groups large and small, and across the life span, emergent at the earliest stages of language development. It is not hard to imagine why the impulse to narrate experience is pervasive. The human condition is such that we not only act in and on the world, we also reflect on our actions and reflect on our reflections. In the middle of experiences, we are myopic and cannot make sense of them in relation to our expectations concerning people, objects, environments, activities, internal states, and other facets of the human condition. In narrating we do not replay an intact experience so much as bring experience into social and psychological focus.

2.5   Narrative Lesson Five: Narrating personal experience consists of two practices

Narrative Practice 1	Narrative Practice 2
Narrators present one consistent logic of experience, including an unexpected/problematic event and resolution.	Narrators question or dispute the meaning or accuracy of a recounted logic of experience.

If we think of narratives of personal experience as raising a dilemma for protagonists, Narrative Practice 1 generates both the dilemma and its resolution. The bank robbery narrative exemplifies Narrative Practice 1, in that it displays both the problematic incident of the bank hold-up and the subsequent means of handling the problem, namely the bullet-proof teller window. While this narrative practice depicts a way out of life's predicaments, Narrative Practice 2 draws narrators into probing multiple logics of experience, calling into question what happened, why, and/or the relevance of an incident for life more generally (Morson 1994; Ochs and Capps 2001), as in excerpt (3) below (Ochs, Taylor, et al. 1992: 52–3). In this excerpt, the co-narrators of the past sequence of events are also the protagonists of the story, and they dispute what each other thought, said, and did in an incident involving photo negatives. They also dispute the moral character of one another; each casts the other as irresponsible, which in turn is rejected:

(3)
Marie: Jon – Do you have those negatives from the (pony?) pictures?
Jon: Yeah –
        They're a:ll in your cabinet ((pointing))
Marie: ((clears throat)) I wish you woulda told (Janie)
        cuz that's why I sent her down
        (cuz/and) Susan wanted em – when she came ↑ –
        (so she could) go (if) she took my roll of film =
Jon: = ((with slight shrug)) Sorry –
        I told Janie I didn't have time to come in –
        Janie didn't ask me that –
        What Janie asked me was –
        Can I get the negative fo:r Susan's picture –
        [That meant I had to go through all those negatives
        [((breathy))
        and I was- I said "Hey I .h – I don't –
        Tell her I don't have time to do that right now"
        . . .
        I did the best I could with the information that I was given
        . . .
        I did not know =
        . . .
        = that you needed to know the location of the – film
        . . .
        ('f) Janie had come out and said to me –
        "Dad will you tell M:Mommy
        where the films- are from the pic↑tures"
        I would have said "Yes? Janie"
Marie: [Well when she's about eight or nine =
Jon: [Janie came out =
Marie: = I bet she'll be able to do that
        . . .
Jon: YOU: are over eight or nine are you not?
Marie: Ye:s – and that's exactly what I told her to say↑ =
Jon: That's right?
Marie: = is to find out where the negatives were. =
        . . .
Marie: = so I could give them to Susan
        (0.2 sec. pause)
Jon: I↑ see –
        Well she didn't she di-
        she didn't give me your message =
        . . .
        = in the form you asked it
        ((narrative continues))

Narrative Practice 2 explores alternative understandings of experience, including the possibility that some life problems such as serious illnesses may be ultimately unresolvable. Across communities everyday narrative practice gives human beings an opportunity to examine facets of life experience and try to piece them together into a temporal, causal, and moral logic.

In recounting narratives of personal experience, tellers are pulled between their desire to arrive at a coherent account of life events and their desire to construct an account that is authentic, that is, that resonates with their understandings and sensibilities of what it was like to participate in the events being narrated. The desire for coherence of life experience is so strong, however, that it often overwhelms the desire for authenticity. Narrators want an explanation of events and moral guidelines for participating in them. In their desire to make sense out of events, they construct for themselves and for their interlocutors narratives that have a beginning, a middle, and an end, wrapped in a cloak of moral certainty (Bernstein 1994; Morson 1994). The most important characteristic of these narratives is that they offer a framework for handling unanticipated situations. Narratives "domesticate" unexpected life events by providing cultural schemata for interpreting them (Bruner 2002). Focal events are organized in terms of cultural genres of experience; precedents are proffered; and breaches and ways of dealing with them are outlined. Coherent narratives may be rhetorically compelling, having the character of what Mary Louise Pratt (1977) calls "display texts." These effective narratives of personal experience create colloquial dramas, which share aesthetic qualities of literary genres.

Authenticity plays second fiddle to these culturally canonical grids for interpreting events. For example, so-called master narratives of war or debilitating illness very often overwhelm individual renderings of these experiences (Morrison 1994). Default narrative models for making sense out of experience are pervasive, from mass media to professional advisers to peers and family offerings of their own parallel experiences and other precedents with which to interpret a specific experience.

Coherent renderings of personal experience, however, may dissolve when narrators exercise a desire to probe further and make sense out of events in a way that captures how they and other protagonists felt, thought, and acted. Coherent canonical narratives may simply not ring true to participants in or analysts of events, as when Vietnamese veterans and peace activists countered official accounts of the war events (O'Brien 1990), or when sufferers of a chronic illness discard medical narratives of recovery (Mattingly 1998). Even or especially in intimate contexts of narrating experiences among friends, family, and healers, tellers may raise doubts about their own and others' versions of what transpired. Interlocutors engaged in reconstructing events through narrative may suggest alternative scenarios or pose queries that leave ambiguous the contours of an experience.

2.6   Narrative Lesson Six: Pursuit of a coherent logic of events and pursuit of authenticity of experience differentially influence the shaping of narrative practices

Narrative practice that veers in the direction of coherence (Narrative Practice 1) is more likely to be dominated by one active primary teller, while narrative practice that involves open-ended probing (Narrative Practice 2) generally involves the active participation of more than one teller who collaboratively author the narrative of personal experience.

Narratives that lean in the direction of coherence lend themselves to *performance* and *didactic modeling*, while narratives that take the path of probing before settling upon coherence lend themselves to open-ended dialogic problem-solving. If we accept that a fundamental motivation to narrate life events is to make sense out of those events, and if we accept that narrative sense-making may reach beyond tidy progressions of events, then the boundaries of narrative can encompass raising and responding to doubts, questions, speculations, challenges, and other evaluative stances.

2.7 Narrative Lesson Seven: These two tendencies in narrating experience – one to display a coherent logic of events and the other to probe alternative logics – have ramifications for the analysis of narrative as a human endeavor

Most social scientists consider narratives of personal experience to be those that assert a logic of events within a consistent evaluative framework (Narrative Practice 1) and ignore narrative activity that draws interlocutors into dialogically piecing together frameworks for ordering and interpreting events (Narrative Practice 2). This asymmetry is startling, in that all over the world people find themselves in the position of beginning to narrate an experience without having a firm grip or consensus on the shape and meaning of that experience. Whether as gossip or as mealtime accounts of the day's events or in some other social context, narrative probings of life events pervade informal social interactions around the world. Moreover, it is precisely this sort of dialogic narrative interaction that lays the foundations for open-ended, problem-solving narrative activity in law and science (Amsterdam and Bruner 2000; Ochs, Taylor, et al. 1992). In laboratory settings, for example, scientific accounts of physical events are vulnerable to challenge. The purported temporal and causal logic of events is probed and revised as a matter of course (Ochs and Jacoby 1997).

2.8 Narrative Lesson Eight: Recognition of distinct narrative practices affects the scholarly conceptualization of competence in narrating life events

The acquisition of the ability to tell narratives, especially narratives of personal experience, entails two forms of competence:

Narrative Competence 1	Narrative Competence 2
Competence to present a certain, consistent logic of events	Competence to probe, challenge, revise a logic of events

Each of these forms of competence is organized by communities of speaker-hearers, and each entails cognitive and social challenges. Narrative Competence 1 involves the ability to articulate a temporal sequence of events; situate the events; compose a coherent plot line with a beginning, middle, and end; and maintain a moral perspective (Berman and Slobin 1994; Nelson 1989; Stein and Glenn 1979). These skills develop throughout childhood, but even young children relate rudimentary coherent narratives of personal experience, as in the following excerpt from a 23-month-old child, Emily, as she recounts life events in her crib at night (Bruner and Lucariello 1989: 87–8):

(4)
Emily: Then Emily got the blanket
         and set the dinner
         Emmy ate one time
         and one time Emmy sick
         Emmy wanted dinner
         Emmy (?)
         and Emmy ate the ice
         and took dinner

In this passage, Emily recalls a problematic event ("one time Emmy sick"). Moreover, she provides a relevant prior circumstance ("Emmy ate one time") and goes on to relate her psychological response ("Emmy wanted dinner"), her attempt to remediate her problem ("and Emmy ate the ice"), and its aftermath ("and took dinner").

Narrative Competence 2, the ability to probe event logics, entails minimally the capacity to conceptualize and evaluate multiple versions of experience. This competence also develops throughout childhood and is evident in early efforts to render experience in narrative form (Feldman 1989). That is, young children ponder facets of what happened, what will happen, or what could happen in their narrative activity, as in the following excerpt by Emily at 24 months of age (Feldman 1989: 109–10):

(5)
Emily: In the bed fall down.
         Actually the bed broken.
         Huh, huuh, Daddy funny.
         The bed broken.
         Anybody can put it away.
         Emmy go to sleep.
         Maybe the baby and the mommy buy a different crib.
         Maybe do that cause the other one broken.
         What be the tree fell down.
         Could be.
         I don't know which.
         Maybe tree fell down and broke that crib.
         I don't know what thing fell down.

         . . .

         The crib did it . . .
         The tree did it.

The crib.
But I don't know which kind of lady bought the crib ...
But that one fell down.
That crib must been,
that tree must have been,
broke that tree.
That must fell down.
I don't know what lady bought it.
But the lady went to get this new crib.
But then this is one was, bring it back (seat) ...
And the you not supposed broke the tree.
(Broke) up.

Emily recounts a narrative about a broken bed that raises uncertainties about exactly what transpired and poses different possibilities of what could have occurred. The narrative is laced with a vocabulary of doubt, e.g. "Maybe," "Could be," "I don't know." One casting of an event alternates with another, e.g. "The crib did it" → "The tree did it." Emily speculates on how the bed broke in the first place and how the family will respond to the problem of the broken bed, e.g. "Maybe the baby and the mommy buy a different crib."

Overwhelmingly, acquisition research has favored a model of narrative in which competence consists of the ability to render experience in terms of a coherent temporal and causal logic. Scant attention has been paid to the equally viable template of narrative competence as the ability to engage in open-ended probing of experience. The remainder of this chapter attempts to redress this lopsided view of narrative competence by suggesting a framework for analyzing the breadth of human narrative variability. The narrative lesson that follows highlights facets of what Lisa Capps and I call a "Dimensional Approach" to narrative (Ochs and Capps 2001).

2.9 Narrative Lesson Nine: Narratives of personal experience can be analyzed in terms of five basic dimensions, each representing a spectrum of possible realizations

While temporal sequentiality is a criterial property of narratives of personal experience, other properties, such as a plot organization with a beginning, middle, and end, do not necessarily apply to all variants of personal narratives across situations and communities. The Dimensional Approach posits five dimensions that are relevant to *all* narratives of personal experience and are realized through a set of features that *variably* characterize different realizations of personal narrative. These variable features allow analysis of a range of narrative practices. The five basic narrative dimensions comprise Tellership, Tellability, Embeddedness, Linearity, and Moral Stance.

Tellership: Oral narratives of personal experience are rarely told apart from other interlocutors, as in the case of young Emily alone in her bed at night. More typically across the world's societies, personal narratives are collaboratively constructed with other interlocutors (Baquedano-López 1998; Blum-Kulka 1997; Goodwin 1986; Haviland 1977; Mattingly and Garro 2000; Miller et al. 1996; Minami 1996). The dimension of Tellership includes the extent and kind of participation in the co-telling of a narrative. As indicated by the arrow, tellership may range from one active co-teller to multiple, active co-tellers.

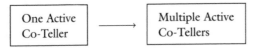

Narrative interaction may be dominated by a primary teller, who recounts events with a relatively passive co-teller. Interviews that elicit personal narratives often have this character, as illustrated in the narrative about diving into a deep pool (example 1). In this relatively informal interview, the interviewee (Meg) is the primary teller and the interviewer (Lisa) provides relatively restricted feedback ("wow," "uh huh," etc.). Alternatively, the narrative about the toy cigarette lighter, toy gun, and bank hold-up (example 2) involves several family members as active co-tellers. Some narrative interactions may start out with one variant of tellership, e.g. one primary co-teller, then shift to another form of teller participation, e.g. multiple active co-tellers.

Tellability. The dimension of Tellability refers to the significance of the narrated experience and the rhetorical style in which it is related. As noted in Lesson Two, narratives of personal experience tend to focus on events that are out of the ordinary, unexpected, or otherwise reportable (Labov 1966; Labov and Waletzky 1968). Everyday narrative activity, however, examines a range of life events, some of which are narrated as highly tellable and others which are less so:

High Tellability	Low Tellability
Experience recounted as highly reportable, in a compelling manner	Experience recounted as moderately reportable, in an uncompelling manner

As linguistic anthropologist Shirley Brice Heath (1985) notes, narratives of personal experience elicited from children by their parents may be delivered reluctantly and with minimal elaboration. Such narratives fall on the low end of the tellability dimension. What counts as a highly tellable incident depends upon personal, local, and community evaluative frameworks. For example, from Meg's perspective, diving into a pool over her head when she couldn't swim is a vivid memory and highly tellable experience. Near-death and other extraordinary experiences (Labov 1966) may be recognized as inherently tellable. Yet, gifted narrators can rhetorically transform even relatively mundane occurrences into highly tellable events. In this sense, tellability resides in narrative style.

Embeddedness. The dimension of Embeddedness captures the relation of a narrative to surrounding discourse and social activity. Narratives of personal experience vary in terms of the extent to which and how they are part of ongoing concerns along a continuum from detached to embedded. Relatively detached and embedded narratives are distinguished in terms of the following features:

Detached Narratives	Embedded Narratives
• distinct conversational turn format • unrelated thematic content • distinct rhetorical format	• continuation of prior conversational turn format • thematic content relevant • rhetorical format of surrounding discourse

Detached narratives of personal experience are recounted in a turn-taking format that differs from prior and subsequent discourse. For example, a detached narrative initiated at some point in informal conversation may be recounted across one or more relatively extended conversational turns, which sets it apart from the surrounding conversational turns of variable length. In addition, detached narratives may introduce an experience unrelated to what interlocutors have been discussing or the ongoing activity in which they are engaged. Finally, tellers of relatively detached narratives may use distinctive rhetorical techniques, such as the use of particular verb tenses, lexicon, voice quality, intonation, sound symbolism, parallelism, slow disclosure, or other available stylistic strategies. As noted, Pratt (1977) refers to these narratives of personal experience as "display texts," in that they are geared more toward performance than communication of information.

Alternatively, embedded narratives tend to continue whatever turn-taking format is in interactional play. Initiated in the course of informal conversation, for example, embedded narratives of personal experience tend to be constructed across turns of variable length and appear part of the ongoing conversational dialogue. Relatively embedded narratives also tend to relate events that extend a current focus of attention. Thus, an instructor may embed a narrative of personal experience into a lesson to illustrate a point; similarly, litigants may use a personal narrative to shore up their argument. In addition, embedded narratives may be shaped by the rhetorical style of surrounding discourse. For example, personal narratives recounted to enhance a point in instruction may be inflected with features of a teaching register or by norms for communicating in classroom contexts (Haroutunian-Gordon 1991). Similarly, personal narratives delivered as part of legal testimony, medical visits, and political arguments may be constrained by institutional norms (Drew and Heritage 1992).

Linearity. The dimension of Linearity attends to the narrative logic organizing a sequence of events and lies at the heart of the distinction between narrative practices that favor coherence and those that favor inquiry. Narratives of personal experience related in the course of informal conversation vary in terms of how tightly events are woven into an integrated plot, as follows:

Closed Temporal and Causal Order	Open Temporal and Causal Order

Human beings are capable of recounting narratives that present an orderly, linear temporal and causal progression of events, as in the following exchange between a working-class Euro-American mother and child (Berko Gleason and Melzi 1997: 220):

(6)

Mother:	Did someone bump you on the head?
	Who bumped you on the head
Child:	Derek
Mother:	Derek?
	What happened?
Child:	I was going to ran into his leg
	An um he hit me

Guided by Mother, the co-tellers of this narrative recount a linear sequence of events, moving back in time from a later event (Derek bumps child's head) to temporally and causally prior events (child going to run/runs into Derek's leg, Derek hits child).

Alternatively, humans are capable of questioning a purported progression of events and speculating alternative scenarios. In non-linear narratives, tellers may evidence confusion, disagreement, or memory lapses. They also may veer off the course of a story line or propose alternative scenarios for life events. Narrating can be an occasion for sorting through a tangle of experiential possibilities, as young Emily displayed in constructing versions of what happened to cause a baby's bed to fall down (example 5) and as the spouses Marie and Jon displayed in their conflicting accounts of what transpired in the events surrounding a search for photo negatives (example 3).

Moral Stance: Central to narratives of personal experience is the dimension of Moral Stance, namely, how tellers articulate a temporal and causal sequence of events in relation to principles of goodness. Narratives or portions of narratives may orient to one of the following propensities:

Certain, Constant Moral Stance	Uncertain, Fluid Moral Stance

Moral stance may be variably realized across narratives in terms of whether tellers posit or explore the moral implications of personal experience. Depending upon situation and community, some tellers may use narrative to affirm a moral perspective; they may elicit and receive supportive feedback from other interlocutors on their position. When the teller is the protagonist, the perspective is often that the teller-protagonist took the moral high ground compared to others involved in the re-counted incident (Bamberg 1996; Ochs, Smith, and Taylor 1989). Alternatively, tellers may launch a narrative precisely because they are unsure of how to morally evaluate a life event, or tellers may disagree on the fairness or appropriateness of a protagonist's behavior. Narrating allows tellers to bring experiences into moral focus.

Moral stance and tellership are related, in that multiple active co-tellers often offer assessments or moral canons rooted in culture and history for understanding personal experience. Moral stance and tellability are intertwined, in that a highly tellable incident often involves a violation of moral standards or canons of behavior

(Amsterdam and Bruner 2000). In addition, imbuing a narrative with a certain, constant moral stance is compatible with linear plot organization, while uncertain, fluid shifting of moral stance is characteristic of non-linear narrative structure (Bernstein 1994).

2.10 Narrative Lesson Ten: The variable realizations of narratives of personal experience play an important role in configuring selves

Formulating a personal experience in narrative form is a species-wide means of enhancing self-awareness. While inside an experience, participants are not able to adequately grasp how they and others are acting, feeling, and thinking in a situation at hand. As Milan Kundera (1995) notes, human beings move through life in a fog. Personal narrative becomes a way to reflect back on experience and give it autobiographical shape. Narrating personal experience allows us to reconcile how we (and others) behaved in the past and how we project ourselves (and others) in an as-yet-unrealized future with current self-understandings. That is, narrating experiences is a way of fashioning a sense of continuity of self. This is all the more true considering that most personal narratives dwell upon experiences that upset tellers' life expectations.

Narrative activity can reinstate a sense of stability of self when tellers engage in Narrative Practice 1. Tellers may be comforted by constructing a uniform account of what transpired and why, and by seeking and securing affiliative moral positions from their interlocutors. Certainly, Narrative Practice 1 is an effective means of socializing novices into who they are and who they can expect to become. As anthropologist Cheryl Mattingly notes, for example, narratives can "emplot" lives (1998). Yet, tellers do not always select this path to redress the uncertainties of life experience (Mattingly 1998; Mattingly and Garro 2000; Ochs and Capps 2001). Rather, they may pursue Narrative Practice 2, wherein they muse, inquire, contradict, revise, or otherwise reconfigure sedimented visions of self and the world. When tellers engage in Narrative Practice 2, they are unsure of themselves, yet this ambiguity affords a heightened self-awareness that serves as a universal springboard to self-transformation. In this manner, analysis of how personal experience is variably rendered yields insight into the narrative impulse.

3 CODA

Narrative provides a medium for construing events experienced in the imagination and in the everyday world. When recounting life events, memory and anticipation are filtered through narrative formats. In particular, narrative links events in temporal and causal sequences. Temporal sequences instantiate and influence how time is sensed by protagonists and narrators rather than time as calculated by scientific observation. This phenomenology of time sometimes leads narrators to leap from a past experience to its implications for present and future existence, or the inverse. In this manner, narrative constructs a framework for charting experiential paths through life. Causal sequences in everyday narratives typically do not make predictions but rather construe how one event afforded or otherwise made probable another event.

Quotidian narrative activity involves narrators in two alternative narrative practices. When engaged in Narrative Practice 1, narrators articulate a plot that is coherent and consistent. Alternatively, narrators may participate in Narrative Practice 2, wherein they raise ambiguities and doubts concerning the experience recounted. Both narrative practices are essential to competent narration in day-to-day social interactions. A Dimensional Approach to analyzing narrative encompasses both of these practices. The dimensions of Tellership, Tellability, Embeddedness, Linearity, and Moral Stance are relevant to all narrative activity, but their properties differ depending upon whether interlocutors are engaged in Narrative Practice 1 or Narrative Practice 2. In particular, Narrative Practice 1 often manifests the following features:

Narrative Practice 1

Dimensional Characteristics
- one active co-teller
- highly tellable experience
- relatively detached
- linear plot line
- certain, constant moral stance

Alternatively, Narrative Practice 2 typically exhibits the following features:

Narrative Practice 2

Dimensional Characteristics
- multiple active co-tellers
- moderately tellable experience
- embedded in ongoing activity
- indeterminate plot line
- uncertain, shifting moral stance

Scholarship has privileged the distinctive features of Narrative Practice 1 as typical of narratives of personal experience. This chapter offers a framework for discerning and analyzing a broader spectrum of narrative practices, in an effort to better understand how narratives of personal experience are variably realized within and across speech communities.

REFERENCES

Amsterdam, A. G., and Bruner, J. (2000). *Minding the Law*. Cambridge, MA: Harvard University Press.

Aristotle (1982 [4th century BCE]). *Poetics* (trans. J. Hutton). New York: W. W. Norton.

Augustine (1961 [4th century CE]). *Confessions* (trans. with an introduction by R. S. Pine-Coffin). Baltimore: Penguin Books.

Bamberg, M. (1996). Perspective and Agency in the Construal of Narrative Events. In A. Stringfellow, D. Cahana-Amitay, E. Hughes, and A. Zukowski (eds.), *Proceedings of the 20th Annual Boston University Conference on Language Development*, vol. 1 (pp. 30–39). Sommerville, MA: Cascadilla Press.

Baquedano-López, S. P. (1998). Language Socialization of Mexican Children in a Los Angeles Catholic Parish. PhD dissertation, University of California, Los Angeles.

Berko Gleason, J., and Melzi, G. (1997). The Mutual Construction of Narrative by Mothers and Children: Cross-cultural Observations. *Journal of Narrative and Life History* 7(1–4): 217–222.

Berman, R. A., and Slobin, D. I. (1994). *Relating Events in Narrative: A Crosslinguistic Developmental Study.* Hillsdale, NJ: Lawrence Erlbaum.

Bernstein, M. A. (1994). *Foregone Conclusions: Against Apocalyptic History.* Berkeley: University of California Press.

Blum-Kulka, S. (1997). *Dinner Talk: Cultural Patterns of Sociability and Socialization in Family Discourse.* Mahwah, NJ: Lawrence Erlbaum.

Bruner, J. (1991). The Narrative Construction of Reality. *Critical Inquiry* 18: 1–21.

Bruner, J. (2002). *Making Stories: Law, Literature, Life.* New York: Farrar, Strauss & Giroux.

Bruner, J., and Lucariello, J. (1989). Monologue as Narrative Recreation of the World. In K. Nelson (ed.), *Narratives from the Crib* (pp. 73–98). Cambridge, MA: Harvard University Press.

Burke, K. (1962). *A Grammar of Motives and a Rhetoric of Motives.* Cleveland and New York: Meridian Books.

Capps, L., and Ochs, E. (1995a). *Constructing Panic: The Discourse of Agoraphobia.* Cambridge, MA: Harvard University Press.

Capps, L., and Ochs, E. (1995b). Out of Place: Narrative Insights into Agoraphobia. *Discourse Processes* 19(3): 407–440.

Deacon, T. W. (1997). *The Symbolic Species: The Co-evolution of Language and the Brain.* New York: Norton.

Drew, P., and Heritage, J. (1992). Analyzing Talk at Work: An Introduction. In P. Drew and J. Heritage (eds.), *Talk at Work.* Cambridge: Cambridge University Press.

Feldman, C. (1989). Monologue as Problem-solving Narrative. In K. Nelson (ed.), *Narratives from the Crib* (pp. 98–119). Cambridge, MA: Harvard University Press.

Goodwin, C. (1984). Notes on Story Structure and the Organization of Participation. In J. M. Atkinson and J. Heritage (eds.), *Structures of Social Action* (pp. 225–246). Cambridge: Cambridge University Press.

Goodwin, C. (1986). Audience Diversity, Participation and Interpretation. *Text* 6(3): 283–316.

Goodwin, M. H. (1990). *He-Said-She-Said: Talk as Social Organization among Black Children.* Bloomington: Indiana University Press.

Gould, J. L., and Gould, C. G. (1988). *The Honey Bee.* New York: W. H. Freeman.

Haroutunian-Gordon, S. (1991). *Turning the Soul: Teaching through Conversation in the High School.* Chicago: University of Chicago Press.

Haviland, J. B. (1977). *Gossip, Reputation, and Knowledge in Zinacantan.* Chicago: University of Chicago Press.

Heath, S. (1985). The Cross-cultural Study of Language Acquisition. *Papers and Reports on Child Language Development* 24: 1–21.

Heidegger, M. (1962). *Being and Time.* New York: Harper & Row.

Husserl, E. (1991). *On the Phenomenology of the Consciousness of Internal Time (1893–1917).* Dordrecht: Kluwer.

Kundera, M. (1995). *Testaments Betrayed.* New York: Harper Collins.

Labov, W. (1966). *The Social Stratification of English in New York City.* Arlington: Center for Applied Linguistics.

Labov, W. (1972). *Language in the Inner City: Studies in the Black English Vernacular.* Philadelphia: University of Pennsylvania Press.

Labov, W., and Waletzky, J. (1968). Narrative Analysis. In W. Labov et al. (eds.), *A Study of the Non-Standard English of Negro and Puerto Rican Speakers in New York City* (pp. 286–338). New York: Columbia University Press.

Mattingly, C. (1998). *Healing Dramas and Clinical Plots: The Narrative Structure of Experience.* Cambridge: Cambridge University Press.

Mattingly, C., and Garro, L. (eds.) (2000) *Narrative and the Cultural Construction of Illness and Healing.* Berkeley: University of California Press.

Miller, P., Fung, H., and Mintz, J. (1996). Self-Construction through Narrative Practices: A Chinese and American Comparison of Socialization. *Ethos* 24: 1–44.

Minami, M. (1996). Japanese Preschool Children's and Adults' Narrative Discourse Competence and Narrative Structure. *Journal of Narrative and Life History* 6(4): 339–363.

Morrison, T. (1994). *The Nobel Lecture in Literature.* New York: Alfred A. Knopf.

Morson, G. S. (1994). *Narrative and Freedom: The Shadows of Time.* New Haven and London: Yale University Press.

Nelson, K. (ed.) (1989). *Narratives from the Crib.* Cambridge, MA: Harvard University Press.

O'Brien, T. (1990). *The Things They Carried.* New York: Penguin.

Ochs, E., and Capps, L. (2001). *Living Narrative: Creating Lives in Everyday Storytelling.* Cambridge, MA: Harvard University Press.

Ochs, E., and Jacoby, S. (1997). Down to the Wire: The Cultural Clock of Physicists and the Discourse of Consensus. *Language in Society* 26(4): 479–506.

Ochs, E., Smith, R., and Taylor, C. (1989). Detective Stories at Dinnertime: Problem-solving through Co-narration. *Cultural Dynamics* 2: 238–257.

Ochs, E., Taylor, C., Rudolph, D., and Smith, R. (1992). Story-telling as a Theory-building Activity. *Discourse Processes* 15(1): 37–72.

Pratt, M. L. (1977). *Toward A Speech Act Theory of Literary Discourse.* Bloomington: Indiana University Press.

Propp, V. (1968). *The Morphology of the Folktale,* 2nd ed. (trans. T. Scott). Austin: University of Texas Press.

Ricoeur, P. (1981). Narrative Time. In W. J. T. Mitchell (ed.), *On Narrative.* Chicago: University of Chicago Press.

Ricoeur, P. (1984). *Time and Narrative,* vol 1. Chicago: University of Chicago Press.

Ricoeur, P. (1985). *Time and Narrative,* vol. 2. Chicago: University of Chicago Press.

Ricoeur, P. (1988). *Time and Narrative,* vol. 3. Chicago: University of Chicago Press.

Sharff, S. (1982). *The Elements of Cinema: Toward a Theory of Cinesthetic Impact.* New York: Columbia University Press.

Stein, N., and Glenn, C. G. (1979). An Analysis of Story Comprehension in Elementary School Children. In R. O. Freedle (ed.), *New Directions in Discourse Processing* (pp. 53–120). Norwood, NJ: Ablex.

Sugiyama, M. S. (1996). On the Origins of Narrative: Storyteller Bias as a Fitness Enhancing Strategy. *Human Nature* 7(4): 403–425.

von Frisch, K. (1967). *The Dance Language and Orientation of Bees.* Cambridge, MA: Harvard University Press.

APPENDIX: TRANSCRIPTION CONVENTIONS

Notational conventions employed in the transcribed excerpts examined in this chapter include the following:

.	The period indicates a falling, or final, intonation contour, not necessarily the end of a sentence.
?	The question mark indicates rising intonation, not necessarily a question.
,	The comma indicates "continuing" intonation, not necessarily a clause boundary.
:::	Colons indicate stretching of the preceding sound, proportional to the number of colons.
-	A hyphen after a word or a part of a word indicates a cut-off or self-interruption.
word	Underlining indicates some form of stress or emphasis on the underlined item.
WOrd	Upper case indicates loudness.
°°	The degree signs indicate the segments of talk which are markedly quiet or soft.
><	The combination of "more than" and "less than" symbols indicates that the talk between them is compressed or rushed.
<>	In the reverse order, they indicate that a stretch of talk is markedly slowed.
=	Equal signs indicate no break or delay between the words thereby connected.
(( ))	Double parentheses enclose descriptions of conduct.
(word)	When all or part of an utterance is in parentheses, this indicates uncertainty on the transcriber's part.
( )	Empty parentheses indicate that something is being said, but no hearing can be achieved.
(1.2)	Numbers in parentheses indicate silence in tenths of a second.
(.)	A dot in parentheses indicates a "micropause," hearable but not readily measurable; ordinarily less than 2/10 of a second.
[	Separate left square brackets, one above the other on two successive lines with utterances by different speakers, indicates a point of overlap onset.
hhh	letter "h" indicates hearable aspiration.

CHAPTER **13** Poetry

Giorgio Banti and Francesco Giannattasio

1 INTRODUCTION

Ethnographic research has shown that "poetic" forms and behaviors are almost universally widespread, and it is a common opinion in Western culture that the term "poetry" refers to something that "anyone who goes deeply into oneself may recognize and understand," as Boethius wrote fifteen centuries ago about music.[1] But looking at the facts more carefully one comes to realize that one of the most defining characteristics of poetry – and significantly of music as well – is the impossibility of defining it in any simple way. First, poetry is a term that underwent constant semantic change and redefinition in the Western literary tradition, and increasingly widened its scope. Indeed, if "Aristoteles already was uncertain in his *Poetics* (47a8–47b28) between several definitions of poetry founded respectively upon rhythm, expression, and representation" (Molino 2002: 17–18), the semantic range of the term "poetry" presently goes well "beyond language," as observed by Hymes (2001: 187), and "can express aesthetic pleasure in almost any sphere." Second, it has been observed that in several cultures there are no specific words for indicating something similar to our notion of poetry. Last but not least, in many traditional (and not only oral) cultures, verse generally is sung verse. This makes it often difficult to distinguish "poetic" from "musical" production within a continuum of activities that include, especially in ritual, ceremonial and representational contexts, different levels of bound discourse and of phonic and rhythmic formalization of speech. This difficulty also has an impact upon what we mean by other terms such as "line," "versification," "lyric," "chant," and by the more general dichotomies "prose" versus "poetry," "ordinary speech" versus "poetic speech." In fact, it is necessary to assess how such concepts are to be used when speaking about a specific culture and to take into account how "poetic" texts are created, how and when they are used, and which social and aesthetic values they draw on.

It was not by chance that the first stimulus to a real discussion of poetic formalization in a linguistic anthropological perspective was due to the so-called "oralist" scholars such as Milman Parry, Albert B. Lord, and later Eric A. Havelock, Walter Ong, Jack Goody, Ruth Finnegan, Paul Zumthor, and others, who brought into the foreground since the 1930s the techniques, the systematic organization, and the ends of composing poetry in contexts of oral tradition and "mentality." Equally important has been the evidence of ethnomusicologists who, starting with the work done by George Herzog during the 1930s on Native American societies, investigated the relationship between music and language and the several levels of rhythmic and phonic formalization of speech in different cultures. Suffice it to mention here the systematic studies by Constantin Brăiloiu on the syllabic *giusto* (1948), Rumanian popular sung verse (1954), and "child rhythm" (1956). However, it has been mainly due to Roman Jakobson's (1960) notion of a "poetic function" of language that poetics has become a full-fledged object of inquiry for linguists.

In fact it is well known that Jakobson (1960: 356) regarded the poetic function of language as the "focus on the message for its own sake" differently from, for example, the so-called emotive or "expressive" function, that is focused on the "addresser." In his view, the poetic function projects into the speech chain "the principle of equivalence" as "the constitutive device of the sequence" (p. 358): in poetry, "syllables are converted into units of measure, and so are morae or stresses" (ibid.); "equivalence in sound [...] inevitably involves semantic equivalence" (p. 368); "in the same way any sequence of semantic units strives to build an equation. Similarity superimposed on contiguity imparts to poetry its thoroughgoing symbolic, multiplex, polysemantic essence [...]" (p. 370).

Jakobson's hypothesis of a poetic function intrinsic to language – and his resulting claim that "the analysis of verse is entirely within the competence of poetics, and the latter may be defined as that part of linguistics which treats the poetic function in its relationship to the other functions of language" (1960: 359) – caused a number of linguists to venture into the field of metric and poetic phenomena. Their results have been conspicuous: careful analyses of individual poetic systems (e.g., Wimsatt 1972; Dixon and Koch 1996; Banti and Giannattasio 1996; Schuh 1989, 1999, in press a, in press b), transcultural typologies of versification systems and of their metric organization (e.g., Lotz 1960, 1972; Halle and Keyser 1980), models of phonological analysis such as metrical phonology (e.g., Kiparsky and Youmans 1989; Goldsmith 1990), and more generally a new attention to the rhythmic, intonational, and melodic features of language and their cognitive aspects, even within the framework of a semantics of emotions (Molino 2002: 22). But does a poetic function, intrinsic to the linguistic system, really exist?

Jakobson acknowledges not only that "verse is primarily a recurrent 'figure of sound' " (1960: 367), but even that "measure in sequences is a device which, outside of poetic function, finds no application in language. Only in poetry [...] is the time of the speech flow experienced, as it is [...] with musical time" (p. 358). In other words, he sees a fundamental difference, a sort of dialectics, between the phonic and metric organization of verse and the general properties of how language works. Even though the syllable can be regarded as a rhythmic unit both in ordinary language and in versification systems, it is only in the latter that there is a measured organization of equivalent units (syllables, prosodic length, stresses, word boundaries, syntactic pauses, etc.), often on the basis of a regular (isochronous) periodicity, just like music. Even if it is possible to identify intonational contours in ordinary speech, it is only in specific systems of versification – or in singing – that such contours pattern into "figures of sound," i.e., sequences of fixed and recurring pitches. Although poetic meter undeniably has "many intrinsically linguistic particularities" (Jakobson 1960: 365), it is difficult not to agree with Jean Molino's recent claim (2002: 31) that "poetry cannot be confused with language or one of its functions: it is the outcome of imposing upon language a structure that has very strong links with music and dance."

It is thus in the frame of a virtual continuum from language to music or, better, from speaking to singing, that one has to try and identify the constitutive elements that underlie the oral and written scatter of the different "poetic" forms and behaviors. The point here is not to assign poetry a definite position within this continuum in a Procrustean and – unavoidably – arbitrary way. Rather, it is to look into the problem of poetic formalization and the typology of poetry across cultures and time in a wider perspective, by studying them not only within the traditional limits of literature and linguistics, but also in the wider horizons of ethnomusicology and anthropology.

2   Speaking of "Poetry": A Few Definitions

The fuzzy relationship between word and music, meaning and sound (cf. Brogan 1993a: 939–40), content and form ("essentialists" versus "formalists"; cf. Brogan 1993b: 1347–8) has been one of the leitmotifs of theoretical debate in Western literary tradition, through steadily changing poetic practices and definitions of poetry that followed upon each other since the times of classical Greece. This complex history will not be pursued here;[2] suffice it to point out that this peculiar relationship is called up by two of the most well-known definitions of poetry in European literature. Indeed, Dante's "it is nothing else than rhetorical and musically set creation"[3] unravels the relationship between word and music by means of a simple and neat -que 'and', while Paul Valéry's (1943) more recent *hésitation prolongée entre le son et le sens* 'protracted hesitation between sound and meaning' gives this relationship the shape of a continuous and irresolvable "either . . . or."

Much has happened since the time when the Greeks used the same word, *mousiké*, to describe dance, music and poetry, and basic education in the fields of art and letters (Winn 1993: 804). Little by little literacy and the ensuing theoretical reflections split music from poetry; they developed into separate art forms, even though they merged during the centuries in several forms of poetry for music, music for poetry, and theatrical plays like melodrama. Poetry retained all this time its character of sound patterning of language especially through its specific features of meter and prosody, even though these increasingly became a set of graphic more than aural rules. Indeed, as pointed out by Brogan (1993a: 938), in the Western tradition "what most readers understand as 'poetry' was, up until 1850, set in lines which were metrical," and the definitions of this word that continue to occur in most Western dictionaries begin with such words as "verbal art realized in metric (or rhythmic) form," "in verse," or "in bound speech." This wording is not much different from the general definitions of poetry that can be read also in many non-Western dictionaries. For instance, in *AlMunjid fī alluġa*,[4] one of the most important Arabic dictionaries, one can read under *šiᶜr*, the general term that is closest to our "poetry": "Discourse that obeys meter and rhyme." The Japanese dictionary *Kōjien*[5] defines *uta* as "words combined to rhythm and regulated number." On the other hand, the first Somali monolingual dictionary defines *maanso* as a "general literary term for several things that are composed in verse."[6]

Yet many Western dictionaries top off their definitions with a specification of the ends of poetry, such as: "[...] which has for its object the creation of intellectual pleasure by means of imaginative and passionate language,"[7] or *género literario exquisito, por la materia, que es el aspecto bello o emotivo de la cosas* "literary genre, extraordinary because of its matter, that is the beautiful or emotional aspect of things."[8] Two additional definitions are generally found under the entry for "poetry": art or work of the poet (or of a poetic school); in a wider sense, elevated spiritual tension that can be expressed by a work of art.

The overall meaning that results from the Western definitions shows that in the course of time there has been a gradual shift of the meaning of poetry from means to ends (cf. Brogan 1993a: 938–9), from its formal features to its content. As a consequence the current definitions of poetry – just like those of music – put together in a rather fuzzy way two separate levels of meaning: the one, more formal and technical, refers to the means and the specific elements of poetic production such as versification, meter, etc.; the other, more conceptual and pragmatic, qualifies poetry mainly on the basis of the skill of its recognized specialists, the poets, in evoking intensified values and meanings and a peculiar aesthetic experience.

Indeed, no literary critic would think of qualifying as poetry the verbal text of a commercial pop song, even though the word used when referring to it, "lyrics," reminds us that it is built upon an attested system of versification and, as a consequence, it displays a special kind of rhetoric organization and metric formalization of discourse that distinguishes it from prose and everyday speech. On the other hand the above definition of poetry fully fits the several forms of "free verse" produced in Western literatures since the second half of the nineteenth century, and characterized by a deliberate departure from the traditional patterns of meter and rhyme. As observed by Brogan (1993b: 1351), this development "is simply one literary index of an age which prefers to avoid [...] distinctions as traditionally drawn, and to prefer overlapping forms, [...] and all more complex or more fluid composites."

In fact, the refusal in contemporary Western culture of traditional forms and structures, regarded as no longer being able to produce new creativity, has touched all forms of art, from painting to music. Yet it could be argued that the refused previous formal structures are present in this new art production *per absentiam*. Suffice it to remember here, as an extreme example, the American musician John Cage's 4'33" (1962), a composition consisting in 4 minutes and 33 seconds of absolute silence to be "performed" on the piano or "in any other way." Here it is only how the piece has been created, i.e., its authoritative composer, and the conventional setting of its public performance with a player on the stage, that confer on it the status and pregnancy of a musical object.

It should be clear at this point that two different levels of definition for poetry have to be taken into consideration:

- a wider level of *poetic procedures*, whose general features broadly correspond to what Jakobson said about his poetic function of language. They not only characterize poetry proper, but also occur in magical spells, prayers and ritual discourse, in proverbs and children's games, and so on, right up to today's advertising jingles and political slogans, and of course in the different forms of chant and song. They all share the fact of being special, not ordinary, speech.

- a narrower level of *poetry in a strict sense*, that is autonomously defined by each culture in the course of its history on the basis of its own choice of genres, specific contents, ways of production, functions, occasions of performance, and aesthetic and social values. This level requires a careful analysis of the different poetical settings with their historical, social, and cultural backgrounds.

This second level does not belong only to Western and other literate cultures, but can also be observed in several mainly oral societies and cultures, as among the Somalis whose language has been provided with a script only since the 1970s. It is interesting to consider how *gabay* – the most prestigious form of Somali *maanso* "poetry" – and *hees* "song" are defined in Yaasiin's dictionary (1976):

> Gabay – Verse composed and formed by measured words and letters, alliterated in the same sound; it has lines of similar length and words that are selected and placed in the most proper positions [. . .] in order to produce a pleasant melody and a cadence together with music, that avoid mistakes in meter and in alliteration. The *gabay*, like the other genres of *maanso* (the *geeraar*, the *jiifto*, etc.), talks about all the things that occur in a person's mind, and has the power of exerting a great influence, much stronger than the other kinds of discourse. It is intoned according to a melody.

> Hees – Short composition in verse that has a specific organization like the *gabay*. It is of different kinds, sung for amusement or at work.

It appears that the difference between the *gabay* and the *hees* regards mainly the second level, in so far as their length – and their complexity – is not the same, they have different functions and uses, and, it should be added here, they deal with different topics and are produced the one by a known author, the other – the *hees* – anonymously in most cases.

Generally speaking, the distinction between the two levels is never clear-cut nor set for ever in a culture. Is Bob Dylan a poet or just a folk singer? Are the short Somali genres known as *wiglo*, *dhaanto*, *hirwo*, and *balwo* – that were composed by specific authors, the *laashin*'s, but were not universally appreciated because of their frequently transgressive topics – properly poetry (*maanso*) or just songs (*hees*)? Or should they be regarded as "miniature-poems" as claimed by Johnson (1974: 26ff.)?

However, it should be pointed out that in several traditional cultures the separateness of the two levels is not apparent. This is the case of, for example, the Dyirbal, a rainforest people of Queensland in northeastern Australia, for whom R. M. W. Dixon and Grace Koch (1996) have published a rich and well-researched corpus of traditional sung genres, that they chose to qualify as *Dyirbal Song Poetry*. Conversely Deng (1973) writes consistently of "songs" in his book about the oral literature of the Dinka in southern Sudan, even though he clearly speaks of "experts" who compose songs for others (pp. 78, 85), of "famous singers whose songs are too difficult to learn or be remembered by the public" (p. 91), and of the "classic quality" (p. 91) some songs have for the Dinka, who prize their "intelligence [. . .], riches in symbolism, metaphor, and historical (often legendary) associations" (p. 91), while regarding as "without depth or force" a "song lacking in imagery or associated literature" (p. 91). These are all typical properties of poetry in a strict sense.

In order to provide a brief and ordered outline of the problems and the variables that have to be taken into consideration when discussing poetry, we have chosen here to discuss separately in the following sections the two levels that define it.

3   MAIN TYPES OF FORMAL ORGANIZATION

3.1   Between speaking and singing

There are in every culture ways of expression that are ideally intermediate between language and music. They result from different levels of formalization of speech by means of timbric, rhythmic, and/or melodic procedures that heighten and specialize its symbolic effect. Suffice it to mention here the pitch range, the timbre, and the melodic contours we use when addressing babies – *in-fants*, that is, non-speaking ones – who don't understand the meaning of our words yet, or the power of *en-chantment* of a magic spell, that slogans, prayers, or religious sermons may acquire.

As for singing in its proper sense, it seems to be a sort of link between language and music, that has not yet been studied adequately under this perspective. Indeed, the sung word is not only the locus of maximal expression for all the musical features of speech – such as intonation, emphasis, onomatopoeia, sound and rhythm correspondences, etc. – but also the source of discourse-like features of music, such as musical phrases and periods, syntactic and strophic structures, refrains, punctuation markers such as breaths and rests, and so on, upon which also the so-called pure, i.e., instrumental, music is mainly based in several cultures.

One may wonder whether it is plausible to set up a clear-cut divide between speaking and singing (cf. List 1963), also because each culture distinguishes the area of language from that of music in a different way.

The main procedures for formalizing speech sounds beyond those used in normal conversation seem to be no more than three:

1 altering intentionally and/or by convention one's voice register, that is, its frequency range, timbre, and intensity;
2 altering the melodic contour, in two opposite directions: (a) its complete deletion by keeping a single pitch (singing *recto tono*); (b) giving it an extreme emphasis, almost to the point of reaching a melodic articulation based on a musical scale;
3 segmenting one's utterances rhythmically into a definite number of elements on the basis of an equivalence between vocalic or syllabic units, stresses, and/or several recurring text or sound units, so as to frame one's speech in a cyclic time, often relying on a periodic measure unit (beat).

Any of these procedures can work as an indexical framing device for picking out an utterance as special in some way. Also, a stretch of silence that precedes and follows it may contribute to this effect.

All the speech forms and genres that can be ideally regarded as intermediate between speaking and singing are the result of one or more of the above procedures. Just to mention one example: the *haka*, well known because it is performed by the New Zealand national rugby team before each match, that actually is an old Maori posture dance performed for frightening the enemy and mustering up courage before a fight. *Haka* is supported by chorally uttering long sequences of slogans with an extreme emphasis of the melodic contour – (2b) above – and a strict metrical and rhythmic organization – (3) above – underlined by hand-clapping and foot-stamping.

The first of the three above formalizing procedures (altering voice register) is widely used in different repertoires of speech styles, from forms of declamation and recitation to the so-called *bel canto*, the Western way of singing lyric operas. But the discussion shall focus here especially on the melodic and rhythmic procedures because of their closer link to poetics proper.

Leveling speech prosody on a flat, monotone, contour (2a) is usually associated with transcendental speech as in prayers and magic spells. For instance, it occurs in the traditional recitation tone and proto-cantillation of prayers and other sacred texts in Hebrew, Christian, and Muslim liturgies, where the flattened intonational contour sets prayer free from any emotional connection to worldly contingencies and confers on it a solemn and timeless framework (see also Keane's chapter in this volume). A substantially monotone contour, often described as chant, has also been observed in other genres and repertoires, as in counting-out verses of children's games.

The issue of the procedures that rely upon emphasizing the intonational contours of ordinary speech (2b) is more complex, partly because of the wide range of expressive forms they give rise to: from registers that simply enclose everyday speech with timbric and intonational quotation marks in recitation, to extreme forms of speech-song (*Sprechgesang*)[9] like the above mentioned Maori *haka*. It has to be remarked that this kind of "heightened voice," based upon particular vocal cues for underlining the meanings of speech in specific settings, is usually aimed at reassuring and persuading: for instance, at making represented actions real (theatre, melodrama, children's games, etc.), at turning real actions into ritual ones (e.g., funerary lamentations), at urging somebody to do something, or at convincing an audience to share a particular view or a decision. The scope is quite wide, from war cries, to the calls of street sellers and sport fans, or different forms of political and religious oratory.

Maurice Bloch (1974) observed that religious preaching and political speeches are characterized by an assertive and highly persuasive language that disposes listeners to identify with the charismatic leader's message and express their immediate approval without reflecting upon it. Typical features of this kind of speaking are (a) a careful choice of the voice timbre; (b) cutting up the utterances into short segments of broadly similar length and intonational contour, with a clear-cut dominance of coordinate and syntactically parallel phrases and clauses separated by deliberate silences that provoke listeners to continuous responses such as *yeah, right, no*, etc.; (c) a mindful use of loud peaks and suspensive formulas characterized by prolonged syllables and often also by glissandos. The way discourse is segmented in such communicational performances is not unlike what takes place in verse.

A well-known example may be found in the sermons of African American Baptist preachers that frequently switch with no breaks from speaking to singing. In such performances the tensely excited speech of the preacher is reinforced by the particular musical dynamics, with its steadily delayed conclusion of the musical period on a more relaxing final cadence. The ensuing pent-up expectations create a mood of paroxysm that may cause deep emotional changes and even trance states in some participants.

Finally, as far as the last formalizing procedure is concerned, it should be remarked that the rhythmic segmentation of utterances on a numerical basis is certainly the most important one in connection to poetry. And yet, despite the aura of ineffable aestheticality that hovers about most current conceptions of poetry, it is not unimportant that the foremost and most cheerful users of this procedure are children all over the world in their – frequently nonsense – tongue-twisters and word games. Brăiloiu (1956) showed that there is an almost universal child metrics, based upon symmetric sequences of syllables organized in a binary rhythm, used by children in their group plays. It does not imply any particular melodic formalization; indeed, children's rhymes, counts, and rounds almost always mix plain speaking, monotone, speech-song, and singing proper. As illustrated by two of the simplest and most widespread patterns in Brăiloiu's examples, these rhythmic structures are not related to any particular linguistic system:

(1)								
Han-	dy,	Span-	dy,	Jack	a	dan-	dy	(English)
Sa	che-	mi-	se	de	Ve-	ni-	se	(French)
Ko-	ti,	ko-	ti,	yo-	ly,	yo-	ly	(Senegal)
Uk-	kuer-	pun-	ga,	au-	i-	wun-	ga	(Eskimo)
Cho-	co-	la-	te_y	mo-	li-	nil-	lo	(Spanish)

Că-	ra-	mi-	dă	nou-	ă	(Romanian)
Nτί-	λι,	vτί-	λι,	vτί-	λι	(Greek)
Hei-	le,	Hei-	le,	Se-	gen	(German)

The following may be added to the examples from Brăiloiu (1956):

Gi-	ro-,	gi-	ro-	ton-	do	(Italian)
Roo-bow	roob	leh	noo	da'		(Somali)

Child metrics basically affects the level of words, independently of their melodic formalization. But it has to be remarked that, among the three above-mentioned procedures for altering the sound of speech, the rhythmic-periodical one is the most distant from plain language because it involves strict regularity of lengths, i.e., the main constitutive feature of the metro-rhythmic organization of music. It is quite likely that this linking with an isochronous pulse originates from group activities such as work, marching, play, and dance, that involve imitative and synchronized gestures. Suffice it to remember here the eurhythmic function of so many work songs.

There is no doubt that poetic discourse developed its own shape on the basis of a measured rhythmics and a melodic formatting quite close to what is commonly regarded as music. It is not by chance that poetry is performed more commonly as sung rather than spoken discourse in all oral traditions. Even Western classical poetry was originally melic and lyric, and had its rhythmic unity in musical performance. It is thus likely that poetry and music are separate developments of an originally common procedure of sound and rhythmic formalization of speech, as suggested by Molino (2002).

3.2 Metrics

Beyond the strictly musical aspects of poetry – that have been pushed into an increasingly marginal role in Western learned literatures – the shape of poetic texts is typically regulated by several kinds of rules, that are frequently referred to by such terms as "meter," "scansion," and "prosody," with partly overlapping ranges of meaning. "Meter" is used here in a broad way to cover the major areas that undergo such metrical regulation. There are three main areas (cf. also Molino and Gardes-Tamine 1987–8; Molino 2002: 23ff.):

(a) phonological units, e.g., consonants, vowels, stresses, tones and designated sequences of these, such as syllables, syllable rhymes, etc.;
(b) morphological, syntactic, and lexico-semantic units such as classes of morphemes, nouns or verbs with meanings that fall into similar classes, noun phrases and other syntactic constituents, etc.;
(c) text units such as the line, the stanza, etc.

The formal effect of metrical rules is to create parallelism, i.e., "recurring patterns in successive sections of the text" as stated by Foley (1997: 366), who elaborated upon Jakobson's (1960) notion of poetic function. For instance, consonant parallelism occurs in several metrical systems as one kind of alliteration, that is, as the requirement that the initial consonants of some words match in the lines of a text, as in the following few lines from a *masafo* poem composed by the famous Somali poet Maxamed Cabdille Xasan in order to counter a number of charges the British had made against him and his Dervishes:[10]

(2)	Adig-aa	dulleey-oo	duunya-di	ka	qaaday-e
	you-FOC	*oppressed*-CONJ	*livestock-the*	*from*	*seized*-CONJ
	Ad-a	dagalla-doodii	digaxaar-ka	mariyay-e	
	you-FOC	*settlements-their*	*flattener-the*	*swept*-CONJ	
	Ad-a	deebla-hoodii	daabaqad	ku	jiiday-e
	you-FOC	*camels-their*	*rope*	*with*	*pulled away*-CONJ
	Diin-k-iyo	dugaag-g-iyo	ad-a	duuf-ka	siiyay-e
	tortoise-the-and	*beast-the-and*	*you*-FOC	*filth-the*	*gave*-CONJ

'It is you who oppressed them and seized their livestock. / It is you who flattened their settlements. / It is you who took away their camels. / It is you who reduced them to eating tortoises, wild beasts and filth!'[11]

It is easy to see how each of the above four lines has two full lexical words that begin with *d*: *dulleey-* and *duunya-*, *dagalla-* and *digaxaar-*, *deebla-* and *daabaqad*. There are even three such words in the last line: *diin-*, *dugaag-*, and *duuf-*. These words occur in text stretches of different lengths that form the two halves or hemistichs of each line. It can be seen that each half-line includes one major syntactic constituent or more, but there is never one constituent set astride two half-lines. For instance, in the first of the four lines one finds the focused subject NP *adig-aa* 'you' and the VP *dulleey-oo* 'oppressed-and' in the first half-line, and a second more complex VP, *duunya-di ka qaaday-e* 'seized the livestock from them (and)', in the second half-line. In the last line, the chain of conjoined object Ns *diin-k-iyo dugaag-g-iyo duuf-ka* 'tortoises-and-beasts-and-filth' is too long to fit a half-line, and is thus split into two syntactic constituents: [*diin-k-iyo dugaag-g-iyo*] in the first half-line, while *duuf-ka* is left in the second half-line after the focused subject NP *ad-a* 'you' and before the V *siiyay-e* 'gave (and)'. The boundary that divides the two halves of a line is called a caesura; in other poetic traditions it also corresponds to a syntactic boundary or, at least, to a word boundary even though it does not always occur exactly at the middle point in a line, as in the Somali *masafo*.

The number of syllables in each half-line in example (2) ranges from 6 to 8, but in other *masafo* lines one finds 5 syllables, as in another line of this poem – *duul haad Amxaaraa kaa dooni maayee* 'the subjects (*duul*) of the Amhara thugs, I don't want (to take them away) from you' – and even 9 syllables, as in the first half-line of another *masafo* by Maxamed Cabdille Xasan, alliterated in *b*: *iyag-iyo Berberi-gu-ba baha gaala weey-ee* 'they and the people of Berbera are infidels' kinsfolk'. Yet if one compares a 5-syllable half-line like *kaa dooni maayee* with the longer half-lines, it appears that there is a pattern underlying the different number of syllables. In order to perceive it, it is necessary to know that vowel length – long versus short – is distinctive in Somali. This feature provides one of the basic elements of the Somali metrical system: the strict regulation of the distribution of long versus short vowels, independently of their occurrence in open or closed syllables.[12] Since the two diphthongs *ow* and *ay ~ ey* scan in this system as metrically short or long, the distribution of long | – | and short | ⏑ | vowels in the four lines in (2) and in the other two lines that were mentioned above is as follows:

(3)   ex. (2) line 1 | ⏑ ⏑ – ⏑ – – | – ⏑ ⏑ ⏑ – ⏑ ⏑ |
        ex. (2) line 2 | ⏑ ⏑ ⏑ ⏑ ⏑ – – | ⏑ ⏑ – ⏑ ⏑ ⏑ ⏑ ⏑ |
        ex. (2) line 3 | ⏑ ⏑ – ⏑ – – | – ⏑ ⏑ ⏑ – ⏑ ⏑ |
        ex. (2) line 4 | – ⏑ ⏑ ⏑ – ⏑ ⏑ | ⏑ ⏑ – ⏑ – ⏑ ⏑ |
        duul etc. | – – ⏑ – – | – – ⏑ – – |
        iyag-iyo etc. | ⏑ ⏑ ⏑ ⏑ ⏑ ⏑ ⏑ ⏑ ⏑ | ⏑ ⏑ – ⏑ – – |

Each of the four long vowels in the pattern of *duul* etc. can be replaced by two short vowels in the other half-lines, the only vowel with a fixed value being the central short one that always remains the same. There is never a replacement whereby two long vowels correspond to a sequence of, say, | ⏑ – ⏑ | in another half-line. The different numbers of syllables result from how many replacements occur: no replacement in *duul haad Amxaaraa* and *kaa dooni maayee*, just one replacement in *adig-aa dulleey-oo*, four replacements in *iyag-iyo Berberi-gu-ba*. This can be represented in a sort of shorthand way, by means of the following scansion model:

| ⏑⏑ ⏑⏑ ⏑ ⏑⏑ ⏑⏑ | .

A system strictly based on vowel length like the Somali *masafo* is an instance of quantitative metrics. Somali poets still perform these poems according to a musical organization based upon a ternary rhythmic model that arranges the nine virtual minimal time units of each half-line into a series 2 + 3 + 3 + 1, with three ictuses falling respectively on the third, sixth, and ninth minimal time unit, as shown in (4a). How vowel quantities are organized in each hemistich with reference to the three ictuses is shown in (4b), where the scansion model of the *masafo* half-line is superimposed on the rhythmic pattern. A transcription of how the last line in (2) was performed by the late sheekh Jaamac Cumar Ciise in 1986 and the line *iyag-iyo* etc. by Xaaji Balbaal in 1985 can be seen in (4c) and (4d).

(4) a.

b.

c.

Diin - ki - yo du - gaag - gi - yo   a - da duuf - ka sii - ya - ye

d.

l - ya - gi - yo Ber - be - ri - gu - ba   ba - ha gaa - la wee - yee

Somali is a pitch accent language, where stress is realized as a high tone on most syllables and sometimes as a falling tone. In ordinary speech, the lines in (4c) and (4d) have the following stresses: *dĩin-k-iyo dugáag-g-iyo ad-á dúuf-ka siiyáy-e*, and *iyág-iyo Berberí-gu-bá baha gaalá wéey-ee*. It is interesting to see how the musical ictuses coincide with the stressed syllables only in *dugáag-*, *dúuf-ka*, *-bá*, and *wéey-*, but not in the other cases.

To conclude, each half-line of this Somali poetic genre displays a virtual set of allowed distributions of phonological units, that is, of syllables containing long versus short vowels as described by the above scansion model, within an overarching or underlying framework of nine virtual minimal time units with three musical ictuses. In addition to this, as seen above, alliteration in a designated sound marks each half-line of a poem and links it to all its other half-lines.

The phonologically relevant units that undergo metrical regulation are not the same in all languages. They can be the two vowel classes of Somali, i.e., short versus long, syllables assigned to two different weight classes – light versus heavy – as in Greek, Latin, Sanskrit, Arabic, and Persian, stressed syllables versus unstressed ones as in English and in Italian, two classes of tones as in Chinese verse, and so on. Sometimes it is not the respective distribution of two classes of phonological units that is regulated, but just the number of such units that has to occur within a designated text unit, such as the number of syllables in each line of Japanese, Chinese, and Dyirbal poetry, as shown below. The choice of such units is linked to the phonological makeup of the individual language. For instance, Latin had phonologically distinct short and long vowels, and shared with Greek a metrical system where this distinction played a role in separating light open syllables with short vowels from open syllables with long vowels, that patterned together with all the closed syllables in a single class of metrically heavy syllables. The phonological distinctiveness of vowel length was lost in spoken Latin during the first centuries CE, with the metrical consequence that the Classical system could survive only as a learned and erudite phenomenon. Some authors tried to replace it with systems based upon an opposition between open and closed syllables, but the prevailing trend in western and central Europe was to develop altogether new systems based upon syllable count and stress (cf. Gasparov 1989). The latter played a role in the phonologies of all the languages of the area, both those that had lost distinctive vowel length like the Romance languages, and those that retained it like most West Germanic languages.

Dyirbal songs provide a good example of how a metrical system strictly based upon the number of syllables interacts with its musical organization. Example (5), adapted from Dixon and Koch (1996: 216f.), shows the first six lines of a song of the *jangala* genre, that can be sung by both men and women to convey personal feelings – of love, jealousy, or revenge, or even just physical discomfort – with the accompaniment of hand-clapping or two sticks.

(5) gubigubi   bunu
     daylight coming up

     ganda-ŋu   gulbarru
     burn-RELAT.CLAUSE   *dawn coming up*

     mabin   birri   gabi
     black cloud PARTICLE *there*

     wulmburrun- ŋunu-   ga
     thin jungle - *out of -* LOCATIVE

     daŋgal   banda-y   mirra
     wing   *flap*-PARTICIPLE *in front*

     bura-n   gulu   ŋaygu
     see-NON FUTURE*not*   *my own*

'As daylight was coming up / as the dawn began to glow / as if through a dark cloud / through the thin jungle foliage / (I saw) a wing flapping in front / (but) I didn't look towards my own land'

Only the number of syllables is regulated here: each line has six of them, while the whole text of a *jangala* song has from 4 to 13 lines, that are repeated in varying order by the same performer. There are no other kinds of obligatory phonological parallelism, even though Dyirbal songs are often embellished by complex and irregular patterns of alliteration. The above song is alliterated in both *g* and *b* in the first, third, and sixth lines, only in *g* in the second line, only in *b* in the fifth line, and has a non-alliterating break in the fourth line. But alliteration is just an optional feature of phonological parallelism here, rather than an obligatory one as in Somali poetry; in the latter it is one of the features of metrical regulation, in Dyirbal song poetry it is not. There is an obligatory syntactic pattern, however: each line must be a major constituent. The first three lines are NPs, the fourth a postpositional phrase, the fifth another NP, while the last line is a transitive clause with an unstated first person singular Agent "I."

The actual performance of these six lines by George Watson in 1964 is shown in example (6), adapted from Dixon and Koch (1996: 266). It appears that they were sung to a very simple quaternary rhythm, each syllable being matched by a musical note. Yet the mismatch between the six syllables of each text line and the eight virtual minimal time units of the musical line caused the last notes in a line to be lengthened, or the filler syllable *o* to be added.

(6)   **Jangala-B, GOONDI HILL**
       George Watson, late 1964

Having a fixed number of syllables per line is a well-known feature of Chinese poetry too, but here it is also associated with other kinds of metrical regulation. A good example of this is the *lü shi*, also known as "regulated verse," a genre of poetry that flourished during the age of the Tang (618–907 CE). It is useful to mention it here, because it also is one of the best-studied instances of tonal meter and, at the same time, a good instance of strict morphosyntactic and lexico-semantic parallelism. Poems of this genre consisted of four couplets of 5- or 7-syllable lines, where the last syllables of the even-numbered lines had the same rhyme. The distribution of the tones in each line was regulated. To this purpose, the four tones of Middle Chinese were divided into two classes, the *ping* 'level' tone versus the three *ze* 'oblique' or contour tones. They don't correspond to four tones of contemporary Peking Chinese and had a different distribution, because the sounds of Chinese changed considerably during the last thousand years, but we know which words had which tones from literary sources. The Middle Chinese tonal classes are indicated in example (7), the second and third couplet of a *lü shi* poem by Cui Hao,[13] by means of the symbols " – " for the "level" tone and " / " for the "oblique" ones. It appears that the distribution of the two classes of tones is different but somehow parallel in the two couplets: line 4 has exactly the opposite tones of line 3, and line 6 the opposite ones of line 5, while the rhyming words *qing* and *ping* at the end of each of the two couplets have the same level tone.

(7) 3.

/	/	–	–	–	/	/
wu	di	ci	qian	yun	yu	san
[[[Martial	Emperor]NP	temple]	in front]PP	[clouds]N	[about to disperse]VP	

4.

–	–	/	/	/	–	–
xian	ren	zhang	shang	yu	chu	qing
[[[Immortal	person]NP	hand]	above]PP	[rain]N	[just	clear up]VP

5.

–	–	/	/	–	–	/
he	shan	bei	zhen	qin	guan	xian
[rivers	mountains]NP	[north]	[support]V	[[Qin	passes]NP	fastness]NP

6.

/	/	–	–	/	/	–
yi	lu	xi	lian	han	zhi	ping
[post-						
stations	roads]NP	[west]	[connect]V	[[Han	altars]NP	plains]NP

"In front of the Martial Emperor's temple, the clouds are about to disperse, / Above the Immortal's hand, the rain has just stopped. / Rivers and mountains support in the north the fastness of the Qin passes, / Post-stations and roads link in the west with the plains of the Han altars'

Strict morphosyntactic and lexico-semantic parallelism is required by *lü shi* regulated verse within the second and third couplets of a poem, like the two couplets in (7). The square brackets in the glosses in (7) show that the phrase structures of lines 3 and 5 are the same as those of lines 4 and 6, respectively. But in addition to this, each word and phrase is paired to another of the same category: a name of a dynasty to a name of a dynasty (*Qin* and *Han*), a cardinal point to a cardinal point (*bei* 'north' and *xi* 'west'), verbs to verbs (*san* 'disperse' and *qing* 'clear up', *zhen* 'support' and *lian* 'connect'), a postposition to a postposition (*qian* 'in front of' and *shang* 'above'), a conjoined NP to a conjoined NP (*he shan* 'rivers (and) mountains' and *yi lu* 'post-stations (and) roads'), etc. The semantic connection between the paired elements was of different kinds, ranging from sameness, to likeness, to difference and even antithesis. In the above example, the only paired items that lack any apparent semantic connection are *ci* 'temple' – *zhang* 'hand', and *xian* 'fastness' – *ping* 'plains'.

As far as the rhythmic scansion of the *lü shi* is concerned, Moira Yip (1980: 108) writes that "in the recitation the verse shows clear iambic rhythm, although the last three syllables allow three possible readings," which are described for the seven-syllable lines as follows:

(8)

a. ♪♪. / ♪♪. / ♪♪. / ♪

b. ♪♪. / ♪♪. / ♪ / ♪♪.

c. ♪♪. / ♪♪. / ♪♪ ♩

Morphosyntactic and lexico-semantic parallelism plays a major role also in several poetic systems that appear to lack any kind of metrical regulation based upon phonological units such as the number of syllables, stress, etc. The best-studied of these are those of ancient West Semitic, as attested in the poetic sections of the Hebrew Bible and in Ugaritic poetry.[14] Despite the joint efforts of generations of scholars through several centuries, it has not been possible to reach a consensus about the phonological regulation of meter in classical Hebrew poetry (cf. Yoder 1972: 58ff., and especially O'Connor 1997, and Watson 2001: 97ff.), nor has it been possible for Ugaritic since its discovery in 1929. According to some scholars, such as O'Connor, classical Hebrew poetry had no metrical regulation based upon any kind of phonological units such as those seen above in the Somali, Dyirbal, and Chinese examples. According to other scholars, instead, lines in this poetic tradition were split into syntactic units or cola – from the Greek word *kôlon* 'member' – with two, three, or even four main stresses, arranged in patterns like 3 + 3, 3 + 4, 3 + 3 + 3, 3 + 2 + 2, etc. Yet no single Psalm or other classical Hebrew poetic text is consistently composed following one accentual pattern, because stress parallelism and contrast was not a basic feature of their metrical organization, but rather a consequence of what has been called the *parallelismus membrorum*, the parallelism of members. There is a general agreement that this played a major role in the metric organization of both Ugaritic and old Hebrew poetry: each line consists of two or, more rarely, three cola with identical, similar, or complementary syntactic structure (cf. Segert 1984: 108ff. for Ugaritic). The full words that are used in the first colon (A-words) of a line are echoed by semantically parallel words in the other cola (B-words). These A–B pairs – and at times triplets – include among other things:

1 synonyms, such as 'mountains' versus 'hills', and 'high' versus 'lofty' in Isaiah ii.14: *wᵉ-ᶜal kol he-hārīm hā-rāmīm | wᵉ-ᶜal kol ha-ggᵉbāᶜōt ha-ggiśśāʔōt* 'and upon all the high mountains, and upon all the lofty hills';

2 complementary or antithetic terms, such as the triplet 'heart' versus 'ears' versus 'eyes' and, respectively, 'make fat' versus 'understand', 'make heavy' versus 'hear', 'shut' versus 'see' in example (9) below;

3 periphrases, such as 'Israel' versus 'the house of Jacob', and 'Egypt' versus 'a people speaking a strange language' in Psalm cxiv.1: *bᵉ-ṣēt Yiśrāʔēl mi-Mmiṣrāyim | bēt Yaᶜᵃqōb mē-ᶜam lōᶜ ēz* 'upon(-the)-exit (of) Israel from-Egypt, (of the) house (of) Jacob from(-a)-people speaking a strange language';

4 plain repetition, such as *nᵉhārōt* '(the) floods', and the two semantically similar 3rd plural masculine forms of *nāśā* 'to lift up' – the perfect *nāsᵉʔū* and the old preterite *yiśᵉʔū* – in the three cola of Psalm xciii.3: *nāśᵉʔū nᵉhārōt YHWH | nāśᵉʔū nᵉhārōt*

qōl-ām | yiśᵉʔū nᵉhārōt doky-ām 'The floods have lifted up, Oh Lord, the floods have lifted up their voice, the floods have lifted up their crushing roar'.

Many of these A–B pairs recur several times in the Bible and in Ugaritic poetry, forming a set of fixed parallel expressions used by poets to compose their lines, like *hārīm* 'mountains' and *gᵉbāᶜōt* 'hills' in (1) above, 'shepherd' and 'lord of the flock', 'wine' and 'blood of vines' or 'blood of trees', etc. Similar highly stylized sets of paired words that replace each other in successive sections of a text are also well known from the contemporary Sumbanese tradition in eastern Indonesia (cf. Fox 1988). Finally, it should be pointed out that these pairs and triplets of parallel terms can also occur in a mirror-image ordering in classical Hebrew poetry, i.e., as a chiasm, as in the following two lines of Isaiah vi.10:

(9) hašmēn lēb   hā-ᶜām   ha-zzeh | wᵉ-ʔoznā-w   hākbēd | wᵉ-ᶜēnā-w   hāšaᶜ
   make fat heart *the-people* *the-this*   *&-ears-their* *make heavy* *&-eyes-their* *shut*

   pen yirʔeh bᵉ-ᶜēnā-w | ū-bᵉ-ʔoznā-w   yišmāᶜ | ū-lᵉbāb-ō   yābin
   lest *sees* *with-eyes-their* *&-with-ears-their* *hears*   *&-heart-their* *under-*
                                                                    stands

'Make the heart of this people fat, and make their ears heavy, and shut their eyes; / lest they see with their eyes, and hear with their ears, and understand with their heart'

The question of the musical performance of biblical verse is not a simple one, because the Jewish liturgical performance changed considerably during the millennia in its different western and eastern traditions. The Talmud stated in the first centuries CE that the Bible should be read in public and made understood to the hearers in a musical and sweet tune. Probably this just codified a well-established behavior because, already before being conceptualized as a "musical discourse," the public readings of the Bible followed a model of "sound signification," the cantillation, that had the function of enhancing the structure and the meaning of the text, highlighting the liturgical context, and conveying emotions (cf. Seroussi 2002: 151ff.). The practice of cantillation goes back at least to the time after the Babylonian exile (cf. Fubini 2002: 143). It involves a clear relation between the accentuation of the sentence constituents and the rhythm – and pauses – of the sound structure and, at the same time, meaningful melodic formulas and motives that enhance the main points of syntactic articulation in the text, moving around the recitation tone. The present-day notation used for Jewish liturgical cantillation goes back to the early Middle Ages; each community follows this shared framework of rhythmic scansion, but has freely developed its own melodic tradition in performing it. Unfortunately, it is still not clear whether and to what extent a pattern of sound signification has been involved since the beginning in the peculiar syntactic and semantic organization of classical Hebrew poetry.

The formal organization of ancient West Semitic poetry has interesting parallels in the Native American verbal arts. Tedlock (1983: 218) pointed out that these rely more on "combined syntactic and semantic parallelism" than upon "recurrent quantifications of stresses, vowel lengths, or syllables." In particular, Mesoamerican and Andean poetics appear to be based upon the quantified or numerically regulated syntactic and semantic parallelism of successive text units, organized in sequences of two, three, and even four cola.[15] For instance, in the following passage from the Mayan Popol Vuh (1v.2–6) an introductory phrase with a demonstrative is followed by two sequences of three cola, each dropping the word *ca* 'still, yet' in its final colon, and a single final phrase that stops the rhythm of what precedes it and finishes the sentence:

(10)   are utzihoxic uae
       ca catzininoc | ca cachamamoc | catzinonic
       ca cazilanic | ca calolinic | catolona puch
       upa cah

       'This is the account, here it is:
       Now it still ripples, now it still murmurs, it ripples, / it still sighs, it still hums, and
       it is empty / under the sky' (adapted from Tedlock 1983 and 1996)

It thus appears that different traditions around the world make use of quite diverse kinds of metrical regulation in order to create recurring patterns in successive sections of poetic texts. What is most typical of poetry to a Western educated mind, i.e., scansion-based upon phonological elements such as syllable weight, number of syllables per line, stress, and so on, is a frequent but not universal formal feature.

3.3   The language of poetry

3.3.1   Special grammar and lexicon

Poetic discourse differs from plain discourse in many traditions not only for its musical and/or metrical organization. Quite frequently, the language used for poetic texts is also characterized as a special register, beyond ordinary speech, by features such as (1) special morphology, (2) special syntax, (3) a special lexicon, as well as by (4) special stylistic features. Speaking of "literary languages" in general, and of the language used in ancient Greek poetry in particular, Meillet (1965: 130) wrote that "archaism and dialectalism" are features that characterize this register, that is, a high occurrence of older forms and words and of borrowings from other dialects. Poetic registers are indeed often more or less supradialectal, in the sense of being less bound to local varieties than ordinary language. This is particularly true when they are used for oral texts that circulate among a wider community, such as epic poems performed by traveling professionals, or poetry composed for political debate among different clans as among the Somalis, as well as for written texts addressed to a large readership.

The supradialectal features of a poetic or literary register often bear witness to the historical roots of its particular tradition; for instance, it is well known that the overwhelmingly Tuscan character of literary Italian is due to the strong influence that the fourteenth-century Tuscan poetry of Dante and Petrarch, as well as the tales of Boccaccio's *Decameron*, had upon later Italian poets and literati. Not dissimilarly, recent research has shown that Swahili poetry makes use of a sizeable body of archaic elements from northern Swahili dialects, a sediment of the Swahili literature's origin in the northern areas of its present-day diffusion and its subsequent southward spread through several centuries (Klein-Arendt 1987; Miehe 1995: 294). But borrowing from other languages and dialects also occurs frequently in poetic diction – as well as in ritual and religious registers – for mystifying and intensifying the verbal message. The use of uncommon and alien forms marks the text as esoteric and "forces a stratification of interpretive knowledge" (Feld 1990: 140), because not all listeners or readers have the same familiarity with such forms. To give just one example out of many, Feld construes precisely to this effect the occurrence of expressions from the neighboring Sonia language in the songs of the Kaluli, a small rainforest people in central Papua New Guinea. In several cases, however, Meillet's notions of archaism and dialectalism are not enough for characterizing what is special in a poetic register. Particularly gifted poets in several traditions freely coin new words and expressions to suit what they are composing. This is one of the aspects of what is commonly known as poetic license. A few examples of it shall be seen below in the fields of syntax and of the lexicon.

When borrowed and archaic forms consist in morphological elements, we have instances of special morphology in a poetic register. These may not only be different forms for the same morpheme or morphemes, for example an alternative inflection such as the older *kine* for *cows*, but also more complex cases such as the old second-person singular forms *sayest* and *thee* still used in English poetic diction when the originally plural forms *say* and *you* have replaced them in everyday language; or the use of the old preterite *yiśⁱⁿʔū* 'they lifted up' in classical Hebrew poetry as an alternative to the perfect *nāśⁱⁿʔū* – as in the example from Psalm xciii.3 seen above – when ordinary biblical prosa had completely replaced the old preterite with the perfect in this kind of sentence. Johnstone (1972) described the language used in the oral poetry of the Jibbali in southern Oman as a variety of Jibbali with heavy morphological – and lexical – borrowing from Mehri, a different Modern South Arabian language spoken in eastern Yemen and the adjoining mountains in Oman.

Special syntax can be of different kinds. For instance, several poetic traditions allow change in the usual order of words, e.g., by splitting the constituents in a phrase. There are well-known examples of this in classical Greek and Latin poetry and in other old Indo-European traditions from India to Medieval Iceland. Watkins (1995: 40) pointed out that split constituents of a noun phrase are met typically adjoining caesuras or other metrical boundaries. The first three lines of Virgil's *Aeneid* provide two examples of this with the split phrases *Troiae...ab oris* 'from the shores of Troy' and *Italiam...Lavinia-que...litora* 'Italy and the Lavinian strands' adjoining the caesuras and some of the outer borders of these lines:

(11) *1.* Arma   virum-que cano | Troiae   qui   primus ab   oris
           arms   man-and   I sing   *of Troy   who   first   from   shores*

     2. Italiam fato   profugus | Lavinia-que   venit
           Italy   by fate   exiled   Lavinian-and   came

     3. litora   .....
           strands

'I sing the arms and the man who first came from the shores of Troy, exiled by fate, to Italy and the Lavinian strands'.

Such split phrases do not occur any more in contemporary Italian or English poetry, but they do occur in unrelated traditions in other parts of the world. An instance of a noun separated from the conjoined nouns that precede it has been pointed out in the Somali example (2) above: *diink-iyo dugaagg-iyo...duufka* 'tortoises, beasts, and filth'.

Special lexis is one of the most easily perceived features that distinguish poetic from other texts in many traditions. For instance, Dixon and Koch (1996: 32) identified *ca.* 300 "song words," i.e., words used only in poetic diction and never in ordinary communication, in Dixon's corpus of 174 Dyirbal song poems. They made up almost one third of the occurring words. Just a tiny amount of them was drawn from another dialect or language, while the rest of them could only be characterized as restricted to the poetic use of this small community of Australian hunter-gatherers. Even more strikingly, Ludovica Koch (1992: xlviii) has pointed out that while the simple adjectives and verbs used in *Beowulf* – the well-known Old English epic poem from the early Middle Ages – are of current usage, more than half of the nouns and compound adjectives that occur in this text are restricted to poetic diction and may often have been coined by its author. As mentioned above, however, also borrowing from other languages or dialects is frequently observed as a means for distinguishing the special lexis of a poetic register, as in the Kaluli songs described by Feld (1990).

3.3.2   Special style

Beyond these aspects, poetic diction frequently involves an indirect or veiled style that adds to its supra-ordinary quality: instead of using a direct and straightforward way of referring to an object or a concept, it is hinted at in a way that requires previous knowledge or some thinking, even to the point of not being easily understood by everybody. This is what the Kaluli of Papua New Guinea refer to when they say that poetic lines have "insides" and "underneaths," according to Feld (1990: 161). At the same time, this indirect and veiled diction is much more evocative than ordinary speech and adds to the complex web of cultural and emotional implications that heighten and intensify the power of what is being said.

Some of the procedures used to this end are similar to those that were mentioned above when speaking about the parallelism of members in classical Hebrew poetry: rather than referring to something in the usual way, it is referred to by means of a synonym, especially a rare or archaic one, or a neologism, or by means of a one-word or multi-word metaphor. They largely fall within such figures of speech as paronomasia, metonymy, and synecdoche, that have been classified by the Western rhetorical and literary tradition since Gorgias first identified some of them in the fifth century BCE. The Arabs systematized them in their *ʿilm al-badīʿ*, "the science of tropes," and adapted them to their language and the peculiarities of their poetic diction. Some of them are particularly important or pervasive in individual traditions. For instance, Aztec poets made frequent use of couplets of nouns – called *difrasismos* in the relevant Spanish literature – as metaphorical expressions for other concepts, such as *in xochitl in cuicatl* 'flower and song' for 'poetry', *in tlilli in tlapalli* 'black and red' for 'knowledge', *in atl in tepetl* 'water and hill' for 'village', etc. (Leander 1972: 62; Segala 1989: 117f.).

One particular kind of metaphor that has been widely used in several old Indo-European poetic traditions is the kenning, formed by two nouns in a genitive relationship (A of B) or forming a compound (B–A), that replace a third concept (C): 'horse of the sea' or 'sea-horse' for 'ship', 'dog of the river' for 'fish', 'shepherd of the people' for 'king', etc. Each of the following four lines from the fourteenth stanza of the "Haustlöng," a ninth-century Old Norse poem by Þjóðólfr ór Hvini, contains a kenning: *ísarn-leikr* 'iron game' for 'battle', *Jarðar sunr* 'the Earth's son' and *Meila blóði* 'Meili's brother' for the god Thor, and *Mána vegr* 'the moon's way' for 'the sky':

(12) *1.* ók   at   ísarn-leiki
         drove   *to*   *iron game*

      2. Jarðar   sunr,   en   dunði
         Earth's *son*   *and*   *thundered*

      3. móðr   svall   Meila   blóða
         wrath   *swelled* *Meili's* *brother*

      4. Mána   vegr   und   hánum
         moon's   *way*   *beneath* *him*

'The son of the Earth drove to the iron game, and the moon's way thundered beneath him, (while) wrath swelled in him.'

Although kennings and other poetic expressions are often created by a particular poet, there are several instances of expressions that recur as poetic formulas in the work of more than one poet, and even in different traditions related to each other through historical origin or cultural contacts. For instance, 'horse of the sea' as a kenning for 'ship' occurs both as Homer's *halòs híppoi* and in the Old Norse compound *vág-marr* 'sea-horse'. They are an important part of the intertextual web that links poetic discourse to the traditions of its genres.

A peculiar stylistic procedure is the *sam-ənnā warq* 'wax and gold' used in the Ethiopian *qene*, a genre of short religious poems with a single rhyme. As the goldsmith pours gold in a wax mould, so the Ethiopian poet gives his subject the form of a simile by collapsing the one and the other in a single statement. This is usually done by using words with double meanings or by adding elements of the simile as appositions or genitival complements to the proper statement. Example (13) is a *qene* in Geez where the statement that the well-known saint Takla Hāymānot became righteous through the tears of his grief is likened to the growth of a tree that is watered by a farmer, i.e., "the tree became firm, because the farmer watered it with fruitful water":

(13) *1.* ṣadqa   Takla   Hāymānot   taklə
         he became righteous / strong   *Takla* *Hāymānot* *tree*

      2. ʔəsma   ʔaṭlal-o   ḥazan   ḥarāsi   ba-māya   ʔanbaᶜ təlulə
         because *watered-him*   *grief* *farmer* *with-water of* *tear* *fruitful*

'Takla Hāymānot, the tree, became holy, / because grief, the farmer, watered him with the fruitful water of tears' (from Moreno 1935: 3)

The initial verb *ṣadqa* means 'he became righteous' if it is construed with Takla Hāymānot as its subject, but 'it became strong' if *takl(ə)* 'tree' is its subject. The latter and *ḥarāsi* 'farmer', two elements from the simile, occur as appositions to, respectively, Takla Hāymānot and *ḥazan* 'grief', while *Ɂanbəᶜ* 'tear' is the genitival complement of *māy(a)…ṭəlul(ə)* 'fruitful water', another element of the simile. Rhyme in the above short *qene* consists in two final syllables *-lə*,[16] but additional embellishing elements of parallelism are (a) the fact that the same word *takl(ə)* 'tree, plant' occurs in the same noun phrase first as the head constituent of the proper name Takla Hāymānot, lit. 'Tree of Faith', and then as an apposition of it; (b) the alliteration of *ḥazan* 'grief' and *ḥarāsi* 'farmer' in the same noun phrase, both pronounced with initial pharyngeal [ḥ] in the traditional pronunciation of Geez.

4   GENRES

4.1   Intermediate genres

The various procedures that have been briefly surveyed in section 3 – a musical and quasi-musical formalization of speech, metrics, and a special grammar, lexicon, and style – are present in several kinds of oral or written discourse in most societies. They are not always found together and, as mentioned above, they often occur also in kinds of texts one would not characterize as poetry in its proper sense. It is thus useful to speak of poetically organized discourse (POD), as a broader category than poetry. Listeners and readers regard as poetry a specific item of POD according to their shared or individual cultural choices, yet not on the basis of purely aesthetic considerations, because there is both good and bad poetry. Some of the better-known kinds of non-poetic discourse that, nevertheless, display several formal procedures of poetry have already been mentioned, such as proverbs, riddles, and children's games, or today's advertising jingles and political slogans like George W. Bush's oxymoron, the alliterative and accentually parallel *compássionate consérvatism*. It is important to point out that in most cultures such genres occur with features of poetic organization optionally, and not obligatorily. For instance, English has rhymed proverbs like *Finders keepers, losers weepers*, with the full accentual parallelism of a trochaic tetrameter, i.e., of a sequence of four trochees – | x́ x x́ x | x́ x x́ x | – and even with the morphological parallelism of the four plural agent nouns in *-er-s*. But it also has proverbs such as *Those who live in glass houses should not throw stones* that lack any of the formal features of poetic organization and rely solely upon the semantic contrast between *glass houses* and *stones*.

The typical features of POD frequently occur also in other genres, such as prayers, blessings, and magical spells, in curses – as among the Somalis – and in ritual languages such as those that are used in Sumba and other islands of eastern Indonesia for political and marriage negotiations, narrating clan histories, communicating with spirits, etc. (Fox 1988; Foley 1997: 369 f.; Keane, this volume). Such ritual languages are used also for divination, indeed a rather frequent function of POD across the world, from the prophets of the Old Testament (cf. Isaiah and example (9) above), to the seers and soothsayers of pre-Islamic Arabia, and the *ginnili* diviners among the Afar in the Horn of Africa. For early medieval northern Europe there are versified law texts from Ireland and judicial formulas in Old Norse, while still earlier, in classical Greece and Rome, it is possible to observe a large use of what has been traditionally called didactic or didascalic poetry, from Hesiod's discussion of agriculture, sailing, and well- and ill-omened days in his *Works and Days*, to Parmenides's philosophical presentation of Truth and the World of Illusion in his *On Nature*, or Lucretius's comprehensive exposition of the Epicurean worldview in his *On the Nature of the Universe*. Even more distant from the Western prototypical concept of poetry are the versified Sanskrit dictionaries from medieval India and the bilingual dictionaries – Turkish–Persian, Turkish–Arabic, Persian–Arabic, etc. – in rhyming verse that were so frequent from India to the Ottoman Empire during the seventeenth to the nineteenth centuries.

A different type of texts that are intermediate between ordinary discourse and poetry is represented by a group of genres that are only partially organized as PODs, i.e., that either alternate prose and POD, or display only some of the features that distinguish poetry in their cultural tradition. An example of the former are the Menippean *saturae*, a genre initiated by Menippus of Gadara in the first half of the third century BCE that alternated prose and poetry in the same text, and that became particularly popular among Latin writers, for example with Varro's *Saturae Menippeae*. Also the Chinese *fu* included prose and poetry in a single text, but the prose sections were additionally required to have a rhythmic organization with parallel and balanced clauses; in other words, they had to display some of the typical features of Chinese poetic discourse.

Metrical and rhythmic prose, i.e., prose with quasi-POD features, is not restricted to China. It can be clearly distinguished when it occurs in a cultural tradition where proper poetry is quite different. For instance, the types of meter and the architecture of lines and/or metric periods clearly distinguishes classical Greek and Latin poetry from the rhythmic prose introduced by Gorgias in the fifth century BCE, with its short cola, its poetic lexicon, and its frequent use of poetic style, as well as from the later metrical prose of Cicero and Quintilian with metrical clauses – or closes – at the end of sentences or major sections. The rhythmic *cursus* continued this practice well into the Western Middle Ages. Also in the Arab cultural tradition, verse has been regarded since the very beginning as something different from the rhythmic speech (*saj'*; cf. Fahd, Heinrichs, and Ben Abdesselem 1995) of the soothsayers and the great orators of pre-Islamic times, as well as from the so-called *fawāṣil*, the rhymed prose of many a sura of the Koran. Example (14) shows the entire text of *Sūratu l-ʔiḫlāṣ*, the sura of the Unity, one of the shortest ones in the Koran. After the initial invocation, the *basmala*, the four verses are of different lengths and don't display any recurrent pattern of distribution of light vs. heavy syllables like Arabic poetry of that time, but they all rhyme in *-d*, the first and the last verse are closed by the same word *ʔaḥad* 'one', the third verse displays a word play between active *lam yalid* 'he does not beget' and passive *lam yūlad* 'he was not begotten', and so on:

(14) | b-ismi | Llāhi | r-raḥmāni | r-raḥīm |
| --- | --- | --- | --- |
| *in-name* | *of God* | *the-Beneficent* | *the-Merciful* |

qul	huwa	Llāhu	ʔaḥad |	Allāhu	ṣ-ṣamad |	lam	yalid	wa-lam
say	*he*	*God*	*one*	*God*	*the-everlasting*	*not*	*begot*	*and-not*

yūlad |	wa-lam	yakun	la-hu	kufuwan	ʔaḥad
was begotten	*and-not*	*was*	*to-him*	*equal*	*one*

'In the name of Allah, the Beneficent, the Merciful.
Say: He, God, is One, | the everlasting God. | He does not beget, nor was He begotten, |
and none is equal to Him'

Another case that should be remembered here is the Indo-European "strophic style" identified by Watkins (1995: 20, 229 ff.) as a separate verse form that had text units of variable length, in many cases no fixed metrical pattern, and a highly elaborate style characterized by kennings, parallel morphological and syntactic structures, and sound plays such as alliteration and assonance. It occurs in the oldest Latin, Umbrian, Iranian, Sanskrit, and Hittite prayers, as well as in several kinds of Old Irish *rosc*, a genre used, for example, for poetico-legal texts that was quite distinct from the early Irish rhyming syllabic verse.

Metrical prose is less easy to identify as a separate genre in cultural traditions that lack features like a metrical system based upon phonological units, as in classical Hebrew and several Native American traditions. One wonders, indeed, whether metrical prose and poetically organized discourse should not be regarded as one and the same thing in such cases. It has sometimes been said that quasi-POD genres like the Arabic *saǰ* represent a more archaic stage than proper poetry (Goldzieher 1899: 59 f.; Frolov 2000: 98). But several of the peculiar features of poetic registers may have developed as a consequence of the severe constraints imposed upon versified speech by its metrical and musical organization, and a more careful consideration should distinguish the features of quasi-POD genres that may have had an independent origin from those that are best regarded as partial extensions of the peculiarities of POD to other kinds of discourse.

4.2 Some common genres

The genres of POD that are more commonly recognized as poetry can be classified into several groups, a few of which are listed below. It is important to point out that these don't occur everywhere: different communities and traditions give more importance to some of them at the expense of others.

(1) *Epic poetry* typically consists in long narrative poems that treat one or more heroic figures, and concerns historical, legendary, or mythical events that are central to the traditions and beliefs of a community (Newman 1993: 361b). In written literatures there are several instances of authored epic poems, such as Virgil's *Aeneid*, Firdawsī's *Shāhnāme*, Ariosto's *Orlando Furioso*, and many others. In oral contexts it is performed by specialists who, in most studied cases, re-adapt the text to the specific audience they are performing to. Such a text can be ascribed to performers, but not to a specific author who composed it. Oral epic poetry is present in a wide belt that stretches from the Chinese folk-literature through Central Asia and Tibet to Europe, where it is still alive and well in the Balkans and among the *cantastorie*, the "story-singers" of Sicily and southern Italy. Through southeastern Asia (e.g., the Javanese epic) this belt also reaches India (the Hindi and Tamil epic), Yemen and modern

Egypt, and several peoples in central and western Africa with the BaNyanga epic of Mwindo from eastern Congo, the Mande epic of Son-Jara or Sundyata, the Fulani epics of Silamaka and Baajankaro, etc. (cf. Biebuyck 1978; Johnson and Fa-Digi Sisòkò 1986; Abu-Manga 1985).

(2) *Dramatic poetry* is strongly entrenched in the Western cultural tradition, where drama has been in dialogic verse since its very beginning in classical Greece and Rome and up to the nineteenth century. Suffice it to mention here Sophocles' tragedies, Aristophanes' and Plautus's comedies, the works by Shakespeare, or Goethe's *Faust*. Drama in verse is known also from classical India and spread through Buddhism and commerce to Tibet, China, and beyond. Quite frequently Oriental drama has sections in poetry that alternate with sections in plain prose, and is thus properly an intermediate genre in the sense of section 4.1 above. It is still quite alive and has spread also to eastern Africa where, for example, contemporary Somali drama is mostly in verse.

(3) *Religious poetry* is typically represented by hymns that are performed during religious rituals. Ancient and well-known instances are the Psalms of the Bible and the old Indian hymns of the Rigveda. Medieval instances are Christian hymns like Thomas of Celano's *Dies irae*, and the Arabic *qaṣīda*s – such as those by Ibn al-Fāriḍ – sung by the worshippers during the *ḥaḍra*s or dhikr ceremonies of Sufi orders. Among the countless other instances of religious poetry, one may mention here the *ijálá*-chants of the Yoruba of southwestern Nigeria, that are closely associated to the worship of the god Ogun (cf. Babalola 1966), and the *gisalo* songs of the spirit medium dances of the Kaluli in New Guinea described by Schieffelin (1976) and Feld (1990).

(4) *Choreutic poetry*, or poetry that is closely associated to a particular dance, has been described especially for several non-Western societies, from the songs of the ox and war dances of the Dinka in southern Sudan and the *diet ke tueeng* 'songs of the *tueng* dance' of their women (Deng 1973: 88 ff., 218), to several genres of Somali poetry like the *dhaanto*, the *saar*, and the *buraambur*, that is danced, sung, and composed exclusively by women. During recent decades, some particularly skilled poets developed the *saar* and the *buraambur* into major genres of long poems that, while still retaining their original metric and musical organization, are well fit for discussing social and political issues. The close connection between sung performances of Aztec poetry and solemn dances in the temples has been pointed out by several authors (cf. Segala 1989: 162). Here it may also be interesting to remember that one of the hypotheses about the origin of classical Greek tragedy is that it arose from dances by a chorus of masked singers performed during religious rituals.

(5) *Praise poetry* is, in its most typical examples, composed for praising important people, like the *izibongo*s that celebrate the kings and war heroes of the Zulu and the Xhosa in South Africa, the heroic panegyrics of the Ankole in Uganda, or the traditional Hausa praise-singing. The early Spanish chronicles of Mexico report that Motecuhzoma of Tenoxtitlán and Nezahualpintli of Texcoco had poems composed under their reigns in celebration of their greatness, their victories, their genealogies, and their richness (Segala 1989: 162). Poetry praising war or agonistic victories is well known also from other places and times; suffice it to mention here Pindar's triumphal odes (*epinicia*) that celebrated the victors in the Olympian, Pythian, Nemean, and Isthmian games in fifth-century BCE Greece, and were sung in processions when they

returned to their home cities. A peculiar genre of praise poetry is the praise of one's self like the Somali *faan*, and a few similar instances from Bantu Africa.

(6) *Abusive poetry* is reported from several parts of the world. The *hijā?* in rhymed prose and in verse was a powerful weapon in pre-Islamic Arabia that humiliated and shattered the honor of one's enemies, and survived – although in less devastating forms – well into modern times (Pellat et al., 1975). The Inuit derisive songs aimed at shaming individuals and groups are often performed in the context of poetic duels that may even turn into outright physical fighting, like the exchanges of ritualized verbal insults in rhymed couplets in the African American game of the dozens. Another example of a poetic abusive duel is the traditional Scottish flyting, examples of which are known already from the fifteenth and sixteenth centuries.

(7) *Social poetry* refers here to poetry whose stated purpose is achieving a political or social effect. This is particularly well known in several African traditions, and is in strong contrast with the more aesthetic and hedonistic function of some genres of poetry in a number of other societies. For instance, Andrzejewski and Lewis (1964: 45) point out that the Somalis assume that "every poem has a purpose when it is composed . . . It may be used for giving moral support to someone, or for undermining his prestige; it may be used as an instrument of war, or of peace and reconciliation," and above all and still now it is used for political debate. Even in modern poems about love one can often perceive the purpose of pleasing the clan of the woman addressed by the poet, and of securing some advantage in clan politics. Not dissimilarly, Deng (1973: 84) remarks that Dinka songs "are based on actual, usually well-known events and are meant to influence people with regard to those events. This means that the owner whose interests are to be served by the songs, the facts giving rise to that song including the people involved, the objectives it seeks to attain whether overtly or subtly and whether directly or indirectly, all combine to give the song its functional force."

(8) *Lyric poetry* is a broad category that has changed its meaning through the centuries. The word comes from the well-known stringed musical instrument called *lýra* 'lyre' by the ancient Greeks. During Alexandrian Hellenism "lyric" came to indicate any poem which had been composed to be sung, with or without musical accompaniment. In the Renaissance the term was increasingly associated with short poems expressing deep personal feelings and emotions like love, nostalgia, or sorrow, that were not necessarily intended for a sung performance, and presently this is the meaning that is more often associated with this term in Western culture. As a typological category, this second meaning suits both Romantic poetry by Coleridge or Leopardi, many genres of Arabic, Chinese, and Japanese poetry (such as the *haiku*), as well as some kinds of poetry from non-literate societies like the *jangala* songs of the Dyirbal (see example (5) above). It should not be overlooked, however, that an expression of personal emotions can have a considerable impact and wide implications in a community, as shown by Lila Abu-Lughod (1986) for the *ghinnāwa* oral poetry of the Bedouins in the Western Desert of Egypt.

The above eight groups of poetic genres are not exhaustive and, like most typologies, are clear in their central areas but may overlap. For instance, the long *gisalo* songs of the Kaluli are religious poetry in so far as they are performed during spirit medium dance ceremonies, but they may also be regarded as a long kind of lyric poetry because they express intense feelings of sorrow and grief to their listeners.

Another well-known example of overlapping is represented by the West African griots, especially in the Mande area, who perform epic poetry in order to praise their hosts or to abuse their foes. What should be stressed here is that most known societies, both the mainly oral and the literate ones, have developed different kinds of poetry, that are generally composed by particularly gifted and skilled people or even by recognized professional specialists. Societies where everybody is required to be able to compose at least some genres of poetry are much rarer than those where most people know some poetic texts and are able to sing or recite them. The particular genres and the occasions for their composition, circulation, and performance vary greatly across time and space, and are a rich field for anthropological, linguistic, musical, and literary research.

There is little space here for discussing the different kinds of chant and song that do not qualify as poetry in a strict sense. In addition to what has been said above in sections 2 and 3.1 one may say that their register is often simpler and less elaborate than the register of true poetry, even though they usually obey similar kinds of metrical regulation. Also the occasions for their performance are usually different: individual or group labor at home or elsewhere, lulling babies to sleep, children's play, adult play and recreation, and so on. There is a broad area of intermediate cases between them and poetry in a strict sense, that cannot be defined with more accuracy without taking into account their specific cultural contexts.

5 Conclusion

Poetically organized discourse (POD) and, in general, poetic procedures may be regarded as a special way of formalizing speech by means of a number of constraints on how the text is organized – such as meter, rhythm, morphosyntactic parallelism, assonance, and other procedures – that affect speech sounds in the voice register, in the melodic and accentual contour, and, especially, in their recurrence through time, on the basis of an equivalence between vocalic or syllabic units, stresses, and/or several recurring text or sound units, so as to frame one's speech in a cyclic time, often relying on a periodic measure unit or beat. Such constraints, that often occur together, heighten and specialize the symbolic impact of an utterance.

On the one hand, the silence that precedes and follows a POD event creates a particular aura for the utterance that is so marked for evidence. On the other hand, submitting linguistic strings to modules and formal requirements that bind, order – not infrequently through repetition – and reinforce each other causes particular levels of emphasis and of condensed meaning that make POD a special register of language. This special register may also involve, and in some cases give rise to a special morphology, a special syntax, a special lexicon, as well as special stylistic features.

It has been seen above that different procedures that characterize POD, such as a musical and quasi-musical formalization of speech, metrics, style, etc., occur in most societies in several kinds of discourse, both oral and written, improvised or composed in advance, anonymous or authorial. They often occur also in kinds of texts one would not characterize as poetry in its proper sense, such as proverbs, political slogans, or songs, and it is for this reason that it has been useful to speak of POD as a broader category than poetry proper.

Most societies use POD and recognize different genres of it on the basis of the practices and the knowledge they have acquired in their cultural and historical settings. Poetry in a strict sense can be defined as a specialized subset of POD according to the criteria that are defined by each culture according to its own choice of genres, specific contents, ways of production, functions, occasions of performance, and aesthetic and social values. Poetry as a form of art crafted by a poet, or a poetic school, "which has for its object the creation of intellectual pleasure by means of imaginative and passionate language" (cf. section 2 above), is a definition that does not even describe fully what actually happens in the literary tradition of the West.

NOTES

The authors are grateful to all those who helped them with their advice in preparing this chapter. The following friends deserve a particular mention: Alessandro Bausi, Yaqob Beyene, Paolo Calvetti, Giorgio Casacchia, Francesca Corrao, Alessandro Duranti, Enrico Fubini, Donatella Izzo, Valeria Micillo, Antonio Perri, Encarnación Sanchez García, Alberto Ventura. Obviously, only the two authors should be blamed for any mistake or misunderstanding.

1 "Humanam vero musicam quisquis in sese ipsum descendit intellegit"; *De institutione musica*, book I, ch. II; written *ca*. 495 CE.

2 It is useful to consult Preminger and Brogan (1993) for more details about these topics.

3 "Nihil aliud est quam fictio rhetorica musicaque posita"; *De vulgari eloquentia*, book II, chapter IV, written about 1304 CE.

4 *AlMunjid fi alluġa*, 19th edition (Beirut: Almaktaba aššarqiya, 1986). The authors are wholly responsible for the translations from the original languages here and elsewhere in this chapter.

5 *Kōjien*, 5th edition (Tokyo: Iwanami Shoken, 1998).

6 Yaasiin C. Keenadiid (1976).

7 *The New Webster Encyclopedic Dictionary of the English Language*, vol. I (New York: Grolier, 1965).

8 Moliner (1971: 790).

9 A compound word created by Arnold Schönberg, the first Western music composer who theorized and used this kind of vocal performance for his *Pierrot Lunaire* (1912). This term is now widely used in ethnomusicology.

10 This poem belongs to the *masafo* genre because of its meter, the melody it is sung to, and its topic. Its Somali text has been published by Sh. Jaamac Cumar Ciise (1974: 82). An English translation of it can be found in Andrzejewski and Lewis (1964: 74 f.), and an Italian translation in Yaasiin C. Kenadiid (1984: 147 f.).

11 Slashes are used to separate lines of poetry when they are written continuously, especially in translations. Vertical lines are used as brackets around representations of scansions, and for line-internal boundaries separating half-lines, rhythmic groups, and cola.

12 Open syllables are those that end in a vowel, like the two in *Aussie*, pronounced as ['ɔsɪ], whereas closed syllables are those that end in one or more consonants, like the two in *intend*, pronounced as [ɪn 'tend]. It will be seen that in other scansion systems this distinction plays a crucial role.

13 This example is drawn from Frankel (1960: 29 ff.), a good introduction to five of the major genres of Chinese poetry. The name of this particular poem is translated as "Passing through Huà-yīn" in Frankel, but is *Huang Ge Lou* in the *Quan Tang Shi*, the well-known collection of Tang poetry. The transcription represents by means of the *pinyin* orthog-

raphy the contemporary Peking pronunciation, that differed in several aspects from the Middle Chinese one.

14 Written in a quasi-alphabetic variety of the cuneiform script during the fourteenth and thirteenth centuries BCE in the ancient town of Ugarit, modern Ras Shamra, on the northern Syrian coast.

15 Tedlock (1983) doesn't use this term, but stresses that "the division between the internal parts of a couplet or triplet should be treated not as a line break but as a caesura, so long as we understand that this is not an interruption in the *sound*, but a transition in the *sense*" (p. 226).

16 Notice that rhyme in Ethiopian poetry is different from that of modern English poetry, where it involves similarity of the vowels, but not of the initial consonants, of the last accented syllables in two lines.

REFERENCES

Abu-Lughod, L. (1986). *Veiled Sentiments: Honor and Poetry in a Bedouin Society.* Berkeley, Los Angeles, and London: University of California Press.

Abu-Manga, A.-A. (ed.) (1985). *Baajankaro. A Fulani Epic from Sudan.* Berlin: Reimer.

Andrzejewski, B. W., and Lewis, I. M. (1964). *Somali Poetry: An Introduction.* Oxford: Oxford University Press.

Babalola, S. A. (1966). *The Content and Form of Yoruba Ijala.* Oxford: Oxford University Press.

Banti, G., and Giannattasio, F. (1996). Music and Metre in Somali Poetry. In R. J. Hayward and I. M. Lewis (eds.), *Voice and Power: Essays in Honour of B. W. Andrzejewski* (pp. 83–127). *African Languages and Cultures,* supplement 3.

Biebuyck, D. (1978). *Hero and Chief. Epic Literature from the Banyanga.* Berkeley: University of California Press.

Bloch, M. (1974). Symbols, Song, Dance and Features of Articulation. Is Religion an Extreme Form of Traditional Authority? *Archives Européennes de Sociologie* XV(1): 55–81.

Brăiloiu, C. (1948). Le giusto syllabique bichrone. Un système rythmique propre à la musique populaire roumaine. *Polyphonie* 2: 26–57 [rev. as "Le giusto syllabique. Un système rythmique populaire roumaine", *Anuario Musical,* 8 (1952): 117–158; repr. in Brăiloiu (1973), pp. 151–194].

Brăiloiu, C. (1954). Le vers populaire roumain chanté. *Revue des Etudes Roumaines* 2: 7–74. Paris: Edition de l'Institut universitaire roumain [repr. in Brăiloiu (1973), pp. 195–264].

Brăiloiu, C. (1956). Le rythme enfantin: notions liminaires. *Le Colloques de Wegimont: Ethnomusicologie* 1 (pp. 64–96). Paris-Bruxelles: Elsevier [repr. as "La rythmique enfantine. Notions liminaires" in Brăiloiu (1973), pp. 265–299].

Brăiloiu, C. (1973). *Problèmes d'ethnomusicologie* (ed. G. Rouget). Geneva: Minkoff Reprint.

Brogan, T. V. F. (1993a). Poetry. In A. Preminger and T. V. F. Brogan (eds.), *The New Princeton Encyclopedia of Poetry and Poetics* (pp. 938–942). Princeton, NJ: Princeton University Press.

Brogan, T. V. F. (1993b). Verse and Prose. In A. Preminger and T. V. F. Brogan (eds.), *The New Princeton Encyclopedia of Poetry and Poetics* (pp. 1346–1351). Princeton, NJ: Princeton University Press.

Deng, F. (1973). *The Dinka and Their Songs.* London: Oxford University Press.

Dixon, R. M. W., and Koch, G. (1996). *Dyirbal Song Poetry: The Oral Literature of an Australian Rainforest People.* St. Lucia, Queensland: University of Queensland Press.

Fahd, T., Heinrichs, D., and Ben Abdesselem, A. (1995). Sadjᶜ. In C. E. Bosworth, E. van Donzel, W. P. Heinrichs, and G. Lecomte (eds.), *Encyclopédie de l'Islam* (nouvelle édition) [Encyclopedia of Islam (new edition)], vol. VIII (pp. 753b–759b). Leiden: E. J. Brill.

Feld, S. (1990). *Sound and Sentiment: Birds, Weeping, Poetics, and Song in Kaluli Expression*, 2nd edn. Philadelphia: University of Pennsylvania Press.

Foley, W. A. (1997). *Anthropological Linguistics: An Introduction*. Malden, MA: Blackwell.

Fox, J. J. (ed.) (1988). *To Speak in Pairs: Essays on the Ritual Languages of Eastern Indonesia*. Cambridge: Cambridge University Press.

Frankel, H. H. (1960). Classical Chinese. In W. K. Wimsatt (ed.), *Versification: Major Language Types* (pp. 22–37). New York : New York University Press.

Frolov, D. (2000). *Classical Arabic Verse: History and Theory of ᶜArūḍ*. Leiden, Boston, and Cologne: Brill.

Fubini, E. (2002). Quale musica ebraica oggi e quale uso nell'ambito della sinagoga. In S. Pozzi (ed.), *La musica sacra nelle chiese cristiane. Atti del Convegno internazionale di studi – Roma, 25–27 gennaio 2001* (pp. 141–147). Bologna: AlfaStudio.

Gasparov, M. L. (1989). *Ocherk istorii evropeiskogo stiha* [Outline of the History of European Verse]. Moscow: Izdatel'stvo Nauka. Transl. *Storia del verso europeo* (Bologna: il Mulino, 1993); *A History of European Versification* (Oxford: Clarendon Press, 1997).

Goldsmith, J. A. (1990). *Autosegmental and Metrical Phonology: A New Synthesis*. Oxford: Blackwell.

Goldzieher, I. (1899). *Abhandlungen zur arabischen Philologie*, 2 vols. Leiden: Brill [repr.: Leiden: Brill, 1976].

Halle, M., and Keyser, S. J. (1980). Metrica. *Enciclopedia Einaudi*, 9 [Einaudi Encyclopedia]. Turin: Einaudi (transl. of Halle and Keyser, "Metrics". Cambridge, MA: MIT, unpublished manuscript).

Hymes, D. (2001). Poetry. In A. Duranti (ed.), *Key Terms in Language and Culture* (pp. 187–189). Malden, MA, and Oxford: Blackwell.

Sh. Jaamac Cumar Ciise (ed.) (1974). *Diiwaanka gabayadii Sayid Maxamed Cabdulle Xasan* [A Collection of the Poems of Maxamed Cabdulle Xasan]. Mogadishu: Akadeemiyada Dhaqanka, Wasaaradda Hiddaha iyo Tacliinta Sare.

Jakobson, R. (1960). Closing Statement: Linguistics and Poetics. In T. A. Sebeok (ed.), *Style in Language* (pp. 350–377). Cambridge, MA: MIT Press.

Johnson, J. W. (1974). *Heellooy Heellellooy: The Development of the Genre Heello in Modern Somali Poetry.* Bloomington: Indiana University Press.

Johnson, J. W., and Fa-Digi Sisòkò (1986). *The Epic of Son-Jara: A West African Tradition*. Bloomington: Indiana University Press.

Johnstone, T. M. (1972). The Language of Poetry in Dhofar. *BSOAS* 35: 1–17.

Jouad, H. (1995). *Le calcul inconscient de l'improvisation. Poésie berbère – rhythme, nombre et sense* [The Unconscious Calculus of Improvisation. Berber Poetry – Rhythm, Number and Meaning]. Paris and Louvain: Éditions Peeters.

Kiparsky, P., and Youmans, G. (eds.) (1989). *Rhythm and Meter. Phonetics and Phonology*, vol. 1. San Diego, CA: Academic Press.

Klein-Arendt, R. (1987). KiNgozi: Extinct Swahili Dialect or Poetic Jargon? A Historical, Dialectological and Contextual Analysis. *Sprache und Geschichte in Afrika* 8: 181–245.

Koch, L. (ed.) (1992). *Beowulf.* Turin: Giulio Einaudi Editore.

Leander, B. (1972). *In xochitl in cuicatl: Flor y canto, la poesía de los aztecas* [In xochitl in cuicatl: Flower and Song, the Poetry of the Aztecs]. Mexico: INI-SEP.

List, G. (1963). The Boundaries of Speech and Song. *Ethnomusicology* 7(1): 1–16.

Lotz, J. (1960). Metric Typology. In T. A. Sebeok (ed.), *Style in Language* (pp. 135–148). Cambridge, MA: MIT Press; New York and London: John Wiley & Sons.

Lotz, J. (1972). Elements of Versification. In W. K. Wimsatt (ed.), *Versification: Major Language Types* (pp. 1–21). New York: New York University Press.

Meillet, A. (1965). *Aperçu d'une histoire de la langue grecque*, 7th edn. Paris: Klincksieck.

Miehe, G. (1995). Stilistische Merkmale der Swahili-Versdichtung. In G. Miehe and W. J. G. Möhlig (eds.), *Swahili-Handbuch* [Swahili-Handbook]. Cologne: Rüdiger Köppe.

Moliner, M. (1971). *Diccionario de uso del Español*. Madrid: Gredos.

Molino, J. (2002). La poesia cantata. Alcuni problemi teorici. In M. Agamennone and F. Giannattasio (eds.), *Sul verso cantato* [On Sung Verse] (pp. 17–33). Padova: il Poligrafo.

Molino, J., and Gardes-Tamine, J. (1987–8). *Introduction à l'analyse de la poésie* [Introduction to the Analysis of Poetry], Parts I and II. Paris: Presses Universitaires de France.

Moreno, M. M. (1935). *Raccolta di qēnē*. Rome: Tipografia del Senato.

Newman, J. K. (1993). Epic. In A. Preminger and T. V. F. Brogan (eds.), *The New Princeton Encyclopedia of Poetry and Poetics* (pp. 361–375). Princeton, NJ: Princeton University Press.

O'Connor, M. (1997). *Hebrew Verse Structure*. Winona Lake, IN: Eisenbrauns.

Pellat, C., Bausani, A., İz, F., and Ahmad, A. (1975). Hidjā'. In B. Lewis, V. L. Ménage, C. Pellat, and J. Schacht (eds.), *Encyclopédie de l'Islam (réimpression anastatique)* [Encyclopedia of Islam (anastatic reprint)], vol. III (pp. 363b–370b). Leiden and Paris: E. J. Brill and G. P. Maisonneuve & Larose S.A.

Preminger, A., and Brogan, T. V. F. (eds.) (1993). *The New Princeton Encyclopedia of Poetry and Poetics*. Princeton, NJ: Princeton University Press.

Schieffelin, E. L. (1976). *The Sorrow of the Lonely and the Burning of the Dancers*. New York: St. Martin's Press.

Schuh, R. (1989). Toward a Metrical Analysis of Hausa Verse Prosody: Mutadaarik. In I. Haïk and L. Tuller (eds.), *Current Approaches to African Linguistics*, vol. 6 (pp. 161–175). Dordrecht: Foris.

Schuh, R. (1999). Metrics of Arabic and Hausa Poetry. In P. F. A. Kotey (ed.), *New Dimensions in African Linguistics and Languages. Trends in African Linguistics*, vol. 3 (pp. 121–130). Trenton and Asmara: Africa World Press.

Schuh, R. (in press a). Text and Performance in Hausa Metrics.

Schuh, R. (in press b). The Metrics of Three Hausa Songs of Marriage by Dan Maraya Jos.

Segala, A. (1989). *Histoire de la littérature nahuatl (sources, identités, représentations)* [History of Nahuatl Literature (Sources, Identities, Representations)]. Rome: Bulzoni Editore.

Segert, S. (1984). *A Basic Grammar of the Ugaritic Language*. Berkeley, Los Angeles, and London: University of California Press.

Seroussi, E. (2002). The Dimension of Sound in the Traditional Synagogue. In S. Pozzi (ed.), *La musica sacra nelle chiese cristiane. Atti del Convegno internazionale di studi – Roma, 25–27 gennaio 2001* (pp. 149–156). Bologna: AlfaStudio.

Tedlock, D. (1983). The Forms of Mayan Verse. In D. Tedlock, *The Spoken Word and the Work of Interpretation* (pp. 216–230). Philadelphia: University of Pennsylvania Press.

Tedlock, D. (1996). *Popol Vuh: The Mayan Book of the Dawn of Life*. New York: Simon and Schuster.

Valéry, P. (1943). Rhumbs. *Tel Quel*, vol. II. Paris: Gallimard.

Watkins, C. (1995). *How to Kill a Dragon: Aspects of Indo-European Poetics*. Oxford and New York: Oxford University Press.

Watson, W. G. E. (2001). *Classical Hebrew Poetry: A Guide to Its Techniques*, 4th edn. Sheffield: Sheffield Academic Press.

Wimsatt, W. K. (ed.) (1972). *Versification: Major Language Types*. New York: New York University Press.

Winn, J. A. (1993). Music and Poetry. In A. Preminger and T. V. F. Brogan (eds.), *The New Princeton Encyclopedia of Poetry and Poetics* (pp. 803–806). Princeton, NJ: Princeton University Press.

Yaasiin C. Keenadiid (1976). *Qaamuuska Af-Soomaaliga*. Xamar: Wasaaradda Hiddaha iyo Tacliinta Sare iyo Akademiyada Dhaqanka.

Yaasiin C. Keenadiid (1984). *Ina Cabdille Xasan e la sua attività letteraria*. Naples: Istituto Universitario Orientale.

Yip, M. (1980). The Metrical Structure of Regulated Verse. *Journal of Chinese Linguistics* 8: 107–124.

Yoder, P. B. (1972). Biblical Hebrew. In W. K. Wimsatt (ed.), *Versification: Major Language Types* (pp. 52–65). New York: New York University Press.

14 Vocal Anthropology: From the Music of Language to the Language of Song

Steven Feld, Aaron A. Fox, Thomas Porcello, and David Samuels

1 INTRODUCTION

There is a considerable history to research exploring relations between music and language. We begin with some of this intellectual background to better locate the research questions taken up in the body of this chapter. While these questions – about the linguistic mediation of musical and especially timbral discourse, and the connections between the singing voice and place, class, ethnicity, and identity – are very contemporary ones, they are clearly prefigured historically, in the overlapping legacies of Franz Boas, Edward Sapir, and Roman Jakobson, all of whom made a place for music in their programs for the study of the mental, semiotic, communicative, expressive, and discursive roles of language. In ethnomusicology it was their student and contemporary George Herzog, also trained as a linguistic anthropologist, who drew out the musical implications of their ideas and elaborated the importance of bringing linguistic sophistication to the social analysis of music.

A review of the key themes in the language and music literature during the formative periods of twentieth-century anthropology, linguistics, and ethnomusicology (Feld and Fox 1994) indicates how those early programs developed into four principal conversations. The first, and perhaps best known of these, is the general and abstract consideration of *music as a language*. This is the perspective that produced formal linguistic models of music, models meant to use linguistic theory to advance the analysis of music. These models have been based on analogies between the distributional character of pitch systems and phonetic inventories, as well as analogies between syntactic structures and the harmonic, metrical, and motival organization of musical pieces. Looking at the products of these efforts, one recognizes critical differences between linguistic approaches to syntax and semantics and musical approaches to form and meaning. From a semiotic point of view, music seems far more syntactically redundant and overdetermined when compared to language. At the same time music is semantically far more diffuse and ambiguous than language. In other words, forms of repetition, cyclicity, and predictable recursiveness dominate musical structure more than language structure. In this sense music may seem a simpler formal system to describe with logical rules. But at the same time, meaning in music is notoriously more complex to formally characterize when compared to the semantic structures of language. Nonetheless, linguistically motivated models for the description and analysis of music have, since the early 1980s, produced a number of intellectually productive developments toward a cognitive science of music (Lerdahl and Jackendoff 1983; Lerdahl 2001).

A second, less theoretical and more strictly empirical conversation focuses on *music about language*, that is, of speech surrogates. As a semiotic for musicking language, speech surrogates involve the transposition of linguistic tonal and temporal contours to surrogate articulatory modes and media. These are principally instrumental, like the phenomena of "talking drums," or involve other secondary signaling systems, for example, "whistled speech" (Umiker-Sebeok and Sebeok 1976).

The substance of this chapter sidesteps these two areas, as they represent both the most general and the most specific poles of all language/music discourses. Instead we concentrate on developments in two other research conversations, the locations where the fully social implications of the language/music issues now most completely emerge. The first of these is devoted to considerations of *language about music*, namely, the intertwining of verbal and musical discourse. This research starts with the simple observation that the dominant Western conceptualization of music as a mental construct and a performance practice obscures one of its most significant social facts. Namely, music is a ubiquitous topic for discourse. Musicians and listeners everywhere spend a great deal of time and productive social energy talking about music (Feld 1994a). Three empirical domains for social analysis have unfolded from this observation. First is research on the relations between musical terminology, local theories of music, and the metaphoric basis of language about music (Feld 1990). Second is research on the intertwining of speaking and musicking as a site of social interaction among musicians. Finally, engaging debates originating in the philosophy of musical aesthetics, there is research investigating the social location of evaluative, critical, and interpretive musical discourse (Feld 1994a).

In the first case study that follows, Thomas Porcello brings together a number of these themes in his research on the management of talk about timbre, a term often glossed by the synaesthetic metaphor of "tone color." This is talk about sound qualities, an area of acoustically and socially complex verbal practices critical to the production of music. Often imagined as an "unspeakable" realm of music, where words are either imprecise or unnecessary, timbre turns out, in Porcello's empirical research, to occupy a far more central location in verbal interactions among musicians and engineers.

The final set of conversations also focus on the centrality of vocal sound to verbal significance. They link the study of *music in language* and *language in music* through a focus on song and on texted vocalization. Here we begin where poetics meets performance, namely, in the voice. Language's musicality – its tonal, timbral, prosodic, and gradient dynamic qualities – highlights the role of vocal performance for linguistic meaning. Music's language – the texted dimensions of songs and other sung poetic genres – highlights verbal art as vocal art. Critical social issues arise in these areas, namely the account of voice and its relationship to social agency, difference, social imagination, and identity. These topics are addressed in two additional case studies, below, from the Texas country song research of Aaron A. Fox, and the Apache country song research of David Samuels.

2   TALK ABOUT TIMBRE IN THE RECORDING STUDIO

Sound recording studios provide a rich locale in which music is the predominant subject of, and reason for, discourse. Contemporary popular music recording sessions involve the intertwining of musical performance and speech – often performative speech – about music (Porcello 1998). All aspects of a musical work, from its melodic, harmonic, and rhythmic structure to its instrumental arrangement and the aesthetics of its performance, are open to discussion. But it is talk about sound quality, or timbre, that receives particular emphasis.

Technological changes since the advent of sound recording have been driven by the twin goals of increased sonic fidelity between live and recorded sounds, and increased control over the manipulation of recorded sounds (Théberge 1994). As the ability to isolate and craft musical sounds has grown, so too has the amount of time and attention devoted to working on the timbral dimension of musical performances and sound recordings. As a result, talk about popular music, especially in its sites and processes of production, is saturated with vocal descriptions and depictions of musical timbre. Among musicians, engineers, producers, and other recording professionals, this timbral dimension is generally glossed by the phrase "the sound," or simply the term "sound," both of which are conceptually separated from considerations such as pitch, performance, and technique.

The prominence of talk about timbre within the sound recording industry is in direct contrast to Western academic and critical discourses about music that emphasize the formal plane of music's harmonic, tonal, and rhythmic dimensions. Musicologists often characterize discussions of timbre as mere verbal imitation or impressionistic metaphor. Alternatively, timbre is imagined as a domain specific to the scientific discourse of acousticians.[1] Such portrayals are clearly problematized in recording sessions by naturally occurring speech, used to actively negotiate the social salience of timbre to music-makers and listeners (present and eventual). In this workplace context, a structured, technical lexicon of timbre circulates publicly; knowledgeable deployment and interpretation of this lexicon provide the essential framework for playing, evaluating, recording, and mixing music. To be ignorant of this lexicon and its rules for deployment is to be seriously disadvantaged as a participant in the music-making process.

2.1 Discursive strategies

Participants in recording sessions rely on numerous strategies for talking about timbre. A careful examination of field tapes I made in studios in the southwestern United States in the mid-1990s (Porcello 1996), as well as extensive review of professional magazines, reveal five common discursive strategies used for talk about timbre during recording sessions (see also the transcriptions in Meintjes 2003, whose work in South African studios shows a remarkably similar set of strategies).

(1) Spoken/sung "vocables" are used in an attempt to iconically mimic in vocalization the timbral features of the musical sound(s) under consideration. Such sound icons include, for example, /dz:::/ to represent the sound of the snare beads vibrating against the lower head of a snare drum, /š::: ts ts/ for a triple-meter maracas pattern, and so forth. These vocables are almost always enunciated with the speaker literally performing the musical part – its pitch and rhythmic dimensions included – as accurately as possible.[2]

(2) Lexical onomatopoeic metaphors, or, lexical items that bear a phonological resemblance to the sound they are describing based upon acoustic properties. Examples of this large class of timbral descriptors include *click*, *buzz*, and *hiss*, which clearly operate on principles of both iconicity and sound symbolism.

(3) "Pure" metaphor, in which timbral features are invoked not via sonic iconicity but with reference, generally, to other sensorial domains. Examples include *wet*, *dry*, *deep*, *bright*, *round*, each a synaesthetic metaphor. The majority of pure metaphors used to describe musical timbre are synaesthetic to touch and sight, the latter set almost always invoking spatial relationships. Many of the pure metaphors are highly codified, especially among sound engineers who recognize, for example, that a sound described as "too boxy" (a negative timbral trait) can regularly be corrected by dampening all frequencies between 250 and 500 Hz.

(4) Association, a strategy involving the citation of other musicians, recordings, sounds, technologies, time periods, etc. (see Feld 1994a). A typical use of association can be seen in this conversation between a producer (DE) and a drum tuner (JM), for example, recorded at the very beginning of a studio session near Austin, Texas:

> 69 DE: I like . . . I . . . you see, snare-wise . . . actually all the way around drum rise..drum wise..I like the sounds that were probably created but not captured in the '60s . . . .a lot of the like..or even early '70s,..a lot of the like Earth, Wind & Fire and uh . . .
>
> 70 JM: Tony Williams type stuff? . . . do you know . . .
>
> 71 DE: I don't know Tony..no.
>
> 72 JM: Oh, the drummer yeah..that sort of . . . what..Zeppelin sound? Real . . . flat? . . . like that?
>
> 73 DE: Nn::::.....
>
> 74 JM: Yeah cause I mean..John Bonham was a good drummer but . . .
>
> 75 DE: Yeah . . . ((skeptically))
>
> 76 JM: Personally I don't like his drums..but that has nothing to do with this job so . . .
>
> 77 DE: Yeah . . . ((thinking))
>
> 78 JM: But I mean you're talking about early '70s type sound? is what you're partial to?
>
> 79 DE: Yeah, some of those . . .

80 JM: ... and that's what you want?
81 DE: No.. not so much the rock stuff but the funkier stuff.
(Porcello 1996)

Rather than attempt to describe the sounds directly, associations index frames of reference external to the session itself and in so doing strongly link musical timbre to linguistically mediated forms of sociability, as association succeeds or fails on the basis of shared cultural knowledge.

(5) Evaluation, in which rather than attempt a description of a musical sound, an assessment of its merit is offered (see, e.g., line 74 in the above transcription, assessing John Bonham's drum sound). Evaluation plays a key role in the microsocial relations of studio practice; it is often used to determine the boundaries of shared stylistic solidarity among session participants, to establish sociable working relationships, and to mark territory of shared or divergent aesthetics.

In extended discussions of specific musical sounds, interlocutors will often utilize a combination of these strategies. In a single turn at talk built around a pure metaphor, for instance, it is not unusual for the speaker to clarify by referencing a particular recording that embodies the timbral feature evoked by the metaphor (e.g., "a clipped snare, you know, like Phil Collins"). Similarly, across turns at talk in a dyadic exchange Speaker B may respond to Speaker A's use of a pure metaphor by supplying an association for purposes of checking Speaker A's intended meaning (e.g., Speaker A: "A clipped snare, you know?" Speaker B: "Like Phil Collins, you mean?") or to forcefully reorient Speaker A's approach (e.g., Speaker B: "You obviously have a sound in mind, but if you could say who it's by I'd have a better idea of what you mean"). Analysis of the moves among these strategies suggests that a great deal of the ability to communicate meaningfully about timbre lies in the metadiscursive work done by interlocutors.

2.2   Onomatopoeic form and semantics

Analysis of a corpus of the one hundred most frequently occurring vocabalic and lexical onomatopoeic metaphor timbral descriptors from recording sessions I taped suggests the utility of a modified version of Rhodes' typology of linguistic sound images (1994). Rhodes' tripartite continuum of linguistic strategies for mapping sound shape includes non-lexical forms (vocables such as /dz:::/ from Strategy (1) above), onomatopoeic forms – phonetic imitations that are nonetheless lexemes (Strategy (2) above) – and fully arbitrary forms (Strategy (3) above). Among ono-matopoeic items, Rhodes suggests a further, two-part distinction between "wild" and "tame" forms. "Wild" forms are closer to simple phonetic imitations, while their "tame" counterparts strongly adhere to the phonological rules of the language in which they are uttered. For items applied to musical sounds in this corpus there is one additional significant point on this continuum linking imitation to arbitrariness: "motivated" arbitrary forms. Motivated arbitrary forms mix partial arbitrariness with partial onomatopoeia (e.g., lexemes *thin, tinny, sibilant,* in which the initial consonant–vowel cluster functions onomatopoeically but the balance of the lexeme resists iconicity). These are, in ways, reminiscent of Bolinger's characterization of phonesthemic (submorphemic sounds or sound clusters with regularly associated meanings) rimes and assonances (1950). As speakers move from vocables to fully arbitrary forms, the tendency to perform the utterance disappears. (See figure 14.1.)

Strategy (2) – use of lexical onomatopoeic metaphors – is of particular interest because the majority of these items, like their pure metaphorical counterparts, are highly codified in studio discourse, deployed and interpreted by sound engineers not as impressionistic but as a technically precise metalanguage that glosses specific physical properties of sound waves. Part of the technical vocabulary of sound engineers and studio musicians, they are a primary means by which musical, engineering, and sonic competence are negotiated in recording sessions (see Bartlett and Bartlett 1994). As such, they powerfully link iconicity to reference as well as to the social roles of those who work in recording studios. Here the limitations of a linguistic ideology in which iconicity is rarely examined in contexts other than poetics or child language development (an ideology critiqued by Nuckolls 1999 and Wescott 1977) are evident; iconicity serves as a crucial, systematic professional linguistic resource in the world of audio production (see also Feld 1981 on the systematicity of metaphors in discourse about music; see Jakobson and Waugh 1979: ch. 4 on the systematicity of sound symbolism in general).

The vast majority of onomatopoeic lexemes will be deployed in adjectival form (e.g., in a syntactic frame such as "that sound is too _____") but derive from a monosyllabic nominal or (more rarely) verbal form. Common examples are *boom*, *hiss*, *grunge*, *click*, *thump*, *honk*, which become *boomy*, *hissy*, *grungy*, *clicky*, *thumpy*, *honky*, etc. In these cases, the noun or verb is treated as the basic analytical unit. The corpus includes a limited number of disyllabic noun or verb forms that remain disyllabic in adjectival form; in each case the second syllable of the nominal form is built around an unstressed syllabic [l]. Thus *rumble*, *crackle*, *muffle* become *rumbly*, *crackly*, *muffled*. The preponderance of monosyllabic onomatopoeic forms in this corpus suggests that monosyllables are employed by speakers as optimal mappings of musically articulated sounds; just as a musical sound consists of an envelope comprising an attack, a sustain, and a decay, so does the monosyllabic utterance.

Non-lexical forms	Onomatopoeic forms		Motivated arbitrariness	Arbitrary words
|	*Wild*	*Tame*	|	|
not "words"	often performed,	not performed,	one + individual	metaphorical,
often sung/	may violate	whole word	segment(s)	no use of
spoken	phonological	adheres to	partakes of	onomatopoeia
|	rules	phonological	onomatopoeia	|
		rules		
|	|	|	|	|
[m:::]	[ʔwæk + nasal	[kwæk]	thin (θ and ɪ)	*deep*
[dz:::]	vowel]	[hɪs]	tinny (t and ɪ)	*bright*
[s:::]	[hɪs::]		sibilant (s) etc.	round
etc.				etc.

Figure 14.1 Continuum of linguistic descriptors of musical sound (modified version of Rhodes 1994)

If one accepts that onomatopoeia involves a fairly direct mapping between the timbral features of the musical sound and the phonetic/phonemic features of the linguistic item that replicates it, then the principles of phonesthemic patterning, particularly within the monosyllabic items, may be summarized as in figure 14.2.[3]

No onomatopoeic items in the corpus are vowel-initial or vowel-final, suggesting that the details of the acoustic properties comprising the onset and decay of musical sounds are just as crucial to speakers as those of the sustain in describing and evaluating musical timbre.

Aside from phonological concerns, certain semantic features appear particularly salient to engineers and musicians working in a Western recording studio context that highly values sonic purity, cleanliness, and the transparent accuracy of recorded sounds. Here a large number of pure metaphors signify undesirable diffuseness of sound. Some are generally applied solely to individual instruments or voices (e.g.,

Principles of phonesthetic patterning

— General structure is CVC (all begin and end with consonants as pronounced)
— Initial and final sounds may be individual consonant or consonant clusters (*Cr-, Cl-, spl-, -nč*, etc.)

A. Syllable-initial sounds (onset) → attack
   1. Abrupt/explosive
         stop only /p, t, k, b, d, g/   (*puff, boom, tick*, etc.)
         stop + liquid /bl, kl, kr/   (*blat, click, crisp*, etc.)
   2. More gradual
         fricatives /h, s, f/   (*hiss, sizzle, fuzz*, etc.)
         affricates /č/   (*chunk*, etc.)

B. Syllable middle (medial vowels) → sustain, pitch
   1. High /ɪ, i/   (*click, crisp, jingle*, etc.)
   2. Neutral /æ/   (*clack, smack*, etc.)
   3. Low /ʌ, u/   (*clunk, thump, boom*, etc.)

C. Final sounds → decay
   1. Abrupt
      a. stops   (*snap, crack, smack*, etc.)
   2. Gradual
      a. non-resonant
         white noise
           – fricatives, affricates   (*crash, splash, smash, hiss*, etc.)
      b. resonant
         fading to infinity
           – nasals /m, ŋ/   (*boom, ring, hum*, etc.)
         brief fading until a moment of truncation
           – nasal + stop   (*clunk, thump*, etc.)

D. Disyllabic words ending with unstressed syllable with /l/ as nucleus
   1. Sustained decay with a point of noticeable fall-off
      a. resonant   (*rumble*, etc.)
      b. non-resonant   (*crackle*, etc.)

Figure 14.2 Structure of onomatopoeic forms

breathy) but the majority can be used to refer to the mix as a whole (e.g., *blurred*, *smeared*, *distant*, *puffy*, *muddy*, *muffled*). A similarly large set of terms concerns the extent to which the performed sound (as heard by a co-present ear) has been modified in the recording and reproduction process, a semantic domain perhaps best labeled "accuracy." The terms *blanketed*, *boxy*, *brittle*, and *thin*, for example, imply that in the recording process something has induced a modification to an original sound as emitted from its source.[4] The large number of terms for accuracy and diffuseness suggest phenomena that are of overriding concern in studio production and which must therefore have a well-developed vocabulary to pinpoint particular sonic features in need of modification or correction.[5]

Musical timbre arguably provides the most important structure of hearing in the process of music-making in sound recording studios. It is therefore incumbent on session participants to develop elaborated, yet precise, discursive means of communicating about a phenomenon notoriously resistant to essentializing statements. This takes place through identifiable and significant principles that structure ways of speaking about timbre; these include the phonetic and phonological structure of onomatopoeic forms, or the semantics of metaphors. This focus on vocality, on the sonic material of articulation, constitutes a critical bridge between the musicality of language and verbal discourse about sound. It further connects to a perspective on singing and song that links music in language to language in music.

3   WORKING-CLASS "COUNTRY"

In South-Central Texas, the art of singing "country" music is highly valued and carefully cultivated, as are critical and aesthetic discourses about singing (Fox 1995). Country singers are musical specialists, responsible – like all folk artists – to their local communities for a wide range of performance skills (Bauman 1977); but they are especially respected for their mastery over (and creative extensions of) a canonical catalogue of vocal techniques. This case study focuses on several of those techniques, in order to consider the larger significance of singing as a cultural practice that presents ramifications for a general theory of music and language.

Many articulatory possibilities are available to working-class country singers. Fully pitched, metrically regularized, and amplitudinally shaped singing (with an expansive and exploitable range of voice qualities and vibratos and phonetic indexes of different modes, registers, genres, and dialects of "ordinary" speech) is of course a predominant "default" modality. Singers also produce heightened speech, which they call "recitation," and which mimics the less rigid meter of speech while retaining a song's original versification (similar to some types of operatic "recitative" and other quasi-spoken idioms in many musical drama traditions).

Country singing style also involves frequent importation of fragments of metrically non-regular and non-pitched speech into song performance (e.g., bits of dialogue between a singer and a "picker" in the band that are performatively spoken against the background of a song). Of course, such "fully spoken" discourse also shapes the boundaries around song performances. Stage patter, bandstand talk, and interactions with audience members (using intonationally and dynamically heightened speech) can also be used to move between the spoken frame of song performance and full singing. Specific transitional gestures between speech and song include "count-offs," which establish the meter of the song, introductory words summoning full attention from audiences (for example, many singers begin songs with the formulaic expression "I said ..."), and stylized formulae for marking reported speech, including elaborate techniques of voice imitation, reflecting a strong preference among Southern working-class Americans for direct discourse over indirect discourse.

Competent singers are often quite consciously aware of this range of articulations. They may refer to a corresponding set of ethnotheoretical concepts to describe specific formulae, articulations, and voice qualities. More commonly, both among singers and among listeners, metamusical discourse proceeds by analogy (usually comparing one singer's style to another well-known singer's example), or through a metaphorical vocabulary that emphasizes qualities of "hardness," "sweetness," "sadness," "volume," "power," "precision," "ordinariness," and appropriateness of singing style to textual content and sociomusical context.

All such evaluations are oriented toward the master-tropes of musical evaluation in South Texas, the sociomusical categories of "feeling" (as noun and verb) and "relating" (as a mode of telling and a mode of social and aesthetic engagement). Singers who perform "with feeling" are said to "relate to" their material, their traditions, and their communities. Likewise, audiences say they can "relate to" singers who sing "with feeling" (or "feel"). In turn, such evaluative tropes are further summarized through strongly inflected tropes of genre identification, typically in phrases like "that's *country*," or (most assertively), "that's *real* country." Such tropes resonate with a matrix of cultural sensibilities and practices for which musical style is a summarizing symbol. Evaluations of song performance thus extend pervasively into assertions of rural, working-class, Southern social identity and cultural continuity.

Vocal style in Texas country singing can be approached analytically through a fine-grained description of particular techniques employed by singers. Many properties of vocal sound (e.g., vibrato, amplitude, articulatory noise, melodic shape, etc.) can be measured and correlated with the communicative and expressive features of song texts (e.g., explicit affective verbs, specific references to feeling states, canonical moods of particular poetic (sub)genres. Similar correlations, considered quite important by most Texas country singers, can be made between vocal techniques and the language-structural properties of song texts (many vocal inflections, such as "cry breaks," appear to be conditioned equally by phonological environments and by affective connotations of the referential text).

A continuum of intonational markedness, ranging from unpitched, metrically irregular, but intonationally heightened speech to full pitched, metrically regular singing, is routinely employed to mark structural divisions in song texts, changes of point of view and narrative voice, contrasting affects, and degrees of expressive engagement by the singer. Timbral quality deserves special attention; Texas singers evoke important affects and moods through distinctive changes in the site and manner of voice production. A pharyngealized tone, for example, can be iconic of the ravaged voice of a character textually narrated explicitly or implicitly as "crying." "Crying" itself can be iconically represented with specific inflections known categorically as "cry breaks" – sharp deformations of the melodic line effected through intermittent falsetto or nasalization, pulsing articulations achieved through glottal stops or diaphragmatic tensing, or the addition of articulatory vocal "noise" to an otherwise "smooth" tone. An enormous range of rhythmic and metric possibilities are suggested by the intertwining of musical and linguistic form in country singing as well, ranging from a relatively "natural" delivery that mimics the variable meters of ordinary speech, to the rigidly metrical delivery characteristic of other locally familiar oral genres such as auctioneering.

Working-class singers (and listeners) themselves often attend to these various dimensions of singing style as analytically and technically distinct. But of course the art of singing well involves a less consciously considered blending of these techniques into expressive syntheses that can be drawn upon for specific aesthetic purposes. Most typically, musicians and listeners use a shorthand terminology for such gestalts that refers to the names of canonical singers like George Jones, Merle Haggard, Patsy Cline, Johnny Cash, and Marty Robbins.

3.1 "He Stopped Loving Her Today"

Since much of the repertoire performed by local singers in Texas comprises "covers" of the classic country canon, the default local practice is to apply (or imitate) the style of the original recording artist associated with each particular song. This is especially true for less accomplished singers, and for those still learning their craft. As Texas singers become more competent and develop individual styles, and as they acquire a repertoire of original songs or covers by obscure artists whose styles are not familiar, they increasingly apply their own distinctive stylistic signature to everything they perform. Eventually they may be said to have "made (even a well-known 'cover') song their own" by fully restyling a canonical song, sometimes with dramatic modifications in affect and meaning from the canonical recording.

Typically, however, such singers retain a special affinity for one or two major stars' styles (and repertoire), and these styles can be instantly recognized as "influences" on their personal styles. Thus, a singer might be classified as singing "in a Marty Robbins (or Merle Haggard, etc.) style." This would not necessarily imply that the singer in question was simply competent in a derivative sense. A rich cultural conception of voice and orality, reminiscent of Bakhtin's theory of voicing in literary discourse (1981), is the basis for such tropes of classification, resonating with the pervasive elaboration in working-class Texas discourse of direct and quasi-direct discourse and extensive voice-imitation in reported speech constructions.

Movements within this range of possible articulations are ubiquitous expressive resources. A careful listening to George Jones's 1980 recording "He Stopped Loving Her Today,"[6] for example, reveals why Jones is widely regarded as the greatest vocalist in the history of country music, especially by his fellow Texans, and why this particular performance is almost universally acclaimed by working-class country fans as among the most important in the history of the genre. What follows is a description of Jones's complex vocal stylization of this song, from beginning to end. Interested readers should have little difficulty locating an audio recording of this legendary song (first released on Jones's 1980 Epic recording "I Am What I Am," but subsequently reissued on many compilations and greatest hits recordings) to supplement the verbal descriptions below.

Jones begins the narration, which is introduced as reported speech ("*He said* 'I'll love you 'til I die'...") by singing lightly, at times coming close to a spoken articulation, glancing off each word with a breathy tone and very delicate vibrato. Subtle changes in pitch quality and metric feel mark the boundaries between verbs of speaking and directly reported discourse. A subtly pharyngealized tone, in which one can hear the ravaging effects of crying on the narrator's voice, conveys the ethos of elegiac sadness that dominates this song. The stressed vowel in the word "slowly" is mimetically elongated as Jones's narrator describes the passage of years during which the protagonist cannot forget his beloved.

Over the course of the song's unusually long sequence of four verses prior to the first refrain, Jones uses modulations in voice quality to intensify the abject poetic scene. These become ever more claustrophobic as the narrator gradually reveals the depth of the male protagonist's obsession with a lost love, as he lives out his "half crazy" life surrounded by objects that serve as shrines to the memory of his beloved (her picture on his wall; her letters, which he keeps by his bed with every "I love you" underlined in red). The vocal line gradually acquires more intensity, with increasingly sustained and amplitudinally shaped notes (i.e., the amplitudinal envelopes of sustained vowels become more elaborate). Jones gradually develops a richer timbre and a broader vibrato as these verses progress. The song modulates up a half-step at the third verse, after Jones reaches for a high note on the desperate line in which we learn the protagonist never stopped "hoping she'd come back again." Jones also gradually increases the use of his trademark melismas, and the entire sequence of verses is characterized by steadily increasing amplitude. These effects combine to create extreme tension and anticipation of a remarkable textual and performative *denouement*.

Finally, in the fourth verse we find out that the narrator has gone to see the protagonist as he is "all dressed up to go away," and finally smiling (marked by the most melismatic articulation yet in the performance) for the first time "in years." At this point, the anticipation of an explosive release of tension is literally unbearable for many listeners.

The long-anticipated refrain, from which the song takes its title, arrives in full-throated, elaborately melismatic, sustained, and vibrato-rich tones as Jones at last reveals the reason why the protagonist "has stopped loving her today": he has died. He is dressed up and smiling because he is at his own funeral. At last, the somber, elegiac tone of the previous melodramatic verses is narratively justified. However, the song contains an additional poetic relaxation and release, in the following verse and refrain.

Withdrawing, after the refrain, to observe the arrival of the protagonist's long-lost beloved at the funeral, Jones suddenly reverts, with an eerie effect, to what country singers call "recitation" – a loosely metric spoken articulation (breathy, with elongated vowels and heightened intonational movement) which preserves the poetic structure of the composition (rhyme, line breaks, and scansion). This sudden distancing of the narrator from the poetic *mise en scène* demands, as it were, a third vocal persona to emerge from Jones's performance: that of the wry observer, personally uninvolved in the immediate emotional drama of the song. Behind this recitation, in which Jones describes the funeral scene, a wordless female voice laments in an operatic melodic descant, layering the most extreme form of singing (fully pitched, wordless, rich vibrato) behind Jones's move into a quasi-spoken recitation, a juxtaposition of non-referential pure song and song straining toward referential speech that is almost didactic in its representation of the speech/song continuum as it is understood in this musical tradition.

This recitation moves, in a manner typical of the genre, from a description of the scene to the first reported inner speech of the narrator himself (who has otherwise been merely a relatively dispassionate reporter of events). This thought is couched as wordplay – indeed, as reported inner speech – and it delivers the final refrain on the heels of a vertiginous joke that plays on a trite romantic cliché: "This time, he's over her for good." But just as this comic moment seems to break the morbid spell of the tale, the refrain returns, one last time, more fully and powerfully sung than previously, in an all-out quasi-operatic apotheosis in which Jones sweeps grandly through his entire vocal range until relaxing on the final line.

Such masterful examples of vocal style lie at the center of an extremely dense network of vocal practices and expressive ideologies that constitute the discursive and experiential world of working-class Texas communities extending from the most casual forms of talk through a rich range of verbal art genres to song. This network is focused and attended to explicitly in singing practice, but it extends well beyond the boundaries of song *per se*. An analysis of the techniques of Texas country singers reveals the dense relationships between song and speech in this culture. When the focus is expanded to incorporate verbal art, ordinary talk, and the soundscapes of everyday working-class life, one sees, or rather hears, a vivid acoustic refraction of a particular form of sociality materialized in every act of vocalization, and every act of listening. Singing is especially privileged in this community because it allows for a ritualized, explicit consideration (both by community members and by analysts) of the voice as the material embodiment of social ideology and experience. Song stands in an explicitly critical and denaturalizing relationship to "ordinary" speech in rural Texas, as in many other societies.

The parameters and microstructural details that emerge from an analysis of Texas singers' technical practice represent only a small portion of the "voice consciousness" of working-class Texans. And this consciousness, in turn, represents only one perspective, either local or ethnographic, on the social life of these communities. But it is a locally privileged perspective, one that is highly cultivated and deeply valued by community members. This suggests that theorists of the speech/song relationship should engage more fully with local understandings of vocal practice across a wide range of expressive genres. It suggests also that close attention to vocal practice and to the speech/song relationship can provide vital insights into the life of language in human society.

4 Voicing Apache Country

Like the rural Texans just discussed, many Apaches living on the San Carlos reservation in southeastern Arizona also love country music.[7] There are songs, such as Johnny Horton's "North to Alaska," that put people in mind of their community's history. There are others, like Merle Haggard's "Silver Wings," that everyone seems to know by heart. Others, like Hal Ketchum's "Past the Point of Rescue," pull people of all ages out onto the dance floor. And still others, like Charlie Daniels's "Long

Haired Country Boy," or George Jones's "One Woman Man," are so closely associated with particular singers in the community as to act almost like fingerprints.

Local bands in San Carlos, Peridot, and Bylas (the main communities of the San Carlos reservation) have played country music since at least the 1950s. Local songwriters have added to the local repertoire, composing country and rockabilly songs – some with English lyrics, some Western Apache – that sing about the places, histories, and experiences that are important to people in the reservation's communities.

There is no doubt that country is a powerfully evocative genre of song on the reservation (Samuels 1998). Yet, when San Carlos Apaches sing country, they do not sing it the way commercial country singers do on discs, cassette tapes, and the radio. In fact, country singers on the reservation assiduously avoid some of the key vocal gestures that are most diagnostic of country singing, reserving them only for joking performances of white singers. This joking linguistic practice is reminiscent of Keith Basso's analysis of joking imitations of "the Whiteman" in the Western Apache community of Cibecue, which is about 100 miles north of San Carlos, on the Fort Apache reservation (Basso 1979). Of what significance are these differences in the manner of sung vocalization between mainstream commercial country singers and local San Carlos performances of country songs?

4.1 Phonation

The body acts as a resonating chamber in the performance of both speech and song. As with any musical instrument, the acoustical qualities of sung or spoken utterances – their tone and timbre – are partly determined by the physical shape and resonance of the cavity through which air passes during vocalization. The subtle and naturalized control of lungs, diaphragm, larynx, pharynx, tongue, sinuses, lips, and teeth, in the production of sung or spoken vocalization, is the end result of conscious or unconscious discipline and socialization. The apparatus of phonation, especially the mouth and the vocal tract, are crucial bodily sites of hegemonic contestation over the indexical and iconic modalities of both language and music (speech and song).

The study of those variations in vocal practices is one of the key areas in which the interests of sociolinguists overlap strongly with those of ethnomusicologists. That study includes the means by which varieties of spoken and sung phonation are produced, the indexical and iconic links associated with them, and the cultural ideologies surrounding the acceptable or unacceptable performance of these vocalizations. On the one hand, the core insights of sociolinguists demonstrate the numerous and complex ways in which language varieties and dialects act as indexical signs of sociopolitical position. That is, sonic features of vocal speech production, such as deletion of postvocalic /r/ in New York City (Labov 1966), deployment of monophthongal /ai/ in the southern United States (Bernstein, Nunnally, and Sabino 1997), and other articulatory phenomena such as nasality (McMillan 1939), rising intonation at the ends of declarative sentences (McConnell-Ginet 1983), or fronting of back vowels (Hinton et al. 1987; Luthin 1987), act as indexes of regional, class, ethnic, gender, or generational group membership or identity.

On the other hand, ethnomusicology has often posited an indexical relationship between singing style and social order. This has included such statistically driven work as Alan Lomax's Cantometrics project (Lomax 1968), but also includes more subtle and open-ended interpretive research, such as Feld's work on Kaluli "lift-up-over sounding" (1994b), Nattiez's explorations of Inuit and Siberian throat-singing (Nattiez 1983, 1999), and Hugo Zemp's comprehensive recorded anthology, *Voices of the World* (1996).

Both of these insights – the sociolinguistic and the ethnomusicological – claim the voice as the central locus in the production of social and cultural being. They are both concerned with the shape of the mouth as well as the placement of sounds within the vocal tract during processes of phonation, and both interpret these differences as enunciations of ideology, or as markers of social and political identity.

Unlike most musical instruments, the size and shape of the vibrating vocal tract in speech and song is not fixed. As the linguist Peter Ladefoged has written, "Different vowels are like different instruments" (2000: 118). Trumpets, guitars, clarinets, and cellos have distinctive timbral characteristics based partly on the size and shape of the chamber in which sound-making air vibrates to produce a note. But the size and shape of the resonant chamber used in speaking and singing – the mouth – is constantly being changed in the articulation of different sounds. The difference between pronouncing the words "hoot" and "heat," for example, involves a shift in the position of the tongue. This positional change in turn changes the shape of the resonant space of the mouth, which causes different clusters of overtones – called "formants" – to be emphasized for different vowel sounds.

The shape of the mouth when speaking is reflected in the diagram of the "vowel triangle" (see figure 14.3). As the tongue moves from being raised in the front to being raised in the back, the vowel sound produced changes from the high-front /i/, as in "heat," to the high-back /u/, as in "hoot." As the jaw is opened and the tongue lowered, the vowel sound produced shifts from the schwa /ə/ to the low-mid /a/. These sonic differences carry social differences, as well, and also culturally meaningful senses of contextual propriety and proper style. The shape of the mouth in singing also implicates numerous cultural values of proper style. The open and rounded mouth of the boy soprano in a church choir, for example, is an almost immediately identifiable visual marker of this vocal quality and this style of singing. These cultural values about proper singing style circulate and are perpetuated through the training and socialization of singers.

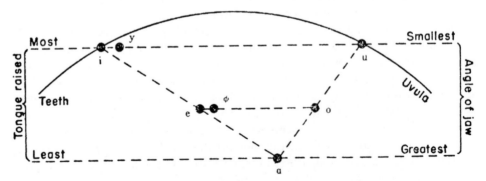

Figure 14.3 Viëtor's vowel triangle, showing the relationship of tongue position and jaw angle to vowel quality (from Heffner 1950: 84). © 1950. Reprinted with permission of the University of Wisconsin Press.

In Western classical forms, for instance, the buttery sound of the operatic soprano is the result of years of training and discipline. Operatic training produces singers who are able to eliminate the upper overtones from their sung performances – like turning the treble on your stereo all the way down. Figure 14.4 is a spectrographic depiction of operatic sopranos Renata Tebaldi and Mirella Freni. A spectrogram is a visual representation of the concentrations of acoustic energy in a spoken or sung utterance, from the lowest to the highest harmonic resonances. Operatic sopranos are able to configure their vocal tract in such a way as to cut most or all acoustic concentrations above around 3,000 cycles per second (Hz). By comparison, figure 14.5 is a spectrographic depiction of legendary Broadway belter Ethel Merman (singing "Bye bye baby, stop your yawnin'/So long baby, day will be dawnin'"). Quite obviously, in distinction to opera singing, Broadway show singing reveals concentrations of resonance well above 10,000 Hz.

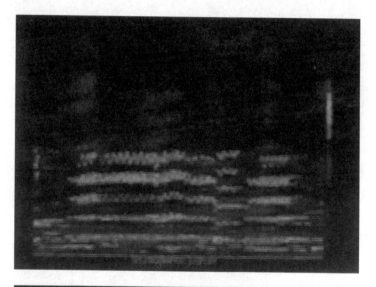

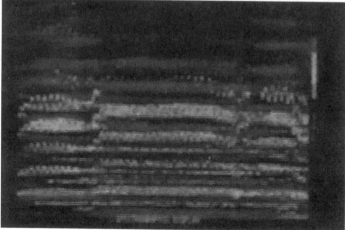

Figure 14.4   Spectrograms of Metropolitan Opera stars Renata Tebaldi and Mirella Freni, showing the extreme tapering of upper partials in the vocal timbre of operatic sopranos (from Miller 2001: 73). Reprinted by permission of the author.

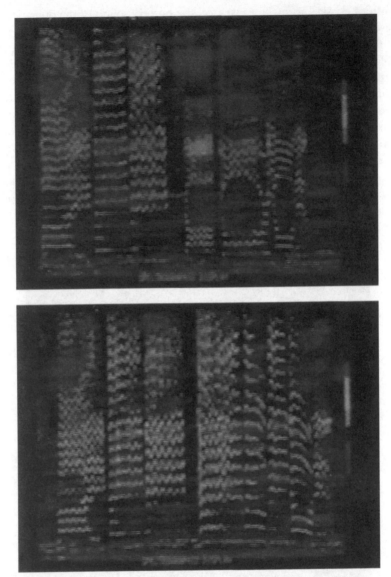

Figure 14.5   Spectrogram of Broadway star Ethel Merman, showing the concentrations of acoustic resonance, to more than 10,000 Hz, that marked the timbre of this showtune belter (from Miller 2001: 74). Reprinted by permission of the author.

4.2   Country vocality

Commercial country singing incorporates a number of distinctive phonological features of Appalachian American English that deviate from a received "standard" dialect (Wolfram and Christian 1976). Among the most important of these, for the present discussion, are a cluster of vowel-glide phenomena. These include long off-glides in diphthongs, found in the "Southern Drawl" (Bailey and Tillery 1996), as well as various forms of diphthongization. "Diphthongization" refers to a process by which diphthongs, or vowel glides, are inserted into phonological segments which, in "standard" dialects, are "pure," or monophthongal, vowels (/hɛɪd/ for /hɛd/, /hɛɪf/ for /hæf/, etc.). In country singing, these vowel glides often take the form of what one could call "twang" – the insertion of a tensing of the vowel followed by an offglide to the lax form (/bɛɪəd/ for /bɛd/, /mɛɪən/ for /mæn/, etc.).[8] Country-western singing includes a network of phonological features, shared by numerous performers, all of which orbit around a collection of Appalachian American English dialectal pronunciations. These dialect features are in turn centered around questions of vowel location, and more specifically around vowel glides, diphthongs, and diph-thongization as embodiments of what Jack Temple Kirby (1995) calls the "counter-cultural values" of southern redneck identity.[9]

The play of vowel quality and dialect in country singing creates opportunities for songwriters, arrangers, producers, and performers to use these Appalachian dialectal features for poetic and artistic effect. Singers often emphasize the offglides of diph-thongs, especially when those diphthongs occur in line-final position. In the Lorrie Morgan song "Watch Me," for example, Morgan consistently stresses the offglides of the line-final words "today," "stay," and "away," creating a great deal of stylistic energy for the textual hook of the song. The songwriter, Gary Burr, conveniently distributes the two parts of the diphthong over a two-note melodic sequence.

Popular singers such as Faith Hill, Andy Griggs, and Reba McEntire consistently employ twanging to index their "country"-ness. Hill, in her hit song "This Kiss," gently modifies the monophthongal vowel /ɪ/ in the word "kiss" in the chorus, into a diphthong /iə/. Griggs, in another example, diphthongizes the second syllable of the word "lonely" in the title song of his debut CD, "You Won't Ever Be Lonely," from monophthongal /i/ to the diphthong /eɪ/. As for Reba McEntire, her stardom and her backwoods identity are due in no small part to the way her vowel segments float in her mouth. One of the hallmarks of McEntire's style is the way she sings long notes, drawing out not only their musical, but also their vocalic potential. In the song "One Honest Heart," for example, Reba performs full-on twangs on the line-final words "sound" and "found," remolding the /au/ diphthongs of Standard English into /æiʉ/s.

Of course, a good deal of Reba's ability to vocalize in this manner is related to her Oklahoma upbringing. But these vocal qualities are identified with a commercial genre of music, and not simply a geographic region. It's not necessary to be from Oklahoma to have twang as part of your vocal style if you're a country singer. The strength of those indexical associations with a musical style give this "regional" dialect a social life that extends well beyond its Appalachian/Ozark regional bound-aries. This kind of appropriation and assimilation is not limited to country singing. As Peter Trudgill pointed out in a well-known discussion of British rock singers appro-priating "American" accents (Trudgill 1983), the mediating technologies of mod-ernity have made multiple styles of singing available – and appealing as a means of expressing identity – to singers around the world. For example, the Canadian country trio the Wilkinsons, Sweden's Inger Nordstrom and the Rhinestone Band, and Raebekah Roycroft from Australia, all feature vocalization styles in which the singers have disciplined their voices to produce the kinds of vowel glide phenomena dis-cussed here, even though these twanging forms are not part of their everyday spoken discourse.

4.3   Real Apaches don't diphthongize

Although singers on the San Carlos reservation love country music deeply, they never (in my experience) diphthongize or twang, except in joking imitations of white singers. Keep in mind the earlier discussion of the prominence of twang in country singing style. These Appalachian features of country singing are so prominent, and so identified with the musical style, that one of linguist Dennis Preston's respondents to his "folk dialectology" project circled the area around North Carolina, Kentucky, and Tennessee, and wrote "Country, As In Music" (Preston 1997). The refusal of San Carlos Apache country singers to discipline their voices in this way is therefore quite radical, given the love for country music exhibited by many in the reservation community.

The Pacers, the band I did the bulk of my fieldwork with in San Carlos, played a number of songs that one might call "signature tunes." The lead singer, Marshall, was known for his renditions of these particular songs, and whenever the band played, or whenever Marshall was present with a guitar, people would always request songs from this special group.

Among those songs was one by Steve Earle, called "Copperhead Road." The story of three generations of bootleggers, sung in the first person, the song is something of an anthem of hardcore, hardscrabble, backwoods, redneck identity. In Marshall's performance, the song became somewhat gentler, more like a two-step than an all-out rock song. But the fact that the song was an expression of marginal resistance, and not a love song, was extremely important to everyone in the band.[10] During my fieldwork, the band members had asked me not to pay them an hourly fee for interviews and so forth. Instead, they wanted me to do something else at the end of my time in San Carlos: to buy studio time for the Pacers so that they could make a cassette tape that the band could sell. And, as the time approached, it was an easy decision to include "Copperhead Road" on the cassette.

Marshall took this all very seriously, and one of the tasks he assigned to me was to make sure that all the words in the songs the Pacers were going to record were right. In the process of transcribing song lyrics from recorded versions, Marshall included a number of "oronyms," or shifting of phonemes so that words change while some kind of sense remains.[11] In live performances this hardly mattered, because the chances were small that anybody would attend to the differences. But for the purposes of making a permanent record, Marshall contracted a bad case of what one might call "lexico-mania." Every word had to be right. As the resident native English-speaking scholar, I was enlisted to double-check Marshall's transcriptions of the lyrics for every song the band was about to record. And in undertaking this task for Marshall, I heard the original Steve Earle version of "Copperhead Road" for the first time. Until that point I had only heard Marshall's rendition of it.

The third verse of the song is about the singer's decision to shift the bootlegging business over from liquor to marijuana, and his decision to rig Copperhead Road with booby traps he had learned about from his experiences fighting the Viet Cong. In Steve Earle's recording of his song, one rhyme in that third verse depends on inserting a particularly strong twang into the first line of the couplet.

I done two tours of duty in Viet Nam (/næiəm/)
I came home with a brand new plan (/plæiən/)

When Marshall sang this same couplet, he pronounced the end of the first line /na:m/, sacrificing the rhyme – and also, in a sense, the cultural identification of the character. The words were right, but the pronunciation was wrong. So when the Pacers went into the studio, thinking that Marshall had wanted everything to be "right," I tried to convince him to sing *Viet Nayum* instead of *Viet Nahm*. In the final take, Marshall was willing to raise his /a/ to an /æ/, in order to make the rhyme scan, but he would go no further. He never explicitly objected, but clearly he was reticent to make his voice twang. On the drive back to San Carlos from the studio in Tucson, Marshall and Pat, the lead guitarist in the band, teased me mercilessly about how I had really made Marshall "sound like a redneck." I could never get Marshall or Pat to talk about this in any detail. They knew what I was talking about when I asked, but the only thing Marshall would say was, "well, you *know* we don't get along with them." And Pat corrected him, saying, "I think it's *them* that doesn't get along with *us*." But that was all.[12]

People in San Carlos love country music. There is no secret to this, and no magical explanation. Music has always been a key institutional expression of assimilation projects on the reservation, from Christian hymns to school bands to Elvis Presley movies. People in San Carlos have been playing guitars at least since the first Sears catalogues circulated in the community, and have been listening to "Hillbilly" and country music since the first radios arrived. And, to be sure, people in this hard-scrabble community have much in common, in terms of the history of economic and social marginalization, with the rednecks in the next town over who also love country music.

But here we can make a distinction between *common* history and *shared* history. The parallax trajectories that have brought "rednecks" and "Indians" to occupy overlapping positions in the American social landscape fill that overlapping space with irony and ambiguity. Country music's sonic and textual evocations of loss, of place, of memories that refuse to recede into the past, and of broken hearts are strong markers of its connections to marginalized, white, redneck social and political exist-ence. That these markers of rural, working-class whiteness can be made iconic with a feelingful experience of Apache social history makes country music an ironic and ambiguous aesthetic form on the San Carlos reservation. But San Carlos is an ironic and ambiguous place. And the historical and cultural ironies of social being in San Carlos saturate vocal expression down to the level of phonetic and phonological production.

In their refusal to twang, people in San Carlos insist that their love of country music grows out of an Apache, and not a "white trash," history of exploitation and marginalization. Through this local style of country singing, San Carlos Apaches perform identities that attempt to maintain an existence outside the American class system at the same time that they are being inexorably pulled into the American socioeconomic system in a class position. One possible question that could frame this vocal practice might be to ask, "What do you do if you love country but you hate rednecks? If you love the music, but you cæin't stæind the sæiund?" And one possible answer might be to sing country music as Marshall and so many others in San Carlos do – in what Mikhail Bakhtin called a "polyphonic" style (Bakhtin 1981). Polyphony in this sense is not musical polyphony, or multi-voiced harmony. Rather, it is a means by which individual speakers, or singers, are able to layer varying attitudes within a single utterance. Through the manipulation of vocal qualities speakers can layer their speech with, for example, sarcasm or irony, making the sense of their words richer and more complex. Through such practices, Apache country singers are able to layer their attitudes about "rednecks" through the way they sing their music.

5   CONCLUSION

Important general works like David Burrows' *Sound, Speech and Music* (1990) or Theo Van Leeuwen's *Speech, Music, Sound* (1999) discuss the historical differences between language and music as sounding modalities, and the semiotic importance of approaching them in a unified framework of sound. The kind of vocal anthropology elaborated here takes the argument to the next level, working at the precise ways that music and language are phenomenally intertwined and socially dialogic. Music and language are fundamentally interrelated domains of expressive culture and human behavior and experience. The case studies presented here indicate some of the richness of verbal discourses about musical timbre and musical meaning, and of voice as the embodied site of both musical and linguistic expressivity, and of social distinction. These ethnographic studies reveal the micropolitics of emplaced, embodied, and voiced identity in particular local lifeworlds. They signal renewed attention to understanding how social identities are indexed and expressed in the intertwining of musical and verbal practices. Above all they demonstrate the poststructuralist commitment to linking the materiality of sound to the sociality of vocal practice.

Thomas Porcello's case study of talk about timbre in the recording studio demonstrates why the musicality of language, the place where sound symbolism and iconicity meets lexical semantics, is critical to understanding the pragmatic role of sound knowledge in language use. We see in this research a detailed application of one of Roman Jakobson's claims about linguistic iconicity (Jakobson and Waugh 1979). Namely, at the level of the lexicon, verbal iconicity is always both partial and systematic in the ways sound might relate to sense. "The vile vomit of the vicious vituperative villain" suggests one systematic relationship between the /v/ sound and a semantic field. But when that phrase is juxtaposed with another, "the voluptuous viscosity of the vivacious vamp," the very partial nature of that suggested relationship is revealed.

When it comes to sound and sense at the lexical and morphological levels, Porcello's analysis underscores Jakobson's profound point, namely, that the whole of language is a field of potentially consummated iconicities, only a small segment of which are ever consummated. But when and where they are consummated they bring sensuous immediacy to the experience of sonic materiality. And that is what matters at the level of their practical and affecting use in discourse, particularly evident in the examples of morpho-iconic coherence, linking the audio envelope of attack/sustain/decay, and a pattern of [c + v] in a distinctive feature package.

Metalanguages of timbre, and talk about timbre in studio shop talk, indicate that timbre's life is as much social as it is acoustic. In other words, it is public and circulates as both general and specialized components of a technical and poetic lexicon. Most critically, this lexicon indexes how knowledge and its practical use is central to the ordinary work that makes music happen – tuning, playing, recording, mixing, listening, commenting, evaluating. All of these dimensions of "getting the sound" can be understood as multiply dialogic relations among musicians and engineers, embedded in a distinct industrial habitus.

The perspectives presented in Fox's case study of rural working-class Texas song and Samuels' case study of Apache country also bring social specificity to questions of timbre and voice, dialogue and practice. Fox's research makes clear that the heightened presence of the singing voice produces a site where speech and song intertwine to produce timbral socialities. The ones he particularly reveals are those of recognized and recognizable agency – artful mastery and its intervocal location in the history of song styles. David Samuels likewise takes up timbre at a crucial bodily site of the voice, where vowel placement is an embodied attitude saturated with a powerful sociality.

These arguments call to mind Roland Barthes's celebrated essay "The Grain of the Voice" (1977). Barthes opposed the structures of language and musical style to what he called "the grain of the voice," by which he means "the materiality of the body" that comes through voice and affects the listener at the level of personal pleasure. Barthes's claim, that this grain is the body in the voice as it sings, has become canonical among humanists and theorists of difference (see Koestenbaum 1993). But the kind of vocal anthropology evident in Fox's and Samuels' essays makes clear the social critique both of the arch humanist position in Barthes, and the arch speech science position on this acoustic materiality, as represented by Johan Sundberg's *The Science of the Singing Voice* (1987): namely, that it is always the body social that is enunciated in and through the voice. In both the settings described by Fox and Samuels, the sonorousness of the voice indexes a clear social agency and a sense of place. Practice-oriented approaches to the phenomenological intertwining of language and music make clear that voice itself is a way of writing against essentialization, a way of writing for performativity, and creative agency. This in no way denies the body or pleasure, any more than it denies acoustics or physiology; rather it insists that these are materially social sites as much as anything else. In other words, the physical grain of the voice has a fundamentally social life.

Voice is the embodied locus of spoken and sung performance, the site where language and music have received closest ethnographic scrutiny. But voice has a more familiar articulation in contemporary anthropology, having also become a metaphor for difference, a key representational trope for identity, power, conflict, social position, and agency. Vocality, in this light, is a social practice that is everywhere locally understood as an implicit index of authority, evidence, and experiential truth.

If voice and vocality constitute a particularly significant site for the articulation of opposition, it may be argued that the root of this articulation is social ontogeny: voice is among the body's first mechanisms of difference. The ability to differentiate one voice from another, the ability to recognize that each and every voice is different, the ability to hear oneself at the same time as hearing others, the ability to silently hear oneself within, the ability to auditorally imagine the voice of another in the absence of their immediate vocalic presence – these are all fundamental human capacities (Idhe 1976; Appelbaum 1990; Feld 2000). It is therefore not surprising that phrases like "giving voice," "taking voice," "having voice" are now routinely linked to the politics of identity, to the production of difference, to the ability of the subaltern to speak, to the ability of indigeneity movements to "talk back" and for class, gender, and race politics to "back talk" the dominant. As feminist historians Leslie Dunn and Nancy Jones write, introducing *Embodied Voices*, their edited volume on female vocality in Western culture: " . . . 'voice' has become a metaphor for textual authority, and alludes to the efforts of women to reclaim their own experience through writing ('having a voice') or to the specific qualities of their literary and cultural self-expression ('in a different voice')" (1994: 1; also see Salvaggio 1999). Linking the histories of *vox populi* to "lift every voice and sing," vocality has become the site where linguistic and musical anthropology most strikingly conjoin a poetics and politics of culture.

NOTES

1 Timbre, unlike melody, harmony, and rhythm, is a non-segmentable feature of music. An important parallel thus exists between its decidedly marginal status within music theory and the secondary status of work on suprasegmentals and acoustic phonetics in much of formal linguistic theory.

2 This is clearly close to the approach used by scat singers in jazz, but the vocalisms of Bobby McFerrin, especially in his evocation of particular musical instruments, are even closer to what is being described here (see especially his CD *The Voice*, 1988).

3 In comparing /Cl/ to /Cr/ in word-initial position (section A1, "stop + liquid" in figure 14.2), the former items all imply re- or deflection of a force off an object without rupturing the object's form, while the latter items all suggest that rupture of the object's form does occur. This makes these terms especially useful for describing certain signal-processing effects, particularly those involving electronic and mechanical distortion, as well as idiophonic instruments.

4 Methodologically, the patterning of meaning within these semantic fields can be pinpointed by examining the particular syntactic frames in which items appear. The most useful frames for the studio corpus involve adverb–adjective pairs such as "too ADJ" or "not enough ADJ," as well as imperatives or request structures such as "Make it more ADJ" or "Can you reduce the NOUN?" For music genres that highly value accuracy, as were most of the sessions from which this data was gathered, for instance, there is something nonsensical about saying *Make it more constricted*, or *That sound is not muffled enough*, or *The kick drum needs to be more boxy*. In other musical styles, however, those may be desirable sonic characteristics.

5 The semantic field of diffuseness is also marked by a comparatively large number of antonymic pairs (blurred/focused, smeared/crisp) that provide explicit contrastive and evaluative information about desired sound quality.

6 "He Stopped Loving Her Today" by Bobby Braddock and Curly Putnam. Copyright 1978, 1980 by American Music. Copyright renewed, assigned to Unichappell Music, Inc. (Rightsong Music, publisher). I choose this example because it is a widely known and easily accessible performance, regarded by my ethnographic consultants as a masterpiece of country singing style. Jones developed his style in Southeast Texas, and his internationally renowned work has in turn strongly influenced vocal practice in Texas.

7   Country and Western are obviously not the only contemporary popular genres that people in San Carlos listen to. Rock, oldies, reggae, chicken scratch, and hiphop are some others. There are generational differences, certainly, at work in some of the differences in individual taste. However, many people are hardly exclusive in their preferences, moving from one genre to another with ease.

8   "Tense" and "lax" are phonetician's terms – /i/ [beat] is the tense form of /I/ [bit], /ʊ/ [pull] the lax form of /u/ [pool] – and don't necessarily imply that the muscles are any more tense during the production of that sound.

9   These vowel glides may be even more prominent now than in the past, as country music's commercial success and growing pop music sensibility make the indexical rustic associations of the singer's accent a more prominent part of the rootedness of the song to the country.

10 Diverging somewhat from the commercial category of "country and western," the band members made a distinction between "country" music and "western" music, preferring the former for its rootedness and its lack of saccharine sweetness. This distinction is akin to that between "Hard Shell" and "Soft Core" country that Richard Peterson (1997) discusses in his history of the commodification of authenticity in Nashville.

11 Rock music is actually fairly famous for these kinds of interpretive errors, making someone who works with language and music sometimes wonder if the lyrics matter at all. One of the more famous oronyms is contained in the Beatles' "Lucy in the Sky with Diamonds," in which the line "the girl with kaleidoscope eyes" is often heard as "the girl with colitis goes by."

12 The band Apache Spirit, from Whiteriver on the Fort Apache reservation, has also recorded "Copperhead Road." In their version, as well, the lead singer, Midnite Ethelbah, does not perform the twang in the word "Viet Nam."

REFERENCES

Appelbaum, D. (1990). *Voice*. Albany: State University of New York Press.

Bailey, G., and Tillery, J. (1996). The Persistence of Southern American English. *Journal of English Linguistics* 24(4): 308–321.

Bakhtin, M. (1981). *The Dialogic Imagination: Four Essays* (ed. M. Holquist, trans. C. Emerson and M. Holquist). Austin: University of Texas Press.

Barthes, R. (1977). The Grain of the Voice. In *Image, Music, Text* (pp. 179–189). London: Fontana.

Bartlett, B., and Bartlett, J. (1994). Engineer's Guide to Studio Jargon. *EQ* 5(2): 36–41.

Basso, K. (1979). *Portraits of the Whiteman*. Cambridge: Cambridge University Press.

Bauman, R. (1977). *Verbal Art as Performance*. Rowley, MA: Newbury House.

Bernstein, C., Nunnally, T., and Sabino, R. (eds.) (1997). *Language Variety in the South Revisited*. Tuscaloosa: University of Alabama Press.

Bolinger, D. (1950). Rime, Assonance, and Morpheme Analysis. *Word* 6: 117–136.

Burrows, D. (1990). *Sound, Speech and Music*. Amherst: University of Massachusetts Press.

Dunn, L., and Jones, N. A. (eds.) (1994). *Embodied Voices: Representing Female Vocality in Western Culture*. New York: Cambridge University Press.

Fabb, N. (1997). *Linguistics and Literature: Language in the Verbal Arts of the World*. Oxford: Blackwell.

Feld, S. (1981). "Flow like a Waterfall": The Metaphors of Kaluli Musical Theory. *Yearbook for Traditional Music* 13: 22–47.

Feld, S. (1990). *Sound and Sentiment: Birds, Weeping, Poetics, and Song in Kaluli Expression* (2nd edn). Philadelphia: University of Pennsylvania Press.

Feld, S. (1994a [1984]). Communication, Music, and Speech about Music. In C. Keil and S. Feld, *Music Grooves* (pp. 77–95). Chicago: University of Chicago Press.

Feld, S. (1994b [1984]). Aesthetics as Iconicity of Style, or "Lift-up-over Sounding": Getting into the Kaluli Groove. In C. Keil and S. Feld, *Music Grooves* (pp. 109–150). Chicago: University of Chicago Press.

Feld, S. (2000). They Repeatedly Lick Their Own Things. In L. Berlant (ed.), *Intimacy* (pp.165–192). Chicago: University of Chicago Press.

Feld, S., and Fox, A. (1994). Music and Language. *Annual Review of Anthropology* 23: 25–53.

Fox, A. (1995). "Out the Country:" Speech, Song and Feeling in Texas Rural Working-class Culture. PhD dissertation, Department of Anthropology, University of Texas at Austin.

Heffner, R.-M. S. (1950). *General Phonetics*. Madison: University of Wisconsin Press.

Hinton, L., Moonwomon, B., Bremner, S., Luthin, H., Van Clay, M., Lerner, J., and Corcoran, H. (1987). It's Not Just the Valley Girls: A Study of California English. In J. Aske, N. Beery, L. Michaelis, and H. Filip (eds.), *Proceedings of the Thirteenth Annual Meeting of the Berkeley Linguistics Society* (pp. 117–128). Berkeley: Berkeley Linguistics Society.

Idhe, D. (1976). *Listening and Voice: A Phenomenology of Sound*. Athens: Ohio University Press.

Jakobson, R., and Waugh, L. R. (1979). *The Sound Shape of Language*. Bloomington: Indiana University Press.

Kirby, J. T. (1995). *The Countercultural South*. Athens: University of Georgia Press.

Koestenbaum, W. (1993). *The Queen's Throat: Opera, Homosexuality and the Mystery of Desire*. New York: Vintage.

Labov, W. (1966). *The Social Stratification of English in New York City*. Arlington: Center for Applied Linguistics.

Ladefoged, P. (2000). The Sounds of Speech. In P. Kruth and H. Stobart (eds.), *Sound* (pp. 112–132). New York: Cambridge University Press.

Lerdahl, F. (2001). *Tonal Pitch Space*. New York: Oxford University Press.

Lerdahl, F., and Jackendoff, R. (1983). *A Generative Theory of Tonal Music*. Cambridge, MA: MIT Press.

Lomax, A. (1968). *Folk Song Style and Culture*. Washington, DC: American Association for the Advancement of Science.

Luthin, H. W. (1987). The Story of California (ow): The Coming-of-Age of English in California. In K. M. Denning, S. Inkelas, F. C. McNair-Knox, and J. R. Rickford (eds.), *Variation in Language: NWAV-XV at Stanford* (pp. 312–324). Stanford: Department of Linguistics, Stanford University.

McConnell-Ginet, S. (1983). Intonation in a Man's World. In B. Thorne, C. Kramarae, and N. Henley (eds.), *Language, Gender, and Society* (pp. 69–88). New York: Newbury House.

McFerrin, B. (1988). *The Voice*. WEA/Elektra Entertainment. CD.

McMillan, J. B. (1939). Vowel Nasality as a Sandhi form of the Morphemes *nt* and *ing* in Southern American. *American Speech* 14: 120–123.

Meintjes, L. (2003). *Sound of Africa! Making Music Zulu in a South African Studio*. Durham, NC: Duke University Press.

Miller, R. (2001). *Training Soprano Voices*. New York: Oxford University Press.

Nattiez, J.-J. (1983). Some Aspects of Inuit Vocal Games. *Ethnomusicology* 27(3): 457–475.

Nattiez, J.-J. (1999). Inuit Throat Games and Siberian Throat Singing: A Comparative, Historical, and Semiological Approach. *Ethnomusicology* 43(3): 399–418.

Nuckolls, J. B. (1999). The Case for Sound Symbolism. *Annual Review of Anthropology* 28: 225–252.

Peterson, R. A. (1997). *Creating Country Music: Fabricating Authenticity*. Chicago: University of Chicago Press.

Porcello, T. (1996). Sonic Artistry: Music, Discourse, and Technology in the Sound Recording Studio. PhD dissertation, Department of Anthropology, University of Texas at Austin.

Porcello, T. (1998). "Tails Out": Social Phenomenology and the Ethnographic Representation of Technology in Music-making. *Ethnomusicology* 42(3): 485–510.

Preston, D. (1997). The South: The Touchstone. In C. Bernstein, T. Nunnally, and R. Sabino (eds.), *Language Variety in the South Revisited*. Tuscaloosa: University of Alabama Press.

Rhodes, R. (1994). Aural Images. In L. Hinton, J. Nichols, and J. J. Ohala (eds.), *Sound Symbolism* (pp. 276–292). New York: Cambridge University Press.

Salvaggio, R. (1999). *The Sounds of Feminist Theory*. Albany: State University of New York Press.

Samuels, D. W. (1998). A Sense of the Past: Music, Place and History in San Carlos and Bylas. PhD dissertation, Department of Anthropology, University of Texas at Austin.

Sundberg, J. (1987). *The Science of the Singing Voice*. Dekalb: Northern Illinois University Press.

Théberge, P. (1994). *Any Sound You Can Imagine: Making Music/Consuming Technology*. Hanover, NH: Wesleyan University Press.

Trudgill, P. (1983). Acts of Conflicting Identity: The Sociolinguistics of British Pop-song Pronunciation. In P. Trudgill, *On Dialect: Social and Geographical Perspectives* (pp. 141–160). Oxford: Blackwell.

Umiker-Sebeok, D. J., and Sebeok, T. A. (eds.) (1976). *Speech Surrogates: Drum and Whistle Languages*, vols. 1 and 2. The Hague: Mouton.

Van Leeuwen, T. (1999). *Speech, Music, Sound*. New York: St Martins Press.

Wescott, R. (1977). Ideophones in Bini and English. *Forum Linguisticum* 2(1): 1–13.

Wolfram, W., and Christian, D. (1976). *Appalachian Speech*. Arlington: Center for Applied Linguistics.

Zemp, H. (ed.) (1996). *Voices of the World: An Anthology of Vocal Expression*. Book with 3 CDs. Paris: Le Chant du Monde.

PART **III** Achieving
Subjectivities and
Intersubjectivities
through Language

CHAPTER **15** Language Socialization

*Don Kulick and Bambi
B. Schieffelin*

1 INTRODUCTION

Language socialization is a theoretical and methodological paradigm concerned with
the acquisition of what Pierre Bourdieu called habitus, or ways of being in the world.[1]
It was articulated and developed in the 1980s (Ochs and Schieffelin 1984; Schieffelin
and Ochs 1986a) as a response to two significant absences in (a) the developmental
psycholinguistic literature on language acquisition and (b) the anthropological literature on child socialization. In the first case – the literature on language acquisition –
the absence at issue was that of culture. In other words, studies of first language
acquisition proceeded as though there were particular sociolinguistic practices that
facilitated children's acquisition of language (for example, the existence of a simplified
"baby talk" register). Linguists asserted that those practices, which they observed in
their subjects and enacted themselves, must be universal and necessary conditions of
first language acquisition.[2] What went unremarked was the fact that the overwhelm-
ing majority of studies of language acquisition were studies of white, middle-class
North American and northern European children. That is to say, they were studies of
children and caregivers who shared not only the linguistic but also the sociocultural
backgrounds of the scholars who studied them. For this reason, culture remained
invisible as a principle that organized speech practices and their acquisition.

It took anthropological studies of language acquisition in non-Western communities[3] and non-middle-class white and African American communities in the United
States (e.g., Miller 1986; Ward 1971; Heath 1983) to demonstrate that aspects of
language acquisition assumed to be universal were in fact variable. Many assumed
prerequisites, such as simplified registers or extensive repetition and paraphrase,
turned out not to be necessary for the acquisition of language.

In studies of child socialization, researchers proceeded as if language was irrelevant.
Classic works, of which Margaret Mead's books on growing up in Samoa and New
Guinea are the best known (Mead 1954 [1928], 1930), examined socialization as a
kind of behaviorist installing of cultural values into children. The Culture and

Personality School worked with the concept of "enculturation," not "socialization." Indeed, the term "socialization" was purposely chosen by the founders of language socialization studies precisely to differentiate and distance their project from that of scholars like Mead.[4] A problem with "enculturation" was that it implied no participation or agency on the part of the child, who was simply an empty vessel into which culture was poured. Another problem was that the enculturation of children was largely assumed to be complete by the time a child reached puberty (conveniently marked by rites of passages in many societies); thus adolescence was often treated as a time when one then began enculturating others. In addition, Mead and her colleagues were more interested in documenting *that* enculturation processes were different in different societies. *How* exactly those processes differed was not their concern. And most seriously, the role that language played in the acquisition of cultural practices and cultural competencies was not imagined to be a problem in its own right. Indeed, reading Mead's work, and many other later anthropological studies of how children "acquire culture," one is left with the impression that language plays little or no role in socializing contexts. In most studies, language is largely disregarded as an aspect of social life. Children acquire habitus and become competent members of their societies through what seems like an unproblematic and predictable process of mimesis.

The language socialization paradigm addresses the lack of culture in language acquisition studies, and the absence of language in child socialization studies by insisting that in becoming competent members of their social groups, children are socialized through language, and they are socialized to use language. Hence, language is not just one dimension of the socialization process; it is the most central and crucial dimension of that process. The language socialization paradigm makes the strong claim that any study of socialization that does not document the role of language in the acquisition of cultural practices is not only incomplete. It is fundamentally flawed.

Language socialization studies should fulfill three criteria. They should be ethnographic in design, longitudinal in perspective, and they should demonstrate the acquisition (or not) of particular linguistic and cultural practices over time and across contexts. These criteria are important to bear in mind when considering whether or not a particular perspective is a language socialization perspective, or if it is a study of language and social interaction. One of the claims made in the books and articles that founded the language socialization paradigm was that "all interactions are potentially socializing contexts" (Schieffelin 1990: 19; Ochs 1988: 6). This was asserted in response to "enculturation" studies, which implied that cultural competence was largely complete after adolescence. It was also stressed to upend the behaviorist implications of previous work on child socialization. The claim was meant to highlight the socializing nature of all human interaction so that attention might be focused on the ways in which subjectivities, stances, and positions are negotiated and achieved, not given. So in mother-child interactions, it is not only the child who is being socialized – the child, through its actions and verbalizations, is also actively (if not necessarily consciously) socializing the mother as a mother. Co-workers socialize one another as co-workers. Lovers socialize one another as lovers. And so on. The point was that multiple agencies are present – and should be accounted for – in any social interaction. These days, the claim about all interactions being potentially socializing contexts could easily be framed in the language of performativity theory: all interactions performatively materialize different kinds of subjects.

What happened, however, is that the idea that all interactions are potentially socializing contexts has given license to a wide range of researchers to claim they are conducting "language socialization" studies, when in our view what they are studying is language and social interaction. This may be due to the increased attention to microanalytical studies of social interaction involving experts and novices, as researchers have sought to ethnographically document how people manage concerted activity "by constantly informing and conforming each other to whatever it is that has to happen next" (McDermott, Gospodinoff, and Aron 1978: 246). There is clearly a great deal we can learn about social life from studies like these. However, we want to caution against claiming that every analysis of social encounters is a language socialization study. As we just reaffirmed, all social interactions are in some sense socializing contexts. But to call studying them "language socialization" is to stretch the brief of the paradigm so far that it risks losing its theoretical and methodological distinctiveness.

That distinctiveness lies in the investment of the language socialization paradigm in long-term ethnography, and its focus on how particular culturally meaningful practices become acquired (or not) by children and other novices. This leads us to what is perhaps the most important contribution that such studies can offer anthropology; namely, a processual account of how individuals come to be particular kinds of culturally intelligible subjects. In a sense, this was Mead's concern. But her question, again, was really "Do people vary cross-culturally?" Language socialization studies ask a different question: "How do different kinds of culturally specific subjectivities come into being?"

Because the central question here is *how*, the language socialization paradigm is a form of ethnomethodology, and is deeply indebted to the theoretical insights and methodological tools developed by such scholars as Howard Garfinkel, Harvey Sacks, and Emanuel Schegloff. However, because it is also a form of anthropology, it is not only interested in the details of what Conversation Analysts call "local management systems" (Sacks, Schegloff, and Jefferson 1974; Keating and Egbert, this volume). Instead, language socialization studies are careful to link the micropractices of socialization to local social structures (such as gender and rank) and to larger, globalizing processes. For example, Don Kulick's study of language shift in a small village in Papua New Guinea linked routines that caregivers used in speaking to babies to the loss of the local language in the face of colonialism, modernity, and encroaching proletarianization (Kulick 1992). Later studies of language socialization in multilingual societies also demonstrate how the languages that children acquire in the remotest of villages are influenced by sociopolitical and economic processes that extend far beyond the scope of the local setting (Garrett 1999; Paugh 2001).

One of the never-remedied (or even adequately addressed) weaknesses in Bourdieu's formulations of habitus, and, more recently, in Judith Butler's claims about the performative power of language, has been that the socialization of habitus, or the early reiterations of language that initiate processes of becoming a culturally intelligible subject, are assumed and asserted more than they are actually demonstrated. So, once again, we know *that* they happen – we know that children come to assume a habitus, and we know that the performative process of boy-ing or girl-ing occurs in socializing contexts – but we don't know *how*. Because the "how" part of these processes remains vague, both Bourdieu and Butler have been repeatedly charged with theorizing reproduction, not change, and entrenching a behaviorist theory of subjectivity, where everyone miraculously becomes what they are supposed to become. We remain agnostic on whether this charge accurately characterizes Bourdieu's work, and we think it is wrong when it comes to Butler. But it is clear that the charge can arise because both theorists pay so little attention to actual socialization practices. Here is where language socialization studies have enormous potential for enriching social theory. By analyzing ways in which praxis comes to be acquired, and performativity actually operates in situated interactions, language socialization studies can document not only how and when practices are acquired, but also how and when they are acquired differently from what was intended, or not acquired at all. Hence, reproduction is not assumed, and unintended consequences of socializing practices, or change, can be documented and accounted for in empirically delineated social contexts.

Programmatic statements about the intellectual history, scope, and goals of the language socialization paradigm can be found in a number of publications.[5] A comprehensive review of two decades of language socialization studies has also recently appeared (Garrett and Baquedano-López 2002). Therefore, instead of offering an overview of the field, we want to illustrate the power of the paradigm by concentrating here on work that demonstrates how different kinds of culturally intelligible subjectivities come into being. The dimensions of subjectivity that interest us most here are desire and fear. In anthropological work, desires and fears are usually addressed under the rubric of "affect," defined broadly as emotion, feelings, moods, dispositions, and attitudes associated with persons and/or situations (Ochs and Schieffelin 1989: 7).

Affect is a central dimension of any theory of becoming, regardless of whether the theory is a scholarly one or a local one. Everyone has ideas about and conventions for displaying, invoking, and interpreting affect. Scholarly work on the topic of affect has consisted of endless debates about whether the conventionalized displays of affective stances actually correspond with, or provide a window into, the "real" feelings of the people who produce the displays. This concern with surface and depth is a profoundly Western problematic, one that has arisen from a long history of meditation on supposedly fundamental binaries (presence versus absence, body versus soul, mind versus body, conscious versus unconscious, etc.). Many social groups do not hypostasize these dichotomies, and they do not recognize, or they have different ideas about, the relationship between the display of an affective stance and the inner sensation that the stance conventionally indexes (Lutz and White 1986). In other words: many groups do not expect or demand sincerity. Whether or not a person "really means" what she or he says or does is not a topic for speculation. In true performative manner, the invocation of a conventionalized affective sign (laughing, or crying, or saying "I'm sorry") is the doing of that emotion, and nobody cares much, or even considers, whether or not that doing corresponds with some privately felt sensation (Besnier 1990; Irvine 1990).

As Hymes (1974) recognized long ago, affect is a core characteristic of communicative competence. Hence the ability to display culturally intelligible affective stances is a crucial dimension of the process of becoming a recognizable subject in any social group. Language socialization studies have demonstrated that these affective stances are attributed to infants from very early on, and that these attributed stances influence how caregivers react to children, and how children come to act and speak.

One striking example of this is the way that caregivers in the Papua New Guinean village of Gapun assume that infants are naturally stubborn, willful, and "big-headed." Caregivers routinely interpret infants' actions as expressing dissatisfaction and anger. A child cooing softly in its mother's lap is likely to be shaken suddenly and asked "Ai! What are you mad about?!" The first words attributed to a baby are *oki*, *mnda*, and *ayata* – words which mean "I'm leaving," "I'm sick of this," and "Stop it," respectively. If a mother notices a baby reaching out toward a dog, she won't tell the child to pet it. Instead, voicing what she takes to be the child's inner state, the mother asserts "Look, she's mad now, she wants to hit the dog," and she moves closer to the animal, thrusting out the child's hand onto the dog's fur, encouraging her "That's it, hit it! Hit it!" Imputed aggression in babies is frequently matched by anyone tending them, and the most common mode of face play with babies involves the caregiver biting her lower lip, widening her eyes, thrusting out her chin sharply, and raising the heel of her hand in a threatening manner, swinging it to within a few inches of the child's face and then suddenly pulling it back again. After pulling several of these punches, the woman or man doing this laughs at the baby and nuzzles its face and body with her or his lips (Kulick 1992: 99–104).

Given these kinds of ideas about the nature of children, and these kinds of routine caregiver–child interactions that foreground anger, it should come as no surprise to discover that anger in Gapun is a structuring principle of social life. It is a crucial component of the village's gender division, for example, in that women are held to be selfish and always ready to publicly vent their anger (in verbal genres such as a *kros*, where women who feel wronged hurl vituperative monologues of abuse at the persons whom they feel have wronged them), whereas men are expected to suppress their anger for the greater social good. The salience of anger is also manifested in the village conviction that imposing on another person and making them angry may cause them, their ancestors, or the supernatural entities associated with their land to ensorcell one and cause one to sicken or die (Kulick 1992, 1993, 1998).

The Kaluli, another group in Papua New Guinea, hold beliefs about the nature of children that strongly contrast with Gapun notions and practices. Instead of willful or stubborn, infants and preverbal children are thought by Kaluli to be *taiyo* 'soft', which translates as helpless, vulnerable, and having no understanding. The first sounds produced by children and recognized by adults as Kaluli words are *no:* and *bo*, 'mother' and 'breast'. These words are significant in that they attest to a social view of language, expressing the child's primary relationship and the giving of food that is central to its constitution. Kaluli say children know how to beg and whine to get what they want, but they must be taught to use language. Kaluli use no baby talk lexicon or simplified speech, but once 'mother' and 'breast' are established, mothers begin to socialize young children using a speech prompting routine, *a:la:ma* 'say it', to elicit the repetition of specific speech forms that convey an assertive demeanor directed to others. So again in stark contrast to Gapun, Kaluli children are understood to need to *acquire* assertive demeanors. Often paying little attention to what the young child might want to do or say at a given point in time, mothers make extensive use of the "say it" routine to direct young children to request, command, tease, and challenge. In so doing, they model what they want the child to say and how it should be said. They also make verbally explicit what they want the child to desire (some food, a particular object). A child's ability to repeat and ultimately produce such speech acts independently is crucial to the desired shift from being *taiyo* 'soft', to *halaido:* 'hard' – "hardness" being a potent cultural trope that signifies verbal and social competence. Once children are able to verbally demand, they too may be asked to give and share, and can enter into the system of reciprocity that defines Kaluli social life and relationships. This is one goal of language socialization in this "egalitarian" society, where the ability to know when to demand, and when to appeal to others to feel sorry and give, is crucial throughout the life cycle.

A final example we can mention in this context is the Hasidic Jewish community in New York that has been studied by Ayala Fader (2000). According to Hasidic belief, each person has a set of God-given inclinations, one for good (*yaytser hatoyv*) and one for evil (*yaytser hure*). Throughout life, these inclinations are expected to be acted upon – through prayer, self-control, obedience, and fulfillment of the command-ments – so that the good inclinations keep the evil ones forever in check. Children enter this Hasidic world in a state of moral innocence. However, throughout infancy and childhood, they are guided or trained in managing their evil inclinations – manifested through immodesty, selfishness, and openly expressed desire – by care-givers' praising and shaming. Children do not receive the inclination for good until the age of 12 or 13, when they reach the transitional age of *bar/bas mitsve* and thereby become responsible for fulfilling all of the Jewish commandments. Before that time, children are not expected to independently exercise the self-control re-quired for subsuming the inclination for evil to that for good.

Socialization in this community is aimed at making children aware of their *yaytser hure* (which they are told is like a little man within themselves who urges unacceptable speech, thought, and action) so that they can counteract it through acts of charity, compassion, and modesty. Because infants and young children are overwhelmingly concerned with physical needs, socialization practices encourage the more spiritual concerns valued in this community. These are accomplished through elaborate prais-ing routines which encourage and prepare the child to form associations between parental love, communal acceptance, and conformity – all of which sets the stage for a more fulfilling relationship with God. For example, through *mevater* ('selflessness') routines, small children are encouraged to give in to another's wishes, and they are given small prizes or rewards when they do so. Children who do not conform are given a series of warnings and if they still do not comply, they are publicly shamed. While children do not grasp the larger spiritual implications of this system of pleasing others, they nonetheless experience culturally valorized emotions and rewards.

2 THE CHALLENGE OF "BAD SUBJECTS"

Framing the language socialization paradigm as we have done until now, and illus-trating it with the examples we have chosen so far, it would be possible to conclude that language socialization can only account for culturally predictable outcomes. That is, it can effectively document reproduction. But what about unexpected or undesirable outcomes, such as children raised in Hasidic families who don't turn out to be so modest and obedient? What about resistance? What about change? That the majority of language socialization studies have focused on reproduction is a strength – they provide us with methodological and analytical tools for investigating and interpreting social reproduction and affective continuity across generations. But the focus on expected and predictable outcomes is a weakness if there is not also an examination of cases in which socialization doesn't occur, or where it occurs in ways that are not expected or desired. To the extent that language socialization studies only document the acquisition of normatively sanctioned practices, they open themselves to the charge that they are merely behaviorism in new clothes.

Documenting the acquisition of normatively proscribed cultural practices is methodologically challenging, because to do so conclusively would involve extensive fieldwork with the same subjects spread over many years. After all, it is one thing to document individual interactions in which children, for example, transgress adult restrictions and do or say things incorrectly from an adult's perspective. This happens all the time, and in fact, one great value of documenting language socialization is that one frequently sees normally taken-for-granted cultural values overtly displayed to children, who, as novices, get things "wrong" (see Bailey, this volume).

It is something else entirely to convincingly document how certain children or other novices come to be what Louis Althusser (1971: 169) would call "bad subjects" – that is, subjects who do not recognize or respond to calls to behave in particular, socially sanctioned ways. Homosexuals in societies that expect and demand heterosexuality are one obvious type of "bad" subjects; tomboys in societies where females are socialized to be demure is another example. Note that "bad" here is not a value term, but a structural label. A subject is "bad" in Althusser's terms if it does not recognize or respond to socially powerful, coercive calls to inhabit certain subject positions. (We discuss the reasons why subjects are structurally able to be "bad" below.) Other examples of "bad" subjects would be social boors in societies that value sensitivity, selfish individuals in societies that stress generosity, mean or criminal people in societies that socialize cooperation, and so on.

There are several ways of approaching this issue. Traditionally, what we are calling "bad subjects" would have been treated as "deviants" – failures, the limit of socialization and culture. To the credit of earlier paradigms, the existence of such "deviants" was not downplayed or ignored. In the very first and still best-known anthropological study of socialization (*Coming of Age in Samoa*), for example, Margaret Mead (1954 [1928]) devoted an entire chapter to "deviant" girls. The problem, however, was the explanation: rather than understanding deviance as something produced by and essential to the social system in which it occurs, analyses like Mead's saw it as the bubbling up of an individual temperament that for some reason went unsuppressed by the "patterns of culture" into which that individual was born.

One might indeed argue that "bad subjects" are the product of individual psychological processes that are either unknowable, or knowable only through methods and tests developed by psychologists or neurologists. Or one might also hypothesize that "bad subjects" are overtly socialized as such, through negligence, abuse, or idiosyncratic caregiving practices. There is something to be said for both those arguments: the most extreme case of a "bad" subject that we can think of – a serial rapist-murderer, say – is clearly the product of a very particular psychological and social history. But to particularize even a case as extreme as this ignores the fact that serial rapist-murderers are cultural products – they do not exist everywhere, as either a culturally imaginable subjectivity or as an actually occurring type of person; nor are they exclusively the children of negligent or abusive parents (see e.g. Cameron and Frazer 1987, 1994). Hence, even here, a cultural analysis is crucial, and a culturally sensitive understanding of socialization has the potential to illuminate key dimensions in the production of even the seemingly most unintelligible subjectivities.

The approach that we want to suggest for meeting the challenge of "bad" subjectivities is one that uses the methods and theories of the language socialization paradigm, but augments them to allow us to account for why socializing messages to behave and feel in particular ways may also produce their own inversion.

Before we proceed, however, we should perhaps say a few words about why we have been speaking about "subjects" and "subjectivities" rather than using terms like "person" or "personhood," which are more common in both anthropology generally and the earlier literature on language socialization specifically (in our own work, for instance). In essence, the two different terminologies reference two different sets of debates. The debates about "persons" and "personhood" are anthropological debates, with roots in the Culture and Personality School's project of showing how different societies promote the development of different temperamental patterns, and also in French sociology's early concerns with the cultural production of "the notion of person" (Marcel Mauss's classic essay (1985) of that name is of course central here). Debates about "subjects," on the other hand, arise most directly from French post-structuralist thought. So if anthropological discussions tended to center on whether or not the (social) person was culturally imagined to be the same as the (individual) actor (e.g. La Fontaine 1985), or on how culturally competent persons came to be socialized in particular cultural settings (e.g. any of the socialization studies we have cited so far), French scholars like Althusser, Jacques Lacan, and Michel Foucault were interested in theorizing the processes by which individuals come to know themselves as such. Even though they used very different theoretical language (Althusser wrote about "interpellation," Lacan discussed "identifications," and Foucault elaborated what he called "subjectification" and "governmentality"), these thinkers were all committed to exploring the ways in which individuals not only come to inhabit particular culturally recognizable places in a social system, but also (a) how those places become made available to inhabit in the first place, and (b) how individuals come to desire to inhabit those subject positions, as opposed to others. This is what Butler, paraphrasing Foucault, means when she defines a subject as one who is "subjected to a set of social regulations, . . . [in which] the law that directs those regulations reside[s] both as the formative principle of one's sex, gender, pleasures, and desires and as the hermeneutic principle of self-interpretation" (1990: 96).

We now believe that the questions asked by French post-structuralists are more compelling, broader in scope, and suggestive in potential than anthropological discussions about persons and personhood. The theorists mentioned above explicitly thematize issues of desire, power, and positionality. In different ways, and to different extents, they also encourage an analysis of socialization: how do individuals come to perceive the subject positions that are available or possible in any given context? How is the taking up of particular positions enabled or blocked by relations of power?

How do particular positions come to be known as intelligible and desirable, while others are inconceivable and undesirable?

The broader question, though, is this: how can these kinds of issues be addressed by the kind of data that linguists and anthropologists interested in language socialization collect and analyze? The answer we suggest is as follows.

Throughout the 1990s, a group of British psychologists and social scientists elaborated an approach to social and psychological life that they call "discursive psychology." As Michael Billig, one of the group's most articulate proponents, explains, discursive psychology differs from orthodox social psychology and psychoanalysis because it discourages speculation about hidden, inner processes. Instead,

> [d]iscursive psychology takes inspiration from the philosophical tradition of Wittgenstein's later philosophy and from the development of ethnomethodology and conversation analysis. These traditions of analysis stress the need to examine in detail the outward accomplishment of social life, showing how social order is produced through discursive interaction. Discursive psychology applies this project to psychological phenomena. It argues that phenomena, which traditional psychological theories have treated as "inner processes" are, in fact, constituted through social, discursive activity. Accordingly, discursive psychologists argue that psychology should be based on the study of this outward activity rather than upon hypothetical, and essentially unobservable, inner states. (Billig 1997: 139–40)

A concrete example of what discursive psychology means in practice is Billig's monograph which reconsiders the Freudian concept of repression in terms of language (Billig 1999). Repression in Freudian theorizing is the idea that certain thoughts, feelings, and emotions are not only hidden and denied (or, as psychoanalysts say, disavowed), but also desired as a source of pleasure *because* they are hidden and denied. In other words, admonitions which are intended to discourage particular desires, in fact often incite and sustain them. As Freud and many others before him recognized, the act of prohibition is a crucial instigator of desire (see Freud 1989; Žižek 1999). Prohibition is always libidinally invested: it fixes desire on the prohibited object and raises the desire for transgression.

Billig agrees with Freud that repression is a fundamental dimension of human existence. But he disagrees with the idea that the roots of repression lie in biologically inborn urges, as Freud thought. Instead, he argues that repression is demanded by language: "in conversing, we also create silences," says Billig (1999: 261). Thus, in learning to speak, children also learn what must remain unspoken and unspeakable. This means two things: first, that repression is not beyond or outside language, but is, instead, the constitutive resource of language; and second, that repression is an interactional achievement.

Billig stresses that repression is accomplished in everyday interactions, and he examines the ways in which repudiations and disavowals are achieved through avoidances, topic changes, and direct commands. For example, in discussing the socialization of polite behavior, Billig remarks that "each time adults tell a child how to speak politely, they are indicating how to speak rudely. 'You must say *please*' . . . 'Don't say *that* word'. All such commands tell the child what rudeness is, pointing to the forbidden phrases. . . . [I]n teaching politeness, [adults provide] a model of rudeness" (1999: 94, 95; emphasis in original).

Although Billig does not situate his own work in the language socialization paradigm, his attention to socializing contexts and the constitutive role that language plays in those contexts invites us to consider the production of silences and desires from the perspective of language socialization. Paying attention to the role that the not-said or the unsayable plays in socializing contexts would enrich the language socialization paradigm, because it would compel analysis to go beyond surface readings of verbal interactions and explore the ways in which utterances necessarily manifest what Kulick (2003) has called "dual indexicality" – that is, they manifest both their surface propositional content and the simultaneous inverse of that content. Appreciation of dual indexicality in socializing contexts would wash away any residual ties to behaviorism that the language socialization paradigm might harbor, and it would encourage an active exploration of the formation of "bad" subjects. From this kind of perspective, the emergence of homosexual subjects, to take just one example, would not be mysterious or problematic in the slightest. Understanding that utterances always simultaneously manifest their inversion makes it possible to see that even in the most homophobic environments – *especially* in the most homophobic environments – messages about the possibility and desirability of homosexual subjectivity are continually conveyed, precisely by all the admonitions directed to children and others to not think or act *that* way. Paraphrasing Billig, we could say that in teaching hatred of homosexuals, adults provide a model of desire for them. Why a particular individual should come to inhabit a homosexual subjectivity will always remain difficult, if not impossible, to answer conclusively. But a study of language socialization in homophobic environments would provide invaluable empirical material about the ways in which particular forms of desire (desire to be or have something) are dialogically incited and socially circulated.

The circulation and incitement of desire is a topic currently being pursued in some of the most exciting work on language socialization now underway. This work does not draw on discursive psychology – indeed, just as the language socialization paradigm seems not to have yet made it over the Atlantic to discursive psychologists in the UK, discursive psychology seems largely unknown to US linguistic anthropologists working with language socialization data. However, we believe it should be, since the two paradigms share many of the same interests and analytical perspectives. A thoughtful amalgamation of the two would be extremely productive.

In the meantime, research is already being done which allows us to see how particular fears and desires are conveyed and acquired through recurring linguistic routines. An early article that examined this is Patricia Clancy's investigation of how Japanese children acquire what she calls communicative style; that is, "the way language is used and understood in a particular culture" (Clancy 1986: 213). Clancy was interested to see how children are socialized to command the strategies of indirection and intuitive understanding that characterize Japanese communicative style. In working with two-year-old children and their mothers, she discovered that these skills were acquired through early socialization routines in which mothers, among other practices, (a) juxtaposed indirect expressions (e.g. "It's already good") with direct ones ("No!"), thus conveying the idea that various forms of expression could be functionally equivalent; (b) attributed speech to others who had not actually spoken, thereby indicating to children how they should read non-verbal behavior; (c) appealed to the imagined reactions of *hito* 'other people', who are supposedly always watching and evaluating the child's behavior; and (d) used strongly affect-laden adjectives like "scary" or "frightening" to describe a child's (mis)behavior, making it clear that such behavior is socially unacceptable and shameful. These kinds of communicative interactions sensitized children to subtle interactional expectations which in adult interactions are not expressed explicitly. They also encouraged children to acquire the specific anxieties and fears (such as the disapproval of *hito*) that undergird Japanese communicative style.

The socialization of fear is also described by Lisa Capps and Elinor Ochs (1995), in their study of an agoraphobic woman in Los Angeles. A central attribute of agoraphobia is a sense of having no control over one's feelings and actions (hence one gets gripped by paralyzing anxiety attacks). Capps and Ochs hypothesize that this sense of being unable to control one's feelings is, at least in part, socialized, and they examine how this might occur by analyzing the interactions that occur between Meg, the agoraphobic woman, and Beth, her eleven-year-old daughter, when Beth talks about how she managed to handle some threatening situation. Whenever this happens, Meg often reframes her daughter's story in ways that undermine Beth's control as protagonist. She does this by portraying people as fundamentally and frighteningly unpredictable, no matter what Beth may think; by casting doubt on the credibility of her daughter's memory of events; by minimizing the threatening dimension of the daughter's narrative, thereby implying that Beth has not truly surmounted danger; and by reframing situations in which Beth asserts herself as situations in which the daughter has done something embarrassing.

Although the studies by Clancy and Capps and Ochs discuss fear and not desire, it is important to remember that from another perspective, *fears are desires* – the desire to avoid shame, embarrassment, danger, punishment, and so on. Another study co-authored by Ochs (Ochs, Pontecorvo, and Fasulo 1996) specifically discusses desire. In this case, the desire is gustatory. Here, the research team investigated how children come to develop taste. One of their main findings was that children's likes and dislikes of different kinds of food are actively socialized at the dinner table.

In a comparison of dinnertime interactions in American and Italian middle-class families, Ochs, Pontecorvo, and Fasulo found that dinners at the American tables were consistently marked by oppositional stances in relation to food, with children complaining that they did not want to eat the food they were served, and parents insisting that they must. One of the reasons why these dinnertime interactions were so oppositional is that they were framed that way by parents. American parents often assumed that children would not like the same kinds of foods that they enjoyed. This could be signaled through the preparation of different dishes, some for children and others for the adults, or by remarks that invited children to align in opposition to adults. For example, when one parent presents a novel food item at the dinner table, the other might remark "I don't know if the kids'll really like it, but I'll give it to them." In addition, the tendency in American homes was to "frame dessert as what their children *want* to eat, and vegetables, meat, etc., as what their children *have* to eat" (1996: 22, emphasis in original), thereby creating a situation in which certain foods were portrayed as tasty and desirable, and others as mere nutrition, or even punishment ("Eat that celery or you'll get no dessert").

Italian families, in contrast, highlighted food as pleasure. Parents did not invite their children to adopt oppositional stances (by creating distinctions between themselves and "the kids" in relation to food); they foregrounded the positive dimensions of the social relations that were materialized through food ("Hey look at this guys! Tonight Mamma delights us. Spaghetti with clams") and they did not portray dessert as a reward to be gained only after one has first performed an onerous duty. The results of these kinds of differences in socializing contexts is that children acquire (rather than simply "discover") different kinds of relationships to food, different kinds of tastes, and different kinds of desires.

Studies of language socialization like those by Clancy and by Ochs, Pontecorvo, and Fasulo do not discuss repression or mention Freud or psychoanalysis. No matter: this kind of work is an important and guiding example of how linguists can link with the project of discursive psychology to demonstrate how "phenomena, which trad-itional psychological theories have treated as 'inner processes' [such as taste, intu-ition, shame, or anxiety] are, in fact, constituted through social, discursive activity" (Billig 1997: 139). Therefore, "the location of desire outside the processes of dialogue and social order is not necessary" (Billig 1997: 151).

3   THE GRAMMAR OF DESIRE

In their book about how the condition of agoraphobia might be illuminated by a close examination of the way agoraphobics use language to narrate their experiences and talk about their feelings, Lisa Capps and Elinor Ochs have noted that even though therapists have long recognized the role that language plays in understanding and alleviating psychological illnesses (psychoanalysis, after all, has been known since Freud's day as "the talking cure"), the tendency in therapy is "to look *through* language rather than *at* its forms" (Capps and Ochs 1995: 186, emphasis in original). A powerful contribution that the language socialization paradigm makes to an understanding of the production of subjects is its close attention to the linguistic forms that are used to socialize children and other novices into expected roles and behaviors.

We referred above to the claim made by Capps and Ochs that Beth, the daughter of the agoraphobic woman they write about, is exposed to socializing messages that may contribute to her one day developing the condition of agoraphobia. Note that Capps and Ochs make no claims about determination or inevitability – no one can know for sure whether or not Beth will eventually become agoraphobic. What we can say, however, is that the language that gets circulated between mother and daughter has specific forms, and that these linguistic structures foreground specific desires and competencies, and background others. One of the many examples analyzed by Capps and Ochs is the following (1995: 160–1):

> Meg's [the agoraphobic mother's] contributions to stories that feature Beth as a protag-onist may also reinforce and even augment a view of people in general, and Beth in particular, as lacking control over their emotions and actions. In telling about her frightening encounter with a boy with a shaved head, for example, Beth frequently uses grammatical forms that emphasize the inexplicability of her feelings and actions. Beth draws on phrases and words such as "for some reason" and "just" to imbue her rendition of this experience with a sense of bewilderment:

For some *reason*, it just scared me.

Throughout this account, Beth also ponders the source of this boy's behavior and of her own fear at the sight of him. Why would anyone shave his head? Why did I feel that way? But she does not come up with answers to these questions. After much deliberation, at the end of this lengthy story, Beth turns to her mother for help:

Why would anyone do that?

Meg at first laughs and then offers the following response:

I don't know.

Capps and Ochs analyze this interaction by pointing out how Meg's response perpetuates Beth's wondering and aligns their worldviews. They observe how, together, Meg and Beth construct the perspective that people behave in ways that are incomprehensible – a perspective that directly contributes to an agoraphobic's fear of ever leaving the restricted zone in which she feels safe and secure.

Implicit in this interaction is a notion of desirability, in which it is desirable to be able to understand why people act like they do, and "scary" to not be able to do so. The underlying structures of desirability that animate talk have been elaborated by Noriko Akatsuka, who proposed an analysis of Japanese conditionals in terms of desirability; in collaboration with Patricia Clancy and Susan Strauss, this analysis has been applied to the way in which Japanese-, Korean-, and English-speaking caregivers use language to socialize children (Akatsuka 1991a, b; Akatsuka and Clancy 1993). In analyzing adult–child interactions, Akatsuka (1991b) and Clancy, Akatsuka, and Strauss (1997) have shown how speech to children is structured according to a particular contingency relationship between antecedent and consequent, such that

DESIRABLE leads to DESIRABLE
UNDESIRABLE leads to UNDESIRABLE

For example, a child who is afraid of the sound of a vacuum cleaner is told by her mother "I won't put the vacuum cleaner on if you drink all your juice" (DESIRABLE → DESIRABLE). An example of UNDESIRABLE → UNDESIRABLE is a father's warning to his child "If I see you with matches, I'll give you a spanking." Note that this underlying structure of desirability is a channel of power. Adults attempt to control the behavior of their child addressees by linking actions that are desirable for the adult (getting the child to drink her juice, having the child avoid matches) to actions that the adult explicitly frames as desirable to the child (not having the vacuum cleaner turned on, avoiding physical punishment).

Clancy, Akatsuka, and Strauss (1997) have observed that different languages rely on different linguistic forms to channel this power and frame these relationships. In Japanese and Korean, prohibitions, instructions, permissions, promises, and threats occur in the form of what they call deontic conditionals. Deontic conditionals are conditionals in which speakers specify a behavior and then evaluate it as good or bad, for example, "If you do it, it's good." This linguistic form is extremely frequent in Japanese and Korean adult–child interactions. It contrasts with the way in which deontic modality is conveyed in a language like English, where modal or modal-like forms (such as *can, should, may, have to*, etc.) are used to convey speaker attitude toward the proposition being expressed. Furthermore, the conditionals, promises, threats, and warnings used by the English speakers often provided children with an explicit reason for complying with the directive that was linked to consequences that they would face (" . . . I'll give you a spanking"). Japanese and Korean adults, on the other hand, did not present children with this kind of information. Instead, they relied on general statements (such as " . . . it won't do," or " . . . it's scary"), which do not assert what will happen if the child does or does not accede to the adult's command to do, or stop doing, something.

In terms of language socialization, Clancy et al. (1997) provide a suggestive framework for analyzing not only how speakers encode desire in language, but also how that desire is articulated with different kinds of authority and power. While the work takes as its analytical starting point the perspective of caregivers, it could be extended to other speakers, in order to examine the way that desirability and power are disseminated across the social field. Once we understand the structures through which this occurs, we are in a better position to also understand the ways in which those structures may be challenged, resisted, changed – or entrenched.

4   LANGUAGE SOCIALIZATION IN ACTION: KALULI SERMONS AND THE PRODUCTION OF NEW SUBJECTS

The idea of entrenchment leads us to the final example that we will discuss, one that highlights the three main themes – change, desire, and the production of subjectivities – that we have been discussing throughout this chapter. Let us return to Bosavi, the home of the Kaluli. In the early 1970s, fundamentalist Christian missionaries from Australia established a mission station in Bosavi with the goal of converting this "Stone Age" population as quickly as possible (Schieffelin 2002). These missionaries viewed most traditional Bosavi cultural practices and beliefs as anathema and antithetical to their evangelical project, and they were determined to change how people looked, thought, felt, and spoke. Local men who knew some Tok Pisin were recruited as pastors, and within a relatively short period of time, these local pastors had been trained to hold frequent village church services, during which they translated and preached New Testament verses in the vernacular.[6]

Church services were the primary context in which pastors entrenched the new desires and fears that were required to transform Kaluli women and men into Christian subjects. In some ways, the language socialization strategies in sermons were pragmatically similar to those that were habitually used between caregivers and young children. In both the church and the home, for example, positive and negative imperatives directed addressees' actions and desires, and rhetorical questions were used to shame and challenge those who did not conform. There were, however, crucial differences. Caregiver speech to children focused on immediate and ongoing activities (using present imperatives, like "Go now!"). Pastor speech addressed future activities, thoughts, and desires, and it relied heavily on the Kaluli grammatical form of future imperatives ("Think in the future!"). This stress on the future was part of the Christian message that all actions and desires in the present had direct and predictable future consequences.

In addition to a heavy use of future imperatives, a series of new discursive techniques were used to convey temporal re-orientation. One striking innovation in this area was the shift from unelaborated, vague, third party threats (e.g., "someone will say something") as the main reason given for prohibitions, to detailed and graphic depictions of the negative consequences that would follow disapproved actions. The emphasis thus shifted from language that foregrounded social relations (anyone hearing the threat that "someone will say something" was invited to wonder who might say something and why they might say something) to language that encouraged fear of something intangible and abstract. Pastors issued conditional threats and warnings that articulated future worlds in which particular antecedent actions (such as not converting to Christianity) would have foreseeable negative consequences – usually painful death, burning Hell, and eternal torture. People were consistently warned against acting proud and strong, and they were warned what would happen if they did not follow Christian messages. For example,

Degelo's sermon in Bona Village, 1975

o:go: walafo: aundoma:lo: o:ngo: kiso:no: siyalega tifa ya:su gelesolo: yan amiyo: e a:ma:la:yo: e dasima:no: aundo:ma
today those acting like they are without sin, going around proud/strong, later when Jesus Christ comes, they will never get up again

ko:sega ge Baibo:lo: to mo:aloba:ndalega ho:len tambo ba da:da:sa:ga: ka to:go:liya: ha:na: lalega walaf a:no: anaya:i ha:na:ga: a:ma: ge sola:ma:ib
but if you do not measure yourself against the Bible every day but just listen; if you keep moving away from it [what the Bible says], sickness/sin will continue to get bigger and it (sickness/sin) will kill you

Conditional threats and warnings ("if you do X, Y will happen") were rare in the traditional Bosavi speaking repertoire. In language socialization activities between caregivers and children, as well as in emotionally charged talk between adults, speakers showed a strong dispreference for mentioning specific consequences if someone violated a social expectation, and they avoided articulating or taking responsibility for any implied action or outcome. On the other hand, the kinds of conditional threats and warnings used by pastors are what Clancy et al. call "prohibitions in disguise" (1997: 37), that make explicit a "logic of desirability" (Akatsuka 1991b) in which good behavior leads to rewards and bad behavior to punishment. As we noted above in our discussion of the work of these scholars, prohibitions of this kind are used to control behavior, and their syntax provides a grammar of desire and fear.

Read for their cultural content, conditionals can be examined for the categories of concern that they express (e.g. personal safety, morality, conventionality), and can thus be viewed as templates for displaying what is culturally desirable, and what is not. In analyzing conditionals, we might ask which templates are expressed and how different categories of concern play out over time, in terms of gender, age, social class, and other relevant categories. A cross-culturally interesting question might also be: what kinds of antecedents/consequences are articulated, and what is left unsaid? We could investigate categories of consequences (the "Y" in "if you do X, Y will happen") in terms of who will be affected, and how and whether such assertions are moral, egocentric, or sociocentric from the perspective of the speaker. What are the propositions of justification and explanation?

Speech acts such as warnings and promises use specific syntactic devices, in this case, conditionals. Conditionals and the speech acts expressed through them provide a framework for using linguistic and discourse data to tap in to cultural and social categories. Cultural strategies of persuasion are linguistically and socially constructed, which means that some social groups may emphasize promising, which expresses positive desires and outcomes, while others may make habitual use of threats and warnings that express negative outcomes. In Bosavi, for example, promising is rare. The main form of social control is implicit threats – and it is these that were transformed into explicit threats by evangelist pastors.

In addition to the expanded use of future imperatives and the modified use of conditionals and threats, a third dimension of language practices also played an important role in Christian language socialization in Bosavi. This was the introduction of new speech genres, namely public prayer and confession. Both these speech genres were designed to resubjectify Kaluli by getting them to expose their private desires and hidden thoughts and actions to the pastor and the entire congregation. This was extremely problematic, and confessions in particular were resisted, largely because Kaluli had been socialized to guard their personal thoughts – not reveal them. What mattered traditionally was that one spoke appropriately, not sincerely. Pastors, however, did not refrain from directly and publicly questioning the thoughts and behavior of congregants, a situation that made most Kaluli uncomfortable and frightened. Pastors had the authority as gatekeepers and evaluators of who would be baptized and saved; thus anyone who wanted to be baptized had to comply with their new rules. This restructuring of social relationships generated new levels of fear in Bosavi society.

In terms of participant structure, talk in church services differed from the highly interactive and dialogic nature of Bosavi verbal genres. In stark contrast to all other speech genres, sermons were monologic. In addition, the behaviors exhorted through these monologues were inversions of what Kaluli traditionally valued. Bosavi pastors told people to go around softly and quietly, as though they were sick, so that they could be "healed." They warned their congregants that displays of assertiveness, pride, competence/strength (halaido:), and anger were barriers to becoming Christian, as were the ways of speaking, such as arguing, that were associated with such stances. Thus, precisely those stances and demeanors through which Kaluli women and men had come to know themselves as subjects were reassigned exclusively negative valences, and anyone who embodied and displayed them was seen as rejecting a Christian identity.

What was at stake in all these practices was the production of new forms of subjectivity. Traditional modes of subjection were explicitly devalued and resolutely replaced with different forms of knowledge, experience, and language. And in producing new, "good" subjects, these missionary practices simultaneously actively materialized new, "bad subjects." This is particularly explicit in one of the expressions used to denote Christians: in Bosavi, Christians spoke about themselves as being "inside" (us). Those who refused to join the church, or who transgressed after conversion, were said to be "to the side" (ha:la:ya). Individuals "to the side" – the ones who did not respond to Christian interpellations – were refigured by the

Christians as unintelligible (how could one not want to be healed and saved?). In addition to the considerable social fragmentation that this produced, these new understandings also generated new modes of knowing oneself as a subject, and new modes of orienting toward the forces that gave meaning and value to those subjectivities.

What does viewing these missionizing practices as language socialization show us? First, it shows us that language socialization is a perspective that can examine more than language directed at children. The language we have examined here was directed at adults, not children. Christianity consists of a number of concrete practices, many of them linguistic, and these practices were what Kaluli women and men had to acquire in order to become known to themselves and others as Christian subjects. This acquisition was socialized – it took place largely through language, and it entailed the learning, over time, of novel ways of using language. Furthermore, what we see very clearly in contexts of change like this is that language socialization is not only about reproduction – the Christian missionaries who came to Bosavi certainly had the goal of socializing the reproduction of their own habitus, their own ways of being in the world. But this reproduction entailed explicit and concerted efforts to change Bosavi people. In this case, what was socialized through language was emphatically *not* culturally predictable outcomes. On the contrary, socialization here resulted in change, not reproduction. Finally, what we see clearly in this case is the way in which language socialization is bound up with the production of particular kinds of subjectivities, which are articulated through different forms of desire. Socialization into Christianity produced new desires and new fears – all of which were materialized through and indexed by novel participant structures, speech genres, and conditional forms. These new forms did not produce only one kind of culturally intelligible subject. On the contrary, what was produced through language were intelligible, "good" subjects, and other subjects – those who refused the hailings of Christianity, and who were increasingly materialized as unintelligible, "bad" subjects.

5 Conclusion

Throughout this chapter, we have argued that the methodological and theoretical perspectives that characterize work on language socialization constitute a distinctive research paradigm. The examples we have discussed demonstrate some of the contributions that the paradigm can make to social theory, and they show how a focus on language socialization can generate insight into processes that effect not only reproduction, but also change. We chose to focus here on subjectivity and desire in order to highlight the potential of language socialization studies to illuminate both culturally predictable and culturally problematic subjectivities, thereby making it clear that this kind of research can be extended into domains that have traditionally appeared problematic or unapproachable for anthropologists and linguists. Socialization through language, and to use language, consists of empirically delineable understandings and practices that are disseminated across social space and enacted in situated contexts. To document those understandings and practices, and to see them as constitutive of power and invested with structures of feeling, is to chart the processes that materialize the social world.

NOTES

1 We mention habitus here as a kind of shorthand: the language socialization paradigm was not developed in response to Bourdieu's theories of social reproduction. Instead, it was developed as a response to the literature we discuss in the main text.

2 For example, "Baby talk seems to exist in every language and culture" (Fromkin and Rodman 1978: 344).

3 See, for example, Clancy 1986; Kulick 1992; Ochs 1985, 1988; Pye 1986; Schieffelin 1985, 1990; Watson-Gegeo and Gegeo 1986.

4 The term "socialization" was also used by many researchers carrying out what they called psychocultural analysis of behavior; verbal behavior was excluded, e.g., Whiting et al. 1966.

5 See Ochs and Schieffelin 1984, 1989, 1995; and Schieffelin and Ochs 1986a, 1986b.

6 Local men were easy to recruit and train as pastors largely because the Bosavi region had been neglected by the national government. The Christian mission was the only source of new and desirable goods, services, and opportunities, in addition to being a conduit of contact with outsiders and information about the outside world. Those who affiliated and became pastors benefited enormously.

REFERENCES

Akatsuka, N. (1991a). Affect and Japanese Conditionals. In P. Clancy and S. Thompson (eds.), *Asian Discourse and Grammar* (pp. 1–8). Santa Barbara Papers in Linguistics, vol. 3.

Akatsuka, N. (1991b). Dracula Conditionals and Discourse. In C. Georgopolous and R. Ishihara (eds.), *Interdisciplinary Approaches to Language: Essays in Honor of S.-Y. Kuroda* (pp. 25–37). Dordrecht: Kluwer.

Akatsuka, N. and Clancy, P. (1993). Conditionality and Deontic Modality in Japanese and Korean: Evidence from the Emergence of Conditionals. In P. Clancy (ed.), *Japanese/Korean Linguistics*, vol. 2 (pp. 177–192). Stanford, CA: CSLI Publications.

Althusser, L. (1971). Ideology and Ideological State Apparatuses (Notes Towards an Investigation). In L. Althusser, *Lenin and Philosophy and Other Essays* (pp. 127–188). London: Monthly Review Press.

Besnier, N. (1990). Language and Affect. *Annual Review of Anthropology* 19: 419–451.

Billig, M. (1997). The Dialogic Unconscious: Psychoanalysis, Discursive Psychology and the Nature of Repression. *British Journal of Social Psychology* 36: 139–159.

Billig, M. (1999). *Freudian Repression: Conversation Creating the Unconscious*. Cambridge: Cambridge University Press.

Butler, J. (1990). *Gender Trouble: Feminism and the Subversion of Identity.* New York: Routledge.

Cameron, D. and Frazer, E. (1987). *The Lust to Kill: A Feminist Investigation of Sexual Murder.* Cambridge: Polity Press.

Cameron, D., and Frazer, E. (1994). Cultural Difference and the Lust to Kill. In P. Harvey and P. Gow (eds.), *Sex and Violence: Issues in Representation and Experience* (pp. 156–171). London: Routledge.

Capps, L. and Ochs, E. (1995). *Constructing Panic: The Discourse of Agoraphobia*. Cambridge, MA: Harvard University Press.

Clancy, P. M. (1986). The Acquisition of Communicative Style in Japanese. In B. B. Schieffelin and E. Ochs (eds.), *Language Socialization across Cultures* (pp. 213–250). Cambridge: Cambridge University Press.

Clancy, P., Akatsuka, N., and Strauss, S. (1997). Deontic Modality and Conditionality in Discourse: A Cross-linguistic Study of Adult Speech to Young Children. In A. Kamio (ed.), *Directions in Functional Linguistics* (pp. 19–57). Amsterdam: John Benjamins.

Fader, A. (2000). Gender, Morality, and Language: Socialization Practices in a Hasidic Community. PhD thesis, New York University.

Freud, S. (1989). *Totem and Taboo.* New York: W.W. Norton.

Fromkin, V. and Rodman, R. (1978). *An Introduction to Language*, 3rd ed. New York: Holt, Rinehart and Winston.

Garrett, P. (1999). Language Socialization, Convergence, and Shift in St. Lucia, West Indies. PhD thesis, New York University.

Garrett, P. and Baquedano-López, P. (2002). Language Socialization: Reproduction and Continuity, Transformation and Change. *Annual Review of Anthropology* 31: 339–361.

Heath, S. B. (1983). *Ways with Words: Language, Life, and Work in Communities and Classrooms.* New York: Cambridge University Press.

Hymes, D. (1974). *Foundations in Sociolinguistics: An Ethnographic Approach.* Philadelphia: University of Pennsylvania Press.

Irvine, J. (1990). Registering Affect: Heteroglossia in the Linguistic Expression of Emotion. In C. Lutz and L. Abu-Lughod (eds.), *Language and the Politics of Emotion* (pp. 126–161). Cambridge: Cambridge University Press.

Kulick, D. (1992). *Language Shift and Cultural Reproduction: Socialization, Self, and Syncretism in a Papua New Guinean Village.* New York: Cambridge University Press.

Kulick, D. (1993). Speaking as a Woman: Structure and Gender in Domestic Arguments in a New Guinea Village. *Cultural Anthropology* 8(4): 510–541.

Kulick, D. (1998). Anger, Gender, Language Shift, and the Politics of Revelation in a Papua New Guinean Village. In B. B. Schieffelin, K. A. Woolard, and P. V. Kroskrity (eds.), *Language Ideologies: Practice and Theory* (pp. 87–102). Oxford: Oxford University Press.

Kulick, D. (2003). Language and Desire. *Language and Communication* 23: 139–151 (Special Issue, ed. D. Cameron and D. Kulick).

La Fontaine, J. S. (1985). Person and Individual: Some Anthropological Reflections. In M. Carrithers, S. Collins, and S. Lukes (eds.), *The Category of the Person: Anthropology, Philosophy, History* (pp. 123–140). Cambridge: Cambridge University Press.

Lutz, C. and White, G. (1986). The Anthropology of Emotions. *Annual Review of Anthropology* 15: 405–436.

Mauss, M. (1985 [1935]). A Category of the Human Mind: The Notion of Person; The Notion of Self. In M. Carrithers, S. Collins, and S. Lukes (eds.), *The Category of the Person: Anthropology, Philosophy, History* (pp. 1–25). Cambridge: Cambridge University Press.

McDermott, R. P., Gospodinoff, K. and Aron, J. (1978). Criteria for an Ethnographically Adequate Description of Concerted Activities and Their Contexts. *Semiotica* 24(3/4): 245–275.

Mead, M. (1930). *Growing up in New Guinea.* Harmondsworth: Penguin.

Mead, M. (1954 [1928]). *Coming of Age in Samoa.* New York: Morrow Quill.

Miller, P. (1986). Teasing as Language Socialization and Verbal Play in a White Working-class Community. In B. B. Schieffelin and E. Ochs (eds.), *Language Socialization across Cultures* (pp. 199–211). Cambridge: Cambridge University Press.

Ochs, E. (1985). Variation and Error: A Sociolinguistic Approach to Language Acquisition in Samoa. In D. Slobin (ed.), *The Crosslinguistic Study of Language Acquisition*, vol. 1, (pp. 783–838). Hillsdale, NJ: Lawrence Erlbaum.

Ochs, E. (1988). *Culture and Language Development: Language Acquisition and Language Socialization in a Samoan Village.* New York: Cambridge University Press.

Ochs, E., Pontecorvo, C., and Fasulo, A. (1996). Socializing Taste. *Ethnos* 61(1–2): 5–42.

Ochs, E., and Schieffelin, B. B. (1984). Language Acquisition and Socialization: Three Developmental Stories and Their Implications. In R. Shweder and R. LeVine (eds.), *Culture Theory: Essays on Mind, Self, and Emotion* (pp. 276–320). New York: Cambridge University Press.

Ochs, E., and Schieffelin, B. B. (1989). Language Has a Heart. *Text* 9(1): 7–25.

Ochs, E., and Schieffelin, B. B. (1995). The Impact of Language Socialization on Grammatical Development. In P. Fletcher and B. MacWhinney (eds.), *The Handbook of Child Language* (pp. 73–94). Oxford: Blackwell.

Paugh, A. (2001). "Creole Day is Every Day": Language Socialization, Shift, and Ideologies in Dominica, West Indies. PhD thesis, New York University.

Pye, C. (1986). Quiche' Mayan Speech to Children. *Journal of Child Language* 13: 85–100.

Sacks, H., Schegloff, E. A. and Jefferson, G. (1974). A Simplest Systematics for the Organization of Turn-Taking for Conversation. *Language* 50(4): 696–735.

Schieffelin, B. B. (1985). The Acquisition of Kaluli. In D. Slobin (ed.), *The Crosslinguistic Study of Language Acquisition*, vol. 1 (pp. 525–593). Hillsdale, NJ: Lawrence Erlbaum.

Schieffelin, B. B. (1990). *The Give and Take of Everyday Life: Language Socialization of Kaluli Children*. New York: Cambridge University Press.

Schieffelin, B. B. (2002). Marking Time: The Dichotomizing Discourse of Multiple Temporalities. *Current Anthropology* 43: S5–17.

Schieffelin, B., and Ochs, E. (1986a). Language Socialization. *Annual Review of Anthropology* 15: 163–191.

Schieffelin, B. and Ochs, E. (ed.) (1986b). *Language Socialization across Cultures*. New York: Cambridge University Press.

Ward, M. C. (1971). *Them Children: A Study in Language Learning*. New York: Holt, Rinehart and Winston.

Watson-Gegeo, K., and Gegeo, D. (1986). Calling Out and Repeating Routines in Kwara'ae Children's Language Socialization. In B. B. Schieffelin and E. Ochs (eds.), *Language Socialization Across Cultures* (pp. 17–50). New York: Cambridge University Press.

Whiting, J., Child, L., Lambert, W., et al. (1966). *Field Guide for a Study of Socialization*. New York: Social Science Research Center.

Žižek, S. (1999). *The Ticklish Subject: The Absent Center of Political Ontology*. London and New York: Verso.

CHAPTER 16 Language and Identity

Mary Bucholtz and Kira Hall

1 INTRODUCTION

In many ways, the study of linguistic anthropology is the study of language and identity. The field's concern with the linguistic production of culture entails a concern with the variety of culturally specific subject positions that speakers enact through language. Thus classic linguistic-anthropological studies of performance and ritual, of socialization and status, describe not merely kinds of speech but kinds of speakers, who produce and reproduce particular identities through their language use.[1] Although the field did not rely heavily on the term *identity* itself until relatively recently, the concept has now taken a central position in linguistic anthropology, serving less as the background for other kinds of investigation and more as a topic meriting study in its own right. This move is important because among the many symbolic resources available for the cultural production of identity, language is the most flexible and pervasive. The fact that so much scholarship on identity in socio-cultural anthropology draws on linguistic evidence – such as life stories, narratives, interviews, humor, oral traditions, literacy practices, and more recently media discourses – attests to the crucial if often unacknowledged role language plays in the formation of cultural subjectivities.

This chapter characterizes some of the most important recent developments in the new anthropological research tradition of language and identity. We begin by exploring two key concepts, sameness and difference, that offer complementary perspectives on identity. The first of these allows for individuals to imagine themselves as a group, while the second produces social distance between those who perceive themselves as unlike. Even together, however, these concepts are inadequate to capture the power relations in which identities are enmeshed. For sameness and difference are not objective states, but phenomenological processes that emerge from social interaction. We therefore turn to the ways in which similarities and differences become organized hierarchically in social contexts. We discuss this process in terms of *markedness*, an originally linguistic concept that is now applied more generally to situations in which normative and non-normative categories are established.

With this background laid, we review the development of identity studies in linguistic anthropology and related fields, and the critiques that such studies have attracted. Anthropological research on identity has long been an overtly political undertaking, focusing on relations of power and subjectivity in local societies and in encounters between cultures, as well as in the ethnographic project itself. Yet precisely because of its political nature, some of this research has been vulnerable to charges of operating within overgeneralized notions of similarity and difference, often referred to as *essentialism*. Despite this criticism, however, the study of identity continues to be both viable and necessary. And because language is central to the production of identity, linguistic anthropology has a vital role to play in the development of new research frameworks.

Recent theoretical work in linguistic anthropology creates the conditions for achieving this goal by foregrounding the complex social and political meanings with which language becomes endowed in specific contexts. We focus in particular on four semiotic processes that are widely discussed in the literature: *practice, indexicality, ideology,* and *performance*. Although identity is not always explicitly at issue in such research, these semiotic processes provide a clear account of how social identities come to be created through language. Indeed, it is on the basis of this scholarship that we are able to propose a definition of identity that avoids essentialism while remaining politically productive. In the final section of the chapter, we build on this definition by offering a framework to explain how such processes are carried out – the social and political relations engendered through semiotic acts of identification. This model, which we term *tactics of intersubjectivity*, provides a more systematic and precise method for investigating how identity is constructed through a variety of symbolic resources, and especially language.[2]

2 IDENTITY: SAME DIFFERENCE?

The term *identity* literally refers to sameness. One might therefore expect that identity would be most salient when people are most similar. Yet this seemingly straightforward formulation is more complex in practice. It is not easy for an outside observer to determine when a group of people should be classified as "alike," nor is it obvious on what grounds such a classification should be made, given the infinitude of ways in which individuals vary from one another. Hence, externally imposed identity categories generally have at least as much to do with the observer's own identity position and power stakes as with any sort of objectively describable social reality. Such issues often come to the fore when linguistic anthropologists and sociolinguists attempt to characterize the membership of a given speech community, for what counts as membership in linguistic terms may differ from equally relevant social, cultural, historical, and political criteria (see Silverstein 1996). This issue has been extensively debated with respect to African American Vernacular English. Some researchers (e.g., Labov 1973, 1980) have privileged linguistic criteria and advocated a restrictive definition of speech community membership as centrally associated with adolescent and pre-adolescent boys in urban street gangs. Other scholars instead take a more anthropological perspective, emphasizing the importance of the perceptions and practices of the full range of speech community members (e.g., Jacobs-Huey 1997; Morgan 1994). While misrecognition of a community's own norms is especially likely when a scholar is not a member of the group she or he studies, even "native" anthropologists may misinterpret what they see and hear. In the 1950s, Edward Dozier, an anthropologist of Santa Clara Tewa and French American parentage, argued that another Tewa group based in Arizona had partly acculturated to its Hopi neighbors, despite plentiful linguistic and cultural evidence of their separate identity (Kroskrity 2000a).

It is therefore crucial to attend closely to speakers' own understandings of their identities, as revealed through the ethnographic analysis of their pragmatic and metapragmatic actions. When individuals decide to organize themselves into a group, they are driven not by some pre-existing and recognizable similarity but by agency and power. In a French-language high school in English-speaking Canada, for example, students whose linguistic, racial, and ethnic identities did not conform to the rigid categories available at the school formed a "multicultural" group that based its identity on ethnoracial diversity and a shared resistant youth style, hiphop (Heller 1999a). Social grouping is a process not merely of discovering or acknowledging a similarity that precedes and establishes identity but, more fundamentally, of inventing similarity by downplaying difference.

Although identity work frequently involves obscuring differences among those with a common identity, it may also serve to manufacture or underscore differences between in-group members and those outside the group. The perception of shared identity often requires as its foil a sense of alterity, of an Other who can be positioned against those socially constituted as the same. Indeed, many studies of language and identity in linguistic anthropology report the most vigorous formation of socially significant identities in contexts of (perceived) heterogeneity rather than of (perceived) homogeneity. Ethnic identity, for example, generally emerges under conditions of contact, whether as a way of reifying distinctions between people who live in juxtaposition to one another (Barth 1986 [1972]; Urciuoli 1995) or as a way for cultural groups to remain apart, voluntarily or involuntarily, from the de-ethnicizing process of citizenship in the nation-state (Fishman 1999). The latter type of situation makes clear that homogeneity is itself a contested ideological achievement that seeks to erase crucial differences in identity. Moreover, the possibility that ethnic identities may be eliminated altogether under nationalism suggests that such identities do not coexist in the kind of multicultural harmony marketed in the mass media and promoted by liberal education, in which physical, cultural, and linguistic specificities become interchangeable and equivalent differences. In reality, in situations of cultural contact, equal status is won, if at all, through bitter struggle. This fact is illustrated by ongoing efforts around the world to gain some form of official state recognition for the languages of people who have experienced subordination and oppression under colonial rule, nationalism, and global capitalism (see e.g., Hornberger 1998; Paulston 1997).

Where difference is not deliberately eradicated, at least at the ideological level, the organization of difference into systematized structures – social categories – is the functional output of identity work. Such structures have been well documented in US high schools, where binary and oppositional local youth identities proliferate. Among these oppositions are Jock versus Burnout, based on class (Eckert 2000); Norteña versus Sureña, based on national allegiance (Mendoza-Denton 1996); and nerdy versus cool, based on engagement in youth culture (Bucholtz 1999). Although these and other contrastive identities may seem to form pairs in which each element is equal, usually there are social inequities associated with such identity choices. In most cases difference implies hierarchy, and the group with the greater power establishes a vertical relation in terms beneficial to itself. Such ideological ranking enables the identities of the more powerful group to become less recognizable as identities; instead, this group constitutes itself as the norm from which all others diverge.

3   POWER AND MARKEDNESS

Within linguistics, this hierarchical structuring of difference has been termed *marked-ness*, a concept that has been borrowed and extended by a number of scholars of identity within the humanities and social sciences to describe the process whereby some social categories gain a special, default status that contrasts with the identities of other groups, which are usually highly recognizable. In many contexts in the United States, such unmarked categories may include whiteness, masculinity, heterosexuality, middle-class status, and Christianity, but in local settings other arrangements are also possible, and of course the particular categories that are unmarked vary across cultures, though not limitlessly. The unmarking of powerful identities is generally supported by a wide network of supralocal ideologies, but the process also crucially involves the local level, at which unmarked identities may be reproduced as well as challenged and reinscribed with identity markings. Marked identities are also ideo-logically associated with marked language: linguistic structures or practices that differ from the norm. In US culture, the politics of markedness plays out among Puerto Ricans in New York in their experiences of imposed racialization and ethnicization and in the stigmatization of their language varieties, both Spanish and English (Urciuoli 1996).

The power of unmarkedness is likewise evident in Zambia, in which the 73 languages spoken in the country are hierarchically organized: the seven dominant ethnic-group languages used in the media are positioned above the other languages, while English, the official state language, is the unmarked and most prestigious code (Spitulnik 1998). Thus despite a rhetoric of pluralistic equality, English's privileged status remains largely immune to challenge, unlike the seven ethnic-group languages. When one category is elevated as an unmarked norm, its power is more pervasive because it is masked. By being construed as both powerful and normative, its special status is naturalized and the effort required to achieve this status is rendered invisible – and, when associated with language, inaudible (cf. Bucholtz 2001; Trechter and Bucholtz 2001). This ideological process of *erasure* (Irvine and Gal 2000) comple-ments and is supported by the erasure of social complexity in those languages and identities that remain marked and subordinate, like the scores of Zambian languages and ethnic groups that have no media outlet.

Because markedness implies hierarchy, differences between groups become socially evaluated as deviations from a norm and, indeed, as failures to measure up to an implied or explicit standard. Hence such differences are used as a justification for social inequality. Those who transgress gender norms in their linguistic and other social practices are often targeted in this way, but members of racialized, ethnicized, or other groups who do not conform to the stereotypical behavior expected of them are also susceptible to accusations of inadequacy or inauthenticity. Until recently, researchers often shared with community members the perception that those who do not conform to ideological expectations are somehow socially deficient, and thus unconventional social actors were marginalized both within their own culture and in scholarly reports (see Hall 2003; Trechter 2003). The charge of deficiency, however, overlooks the important fact that speakers who resist, subvert, or otherwise challenge existing linguistic and social norms are vital to the theoretical understanding of identity as the outcome of agency, through which language users creatively respond to and interrogate social constraints they cannot disregard or dismantle (for a fuller discussion of agency, see Ahearn 2001; Duranti, this volume). To understand why earlier studies of identity tended to miss this fact, it is necessary to consider the development of identity as a scholarly and political concept.

4 IDENTITY AND ITS CRITICS IN LINGUISTIC ANTHROPOLOGY

The trend to focus on identity in linguistic anthropology is in part a response to similar intellectual developments elsewhere in anthropology, as well as in the social sciences and humanities more widely. At the center of this scholarly endeavor are some dimensions of identity that are currently the most contested and politicized: race, ethnicity, gender, sexuality. Arising from struggles for equal rights for marked members of these categories, the study of identity has always been highly political.

Although the study of identity has been most closely associated with other fields, especially psychology and sociology, anthropologists have also found the concept to be a valuable tool for understanding local cultural workings of and responses to sexism, racism, (neo)colonialism, and other kinds of power relations. The study of identity has also led anthropology to greater reflexivity, as indicated both by scholars' fuller consciousness of their own positionality in the research process (Briggs 1986; Clifford and Marcus 1986) and by the increased attention to the anthropology of late modern societies and the identities that emerge from them (Marcus 1999). Though its role in providing the impetus for this shift in the field is sometimes overlooked, feminist anthropology has been especially important in moving the discipline in these directions, given its central concerns with researcher subjectivity and in drawing connections between gender in Western and non-Western societies (Behar and Gordon 1995; Visweswaran 1994). In linguistic anthropology, studies of identity have addressed questions of contact, colonialism, and power between societies as well as political and social inequities within a given culture (see also Garrett, this volume; Philips, this volume); hence gender has been central here as well (e.g., Gal 1978; Keenan 1989 [1974]; Philips, Steele, and Tanz 1987). Critical anthropological work on race and ethnicity has been equally important in this regard (e.g., Bucholtz and Trechter 2001; Harrison 1988; Morgan, forthcoming; Twine and Warren 2000), and the study of sexuality in sociocultural and linguistic anthropology has also made significant contributions to the understanding of the identity of self and other (e.g., Herdt 1997; Kulick and Willson 1995; Livia and Hall 1997; Weston 1998).

But just as questions of identity have come into focus in linguistic anthropology, such research has experienced a backlash both within the field and in adjacent areas of research. The study of identity has been subject to critique on both theoretical and political grounds. Critics have charged researchers of identity with *essentialism*, a theoretical position that maintains that those who occupy an identity category (such as women, Asians, the working class) are both fundamentally similar to one another and fundamentally different from members of other groups. Essentialism takes as its starting point that these groupings are inevitable and natural, and that they are separated from one another by sharp boundaries. Although essentialism is often understood as biologically based, it may also be interpreted as a cultural phenomenon. Hence, some who reject the claim that African Americans, say, are biologically distinctive as a group (a claim that has been thoroughly discredited in anthropology; see Harrison 1995; Keita and Kittles 1997) may nonetheless argue that African American culture is relatively homogeneous and clearly different from other cultures, a position that was put forward in much of the early research (e.g., Kochman 1981; for a critique of this view, see Morgan 1994).

From this description, two things will be obvious to students of linguistic anthropology: first, until quite recently, essentialism served as the basis of anthropology as a discipline; and second, in most of its forms, cultural essentialism relies on language as a central component. The essentialist origins of anthropology may be found not only in the fruitless nineteenth-century quest to find biological correlates of race but also in the forging of a close ideological connection between language and identity, especially ethnic identity. The scholarly tradition of Romanticism, motivated by the emergence of nationalism, indelibly linked language to ethnicity in a quasi-biological fashion (see also Bauman and Briggs 2000). In this version of ethnicity, which endures both in academic and in popular discourse, identity is rooted not in genetics but in heritable cultural forms, especially language, which symbolize and, in more extreme essentialist modes, iconically embody an ethnic group's distinctive cultural identity. The Romantic understanding of language tied it to the spiritual essence of its speakers: hence languages, like the cultural identities that gave rise to them, were thought to be necessarily separate and non-overlapping. Conversely, perceived or asserted cultural similarity produced an expectation of linguistic similarity (and vice versa). In the twentieth century, cultural essentialism was most evident in the study of ethnic minorities within the nation-state. In the US context, the primary focus of such work was the language and culture of African Americans; as noted above, the essentialism of much of this research was challenged by later scholars.

Even when ethnicity is not the focus of analysis, social identities have often been represented in scholarship as clearly delineated from one another, internally homogeneous, and linked to distinctive linguistic practices. In particular, this perspective dominated much early work on language and gender, which for many years viewed the categories of female and male as dichotomous and the corresponding linguistic practices of each gender as vastly different ("women's language" and "men's language"). While this approach was valuable for both intellectual and political reasons in calling attention to understudied linguistic and social phenomena, it overlooked the extent of intra-gender variation and inter-gender similarity in language use. This preoccupation with gender difference to the exclusion of other kinds of analyses has been critiqued by language and gender scholars for some years (e.g., Bing and Bergvall 1996; Cameron 1996; Crawford 1995; Eckert and McConnell-Ginet 1992; Gal 1991, 1995; Trechter 1999).

Ironically, the lure of essentialism is so attractive that even some of its most vehement opponents draw on it in their argumentation. As a case in point, in a series of publications, Kulick (1999, 2000, 2002, 2003) offers several versions of what is fundamentally the same critique: that the study of language and sexuality (a term which for him is often synonymous with *sexual identity*) is unproductive and must be replaced by the study of language and desire. He argues that research on language and sexuality, or what he calls "gay and lesbian language," relies on unwarranted essentialist assumptions. Despite his reduction of a broad field of study to a much narrower realm, Kulick's basic objection is well taken in so far as it calls into question any necessary link between gay or lesbian identity and unique language use. Indeed, in this regard his discussion echoes the extensive critique of the notions of "women's language" and "men's language" in language and gender studies. Yet at the same time, Kulick maintains that it is only from such an essentialist vantage point that identity can be studied. He asserts, for example, that "any discussion that wants to make claims about gay or lesbian language must [. . .] establish that those ways of using language are unique to gays and lesbians" (Kulick 2000: 259). This insistence on difference as the basis of identity is the very claim that language and gender scholars have been working against for several years. Since such a strong criterion can never be met, the conclusion to be drawn is that the study of language and sexuality, and by extension any study of language and identity, is illegitimate.[3] While Kulick is not advocating an essentialist approach to language and identity, he fails to understand that identity – including sexual identity – is constituted by much more than difference. As the wealth of research surveyed in this chapter indicates, the interconnections between language and identity are multiple, complex, and context-ually specific (Hall 1995; Hall and O'Donovan 1996).

The answer to the problem of essentialism, then, is not to eliminate the study of identity. Without identity, we argue, there can be no anthropology, since cultural processes are intimately bound up with socially located cultural subjects. The solution is instead to develop better theoretical frameworks. While recognizing the difficulties with research that accepts the essentialist or binary models of identity that community members may eagerly offer up, we also want to emphasize that such research provides a starting point for understanding the ideological underpinnings of language, iden-tity, and their interrelationship. Previous research often failed to distinguish between essentialism as a theoretical position and as an ethnographic fact. But to recognize that essentialism is frequently operative in the formation of social identities, as many researchers do, is not necessarily to embrace it as one's own theoretical stance. A great deal of work within linguistic anthropology addresses itself to essentialism as a one-to-one mapping between language and identity, whether to explore how this ideol-ogy works in a particular cultural context; to exploit it as part of an activist endeavor to protect communities in jeopardy; or to explode it by revealing the many other ways in which identity and language may intersect. Inevitably, linguistic anthropologists often find themselves drawing on more than one of these perspectives in their research. A non-essentialist approach to identity within linguistic anthropology cannot dispense with the ideology of essentialism as long as it has salience in the lives of the speakers we study. Moreover, a researcher may deliberately engage in essentialist analysis for specific political or intellectual purposes, such as calling attention to identities that would otherwise be ignored; this "strategic essentialism" (Spivak 1995; see also McElhinny 1996) purposefully oversimplifies complex situations in order to initiate a discussion that will later become more nuanced. While researchers will disagree as to when and whether such moves are appropriate, it is important not to essentialize essentialism itself: like all ideologies, it is situated and strategic (see also Herzfeld 1996; Jaffe 1999; Woolard 1998a).

One of the greatest weaknesses of previous research on identity, in fact, is the assumption that identities are attributes of individuals or groups rather than of situations. Correlational approaches to language and identity, such as those commonly taken in some areas of sociolinguistics, associate rates of use of particular linguistic forms with particular kinds of speakers. Although more recent approaches have complicated this simple picture (see Mendoza-Denton 2002), much work within variationist sociolinguistics assumes not only that language use is distinctive at some level but that such practices are reflective, not constitutive, of social identities. Correlational perspectives on language often emphasize the distinctiveness of group patterns at the expense of variation across individuals within the group, or even variation within a single individual. But identity inheres in actions, not in people. As the product of situated social action, identities may shift and recombine to meet new circumstances. This dynamic perspective contrasts with the traditional view of identities as unitary and enduring psychological states or social categories.

The extent to which identities are forged in action rather than fixed in categories is evident in studies of status. Although this term quite literally defines power as residing in unchanging ("static") roles that individuals inhabit across social contexts, anthropological research on the linguistic dimensions of status demonstrates that high-status identities are not entirely given in advance but are interactionally negotiated. One of the earliest studies to make this point is Irvine's (1989 [1974]) analysis of greetings among Wolof-speaking people in West Africa, who may artfully use greetings to impose higher status on addressees for social purposes such as eliciting the financial support that this status entails. Similarly, Duranti (1992) demonstrates that Samoan respect vocabulary does not always map neatly onto pre-existing social categories that merit respect, namely, titled persons such as chiefs. Instead, respectful words are used to create contextually relevant status relations depending on the needs of the interactional moment. Referents of high status may be assigned ordinary lexical items, while non-titled individuals may be referred to respectfully, in order to position the speaker, the addressee, and/or the reference in temporarily salient statuses for strategic purposes such as flattery.

Recent attention in linguistic anthropology to language as social semiotic action also provides an approach to identity that does not fall into the trap of essentialism. The deterministic outlook on identity is here replaced with a more agentive perspective. Because in this body of scholarship identity is better understood as an outcome of language use rather than as an analytic prime, traditional identity categories do not drive the analysis and are often invoked obliquely, if at all. The semiotics of language concerns not identity as a set of fixed categories but identification as an ongoing social and political process.

5   SEMIOTIC PROCESSES OF IDENTIFICATION

Given its focus on the social and cultural, linguistic anthropology considers identity a quintessentially social phenomenon. This view contrasts with Freudian-influenced psychological perspectives, which understand selfhood as a pre-cultural object that resides in the individual mind and develops within the (psycho)social drama of the family, the broad outlines of which are thought to be similar across cultures. Such psychoanalytic approaches are often overly deterministic and overly universalizing, and at best account for only a narrow set of the identities that emerge even in a single cultural context. Yet psychology is also cultural, as Sapir (1949, 1994) long ago recognized, and recent efforts in linguistic anthropology to consider individual subjectivity and social agency in the linguistic construction of selfhood (e.g., Ochs and Capps 1996; Wortham 2001) are an important counterbalance to previous studies of social identity as largely monolithic, such as the early sociolinguistic work on race and gender.

Semiotics, or the study of systems of meaning, offers a valuable perspective from which to view identity. Semiotics investigates the association created between social or natural objects and the meanings they bear. While language is often taken as the prototypical semiotic system, it is more complex than many other systems because it has social meaning as well as referential meaning. It is precisely this duality of language – its ability to convey meaning at two levels, one semantic or referential and one pragmatic or contextual – that makes it such a rich resource for semiotic production within human societies. To take a simple example, at the referential level the contemporary slang word *props* means (refers to) respect, but at the broader sociocultural level it means (is associated with) hiphop culture, and hence a speaker who uses the word may indirectly invoke this identity. Such semiotic associations are created in a number of ways. We consider four interrelated and overlapping processes whose study has been especially fruitful for the anthropological understanding of language and identity: practice, indexicality, ideology, and performance.

5.1   Practice

Practice is habitual social activity, the series of actions that make up our daily lives. The notion of practice (or praxis) emerges from Marxism, and while this influence is apparent in the frequent use of the concept to understand the political economy of everyday life, the term now has a wider range of use. For linguistic anthropologists, one of the most important practice theorists is Bourdieu, not only because he considers language a practice rather than merely an abstract system of rules, as many theoretical linguists maintain, but also because he recognizes that linguistic practice is not distinct from other forms of everyday social activity (Bourdieu 1977b). Thus through sheer repetition language, along with other social practices, shapes the social actor's way of being in the world, what Bourdieu calls *habitus*. However, the specific practices in which one engages, and which in turn constitute the habitus, are not the same for everyone: gender, social class, age, and many other dimensions of life experience are culturally reified as the basis for the inculcation of differentiated practice, and these are associated with differential values as "symbolic capital" – that is, as resources that may be drawn upon to build social and economic success.

Here we see the beginnings of identity forming through the sedimentation of habitual action. But although Bourdieu (1977a [1972]) argues that practice, including linguistic practice, is more often rooted in embodied repetition than in deliberate action, this does not preclude the possibility that it may be the outcome of social agency. Speakers may elect to engage in certain activities or to affiliate with social groupings in which particular practices are expected, or "communities of practice" (Lave and Wenger 1991; Wenger 1998). Thus while the process of socialization into our first community of practice is particularly significant for the acquisition of both communicative and other cultural competence, such socialization is not a one-time event but a phenomenon that happens throughout our lives (Ochs and Schieffelin 1995; Kulick and Schieffelin, this volume).

The relevance of this framework for sociolinguistic research on identity has been most fully explored by feminist scholars, who note its potential to examine speaker agency within social constraints (Eckert and McConnell-Ginet 1992; McElhinny 1998). Eckert (1989) argues that because of gender subordination, women in many cultures are not permitted to strive for real-world accomplishments to the same extent as men; they therefore must rely more heavily on symbolic resources, such as language, appearance, and personality, to display themselves as acceptable cultural members. It is for this reason, Eckert suggests, that many studies of variationist sociolinguistics find that women's speech more closely approximates the standard or prestigious form of a language. But speakers are not entirely locked into particular subject positions based on gender or other dimensions of social inequality; as social actors move between different communities of practice in their daily lives different dimensions of identity come to the fore, including identities based on activities rather than categories (Goodwin 1990). Moreover, the fact that a suburban American high-school girl, for example, can become a popular Jock or a rebellious Burnout through her habitual choice of everything from blue jeans to vowels means that practices can converge not just around macrolevel social categories but around local identities based on style, or distinctive practice (Eckert and McConnell-Ginet 1995).

5.2   Indexicality

Practice, as repetition, is instrumental to a second semiotic process associated with identity: indexicality. *Indexicality* is the semiotic operation of juxtaposition, whereby one entity or event points to another. The basic insight, first developed by semiotician Charles Peirce, is that some signs, which he called indices, function via repeated and non-accidental cooccurrence: smoke is an index of fire, clouds of rain. This process of extracting meaning from juxtaposed events or entities has been generalized for the analysis of the social and ideological realm by Michael Silverstein (e.g., 1985).

The fullest treatment of indexicality in relation to identity is Elinor Ochs's (1992) exposition of the linguistic indexing of gender. Ochs notes that linguistic structures become associated with social categories not directly but indirectly, through a chain of semiotic associations. An example of this phenomenon is the process by which certain sentence-final particles in Japanese have come to be thought of by Japanese speakers as "women's language." Some particles, Ochs observes, are used to mitigate the force of an utterance; this linguistic form is therefore directly associated not with an identity category but with a stance, an orientation to the ongoing interaction. However, because the speakers who tend to take up this "deferential" stance are usually female, the same linguistic form has become indirectly associated with women, and this connection is now so widely recognized that the intermediate step from stance to identity has become obscured. The direct indexical relationship is still readily recoverable in actual linguistic practice, since speakers of Japanese and other languages said to have "gender-exclusive" forms can in fact draw on the linguistic elements associated with the other gender to index particular interactional stances (Trechter 1999). Thus so-called women's language is often used by men in order to convey a general interactional stance that has no necessary association with femininity.

This ambiguity between direct and indirect indexicality is an important source for establishing and justifying power inequities between groups. Hill (1995) argues that Anglo-Americans who do not speak Spanish may use "mock Spanish" forms like *No problemo* (cf. Spanish *No problema*) in their speech to directly index a jocular stance, but because it is ungrammatical the same form may indirectly index an identity that covertly defines itself over and against Spanish speakers (on this point, see further below). In both of these examples, the accretion of social meanings through repeated occurrence, together with the denotational meaning of these linguistic forms, results in the formation of social stereotypes based on language: the demure middle-class Japanese woman, the laid-back Mexican. Such stereotypes are not neutral but highly politicized. Attention to the semiotic processes through which language enters into power relations has become one of the most productive areas of research in linguistic anthropology via the study of language ideologies (Kroskrity, this volume). This issue is also closely tied to identity, for beliefs about language are also often beliefs about speakers.

5.3   Ideology

Sociolinguistic research has long used concepts such as stereotypes or attitudes to characterize sociocultural beliefs about languages and their speakers. Yet these notions emphasize individual psychology at the expense of the sociocultural level at which belief systems contribute to the structuring logics of power. The issue of power as a social phenomenon is central in the concept of ideology, which has become the preferred term of art for linguistic anthropologists concerned with how language accrues sociopolitical meaning (e.g., Blommaert 1999; Kroskrity 2000b; Schieffelin, Woolard, and Kroskrity 1998).

Like *practice*, the term *ideology* originates in Marxist thought, but it too has undergone extensive revision in the hands of later scholars. The conventional understanding of ideology as a process of mystification that distorts subjects' perception of political-economic realities has been replaced in most linguistic-anthropological research by a more nuanced view in which ideology organizes and enables all cultural beliefs and practices as well as the power relations that result from these.

The concept of ideology in linguistic anthropology has been given further analytic force by Irvine and Gal (2000), who have developed a highly influential model for how language ideologies become instantiated. As we noted briefly above, one of the processes they document is *erasure*, or the elimination of details that are inconsistent with a given ideological position. Another process is *iconization*, a concept that expands Peirce's notion of the iconic sign into the ideological domain, much as Silverstein and Ochs did for the index. Irvine and Gal characterize the semiotic process of iconization as the ideological representation of a given linguistic feature or variety as formally congruent with the group with which it is associated. Thus iconization is also a process of *essentialization* (see also Kuipers 1998): the creation of a naturalized link between the linguistic and the social that comes to be viewed as even more inevitable than the associations generated through indexicality. Irvine (2001a), for example, details the ways in which European linguists' classification of African languages in the nineteenth century relied on assumptions about the corres-pondence of linguistic gender (i.e., a system of noun classification) and cultural practices, gender relations, and family structure. Because linguistic gender was be-lieved to be "lacking" in African languages, African social gender was thought to be equally defective. In this way, European languages, which tend to have gender-based noun classification, could be elevated above "inadequate" African languages, and accordingly, European cultures could be considered superior to African cultures. Such reasoning was used to represent colonialism as not simply justifiable but even necessary and beneficent. Irvine and Gal note that such oppositions can be replicated at various levels of social structure, a phenomenon they term *fractal recursivity*, and hence can produce multiple identity positions at once: the asserted superiority of Europeans over Africans could be played out at the level of languages, nations, communities, and individuals. In principle, then, there is no end to the differentiation of identity.

Iconization and indexicality are converse processes of identity formation: indexi-cality produces ideology through practice, while iconization represents practice through ideology. In the first instance, ideologies of culturally intelligible identities emerge from social actors' habitual practice; in the second instance, actual practice may be far removed from the imagined practices that ideology constructs on the basis of perceived and literalized metaphorical resemblance between language and social organization. In both situations, however, ideology remains in the shadows. In fact, these processes cannot operate successfully if their ideological foundation is exposed. By contrast, the final semiotic process of identification that we consider here, per-formance, often calls attention to ideology and thus renders it hypervisible.

5.4   Performance

Whereas practice is habitual and oftentimes less than fully intentional, *performance* is highly deliberate and self-aware social display. In everyday speech, as in much linguis-tic anthropology, the type of display that *performance* refers to involves an aesthetic component that is available for evaluation by an audience (Bauman 1977). In this sense, performances are marked speech events that are more or less sharply differen-tiated from more mundane interaction.

But as linguistic anthropologists have long recognized, performance occurs not only on stages and under spotlights but in frequent and fleeting interactional moments throughout daily life (e.g., Bauman 1986; Hymes 1975). This broader notion of performance is also compatible with the concept of the performative in the philosophy of language, which has gone on to a long and influential afterlife in gender theory. According to Austin (1962), performative verbs effect change in the world through language under appropriate social conditions, such as the jury statement "We find the defendant not guilty." This concept was introduced to gender theory as *performativity* through the work of Butler (1990), who observed that gender is accomplished in much the same way as a performative speech act: through its very invocation under felicitous conditions. Performance, then, does not merely refer to the social world but actually brings it into being, although performances may be evaluated as more or less felicitous, more or less successful. The production of gender – or any identity – thus depends crucially on ideology to render that identity recognizable and legitimate. And although Butler maintains that most gender performances are not intentional acts but reiterations of hegemonic practices, she also acknowledges that an element of deliberate action is potentially present in those performances that challenge or subvert dominant ideologies, an insight that brings her notion of gender performance closer to the usual linguistic-anthropological meaning of the term, in which agency and individual action are often central.

Performance in both senses often involves *stylization*, the highlighting and exaggeration of ideological associations. An illustration of both aspects of performance is found in Barrett's (1999) research on African American drag queen performers in a Texas gay bar. Although they dress and talk like wealthy European women in their stage performances, these men wish to be neither female nor white. Instead, their stylized use of features of "women's language" (Lakoff 1975), African American Vernacular English, and gay double-entendres, like their elegant yet flamboyant clothing, is meant to question ideologies of sexuality, race, and class by ironically underscoring them through an exaggerated performance of (white, middle-class, heterosexual, female) gender that clashes with simultaneous performances of blackness and gayness. Such performances are highly political in that they demand recognition of identities – poor, gay, black – that are marginalized in hegemonic culture. Performance is therefore a way of bringing identities to the fore, often in subversive or resistant ways (e.g., Bauman and Briggs 1990; Pagliai and Farr 2000).

5.5   Identity and culture

As the foregoing discussion indicates, practice, performance, indexicality, and ideology do not operate separately in the creation of identity. Ideology is the level at which practice enters the field of representation. Indexicality mediates between ideology and practice, producing the former through the latter. Performance is the highlighting of ideology through the foregrounding of practice. Yet it is also important to keep these processes conceptually distinct. What we find repeatedly in studies of language and identity is a clear difference between cultural ideologies and social practices: cultural beliefs about how people of various social backgrounds should, must, or do speak and act (generated through indexicality) are generally reductive and inflexible, while the actual linguistic and social practices in which people engage in specific social contexts (including the display of practice in performance) are highly complex and strategic.[4] Ethnographers have often relied too heavily on cultural ideologies, mistaking them for accurate descriptions of cultural practice. Such errors are easy to make given that ideologies about practice usually bear some relation to practice, however distorted, and that practice often reproduces ideological expectations.

The semiotic processes detailed above reveal the extent to which identity is not simply the source of culture but the outcome of culture: in other words, it is a cultural effect. And language, as a fundamental resource for cultural production, is hence also a fundamental resource for identity production. This assertion challenges the common understanding of language as a mirror reflecting one's culture and identity. The following working definition of identity captures these key insights:

> *identity*: an outcome of cultural semiotics that is accomplished through the production of contextually relevant sociopolitical relations of similarity and difference, authenticity and inauthenticity, and legitimacy and illegitimacy

The remainder of the chapter explains each element of this definition and offers illustrations of how linguistic anthropology has examined the various dimensions of identity as a social, cultural, and political construct.

6   TACTICS OF INTERSUBJECTIVITY

While the various semiotic actions described above are all undertaken for the sake of identity, they do not always perform the same sort of identity work. As an explanation for social action, then, identity is not an analytical primitive. Just as important as understanding *how* identities are formed is understanding *why* they are formed, the purpose for which particular semiotic processes are put to use. Yet there has been very little theorization of the various purposes for which such identity work is accomplished. Some of this work has been done within sociolinguistics and related fields, where several different but overlapping models of identity have been developed: accommodation theory within social psychology (Giles and Smith 1979); audience and referee design within sociolinguistic studies of mass media (Bell 1984, 1992); and acts of identity within creole studies (Le Page and Tabouret-Keller 1985). However, these models do not completely address the issues of culture, power, and agency that are crucial to much of contemporary linguistic anthropology.

Recognizing this gap, we have developed a framework for describing the social relations established through semiotic processes.[5] We call these often overlooked and underdiscussed components of identity *tactics of intersubjectivity*. Tactics of intersubjectivity are the relations that are created through identity work. We have chosen the term *tactics*, following Certeau (1984 [1974]), to invoke the local, situated, and often improvised quality of the everyday practices through which individuals, though restricted in their freedom to act by externally imposed constraints, accomplish their social goals. Our second term, *intersubjectivity*, is meant to highlight the place of agency and interactional negotiation in the formation of identity. As with *tactics*, however, we wish to emphasize the limits that are placed on social agency, a tension that is captured in the polysemy of *subject* as both the agent and the patient of social action.

We propose three different pairs of tactics, which we term *adequation* and *distinction*, *authentication* and *denaturalization*, and *authorization* and *illegitimation*. Each of these tactics foregrounds a different use to which identity may be put: the establishment of relations of similarity and difference, of genuineness and artifice, and of legitimacy and disempowerment *vis-à-vis* some reference group or individual. They thus pertain to three different but interrelated concepts central to identity: markedness, essentialism, and institutional power. These relations may operate singly or in tandem within particular semiotic processes. Moreover, given the frequent ambiguity and indeterminacy of interaction, the same linguistic act may be understood by speaker, hearer, or other participants as motivated by different tactics, and the tactical outcome may be negotiated by all those involved rather than established in advance.

The framework we sketch here is not intended as an exhaustive model of identity but as a way to examine the relational dimension of identity categories, practices, and ideologies. These relations may be enacted via any aspect of identity, such as ethnicity, nationality, gender, or status, and they may be forged through any of the semiotic processes described above. Tactics of intersubjectivity therefore do not replace these other perspectives, but rather provide a more complete picture of how and why identity is created through language and other semiotic systems.

6.1 Adequation and Distinction

We focus in most detail on the first pair of tactics, adequation and distinction, because processes of similarity and difference have been the most thoroughly examined aspects of identity formation. The first of these, *adequation*, involves the pursuit of socially recognized sameness. In this relation, potentially salient differences are set aside in favor of perceived or asserted similarities that are taken to be more situationally relevant. The term *adequation* denotes both equation and adequacy; the relation thus establishes sufficient sameness between individuals or groups. The relation of adequation suggests that likeness, which as discussed above is often taken to be the basis of identity, is not an objective and permanent state but a motivated social achievement that may have temporary or long-term effects. For instance, adequation may be a means of preserving community identity in the face of dramatic cultural change. Thus as the indigenous Mexicano language is supplanted by Spanish in the Malinche region of Mexico, many people maintain the community standing of younger non-speakers of Mexicano by invoking a "rhetoric of continuity" in which language differences are subsumed under the discourse of kinship (Hill and Hill 1986: 418). Adequation also allows Mexicano speakers of both languages to locate themselves simultaneously within two different identity frames, by syncretically combining elements of each language into a single sociolinguistic system (cf. Woolard 1998b, this volume).

Adequation is often the basis of political organization and alliance. It may involve coalition-building across lines of difference, or it may collapse these boundaries altogether for the sake of a politically motivated strategic essentialism. This situation is seen in a radio panel discussion that aired in response to the Los Angeles uprisings following the trial of the police officers who beat black motorist Rodney King. In the interaction, several panelists, though of different professional backgrounds, genders, and experiences, united around what was constructed as a shared and, under the circumstances, highly salient, African American identity (Bucholtz 1996); this temporary unity was conditioned by political events and should be taken as an indication not that the panelists are committed to essentialism but rather that a common identity is a social achievement rather than a social artifact.

It is important to recognize that the assertion of similarity through adequation does not necessarily involve solidarity. In Guatemala markets, Mayan vendors may meet their non-Mayan customers' insulting comments with equally insulting responses; in this situation Mayan women's use of the tactic of adequation to insist on social equality challenges longstanding power asymmetries in Guatemalan society (French 2000). Thus adequation may be a process of contested equalization rather than a consensual process of equation.

Like similarity, difference does not exist as a social reality prior to its deployment for social ends. The second tactic, *distinction*, is the mechanism whereby salient difference is produced. Distinction is therefore the converse of adequation, in that in this relation difference is underscored rather than erased. And like adequation, distinction involves partiality or sufficient difference. Our terminology echoes that of Bourdieu (1984), whose analysis of how class distinction is reproduced through the cultivation of taste demonstrates that social differences are made, not found. Distinction is one of the sociopolitical relations most fully explored in linguistic anthropology, particularly in studies that address hierarchy and stratification (e.g., Keating 1998; Duranti 1994). Irvine (2001b) has also described how linguistic and other semiotic resources may cluster together to form styles, or distinctive sets of cultural practices.

While distinction may be a strategy of domination, as in the case of the non-Mayan market customers just discussed, it is also a tactic of those with little access to hegemonic power. We have already pointed out that differentiation of identity is a way of resisting the relentless march of the assimilating forces of modernity and the nation-state. Hence speakers of minority or unofficial languages often elaborate linguistic differences between their own language and the language of the state. This tactic is well developed on Corsica, where Corsican identity is closely linked to language and an ideology of linguistic essentialism positions Corsican as naturally oppositional to the state language, French. Although in practice Corsican and French are often mixed, powerful ideologies, promoted in Corsican discourses and enforced in Corsican institutions, maintain the structural integrity of the language as an autonomous code (Jaffe 1999).

As both these examples indicate, distinction most often operates in a binary fashion, establishing a dichotomy between social identities constructed as oppositional or contrastive. It thus has a tendency to reduce complex social variability to a single dimension: us versus them. But distinction may also allow groups to create an alternative to either pole of a dichotomous social relation. Radical Basque youth in free radio broadcasts use creative linguistic practices to align themselves against both the political oppressiveness of Castilian Spanish and the rigid hierarchies and accommodationism of other forms of Basque nationalism (Urla 2001). Yet while such identities are complex and non-dichotomous, they are usually realized through a binary logic. Dominican American teenagers, for example, occupy a subject position outside of the regulative structures of race, ethnicity, and language in force in much of the United States, since they are Spanish speakers who are phenotypically black (Bailey 2000). Such speakers negotiate their identities with their peers by using language to variously play off dichotomies of race (non-white versus white), language (Spanish-speaking versus English-speaking), and immigrant generation (English-dominant second generation versus Spanish-dominant first generation). Distinction, then, may erase other axes of difference or it may produce differentiation along multiple axes simultaneously.

6.2   Authentication and denaturalization

Authentication and *denaturalization*, the second pair of tactics, respectively concern the construction of a credible or genuine identity and the production of an identity that is literally incredible or non-genuine. We have chosen the term *authentication* in deliberate contrast with *authenticity*, another term that circulates widely in scholarly discourses of identity and its critique. Where authenticity has been tied to essentialism through the notion that some identities are more "real" than others, authentication highlights the agentive processes whereby claims to realness are asserted. Such claims often surface in nationalist movements, where a shared language becomes a powerful force in the formation and articulation of an imagined national unity (Anderson 1983; Gellner 1983). Here the process of authentication often involves the rewriting of linguistic and cultural history. In the standardization of a national language, for instance, a single language variety, and the people who speak it, are frequently repositioned as more central, fundamental, or "authentic" to the historical workings of the nation-state. The nationalistic rhetoric deployed in Muslim and Hindu political movements since the late eighteenth century in north India is a case in point (King 1994). While Hindu nationalists have adopted a *śuddh* or "pure" Sanskritic Hindi in the constitution of a historically situated Hindu identity, Muslim nationalists have embraced a variety of Urdu that draws more exclusively from Perso-Arabic sources. The linguistic correlate has been an ever-increasing divergence between Hindi on the one hand and Urdu on the other, with non-comprehensibility sometimes existing between radical versions of each. The authentication of identity in nationalistic movements like these tends to personify the language as much as it imagines a people, leading to situations like that in southern India where nationalist rhetoric is responsible for the transformation of the Tamil language into goddess, mother, and maiden (Ramaswamy 1998). Through this ideological reconstitution, Tamil speakers are accordingly authenticated as a people whose search for political and social empowerment is motivated by devotion, love, and purity.

   In the above cases, language contributes to nationalist identity formation by providing a sense of cohesion and unity for its speakers. Once the identity of a language and its speakers becomes authenticated through nationalistic rhetoric, the language variety itself comes to index particular ways of being in and belonging to the nation-state. Everyday conversation then becomes the vehicle for authentication practices, as speakers are able to index various ethnic and nationalist stances through language choice. Research on bilingualism in multilingual nation-states, such as

Errington's (1998) study of bilingual Javanese and Indonesian speakers in Central Java, illustrates how speakers convey ethnic, nationalist, and political alliances through everyday codeswitching practices. But authentication can be achieved through stylistic choice as well, as when female participants on a feminist separatist Internet discussion list collaboratively construct a "female culture" through the required use of textual features stereotypically associated with women's communication (Hall 1996). The fact that many male-to-female transsexuals in the United States appropriate the stereotypical features of what Lakoff identified as "women's language" (see Bucholtz and Hall 1995) suggests that authentication necessarily works through singular and essentialist readings of particular identities and their language practices. The term *authentication*, then, as we use it in this model, refers to how speakers activate these essentialist readings in the articulation of identity.

Much less frequently discussed, but no less frequent in occurrence, is the process whereby identities come to be severed from or separated from claims to "realness," a process we term *denaturalization* because it often tends to highlight the artificiality and non-essentialism of identity. Again, research on gender offers a powerful example. By contrast with much of the research on transsexuals, who are often argued to use language and other social practices to authenticate a gender identity that does not conform to the one biologically assigned to them, the black drag queens studied by Barrett (1999) discussed above regularly disrupt their performance of white femaleness in order to question the naturalness of categories of race and gender. Performance is an especially rich site for the study of the tactic of denaturalization, but such de-essentializing moves are also found in everyday life, as when the Dominican American teenagers that Bailey (2000) studied playfully challenge their schoolmates' essentialist assumptions about the relationship between race, language, and immigrant generation. Thus denaturalization frequently operates to destabilize the essentialist claims enacted by authentication.

6.3   Authorization and illegitimation

The final pair of tactics are *authorization* and *illegitimation*, which involve the attempt to legitimate an identity through an institutional or other authority, or conversely the effort to withhold or withdraw such structural power. Authorization may involve invoking language in ways recognized by the state. Thus highly multilingual Australian Aborigines, for whom language is not strongly associated with identity, nonetheless have sought to use linguistic evidence of "community" in legal struggles over land rights (Haviland 1996). The most discussed forms of authorization in linguistic anthropology, however, are those associated with linguistic standardization. The authorization of a single, often highly artificial, form of language as the standard may be central to the imposition of a homogeneous national identity in which modern elites and speakers who once held traditional authority have very different roles (Errington 1998; Kuipers 1998). Yet the imagined identities thought to emerge from nationalist discourse are far from uncontested (Gal 2001; Silverstein 2000). An authoritative identity may also be constructed through the strategic use of linguistic markers of expertise, such as formal language and specialized jargon. In this way, in a much-publicized US court case in 1991, William Kennedy

Smith, a physician accused of rape, was able to position himself on the witness stand as simultaneously a medical expert and an (innocent) criminal defendant in order to respond persuasively to the accusation against him (Matoesian 1999).

But while authorization may depend on using language sanctioned by a hegemonic authority, legitimation is not always limited to those who control the most prestigious or powerful linguistic variety. In Senegal, the valorization of French is diminishing, despite its status as the official language of the state, and a hybrid form of Wolof is taking its place in practice if not in official ideology. This form of Wolof indexes an urban, sophisticated identity and is used in government, the informal economic sector, the media, and advertising; such uses may be understood to confer an "alternative legitimacy" on speakers of this variety (Swigart 2000: 91). Despite hegemonic structures, then, authorization is also a local practice that can contest as well as confirm dominant forms of power.

Similarly, illegitimation, or the process of removing or denying power, may operate either to support or to undermine hegemonic authority. In so far as every establishment of a standard or official language strips authority from those languages or varieties classified as non-standard or non-official, such language planning is an act of illegitimation as well as authorization, as shown by many researchers (e.g., Dorian 1989; Milroy 2000). On the other hand, illegitimation may also serve as a form of resistance to the state or another dominant authority. For example, a transnational language ideology that emphasizes the economic benefits of German allows German Hungarians to discount the local and national authority of the Hungarian language (Gal 1993). Thus, as also demonstrated by studies on the institutionalization of French in Canada (Heller 1999b) and of German dialect in Switzerland (Watts 1999), illegitimation may in turn result in a new set of authorizing practices.

7 CONCLUSION

In this chapter we have argued for the necessity of continued research on identity in linguistic anthropology. Despite a long history of scholarship that relies implicitly on identity to understand the relationship between language and culture, the field has only recently begun to address the topic overtly. The efflorescence of identity research in other fields, which informs and inspires recent work on language and identity, is an important resource for linguistic anthropologists; however, critiques of identity in our own discipline and others require that the analytic value of identity be made clear and that identity as a concept be more fully theorized.

The tactics of intersubjectivity that we propose here are meant to illuminate the motivations for identity work, in the same way that research on the semiotic processes of practice, indexicality, ideology, and performance helps to account for the mechanisms whereby identities are produced. Together, these two kinds of phenomena move us closer to a full picture of identity as the sociopolitical distillation of cultural processes. A working model of identity must accommodate such issues as markedness, essentialism, and institutional power as central components of identity. Such a model also addresses the critiques of language and identity research as well as the objections leveled against identity more generally by recognizing that sameness and difference, the raw material of identity, do not exist apart from the ideologies and practices through which they are constructed.

NOTES

Our thanks to Alessandro Duranti for his patience and insightful suggestions. We are also grateful to James Fernandez and to audiences at the conference on Lavender Languages and Linguistics in Washington, DC, and the International Gender and Language Association conference in Lancaster, to whom we first introduced a number of the ideas in this chapter.

1   For convenience, this chapter, following longstanding custom in linguistic anthropology and linguistics generally, refers primarily to speech and speakers, but these terms should also be understood to include other kinds of linguistic systems such as sign languages and writing, which are equally available for the construction of identity (Baquedano-López, this volume; LeMaster and Monaghan, this volume).

2   Although in this chapter we focus on the linguistic production of identity, the processes we describe are not restricted to language and may be carried out through other semiotic means as well. Indeed, even linguistic identity projects are often supported by non-linguistic identity work, as many of our illustrative examples show.

3   In fact, it is not clear if Kulick intends this conclusion to be drawn, given his own work on Brazilian transgendered prostitutes, which makes precisely such a link between social practices – including language – and identity (Kulick 1998). We discuss this and other problems with Kulick's critique of identity research at greater length elsewhere (Bucholtz and Hall 2004).

4   Here and elsewhere we use the collocation *ideologies and practices* as a shorthand for the complex set of semiotic processes described above.

5   Our framework owes a great deal to the work of Judith Irvine and Susan Gal, whose model of ideological processes inspires our own formulation of semiotics and social relations of identity.

REFERENCES

Ahearn, L. (2001). Language and Agency. *Annual Review of Anthropology* 30: 109–137.

Anderson, B. (1983). *Imagined Communities*. New York: Verso.

Austin, J. L. (1962). *How to Do Things with Words*. Cambridge, MA: Harvard University Press.

Bailey, B. (2000). The Language of Multiple Identities among Dominican Americans. *Journal of Linguistic Anthropology* 10(2): 190–223.

Barrett, R. (1999). Indexing Polyphonous Identity in the Speech of African American Drag Queens. In M. Bucholtz, A. C. Liang, and L. Sutton (eds.), *Reinventing Identities: The Gendered Self in Discourse* (pp. 313–331). New York: Oxford University Press.

Barth, F. (1986 [1972]). Ethnic Processes on the Pathan–Baluch boundary. In J. J. Gumperz and D. Hymes (eds.), *Directions in Sociolinguistics: The Ethnography of Communication* (pp. 454–464). Oxford: Blackwell.

Bauman, R. (1977). *Verbal Art as Performance*. Prospect Heights, IL: Waveland Press.

Bauman, R. (1986). *Story, Performance, and Event: Contextual Studies of Oral Narrative*. Cambridge: Cambridge University Press.

Bauman, R., and Briggs, C. L. (1990). Poetics and Performance as Critical Perspectives on Language and Social Life. *Annual Review of Anthropology* 19: 59–88.

Bauman, R., and Briggs, C. L. (2000). Language Philosophy as Language Ideology: John Locke and Johann Gottfried Herder. In P. V. Kroskrity (ed.), *Regimes of Language: Ideologies, Polities, and Identities* (pp. 139–204). Santa Fe, NM: School of American Research Press.

Behar, R., and Gordon, D. (eds.) (1995). *Women Writing Culture*. Berkeley: University of California Press.

Bell, A. (1984). Language Style as Audience Design. *Language in Society* 13: 145–204.

Bell, A. (1992). Hit and Miss: Referee Design in the Dialects of New Zealand Television Advertisements. *Language and Communication* 12(3/4): 327–340.

Bing, J. M., and Bergvall, V. L. (1996). The Question of Questions: Beyond Binary Thinking. In V. L. Bergvall, J. M. Bing, and A. F. Freed (eds.), *Rethinking Language and Gender Research: Theory and Practice* (pp. 1–30). London: Longman.

Blommaert, J. (ed.) (1999). *Language Ideological Debates*. Berlin: Mouton de Gruyter.

Bourdieu, P. (1977a [1972]). *Outline of a Theory of Practice* (trans. R. Nice). Cambridge: Cambridge University Press.

Bourdieu, P. (1977b). The Economics of Linguistic Exchanges. *Social Science Information* 16(6): 645–668.

Bourdieu, P. (1984). *Distinction: A Social Critique of the Judgment of Taste*. Cambridge, MA: Harvard University Press.

Briggs, C. L. (1986). *Learning How to Ask: A Sociolinguistic Appraisal of the Role of the Interview in Social Science Research*. Cambridge: Cambridge University Press.

Bucholtz, M. (1996). Black Feminist Theory and African American Women's Linguistic Practice. In V. L. Bergvall, J. M. Bing, and A. F. Freed (eds.), *Rethinking Language and Gender Research: Theory and Practice* (pp. 267–290). London: Longman.

Bucholtz, M. (1999). "Why Be Normal?": Language and Identity Practices in a Community of Nerd Girls. *Language in Society* 28(2): 203–223.

Bucholtz, M. (2001). The Whiteness of Nerds: Superstandard English and Racial Markedness. *Journal of Linguistic Anthropology* 11(1): 84–100.

Bucholtz, M., and Hall, K. (1995). Introduction: Twenty Years after *Language and Woman's Place*. In K. Hall and M. Bucholtz (eds.), *Gender Articulated: Language and the Socially Constructed Self* (pp. 1–22). New York: Routledge.

Bucholtz, M., and Hall, K. (2004). Theorizing Identity in Language and Sexuality Research. *Language in Society*.

Bucholtz, M., and Trechter, S. (eds.) (2001). *Journal of Linguistic Anthropology* 11(1). Special Issue: Discourses of Whiteness.

Butler, J. (1990). *Gender Trouble: Feminism and the Subversion of Identity*. New York: Routledge.

Cameron, D. (1996). The Language–Gender Interface: Challenging Co-optation. In V. L. Bergvall, J. M. Bing, and A. F. Freed (eds.), *Rethinking Language and Gender Research: Theory and Practice* (pp. 31–53). London: Longman.

Certeau, M. de (1984 [1974]). *The Practice of Everyday Life* (trans. S. Rendall). Berkeley: University of California Press.

Clifford, J., and Marcus, G. E. (eds.) (1986). *Writing Culture: The Poetics and Politics of Ethnography*. Berkeley: University of California Press.

Crawford, M. (1995). *Talking Difference: On Gender and Language*. Thousand Oaks, CA: Sage.

Dorian, N. C. (ed.) (1989). *Investigating Obsolescence: Studies in Language Contraction and Death*. Cambridge: Cambridge University Press.

Duranti, A. (1992). Language in Context and Language as Context: The Samoan Respect Vocabulary. In A. Duranti and C. Goodwin (eds.), *Rethinking Context: Language as an Interactive Phenomenon* (pp. 77–99). Cambridge: Cambridge University Press.

Duranti, A. (1994). *From Grammar to Politics: Linguistic Anthropology in a Western Samoan Village*. Berkeley: University of California Press.

Eckert, P. (1989). The Whole Woman: Sex and Gender Differences in Variation. *Language Variation and Change* 1: 245–267.

Eckert, P. (2000). *Linguistic Variation as Social Practice*. Oxford: Blackwell.

Eckert, P., and McConnell-Ginet, S. (1992). Think Practically and Look Locally: Language and Gender as Community-based Practice. *Annual Review of Anthropology* 21: 461–490.

Eckert, P., and McConnell-Ginet, S. (1995). Constructing Meaning, Constructing Selves: Snapshots of Language, Gender, and Class from Belten High. In K. Hall and M. Bucholtz (eds.), *Gender Articulated: Language and the Socially Constructed Self* (pp. 469–507). New York: Routledge.

Errington, J. (1998). *Shifting Languages: Interaction and Identity in Javanese Indonesia*. Cambridge: Cambridge University Press.

Fishman, J. A. (ed.) (1999). *The Handbook of Language and Ethnic Identity.* New York: Oxford University Press.

French, B. M. (2000). The Symbolic Capital of Social Identities: The Genre of Bargaining in an Urban Guatemalan Market. *Journal of Linguistic Anthropology* 10(2): 155–189.

Gal, S. (1978). Peasant Men Can't Get Wives: Language Change and Sex Roles in a Bilingual Community. *Language in Society* 7: 1–16.

Gal, S. (1991). Between Speech and Silence: The Problematics of Research on Language and Gender. In M. DiLeonardo (ed.), *Gender at the Crossroads of Knowledge: Toward a New Anthropology of Gender*. Berkeley: University of California Press.

Gal, S. (1993). Diversity and Contestation in Linguistic Ideologies: German Speakers in Hungary. *Language in Society* 22(3): 337–359.

Gal, S. (1995). Language, Gender, and Power: An Anthropological Review. In K. Hall and M. Bucholtz (eds.), *Gender Articulated: Language and the Socially Constructed Self* (pp. 169–182). New York: Routledge.

Gal, S. (2001). Linguistic Theories and National Images in Nineteenth-century Hungary. In S. Gal and K. A. Woolard (eds.), *Languages and Publics: The Making of Authority* (pp. 30–45). Manchester: St. Jerome.

Gellner, E. (1983). *Nations and Nationalism*. Ithaca: Cornell University Press.

Giles, H., and Smith, P. (1979). Accommodation Theory: Optimal Levels of Convergence. In H. Giles and R. N. St. Clair (eds.), *Language and Social Psychology* (pp. 45–65). Oxford: Blackwell.

Goodwin, M. H. (1990). *He-Said-She-Said: Talk as Social Organization Among Black Children*. Bloomington: Indiana University Press.

Hall, K. (1995). Lipservice on the Fantasy Lines. In K. Hall and M. Bucholtz (eds.), *Gender Articulated: Language and the Socially Constructed Self* (pp. 183–216). New York: Routledge.

Hall, K. (1996). Cyberfeminism. In S. C. Herring (ed.), *Computer-mediated Communication: Linguistic, Social, and Cross-cultural Perspectives* (pp. 147–170). Amsterdam: John Benjamins.

Hall, K. (2003). Exceptional Speakers: Contested and Problematized Gender Identities. In J. Holmes and M. Meyerhoff (eds.), *The Handbook of Language and Gender*. Oxford: Blackwell.

Hall, K., and O'Donovan, V. (1996). Shifting Gender Positions among Hindi-Speaking Hijras. In V. L. Bergvall, J. M. Bing, and A. F. Freed (eds.), *Rethinking Language and Gender Research: Theory and Practice* (pp. 228–266). London: Longman.

Harrison, F. V. (ed.) (1988). *Urban Anthropology* 17(2/3). Special Issue: Black Folks in Cities Here and There: Changing Patterns of Domination and Response.

Harrison, F. V. (1995). The Persistent Power of "Race" in the Cultural and Political Economy of Racism. *Annual Review of Anthropology* 24: 47–74.

Haviland, J. B. (1996). Owners versus Bubu Gujin: Land Rights and Getting the Language Right in Guugu Yimithirr Country. *Journal of Linguistic Anthropology* 6(2): 145–160.

Heller, M. (1999a). *Linguistic Minorities and Modernity: A Sociolinguistic Ethnography.* London: Longman.

Heller, M. (1999b). Heated Language in a Cold Climate. In J. Blommaert (ed.), *Language Ideological Debates* (pp. 143–170). Berlin: Mouton de Gruyter.

Herdt, G. (1997). *Same Sex, Different Cultures: Gays and Lesbians across Cultures.* Boulder, CO: Westview Press.

Herzfeld, M. (1996). National Spirit or Breath of Nature? The Expropriation of Folk Positivism in the Discourse of Greek Nationalism. In M. Silverstein and G. Urban (eds.), *Natural Histories of Discourse* (pp. 277–298). Chicago: University of Chicago Press.

Hill, J. H. (1995). Mock Spanish: A Site for the Indexical Reproduction of Racism in American English. Language–Culture Symposium 2, October 9. <http://www.language-culture.org/colloquia/symposia/hill-jane/>

Hill, J. H., and Hill, K. C. (1986). *Speaking Mexicano: Dynamics of a Syncretic Language in Central Mexico.* Tucson: University of Arizona Press.

Hornberger, N. H. (1998). Language Policy, Language Education, Language Rights: Indigenous, Immigrant, and International Perspectives. *Language in Society* 27(4): 439–458.

Hymes, D. (1975). Breakthrough into Performance. In D. Ben-Amos and K. S. Goldstein (eds.), *Folklore: Performance and Communication* (pp. 11–74). The Hague: Mouton.

Irvine, J. T. (1989 [1974]). Strategies of Status Manipulation in the Wolof Greeting. In R. Bauman and J. Sherzer (eds.), *Explorations in the Ethnography of Speaking,* 2nd edn. (pp. 167–191). Cambridge: Cambridge University Press.

Irvine, J. T. (2001a). The Family Romance of Colonial Linguistics: Gender and Family in Nineteenth-century Representations of African Languages. In S. Gal and K. A. Woolard (eds.), *Languages and Publics: The Making of Authority* (pp. 13–29). Manchester: St. Jerome.

Irvine, J. T. (2001b). "Style" as Distinctiveness: The Culture and Ideology of Linguistic Differentiation. In P. Eckert and J. R. Rickford (eds.), *Style and Sociolinguistic Variation* (pp. 21–43). Cambridge: Cambridge University Press.

Irvine, J. T., and Gal, S. (2000). Language Ideology and Linguistic Differentiation. In P. V. Kroskrity (ed.), *Regimes of Language: Ideologies, Polities, and Identities* (pp. 35–84). Santa Fe, NM: School of American Research Press.

Jacobs-Huey, L. (1997). Is There an Authentic African American Speech Community? Carla Revisited. *University of Pennsylvania Working Papers in Linguistics* 4(1): 331–370.

Jaffe, A. (1999). *Ideologies in Action: Language Politics on Corsica.* Berlin: Mouton de Gruyter.

Keating, E. (1998). *Power Sharing: Language, Rank, Gender, and Social Space in Pohnpei, Micronesia.* New York: Oxford University Press.

Keenan, E. (1989 [1974]). Norm-Makers, Norm-Breakers: Uses of Speech by Men and Women in a Malagasy Community. In R. Bauman and J. Sherzer (eds.), *Explorations in the Ethnography of Speaking,* 2nd edn. (pp. 125–143). Cambridge: Cambridge University Press.

Keita, S. O. Y., and Kittles, R. A. (1997). The Persistence of Racial Thinking and the Myth of Racial Divergence. *American Anthropologist* 99(3): 534–544.

King, C. R. (1994). *One Language, Two Scripts: The Hindi Movement in Nineteenth-Century North India.* New Delhi: Oxford University Press.

Kochman, T. (1981). *Black and White Styles in Conflict.* Chicago: University of Chicago Press.

Kroskrity, P. (2000a). Language Ideologies in the Expression and Representation of Arizona Tewa Ethnic Identity. In P. V. Kroskrity (ed.), *Regimes of Language: Ideologies, Polities, and Identities* (pp. 329–359). Santa Fe, NM: School of American Research Press.

Kroskrity, P. V. (ed.) (2000b). *Regimes of Language: Ideologies, Polities, and Identities.* Santa Fe, NM: School of American Research Press.

Kuipers, J. C. (1998). *Language, Identity, and Marginality in Indonesia.* Cambridge: Cambridge University Press.

Kulick, D. (1998). *Travesti.* Chicago: University of Chicago Press.

Kulick, D. (1999). Language and Gender/Sexuality. Paper presented at the Sixth Language and Culture Online Symposium. http://www.language-culture.org/colloquia/symposia/kulick-don/

Kulick, D. (2000). Gay and Lesbian Language. *Annual Review of Anthropology* 29: 243–285.

Kulick, D. (2002). Queer Linguistics? In K. Campbell-Kibler, R. J. Podesva, S. J. Roberts, and A. Wong (eds.), *Language and Sexuality: Contesting Meaning in Theory and Practice* (pp. 65–68). Stanford: CSLI Publications.

Kulick, D. (2003). Language and Desire. In J. Holmes and M. Meyerhoff (eds.), *The Handbook of Language and Gender.* Oxford: Blackwell.

Kulick, D., and Willson, M. (eds.) (1995). *Taboo: Sex, Identity and Erotic Subjectivity in Anthropological Fieldwork.* New York: Routledge.

Labov, W. (1973). The Linguistic Consequences of Being a Lame. *Language in Society* 2(1): 81–115.

Labov, W. (1980). Is There a Creole Speech Community? In A. Valdman and A. Highfield (eds.), *Theoretical Orientations in Creole Studies* (pp. 369–388). New York: Academic Press.

Lakoff, R. (1975). *Language and Women's Place.* New York: Harper & Row.

Lave, J., and Wenger, E. (1991). *Situated Learning: Legitimate Peripheral Participation.* Cambridge: Cambridge University Press.

Le Page, R. B., and Tabouret-Keller, A. (1985). *Acts of Identity: Creole-based Approaches to Language and Ethnicity.* Cambridge: Cambridge University Press.

Livia, A., and Hall, K. (eds.) (1997). *Queerly Phrased: Language, Gender, and Sexuality.* New York: Oxford University Press.

Marcus, G. E. (ed.) (1999). *Critical Anthropology Now: Unexpected Contexts, Shifting Constituencies, Changing Agendas.* Santa Fe, NM: School of American Research Press.

Matoesian, G. M. (1999). The Grammaticalization of Participant Roles in the Constitution of Expert Identity. *Language in Society* 28(4): 491–521.

McElhinny, B. (1996). Strategic Essentialism in Sociolinguistic Studies of Gender. In N. Warner, J. Ahlers, L. Bilmes, et al. (eds.), *Gender and Belief Systems: Proceedings of the Fourth Berkeley Women and Language Conference* (pp. 469–480). Berkeley: Berkeley Women and Language Group.

McElhinny, B. (1998). Genealogies of Gender Theory: Practice Theory and Feminism in Sociocultural and Linguistic Anthropology. *Social Analysis* 42(3): 164–189.

Mendoza-Denton, N. (1996). "Muy macha": Gender and Ideology in Gang-Girls' Discourse about Makeup. *Ethnos* 61(1/2): 47–63.

Mendoza-Denton, N. (2002). Language and Identity. In J. K. Chambers, P. Trudgill, and N. Schilling-Estes (eds.), *The Handbook of Language Variation and Change* (pp. 475–499). Oxford: Blackwell.

Milroy, L. (2000). Britain and the United States: Two Nations Divided by the Same Language (and Different Language Ideologies). *Journal of Linguistic Anthropology* 10(1): 56–89.

Morgan, M. (1994). Theories and Politics in African American English. *Annual Review of Anthropology* 23: 325–345.

Morgan, M. (forthcoming). *Language and Verbal Style in African American Culture.* Cambridge: Cambridge University Press.

Ochs, E. (1992). Indexing Gender. In A. Duranti and C. Goodwin (eds.), *Rethinking Context: Language as an Interactive Phenomenon* (pp. 335–358). Cambridge: Cambridge University Press.

Ochs, E., and Capps, L. (1996). Narrating the Self. *Annual Review of Anthropology* 25: 19–43.

Ochs, E., and Schieffelin, B. B. (1995). The Impact of Language Socialization on Grammatical Development. In P. Fletcher and B. MacWhinney (eds.), *The Handbook of Child Language* (pp. 73–94). Oxford: Blackwell.

Pagliai, V., and Farr, M. (eds.) (2000). *Pragmatics* 10(1). Special Issue: Art and the Expression of Complex Identities: Imagining and Contesting Ethnicity in Performance.

Paulston, C. B. (1997). Language Policies and Language Rights. *Annual Review of Anthropology* 26: 73–85.

Philips, S. U., Steele, S., and Tanz, C. (eds.) (1987). *Language, Gender and Sex in Comparative Perspective.* Cambridge: Cambridge University Press.

Ramaswamy, S. (1998). *Passions of the Tongue: Language Devotion in Tamil India, 1891–1970.* Berkeley: University of California Press.

Sapir, E. (1949). Why Cultural Anthropology Needs the Psychiatrist. In D. G. Mandelbaum (ed.), *Selected Writings of Edward Sapir in Language, Culture, and Personality* (pp. 569–577). Berkeley: University of California Press.

Sapir, E. (1994). *The Psychology of Culture: A Course of Lectures* (ed. J. T. Irvine). Berlin: Mouton de Gruyter.

Schieffelin, B. B., and Ochs, E. (eds.) (1986). *Language Socialization across Cultures.* Cambridge: Cambridge University Press.

Schieffelin, B. B., Woolard, K. A., and Kroskrity, P. V. (eds.) (1998). *Language Ideologies: Practice and Theory.* New York: Oxford University Press.

Silverstein, M. (1985). Language and the Culture of Gender: At the Intersection of Structure, Usage, and Ideology. In E. Mertz and R. J. Parmentier (eds.), *Semiotic Mediation: Sociocultural and Psychological Perspectives* (pp. 219–259). Orlando, FL: Academic Press.

Silverstein, M. (1996). Encountering Languages and Languages of Encounter in North American Ethnohistory. *Journal of Linguistic Anthropology* 6(2): 126–144.

Silverstein, M. (2000). Whorfianism and the Linguistic Imagination of Nationality. In P. V. Kroskrity (ed.), *Regimes of Language: Ideologies, Polities, and Identities* (pp. 85–138). Santa Fe, NM: School of American Research Press.

Spitulnik, D. (1998). Mediating Unity and Diversity: The Production of Language Ideologies in Zambian Broadcasting. In B. B. Schieffelin, K. A. Woolard, and P. V. Kroskrity (eds.), *Language Ideologies: Practice and Theory* (pp. 163–188). New York: Oxford University Press.

Spivak, G. (1995). Subaltern Studies: Deconstructing Historiography. In D. Landry and G. MacLean (eds.), *The Spivak Reader.* New York: Routledge.

Swigart, L. (2000). The Limits of Legitimacy: Language Ideology and Shift in Contemporary Senegal. *Journal of Linguistic Anthropology* 10(1): 90–130.

Trechter, S. (1999). Contextualizing the Exotic Few: Gender Dichotomies in Lakhota. In M. Bucholtz, A. C. Liang, and L. A. Sutton (eds.), *Reinventing Identities: The Gendered Self in Discourse* (pp. 101–119). New York: Oxford University Press.

Trechter, S. (2003). A Marked Man: The Contexts of Gender and Ethnicity. In J. Holmes and M. Meyerhoff (eds.), *The Handbook of Language and Gender.* Oxford: Blackwell.

Trechter, S., and Bucholtz, M. (2001). White Noise: Bringing Language into Whiteness Studies. *Journal of Linguistic Anthropology* 11(1): 3–21.

Twine, F. W., and Warren, J. W. (eds.) (2000). *Racing Research, Researching Race: Methodological Dilemmas in Critical Race Studies.* New York: New York University Press.

Urciuoli, B. (1995). Language and Borders. *Annual Review of Anthropology* 24: 525–546.

Urciuoli, B. (1996). *Exposing Prejudice: Puerto Rican Experiences of Language, Race, and Class.* Boulder, CO: Westview Press.

Urla, J. (2001). Outlaw Language: Creating Alternative Public Spheres in Basque Free Radio. In S. Gal and K. A. Woolard (eds.), *Languages and Publics: The Making of Authority* (pp. 141–163). Manchester: St. Jerome.

Visweswaran, K. (1994). *Fictions of Feminist Ethnography.* Minneapolis: University of Minnesota Press.

Watts, R. (1999). The Ideology of Dialect in Switzerland. In J. Blommaert (ed.), *Language Ideological Debates* (pp. 67–103). Berlin: Mouton de Gruyter.

Wenger, E. (1998). *Communities of Practice.* Cambridge: Cambridge University Press.

Weston, K. (1998). *Longslowburn: Sexuality and Social Science.* New York: Routledge.

Woolard, K. A. (1998a). Introduction: Language Ideology as a Field of Inquiry. In B. B. Schieffelin, K. A. Woolard, and P. V. Kroskrity (eds.), *Language Ideologies: Practice and Theory* (pp. 3–47). New York: Oxford University Press.

Woolard, K. A. (1998b). Simultaneity and Bivalency as Strategies in Bilingualism. *Journal of Linguistic Anthropology* 8(1): 3–29.

Wortham, S. (2001). *Narratives in Action: A Strategy for Research and Analysis.* New York: Teachers College Press.

Benjamin Bailey

1 INTRODUCTION

A degree of intersubjective understanding is the foundation of social life. It represents a link between conscious minds in distinct bodies, and it is implicit in the achievement of coordinated social action and the constitution of larger social structures and institutions. Language, our primary symbolic medium, is intertwined with the achievement of understanding, and language-in-use is itself an exemplar of coordinated social action.

The fact that we regularly coordinate social action in our daily lives can make understanding seem transparent and a natural condition. It is when we *mis*understand each other – when we encounter "problems" in interaction or undesirable consequences of interactions – that we examine the process of understanding. Examining *mis*understanding can thus help to illuminate processes of understanding by rescuing them from an underanalyzed naturalness.

As a marked form – the negation of the affirmative "understanding" – misunderstanding points to an implicit ideology of communication: that to "understand" is normal, and to "misunderstand" represents a breakdown or failure of something that is natural. The positive value assigned to understanding veils the conflict, ambiguity, and uncertainty that are part-and-parcel of social and communicative worlds. This ideology backgrounds the material and political conflicts that are inherent in a socially and economically stratified world, serving the interests of those who would portray the status quo as equitable and harmonious.

While folk notions of communication and understanding center on referential, or propositional, meanings, misunderstandings at this level are relatively easily recognized as such and are commonly repaired by interlocutors. In the following segment, for example, interlocutors quickly attend to a problematic reference to A's employer, and clarify it:

(1) (adapted from Schegloff, Jefferson, and Sacks 1977: 368):
A: Well I'm working through the Amfat Corporation.

B: The *who?*
A: Amfah Corporation. T's a holding company.
B: Oh.

The very frequency and distinctive structure of such everyday conversational repair procedures highlights our ability to achieve a degree of intersubjective understanding (Schegloff 1992). Misunderstandings along more pragmatic dimensions of communication, in contrast, are often more persistent, confounding, and linked to debilitated social relationships.

Analysis of inter-group misunderstanding provides a window onto the workings of larger-scale social processes and relationships. Notions of understanding are commonly seen as undergirding social commonalty, i.e. common social identities, while misunderstanding is seen as both a cause and an emblem of social difference. By looking at misunderstandings in interactions across boundaries of apparent social difference (e.g. race or culture) we can see some of the ways in which power, culture, and social identities are negotiated through talk and social interaction.

In this chapter, I first address questions of what it means to understand, highlighting the impossibility of complete intersubjectivity and reviewing communicative practices through which a degree of intersubjective understanding is constituted. I then review several non-referential levels of meaning and activity in talk and interaction that are central to pragmatic notions of understanding. Everyday communicative behavior includes multiple levels and dimensions of meaning-making and interpretation, which means that understanding and misunderstanding are neither monolithic nor entirely discrete. Finally I consider how "misunderstanding" or "miscommunication" has been addressed in two strands of research in inter-cultural and inter-gender communication. In the first of these strands of research, misunderstandings are explained as communicative phenomena resulting from cultural and linguistic differences between groups. In the second of these traditions, misunderstandings are seen as local, linguistic enactments of larger-scale, pre-existing conflicts. In both types of analysis, communicative behavior at the local level is linked to social relationships and structure at a larger level, making such analyses of particular interest for students of culture and communication.

2   UNDERSTANDING

Everyday notions of understanding assume that conscious minds that exist in separate bodies can experience an intersubjective link. At the most fundamental level, "understanding" and "misunderstanding" are about the nature of this intersubjective connection. To what extent can two minds share a common perspective, idea, experience, or emotion? The notion of an intersubjective link can be difficult to reconcile with the individualist theories of person and mind that are common in Western cultures. The individualist perspective privileges the privacy, inviolability, and continuity of the individual's mind, conditions which are at odds with the idea of intersubjective understandings.

Language is popularly conceptualized as a symbolic means of overcoming this isolation and linking individual minds, and in many ways it serves this function.

The human capacity for the use of signs that bear arbitrary, conventional connections to meanings enables our communicative interactions ranging from using sign language, to reading, to verbal talk. Words, for example, are a powerful reference system for invoking aspects of the world. The arbitrary nature of the relationship between a string of phonemes, e.g. /kæt/ 'cat', and a mental representation of an entity in the world makes language an extremely compact, convenient, and flexible semiotic system. This referential, or propositional, character of language has long been the subject of attention of formal linguists (e.g. Lyons 1977) and of philosophers interested in logic and truth-values.

The referential power of language and our faculty for its use (Chomsky 1977; Pinker 1994) are not sufficient, in and of themselves, to ensure intersubjective understandings, however. What a given person understands by the word "cat," for example, may be very different from what another person understands by it. A veterinary surgeon, a child keeping a cat as a pet, the bird-loving neighbor of cats, and a pet shop owner may all have different understandings of "cat." Even for a single actor, the meaning of "cat" will vary across contexts according to his/her practical purposes in using the term; for example, "Did you feed the cat?" versus "Cats are mammals" (cf. Schutz 1962: 21).

These differences in perspective on "cat" are a result of the inherently individual, subjective perception and structuring of the world. From a phenomenological perspective, our mental worlds are not reflections of an independently existing reality, but are constituted through our individual acts of consciousness (Husserl 1970 [1901]). Given individual and situational differences in subjective structuring and experiencing of the world, no two individuals share identical perspectives or understanding of any subjectively constituted phenomenon, including linguistic signs. Communication via linguistic and other signs can thus only approximate an absolute form of understanding. While the word "cat," for example, may provoke *similar* constitutive acts of consciousness in two individuals, it will not provoke identical ones:

> 'Intended meaning' is therefore essentially subjective and is in principle confined to the self-interpretation of the person who lives through the experience to be interpreted. Constituted as it is within the unique stream of consciousness of each individual, *it is essentially inaccessible to every other individual.* (Schutz 1967 [1932]: 99)

Intersubjectivity, as an ideal form of understanding, in which subjective experiences are held in common, is impossible. Thus, even when participants in an interaction – and analytical observers of that interaction – find no evidence of "misunderstanding," the understandings that do occur are necessarily incomplete or partial.

While intersubjective understanding is impossible as an ideal form, we know that we constantly and successfully approximate understanding as we lead our lives. We greet our neighbors, talk to our bosses, and give advice to friends. Following Husserl (1970 [1901]) and Schutz (1967), Garfinkel (1967) and ethnomethodologically oriented researchers have conceptualized intersubjectivity and understanding precisely in terms of such everyday, practical action. Approaching intersubjectivity in terms of social activity helps to avoid the theoretical impasse posed by the impossibility of intersubjectivity as an ideal type. From this ethnomethodological perspective, the goal of the researcher is to explore the means by which interlocutors coordinate the social actions of which intersubjectivity is a characteristic. Thus, understanding is not an independent state that precedes and affords coordinated social action, but rather a dimension of coordinated social action itself: "The appropriate image of a common understanding is therefore an operation rather than a common intersection of overlapping sets" (Garfinkel 1967: 30). Thus, understanding is not a state or condition in which minds have common content – or pass information back and forth, as in a conduit metaphor (Reddy 1979) for communication – but rather a contingent dimension of particular communicative activities and procedures.

Conversation analysts (see Goodwin and Heritage 1990 for a review) have approached everyday conversation as just such a form of coordinated social action. In analyzing the structures and patterns of this coordinated action, they identify a structural basis of intersubjectivity. In their seminal piece on turn-taking in everyday conversation, for example, Sacks, Schegloff, and Jefferson (1974) identify *turns* as a fundamental unit of social interaction and coordinated social activity. Because everyday talk proceeds on a turn-by-turn basis, interactions are built up *incrementally, sequentially,* and *interactionally.*

This turn-by-turn process of building a conversation can be likened to individuals jointly building a column of wooden blocks. The building of the column is incremental (with blocks as units) and sequential, with blocks higher in the column placed after those that are lower in the column. The building of the column is also necessarily interactional, in that each person's placement of a block is made with reference to previously placed blocks, and each newly placed block simultaneously shapes future block placements.

Building a conversation, like building a tower of blocks, is a sequential, interactional project, in which turns at talk are *doubly contextual* (Heritage 1984: 242). Each turn at talk depends for its interpretation on the context created by prior utterances, while at the same time each utterance creates a new context in which subsequent turns and social action will be understood.

The orientation of turns to immediately prior ones is crucial to achieving a degree of intersubjectivity, because it is a means for interlocutors to display incremental understandings of ongoing talk. In the following sequence, for example, a mother's turn displays her understanding of her child's initial turn as a *summons* to attract her attention:

(2) (adapted from Atkinson and Drew 1979: 46)
Child: Mummy
Mother: Yes dear.
Child: I want a cloth to clean the windows.

The child's second turn ("I want a cloth . . . ") similarly displays an implicit understanding of the mother's immediately preceding turn: by proceeding with a request, the child treats the mother's turn as a satisfactory response to the child's initial summons. There is thus a continuously updated, and incremental, display of understandings at each turn in the conversation (Heritage and Atkinson 1984: 11). It is through the step-by-step structure of turns that interlocutors negotiate and approximate common understandings of the activities in which they are engaged.

The incremental and interactional structuring of conversation provides participants with regular opportunities to *repair* or head-off potential misunderstandings (Schegloff, Jefferson, and Sacks 1977). Repair includes a range of techniques used by both parties in interaction to resolve what they perceive as some problematic aspect of the talk. This repair can be initiated by speaker or hearer, and the repair itself, for example the correction of a name on the repetition of a phrase, can be executed by either the speaker or a hearer of the problematic bit of talk.

In the following bit of talk, for example, Louise uses her turn to draw attention to a potentially problematic aspect of Ken's first turn, his use of the word "selling." Ken then uses his subsequent turn, the third in the segment, to repair the problem to which Louise had alluded:

(3) (adapted from Jefferson 1987: 86)
Ken: Hey, the first time they stopped me from selling cigarettes was this morning.
Louise: From selling cigarettes?
Ken: Or buying cigarettes.

The turn-by-turn structuring of talk, in which turns both display interpretations of prior turns and project future ones, affords this interactive, joint construction of meanings. This example also points to the sociocultural matrix of knowledge and practices of which social interaction is a part. Although Ken's initial turn is well-formed grammatically and semantically, Louise finds the proposition that it expresses problematic. Louise's initiation of repair is based not on linguistic knowledge as such, but on social knowledge: of Ken, of buying and selling cigarettes, and/or of the activities in which this utterance is produced. Paradoxically, Louise appears to have "understood" a meaning of Ken's initial utterance that was directly contrary to the conventional meaning of the words that he was using. It is only through such prior, sociocultural understanding that Louise could initiate repair on the phrase "from selling cigarettes." At the same time, however, this sociocultural knowledge (that Ken meant "buying") does not obviate the need for a repair procedure. In this case, sociocultural knowledge is activated and a local conversational repair procedure is initiated, which allows interlocutors to achieve a joint construction of meaning and understanding.

Even when a turn at talk is not explicitly problematic, interlocutors do repair-like work to display and confirm understandings of their ongoing talk. In the following segment, Marcia explains to her husband that her son cannot drive home because the top of his (convertible) car was "ripped off." The phrase "ripped off" could mean "stolen" or it could refer to the kind of tearing that might happen to a convertible car's fabric top. All three of the turns in this sequence display possible efforts to disambiguate the phrase "ripped off" and to thereby achieve a common understanding.

(4) (adapted from Schegloff 1992: 1302)
Marcia: Because the top was ripped off of his car, which is to say somebody helped
          themselves.

Tony: Stolen.
Marcia: Stolen. Right out in front of my house.

In her first turn, Marcia clarifies her use of "ripped off" by specifying "somebody helped themselves," which helps make clear that the top of the car wasn't torn off by some accident. In his turn, Tony displays an even more specific candidate understanding ("Stolen") of Marcia's turn, in repair-like form, and in her final turn, Marcia confirms this candidate understanding ("Stolen. Right out ...''). The task of achieving a degree of understanding is an omnipresent one, and interlocutors regularly do work to make it possible, even in the absence of apparent errors or misunderstandings.

In examples (3) and (4), aspects of new information that speakers were presenting were treated as potentially problematic: Ken's use of "selling" and Marcia's use of the ambiguous "ripped off." As described above, however, turns at talk not only present new information and project future action, they also display understandings of prior turns. Repair can also thus be directed at the dimension of a turn that displays a potentially problematic understanding of a prior turn.

Such initiation of repair on displays of (potential) misunderstanding typically occurs in the turn immediately following the problematic display (Schegloff 1992). In the following segment of interaction, for example, a caller to a radio show expresses fear about driving over a bridge. Repair is initiated by the radio host in the fourth turn, based on a potentially problematic display of understanding in the third turn.

(5) (adapted from Schegloff 1987: 211)
Caller: I have fears of driving over a bridge. And seems I just can't uh- if I ever have to
           cross a bridge, I just don't (do the) trip at all.
Host: What are you afraid of?
Caller: I don't know, see uh-
Host: Well, I mean wait a minute. What kind of fear is it? Are you afraid you're going
           to drive off the edge? Are you afraid that you're going to get hit while you're on
           it?
Caller: Off the edge or something.

The radio host's "What are you afraid of?" could be interpreted as either (a) a rhetorical question that is a reprimand for having irrational fears, or (b) a request for the details of the feeling of fear. When the caller's response ("I don't know...") suggests that the question is interpreted as a reprimand, the host takes action ("wait a minute. What kind of fear is it? ... ") to engender a different kind of sequence, one in which the caller will specify a type of fear.

Because interlocutors display their (mis)understandings of prior turns to each other on an ongoing, turn-by-turn basis, they have an opportunity at each turn to confirm or make problematic the understanding that has just been displayed. These built-in locations for self-righting in talk enable interlocutors to coordinate their talk and achieve a degree of intersubjective understanding. Paradoxically, talk that is treated by participants as containing (potential) misunderstandings clearly illustrates the self-righting processes in talk of which intersubjective understanding is a dimension.

3   LEVELS OF (MIS)UNDERSTANDING

> The number of ambiguities associated with the notion of "understanding another person" becomes even greater when we bring in the question of understanding the signs he is using. On the one hand, what is understood is the sign itself, then again *what* the other person means by using this sign, and finally the significance of the fact *that* he is using the sign, here, now, and in this particular context. (Schutz 1967: 102)

Communicative behavior is inherently polysemous and multi-functional, and speakers engage in multiple activities, at multiple levels, as they speak (Goodwin 1981). In the above quote, Schutz suggests three levels at which understanding (and presumably misunderstanding) takes place. The first level, "the sign itself," corresponds roughly to the referential meaning of language; the second level, what a "person means by using this sign," is similar to the level of activity addressed by philosophers of language in speech act theory and related traditions; and the third level, "the significance of the fact *that* he is using the sign, here, now, and in this particular context," links understanding to a broader range of sociocultural meanings and sociohistorical relations among people. In this section, I focus on the second of these levels of meaning or understanding, with some overlap into the third.

In the three examples of repair given above, interlocutors were *oriented* toward each other's words – they displayed understanding of those words – but they were also oriented toward what their interlocutors were *doing* with words. In example (5), for example, the fundamental issue that needed clarifying was not the words used by the radio host, but the activity in which he was engaged. Was he (a) reprimanding, or (b) relatively sympathetically asking for details?

Such seeming disjuncture between the literal meanings of words or utterances, and what interlocutors treat them as doing, are not uncommon. Indirect requests, for example, regularly take the form of questions about a state of knowledge ("Do you know what time it is?"), but they are generally treated as requests for action (in this case, to tell the asker the time). This discrepancy between propositional meanings and interactional behavior suggests the need for units of analysis other than words. Philosophers, anthropologists, and sociologists have proposed overlapping ways of conceptualizing some of the utterance- and discourse-level activities in which speakers engage.

Philosopher John Austin (1962), in his theory of performatives, focused on the social action inherent in utterances. Austin argued that when we speak, we are not just describing, or reporting on, the world, we are also *doing* an activity. Thus when we say "Be careful!" we are not just talking about a pre-existing world, we are doing something, namely, warning a person. Thus, besides conventional meanings based on propositional content, our utterances have particular forces rooted in the activity (e.g. warnings) that they instantiate as well as potential wider social effects, depending on social circumstances (see also Searle 1969 for related speech act theory). Philosopher Ludwig Wittgenstein uses the metaphor of "language game," which emphasizes the social situatedness of the activities in which we engage when we speak. The metaphor of game captures the sense of social rules and roles and unconscious practices that we follow in everyday talk and interaction, just as players in a game negotiate a playing field within a certain set of accepted rules or procedures.

In anthropology, Dell Hymes (1972: 56) defined a unit of analysis, the "speech event," as "activities, or aspects of activities that are directly governed by rules or norms for the use of speech." The speech event is a social unit, emphasizing that we do not just speak to describe the world but that we engage in social and cultural activities through speech. In conversation analysis, the units of analysis, such as turns and sequences, have been interactionally achieved activities, rather than words themselves. In analyses of misunderstandings in conversation analysis, it is difficulties in coordinating sequences, rather than understanding words, which is presented as the source of problems (Schegloff 1987; Whalen, Zimmerman, and Whalen 1988). Each of these analytical traditions has emphasized the activity(ies) inherent in talk and interaction, shifting attention from referential and purely ideational functions of language to the activities of human agents, and, to varying degrees, the sociocultural embeddedness of these activities.

As argued by Schutz in the above quote, the ambiguities inherent to signs become even greater when we consider what a person is doing with those signs, the communicative activities in which he/she is engaging. Sequences of interactional behavior do not have one, unambiguous, explicit meaning, and activities that are very similar in form can have very different meanings and implications. What differentiates a wink from a blink (Geertz 1973: 6)? How do we know if a person is engaging in a joking activity or a serious one? On what basis can we achieve mutual understanding of interactional activities if the form of disparate activities, such as winking and blinking, is essentially the same?

Several students of social interaction have emphasized that our communicative activities include a metacommunicative dimension that helps to disambiguate them. As we engage in talk and interaction, a dimension of our very talk comments upon itself, giving clues as to what activities are being done and how they should be interpreted. Framing/keying (Bateson 1972; Goffman 1974), footing (Goffman 1981), contextualization (Gumperz 1982a, 1992), and metapragmatics (Silverstein 1993) are closely overlapping ways of conceptualizing this metacommunicative dimension through which interlocutors mutually coordinate the conversational activities in which they are engaging.

John Gumperz (1982a, 1992), for example, argues that we communicate rapidly shifting communicative/interpretive frames through conventionalized surface forms, which he calls *contextualization cues*. These contextualization cues – "constellations of surface features of message form" – are "the means by which speakers signal and listeners interpret what the activity is, how semantic content is to be understood and *how* each sentence relates to what precedes or follows" (1982a: 131). These surface forms vary greatly, ranging from prosody, to code and lexical choice, from formulaic expressions or sequencing choices, to visual and gestural phenomena. They are united in a common, functional category by their use, commonly in constellations of multiple features, to instantiate particular frameworks in which inherently ambiguous communicative behavior can be interpreted to have more particular meanings. As described in the section below, contextualization cues have been a key construct in one tradition of explaining inter-group miscommunication and misunderstanding.

4 Inter-cultural and Inter-gender Misunderstanding

Among students of language and social life, research on misunderstanding, particularly under the rubric "miscommunication," has focused largely on *inter-cultural* and *male–female* miscommunication and misunderstanding. In such research, the problematic communication is across lines of apparent social difference, and the misunderstandings are linked, sometimes causatively, to the poor quality of inter-group relations. This type of misunderstanding is thus different from those that are recognized and locally repaired by participants. In examples (3–5) of repair above, for example, the misunderstandings served to illustrate the structures by which intersubjective understandings were instantiated. Studies of inter-group miscommunication, in contrast, commonly focus on misunderstandings that (a) are not explicitly treated as misunderstandings as they occur, (b) are not successfully repaired, and (c) are seen as related to poor inter-group relations on a larger scale (cf. Banks, Ge, and Baker 1991: 105).

Examples of such inter-group miscommunication commonly include asynchronies and asymmetries, rather than explicitly referenced misunderstandings and repair procedures, and participants appear to have difficulties achieving satisfactory, joint activities. When one participant initiates an activity, for example making an assessment such as "It was so good" (Goodwin and Goodwin 1992: 166), the other participants may not respond with a turn that complements or builds on the initiated activity in an unmarked way.

In the following sequence, a Korean immigrant storekeeper in Los Angeles asks an African American customer who had just returned from Chicago about the weather in Chicago. When the customer emphasizes the cold of Chicago with considerable affect, including an exclamation, lateral headshakes, a potentially humorous anecdote, and laughter, the storeowner responds with a factual comment:

(6) (adapted from Bailey 1997: 340)
Owner: Is Chicago cold?
Customer: Uh! ((lateral headshakes)) Man I got off the plane and walked out the airport I said 'Oh shit'.
Customer: heh heh heh
Owner: ((no smile or laughter)) I thought it's gonna be nice spring season over there.

The customer repeatedly displays his affective stance toward the extreme cold of Chicago, which provides an opportunity for the storekeeper to engage in complementary displays, but the storekeeper does not do so. The two interlocutors demonstrably understand each other's words, but they fail to construct a culturally appropriate joint activity of assessing. Over the course of this entire encounter, multiple instances of such exchanges initiated by the customer give the interaction a stilted, one-sided feeling.

Chick (1990: 227) likens the coordination of intra-cultural interactions to the synchrony of "ballroom dancing partners of long standing, confident in the mutual knowledge of the basic sequence of dance steps and of the signals by which they inform one another of changes in direction or tempo, moving in smooth harmony."

Inter-cultural encounters, in contrast, are more like ballroom dances between strangers who "misinterpret one another's signals, struggle to develop a sequence or theme, or establish a rhythm, quarrel over rights to lead, and, metaphorically speaking, trample one another's toes." It is thus the seeming inability to engage in coordinated discourse activities, rather than the occurrence of sequences that interlocutors explicitly treat as misunderstandings, which is characteristic of these encounters (cf. Erickson and Shultz 1982).

The combination of (a) problematic communicative interactions, (b) boundaries of apparent social difference, and (c) debilitated inter-group relationships make such misunderstandings particularly interesting to students of language and social processes. While agreeing on the empirical characteristics of such encounters and intergroup relations, analysts have differed in their explanations of causal relations. Communicative behavior is both reflective of social worlds and also constitutive of them. Because of this dual functioning of language, it can be difficult to determine whether particular social relations cause particular communicative patterns, or whether particular communicative patterns partially cause particular social relationships (Bailey 2000).

One tradition, associated with the work of Gumperz (1982a, 1982b) and his students, has emphasized the constitutive power of face-to-face interaction in the shaping of inter-group relations. In exploring the contingent details of face-to-face interaction such researchers have argued that problematic communicative interactions at the microlevel contribute to poor inter-group relations at the macrolevel. A second tradition, which emphasizes social inequality at the macrolevel, has interpreted the same data as simply reflections of pre-existing social conflicts (e.g. Park 1996). Asynchronous and stilted inter-group interactions are seen as local enactments of more long standing, structural, conflicts rooted in inequality, whether ethnic, racial, national, gender, etc. In simplified form, these two contrasting explanations for inter-group misunderstanding can be represented by "A" and "B," respectively, in figure 17.1.

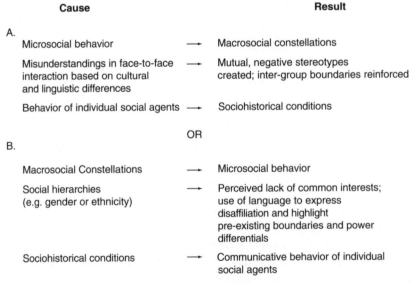

Figure 17.1   Directions of causality between microsocial behavior and inter-group relations

In this first tradition, Gumperz's (1982a, 1992) seminal work on discourse strategies illustrated how sociocultural background shapes the moment-to-moment management of interaction and achievement of intersubjectivity. His use of audio recordings of inter-group interactions in conjunction with analyses by native consultants enabled him to link specific surface forms of discourse with broader communicative activities and interpretive patterns. When consultants from given social groups consistently provide a group-specific interpretation of behavior and cite group-specific surface linguistic bases for that interpretation, it provides evidence for socioculturally specific contextualization conventions. Thus, while two groups may "speak the same language," i.e. share syntax, phonology, and vocabulary, they may differ in the ways they metacommunicatively define the moment-to-moment activities in which they are engaging.

According to Gumperz, cultural differences in contextualization conventions can undermine inter-group communication insidiously because individuals tend to be unconscious of this dimension of interaction (1982a: 131). The cues tend to be scalar rather than discrete in form, most are non-referential, and their meanings are a function of the context of their use. Pragmatic phenomena with these features are particularly difficult for individuals to consciously articulate and explicitly identify (Silverstein 2001). Gumperz (1982a: 173) reports, for example, how intonation affected interactions between South Asian immigrant cafeteria workers and Anglo-British workers at a British airport. When cafeteria workers asked employees if they wanted gravy, they said "Gravy" with a falling intonation contour rather than the rising one associated with Anglo-British question-asking. Because Anglo-British workers interpreted the falling intonation as contextualizing a statement ("This is gravy."), they found the utterance "Gravy" (with falling intonation) redundant and rude. Neither British nor South Asian workers were able to articulate the role that intonation played in their problematic interactions until it was pointed out by outside researchers/trainers.

Because sociocultural differences in contextualization conventions are unconscious, they are not a readily available explanation to participants for breakdowns in communication or for stilted, asynchronous interactions. When a person recognizes the failure to achieve a synchronous interaction with another, a personality/psychological idiom is readily available to explain an interlocutor's behavior: the other's behavior is explained in terms of his/her rudeness, insensitivity, selfishness, etc. When such problematic interactions come to be associated with inter-group interactions, rather than just particular individuals, it can result in pejorative stereotyping of entire groups and the reinforcement of inter-group boundaries.

Scollon and Scollon (1981) followed this tradition in analyzing inter-cultural communication between Athabaskans socialized in Athabaskan communities and Canadians/Americans who had been socialized in dominant, Anglo-American communities. Although many of the Athabaskan subjects were monolingual in English, their discourse patterns reflected traditional Athabaskan ones. Among the differences in discourse patterns and expectations, Scollon and Scollon found that:

(a) While English speakers are relatively voluble in social situations with non-intimates, Athabaskans are relatively taciturn in such situations, becoming more voluble among intimates.

(b) While American English speakers expect supplicants such as job interviewees and students to highlight their best qualities and abilities and project future accomplishments, Athabaskans avoid these self-displays and find it inappropriate and bad luck to anticipate and describe favorable future events.
(c) Because of differences in the way topics are introduced and turns exchanged – non-Athabaskans are generally quicker to initiate topics and consider a turn finished after a relatively brief period of silence – non-Athabaskans generally control topics and dominate conversations.

In interactions between Athabaskans and non-Athabaskan English speakers, these differences contribute to negative stereotyping and outcomes that generally disfavor the Athabaskans. In such petitioning situations as job and social service interviews, for example, Athabaskans often end up feeling that they have not gotten served despite having

> taken the proper subordinate, petitioning position by not speaking and carefully observing the English speaker. English speakers, on the other hand, feel that Athabaskans being interviewed do not display enough of themselves for the interviewer to evaluate their need, that they have become sullen and withdrawn or perhaps even acted superior, as if they needed no help. (Scollon and Scollon 1981: 19)

Contrasts in discourse patterns in such encounters can become greater and greater as interactions progress, in what Tannen (1981), in a term borrowed from Bateson (1936), refers to as "complementary schismogenesis." As each party pursues discourse patterns that seem illogical, confusing, or inappropriate to the other, each party clings more closely to its own, trying to build an intersubjective world through familiar patterns. As communicative patterns diverge more and more, the level of misunderstanding, and accompanying negative attribution, increases.

The model of inter-group misunderstanding based on cultural and linguistic difference has also been applied to inter-gender communication. Maltz and Borker (1982), for example, argue that males and females in the USA are socialized in different subcultures and follow distinctive interaction patterns, which make inter-gender communication problematic: "What we are suggesting is that women and men have different cultural rules for friendly conversation and that these rules come into conflict when women and men attempt to talk to each other as friends and equals in casual conversation" (1982: 212). They point out a number of differences between male and female communicative patterns that are particularly implicated in cross-gender misunderstandings, including the following:

(a) Men use and interpret minimal responses such as nods and "mm hmm" to mean "I agree" or "I follow your argument so far," while women use them to indicate that they are listening.
(b) Women tend to treat questions as part of maintaining the flow of interaction, while men view them primarily as requests for information.
(c) Women tend to discuss problems with each other as a means of personal sharing and offering reassurance, while men tend to interpret stated problems as requests for explicit advice or solutions.

In each of these cases, contrasting uses and interpretations of surface forms can lead to misunderstandings. The difference in use and interpretation of minimal responses, for example, can explain contrasting perspectives expressed in both male and female complaints regarding male–female interaction: men think that "women are always agreeing with them and then conclude that it's impossible to tell what a woman really thinks" while women "get upset with men who never seem to be listening" (1982: 202). This cultural approach to male–female communication became well known through the work of Deborah Tannen (1986, 1990), particularly her best-selling book *You Just Don't Understand: Women and Men in Conversation* (1990).

This model of inter-group misunderstanding based on linguistic and cultural difference privileges the power of primary language socialization (Ochs and Schieffelin 1984) and associated (and idealized) cultural beliefs and practices. Interlocutors are seen as reproducing cultural scripts for speech behavior and interpretation in inter-group encounters, even as these scripts appear to be less effective than in intra-group encounters. Larger-scale sociohistorical phenomena such as ethnic/racial identity formation processes and power differentials are backgrounded in this explanation.

Critics of this approach have argued that it mistakes *power differentials* for *cultural differences* and *sociopolitical conflicts* for *linguistic-interactional problems*. In this second approach, problematic interactions are seen as local enactments of larger-scale, pre-existing conflicts. From this perspective, individual social actors are not unwittingly reproducing culturally determined scripts in a politically neutral environment, but are using language to assert the legitimacy and positive value of their social identities and associated social perspectives. Problematic interactions are thus seen not as "misunderstandings," but as a form of communication that highlights on-going differences in perspective and sociopolitical interests.

These critics point out that most of the work in the linguistic/cultural difference tradition has looked at interaction between a dominant group and a less powerful group: Anglo-Americans and Native Americans (Philips 1983; Scollon and Scollon 1981); Anglo-Americans and African Americans (Kochman 1981; Akinnaso and Ajirotutu 1982); Anglo-Americans and Chinese (Young 1982, 1994; Scollon and Scollon 1995); males and females (Maltz and Borker 1982; Tannen 1986, 1990); Anglo-British and South Asians (Gumperz 1982a; Jupp, Roberts, and Cook-Gumperz 1982); and white and black South Africans (Chick 1990). Because of this discrepancy in power between the groups studied, it is difficult to determine whether inter-group conflict is influenced by discourse patterns or simply resides in pre-existing inequality (cf. Murray and Sondhi 1987: 31).

Singh, Lele, and Martohardjono (1996: 240–1) ask rhetorically why "intercultural encounters involving, for instance, Swedish or German speakers of English have not been studied. . . . Such studies will, we believe, allow us to separate the linguistic from the nonlinguistic factors that throw discourse harmony out of gear." They argue that the ability to avoid persistent misunderstandings – and to avoid their long-term damage to inter-group relationships – seems to depend crucially on *non*-linguistic factors. The differences in discourse patterns that appear to undermine relationships between ethnic/racial groups in relationships of domination or dependence do not appear to undermine relationships among groups of similar or equal power. They note, for example, that the reparability threshold of American business people "can be shown to increase in proportion to the wealth of the Arab sheiks they deal with"

(1996: 251). When there is significant social incentive to overcome differences in communicative patterns, they can be overcome. In the types of situations most often addressed by cultural/linguistic difference researchers, however, neither dominant nor dominated groups have such unambiguous social incentive to accommodate communicative patterns to each other.

Similar critical arguments have been advanced by researchers to counter linguistic/cultural explanations of male–female interactions. Henley and Kramarae (1991) and Troemel-Ploetz (1991) argue that the *types* of male–female discourse differences cited by Maltz and Borker (1982) are the very types of difference typical of dominant–subordinate relationships more generally. For example, men are constructed as experts (by treating questions and stated problems as requests for information and expertise) and as judgers of women's talk (through restricted and delayed use of minimal responses). If male–female differences in discourse patterns were merely cultural, discourse patterns associated with superior power would be equally shared by men and women. Henley and Kramarae (1991) further point out that the mis-understandings cited by linguistic/cultural difference researchers in male–female talk do not occur across all communicative activities. Instead, it is in activities such as requests, excuses, and explanations, where there are issues of exercising one's will and projecting one's vision of the world, that these misunderstandings occur, suggesting that contestations of power are at issue, not cultural habits.[1]

This "domination" explanation of misunderstanding can account for the very same data – asynchronous, stilted interactions – that are explained by linguistic and cultural differences. Awkward interactional sequences, in which divergent discourse patterns are used by members of different groups, are seen as symbolic struggles related to differences in power. Language is our primary symbolic system for organizing and constituting the social world and it is a primary locus for conflict and struggle over how the world is and how it should be represented (Gal 1989).

More specifically, language practices are a primary means of marking and maintaining group social identity. Ways of speaking are commonly associated with group identities and may be experienced by both members and non-members as *extensions* of those identities. Maintenance of distinctive ways of speaking in inter-group interaction can be seen as attesting to the validity and value of the associated identities. In contrast, accommodation to ways of speaking associated with other groups can be seen as a relative devaluing of one's own ways of speaking and relative valorization of the other's (Ferguson and Gumperz 1960; Labov 1972).

Speech accommodation theorists such as Howard Giles have shown that speakers can actively accommodate linguistic aspects of their speech to each other ("convergence") or that they can actively accentuate differences in linguistic features ("divergence"). They argue that such accommodation or divergence depends on the social goals, rather than the socialized patterns, of interlocutors:

> Central to this [speech accommodation theory] framework is the notion that during social interaction, participants are motivated to adjust (or to accommodate) their speech styles as a means of gaining one or more of the following goals: evoking listeners' social approval, attaining communicational efficiency between interactants and maintaining speakers' positive social identities. (Thakerar, Giles, and Cheshire 1982: 207)

An implicit assumption of much work in the linguistic/cultural difference tradition is that "communicational efficiency" and "evoking listeners' social approval" are high priorities for speakers, but this is not necessarily the case. When individuals who see themselves as having disparate economic or political interests encounter each other, there is often more at stake than achieving symmetrical, synchronous inter-actions. In such inter-group interactions, speakers may even select group-specific linguistic markers of social identity at a greater rate than in intra-group interaction (Morgan 1994: 132). Thus, interactions in which participants are unable to coordinate activities may not represent "misunderstanding" at all, but rather effective communication of difference: difference in experience, beliefs, perspectives, and power.

Even when there are not explicit differences in political interests between individ-uals or groups, misunderstandings are a way for humans to negotiate and constitute sociocultural worlds. Ochs (1991), for example, argues that apparent breakdowns in communication are part of language socialization. In analyzing misunderstandings between adults and children, she finds that: "misunderstandings are not loci in which social life breaks down. Rather, to the contrary misunderstandings structure social life. Each misunderstanding is an opportunity space for instantiating local epistemol-ogy and for structuring social identities of interactants" (Ochs 1991: 60). Misun-derstandings between adults and children are a way for children to be socialized into a local epistemology, rather than a failure of social interaction.

Language socialization – as an omnipresent and life-long process – provides a perspective from which to view misunderstandings as a form of social negotiations. At the center of language socialization are indexical relationships among social identities, situations, social/linguistic acts, and affective and epistemic stances (Ochs 1996: 410, 431). These indexical relations must be negotiated, whether in adult–child, intra-group, or inter-group interaction. Fundamental social questions are thus addressed through seeming misunderstandings: What indexical meanings, con-ventions, and identities will hold in interaction? Whose vision of how the world is – and should be – will be validated through talk?

5 CONCLUSION

Misunderstandings, as a contingent outcome of any interaction, encourage us to analyze the practices that afford a degree of intersubjective understanding. In our subjectively constituted world, "understanding" is not a state in which minds share the same content, but is rather a dimension of coordinated social interaction itself. The turn-by-turn structure of everyday talk helps make this coordination possible, enabling us to display, confirm, and make problematic our incremental, ongoing understandings of the very activities in which we are engaged. Paradoxically, those interactions in which apparent misunderstandings are explicitly addressed and repaired most clearly highlight our ability to achieve a degree of intersubjective understanding.

As analytical focus moves from propositional meanings to the multiple levels of activity and indexical meanings in everyday talk, misunderstandings increasingly link social and linguistic worlds. Coordination of conversational activities involves notions of social identities, situation, conventional conversational sequences and activities, and cultural beliefs about the interrelationships among these elements and linguistic forms. Understanding, then, includes understanding not only utterances, but also sociocultural worlds. Researchers have repeatedly documented patterns of relatively awkward, disjointed interaction in conversations across boundaries of apparent social difference, such as gender or ethnicity. These patterns – like other forms of language use – can be seen as resulting from social differences, but simultaneously as contributing to the constitution of such difference.

As a linguistically marked form, *mis*understanding suggests the failure of a process that is natural, but misunderstandings can be viewed more profitably as normal instances of the negotiations of social and linguistic lives. Our interactions – and misunderstandings – take place in cultural and sociohistorical contexts that are never neutral or natural, and they reflect and reproduce a world that includes conflict, ambiguity, and uncertainty.

NOTE

1   Other research suggests that the patterns addressed here are neither cross-cultural nor as monolithic as has been implied in some of the debate on "difference" or "dominance" in inter-gender interaction. Elinor (Ochs) Keenan (1974) found that Malagasy-speaking women in a Madagascar village used a relatively direct style of speaking even though they were socially subservient to men, who used a more indirect style, so directness cannot always be linked with power. A number of researchers (e.g. Tannen 1993; Gal 1995; Cameron 1998; Kulick 2000) have argued that there are not entirely discrete male and female ways of speaking, but rather semiotic resources to which both males and females have access.

REFERENCES

Akinnaso, F. N. and Ajirotutu, C. S. (1982). Performance and Ethnic Style in Job Interviews. In J. J. Gumperz (ed.), *Language and Social Identity.* Cambridge: Cambridge University Press, pp. 119–144.
Atkinson, J. M. and Drew, P. (1979). *Order in Court.* London: Macmillan.
Austin, J. L. (1962). *How to Do Things with Words.* Oxford: Oxford University Press.
Bailey, B. (1997). Communication of Respect in Interethnic Service Encounters. *Language in Society* 26(3): 327–356.
Bailey, B. (2000). Communicative Behavior and Conflict between African-American Customers and Korean Immigrant Retailers in Los Angeles. *Discourse and Society* 11(1): 87–108.
Banks, S. Ge, G., and Baker, J. (1991): Intercultural Encounters and Miscommunication. In N. Coupland, H. Giles, and J. Wiemann (eds.), *Miscommunication and Problematic Talk.* Newbury Park, CA: Sage, pp. 103–120.
Bateson, G. (1936). *Naven, a Survey of the Problems Suggested by a Composite Picture of the Culture of a New Guinea Tribe Drawn from Three Points of View.* Cambridge: Cambridge University Press.
Bateson, G. (1972). *Steps to an Ecology of Mind.* New York: Ballantine Books.
Cameron, D. (1998). Gender, Language, and Discourse: A Review Essay. *Signs* 23(4): 945–973.

Chick, J. K. (1990). The Interactional Accomplishment of Discrimination in South Africa. In D. Carbaugh (ed.), *Cultural Communication and Intercultural Contact*. Hillsdale, NJ: Lawrence Erlbaum, pp. 225–252.

Chomsky, N. (1977). *Essays on Form and Interpretation*. New York: North Holland.

Erickson, F., Shultz, J. (1982). *The Counselor as Gatekeeper: Social Interaction in Interviews*. New York: Academic Press.

Ferguson, C., and Gumperz, J. J. (1960). Introduction. In C. Ferguson and J. J. Gumperz (eds.), *Linguistic Diversity in South Asia: Studies in Regional, Social and Functional Variation*. Indiana University Research Center in Anthropology, Folklore, and Linguistics. Bloomington: Indiana University Press, pp. 1–26.

Gal, S. (1989). Language and Political Economy. *Annual Review of Anthropology* 18: 345–367.

Gal, S. (1995). Language, Gender and Power: An Anthropological Review. In K. Hall and M. Bucholtz (eds.), *Gender Articulated: Language and the Socially Constructed Self*. New York and London: Routledge, pp. 169–182.

Garfinkel, H. (1967). *Studies in Ethnomethodology*. Englewood Cliffs, NJ: Prentice-Hall.

Geertz, C. (1973). Thick Description: Toward an Interpretive Theory of Culture. In C. Geertz, *The Interpretation of Cultures*. New York: Basic Books, pp. 3–30.

Goffman, E. (1974). *Frame Analysis: An Essay on the Organization of Experience*. New York: Harper and Row.

Goffman, E. (1981). Footing. *Semiotica* 25: 1–29.

Goodwin, C. (1981). *Conversational Organization: Interaction between Speakers and Hearers*. New York: Academic Press.

Goodwin, C., and Goodwin, M. H. (1992). Assessments and the Construction of Context. In A. Duranti and C. Goodwin (eds.), *Rethinking Context: Language as an Interactive Phenomenon*. Cambridge: Cambridge University Press, pp. 147–189.

Goodwin, C., and Heritage, J. (1990). Conversation Analysis. *Annual Review of Anthropology* 19: 283–307.

Gumperz, J. J. (1982a). *Discourse Strategies*. New York and Cambridge: Cambridge University Press.

Gumperz, J. J. (ed.) (1982b). *Language and Social Identity*. Cambridge: Cambridge University Press.

Gumperz, J. J. (1992). Contextualization and Understanding. In A. Duranti and C. Goodwin (eds.), *Rethinking Context: Language as an Interactive Phenomenon*. Cambridge: Cambridge University Press, pp. 230–252.

Henley, N., and Kramarae, C. (1991). Gender, Power, and Miscommunication. In N. Coupland, H. Giles, and J. Wiemann (eds.), *Miscommunication and Problematic Talk*. Newbury Park, CA: Sage, pp. 18–43.

Heritage, J. (1984). *Garfinkel and Ethnomethodology*. Cambridge: Polity Press.

Heritage, J., and Atkinson, J. M. (1984). Introduction. In J. M. Atkinson and J. Heritage (eds.), *Structures of Social Action: Studies in Conversation Analysis*. Cambridge and New York: Cambridge University Press, pp. 1–15.

Husserl, E. (1970 [1901]). *Logical Investigations*. London: Routledge and Kegan Paul.

Hymes, D. (1972). Models of the Interaction of Language and Social Life. In J. J. Gumperz and D. Hymes (eds.), *Directions in Sociolinguistics: The Ethnography of Communication*. New York: Holt, Rinehart, & Winston, pp. 35–71.

Jefferson, G. (1987). On Exposed and Embedded Correction in Conversation. In G. Button and J. R. Lee (eds.), *Talk and Social Organisation*. Clevedon: Multilingual Matters, pp. 86–100.

Jupp, T. C., Roberts, C., and Cook-Gumperz, J. (1982). Language and Disadvantage: The Hidden Process. In J. J. Gumperz (ed.), *Language and Social Identity*. Cambridge: Cambridge University Press, pp. 232–256.

Keenan, E. O. (1974). Conversation and Oratory in Vaninankaratra Madagascar. Unpublished PhD dissertation, University of Pennsylvania.

Kochman, T. (1981). *Black and White Styles in Conflict.* Chicago: University of Chicago Press.

Kulick, D. (2000). Gay and Lesbian Language. *Annual Review of Anthropology* 29: 243–285.

Labov, W. (1972). *Sociolinguistic Patterns.* Philadelphia: University of Pennsylvania Press.

Lyons, J. (1977). *Semantics.* Cambridge: Cambridge University Press.

Maltz, D., and Borker, R. (1982). A Cultural Approach to Male-Female Miscommunication. In J. J. Gumperz (ed.), *Language and Social Identity.* Cambridge: Cambridge University Press, pp. 196–216.

Morgan, M. (1994). The African-American Speech Community: Reality and Sociolinguists. In M. Morgan (ed.), *Language and the Social Construction of Identity in Creole Situations.* Los Angeles: Center for Afro-American Studies, UCLA.

Murray, A., and Sondhi, R. (1987). Socio-political Influences on Cross-cultural Encounters. In K. Knapp, W. Enninger, and A. Knapp-Potthoff (eds.), *Analyzing Intercultural Communication.* New York: Mouton de Gruyter, pp. 17–33.

Ochs, E. (1991). Misunderstanding Children. In N. Coupland, H. Giles, and J. Wiemann (eds.), *Miscommunication and Problematic Talk.* Newbury Park, CA: Sage, pp. 44–60.

Ochs, E. (1996). Linguistic Resources for Socializing Humanity. In J. J. Gumperz and S. Levinson (eds.), *Rethinking Linguistic Relativity.* Cambridge: Cambridge University Press, pp. 407–437.

Ochs, E., and Schieffelin, B. B. (1984). Language Acquisition and Socialization: Three Developmental Stories and Their Implications. In R. Shweder and R. LeVine (eds.), *Culture Theory: Essays on Mind, Self, and Emotion.* New York: Cambridge University Press, pp. 276–320.

Park, K. (1996). Use and Abuse of Race and Culture: Black–Korean Tension in America. *American Anthropologist* 98(3): 492–498.

Philips, S. U. (1983). *The Invisible Culture: Communication in Classroom and Community on the Warm Springs Indian Reservation.* New York: Longman.

Pinker, S. (1994). *The Language Instinct: How the Mind Creates Language.* New York: William Morrow.

Reddy, M. (1979). The Conduit Metaphor: A Case of Frame Conflict in Our Language about Language. In A. Ortony (ed.), *Metaphor and Thought.* Cambridge: Cambridge University Press, pp. 284–324.

Sacks, H., Schegloff, E. A., and Jefferson, G. (1974). A Simplest Systematics for the Organization of Turn-Taking for Conversation. *Language* 50: 696–735.

Schegloff, E. A. (1987). Some Sources of Misunderstanding in Talk-in-Interaction. *Linguistics* 25: 201–218.

Schegloff, E. A. (1992). Repair after Next Turn: The Last Structurally Provided Defense of Intersubjectivity in Conversation. *American Journal of Sociology* 97(5): 1295–1345.

Schegloff, E. A., Jefferson, G., and Sacks, H. (1977). The Preference for Self-correction in the Organization of Repair in Conversation. *Language* 53: 361–382.

Schutz, A. (1962). Commonsense and Scientific Interpretations of Human Action. In *Collected Papers,* vol. 1. The Hague: Martinus Nijhoff, pp. 3–21.

Schutz, A. (1967 [1932]). *The Phenomenology of the Social World* (trans. G. Walsh and F. Lehnert). Evanston, IL: Northwestern University Press.

Scollon, R., and Scollon, S. W. (1981). *Narrative, Literacy, and Face in Interethnic Communication.* Norwood, NJ: Ablex.

Scollon, R., and Scollon, S. W. (1995). *Intercultural Communication: A Discourse Approach.* Cambridge, MA: Blackwell.

Searle, J. (1969). *Speech Acts: An Essay in the Philosophy of Language.* Cambridge: Cambridge University Press.

Silverstein, M. (1993). Metapragmatic Discourse and Metapragmatic Function. In J. Lucy (ed.), *Reflexive Language: Reported Speech and Metapragmatics*. Cambridge: Cambridge University Press, pp. 33–58.

Silverstein, M. (2001). The Limits of Awareness. In A. Duranti (ed.), *Linguistic Anthropology: A Reader*. Oxford: Blackwell, pp. 386–401.

Singh, R., Lele, J., and Martohardjono, G. (1996). Communication in a Multilingual Society: Some Missed Opportunities. In R. Singh (ed.), *Towards a Critical Sociolinguistics*. Amsterdam: John Benjamins, pp. 237–254.

Tannen, D. (1981). NY Jewish Conversational Style. *International Journal of the Sociology of Language* 30: 133–149.

Tannen, D. (1986). *That's Not What I Meant!* London: Dent.

Tannen, D. (1990). *You Just Don't Understand: Women and Men in Conversation*. New York: William Morrow.

Tannen, D. (1993). The Relativity of Linguistic Strategies: Rethinking Power and Solidarity in Gender and Dominance. In D. Tannen (ed.), *Gender and Conversational Interaction*. New York: Oxford University Press, pp. 165–188.

Thakerar, J. N., Giles, H., and Cheshire, J. (1982). Psychological and Linguistic Parameters of Speech Accommodation Theory. In C. Fraser and K. R. Scherer (eds.), *Advances in the Social Psychology of Language*. Cambridge: Cambridge University Press, pp. 205–255.

Troemel-Ploetz, S. (1991). Selling the Apolitical. *Discourse and Society* 2(4): 489–502.

Whalen, J., Zimmerman, D., and Whalen, M. (1988). When Words Fail: A Single Case Analysis. *Social Problems* 35(4): 335–360.

Young, L. W. (1982). Inscrutability Revisited. In J. J. Gumperz (ed.), *Language and Social Identity*. Cambridge: Cambridge University Press, pp. 72–84.

Young, L. W. (1994). *Crosstalk and Culture in Sino-American Communication*. New York: Cambridge University Press.

CHAPTER 18

Language and Madness

James M. Wilce

1 INTRODUCTION

Madness inevitably involves language. Admittedly, speech-related symptoms come and go and rarely involve grammar, and many disturbing non-linguistic symptoms remind us that madness is by no means strictly linguistic. Still, deviant speech helps define madness.

Why "madness" – an old folk term, a shifting social construction? I address suffering and deviance under that rubric, rather than "mental illness," because the latter term comes culturally shrink-wrapped in the perspective of biomedical psychiatry. Cultural views of madness, while constrained by some universals, vary more than concepts of universal disease processes allow for. (For instance, rural Bangladeshis whom I asked to list all the illnesses they could think of did not mention *pāgalāmi*, madness; Bengali religious traditions have defined it as a gift, McDaniel 1989). Then, too, using an older folk term rather than a biomedical term avoids the misimpression that linguistic anthropological fieldwork results in data transparently related to psychiatric nosologies (diagnostic categories).

This chapter draws from psychology, philosophy, linguistics, and evolutionary biology – as well as other subfields of anthropology – to explore madness as a human linguacultural phenomenon. I cast my net widely because of the paucity of studies of madness by linguistic anthropologists (the few that come to mind are Bateson 1972; Beeman 1985; Capps and Ochs 1995; Goffman 1969; Ribeiro 1995; Wilce, in press; Ochs et al., in press). This shortage prompts me to stretch my topic to cover personality disorders as well as the "true" forms of madness – in psychiatric parlance, bipolar disorder, schizophrenia, and perhaps autism. This broader view allows me to make important points about the role of language in organizing concepts of suffering and constructing psychiatric categories.

Before I begin, I must briefly mention a long debate over whether schizophrenia – which in many ways epitomizes madness – is a disorder of thought or of speech. It is fruitless because schizophrenia precipitates the perceived collapse of that distinction (Crow 2000); to reify it at the outset of investigation cuts us off from a phenomeno-logical exploration. More importantly, the debate assumes that speech expresses private thoughts, precluding an interactionist perspective on the joint construction of understanding and even breakdowns therein. Linguistic anthropologists in the interactionist tradition have worked to overcome the thought–speech dichotomy (Beeman 1985; Gumperz and Levinson 1996). Other anthropologists adopt a semiotic perspective that encompasses and links speech and thought (Desjarlais 1997; Martínez-Hernáez 2000).

My argument begins by describing the common sense that makes normal speech interaction a sign of full humanness and thus construes madness as a loss of human-ness. Sections 3 and 4 explore two ways to transcend that apprehension of madness and sociality.

2   MADNESS COMPROMISING THE LINGUISTIC CAPACITIES OF HUMAN BEINGS

The ability to speak coherently enough to respond appropriately to, and help create, recognizable social contexts helps define our sense of full humanness. From primat-ologist Jane Goodall to linguist John Lyons (1982), many have built concepts of humanness upon the capacity for linguistic interaction. Radical deviation from normal speech interaction can cause interlocutors to judge one not only insane but less than completely human. This section explores the link between madness and fundamental human linguistic and intersubjective capacities.

The capacity for language as we know it probably emerged with anatomically modern *Homo sapiens* roughly 200,000 years ago (Dunbar 1998: 104). This capacity is not reducible to the grammatical delivery of information but must serve diverse social and semiotic needs. The prototypical site of language use is in social interaction. Such interaction requires a "theory of mind" (ToM), the ability to make continual inferences about others' internal dispositions (feelings, intentions, etc.). Linguistic anthropolo-gist Ochs and her colleagues (in press) review the importance of ToM in relation to autism and call for richer theorization of the social in relation to such conditions: "A study of autism . . . holds promise for enhancing theories of society and culture, in that both the struggles and the successes of persons diagnosed with autism make evident what is most essential to participation in human society." To think about ToM is to think about intentionality. Whether or not we see intentionality as conscious planning (see Duranti, this volume), we can hardly account for normal language use without modeling some intention to do something in relation to interlocutors – persuade, deceive, amuse, etc. – by speaking. But if this is fundamental to our humanity, and if Sass is correct in finding in some persons with schizophrenia "an experiential attitude that would sever the word from any intention-to-signify" (1992: 203), then such madness severely compromises the socially and linguistically engaged mind.

2.1   Madness as human linguistic gifts run amok

Using language in face-to-face interaction requires more than just deploying symbols (arbitrary, invariant signs). It requires pragmatic or indexical competence – fitting speech to context, e.g. through appropriate use of deictics (pronouns and demonstratives) and politeness markers. Where would conversation be without deictics like "you" or "I"? Talk works from a "deictic origo" or center to locate "close" and "far," "self" and "other," even while speakers exchange turns and move about in space. Indexicality is key to an anthropological approach to language (Duranti 1997). But madness compromises the capacity to grasp what is indexed, i.e. "the range of socio-cultural dispositions, acts, identities, activities, and institutions indexed moment-by-moment by linguistic and other conventional semiotic features of shifting social situations" (Ochs et al., in press).

Linguistic anthropologists know that "the self" is decentered in much talk; for example, "I" does not index the speaker when (s)he is directly quoting someone else. But schizophrenia radically weakens the integrity of the self. Therefore many experts (including sufferers themselves) describe it as one of the most terrifying of all forms of human suffering. Some sufferers feel "their" thoughts are not "their own" – a feeling so foreign to most of us as to be inconceivable. British psychiatrist Crow attributes this crisis to a disturbance in the way the brain makes the indexical distinctions between thought, one's own speech production, and others' speech. This disturbance is potentiated by the way language and the brain evolved. The "speciation event" or split from the hominid line that produced *Homo sapiens* involved the lateralization of the brain's language-related functions (two hemispheres, specialized but integrated). Lateralization of brain function is less marked in those with schizophrenia (Crow 2000: 122–3).

Our ability to index speaker and addressee with "I" and "you" presupposes clear perception of the difference between speech as heard (from others), as produced, and as thought. Brains are able to distinguish the source of words because they are lateralized. Unfortunately, this means that compromised lateralization distorts speech interaction. In arguing that this is precisely what schizophrenia does, Crow (2000) is proposing a model of the brain and its evolution that explains the neuropsychological grounds of indexicality. His model posits schizophrenia as a breakdown therein, with severe repercussions for success in life and reproduction. And yet the disease represents a common genetic inheritance of our species (occurring in about 1 percent of adults around the world). What possible selective advantage could lateralization confer if it potentiates schizophrenia? Language: the genetic mutations that led to functional lateralization (and the possibility of dysfunction) also give us linguistic capacities, including indexicality. Crow's neurolinguistic vision links a central focus of linguistic anthropology – indexicality – with the evolution and modern function of the brain in a way that clarifies the significance of schizophrenia for anthropology.

2.1.1   Metacommunication and madness

Indexicality includes more complex contextual engagements than simply perceiving who is speaking and thus distinguishing "I" from "you." It presupposes sociocultural perspective-taking, including awareness of what implicit rules and messages, indirect indexes, or veiled insults are relevant to the "language game" being played in a given context. Gaps between culturally preferred states (such as approving of others) and actual states (such as disapproval) lead to indirect insults, such as damning with faint praise. Decoding these requires taking the speaker's perspective and imagining other utterances (fuller praise) in comparable contexts. Subtle cues in intonation or rhythm guide the decoding of such messages; that is, they are metacommunicative signs, serving framing functions. Autistic and schizophrenic listeners are significantly more likely to misperceive such cues and miss indirect indexes (Ochs et al., in press; Tényi et al. 2000).

Some awareness of how speech relates to context – of pragmatics – is required for successful talk. But "metapragmatic awareness" – a subtype of metalinguistic awareness or the ability to reflect, in language, about language – is a mixed blessing. Linguistic self-consciousness can paralyze. Madness (particularly schizophrenia) can be viewed as deviance affecting all metalinguistic usage. Schizophrenic speech involves a tendency to reflect so much on words that "normal" conversation bogs down in language play. Extreme linguistic self-consciousness does not necessarily help persons achieve contextual appropriateness. The self-reflexive linguistic capacity, so basic to our humanness and to our play, becomes "madness" when it swamps basic functions like achieving shared reference and thus a shared reality.

2.1.2 Metacommunication in Rani's family

Rani is a young Bangladeshi woman with schizophrenia; I talked with her and her family in 1992 (Wilce 1998a, in press). In the following lines, Rani fails to answer my questions (1–2, 18–19), then says something about direction and the house near which we (her family and I) spoke – which, to us as her interlocutors, bore no relation to the previous turns. Then, Rani's family and I felt the pragmatic disconnect worsen when she began to pun on *dik-e*, which can mean "in [some] direction" but also "let [someone] give this." J is Jim, the author; R is Rani; S is her sister Shapla; M is their mother.

1J	tomār keman ghum haiyechilo (0.8)	How did you sleep (0.8)
2J	gato rātre? (2)	last night? (2)
3R	(??) /man-iyā/	/(?? in my mind??)/
4J	/ghum haiyechilo?/	/Did you sleep?/
5R	man-iyā jvā lā -y je din	On the day my mind was burning.
6J	(1.5) Hm?	(1.5) Hm?
3 lines	[omitted]	[omitted]
10S	/bal (paṛār matan)/ ki nā kathā kaite / pāra-s/?	/Speak (like a recitation)/. Can't you speak like that?
11R	/niye/jā-y nā (??)	/[They]/ don't take [it]./
12S	Rani! bal! (0.5)	Rani, Speak! (0.5)
13S	sundar kare bal.	Speak beautifully.
4 lines	[omitted]	[omitted]
18J	ekhan (0.2) tumi ki chāo (1.5)	What do you [yourself] want now (1.5)
19J	Rani =	[to happen] Rani?

20M	= kaw "āmi bhālo haite /chāi/." (2)	Say, "I want to get better."
21R	((to Shapla, laughing voice)) /(xxxxx)/	((to Shapla, laughing voice)) /(xxxxx)/
22R	(he jāgār māṭi je dik)	(Whatever direction the mud of this homestead)
23R	dik-e	(Let [someone] give this, or direction-this)
24R	dik ā /da/\/	(Direction, or Let [someone] give this.
7 lines	[omitted]	[omitted]
32J	āchā	Well . . .
33R	dikāṭā ḍi	(? The direction? Or Let someone give)
34J	Rani	Rani.
35R	dite balle	. . . if someone says give.
36J	kabi-kabirājke tomār keman lāgsilo	How did you feel about the healers?
37J	(0.8)	(0.8)
38J	kabi-kabirājer cikitsā	The healers' treatment—
39J	keman lāglo	how was it?
40R	[smiles] °(?) haiye gesegā°	[smiles] °It went like (x)°
41S	bal	Speak.
42M	bal!	Speak!
43S	Rani!	Rani!
44M	[leaning forward] kabirājer cikitsā	[leaning forward] The healer's treatment—
45M	/keman/?	/how was it/?
46R	[shaking head negatively] /kabirāj/	[shaking head negatively] /Healers/
47R	bhālo hay nā =	don't succeed
48M	= bal "bhālo hay nā" [starts echoing R's head shake]	Say "don't succeed" [starts echoing R's head shake]

What sort of odd interchange is this? If Rani answered my questions (1, 18–19) at all it was in metaphors (3–5) and puns. Punning is metalinguistic; it reflects a high awareness of language. If Rani was indeed playing with two homonyms meaning "let [someone] give" and "in [some] direction," that was creative but purely self-engaged, not engaged in the conversation we thought we were having. Such communication problems often prompted Rani's family to attempt repairs (10, 12, 20, 41–48). These were other-initiated and other-completed repairs (Keating and Egbert, this volume). The family's repair efforts included statements about how one should speak – viz., *beautifully* (13; see Wilce, in press). Rani's self-reflexive linguistic play run amok prompted her family's intervention. For them – as for Sass (1992) and Crow (2000) – such pervasive contextual disconnects constitute madness. Rani and her family used different frames to signal competing stances toward language.

Anthropologist Gregory Bateson pioneered the study of such metacommunicative frames, and applied the notion to schizophrenia. Bateson speculated that a "double bind" – in which someone hears words framed in a conflicting metamessage, within a context allowing no escape (as when a child hears words of love but experiences violence from its parents) – could be "schizophrenogenic." The victim of such a bind "spirals into never-ending, but always systematic, distortion" characterizing schizophrenia (1972: 212). Bateson also saw the potential in such binds for the creative generation of insight and new metaphorical worlds.

Research on madness inside and beyond linguistic anthropology reflects Bateson's interest in metacommunication. His work has proved relevant to bipolar psychosis as well as schizophrenia. Erving Goffman drew on Bateson when he wrote of the "atypical framing practices" and rapidly shifting "footings" – the way one person's speech projects various selves – that characterize psychotic discourse. Brazilian applied linguist Branca Ribeiro (1995: 54) invokes Goffman's notions to explain why a woman diagnosed as "manic," Dona Jurema, is so hard to follow. As Woolard explains (this volume), codeswitching often signals such shifts. Dona Jurema rapidly shifted footing without changing code – she spoke Portuguese – and still managed to confuse her interlocutors and earn the label "mad." The rapidity with which she changed footings is isomorphic with her diagnosis (mania).

Linguistic play manifests metalinguistic consciousness that can become excessive. Such play can obsess those considered mad, leaving them entranced and their inter-locutors alienated (Sass 1992: 214, 241). The reflexive potential of language – one of the most creative features of language, distinguishing it from animal communication – becomes, in psychosis, a kind of trap.

2.2   Madness as compromised intersubjectivity

Hominid evolution is, simultaneously, the evolution of culture, and one way to define culture is as a pattern of shared contexts and meanings, in other words, in terms of intersubjectivity. Yet, theories of social life arising straightforwardly from a vision of this shared, commonsense world are limited in so far as common sense is precisely what is *not* typical of interactions involving the mad (Van Dongen 1997). Schutz, who described that world (1962–66), held that intersubjectivity is always a tenuous achievement. Yet, taking the always tenuous achievement of intersubjectivity for granted might meet a universal need. Social science discourse uses intersubjectivity to define sociality, and makes sociality definitive of humanity. But to take the mutual attunement of social actors as an unproblematic given is harmful in so far as it excludes some people from the social world.

The speech of the mad is hard to understand. Odd speech is a diagnostic feature of madness in many societies, and is a key criterion for schizophrenia in the DSM-IV, psychiatry's diagnostic manual (APA 2000). Schizophrenia's challenge to mutual understanding shakes the foundations of sociality and brings grief to families. Para-doxically, psychosis is less a loss of mind and its capacity for speech than a hypertrophy of the capacity for self-reflection. Those with schizophrenia seem to see language as Wittgenstein and Derrida did, in one of two ways: either language is not produced by minds but emerges autonomously, or (conventional) language cannot be a fitting vessel for the contents of private minds (Sass 1992).

These voices disagree with psychologists regarding the importance of a ToM, perhaps rightly so. Psychologists tend to assess ToM outside of any sociocultural matrix, and perhaps assign it an exaggerated importance. In order to assert its biological innateness, they claim that speculative talk about others' inner states is common around the world. Linguistic anthropology problematizes such claims; among many possible approaches to agency, they reflect an "intentionalist stance" (Duranti, this volume). Astington argues that "ToM is a cultural invention":

"Children do not really acquire any theory of their own but, through participation in cultural activities, they come to share their culture's way of regarding and talking about people's relations to one another and to the world" (1999). Ochs et al.'s (in press) proposed modification of ToM would incorporate a more richly theorized modeling of the social processes through which others' minds come to be imagined and local theories of mind internalized. Yet, however it is acquired or defined, ToM-like perspective-taking is undeniably compromised in madness.

Cultures (or ways of interacting) are "organizations of diversity" (Wallace 1965), and even in the same society social actors use language for very different purposes. Conflict over Rani's use of language evokes the topic of language ideologies like those addressed by Kroskrity (this volume). Such ideologies – understandings of, and evaluative criteria for, speech – are contested, even if one ideology achieves dominance in and perhaps even beyond one society. The drive toward transparent reference reflects an ideology of language that has dominated Western thought, at least in academic if not political discourses. Yet it is as alien to those with schizophrenia as it is to many poets and lovers. Madness highlights the fragility of any apparent agreements about language, even within one family like Rani's (Wilce, in press).

In the following section I describe asynchronous interactions involving those considered mad as breakdowns in agreements about timing, one manifestation of intersubjectivity.

2.2.1   Intersubjectivity and interactive rhythmicity

Interactive rhythmic harmony typifies talk universally, though the nature of the rhythms – and levels of awareness of rhythmicity as a cultural value – varies markedly. Bailey (this volume) notes how multiple levels of synchrony characterize intra-cultural interactions, while asynchrony plagues inter-cultural interactions (Gumperz 1982). Interactants might well take the ability to achieve rhythmic synchrony in talk and movement (including gesture – Haviland, this volume) as a key sign of sharing a language, in the sense of a coherent set of skills for using language and body together in face-to-face interaction. This rhythmic attunement, however, is as unlikely in interactions with those considered mad as it is in inter-cultural encounters.

2.2.2   Culture, rhythm, and depression

Intersubjectivity is enacted in sense and rhythm more commonly than it is discussed in the abstract. Its manifestations include synchrony and tight sequentiality. Making music together (Schutz 1962–66) exemplifies and metaphorically represents making sense together conversationally. "Conversational duetting" (Falk 1979), in which enthusiastic interlocutors co-construct utterances in partly overlapping speech, is an example of synchrony, and the achievement of no gaps or overlaps between different speakers' turns at talk epitomizes tight sequentiality.

Depression and mania can be seen as rhythmic disturbances. Mania speeds speech rhythms; clinical depression slows the pace of speech (Siegman 1987). Both can disrupt interaction. Indeed, mother–infant dyads in psychologist Maya Gratier's study rarely achieved synchrony when the mother was depressed – not surprisingly, since the depressed mothers' speech showed a slower, *irregular* "beat" with flattened prosody. Such irregularities, and the loss of prosodic marking such as the falling intonation that typically comes at the end of utterances, make predicting turn-transitions harder (see Keating and Egbert, this volume). Gratier locates interactive rhythm within the orb of culture, and finds depression and interactive disharmony more frequent among immigrant mothers (Gratier 1999). Secure attachment develops through healthy interaction, measured more in rhythmicity than in the particular words exchanged; insecure attachment hinders normal brain growth (Schore 2001). So we need to learn more about what constitutes healthy caregiver–child interaction in a variety of sociocultural settings in order to better understand the roots of disturbance (beyond genetics).

2.2.3   Dyssynchrony and schizophrenia

Studies of schizophrenia and interactive rhythm date back to the 1960s. Bateson's collaborator Condon found synchrony at intra- and inter-personal levels – in the relations between one speaker's words and bodily acts ("self-synchrony"), and in the movements of two interlocutors ("interactional synchrony"). "In [a] schizophrenic patient the right arm and right leg appear at times to be dyssynchronous with the speech, head and the left aspect of the body, including the left arm and leg" (Condon and Ogston 1966: 343–4). Parts of the patient's body that were out of synch with each other were also out of synch with her interlocutor, a therapist. Schizophrenia, then, disrupts synchronies observable in same-culture interactions between people without such a diagnosis.

Interactional rhythm is organized by turns, and cultural norms of politeness may focus on maintaining orderly turn-taking. Such rhythms are learned along with other cultural knowledge, so cultural outsiders can normally learn new interactive rhythms. Rani's mother, sister, and I (a foreigner) were able to achieve such rhythmic attunement that our turns had few overlaps or gaps between them, and we jointly produced one utterance (lines 19–20, where Rani's mother completed my sentence). But madness disrupts turn-taking. Rani allowed long pauses before responding to questions (lines 2–3), and often responded only in a mumble that was hard to hear and transcribe. Sometimes Rani would completely ignore questions. Her mother would then try to repair this omission, as she did in line 20, answering my question (18–19; note my pause of 1.5 seconds in waiting for Rani after line 18) on Rani's behalf.

I asked another question (lines 38–9) – about Rani's experience with traditional healers. When Rani did finally answer (46–47) after hearing her mother recycle the question, her mother celebrated – and compensated for the loss of face Rani might have caused, through a sequence of acts closely coordinated with Rani's. Mother echoed Rani's responses visibly and audibly. In close order (47–48), the two said "don't succeed" and shook their heads from side to side. As an icon of their deeper disconnection, however, Rani kept her back turned to her mother in this sequence. She heard her mother but did not see her "bodily echo." This "coordination" was remedial, the achievement of Mother alone.

So the excess of linguistic self-reflexivity often associated with schizophrenia does not engender greater sensitivity to the requirements of polite engagement with interlocutors. Family members' efforts to connect with those suffering from psychosis indicate that they experience madness as disengagement. Rani's flights from context included her failure to answer questions or to do so in a manner recognized as relevant (lines 3–5). Under a culture of individualism such failures are bad, but might be overlooked in settings involving distanced or bureaucratic relationships, perhaps even in a psychiatric hospital. In rural Bangladesh, where most interactions are with kin and close friends, failure to respond (to offer a second move in an adjacency pair: see Keating and Egbert, this volume) is clearly a problem.

Rani's family's attempts to control how she spoke and engaged others included her mother's bodily attempts to compensate for, and to restart, absent responses (line 48). They also included her sister's metalinguistic command, "Speak beautifully" (13). For them, speaking beautifully meant achieving interactive harmony in polite exchanges. This family's coping style is not unique. Another family affected by schizophrenia in Bangladesh – "Bimal," the "patient," is one of four middle-aged brothers – told me in 2001 how they took his early attempts to shut out the voices he was hearing (decades ago) as defiant refusal to hear *them*. In my videotape of the four, two "normal" brothers repeated Bimal's words several times until they finally said the words – the name of the hospital where Bimal is an outpatient – simultaneously. Bimal did not share this achievement of rhythmic harmony. Such achievements, tenuous even in "normal" interaction, are much rarer in the face of madness. The fact that such disruption occurs both in psychosis and in inter-ethnic communication (Gumperz 1982) raises questions ideally suited for linguistic anthropologists.

3   LANGUAGE AND THE CONSTITUTION OF MADNESS

Madness *appears* to be an objective label for deviant speech and related symptoms. How objective is that appearance, and what do powerful metadiscourses have to do with shaping it? How is it that observers perceive certain ways of speaking to perform and confirm madness as an essential identity (see Keane, and Bucholtz and Hall, this volume)? Michel Foucault's work (1973) has prompted anthropologists to investigate the possibility that discourses that invoke madness do not simply reflect a pre-existing condition – they help constitute not only its meaning for the larger society but perhaps the very experience of madness. Writing in the abstract, Scandinavian psychologist Rommetveit is able to claim that a "reflective detachment would by Buber and Gadamer be conceived of as *immoral*" (1998: 366). Rani's and Bimal's families apparently considered their detachment a moral violation, too. If we can uncover how metacommunicative processes help constitute the detachment of madness as immoral, we can problematize the dichotomization of madness and essential humanity.

Erving Goffman (1969) laid the groundwork for a critical anthropology of madness, defining psychotic symptoms as deviance *vis-à-vis* the social organizations in which they occurred. Deviance is constituted in relation to social-semiotic rules. Building on Goffman's work, Catalonian psychiatric anthropologist Martínez-

Hernáez (2000: 138–41, 235) catches psychiatry up in a contradiction as it constructs deviance as objective. Modern medicine defines *symptoms* as "what patients say" – expressing subjective experiences of disease – opposing symptoms with *signs*, defined as the natural indexes of disease that experts can objectively observe. Is psychotic speech a symptom? It cannot be subjectively perceived as a problem as long as psychiatry makes patients' "lack of insight" into the problematic nature of their speech a hallmark of psychosis. Is psychotic speech then an objective sign, despite its prompting subjective concern for psychiatrists and families? To raise such questions points to the dialogical nature of disease-signs and socially construed symptoms. In the case of madness, symptoms appear in the eye of the beholder. Locating the meaning of behavior somewhere between patient and observer, as Martínez-Hernáez does, gives intersubjectivity a new sense, one that implicates it in power relations.

3.1   Psychiatric nosologies: Categories for (mis)understanding?

Assessing the relation of madness to language – and power – should include accounting for the language of psychiatry. Linguistic anthropologists scrutinize folk theories of language, including those dressed up as academic theories (see critiques of speech act theory: Duranti, this volume). The founding generations of linguistic anthropologists engaged in an implicit critique of Western knowledge. Whorf (1956) claimed that the categories of "standard average European" languages constrained speakers' habitual perceptions, disadvantaging us *vis-à-vis* Hopi speakers, better equipped to grasp physicists' concepts of time. The DSM's categories of psychiatric diagnosis (APA 2000), terms like "schizophrenia" and "alexithymia," reflect and constrain Western perceptions. Such taxonomies are the rusty remnants of chains of discourse deserving critical investigation. Psychological anthropologists engaged in such investigations offer critical insights for an anthropology of language and madness by exposing the culture-bound nature of the DSM as a taxonomy. For example, the DSM sharply divides "affective" and "cognitive" disorders, reproducing a Western dichotomy that is blurred in Bengali, Nepali, and Balinese (for example), which use a simple, single term to refer to feeling-thinking. Linguistic anthropological investigations of madness could further the critique.

Eugen Bleuler advanced the term "schizophrenia" in 1907, objectifying the "split" perceived at the heart of the illness and defining it as necessarily chronic. Bleuler's definition – echoed in the DSM-IV (APA 2000) – makes "short-term schizophrenia" impossible and recovery almost unthinkable. As the West constructs itself in relation to rationality, it needs madness within and abroad as the Other against which it confirms its identity (Lucas and Barrett 1995). Discourse that makes schizophrenia exemplify liminality as well as danger might well shape its symptoms: "If liminality is an issue, patients may feel as if they are neither sick nor well but stuck, ambiguously, somewhere betwixt and between: By exploring these metaphors with patients it may be possible to gain a better understanding of the phenomenal experience of schizophrenia" (Barrett 1998: 28).

Fewer know or feel the effects of the construct "alexithymia," but it illustrates both the potential power of diagnostic labels to impact the experience of patients and the centrality of ideologies of language and emotion in psychiatric nosologies. "Alexithymia" is a recent coinage, combining Greek roots – *a* (no), *thumos* (feeling), and *lexis* (word) – to construct the pathology, "having no words for feelings." So the term medicalizes difficulties some persons ostensibly have in "putting feelings into words." Reproducing key structures of Western philosophy, the term presupposes a sharp distinction between feeling and thought. Then, it reifies feelings as substances that require container-like words to give them shape and expression (Reddy 1993). Reanalyzing attempts to make alexithymia fit Japanese clinical settings, Fukunishi et al. reached the conservative conclusion that "the possibility remains that alexithymia is a culture-bound construct" (1997).

3.2 Labeling Mania

Like schizophrenia and alexithymia, mania is caught in complex webs of significance. In the case of mania these webs include codeswitching and reactions to it. Several accounts of mania – from Brazil (Ribeiro 1995), Papua New Guinea (Goddard 1998), South Africa (Swartz and Swartz 1987), and Bangladesh (Wilce 2000) – mention codeswitching. People who, along with other unusual behaviors, rapidly shift footings – typically signaled by codeswitching – sometimes attract the label "mad." In itself the rapid codeswitching is a kind of performance of metalinguistic playfulness. Psychiatrists around the world (Reddy et al. 1997) might interpret it as one of the tell-tale signs of manic behavior in bipolar disorder, "pressure of speech" – the sense that words pile up too quickly and then spill out (often in lists) in the manic phase. Whereas they would want to encounter a codeswitching patient clinically before assigning a label, in other contexts, less cautious audiences label such performances signs of madness.

Goddard (1998) describes Hari, a Kaugel man of highland Papua New Guinea who has a great excess of energy and strength and whose speech is odd in two respects: he has difficulty with pronouns (especially "I" and "you"), and shifts rapidly between Tok Pisin and English. For Goddard, the community's decision to ostracize Hari reflected his unpredictability, and his identification – indexed by his codeswitching among many other things – with European people and culture. For some, such codeswitching constitutes a dangerous liminality. Swartz and Swartz (1987) describe a South African woman, "B," who was hospitalized in a manic state. Contrary to hospital records, the authors describe B's speech as coherent. In a startling display of linguistic one-upmanship, B shifted from English to French, Italian, and finally Afrikaans, in which she told the interviewer (who did not speak Afrikaans), "You have big ears." The authors interpret B's remark as a clear and powerful reframing of therapy as surveillance.

The speech of B and Hari appeared deviant only in particular social contexts. Codeswitching marked it as playful, perhaps liminal, but not incoherent or transparently psychotic. Codeswitching keeps in play a broader range of identities than their interlocutors found manageable (Wilce 2000). Their performances, as co-constructed with audiences imbued with narrower senses of appropriateness, marginalize them. But marginalization is but one of several somewhat arbitrary cultural processes in response to manic acts (including speech). The "late capitalist" culture of the contemporary USA embraces mania as an epitomization of the excess of energy and creativity required for high productivity (Martin 2000). Human audiences interpret speech performances as mad or rational in interpretive contexts that reflect economic, social, and cultural histories.

Thus, what is labeled mad is broader than what meets DSM critieria for psychotic illness. For example, many in Bangladesh interpret madness as a deviant egocentricity – a willfulness that may be part of a syndrome in which the *māthā* (head) is made *garam* (hot) by words and actions that are under conscious control. Latifa, whom I describe at length elsewhere (Wilce 1998b), was a young woman whose "excessive" lamenting over her divorce was taken as a sign of madness, though she would never have been diagnosed psychotic by any psychiatrist. Instead, labeling her *pāgal* was simply a way of pointing out her deviance. At the emotional peak of one of Latifa's performances of tearful singing (lamentation) (described in detail in Wilce 1998b, 2002), her female cousin said:

> *he Latifa, cup karas nā? cheḍir māthā āro pāgal haybo besî,*
> Hey Latifa, won't you shut up? The girl's head will get even crazier!

Latifa's cousin spun her acts as "performative" (see Keane, and Bucholtz and Hall, this volume), holding her responsible for doing things (lamenting) that *"made her* crazy" by heating her head. Since Austin began calling some utterances performative, linguistic anthropologists have noted how easily the perceived efficacy of "performative utterances" is attributed to magic rather than identifiable metacommunicative processes (Duranti, this volume; Lee 1997). Latifa shares with these critics greater insight into the political nature of claims that certain utterances are performative. What her cousin's words immediately followed, if not responded to, were these words of Latifa:

> *āmāre diye pāgal kaiyā kaite dilo nā go!*
> By calling me "mad" they prevented me from speaking! (Wilce 1998b: 214)

Claims that some bit of speech is performative of some contested state of being are themselves contested. The conflict over Latifa's words and their relation to her "diagnosis" is the kind of conflict that has made involuntary commitment to mental institutions more difficult in the USA in recent decades. Competing claims over the performative nature of certain speech acts of clients interacting with their attorneys have made trials of accused criminals with a history of schizophrenia – particularly "Twentieth Hijacker" Zacarias Moussaoui and Ted "Unabomber" Kaczynski – so problematic.

3.3   Interactive/discursive constitution of madness: A generalizable possibility

So diagnostic *categories* might call forth the conditions they represent. It is even easier to make a constructivist argument about *interactions*, such as psychotherapy – for many, an unfamiliar and potentially off-putting form of talk (Kirmayer 1987). The alexithymia construct locates feelings strictly *inside* of persons, as if social interaction did not constitute them but simply allowed them to see the light of day. Kirmayer noted in 1987 what recent work has reasserted – that this "problem" tends to show up in men with low incomes and relatively little education. Alexithymia, then, may be little more than a medicalization of a class-specific way of speaking – or *not* speaking – about feelings (compare Kusserow 1999). Psychotherapists and psychiatrists expect – sometimes inspire or demand – a certain way of speaking in which feelings receive lexical labels (e.g. "I'm feeling *sad*"), and regard those unwilling to use them as lacking "insight."

The possibility of an interactive basis of psychopathology extends well beyond therapist–client interaction. Linguistic anthropologist William Beeman asserted the interactive basis of depression in 1985. Could psychosis also emerge interactively? Bateson's now rejected double-bind model of schizophrenia (1972) asserted this. The current popularity of genetic and biochemical models has cost the double-bind model its support. One niche, however, in which we see persisting attention to interaction with persons with schizophrenia is in regards to familial "expressed emotion." "EE" refers to familial expressions of excessive, overbearing, or critical concern in relation to the person with schizophrenia; high EE correlates with poor prognosis. Janis Jenkins (Karno, Jenkins, et al. 1987; Jenkins 1991) developed a Batesonian anthropology of expressed emotion. This promising work invites collaboration with those who could contribute a finer-grained linguistic analysis of interactive conditions affecting the prognosis if not the very nature of schizophrenia. Though there is strong evidence of breakdowns in intersubjectivity attributable to conditions like autism and schizophrenia, Ochs and colleagues (in press) found high functioning children with autism engaging in the joint construction of a proposition, a task requiring a fine level of interactive attunement. Some of the misunderstandings that surround madness arise interactively (Swartz and Swartz 1987). And the feedback effects of others' alienation can exacerbate psychological disturbances.

Are panic disorders interactively constructed? Capps and Ochs's (1995) study of panic disorder (agoraphobia) is one of the few book-length studies of any psychological disorder by linguistic anthropologists. The authors' conviction that Meg's (the subject) language, and the talk exchanged in her psychotherapy sessions, plays a role in the perpetuation of her diagnosis and of her suffering leads them to explore how therapy could work better for such patients. Therapy might become a context for learning to speak differently, specifically, for "revising one's life story to place individual agency in the foreground" (1995: 179–80). Capps and Ochs's analysis includes interlocutors; talk (even talk judged panicky or otherwise pathological) emerges in interpersonal engagement, not from disengaged minds. Therapists who learn to listen differently could interrupt the interactive cycle that reproduces panic (1995: 187–8).

3.4   Entextualization and the construction of post-traumatic stress disorder

Psychiatrists do not consider PTSD (unlike schizophrenia) to be in any sense a communicative disorder. Young's (1995) study of the National Center for the

Treatment of War-Related PTSD thus reveals more about the discursive means of constituting an "authentic case" of the disorder than about PTSD's effects on discourse. Men at the Center produce stories that are far too messy for medical records. In diagnostic meetings, however, staff members rework them into tidy three-part narratives – the patient's "premorbid adjustment," his military life, and his postmilitary life. If the staff presentation must culminate in a recommendation for diagnosis of PTSD, it thematizes distressing re-experiences of the traumatic event. Young notes how easy it would be for outsiders to think of the narrative structure produced in staff meetings as intrinsic to the patient's own stories. In fact what pre-exists the session is not an objectively observable disease with a clear course, but a narrative structure – a model of PTSD – created in psychiatric clinics and textbooks. It is a structure hinging on relatively recent concepts of "experience."

4 CONTEXTUALLY COMPROMISED NARRATIVITY

Between the claim that objective mental illness can rob persons of the humanness manifested in normal interaction, and the counterclaim that powerful discursive structures constitute madness itself, is a third position: the environment in which some mentally ill people live does not support the kinds of interaction upon which normal "experience" depends. All human life has subjective depth, but what sort of subjectivity do we mean when we speak of "having an experience"? In surveying the history of this notion in English, Desjarlais (1997) finds that "experience" evokes something endlessly interpretable, something leading to internal self-reflection and coherently narratable as a temporally ordered transformation (on temporality in narrative, see Ochs, this volume). Desjarlais finds these defining features absent from the talk of those in a Boston shelter for the homeless mentally ill. He attributes their "experience-less" form of subjectivity to their homelessness rather than their diagnostic categories.

Desjarlais's problematization of "experience" opens new perspectives on self, narrative, and the fog through which some or all of us move (Ochs, this volume). In my view, the three features of experience Desjarlais highlights all pertain to narrative – its temporality, its focus on transformation, and the multiple meanings it affords. We can paraphrase his argument as follows: if I do not (or perhaps cannot) narratively organize the key events of my life, I cannot convincingly perform the role of person (social actor, culturally recognizable agent – Duranti, this volume). This is evidence, albeit of a negative sort, of the key role narrative plays in constructing coherent self-awareness (Ochs, this volume).

What of those with similar diagnoses (such as schizophrenia) who stay off the streets and participate in a more stable discursive community? For psychiatric anthro-pologist Ellen Corin (Corin and Lauzon 1994), as for Capps and Ochs (1995), discursive style is not determined by diagnosis. Among a population of non-homeless persons diagnosed with schizophrenia, Corin found a difference in narratives of those who did and did not need rehospitalization after their initial psychotic episodes. The non-rehospitalized group engaged in just as much metalinguistic play; in fact, their play involved positively recontextualizing stigmatizing terms used about them. Their narratives uniquely emphasized pleasure in friendships, and recaptured the

temporality that seems so fragile in schizophrenia (Van Dongen 1997). They reintro-
duced "the present mode of being within a historical frame, contrasting now with
'before'" (Corin and Lauzon 1994: 30). Like Desjarlais, these authors attribute
much to sociocultural environment, and – drawing on Corin's fieldwork in African
possession groups – lament the lack of Western stages for performing other subjectivities in a therapeutic social context (compare Van Dongen 1997: 94).

5   CONCLUSION

To uncritically reproduce widespread perceptions that madness entails linguistically
signaled disengagement from others contributes to the construction of madness that
Foucault (1973) ascribed to modern forms of power. It cuts off the dialogue between
madness and sanity. On the other hand, this chapter's first section presents ample
evidence to problematize romanticizing views of madness as creativity. Madness is
suffering. To the extent that it entails a failure of intersubjectivity, it is interactively
achieved. The suffering is shared. It is all too easy to regard linguistic signals such as
"excessive" word play or "pressure of speech" as performative in some automatic or
magical way, as if they either betrayed the essence of the mad self or brought about
the madness that they seem merely to indicate. (People said, for example, that Latifa's
laments heated her head and made her crazier.) But the fragmentation of the narrative
capacity that would appear native to schizophrenia may instead reflect environments
that are unfriendly to recovering intersubjectivity.

Thus, linguistic anthropologists should devote more thought to madness for at
least two reasons. Madness involves language so profoundly as to spread awareness of
issues central to this subdiscipline. Moreover, linguistic anthropologists have a political impact on the world. We are well positioned to raise helpful questions about the
relationship between humanness, interactive norms, and sanity, and about language
and power in institutions.

REFERENCES

APA (American Psychiatric Association) (2000). Diagnostic and Statistical Manual of Mental
    Disorders : DSM-IV-TR. Washington, DC: APA.
Astington, J. W. (1999). What Is Theoretical about the Child's Theory of Mind? A Vygotskian
    View of Its Development. In P. Lloyd and C. Fernyhough (eds.), Lev Vygotsky: Critical
    Assessments: Future Directions (pp. 401–418). Florence, KY: Taylor & Francis/Routledge.
Barrett, R. J. (1998). The "Schizophrenic" and the Liminal Persona in Modern Society.
    Culture, Medicine and Psychiatry 22(4): 464–503.
Bateson, G. (1972). Steps to an Ecology of Mind. Scranton, PA: Chandler.
Beeman, W. O. (1985). Dimensions of Dysphoria: The View from Linguistic Anthropology. In
    A. Kleinman and B. Good (eds.), Culture and Depression (pp. 216–243). Berkeley: Univer-
    sity of California Press.
Capps, L., and Ochs, E. (1995). Constructing Panic: The Discourse of Agoraphobia. Cambridge,
    MA: Harvard University Press.
Condon, W. S., and Ogston, W. D. (1966). Sound Film Analysis of Normal and Pathological
    Behavior Patterns. Journal of Nervous and Mental Disease 143: 338–347.

Corin, E., and Lauzon, G. (1994). From Symptoms to Phenomena: The Articulation of the Experience in Schizophrenia. *Journal of Phenomenological Psychology* 25(1): 3–50.

Crow, T. J. (2000). Schizophrenia as the Price that *Homo sapiens* Pays for Language: A Resolution of the Central Paradox in the Origin of the Species. *Brain Research Reviews* 31: 118–129.

Desjarlais, R. (1997). *Shelter Blues: Homelessness and Sanity in a Boston Shelter.* Philadelphia: University of Pennsylvania Press.

Dunbar, R. (1998). Theory of Mind and the Evolution of Language. In J. R. Hurford, M. Studdert-Kennedy, and C. Knight (eds.), *Approaches to the Evolution of Language: Social and Cognitive Bases* (pp. 92–110). Cambridge: Cambridge University Press.

Duranti, A. (1997). *Linguistic Anthropology.* Cambridge Textbooks in Linguistics. Cambridge: Cambridge University Press.

Falk, J. (1979). The Conversational Duet. PhD dissertation, Princeton University.

Foucault, M. (1973). *Madness and Civilization: A History of Insanity in the Age of Reason.* New York: Vintage.

Fukunishi, I., et al. (1997). Is Alexithymia a Culture-bound Construct? Validity and Reliability of the Japanese Versions of the 20-item Toronto Alexithymia Scale and Modified Beth Israel Hospital Psychosomatic Questionnaire. *Psychological Reports* 80(3, Pt 1): 787–799.

Goddard, M. (1998). What Makes Hari Run? The Social Construction of Madness in a Highland Papua New Guinea Society. *Critique of Anthropology* 18(1): 61–81.

Goffman, E. (1969). The Insanity of Place. *Psychiatry* 32: 357–388.

Goffman, E. (1974). *Frame Analysis: An Essay on the Organization of Experience.* Cambridge, MA: Harvard University Press.

Gratier, M. (1999). Expressions of Belonging: The Effect of Acculturation on the Rhythm and Harmony of Mother–Infant Vocal Interaction. In *Musicae Scientiae* 1999, Special Issue on "Rhythm, Musical Narrative, and Origins of Human Communication".

Gumperz, J. J. (1982). Interethnic Communication. In J. J. Gumperz, *Discourse Strategies* (pp. 172–186). Cambridge: Cambridge University Press.

Gumperz, J. J., and Levinson, S. C. (eds.) (1996). *Rethinking Linguistic Relativity.* Cambridge: Cambridge University Press.

Jenkins, J. H. (1991). Anthropology, Expressed Emotion, and Schizophrenia. *Ethos* 19(4): 387–431.

Karno, M., et al. (1987). Expressed Emotion and Schizophrenic Outcome among Mexican-American Families. *Journal of Nervous and Mental Disease* 175(3): 143–151.

Kirmayer, L. J. (1987). Languages of Suffering and Healing: Alexithymia as a Social and Cultural Process. *Transcultural Psychiatric Research Review* 24(2): 119–136.

Kusserow, A. S. (1999). De-Homogenizing American Individualism: Socializing Hard and Soft Individualism in Manhattan and Queens. *Ethos* 27(2): 210–234.

Lee, B. (1997). *Talking Heads: Language, Metalanguage, and the Semiotics of Subjectivity.* Durham, NC: Duke University Press.

Lucas, R. H., and Barrett, R. J. (1995). Interpreting Culture and Psychopathology: Primitivist Themes in Cross-Cultural Debate. *Culture, Medicine and Psychiatry* 19: 287–326.

Lyons, J. (1982). Deixis and Subjectivity: *Loquor, ergo sum?* In R. J. Jarvella and W. Klein (eds.), *Speech, Place, and Action: Studies in Deixis and Related Topics* (pp. 101–124). Chichester: John Wiley & Sons.

Martin, E. (2000). The Rationality of Mania. In R. Reid and S. Traweek (eds.), *Doing Science + Culture,* (pp. 177–196). New York and London: Routledge.

Martínez-Hernáez, A. (2000). *What's Behind the Symptom? On Psychiatric Observation and Anthropological Understanding.* Amsterdam: Harwood Academic Publishers.

McDaniel, J. (1989). *The Madness of the Saints: Ecstatic Religion in Bengal.* Chicago: University of Chicago Press.

Ochs, E., Kremer-Sadlik, T., and Solomon, O. (in press). Autism and the Social World: An Anthropological Perspective. *Discourse Studies.*

Reddy, M. (1993 [1979]). The Conduit Metaphor: A Case of Frame Conflict in Our Language about Language. In A. Ortony (ed.), *Metaphor and Thought* (pp. 164–201). Cambridge: Cambridge University Press.

Reddy, Y., Girimaji, S., and Srinath, S. (1997). Clinical Profile of Mania in Children and Adolescents from the Indian Subcontinent. *Canadian Journal of Psychiatry* 42(8): 840–846.

Ribeiro, B. T. (1995). *Coherence in Psychotic Discourse.* New York: Oxford University Press.

Rommetveit, R. (1998). Intersubjective Attunement and Linguistically Mediated Meaning in Discourse. In S. Bråten (ed.), *Intersubjective Communication and Emotion in Early Ontogeny* (pp. 354–371). Cambridge: Cambridge University Press.

Sass, L. A. (1992). *Madness and Modernism: Insanity in the Light of Modern Art, Literature, and Thought.* New York: Basic Books.

Schore, A. N. (2001). Effects of a Secure Attachment Relationship on Right Brain Development, Affect Regulation, and Infant Mental Health. *Infant Mental Health* 22(1–2): 7–66.

Schutz, A. (1962–66). Making Music Together: A Study in Social Relationship. In *Collected Papers*, ed. A. Brodersen, vol. 2, *Studies in Social Theory* (pp. 159–178). The Hague: Martinus Nijhoff.

Siegman, A. (1987). Pacing of Speech in Depression. In J. D. Maser (ed.), *Depression and Expressive Behavior.* Hillsdale, NJ: Lawrence Erlbaum.

Silverstein, M., and Urban, G. (eds.) (1996). *Natural Histories of Discourse.* Chicago and London: University of Chicago Press.

Swartz, S., and Swartz, L. (1987). Talk about Talk: Metacommentary and Context in the Analysis of Psychotic Discourse. *Culture, Medicine, and Psychiatry* 11(4): 395–415.

Tényi, T., et al. (2000). Schizophrenics Show a Failure in the Decoding of Violations of Conversational Implicatures. *Psychopathology* 35(1): 25–27.

Van Dongen, E. (1997). Space and Time in the Lives of People with Long-standing Mental Illness: An Ethnographic Account. *Anthropology and Medicine* 4(1): 89–103.

Wallace, A. F. C. (1965). *Culture and Personality.* New York: Random House.

Whorf, B. L. (1956). *Language, Thought, and Reality: Selected Writings of Benjamin Lee Whorf.* Cambridge, MA: MIT Press.

Wilce, J. M. (1998a). Coping with the Language of Madness in Rural Bangladesh: Aesthetics and Language Ideologies. In *Proceedings of the 6th International Pragmatics Conference*, Reims, France (pp. 584–595). International Pragmatics Association.

Wilce, J. M. (1998b). *Eloquence in Trouble: The Poetics and Politics of Complaint in Rural Bangladesh.* Oxford Studies in Anthropological Linguistics. New York: Oxford University Press.

Wilce, J. M. (2000). The Poetics of "Madness": Shifting Codes and Styles in the Linguistic Construction of Identity in Matlab, Bangladesh. *Cultural Anthropology* 15(1): 3–34.

Wilce, J. M. (2002). Tunes Rising from the Soul and Other Narcissistic Prayers: Contested Realms in Bangladesh. In D. Mines and S. Lamb (eds.), *Everyday Life in South Asia* (pp. 289–302). Bloomington: Indiana University Press.

Wilce, J. M. (in press). To "Speak Beautifully" in Bangladesh: Subjectivity as *pāgalāmi.* In J. Jenkins and R. Barrett (eds.), *The Edge of Experience: Culture, Subjectivity, and Schizophrenia.* New York: Cambridge University Press.

Young, A. (1995). *The Harmony of Illusions: Inventing Post-Traumatic Stress Disorder.* Princeton, NJ: Princeton University Press.

CHAPTER 19 Language and Religion

Webb Keane

1 INTRODUCTION: "RELIGIOUS LANGUAGE" AS AN ANTHROPOLOGICAL TOPIC

Despite long-standing interest in subjects such as ritual speech, oratory, magic, myth, exorcism, divination, possession, oaths, prophecy, and more recently, textuality, reading, and performativity, "religious language" *per se* has not been a commonly recognized anthropological topic (one exception is Samarin 1976). But taken as the intersection of the studies of religion and language, it can bring insight into key questions that have usually been treated from more restricted perspectives. Religious contexts can be especially revealing for the study of linguistic form and action since they can involve people's most extreme and self-conscious manipulations of language, in response to their most powerful intuitions about agency.

For the purposes of this chapter, I propose that an anthropological study of "religious language" concerns linguistic practices that are taken *by practitioners themselves* to be marked or unusual in such a way as to suggest that they involve entities or modes of agency which are considered by those practitioners to be consequentially distinct from more "ordinary" experience, or situated across some sort of ontological divide from something understood as a more everyday "here and now."[1] This definition aims to take indigenous perceptions as a guide, without foreclosing the possibility of comparison and generalization. I argue that religious language practices exploit a wide range of the formal and pragmatic features of everyday language in ways that help make available to experience and thought the very ontological divides to which they offer themselves as a response. These practices can assist the construction of forms of agency that are expanded, displaced, distributed or otherwise different from – but clearly related to – what are otherwise available.

This approach does *not* presuppose belief, since it starts from the existence of signifying practices rather than pre-existing concepts. Many religious traditions have little interest in either individual belief or public statements of doctrine (Asad

1993; Needham 1972), and may accept differences of interpretation as long as practices themselves remain consistent. Moreover, even religions that do stress belief may still object to the subordination of material practices to inner states. For instance, Blaise Pascal insisted, "The external must be joined to the internal to obtain anything from God, that is to say, we must kneel to pray with the lips, etc., in order that proud man, who would not submit himself to God, may be now subject to the creature. ... [To] refuse to join [externals] to the internal is pride" (no. 250, 1958: 73).

Such "externals" as ritual have been the stuff of ethnography. One recent theory of religion asserts that "the sacred, the numinous, the occult and the divine" are all ultimately generated in ritual (Rappaport 1999: 23). This reflects a common anthropological view that to count as "religion" something must take forms that can be shared and reproduced as sociological realities (Geertz 1973). That is, religion is approached in its modes of "semiotic mediation," the ways in which social relations, cultural meanings, even subjective experience, are not just transmitted by signs but are constrained, made available for embodiment and circulation, and transformed by them (see Lee 1997; Urban 1996).

The approach taken here presupposes that people have some intuitions, or language ideologies (see Kroskrity 2000 and this volume), about distinctions of markedness among different linguistic forms and practices. As Roman Jakobson suggested for poetics (1960), since religious language practices may involve practitioners' heightened awareness of language (among other things), they offer analysts insight into that awareness and its linguistic and, by extension, conceptual and social consequences. Although such intuitions presumably involve cognitive input (Boyer 1993), the best evidence suggests that their concrete realizations are irreducibly mediated by specific cultural, social, and historical formations.

2   RELIGIOUS LANGUAGE AS ACTION: FROM GAME TO PERFORMATIVE

An important theological question in several monotheistic traditions has been how words, which normally denote objects of experience, could have meaning when applied to a God who transcends experience. The question tends to assume that the primary function of language is to denote entities and say something about them. One response has been to focus on linguistic functions *other* than denotation. For instance, words that are apparently statements about God could actually be affirming the speaker's faith. This led many Western theologians to concepts that have been foundational for contemporary linguistic anthropology, Ludwig Wittgenstein's "language game" (1953) and J. L. Austin's "performative" (1962) (see Duranti, this volume). Wittgenstein claimed that different language games are governed by their own, distinct conventions. One would not hold a sonnet, shaggy-dog story, instruction manual, scientific proof, declaration of love, or memorized liturgy to identical standards of verifiability or sincerity. As Bronislaw Malinowski (1935) suggested, when Trobriand magic spells include semantically opaque speech, the resulting "coefficient of weirdness" shows that their "context of action" is distinct from that of other verbal acts.

The notion of language games drew attention to the interactive, socially conventional, and multi-functional character of speech practices. But it fell short of explaining their authority, specific forms, or how they change. Many students of religion turned to Austin's account of speech acts or performativity. Austin observed that certain expressions, such as "I hereby do thee wed," when spoken under certain conditions, serve not to make statements about things, but to effect changes in a state of affairs, such as transforming two persons into husband and wife. He eventually suggested that *all* statements have a performative (or "illocutionary") dimension.

The idea of the performative seemed to offer a way of understanding how talk "about" God could be doing something else. But if such talk is really performative, why should its linguistic forms have *looked* so much like an assertion as to have given rise to that mistaken impression (see Keane 1995)? After all, affirmations of faith take many forms such as words addressed *to* rather than *about* God, bodily gestures (Mahmood 2001), or semantically opaque utterances like mantra (Staal 1990). The role of explicit belief statements in certain traditions requires analysis of "language ideology," to which I will turn below.

In a different line of development, some anthropologists (Ahern 1979; Rappaport 1990; Tambiah 1979) took a cue from the fact that Austin's key examples are rituals. They suggested that the specific nature of ritual efficacy is performative, its results being due to the social convention that a certain form constitutes a certain action. The logical necessity linking act and consequence is like that between saying "I promise" under the right conditions, and the making of a promise. The saying *is* the making of a promise.

The performative approach to ritual seemed useful in explaining several things about ritual. One is that by removing its efficacy from the domain of physical causality, ritual escaped the accusation of being bad science, of trying to accomplish material results (such as making rain) on the basis of faulty premises (the magical power of words). Another is that the emphasis on conventionality fits the empirical observation that actors often consider it important that they themselves did not invent the ritual. As in many traditions, ritualists in Sumba, Indonesia, insist that "there are no longer any who really know" the rites, for the living are merely "new lips and new eyes" who did not create the ancestral words but just follow the traces of "Lord's tracks in the twigs, Lady's cutting-marks on the stump" (Keane 1997b). The poetic structure of their ritual speech and the highly salient pragmatic norms governing its performance reinforce the sense that these words are independent of their speakers, and that this contributes to their power. Finally, the conventionality of performatives seemed to justify the common ritual emphasis on repetition of forms. Adherence to a certain form (such as the parallelisms in the Sumbanese couplets just quoted, or, in English, a "hereby" in a proclamation) can help determine that a given utterance is a token of a certain performative type.

But the performative approach is also subject to an important criticism. In many cases, the practitioners themselves do *not* see their rituals as achieving their effects simply by convention. They may, for instance, be concerned with influencing the spirit world through emotional effects or magical causality (Gardner 1983). Some further explanation is required of how practitioners commonly define ritual as having special powers, or as able to bring about social interaction with extra-ordinary agents.

2.1   Ritual as authoritative action

If language games and performativity concern the *logic* of symbolic action, anthropology has increasingly been interested in its relation to *power*. The observation that participants in ritual can experience its regimentation of vocal and bodily movements as an external force was, of course, central to Emile Durkheim's (1915) account of its function in creating social solidarity. Similarly, as Gladys Reichard (1944) proposed of Navaho prayer, poetic patterning has "compulsive force," and linguistic anthropology has long tried to specify the emotional and social effects of ritual's formal properties more broadly (Duranti 1994: chapt. 4; Irvine 1989).

Maurice Bloch (1989 [1974], 1975) looked at several dimensions of structure to explain the distinctive character of ritual authority. He defined ritual in terms of its formality and repetitiousness, understood these to be markedly apart from the norms of everyday interaction, and looked to them for its special power. Since ritual, as he defines it, severely restricts the participants' choices of intonation, vocabulary, syntactic forms, and acceptable illustrations (such as scriptural or mythological allusions), it wields what he claims is necessarily a highly impoverished kind of propositional language. Therefore he concludes that ritual cannot primarily function to make statements. Rather, it is coercive: once participants have entered the ritual frame, they are committed to a pre-ordained sequence of events. The only alternative is the extreme act of rejecting the very premises of the ritual. Moreover, this coercion is all the more effective in so far as it tends to operate beneath the level of individual awareness, and includes the pressures of ordinary politeness norms – that to interrupt or speak in the wrong register, for instance, is vulgar or insulting.

In contrast to many "language-game" theorists, therefore, Bloch did not simply situate ritual as one game alongside, and neutral with respect to, others. Ritual words gain their power to suppress "reality" by being detached from context and from any association with the particular speaker. This makes it possible for the ritualists to speak on behalf of experience-distant entities, such as impersonal ancestor spirits.

Bloch drew criticism for too directly associating form with a particular social function. Judith Irvine (1979) showed that the word "formality" often conflates a wide range of meanings which do not necessarily correlate, and may even work at odds with one another. She argued that our analytic vocabulary must distinguish among at least four kinds of formality: increased code structuring, heightened cooccurrence rules, invocation of positional identities, and the emergence of a central situational focus. In particular, the structuring of linguistic code is relatively independent of the other three aspects of formality, which are more sociolinguistic and pragmatic in character. Moreover, in any empirical instance, local ideologies play a crucial role in mediating any actual social consequences of ritualization. Form alone is not fully determinative.

The high formality of poetic structure and interactive norms in Sumbanese ritual genres, for instance, can undermine rather than simply reinforce the smooth workings of hegemonic authority, fostering the participants' sense that ritual actions involve grave risks (Keane 1997b). The sense of risk operates at several levels. Foregrounding the rule-governed character of ritual implies that errors in performance can bring dangerous consequences. Tight constraints on interaction imply that the spirits themselves are difficult to reach, and potentially dangerous. The sense of risk makes palpable two things. First is the effort needed to communicate across an ontological gap; second, that such communications face inescapable potential for pragmatic and semantic slippage. Since ritual forms are seen to have an existence independent of their users, they can never be fully under their control. Even the most knowledgeable elders must insist that they possess only fragments of the ritual – or risk being stricken down by spirits for their presumption. In cases like this, there seems to be a positive correlation between a highly formalistic understanding of ritual and the relative lack of stable human authority.

3   RITUAL AS A SPEECH GENRE

The development of the ethnography of speaking (Gumperz and Hymes 1964; Bauman and Sherzer 1974) helped direct attention to speech genres (Bakhtin 1986; Briggs 1988). Genre is "one order of speech style, a constellation of systemically related, co-occurrent formal features and structures that serves as a conventionalized orienting framework for the production and reception of discourse" (Bauman 2001: 79). Ritual can thus be situated in a multi-dimensional field rather than at one end of a line ranging from formal to not-formal. A given genre, such as liturgical chanting, will share some but not all features with others, such as oratory (Bloch 1975) or poetry (Leavitt 1997). Part of ritual's distinctive power, then, might derive from the complex of such linking and distinguishing features articulating it with its verbal surroundings. In this context even highly rule-governed ritual forms turn out to provide more creative resources than might be apparent when viewed in isolation (Gill 1981).

This observation draws support from the growing interest in less obviously formalized activities, such as Muslim sermons on cassette, a moment of evangelical "witnessing" in a conversation, or charismatic Catholic social gatherings, which show that ritual actively contrasts with and borrows from other genres. This weakens any claims about the necessary effects of form on authority, since ritual actions depend on their relation to what happens outside the ritual frame. A televised jeremiad by Jerry Falwell (Harding 2000; cf. Crapanzano 2000; Meigs 1995), spoken in the context of American traditions of religiously inflected political oratory, may have much greater relevance than in societies where political rhetoric has been more secular. Verbal productions that in Taiwan might index a state of potentially benevolent spirit possession would in Canada be likely to lead to a diagnosis of mental illness – even in Taiwan they may end up socially classified as madness (Irvine 1982; Wolf 1990; Wilce, this volume). Moreover, since genres must be identifiable by features that exist independent of any particular context (Bauman 2001), ritual genres are inherently vulnerable to being quoted, parodied, performed insincerely, reframed as art forms, and so forth. The fact that in themselves semiotic forms such as word morphology, poetic structure, or the pragmatic sequence cannot guarantee particular intentions or effects has also been a perennial source of difficulty and reformist efforts within many religious traditions.

3.1 Form and function in ritual speech genres

Ritual speech commonly displays a degree of repetition and elaboration far out of proportion to any obvious propositional requirements. For example, one typical Sumbanese prayer sequence involving two speakers and taking about 113 lines of verse might be reduced to this: "we are following the rules, so please accept this offering and hear our words" (Keane 1997b: 122–4). Couplets such as

followed path there	*lara liya*
for horses to follow	*pali waingu jaraya*
going the Laboyan way	*ta pali Laboya*
crossing trail there	*ada palaya*
for people to cross	*papala waingu tauya*
crossing the Wanukakan way	*ta papala Wanukaka*

(Keane 1997b: 103) amount to "we are performing a ritual properly." These are instances of the framing function (Bateson 1972) that can, in principle, be achieved by any linguistic property, such as esoteric vocabulary or unusual intonation, that marks off a stretch of discourse from its surround.

A frame is "indexical," that is, it points out something in the immediate context – indicating, for instance, "this, now" is a ritual (Hanks 1990; Peirce 1955; Silverstein 1976). It is thus "metapragmatic" (Silverstein 1993), saying something about the linguistic act being undertaken. But indexes alone merely point to the presence of something and cannot themselves offer any information about it. Some acts, such as "I hereby do thee wed," use explicit metapragmatic verbs ("to wed") to state what they are doing. Commonly, however, more guidance from semiotic form is needed, such as iconism or resemblance (Jakobson 1990). For instance, because the strongly dualistic couplet forms just quoted manifest a Sumbanese aesthetic of completeness and balance, they are iconic of the desired ritual outcome – sacred wholeness – without actually denoting it. And, over the course of the ritual, speakers' utterances tend increasingly to take strict parallelistic form. This is one example of how changes in linguistic form may realize the progression of the ritual action by resembling it, an instance of a "metapragmatic icon" (Silverstein 1981).

The observation is significant because it goes beyond imputing the effects of ritual simply to convention, to show they can derive from formal properties as they unfold in real time. For example, rituals may display increasing depersonalization over the course of the event (Bloch 1989 [1974]; Kuipers 1990). Indexes of the present time, place, or participants such as personal pronouns may be progressively eliminated, with poetic formulae, prosodic regularity, and other regimentations of discourse becoming more stringent, such that the participants come increasingly to speak not as individuated, complex, politically interested, and temporally finite parties, but as more abstract, disinterested, and timeless elders or spirits. The outcome is due not wholly to convention or conscious intention but to subliminal effects of linguistic and pragmatic forms.

Indexes and metapragmatic icons can make use of a wide range of linguistic properties in mutually reinforcing ways. For instance, the appearance of phonological or morphological forms markedly different from those found in colloquial speech may be taken by participants to be an irruption of divine speech. Entire stretches of discourse may take on greater poetic structuring, or shift their tense markings, reinforcing the intuitive sense that, as in the case of Zuni prayer, the words are being repeated exactly "according to the first beginning" (Bunzel 1932: 493).

Regardless of the varying conscious intentions of ritual performers, the properties of ritual speech tend to mark it as different from more "ordinary" ways of using language. But the examples of metapragmatic iconism imply that there are more specific functions involved in these marked forms than the mere framing as "ritual." This may help explain the recurrence of certain features in ritual speech across the ethnographic record. John Du Bois (1986) identified some of these as follows:

- use of a ritual register
- archaistic elements
- elements borrowed from other languages
- euphemism and metaphor
- semantic opacity
- semantic-grammatical parallelism
- marked voice quality
- stylized and restricted intonation contours
- unusual fluency of speech
- gestalt knowledge
- personal volition disclaimers
- avoidance of first and second person pronouns
- speech style attributed to ancestors
- use of mediating speakers

Some of these are mutually determined. Fluent speaking style and gestalt knowledge, for instance, can both result from learning entire texts as seamless, and sometimes semantically opaque, wholes. Overall, however, these features must be understood as bearing what Wittgenstein called family resemblances, in so far as they do not constitute necessary and sufficient conditions for membership in a set, but form linked clusters such that no single member of the family need possess every feature. But viewing this cluster in terms of pragmatic functions and semiotic characteristics may offer a way of widening our scope from ritual speech to religious language practices more generally.

4 RELIGIOUS LANGUAGE AS ALTERING CONVERSATIONAL ASSUMPTIONS

As the concept of the metapragmatic icon suggests, rituals may derive some of their efficacy by linking formal properties to expected outcomes. One comparative question that arises, then, is whether there is something that motivates this common feature of ritual speech across the ethnographic spectrum. I have suggested that religious language commonly helps make present what would otherwise, in the course of ordinary experience, be absent or imperceptible, or makes that absence presupposable by virtue of the special means used to overcome it. In pragmatic terms, ritual suspends certain presuppositions of ordinary interaction, such as the assumption that one's interlocutors can see and hear one, that they share one's language, and that the relevant shared context and conversational goals are unproblematic (Grice 1975). The special character of interaction across an ontological gap is made explicit in the question posed by some prayers of the Berawan of Indonesia (Metcalf 1989), "where are you spirits?"

Face-to-face interactions commonly build up an indexical ground, a emergent consensus among the participants about the nature of the shared here-and-now that forms the center of their conversation. Much interactive work is devoted to coordinating speakers (see Keating and Egbert, this volume; Bailey, this volume) and determining the relevant context and the identities of the participants (Duranti and Brenneis 1986; Mannheim and Tedlock 1995). The outsider to the conversation may not know whether "we," at the moment, includes, for instance, only those people within earshot, all Canadian citizens, or the dead ancestors, whether "now" contrasts with yesterday, the era before feminism, or the afterlife (see Urban 1996), but what Erving Goffman called "ratified participants" (1981) normally come to some consensus very quickly. In contrast to such default assumptions, many of the formal properties of ritual speech play down the indexical grounding of the utterances in the immediate context. As Goffman (1967, 1981) observed, problems in coordination during ordinary conversation may be clues to trouble with, or new threats to, participants' identities and their sense of shared assumptions. In some religious contexts, however, it may be precisely the function of language to raise questions like "what's going on here?" and "who's speaking now?"

4.1   The dialectics of text and context

Forms that decontextualize discourse help create a perception that certain chunks of speech are self-contained, belong together, and could be reproduced in different contexts without substantive consequences for the discourse itself. This results in what has been called a "decentering of discourse" through "entextualization," the process of foregrounding its text-like properties, and the sense that it is relatively context-independent (Silverstein and Urban 1996). The words will seem to come from some source beyond the present situation in which they are being spoken and heard. Often the speakers seem to others or even themselves to have relatively little volition in producing their speech. They may be supposed, for instance, to be speaking exactly as the ancestors did, as the spirits who possess them dictate, or as has been written. The textual character of scripture can support the trans-contextual efforts of some Christians to find Biblical prototypes for every aspect of life (Harding 2000; Stromberg 1993). Effects of linguistic form are likely to seem especially persuasive and realistic because they are not derived from explicit doctrines, which one might doubt or deny, but seem to come directly from experience.

The decentering of discourse is one moment in a larger set of dialectical processes that also include the centering or contextualizing of discourse, which stress the relatively objective and subjective experiences of language. On the one hand, language is associated with the experience of inner speech and speaker's intentionality. On the other hand, it consists of pre-existing forms that one has learned from others, and, in addressing and being addressed, remains "on the borderline between oneself and the other" (Bakhtin 1981: 293; see also Benveniste 1971; Mead 1934; Vygostky 1978).

Taken as objectified forms, language has been an important target of religious critiques. One, stressing the propositional function, is that human language is an innately limited imposition on the ineffable or infinite, a position developed, for example, by Buddhism (Gómez 2000), some Christian mystics (Katz 1992), and Jewish Kabbalah (which treats scriptural language as divine emanation – but its communicative function as merely human (Scholem 1969)). The other, more socio-linguistic, is that language is inescapably implicated in politics or social vanities, as claimed by early Quakers (Bauman 1983). The latter critique in particular has tended to be associated with an emphasis on (apparently) plain or spontaneous speech, and language ideologies that stress the subjective intimacy of inner speech, and the norm of sincerity (Keane 1997c, 2002; Robbins 2001).

4.2 Reported speech

Suspicions of language in some religious traditions focus on the very same linguistic and pragmatic properties that other traditions may seek to exploit. To the extent that religious practices respond to or contribute to the perception of an ontological gap contrary to the assumptions of ordinary interaction, they may be prone to draw on the decentering and recentering possibilities of entextualization processes. For religions "of the book," the very existence of a written scripture is often taken as evidence for claims to an authority that transcends any particular context, and provides semiotic grounds for their intuitive verification. But the same decontextual-izing objectivity may become the target of reformers and critics who seek unmediated access to divinity (Bauman 1983; Keane 1997c).

Compelling examples of the dialectic of recontextualization are found in the use of scriptures among contemporary Christians. Certain parts of scripture, such as Christ's Sermon on the Mount or the Lord's Prayer, are taken by many believers to reproduce words that were originally spoken in a particular context. Circulating in textual form, the words are now available for broad dissemination. Indeed, some believers take a capacity for wide circulation found, for example, in videotaped sermons, as evidence of the divinity of words even when they are not themselves sacred scripture (Coleman 2000; cf. Besnier 1995).

As they circulate, entextualized words are subject to recontextualization, as, for example, they are performed, read out loud, quoted, alluded to, or made the objects of silent meditation. The formal means by which words are introduced into new contexts have significant implications for the imputed relations not only between text and context, but also between different participants in the event (Boyarin 1993). Direct quotation, in which the words are supposed to retain the forms of the original utterance, tends to sharpen the distinction between the quoter and the person quoted. According to Vološinov, "The stronger the feeling of hierarchical eminence in another's utterance, the more sharply defined will its boundaries be, and the less accessible will it be to penetration by reporting and commenting tendencies from outside" (1973: 123). In contrast, indirect quotation, in which the original words are rephrased, permits the person doing the quoting to interpret the original words and their intended effects from the perspective of the subsequent context (Lucy 1993). As a result, direct quotation is often felt to be more deferential to the original speaker, since it does not impose an interpretation or mingle voices (Hanks 1996; Urban 1989).

Linguistic form alone, however, does not fully determine the nature of the relationship between quoter and quoted source, for under some ideological interpretations, direct quotation can come to identify the two. Naomi Janowitz (1989) argues that the words of some Jewish mystical texts were supposed to be identical to those sung by angels, so the human reciting them joins the angelic chorus. Similar efforts to eliminate the distinction between quoting context and quoted original are found in some Buddhist meditation practices that aim at the internalization of texts such that the meditator identifies with their divine source (Gómez 2000). For many Christian fundamentalists the process of becoming saved is inseparable from the ongoing penetration of their everyday speech by scripture (Harding 2000; Stromberg 1993). Citations can become so thoroughly part of the speaker's consciousness as to lose at least some of their character as quoted text and become difficult to separate from the speaker's "own words."

4.3   Participation roles

Ways of reporting speech commonly express aspects of the relations among participants in a speech event or text. Quotation indexes the participant role of "animator." In Goffman's (1981) terminology, conversational roles can be analyzed into *principal,* who bears responsibility for what is said, *author* who formulates the words, *animator* who utters them, *proximal addressee* of the utterance, *target* to whom the words are ultimately directed, and *overhearer.* Sumbanese rituals institutionalize such distinctions, as speakers pray and orate on behalf of silent sponsors, animating couplets whose ultimate authorship is attributed to ancestors, but whose selection and sequence must be determined by a different ritual specialist. The speakers address these words to yet other ritualists (the proximal addressees) thus casting both spirits and humans as overhearers, the former also being ratified as targets, and, overall, creating a manifestly supra-individual "speaker" (Keane 1997b).

The distinction between author and animator encompasses a wide range of possible relationships. Responsibility for words can range from a sharp hierarchical distinction between author and animator, to some degree of co-authorship or ambiguity (Duranti and Brenneis 1986). Early Islam apparently did not differentiate between the authority of words spoken by God and those spoken by the Prophet Muhammed (W. Graham 1977). In the Qur'an, God's words appear as reported speech, and so are also the Prophet's words, as he is their animator. But Muhammed also animates prophetic speech of which he is the author – although its principal remains the divine source of his inspiration. Eventually, however, it became theologically important to distinguish prophetic speech from direct revelation, sharpening the boundary between reported speech and its frame, and thus between animator and author. This placed the original prophecy and its divine author at a greater remove from historical events, in order to accentuate the otherworldliness of the divinity and prevent the deification of the prophet.

Often what is at stake in the precise distinction between author and animator is the degree of agency, authority, and responsibility a performer is willing or permitted to assume. As Sumbanese ritualists would insist, powerful words come from absent authors. The forms of reported speech help make such distance (or its reverse) presupposable. In Lowland South America, narrators may gradually shift the extent of their identification with the protagonists in the myth they are narrating, positioning themselves either as commentators on absent spirits or as the spirit itself, bringing the otherworld into the present (Urban 1989; see also L. Graham 1995). Such "breakthroughs into performance" (Hymes 1981) are crucial for the capacity of religious practices to transform their contexts.

Even subtle alterations in speaking role can be crucial. For example, evangelical Protestants often describe their conversion as a call to witness, testify, or preach to others (Titon 1988; Peacock and Tyson 1989). Notice that this may not involve any particular change in *belief* itself – the individual may have subscribed to the same doctrines before and after being "saved." Rather, in such cases, full conversion consists in taking on a specific kind of authority – being transformed, as Susan Harding (2000) puts it, from a listener into a speaker, with a greater responsibility for and even authorship of words.

Bakhtin identified heteroglossia, or the capacity for coexisting linguistic styles to index multiple social identities, as pervasive in everyday speech. Many religious practices systematically take advantage of this capacity to alter the salient identities and relationships among authors and animators over the course of a performance. As the participant roles taken on by performers change, they index the absence, presence, or emergence of divine or spirit participants. The progressive transformation of these indexes is itself iconic of the transformation being effected by the religious event, for example the gradual appearance and then departure of the Quaker's Inner Light, the Pentecostal's glossolalia or speaking in tongues, the ritualist's ancestral spirit, or a shaman's spirit familiar. In contrast to more intellectualist and conventionalist aspects of ritual, the power of such semiotic forms seems to lie in the sense of realism they create by their direct availability to the senses and intuitions of participants and witnesses.

In general, where relatively egalitarian relationships prevail, the living may be expected to speak to the spirits in their "own" voices (Metcalf 1989), that is, as simultaneously author, animator, and principal. But in taking on individual agency, these speakers also expose themselves to the risks that attend interaction with spirits. In a less egalitarian situation, divine inspiration may provide speakers with an acceptable voice for public speaking that would not be available were they taken to be the authors of their own words (Lawless 1988; Lewis 1971).

Such examples show imputed authorship to have creative effects, by making available to speakers an identity or a relationship to some special agent. This is an instance of the broader point, that one widespread effect of religious language is the creation or extension of agents and forms of agency beyond what is commonly available in unmarked interaction. It is also one reason why "religious" speech has often been appropriated in "political" ways.

5   INTENTIONS AND THE IDENTITY OF THE ACTORS

The denial or displacement of individual intentionality can occur at several levels, from explicit propositions to the implications of linguistic form and the pragmatics of participation. The analysis of participant roles is only one instance of the collaborative and distributed nature of linguistic intentionality (Duranti 1993) and responsibility (Hill and Irvine 1993). Many of the effects of religious language can be better understood as expanding the presumptive speaker *above* the level of the individual, or, conversely, distinguishing among different voices *below* that level, emanating from a single body (Irvine 1996).

The distinctions among participation roles are of particular significance in many religious activities, given that the character and even the very presence of some participants is not guaranteed or readily determined by immediate observation, and that often the focus of the activity is the transformation of the identity of human actors, making present and bringing into engagement non-human ones. Therefore religious practices often elaborate on these distinctions to develop or respond to the purported nature, powers, and responsibilities of both practitioners and the entities with which they are interacting. In many cases where the authorship, performance, and responsibility for speech is distributed among different actors, it might be most accurate to describe the result as the creation of a supra-individual speaking subject (Keane 1997b). The reverse is also possible, the combining of distinct roles in a single bodily individual. As American folk preachers come to be "filled with the spirit," their performances display emergent features such as highly rhythmical, repetitive utterances, marked vocabulary, and gasping and shouting (Pitts 1993). When these are taken to index the individual's loss of personal control in favor of a divine agent, they verge on "possession," although this definition depends on local categories and participants' willingness to ascribe them in a given case (Irvine 1982). More generally, spirit possession (Boddy 1994) and glossolalia (Goodman 1972; Samarin 1972) involve both a deity and a human being using the same body but speaking in different voices, marked by contrasting prosodic and paralinguistic features, and sometimes distinct linguistic codes.

5.1   Objectifications of language and the construction of agency

The formal properties of highly ritualized performances often play down the agency of the living human participants in favor of powers ascribed to other entities. The social results may vary from the reinforcement of hierarchies to the making available of "other" voices that marginal or subaltern speakers may appropriate to subversive effect. In general, the formal means by which different religions propose to interact with their respective otherworlds can be diagnostic of their basic assumptions about the nature of the beings to be found there, as well as of living humans themselves. To this extent, linguistic practice may *reflect* ontological assumptions. For example, some beings do not require deference. Ruth Bunzel (1932: 618) claimed that in praying, Zuni "do not humble themselves before the supernatural; they bargain with it." This is strikingly different from Calvinists who try to avoid implying by their words that they could actually influence God (Keane 1997c). And these both differ from forms of address that beseech or flatter (Calame-Griaule 1986) or influence by displaying the speaker's esoteric knowledge about the spirit addressee (Sherzer 1990). Modernist or reformist movements may place a great emphasis on cultivating sincere speaker intentionality, as in the demand that prayer be spontaneous. But even when highly scripted texts are followed, as in the daily prayers of Muslims, reformers may insist that the speakers utter them with "powerful depictive imagination" (Bowen 1993: 84). One may not be able to detect simply on the basis of speech forms whether the ideological emphasis is on personal intention or divine inspiration. In this respect, religious language does *not* necessarily reflect prior beliefs. Doctrine can be in tension with and even be constrained by linguistic practice.

The emphasis on sincere intentions usually manifests language ideology that privileges individual interiority (Keane 2002). The encounter between this ideology and actual linguistic activities can have interesting consequences. For example, Swedish Evangelicals expect conscious individual intentions to be the source of human linguistic expressions. Therefore, when people under stress utter words they claim not to have intended, they assume that divine agency is at work (Stromberg 1993). Similarly, Catholic Charismatics tell rounds of stories that, like many group conversations, tend to develop a thematic unity over time. In light of their assumption that speech derives from individual volition, they find the unintended emergence of this collective unity to be inexplicable without divine intervention (Szuchewycz 1994; cf. Csordas 1997). Language ideology is crucial to the interpretation of discursive forms.

The action being performed by a rite is, in principle, not created anew by the performers. Its efficacy depends on being accepted as an instance of something that can be repeated, and that cannot be derived solely from the speaker's intentions. One reason that some ritualists insist they are merely following the procedures laid down by ancestors is precisely to stress that link, forged by linguistic means, between an absence of intentionality on their part, and efficacy due to more distance powers. More generally, religious uses of language often work to suppress, constrain, deny, or otherwise displace what in other contexts might be intentions imputed to the immediate speakers (divination possibly presenting an extreme case; see Du Bois 1993).

6 Conclusion: Form, Function, and Mediation

Perhaps the single most important and widespread effect of the various formal and pragmatic devices by which religious language is distinguished from more unmarked language practices is the transformation of intentionality and agency. This claim, however, is not intended to reduce the phenomena to a single "explanation," if only because of the emphasis on language as a component of social practice. Being by their very nature heterogeneous, social practices include elements that are subject to determinants and constraints operating at distinct structural levels or domains (Bourdieu 1977). Where religious doctrines exist, for example, they can only become real to the extent that there exist concrete semiotic practices by which they can be enacted, embodied, experienced, and transmitted. But those practices will be subject to such factors as logistics, aesthetics, economics, or prior history, that are independent of the logical, political, or emotional demands of and constraints on doctrine itself. Their push and pull must be understood within what could be called an economy of language practices and ideologies. Even textual forms as relatively autonomous, portable, and durable as written scriptures depend for their persistence and power on social dynamics surrounding contextualization and entextualization. Religious language is subject to the constraints imposed both by linguistic principles and by the practical requirements of action or performance, and its interpretation is subject to negotiation. Formal features of language do not achieve their effects alone or automatically.

Religious practices therefore require an appreciation of mediation in at least two respects. First, beliefs are mediated by the linguistic forms and practices through which they are remembered, transmitted, and made available for acts and reflections. The semiotic forms of those practices may constrain the production of beliefs and give direction to their transformations, as, for example, when fundamentalists draw conclusions from texts or reformers rebel against liturgies. Even a bald statement of faith depends on local conventions for expressing "beliefs" in the form of propositions, and for their hearers' acceptance of them as a recognizable and sensible activity. Second, those linguistic forms are not fully deterministic but are subject to reinterpretations within particular social and historical circumstances. As the historical adaptability of scriptures and liturgies suggests, form may persist while function or interpretation changes (e.g. Keane 1995).

From the first point it follows that close attention to language is required for any ethnographer who wants to gain insight into what people "believe," or even identify "who" the actors are in any particular situation – neither the invisible spirits presupposed by some acts nor the collective entities entailed by others may be immediately apparent to the external observer. It follows from the second point that linguists must bear in mind the importance of the social field for the interpretation of linguistic form in its ethnographic realizations. This means that we not attempt to reduce pragmatic function to linguistic form, conflate practice with some prior social function, reduce either form or function to cognitive determinants, or otherwise foreclose the role of social dynamics. Any account of social action requires attention to its semiotic mediation. And, conversely, any account of the effects of linguistic form in actual settings requires analysis of their social mediation.

NOTE

This chapter develops some of the arguments made in an earlier form, with more detail, in Keane 1997a. I have benefited from conversations with Luis Gómez and the participants in the Michicagoan Linguistic Anthropology Faculty Workshop, and especially Judith Irvine and Robert Scharf for comments on the manuscript, and Alessandro Duranti for his sure editorial hand.

1 On the problem of defining "religion" see Asad 1993; Smith 1982. By "ontological divide" I mean that practitioners understand the difference to be a qualitative one, as between kinds of things, rather than, say, simple spatial distance. The distinction is not, of course, always clear – the lines separating elders, ancestors, and deities may be quite blurred indeed. For the linguistic mediation of agency see Ahearn (2001), Duranti (this volume).

LANGUAGE AND RELIGION   445

REFERENCES

Ahearn, L. M. (2001). Language and Agency. *Annual Review of Anthropology* 30: 109–137.
Ahern, E. (M.) (1979). The Problem of Efficacy: Strong and Weak Illocutionary Acts. *Man* (ns) 14(1): 1–17.
Asad, T. (1993). *Genealogies of Religion: Discipline and Reasons of Power in Christianity and Islam*. Baltimore and London: Johns Hopkins University Press.
Austin, J. L. (1962). *How to Do Things with Words*. Oxford: Oxford University Press.
Bakhtin, M. (1981). *The Dialogic Imagination: Four Essays* (ed. M. Holquist, trans. C. Emerson and M. Holquist). Austin: University of Texas Press.
Bakhtin, M. (1986). The Problem of Speech Genres. In *Speech Genres and Other Late Essays*. Austin: University of Texas Press.
Bateson, G. (1972 [1955]). A Theory of Play and Fantasy. In *Steps to an Ecology of Mind*. New York: Ballantine Books.
Bauman, R. (1983). *Let Your Words Be Few: Symbolism of Speaking and Silence among Seventeenth Century Quakers*. Cambridge: Cambridge University Press.
Bauman, R. (2001). Genre. In A. Duranti (ed.), *Key Terms in Language and Culture* (pp. 79–82). Malden, MA: Blackwell.
Bauman, R., and Sherzer, J. (1974). *Explorations in the Ethnography of Speaking*. Cambridge: Cambridge University Press.
Benveniste, É. (1971 [1958]). Subjectivity in Language. In *Problems in General Linguistics* (trans. M. E. Meek). Coral Gables: University of Miami Press.
Besnier, N. (1995). *Literacy, Emotion, and Authority: Reading and Writing on a Polynesian Atoll*. Cambridge: Cambridge University Press.
Bloch, M. (1989 [1974]). Symbols, Song, Dance, and Features of Articulation: Is Religion an Extreme Form of Traditional Authority? In M. Bloch (ed.), *Ritual, History, and Power: Selected Papers in Anthropology*. London School of Economics Monographs on Social Anthropology 58. London: Athlone Press.
Bloch, M. (1975). Introduction. In M. Bloch (ed.), *Political Language and Oratory in Traditional Society*. New York: Academic Press.
Boddy, J. (1994). Spirit Possession Revisited: Beyond Instrumentality. *Annual Review of Anthropology* 23: 407–434.
Bourdieu, P. (1977 [1972]). *Outline of a Theory of Practice* (trans. R. Nice). Cambridge: Cambridge University Press.
Bowen, J. R. (1993). *Muslims Through Discourse: Religion and Ritual in Gayo Society*. Princeton, NJ: Princeton University Press.
Boyarin, J. (ed.) (1993). *The Ethnography of Reading*. Berkeley: University of California Press.
Boyer, P. (ed.) (1993). *Cognitive Aspects of Religious Symbolism*. Cambridge: Cambridge University Press.
Briggs, C. L. (1988). *Competence in Performance: The Creativity of Tradition in Mexicano Verbal Art*. Philadelphia: University of Pennsylvania Press.
Bunzel, R. L. (1932). Zuni Ritual Poetry. *47th Report of the Bureau of American Ethnology, 1929–1930*. Washington, DC: Smithsonian Institution Press.
Calame-Griaule, G. (1986 [1965]). *Words and the Dogon World*. Philadelphia: Institute for the Study of Human Issues.
Coleman, S. (2000). *The Globalisation of Charismatic Christianity: Spreading the Gospel of Prosperity*. Cambridge: Cambridge University Press.
Crapanzano, V. (2000). *Serving the Word: Literalism in America from the Pulpit to the Bench*. New York: New Press.

Csordas, T. J. (1997). *Language, Charisma, and Creativity: The Ritual Life of a Religious Movement*. Berkeley: University of California Press.

Du Bois, J. W. (1986). Self-Evidence and Ritual Speech. In W. Chafe and J. Nichols (eds.), *Evidentiality: The Linguistic Coding of Epistemology*. Norwood, NJ: Ablex.

Du Bois, J. W. (1993). Meaning without Intention: Lessons from Divination. In J. Hill and J. Irvine (eds.), *Responsibility and Evidence in Oral Discourse*. Cambridge: Cambridge University Press.

Duranti, A. (1993). Intentionality and Truth: An Ethnographic Critique. *Cultural Anthropology* 8: 214–245.

Duranti, A. (1994). *From Grammar to Politics: Linguistic Anthropology in a Western Samoan Village*. Berkeley and Los Angeles: University of California Press.

Duranti, A., and Brenneis, D. L. (eds.) (1986). The Audience as Co-Author. Special Issue, *Text* 6(3): 239–347.

Durkheim, E. (1915 [1912]) *The Elementary Forms of the Religious Life* (trans. J. W. Swain). London: George Allen & Unwin.

Gardner, D. S. (1983). Performativity in Ritual: The Mianmin Case. *Man* (ns) 18: 346–360.

Geertz, C. (1973). Religion as a Cultural System. In *The Interpretation of Cultures*. New York: Basic Books.

Gill, S. D. (1981). *Sacred Words: A Study of Navajo Religion and Prayer*. Westport, CT: Greenwood Press.

Goffman, E. (1967). *Interaction Ritual: Essays on Face-to-Face Behavior*. New York: Anchor Books.

Goffman, E. (1981). Footing. In *Forms of Talk* (pp. 124–157). Philadelphia: University of Pennsylvania Press.

Gómez, L. O. (2000). Prayer: Buddhist Perspectives. In W. M. Johnston (ed.), *Encyclopedia of Monasticism*, vol. 2. Chicago: Fitzroy Dearborn.

Goodman, F. D. (1972). *Speaking in Tongues: A Cross-cultural Study in Glossolalia*. Chicago: University of Chicago Press.

Graham, L. R. (1995). *Performing Dreams: Discourses of Immortality among the Xavante of Central Brazil*. Austin: University of Texas Press.

Graham, W. A. (1977). *Divine Word and Prophetic Word in Early Islam: A Reconsideration of the Sources with Special Reference to the Divine Saying or Hadith Qudsi*. The Hague: Mouton.

Grice, H. P. (1975). Logic and Conversation. In P. Cole and N. L. Morgan (eds.), *Syntax and Semantics*, vol. 3: *Speech Acts* (pp. 41–58). New York: Academic Press.

Gumperz, J. J., and Hymes, D. (eds.) (1964). The Ethnography of Communication. Special Issue, *American Anthropologist*. 66, part 2.

Hanks, W. F. (1990). *Referential Practice: Language and Lived Space among the Maya*. Chicago: University of Chicago Press.

Hanks, W. F. (1996). Exorcism and the Description of Participant Roles. In M. Silverstein and G. Urban (eds.), *Natural Histories of Discourse*. Chicago: University of Chicago Press.

Harding, S. F. (2000). *The Book of Jerry Falwell: Fundamentalist Language and Politics*. Princeton, NJ: Princeton University Press.

Hill, J. H., and Irvine, J. T. (eds.) (1993). *Responsibility and Evidence in Oral Discourse*. Cambridge: Cambridge University Press.

Hymes, D. (1981). Breakthrough into Performance. *"In Vain I Tried to Tell You": Essays in Native American Ethnopoetics*. Philadelphia: University of Pennsylvania Press.

Irvine, J. T. (1979). Formality and Informality in Communicative Events. *American Anthropologist* 81(4): 773–790.

Irvine, J. T. (1982). The Creation of Identity in Spirit Mediumship and Possession. In D. Parkin (ed.), *Semantic Anthropology*. London: Academic Press.

Irvine, J. T. (1989). When Talk Isn't Cheap: Language and Political Economy. *American Ethnologist* 16(2): 248–267.

Irvine, J. T. (1996). Shadow Conversations: The Indeterminacy of Participant Roles. In M. Silverstein and G. Urban (eds.), *Natural Histories of Discourse* (pp. 131–159). Chicago: University of Chicago Press.

Jakobson, R. (1960). Closing Statement: Linguistics and Poetics. In T. A. Sebeok (ed.), *Style in Language*. Cambridge, MA: MIT Press.

Jakobson, R. (1990). Quest for the Essence of Language. In L. R. Waugh and M. Monville-Burston (eds.), *On Language*. Cambridge, MA: Harvard University Press.

Janowitz, N. (1989). *Poetics of Ascent: Theories of Language in a Rabbinic Ascent Text*. Albany: SUNY Press.

Katz, S. T. (ed.) (1992). *Mysticism and Language*. New York: Oxford University Press.

Keane, W. (1995). The Spoken House: Text, Act, and Object in Eastern Indonesia. *American Ethnologist* 22: 102–124.

Keane, W. (1997a). Religious Language. *Annual Review of Anthropology* 26: 47–71.

Keane, W. (1997b). *Signs of Recognition: Powers and Hazards of Representation in an Indonesian Society*. Berkeley: University of California Press.

Keane, W. (1997c). From Fetishism to Sincerity: On Agency, the Speaking Subject, and Their Historicity in the Context of Religious Conversion. *Comparative Studies in Society and History* 39: 674–693.

Keane, W. (2002). Sincerity, "Modernity," and the Protestants. *Cultural Anthropology* 17: 65–92.

Kroskrity, P. V. (ed.) (2000). *Regimes of Language: Ideologies, Polities and Identities*. Santa Fe, NM: School of American Research Press.

Kuipers, J. C. (1990). *Power in Performance: The Creation of Textual Authority in Weyewa Ritual Speech*. Philadelphia: University of Pennsylvania Press.

Lawless, E. J. (1988). *Handmaidens of the Lord: Pentecostal Women Preachers and Traditional Religion*. Philadelphia: University of Pennsylvania Press.

Leavitt, J. (ed.) (1997). *Poetry and Prophecy: The Anthropology of Inspiration*. Ann Arbor: University of Michigan Press.

Lee, B. (1997). *Talking Heads: Language, Metalanguage, and the Semiotics of Subjectivity*. Durham, NC: Duke University Press.

Lewis, I. M. (1971). *Ecstatic Religion: A Study of Shamanism and Spirit Possession*. London and New York: Routledge.

Lucy, J. A. (ed.) (1993). *Reflexive Language: Reported Speech and Metapragmatics*. Cambridge: Cambridge University Press.

Mahmood, S. (2001). Rehearsed Spontaneity and the Conventionality of Ritual: Disciplines of *Salat*. *American Ethnologist* 28: 827–853.

Malinowski, B. (1935). *Coral Gardens and Their Magic*. London: Allen and Unwin.

Mannheim, B., and Tedlock, D. (1995). Introduction. In B. Mannheim and D. Tedlock (eds.), *The Dialogic Emergence of Culture*. Urbana and Chicago: University of Illinois Press.

Mead, G. H. (1934). *Mind, Self, and Society from the Standpoint of a Social Behaviorist*. Chicago: University of Chicago Press.

Meigs, A. (1995). Ritual Language in Everyday Life: The Christian Right. *Journal of the American Academy of Religion* 63: 85–103.

Metcalf, P. (1989). *Where Are You Spirits? Style and Theme in Berawan Prayer*. Washington, DC: Smithsonian Institution Press.

Needham, R. (1972). *Belief, Language, and Experience*. Chicago: University of Chicago Press.

Pascal, B. (1958). *Pascal's Pensées* (trans. W. F. Trotter). New York: E. P. Dutton.

Peacock, J. L., and Tyson, R. W., Jr. (1989). *Pilgrims of Paradox: Calvinism and Experience among the Primitive Baptists of the Blue Ridge.* Washington, DC: Smithsonian Institution Press.

Peirce, C. S. (1955). Logic as Semiotic: The Theory of Signs. In J. Buchler (ed.), *Philosophical Writings of Peirce.* New York: Dover.

Pitts, W. F. (1993). *Old Ship of Zion: The Afro-Baptist Ritual in the African Diaspora.* New York and Oxford: Oxford University Press.

Rappaport, R. A. (1999). *Ritual and Religion in the Making of Humanity.* Cambridge: Cambridge University Press.

Reichard, G. A. (1944). *Prayer: The Compulsive Word.* Monographs of the American Ethnological Society, No. 7. New York: Augustin.

Robbins, J. (2001). God Is Nothing but Talk: Modernity, Language, and Prayer in a Papua New Guinea Society. *American Anthropologist* 103: 901–912.

Samarin, W. J. (1972). *Tongues of Men and Angels: The Religious Language of Pentecostalism.* New York: Macmillan.

Samarin, W. J. (ed.) (1976). *Language in Religious Practice.* Rowley, MA: Newbury House.

Scholem, G. (1969 [1960]). *On the Kabbalah and Its Symbolism.* (trans. Ralph Manheim). New York: Schocken Books.

Sherzer, J. (1990). *Verbal Art in San Blas: Kuna Culture through Its Discourse.* Cambridge: Cambridge University Press.

Silverstein, M. (1976). Shifters, Linguistic Categories, and Cultural Description. In K. H. Basso and H. A. Selby (eds.), *Meaning in Anthropology* (pp. 11–56). Albuquerque: University of New Mexico Press.

Silverstein, M. (1981). Metaforces of Power in Traditional Oratory. (Unpublished MS.)

Silverstein, M. (1993). Metapragmatic Discourse and Metapragmatic Function. In J. Lucy (ed.) *Reflexive Language* (pp. 33–58). New York: Cambridge University Press.

Silverstein, M., and Urban, G. (eds.) (1996). *Natural Histories of Discourse.* Chicago: University of Chicago Press.

Smith, J. Z. (1982). *Imagining Religion: From Babylon to Jonestown.* Chicago: University of Chicago Press.

Staal, F. (1990). *Rules without Meaning: Ritual, Mantra, and the Human Sciences.* Toronto Studies in Religion, vol. 4. New York: Lang.

Stromberg, P. G. (1993). *Language and Self-Transformation: A Study of the Christian Conversion Narrative.* Cambridge, MA: Harvard University Press.

Szuchewycz, B. (1994). Evidentiality in Ritual Discourse: The Social Construction of Religious Meaning. *Language in Society* 23: 389–410.

Tambiah, S. J. (1979). *A Performative Approach to Ritual.* Oxford: Oxford University Press.

Titon, J. T. (1988). *Powerhouse for God: Speech, Chant, and Song in an Appalachian Baptist Church.* Austin: University of Texas Press.

Urban, G. (1989). The "I" of Discourse. In B. Lee and G. Urban (eds.), *Semiotics, Self, and Society.* Berlin: Mouton de Gruyter.

Urban, G. (1996). *Metaphysical Community: The Interplay of the Senses and the Intellect.* Austin: University of Texas Press.

Vološinov, V. N. (1973 [1930]) *Marxism and the Philosophy of Language* (trans. L. Matejka and I. R. Titunik). New York: Seminar Press.

Vygotsky, L. S. (1978). *Mind in Society: The Development of Higher Psychological Processes* (eds. M. Cole, V. John-Steiner, S. Scribner, and E. Souberman). Cambridge, MA: Harvard University Press.

Wittgenstein, L. (1953). *Philosophical Investigations* (trans. G. E. M. Anscombe). New York: Macmillan.

Wolf, M. (1990). The Woman Who Didn't Become a Shaman. *American Ethnologist* 17: 419–430.

PART **IV** The Power in Language

CHAPTER **20** # Agency in Language

Alessandro Duranti

1 INTRODUCTION

The goal of this chapter is to sketch a model of how agency is enacted and represented in (and through) language. I have chosen to talk about agency *in* language as opposed to the agency *of* language because the latter description might assume the uncritical reification of language as an agent with its own (independent) goals and even with its own will. While it is important to recognize the role that any language has in providing the communicative resources for the definition and enactment of (past, present, and future) realities, it is equally important to develop an analytical framework for distinguishing between speakers' conceptualization of what a language "does" and the conditions that make such a conceptualization possible (see also Kroskrity, this volume; Philips, this volume). As part of the discussion of "linguistic relativity," the issue of the agency *of* language has a long tradition within linguistic anthropology (Duranti 2001; Gumperz and Levinson 1996; Hill and Mannheim 1992). There is also a considerable body of literature on the impact that forces external to a language have on its structure (e.g. phonology) and its meaning – a great deal of sociolinguistics is devoted to these issues. In this chapter, however, I go in a different direction. I start from a working definition of agency and, on its basis, I reconsider two related and yet analytically distinct dimensions of agency: its linguistic realization (performance) and its linguistic representation (grammatical encoding).

As I will discuss below, any act of speaking involves some kind of agency, often regardless of the speaker's intentions and the hearer's interest or collaboration. This is due to the fact that by speaking we establish a reality that has at least the potential for affecting whoever happens to be listening to us, regardless of the originally intended audience. We not only affect the mind and future actions of our listeners by providing new information about the world (e.g. *the house is on fire! This cheese is scrumptious*), we also affect them when we repeat what our listener already knows (e.g. *we live in a democracy, Rome wasn't built in a day, I used to know you when you were this tall*).

Furthermore, language use is a primary example of what Giddens called the "duality of structure":[1]

> when I utter a grammatical English sentence in a casual conversation, I contribute to the reproduction of the English language as a whole. This is an unintended consequence of my speaking the sentence, but one that is bound indirectly to the recursiveness of the duality of structure. (Giddens 1979: 77–8)

Through linguistic communication, we display our attitudes, feelings, beliefs, and wishes. Once expressed, this type of information has an impact on others, as well as on us (e.g. we proudly reaffirm our convictions or, conversely, we prove to ourselves that we can embrace new ideas and attitudes).

Another challenge in the discussion of agency is due to the problems associated with combining the intuitions expressed in linguistic studies with those expressed by social theorists dealing with human action abstracted from verbal interaction. Despite the fact that the issue of the understanding and control that individuals have *vis-à-vis* their group's (or groups') cultural assumptions has long been the object of study of psychological anthropology, the term "agency" itself has been only recently brought into the social sciences by post-structuralist social theorists such as Anthony Giddens (1979, 1984) and Pierre Bourdieu (1977, 1990, 2000), who tried to define a theory of social action that would recognize the role played by social actors, viz. agents, in the production and reproduction of social systems, and thus overcome the structuralist and Marxist tendency to see human action as produced by a logic (in structuralism) or historical laws (in Marxism) that human subjects can neither control nor understand. Social theorists, however, have not elaborated on the linguistic implications of their theories beyond a number of provoking but generic claims regarding the social implications of language usage (Bourdieu 1982). Linguists, in turn, have been dealing with agency as a semantic notion since the mid-1960s, but have kept their models largely devoid of social implications. This is not surprising, given that the interest in semantic (or thematic) roles like Agent[2] (see below) came out of the generative paradigm established by Chomsky in the late 1950s and early 1960s and has remained influenced by his vision of linguistic theory as separate and separable from social theory (see for example his dismissal of sociolinguistics in Chomsky 1977). Issues of the social functions of permission and obligation are mentioned in more recent and functionally oriented studies of modality (Bybee and Fleischman 1995b: 4) but much more needs to be done to integrate those studies with a more general theory of agency. The institutional separation among the fields of linguistics, anthropology, and sociology in the second part of the twentieth century has certainly contributed to their intellectual separation and the ensuing lack of public debates around common issues. Discourse analysts, linguistic anthropologists, sociolinguists, and other interdisciplinary researchers have tried to bridge the gap with limited success, due in part to the difficulty of communicating across discipline boundaries and in part to the paucity of clear theoretical statements that could be either adopted or challenged by scholars in other fields. I will here argue, however, that there are a number of claims made on agency based on language use and language structure that can be integrated with a social theory of agency (see also Ahearn 1999, 2001 for earlier attempts to systematize the available literature).

2   TOWARD A DEFINITION OF AGENCY

Any attempt to arrive at a definition of agency is a difficult task because it forces us to take a stand with respect to a number of thorny issues including the role of intentionality and the ontological status of the semantic (or thematic) role of Agent and other, related notions (e.g. Patient, Instrument). For example, should they be treated as basic or primitive notions (e.g. Fillmore 1968) or as derived concepts to be defined in terms of entailments associated with certain types of events (e.g. Chierchia 1989; Dowty 1989)?

Another obstacle faced by any attempt at a general definition of agency is the difficulty of combining the intuitions expressed in strictly semantic theories (dealing with linguistic structures, abstracted from social processes) with those expressed in social theories (dealing with social processes, abstracted from verbal interaction) or with those expressed in philosophical theories (based on ideal situations and often purposely devoid of any anthropological understanding). Despite these unresolved issues, however, I will attempt a working definition of agency that tries to take into consideration the intuitions as well as the explicit definitions provided by authors in different fields.

2.1   A working definition of agency

I propose the following working definition of agency:

> (1) Agency is here understood as the property of those entities (i) that have some degree of control over their own behavior, (ii) whose actions in the world affect other entities' (and sometimes their own), and (iii) whose actions are the object of evaluation (e.g. in terms of their responsibility for a given outcome).

The three properties of agency included in (1) are obviously interconnected. For example, the first property of agency (degree of control over one's own behavior) is closely related to but not identical with the notion of intentionality, a term that is often evoked in the discussion of agency. However, there is often confusion or at least lack of clarity regarding what intentionality means for each author. If by intentionality we mean, with Husserl (1931: 223), the property of an entity of being directed-toward or being about something – e.g. the "aboutness" of human mental life – there is no question that such a property is at work in those actions or events that we recognize as involving agency. If, on the other hand, by intentionality we mean the conscious planning of a given act (or sequence of acts) by someone (or something?), we start to run into trouble. One of the problems in this case is that the attribute of conscious planning as a prerequisite for agency would immediately exclude institutions from the discussion of agency given that, as pointed out by Giddens (1979, 1984), institutions have no consciousness and yet, they do have the power – a power of a kind that is different from the sum of the powers of the individuals involved – to "make a difference," that is, to have an effect (on themselves, on other institutions, on individuals, on the environment).

Another reason to resist a definition of intentionality that implies conscious planning is that, as pointed out by a number of social theorists (most effectively by Garfinkel 1967), there is a type of routine monitoring of one's actions in the (familiar) world that is not subject to the same level of analytical rationalization that becomes necessary when we are asked to provide an after-the-fact account of those actions. The notion of control over one's actions is closely connected not only with the already invoked notion of power (implicit in the second criterion), but also with the notion of evaluation (the third criterion) through the notion of freedom understood as the possibility of having acted otherwise. This possibility must be maintained as a feature of agency in spite of the fact that there are situations in which human actors might feel (or be judged) unable to act otherwise.

A crucial aspect of (1.ii) is that agents are entities whose actions have consequences for themselves or others. In other words, they "affect" themselves or some other entities (e.g. Lyons 1977; Jackendoff 1990) or, we could say, they are involved in a causative chain (Talmy 1976, 2000; Lakoff and Johnson 1980). The extent to which such actions are performed willfully and with specific goals in mind varies. Such variation is responsible for the *degree* of agency that is attributed to a given entity and also for the type of evaluation they may receive.

To fully appreciate the importance of evaluation in the construction of agency, we must connect it not only to morality (e.g. as Taylor 1985 does) but also to performance, in its various meanings and connotations (Duranti 1997b: 14–17). First, there is an evaluation of someone's words as they contribute to the presentation and realization of a self (the speaker) who is always also a moral subject (Kant 1785: 445). Second, there is the evaluation of someone's words as they contribute toward the constitution of culture-specific acts and activities (what I would call the ethno-pragmatic level). Third, there is the evaluation of someone's words as they display their knowledge (linguistic competence), the sources of such knowledge (evidentiality, modality), and its use for specific ends, including aesthetic ones (Bauman 1975, 1993; Chafe and Nichols 1986; Hymes 1975). In all three types of evaluation – regarding the accumulation of knowledge, the sources of knowledge, and the artful display of knowledge – speakers are engaged with an audience (whether real or imaginary) without which the very notion of evaluation would lose its meaning.

3   TWO DIMENSIONS OF AGENCY

Keeping in mind the working definition provided in (1), I will here propose that there are two basic dimensions of agency in language: *performance* and *encoding*. Although I will discuss these two dimensions separately, the two dimensions are in fact mutually constitutive, that is, it is usually the case that performance – the enacting of agency, its coming into being – relies on and simultaneously affects the encoding – how human action is depicted through linguistic means. Conversely, encoding always serves performative functions, albeit in different ways and with varying degrees of effectiveness. By describing agentive relationships among different entities (e.g. participants in a speech event, characters in a story) and affective and epistemic stances toward individuals and events, speakers routinely participate in the construction of certain types of beings, including moral types, and certain types of social realities in which those beings can exist and make sense of each other's actions.

3.1   The performance of agency

Agency is performed at a number of levels. The first level is what I call (for lack of a better term) "ego-affirming." A second level is "act-constituting." In the past, it is the latter that has been highlighted, even by authors who were concerned with identity and identity formation. Students of language were so anxious to prove the axiom that "language is action (too)" that they forgot to recognize that language already does something by *being*, before *doing*.

3.1.1   Ego-affirming agency

A basic and recurrent type of agency expressed and realized by language is what we might call "self-" or "ego-affirming." This type of agency is usually achieved, albeit in different degrees, any time language is used. The very act of speaking in front of others who can perceive such an act establishes the speaker as a being whose existence must be reckoned with in terms of his or her communicative goals and abilities. As the most sophisticated form of human expression, language use implies that its users are entities that must also possess other human qualities including the ability to affect their own and others' ways of being. Hence, this most basic level of agency – an agency of an existential sort which, however, needs others (whether as a real or imaginary audience) – does not need to rely on referential or denotational meaning. It is language *per se* as a human faculty rather than the meaning of its words that is sufficient for agency as ego-affirming to be at work. This basic and yet already complex level of agency is achieved, for example, when we hear the sounds produced by an individual (or group) well enough to know that *a* language is being used but not distinctly enough to identify the words that are being uttered or even the specific language that is spoken. Even though we cannot interpret what is being talked about, we grant the speaker the performance of a special type of self-assertion, one that goes even beyond the slogan *loquor ergo sum* (Lyons 1982) to something that is best represented as *loquor, ergo agens sum*.

   At first, the identification of this type of agency-through-language might seem redundant or superfluous. One might argue that the use of language is not necessary for human beings to assert their existence as agents. Any sign of life including such natural and usually unconscious acts as blinking or breathing should suffice to establish that a body is alive and, even if not fully active at the moment, at least endowed with the faculties that will allow it to become an agent (although such an assumption is not necessarily warranted if the person is lying in a bed in a hospital). One might thus object that this first type of agency-through-language is no different from any other human act, including those that do not rely on language, such as walking, glancing, or even snoring. Mere human existence, or rather, human *presence* is something that must be reckoned with by others and therefore implies the power to affect others. If people are standing or sitting next to us or close enough to be able to monitor our actions or to be awakened by the noises we make, we must in some way take their presence into consideration and therefore, one might argue, they are potential or actual agents. In other words, one might argue that humans don't have to *do* anything special to affirm, assert, or enforce their potential for various forms of agency. We cannot but *be*, and being for humans typically means *doing*. When we enter a social space occupied by others, they do not need to do or say anything for us to act according to expectations that take into consideration their presence (and hence their gazing at us, their monitoring of our actions). While agreeing with these observations, I would still argue that the type of self-affirming done through language – even when the meaning of what is said is not (fully) understood – is of a different nature from mere physical presence or even physical acts other than gestures (which are of course a type of language: Kendon 1997). The difference lies in the most basic qualities of language as both a human faculty and a human potential (performance).

3.1.1.1 *Greetings as a recognition of an Other as a potential agent*

Although this kind of existential agency-through-language is always at work when language is used, there are particular speech activities that, by being dedicated to the establishment of a person's presence and its recognition by others, foreground this first kind of ego-affirming agency. This is the case, for example, in greetings. By identifying the interlocutor as a distinct being worth recognizing (Duranti 1997a: 71), greetings also acknowledge the Other as a possible agent, that is, someone whose actions have potential consequences for our own – this is, by the way, a dimension of greetings that is usually missed if we categorize them as *phatic communion* (Malinowski 1923), that is, as having the main function of establishing or maintaining contact between interactants. That greetings constitute a type of agency-recognition is made particularly obvious by their absence, which may be interpreted in certain contexts not so much as a denial of the Other's presence but as a denial of the Other's actual or potential power to affect us or be relevant to our ways of being.

This hypothesis can be tested by examining who gets greeted when and by whom. In all communities there are individuals or groups, such as children or servants, who are not greeted even though they inhabit places and are present in situations where greetings *are* routinely exchanged. For example, in Samoan communities, children are usually not greeted when one enters a house. This absence of greetings might even include young unmarried adults – as shown by the semantic extension of the term *teine* 'girl' to unmarried women, even those in their late thirties. On the other hand, in the USA, especially among the white middle class, there is a tendency to engage in greetings even with newborn babies and very young infants who are unable to be either cognizant of or full participants in the greeting exchange. In both cases, whether consciously or not, adults are implying and enforcing specific ideologies of agency (and, in this case, ideologies of childhood) (see Kulick and Schieffelin, this volume). In one case (Samoa), children are being defined as having a weak (or derived) agency: they might be seen as instrumental to (or dependent upon) the agency of others. In the other case (white middle-class communities in the USA), children's agency is raised to a level beyond their actual capability to control their own actions. These specific behaviors correspond rather closely to different conceptions of the relationship between children and adults in the two societies: the adult-centered perspective of most activities in Samoa (excluding imported literacy practices) and the child-centered perspective of many activities in middle-class families in the USA (Ochs and Schieffelin 1984). In both cases, it is a stance *vis-à-vis* agency that plays a major role in the type of participation that is expected and allowed in greetings.

3.1.2   Act-constituting agency

The view that language not only describes an already-made world but constitutes real and imaginary worlds through culture-specific and contextually designed (mostly, but not necessarily, appropriate) *acts* is at the foundation of a number of contemporary philosophical, linguistic, and anthropological theories, with roots in the European intellectual tradition represented by authors as diverse as Ludwig Wittgenstein (1958) and Bronislaw Malinowski (1923, 1935). It was, however, the British philosopher John L. Austin who, in the late 1940s and early 1950s, articulated in a more systematic fashion a formal apparatus for a theory of acts-through-language (Austin 1962, 1975), which laid the foundations for what came to be known as Speech Act Theory (Searle 1965, 1969). Starting from a fictitious distinction between *constative* utterances (e.g. "the sky is blue") and *performative* utterances (e.g. "you're fired!"), Austin argued that all utterances are in fact *acts*, and therefore (in plain language) *words always do things*. It is thus necessary to distinguish between the utterance as it can be interpreted according to grammatical rules and truth-values (the *locutionary* act) – traditionally the object of study of grammarians and logicians respectively – and the utterance as an act the speaker *intends* to perform by means of conventional expressions typically used to perform such an act, for example a promise, a threat, a declaration, an apology, a suggestion, a compliment, a complaint, etc. The latter type of act, which Austin called *illocutionary*, can be made explicit by means of a special class of verbs which he called *performatives* (i.e. expressions that do things, perform deeds). By conjugating these verbs in the first person singular, we obtain a method for analyzing the type of act intended by the speaker for any given utterance. An assertion would be represented by preceding it with *I inform you that* ..., a command by *I order you to* ..., a promise by *I promise you that* ..., and so forth. Austin was also aware of the fact that utterances may have consequences that are different from the speakers' intentions and coined the term *perlocutionary act* for the effects of a given utterance, irrespective of its intended and conventional force; for example, your telling me that you just sent in an application for a certain job might have the intended effect of informing me of this decision of yours and the unintended effect of making me decide that I should also apply for the same job.

Austin's analysis of what words can do was complemented by Grice's (1975) theory of the meaning of the unsaid (Levinson 1983). Grice proposed four universal maxims that are meant to guide our interpretation of what is being said: (1) Quality (say the truth and don't provide information for which you lack evidence), (2) Quantity (give the right amount of information), (3) Relation (be relevant), (4) Manner (avoid obscurities). In other words, according to Grice, we usually assume that people tend to tell the truth (quality), give the contextually appropriate amount of information (quantity), say things that are relevant to the ongoing activity, and say things in ways that can be understood without too much work. Thus, if I ask someone "Has the meeting started?" and he answers "I don't think everyone has arrived yet," I can infer that he thinks that the meeting hasn't started but has no strong evidence for it. This inference is based on a set of *implicatures* that I can draw on the basis of what the person said as well as on the basis of what he *did not* say. For example, I assume that he is telling me information for which he has evidence (he must be able to monitor who comes into the meeting) and he is not hiding information from me (e.g. the fact that the meeting usually starts even though not everyone is present). I can also assume that the statement that not everyone has arrived yet is relevant to my question (e.g. it is not about people who are not meant to participate at the meeting). And so on. According to Grice, certain social phenomena (e.g. politeness) would be precisely conveyed by the violation of one or more of these maxims. To be polite, we might not tell the truth (quality), might take a long time to say something (quantity), bring up apparently irrelevant information (relevance), and introduce some ambiguous or obscure expressions (manner) (Brown and Levinson 1987).

Austin, Searle, and Grice made a number of assumptions about truth, intentions, and conventions that have been criticized by a number of authors (e.g. Derrida 1982; Duranti 1997b: 227–44; Schegloff 1992; Streeck 1980). Within linguistic anthropology, Michelle Rosaldo (1982) criticized the universality of the notion of person presupposed by Speech Act Theory, including its strong commitment to sincerity. Michael Silverstein (1977) suggested that Austin's notion of what language can do relies too heavily on the ability that speakers have to identify certain acts by means of verbs describing those acts (e.g. English verbs *inform, claim, suggest, request, warn, apologize, congratulate, greet, nominate, bless, promise, threaten*). Silverstein rightly pointed out that the illocutionary force of speech is only one type of social action. There are other types of actions performed by linguistic signs that are not conceived as or represented by performative verbs. A large category of such acts includes *indexes* (a term borrowed from the writings of the philosopher Charles Peirce), that is, expressions through which some aspect of the situation-at-hand is *presupposed* or even *created* (Silverstein 1976b). For example, certain linguistic features (such as pronunciation, use of linguistic expressions) presuppose an existential connection between the speaker and a particular place (for example, people from Northern Italy quickly recognize my Italian as "from Rome"), although sometimes the inference may be factually wrong, thereby establishing a temporary fictional identity (as when people from Southern Italy hear my accent as "not-Southern" and sometimes mistakenly place me a bit too far north, such as "from Tuscany"). The use of a particular title (e.g. Doctor, Professor, Senator) can presuppose the status of the addressee in a particular profession or public office. Other times indexical expressions can *de facto* help create an identity or position (e.g. Ochs 1992), as when speakers exaggerate or fake a regional accent, sometimes unconsciously and other times consciously (e.g. to create co-membership with their listeners), or when addressees are contingently assigned a title or status so as to induce them to act according to whatever cultural expectation is associated with such a title or status, for example being gracious, generous, or forgiving (see Irvine 1974; Duranti 1992). In Rome, in the 1960s, unlicensed parking attendants hoping for a tip used to address all the men who went to park in the attendants' self-ascribed lot with the term *dotto'* (short for the Standard Italian *dottore*), a title implying the possession of a university degree, even when their addressee was visibly too young to have such a title. In the late 1970s, while living in Samoa, I learned to predict when people were going to ask me for a favor from the fact that they would come into our house, sit down, lower their voice, and start addressing me with such forms as *Lau Afioga* 'Your Highness' (usually said to an *ali'i* or 'chief') instead of using the Samoan version of my first name (Alesana). In all of these cases, speakers are *doing things with language* (e.g. evoking social identities, invoking solidarity, elevating someone's status in the attempt to create a sense of obligation) even though there might be no specific performative verbs that identify such acts. In fact, when we look at spontaneous interaction, we find that there is a great deal that is being accomplished (or at least attempted) with language beyond the illocutionary force identified by means of explicit or implicit performative verbs.

There are other important dimensions of the performance of agency that are often left out of the linguistic and philosophical literature (Duranti 1997b: 14–17). One of them is the creative power of language as realized in poetry, songs, theater, everyday humor, and story-telling (see Banti and Giannattasio, this volume). This is a dimension where speakers/singers/actors/story-tellers exploit some taken for granted or hidden properties of language, transforming our ordinary understanding of language and its relation to reality.[3] It is also a dimension where the aesthetic function of language dominates (Jakobson 1960), making language users accountable for the form of their expressions and the style of delivery.[4] In this realm, a wide range of usually ignored properties or configurations of language become very relevant, among them the human voice (De Dominicis 2002), which both affirms the speaker qua speaker (see Section 2.1) and reveals human qualities and emotions that can be equally or more powerful than the propositional content or the explicit performative verbs (e.g. *promise, warn, declare, request*, etc.) discussed by speech act theorists.

More generally, the doing of things through language always entails the accountability of the language user(s). It is precisely when our labor is recognized that we also become accountable for the implications and consequences of such labor. Linguistic labor is no exception, hence the importance of the disclaimers for those speakers who are in a positional role that requires them to say something for which they do not want to claim responsibility (Bauman 1993; Du Bois 1986; Hill and Irvine 1993).

The act-constituting agency of language is the most studied type of agency within linguistic anthropology and therefore all of the chapters in this volume have something relevant on the topic.

4   ENCODING OF AGENCY

I start from the assumption that the grammatical systems of known languages provide us with a record of the range of solutions that past speakers found to particular communicative problems. One such problem is the encoding of agency. Based on the existing literature on how agency is represented through grammatical and discourse devices, we can draw the following generalizations (to be understood as putative universals of language structure and language use):

(2a) *Centrality of agency in languages:* All languages have ways of representing agency.

(2b) *Diversity of encoding of agency:* There is variation both across languages and within the same language in the way in which agency is represented.

(2c) *Mitigation of agency:* All languages have ways of mitigating, that is, modulating some of the properties of agency as defined in (1) by means of a number of grammatical and discourse strategies, including omission (i.e. no mention of agent at all) and alternative grammatical framings (e.g. variation in the expressed connection between an event and the entity that might have caused it).

4.1   Agency and transitivity

There is substantial evidence that agency plays an important role in the grammatical organization of the world's languages and languages are often classified in terms of how they encode agency (e.g. Foley and Van Valin 1984; Grimshaw 1990; Hopper and Thompson 1980; Sánchez 1997). For example, grammarians distinguish among the following three types of languages:

(3a) nominative-accusative (e.g. English, Hawai'ian, Quechua);
(3b) ergative-absolutive (e.g. Basque, Dyirbal, Samoan); and
(3c) stative-active (also called "split-subject") (e.g. Acehnese, Guaraní, Lakhota).

Agency plays a crucial role in this classification because the difference among the three types is based on the ways in which a language encodes the Agent NP (noun phrase) (that is, *the boy* in *the boy broke the window*) *vis-à-vis* other types of NP arguments of the verb.

In nominative-accusative languages what we call "subject" (in the nominative case in languages like Latin) may represent a range of participants in the event (Keenan 1984). For example, in English the subject of transitive sentences like (4) is treated in the same way (e.g. it occupies the same position, it governs rules such as subject–verb agreement) as the subject of sentences like (5)–(8), regardless of the differences among the types of participants it represents. Grammarians have used a number of names for such participant roles, including: Case (with a capital "C" to distinguish it from the morphological "case" of languages like Latin) (Fillmore 1968), thematic role (Jackendoff 1972), and theta-role (Chomsky 1982). The most commonly used names for such roles are: Agent, Actor, Object (or Patient, or Theme, or Undergoer), Instrument, Experiencer, Goal, and Source.

(4) The boy broke the window.   (The boy = Agent)
(5) The window broke.   (The window = Object)
(6) The rock broke the window.   (The rock = Instrument)
(7) The boy walks to the house. (The boy = Actor)
(8) The boy is happy.   (The boy = Experiencer)

In English, when present, the NP with the Agent role is typically chosen to be the Subject, unless the verb is in the passive voice (e.g. *the window was broken by the boy*), whereas the Instrument NP can be the subject of an active sentence only if the Agent is not present, as shown in example (6) above (Fillmore 1968: 33; Jackendoff 1990).

In ergative-absolutive and stative-active languages, agency (or a certain degree of agency) is encoded directly and often overtly in the grammar.

In an ergative-absolutive language, the Agent NP (corresponding to the subject of a transitive clause in English) is marked differently from the Object/Patient/Under-goer NP (corresponding to either subject or object in English). This pattern is here reproduced in (9)–(13), from Samoan, where only the Agent NP is marked by the preposition *e* (the ergative marker), whereas the Object is marked by zero or no preposition (which is the marking of the absolutive in Samoan) regardless of whether there is an Agent present:[5]

(9) *na ta`e   e    le   tama le  fa`amalama.*   (le tama = Agent)
    PST break ERG ART boy   the window
    'the boy broke the window.'

(10) *na ta`e   le   fa`amalama.*   (le fa`amalama = Object)
    PST break ART window
    'the window was broken.'

(11) *na ta`e   le   fa`amalama`i    le    ma`a.* (le ma`a = Instrument)
    PST break ART window   INST ART rock
    'the window broke with/because of the rock.'

(12) *na alu le   tama.*   (le tama = Actor)
    PST go ART boy
    'the boy left/went.'

(13) *e   fiafia le   tama.*   (le tama = Experiencer)
    PRES happy ART boy
    'the boy is happy.'

This pattern can be seen at work in example (14), from a conversation, where a speaker uses both the ergative *e* with an NP representing a human referent and the instrumental `*i* for a (non-human) Instrument (*se ma`a* 'a rock'):[6]

(14) ("Inspection"; audio-recorded, December 1978)
S: [. . .]*`age`ua   kogi e   se   isi - `i    se    ma`a.*
        if   PERF hit   ERG ART other INST ART rock
    'if (it) is hit by another- by a rock' (self-repair) or 'if (it) is hit by someone with a rock'

The ergative-absolutive pattern is the closest realization of the definition of agency presented in (1) above not only because the Agent is singled out, but because its status is partly defined by the presence of an Object, that is, an entity that is affected by the actions of the Agent (conversely, we could say that part of the definition of an Agent is that it affects an Object). This is demonstrated in Samoan by the fact that the ergative marker only appears if the event that is being represented includes an Object (although the Object NP may not be expressed). For example, in (15), from a conversation among young men about a Dracula movie, the highly agentive participant Dracula, here called *le kama*, literally 'the boy', is given the ergative marker to describe his despicable action on young women:

(15) ("Dracula"; audio-recorded in 1978)
1 T: *leaga le amio o le kama sole gai keige sole*
    'the behavior of the guy (was) bad, those poor girls, man'

2   (*0.6 second pause*)

3 S: `ai   e    le    **kama** `ā?
    bite ERG ART boy   TAG
    'the guy (lit. 'the boy') bites (them), doesn't he?'

The presence of the Agent (*e le kama* 'Ergative the boy') in line 3 entails an identifiable and malleable Object, which is not realized phonologically but is semantically implied (through zero anaphora) and identifiable from the discourse context – i.e. "those poor girls" mentioned by speaker T in the prior turn. Contrast the use of the verb `ai 'bite, eat' in (15) with its use in example (16), where there is no specific Object entailed – and, by definition, the prototypicality[7] of the agency of the human actor diminishes:

(16) ("Dinner 3," video-recorded in 1988; Mother (Mo) complains about lack of
    proper etiquette at dinner time)
1 Mo: *e   fai ā,*
    TA do EMP
    '(grace) is being done'
2   `ae lā    e   `ai ā   Oiko.
    but there TA eat EMP Oiko
    'and Oiko is (already) eating.'

In stative-active languages, intransitive verbs are divided in two categories, those that mark their subject like the subject of transitive clauses (the Agent) and those that mark their subjects like the direct object of a transitive clause (Object/Patient) (Kibrik 1985; Merlan 1985; Mithun 1991). For example, in Guaraní and Lakhota the first singular personal pronoun has two forms. One is used for subjects of intransitive verbs of actions (e.g. **I** go, **I** get up) and transitive verbs (e.g. **I** bring it, **I** catch it) and the other form is used for subjects of stative verbs (e.g. **I** am sick, **I** am sleepy) and for the direct object (Object/Patient) of transitive verbs (e.g. it will carry **me** off, he'll kill **me**) (see Mithun 1991).

Data from stative-active languages have been used for a number of arguments in linguistics, including the proposal by Mark Durie (1988), based on Acehnese, to avoid altogether the category "intransitive subject" and use only two roles: Actor and Undergoer (from Foley and Van Valin 1984). Working on Lhasa Tibetan, a language with an active type of structure (it is described as a language where the ergative marker is extended to volitionally acting intransitive subjects), Scott DeLancey (1982, 1990) argued for the interconnection among case marking, aspect, and evidential particles, reinforcing the idea that the encoding of agency is not something that affects only nominal arguments (NPs) but is the combination of a number of linguistic features that, together, provide a perspective on an event, based on the relation between the represented event and the speech event, the source of knowledge the speaker has, and expectations about the way the world is or should be.

At first, stative-active languages seem more similar to nominative-accusative languages like English than to ergative languages like Samoan because they do not distinguish (in some recurrent grammatical patterns) between an entity (called Agent by grammarians) that acts on another entity (Object/Undergoer), such as *the girl* in (17), and an entity (called Actor) that has control over its actions and acts of its own will but without necessarily affecting an Object (or Undergoer), as *the girl* in (18):

(17) The girl brought the book.
(18) The girl left.

But if we think about the action of the girl in (18) as something that affects her, it would conform to the definition of agency in (1). This is in fact Jackendoff's (1990) and Talmy's (2000) view of certain types of apparently intransitive constructions such as (19) when the referent of the subject is understood as having done the action intentionally:

(19) The girl rolled down the hill.

It is relevant that some stative-active languages do in fact distinguish between the intentional and unintentional reading of (19) (e.g. Mithun 1991: 541).[8] The terminological decision over Agent versus Actor as a fundamental semantic notion reflects a theoretical stance with respect to the most basic type of agency in linguistic encoding.

Finally, it is important to remember that both ergative-absolutive and stative-active languages tend to have "split systems" whereby a distinction that is made in one part of the grammatical system (e.g. between Agent and Actor) is not made in another (e.g. full nouns may require ergative marking whereas pronouns may function as if the language were nominative-accusative) (Dixon 1994; Mithun 1991). This means, then, that within the same language agency plays different roles, depending on the type of referent and the type of grammatical form available for a particular referent. A considerable body of literature in fact exists on ergative languages (Comrie 1978, 1981; Dixon 1979, 1994; Silverstein 1976a) and nominative-accusative languages (e.g. Hawkinson and Hyman 1974) on various "hierarchies" that try to capture precisely this type of phenomena, showing a recurrent continuum of "animacy" from first and second person pronouns (high animacy) to inanimate referents expressed through indefinite NPs (low animacy). One implication from these studies is that there are a number of (sometimes conflicting) factors conspiring toward making no grammatical system perfectly coherent from the point of view of the encoding of agency. The issue is where to look for a general theory that might account for these apparent inconsistencies (see Du Bois 1987 for an attempt to sketch out the discourse factors involved).

Much of the discussion of the encoding of agency and other semantic and pragmatic notions tends to be based on made-up examples and intuitions rather than on actual language usage. When we examine what people actually say, we end up with a different picture from the one drawn on the basis of linguistic intuitions.

For example, it is true that when expressed, Agents tend to appear as subjects in English; however, it is also true that they often do not appear at all. That is, contrary to what is often argued or implied in the literature on agency and thematic roles, it is not true that "[i]n most English sentences the subject is the agent" (Bates and MacWhinney 1982). On the contrary, most clauses in spoken English are intransitive and therefore have no Agent role expressed (Du Bois 1987; Thompson and Hopper 2001).[9] Furthermore, the fact that English allows for a wide range of referents in addition to Agents to be represented in the subject position of transitive clauses creates agents out of non-human entities like plants and bureaucratic processes.[10] For example, newspaper articles in the USA are full of sentences in which a non-human participant is placed in the subject position of a transitive clause with a predicate that entails properties (of action, attitudes, feelings) we normally associate with people. Here are some examples from the *Los Angeles Times* (May 5, 2001):[11]

(20) A huge falling tree **injured** 20 people at Disneyland's Frontierland on Friday [...]
(21) Rents **jumped** to record highs in Southland [...]
(22) Arbitration claims against brokerage firms **jumped** sharply in April [...]
(23) Tight security will **keep** the insects **in**.
(24) Those funds **helped support** party activities [...]
(25) The decision **dealt another blow** to claims by former senior TRW engineer Nina Schwartz [...]

There are at least two observations that can be made on the basis of these examples. The first is that English speakers/writers are allowed to treat certain events that in some cases *may* have (example (20)) and in other cases *must* have (examples (21)–(25)) involved human agency as if no humans were involved. Sentences (20)–(25) illustrate the phenomenon of "mitigation" of agency discussed in section 5 below. The second observation is of a (weak) Whorfian kind, in the sense that it focuses on the implicit analogy that is being drawn in such constructions between non-human and human referents (Whorf 1941, 1956). We should take into consideration the possibility that, by representing actions and events typically generated by human beings *as if* they were generated by inanimate objects or abstract sources, English speakers might be giving these non-human entities a quasi-agentive status (Schlesinger 1989 argues for an agentive interpretation of structures similar to the ones mentioned in (15)–(20)). In Lakoff and Johnson's (1980) terms, we could say that in these examples, speakers are extending the prototype of "causation" (roughly equivalent to my definition of "agency") to less prototypical situations, that is, they are using human agency to think about the role of non-human entities in affecting the world. This second observation (which needs to be corroborated by more robust analysis) opens up the possibility of rethinking one of the prevailing cognitive theories of our time, succinctly named "the intentional stance" by Daniel Dennett, as a corollary of English grammatical usage: "the intentional stance consists of treating the object whose behavior you want to predict as a rational agent with beliefs and desires and other mental stages exhibiting what Brentano and others call *intentionality*" (Dennett 1987: 15).

It might not be accidental that the theory according to which we, as rational beings, make predictions about the behavior of a tool (e.g. the thermostat) by treating it as having beliefs and even intentions has been proposed by philosophers whose native language, English, allows for constructions like those in (20)–(25). A possible (Whorfian) project would be to find out whether speakers of different grammatical systems that do not as easily allow for similar constructions (e.g. Japanese, Samoan, Turkish) are less likely to accept the "intentionalist stance."

5 MITIGATION OF AGENCY

Any attempt to fully understand how agency is represented in any given language cannot stop at the examples and types of sentences in which Agents are expressed. We also need to get a sense of those cases in which agents *could have been* expressed as such but were not. This is a difficult task because it is always dangerous to make hypotheses on the basis of what is *not* there. However, the need for such an approach is implicit in a number of proposals made by formal linguists. For example, Fillmore (1977) and Talmy (1976, 2000), among others, tried to account for the fact that the same event can be represented by different grammatical frames and with the subject in a number of different thematic roles. Other linguists have dealt with different grammatical framings through the notion of *empathy* (Kuno and Kaburaki 1977; Kuroda 1974) and *viewpoint* (DeLancey 1982). All of these contributions are concerned with the expressive power of language, including the ability that speakers have to present the same event or series of events in a different perspective, from a different stance, and with different emphasis on different participants. In terms of agency, this means that in addition to a range of options for its representation, languages also offer a range of options for its absence, that is, for the obfuscation or mitigation of agency. Whether or not speakers are conscious of how they are framing a given event, we know that all languages allow the choice between mentioning or not mentioning who is responsible for a given event or for a causal chain of events. There is a considerable body of literature on this subject, especially within the fields of pragmatics and functional linguistics. There seems to be some cross-linguistic evidence for the use of impersonal constructions as a means of mitigation (Berk-Seligson 1990: 99–100) and for the use of passive or passive-like constructions to avoid assigning blame to specific parties (Costa 1975; Kirsner 1976). We know, for example, that passive-like constructions in many languages are agent-less (e.g. Schlesinger 1989; Shibatani 1985) and that the majority of examples of passives in English discourse are also agent-less (Stubbs 1994). Here are three examples in a row from a passage in which a Teaching Assistant, addressing the students in a large auditorium, briefly discusses the problem of finding copies of the text(s) for the course:

(26) (UCSB, 11/14/95)
1   TA: the books came in and **they were sent back**.
2   there was a mistake and **they were sent back** and
3   **they had to be sent again**

Given that the same speaker in a previous utterance was trying to make the students themselves responsible for getting the books (he had said: *there were problems getting the book but at no time was it ever said that you would not be responsible for it*), we could reasonably argue that in this type of situation the use of the agent-less passive construction (e.g. *they were sent back*) allows the speaker to avoid blaming anyone in particular about the problem of the missing textbooks.

These observations should not be understood as implying that passives are the best solution to the problem of avoiding mentioning the Agent (and thus avoiding the issue of assigning responsibility to a party) or that the avoidance of the Agent NP is the only function of the passive (Stubbs 1994: 204). There is a range of other grammatical resources that augment or reduce a speaker's or a referent's agency, including deontic modality, that is, the encoding of the possibility or necessity of acts performed by morally responsible agents (Bybee and Fleischman 1995b; Lyons 1977: 823) and alternative expressions of the role of Agent.

Bybee, Perkins, and Pagliuca (1994) identify four types of "agent-oriented modality"[12] expressed in languages: (i) obligation, (ii) necessity, (iii) ability, and (iv) desire. They discuss a number of resources for representing speakers' knowledge as well as speakers' stance with respect to events and states of affairs. For example, the use of modal verbs such as the English *must, should, may* provides hearers with a sense of how speakers are representing their own as well as others' obligations within a primarily language-constructed (actually discourse-constructed) moral world. The use of volition predicates like *want, would, would like, wish* make certain internal psychological states available to others for understanding and evaluation.

The notion of mitigation also helps us look at discourse to search for would-be Agents, that is, referential NPs that could have been expressed as Agent NPs but were not. This is a strategy followed in Duranti and Ochs (1990) and Duranti (1994: 129–38) for Samoan, but it could be easily extended to other languages. For example, it is not uncommon for a potential Agent to appear as a modifier of a non-Agent NP. Compare (a) and (b) in the following examples:

(27) a. John's speech was very long.
    b. John gave a very long speech.
(28) a. This plate of fruit came from our neighbors.
    b. Our neighbors sent/brought us this plate of fruit.

Too little is known at the moment about the context of use of constructions of this kind across languages for us to build a model of exactly how they play a role in the mitigation of agency, but there is no question that perspective or point of view is at work here.

A possible direction for future research is to expand our horizon of theoretical and empirical research to include an understanding of these phenomena not only from the point of view of the type of information that is being encoded (e.g. is the agent of this event expressed and, if so, how?) but also from the point of view of the type of persons and the type of world that speakers build through their typically unconscious but nevertheless careful choice of words. It is in this sense that the notion of representation of agency is intimately tied to the notion of performance. In using language, we are constantly monitoring the type of person we want to be (Self) for Others and the type of Others we want to be there for us. The way we handle the expression of agency has a major role in this routine and yet complex enterprise. In constructing our daily discourse, we are constantly monitoring several types of "flows," including the flow of information (Chafe 1987) and the flow of moral stances and moral characters we implicitly establish by using any kind of grammatical framing (Duranti 1994).

6 CONCLUSIONS

In this chapter I have brought together a number of traditions in the study of agency, including the work of sociologists, anthropologists, philosophers, and grammarians. On the basis of these studies, I have proposed a working definition of agency that should apply across the spectrum, that is, that should satisfy those interested in social structure and those interested in linguistic framing. Starting from the definition of agency given in (1), I have identified two types of agency, which I called *performance* and *encoding*. I have suggested that although it is important to separate these two types for analytical purposes, they are actually mutually dependent, with encoding being an important element of performance and vice versa. Within the performance type, I have identified two subtypes: *ego-affirming* and *act-constituting* agency. Within the encoding of agency, I have concentrated on the role of agency in defining different types of grammatical patterns (e.g. nominative-accusative versus ergative-absolutive) offered by typologically different languages. I used English as an example of a language in which the subject position is quite open to a variety of semantic roles and in which, therefore, agency can be metaphorically extended to semantic roles and situations in ways that would not be possible to conceive in other languages. I have used Samoan as an example of an ergative-absolutive language in which (for full NPs) a sharp distinction is made between Agent NPs and other kinds of roles. I have also briefly looked at so-called stative-active languages and suggested that their existence provides support for a wider, more open category of agency (and Agent), where we might include entities that do not have an obvious impact on others or on their environment (i.e. that the presence of a malleable Object other than the participant in the Subject role might not be a necessary condition for agency to be recognized). I have also pointed out that no language is perfectly consistent in any given type and the same language might in fact encode agency in different ways, according to the type of referent NPs that are being talked about.

Finally, on the basis of the existing typology of grammatical systems, I have proposed two generalizations (potential universals of language structure): (i) the centrality of agency in languages (all languages have grammatical structures that seem designed to represent agency) and (ii) the diversity of the encoding of agency (alternative ways of marking agency are available both across languages and within the same language). On the basis of existing data on how grammatical systems are actually used by speakers in spoken and written discourse, two further generalizations can be added: (iii) the universality of the mitigation of agency (all languages have ways of reducing or "modulating" the level of agency of certain participants) and (iv) the universality of the omission of agency (all languages have ways of omitting altogether the sources of agency).

When seen together, these four generalizations suggest that the encoding of agency is both an important and a potentially problematic act for speakers. These two qualities are tied to what I would call the *inevitability of agency* for humans. There is inevitability at the existential level (ego-affirming), performative level (act-constituting), and grammatical level (encoding). At each of these three levels, agency is either the goal or the result of a person's being-in-the-world. It is this multi-level inevitability that, more than anything else, gives language its claim to power and it is this claim that linguistic anthropologists have been studying for over a century. The integration of social theory and linguistic analysis offered in this chapter continues in that tradition.

NOTES

An earlier version of this chapter was presented at the 2001 SALSA (Symposium about Language and Society) Conference at the University of Texas, Austin, and at one of the weekly UCLA Anthropology "Discourse Labs." I am grateful to the participants at those two events who provided insightful comments and to Adrienne Lo for reading and commenting on earlier drafts of this chapter. I also benefited from written comments by Laura Ahearn, Vincent Barletta, Ken Cook, Doug Hollan, Webb Keane, Matt Shibatani, and Laura Sterponi, and from conversations with Elinor Ochs and Sandra Thompson. My students' interest in agency was a major factor in my decision to address the issues discussed here.

1 "By the duality of structure, I mean the essential recursiveness of social life, as constituted in social practices: structure is both medium and outcome of the reproduction of practices. Structure enters simultaneously into the constitution of the agent and social practices, and 'exists' in the generating moments of this constitution" (Giddens 1979: 5).

2 I will use the standard linguistic convention of capitalizing the names of semantic roles like Agent, Object (or Patient), Instrument, etc.

3 For a series of succinct statements and references to these concepts, see Banti (2001), Beeman (2001), Ben-Amos (2001), Feld and Fox (1994, 2001), Hoëm (2001).

4 There is a long tradition of studies in folklore, linguistic anthropology, and literary studies on this dimension, e.g. Bauman (1975); Briggs and Bauman (1992); Hymes (1975); Palmer and Jankowiak (1996).

5 Abbreviations used in interlinear glosses: ART = article; ERG = ergative; INST = Instrument/Cause; PRES = present; PST = past; TA = tense/aspect marker; EMP = emphatic particle.

6 In some ergative languages (e.g. Dyirbal and some other Australian Aboriginal languages), the ergative marker has the same phonological shape as the instrumental marker. This coincidence of form suggests a possible conceptualization based on a larger category of causality, which does not involve volition or control. At the same time, it is also possible that the similarity is only very superficial and a more detailed analysis may reveal that although marked by the same surface form, Agents and Instruments display certain important differences. This is indeed the argument presented by Dixon (1972) for Dyirbal.

7 Dowty (1991) provides a prototype definition of Agent:
    a. volitional involvement in the event or state
    b. sentence [sic, read "sentience"] (and/or perception)
    c. causing an event or change of state in another participant
    d. movement (rel. to the position of another participant)
    e. exists independently of the event named by the verb.
    For a prototypical definition of causation, see Lakoff and Johnson (1980). On Agents within the context of the grammar and meaning of causation, see also Talmy (1976, 2000).

8   Even though he does not use cross-linguistic comparison in his discussion, Jackendoff's more recent use of the term "Actor" (1990) over "Agent" (1972) suggests that he sees agency along lines similar to the conceptualization found in active-stative languages.

9   This lack of Agents in discourse has been documented for other languages as well. For Samoan, see Duranti (1981, 1990, 1994), Duranti and Ochs (1990), Ochs (1988). However, cross-linguistic comparison is made difficult in this area because in languages with so-called "zero anaphora" (i.e. with no overt pronouns to represent certain NP arguments of the verb, at least in some constructions) it is often difficult to tell whether the unexpressed Agent is identifiable or not.

10   I am treating here what Levinson (1995: 224) calls "animistic and interactional thinking" as a by-product of the syntax and semantics of English (and presumably other languages, but not all).

11   "[...]" indicates that a portion of the longer sentence or paragraph has been omitted.

12   "Agent-oriented modality reports the existence of internal and external conditions on an agent with respect to the completion of the action expressed in the main predicate. As a report, the agent-oriented modality is part of the propositional content of the clause and thus would not be considered a modality in most frameworks" (Bybee, Perkins, and Pagliuca 1994: 177).

REFERENCES

Ahearn, L. M. (1999). Agency. *Journal of Linguistic Anthropology* 9: 12–15.

Ahearn, L. M. (2001). Language and Agency. *Annual Review of Anthropology* 30: 109–137.

Austin, J. L. (1962). *How to Do Things with Words*. Oxford: Oxford University Press.

Austin, J. L. (1975). *How to Do Things with Words*, 2nd edn. (ed. J. O. Urmson and M. Sbisà). Cambridge, MA: Harvard University Press.

Banti, G. (2001). Meter. In A. Duranti (ed.), *Key Terms in Language and Culture* (pp. 150–153). Malden, MA: Blackwell.

Bates, E., and MacWhinney, B. (1982). Functionalist Approaches to Grammar. In E. Wanner and L. Gleitman (eds.), *Language Acquisition: The State of the Art* (pp. 173–218). Cambridge: Cambridge University Press.

Bauman, R. (1975). Verbal Art as Performance. *American Anthropologist* 77: 290–311.

Bauman, R. (1993). Disclaimers of Performance. In J. Hill and J. T. Irvine (eds.), *Responsibility and Evidence in Oral Discourse* (pp. 182–196). Cambridge: Cambridge University Press.

Beeman, W. (2001). Humor. In A. Duranti (ed.), *Key Terms in Language and Culture* (pp. 98–101). Malden, MA: Blackwell.

Ben-Amos, D. (2001). Metaphor. In A. Duranti (ed.), *Key Terms in Language and Culture* (pp. 147–149). Malden, MA: Blackwell.

Berk-Seligson, S. (1990). *The Bilingual Courtroom: Court Interpretation in the Judicial Process*. Chicago: University of Chicago Press.

Bourdieu, P. (1977). *Outline of a Theory of Practice* (trans. R. Nice). Cambridge: Cambridge University Press.

Bourdieu, P. (1982). *Ce que parler veut dire*. Paris: Fayard.

Bourdieu, P. (1990). *The Logic of Practice*. Stanford: Stanford University Press.

Bourdieu, P. (2000). *Pascalian Meditations*. Stanford: Stanford University Press.

Briggs, C. L., and Bauman, R. (1992). Genre, Intertextuality, and Social Power. *Journal of Linguistic Anthropology* 2: 131–172.

Brown, P., and Levinson, S. C. (1987). *Politeness: Some Universals in Language Use*. Cambridge: Cambridge University Press.

Bybee, J., and Fleischman, S. (eds.) (1995a). *Modality in Grammar and Discourse*. Amsterdam and Philadelphia: John Benjamins.

Bybee, J., and Fleischman, S. (1995b). Modality in Grammar and Discourse: An Introductory Essay. In J. Bybee and S. Fleischman (eds.), *Modality in Grammar and Discourse* (pp. 1–14). Amsterdam and Philadelphia: John Benjamins.

Bybee, J., Perkins, R., and Pagliuca, W. (1994). *The Evolution of Grammar: Tense, Aspect, and Modality in the Languages of the World*. Chicago: University of Chicago Press.

Chafe, W. L. (1987). Cognitive Constraints on Information Flow. In R. S. Tomlin (eds.), *Coherence and Grounding in Discourse*. Amsterdam: John Benjamins.

Chafe, W., and Nichols, J. (1986). *Evidentiality: The Linguistic Coding of Epistemology*. Norwood, NJ: Ablex.

Chierchia, G. (1989). Structured Meanings, Thematic Roles and Control. In G. Chierchia, B. H. Partee, and R. Turner (eds.), *Properties, Types, and Meaning*, vol. II: *Semantic Issues* (pp. 131–166). Dordrecht: Kluwer.

Chomsky, N. (1977). *Language and Responsibility*. Based on Conversations with Mitsou Ronat (trans. J. Viertel). New York: Pantheon Books.

Chomsky, N. (1982). *Lectures on Government and Binding: The Pisa Lectures* (2nd edn.). Dordrecht: Foris.

Comrie, B. (1978). Ergativity. In W. P. Lehmann (ed.), *Syntactic Typology*. Austin: University of Texas Press.

Comrie, B. (1981). *Language Universals and Linguistic Typology: Syntax and Morphology*. Chicago: University of Chicago Press.

Costa, R. (1975). Functional Solution for Illogical Reflexes in Italian. In R. E. Grossman, L. J. San, and T. J. Vance (eds.), *Papers from the Parasession on Functionalism*. Chicago: Chicago Linguistic Society.

De Dominicis, A. (ed.) (2002). *La voce come bene culturale*. Rome: Carocci.

DeLancey, S. (1982). Aspect, Transitivity and Viewpoint. In P. J. Hopper (ed.), *Tense-Aspect: Between Semantics and Pragmatics* (pp. 167–183). Amsterdam and Philadelphia: John Benjamins.

Delancey, S. (1990). Ergativity and the Cognitive Model of Event Structure in Lhasa Tibetan. *Cognitive Linguistics* 1: 289–321.

Dennett, D. C. (1987). *The Intentional Stance*. Cambridge, MA: MIT Press.

Derrida, J. (1982). Signature Event Context. In *Margins in Philosophy* (trans. and with additional notes by A. Bass) (pp. 307–330). Chicago: University of Chicago Press.

Dixon, R. M. W. (1972). *The Dyirbal Language of North Queensland*. Cambridge: Cambridge University Press.

Dixon, R. M. W. (1979). Ergativity. *Language* 55: 59–138.

Dixon, R. M. W. (1994). *Ergativity*. Cambridge: Cambridge University Press.

Dowty, D. R. (1989). On the Semantic Content of the Notion "Thematic Role". In G. Chierchia, B. H. Partee, and R. Turner (eds.), *Properties, Types, and Meaning*, vol. II: *Semantic Issues* (pp. 69–129). Dordrecht: Kluwer.

Dowty, D. R. (1991). Thematic Proto-roles and Argument Selection. *Language* 67(3): 547–619.

Du Bois, J. (1986). Self-Evidence and Ritual Speech. In W. Chafe and J. Nichols (eds.), *Evidentiality: The Linguistic Coding of Epistemology* (pp. 313–336). Norwood, NJ: Ablex.

Du Bois, J. (1987). The Discourse Basis of Ergativity. *Language* 63: 805–855.

Duranti, A. (1981). *The Samoan Fono: A Sociolinguistic Study*. Pacific Linguistics Monographs, Series B. Vol. 80. Canberra: Australian National University, Department of Linguistics, Research School of Pacific Studies.

Duranti, A. (1990). Politics and Grammar: Agency in Samoan Political Discourse. *American Ethnologist* 17: 646–666.

Duranti, A. (1992). Language in Context and Language as Context: The Samoan Respect Vocabulary. In A. Duranti and C. Goodwin (eds.), *Rethinking Context: Language as an Interactive Phenomenon* (pp. 77–99). Cambridge: Cambridge University Press.

Duranti, A. (1993). Intentions, Self, and Responsibility: An Essay in Samoan Ethnopragmatics. In J. Hill and J. Irvine (eds.), *Responsibility and Evidence in Oral Discourse* (pp. 24–47). Cambridge: Cambridge University Press.

Duranti, A. (1994). *From Grammar to Politics: Linguistic Anthropology in a Western Samoan Village*. Berkeley and Los Angeles: University of California Press.

Duranti, A. (1997a). Universal and Culture-specific Properties of Greetings. *Journal of Linguistic Anthropology* 7: 63–97.

Duranti, A. (1997b). *Linguistic Anthropology*. Cambridge: Cambridge University Press.

Duranti, A. (2001). Relativity. In A. Duranti (ed.), *Key Terms in Language and Culture* (pp. 129–131). Malden, MA: Blackwell.

Duranti, A., and Ochs, E. (1990). Genitive Constructions and Agency in Samoan Discourse. *Studies in Language* 14: 1–23.

Durie, M. (1988). Preferred Argument Structure in an Active Language. *Lingua* 74: 1–25.

Feld, S., and Fox, A. (1994). Music and Language. *Annual Review of Anthropology* 23: 25–53.

Feld, S., and Fox, A. (2001). Music. In A. Duranti (ed.), *Key Terms in Language and Culture* (pp. 154–157). Malden, MA: Blackwell.

Fillmore, C. J. (1968). The Case for Case. In E. Bach and E. T. Harms (eds.), *Universals of Linguistic Theory*, (pp. 1–88). New York: Holt.

Fillmore, C. J. (1977). Topics in Lexical Semantics. In R. Cole (ed.), *Current Issues in Linguistic Theory* (pp. 76–138). Bloomington: Indiana University Press.

Foley, W., and Van Valin, R. (1984). *Functional Syntax and Universal Grammar*. Cambridge: Cambridge University Press.

Garfinkel, H. (1967). *Studies in Ethnomethodology*. Englewood Cliffs, NJ: Prentice-Hall.

Giddens, A. (1979). *Central Problems in Social Theory: Action, Structure and Contradiction in Social Analysis*. Berkeley: University of California Press.

Giddens, A. (1984). *The Constitution of Society: Outline of the Theory of Structuration*. Berkeley: University of California Press.

Grice, H. P. (1975). Logic and Conversation. In P. Cole and N. L. Morgan (eds.), *Syntax and Semantics*, vol. 3: *Speech Acts* (pp. 41–58). New York: Academic Press.

Grimshaw, J. (1990). *Argument Structure*. Cambridge, MA: MIT Press.

Gumperz, J. J., and Levinson, S. C. (eds.) (1996). *Rethinking Linguistic Relativity*. Cambridge: Cambridge University Press.

Hall, K. (1999). Performativity. *Journal of Linguistic Anthropology* 9: 184–187.

Hawkinson, A., and Hyman, L. M. (1974). Hierarchies of Narual Topic in Shona. *Studies in African Linguistics* 5: 147–170.

Hill, J. H., and Irvine, J. T. (eds.) (1993). *Responsibility and Evidence in Oral Discourse*. Cambridge: Cambridge University Press.

Hill, J. H., and Mannheim, B. (1992). Language and World View. *Annual Review of Anthropology* 21: 381–406.

Hoëm, I. (2001). Theater. In A. Duranti (ed.), *Key Terms in Language and Culture* (pp. 244–247). Malden, MA: Blackwell.

Hopper, P. J., and Thompson, S. A. (1980). Transitivity in Grammar and Discourse. *Language* 56: 251–299.

Husserl, E. (1931). *Ideas: General Introduction to Pure Phenomenology* (trans. W. R. Boyce Gibson). New York: Collier.

Hymes, D. (1975). Breakthrough into Performance. In D. Ben-Amos and K. S. Goldstein (eds.), *Folklore: Performance and Communication* (pp. 11–74). The Hague: Mouton.

Irvine, J. T. (1974). Strategies of Status Manipulation in Wolof Greeting. In R. Bauman and J. Sherzer (eds.), *Explorations in the Ethnography of Speaking* (pp. 167–191). Cambridge: Cambridge University Press.

Jackendoff, R. (1972). *Semantic Interpretation in Generative Grammar.* Cambridge, MA: MIT Press.

Jackendoff, R. (1990). *Semantic Structures.* Cambridge, MA: MIT Press.

Jakobson, R. (1960). Closing Statement: Linguistics and Poetics. In T. A. Sebeok (ed.), *Style in Language* (pp. 350–377). Cambridge, MA: MIT Press.

Kant, I. (1785). *Grundlegung zur Metaphysik der Sitten.* Leipzig: Hartknoch.

Keenan, E. L. (1984). Semantic Correlates of the Ergative/Absolutive Distinction. *Linguistics* 22: 197–223.

Kendon, A. (1997). Gesture. *Annual Review of Anthropology* 26: 109–128.

Kibrik, A. E. (1985). Toward a Typology of Ergativity. In J. Nichols and A. Woodbury (eds.), *Grammar Inside and Outside the Clause: Some Approaches to Theory from the Field* (pp. 268–323). Cambridge: Cambridge University Press.

Kirsner, R. S. (1976). On the Subjectless "Pseudo-Passive" in Standard Dutch and the Semantics of Background Agents. In C. N. Li (ed.), *Subject and Topic.* New York: Academic Press.

Kuno, S., and Kaburaki, E. (1977). Empathy and Syntax. *Linguistic Inquiry* 8: 627–673.

Kuroda, S.-Y. (1974). Where Epistemology, Style, and Grammar Meet: A Case Study from Japanese. In S. R. Anderson and P. Kiparsky (eds.), *A Festschrift for Morris Halle* (pp. 377–391). New York: Holt, Rinehart and Winston.

Lakoff, G., and Johnson, M. (1980). *Metaphors We Live By.* Chicago: University of Chicago Press.

Levinson, S. C. (1983). *Pragmatics.* Cambridge: Cambridge University Press.

Levinson, S. C. (1995). Interaction Biases in Human Thinking. In E. Goody (ed.), *Social Intelligence and Interaction* (pp. 221–259). Cambridge: Cambridge University Press.

Lyons, J. (1977). *Semantics.* Cambridge: Cambridge University Press.

Lyons, J. (1982). Deixis and Subjectivity: *Loquor, ergo sum?* In R. J. Jarvella and W. Klein (eds.), *Speech, Place, and Action: Studies in Deixis and Related Topics* (pp. 101–125). New York: John Wiley and Sons.

Malinowski, B. (1923). The Problem of Meaning in Primitive Languages. In C. K. Ogden and I. A. Richards (eds.), *The Meaning of Meaning* (pp. 296–336). New York: Harcourt, Brace and World.

Malinowski, B. (1935). *Coral Gardens and Their Magic.* London: Allen and Unwin.

Merlan, F. (1985). Split Intransitivity: Functional Oppositions in Intransitive Inflection. In J. Nichols and A. Woodbury (eds.), *Grammar Inside and Outside the Clause: Some Approaches to Theory from the Field* (pp. 324–362). Cambridge: Cambridge University Press.

Mithun, M. (1991). Active/Agentive Case Marking and Its Motivation. *Language* 67: 510–546.

Ochs, E. (1988). *Culture and Language Development: Language Acquisition and Language Socialization in a Samoan Village.* Cambridge: Cambridge University Press.

Ochs, E. (1992). Indexing Gender. In A. Duranti and C. Goodwin (eds.), *Rethinking Context,* (pp. 335–358). Cambridge: Cambridge University Press.

Ochs, E., and Schieffelin, B. B. (1984). Language Acquisition and Socialization: Three Developmental Stories and Their Implications. In R. A. Shweder and R. A. LeVine (eds.), *Culture Theory: Essays on Mind, Self, and Emotion* (pp. 276–320). Cambridge: Cambridge University Press.

Palmer, G. B., and Jankowiak, W. R. (1996). Performance and Imagination: Toward an Anthropology of the Spectacular and the Mundane. *Cultural Anthropology* 11: 225–258.

Rosaldo, M. Z. (1982). The Things We Do With Words: Ilongot Speech Acts and Speech Act Theory in Philosophy. *Language in Society* 11: 203–237.

Sánchez, A. R. (1997). Reflexiones en torno a la agencia y la afección en Español. *Anuario de Estudios Filológicos* 20: 365–387.

Schegloff, E. A. (1992). To Searle on Conversation: A Note in Return. In J. R. Searle, *(On) Searle on Conversation* (pp. 113–128). Amsterdam and Philadelphia: John Benjamins.

Schlesinger, I. M. (1989). Instruments as Agents: On the Nature of Semantic Relations. *Journal of Linguistics* 25: 189–210.

Searle, J. R. (1965). What Is a Speech Act? In M. Black (ed.), *Philosophy in America* (pp. 221–239). London: George Allen and Unwin.

Searle, J. R. (1969). *Speech Acts: An Essay in the Philosophy of Language.* Cambridge: Cambridge University Press.

Shibatani, M. (1985). Passives and Related Constructions: A Prototype Analysis. *Language* 61: 821–848.

Silverstein, M. (1976a). Hierarchy of Features of Ergativity. In R. M. W. Dixon (ed.), *Grammatical Categories in Australian Languages* (pp. 112–171). Canberra: Australian Institute of Aboriginal Studies.

Silverstein, M. (1976b). Shifters, Linguistic Categories, and Cultural Description. In K. H. Basso and H. A. Selby (eds.), *Meaning in Anthropology* (pp. 11–56). Albuquerque: University of New Mexico Press.

Silverstein, M. (1977). Cultural Prerequisites to Grammatical Analysis. In M. Saville-Troike (ed.), *Linguistics and Anthropology: Georgetown University Round Table on Languages and Linguistics 1977* (pp. 139–151). Washington, DC: Georgetown University Press.

Streeck, J. (1980). Speech Acts in Interaction: A Critique of Searle. *Discourse Processes* 3: 133–154.

Stubbs, M. (1994). Grammar, Text and Ideology. *Applied Linguistics* 15: 201–223.

Talmy, L. (1976). Semantic Causative Types. In M. Shibatani (ed.), *Syntax and Semantics*, vol. 6: *Causatives* (pp. 43–116). New York: Academic Press.

Talmy, L. (2000). *Toward a Cognitive Semantics*, vol. 1: *Concept Structuring Systems.* Cambridge, MA: MIT Press.

Taylor, C. (1985). *Human Agency and Language.* Cambridge: Cambridge University Press.

Thompson, S. A., and Hopper, P. J. (2001). Transitivity, Clause Structure, and Argument Structure: Evidence from Conversation. In J. Bybee and P. J. Hopper (eds.), *Frequency and the Emergence of Linguistic Structure* (pp. 27–60). Amsterdam: John Benjamins.

Whorf, B. L. (1941). The Relation of Habitual Thought and Behavior in Language. In L. Spier, A. I. Hallowell, and S. S. Newman (eds.), *Language, Culture, and Personality: Essays in Honor of Edward Sapir* (pp. 75–93). Menasha, WI: Sapir Memorial Publication.

Whorf, B. L. (1956). Linguistics as an Exact Science. In J. B. Carroll (ed.), *Language, Thought, and Reality: Selected Writings of Benjamin Lee Whorf* (pp. 220–232). Cambridge, MA: MIT Press.

Wittgenstein, L. (1958). *Philosophical Investigations* (ed. G. E. M. Anscombe and R. Rhees; trans. G. E. M. Anscombe, 2nd edn.). Oxford: Blackwell.

CHAPTER 21 Language and Social Inequality

Susan U. Philips

1 INTRODUCTION

At the heart of the relationship between language and social inequality is the idea that some expressions of language are valued more than others in a way that is associated with some people being more valued than others and some ideas expressed by people through language being more valued than others. The purpose of this chapter is to explore the range of ways that these connections are articulated in linguistic anthropology.

Dell Hymes expressed this general view of language and social inequality in his essay on the origins of inequality among speakers (Hymes 1973). Hymes envisions a human condition in which, at any given point in time, people will desire to use some forms of talk more than others. Whatever language those forms of talk are conducted in will gain speakers and spread in use. The languages of the forms of talk that people less desire to engage in will correspondingly lose speakers and shrink in their functional ranges. Hymes stresses the coercive and power-laden forces through which some languages and forms of talk thrive while others fail to thrive or decline, so that while people voluntarily take up and discard forms of talk, they also are forced to do so. While Hymes uses a variety of examples to illustrate the processes he is talking about, no one could fail to think most of the rapid extinction of North American Indian languages that has been with us since the beginning of American anthropology at the turn of the twentieth century (see Mithun, this volume). At that time Boas (1911) painstakingly developed arguments to counter the widespread notion that languages are not equal, that some languages, specifically European languages, were superior to others in their complexity and range of expression.[1] He was opposing a climate in which North American Indians were under pressure to give up speaking their languages and to instead speak English; because the Indians were little valued, their languages and the social acts and ideas entailed in and expressed through their languages were little valued. That same climate exists today. This North American Indian situation has been the point of departure for linguistic anthropological interest in the relation between language and social inequality and it is still a key concern today.

Bourdieu (1977) has been the theoretical successor to Hymes in the promulgation of a broad theoretical conceptualization of language and social inequality with his concept of symbolic capital. He has argued that just as humans can deploy material capital to enhance their situations economically, so too may they deploy non-material symbolic capital to that same end. Symbolic capital is cultural capital. It refers to sociocultural attributes, both acquired and achieved, that are highly valued in a society, bring prestige to the individual, and can be converted into material capital. Bourdieu's canonical example of symbolic capital is language. Some forms of language are more highly valued than others. Most concretely, in Western European contexts, those who speak the standard dialect of their national language will be able to get higher-paying jobs than those who do not speak it, because of its prestige. Bourdieu envisioned a unified or integrated market for symbolic capital created for a given nation through its education system, which would teach the prestige dialect, as dictated by the state. In this way all would be inculcated in the value of the prestige dialect. Some have disagreed with Bourdieu's assumption of a unified market, but few have disagreed with his emphasis on an inequality of codes associated with a socio-economic inequality among speakers.

Bourdieu brings actual *people* more to the fore than Hymes did by more explicitly linking the valuing of some ways of speaking over others to the valuing of some people over others. There are, however, additional theoretical constructs in linguistic anthropology that foreground the *strategic activity* of using prestigious forms of talk as a way of persuading others to one's view, i.e. that stress that ideas can be inculcated through speech that is persuasive in part because of its prestigious nature. Variants of a concept of "authoritative speech" that take up this idea have been around for some time (e.g. Bloch 1975; Hanks 1987; Parmentier 1993; Duranti 1994; Gal and Woolard 1995), though no version of the concept has been developed in a sustained way until quite recently. Authoritative speech refers to the idea that by speaking in a particular style which is highly valued and/or associated with authority, or by speaking from within a particular discourse genre that is authoritative or associated with authoritative people, a speaker is more persuasive, more convincing, and more attended to. Thus Parmentier argues that a Belauan chief making a speech in a traditional format using traditional rhetorical strategies invokes the authority associated with these qualities to persuade his audience to his point of view. He also points out, as do others, that the style and format themselves derive their authority in part from their indexical connections to the people typically thought of as being in authority, in this case chiefs. Further, not all Belauans will have access to such speech in a way that will enable them to learn to control and produce it. Nor will all be seen as having the right to deploy such speech. There is, then, a reflexive quality to authoritative speech – it is authoritative because of who uses it, and those who use it are authoritative because they are able to use it.[2]

There are also other concepts related to the idea of authoritative speech that show us there is flexibility, creativity, and emergence in making speech authoritative, and not just the invocation of traditional authority. First, some forms of evidence are considered more reliable than others. For example, reported or quoted speech is imported into talk as a way of drawing on the authority of the person whose speech is being reported (Hill and Irvine 1993). The Bakhtinian (1981) concept of "voices" more broadly develops similar ideas. Intertextuality, or the linking of texts in various ways, has similarly been argued to bring the authority of one textual rendering into another (Bauman and Briggs 1990).

The importance of ideas about authoritative speech resides in the emphasis on persuasiveness via authority because this points to the capacity of some forms of speech and language to have a greater impact on the constitution of reality than others, rather than simply to have a greater or lesser presence, or greater or lesser valuing.

We have begun here, then, with a set of very general ideas about the role of language in the creation and reproduction of social inequalities. Basically, language forms are differentiated in their value and persuasiveness, and this differentiation plays a major role in the constitution of social inequalities and in the actual shaping of social reality. We will turn now to the examination of several prominent schools of thought that have developed such ideas more concretely, in a way that ties them to specific aspects of culture and social organization. Four coherent areas of linguistic anthropological research in which concepts of language and social inequality are theoretically central will be considered: language use in bureaucratic settings, gender and language, language and political economy, and language and colonialism.

These four topics were selected for two reasons. First, for each of these there is a coherent body of work with multiple scholars who share a common orientation theoretically and methodologically. Second, in each tradition there is an explicit or overt orientation toward power relations, or relations of domination and subordination. (Other chapters in this volume that deal with related topics include Agha on Registers, Duranti on Agency in Language, Bucholtz and Hall on Language and Identity, and Kroskrity on Language Ideologies.)

2 LANGUAGE AND SOCIAL INEQUALITY IN BUREAUCRATIC SETTINGS

The 1960s was a critical period for the crystallization of a certain kind of awareness of language and social inequality that has been with us since that time. That awareness developed in the context of the emergence of sociolinguistics, itself a mix of approaches from scholars of language in linguistics, anthropology, and sociology, who were talking to each other and assigning each other's work to their students. A brief examination of William Labov's writing on Black English during this period (Labov 1972) can help clarify how certain concerns came to the fore and stayed there.

Civil Rights issues in communities and schools that centered around equality for blacks created an awareness that the English being spoken by black children was being treated as not equal to that of white children. Their non-standard dialects were conceptualized as broken, corrupted versions of Standard English and blamed for the children's failure to participate and thrive in schools. Labov famously argued for the rule-governedness and systematicity of Black English and for the inappropriateness of thinking of the dialect as broken or corrupted. But he also argued that the typical classroom was not a comfortable place for black children, because there they interacted with white teachers with whom they were unfamiliar at best, in ways of speaking, and about topics that were also unfamiliar. He illustrated the facility with language of black children when they were given opportunities to interact with black interviewers in black community contexts.

Labov's argument for the inappropriateness of blaming Black English for the school problems of the children who spoke it entailed all of the elements involved in the relation between language and social inequality that have been central to discussions of this topic in linguistic anthropology since the mid-twentieth century. His argument entails *language features*, in this case a dialect, a dialect that was *ideologically* disvalued by the wider society, compared with a dialect that was valued. These dialects, and their positive and negative valuing, were associated with particular *social identities*, in this case the racially opposed identities of black and white. The ideological disparagement of the code took place in a particular *social context*, in this case the classroom, through which an identifiable subordinated community, blacks, was articulated with the wider nation-state. But in addition to the expressed disparagement of the code, Black English, there was also, in that institutional setting, a more covert and implicit disparagement, through exclusion, of other language features: ways of speaking and topics to be spoken about associated with the community and its code.

This focus on ethnic minority children in American classrooms stimulated a series of studies of language inequalities in institutional settings, particularly in schools, but also courts and medical clinics. Not all of these studies have been concerned with African American or even ethnic minority identities, although many are. And, whereas Labov works out of the language variationist tradition, the studies of language inequalities that followed his were more rooted in the interactional sociolinguistic traditions of symbolic interactionism associated with Erving Goffman, ethnomethodology associated with Harold Garfinkel and Aaron Cicourel, and conversation analysis associated with Harvey Sacks, Emanuel Schegloff, and Gail Jefferson. These traditions have in common with ethnography in anthropology a methodological commitment to the study of naturally occurring activities through participant observation and, as the technology has emerged, through the tape recording and transcription of speech. Goffman, Garfinkel, and Cicourel are sociologists who were initially interested in how stigmatized populations were socially defined and constituted through their treatment in institutional contexts such as psychiatric and medical encounters, prisons, and mental hospitals. (Note that these are precisely the institutional contexts also taken up by Michel Foucault, whose influence on anthropologists has been more recent.) The work of these sociologists came into anthropology largely through the efforts of Dell Hymes and John Gumperz to link it to that of anthropologists in the ethnography of communication tradition.

Studies in schools (Erickson and Shultz 1982; Philips 1983; Mehan 1979) focus on the ways in which children were culturally defined as succeeding or failing by teachers and counselors. This work represented teachers as exercising power over students through the way in which language was used in interaction. Studies in courts (Danet et al. 1976) display the ways that lawyers control the production of legal realities elicited from witnesses. And studies in medical clinics (West 1984; Fisher 1986; Ainsworth-Vaughn 1998) focus attention on the power that doctors have to define the medical realities constituted in doctor–patient interactions by virtue of their control over patients.

The people working on these topics have varied in the issues they focus on, but there are several particular aspects of language use that have been returned to again and again as central devices through which bureaucrats define the realities of their clients, or those being processed by the bureaucracies. I will focus here on turn economies, question–answer sequences, and ratification.

In classrooms, courtrooms, and clinics, turn economies are such that teachers, judges, and doctors, who are the representatives of their respective institutional complexes, control the turns at talk of those in their settings. They determine who talks next, or delegate that control by deciding who will determine who speaks next, as when judges turn control over to lawyers to question witnesses. They can also interrupt and take the floor back whenever they wish to do so.

Question and answer sequences are also under the control of these bureaucrats. They ask the questions to whomever they choose, and others are required to answer. In research on courtrooms in particular, questions have been characterized as coercive, as requiring an answer, with the form of the question, for example a yes–no question versus a *wh*-question ("who/what/where/when/why"), also determining the form that the answer will take. In actuality, it is important to recognize that it is not so much the uttering of a question that coerces an answer as it is the authority of the person asking the question that creates the coercion. This can be seen in evidence that when judges and lawyers are asked questions, particularly by non-lawyers, they do not necessarily allow the form of the question to dictate a response. Yet they are not seen as being uncooperative in the way that witnesses and defendants are when they fail to submit to question forms (Philips 1987). Note that control through question and answer sequences also entails control of topics, or of the content of what is discussed.

In such contexts, by virtue of control of the floor for talk control and question–answer sequences, bureaucrats also are in a position to ratify or fail to ratify what others say. Through this they are able to determine whether and how what others say gets incorporated into the social reality that emerges through the taking of turns at talk. Awareness of this most fundamental capacity for ratification was developed in conversation analysis through Sacks' (1967) idea that in a current turn at talk, a speaker gives evidence of "having heard" what went before. To illustrate this idea, I draw on transcript excerpts from my research in a first-grade classroom on the Warm Springs Indian Reservation. In the first excerpt, a student gives evidence of having heard the teacher:

(1)   (from Philips 1983: 86)
Teacher: Alright, Larry? Why would you rather sleep in a camper than a tent?
Student: 'Cause if you sleep in a tent all the animals can get in.
Teacher: Alright, Shane?

The student gives evidence of having heard the teacher by virtue of the fact that the student's response cannot be made sense of without having heard the teacher, and it does make sense if one has heard the teacher. The teacher's and student's turns are interdependent. We also see that the teacher accepts the answer and moves on to the next student. However, sometimes the evidence that the next speaker has heard the first speaker is more ambiguous, as in the following example:

(2)   (from Philips 1983: 88)
Teacher: The lark what to the tree?
Student: Song.
Teacher: Flew to the tree. It's a bird. It flew to the tree.

It is this inability to read an utterance as a response to what went before that Schegloff (1972) argued causes people to repeat what they said, or to cycle back through turns until what the next speaker says can be heard as a response. In this case, however, the teacher simply provides an answer to her own question that gives evidence of having heard the question.

Analyses of speech in classrooms is full of examples of situations where teachers fail to ratify students' responses, and this commonly occurs in courtrooms as well. For example, in my study of judges' use of language in the Tucson courts (Philips 1998), when defendants pleading guilty offered excuses for their crimes, judges rarely gave responses that signaled evidence of having heard the specific excuse. For example, in the following transcript excerpt, the judge is questioning a defendant who has stolen some cigarettes from a grocery store:

(3)   (from Philips 1998: 103)
Judge: And what did you intend to do, sell the cigarettes?
Defendant: Yes, sir.
Judge: Keep the money?
Defendant: No. I was-w-w- in need of money, you know. And I was waiting to go to school, and I was just broke, I was uh in need of money.
Judge: All right. Well, the Court finds there's a factual basis for the defendant's plea.

Here the judge acknowledges that the defendant has spoken, but shows no evidence of having heard the defendant's excuse for his crime. Doctors also regularly are perceived by patients to have failed to hear their complaints. Of course failure to ratify can also take the form of outright rejection, as for example when a child speaks in a language other than English in the classroom and is rebuked or punished by the teacher for having done so (e.g. Dorian 1981).

In the bureaucratic settings I have identified as prototypical, these three interactional strategies, i.e. turn control, question control, and control of ratification, have been shown to play a role in the creation of inequality in more than one way. It is easiest to see that the bureaucratic turn economy and question–answer format, taken together, create a systematic inequality between representatives of powerful institutions and the individuals they are supposed to serve, or what I have referred to as the bureaucrat and the client. In a purportedly egalitarian society such as America these two discourse organizational devices are fundamental strategies for constituting status differentiation in organizational life. Some find this differentiation unobjectionable, and view it as a consequence of specialization of knowledge and labor that is characteristic of modern life. Others have seen such institutional role differentiation as a consequence of the rise of the authority of professional classes – doctors, lawyers, and teachers – that has gotten out of control in a way that calls for amelioration. The idea that professional expertise justifies control of discourse in bureaucratic settings can be seen as the ideology that gives the professionals the authority they have in these settings.

However, a second level of creating of inequalities is added to this basic differentiation through bureaucratic control of ratification, a control that renders some clients more subordinated than others. All students enter the classroom as equals in the sense that no student is more or less subject than any other to the control of turns and questions by the teacher. But they become differentiated through the process of ratification in which some students' turns at talk are validated and incorporated more than others. Most particularly, classroom studies show that ethnic minority children's contributions are not incorporated in the ongoing creation of educational realities in the way that Anglo children's are. By analogy, there is a concern for the possibility that ethnic minority criminal defendants, job interviewees, and medical patients have the same experience.

On one hand, the three strategies I have identified for rendering participants in an encounter unequal are abstract and content-free, and this is part of their potential power. In any situation, a cultural schema of social identities can be used to differentiate speakers' access to turns at talk and to differentiate questioner and answerer. Speakers can take turns by going around in a circle, or be ordered sequentially from youngest to oldest, or oldest to youngest. In a circle, you may question the person to your left, while the person to your right questions you. The younger can question the older or the older can question the younger. Only when the differentiation is asymmetrical rather than symmetrical (Goffman 1956), as when questioner and answerer cannot change positions, do we have a basis for the emergence of inequality.

While there is the potential for inequalities to emerge in all interactions, in the settings I have identified the inequalities are pervasively routinized. The strategies I have identified are used to rigorously enforce the interpretive perspectives of the institutional complexes and the professional classes associated with them. The turn economies and question–answer formats assure that this will be done systematically. The selective ratification of some participants more than others means that the ideological regimentation in classrooms, courtrooms, and clinics is greater for some people being articulated into bureaucracies than for others.

In practice, it seems that sociolinguists have been more concerned with the general capacity of interactional strategies to create inequalities than with the ideological or cultural consequences of their deployment. This may be one reason why cultural anthropologists have been less drawn to our work and more drawn to the work of Foucault, which is fundamentally concerned with the general ideological content and consequences of institutional regimentation.

3 GENDER, INEQUALITY, AND LANGUAGE

The gender and language literature in linguistics, sociology, and anthropology developed in response to the Women's Liberation Movement of the 1970s, a social movement that focused on changing women's inferior position relative to men in American society. The earlier Civil Rights movement, intended to bring parity to blacks relative to whites, concentrated on the public sphere – on legal rights in education, politics, and law. The women's movement, in contrast, was as politically concerned with women's personal home lives as it was with their situations in the public sphere. From the beginning, this political movement put forth an ideological critique of women's roles in society in which there was an important place for language. This critique was quickly picked up by academic linguists, most notably Robin Lakoff (1975). The basic idea of the ideological critique was that the inequality of women relative to men is sustained in part through a false belief in the inferiority of females. This belief was held to provide the basis for women's exclusion from political and work-related roles, and for their subordination to males in kinship and household relationships. Ideology, then, is central to analyses of language and gender inequality in a way that is not true of analyses of language in bureaucratic settings.

Language is implicated in the feminist critique in several ways. First there is the idea that the semantic structure of English derogates women, and renders them invisible, among other things. Examples of these ideas include the proliferation of terms that disparaged women sexually, such as "whore" and "bitch," that dimunized them, as in "baby," "chickie," and "cutie," and that rendered them invisible, as in the use of the pronouns "he," "him," and "his" to refer to both women and men.

Second there is the idea that women's language style is perceived as powerless, compared to the powerful language of men. Lakoff characterized women's language as more polite, and her work opened up the development of politeness theory more generally (Brown and Levinson 1987), and the development of comparative inquiry on whether women's language is cross-linguistically more polite than men's. Powerlessness means not being attended to, and accordingly involved a kind of silencing of women (Gal 1991).

Third, women in conversation were thought to be disadvantaged compared with men in the regulation of turns at talk by being interrupted more than men (Zimmerman and West 1975) and by not having the topics they introduced into conversation developed to the same extent that men's are (Fishman 1983). In this way there was overlap between the literature on language use in bureaucratic settings that I have just discussed and the literature on gender and language. This too was seen as a way of silencing women.

Some of these claims about differences in women's and men's speech have been challenged as conceptually inadequate, as varying contextually, as having undergone change as a result of the critique of patriarchy, or as simply empirically undemonstrable, most notably the idea that men interrupt more than women (e.g. James and Clarke 1993). Yet all of the features I have discussed continue to be perceived by women as sources of inequality in their daily lives.

Feminist anthropological research and research in the ethnography of communication also has given rise to the idea that a gendered social organization of speech entails the exclusion of women from speech events and speech genres in public domains, as opposed to private domains of language use (Keenan 1974; Sherzer 1987; Briggs 1992), and it is this theoretical perspective that is most unique to linguistic anthropology. The kind of speech community anthropologists envisioned when they developed this idea was at the level of the kinship group or village, not the nation. And the kind of speech event from which women were excluded that they most had in mind was the political meeting.

Here too, as in the other ideas about gender inequality and language, there is thought to be a significant ideological dimension to women's exclusion from the public sphere such that a disvaluing of women and their speech provided the rationale for that exclusion (Philips 2003). And again, women are seen as silenced, although here the concept of silencing is a little more complex. In this model of domain differentiation women certainly speak in private, in the household. But by being denied access to the public sphere, they are denied larger audiences for their words and views, and denied access to forms of talk or speech genres that carry greater prestige or weight in society.

For example, in Tonga, a Polynesian society in the south Pacific, women do not normally attend or participate in village *fonos*, meetings where male political leaders give directions to and make plans with villagers regarding various projects to be carried out by them. This is true even though much of the work for the projects, such as the preparation of *polas*, large sleds of food for feasts, will be carried out by women. Nor are women *matāpule*, titled orators who represent chiefs and families, making speeches and engaging in highly metaphorical and allusive verbal exchanges on occasions such as funerals and weddings. This is true even though, once again, women are deeply and intimately involved in the planning and execution of such events.

In more recent years the idea has become more prominent that women's views were different from the men's views that dominated in the public sphere, and were often in opposition or resistance to men's, even if only in private (Martin 1987; Abu-Lughod 1986). In other words, the exclusion of women from participation in political public spheres does not just mean that they don't get to talk, but also that they have perspectives on important issues that communities as a whole do not have the opportunity to be exposed to and influenced by.

Since the early 1980s, these ideas have been criticized and have undergone change. Some feminist scholars have a more sociological rather than anthropological concept of the public sphere. They have taken exception to the idea that women were excluded from public activities, seeing work, for example, as taking place in the public sphere. They also want women to be credited for the contributions they have made historically to twentieth-century American religion and politics, as in the temperance movement, the reform of child labor, and the development of social welfare protection of the poor. Through these and other developments, such as the influence of the Frankfurt School's concept of media (newspapers, television) as vehicles for public discourse, we now have a much more multi-faceted concept of multiple public spheres (Hanson 1993).

Gender itself has also been reconceptualized. Criticisms that a simple man–woman dichotomy essentializes women and obscures the diversity in their experiences has led to analysis of the ways in which gender intersects with race, class, ethnicity, and sexual orientation. This view in turn has been seen by some as too static and deterministic, and as failing to give women agency in the constitution of their own identities. So now we see phenomenological approaches to gender coming to the fore, approaches that emphasize the more transitory and fleeting performance of gender. This is connected to the idea that situations vary in the extent to which gender and other aspects of identity are made salient. Add to this an active rejection of the assumption of a link between sex and gender, and we have gender being very much constituted at will, particularly in studies of the cultural semiotic strategies deployed by biological males who assume female gendered identities (Kulick 1998; Besnier 1997). The interest in gender as a cultural system, as important an anthropological dimension of culture in all societies as this is, has not, however, kept with it the real focus on gender inequality out of which this interest grew.

When we compare the work on gender inequality and language with that of the inequalities between bureaucrat and client discussed in the previous section, some distinctive contributions of the gender research can be identified. First, it focuses on one specific aspect of social identity, rather than on a cluster of institutional complexes.

Second, the gender work brought to the study of language and social inequality a concept of a whole society organized into domains, rather than focusing on a single setting of a usually undescribed institutional complex, as in focusing on a classroom rather than a school. It is true that in linguistic anthropology this whole society tended not to be more than a kinship group or a village, as I have already noted, but the gender work still has contributed a new approach to the social organization of social inequality and language. It was through this work that the issue of who has access to speaking roles and speech genres first became prominent, along with the idea that access itself or the lack thereof could be a form of social inequality in language use.

Third, the research on gender developed the idea that stylistic differences in language use could be the basis for social inequality. The work developed this idea both theoretically and empirically. There has been considerable innovation in research methods as part of the effort to examine the actual linguistic nature of the differences in men's and women's styles (Philips, Steele, and Tanz 1987; Hall and Bucholtz 1995; Eckert 2000).

Finally, and most importantly, the research on language and gender inequality has played an important role in developing the concept of ideology in language-related research by making the negative evaluation of women's language and speech a central factor in their silencing. Silencing through inattention to women's speech because it was perceived as powerless, silencing through the deployment of conversational strategies in taking turns at talk that discourage women's participation, and silencing through the exclusion of women's speech in public domains, events, and genres all have been justified by language ideologies about men's and women's speech that negatively evaluated women's contributions.

4   LANGUAGE AND POLITICAL ECONOMY

A third coherent approach to language and inequality treats economic relations as the basic source of inequality among languages and their speakers. Most simply stated, this approach argues that economically disadvantaged persons have less prestige, and so do the codes they use. Conversely, economically advantaged persons have more prestige, and therefore so do the codes they use. A consequence of this is that codes associated with the economically advantaged, or dominant, flourish and expand in interaction. And codes associated with the economically disadvantaged are used less. In a process referred to as language shift, their functional range shrinks, relative to that of the more prestigious codes, sometimes to the point of language extinction. This theory, then, highlights as interconnected the economic positions of particular social groups, the attitudes toward those social groups, attitudes toward the languages they speak, and actual use of those languages.

At the most general level, political economists such as Andre Gundar Frank, Emmanual Wallerstein, and Eric Wolf argue that a global capitalist economic order has emerged over the last five hundred years out of European colonial economic exploitation of the rest of the world. This process has been characterized as one in which wealth moves from economic peripheries to centers, prototypically and historically European centers. In this model, the extraction of wealth enriches the centers and impoverishes the peripheries. It is this fundamental economic inequality that in turn influences the relative prestige of languages and their speakers. It creates pressures that in the broader global picture expand the use of European languages and contract the use of non-European languages.

At the same time as there are absolute centers in this model, however, centers and peripheries are also relative, so that, for example, while Lima may be a center for the extraction of wealth from interior Peru, wealth and prestige will still flow from Lima to Europe and the United States. For this reason, non-European languages of wider communication that become associated with economic regional centers may also gain prestige and speakers relative to related languages that do not come to have such an association. Examples of this include Tagalog in the Philippines, Indonesian in Indonesia, and Swahili in Tanzania. However, it is important to note that in spite of the political dimension to political economic theories of language inequality, ideas about the role of the state in shaping economic and linguistic processes, both independently and interdependently, are not always well integrated into such theories.

The work of the linguistic anthropologists who laid the foundations of the political economic approach to language and social inequality – Susan Gal, Kathryn Woolard, and Jane and Kenneth Hill – can be seen as significantly influenced both theoretically and methodologically by the earlier research of John Gumperz (1958) and William Labov (1963) on language variation. Gumperz's work on dialect variation in India and in Norway recognized both local and national dimensions to dialect variation. Labov's work on Martha's Vineyard was oriented in detail not only to the general historical economic stratification of the island, but also to the salience of occupational role identities on the island, in his explanation of dialect variation there. And his subsequent work on dialect variation in New York City, focused as it was on class-based variation, also drew attention to the underlying influence of economic differentiation on both language attitudes and phonological variation. However, as I will further explain, Gal, Hill and Hill, and Woolard do all have a more political economic conceptualization of the organization of economic processes than their predecessors in this much: they conceptualize national economies as internally differentiated into more central and profitable and less central and less profitable economic spheres; they conceptualize particular ethnic groups as articulated into those economies in and through specific economic sectors; they relate the economic positioning of the ethnic groups to language attitudes and code choices; and finally they conceptualize political economy as processual, as changing over time in a way that clearly allows some codes to expand or sustain their functional range while others contract in their functional range.

Susan Gal's (1979) study of bilingual speakers of German and Hungarian in Oberwart, a town in eastern Austria, documents a language shift taking place in which Hungarian was being used less and less while German was being used more and more by a Hungarian ethnic minority. At the time of Gal's study in the 1970s, young men were in the process of shifting from farming to industrial labor, as farming became less economically advantageous. Gal argues that the shift away from Hungarian to German after a long period of stable bilingualism was due to the attitudinal association of German with the increasingly positive identity of industrial worker.

Kathryn Woolard's (1989) research from the same period focuses on the relative status of the Catalonian and Castilian languages in the Catalan region of Spain around Barcelona. Woolard found that in spite of pressure from the central state government of Spain to eliminate Catalonian through education in Castilian, a regional loyalty of Catalonian speakers to Catalonian and positive attitudes toward it were being sustained in Barcelona. She attributes this language loyalty to the continued control by speakers of Catalonian over the prosperous regional industrial economy. She found that while Castilian gives its speakers access to government positions, Catalans "continue to be predominant in ownership and management of the private sector, which is still charac-terized by small and mid-sized industries" (Woolard 1985: 742). Catalonian speakers occupy managerial positions, while Castilian-speaking immigrants into the area engage in manual labor. Catalonian speakers own homes in more upscale neighborhoods and speak Catalan in their privately owned shops and service-providing businesses. Woolard's work complicates the concepts of center and periphery because while the agricultural and governmental center of Spain, Madrid, was Castilian, the industrial economic center was Catalonian. And she challenges Bourdieu's idea of an integrated national symbolic economy by documenting the presence of more than one system for the relative prestige or valuing of codes in Spain, and of resistance to the Spanish state's efforts to impose linguistic hegemony on the nation.

Jane and Kenneth Hill's (1986) research contrasts with these other two studies in its focus on a New World situation of a colonized group, Mexicano peasants in central Mexico. The Hills examine the factors influencing the role of Spanish and Nahuatl (Mexicano) in the lives of these descendants of Native Americans conquered by the Spanish. The picture they paint is quite complex. One can see a global political economy at work in the lives of these people. Mexicano peasants are undercapitalized small-scale agriculturalists who have been pushed into the least profitable farming areas by the members of the dominant Mexican culture who are identified with the Spanish colonial heritage of conquest. At the local village level, the prestige of Spanish is evident in ritual language use, but also in the way Mexicano grammar and lexicon have been deeply penetrated by Spanish lexicon and grammar. As young men make the transition from farming to industrial labor in the city of Puebla, they experience further loss of Mexicano, but counter their loss with an ideology of language purism that stresses the importance of producing certain key features of Mexicano in the correct way.

In each of these studies, the nation-state is the largest maximal political economic unit. In each, industry functions as the dominant economic activity to which agricul-ture is subordinate. In each, the language of urban industrial activity has or gains prestige relative to the language of rural farming or manual labor and sustains or gains ground in the actual use practices of a particular ethnic group. In sum, the political economic position of a group determines its attitudes toward the codes in the group's multilingual repertoire, the group's code choices, and the ultimate survival of the codes being spoken. The inequality of languages originates in economic inequality.

When we compare the political economic approach to language and social inequality to the other two traditions I have already documented, some interesting differences emerge. First, this is our first truly macrosocietal theory of language inequality in linguistic anthropology. It encompasses the nation, if not the entire globe. Face-to-face interaction moves to the background, and is no longer the focus in the way it is in the earlier two traditions, though it does not entirely disappear. The analytical focus is on codes as the aspect of language drawn into a framework of inequality, rather than turns at talk or genres, as in the studies of bureaucratic language use and gendered language respectively. Speakers' contributions of ideas or meaning are lost through loss of turns, and loss of participation in domain-organized speech genres in the earlier theories. Here, in contrast, we have to say that the political economic theory of language inequality focuses on the loss or threat of loss of whole linguistic codes to particular speech communities, and possibly, as with very many Native American languages, to the world and to history forever as well. This does not mean that whole speech genres are not also being lost, a point to which I will return. Rather, it means that speech genres are not the focus in the political economic approach.

In recent years, research that builds on the political economic model of language and social inequality has increasingly elaborated the ideological dimensions of the prestige of the languages involved (e.g. Hill 1998). The current interest in language revitalization that has been growing since the 1970s has led to the documentation of the reversal of language shifts of the kind held to be caused by political economic processes, as for example in northern Italy (Fellin 2001) and Corsica (Jaffe 1999). While new economic prosperity in these situations is acknowledged as a factor in the analysis of these reversals, other factors such as long-term antagonism toward weakly sustained nation-state hegemony, accompanied by ideological regionalism, challenge the primacy of economic causality in this theoretical tradition.

5   The Colonial Transformation of Language and Social Inequality

As I have noted, political economy broadly conceived includes the view that European colonialism set into motion a historically specific capitalist constitution of uneven economic development and accumulation of wealth. It is thus appropriate to see European colonialism as a fundamentally economically motivated process (as opposed, for example, to the American political ideological emphasis on the motivation of a search for religious freedom). It is also important, however, to recognize a political dimension to colonialism that has led to the formation of nation-states around the world. That political dimension has entailed the imposition of European forms of governmental organization and political ideologies on European colonies in the exercise of control over colonized peoples. This in turn also entails the element of direct brute force or conquest in the exercise of control over such populations.

The final anthropological conceptualization of language and inequality to be considered here, then, is the recent vision of the transformation of systems of language and inequality that have resulted from and continue to be influenced by

European colonization of non-European parts of the world, with particular attention to the emergence of a global order of nation-states that is a consequence of this broad process.

Two very general dimensions of this transformation can be identified. First, there has been a reorganization of linguistic codes, of their ecological distribution, and of the ideological or symbolic valuing of codes throughout the world. Many whole languages have been eradicated as the result of both the death and the re-education of populations, particularly in North and South America, Australia, New Zealand, and the Khoisan-speaking area of Southern Africa. These eradications most strikingly occurred in areas that were relatively thinly populated by hunters and gatherers, enabling deep penetration inland by colonizers. Compare the areas mentioned with areas that were relatively densely populated by agriculturalists as in East Asia, Southeast Asia, and South Asia, where the same scale of European penetration and eradication of peoples and languages did not take place.

The emergence of pidgin and creole languages with a distinct configuration of European vocabularies and indigenous language grammars has also been a consequence of European plantation economies in the circum-Caribbean area and the Pacific. These mixed languages are typically associated with the mass importation and concentration of populations from elsewhere for plantation labor. For example, in the Caribbean this took the form of slave labor from Africa. In Hawai'i indentured laborers from Japan and other parts of East Asia were brought in to work the sugar cane.

In areas where there has been massive eradication of languages, those languages have been replaced by European languages spoken by people of European descent, as in the domination of English in North America, Australia, and New Zealand, and the domination of Spanish and Portuguese in Central and South America.

In many areas where local languages were not eradicated, they were overlain by European languages introduced by colonizers, as in India, and many countries in the Middle East, sub-Saharan Africa, and the Pacific. In these contexts former European colonial administrative units eventually became independent nations, and the nature of the overlay is nation-specific. In such countries, a part of the population is bilingual in an indigenous language and a European language. Those who are bilingual are those most closely involved with nation-state-constituting and transnational economic and political processes, i.e. with centers rather than peripheries of nations. The symbolic economies of the language varieties in these former colonies has been transformed in such a way that the European languages have come to have a highly valued place in the economies.

This same pattern is sometimes reproduced with non-European languages too. In other words, in some nations, an indigenous language of the area that became a language of wider communication in colonial economic and political processes was chosen as a national language at the time that national independence was achieved, gaining prestige in the process. Here members of the educated elite speak the national language or are bilingual in a local language and the national language. Swahili became the national language of Tanzania in this way (Fabian 1986). In Indonesia, Malaysian, a language of wider communication under Dutch rule, became the national language now referred to as Indonesian. Errington (1998) has documented the ongoing penetration of Indonesian into new areas of the country and its replacement of other indigenous languages in a range of activities as a consequence of Indonesian state sponsorship of Indonesian. A creole language can also become the language of prestige and a national language, as Tok Pisin has in New Guinea (Kulick 1992).

In this expansion of national languages, it is possible to see the promulgation of European language ideologies that conceptualize local populations and their languages through European lenses (Irvine and Gal 2000; Errington 2001) and envision the ideal or most stable nation as one in which everyone speaks the same language (Blommaert and Verschueren 1998). As nationalist movements emerged in European colonial units, European colonizers often imposed conditions for the gaining of independence that included not only European-like political processes and governmental organization, but also plans for educational systems that would foster a national language in schools. Significantly, these European language ideologies have assumed the central importance of the written word (Besnier 1995) and the choice of a national language which is written, or for which a writing system is developed (Schieffelin and Doucet 1998). And today, pressure from European and North American economic centers for international communication in European languages continues the hegemony of European languages, particularly English.

Overall there is a strong historical trend toward larger numbers of people speaking smaller numbers of languages.

A second major consequence of colonialism in addition to that of code reorganization is that wholly and partly new "discourses" emerged in colonial contexts that are now characteristic of nation-states. Foucault (1972) has used the term "discourse" to talk about whole ideological regimes that permeate consciousness to the degree that they become the lived reality of the people who participate in the institutions that constitute and reproduce those discourses. Thus colonialism entailed the introduction and imposition of the key institutional and ideological complexes or discourses of European religion (e.g. Gordon 2002; Besnier 1995; Hanks 1987), education (Watson-Gegeo and Gegeo 1992; Schieffelin 2000), law (Philips 2000), and media (Spitulnik 1998). Drawing on a more linguistic anthropological sense of discourse, anthropologists have documented the emergence of wholly new *genres* of discourse in what Pratt (1992) refers to as the "contact zone." These have been produced by colonizers appropriating the cultural forms of knowledge of those they colonized, such as the production of authoritative interpretations of Sanskrit texts by British colonial administrators in India (Cohen 1985). More pervasively, local colonized people take on the genres associated with the new institutional complexes introduced by colonizers, such as legal procedures, school lessons, and hymns and sermons. The authority of indigenous genres has also been transformed and weakened under European influence (Kuipers 1998). The acquisition and sometimes imposition of literacy has been central to these processes, often resulting in the production of speech genres with characteristics of both European and local forms of language use, as has been documented for letter-writing (Hanks 1987; Besnier 1995; Ahearn 2001).

There are also examples of very dynamic situations in which colonizers have appropriated forms, only to find that appropriation being resisted by the colonized in ways that lead to the reinvigoration of the indigenous forms among the colonized. My best and most hopeful example of this is the appropriation of the hula as a song and dance form by the tourist industry in Hawai'i, and its reclamation by local

Hawai'ians. This reclamation has led to the burgeoning of hula dance schools and dance competitions like the annual week-long Merry Monarch Festival that is broadcast on television throughout the state.

There are, then, many and diverse syncretic or hybrid discourse genres from both the past and the present consequences of European colonialism throughout the world, and the overall picture of those consequences for codes and for discourse is complex. Europeans don't "own" all of those changes any more than Saudi Arabians, for example, still "own" the manifestations of Islam across Asia after its spread over the centuries since Mohammed's birth. Still, however much agency can be attributed to people and processes at local levels in non-European societies, the reorganization of codes and discourse genres into new systems of inequality in which European form and content have acquired great value in non-European systems of symbolic capital is inescapable.

A theoretical focus on the colonial transformation of systems of language and inequality sustains the orientation of political economic approaches to local manifestations of macrosocietal processes, but also brings some new issues into the foreground. The researchers in this tradition are more inclined than those in the political economic tradition to view present inequalities involving language as the result of social processes that have been going on for hundreds of years. In other words these researchers are more inclined to take a strongly historical perspective in explaining these inequalities. This work also foregrounds political and ideological, as well as economic, processes as causal, particularly the politics associated with constituting nation and state. As in the study of language use in bureaucratic contexts, it is common to analyze the effects of colonialism in specific institutional complexes such as religion, education, and law. Those complexes are often treated as if they are bounded, much as villages were treated by anthropologists as bounded at one time, even though we know this is an analytical strategy rather than the only reality. Work on the consequences of colonialism endeavors to treat effects on codes and effects on discourse or forms of talk together, rather than dealing primarily with discourse genres, as was true of the gender and language research, or dealing primarily with codes, as in the political economic tradition. Above all, we are acutely aware of the ideological transformation of local cultures that has come about as a consequence of the imposition of colonial orders of new systems of language and inequality.

6 CONCLUSION

At the heart of the study of language and social inequality is the *ideological* valuing of some *features of language* over others. The relative value of features of language is in turn related in part to the *social contexts*, particularly the *social identities*, with which the forms of talk are associated. Because forms of talk carry meaning, information, or ideas, when some forms of talk are valued over others, this also entails the valuing of some *ideologies* or ways of thinking over others. Ideas about the *causes* of the emergence and maintenance of systems of social inequality also figure prominently in theories of language and social inequality.

In this chapter I have discussed four major areas of coherent research that develop ideas about language and social inequality in linguistic anthropology: inequalities created in bureaucratic contexts through the regulation of turns at talk between bureaucrats and the people they serve; inequalities between women and men created through men's greater involvement in public genres of discourse; inequalities created through the greater economic valuing of some kinds of economic activity, people who carry out the activity, and the codes used by those people to communicate; and finally inequalities created through European colonization of other parts of the world through which European codes and institutional complexes of discourse were imposed on and came to be valued more than those of the indigenous populations colonized.

These theories are similar in that each focuses on a particular social basis for inequality. Each identifies some aspect of language that is implicated in the social inequality. Each theory has some kind of concept of the causes of the particular socially based kind of inequality that is at issue. And each theory develops some account of the way that ideas associated with the aspects of language at issue are affected by inequality. *In all of these theories, the forms of language and the ideas associated with the dominant or more highly valued social category flourish, while the forms of language and ideas associated with the subordinate or less highly valued social category are constricted and disattended.*

At the same time, these theories differ in the aspects of social life that are seen as critical bases of social inequality: bureaucratic role, gender identity, economic position, and colonial role. They also vary in the aspects of language that are seen as central to the creation of inequality: turns at talk, genres of discourse, and linguistic codes are all affected by social inequality. These theories also differ in the extent to which they give attention to causes of inequality and in the kinds of causes that are treated as central. In addition, we have also seen different ways in which the ideas of the subordinate or less valued people are suppressed through the suppression of their forms of talk (figure 21.1 highlights these similarities and differences).

Yet these theories are not so very different. Basically turns at talk, genres of speech, and codes of people who are relatively little appreciated are shut down and not allowed expression. And when the language forms of the subordinate or lesser valued people *are* allowed expression, they are ignored, go unratified, and are not incorporated into the ongoing process of the creation of social realities that is characteristic of human communication.

It may be that it is human to constantly seek to differentiate among ourselves and our symbolic behaviors in ways that hierarchize or create social inequalities. If so, it is certainly equally human to resist those same processes. The analysis of the ways language plays a role in the maintenance of social inequalities offered in this chapter can be viewed as a form of ideological critique of social inequality and can contribute to the resistance to and amelioration of such inequalities.

NOTES

1   For a critique of Boas, see Briggs (2002).
2   A new and distinctive approach to authoritative speech has emerged in linguistic anthropology since the 1990s. It involves analysis of language ideologies implicit in written texts produced in the historical past by linguists and language philosophers. This approach

	Social identities	Social contexts	Language features	Dominant ideologies	Causes
Language in bureaucratic settings	Bureaucrat and client Ethnic minorities	Classrooms Courtrooms Clinics	Turn economies Question–Answer Ratification	Professional/bureaucratic expertise	Institutional
Gender and language	Men and women	Public and private domains	Speech genres Speech styles	Intrinsic inferiority of women	Ideological
Language and political economy	Ethnic groups	Industrial and agricultural	Whole languages	Prestige of standard language	Economic
Language and colonialism	Colonizer and colonized	(Imagined) colonial encounters, e.g. plantations, mines Texts	Linguistic codes "Discourses" Genres Modes (written and spoken)	Intrinsic inferiority of colonized	Economic Political Ideological

Figure 21.1 Comparative framework for language and social inequality

entails ideological critique of the authoritative contributions of language-focused scholars to culturally European ideological "projects" of colonialism (Irvine 1995; Errington 2001), nation-state formation and maintenance (Silverstein 1995, 2000; Gal 1995), and modernity (Briggs and Bauman 1999; Bauman and Briggs 2000; Briggs 2002). Bauman and Briggs specifically argue that linguists and philosophers from the seventeenth century through the twentieth century have played an important role in the ideological constitution of new forms of social inequality through their language-focused representations of modernity. This new general approach to language and authority builds on the traditions I have identified, but contrasts with them in several key ways, most notably for our present purposes in its focus on written texts of what is framed as the historical past, rather than the spoken language use of what is framed as the present. This chapter is primarily concerned with the latter rather than the former, but it is important to note the connections of this new approach to traditions documented in this chapter.

REFERENCES

Abu-Lughod, L. (1986). *Veiled Sentiments*. Berkeley: University of California Press.

Ahearn, L. M. (2001). *Invitations to Love: Literacy, Love Letters, and Social Change in Nepal*. Ann Arbor: University of Michigan Press.

Ainsworth-Vaughn, N. (1998). *Claiming Power in Doctor–Patient Talk*. New York: Oxford University Press.

Bakhtin, M. (1981). *The Dialogic Imagination*. Austin: University of Texas Press.

Bauman, R., and Briggs, C. L. (1990). Poetics and Performance as Critical Perspectives on Language and Social Life. *Annual Review of Anthropology* 19: 59–88.

Bauman, R., and Briggs, C. L. (2000). Language Philosophy as Language Ideology: John Locke and Johann Gottfried Herder. In P. V. Kroskrity (ed.), *Regimes of Language: Ideologies, Polities, and Identities* (pp. 139–204). Santa Fe, NM: School of American Research Press.

Besnier, N. (1995). *Literacy, Emotion, and Authority: Reading and Writing on a Polynesian Atoll*. Cambridge: Cambridge University Press.

Besnier, N. (1997). Sluts and Superwomen: The Politics of Gender Liminality in Urban Tonga. *Ethnos* 62: 5–31.

Bloch, M. (1975). Introduction. In M. Bloch (ed.), *Political Language and Oratory in Traditional Society* (pp. 1–28). London: Academic Press.

Blommaert, J., and Verschueren, J. (1998). The Role of Language in European Nationalist Ideologies. In B. B. Schieffelin, K. A. Woolard, and P. V. Kroskrity (eds.), *Language Ideologies: Practice and Theory* (pp. 189–210). New York: Oxford University Press.

Boas, F. (1911). Introduction. In F. Boas (ed.), *Handbook of American Indian Languages*, Part 1. Bureau of American Ethnology, Bulletin 40. Washington, DC: Smithsonian Institution and Bureau of American Ethnology.

Bourdieu, P. (1977). The Economics of Linguistic Exchanges. *Social Science Information* 16(6): 645–668.

Briggs, C. (1992). "Since I am a Woman, I will Chastise My Relatives": Gender, Reported Speech, and the (Re)production of Social Relations in Warao Ritual Wailing. *American Ethnologist* 19: 337–361.

Briggs, C. L. (2002). Linguistic Magic Bullets in the Making of a Modernist Anthropology. *American Anthropologist* 104: 481–498.

Briggs, C. L., and Bauman, R. (1999). The Foundation of all Future Researches: Franz Boas, George Hunt and the Textual Construction of Modernity. *American Quarterly* 51: 479–528.

Brown, P., and Levinson, S. C. (1987). *Politeness: Some Universals in Language Usage.* Cambridge: Cambridge University Press.

Cohen, B. (1985). The Command of Language and the Language of Command. In R. Guha (ed.), *Subaltern Studies IV: Writings on South Asian History and Society* (pp. 276–329). Delhi: Oxford University Press.

Danet, B., Hoffman, K., Kermish, N., Rafn, H. J., and Stayman, D. (1976). An Ethnography of Questioning in the Courtroom. In R. R. Shuy and A. Shnukal (eds.), *Language Use and the Uses of Language*, NWAVE 5 (pp. 222–234). Washington, DC: Georgetown University Press.

Dorian, N. C. (1981). *Language Death: The Life Cycle of a Scottish Gaelic Dialect.* Philadelphia: University of Pennsylvania Press.

Duranti, A. (1994). *From Grammar to Politics: Linguistic Anthropology in a Western Samoan Village.* Berkeley and Los Angeles: University of California Press.

Eckert, P. (2000). *Linguistic Variation as Social Practice.* Cambridge, MA: Blackwell.

Erickson, F., and Shultz, J. (1982). *The Counselor as Gatekeeper: Social Interaction in Interviews.* New York: Academic Press.

Errington, J. J. (1998). *Shifting Languages: Interaction and Identity in Javanese Indonesia.* Cambridge: Cambridge University Press.

Errington, J. J. (2001). Colonial Linguistics. *Annual Review of Anthropology* 30: 19–39. Palo Alto: Annual Reviews.

Fabian, J. (1986). *Language and Colonial Power.* Berkeley: University of California Press.

Fellin, L. (2001). Language Ideologies, Language Socialization and Language Revival in an Italian Alpine Community. PhD dissertation, University of Arizona.

Fisher, S. (1986). *In the Patient's Best Interest: Women and the Politics of Medical Decisions.* New Brunswick: Rutgers University Press.

Fishman, P. M. (1983). Interaction: The Work Women Do. In B. Thorne, C. Kramarae, and N. Henley (eds.), *Language, Gender and Society* (pp. 89–101). Rowley, MA: Newbury House.

Foucault, M. (1972). The Discourse on Language. In *The Archaeology of Knowledge* (pp. 215–237). New York: Pantheon.

Gal, S. (1979). *Language Shift: Social Determinants of Linguistic Change in Bilingual Austria.* New York: Academic Press.

Gal, S. (1991). Between Speech and Silence: The Problematics of Research on Language and Gender. In M. DiLeonardo (ed.), *Gender at the Crossroads of Knowledge: Toward a New Anthropology of Gender* (pp. 175–203). Berkeley: University of California Press.

Gal, S. (1995). Lost in a Slavic Sea: Linguistic Theories and Expert Knowledge in 19th Century Hungary. *Pragmatics* 5: 155–166.

Gal, S., and Woolard, K. A. (1995). Constructing Languages and Publics: Authority and Representation. *Pragmatics* 5: 129–138.

Goffman, E. (1956). On the Nature of Deference and Demeanor. *American Anthropologist* 58: 473–502.

Gordon, T. (2002). *Mormons and Modernity in Tonga: The Politics of Religion, Identity and Tradition.* Durham, NC: Duke University Press.

Gumperz, J. J. (1958). Dialect Differences and Social Stratification in a North Indian Village. *American Anthropologist* 60: 668–682.

Hall, K., and Bucholtz, M. (eds.) (1995). *Gender Articulated: Language and the Socially Constructed Self.* New York: Routledge.

Hanks, W. F. (1987). Discourse Genres in a Theory of Practice. *American Ethnologist* 14(4): 668–692.

Hanson, M. (1993). Foreword. In O. Negt and A. Kluge (eds.), *Public Sphere and Experience* (pp. ix–xlix). Minneapolis: University of Minnesota Press.

Hill, J. H. (1998). "Today There Is no Respect": Nostalgia, "Respect," and Oppositional Discourse in Mexicano (Nahuatl) Language Ideology. In B. B. Schieffelin, K. A. Woolard, and P. V. Kroskrity (eds.), *Language Ideologies: Practice and Theory* (pp. 68–86). New York: Oxford University Press.

Hill, J., and Hill, K. C. (1986). *Speaking Mexicano: Dynamics of a Syncretic Language in Central Mexico.* Tucson: University of Arizona Press.

Hill, J. H., and Irvine, J. T. (eds.) (1993). *Responsibility and Evidence in Oral Discourse.* Cambridge: Cambridge University Press.

Hymes, D. (1973). Speech and Language: On the Origins and Foundations of Inequality among Speakers. *Daedalus* 102: 59–80.

Irvine, J. (1995). The Family Romance of Colonial Linguistics: Gender and Family in Nineteenth-century Representations of African Languages. *Pragmatics* 5: 139–154.

Irvine, J. T., and Gal, S. (2000). Regimenting Languages: Language Ideological Perspectives. In P. V. Kroskrity (ed.), *Regimes of Language* (pp. 1–34). Santa Fe, NM: School of American Research Press.

Jaffe, A. (1999). *Ideologies in Action: Language Politics on Corsica.* Berlin: Mouton de Gruyter.

James, D., and Clarke, S. (1993). Women, Men and Interruptions: A Critical Review. In D. Tannen (ed.), *Gender and Conversational Interaction* (pp. 231–280). New York: Oxford University Press.

Keenan, E. O. (1974). Norm-Makers, Norm-Breakers: Uses of Speech by Men and Women in a Malagasy Community. In R. Bauman and J. Sherzer (eds.), *Explorations in the Ethnography of Speaking* (pp. 125–143). Cambridge: Cambridge University Press.

Kuipers, J. C. (1998). *Language, Identity, and Marginality in Indonesia: The Changing Nature of Ritual Speech on the Island of Sumba.* Cambridge: Cambridge University Press.

Kulick, D. (1992). *Language Shift and Cultural Reproduction: Socialization, Self, and Syncretism in a Papua New Guinean Village.* Cambridge: Cambridge University Press.

Kulick, D. (1998). *Travesti: Sex, Gender, and Culture among Brazilian Transgendered Prostitutes.* Chicago: University of Chicago Press.

Labov, W. (1963). The Social Motivation of a Sound Change. *Word* 19: 273–309.

Labov, W. (1972). *Language in the Inner City: Studies in the Black English Vernacular.* Philadelphia: University of Pennsylvania Press.

Lakoff, R. (1975). *Language and Women's Place.* New York: Holt, Rinehart and Winston.

Martin, E. (1987). *The Woman in the Body: A Cultural Analysis of Reproduction.* Boston: Beacon Press.

Mehan, H. (1979). *Learning Lessons: Social Organization in the Classroom.* Cambridge, MA and London: Harvard University Press.

Parmentier, R. (1993). The Political Function of Reported Speech: A Belauan Example. In J. Lucy (ed.), *Reflexive Language: Reported Speech and Metapragmatics* (pp. 261–286). New York: Cambridge University Press.

Philips, S. U. (1983). *The Invisible Culture: Communication in Classroom and Community on the Warm Springs Indian Reservation.* New York: Longman.

Philips, S. U. (1987). The Social Organization of Questions and Answers in Courtroom Discourse. In L. Kedar (ed.), *Power through Discourse* (pp. 83–112). Norwood, NJ: Ablex.

Philips, S. U. (1998). *Ideology in the Language of Judges: How Judges Practice Law, Politics and Courtroom Control.* New York: Oxford University Press.

Philips, S. U. (2000). Constructing a Tongan Nation State through Language Ideology in the Courtroom. In P. V. Kroskrity (ed.), *Regimes of Language* (pp. 229–257). Santa Fe, NM: School of American Research Press.

Philips, S. U. (2003). The Power of Gender Ideologies in Discourse. In J. Holmes and M. Meyerhoff (eds.), *The Handbook of Language and Gender.* Oxford: Blackwell.

Philips, S. U., Steele, S., and Tanz, C. (eds.) (1987). *Language, Gender and Sex in Comparative Perspective*. Cambridge: Cambridge University Press.

Pratt, M. L. (1992). *Imperial Eyes: Travel Writing and Transculturation*. London: Routledge.

Sacks, H. (1967). On Proving Hearership. Lecture 3, Spring Quarter, April 10, 1967; Lecture 4, Spring Quarter, April 12, 1967. Unpublished mimeograph copy.

Schegloff, E. A. (1972). Sequencing in Conversational Openings. In J. J. Gumperz and D. Hymes (eds.), *Directions in Sociolinguistics: The Ethnography of Communication* (pp. 346–380). New York: Holt, Rinehart and Winston.

Schieffelin, B. B. (2000). Introducing Kaluli Literacy: A Chronology of Influences. In P. V. Kroskrity (ed.), *Regimes of Language* (pp. 293–327). Santa Fe, NM: School of American Research Press.

Schieffelin, B. B., and Doucet, R. C. (1998). The "real" Haitian Creole: Ideology, Metalinguistics, and Orthographic Choice. In B. B. Schieffelin, K. A. Woolard, and P. V. Kroskrity (eds.), *Language Ideologies: Practice and Theory* (pp. 285–316). New York: Oxford University Press.

Sherzer, J. (1987). A Diversity of Voices: Men's and Women's Speech in Ethnographic Perspective. In S. U. Philips, S. Steele, and C. Tanz (eds.), *Language, Gender, and Sex in Comparative Perspective* (pp. 95–120). Cambridge: Cambridge University Press.

Silverstein, M. (1995). From the Meaning of Meaning to the Empires of the Mind: Ogden's Orthological English. *Pragmatics* 5: 185–196.

Silverstein, M. (2000). Whorfianism and the Linguistic Imagination of Nationality. In P. V. Kroskrity (ed.), *Regimes of language* (pp. 85–138). Santa Fe, NM: School of American Research Press.

Spitulnik, D. (1998). Mediating Unity and Diversity: The Production of Language Ideologies in Zambian Broadcasting. In B. B. Schieffelin, K. A. Woolard, and P. V. Kroskrity (eds.), *Language Ideologies: Practice and Theory* (pp. 163–188). New York: Oxford University Press.

Watson-Gegeo, K. A., and Gegeo, D. W. (1992). Schooling, Knowledge and Power: Social Transformation in the Solomon Islands. *Anthropology and Education Quarterly* 23: 10–229.

West, C. (1984). Questions and Answers between Doctors and Patients. In C. West, *Routine Complications: Troubles with Talk between Doctors and Patients* (pp. 71–96). Bloomington: Indiana University Press.

Woolard, K. A. (1985). Language Variation and Cultural Hegemony: Toward an Integration of Sociolinguistic and Social Theory. *American Ethnologist* 12: 738–748.

Woolard, K. A. (1989). *Double Talk: Bilingualism and the Politics of Ethnicity in Catalonia*. Stanford, CA: Stanford University Press.

Zimmerman, D. H., and West, C. (1975). Sex Roles, Interruptions and Silences in Conversation. In B. Thorne and N. Henley (eds.), *Language and Sex: Difference and Dominance* (pp. 105–129). Rowley, MA: Newbury House.

CHAPTER 22 Language Ideologies

Paul V. Kroskrity

1 INTRODUCTION

Though the relationship of language and thought has received much academic and popular attention, "thoughts about language" by their speakers have, by comparison, been neglected, dismissed, denigrated, or proscribed as objects of study and concern until relatively recently. Language ideology, as succinctly defined by Errington (2001a: 110), "refers to the situated, partial, and interested character of conceptions and uses of language." These conceptions, whether explicitly articulated or embodied in communicative practice, represent incomplete, or "partially successful," attempts to rationalize language usage; such rationalizations are typically multiple, context-bound, and necessarily constructed from the sociocultural experience of the speaker.

At the outset it is important to note that although interdisciplinary scholarship on language ideologies has been extremely productive in recent decades (Woolard 1998), there is no particular unity in this immense body of research, no single core literature, and a range of definitions. One of the most straightforward, though controversial, definitions is that of Alan Rumsey (1990: 346): "shared bodies of commonsense notions about the nature of language in the world." This definition properly highlights the informal nature of cultural models of language but – and here is the controversy – does not problematize language ideological variation (by age, gender, class, etc.) and therefore promotes an overly homogeneous view of language ideologies within a cultural group. Why is this unsatisfactory? Since social and linguistic variation provide some of the dynamic forces which influence change, it is more useful to have an analytical device which captures diversity rather than emphasizing a static, uniformly shared culture. Used in opposition to culture, language ideologies provide an alternative for exploring variation in ideas, ideals, and communicative practices.

A graphic example of the importance of multiplicity and contention in language-ideological processes, one that has noticeably changed the grammar of English within my generation's lifetime, resulted from the feminist challenge to the once standard "generic he" (Silverstein 1985). Once upon a time, a sentence like (1) below would have been regarded as needlessly redundant and viewed as the dispreferred version of (2):

(1) If a student wishes to be considered for financial assistance, he or she must complete an application.
(2) If a student wishes to be considered for financial assistance, he must complete an application.

But American feminist objections to generic "he," as in (2) above, sought to define it as untrue by virtue of referential exclusion and therefore emblematic of being unfair, viewing a previously accepted grammatical convention of the standard register as not just a neutrally arbitrary grammatical convention but as a discriminatory, gendered practice (Silverstein 1985). Relevant interest groups, in this case feminists, con-structed a stance against a rule of grammar that speakers of Standard English had been following for hundreds of years.

Other sensitizing definitions of linguistic/language ideologies have often shown a tension between emphasizing speakers' "awareness," as a form of agency, and fore-grounding their "embeddedness" in the social and cultural systems in which they are enveloped. In addition these definitions also illustrate the mediating role of linguistic anthropology as an interdisciplinary field concerned with relevances of both linguis-tics and sociocultural anthropology, including notions about the structure and rela-tionships of both linguistic and social systems. Michael Silverstein (1979: 193), for example, defined linguistic ideologies as "sets of beliefs about language articulated by users as a rationalization or justification of perceived language structure and use." This definition emphasizes the role of linguistic awareness as a condition which permits speakers to rationalize and otherwise influence a language's structure. Ex-hibiting a more sociocultural emphasis is Judith Irvine's (1989: 255) definition of language ideologies as "the cultural system of ideas about social and linguistic relationships, together with their loading of moral and political interests." Here language ideologies are viewed as multiple and constructed from specific political economic perspectives which, in turn, influence "the cultural ideas about language." Certainly language ideologies are not merely those ideas which stem from the "offi-cial culture" of the ruling class but rather a more ubiquitous set of diverse beliefs, however implicit or explicit they may be, used by speakers of all types as models for constructing linguistic evaluations and engaging in communicative activity. They are beliefs about the superiority/inferiority of specific languages, such as the sentiments expressed, during the so-called "Ebonics Debate," by many African and non-African Americans, that African American Vernacular English is not a legitimate language and therefore an inappropriate medium for any educational discourse, or the sentiments behind so-called "English-only" legislation that English is somehow a "threatened" language. They are beliefs about the linguistic adequacy of ASL (American Sign Language) and other sign languages for Deaf communities (LeMaster and Monaghan, this volume) or the transparency of gestural communication (Haviland, this volume). They are beliefs about how languages are acquired, such as the Samoan and Kaluli belief that very young children are not appropriate targets for verbal interaction by adults (Ochs and Schieffelin 1984) or the Gapun idea that children should learn their ancestral language, Taiap, even if it is not regularly spoken in their homes (Kulick 1992: 248). They are beliefs about language contact (Garrett, this volume) and multilingualism including, for example, deliberate attempts by the Arizona Tewa, a Pueblo Indian community, to avoid loanwords from other languages, or celebrations of bilingualism through conversational codeswitching by Puerto Rican New Yorkers, and expressions of dismay by some Nahuatl speakers of Northern Mexico that they speak neither Mexicano nor Spanish "correctly" – in their "proper" purist forms. In sum, language ideologies are beliefs, or feelings, about languages as used in their social worlds.[1]

This chapter briefly explores this relatively recent trend in linguistic anthropological work – the analysis of language and discourse as a political economic resource used by individual speakers, ethnic and other interest groups, and nation-states. It provides an overview of its conceptual development and identifies and illustrates some of its main themes. I understand this characterization of "language ideologies," which I use as a default plural concept (for reasons which will be explicated later), to circumscribe a body of research which simultaneously problematizes speakers' consciousness of their language and discourse as well as their positionality (in political economic systems) in shaping beliefs, proclamations, and evaluations of linguistic forms and discursive practices (Kroskrity 2000b). In so doing, I restrict the scope of this chapter to a body of research centered largely within linguistic anthropology, focusing on research which has emerged within linguistic anthropology beginning with the publication of Michael Silverstein's (1979) "Language Structure and Linguistic Ideology."[2]

2 THE CONCEPTUAL DEVELOPMENT OF LANGUAGE IDEOLOGIES

Silverstein's pioneering article, first presented in a Parasession on Linguistic Units and Levels at the Chicago Linguistic Society, argued for the recognition of a more central, mediating role for linguistic ideology as an influential part, or "level," of language. He argued that speakers' awareness of language and their rationalizations of its structure and use were often critical factors in shaping the evolution of a language's structure. In a later formulation of this position, he summarized: "The total linguistic fact, the datum for a science of language, is irreducibly dialectic in nature. It is an unstable mutual interaction of meaningful sign forms, contextualized to situations of interested human use and mediated by the fact of cultural ideology" (Silverstein 1985: 220). Demonstrating the role of ideology in shaping and influencing such linguistic structures as gendered pronouns and pronominal alternation and change in English as well as Javanese speech levels (Errington 1988), he clearly revealed the role of such "partially successful" folk analyses in contributing to significant analogic change (Silverstein 1979, 1985). This change alters, regularizes, and rationalizes such linguistic changes as the rejection of generic "he" (in the second half of the twentieth century) and the shift to "you," thus eliminating "thou" from non-Quaker English speech (since the beginning of the eighteenth century).

It should be emphasized that this recognition of a more central role for linguistic ideology represented a dramatic reversal of scholarly assumptions within both anthropology and linguistics. Within anthropology, the foundational figure of Franz Boas was more concerned with the description and analysis of languages as categorization systems and with historical linguistics rather than with the understanding of culturally contexted speech. In his view, the linguistic consciousness of natives produced nothing of analytic value but only "the misleading and disturbing factors of second-ary explanations" (Boas 1911: 69). He clearly favored a "direct method" which privileged the linguist's expertise and bypassed what could be termed the "linguistic false consciousness" of culturally deluded natives who could not adequately interpret the linguistic facts. Thus though Boas is properly credited with viewing language as an indispensable part of the totalizing analysis of anthropology, his preoccupation with linguistic structure as the locus of the cultural mind of natives led him to dismiss any local notions about language as unworthy of attention.

In linguistics of the early and mid-twentieth century, a similar marginalization or proscription of linguistic ideology also dominated the field. Modern linguistics, since Saussure, has tended to exhibit what Vološinov (1973) has described as its "abstract objectivist" emphasis – "they are interested only in the inner logic of the system of signs itself, taken . . . independently of the meaning that gives signs their content." For him, such an emphasis ignores the position that meaningful signs are inherently ideological. Since American structuralist linguistics under scholars like Leonard Bloomfield (1933) largely ignored meaning, this neglect of ideology was paradigmat-ically propagated. Though Bloomfield occasionally addressed such "secondary re-sponses" of speakers in a variety of publications (e.g. 1987 [1927], 1933: 22, 1944), in each case he ultimately concluded that speakers' linguistic ideologies – even those cast as prescriptive norms – had a negligible effect on their actual speech.

As Bloomfield's taxonomic structuralism was replaced by Chomsky's (1957, 1965) transformational-generative version and its various successors in the second half of the twentieth century, the pattern of dismissing speakers' linguistic ideologies was main-tained. Even though Chomsky appealed to the "linguistic intuitions" of native speakers in asserting the greater "descriptive adequacy" of language models with "deep structures," these intuitions were highly circumscribed in a manner befitting a model which consistently "bracketed" (i.e. heuristically ignored) the social world through such tropes as "the ideal speaker-hearer," "the perfectly homogenous speech community," and "the single-style speaker." This model limited speakers' "linguistic intuitions" to purely grammatical judgments such as speakers' awareness that a "structurally homonymous" sentence like "Visiting anthropologists can be amusing" had two possible readings, or that English passive constructions and their "active voice" counterparts were "logically equivalent" in meaning.[3] Clearly such intuitive glimpses of structural knowledge were, for Chomsky and his followers, not rationalizations but rather revelations of structure. Speakers, through their linguistic ideologies, were neither part of language nor capable of being agents of linguistic change. Rather than being viewed as partially aware or as potentially agentive, speakers – in Chomskyan models – were merely hosts for language.

Given this marginalization and dismissal in both anthropological and linguistic treatments of linguistic ideologies, Silverstein's (1979) article represents a dramatic reversal of traditional linguistic theorizing, one which rescued linguistic awareness from ongoing scholarly neglect. But a single emphasis on native consciousness of linguistic structures would not suffice in explaining the genesis of the linguistic anthropological approach to language ideologies. Another neglected topic which was inadequately explored was the non-referential functions of language. Most models, including Chomsky's linguistic models and those of ethnoscience within anthropology, reduced linguistic meaning to denotation, or "reference," and predication.[4] This kind of meaning emphasizes the work of language in providing "words for things." But semiotic models of communication based on the theories of C. S. Peirce (1931–58) recognized a broad variety of sign-focused "pragmatic" relations between language users, the signs themselves, and the connections between these signs and the world. One of the key theoretical advantages, for researchers, of these semiotic-functional models is their recognition that many "meanings" that linguistic forms have for their speakers emerge from "indexical" connections between the linguistic signs and the contextual factors of their use.[5] This theoretical orientation, especially as formulated by Jakobson (1957, 1960) and later translated into a functional idiom by Hymes (1964), created the foundation for "an ethnography of communication" – for the long overdue examination of language use in regard to settings, topics, institutions, and other aspects of speakers and their relevant sociocultural worlds.

This inclusion of speakers along with their languages began a period in linguistic anthropology of greater integration with the concerns of sociocultural anthropology and general social theory. The pioneering figures of ethnography of communication and interactional sociolinguistics created important precedents for developing interests in language ideologies. Dell Hymes (1974: 33), for example, called for the inclusion of a speech community's local theories of speech, and John Gumperz (e.g. Blom and Gumperz 1972: 431) often considered local theories of dialect differences and discourse practices and how linguistic forms derived their "social meaning" through interactional use.

This movement continued in the late 1970s and into the 1980s as linguistic anthropologists were becoming increasingly influenced by the same concerns that were sweeping sociocultural anthropology. These include an emphasis on practice theory and the agency of social actors as well as a syncretic attempt to wed Marxist materialism with a Weberian idealism (Ortner 1984: 147) in an attempt to achieve analytical balance in the representation of human agency within the structure of social systems (Giddens 1979). As Marxist and other political economic perspectives became staples for the then contemporary sociocultural theory, they also inspired some of the earliest work in the linguistic anthropological tradition of language ideologies to integrate these concerns with the legitimated interests in speakers' awareness of the linguistic system. These works include Susan Gal's (1979) *Language Shift* and "Language and Political Economy"(1989); Jane H. Hill's (1985) "The Grammar of Consciousness and the Consciousness of Grammar" and Jane H. and Kenneth C. Hill's *Speaking Mexicano: Dynamics of a Syncretic Language in Central Mexico* (Hill and Hill 1986); Judith Irvine's (1989) "When Talk Isn't Cheap: Language and Political Economy," and Kathryn A. Woolard's (1985) "Language Variation and Cultural Hegemony: Toward an Integration of Sociolinguistic and Social Theory." These works adumbrated many key concerns which have since flourished through the remainder of the twentieth century and into the twenty-first, producing a number of anthologies devoted to language ideological work (e.g. Schieffelin, Woolard, and Kroskrity 1998; Blommaert 1999a; Kroskrity 2000a; Gal and Woolard 2001).

3   LANGUAGE IDEOLOGIES: FIVE LEVELS OF ORGANIZATION

To further explore the significance and utility of this notion, which has moved from a marginalized topic to an issue of central concern, it is useful to regard language ideologies as a cluster concept, consisting of a number of converging dimensions. Here, I will consider five of these partially overlapping but analytically distinguishable layers of significance, in an attempt to identify and exemplify language ideologies – both as beliefs about language and as a concept designed to assist in the study of those beliefs. The five levels are (1) group or individual interests, (2) multiplicity of ideologies, (3) awareness of speakers, (4) mediating functions of ideologies, and (5) role of language ideology in identity construction.

One, *language ideologies represent the perception of language and discourse that is constructed in the interest of a specific social or cultural group.* A member's notions of what is "true," "morally good," or "aesthetically pleasing" about language and discourse are grounded in social experience and often demonstrably tied to polit-ical-economic interests. These notions often underlie attempts to use language as the site at which to promote, protect, and legitimate those interests. Nationalist programs of language standardization, for example, may appeal to a modern metric of commu-nicative efficiency, but such language development efforts are pervasively underlain by political-economic considerations since the imposition of a state-supported hege-monic standard will always benefit some social groups over others (see Woolard 1985, 1989; Errington 1998, 2000). What this proposition refutes is the myth of the sociopolitically disinterested language user or the possibility of unpositioned knowledge, even of one's own language. Thus when judges of Pima County Superior Court in Tucson represent themselves as "implementers of the law, uninfluenced by their own political and social backgrounds" (Philips 1998: 14), their denial of any connection between their political ideologies and their ideologies of courtroom procedure and control is, as Susan Philips (1998) has carefully revealed, better understood as a professional language ideology rather than as an accurate depiction of the intricate connections between their beliefs and actual courtroom practices.

Though interests are rendered more visible when they are embodied by overtly contending groups – as in the struggle for airtime on Zambian radio (Spitulnik 1998), the disputes of Warao shamans (Briggs 1998), the public "duels" of Tuscan "contrasto" singers (Pagliai 2000), the political debates in Corsica about the insti-tutional status or cultural role of the Corsican language (Jaffe 1999), or – as discussed above – the confrontations of feminists with the traditional grammarian defenders of the generic "he" (Silverstein 1985), one can also extend this emphasis on grounded social experience to seemingly homogeneous cultural groups by recognizing that cultural conceptions "are partial, contestable, and interest-laden" (Woolard and Schieffelin 1994: 58). Even shared cultural language practices, such as Arizona Tewa kiva speech (Kroskrity 1998), can represent the constructions of particular elites who obtain the required complicity (Bourdieu 1991: 113) of other social groups and classes. Viewed in this manner, the distinction between *neutral ideological analysis* (focusing on "culturally shared" beliefs and practices) and *critical ideological analysis* that emphasizes the political use of language as a particular group's instrument of symbolic domination may seem more gradient than dichotomous.[6]

But even though so-called neutral ideologies contribute to our understanding of members' models of language and discourse, an emphasis on the dimension of interest, taken in the political-economic sense, can stimulate a more penetrating sociocultural analysis by rethinking supposedly irreducible cultural explanations. In studies of the indigenous languages of the Pueblo Southwest, for example, a scholarly tradition of explaining such practices as indigenous purism by attributing "linguistic conservatism" as an essential feature of Pueblo culture had obscured the relevant association between such purism and the discourse of kiva speech that is controlled or regimented by a ceremonial elite (Kroskrity 1998).

A language-ideological emphasis on the worldly interests of scholars and philosophers of language permits the reader to recognize such interests in domains that are both purportedly non-ideological and culturally proximate to those of the analysts (as in the case of judges mentioned above). Judith T. Irvine and Susan Gal (2000) examined European linguistic confrontations with multilingual Senegalese and Macedonian speech communities. They revealed the ideological bias of this linguistic scholarship and its effects on such practices as linguistic mapping, historical linguistic interpretation, and imputation of nationality. Their several case studies revealed different kinds of interests, ranging from a relatively unconscious colonial importation of European models of language (and of identity) to a more strategic representation of the subject non-Europeans as inferior Others, to outright politically motivated linguistic gerrymandering used as justification for redrawing national boundaries. Clearly this, and other forms of colonial linguistics (Errington 2001b), demonstrate the profound ways in which language ideologies can shape presumably "objective" linguistic analysis.

Rosina Lippi-Green's (1997) *English With an Accent: Language, Ideology, and Discrimination* explicitly emphasizes language ideologies in her examination of contemporary educational and other institutionalized policies and practices, by demonstrating the class-based interests behind what she calls, following Milroy and Milroy (1999), the *standard language ideology*. She defines it as "a bias toward an abstracted, idealized, homogenous spoken language which is imposed and maintained by dominant bloc institutions and which names as its model the written language, but which is drawn primarily from the speech of the upper, middle class" (Lippi-Green 1997: 64). This language ideology promotes "the language subordination process" which amounts to a program of linguistic mystification undertaken by dominant institutions designed to simultaneously valorize the standard language and other aspects of "mainstream culture" while devaluing the non-standard and its associated cultural forms. She demonstrates that most of the differences between the standard and non-standard dialects of English are, from a comparative linguistic perspective, trivial and invalid evidence of structural inferiority or deficiency. But most speakers of English are not informed by such comparative perspectives; rather they are preoccupied by the standard-based prescriptivism which hierarchically ranks both speakers and linguistic forms, using Standard English as a metric. So-called "double negatives" (as in "He does not have no money," for example) may seem repulsive embodiments of ignorance to those of us trained to the norms of the standard, and yet its supposed deficiency is not traceable to any logical flaw which obscures its "meaning" but rather comes from its association with a class of speakers who use it. For Lippi-Green, then, the proclaimed superiority of Standard English rests not on its structural properties or its communicative efficiency but rather on its association with the political-economic influence of affluent social classes who benefit from a social stratification which consolidates and continues their privileged position.

Michael Silverstein (1996), in his "Monoglot 'Standard' in America," has also provided a close, language-ideological analysis of both the authorizing and deauthorizing moves associated with Standard English. Through "referential displacement," champions of the standard celebrate its clarity and precision and invoke its supposedly superior ability to achieve "truthful" reference – which becomes a paramount measure of language. Languages other than the standard (such as Ebonics) are claimed to "lack vocabulary," or "fail to make [or hear] certain sounds" (Collins 1999). Rather than being understood as linguistic differences, such perceived inadequacies are instead naturalized and hierarchized in a manner which replicates the social hierarchy. Finally the standard language, which is presented as universally available, is commodified and presented as the only resource which permits full participation in the capitalist economy and an improvement of one's place in its political economic system.

Two, *language ideologies are profitably conceived as multiple* because of the plurality of meaningful social divisions (class, gender, clan, elites, generations, and so on) within sociocultural groups that have the potential to produce divergent perspectives expressed as indices of group membership. Language ideologies are thus grounded in social experience which is never uniformly distributed throughout polities of any scale. Thus, in Jane H. Hill's (1998) study of Mexicano linguistic ideologies, when older Mexicano speakers in the Malinche Volcano area of Central Mexico say the Mexicano equivalent of "Today there is no respect," this nostalgic view is more likely to be voiced by men. Although both genders recognize the increased "respect" once signaled by a tradition of using Nahuatl honorific registers and other polite forms, "successful" men are more likely to express this sense of linguistic deprivation of earned deference. Mexicano women, on the other hand, are more likely to express ambivalence; having seen their own lot in life improve during this same period of declining verbal "respect," some women are less enthusiastic in supporting a symbolic return to practices of former times (Hill 1998: 78–9).

Viewing language ideologies as "normally" (or unmarkedly) multiple within a population focuses attention on their potential conflict and contention in social space and on the elaborate formulations that contestation can encourage (Gal 1992, 1993). This emphasis can also be maintained in the analysis of "dominant" ideologies (Kroskrity 1998) or those that have become successfully "naturalized" by the majority of the group (Bourdieu 1977: 164). As in Gramscian (1971) models of state-endorsed hegemonic cultures, there is always struggle and adjustment between states and their adversaries, so that even those "dominant" ideologies are dynamically responsive to ever-changing forms of opposition. By viewing multiplicity, and its attendent contestations and debates, as the sociological baseline, we are challenged to understand the historical processes employed by specific groups to have their ideologies become the taken-for-granted aspects and hegemonic forces of cultural life for a larger society (Blommaert 1999b). As demonstrated by Swigert (2000) in an instructive study of contemporary Senegal, the multiplicity available in language-ideological approaches confers an analytical advantage to that perspective over one, like Bourdieu's (1991), which is more singularly preoccuppied with notions of "legitimate language" and "symbolic capital" and less attuned to understanding the development of an alternative (to French) in the form of an authorization of an urban, indigenous lingua franca – Urban Wolof.[7]

Another very revealing application of multiplicity is the exploration of internal diversity as a driving force in linguistic change, as in Joseph Errington's (1998, 2000) research on the complementary, if not contradictory, language ideologies underlying the development of standard Indonesian. Errington examines the "conflicted efforts of the New Order to domesticate exogenous modernity and modernize domestic traditions." Though often viewed as a success story in terms of "the national language problem," standardized Indonesian does not readily conform to a number of facile claims by scholars and policymakers who share an instrumentalist ideology of language development in nationalism. Gellner (1983), for example, sees development of a national standard language as a key element in making the transformation to national-ism. According to Gellner, state-level polities typically emerge from a religiously based society anchored in local communities controlled by literate elites who derive their authority from knowledge of a sacred script. Here Gellner portrays standardized Indonesian as an "ethnically uninflected, culturally neutral language" that is both universally available to its citizens and itself subject to development by the state.

But Errington provides several key examples suggesting that the "instrumentalist" ideals of creating a linguistically homogeneous tool for economic development are clearly not resulting in a culturally neutral national language. Though the New Order attempts to efface the derivativeness of national high culture and national language by erasure of its ethnic and class sources, the language itself provides a key example of an apparent contradiction. Errington examines recent lexical change and finds product-ive use of both archaic or archaicized terms traceable to Old Javanese and Sanskrit, as well as the incorporation of almost one thousand terms from English. This dual development of the lexicon can hardly be defended as "communicatively efficient" or as contributing to some neutral language widely available to all as an emblem of national identity. Rather, it represents continuity with a supposedly abandoned linguistic past in which exemplary elites rule through a language over which they have specialized control. And since knowledge of the local prestige charismatic languages (Javanese and Sanskrit) and the prestige international language, English, is socially distributed, this standardizing project joins other nationalist projects in both creating and legitimating a state-endorsed social inequality (Alonso 1994; Philips, this volume).

Another trend in this emphasis on multiplicity is to focus on contestation, clashes or disjunctures in which divergent ideological perspectives on language and discourse are juxtaposed, resulting in a wide variety of outcomes. In one such example from Alexandra Jaffe's research on language politics in Corsica (1999a, b), she examines the ideological debate regarding the translation of French literature into Corsican – a language which has undergone language shift and has lost many functions to the state's official, written language – French. The contestation which emerges is between instrumentalists who see such translations as acts of promotion or enhancement for the symbolic value of Corsican, and romanticists who adopt a more classic language and identity perspective. For them, such translations are a perversion of language and identity relationships because the act of translation suggests a common or colonized identity rather than an expression of a uniquely Corsican identity.

In another case involving language shift, I (Kroskrity 1999) have examined dia-chronic shift in Western Mono language ideologies as the powerful, hegemonic influence of the nation-state. A small indigenous group in Central California, the Western Mono precolonial language ideologies included a strong emphasis on lin-guistic utilitarianism rather than a well-developed and singular association of a particular language with tribal identity. But now in the postcolonial period, Western Monos have been persuaded by such developments as federally sponsored educational initiatives emphasizing indigenous languages and cultures, practices of federal recog-nition, the passage of the Native American Languages Acts of 1990 and 1992, and their own experience of US linguistic nationalism, that language is indeed inexorably linked to group identity. In James Collins's (1998) article, "Our Ideologies and Theirs," he examines critical differences in language ideologies by tribal members of the Tolowa (a Native American community in northern California), linguistic experts, and state officials involved in processes of a legal and regulatory nature. Fundamental questions involving the very nature of the language to be rescued from obsolescence reveal a multiplicity of language ideologies. Whereas most Tolowa consider the language to be a storehouse of cultural knowledge, largely lexical in nature, linguists emphasize the grammatical and phonological patterns as the identi-fying core of the language. Finally there are those bureaucrats who merely want a definitive basis by which to authorize the linguistically knowledgeable.

In all these works, contestation and disjuncture disclose critical differences in ideological perspectives that can more fully reveal their distinctive properties as well as their scope and force (Kroskrity 1998).

Three, *members may display varying degrees of awareness of local language ideologies.* While the Silverstein (1979) definition quoted above suggests that language ideolo-gies may often be explicitly articulated by members, researchers also recognize ideologies of practice that must be read from actual usage. Sociological theorists, such as Giddens (1984: 7), who are concerned with human agency and the linkage of micro and macro, allow for varying degrees of members' consciousness of their own rule-guided activities, ranging from discursive to practical consciousness.[8] I have suggested (Kroskrity 1998) a correlational relationship between high levels of discur-sive consciousness and active, salient contestation of ideologies and, by contrast, the correlation of practical consciousness with relatively unchallenged, highly naturalized, and definitively dominant ideologies.

The types of sites in which language ideologies are produced and commented upon constitute another source of variation in awareness. Silverstein (1998a: 136) de-veloped the notion of *ideological sites* "as institutional sites of social practice as both object and modality of ideological expression." One type of especially authorizing sites are religious ceremonies such as those performed in Pueblo kivas (Kroskrity 1998) or other similarly contexted displays of religious speech (Keane, this volume). Sites may also be secular, institutionalized, interactional rituals that are culturally familiar loci for the expression and/or explication of ideologies that indexically ground them in identities and relationships. Susan Philips (2000) clarifies the rela-tionship between different types of sites and ideological awareness. She develops the notion of *multi-sitedness* to recognize how language ideologies may be indexically tied, in complex and overlapping ways, to more than a single site – either a *site of ideological production* or a *site of metapragmatic commentary.* This distinction becomes especially important in the case of Tongan *lea kovi* 'bad language' (Philips 2000). Since "bad language" is a profaning topic, there are few opportunities for its explicit ideological elaboration in its prototypical family contexts of use in which members display "mutual respect" by strictly adhering to a variety of proscriptions on their discourse (including one against "bad language"). Though *lea kovi* is not explicitly discussed in this domestic "site of use," its elaboration does occur in the courts, where such notions must be clearly discussed as part of the legal process. The legal setting thus becomes a site of "metapragmatic commentary" on *lea kovi*, in which Tongan magistrates explicitly rationalize why a cultural proscription on intra-familial interaction should be generalized to larger Tongan society. Thus a language ideology which would normally be tacit, embodied in interaction which conforms to the cultural norm but very rarely brought up to the level of discursive consciousness, is fully explicated in the one social context in which, by law, it must be verbally elaborated.

By further refining the concept of ideological sites, Philips permits us to see ideological awareness as related to the number and nature of sites in which members deploy and explicate their language ideologies. Sites of ideological production are not necessarily sites of metapragmatic commentary and it is only the latter which both requires and demonstrates the discursive consciousness of speakers. In cases where the government monopolizes state resources, sites of ideological production and explication are one and the same. Under the influence of Ujamaa, the socialist ideology of the Tanzanian state, explicit state language ideologies promoted Swahili and encouraged bilingual writers to develop new genres of Swahili literature (Blommaert 1999c) designed to develop indigenous forms and reject foreign litera-ture. Having a monopoly on publishing, the state could use state-controlled media to explicate the state-endorsed language ideologies and then publish only those works which exemplified those ideologies.

Awareness is also a product of the kind of linguistic or discursive phenomena that speakers, either generically or in a more culturally specific manner, can identify and distinguish (Silverstein 1981). Nouns, our "words for things," display an unavoid-able referentiality that makes them more available for folk awareness and possible folk theorizing than, say, a rule for marking "same subject" as part of verb morphology. While Silverstein's (1979, 1981) early research on awareness clearly established the need to view speakers' awareness of the linguistic system as part of language – one which has repeatedly influenced analogic and other linguistic changes – and demon-strated general tendencies regarding differential awareness of various types of linguis-tic structures (e.g. lexical, morphological, syntactic), additional work still needs to be done in this area to test and perfect what is known about the potential for certain structures of language to become objects of awareness which can be made subject to speakers' ideological treatment.

In my own analysis (Kroskrity 1993, 1998) of the contact history of the Southern Tewa, now generally known as the Arizona Tewa, a consistent pattern of indigenous purism can be established as both a local language ideology of the group and an established fact of language contact. I have traced the efficacy of this purist project to the pervasive influence of *te'e hiili* 'kiva speech' – the prestigious code associated with a theocratic elite. But this program of purism is selectively imposed on linguistic phenomena that are more word-like while grammatical diffusion from Apachean and

Hopi seems to have evaded Tewa folk scrutiny (Kroskrity 1998). In a similar fashion, Tewa speakers have scrupulously avoided borrowing the Hopi evidential *yaw* 'so they say' in their traditional narratives, but they now use a similar Tewa evidential (*ba*), in precisely the same manner that Hopis use *yaw* in their narratives.[9] Thus an ideology of Tewa indigenous purism is demonstrably successsful in halting the borrowing of Hopi vocabulary but not in deflecting more general, and apparently less visible, patterns of grammatical and discourse convergence. But this does not mean that discourse patterns necessarily evade popular rationalization. In Marcyliena Morgan's (1993, 1996) effective analysis of African American "indirection" as a form of "counterlanguage" in which the seeds of African speech preferences were exaggerated during the period of slavery to create an insider code, she illustrates how discursive forms and styles can be ideologized.

Clearly we still have much to learn about folk awareness and cultural and historical variation in the popular salience of aspects of linguistic and discursive structures. Yet the importance of attending to awareness as a dimension of ideology is both the reversal of a long-standing scholarly tradition of delegitimating common people's views of language – a tradition extending back at least as far as Locke and Herder (Bauman and Briggs 2000) and relevantly manifested in the modern period by Boas's dismissal of folk understandings of language as superfluous and "misleading" (Boas 1911: 67–71) – and the recognition that when speakers rationalize their language they take a first step toward changing it (Silverstein 1979).

Four, *members' language ideologies mediate between social structures and forms of talk*. Language users' ideologies bridge their sociocultural experience and their linguistic and discursive resources by constituting those linguistic and discursive forms as indexically tied to features of their sociocultural experience. These users, in constructing language ideologies, display the influence of their consciousness in their selection of features of both linguistic and social systems that they do distinguish and in the linkages between systems that they construct.

The mediating role of language ideologies is further explored and analyzed in research by Irvine and Gal (2000). Using a semiotically inspired orientation, they develop three especially useful analytical tools for revealing productive patterns in language-ideological understanding of linguistic variability over populations, places, and times. Irvine and Gal regard these language-ideological processes as universal and "deeply involved in both the shaping of linguistic differentiation and the creating of linguistic description."

The three productive semiotically based features underlying much language-ideological reasoning are *iconization, fractal recursivity*, and *erasure*. Irvine and Gal illustrate these processes in each of three sections devoted to detailed examinations of specific historical situations in Africa and Europe. Iconization, for example, emerges as a highly productive feature of folk linguistic ideologies as well as those imported by European linguists attempting to interpret the exotic languages of Africa and the Balkan frontier. Here iconization is a feature of the representation of languages and aspects of them as pictorial guides to the nature of groups. It becomes a useful tool for understanding how Western European linguists misinterpreted the South African Khoisan clicks as degraded animal sounds rather than phonological units, and viewed the linguistic and ethnic diversity of the Balkans as a pathological sociolinguistic chaos that could only be opposed to Western Europe's transparent alignment of ethnic nation, standardized national language, and state. Irvine and Gal also see iconization as a typical feature of folk linguistic models in their account of how click sounds enter the Nguni languages through their expressions of politeness or formality – what linguists usually refer to as "respect" or "avoidance" registers – from neighboring Khoisan languages. By first viewing the clicks as sounds produced by foreign and subordinate others, Nguni language speakers can "recursively" incorporate such iconic linkages for use as a linguistic marker of a Nguni language register, or speech level, designed to show respect and deference under various culturally prescribed situations.

Erasure of differentiation is a selective disattention to often unruly forms of variation that do not fit the models of speakers and/or linguists. In their study of nineteenth-century European linguistic treatment of Senegalese languages, Irvine and Gal document the erasure of multilingualism and linguistic variation required to produce linguistic maps analogous to those of Europe. Erasure permits us to measure the difference between comprehensive analytical models, which attempt to understand a broad spectrum of linguistic differentiation and variation, and a more dominating or even hegemonic model in which analytical distinctions are glossed over in favor of attending to more selective yet locally acknowledged views. Erasure, like iconization and recursivity, is a sensitizing concept, inspired by semiotic models of communication, for tracking and ultimately locating the perspectivally based processes of linguistic and discursive differentiation that inevitably represent the products of ideological influence on positioned social actors. All three processes provide useful means of describing and comparing the productive features of language ideologies employed by both nation-states, the social groups within them, and even individuals within those groups.

Attending to such ideological processes, Joel Kuipers's research on a type of language shift involving the register of Weyewa ritual speech on the Indonesian island of Sumba, provides a detailed study of the mediating roles of language ideologies (both those of the Weyewa as well as those of the Indonesian state), relating discursive forms to the positioned interests of these groups and their participation in socio-economic patterns. He details how the many genres of ritual speech which once included the "angry" character of the speech of charismatic leaders have been systematically eliminated both through the use of force (by both the Dutch colonizers and the Indonesian nation-state) and through hegemonic institutions. The Indonesian state has suppressed many ritual events which are tied to indigenous displays of authority and prestige and is quite selective in its incorporation of Weyewa forms of verbal art that are taught in its Sumba-based schools. As Kuipers (1998: 152) notes, "By only teaching 'laments,' Indonesian schools render the more authoritative and potentially challenging forms of ritual speech invisible. Increasingly laments are coming to stand for ritual speaking as a whole." This "erasure" of specific ritual speech forms (and their connection to an indigenous authority) demonstrates both the way language ideologies guide local understandings of discursive forms as well as the embeddedness of language-ideological processes in the political economic incorporation of Sumba by the Indonesian state. Thus ideas about language emerge from social experience and profoundly influence the perception of linguistic and discursive forms and these forms, in turn, now saturated by cultural ideologies, provide a microcultural reproduction of the political economic world of the language user.

Five, *language ideologies are productively used in the creation and representation of various social and cultural identities (e.g. nationality, ethnicity)*. Language, especially shared language, has long served as the key to naturalizing the boundaries of social groups (see Bucholtz and Hall, this volume). The huge volume of scholarship on nationalism and ethnicity typically includes language as a criterial attribute. Though much has changed since Herder and other European language philosophers valorized and naturalized the primordial unity of language, nation, and state, there are still features of contemporary Western European ideologies, such as "homogenism" (Blommaert and Verschueren 1998), with more than a family resemblance to their eighteenth-century conceptual ancestors. Contemporary scholars of nationalism use tropes of "invention," "imagination," or "narration" (Hobsbawm and Ranger 1983; Anderson 1991; Bhabha 1990) to understand that complex social formation known as the nation-state. They appeal to the role of language and discursive forms in such nation-making processes (Foster 1995) as the invention of national traditions, the production of news reports and popular fiction, and the creation of state-produced narratives that locate citizens in the flow of national time (Anderson 1991; Kelly 1995). Though overtly different from Herder's preference for poetry from the *Volk* as a nation-nucleating force, these contemporary tropes and their associated theories all presuppose the existence and efficacy of shared language forms as a basis for making discursive genres which, in turn, make the nation.

Language-ideological research counters or complements this focus on shared linguistic forms by reminding us that when language is used in the making of national or ethnic identities, the unity achieved is underlain by patterns of linguistic stratification which subordinates those groups who do not command the standard. Thus, Lippi-Green (1997) and Joseph Errington (2000) respectively remind us that Standard English and Standardized Indonesian, like other hegemonic standards, may symbolize a nation but they disproportionately represent the interests of specific groups within those nations. In the creation and maintenance of Arizona Tewa ethnicity, I (Kroskrity 1998) have emphasized the importance of *te'e hiili*, 'kiva speech' as both a source of group unity, through the "erasure" of clan and class differences, and a legitimation of the theocratic rule of a priestly elite.

By using a language-ideological emphasis on both indigenous purism and compartmentalization of languages which is traceable to the influence of kiva speech as a model, Arizona Tewa people have controlled and minimized borrowing from other languages – at least at the level of the lexicon, which seems to enjoy maximal ideological monitoring. This discursive strategy, in the multilingual adaptation of the Arizona Tewa, maintains a linguistic repertoire of maximally distinctive languages by discouraging mixing and iconizing each language with a corresponding identity (as Tewa, Hopi, "American") in a variety of groups. This "discourse of difference" is naturalized in a culturally specific manner by a senior Arizona Tewa man when he relates the maintenance of linguistic diversity to the need for maintaining different colors of corn (required for ceremonial purposes) by planting separate fields for each color: "If you mix them they are no longer as good and useful. The corn is a lot like our languages – we work to keep them separate" (Kroskrity 2000c: 338–9).

But while the language ideologies of the Arizona Tewa have deterred "mixing" of both languages and their associated identities, many ethnic groups exploit or celebrate their hybridity through mixing. In Tsitsipis's (1998) treatment of the bilingual, youngest generation of the Arvanítika-speaking community in Greece, he describes how these low-proficiency Arvanítika speakers who use Greek as a dominant language nevertheless attempt to display sufficient ethnic language conversance to display the "across-the-border voice," claiming the rights and resources associated with dual membership in their ethnic community and in Greek society. In other communities, fluency in two languages permits forms of discourse which represent celebrations of hybridity. For example, in the Puerto Rican community of El Barrio in New York City's East Harlem (Zentella 1997), speaking both languages in the form of intra-sentential codeswitching is a valued expression of their status as bilingual "Nuyor-icans." "She have [sic] a brother in the hospital, *en el Bellevue* ("in Bellevue"), and he was crazy" is one of many examples provided by Zentella (1997: 96). This use of Spanish as a parenthetical expression – one containing background as opposed to more central or "foregrounded" information – is representative of many codeswitch-ing examples between the two languages in which the switch is not required because of limited knowledge of the other language but rather part of a pattern in which language switches are explicable as strategies of emphasis (see Woolard, this volume, section 3.3). For the children who grew up during Zentella's longitudinal study, "the frequent interspersal of sentences and words from both languages was the primary symbol of membership in el bloque and reflected the children's dual cultural identifi-cation" (1997: 79). But this positive view of their linguistic adaptation is balanced by alternating negative self-assessments of their linguistic abilities. As children become more exposed to the pejorative view of their language skills that is promoted by educational and other dominant bloc institutions which strongly endorse the stand-ard, the children also learn to see deficiency in their language skills and view the linguistic feat of their codeswitching as nothing more than a crutch-like compen-sation for their imperfect command of either language. By so doing they display the language-ideological compliance of subordinated groups by accepting, even partially, the negative images of themselves presented by the dominant society and its myriad collaborative institutions.

Also relevant to appreciating the role of language ideologies in producing ethnic stratification are explicit attempts to direct culture change and to alter the identities of people through either imposed assimilation or conversion. Bambi Schieffelin's (2000) study of the missionary introduction of Kaluli literacy examines the disjunc-ture between indigenous language ideologies of a cultural group in Papua New Guinea and the "modernizing" and Christianizing ideologies embodied in a mission-ary-introduced literacy program. A small community in the Mt. Bosavi area of south-western Papua New Guinea, the Kaluli did not experience significant foreign influence until the 1960s, when the missionaries exposed the area to both Christian-ization and modernization (see Kulick and Schieffelin, this volume).

Among the *literacy products* and practices Schieffelin examined are Kaluli primers written by missionaries, with the assistance of Kaluli speakers, to further their own objectives of Westernization. In her careful analysis Schieffelin effectively demon-strates how these primers "(re)presented and (re)constituted social identity." From the first, this promotion of "missionary literacy" within the oral tradition of the

Kaluli introduced not only a new metalanguage of literacy for "books," "reading," and so on but also a fragmentation of language and a decentering of identity. In ways unfamiliar to pre-existing Kaluli language ideology but seemingly naturalized by both Kaluli orthography and newly introduced literacy practices, the vernacular language was stripped of its cultural practices and severed from Kaluli discourses in church and school settings. The primers produced in the 1970s began to juxtapose Kaluli local culture to the innovations of a Christian modernity. By referring to the Kaluli themselves as *ka:na:ka:* (a derogatory term for Pacific Island native from Tok Pisin) and systematically depicting Kaluli practices as backward and inferior, these texts influenced the Kaluli to construct themselves from the pejorative perspective of outsiders.

As a novel *literary practice* (see Baquedano-López, this volume), the production of a coordinated, unison vocal repetition of passages from authoritative books challenged traditional ideological preferences for locating "truth" in collective, multi-party, polyphonic discourse. In this clash of ideologies regarding authoritative speech, missionaries had a double advantage: they controlled the new technology of native language literacy and enjoyed the hegemonic support of the nation-state. Their ability to effect radical culture change through introducing Kaluli literacy thus linked modernity, Christianity, and the economic resources of the nation-state to deliberately transmute Kaluli identities into modern Christian ones. Since a group's beliefs about language, often unexamined beliefs at that, are typically at the heart of its sense of group identity, language-ideological concerns will always matter not only to scholars of these processes but also to nation-states, ethnic groups, and others that would variously define themselves through language and/or resist the definitions of identity imposed by others.

4 CONCLUSION

The topic of identity just broached provides a useful segue into a retrospective rethinking of the brief history of language-ideological research outlined earlier. There I traced its genesis to the reopening of such formerly closed topics as the functions of language and the role of speakers' awareness of linguistic and discursive systems. But an alternative account of the origin and development of language-ideological research would focus less on the growing sophistication of researchers' models and more on the radically changed nature of their objects of study, "the transformation of local linguistic communities" (Silverstein 1998b). As Appadurai (1991: 191) has observed: "The landscapes of group identity – the ethnoscapes – around the world are no longer familiar anthropological objects, insofar as groups are no longer tightly territorialized, spatially bounded, historically unselfconscious, or culturally homogeneous. We have fewer cultures in the world and more 'internal cultural debates'." Though it would be wrong to suggest that processes such as nationalism and state formation, the emergence of global economies and international communication, transnational migration, and diasporic population movements are without precedent, it is certainly true that linguistic communities in the contemporary period have experienced these forces on an unprecedented scale. In order to more adequately perform the art and science of cultural representation, anthropologists have shifted their focal glance from the uniformity of stable, cultural "centers" to what Rosaldo (1988: 85) calls the emergent "border zones" within and between social groups. Rejecting the practice of describing autonomous, homogeneous cultures in a postcolonial world, he writes, "All of us inhabit an interdependent ... world, which is marked by borrowing and lending across porous cultural boundaries, and saturated with inequality, power, and domination" (Rosaldo 1988: 87).

Just as modes of cultural representation have been reshaped by a confrontation with the increasing complexity of the sociocultural world so, too, linguistic anthropologists have turned to language-ideological perspectives as an increasingly important means of understanding this complexity and the way that speakers, groups, and governments use languages – *and their ideas about languages* – to create and negotiate those sociocultural worlds. Because language-ideological approaches emphasize political economic forces (and other interest-informed action), diversity and contestation, the influence of speakers' consciousness on both linguistic and social systems, the constitutive role of language in social life, and the myriad ways that ideologies of language and discourse construct identity, they should continue to provide very useful tools for researchers who must recognize a larger context for the grammatical, textual, microinteractional, and microcultural phenomena that continue to comprise the staples of linguistic anthropological scholarship.

NOTES

1   By glossing language ideologies as "beliefs or feelings" about languages, I am hoping to capture a wide range of analytical possibilities. In language ideological discussions it is perhaps more customary to regard the former as local understandings, whether explicit or tacit, about language. But I use "feelings" here to connect with the less acknowledged aspect of language ideologies as relatively automatic aesthetic response. By doing so, I hope to connect with Williams's (1977: 128) notion of "structures of feeling" and the promise of such concepts to go beyond the analytical dichotomies of consciousness – practical and discursive (see Giddens 1984, n. 8 below). I am indebted to Jennifer Reynolds for suggesting the promise of this concept in her own dissertation research (Reynolds 2002).

2   Thus rather than attempting to explore relationships between research on language ideologies and similar movements, such as Critical Discourse Analysis (e.g. Fairclough 1989, 1992; van Dijk 1998; Wodak 1989; Blommaert and Bulcaen 2000) or Cultural Cognitive Models (e.g. Dirven, Frank, and Ilie 2001) which have convergent interests in power, ideology, and social inequality, I will merely note their existence here. Another related topic which can be mentioned but not examined because of the need for a sharply delimited focus here is research on "language policy" (e.g. Schiffman 1996; May 2001).

3   "Logical equivalence," a notion from early transformational grammar theory (e.g. Chomsky 1965), meant that two sentences had the "same meaning" with meaning being reduced to "truth value." In other words, two sentences – like active and passive counterparts – have the same meaning if when S1 is true S2 is also true. This type of semantic analysis ignores the important fact that speakers do not use these sentences interchangeably, in part because each foregrounds a different argument.

4   In linguistics, "denotation" is usually understood to be the property of linguistic expressions to identify a particular class of objects, whereas "reference" identifies a particular object (Lyons 1977; Duranti 1997).

5   One of the important conceptual distinctions which semiotic models provide is a typology of signs which trichotomizes signing activity into symbols, icons, and indexes. One way to understand these different types of sign is to focus on the relationship of a particular linguistic form to its meaning. In the case of symbols we find an arbitrary relationship between form and meaning (e.g. the pronunciation of the word "table" and its denotation of that class of furniture) whereas in the case of icons we see a principle of formal resemblance in the form of the sign ("buzz," for example, phonetically imitates the sound of bees). In the case of indexes, their meaning comes from some contiguity, or association, between a linguistic form and a pragmatic context. Thus words like "here," "now," and "I" index a particular speech context. It is important to realize that these are not mutually exclusive types of sign and that the addition of "indexical" sign relations is an important step in recognizing how speakers, in part, construe the meaning of linguistic forms and discursive practices from the way they are indexically connected to particular speakers (e.g. relevant gender and/or ethnic identities), to contexts (e.g. formal and informal), and to activities (e.g. prayer, political protest), to name but a few.

6   Note that by "culturally shared," I mean something like uniformly distributed within cultural groups, as in the Rumsey definition cited above. For more on the neutral/critical distinction, see Woolard (1998: 7–9).

7   One can metaphorically extend the "legitimate language" of Bourdieu (1991) as Gross (1993: 200) has done by appealing to "popular legitimacy" which derives from "the palpable exercise of power" and gain some of the analytical flexibility associated with multiplicity. What of course would be lost would be the local perspective on what acts are locally recognized as power displays.

8   I follow Giddens (1984) in distinguishing "discursive" consciousness and "practical" consciousness. The former is a form of reflexive monitoring that would permit speakers' explicit discussion of language ideologies, while the latter represents those ideologies which are embodied in actual and relatively automatic conduct. Language ideologies of the latter type may be so taken for granted that they represent "unsaid" background knowledge. Also relevant here is the discussion of types of agency, given such important distinctions as those between evaluation, influence, and control (see Duranti, this volume).

9   For more on this case of discursive convergence, including the comparative data which suggests that the Southern Tewa ancestors of the Arizona Tewa used evidential particles differently in their narratives than their descendants do now, see Kroskrity 1997.

REFERENCES

Alonso, A. M. (1994). The Politics of Space, Time, and Substance: State Formation. *Annual Review of Anthropology* 23: 379–405.

Anderson, B. (1991 [1983]). *Imagined Communities: Reflections on the Origins and Spread of Nationalism*. London: Verso.

Appadurai, A. (1991). Global Ethnoscapes: Notes and Queries for a Transnational Anthropology. In R. G. Fox (ed.), *Recapturing Anthropology* (pp. 191–210). Santa Fe, NM: School of American Research Press.

Bauman, R., and Briggs, C. L. (2000). Language Philosophy as Language Ideology: John Locke and Johann Gottfried Herder. In P. V. Kroskrity (ed.), *Regimes of Language* (pp. 139–204). Santa Fe, NM: School of American Research Press.

Bhabha, H. (1990). *Nation and Narration*. New York: Routledge.

Blom, J.-P., and Gumperz, J. J. (1972). Social Meaning in Linguistic Structure: Codeswitching in Norway. In J. J. Gumperz and D. H. Hymes (eds.), *Directions in Sociolinguistics* (pp. 407–434). New York: Holt.

514   PAUL V. KROSKRITY

Blommaert, J. (ed.) (1999a). *Language Ideological Debates*. Berlin: Mouton de Gruyter.

Blommaert, J. (1999b). The Debate is Open. In J. Blommaert (ed.), *Language Ideological Debates* (pp. 1–38). Berlin: Mouton de Gruyter.

Blommaert, J. (1999c). *State Ideology and Language in Tanzania*. Cologne: Rudiger Koppe Verlag.

Blommaert, J., and Bulcaen, C. (2000). Critical Discourse Analysis. *Annual Review of Anthropology* 29: 447–466.

Blommaert, J., and Verschueren, J. (1998). The Role of Language in European Nationalist Ideologies. In B. B. Schieffelin, K. A. Woolard, and P. V. Kroskrity (eds.), *Language Ideologies* (pp. 189–210). New York: Cambridge University Press.

Bloomfield, L. (1933). *Language*. New York: Henry Holt.

Bloomfield, L. (1944). Secondary and Tertiary Responses to Language. *Language* 20: 44–55.

Bloomfield, L. (1987 [1927]). Literate and Illiterate Speech. In C. F. Hockett (ed.), *A Leonard Bloomfield Anthology* (pp. 84–93). Chicago: University of Chicago Press.

Boas, F. (1911) Introduction. In F. Boas (ed.), *Handbook of American Indian Languages* (pp. 1–83). Bulletin of the Bureau of American Ethnology, vol. 40. Washington, DC: U.S. Government Printing Office.

Bourdieu, P. (1977). *Outline of a Theory of Practice* (trans. R. Nice). Cambridge: Cambridge University Press.

Bourdieu, P. (1991). *Language and Symbolic Power*. Cambridge, MA: Harvard University Press.

Briggs, C. L. (1998). "You're a Liar – You're Just Like a Woman!" Constructing Dominant Ideologies of Language in Warao Men's Gossip. In B. B. Schieffelin, K. A. Woolard, and P. V. Kroskrity (eds.), *Language Ideologies* (pp. 229–255). New York: Oxford University Press.

Chomsky, N. (1957). *Syntactic Structures*. The Hague: Mouton.

Chomsky, N. (1965). *Aspects of the Theory of Syntax*. Cambridge, MA: MIT Press.

Collins, J. T. (1998). Our Ideologies and Theirs. In B. B. Schieffelin, K. A. Woolard, and P. V. Kroskrity (eds.), *Language Ideologies* (pp. 256–270). New York: Oxford University Press.

Collins, J. T. (1999). The Ebonics Controversy in Context: Literacies, Subjectivities, and Language Ideologies in the United States. In J. Blommaert (ed.), *Language Ideological Debates* (pp. 201–234). Berlin: Mouton de Gruyter.

Dirven, R., Frank, R., and Ilie, C. (2001). *Language and Ideology*, vol. II: *Descriptive and Cognitive Approaches*. Amsterdam: John Benjamins.

Duranti, A. (1997). *Linguistic Anthropology*. Cambridge: Cambridge University Press.

Errington, J. (1988). *Structure and Style in Javanese: A Semiotic View of Linguistic Etiquette*. Philadelphia: University of Pennsylvania Press.

Errington, J. (1998). *Shifting Languages: Interaction and Identity in Javanese Indonesian*. Cambridge: Cambridge University Press.

Errington, J. (2000). Indonesian('s) Authority. In P. V. Kroskrity (ed.), *Regimes of Language* (pp. 205–227). Santa Fe, NM: School of American Research Press.

Errington, J. (2001a). Ideology. In A. Duranti (ed.), *Key Terms in Language and Culture* (pp. 110–112). Malden, MA: Blackwell.

Errington, J. (2001b). Colonial Linguistics. *Annual Review of Anthropology* 30: 19–39.

Fairclough, N. (1989). *Language and Power*. London: Longman.

Fairclough, N. (1992). *Critical Language Awareness*. London: Longman.

Foster, R. J. (ed.) (1995). *Nation Making: Emergent Identities in Postcolonial Melanesia*. Ann Arbor: University of Michigan Press.

Gal, S. (1979). *Language Shift: Social Determinants of Linguistic Change in Bilingual Austria*. New York: Academic Press.

Gal, S. (1989). Language and Political Economy. *Annual Review of Anthropology* 18: 345–367.

Gal, S. (1992). Multiplicity and Contention among Ideologies. *Pragmatics* 2: 445–450.

Gal, S. (1993). Diversity and Contestation in Linguistic Ideologies: German Speakers in Hungary. *Language in Society* 22: 337–359.

Gal, S., and Woolard, K. A. (eds.) (2001). *Languages and Publics: The Making of Authority.* Manchester: St. Jerome.

Gellner, E. (1983). *Nations and Nationalism.* Ithaca: Cornell University Press.

Giddens, A. (1979). *Central Problems in Social Theory: Action, Structure, and Contradiction in Social Analysis.* London: Macmillan.

Giddens, A. (1984). *The Constitution of Society.* Berkeley: University of California Press.

Gramsci, A. (1971). *Selections from the Prison Notebooks.* New York: International Press.

Gross, J. E. (1993). The Politics of Unofficial Language Use: Walloon in Belgium, Tamazight in Morocco. *Critique of Anthropology* 13: 177–208.

Hill, J. H. (1985). The Grammar of Consciousness and the Consciousness of Grammar. *American Ethnologist* 12: 725–737.

Hill, J. H. (1998). "Today There Is no Respect": Nostalgia, "Respect," and Oppositional Discourse in Mexicano (Nahuatl) Language Ideology. In B. B. Schieffelin, K. A. Woolard, and P. V. Kroskrity (eds.), *Language Ideologies* (pp. 68–86). New York: Oxford University Press.

Hill, J. H., and Hill, K. C. (1986). *Speaking Mexicano: Dynamics of a Syncretic Language in Central Mexico.* Tucson: University of Arizona Press.

Hobsbawm, E., and Ranger, T. (1983). *The Invention of Tradition.* Cambridge: Cambridge University Press.

Hymes, D. H. (1964). Introduction: Toward Ethnographies of Communication. In J. J. Gumperz and D. H. Hymes (eds.), *The Ethnography of Communication* (pp. 1–34). Special Issue, *American Anthropologist* 66(6), part 2.

Hymes, D. H. (1974). *Foundations in Sociolinguistics: An Ethnographic Approach.* Philadelphia: University of Pennsylvania Press.

Irvine, J. T. (1989). When Talk Isn't Cheap: Language and Political Economy. *American Ethnologist* 16: 248–267.

Irvine, J. T., and Gal, S. (2000). Language Ideology and Linguistic Differentiation. In P. V. Kroskrity (ed.), *Regimes of Language* (pp. 35–83). Santa Fe, NM: School of American Research Press.

Jaffe, A. (1999a). Locating Power: Corsican Translators and Their Critics. In J. Blommaert (ed.), *Language Ideological Debates* (pp. 1–38). Berlin: Mouton de Gruyter.

Jaffe, A. (1999b). *Ideologies in Action: Language Politics on Corsica.* Berlin: Mouton de Gruyter.

Jakobson, R. (1957). *The Framework of Language.* Ann Arbor: University of Michigan Press.

Jakobson, R. (1960). Closing Statement: Linguistics and Poetics. In T. A. Sebeok (ed.), *Style in Language* (pp. 350–377). Cambridge, MA: MIT Press.

Kelly, J. D. (1995). The Privileges of Citizenship: Nations, States, Markets, and Narratives. In R. J. Foster (ed.), *Nation Making: Emergent Identities in Postcolonial Melanesia* (pp. 253–273). Ann Arbor: University of Michigan Press.

Kroskrity, P. V. (1993). *Language, History, and Identity: Ethnolinguistic Studies of the Arizona Tewa.* Tucson: University of Arizona Press.

Kroskrity, P. V. (1997). Discursive Convergence with an Evidential Particle. In J. H. Hill, P. J. Mistry, and L. Campbell (eds.), *The Life of Language: Papers in Honor of William Bright* (pp. 25–34). Berlin: Mouton de Gruyter.

Kroskrity, P. V. (1998). Arizona Tewa Kiva Speech as a Manifestation of a Dominant Language Ideology. In B. B. Schieffelin, K. A. Woolard, and P. V. Kroskrity (eds.), *Language Ideologies* (pp. 103–122). New York: Oxford University Press.

Kroskrity, P. V. (1999). Language Ideologies, Language Shift, and the Imagination of a Western Mono Community: The Recontextualization of a Coyote Story. In *Language and Ideology*, vol. 1: *Selected Papers from the 6th International Pragmatics Conference* (pp. 270–289). Antwerp: International Pragmatics Association.

Kroskrity, P. V. (ed.) (2000a). *Regimes of Language: Ideologies, Polities, and Identities.* Santa Fe, NM: School of American Research Press.

Kroskrity, P. V. (2000b). Regimenting Languages. In P. V. Kroskrity (ed.), *Regimes of Language* (pp. 1–34). Santa Fe, NM: School of American Research Press.

Kroskrity, P. V. (2000c). Language Ideologies in the Expression and Representation of Arizona Tewa Ethnic Identity. In P. V. Kroskrity (ed.), *Regimes of Language* (pp. 329–359). Santa Fe, NM: School of American Research Press.

Kuipers, J. C. (1998). *Language, Identity, and Marginality in Indonesia.* Cambridge: Cambridge University Press.

Kulick, D. (1992). *Language Shift and Cultural Reproduction.* Cambridge: Cambridge University Press.

Lippi-Green, R. (1997). *English With an Accent: Language, Ideology, and Discrimination in the United States.* London: Routledge.

Lyons, J. (1977). *Semantics.* Cambridge: Cambridge University Press.

May, S. (2001). *Language and Minority Rights: Ethnicity, Nationalism, and the Politics of Language.* London: Longman.

Milroy, J., and Milroy, L. (1999). *Authority in Language: Investigating Language Prescription and Standardisation.* London: Routledge.

Morgan, M. (1993). The Africanness of Counterlanguage among African Americans. In S. Mufwene (ed.), *Africanisms in Afro-American Language Varieties* (pp. 423–435). Athens: University of Georgia Press.

Morgan, M. (1996). Conversational Signifying: Grammar and Indirectness among African American Women. In E. Ochs, E. A. Schegloff, and S. A. Thompson (eds.), *Interaction and Grammar* (pp. 405–434). New York: Cambridge University Press.

Ochs, E., and Schieffelin, B. B. (1984). Language Acquisition and Socialization: Three Developmental Stories and Their Implications. In R. A. Shweder and R. A. LeVine (eds.), *Culture Theory: Essays on Mind, Self, and Emotion* (pp. 276–320). Cambridge: Cambridge University Press.

Ortner, S. (1984). Theory in Anthropology since the Sixties. *Comparative Studies in Society and History* 26: 126–166.

Pagliai, V. (2000). Lands I Came to Sing: Negotiating Identities and Places in the Tuscan "Contrasto." *Pragmatics* 10: 125–146.

Peirce, C. S. (1931–58). *Collected Papers of Charles Sanders Peirce* (C. Hartshorne and P. Weiss, eds., vols. 1–6; A. W. Burks, ed., vols. 7–8). Cambridge, MA: Harvard University Press.

Philips, S. U. (1998). *Ideology in the Language of Judges.* New York: Oxford University Press.

Philips, S. U. (2000). Constructing a Tongan Nation-state through Language Ideology in the Courtroom. In P. V. Kroskrity (ed.), *Regimes of Language* (pp. 229–257). Santa Fe, NM: School of American Research Press.

Reynolds, J. F. (2002). Maya Children's Practices of the Imagination: (Dis)Playing Childhood and Politics in Guatemala. Unpublished doctoral dissertation, University of California, Los Angeles.

Rosaldo, R. (1988). Ideology, Place, and People without Culture. *Cultural Anthropology* 3: 77–87.

Rumsey, A. (1990). Wording, Meaning, and Linguistic Ideology. *American Anthropologist* 92: 346–361.

Schieffelin, B. B. (2000). Introducing Kaluli Literacy: A Chronology of Influences. In P. V. Kroskrity (ed.), *Regimes of Language* (pp. 293–327). Santa Fe, NM: School of American Research Press.

Schieffelin, B. B., Woolard, K. A., and Kroskrity, P. V. (eds.) (1998). *Language Ideologies: Practice and Theory.* New York: Oxford University Press.

Schiffman, H. E. (1996). *Linguistic Culture and Language Policy.* London: Routledge.

Silverstein, M. (1979). Language Structure and Linguistic Ideology. In P. Clyne, W. Hanks, and C. Hofbauer (eds.), *The Elements* (pp. 193–248). Chicago: Chicago Linguistic Society.

Silverstein, M. (1981). *The Limits of Awareness.* Working Papers in Sociolinguistics, no. 84. Austin, TX: Southwest Educational Development Laboratory. [Reprinted in A. Duranti (ed.), *Linguistic Anthropology: A Reader* (pp. 382– 402). Malden, MA: Blackwell, 2001.]

Silverstein, M. (1985). Language and the Culture of Gender. In E. Mertz and R. Parmentier (eds.), *Semiotic Mediation* (pp. 219–259). New York: Academic Press.

Silverstein, M. (1996). Monoglot "Standard" in America. In D. Brenneis and R. Macaulay (eds.), *The Matrix of Language: Contemporary Linguistic Anthropology* (pp. 284–306). Boulder, CO: Westview Press.

Silverstein, M. (1998a). The Uses and Utility of Ideology: A Commentary. In B. B. Schieffelin, K. A. Woolard, and P. V. Kroskrity (eds.), *Language Ideologies* (pp. 23–45). New York: Oxford University Press.

Silverstein, M. (1998b). Contemporary Transformations of Local Linguistic Communities. *Annual Review of Anthropology* 27: 401–426.

Spitulnik, D. (1998). Mediating Unity and Diversity: The Production of Language Ideologies in Zambian Broadcasting. In B. B. Schieffelin, K. A. Woolard, and P. V. Kroskrity (eds.), *Language Ideologies* (pp. 163–188). New York: Oxford University Press.

Swigart, L. (2000). The Limits of Legitimacy: Language Ideology and Shift in Contemporary Senegal. *Journal of Linguistic Anthropology* 10: 90–130.

Tsitsipis, L. D. (1998). *A Linguistic Anthropology of Praxis and Language Shift: Arvanítika (Albanian) and Greek in Contact.* Oxford: Clarendon Press.

van Dijk, T. (1998). *Ideology: A Multidisciplinary Approach.* London: Sage.

Vološinov, V. N. (1973). *Marxism and the Philosophy of Language* (trans. L. Matejka and I. R. Titunik). New York: Seminar Press.

Williams, R. (1977). *Marxism and Literature.* Oxford: Oxford University Press.

Wodak, R. (1989). *Language, Power, and Ideology: Studies in Political Discourse.* Amsterdam: Walter Benjamins.

Woolard, K. A. (1985). Language Variation and Cultural Hegemony: Toward an Integration of Sociolinguistic and Social Theory. *American Ethnologist* 2: 738–748.

Woolard, K. A. (1989). *Double Talk: Bilingualism and the Politics of Ethnicity in Catalonia.* Stanford: Stanford University Press.

Woolard, K. A. (1998). Introduction: Language Ideology as a Field of Inquiry. In B. B. Schieffelin, K. A. Woolard, and P. V. Kroskrity (eds.), *Language Ideologies* (pp. 3–47). New York: Oxford University Press.

Woolard, K. A., and Schieffelin, B. B. (1994). Language Ideology. *Annual Review of Anthropology* 23: 55–82.

Zentella, A. C. (1997). *Growing Up Bilingual: Puerto Rican Children in New York.* Malden, MA: Blackwell.

General Bibliography

Aarons, D., and Reynolds, L. (2003). South African Sign Language: Changing Policies and Practice. In L. Monaghan, C. Schmaling, K. Nakamura, and G. H. Turner (eds.), *Many Ways to be Deaf*. Washington, DC: Gallaudet University Press.

Abrahams, R. D. (1970). A Performance-Centered Approach to Gossip. *Man* 5: 290–301.

Abrahams, R. D. (1972). Folklore and Literature as Performance. *Journal of the Folklore Institute* 9: 75–91.

Abrahams, R. D. (1974). Black Talking on the Streets. In R. Bauman and J. Sherzer (eds.), *Explorations in the Ethnography of Speaking* (pp. 337–353). Cambridge: Cambridge University Press.

Abrahams, R. D. (1975a). Folklore and Communication in St. Vincent. In D. Ben-Amos and K. S. Goldstein (eds.), *Folklore: Performance and Communication* (pp. 287–300). The Hague: Mouton.

Abrahams, R. D. (1975b). Negotiating Respect: Patterns of Presentation among Black Women. *Journal of American Folklore* 88: 58–80.

Abrahams, R. D. (1983). *The Man-of-Words in the West Indies*. Baltimore: Johns Hopkins University Press.

Abu-Lughod, L. (1986). *Veiled Sentiments: Honor and Poetry in a Bedouin Society*. Berkeley, Los Angeles, and London: University of California Press.

Abu-Manga, A.-A. (ed.) (1985). *Baajankaro. A Fulani Epic from Sudan*. Berlin: Reimer.

Adger, C. T. (1998). Register Shifting and Dialect Resources in Instructional Discourse. In S. Hoyle and C. T. Adger (eds.), *Kids Talk: Strategic Language Use in Later Childhood* (pp. 151–169). Oxford: Oxford University Press.

Agawu, K. (1984). The Impact of Language on Musical Composition in Ghana: An Introduction to the Compositional Style of Ephraim Amu. *Ethnomusicology* 28(1): 37–74.

Agha, A. (1994). Honorification. *Annual Review of Anthropology* 23: 277–302.

Agha, A. (1997). "Concept" and "Communication" in Evolutionary Terms. *Semiotica* 116(2–4): 189–215.

Agha, A. (1998). Stereotypes and Registers of Honorific Language. *Language in Society* 27(2): 151–194.

Agha, A. (2002). Honorific registers. In K. Kataoka and S. Ide (eds.), *Culture, Interaction and Language* (pp. 21–63). Tokyo: Hituzisyobo.

Ahearn, L. (1999). Agency. *Journal of Linguistic Anthropology* 9: 12–15.

Ahearn, L. (2001a). Language and Agency. *Annual Review of Anthropology* 30: 109–137.

Ahearn, L. (2001b). *Invitations to Love: Literacy, Love Letters, and Social Change in Nepal*. Ann Arbor: University of Michigan Press.

Ainsworth-Vaughn, N. (1998). *Claiming Power in Doctor–Patient Talk*. New York: Oxford University Press.

Akatsuka, N. (1991a). Affect and Japanese Conditionals. In P. Clancy and S. Thompson (eds.), *Asian Discourse and Grammar* (pp. 1–8). Santa Barbara Papers in Linguistics, vol. 3.

Akatsuka, N. (1991b). Dracula Conditionals and Discourse. In C. Georgopolous and R. Ishihara (eds.), *Interdisciplinary Approaches to Language: Essays in Honor of S.-Y. Kuroda* (pp. 25–37). Dordrecht: Kluwer.

Akatsuka, N., and Clancy, P. (1993). Conditionality and Deontic Modality in Japanese and Korean: Evidence from the Emergence of Conditionals. In P. Clancy (ed.), *Japanese/Korean Linguistics*, vol. 2 (pp. 177–192). Stanford, CA: CSLI Publications.

Akinnaso, F. N. (1989). One Nation, Four Hundred Languages: Unity and Diversity in Nigeria's Language Policy. *Language Problems and Language Planning* 13: 133–146.

Akinnaso, F. N., and Ajirotutu, C. S. (1982). Performance and Ethnic Style in Job Interviews. In J. J. Gumperz (ed.), *Language and Social Identity* (pp. 119–144). Cambridge: Cambridge University Press.

Allen, J. (1994). Can English Loanwords Create New Phonemes in St. Lucian French Creole? Paper presented at the Workshop on Developmental Issues in Creole Languages and Linguistics, University of Westminster, London.

Alleyne, M. C. (1985). A Linguistic Perspective on the Caribbean. In S. W. Mintz and S. Price (eds.), *Caribbean Contours* (pp. 155–179). Baltimore: Johns Hopkins University Press.

Allsop, L., Woll, B., and Brauti, J. M. (1995). International Sign: The Creation of an International Deaf Community and Sign Language. In H. Bos and G. M. Schermer (eds.), *Sign Language Research 1994* (pp. 171–188). Hamburg: Signum.

Alonso, A. M. (1994). The Politics of Space, Time, and Substance: State Formation. *Annual Review of Anthropology* 23: 379–405.

Alper, H. P. (ed.) (1988). *Understanding Mantras*. Albany: SUNY Press.

Alrabaa, S. (1985). The Use of Address Pronouns by Egyptian Adults. *Journal of Pragmatics* 9: 645–657.

Althusser, L. (1971). Ideology and Ideological State Apparatuses (Notes towards an Investigation). In L. Althusser, *Lenin and Philosophy and Other Essays* (pp. 127–188). London: Monthly Review Press.

Alvarez-Cáccamo, C. (1990). Rethinking Conversational Code-switching. *Proceedings of the Berkeley Linguistics Society* 16: 3–16.

Alvarez-Cáccamo, C. (1996). Building Alliances in Political Discourse: Language Institutional Authority and Resistance. In *Folia Linguistica* XXX 3/4, Special Issue on Interactional Sociolinguistics (ed. H. Kotthoff).

Alvarez-Cáccamo, C. (1998). From "Switching Code" to "Codeswitching": Toward a Reconceptualization of Communicative Codes. In P. Auer (ed.), *Code-switching in Conversation: Language, Interaction and Identity* (pp. 29–50). London: Routledge.

Alvarez-Cáccamo, C. (1999). Codes. *Journal of Linguistic Anthropology* 9(1–2): 28–31.

Amsterdam, A. G., and Bruner, J. (2000). *Minding the Law*. Cambridge, MA: Harvard University Press.

Andersen, E. S. (1990). *Speaking with Style: The Sociolinguistic Skills of Children*. London and New York: Routledge.

Andersen, R. W. (1990). Papiamentu Tense-Aspect With Special Attention to Discourse. In J. V. Singler (ed.), *Pidgin and Creole Tense-Mood-Aspect Systems*. Amsterdam: John Benjamins.

Anderson, B. (1983). *Imagined Communities*. London: Verso.

Andreasen, N. C. (1982). There *May Be* a "Schizophrenic Language" [response to Schwartz, S. (1982). Is There a Schizophrenic Language?]. *Behavioral and Brain Sciences* 5: 588–589.

Andreasen, N. C. (1999). Defining the Phenotype of Schizophrenia: Cognitive Dysmetria and its Neural Mechanisms. *Biological Psychiatry* 46(7): 908–920.

Andrews, E. (1990). *Markedness Theory: The Union of Asymmetry and Semiosis in Language*. Durham, NC: Duke University Press.

Andrzejewski, B. W., and Lewis, I. M. (1964). *Somali Poetry: An Introduction*. Oxford: Oxford University Press.

Anis, J., Chiss, J.-L., and Puech, Ch. (1988). *L'écriture: théories et descriptions*. Brussels: de Boeck.

Ann, J. (2003). The Chiying School of Taiwan: A Foreigner's Perspective. In L. Monaghan, C. Schmaling, K. Nakamura and G. H. Turner (eds.), *Many Ways to be Deaf*. Washington, DC: Gallaudet University Press.

Annamalai, E. (1989). The Linguistic and Social Dimensions of Purism. In B. Jernudd and M. Shapiro (eds.), *The Politics of Language Purism* (pp. 225–231). Berlin: Mouton de Gruyter.

Anzaldúa, G. (1987). *Borderlands / La Frontera: The New Mestiza*. San Francisco: Spinsters/Aunt Lute.

Anzaldúa, G. (1990). How to Tame a Wild Tongue. In R. M. Ferguson, T. Trin Min-ha

Geve, and C. West (eds.), *Out There: Marginalization and Contemporary Cultures* (pp. 203–211). New York: The New Museum of Contemporary Art.

Appadurai, A. (1990). Topographies of the Self: Praise and Emotion in Hindu India. In C. A. Lutz and L. Abu-Lughod (eds.), *Language and the Politics of Emotion* (pp. 92–112). Cambridge: Cambridge University Press.

Appadurai, A. (1991). Global Ethnoscapes: Notes and Queries for a Transnational Anthropology. In R. G. Fox (ed.), *Recapturing Anthropology* (pp. 191–210). Santa Fe, NM: School of American Research Press.

Appadurai, A. (1996). *Modernity at Large: Cultural Dimensions of Globalization*. Minneapolis: University of Minnesota Press.

Appel, R., and Muysken, P. (1987). *Language Contact and Bilingualism*. London: Edward Arnold.

Appelbaum, D. (1990). *Voice*. Albany: SUNY Press.

Applebee, A. N. (1978). *The Child's Concept of a Story: Ages Two to Seventeen*. Chicago: University of Chicago Press.

Aramburo, A. (1989). Sociolinguistic Aspects of the Black Deaf Community. In C. Lucas (ed.), *The Sociolinguistics of the Deaf Community* (pp. 103–119). San Diego, CA: Academic Press.

Aristotle (1982 [4th century BCE.]). *Poetics* (trans. J. Hutton). New York: W. W. Norton.

Aronoff, M. (1985). Orthography and Linguistic Theory. *Language* 61: 28–72.

Aronsson, K., and Cederborg, A. C. (1997). A Love Story Retold: Moral Order and Intergenerational Negotiations. *Semiotica* 114: 83–110.

Arthur, B., Weiner, R., Culver, M., Lee, Y.J., and Thomas, D. (1980). The Register of Impersonal Discourse to Foreigners: Verbal Adjustments to Foreign Accent. In D. Larsen-Freeman (ed.), *Discourse Analysis in Second Language Research* (pp. 111–124). Rowley, MA: Newbury House.

Asmuß, B. (2002). *Strukturelle Dissensmarkierungen in interkultureller Kommunikation: Analysen deutsch–dänischer Verhandlungen* [Structural Disaffiliation Markers in Intercultural Communication: Analyses of German–Danish Negotiations]. Tübingen: Niemeyer.

Aspden, P., Devere, J., Hunt, J., Monaghan, L., and Pivac, L. (1992). *Celebrating 50 Years of Deaf Schools in Auckland*. Auckland, NZ: Kelston Deaf Education Centre.

Astbury, Jill (1996) *Crazy for You: The Making of Women's Madness*. Melbourne and Oxford: Oxford University Press.

Atkinson, J. M. (1979). Sequencing and Shared Attentiveness to Court Proceedings. In G. Psathas (ed.), *Everyday Language: Studies in Ethnomethodology* (pp. 257–286). New York: Irvington.

Atkinson, J. M. (1992). Displaying Neutrality: Formal Aspects of Informal Court Proceedings. In P. Drew and J. Heritage (eds.), *Talk at Work: Interaction in Institutional Settings* (pp. 199–211). Cambridge: Cambridge University Press.

Atkinson, J. M., and Drew, P. (1979). *Order in Court*. London: Macmillan.

Atkinson, J. M. and Heritage, J. (eds.) (1984). *Structures of Social Action: Studies in Conversation Analysis*. Cambridge: Cambridge University Press.

Atkinson, J. M. (1989). *The Art and Politics of Wana Shamanism*. Berkeley: University of California Press.

Atkinson, M. A., and Cuff, E. C. (1978). The Recommencement of a Meeting as a Member's Accomplishment. In J. Schenkein (ed.), *Studies in the Organization of Conversational Interaction* (pp. 133–153). New York: Academic Press.

Auer, P. (1984a). *Bilingual Conversation*. Amsterdam: John Benjamins.

Auer, P. (1984b). On the Meaning of Conversational Code-switching. In J. P. Auer and A. di Luzio (eds.), *Interpretive Sociolinguistics* (pp. 87–108). Tübingen: Gunter Narr Verlag.

Auer, P. (1990). Rhythm in Telephone Closings. *Human Studies* 13: 361–392.

Auer, P. (1991). Vom Ende deutscher Sätze. *Zeitschrift für Germanistische Linguistik* 19: 139–157.

Auer, P. (1998a). Introduction: *Bilingual Conversation* Revisited. In J. C. P. Auer (ed.), *Code-switching in Conversation* (pp. 1–24). London: Routledge.

Auer, P. (ed.) (1998b). *Code-switching in Conversation: Language, Interaction and Identity*. London: Routledge.

Auer, P., Couper-Kuhlen, E., and Müller, F. (1999). *Language in Time: The Rhythm and Tempo of Spoken Interaction*. Oxford: Oxford University Press.

Auer, P., and di Luzio, A. (eds.) (1992). *The Contextualization of Language*. Amsterdam: John Benjamins.

Auer, P., and Kern, F. (2000). Three Ways of Analysing Communication between East and

West Germans as Intercultural Communication. In A. di Luzio, S. Günthner and F. Orletti (eds.), *Culture in Communication: Analyses of Intercultural Situations* (pp. 89–116). Amsterdam: John Benjamins.

Auer, P., and Uhmann, S. (1982). Aspekte der konversationellen Organisation von Bewertungen [Aspects of the Conversational Organization of Assessments]. *Deutsche Sprache* 10: 1–32.

Austerlitz, R. (1983). Meaning in Music: Is Music Like a Language and If So, How? *American Journal of Semiotics* 2(3): 1–11.

Austin, J. L. (1961). *Philosophical Papers.* London: Oxford University Press.

Austin, J. L. (1962). *How to Do Things with Words.* Oxford: Oxford University Press.

Austin, J. L. (1975). *How to Do Things with Words* (2nd edn., J. O. Urmson and Marina Sbisà, eds.). Cambridge, MA: Harvard University Press.

Azhar, M. Z., and Varma, S. L. (1996). Relationship of Expressed Emotion with Relapse of Schizophrenia Patients in Kelantan. *Singapore Medical Journal* 37(1): 82–85.

Babalola, S. A. (1966). *The Content and Form of Yoruba Ijala.* Oxford: Oxford University Press.

Bagner, D. M., Melinder, R. D., and Barch, D. M. (2003). Language Comprehension and Working Memory Deficits in Patients with Schizophrenia. *Schizophrenia Research* 60(2–3): 299–309.

Bailey, B. (1997). Communication of Respect in Interethnic Service Encounters. *Language in Society* 26(3): 327–356.

Bailey, B. (1999). Switching. *Journal of Linguistic Anthropology* 9(1–2): 241–243.

Bailey, B. (2000a). Communicative Behavior and Conflict between African-American Customers and Korean Immigrant Retailers in Los Angeles. *Discourse & Society* 11(1): 87–108.

Bailey, B. (2000b). The Language of Multiple Identities among Dominican Americans. *Journal of Linguistic Anthropology* 10(2): 190–223.

Bailey, B. H. (2002). *Language, Race, and Negotiation of Identity: A Study of Dominican Americans.* New York: LFB Scholarly Publishing LLC.

Bailey, G., and Tillery, J. (1996). The Persistence of Southern American English. *Journal of English Linguistics* 24(4): 308–321.

Baker, C., and Battison, R. (eds.) (1980). *Sign Language and the Deaf Community: Essays in Honor of William C. Stokoe.* Silver Spring, MD: National Association of the Deaf.

Baker, C., and Cokely, D. (1980). *American Sign Language: A Teacher's Resource Text on Grammar and Culture.* Silver Spring, MD: TJ Publishers.

Baker, P. (1990). Off Target? *Journal of Pidgin and Creole Languages* 5(1): 107–120.

Bakhtin, M. (1981). *The Dialogic Imagination: Four Essays* (ed. M. Holquist, trans. C. Emerson and M. Holquist). Austin: University of Texas Press.

Bakhtin, M. (1984). *Problems of Dostoevsky's Poetics* (ed. and trans. C. Emerson. Introduction by W. C. Booth). Minneapolis: University of Minnesota Press.

Bakhtin, M. (1986). *Speech Genres and Other Late Essays* (trans. V. W. McGee). Austin: University of Texas Press.

Bakker, P., and Mous, M. (eds.) (1994). *Mixed Languages.* Amsterdam: Institute for Functional Research into Language and Language Use [IFOTT], University of Amsterdam.

Bakker, P., and Muysken, P. (1995). Mixed Languages and Language Intertwining. In J. Arends, P. Muysken, and N. Smith (eds.), *Pidgins and Creoles: An Introduction* (pp. 41–52). Amsterdam: John Benjamins.

Bamberg, M. (1996). Perspective and Agency in the Construal of Narrative Events. In A. Stringfellow, D. Cahana-Amitay, E. Hughes, and A. Zukowski (eds.), *Proceedings of the 20th Annual Boston University Conference on Language Development* (pp. 30–39). Sommerville, MA: Cascadilla Press.

Bamberg, M. (ed.) (1997). Oral Versions of Personal Experience: Three Decades of Narrative Analysis. *Journal of Narrative and Life History* 7(1–4) (Special Issue).

Banks, S., Ge, G., and Baker, J. (1991). Intercultural Encounters and Miscommunication. In N. Coupland, H. Giles, and J. Wiemann (eds.), *Miscommunication and Problematic Talk* (pp. 103–120). Newbury Park, CA: Sage.

Banti, G. (2001). Meter. In A. Duranti (ed.), *Key Terms in Language and Culture* (pp. 150–153). Malden, MA: Blackwell.

Banti, G., and Giannattasio, F. (1996). Music and Metre in Somali Poetry. In R. J. Hayward and I. M. Lewis (eds.), *Voice and Power: Essays in Honour of B. W. Andrzejewski* (pp. 83–127). *African Languages and Cultures*, supplement 3.

Baquedano-López, P. (1997). Creating Social Identities through *Doctrina* Narratives. *Issues in Applied Linguistics* 8(1): 27–45.

Baquedano-López, P. (1998). Language Socialization of Mexican Children in a Los Angeles

Catholic Parish. PhD thesis, University of California, Los Angeles.

Baquedano-López, P. (2000). Narrating Community in *doctrina* Classes. *Narrative Inquiry* 10(2): 1–24.

Baquedano-López, P., and Alvarez, H. (1999). Play, Challenge, and Collaboration at an Urban Elementary After-school Program. Paper presented at the American Educational Research Association (AERA) Conference, Montreal, Canada, April 23.

Baquedano-López, P., Alvarez, H., and Gutiérrez, K. (1998). Negotiating Fairness at an After-school Club. Paper presented at the 98th annual meeting of the American Anthropological Association, Philadelphia, December 5.

Bar-Hillel, Y. (1954). Indexical Expressions. *Mind* 63: 359–379.

Barrett, R. (1999). Indexing Polyphonous Identity in the Speech of African American Drag Queens. In M. Bucholtz, A. C. Liang, and L. Sutton (eds.), *Reinventing Identities: The Gendered Self in Discourse* (pp. 313–331). New York: Oxford University Press.

Barrett, R. J. (1988a). Clinical Writing and the Documentary Construction of Schizophrenia. *Culture, Medicine, and Psychiatry* 12: 265–299.

Barrett, R. J. (1988b). Interpretations of Schizophrenia. *Culture, Medicine, and Psychiatry* 12: 357–388.

Barrett, R. J. (1997) Cultural Formulation of Psychiatric Diagnosis. *Culture, Medicine, and Psychiatry* 21: 365–379.

Barrett, R. J. (1998). The "Schizophrenic" and the Liminal Persona in Modern Society. *Culture, Medicine, and Psychiatry* 22(4): 464–503.

Barth, F. (1986 [1972]). Ethnic Processes on the Pathan–Baluch Boundary. In J. Gumperz and D. Hymes (eds.), *Directions in Sociolinguistics: The Ethnography of Communication* (pp. 454–464). Oxford: Blackwell.

Barth, F. (1990). The Guru and the Conjurer: Transactions in Knowledge and the Shaping of Culture in Southeast Asia and Melanesia. *Man* (n.s.) 25: 640–653.

Barthes, R. (1977). The Grain of the Voice. In *Image, Music, Text* (pp. 179–189). London: Fontana.

Bartlett, B., and Bartlett, J. (1994). Engineer's Guide to Studio Jargon. *EQ* 5(2): 36–41.

Barwise, J., and Perry, J. (1983). *Situations and Attitudes*. Cambridge, MA: MIT Press.

Basso, E. B. (1985). *A Musical View of the Universe: Kalapalo Myth and Ritual Performances*. Philadelphia: University of Pennsylvania Press.

Basso, K. (1972). "To Give up on Words": Silence in Western Apache Culture. In P. P. Giglioli (ed.), *Language and Social Context* (pp. 67–86). Harmondsworth, Middlesex: Penguin Books.

Basso, K. (1974). The Ethnography of Writing. In R. Bauman and J. Sherzer (eds.), *Explorations in the Ethnography of Speaking* (pp. 425–432). Cambridge: Cambridge University Press.

Basso, K. (1979). *Portraits of the Whiteman*. Cambridge: Cambridge University Press.

Basso, K. (1988). "Speaking with Names": Language and Landscape among the Western Apache. *Cultural Anthropology* 3: 99–130.

Basso, K. H. (1990). *Western Apache Language and Culture: Essays in Linguistic Anthropology*. Tucson: University of Arizona Press.

Bateman, G. C. (1996). Attitudes of the Deaf Community towards Political Activism. In I. Parasnis (ed.), *Cultural and Language Diversity and the Deaf Experience* (pp. 146–159). Cambridge: Cambridge University Press.

Bates, E., Bretherton, I., Shore, C., and McNew, S. (1983). Names, Gestures, and Objects: Symbolization in Infancy and Aphasia. In K. E. Nelson (ed.), *Children's Language*, vol. 4 (pp. 59–123). Hillsdale, NJ: Lawrence Erlbaum.

Bates, E., and MacWhinney, B. (1982). Functionalist Approaches to Grammar. In E. Wanner and L. Gleitman (eds.), *Language Acquisition: The State of the Art* (pp. 173–218). Cambridge: Cambridge University Press.

Bateson, G. (1936). *Naven. A Survey of the Problems Suggested by a Composite Picture of the Culture of a New Guinea Tribe Drawn from Three Points of View*. Cambridge: Cambridge University Press [2nd edn, Stanford University Press, 1958].

Bateson, G. (1972). *Steps to an Ecology of Mind*. New York: Ballantine Books.

Battison, R. (1978). *Lexical Borrowing in American Sign Language*. Silver Spring, MD: Linstok Press.

Battistella, E. L. (1990). *Markedness: The Evaluative Superstructure of Language*. Albany: SUNY Press.

Battistella, E. L. (1996). *The Logic of Markedness*. New York: Oxford University Press.

Baugh, J. (1983). *Black Street Speech: Its History, Structure, and Survival*. Austin: University of Texas Press.

Baugh, J. (1999). *Out of the Mouths of Slaves. African American Language and Educational Malpractice*. Austin: University of Texas Press.

Baugh, J., and Sherzer, J. (eds.) (1984). *Language Use: Readings in Sociolinguistics*. Englewood Cliffs, NJ: Prentice-Hall.

Bauman, R. (1975). Verbal Art as Performance. *American Anthropologist* 77: 290–311.

Bauman, R. (1977). *Verbal Art as Performance*. Rowley, MA: Newbury House.

Bauman, R. (1983). *Let Your Words Be Few: Symbolism of Speaking and Silence among Seventeenth Century Quakers*. Cambridge: Cambridge University Press.

Bauman, R. (1986). *Story, Performance, and Event*. Cambridge: Cambridge University Press.

Bauman, R. (ed.) (1992a). *Folklore, Cultural Performances, and Popular Entertainments: A Communications-Centered Handbook*. New York: Oxford University Press.

Bauman, R. (1992b). Contextualization, Tradition and the Dialogue of Genres: Icelandic Legends of the *Kraftaskáld*. In A. Duranti and C. Goodwin (eds.), *Rethinking Context: Language as an Interactive Phenomenon* (pp. 125–145). Cambridge: Cambridge University Press.

Bauman, R. (1993). Disclaimers of Performance. In J. Hill and J. T. Irvine (eds.), *Responsibility and Evidence in Oral Discourse* (pp. 182–196). Cambridge: Cambridge University Press.

Bauman, R. (1996). "Any Man Who Keeps More'n One Hound'll Lie to You": A Contextual Study of Expressive Lying. In D. Brenneis and R. Macaulay (eds.), *The Matrix of Language* (pp. 160–181). Boulder, CO: Westview Press.

Bauman, R., and Briggs, C. L. (1990). Poetics and Performance as Critical Perspectives on Language and Social Life. *Annual Review of Anthropology* 19: 59–88.

Bauman, R., and Briggs, C. L. (2000). Language Philosophy as Language Ideology: John Locke and Johann Gottfried Herder. In P. V. Kroskrity (ed.), *Regimes of Language: Ideologies, Polities, and Identities* (pp. 139–204). Santa Fe, NM: School of American Research Press.

Bauman, R., and Briggs, C. L. (2003). *Voices of Modernity: Language Ideologies and the Politics of Inequality*. Cambridge: Cambridge University Press.

Bauman, R., and Sherzer, J. (1974). *Explorations in the Ethnography of Speaking*. Cambridge: Cambridge University Press [2nd edn, 1989].

Bauman, R., and Sherzer, J. (eds.) (1975). The Ethnography of Speaking. *Annual Reviews* 4: 95–119.

Baynton, D. (1996). *Forbidden Signs: American Culture and the Campaign against Sign Language*. Chicago: University of Chicago Press.

Beach, W. (2001). Lay Diagnosis. *Text* 21(1/2).

Becka, S. (1987). Interkulturelle Probleme in der Beratung – eine Fallstudie. *Osnabrücker Beiträge zur Sprachtheorie (OBST)* 38: 53–67.

Becker, A. L. (1979). Text-building, Epistemology, and Aesthetics in Javanese Shadow Theatre. In A. L. Becker and A. Yengoyan (eds.), *The Imagination of Reality* (pp. 211–243). Norwood, NJ: Ablex.

Becker, A. L., and Becker, J. (1979). A Grammar of the Musical Genre Srepegan. *Journal of Music Theory* 23(1): 1–43.

Beebe, L.M., and Giles, H. (1984). Speech Accommodation Theories: A Discussion in Terms of Second Language Acquisition. *International Journal of the Sociology of Language* 46: 5–32.

Beeman, W. (1993). The Anthropology of Theater and Spectacle. *Annual Review of Anthropology* 22: 369–393.

Beeman, W. (2001). Humor. In A. Duranti (ed.), *Key Terms in Language and Culture* (pp. 98–101). Malden, MA: Blackwell.

Behar, R., and Gordon, D. (eds.) (1995). *Women Writing Culture*. Berkeley: University of California Press.

Beier, L. (1995). Anti-language or Jargon? Canting in the English Underworld in the Sixteenth and Seventeenth Centuries. In P. Burke and R. Porter (eds.), *Languages and Jargons: Contributions to a Social History of Language* (pp. 64–101). Cambridge: Polity Press.

Bell, A. (1984). Language Style as Audience Design. *Language in Society* 13: 145–204.

Bell, A. (1992). Hit and Miss: Referee Design in the Dialects of New Zealand Television Advertisements. *Language and Communication* 12(3/4): 327–340.

Bell, C. (1987). Ritualization of Texts and the Textualization of Religion. *History of Religions* 27: 366–392.

Ben-Amos, D. (1972). Toward a Definition of Folklore in Context. In A. Parades and R. Bauman (eds.), *Toward New Perspectives in Folklore* (pp. 3–15). Austin: University of Texas Press.

Ben-Amos, D. (1975). *Sweet Words: Storytelling Events in Benin*. Philadelphia: ISHI.

Ben-Amos, D. (2001). Metaphor. In A. Duranti (ed.), *Key Terms in Language and Culture* (pp. 147–149). Malden, MA: Blackwell.

Ben-Amos, D., and Goldstein, K. (1975). *Folklore: Performance and Communication*. The Hague: Mouton.

Benveniste, É. (1946). Les relations de personne dans le verbe. *BSL* 43: 1–12.

Benveniste, É. (1966). *Problèmes de linguistique générale*. Paris: Gallimard.

Benveniste, É. (1969). *Le Vocabulaire des insitutions indo-européenes*. Paris: Éditions de Minuit.

Benveniste, É. (1971). *Problems of General Linguistics*. Miami: University of Miami Press.

Berdan, F., and Anawalt, P. R. (1992). *Codex Mendoza*, 4 vols. Berkeley: University of California Press.

Berens, F. J. (1981). Dialogeröffnungen in Telefongesprächen: Handlungen und Handlungsschemata der Herstellung sozialer und kommunikativer Beziehungen. In P. Schröder and H. Steger (eds.), *Dialogforschung* (pp. 402–417). Jahrbuch 1980 des Instituts für deutsche Sprache. Düsseldorf: Pädagogischer Verlag Schwann.

Bergmann, J. R. (1981). Ethnomethodologische Konversationsanalyse. In P. Schröder and H. Steger (eds.), *Dialogforschung* (pp. 9–51). Jahrbuch 1980 des Instituts für deutsche Sprache. Düsseldorf: Pädagogischer Verlag Schwann.

Bergmann, J. R. (1987). *Klatsch. Zur Sozialform der diskreten Indiskretion*. Berlin and New York: de Gruyter.

Bergmann, J. R. (1988). Haustiere als kommunikative Ressourcen. Soziale Welt. *Zeitschrift für sozialwissenschaftliche Forschung und Praxis* Special Issue 6: *Kultur und Alltag*.

Bergmann, J. R. (1990). On the Local Sensitivity of Conversation. In I. Markovà and K. Foppa (eds.), *The Dynamics of Dialogue* (pp. 201–226). New York: Harvester Wheatsheaf.

Bergmann, J. R. (1992). Veiled Morality: Notes on Discretion in Psychiatry. In P. Drew and J. Heritage (eds.), *Talk at Work: Interactions in Institutional Settings* (pp. 137–162). Cambridge: Cambridge University Press.

Bergmann, J. R. (1993). *Discreet Indiscretions: The Social Organization of Gossip*. New York: Aldine de Gruyter.

Bergmann, J. R. (1998). Das Subsidiaritätsprinzip – zwischen Sozialstaat und Lebenswelt. In A. Evers (ed.), *Sozialstaat* (pp. 240–263). Gießen: Ferber.

Bergmann, J. R., and Linnell, P. (eds.) (1998). Morality in Discourse. In Special Issue of *Research on Language and Social Interaction* 31(3/4): 279–472.

Bergmann, J. R., and Luckmann, T. (eds.) (1999). *Kommunikative Konstruktion von Moral*, Bd. 1: *Struktur und Dynamik der Formen moralischer Kommunikation*. Opladen: Westdeutscher Verlag.

Berko Gleason, J., and Melzi, G. (1997). The Mutual Construction of Narrative by Mothers and Children: Cross-cultural Observations. *Journal of Narrative and Life History* 7(1–4): 217–222.

Berk-Seligson, S. (1990). *The Bilingual Courtroom: Court Interpretation in the Judicial Process*. Chicago: University of Chicago Press.

Berlim, M. T., Mattevi, B. S., Belmonte-DeAbreu, P., and Crow, T. J. (2003). The Etiology of Schizophrenia and the Origin of Language: Overview of a Theory. *Comprehensive Psychiatry* 44: 7–14.

Berlin, B. (1974). Further Notes on Covert Categories and Folk Taxonomies: A Reply to Brown. *American Anthropologist* 76: 327–331.

Berlin, B. (1975). Speculations on the Growth of Ethnobotanical Nomenclature. In B. G. Blount and M. Sanchez (eds.), *Sociocultural Dimensions of Language Change* (pp. 63–101). New York: Academic Press.

Berlin, B. (1992). *Ethnobiological Classification: Principles of Categorization of Plants and Animals in Traditional Societies*. Princeton, NJ: Princeton University Press.

Berlin, B. (1994). Evidence for Pervasive Synesthetic Sound Symbolism in Ethnozoological Nomenclature. In L. Hinton, J. Nichols, and J. Ohala (eds.), *Sound Symbolism* (pp. 76–93). Cambridge: Cambridge University Press.

Berlin, B., and Kay, P. (1967). *Universality and Evolution of Basic Color Terms*. Working Paper #1, Laboratory for Language Behavior Research, University of California, Berkeley.

Berlin, B., and Kay, P. (1969). *Basic Color Terms: Their Universality and Evolution*. Berkeley: University of California Press.

Berlin, B., and O'Neill, J. (1981). The Pervasiveness of Onomatopoeia in the Jivaroan

Language Family. *Journal of Ethnobiology* 1: 95–108.

Berman, R. (1995). Narrative Competence and Storytelling Performance: How Children Tell Stories in Different Contexts. *Journal of Narrative and Life History* 5(4): 285–314.

Berman, R. A., and Slobin, D. I. (1994). *Relating Events in Narrative: A Crosslinguistic Developmental Study.* Hillsdale, NJ: Lawrence Erlbaum.

Bernardelli, A., and Blasi, G. (1995). Introduction. Semiotics and the Effects-of-Media-Change Research Programmes. An Overview of Methodology and Basic Concepts. In G. Blasi and A. Bernardelli (eds.), *Semiotics and the Effect-of-Media-Change Research Programmes.* Special Issue, *Versus. Quaderni di studi semiotici* 72: 3–28.

Bernstein, B. (1972). Social Class, Language and Socialization. In P. P. Giglioli (ed.), *Language and Social Context* (pp. 157–179). New York: Penguin.

Bernstein, C., Nunnally, T., and Sabino, R. (eds.) (1997). *Language Variety in the South Revisited.* Tuscaloosa: University of Alabama Press.

Bernstein, M. A. (1994). *Foregone Conclusions: Against Apocalyptic History.* Berkeley: University of California Press.

Berthoff, A. (ed.) (1984). *Reclaiming the Imagination: Philosophical Perspectives for Writers and Teachers of Writing.* Montclair, NJ: Boynton Cook.

Besnier, N. (1989). Information Withholding as a Manipulative and Collusive Strategy in Nukulaelae Gossip. *Language in Society* 18: 315–341.

Besnier, N. (1990). Language and Affect. *Annual Review of Anthropology* 19: 419–451.

Besnier, N. (1993). The Demise of the Man Who Would Be King: Sorcery and Ambition on Nukulaelae Atoll. *Journal of Anthropological Research* 49: 185–215.

Besnier, N. (1994). The Truth and Other Irrelevant Aspects of Nukulaelae Gossip. *Pacific Studies* 17(3): 1–39.

Besnier, N. (1995). *Literacy, Emotion, and Authority: Reading and Writing on a Polynesian Atoll.* Cambridge: Cambridge University Press.

Besnier, N. (1997). Sluts and Superwomen: The Politics of Gender Liminality in Urban Tonga. *Ethnos* 62: 5–31.

Besnier, N. (2000). *Tuvaluan: A Polynesian Language of the Central Pacific.* London and New York: Routledge.

Besnier, N. (2001). Literacy. In A. Duranti (ed.), *Key Terms in Language and Culture* (pp. 136–138). Malden, MA: Blackwell.

Bex, T. (1996). Cohesion, Coherence and Register. In T. Bex, *Variety in Written English*, ch. 5 (pp. 90–112). London: Routledge.

Bhabha, H. (1990). *Nation and Narration.* New York: Routledge.

Bhabha, H. (1994). *The Location of Culture.* London: Routledge.

Bhattacharyya, D. (1986). *Pagalami: Ethnopsychiatric Knowledge in Bengal*, vol. 11. Syracuse: Maxwell School of Citizenship and Public Affairs.

Bhimji, F. (2002). "*Dile* family": Socializing Language Skills with Directives in Three Mexican Families in South Central Los Angeles. PhD dissertation, University of California, Los Angeles.

Bialystok, E. (1984). Strategies in Interlanguage Learning and Performance. In A. Davies, C. Criper, and A. P. R. Howatt (eds.), *Interlanguage* (pp. 37–48). Edinburgh: Edinburgh University Press.

Bialystok, E. (1990). *Communication Strategies: A Psychological Analysis of Second-Language Use.* Oxford: Blackwell.

Biber, D. (1988). *Variation across Speech and Writing.* Cambridge: Cambridge University Press.

Biber, D. (1994). An Analytic Framework for Register Studies. In D. Biber and E. Finegan (eds.), *Sociolinguistic Perspectives on Register* (pp. 31–56). New York: Oxford University Press.

Biber, D., and Finegan, E. (eds.) (1994). *Sociolinguistic Perspectives on Register.* New York: Oxford University Press.

Bickerton, D. (1981). *Roots of Language.* Ann Arbor: Karoma.

Bickerton, D. (1984). The Language Bioprogram Hypothesis. *The Behavioral and Brain Sciences* 7: 173–221.

Biesold, H. (1999). *Crying Hands: Eugenics and Deaf People in Nazi Germany* (trans. W. Sayers). Washington, DC: Gallaudet University Press.

Billig, M. (1997). The Dialogic Unconscious: Psychoanalysis, Discursive Psychology and the Nature of Repression. *British Journal of Social Psychology* 36: 139–159.

Billig, M. (1999). *Freudian Repression: Conversation Creating the Unconscious.* Cambridge: Cambridge University Press.

Bing, J. M., and Bergvall, V. L. (1996). The Question of Questions: Beyond Binary Thinking. In V. L. Bergvall, J. M. Bing, and A. F. Freed (eds.), *Rethinking Language and Gender Research: Theory and Practice* (pp. 1–30). London: Longman.

Blacking, J. (1971). Deep and Surface Structures in Venda Music. *Yearbook of the International Folk Music Council,* 3: 91–108.

Blacking, J. (1981). The Problem of "Ethnic" Perceptions in the Semiotics of Music. In W. Steiner (ed.), *The Sign in Music and Literature* (pp. 184–194). Austin: University of Texas Press.

Blacking, J. (1982). The Structure of Musical Discourse: The Problem of the Song Text. *Yearbook for Traditional Music* 14: 15–23.

Blackmer, E. R., and Mitton, J. L. (1991). Theories of Monitoring and the Timing of Repairs in Spontaneous Speech. *Cognition* 39: 173–194.

Blackshire-Belay, C. (1993). Foreign Workers' German: Is It a Pidgin? In F. Byrne and J. Holm (eds.), *Atlantic Meets Pacific: A Global View of Pidginization and Creolization* (pp. 431–440). Amsterdam: John Benjamins.

Bloch, M. (1974). Symbols, Song, Dance and Features of Articulation. Is Religion an Extreme Form of Traditional Authority? *Archives Européennes de Sociologie* XV(1): 55–81.

Bloch, M. (1975a). Introduction. In M. Bloch (ed.), *Political Language and Oratory in Traditional Society* (pp. 1–28). London: Academic Press.

Bloch, M. (1975b). *Political Language and Oratory in Traditional Society.* London: Academic Press.

Bloch, M. (1976). Review of R. Bauman and J. Sherzer (eds.), *Explorations in the Ethnography of Speaking. Language in Society* 5: 229–234.

Blom, J. P., and Gumperz, J. J. (1972). Social Meaning in Linguistic Structures: Code Switching in Norway. In J. J. Gumperz and D. Hymes (eds.), *Directions in Sociolinguistics: The Ethnography of Communication* (pp. 407–434). New York: Holt.

Blommaert, J. (ed.) (1999a). *Language Ideological Debates.* Berlin: Mouton de Gruyter.

Blommaert, J. (1999b). The Debate is Open. In J. Blommaert (ed.), *Language Ideological Debates* (pp. 1–38). Berlin: Mouton de Gruyter.

Blommaert, J. (1999c). *State Ideology and Language in Tanzania.* Cologne: Rudiger Koppe Verlag.

Blommaert, J., and Bulcaen, C. (2000). Critical Discourse Analysis. *Annual Review of Anthropology* 29: 447–466.

Blommaert, J., Collins, J., Heller, M., Rampton, B., Slembrouck, S., and Verschueren, J. (2001). Introduction to Discourse and Critique: Part One. *Critique of Anthropology* 21(1): 5–12.

Blommaert, J., and Verschueren, J. (1998). The Role of Language in European Nationalist Ideologies. In B. B. Schieffelin, K. A. Woolard, and P. V. Kroskrity (eds.), *Language Ideologies: Practice and Theory* (pp. 189–210). New York: Oxford University Press.

Bloomfield, L. (1935). *Language.* London: Allen & Unwin.

Bloomfield, L. (1944). Secondary and Tertiary Responses to Language. *Language* 20: 44–55.

Bloomfield, L. (1987 [1927]). Literate and Illiterate Speech. In C. F. Hockett (ed.), *A Leonard Bloomfield Anthology* (pp. 84–93). Chicago: University of Chicago Press.

Blount, B. G. (1995a). Parental Speech and Language Acquisition: An Anthropological Perspective. In B. G. Blount (ed.), *Language, Culture, and Society. A Book of Readings* (pp. 551–566). Prospect Heights, IL: Waveland Press.

Blount, B. G. (ed.) (1995b). *Language, Culture, and Society. A Book of Readings* (2nd edn). Prospect Heights, IL: Waveland Press.

Blum-Kulka, S., Danet, B., and Gerson, R. (1985). The Language of Requesting in Israeli Society. In J. Forgas (ed.), *Language in Social Situations* (pp. 113–139). Berlin: Springer.

Blum-Kulka, S., and Olshtain, E. (1984). Requests and Apologies: A Cross-Cultural Study of Speech Act Realization Patterns. *Applied Linguistics* 5: 196–213.

Blum-Kulka, S., and Snow, C. E. (1992). Developing Autonomy for Tellers, Tales, and Telling in Family Narrative Events. *Journal of Narrative and Life History* 2: 187–217.

Blust, R. (1995). The Prehistory of the Austronesian-Speaking Peoples: A View from Language. *Journal of World Prehistory* 9: 453–510.

Boas, F. (1889). On Alternating Sounds. *American Anthropologist* 2 (o.s.): 47–53.

Boas, F. (1900). Sketch of the Kwakiutl Language. *American Anthropologist* 2(4): 708–721.

Boas, F. (ed.) (1911a). *Handbook of American Indian Languages*, Part 1. Bureau of American Ethnology Bulletin 40. Washington, DC: Smithsonian Institution and Bureau of American Ethnology.

Boas, F. (1911b). Introduction. In F. Boas (ed.), *Handbook of American Indian Languages*, Part 1. Bureau of American Ethnology Bulletin 40. Washington, DC: Smithsonian Institution and Bureau of American Ethnology.

Boas, F. (1917). Introduction. *International Journal of American Linguistics* 1: 1–8.

Boas, F. (ed.) (1922). *Handbook of American Indian Languages*, Part 2. Bureau of American Ethnology Bulletin 40. Washington, DC: Government Printing Office.

Boas, F. (1925). Stylistic Aspects of Primitive Literature. *Journal of American Folk-Lore* 38: 329–339.

Boas, F. (1940). *Race, Language, and Culture*. New York: The Free Press.

Boden, D., and Zimmerman, D. H. (eds.) (1991). *Talk and Social Structure: Studies in Ethnomethodology and Conversation Analysis*. Berkeley: University of California Press.

Boggs, S. (1972). The Meaning of Questions and Narratives to Hawaiian Children. In C. Cazden, V. John, and D. Hymes (eds.), *Functions of Language in the Classroom*. Prospect Heights, IL: Waveland Press.

Boiles, C. (1982). Processes of Musical Semiosis. *Yearbook for Traditional Music* 14: 24–44.

Bolinger, D. (1950). Rime, Assonance, and Morpheme Analysis. *Word* 6: 117–136.

Bolinger, D. (1989). *Intonation and its Uses*. Stanford: Stanford University Press.

Bolinger, D. (1992). Sound Symbolism. In W. Bright (ed.), *International Encyclopedia of Linguistics*, vol. 4 (pp. 28–30). Cambridge: Cambridge University Press.

Bonner, D. (2001). Garifuna Children's Language Shame: Ethnic Stereotypes, National Affiliation, and Transnational Migration as Factors in Language Choice in Southern Belize. *Language in Society* 30: 81–96.

Borker, R. A. (1986) "Moved by the Spirit": Constructing Meaning in a Brethren Breaking of Bread Service. *Text* 6: 317–337.

Bourdieu, P. (1972). *Esquisse d'une theorie de la pratique. Précédée de trois études d'ethnologie kabyle*. Geneva: Droz.

Bourdieu, P. (1977a). The Economics of Linguistic Exchanges. *Social Science Information* 16(6): 645–668.

Bourdieu, P. (1977b). *Outline of a Theory of Practice* (trans. R. Nice). Cambridge: Cambridge University Press.

Bourdieu, P. (1982). *Ce que parler veut dire*. Paris: Fayard.

Bourdieu, P. (1984). *Distinction: A Social Critique of the Judgment of Taste*. Cambridge, MA: Harvard University Press.

Bourdieu, P. (1986). The Forms of Capital. In J. Richardson (ed.), *Handbook of Theory and Research for the Sociology of Education* (pp. 241–258). New York: Greenwood Press.

Bourdieu, P. (1990). *The Logic of Practice*. Stanford: Stanford University Press.

Bourdieu, P. (1991). *Language and Symbolic Power* (trans. G. Raymond and M. Adamson). Cambridge, MA: Harvard University Press.

Bourdieu, P. (2000). *Pascalian Meditations*. Stanford: Stanford University Press.

Bourdieu, P., and Passeron, J.-C. (1977). *Reproduction in Education, Society, and Culture*. London: Sage.

Bowen, J. R. (1993). *Salat* in Indonesia: The Social Meaning of an Islamic Ritual. *Man* (n.s.) 24: 600–619.

Boyer, P. (1994). *The Naturalness of Religious Ideas: A Cognitive Theory of Religion*. Berkeley: University of California Press.

Boyes Braem, P., Caramore, B., Hermann, R., and Hermann, P. (2003). Romance and Reality: Sociolinguistic Similarities and Differences between Swiss German Sign Language and Rhaeto-Romansh. In L. Monaghan, C. Schmaling, K. Nakamura, and G. H. Turner (eds.), *Many Ways to be Deaf*. Washington, DC: Gallaudet University Press.

Bradshaw, J. L. (1998). Schizophrenia as Failure of Hemispheric Dominance for Language: Comment on Crow. *Trends in Neurosciences* 21(4): 145–146.

Brăiloiu, C. (1948). Le giusto syllabique bichrone. Un système rythmique propre à la musique populaire roumaine. *Polyphonie* 2: 26–57 [rev. as "Le giusto syllabique. Un système rythmique populaire roumaine", *Anuario Musical* 8 (1952): 117–158; repr. in Brăiloiu (1973), pp. 151–194].

Brăiloiu, C. (1954). Le vers populaire roumain chanté. *Revue des Etudes Roumaines* 2: 7–74. Paris: Edition de l'Institut universitaire roumain [repr. in Brăiloiu (1973), pp. 195–264].

Brăiloiu, C. (1956). Le rythme enfantin: notions liminaires. *Le Colloques de Wegimont: Eth-*

nomusicologie 1 (pp. 64–96). Paris-Bruxelles: Elsevier [repr. as "La rythmique enfantine. Notions liminaires" in Brăiloiu (1973), pp. 265–299].

Brăiloiu, C. (1973). *Problèmes d'ethnomusicologie* (ed. G. Rouget). Geneva: Minkoff Reprint.

Branson, J., Miller, D., Marsaja, I G., and Negara, I W. (1996). Everyone Here Speaks Sign Language, Too: A Deaf Village in Bali, Indonesia. In C. Lucas (ed.), *Multicultural Aspects of Sociolinguistics in Deaf Communities*. Washington, DC: Gallaudet University Press.

Bråten, S. (ed.) (1998a). *Intersubjective Communication and Emotion in Early Ontogeny*. Studies in Emotion and Social Interaction (Second Series). Cambridge: Cambridge University Press/Editions de la Maison de Sciences de l'Homme.

Bråten, S. (1998b). Infant Learning by Altercentric Participation: The Reverse of Egocentric Observation in Autism. In S. Bråten (ed.), *Intersubjective Communication and Emotion in Early Ontogeny* (pp. 105–124). Studies in Emotion and Social Interaction (Second Series). Cambridge: Cambridge University Press/Editions de la Maison de Sciences de l'Homme.

Braunschweig, A. (1983). Zum Verhältnis von Haupt-und Nebenkommunikation im Unterricht. In K. Ehlich and J. Rehbein (eds.), *Kommunikation in Schule und Hochschule: Linguistische und ethnomethodologische Analysen* (pp. 102–129). Tübingen: Gunter Narr Verlag.

Brennan, M. (1992). The Visual World of British Sign Language: An Introduction. In D. Brien (ed.), *Dictionary of British Sign Language/English* (pp. 1–133). London: Faber and Faber.

Brenneis, D. (1978). The Matter of Talk: Political Performance in Bhatgaon. *Language in Society* 7: 159–170.

Brenneis, D. (1980). Fighting Words. In J. Cherfas and R. Lewin (eds.), *Not Work Alone: A Cross-Cultural View of Activities Superfluous to Survival* (pp. 166–180). London: Temple Smith.

Brenneis, D. (1986a). Shared Territory: Audience, Indirection and Meaning. *Text* 6(3): 339–347.

Brenneis, D. (1986b). The Fiji Pancayat as Therapeutic Discourse. *IPrA Papers in Pragmatics* 1(1): 55–78.

Brenneis, D. (1987). Performing Passions: Aesthetics and Politics in an Occasionally Egali-

tarian Community. *American Ethnologist* 14: 236–250.

Brenneis, D. (1988). Language and Disputing. *Annual Review of Anthropology* 17: 221–237.

Brenneis, D. (1996). Grog and Gossip in Bhatgaon: Style and Substance in Fiji Indian Conversation. In D. Brenneis and R. Macaulay (eds.), *The Matrix of Language: Contemporary Linguistic Anthropology* (pp. 209–233). Boulder, CO: Westview Press.

Brenneis, D., and Lein, L. (1977). "You Fruithead": A Sociolinguistic Approach to Children's Disputes. In S. Ervin-Tripp and C. Mitchell-Kernan (eds.), *Child Discourse* (pp. 49–66). New York: Academic Press.

Brenneis, D., and Macaulay, R. H. S. (eds.) (1996). *The Matrix of Language: Contemporary Linguistic Anthropology*. Boulder, CO: Westview Press.

Brenneis, D. L., and Myers, F. (eds.) (1984). *Dangerous Words: Language and Politics in the Pacific*. New York: New York University.

Briggs, C. L. (1986). *Learning How to Ask: A Sociolinguistic Appraisal of the Role of the Interview in Social Science Research*. Cambridge: Cambridge University Press.

Briggs, C. L. (1992a). Linguistic Ideologies and the Naturalization of Power in Warao Discourse. *Pragmatics* 2: 387–404.

Briggs, C. L. (1992b). "Since I am a Woman I will Chastise My Relatives": Gender, Reported Speech, and the (Re)production of Social Relations in Warao Ritual Wailing. *American Ethnologist* 19(2): 337–361.

Briggs, C. L. (1993a). Generic versus Metapragmatic Dimensions of Warao Narratives: Who Regiments Performance. In J. A. Lucy (ed.), *Reflexive Language: Reported Speech and Metapragmatics*. Cambridge: Cambridge University Press.

Briggs, C. L. (1993b). Personal Sentiments and Polyphonic Voices in Warao Women's Ritual Wailing: Music and Poetics in a Critical and Collective Discourse. *American Anthropologist* 95(4): 929–957.

Briggs, C. L. (1998). "You're a Liar – You're Just Like a Woman!" Constructing Dominant Ideologies of Language in Warao Men's Gossip. In B. B. Schieffelin, K. A. Woolard, and P. V. Kroskrity (eds.), *Language Ideologies: Practice and Theory* (pp. 229–255). New York: Oxford University Press.

Briggs, C. L. (2002). Linguistic Magic Bullets in the Making of a Modernist Anthropology. *American Anthropologist* 104: 481–498.

Briggs, C. L., and Bauman, R. (1992). Genre, Intertextuality, and Social Power. *Journal of Linguistic Anthropology* 2(2): 131–172.

Briggs, C. L., and Bauman, R. (1999). The Foundation of All Future Researches: Franz Boas, George Hunt and the Textual Construction of Modernity. *American Quarterly* 51: 479–528.

Briggs, J. (1998). *Inuit Morality Play: The Emotional Education of a Three-Year-Old.* New Haven: Yale University Press.

Bright, W. (1960a). Animals of Acculturation in the California Indian Languages. *University of California Publications in Linguistics* 4: 215–246.

Bright, W. (1960b). Linguistic Change in Some Indian Caste Dialects. In C. A. Ferguson and J. J. Gumperz (eds.), *Linguistic Diversity in South Asia: Studies in Regional, Social and Functional Variation* (pp. 19–26). Indiana University Research Center in Anthropology, Folklore, and Linguistics: *International Journal of American Linguistics* 26.

Bright, W. (1963). Language and Music: Areas for Cooperation. *Ethnomusicology* 7(1): 23–32.

Bright, W. (ed.) (1966). *Sociolinguistics: Proceedings of the UCLA Sociolinguistics Conference, 1964.* The Hague: Mouton.

Bright, W. (1984). *American Indian Linguistics and Literature.* Berlin and New York: Mouton.

Bright, W. (1990). *Language Variation in South Asia.* New York: Oxford University Press.

Brinker, K., and Sager, S. F. (1996). *Linguistische Gesprächsanalyse: eine Einführung.* Berlin: Erich Schmidt Verlag.

Brison, K. J. (1992). *Just Talk: Gossip, Meetings, and Power in a Papua New Guinea Village.* Berkeley: University of California Press.

Brison, K. J. (2001). Constructing Identity through Ceremonial Language in Rural Fiji. *Ethnology* 40: 309–327.

Brogan, T. V. F. (1993a). Poetry. In A. Preminger and T. V. F. Brogan (eds.), *The New Princeton Encyclopedia of Poetry and Poetics* (pp. 938–942). Princeton, NJ: Princeton University Press.

Brogan, T. V. F. (1993b). Verse and Prose. In A. Preminger and T. V. F. Brogan (eds.), *The New Princeton Encyclopedia of Poetry and Poetics* (pp. 1346–1351). Princeton, NJ: Princeton University Press.

Brose, H.-G., and Holtgrewe, U. (in progress). *Call Centers: Organisational Interfaces in between Neo-Taylorism and Customer Orientation.* DFG-Projekt.

Brown, C. H. (1974). Unique Beginners and Covert Categories in Folk Biological Taxonomies. *American Anthropologist* 76: 325–327.

Brown, C. H. (1999). *Lexical Acculturation in Native American Languages.* New York: Oxford University Press.

Brown, G., and Yule, G. (1983). *Discourse Analysis.* Cambridge: Cambridge University Press.

Brown, P. (1993). Gender, Politeness, and Confrontation in Tenejapa. In D. Tannen (ed.), *Gender and Conversational Interaction* (pp. 144–162). New York: Oxford University Press.

Brown, P. (1998). Conversational Structure and Language Acquisition: The Role of Repetition in Tzeltal. *Journal of Linguistic Anthropology* 8(2): 197–221.

Brown, P., and Levinson, S. C. (1978). Universals of Language Usage: Politeness Phenomena. In E. N. Goody (ed.), *Questions and Politeness Strategies in Social Interaction* (pp. 56–289). Cambridge: Cambridge University Press.

Brown, P., and Levinson, S. C. (1987). *Politeness: Some Universals in Language Usage.* Cambridge: Cambridge University Press. [Reprint of Brown and Levinson 1987, with new Introduction.]

Brown, R. (1973). Schizophrenia, Language, and Reality. *American Psychologist* 28: 395–403.

Bruner, J. (1990). *Acts of Meaning.* Cambridge, MA: Harvard University Press.

Bruner, J. (1991). The Narrative Construction of Reality. *Critical Inquiry* 18: 1–21.

Bruner, J. (2002). *Making Stories: Law, Literature, Life.* New York: Farrar, Strauss & Giroux.

Bruner, J., and Lucariello, J. (1989). Monologue as Narrative Recreation of the World. In K. Nelson (ed.), *Narratives from the Crib* (pp. 73–98). Cambridge, MA: Harvard University Press.

Bucholtz, M. (1996). Black Feminist Theory and African American Women's Linguistic Practice. In V. L. Bergvall, J. M. Bing, and A. F. Freed (eds.), *Rethinking Language and Gender Research: Theory and Practice* (pp. 267–290). London: Longman.

Bucholtz, M. (1999a). "Why Be Normal?": Language and Identity Practices in a Community of Nerd Girls. *Language in Society* 28(2): 203–223.

Bucholtz, M. (1999b). You Da Man: Narrating the Racial Other in the Linguistic Production of White Masculinity. *Journal of Sociolinguistics* 3: 443–460.

Bucholtz, M. (2001). The Whiteness of Nerds: Superstandard English and Racial Markedness. *Journal of Linguistic Anthropology* 11(1): 84–100.

Bucholtz, M., and Hall, K. (1995). Introduction: Twenty Years after *Language and Woman's Place*. In K. Hall and M. Bucholtz (eds.), *Gender Articulated: Language and the Socially Constructed Self* (pp. 1–22). New York: Routledge.

Bucholtz, M., and Hall, K. (2004). Theorizing Identity in Language and Sexuality Research. *Language in Society*.

Bucholtz, M., and Trechter, S. (eds.) (2001). *Journal of Linguistic Anthropology* 11(1): Special Issue, Discourses of Whiteness.

Budwig, N. (2001). Language Socialization and Children's Entry into Schooling (Preface to Special Issue). *Early Education and Development* 12(3): 295–302.

Bühler, K. (1934). *Sprachtheorie. Die Darstellungsfunktion der Sprache*. Jena: Gustav Fischer.

Bühler, K. (1990). *Theory of Language: The Representational Function of Language* (trans. D. F. Goodwin). Amsterdam and Philadelphia: John Benjamins.

Bunzel, R. L. (1932). Zuni Ritual Poetry. *47th Report of the Bureau of American Ethnology, 1929–1930*. Washington, DC: Smithsonian Institution Press.

Burke, K. (1962). *A Grammar of Motives and a Rhetoric of Motives*. Cleveland and New York: Meridian Books.

Burns, S. E. (1998). Ireland's Second Minority Language. In C. Lucas (ed.), *Pinky Extension and Eye Gaze: Language Use in Deaf Communities* (pp. 233–273). Washington, DC: Gallaudet University Press.

Burrows, D. (1990). *Sound, Speech and Music*. Amherst: University of Massachusetts Press.

Busnel, R. (1966). Information in the Human Whistled Language and Sea Mammal Whistling. In K. Norris (ed.), *Whales, Dolphins, and Porpoises* (pp. 544–568). Berkeley: University of California Press.

Butler, J. (1990). *Gender Trouble: Feminism and the Subversion of Identity*. New York: Routledge.

Butler, J. (1993). *Bodies That Matter*. New York: Routledge.

Button, G. (1987a). Moving Out of Closings. In G. Button and J. R. Lee (eds.), *Talk and Social Organisation* (pp. 101–151). Clevedon and Philadelphia: Multilingual Matters.

Button, G. (1987b). Answers as Interactional Products: Two Sequential Practices Used in Interviews. *Social Psychology Quarterly* 50(2): 160–171.

Button, G. (1990a). On Varieties of Closings. In G. Psathas (ed.), *Interactional Competence* (pp. 93–147). Washington, DC: University Press of America.

Button, G. (1990b). A Clash of Ideas: A Response to Auer. *Human Studies* 13: 393–404.

Button, G. (1992). Answers as Interactional Products: Two Sequential Practices Used in Job Interviews. In P. Drew and J. Heritage (eds.), *Talk at Work: Interaction in Institutional Settings* (pp. 212–231). Cambridge: Cambridge University Press.

Button, G. (ed.) (1993). *Technology in Working Order*. New York: Routledge.

Button, G., and Casey, N. (1984). Generating Topic: The Use of Topical Initial Elicitors. In J. M. Atkinson and J. Heritage (eds.), *Structures of Social Action: Studies in Conversation Analysis* (pp. 167–190). Cambridge: Cambridge University Press.

Button, G., and Casey, N. (1985). Topic Nomination and Topic Pursuit. *Human Studies* 8: 3–55.

Bybee, J., and Fleischman, S. (eds.) (1995a). *Modality in Grammar and Discourse*. Amsterdam and Philadelphia: John Benjamins.

Bybee, J., and Fleischman, S. (1995b). Modality in Grammar and Discourse: An Introductory Essay. In J. Bybee and S. Fleischman (eds.), *Modality in Grammar and Discourse* (pp. 1–14). Amsterdam and Philadelphia: John Benjamins.

Bybee, J., Perkins, R., and Pagliuca, W. (1994). *The Evolution of Grammar: Tense, Aspect, and Modality in the Languages of the World*. Chicago: University of Chicago Press.

Caffi, C. (1999). On Mitigation. *Journal of Pragmatics* 31(7): 881–909.

Caffi, C. (2001). *La mitigazione: Un approccio pragmatico alla comunicazione nei contesti terapeutici*. Münster: Lit Verlag.

Calbris, G. (1990). *The Semiotics of French Gesture*. Bloomington: University of Indiana Press.

Cameron, D. (1996). The Language-Gender Interface: Challenging Co-optation. In V. Bergvall, J. Bing, and A. Freed (eds.), *Rethinking Language and Gender Research: Theory and Practice* (pp. 31–53). London: Longman.

Cameron, D. (1998). Gender, Language, and Discourse: A Review Essay. *Signs* 23(4): 945–973.

Cameron, D., and Frazer, E. (1987). *The Lust to Kill: A Feminist Investigation of Sexual Murder.* Cambridge: Polity Press.

Cameron, D., and Frazer, E. (1994). Cultural Difference and the Lust to Kill. In P. Harvey and P. Gow (eds.), *Sex and Violence: Issues in Representation and Experience* (pp. 156–171). London: Routledge.

Cameron, D., and Kulick, D. (2003). *Language and Sexuality.* Cambridge: Cambridge University Press.

Caminero-Santangelo, M. (1998). *The Madwoman Can't Speak, or, Why Insanity is not Subversive.* Ithaca: Cornell University Press.

Capps, L., and Ochs, E. (1995a). *Constructing Panic: The Discourse of Agoraphobia.* Cambridge, MA: Harvard University Press.

Capps, L., and Ochs, E. (1995b). Out of Place: Narrative Insights into Agoraphobia. *Discourse Processes* 19(3): 407–440.

Cardona, G. R. (1976). *Introduzione all'etnolinguistica.* Bologna: Il Mulino.

Cardona, G. R. (1981). *Antropologia della scrittura.* Turin: Loescher.

Cardona, G. R. (1986). *Storia universale della scrittura.* Milan: Mondadori.

Cardona, G. R. (2001). I percorsi della scrittura. Aspetti conoscitivi di uno strumento di comunicazione. In *I linguaggi del sapere* (pp. 182–192). Rome-Bari: Laterza.

Carpenter, D. (1992). Language, Religion, and Society: Reflections on the Authority of the Veda in India. *Journal of the American Academy of Religion* 60: 57–78.

Carrington, J. (1971). The Talking Drums of Africa. *Scientific American* 225(6): 90–94.

Carroll, J. B. (1956). Introduction. In J. B. Carroll (ed.), *Language, Thought, and Reality: Selected Writings of Benjamin Lee Whorf* (pp. 1–34). Cambridge, MA: MIT Press.

Carter, A. L. (1975). The Transformation of Sensorimotor Morphemes into Words: A Case Study of the Development of "More" and "Mine". *Journal of Child Language* 2: 233–250.

Carter, R. (1988). Front Pages: Lexis, Style and Newspaper Reports. In M. Ghadessy (ed.), *Registers of Written English* (pp. 8–16). London: Pinter.

Cassell, J., and McNeill, D. (1991). Gesture and the Poetics of Prose. *Poetics Today* 12(3): 375–404.

Cassidy, F. G. (1961). *Jamaica Talk: Three Hundred Years of the English Language in Jamaica.* London: Macmillan.

Caton, S. C. (1990). *"Peaks of Yemen I Summon": Poetry as Cultural Practice in a North Yemeni Tribe.* Berkeley: University of California Press.

Cazden, C. (1988). *Classroom Discourse: The Language of Teaching and Learning.* Portsmouth, NH: Heinemann.

Cazden, C. B., John, V. P., and Hymes, D. (eds.) (1972). *The Functions of Language in the Classroom.* New York: Teachers College Press.

Certeau, M. de (1984 [1974]). *The Practice of Everyday Life* (trans. S. Rendall). Berkeley: University of California Press.

Chadwick, J. (1987). *Linear B and Related Scripts.* London: The Trustees of The British Museum.

Chafe, W. L. (1987). Cognitive Constraints on Information Flow. In R. S. Tomlin (ed.), *Coherence and Grounding in Discourse.* Amsterdam: John Benjamins.

Chafe, W., and Nichols, J. (1986). *Evidentiality: The Linguistic Coding of Epistemology.* Norwood, NJ: Ablex.

Chao, Y. R. (1956). Tones, Intonation, Singsong, Chanting, Recitative, Tonal Composition, and Atonal Composition in Chinese. In M. Halle, H. G. Lunt, H. McLean, and C. H. Van Schooneveld (eds.), *For Roman Jakobson: Essays on the Occasion of His Sixtieth Birthday* (pp. 52–59). The Hague: Mouton.

Chau, C. M., Chu, H.-H., and Liu, C.-C. (1988). *Taiwan Natural Sign Language.* Taipei, Taiwan: Deaf Sign Language Research Association of the Republic of China.

Chaudenson, R. (1992). *Des Iles, des Hommes, des Langues.* Paris: l'Harmattan.

Chaudenson, R. (2001). *Creolization of Language and Culture.* New York: Routledge.

Cheng, S., and Kuo, W. (2000). Family Socialization of Ethnic Identity among Chinese American Pre-adolescents. *Journal of Comparative Family Studies* 31(4): 463–484.

Chenoweth, V. (1972). Melodic Perception and Analysis. Summer Institute of Linguistics, Papua New Guinea.

Chick, J. K. (1990). The Interactional Accomplishment of Discrimination in South Africa. In D. Carbaugh (ed.), *Cultural Communication and Intercultural Contact* (pp. 225–252). Hillsdale, NJ: Lawrence Erlbaum.

Chierchia, G. (1989). Structured Meanings, Thematic Roles and Control. In G. Chierchia, B. H. Partee, and R. Turner (eds.), *Properties, Types, and Meaning*, vol. II: *Semantic Issues* (pp. 131–166). Dordrecht: Kluwer.

Chomsky, N. (1957). *Syntactic Structures*. The Hague: Mouton.

Chomsky, N. (1959). Review of *Verbal Behavior* by B. F. Skinner. *Language* 35: 26–58.

Chomsky, N. (1965). *Aspects of the Theory of Syntax*. Cambridge, MA: MIT Press.

Chomsky, N. (1966). *Cartesian Linguistics*. New York: Harper & Row.

Chomsky, N. (1973). Introduction to Adam Schaff's *Language and Cognition*. New York: McGraw-Hill.

Chomsky, N. (1977a). *Essays on Form and Interpretation*. New York: North Holland.

Chomsky, N. (1977b). *Language and Responsibility*. Based on Conversations with Mitsou Ronat (trans. J. Viertel). New York: Pantheon Books.

Chomsky, N. (1982). *Lectures on Government and Binding: The Pisa Lectures* (2nd edn.). Dordrecht: Foris.

Chomsky, N. (1986). *Knowledge of Language: Its Nature, Origin and Use*. New York: Praeger.

Chomsky, N. (1995). *The Minimalist Program*. Cambridge, MA: MIT Press.

Chomsky, N., Halle, M., and Lukoff, F. (1956). On Accent and Juncture in English. In M. Halle et al. (eds.), *For Roman Jakobson: Essays on the Occasion of His Sixtieth Birthday*. The Hague: Mouton.

Cicourel, A. V. (1973). *Cognitive Sociology*. Harmondsworth: Penguin.

Cicourel, A. V. (1992). The Interpenetration of Communicative Contexts: Examples from Medical Encounters. In A. Duranti and C. Goodwin (eds.), *Rethinking Context: Language as an Interactive Phenomenon* (pp. 291–310). Cambridge: Cambridge University Press.

Clancy, P. M. (1986). The Acquisition of Communicative Style in Japanese. In B. B. Schieffelin and E. Ochs (eds.), *Language Socialization across Cultures* (pp. 213–250). Cambridge: Cambridge University Press.

Clancy, P. M. (1999). The Socialization of Affect in Japanese Mother-Child Conversation. *Journal of Pragmatics* 31(11): 1397–1421.

Clancy, P., Akatsuka, N., and Strauss, S. (1997). Deontic Modality and Conditionality in Discourse: A Cross-linguistic Study of Adult Speech to Young Children. In A. Kamio (ed.), *Directions in Functional Linguistics* (pp. 19–57). Amsterdam: John Benjamins.

Clark, H. H. (1992). *Arenas of Language Use*. Chicago: University of Chicago Press.

Clark, H. H. (1996). *Using Language*. Cambridge: Cambridge University Press.

Clark, H. H. (1997). Indicating and Placing. Paper presented at the workshop "Pointing," Max Planck Institute for Psycholinguistics, Oud Turnhout, Belgium, June 1997.

Clark, H. H., and Gerrig, R. J. (1990). Quotations as Demonstrations. *Language* 66(4): 764–805.

Clark, H., and Wilkes-Gibbs, D. (1986). Referring as a Collaborative Process. *Cognition* 22: 1–39.

Clayman, S. E. (1989). The Production of Punctuality: Social Interaction, Temporal Organization, and Social Structure. *American Journal of Sociology* 95: 659–691.

Clayman, S., and Heritage, J. (2002). *The News Interview: Journalists and Public Figures on the Air*. Cambridge: Cambridge University Press.

Clayman, S. E., and Whalen, J. (1988/89). When the Medium Becomes the Message: The Case of the Rather-Bush Encounter. *Research on Language and Social Interaction* 22: 241–272.

Clifford, J. (1990). Notes on (Field)notes. In R. Sanjek (ed.), *Fieldnotes: The Makings of Anthropology* (pp. 47–70). Ithaca: Cornell University Press.

Clifford, J., and Marcus, G. E. (eds.) (1986). *Writing Culture: The Poetics and Politics of Ethnography*. Berkeley: University of California Press.

Coates, J. (1994). Discourse, Gender, and Subjectivity: The Talk of Teenage Girls. In M. Bucholtz, A. C. Liang, L. A. Sutton, and C. Hines (eds.), *Cultural Performances* (pp. 116–132). Berkeley: Berkeley Women and Language Group.

Coe, M. D., and Kerr, J. (1998). *The Art of the Maya Scribe*. New York: Harry N. Abrams.

Cohen, B. (1985). The Command of Language and the Language of Command. In R. Guha (ed.), *Subaltern Studies IV: Writings on South*

Asian History and Society (pp. 276–329). Delhi: Oxford University Press.

Cohen, L. H. (1994). *Train Go Sorry: Inside a Deaf World*. Boston: Houghton Mifflin.

Cohen, M. (1958). *La grande invention de l'écriture et son evolution* (2 vols.). Paris: Klincksieck.

Cohen, P. R., Morgan, J., and Pollack, M. E. (eds.) (1990). *Intentions in Communication*. Cambridge, MA: MIT Press.

Cokely, D., and Baker, C. (1980). *American Sign Languages: A Teacher's Resource on Curriculum, Methods, and Evaluation*. Silver Spring, MD: TJ Publishers.

Cole, M. (1985). The Zone of Proximal Development: Where Culture and Cognition Create Each Other. In J. Wertsch (ed.), *Culture, Communication and Cognition: Vygotskian Perspectives* (pp. 146–161). Cambridge: Cambridge University Press.

Cole, M. (1996). *Cultural Psychology: A Once and Future Discipline*. Cambridge, MA: The Belknap Press of Harvard University Press.

Coleman, J. (1988). Social Capital in the Creation of Human Capital. *American Journal of Sociology* 94, Supplement, S95–S120.

Coleman, J. (1990). *Foundations of Social Theory*. Cambridge, MA: Harvard University Press.

Coleman, S. (1996). Words as Things: Language, Aesthetics, and the Objectification of Protestant Evangelicalism. *Journal of Material Culture* 1: 107–128.

Collins, J. (1995). Literacy and Literacies. *Annual Review of Anthropology* 24: 75–93.

Collins, J. (1996). Socialization to Text: Structure and Contradiction in Schooled Literacy. In M. Silverstein and G. Urban (eds.), *Natural Histories of Discourse* (pp. 203–228). Chicago: University of Chicago Press.

Collins, J. (1998). Our Ideologies and Theirs. In B. B. Schieffelin, K. A. Woolard, and P. V. Kroskrity (eds.), *Language Ideologies: Practice and Theory* (pp. 256–270). New York: Oxford University Press.

Collins, J. (1999). The Ebonics Controversy in Context: Literacies, Subjectivities, and Language Ideologies in the United States. In J. Blommaert (ed.), *Language Ideological Debates* (pp. 201–234). Berlin: Mouton de Gruyter.

Collins, J., and Blot, R. K. (2003). *Literacy and Literacies: Texts, Power, and Identity*. Cambridge: Cambridge University Press.

Collins-Ahlgren, M. (1989). Aspects of New Zealand Sign Language. Unpublished PhD dissertation, Victoria University, Wellington, NZ.

Comrie, B. (1978). Ergativity. In W. P. Lehmann (ed.), *Syntactic Typology*. Austin: University of Texas Press.

Comrie, B. (1981). *Language Universals and Linguistic Typology: Syntax and Morphology*. Chicago: University of Chicago Press.

Conklin, H. (1955). Hanunoo Color Categories. *Southwestern Jounal of Anthropology* 11: 339–344.

Conklin, H. C. (1962). Lexicographical Treatment of Folk Taxonomies. In F. W. Household and S. Saporta (eds.), *Problems in Lexicography*. Bloomington: Indiana University Research Center in Anthropology, Folklore, and Linguistics.

Constantinidou, E. (1994). The "Death" of East Sutherland Gaelic: Death by Women? In P. Burton, K. Kushari-Dyson, and S. Ardener (eds.), *Bilingual Women: Anthropological Approaches to Second Language Use* (pp. 111–127). Oxford: Berg Publishers.

Cook, H. M. (1996). Japanese Language Socialization: Indexing the Modes of Self. *Discourse Processes* 22(2): 171–197.

Cooke, D. (1959). *The Language of Music*. London: Oxford University Press.

Cook-Gumperz, J. (ed.) (1986). *The Social Construction of Literacy*. Cambridge: Cambridge University Press.

Cook-Gumperz, J., Corsaro, W. A., and Streeck, J. (1986). *Children's Worlds and Children's Language*. Berlin: Mouton de Gruyter.

Cook-Gumperz, J., and Keller-Cohen, D. (1993). Alternative Literacies in School and Beyond: Multiple Literacies of Speaking and Writing. *Anthropology & Education Quarterly* 24(4): 283–287.

Coplan, D. (1987). Eloquent Knowledge: Lesotho Migrants' Songs and the Anthropology of Experience. *American Ethnologist* 14(3): 413–433.

Coplan, D. (1988). Musical Understanding: The Ethnoaesthetics of Migrant Workers' Poetic Song in Lesotho. *Ethnomusicology* 32(3): 337–368.

Coplan, D. (1994). *In The Time of Cannibals: The Word Music of South Africa's Basotho Migrants*. Chicago: University of Chicago Press.

Corin, E. E. (1990). Facts and Meaning in Psychiatry: An Anthropological Approach to the Lifeworld of Schizophrenics. *Culture, Medicine and Psychiatry* 14: 153–188.

Corin, E., Bibeau, G., and Uchôa, E. (1993). Eléments d'une sémiologie anthropologique des troubles psychiques chez les Bambara, Soninke, et Bwa du Mali. *Anthropologie et sociétés* 17(1–2): 125–156.

Corin, E., and Rousseau, C. (1997). Sens et contexte dans l'étude des problèmes psychiatriques. À la recherche de nouveaux modèles. *Médecine/Sciences* 13(4): 527–533.

Corin, E., Thara, R., and Padmavati, R. (2003). Living through a Staggering World: The Play of Signifiers in Early Psychosis in South India. In J. H. Jenkins and R. J. Barrett (eds.), *The Edge of Experience: Culture, Subjectivity, and Schizophrenia*. New York: Cambridge University Press.

Corsaro, W., and Rizzo, T. (1990). Disputes in the Peer Culture of American and Italian Nursery-School Children. In A. Grimshaw (ed.), *Conflict Talk* (pp. 21–66). New York: Cambridge University Press.

Costa, R. (1975). Functional Solution for Illogical Reflexes in Italian. In R. E. Grossman, L. J. San, and T. J. Vance (eds.), *Papers from the Parasession on Functionalism*. Chicago: Chicago Linguistic Society.

Coulmas, F. (1989). *The Writing Systems of the World*. Oxford: Blackwell.

Coulmas, F. (1996). *The Blackwell Encyclopaedia of Writing Systems*. Oxford: Blackwell.

Couper-Kuhlen, E., and Selting, M. (eds.) (1996). *Prosody in Conversation*. Cambridge: Cambridge University Press.

Cowan, G. M. (1948). Mazateco Whistle Speech. *Language* 24: 280–286.

Coyaud, M. (1988). *La pertinence en graphémique*. In N. Catach (ed.), *Pour une théorie de la langue écrite* (pp. 157–163). Paris: CNRS.

Crago, M. (1988). Cultural Context in Communicative Interaction of Inuit Children. PhD dissertation, McGill University, Montreal.

Crago, M. B, Annahatak, B., and Ningiuruvik, L. (1993). Changing Patterns of Language Socialization in Inuit Homes. *Anthropology and Education Quarterly* 24(3): 205–223.

Crapanzano, V. (1996). Self-Centering Narratives. In M. Silverstein and G. Urban (eds.), *Natural Histories of Discourse* (pp. 106–127). Chicago: University of Chicago Press.

Crawford, M. (1995). *Talking Difference: On Gender and Language*. Thousand Oaks, CA: Sage.

Crow, T. J. (1997a). Is Schizophrenia the Price that *Homo sapiens* Pays for Language? *Schizophrenia Research* 28(2–3): 127–141.

Crow, T. J. (1997b). Schizophrenia as Failure of Hemispheric Dominance for Language. *Trends in Neurosciences* 20(8): 339–343.

Crow, T. J. (1998a). Commentary: From Kraepelin to Kretschmer Leavened by Schneider. The Transition from Categories of Psychosis to Dimensions of Variation Intrinsic to *Homo sapiens*. *Archives of General Psychiatry* 55(6).

Crow, T. J. (1998b). Precursors of Psychosis as Pointers to the *Homo sapiens*-specific Mate Recognition System of Language. *British Journal of Psychiatry* 173 (April): 183.

Crow, T. J. (2000a). The Genetics of Cerebral Asymmetry and the Structure of Language – What's the Alternative? An Organizer's Viewpoint. The 10th Biennial Winter Workshop on Schizophrenia, Davos, 5–11 February 2000. *Schizophrenia Research* 46(1): 73–76.

Crow, T. J. (2000b). Schizophrenia as the Price that *Homo sapiens* Pays for Language: A Resolution of the Central Paradox in the Origin of the Species. *Brain Research Reviews* 31: 118–129.

Cruttendon, A. (1997). *Intonation*. New York: Cambridge University Press.

Crystal, D. (1987). *The Cambridge Encyclopedia of Language*. Cambridge: Cambridge University Press.

Crystal, D. (1997). *A Dictionary of Linguistics and Phonetics* (4th edn.). Oxford: Blackwell.

Crystal, D. (2000). *Language Death*. Cambridge: Cambridge University Press.

Crystal, D., and Davy, D. (1969). *Investigating English Style*. Bloomington: Indiana University Press.

Cutler, C. A. (1999). Yorkville Crossing: White Teens, Hip Hop, and African American English. *Journal of Sociolinguistics* 3: 428–442.

Daiute, C., and Nelson, K. (1997). Making Sense of the Sense Making Function of Narrative. *Journal of Narrative and Life History* 7: 207–216.

Dalby, D. (1986). *L'Afrique et la lettre*. Paris: Éditions Karthala.

Danet, B., Hoffman, K., Kermish, N., Rafn, H.J., and Stayman, D. (1976). An Ethnography of Questioning in the Courtroom. In R. R. Shuy and A. Shnukal (eds.), *Language Use and the Uses of Language*, NWAVE 5 (pp. 222–234). Washington, DC: Georgetown University Press.

Daniels, T. P., and Bright, W. (eds.) (1996). *The World's Writing Systems*. Oxford: Oxford University Press.

Darnell, R. (1990). *Edward Sapir: Linguist, Anthropologist, Humanist*. Berkeley: University of California Press.

Darnell, R. (1998a). *And along Came Boas: Continuity and Revolution in Americanist Anthropology*. Amsterdam and Philadelphia: John Benjamins.

Darnell, R. (1998b). Camelot at Yale: The Construction and Dismantling of the Sapirian Synthesis, 1931–39. *American Anthropologist* 100(2): 361–372.

Darnell, R. (1998c). Toward a History of Canadian Departments of Anthropology: Retrospect, Prospect and Common Cause. *Anthropologica* 40: 153–168.

Dauenhauer, N. M., and Dauenhauer, R. (1998). Technical, Emotional, and Ideological Issues in Reversing Language Shift. In L. A. Grenoble and L. J. Whaley (eds.), *Endangered Languages* (pp. 57–98). Cambridge: Cambridge University Press.

Davidson, J. A. (1984). Subsequent Versions of Invitations, Offers, Requests, and Proposals Dealing with Potential or Actual Rejection. In J. M. Atkinson and J. Heritage (eds.), *Structures of Social Action: Studies in Conversation Analysis* (pp. 102–128). Cambridge: Cambridge University Press.

Davidson, J. A. (1990). Modifications of Invitations, Offers and Rejections. In G. Psathas (ed.), *Interaction Competence* (pp. 149–179). Washington, DC: International Institute for Ethnomethodology and Conversation Analysis, and University Press of America.

Davis, G. L. (1985). *I Got the Word in Me and I Can Sing It, You Know: A Study of the Performed African-American Sermon*. Philadelphia: University of Pennsylvania.

Davis, J. (1989). Distinguishing Language Contact Phenomena in ASL Interpretation. In C. Lucas (ed.), *The Sociolinguistics of the Deaf Community*. San Diego, CA: Academic Press.

Davis, J., and Supalla, S. (1995). A Sociolinguistic Description of Sign Language Use in a Navajo Family. In C. Lucas (ed.), *Sociolinguistics in Deaf Communities* (pp. 77–108). Washington, DC: Gallaudet University Press.

Davis, L. (1995). *Enforcing Normalcy: Disability, Deafness, and the Body*. London: Verso.

de Condillac, E. B. (ed.) (1971 [1756]). *An Essay on the Origin of Human Knowledge; Being a Supplement to Mr. Locke's Essay on the Human Understanding*. Gainesville, FL: Scholars' Facsimile and Reprint.

De Dominicis, A. (ed.) (2002). *La voce come bene culturale*. Rome: Carocci.

de León, L. (1998). The Emergent Participant: Interactive Patterns in the Socialization of Tzotzil (Mayan) Infants. *Journal of Linguistic Anthropology*, 8(2): 131–161.

de Saussure, F. (1922). *Cours de linguistique générale*. Paris: Payot.

de Zulueta, F. I., Gene-Cos, N., and Grachev, S. (2001). Differential Psychotic Symptomatology in Polyglot Patients: Case Reports and Their Implications. *British Journal of Medical Psychology*, 74: 277–292.

Deacon, H. (1996). Racial Segregation and Medical Discourse in Nineteenth-Century Cape Town. *Journal of Southern African Studies*, 22(2): 287–308.

Deacon, T. W. (1997). *The Symbolic Species: The Co-evolution of Language and the Brain*. New York: Norton.

DeFrancis, J. (1989). *Visible Speech: The Diverse Oneness of Writing Systems*. Honolulu: University of Hawai'i Press.

DeGraff, M. (ed.) (1999). *Language Creation and Language Change: Creolization, Diachrony and Development*. Cambridge, MA: MIT Press.

DeLancey, S. (1982). Aspect, Transitivity and Viewpoint. In D. J. Hopper (ed.), *Tense-Aspect: Between Semantics and Pragmatics* (pp. 167–183). Amsterdam and Philadelphia: John Benjamins.

DeLancey, S. (1990). Ergativity and the Cognitive Model of Event Structure in Lhasa Tibetan. *Cognitive Linguistics*, 1: 289–321.

Deleuze, G., and Guattari, F. (1977). *Anti-Oedipus: Capitalism and Schizophrenia* (trans. from the French by R. Hurley, H. R. Lane, and M. Seem). New York: Viking Press.

DeLisi, L. E. (2001). Speech Disorder in Schizophrenia: Review of the Literature and Exploration of its Relation to the Uniquely Human Capacity for Language. *Schizophrenia Bulletin*, 26: 709–721.

Deng, F. (1973). *The Dinka and Their Songs*. London: Oxford University Press.

Denison, N. (1977). Language Death or Language Suicide? *International Journal of the Sociology of Language* 12: 13–22.

Dennett, D. C. (1987). *The Intentional Stance*. Cambridge, MA: MIT Press.

Derrida, J. (1982 [1972]). Signature Event Context (trans. A. Bass). In *Margins of Phil-*

osophy (pp. 307–330). Chicago: University of Chicago Press.

Desjarlais, R. (1994). Struggling Along: The Possibilities for Experience Among the Homeless Mentally Ill. *American Anthropologist* 96(4): 886–901.

deVries, M. W. (ed.) (1992). *The Experience of Psychopathology: Investigating Mental Disorders in Their Natural Setting.* Cambridge: Cambridge University Press.

DiGiacomo, S. M. (1999). Language Ideological Debates in an Olympic City: Barcelona 1992–1996. In J. Blommaert (ed.), *Language Ideological Debates* (pp. 105–142). Berlin: Mouton de Gruyter.

Diringer, D. (1949). *The Alphabet.* London: Hutchinson.

Diringer, D. (1962). *Writing.* New York: Praeger.

Dirven, R., Frank, R., and Ilie, C. (2001). *Language and Ideology,* vol. II: *Descriptive and Cognitive Approaches.* Amsterdam: John Benjamins.

Dixon, R. M. W. (1971). A Method of Semantic Description. In D. D. Steinberg and L. J. Jakobovitz (eds.), *Semantics: An Interdisciplinary Reader in Philosophy, Linguistics and Psychology* (pp. 436–471). Cambridge: Cambridge University Press.

Dixon, R. M. W. (1972). *The Dyirbal Language of North Queensland.* Cambridge: Cambridge University Press.

Dixon, R. M. W. (1977). *A Grammar of Yidin.* Cambridge: Cambridge University Press.

Dixon, R. M. W. (1979). Ergativity. *Language,* 55: 59–138.

Dixon, R. M. W. (1994). *Ergativity.* Cambridge: Cambridge University Press.

Dixon, R. M. W., and Aikhenvald, A. Y. (eds.) (1999). *The Amazonian Languages.* Cambridge: Cambridge University Press.

Dixon, R. M. W., and Koch, G. (1996). *Dyirbal Song Poetry: The Oral Literature of an Australian Rainforest People.* St. Lucia, Queensland: University of Queensland Press.

Dolnick, E. (1993). Deafness as Culture. *The Atlantic Monthly* (September): 37–53.

Dorian, N. C. (1981). *Language Death: The Life Cycle of a Scottish Gaelic Dialect.* Philadelphia: University of Pennsylvania Press.

Dorian, N. C. (1982). Defining the Speech Community to Include its Working Margins. In S. Romaine (ed.), *Sociolinguistic Variation in Speech Communities* (pp. 25–33). London: Edward Arnold.

Dorian, N. C. (ed.) (1989). *Investigating Obsolescence: Studies in Language Contraction and Death.* Cambridge: Cambridge University Press.

Dorian, N. C. (1993). A Response to Ladefoged's Other View of Endangered Languages. *Language,* 69(3): 575–579.

Dorian, N. C. (1994). Purism vs. Compromise in Language Revitalization and Language Revival. *Language in Society* 23(4): 479–494.

Dorian, N. C. (1998). Western Language Ideologies and Small-Language Prospects. In L. A. Grenoble and L. J. Whaley (eds.), *Endangered Languages* (pp. 3–21). Cambridge: Cambridge University Press.

Doubt, K. (1996). *Towards a Sociology of Schizophrenia: Humanistic Reflections.* Toronto: University of Toronto Press.

Dowty, D. R. (1989). On the Semantic Content of the Notion "Thematic Role". In G. Chierchia, B. H. Partee, and R. Turner (eds.), *Properties, Types, and Meaning,* vol. II: *Semantic Issues* (pp. 69–129). Dordrecht: Kluwer.

Dowty, D. R. (1991). Thematic Proto-roles and Argument Selection. *Language* 67(3): 547–619.

Drechsel, E. J. (1988). Wilhelm von Humboldt and Edward Sapir: Analogies and Homologies in Their Linguistic Thoughts. In W. Shipley (ed.), *In Honor of Mary Haas: From the Haas Festival Conference on Native American Linguistics* (pp. 225–264). Berlin: Mouton de Gruyter.

Drennan, G., Levett, A., and Swartz, L. (1991). Hidden Dimensions of Power and Resistance in the Translation Process: A South African Study. *Culture, Medicine, and Psychiatry* 15: 361–381.

Drennan, G., and Swartz, L. (2002). The Paradoxical Use of Interpreting in Psychiatry. *Social Science & Medicine* 54(12): 1853–1866.

Drew, P. (1984). Speaker's Reportings in Invitation Sequences. In J. M. Atkinson and J. Heritage (eds.), *Structures of Social Action: Studies in Conversation Analysis* (pp. 152–164). Cambridge: Cambridge University Press.

Drew, P. (1992). Contested Evidence in Courtroom Cross-examination: The Case of a Trial for Rape. In P. Drew and J. Heritage (eds.), *Talk at Work: Interaction in Institutional Settings* (pp. 470–520). Cambridge: Cambridge University Press.

Drew, P. (1997a). "Open" Class Repair Initiators in Response to Sequential Sources of

Troubles in Conversation. *Journal of Pragmatics* 28: 69–101.

Drew, P. (1997b). Contested Evidence in Courtroom Cross-examination: The Case of a Trial for Rape. In M. Travers and J. F. Manzo (eds.), *Law in Action: Ethnomethodological and Conversation Analytic Approaches to Law* (pp. 51–76). Aldershot, UK, and Brookfield, VT: Ashgate/Dartmouth.

Drew, P., and Heritage, J. (1992a). Analyzing Talk at Work: An Introduction. In P. Drew and J. Heritage (eds.), *Talk at Work: Interaction in Institutional Settings* (pp. 3–65). Cambridge: Cambridge University Press.

Drew, P., and Heritage, J. (eds.) (1992b). *Talk at Work: Interaction in Institutional Settings*. Cambridge: Cambridge University Press.

Drew, P., and Holt, E. (1988). Complainable Matters: The Use of Idiomatic Expressions in Making Complaints. *Social Problems*, 35: 398–417.

Drew, P., and Sorjonen, M.-L. (1997). Institutional Dialogue. In T. van Dijk (ed.), *Discourse as Social Interaction*. London: Sage.

Drew, P., and Wootton, A. (eds.) (1988). *Erving Goffman: Exploring the Interaction Order*. Cambridge: Polity Press.

Drummond, K. (1989). A Backward Glance at Interruptions. *Western Journal of Speech Communication* (Special Issue: Sequential Organization of Conversational Activities) 53: 150–166.

Drummond, L. (1980). The Cultural Continuum: A Theory of Intersystems. *Man* (n.s.) 15: 352–374.

Du Bois, J. (1986). Self-Evidence and Ritual Speech. In W. Chafe and J. Nichols (eds.), *Evidentiality: The Linguistic Coding of Epistemology* (pp. 313–336). Norwood, NJ: Ablex.

Du Bois, J. (1987). The Discourse Basis of Ergativity. *Language*, 63: 805–855.

Du Bois, J. W. (1993). Meaning without Intention: Lessons from Divination. In J. H. Hill and J. T. Irvine (eds.), *Responsibility and Evidence in Oral Discourse* (pp. 48–71). Cambridge: Cambridge University Press.

Duff, P. (1993). Changing Times, Changing Minds: Language Socialization in Hungarian English Schools. PhD dissertation, University of California, Los Angeles.

Dunn, C. D. (1999a). Toward the Study of Communicative Development as a Life-span Process. *Anthropology and Education Quarterly* 30(4): 451–454.

Dunn, C. D. (1999b). Coming of Age in Japan: Language Ideology and the Acquisition of Formal Speech Registers. In J. Verschueren (ed.), *Language and Ideology: Selected Papers from the Sixth International Pragmatics Conference, 1* (pp. 89–97). Antwerp: International Pragmatics Association.

Dunn, L. C., and Jones, N. A. (eds.) (1994). *Embodied Voices: Representing Female Vocality in Western Culture*. Cambridge: Cambridge University Press.

Duranti, A. (1981). *The Samoan Fono: A Sociolinguistic Study*. Pacific Linguistics Monographs, Series B. Vol. 80. Canberra: Australian National University, Department of Linguistics, Research School of Pacific Studies.

Duranti, A. (1983). Samoan Speechmaking across Social Events: One Genre in and out of a Fono. *Language in Society* 12(1): 1–22.

Duranti, A. (1985). Sociocultural Dimensions of Discourse. In T. A. van Dijk (ed.), *Handbook of Discourse Analysis*, vol. 1: *Disciplines of Discourse* (pp. 193–230). New York: Academic Press.

Duranti, A. (1988a). The Ethnography of Speaking: Toward a Linguistics of the Praxis. In F. J. Newmeyer (ed.), *Linguistics: The Cambridge Survey*. Vol. IV, *Language: The Socio-Cultural Context* (pp. 210–228). Cambridge: Cambridge University Press.

Duranti, A. (1988b). Intentions, Language and Social Action in a Samoan Context. *Journal of Pragmatics* 12: 13–33.

Duranti, A. (1990). Politics and Grammar: Agency in Samoan Political Discourse. *American Ethnologist* 17: 646–666.

Duranti, A. (1992a). Language and Bodies in Social Space: Samoan Ceremonial Greetings. *American Anthropologist* 94: 657–691.

Duranti, A. (1992b). *Etnografia del parlare quotidiano*. Rome: La Nuova Italia Scientifica/Carocci.

Duranti, A. (1992c). Language in Context and Language as Context: The Samoan Respect Vocabulary. In A. Duranti and C. Goodwin (eds.), *Rethinking Context: Language as an Interactive Phenomenon* (pp. 77–99). Cambridge: Cambridge University Press.

Duranti, A. (1993a). Intentionality and Truth: An Ethnographic Critique. *Cultural Anthropology* 8: 214–245.

Duranti, A. (1993b). Intentions, Self, and Responsibility: An Essay in Samoan Ethnopragmatics. In J. H. Hill and J. T. Irvine (eds.), *Responsibility and Evidence in Oral Discourse* (pp. 24–47). Cambridge: Cambridge University Press.

Duranti, A. (1994). *From Grammar to Politics: Linguistic Anthropology in a Western Samoan Village*. Berkeley and Los Angeles: University of California Press.

Duranti, A. (1997a). Indexical Speech across Samoan Communities. *American Anthropologist* 99(2): 342–354.

Duranti, A. (1997b). *Linguistic Anthropology*. Cambridge: Cambridge University Press.

Duranti, A. (1997c). Universal and Culture-specific Properties of Greetings. *Journal of Linguistic Anthropology* 7: 63–97.

Duranti, A. (1997d). Polyphonic Discourse: Overlapping in Samoan Ceremonial Greetings. *Text* 17(3): 349–381.

Duranti, A. (ed.) (2001a). *Key Terms in Language and Culture*. Malden, MA: Blackwell.

Duranti, A. (2001b). Intentionality. In A. Duranti (ed.), *Key Terms in Language and Culture* (pp. 129–131). Malden, MA: Blackwell.

Duranti, A. (ed.) (2001c). *Linguistic Anthropology: A Reader*. Malden, MA: Blackwell.

Duranti, A. (2001d). Linguistic Anthropology: History, Ideas, and Issues. In A. Duranti (ed.), *Linguistic Anthropology* (pp. 1–38, 465–479). Malden, MA: Blackwell.

Duranti, A. (2003). Language as Culture in U.S. Anthropology: Three Paradigms. *Current Anthropology* 44(3): 323–347.

Duranti, A., and Brenneis, D. (eds.) (1986). The Audience as Co-Author. Special Issue of *Text* 6(3): 239–347.

Duranti, A., and Goodwin, C. (eds.) (1992). *Rethinking Context: Language as an Interactive Phenomenon*. Cambridge: Cambridge University Press.

Duranti, A., and Ochs, E. (1990). Genitive Constructions and Agency in Samoan Discourse. *Studies in Language* 14: 1–23.

Duranti, A., and Ochs, E. (1997). Syncretic Literacy in a Samoan American Family. In L. Resnick, R. Säljö, C. Pontecorvo, and B. Burge (eds.), *Discourse, Tools, and Reasoning* (pp. 169–202). Heidelberg: Springer Verlag.

Duranti, A., Ochs, E., and Ta'ase, E. (1995). Change and Tradition in Literacy Instruction in a Samoan American Community. *Educational Foundations* Fall issue: 57–74.

Durbin, M. A. (1971). Transformational Models Applied to Musical Analysis: Theoretical Possibilities. *Ethnomusicology* 15(3): 353–362.

Durie, M. (1988). Preferred Argument Structure in an Active Language. *Lingua* 74: 1–25.

Dusenbery, V. A. (1992). The Word as Guru: Sikh Scripture and the Translation Controversy. *History of Religions* 31: 385–402.

Eble, C. (1996). *Slang and Sociability: In-group Language among College Students*. Chapel Hill: University of North Carolina Press.

Eckert, P. (1980). Diglossia: Separate and Unequal. *Linguistics* 18: 1053–1064.

Eckert, P. (1989a). *Jocks and Burnouts: Social Categories and Identity in the High School*. New York: Teachers College Press.

Eckert, P. (1989b). The Whole Woman: Sex and Gender Differences in Variation. *Language Variation and Change* 1: 245–267.

Eckert, P. (2000). *Linguistic Variation as Social Practice*. Cambridge, MA: Blackwell.

Eckert, P., and McConnell-Ginet, S. (1992a). Think Practically and Look Locally: Language and Gender as Community-based Practice. *Annual Review of Anthropology* 21: 461–490.

Eckert, P., and McConnell-Ginet, S. (1992b). Communities of Practice: Where Language, Gender, and Power All Live. In K. Hall, M. Bucholtz, and B. Moonwomon (eds.), *Locating Power: Proceedings of the Second Berkeley Women and Language Conference* (vol. 1, pp. 89–99). Berkeley: Berkeley Women and Language Group.

Eckert, P., and McConnell-Ginet, S. (1995). Constructing Meaning, Constructing Selves: Snapshots of Language, Gender, and Class from Belten High. In K. Hall and M. Bucholtz (eds.), *Gender Articulated: Language and the Socially Constructed Self* (pp. 469–507). New York: Routledge.

Eckert, P., and McConnell-Ginet, S. (1999). New Generalizations and Explanations in Language and Gender Research. *Language in Society* 28: 185–201.

Eco, U. (1976). *A Theory of Semiotics*. Bloomington: Indiana University Press.

Eco, U. (1986). *Semiotics and the Philosophy of Language*. Bloomington: Indiana University Press.

Eco, U. (2000). *Kant and the Platypus: Essays on Language and Cognition*. New York: Harcourt Brace.

Edelsky, C. (1981). Who's Got the Floor? *Language in Society* 10: 383–421.

Egbert, M. (1996). Context Sensitivity in Conversation Analysis: Eye Gaze and the German Repair Initiator "bitte." *Language in Society* 25: 587–612.

Egbert, M. (1997a). Schisming: The Collaborative Transformation from a Single Conversation to Multiple Conversation. *Research in Language and Social Interaction* 30(1).

Egbert, M. (1997b). Some Interactional Achievements of Other-initiated Repair in Multiperson Conversation. *Journal of Pragmatics* 27: 611–634.

Egbert, M. (1998). Miscommunication in Language Proficiency Interviews of First-year German Students: A Comparison with Natural Conversation. In R. Young and A. W. He (eds.), *Talking and Testing: Discourse Approaches to the Assessment of Oral Proficiency* (pp. 147–172). Amsterdam and Philadelphia: John Benjamins.

Ehlich, K., and Rehbein, J. (1976). Halbinterpretative Arbeitstranskriptionen (HIAT). *Linguistische Berichte* 45: S. 21–41.

Ehlich, K., and Rehbein, J. (1981). Die Wiedergabe intonatorischer Phänomene im Verfahren HIAT. In A. Lange-Seidl (ed.), *Zeichenkonstitution*, vol. 2 (pp. 174–186). Berlin: de Gruyter (Akten des 2. Semiotischen Kolloquiums).

Eisenberg, A. (1985). Learning to Describe Past Experience in Conversation. *Discourse Processes* 8: 177–204.

Eisenstein, E. (1979). *The Printing Press as an Agent of Change: Communication and Cultural Transformations in Early-Modern Europe.* Cambridge: Cambridge University Press.

Ekman, P. (1980). Facial Signals. In I. Rauch and G. Carr (eds.), *The Signifying Animal* (pp. 227–239). Bloomington: Indiana University Press.

Ekman, P. (1988). *Gesichtsausdruck und Gefühl.* Paderborn: Junfermann.

Ekman, P. (1989). *Weshalb Lügen kurze Beine haben.* Berlin: de Gruyter.

Ensink, K., Robertson, B. A., Ben-Arie, O., Hodson, P., and Tredoux, C. (1998). Expression of Schizophrenia in Black Xhosa-speaking and White English-speaking South Africans. *South African Medical Journal* 88(7): 883–887.

Erickson, F. (1979). Talking Down: Some Cultural Sources of Miscommunication in Interracial Interviews. In Aaron Wolfgang (ed.), *Nonverbal Communication: Applications and Cultural Implications* (pp. 99–126). New York: Academic Press.

Erickson, F., and Mohatt, G. (1982). Cultural Organization of Participation Structures in Two Classrooms of Indian Students. In G. Spindler (ed.), *Doing the Ethnography of Schooling* (pp. 132–174). New York: Holt, Rinehart & Winston.

Erickson, F., and Shultz, J. (1982). *The Counselor as Gatekeeper: Social Interaction in Interviews.* New York: Academic Press.

Ernst, W. (1997). Idioms of Madness and Colonial Boundaries: The Case of the European and "Native" Mentally Ill in Early Nineteenth-Century British India. *Comparative Studies in Society and History* 39: 153–181.

Errington, J. J. (1988). *Structure and Style in Javanese: A Semiotic View of Linguistic Etiquette.* Philadelphia: University of Pennsylvania Press.

Errington, J. J. (1998a). Indonesian('s) Development: On the State of a Language of State. In B. B. Schieffelin, K. A. Woolard, and P. V. Kroskrity (eds.), *Language Ideologies: Practice and Theory* (pp. 271–284). New York: Oxford University Press.

Errington, J. J. (1998b). *Shifting Languages: Interaction and Identity in Javanese Indonesia.* Cambridge: Cambridge University Press.

Errington, J. J. (2000). Indonesian('s) Authority. In P. V. Kroskrity (ed.), *Regimes of Language* (pp. 205–227). Santa Fe, NM: School of American Research Press.

Errington, J. J. (2001a). Colonial Linguistics. *Annual Review of Anthropology* 30: 19–39. Palo Alto: Annual Reviews.

Errington, J. J. (2001b). Ideology. In A. Duranti (ed.), *Key Terms in Language and Culture* (pp. 110–112). Malden, MA: Blackwell.

Erting, C. (1981). An Anthropological Approach to the Study of the Communicative Competence of Deaf Children. *Sign Language Studies* 32: 221–238.

Erting, C. (1985). Sociocultural Dimensions of Deaf Education: Belief Systems and Communicative Interaction. *Sign Language Studies* 47: 111–126.

Erting, C., Johnson, R., Smith, D., and Snider, B. D. (eds.) (1994). *The Deaf Way: Perspectives from the International Conference on Deaf Cultures.* Washington, DC: Gallaudet University Press.

Erting, C., and Woodward, J. (1979). Sign Language and the Deaf Community: A Sociolinguistic Profile. *Discourse Processes* 2: 283–300.

Ervin-Tripp, S. (1972a). On Sociolinguistic Rules: Alternation and Co-occurrence. In J. J. Gumperz and D. Hymes (eds.), *Directions in Sociolinguistics: The Ethnography of Communication* (pp. 213–250). New York: Holt.

Ervin-Tripp, S. (1972b). Sociolinguistic Rules of Address. In J. B. Pride and J. Holmes (eds.), *Sociolinguistics* (pp. 225–240). Harmondsworth: Penguin Books.

Ervin-Tripp, S. (1976). Is Sybil There? The Structure of Some American English Directives. *Language in Society* 5: 25–66.

Ervin-Tripp, S. (1992). Gender Differences in the Construction of Humorous Talk. In K. Hall, M. Bucholtz, and B. Moonwomon (eds.), *Locating Power*. Berkeley: Berkeley Women and Language Group.

Ervin-Tripp, S., O'Connor, M. C., and Rosenberg, J. (1984). Language and Power in the Family. In C. Kramarae, M. Schulz, and W. O'Barr (eds.), *Language and Power* (pp. 116–135). Los Angeles: Sage.

Ervin-Tripp, S., and Strage, A. (1985). Parent–Child Interaction. In T. A. van Dijk (ed.), *Handbook of Discourse Analysis*, vol. 3: *Discourse and Dialogue* (pp. 67–77). London: Academic Press.

Esposito, E. (1995). Computers and the Asymmetrization of Communication. In *Semiotics and the Effect-of-Media-Change Research Programmes* (ed. G. Blasi and A. Bernardelli). Special Issue, *Versus. Quaderni di studi semiotici* 72: 77–106.

Esselman, M., and Velez, E. (1994). Silent Screams: A People Report on Sexual Assault at the Nation's Only University for Deaf Students. *People*, June 20, 37–41.

Estroff, S. (1994). Identity, Disability, and Schizophrenia: The Problem of Chronicity. In S. Lindenbaum and M. Lock (eds.), *Knowledge, Power, and Practice: The Anthropology of Medicine and Everyday Life* (pp. 247–286). Berkeley/Los Angeles: University of California Press.

Estroff, S., Lachicotte, W., Illingworth, L., and Johnston, A. (1991). Everybody's Got a Little Mental Illness: Accounts of Illness and Self among People with Severe, Persistent Mental Illnesses. *Medical Anthropology Quarterly* 5: 331–369.

Evans, A. D., and Falk, W. (1986). *Learning to be Deaf*. Berlin: Mouton de Gruyter.

Evans, J. R., and Clynes, M. (eds.) 1986. *Rhythm in Psychological, Linguistic, and Musical Processes*. Springfield, IL: Charles C. Thomas.

Fabb, N. (1997). *Linguistics and Literature: Language in the Verbal Arts of the World*. Oxford: Blackwell.

Fabian, J. (1986). *Language and Colonial Power: The Appropriation of Swahili in the Former Belgian Congo 1880–1938*. Berkeley: University of California Press.

Fabrega, H. (1989). The Self and Schizophrenia: A Cultural Perspective. *Schizophrenia Bulletin* 15: 2770–2790.

Fader, A. (2000). Gender, Morality, and Language: Socialization Practices in a Hasidic Community. PhD thesis, New York University.

Fader, A. (2001). Literacy, Bilingualism and Gender in a Hasidic community. *Linguistics and Education* 12(3): 261–283.

Faerch, C., and Kasper, G. (eds.) (1983). *Strategies in Interlanguage Communication*. London: Longman.

Faerch, C., and Kasper, G. (1984). Two Ways of Defining Communication Strategies. *Language Learning* 34: 45–63.

Fairclough, N. (1989). *Language and Power*. London: Longman.

Fairclough, N. (1992). *Critical Language Awareness*. London: Longman.

Fairclough, N. (1995). *Critical Discourse Analysis*. London: Longman.

Fairclough, N., and Graham, P. (2002). Marx as a Critical Discourse Analyst: The Genesis of a Critical Method and its Relevance to the Critique of Global Capital. *Estudios de Sociolingüística* 3(1): 185–229.

Fan Wenlan (ed.) (1978). *Wen xin diao long zhu*. Beijing.

Fardon, R., and Furniss, G. (eds.) (1994). *African Languages, Development, and the State*. London: Routledge.

Farnell, B. (1995). *Do You See What I Mean? Plains Indian Sign Talk and the Embodiment of Action*. Austin: University of Texas Press.

Farr, M. (1994). *En los dos idiomas*: Literacy Practices among Chicago Mexicanos. In B. Moss (ed.), *Literacy across Communities* (pp. 9–47). Cresskill, NJ: Hampton Press.

Farris, C. (1991). Gender of Child Discourse: Same-sex Peer Socialization through Language Use in a Taiwanese Preschool. *Journal of Linguistic Anthropology* 1(2): 198–224.

Fasold, R. (1990). *The Sociolinguistics of Language*. Oxford: Oxford University Press.

Fasulo, A., and Zucchermaglio, C. (2002). Myselves and I: Identity Markers in Work Meeting Talk. *Journal of Pragmatics* 1119–1144.

Fatigante, M., Fasulo, A., and Pontecorvo, C. (1998). Life with the Alien: Role Casting and Face Saving Techniques in Family Conversations with Young Children. *Issues in Applied Linguistics* 9(2): 97–121.

Feld, S. (1974). Linguistic Models in Ethno-musicology. *Ethnomusicology* 18(2): 197–217.

Feld, S. (1981). "Flow like a Waterfall": The Metaphors of Kaluli Musical Theory. *Yearbook for Traditional Music* 13: 22–47.

Feld, S. (1982). *Sound and Sentiment: Birds, Weeping, Poetics, and Song in Kaluli Expression*. Philadelphia: University of Pennsylvania Press.

Feld, S. (1984). Communication, Music, and Speech about Music. *Yearbook for Traditional Music* 16: 1–18.

Feld, S. (1990a). *Sound and Sentiment: Birds, Weeping, Poetics and Song in Kaluli Expression* (2nd edn.). Philadelphia: University of Pennsylvania Press.

Feld, S. (1990b). Wept Thoughts: The Voicing of Kaluli Memories. *Oral Tradition* 5(2–3): 241–266.

Feld, S. (1994a [1984a]). Communication, Music, and Speech about Music. In C. Keil and S. Feld, *Music Grooves* (pp. 77–95). Chicago: University of Chicago Press.

Feld, S. (1994b [1984]). Aesthetics as Iconicity of Style, or "Lift-up-over Sounding": Getting into the Kaluli Groove. In C. Keil and S. Feld, *Music Grooves* (pp. 109–150). Chicago: University of Chicago Press.

Feld, S. (2000). They Repeatedly Lick Their Own Things. In L. Berlant (ed.), *Intimacy* (pp. 165–192). Chicago: University of Chicago Press.

Feld, S., and Fox, A. (1994). Music and Language. *Annual Review of Anthropology* 23: 25–53.

Feld, S., and Fox, A. (2001). Music. In A. Duranti (ed.), *Key Terms in Language and Culture* (pp. 154–157). Malden, MA: Blackwell.

Feld, S., and Schieffelin, B. B. (1996 [1981]). Hard Words: A Functional Basis for Kaluli Discourse. In D. Brenneis and R. Macaulay (eds.), *The Matrix of Language: Contemporary Linguistic Anthropology* (pp. 56–73). Boulder, CO: Westview Press.

Feldman, C. (1989). Monologue as Problem-solving Narrative. In K. Nelson (ed.), *Narratives from the Crib* (pp. 98–119). Cambridge, MA: Harvard University Press.

Feldmann, H. (1995). Trans-subjective Practice in Schizophrenic Delusions. *Fortschrift des Neurologische Psychiatie* 63(7): 289–294.

Fellin, L. (2001). Language Ideologies, Language Socialization and Language Revival in an Italian Alpine Community. PhD dissertation, University of Arizona.

Ferber, R. (1991). Slip of the Tongue or Slip of the Ear? On the Perception and Transcription of Naturalistic Slips of the Tongue. *Journal of Psycholinguistic Research* 20: 105–122.

Ferguson, C. A. (1959). Diglossia. *Word* 15: 325–340.

Ferguson, C. (1964). Baby Talk in Six Languages. *American Anthropologist* 66(6): 103–114.

Ferguson, C. A. (1976). The Structure and Use of Politeness Formulas. *Language in Society* 5: 137–151.

Ferguson, C. (1977). Baby Talk as a Simplified Register. In C. E. Snow & C. A. Ferguson (eds.), *Talking to Children: Language Input and Acquisition* (pp. 209–235). Cambridge: Cambridge University Press.

Ferguson, C. A. (1978). Talking to Children: A Search for Universals. In J. H. Greenberg (ed.), *Universals of Human Language* (pp. 205–224). Stanford: Stanford University Press.

Ferguson, C. A. (1983). Sports Announcer Talk: Syntactic Aspects of Register Variation. *Language in Society* 12: 153–172.

Ferguson, C. A. (1986). The Study of Religious Discourse. In D. Tannen and J. E. Alatis (eds.), *Languages and Linguistics: The Interdependence of Theory, Data, and Application*. Washington, DC: Georgetown University Press.

Ferguson, C. A. (1991). Diglossia Revisited. *Southwest Journal of Linguistics* 10(1): 214–234.

Ferguson, C. A. (1994). Dialect, Register and Genre: Working Assumptions about Conventionalization. In D. Biber and E. Finegan (eds.), *Sociolinguistic Perspectives on Register* (pp. 15–30). New York: Oxford University Press.

Ferguson, C. A., and Gumperz, J. J. (eds.) (1960a). *Linguistic Diversity in South Asia: Studies in Regional, Social and Functional Variation*. Indiana University Research Center in Anthropology, Folklore, and Linguistics. Bloomington: Indiana University Press.

Ferguson, C. A., and Gumperz, J. J. (1960b). Introduction. In C. A. Ferguson and J. J. Gumperz (eds.), *Linguistic Diversity in South Asia: Studies in Regional, Social and Functional Variation* (pp. 1–26). Indiana University Research Center in Anthropology, Folklore, and Linguistics. Bloomington: Indiana University Press.

Fernandez, J. W. (1986). Syllogisms of Association: Some Modern Extensions of Asturian

Deepsong. In J. Fernandez, *Persuasions and Performances: The Play of Tropes in Culture* (pp. 103–128). Bloomington: Indiana University Press.

Février, J. G. (1984). *Histoire de l'écriture*. Paris: Payot.

Field, M. (1999). Maintenance of Indigenous Ways of Speaking despite Language Shift: Language Socialization in a Navajo Preschool. PhD thesis, University of California, Santa Barbara.

Field, M. (2001). Triadic Directives in Navajo Language Socialization. *Language in Society* 30(2): 249–263.

Fiez, J. (2000). Sound and Meaning: How Native Language Affects Reading Strategies. *Nature Neuroscience* 3(1): 3–5.

Fillmore, C. J. (1968). The Case for Case. In E. Bach and E. T. Harms (eds.), *Universals of Linguistic Theory* (pp. 1–88). New York: Holt.

Fillmore, C. J. (1975). An Alternative to Checklist Theories of Meaning. In *First Annual Meeting of the Berkeley Linguistic Society* (pp. 123–131). Berkeley: Department of Linguistics, University of California at Berkeley.

Fillmore, C. J. (1977a). The Case for Case Reopened. In P. Cole and J. M. Sadock (ed.), *Syntax and Semantics*, vol. 8: *Grammatical Relations* (pp. 59–81). New York: Academic Press.

Fillmore, C. J. (1977b). Topics in Lexical Semantics. In R. Cole (ed.), *Current Issues in Linguistic Theory* (pp. 76–138). Bloomington: Indiana University Press.

Fillmore, C. J. (1982). Towards a Descriptive Framework for Spatial Deixis. In R. Jarvella and W. Klein (eds.), *Speech, Place, and Action: Studies in Deixis and Related Topics* (pp. 31–59). New York: John Wiley and Sons.

Fillmore, C. J. (1985). Frames and the Semantics of Understanding. *Quaderni di Semantica* 6(2): 222–253.

Fine, J. (1994). *How Language Works: Cohesion in Normal and Nonstandard Communication*. Norwood, NJ: Ablex.

Finegan, E. (1980). *Attitudes Toward English Usage: The History of a War of Words*. New York: Teachers College Press.

Finnegan, R. (1992). *Oral Traditions and the Verbal Arts: A Guide to Research Practices*. London: Routledge.

Firth, A., and Wagner, J. (1997). On Discourse, Communication, and (Some) Fundamental Concepts in SLA. *Modern Language Journal* 81(3): 285–300.

Firth, R. (1979). The Sacredness of Tikopia Chiefs. In W. A. Shack and P. S. Cohen (eds.), *Politics in Leadership: A Comparative Perspective* (pp. 139–168). Oxford: Clarendon Press.

Firth, R., with McLean, M. (1990). *Tikopia Songs: Poetic and Musical Art of a Polynesian People of the Solomon Islands*. Cambridge: Cambridge University Press.

Fischer, R. (1993). Abbé de l'Epée and the Living Dictionary. In J. V. Van Cleve (ed.), *Deaf History Unveiled* (pp. 13–26). Washington, DC: Gallaudet University Press.

Fischer, R., and Lane, H. (eds.) (1993). *Looking Back: A Reader on the History of Deaf Communities and Their Sign Languages*. Hamburg: Signum.

Fischer, S. (1975). Influences on Word Order Change in American Sign Language. In C. N. Li (ed.), *Word Order and Word Order Change* (pp. 1–25). Austin: University of Texas Press.

Fischer, S. (1978). Sign Language and Creoles. In P. Siple (ed.), *Understanding Language through Sign Language Research* (pp. 309–332). New York: Academic Press.

Fisher, S. (1986). *In the Patient's Best Interest: Women and the Politics of Medical Decisions*. New Brunswick: Rutgers University Press.

Fishman, J. (1967). Bilingualism with and without Diglossia; Diglossia with and without Bilingualism. *Journal of Social Issues* 23(2): 29–38.

Fishman, J. (1968). Nationality-nationalism and Nation-nationism. In J. Fishman, C. Ferguson, and J. DasGupta (eds.), *Language Problems of Developing Nations* (pp. 39–51). New York: Wiley & Sons.

Fishman, J. (ed.) (1999). *The Handbook of Language and Ethnic Identity*. New York: Oxford University Press.

Fishman, P. M. (1983). Interaction: The Work Women Do. In B. Thorne, C. Kramarae, and N. Henley (eds.), *Language, Gender and Society* (pp. 89–101). Rowley, MA: Newbury House.

Fivush, R. (1991). The Social Construction of Personal Narratives. *Merrill-Palmer Quarterly* 37(1): 59–81.

Fjord, L. (2001). Contested Signs: Discursive Disputes in the Geography of Pediatric Cochlear Implants, Language, Kinship, and Embodiment. PhD dissertation, University of Virginia.

Flap, H. (1996). Creation and Returns of Social Capital. Unpublished Paper. Presented at the Conference of the European Consortium for

Political Research on Social Capital and Democracy, Milan.

Fletcher, P., and MacWhinney, B. (eds.) (1995). *The Handbook of Child Language*. Oxford: Blackwell.

Flinn, J. (1990). We Still Have Our Customs: Being Pulapese in Truk. In J. Linnekin and L. Poyer (eds.), *Cultural Identity and Ethnicity in the Pacific* (pp. 103–126). Honolulu: University of Hawai'i Press.

Foley, J. M. (1988). *The Theory of Oral Composition*. Bloomington: Indiana University Press.

Foley, W. (1986). *The Papuan Languages of New Guinea*. New York: Cambridge University Press.

Foley, W. A. (1997). *Anthropological Linguistics: An Introduction*. Malden, MA: Blackwell.

Foley, W. A. (2000). The Languages of New Guinea. *Annual Review of Anthropology* 29: 357–404.

Foley, W., and Valin, R. V. (1984). *Functional Syntax and Universal Grammar*. Cambridge: Cambridge University Press.

Fonagy, I. (1981). Emotions, Voice, and Music. *Research Aspects of Singing* 3: 51–79. Royal Swedish Academy of Music.

Ford, C. (1993). *Grammar in Interaction: Adverbial Clauses in American English Conversations*. Cambridge: Cambridge University Press.

Ford, C., Fox, B., and Thompson, S. A. (eds.) (2002). *The Language of Turn and Sequence*. New York: Oxford University Press.

Ford, C. E., and Mori, J. (1994). Causal Markers in Japanese and English conversations: A Cross-linguistic Study of Interactional Grammar. *Pragmatics* 4: 31–61.

Ford, C., and Wagner, J. (eds.) (1996). Interaction-based Studies of Language [Special Issue]. *Pragmatics* 6(3).

Foster, G. M. (1948). *Empire's Children, The People of Tzintzuntzan*. Washington, DC: Smithsonian Institution. Institute of Social Anthropology, Publication No. 6.

Foucault, M. (1970). *The Order of Things: An Archaeology of the Human Sciences*. New York: Random House.

Foucault, M. (1972a). *The Archaeology of Knowledge & The Discourse on Language*. New York: Pantheon.

Foucault, M. (1972b). The Discourse on Language. In *The Archaeology of Knowledge* (pp. 215–237). New York: Pantheon.

Foucault, M. (1973). *Madness and Civilization: A History of Insanity in the Age of Reason*. New York: Vintage.

Foucault, M. (1979). *Discipline and Punish: The Birth of the Prison*. New York: Random House.

Foucault, M. (1980). *Power/Knowledge: Selected Interviews & Other Writings 1972–1977* (ed. and trans. C. Gordon). New York: Pantheon.

Foucault, M. (1984). The Birth of the Asylum. In P. Rabinow (ed.), *The Foucault Reader* (pp. 141–168). New York: Pantheon.

Fox, A. (1992). The Jukebox of History: Narratives of Loss and Desire in the Discourse of Country Music. *Popular Music* 11(1): 53–72.

Fox, A. (1995). "Out the Country:" Speech, Song and Feeling in Texas Rural Working-class Culture. PhD dissertation, Department of Anthropology, University of Texas at Austin.

Fox, A. (1997). Ain't it Funny How Time Slips Away? Talk, Trash, and Technology in a Texas "Redneck" Bar. In B. Ching and G. W. Creed (eds.), *Knowing Your Place: Rural Identity and Cultural Hierarchy* (pp. 105–130). New York: Routledge.

Fox, B. A., Hayashi, M., and Jasperson, R. (1996). Resources and Repair: A Cross-linguistic Study of Syntax and Repair. In E. Ochs, E. A. Schegloff, and S. A. Thompson (eds.), *Interaction and Grammar* (pp. 185–237). Cambridge: Cambridge University Press.

Fox, B., and Jasperson, R. (1995). A Syntactic Exploration of Repair in Conversation. In P. Davis (ed.), *Descriptive and Theoretical Modes in the Alternative Linguistics* (pp. 77–134). Amsterdam: John Benjamins.

Fox, J. J. (ed.) (1988). *To Speak in Pairs: Essays on the Ritual Languages of Eastern Indonesia*. Cambridge: Cambridge University Press.

Frake, C. O. (1969). The Ethnographic Study of Cognitive Systems. In S. A. Tyler (ed.), *Cognitive Anthropology* (pp. 28–41). New York: Holt, Rinehart, and Winston.

Frake, C. O. (1972). "Struck by Speech": The Yakan Concept of Litigation. In J. J. Gumperz and D. Hymes (eds.), *Directions in Sociolinguistics: The Ethnography of Communication* (pp. 106–129). New York: Holt, Rinehart and Winston.

Frank, A. W. (1995). *The Wounded Storyteller: Body, Illness, and Ethics*. Chicago: University of Chicago Press.

Frankel, H. H. (1960). Classical Chinese. In W. K. Wimsatt (ed.), *Versification: Major Language Types* (pp. 22–37). New York: New York University Press.

Frankel, R. (1990). Talking in Interview: A Dispreference for Patient-Initiated Questions in Physician–Patient Encounters. In G. Psathas (ed.), *Interaction Competence* (pp. 231–62). Washington, DC: International Institute for Ethnomethodology and Conversation Analysis, and University Press of America.

French, B. M. (2000). The Symbolic Capital of Social Identities: The Genre of Bargaining in an Urban Guatemalan Market. *Journal of Linguistic Anthropology* 10(2): 155–189.

French, P., and Local, J. (1983). Turn-competitive Incomings. *Journal of Pragmatics* 7: 17–38.

Freud, S. (1954 [1904]). *Zur Psychopathologie des Alltags. Über Vergessen, Versprechen, Vergreifen, Aberglaube und Irrtum. Mit einem Vorwort von Alexander Mitscherlich.* Frankfurt/Main: Fischer.

Freud, S. (1989). *Totem and Taboo.* New York: W.W. Norton.

Friedrich, P. (1966). Structural Implications of Russian Pronominal Usage. In W. Bright (ed.), *Sociolinguistics: Proceedings of the UCLA Sociolinguistics Conference, 1964* (pp. 214–259). The Hague: Mouton.

Friedrich, P. (1971). *The Tarascan Suffixes of Locative Space: Meaning and Morphotactics.* Bloomington: Indiana University Press.

Friedrich, P. (1986). *The Language Parallax: Linguistic Relativism and Poetic Indeterminacy.* Austin: University of Texas Press.

Friedrich, P. (1989). Language Ideology and Political Economy. *American Anthropologist* 91: 295–312.

Friess, S. (1998). Silence = Deaf. *POZ Magazine* (April): 60–63.

Frisbie, C. (1980a). Vocables in Navajo Ceremonial Music. *Ethnomusicology* 24(3): 347–392.

Frisbie, C. J. (ed.) (1980b). *Southwestern Indian Ritual Drama.* Albuquerque: University of New Mexico Press.

Frishberg, N. (1977). Arbitrariness and Iconicity: Historical Change in American Sign Language. *Language* 51: 696–719.

Frishberg, N. (1987a). Ghanaian Sign Language. In J. V. Van Cleve (ed.), *Gallaudet Encyclopedia of Deaf People and Deafness,* vol. 3 (pp. 778–779). New York: McGraw-Hill.

Frishberg, N. (1987b). Home Sign. In J. V. Van Cleve (ed.), *Gallaudet Encyclopedia of Deaf People and Deafness,* vol. 3 (pp. 128–131). New York: McGraw-Hill.

Frith, C. D., and Corcoran, R. (1996). Exploring "Theory of Mind" in People with Schizophrenia. *Psychological Medicine* 26(3): 521–530.

Frith, S. (1988). Why Do Songs Have Words? In S. Frith, *Music for Pleasure* (pp. 105–128). London: Routledge.

Frolov, D. (2000). *Classical Arabic Verse: History and Theory of 'Arūḍ.* Leiden, Boston, and Cologne: Brill.

Fromkin, V. A. (1973a). The Non-anomalous Nature of Anomalous Utterances. In V. A. Fromkin (ed.), *Speech Errors as Linguistic Evidence* (pp. 157–163). The Hague: Mouton.

Fromkin, V. A. (1973b). Introduction. In V. A. Fromkin (ed.), *Speech Errors as Linguistic Evidence* (pp. 11–45). The Hague: Mouton.

Fromkin, V. A. (1975). A Linguist Looks at "Schizophrenic Language". *Brain & Language* 2: 498–503.

Fromkin, V. A. (ed.) (1980). *Errors in Linguistic Performance: Slips of the Tongue, Ear, Pen and Hand.* New York: Academic Press.

Fromkin, V., and Rodman, R. (1978). *An Introduction to Language* (3rd edn.). New York: Holt, Rinehart and Winston.

Fubini, E. (2002). Quale musica ebraica oggi e quale uso nell'ambito della sinagoga. In S. Pozzi (ed.), *La musica sacra nelle chiese cristiane. Atti del Convegno internazionale di studi – Roma, 25–27 gennaio 2001* (pp. 141–147). Bologna: AlfaStudio.

Fukuyama, F. (1995). *Trust: The Social Virtues and the Creation of Prosperity.* New York: Free Press.

Fung, H. (1999). Becoming a Moral Child: The Socialization of Shame among Young Chinese Children. *Ethnos* 27(2): 180–209.

Gadamer, H.-G. (1976). *Philosophical Hermeneutics* (trans. D. E. Linge). Berkeley: University of California Press.

Gadamer, H.-G. (1986). *Truth and Method.* New York: Continuum.

Gaines, A. (1992). From DSM-I to DSM-R; Voices of Self, Mastery and the Other: A Cultural Constructivist Reading of U.S. Psychiatric Classification. *Social Science and Medicine* 35: 3–24.

Gal, S. (1978). Peasant Men Can't Get Wives: Language Change and Sex Roles in a Bilingual Community. *Language in Society* 7: 1–16.

Gal, S. (1979). *Language Shift: Social Determinants of Linguistic Change in Bilingual Austria.* New York: Academic Press.

Gal, S. (1987). Codeswitching and Consciousness in the European Periphery. *American Ethnologist* 14(4): 637–653.

Gal, S. (1988). The Political Economy of Code Choice. In M. Heller (ed.), *Codeswitching* (pp. 245–265). Berlin: Mouton de Gruyter.

Gal, S. (1989). Language and Political Economy. *Annual Review of Anthropology* 18: 345–367.

Gal, S. (1991). Between Speech and Silence: The Problematics of Research on Language and Gender. In M. DiLeonardo (ed.), *Gender at the Crossroads of Knowledge: Toward a New Anthropology of Gender* (pp. 175–203). Berkeley: University of California Press.

Gal, S. (1992a). Language, Gender, and Power: An Anthropological Perspective. In K. Hall, M. Bucholtz, and B. Moonwomon (eds.), *Locating Power: Proceedings of the Second Berkeley Women and Language Conference, April 4 and 5, 1992* (vol. 1, pp. 153–161). Berkeley: Berkeley Women and Language Group.

Gal, S. (1992b). Multiplicity and Contention among Ideologies. *Pragmatics* 2: 445–450.

Gal, S. (1993). Diversity and Contestation in Linguistic Ideologies: German Speakers in Hungary. *Language in Society* 22(3): 337–359.

Gal, S. (1995a). Language, Gender, and Power: An Anthropological Review. In K. Hall and M. Bucholtz (eds.), *Gender Articulated: Language and the Socially Constructed Self* (pp. 169–182). New York: Routledge.

Gal, S. (1995b). Lost in a Slavic Sea: Linguistic Theories and Expert Knowledge in 19th Century Hungary. *Pragmatics* 5: 155–166.

Gal, S. (2001). Linguistic Theories and National Images in Nineteenth-century Hungary. In S. Gal and K. A. Woolard (eds.), *Languages and Publics: The Making of Authority* (pp. 30–45). Manchester: St. Jerome.

Gal, S., and Woolard, K. A. (1995). Constructing Languages and Publics: Authority and Representation. *Pragmatics* 5: 129–138.

Gal, S., and Woolard, K. A. (eds.) (2001). *Languages and Publics: The Making of Authority.* Manchester: St. Jerome.

Galarza, J. (1979). *Estudios de escritura indígens tradicional (Azteca-Nahuatl).* México: Archivo General de la Nación.

Gallaudet Research Institute (2000). What Is the Reading Level of Deaf and Hard of Hearing People? http://gri.gallaudet.edu/literacy/#reading, Gallaudet University.

Gannon, J. R. (1981). *Deaf Heritage: A Narrative History of Deaf America.* Silver Spring, MD: NAD Publishers.

Gardiner, D. B. (1980). *Intonation and Music: The Semantics of Czech Prosody.* Bloomington: Physsardt.

Gardner, R. J. (1995). On Some Uses of the Conversational Token Mm. Dissertation, University of Melbourne.

Gardner-Chloros, P. (1995). Code-switching in Community, Regional and National Repertoires: The Myth of the Discreteness of Linguistic Systems. In L. Milroy and P. Muysken (eds.), *One Speaker, Two Languages* (pp. 68–89). Cambridge: Cambridge University Press.

Garfinkel, H. (1967). *Studies in Ethnomethodology.* Englewood Cliffs, NJ: Prentice-Hall.

Garfinkel, H. (1972). Remarks on Ethnomethodology. In J. J. Gumperz and D. Hymes (eds.), *Directions in Sociolinguistics: The Ethnography of Communication* (pp. 301–324). New York: Holt, Rinehart & Winston.

Garretson, M. (1976). Total Communication. *Volta Review* 78: 88–95.

Garrett, P. B. (1999). Language Socialization, Convergence, and Shift in St. Lucia, West Indies. PhD thesis, New York University.

Garrett, P. B. (2000). "High" Kwéyòl: The Emergence of a Formal Creole Register in St. Lucia. In J. H. McWhorter (ed.), *Language Change and Language Contact in Pidgins and Creoles* (pp. 63–101). Amsterdam: John Benjamins.

Garrett, P. B. (2003). An "English creole" That Isn't: On the Sociohistorical Origins and Linguistic Classification of the Vernacular English of St. Lucia. In M. Aceto and J. Williams (eds.), *Contact Englishes of the Eastern Caribbean* (pp. 155–210). Amsterdam: John Benjamins.

Garrett, P. B., and Baquedano-López, P. (2002). Language Socialization: Reproduction and Continuity, Transformation and Change. *Annual Review of Anthropology* 31: 339–361.

Garro, L. C. (2000). The Remembered Past in a Culturally Meaningful Life: Remembering as Cultural, Social and Cognitive Process. In H. Matthews and C. Moore (eds.), *The Psychology of Cultural Experience.* Cambridge: Cambridge University Press.

Garro, L. C., and Mattingly, C. (2000). Narrative as Construct and as Construction. In C. Mattingly and L. C. Garro (eds.), *Narrative and the Cultural Construction of Illness and*

Healing. Berkeley: University of California Press.

Garvin, P. L., and Riesenberg, S. H. (1952). Respect Behavior in Ponape: An Ethnolinguistic Study. *American Anthropologist* 54: 201–220.

Gasparov, M. L. (1989). *Ocherk istorii evropeiskogo stiha* [Outline of the History of European Verse]. Moscow: Izdatel'stvo Nauka. Trans. *Storia del verso europeo* (Bologna: il Mulino, 1993); *A History of European Versification* (Oxford: Clarendon Press, 1997).

Gass, S. M. (1998). Apples and Oranges: Or, Why Apples are not Oranges and Don't Need to Be: A Response to Firth and Wagner. *Modern Language Journal* 82: 83–90.

Gass, S., and Varonis, E. M. (1984). The Effect of Familiarity on the Comprehensibility of Nonnative Speech. *Language Learning* 34: 65–90.

Gates, H. L. (1984). The Blackness of Blackness: A Critique of the Sign and the Signifying Monkey. In H. L. Gates (ed.), *Black Literature and Literary Theory* (pp. 285–322). New York: Methuen.

Gates, H. L. (1988). *The Signifying Monkey: A Theory of Afro-American Literary Criticism.* New York: Oxford University Press.

Gatschet, A. S. (1899). "Real," "True," or "Genuine," in Indian Languages. *American Anthropologist* 1: 155–161.

Gaur, A. (1992). *A History of Writing.* New York: Cross River Press.

Geertz, C. (1960). *The Religion of Java.* Chicago: University of Chicago Press.

Geertz, C. (1973a). *The Interpretation of Cultures.* New York: Basic Books.

Geertz, C. (1973b). Thick Description: Toward an Interpretive Theory of Culture. In *The Interpretation of Cultures* (pp. 3–30). New York: Basic Books.

Gelb, I. J. (1963). *A Study of Writing.* Chicago: University of Chicago Press.

Gellner, E. (1983). *Nations and Nationalism.* Ithaca: Cornell University Press.

Geoghegan, W. H. (1969). The Use of Marking Rules in Semantic Systems. *Language Behavior Research Laboratory Working Paper 26.* Berkeley: University of California.

Geoghegan, W. H. (1970). A Theory of Marking Rules. *Language Behavior Research Laboratory Working Paper 37.* Berkeley: University of California.

Geoghegan, W. H. (1971). Information Processing Systems in Culture. In P. Kay (ed.), *Explorations in Mathematical Anthropology.* Cambridge, MA: MIT Press.

Geraci, M. (2002). *Il silenzio svelato. Rappresentazioni dell'assenza nella poesia popolare in Sicilia.* Rome: Meltemi.

Ghadessy, M. (ed.) (1988). *Registers of Written English: Situational Factors and Linguistic Features.* London: Pinter.

Giacalone Ramat, A. (1995). Code-switching in the Context of Dialect/Standard Language Relations. In L. Milroy and P. Muysken (eds.), *One Speaker, Two Languages* (pp. 45–67). Cambridge: Cambridge University Press.

Gibson, J. J. (1986). The Theory of Affordances. In J. J. Gibson (ed.), *The Ecological Approach to Visual Perception* (pp. 127–143). Hillsdale, NJ: Lawrence Erlbaum.

Giddens, A. (1979). *Central Problems in Social Theory: Action, Structure and Contradiction in Social Analysis.* Berkeley: University of California Press.

Giddens, A. (1984). *The Constitution of Society: Outline of the Theory of Structuration.* Berkeley: University of California Press.

Giglioli, P. P. (1972). *Language and Social Context.* Baltimore: Penguin.

Gilbert, S. M., and Gubar, S. (2000). *The Madwoman in the Attic: The Woman Writer and the Nineteenth-century Literary Imagination.* New Haven and London: Yale University Press.

Giles, H., Coupland, J., and Coupland, N. (eds.) (1991). *Contexts of Accommodation.* Cambridge: Cambridge University Press.

Giles, H., and Smith, P. (1979). Accommodation Theory: Optimal Levels of Convergence. In H. Giles and R. N. St. Clair (eds.), *Language and Social Psychology* (pp. 45–65). Oxford: Blackwell.

Gilligan, C. (1982). *In a Different Voice: Psychological Theory and Women's Development.* Cambridge, MA: Harvard University Press.

Giroux, H. (1992). *Border Crossings: Cultural Workers and the Politics of Education.* New York: Routledge.

Givón, T. (ed.) (1979). *Syntax and Semantics,* vol. 12: *Discourse and Syntax.* New York: Academic Press.

Givón, T. (1989). *Mind, Code, and Context: Essays in Pragmatics.* Hillsdale, NJ: Lawrence Erlbaum.

Glinert, L., and Shilhav, Y. (1991). Holy Land, Holy Language: A Study of Ultraorthodox Jewish Ideology. *Language in Society* 20: 59–86.

Gnerre, M. (1981). Dita, parole e numeri. Note sulla crescita della serie di numerali in shuar. *La ricerca folklorica* 4: 43–49.

Gnerre, M. (1986). The Decline of Dialogue: Ceremonial and Mythological Discourse among the Shuar and Achuar. In J. Sherzer and G. Urban (eds.), *Native South American Discourse* (pp. 307–341). Berlin: Mouton de Gruyter.

Godard, D. (1977). Same Setting, Different Norms: Phone Call Beginnings in France and the United States. *Language in Society* 6: 209–219.

Goddard, M. (1998). What Makes Hari Run? The Social Construction of Madness in a Highland Papua New Guinea Society. *Critique of Anthropology* 18(1): 61–81.

Godelier, M. (1986). *The Making of Great Men: Male Domination and Power among the New Guinea Baruya* (trans. R. P. Swyer). Cambridge: Cambridge University Press; Paris: Editions de la Maison des Sciences de l'Homme.

Goffman, E. (1956). On the Nature of Deference and Demeanor. *American Anthropologist* 58: 473–502.

Goffman, E. (1959). *The Presentation of Self in Everyday Life*. Garden City, NY: Doubleday.

Goffman, E. (1961). *Asylums: Essays on the Social Situation of Mental Patients and Other Inmates*. New York: Doubleday Anchor.

Goffman, E. (1963a). *Behavior in Public Places: Notes on the Social Organization of Gathering*. New York: Free Press.

Goffman, E. (1963b). *Stigma: Notes on the Management of Spoiled Identity*. Englewood Cliffs, NJ: Prentice-Hall.

Goffman, E. (1964a). The Neglected Situation. *American Anthropologist* 66: 133–135.

Goffman, E. (1964b). The Neglected Situation. In J. J. Gumperz and D. Hymes (eds.), *The Ethnography of Communication* (pp. 133–136). Special Issue of *American Anthropologist* 66, 6, Part II.

Goffman, E. (1967). On Facework: An Analysis of Ritual Elements in Social Interaction. In E. Goffman, *Interactional Ritual: Essays on Face-to-Face Behavior* (pp. 5–45). New York: Anchor Books.

Goffman, E. (1971). *Relations in Public: Microstudies of the Public Order*. New York: Harper and Row.

Goffman, E. (1974). *Frame Analysis: An Essay on the Organization of Experience*. New York: Harper and Row.

Goffman, E. (1981). Footing. *Semiotica* 25: 1–29. [Reprinted in E. Goffman, *Forms of Talk* (pp. 124–159). Philadelphia: University of Pennsylvania Press.]

Goffman, E. (1981c). *Forms of Talk*. Philadelphia: University of Pennsylvania Press.

Goffman, E. (1983). The Interaction Order. *American Sociological Review* 48: 1–17.

Goldin-Meadow, S. (1993). When Does Gesture Become Language? A Study of Gesture Used as a Primary Communication System by Deaf Children of Hearing Parents. In K. R. Gibson and T. Ingold (eds.), *Tools, Language, and Cognition in Human Evolution* (pp. 63–85). Cambridge: Cambridge University Press.

Goldman, I. (1970). *Ancient Polynesian Society*. Chicago: University of Chicago Press.

Goldman, L. (1983). *Talk Never Dies: The Language of Huli Disputes*. London: Tavistock.

Goldsmith, J. A. (1990). *Autosegmental and Metrical Phonology: A New Synthesis*. Oxford: Blackwell.

Goldziher, I. (1899). *Abhandlungen zur arabischen Philologie*, 2 vols. Leiden: Brill [repr.: Leiden: Brill, 1976].

González, N. (2001). *I Am My Language: Discourses of Women and Children in the Borderlands*. Tucson: University of Arizona Press.

Good, B. (1977). The Heart of What's the Matter: The Semantics of Illness in Iran. *Culture, Medicine, and Psychiatry* 1: 25–58.

Good, B. J., and Good, M.-J. D. (1994). In the Subjunctive Mode: Epilepsy Narratives in Turkey. *Social Science and Medicine* 38: 835–842.

Goodenough, W. H. (1956). Componential Analysis and the Study of Meaning. *Language* 32: 195–216.

Goodenough, W. H. (1965). Rethinking "Status" and "Role": Toward a General Model of the Cultural Organization of Social Relationships. In M. Banton (ed.), *The Relevance of Models for Social Anthropology* (pp. 1–24). London: Tavistock.

Goodman, M. F. (1971). The Strange Case of Mbugu. In D. Hymes (ed.), *Pidginization and Creolization of Languages* (pp. 243–254). Cambridge: Cambridge University Press.

Goodman, N. (1968). *The Languages of Art*. New York: Bobbs-Merrill.

Goodwin, C. (1979). The Interactive Construction of a Sentence in Natural Conversation. In G. Psathas (ed.), *Everyday Language: Studies in Ethnomethodology* (pp. 97–121). New York: Irvington.

Goodwin, C. (1980). Restarts, Pauses, and the Achievement of a State of Mutual Gaze at Turn Beginning. *Sociological Inquiry* 50(3–4): 272–302.

Goodwin, C. (1981). *Conversational Organization: Interaction between Speakers and Hearers.* New York: Academic Press.

Goodwin, C. (1984). Notes on Story Structure and the Organization of Participation. In J. M. Atkinson and J. Heritage (eds.), *Structures of Social Action* (pp. 225–246). Cambridge: Cambridge University Press.

Goodwin, C. (1986a). Audience Diversity, Participation and Interpretation. *Text* 6(3): 283–316.

Goodwin, C. (1986b). Gestures as a Resource for the Organization of Mutual Orientation. *Semiotica* 62(1/2): 29–49.

Goodwin, C. (1986c). Between and Within: Alternative Treatments of Continuers and Assessments. *Human Studies* 9(2/3): 205–218.

Goodwin, C. (1987a). Unilateral Departure. In G. Button and J. R. E. Lee (eds.), *Talk and Social Organization* (pp. 206–216). Clevedon: Multilingual Matters.

Goodwin, C. (1987b). Forgetfulness as an Interactive Resource. *Social Psychology Quarterly* 50(2): 115–131.

Goodwin, C. (1993). Recording Human Interaction in Natural Settings. *Pragmatics* 3: 181–209.

Goodwin, C. (1994). Professional Vision. *American Anthropologist* 96(3): 606–633.

Goodwin, C. (1995a). Co-constructing Meaning in Conversations with an Aphasic Man. *Research on Language and Social Interaction* 28(3): 233–260.

Goodwin, C. (1995b). Seeing in Depth. *Social Studies of Science* 25: 237–274.

Goodwin, C. (1996a). Practices of Color Classification. *Ninchi Kagaku (Cognitive Studies: Bulletin of the Japanese Cognitive Science Society)* 3(2): 62–81.

Goodwin, C. (1996b). Transparent Vision. In E. Ochs, E. Schegloff, and S. A. Thompson (eds.), *Interaction and Grammar* (pp. 370–404). Cambridge: Cambridge University Press.

Goodwin, C. (1997). The Blackness of Black: Color Categories as Situated Practice. In L. Resnick, R. Säljö, C. Pontecorvo, and B. Burge (eds.), *Discourse, Tools, and Reasoning* (pp. 111–140). Heidelberg: Springer Verlag.

Goodwin, C. (2000a). Action and Embodiment within Situated Human Interaction. *Journal of Pragmatics* 32: 1489–1522.

Goodwin, C. (2000b). Gesture, Aphasia, and Interaction. In D. McNeill (ed.), *Language and Gesture* (pp. 84–98). Cambridge: Cambridge University Press.

Goodwin, C. (2002a). Conversational Frameworks for the Accomplishment of Meaning in Aphasia. In C. Goodwin (ed.), *Conversation and Brain Damage.* Oxford and New York: Oxford University Press.

Goodwin, C. (2002b). Time in Action. *Current Anthropology* 43: S16–S35.

Goodwin, C. (2003). Pointing as Situated Practice. In S. Kita (ed.), *Pointing: Where Language, Culture and Cognition Meet.* Hillsdale, NJ: Lawrence Erlbaum.

Goodwin, C., and Duranti, A. (1992). Rethinking Context: An Introduction. In A. Duranti and C. Goodwin (eds.), *Rethinking Context: Language as an Interactive Phenomenon* (pp. 1–42). Cambridge: Cambridge University Press.

Goodwin, C., and Goodwin, M. H. (1987). Concurrent Operations on Talk: Notes on the Interactive Organization of Assessments. *IPrA Papers in Pragmatics* 1(1): 1–52.

Goodwin, C., and Goodwin, M. H. (1990). Interstitial Argument. In A. D. Grimshaw (ed.), *Conflict Talk: Sociolinguistic Investigations of Arguments in Conversation* (pp. 85–117). Cambridge: Cambridge University Press.

Goodwin, C., and Goodwin, M. H. (1992a). Assessments and the Construction of Context. In A. Duranti and C. Goodwin (eds.), *Rethinking Context: Language as an Interactive Phenomenon* (pp. 147–189). Cambridge: Cambridge University Press.

Goodwin, C., and Goodwin, M. H. (1992b). Context, Activity and Participation. In P. Auer and A. di Luzio, *The Contextualization of Language* (pp. 77–99). Amsterdam: John Benjamins.

Goodwin, C., and Goodwin, M. H. (1996). Seeing as a Situated Activity: Formulating Planes. In Y. Engeström and D. Middleton (eds.), *Cognition and Communication at Work* (pp. 61–95). Cambridge: Cambridge University Press.

Goodwin, C., Goodwin, M. H., and Olsher, D. (2002). Producing Sense with Nonsense Syllables: Turn and Sequence in the Conversations of a Man with Severe Aphasia. In C. Ford, B. Fox, and S. Thompson (eds.), *The*

Language of Turn and Sequence (pp. 56–80). Oxford and New York: Oxford University Press.

Goodwin, C., and Heritage, J. (1990). Conversation Analysis. *Annual Review of Anthropology* 19: 283–307.

Goodwin, M. H. (1980a). Directive–Response Speech Sequences in Girls' and Boys' Task Activities. In S. McConnell-Ginet, R. Borker, and N. Furman (eds.), *Women and Language in Literature and Society* (pp. 157–173). New York: Praeger.

Goodwin, M. H. (1980b). Processes of Mutual Monitoring Implicated in the Production of Description Sequences. *Sociological Inquiry* 50: 303–317.

Goodwin, M. H. (1990a). Byplay: Participant Structure and the Framing of Collaborative Collusion. In B. Conein, M. d. Fornel, and L. Quéré (eds.), *Les Formes de La Conversation* vol. 2 (pp. 155–180). Paris: CNET.

Goodwin, M. H. (1990b). *He-Said-She-Said: Talk as Social Organization among Black Children*. Bloomington: Indiana University Press.

Goodwin, M. H. (1995). Co-construction in Girls' Hopscotch. *Research on Language and Social Interaction* 28(3): 261–282.

Goodwin, M. H. (1997a). By-Play: Negotiating Evaluation in Story-telling. In G. R. Guy, C. Feagin, D. Schriffin, and J. Baugh (eds.), *Towards a Social Science of Language: Papers in Honor of William Labov*, vol. 2: *Social Interaction and Discourse Structures* (pp. 77–102). Amsterdam/Philadelphia: John Benjamins.

Goodwin, M. H. (1997b). Children's Linguistic and Social Worlds: The Knowns and Unknowns. *Anthropology Newsletter* 38(4): 1, 4–5.

Goodwin, M. H. (1998). Games of Stance: Conflict and Footing in Hopscotch. In S. Hoyle and C. T. Adger (eds.), *Kids Talk: Strategic Language Use in Later Childhood* (pp. 23–46). New York: Oxford University Press.

Goodwin, M. H. (1999). Constructing Opposition within Girls' Games. In M. Bucholtz, A. C. Liang, and L. A. Sutton (eds.), *Reinventing Identities: The Gendered Self in Discourse* (pp. 388–409). New York: Oxford University Press.

Goodwin, M. H. (2001). Organizing Participation in Cross-Sex Jump Rope: Situating Gender Differences within Longitudinal Studies of Activities. *Research on Language and Social Interaction*, Special Issue entitled "Gender Construction in Children's Inter-actions: A Cultural Perspective", 34(1): 75–106.

Goodwin, M. H., and Goodwin, C. (1986). Gesture and Coparticipation in the Activity of Searching for a Word. *Semiotica* 62: 51–75.

Goodwin, M. H., and Goodwin, C. (1987). Children's Arguing. In S. Philips, S. Steele, and C. Tanz (eds.), *Language, Gender, and Sex in Comparative Perspective* (pp. 200–248). Cambridge: Cambridge University Press.

Goodwin, M. H., and Goodwin, C. (2000). Emotion within Situated Activity. In N. Budwig, I. C. Uzgiris, and J. V. Wertsch (eds.), *Communication: An Arena of Development* (pp. 33–54). Stamford, CT: Ablex [repr. in Duranti (ed.) (2001c), pp. 239–257].

Goody, E. (1972). "Greeting", "Begging", and the Presentation of Respect. In J. S. La Fontaine (ed.), *The Interpretation of Ritual* (pp. 39–71). London: Tavistock.

Goody, J. (1977). *The Domestication of the Savage Mind*. Cambridge: Cambridge University Press.

Goody, J., and Watt, I. (1962). The Consequences of Literacy. *Comparative Studies in Society and History* 5: 304–326.

Goody, J., and Watt, I. (1968). The Consequences of Literacy. In J. Goody (ed.), *Literacy in Traditional Society* (pp. 27–68). Cambridge: Cambridge University Press.

Gopnik, A., Meltzoff, A. N., and Kuhl, P. K. (1999). *The Scientist in the Crib: Minds, Brains, and How Children Learn*. New York: William Morrow.

Gordon, D. P. (1983). Hospital Slang for Patients: Crocks, Gomers, Gorks and Others. *Language in Society* 13: 173–185.

Gordon, T. (2002). *Mormons and Modernity in Tonga: The Politics of Religion, Identity and Tradition*. Durham, NC: Duke University Press.

Gould, J. L. and Marler, P. (1987). Learning by Instinct. *Scientific American* 256(1): 74–85.

Graf, F. (1992). Gestures and Conventions: The Gestures of Roman Actors and Orators. In J. Bremmer and H. Roodenburg (eds.), *A Cultural History of Language* (pp. 36–58). Ithaca: Cornell University Press.

Graham, L. (1993). A Public Sphere in Amazonia? The Depersonalized Collaborative Construction of Discourse in Xavante. *American Ethnologist* 20: 717–741.

Graham, L. R. (1995). *Performing Dreams: Discourses of Immortality among the Xavante of Central Brazil*. Austin: University of Texas Press.

Graham, W. A. (1987). *Beyond the Written Word: Oral Aspects of Scripture in the History of Religion*. Cambridge: Cambridge University Press.

Gramsci, A. (1971). *Selections from the Prison Notebooks* (ed. and trans. Q. Hoare and G. Nowell Smith). New York: International Publishers.

Gramsci, A. (1975). *Gli intellettuali e l'organizzazione della cultura*. Rome: Editori Riuniti.

Gray, D. E. (2001). Accommodation, Resistance and Transcendence: Three Narratives of Autism. *Social Science & Medicine* 53(9): 1247–1257.

Gray, D. E. (2003). Gender and Coping: The Parents of Children with High Functioning Autism. *Social Science & Medicine* 56(3): 631–642.

Greatbatch, D. (1988). A Turn-Taking System for British News Interviews. *Language in Society* 17: 401–430.

Greatbatch, D. (1992). On the Management of Disagreement between News Interviewees. In P. Drew and J. Heritage (eds.), *Talk at Work: Interaction in Institutional Settings* (pp. 268–301). Cambridge: Cambridge University Press.

Greenberg, J. (1966). *Language Universals: With Special Reference to Feature Hierarchies*. The Hague: Mouton.

Greenberg, J. (1968). *Anthropological Linguistics: An Introduction*. New York: Random House.

Greenberg, J. H., Hoijer, H., Maquet, J. J. P., Hymes, D. H., and Friedrich, P. (1980). *On Linguistic Anthropology: Essays in Honor of Harry Hoijer, 1979*. Malibu: published for the UCLA Dept. of Anthropology by Undena Publications.

Grenoble, L. A., and Whaley, L. J. (eds.) (1998). *Endangered Languages: Language Loss and Community Response*. Cambridge: Cambridge University Press.

Grice, H. P. (1975). Logic and Conversation. In P. Cole and N. L. Morgan (eds.), *Syntax and Semantics*, vol. 3: *Speech Acts* (pp. 41–58). New York: Academic Press.

Griffin, P., and Cole, M. (1984). Current Activity for the Future: The Zo-ped. In B. Rogoff and J. Wertsch (eds.), *New Directions for Child Development* (pp. 45–63). San Francisco: Jossey-Bass.

Grima, B. (1992). *The Performance of Emotion among Paxtun Women*. Austin: University of Texas Press.

Grimshaw, A. D. (1980). Mishearings, Misunderstandings, and Other Nonsuccesses in Talk: A Plea for Redress of Speaker-oriented Bias. *Sociological Inquiry* 50(3–4): 31–74.

Grimshaw, A. D. (ed.) (1990). *Conflict Talk: Sociolinguistic Investigations of Arguments in Conversation*. Cambridge: Cambridge University Press.

Grimshaw, J. (1990). *Argument Structure*. Cambridge, MA: MIT Press.

Groce, N. E. (1985). *Everyone Here Spoke Sign Language: Hereditary Deafness on Martha's Vineyard*. Cambridge, MA: Harvard University Press.

Gross, J. E. (1993). The Politics of Unofficial Language Use: Walloon in Belgium, Tamazight in Morocco. *Critique of Anthropology* 13: 177–208.

Gross, P. (1983). *Die Verheißungen der Dienstleistungsgesellschaft: soziale Befreiung oder Sozialherrschaft?* Opladen: Westdeutscher Verlag.

Gross, P. (1995). *Die Multioptionsgesellschaft*. Frankfurt/Main: Suhrkamp.

Gross, P., Garhammer, M., and Eckardt, J. (1983). *Freizeitmarkt, Dienstleistungen und häuslicher Freizeitpfad*. Dortmund: Institut für Landes- und Stadtentwicklung des Landes Nordrhein-Westfalen (ILS).

Gross, S. (2000). Intentionality and the Markedness Model in Literary Codeswitching. *Journal of Pragmatics* 32: 1283–1303.

Grushkin, D. A. (1996). Academic, Linguistic, Social and Identity Development in Hard-of-Hearing Adolescents Educated within an ASL/English Bilingual/Bicultural Educational Setting for Deaf and Hard-of-Hearing Students. PhD dissertation, University of Arizona, Tucson.

Guerra, J. (1998). *Close to Home: Oral and Literate Practices in a Transnational Mexicano Community*. New York: Teachers College Press.

Guerra, J., and Farr, M. (2002). Writing on the Margins: The Spiritual and Autobiographical Discourse of Two Mexicanas in Chicago. In G. Hull and K. Schultz (eds.), *School's Out! Bridging Out-of-School Literacies with Classroom Practice* (pp. 96–123). New York: Teachers College, Columbia University.

Gumperz, J. J. (1958). Dialect Differences and Social Stratification in a North Indian Village. *American Anthropologist* 60: 668–682.

Gumperz, J. J. (1962). Types of Linguistic Community. *Anthropological Linguistics* 4: 28–40.

Gumperz, J. J. (1964). Linguistic and Social Interaction in Two Communities. *American Anthropologist* 66(6): 137–153.

Gumperz, J. J. (1968a). The Speech Community. *International Encyclopedia of the Social Sciences* (pp. 381–386). New York: Macmillan.

Gumperz, J. J. (1968b). Types of Linguistic Communities. In J. A. Fishman (ed.), *Readings in the Sociology of Language* (pp. 460–472). The Hague: Mouton.

Gumperz, J. J. (1972a). Introduction. In J. J. Gumperz and D. Hymes (eds.), *Directions in Sociolinguistics: The Ethnography of Communication* (pp. 1–25). New York: Holt, Rinehart and Winston.

Gumperz, J. J. (1972b). The Speech Community. In P. P. Giglioli (ed.), *Language and Social Context* (pp. 219–231). Harmondsworth: Penguin.

Gumperz, J. J. (1977). Sociocultural Knowledge in Conversational Inference. In M. Saville-Troike (ed.), *Georgetown University Round Table on Languages and Linguistics 1977*. Washington, DC: Georgetown University Press.

Gumperz, J. J. (1982a). *Discourse Strategies*. Cambridge: Cambridge University Press.

Gumperz, J. J. (ed.) (1982b). *Language and Social Identity*. Cambridge: Cambridge University Press.

Gumperz, J. J. (1984). Comments. In J. P. Auer and A. di Luzio (eds.), *Interpretive Sociolinguistics* (pp. 108–112). Tübingen: Gunter Narr Verlag.

Gumperz, J. J. (1992a). Contextualization and Understanding. In A. Duranti and C. Goodwin (eds.), *Rethinking Context: Language as an Interactive Phenomenon* (pp. 229–252). Cambridge: Cambridge University Press.

Gumperz, J. J. (1992b). Contextualization Revisited. In P. Auer and A. di Luzio (eds.), *The Contextualization of Language*. Amsterdam: John Benjamins.

Gumperz, J. J. (1997). On the Interactional Bases of Speech Community Membership. In G. R. Guy, C. Feagin, D. Schiffrin, and J. Baugh (eds.), *Towards a Social Science of Language: Papers in Honor of William Labov*, vol. 2. Philadelphia: John Benjamins.

Gumperz, J. J., and Hymes, D. (eds.) (1964). The Ethnography of Communication. Special Issue of *American Anthropologist*, 66, 6, Part II.

Gumperz, J. J., and Hymes, D. (1972). *Directions in Sociolinguistics: The Ethnography of Communication*. New York: Holt, Rinehart and Winston.

Gumperz, J. J., and Levinson, S. (1991). Rethinking Linguistic Relativity. *Current Anthropology* 32: 613–623.

Gumperz, J. J., and Levinson, S. C. (eds.) (1996). *Rethinking Linguistic Relativity*. Cambridge: Cambridge University Press.

Gumperz, J. J., and Tannen, D. (1979). Individual and Social Differences in Language Use. In C. Fillmore et al. (eds.), *Individual Differences in Language Ability and Language Behavior* (pp. 305–325). New York: Academic Press.

Gumperz, J. J., and Wilson, R. (1971). Convergence and Creolization: A Case from the Indo-Aryan/Dravidian Border. In D. Hymes (ed.), *Pidginization and Creolization of Languages* (pp. 151–167). Cambridge: Cambridge University Press.

Günthner, S. (1986). Scherzen und Lachen in Gesprächen von Frauen und Männern. *Der Deutschunterricht* 3: 16–29.

Günthner, S. (1992a). Die interaktive Konstruktion von Geschlechterrollen, kulturellen Identitäten und institutioneller Dominanz. Sprechstundengespräche zwischen Deutschen und Chinesen/innen [1]. In S. Günthner and H. Kotthoff (eds.), *Die Geschlechter im Gespräch: Kommunikation in Institutionen* (pp. 91–125). Stuttgart: Metzler.

Günthner, S. (1992b). Sprache und Geschlecht: Ist Kommunikation zwischen Frauen und Männern interkulturelle Kommunikation? *Linguistische Berichte* 138: 123–142.

Günthner, S. (1992c). The Construction of Gendered Discourse: An Analysis of German–Chinese Interactions. *Discourse & Society* 3: 167–191.

Günthner, S. (1993). *Diskursstrategien in der interkulturellen Kommunikation. Analysen deutsch–chinesischer Gespräche*. Linguistische Arbeiten 286. Tübingen: Niemeyer.

Günthner, S. (1994). "Also moment SO seh ich das NICHT". *Zeitschrift für Literaturwissenschaft und Linguistik* 93: 97–122.

Günthner, S. (1996). Male–Female Speaking Practices across Cultures. In M. Hellinger and U. Ammon (eds.), *Contrastive Sociolinguistics* (pp. 447–474). New York: Mouton.

Günthner, S. (1998). Witzige Darbietungen auf eigene Kosten. Über Komplexitäten weiblicher Imagepolitik in der Scherzkommunikation. *Zeitschrift für germanistische Linguistik* 139/140: 253–279.

Günthner, S. (2000a). From Concessive Connector to Discourse Marker: The Use of *obwohl* in Everyday German Interaction. In E. Couper-Kuhlen and B. Kortmann (eds.), *Cause – Condition – Concession – Contrast. Cognitive and Discourse Perspectives* (pp. 439–468). Berlin: de Gruyter.

Günthner, S. (2000b). *Vorwurfsaktivitäten in der Alltagsinteraktion*. Tübingen: Niemeyer.

Günthner, S., and Christmann, G. B. (1996). Sprache und Affekt. Die Inszenierung von Entrüstungen im Gespräch. *Deutsche Sprache* 1: 1–33.

Günthner, S., and Kotthoff, H. (eds.) (1992). *Die Geschlechter im Gespräch: Kommunikation in Institutionen*. Stuttgart: Metzler.

Gutiérrez, K., Baquedano-López, P., and Alvarez, H. (2001). Literacy as Hybridity: Moving beyond Bilingualism in Urban Classrooms. In M. Reyes and J. Halcón (eds.), *The Best for Our Children: Latina/Latino Voices in Literacy* (pp. 122–141). New York: Teachers College Press.

Gutiérrez, K., Baquedano-López, P., Alvarez, H., and Chiu, M. (1999). Building a Culture of Collaboration through Hybrid Language Practices. *Theory into Practice* 38(2): 87–93.

Gutiérrez, K., Baquedano-López, P., and Tejeda, C. (1999). Rethinking Diversity: Hybridity and Hybrid Language Practices in the Third Space. *Mind, Culture, and Activity* 6(4): 286–303.

Gutiérrez, K., Baquedano-López, P., and Turner, M. G. (1997). Putting Language back into the Language Arts: When the Radical Middle Meets the Third Space. *Language Arts* 74(5): 368–378.

Gutiérrez, K., Rymes, B., and Larson, J. (1995). Script, Counterscript, and Underlife in the Classroom: James Brown versus Brown v. Board of Education. *Harvard Educational Review* 65(3): 445–471.

Gutiérrez, K., and Stone, L. (1997). A Cultural-historical View of Learning and Learning Disabilities: Participating in a Community of Learners. *Learning Disabilities: Research and Practice* 12(2): 123–131.

Gutiérrez, K., and Stone, L. (2000). Synchronic and Diachronic Dimensions of Social Practice: An Emerging Methodology for Cultural-historical Perspectives on Literacy Learning. In C. Lee and P. Smagorinsky (eds.), *Vygotskian Perspectives on Literacy Research: Con-structing Meaning through Collaborative Inquiry* (pp. 150–164). Cambridge: Cambridge University Press.

Gutiérrez, K. D., Stone, L., and Larson, J. (in press). Hypermediating in the Urban Classroom: When Scaffolding Becomes Sabatoge in Narrative Activity. In C. D. Baker, J. Cook-Gumperz, and A. Luke (eds.), *Literacy and Power*. Oxford: Blackwell.

Guy, G. (1988). Language and Social Class. In F. J. Newmeyer (ed.), *Linguistics: The Cambridge Survey – IV. Language: The Socio-cultural Context* (pp. 37–63). Cambridge: Cambridge University Press.

Haakana, M. (1999). Laughing Matters. A Conversation Analytic Study of Laughter in Doctor–Patient Interaction. Unpublished doctoral dissertation, University of Helsinki, Department of Finnish.

Haas, M. (1953). Sapir and the Training of Anthropological Linguistics. *American Anthropologist* 55: 447–449.

Haas, M. (1964). Men's and Women's Speech in Koasati. In D. Hymes (ed.), *Language in Culture and Society* (pp. 228–233). New York: Harper and Row.

Haas, M. R. (1977). Anthropological Linguistics: History. In A. F. C. Wallace (ed.), *Perspectives in Anthropology 1976* (pp. 33–47). A Special Publication of the American Anthropological Association.

Haas, M. R. (1978). Boas, Sapir, and Bloomfield: Their Contribution to American Indian Linguistics. In *Language, Culture, and History: Essays by Mary R. Haas. Selected and Introduced by Anwar S. Dil* (pp. 194–206). Stanford, CA: Stanford University Press.

Haiman, J. (ed.) (1985). *Iconicity in Syntax: Proceedings of a Symposium on Iconicity in Syntax, Stanford, June 24–6, 1983*. Amsterdam: John Benjamins.

Hak, T. (1998). "There Are Clear Delusions." The Production of a Factual Account. *Human Studies* 21: 419–436.

Hakulinen, A. (1993). The Grammar of Opening Routines. In S. Shore and M. Vilkuna (eds.), *SKY 1993. 1993 Yearbook of the Linguistic Association of Finland* (pp. 149–170). Helsinki: Linguistic Association of Finland.

Hakulinen, A. (2001). On Some Uses of the Discourse Particle *kyllä* in Finnish Conversations. In M. Selting and E. Couper-Kuhlen (eds.), *Studies in Interactional Linguistics* (pp. 171–198). Amsterdam: John Benjamins.

Hale, K. (1971). A Note on a Walbiri Tradition of Antonymy. In D. D. Steinberg and L. J.

Jakobovitz (eds.), *Semantics: An Interdisciplinary Reader in Philosophy, Linguistics and Psychology* (pp. 472–482). Cambridge: Cambridge University Press.

Hale, K. (1983). Warpiri and the Grammar of Non-configurational Languages. *Natural Languages and Linguistic Theory* 1: 5–48.

Hale, K., Krauss, M., Watahomigie, L. J., Yamamoto, A. Y., Craig, C., Jeanne, L. M., and England, N. C. (1992). Endangered Languages. *Language* 68(1): 1–62.

Hall, E. T. (1983). *The Dance of Life: The Other Dimensions of Time*. New York: Anchor Books/Doubleday.

Hall, K. (1995). Lipservice on the Fantasy Lines. In K. Hall and M. Bucholtz (eds.), *Gender Articulated: Language and the Socially Constructed Self* (pp. 183–216). New York: Routledge.

Hall, K. (1996). Cyberfeminism. In S. C. Herring (ed.), *Computer-mediated Communication: Linguistic, Social, and Cross-cultural Perspectives* (pp. 147–170). Amsterdam: John Benjamins.

Hall, K. (1999). Performativity. *Journal of Linguistic Anthropology* 9: 184–187.

Hall, K. (2003). Exceptional Speakers: Contested and Problematized Gender Identities. In J. Holmes and M. Meyerhoff (eds.), *The Handbook of Language and Gender*. Oxford: Blackwell.

Hall, K., and Bucholtz, M. (eds.) (1995). *Gender Articulated: Language and the Socially Constructed Self.* New York: Routledge.

Hall, K., Bucholtz, M., and Moonwomon, B. (eds.) (1992). *Locating Power: Proceedings of the Second Berkeley Women and Language Conference.* Berkeley: Berkeley Women and Language Group.

Hall, K., and O'Donovan, V. (1996). Shifting Gender Positions among Hindi-Speaking Hijras. In V. L. Bergvall, J. M. Bing, and A. F. Freed (eds.), *Rethinking Language and Gender Research: Theory and Practice* (pp. 228–266). London: Longman.

Hall, R. A. Jr. (1962). The Life Cycle of Pidgin Languages. *Lingua* 11: 151–156.

Hall, S. (1996). The West and the Rest: Discourse and Power. In S. Hall, D. Held, D. Hubert, and K. Thompson (eds.), *Modernity: An Introduction to Modern Societies* (pp. 118–227). Oxford: Blackwell.

Halle, M., and Keyser, S. J. (1980). Metrica. *Enciclopedia Einaudi*, 9 [Einaudi Encyclopedia]. Turin: Einaudi (transl. of Halle and Keyser, "Metrics". Cambridge, MA: MIT, unpublished manuscript).

Halliday, M. A. K. (1964). The Users and Uses of Language. In M. A. K. Halliday, A. Macintosh, and P. Strevens (eds.), *The Linguistic Sciences and Language Teaching* (pp. 75–110). Bloomington: Indiana University Press.

Halliday, M. A. K. (1973). *Explorations in the Functions of Language*. London: Arnold.

Halliday, M. A. K. (1976). Anti-languages. *American Anthropologist* 78: 570–583.

Halliday, M. A. K. (1978). *Language as a Social Semiotic: The Social Interpretation of Language and Meaning*. Baltimore, MA: University Park Press.

Halliday, M. A. K. (1985a). *Learning How to Mean*. London: Edward Arnold.

Halliday, M. A. K. (1985b). *Spoken and Written Language*. Victoria: Deakin University.

Halliday, M. A. K. (1988). On the Language of Physical Science. In M. Ghadessy (ed.), *Registers of Written English* (pp. 162–178). London: Pinter.

Hamers, J. F. and Blanc, M. H. A. (2000). *Bilinguality and Bilingualism* (2nd edn.). Cambridge: Cambridge University Press.

Hancock, I. (1984). Romani and Anglo-Romani. In P. Trudgill (ed.), *Language in the British Isles* (pp. 367–383). Cambridge: Cambridge University Press.

Hanks, W. F. (1986). Authenticity and Ambivalence in the Text: A Colonial Maya Case. *American Ethnologist* 13(4): 721–744.

Hanks, W. F. (1987). Discourse Genres in a Theory of Practice. *American Ethnologist* 14(4): 668–692.

Hanks, W. F. (1990). *Referential Practice: Language and Lived Space among the Maya*. Chicago: University of Chicago Press.

Hanks, W. F. (1993). Notes on Semantics in Linguistic Practice. In C. Calhoun, E. LiPuma, and M. Postone (eds.), *Bourdieu: Critical Perspectives* (pp. 139–155). Cambridge: Polity Press.

Hanks, W. F. (1996a). Exorcism and the Description of Participant Roles. In M. Silverstein and G. Urban (eds.), *Natural Histories of Discourse* (pp. 160–202). Chicago: University of Chicago Press.

Hanks, W. F. (1996b). *Language and Communicative Practices*. Boulder, CO: Westview Press.

Hanks, W. F. (2000). *Intertexts: Writings on Language, Utterance, and Context*. Lanham, MD: Rowman & Littlefield.

Hannan, T. E. (1992). An Examination of Spontaneous Pointing in 20- to 50-month-old Children. *Perceptual and Motor Skills* 74 (April 1992): 651–658.

Hannerz, U. (1987). The World in Creolisation. *Africa* 57(4): 546–559.

Hannerz, U. (1996). *Transnational Connections: Culture, People, Places*. London: Routledge.

Hanson, M. (1993). Foreword. In O. Negt and A. Kluge (eds.), *Public Sphere and Experience* (pp. ix–xlix). Minneapolis: University of Minnesota Press.

Hanzeli, V. E. (1969). *Missionary Linguistics in New France*. The Hague: Mouton.

Haroutunian-Gordon, S. (1991). *Turning the Soul: Teaching through Conversation in the High School*. Chicago: University of Chicago Press.

Harries, P. (1988). The Roots of Ethnicity: Discourse and the Politics of Language Construction in South-East Africa. *African Affairs* 87: 25–52.

Harris, R. (1986). *The Origin of Writing*. London: Duckworth.

Harris, R. (1993). *La sémiologie de l'écriture*. Paris: CNRS.

Harris, R. (1995). *Signs of Writing*. London: Routledge.

Harris, R. (2000). *Rethinking Writing*. London: Athlone Press.

Harrison, F. V. (ed.) (1988). *Urban Anthropology* 17(2/3). Special Issue: Black Folks in Cities Here and There: Changing Patterns of Domination and Response.

Harrison, F. V. (1995). The Persistent Power of "Race" in the Cultural and Political Economy of Racism. *Annual Review of Anthropology* 24: 47–74.

Harweg, R. (1968). Language and Music: An Immanent and Sign Theoretic Approach. *Foundations of Language* 4: 270–281.

Häußermann, H., and Siebel, W. (1995). *Dienstleistungsgesellschaften*. Frankfurt/Main: Suhrkamp.

Have, P. ten (1991). Talk and Institution: A Reconsideration of the "Asymmetry" of Doctor–Patient Interaction. In D. Boden and D. H. Zimmerman (eds.), *Talk and Social Structure* (pp. 138–163). Cambridge: Polity Press.

Havel, V. (1989). *Letters to Olga* (trans. P. Wilson). New York: Henry Holt.

Havelock, E. A. (1976). *Origins of Western Literacy*. Toronto: Ontario Institute for Studies in Education.

Haviland, J. (1977). *Gossip, Reputation, and Knowledge in Zinacantán*. Chicago: University of Chicago Press.

Haviland, J. (1993). Anchoring, Iconicity, and Orientation in Guugu Yimithirr Pointing Gestures. *Journal of Linguistic Anthropology* 3(1): 3–45.

Haviland, J. (1996a). Owners versus Bubu Gujin: Land Rights and Getting the Language Right in Guugu Yimithirr Country. *Journal of Linguistic Anthropology*, 6(2): 145–160.

Haviland, J. (1996b). Projections, Transpositions, and Relativity. In J. J. Gumperz and S. C. Levinson (eds.), *Rethinking Linguistic Relativity* (pp. 271–323). Cambridge: Cambridge University Press.

Haviland, J. (1998). Early Pointing Gestures in Zinacantán. *Journal of Linguistic Anthropology* 8(2): 162–196.

Haviland, J. (2000). Pointing, Gesture Spaces, and Mental Maps. In D. McNeill (ed.), *Language and Gesture: Window into Thought and Action* (pp. 13–46). Cambridge: Cambridge University Press.

Haviland, J. (2001). Gesture. In A. Duranti (ed.), *Key Terms in Language and Culture* (pp. 83–86). Oxford: Blackwell.

Hawkinson, A., and Hyman, L. M. (1974). Hierarchies of Narual Topic in Shona. *Studies in African Linguistics* 5: 147–170.

Hayashi, M. (1999). Where Grammar and Interaction Meet: A Study of Co-participant Completion in Japanese Conversation. *Human Studies* 22: 475–499.

Hayashi, M., Mori, J., and Takagi, T. (2002). Contingent Achievement of Co-tellership in a Japanese Conversation: An Analysis of Talk, Gaze, and Gesture. In C. Ford, B. A. Fox, and S. A. Thompson (eds.), *The Language of Turn and Sequence* (pp. 81–122). New York: Oxford University Press.

He, A. W. (2001). The Language of Ambiguity: Practices in Chinese Heritage Language Classes. *Discourse Studies* 3(1): 75–96.

Heath, C. (1984). Talk and Recipiency: Sequential Organization in Speech and Body Movement. In J. M. Atkinson and J. Heritage (eds.), *Structures of Social Action: Studies in Conversation Analysis* (pp. 247–265). Cambridge: Cambridge University Press.

Heath, C. (1986). *Body Movement and Speech in Medical Interaction*. Cambridge: Cambridge University Press.

Heath, C., and Luff, P. (1996). Convergent Activities: Line Control and Passenger

Information on the London Underground. In Y. Engeström and D. Middleton (eds.), *Cognition and Communication at Work* (pp. 96–129). Cambridge: Cambridge University Press.

Heath, S. (1983). *Ways with Words: Language, Life and Work in Communities and Classrooms.* Cambridge: Cambridge University Press.

Heath, S. (1985). The Cross-cultural Study of Language Acquisition. *Papers and Reports on Child Language Development* 24: 1–21.

Heath, S. (1986). What No Bedtime Story Means: Narrative Skills at Home and School. In B. B. Schieffelin and E. Ochs (eds.), *Language Socialization across Cultures* (pp. 97–124). New York: Cambridge University Press.

Heath, S. (1988). Protean Shapes in Literacy Event: Ever-Shifting Oral and Literate Traditions. In E. Kintgen, B. M. Kroll, and M. Rose (eds.), *Perspectives on Literacy* (pp. 348–370). Carbondale and Edwardsville: Southern Illinois University Press.

Heffner, R.-M. S. (1950). *General Phonetics.* Madison: University of Wisconsin Press.

Heidegger, M. (1962). *Being and Time.* New York: Harper & Row.

Heidegger, M. (1971a). *On the Way to Language.* New York: Harper & Row.

Heidegger, M. (1971b). *Poetry, Language, Thought.* New York: Harper & Row.

Heidegger, M. (1977). Letter on Humanism. In D. F. Krell (ed.), *Martin Heidegger: Basic Writings* (pp. 193–242). New York: Harper & Row.

Heider, E. R. (1972). Universals in Color Naming and Memory. *Journal of Experimental Psychology* 93: 10–20.

Heinemann, F., and Assion, H. J. (1996). Language Regression to the Mother Tongue in Polyglot Patients with Acute Psychosis [German]. *Nervenarzt* 67(7): 599–601.

Heller, M. (1988). Strategic Ambiguity: Codeswitching in the Management of Conflict. In M. Heller (ed.), *Codeswitching* (pp. 77–96). Berlin: Mouton de Gruyter.

Heller, M. (1995a). Code-switching and the Politics of Language. In L. Milroy and P. Muysken (eds.), *One Speaker, Two Languages* (pp. 158–174). Cambridge: Cambridge University Press.

Heller, M. (1995b). Language Choice, Social Institutions, and Symbolic Domination. *Language in Society* 24: 373–405.

Heller, M. (1999a). *Linguistic Minorities and Modernity: A Sociolinguistic Ethnography.* London: Longman.

Heller, M. (1999b). Heated Language in a Cold Climate. In J. Blommaert (ed.), *Language Ideological Debates* (pp. 143–170). Berlin: Mouton de Gruyter.

Henley, N., and Kramarae, C. (1991). Gender, Power, and Miscommunication. In N. Coupland, H. Giles, and J. Wiemann (eds.), *Miscommunication and Problematic Talk* (pp. 18–43). Newbury Park, CA: Sage.

Henrotte, G. A. (1988). Language, Linguistics, and Music: A Source Study. PhD thesis. University of California, Berkeley.

Henson, H. (1974). *British Social Anthropologists and Language: History of Separate Development.* Oxford: Clarendon Press.

Herder, J. G. (1965). *Über den Ursprung der Sprache.* Stuttgart: Verlag Freies Geistesleben.

Herder, J. G. (1966 [1787]). Essay on the Origin of Language. In *On the Origin of Language* (pp. 85–166). Chicago: University of Chicago Press.

Herdt, G. (1997). *Same Sex, Different Cultures: Gays and Lesbians across Cultures.* Boulder, CO: Westview Press.

Heritage, J. (1984a). *Garfinkel and Ethnomethodology.* Cambridge: Polity Press.

Heritage, J. (1984b). A Change-of-State Token and Aspects of its Sequential Placement. In J. M. Atkinson and J. Heritage (eds.), *Structures of Social Action: Studies in Conversation Analysis* (pp. 299–345). Cambridge: Cambridge University Press.

Heritage, J. (1990/1). Intention, Meaning and Strategy: Observations on Constraints on Interaction Analysis. *Research on Language and Social Interaction* 24: 311–332.

Heritage, J., and Atkinson, J. M. (1984). Introduction. In J. M. Atkinson and J. Heritage (eds.), *Structures of Social Action: Studies in Conversation Analysis* (pp. 1–15). Cambridge: Cambridge University Press.

Heritage, J., and Greatbatch, D. (1991). On the Institutional Character of Institutional Talk: The Case of News Interviews. In D. Boden and D. H. Zimmerman (eds.), *Talk and Social Structure* (pp. 93–137). Berkeley and Los Angeles: University of California Press.

Heritage, J., and Sorjonen, M.-L. (1994). Constituting and Maintaining Activities across Sequences: *and*-prefacing as a Feature of Question Design. *Language in Society* 23: 1–29.

Herzfeld, M. (1996). National Spirit or Breath of Nature? The Expropriation of Folk Positivism in the Discourse of Greek Nationalism. In M. Silverstein and G. Urban (eds.), *Natural Histories of Discourse* (pp. 277–298). Chicago: University of Chicago Press.

Herzog, G. (1934). Speech Melody and Primitive Music. *Musical Quarterly* 20: 452–466.

Herzog, G. (1942). Text and Melody in Primitive Music. *Bulletin of the American Musicological Society* 6: 10–11.

Herzog, G. (1945). Drum Signalling in a West African Tribe. *Word* 1: 217–238.

Herzog, G. (1950). Song. In M. Leach (ed.), *Funk & Wagnalls Dictionary of Folklore, Mythology and Legend*, vol. 2 (pp. 1032–1050).

Higgins, P. (1980). *Outsiders in a Hearing World: A Sociology of Deafness*. Beverly Hills, CA: Sage.

Hill, A. A. (1964). A Note on Primitive Languages. In D. Hymes (ed.), *Language in Culture and Society: A Reader in Linguistics and Anthropology* (pp. 86–89). New York: Harper & Row.

Hill, C. A., and Podstavsky, S. (1976). The Interfacing of Language and Music in Hausa Praise-singing. *Ethnomusicology* 20(3): 535–540.

Hill, J. D. (1993). *Keepers of the Sacred Chants: The Poetics of Ritual Power in an Amazonian Society*. Tucson: University of Arizona Press.

Hill, J. H. (1985). The Grammar of Consciousness and the Consciousness of Grammar. *American Ethnologist* 12(4): 725–737.

Hill, J. H. (1990). Weeping as a Meta-signal in a Mexicano Woman's Narrative. In E. B. Basso (ed.), *Native Latin American Cultures through Their Discourse* (pp. 29–49). Bloomington: Folklore Institute, Indiana University.

Hill, J. H. (1993). Hasta la Vista, Baby: Anglo Spanish in the American Southwest. *Critique of Anthropology* 13: 145–176.

Hill, J. (1995). Mock Spanish: A Site for the Indexical Reproduction of Racism in American English. (http://www.language-culture.org/colloquia/symposia/hill-jane)

Hill, J. H. (1998a). Language, Race, and White Public Space. *American Anthropologist* 100(3): 680–689 [reprinted in A. Duranti (ed.) 2001c, pp. 450–464].

Hill, J. H. (1998b). "Today There Is no Respect": Nostalgia, "Respect," and Oppositional Discourse in Mexicano (Nahuatl) Language Ideology. In B. B. Schieffelin, K. A. Woolard, and P. V. Kroskrity (eds.), *Language Ideologies: Practice and Theory* (pp. 68–86). New York: Oxford University Press.

Hill, J. H. (1999). Syncretism. *Journal of Linguistic Anthropology* 9(1–2): 244–246.

Hill, J., and Hill, K. C. (1986). *Speaking Mexicano: Dynamics of a Syncretic Language in Central Mexico*. Tucson: University of Arizona Press.

Hill, J. H., and Irvine, J. T. (eds.) (1993). *Responsibility and Evidence in Oral Discourse*. Cambridge: Cambridge University Press.

Hill, J. H., and Mannheim, B. (1992). Language and World View. *Annual Review of Anthropology* 21: 381–406.

Hill Boone, E. (2000). *Stories in Red and Black: Pictorial Histories of the Aztecs and Mixtecs*. Austin: University of Texas Press.

Hinnenkamp, V. (1994a). Interkulturelle Kommunikation – Strange Attractions. *Zeitschrift für Literaturwissenschaft und Linguistik* 93: 46–74.

Hinnenkamp, V. (1994b). *Interkulturelle Kommunikation*. Heidelberg: Gross.

Hinnenkamp, V. (1998). *Missverständnisse in Gesprächen. Eine empirische Untersuchung im Rahmen der Interpretativen Soziolinguistik*. Opladen: Westdeutscher Verlag.

Hinton, L. (1984). *Havasupai Songs: A Linguistic Perspective*. Tübingen: Gunter Narr Verlag.

Hinton, L. (1990). Song Metrics. In *Berkeley Linguistics Society: Proceedings of the 16th Annual Meeting, Special Session on General Topics in American Indian Linguistics* (pp. 51–60). Berkeley: Dept. of Linguistics, University of California, Berkeley.

Hinton, L., Moonwomon, B., Bremner, S., Luthin, H., Van Clay, M., Lerner, J., and Corcoran, H. (1987). It's Not Just the Valley Girls: A Study of California English. In J. Aske, N. Beery, L. Michaelis, and H. Filip (eds.), *Proceedings of the Thirteenth Annual Meeting of the Berkeley Linguistics Society* (pp. 117–128). Berkeley: Berkeley Linguistics Society.

Hinton, L., Nichols, J., and Ohala, J. (eds.) (1994). *Sound Symbolism*. Cambridge: Cambridge University Press.

Hjelmslev, L. (1961 [1943]). *Prolegomena to a Theory of Language*. Madison: University of Winsconsin.

Hobsbawm, E., and Ranger, T. (1983). *The Invention of Tradition*. Cambridge: Cambridge University Press.

Hochschild, A. (1983). *The Managed Heart: Commercialization of Human Feeling*. Berkeley: University of California Press.

Hoëm, I. (2001). Theater. In A. Duranti (ed.), *Key Terms in Language and Culture* (pp. 244–247). Malden, MA: Blackwell.

Hoffman, R. E., et al. (1982). Apprehending Schizophrenic Discourse: A Structural Analysis of the Listener's Task. *Journal of Brain and Language* 15: 207–233.

Hoijer, H. (1961). Anthropological Linguistics. In C. Mohrmann, A. Sommerfelt, and J. Whatmough (eds.), *Trends in European and American Linguistics 1930–1960* (pp. 110–125). Utrecht and Antwerp: Spectrum Publishers.

Holland, D. and Quinn, N. (eds.) (1987). *Cultural Models in Language and Thought*. Cambridge: Cambridge University Press.

Holm, J. A. (1988). *Pidgins and Creoles*, vol. I: *Theory and Structure*. New York: Cambridge University Press.

Holm, J. A. (1989). *Pidgins and Creoles*, vol. II: *Reference Survey*. New York: Cambridge University Press.

Holst-Warhaft, G. (1992). *Dangerous Voices: Women's Laments and Greek Literature*. London and New York: Routledge.

Holt, J. A., Traxler, C. B., and Allen, T. E. (1992). Interpreting the Scores: A User's Guide to the 8th Edition Stanford Achievement Test for Educators of Deaf and Hard of Hearing Students. *GRI Technical Report: 92–1*. Washington, DC: Gallaudet University.

Honey, J. (1989). *Does Accent Matter? The Pygmalion Factor*. London: Faber and Faber.

Hopper, K. (1991). Some Old Questions for the New Cross-cultural Psychiatry. *Medical Anthropology Quarterly* 5: 299–330.

Hopper, P., and Thompson, S. A. (1980). Transitivity in Grammar and Discourse. *Language* 56: 251–299.

Hopper, P. J., and Traugott, E. C. (1993). *Grammaticalization*. Cambridge: Cambridge University Press.

Hornberger, N. H. (1998). Language Policy, Language Education, Language Rights: Indigenous, Immigrant, and International Perspectives. *Language in Society* 27(4): 439–458.

Hosokawa, S. (1984). How Saussurian is Music? In M. Baroni and L. Callegari (eds.), *Musical Grammars and Computer Analysis* (pp. 155–163). Firenze: Leo S. Olschki Editore.

House, D. (2002). *Language Shift among the Navajos*. Tucson: University of Arizona Press.

Houtkoop-Steenstra, H. (1991). Opening Sequences in Dutch Telephone Conversations. In D. Boden and D. H. Zimmerman (eds.), *Talk and Social Structure* (pp. 232–252). Cambridge: Polity Press.

Hoyle, S. M. (1993). Participation Frameworks in Sportscasting Play: Imaginary and Literal Footings. In D. Tannen (ed.), *Framing in Discourse* (pp. 114–145). New York: Oxford University Press.

Hudson, A. (ed.) (1991). *Studies in Diglossia*. Special Theme Issue of *Southwest Journal of Linguistics* 10(1).

Hudson, A. (1992). Diglossia: A Bibliographic Review. *Language in Society* 21: 611–674.

Hudson, K. (1983). Pop Music as Cultural Carrier. In K. Hudson, *The Language of the Teenage Revolution* (ch. 3, pp. 36–52). London: Macmillan.

Hudson, R. A. (1980). *Sociolinguistics*. Cambridge: Cambridge University Press.

Hughes, D. W. (1988). Deep Structure and Surface Structure in Javanese Music: A Grammar of Gendhing Lampah. *Ethnomusicology* 32(1): 23–74.

Hull, G., and Schultz, K. (2002). Connecting Schools with Out-of-School Worlds: Insights from Research on Literacy in Non-school Settings. In G. Hull and K. Schultz (eds.), *School's Out! Bridging Out-of-School Literacies with Classroom Practice* (pp. 32–57). New York: Teachers College, Columbia University.

Humboldt, W. von (1836). *Über die Verschiedenheit des menschlichen Sprachbaues: und ihren Einfluss auf die geistige Entwickelung des Menschengeschlechts*. Berlin: Druckerei der Königlichen Akademie der Wissenschaften.

Humboldt, W. von (1973). *Schriften zur Sprache*. Stuttgart: Philipp Reclam.

Humboldt, W. von (1999). *On Language: On the Diversity of Human Language Construction and Its Influence on the Mental Development of the Human Species*. New York: Cambridge University Press.

Humphrey, N. (1998). Cave Art, Autism, and the Evolution of the Human Mind. *Cambridge Archaeological Journal* 8(2): 165–191.

Husserl, E. (1931). *Ideas: General Introduction to Pure Phenomenology* (trans. W. R. Boyce Gibson). New York: Collier.

Husserl, E. (1950 [1913]). *Die Idee der Phänomenologie*. The Hague: Martinus Nijhoff.

Husserl, E. (1970 [1910]). *Logical Investigations*. London: Routledge and Kegan Paul.

Husserl, E. (1991). *On the Phenomenology of the Consciousness of Internal Time (1893–1917)* (trans. J. B. Brough). Dordrecht: Kluwer.

Hutchins, E., and Palen, L. (1997). Constructing Meaning from Space, Gesture, and Speech. In L. Resnick, R. Säljö, C. Pontecorvo, and B. Burge (eds.), *Discourse, Tools, and Reasoning* (pp. 23–40). Berlin, Heidelberg, and New York: Springer Verlag.

Hymes, D. (1962). The Ethnography of Speaking. In T. Gladwin and W. C. Sturtevant (eds.), *Anthropology and Human Behavior* (pp. 13–53). Washington, DC: Anthropological Society of Washington (reprinted in J. A. Fishman (ed.), *Readings in the Sociology of Language*, pp. 99–138. The Hague: Mouton, 1968).

Hymes, D. (ed.) (1964a). *Language in Culture and Society: A Reader in Linguistics and Anthropology*. New York: Harper & Row.

Hymes, D. (1964b). General Introduction. In D. Hymes (ed.), *Language in Culture and Society: A Reader in Linguistics and Anthropology* (pp. xxi–xxxii). New York: Harper & Row.

Hymes, D. (1964c). Introduction to Part I. In D. Hymes (ed.), *Language in Culture and Society: A Reader in Linguistics and Anthropology* (pp. 3–14). New York: Harper & Row.

Hymes, D. (1964d). Introduction: Toward Ethnographies of Communication. In J. J. Gumperz and D. Hymes (eds.), *The Ethnography of Communication* (pp. 1–34). Washington, DC: *American Anthropologist* 66 (Special Issue).

Hymes, D. (1966). Two Types of Linguistic Relativity. In W. Bright (ed.), *Sociolinguistics* (pp. 114–167). The Hague: Mouton.

Hymes, D. (ed.) (1971a). *Pidginization and Creolization of Languages*. Cambridge: Cambridge University Press.

Hymes, D. (1971b). Sociolinguistics and the Ethnography of Speaking. In E. Ardener (ed.), *Social Anthropology and Language* (pp. 47–93). London: Tavistock.

Hymes, D. (1972a). Models of the Interaction of Language and Social Life. In J. J. Gumperz and D. Hymes (eds.), *Directions in Sociolinguistics: The Ethnography of Communication* (pp. 35–71). New York: Holt, Rinehart and Winston.

Hymes, D. (1972b). On Communicative Competence. In J. B. Pride and J. Holmes (eds.), *Sociolinguistics* (pp. 269–293). Harmondsworth: Penguin.

Hymes, D. (1973). Speech and Language: On the Origins and Foundations of Inequality among Speakers. *Daedalus* 102: 59–80.

Hymes, D. (1974a). *Foundations in Sociolinguistics: An Ethnographic Approach*. Philadelphia: University of Pennsylvania Press.

Hymes, D. (1974b). Ways of Speaking. In R. Bauman and J. Sherzer (eds.), *Explorations in the Ethnography of Speaking* (pp. 433–451). Cambridge: Cambridge University Press.

Hymes, D. (1975). Breakthrough into Performance. In D. Ben-Amos and K. S. Goldstein (eds.), *Folklore: Performance and Communication* (pp. 11–74). The Hague: Mouton.

Hymes, D. (1981). *"In Vain I Tried to Tell You": Essays in Native American Ethnopoetics*. Philadelphia: University of Pennsylvania Press.

Hymes, D. (1996). *Ethnography, Linguistics, Narrative Inequality*. Bristol, PA: Taylor & Francis.

Hymes, D. (1999). Boas on the Threshold of Ethnopoetics. In L. P. Valentine and R. Darnell (eds.), *Theorizing the Americanist Tradition* (pp. 84–107). Toronto: University of Toronto Press.

Hymes, D. (2001). Poetry. In A. Duranti (ed.), *Key Terms in Language and Culture* (pp. 187–189). Malden, MA: Blackwell.

Ide, R. (forthcoming). *Friendly but Strangers: Small Talk and the Creation of Self through Talk in America*. Amsterdam: John Benjamins.

Idhe, D. (1974). *Listening and Voice: A Phenomenology of Sound*. Athens: Ohio University Press.

Irvine, J. T. (1974). Strategies of Status Manipulation in Wolof Greeting. In R. Bauman and J. Sherzer (eds.), *Explorations in the Ethnography of Speaking* (pp. 167–191). Cambridge: Cambridge University Press.

Irvine, J. T. (1979). Formality and Informality in Communicative Events. *American Anthropologist* 81(4): 773–790.

Irvine, J. T. (1989a [1974]). Strategies of Status Manipulation in the Wolof Greeting. In R. Bauman and J. Sherzer (eds.), *Explorations in the Ethnography of Speaking* (2nd edn., pp. 167–191). Cambridge: Cambridge University Press.

Irvine, J. T. (1989b). When Talk Isn't Cheap: Language and Political Economy. *American Ethnologist* 16: 248–267.

Irvine, J. T. (1990). Registering Affect: Heteroglossia in the Linguistic Expression of Emotion. In C. A. Lutz and L. Abu-Lughod (eds.), *Language and the Politics of Emotion* (pp. 126–161). Cambridge: Cambridge University Press.

Irvine, J. T. (1995). The Family Romance of Colonial Linguistics: Gender and Family in Nineteenth-century Representations of African Languages. *Pragmatics* 5: 139–154.

Irvine, J. T. (1996). Shadow Conversations: The Indeterminacy of Participant Roles. In M. Silverstein and G. Urban (eds.), *Natural Histories of Discourse* (pp. 131–159). Chicago: University of Chicago Press.

Irvine, J. T. (2001a). The Family Romance of Colonial Linguistics: Gender and Family in Nineteenth-century Representations of African Languages. In S. Gal and K. A. Woolard (eds.), *Languages and Publics: The Making of Authority* (pp. 13–29). Manchester: St. Jerome.

Irvine, J. T. (2001b). "Style" as Distinctiveness: The Culture and Ideology of Linguistic Differentiation. In P. Eckert and J. R. Rickford (eds.), *Style and Sociolinguistic Variation* (pp. 21–43). Cambridge: Cambridge University Press.

Irvine, J. T., and Gal, S. (2000a). Language Ideology and Linguistic Differentiation. In P. V. Kroskrity (ed.), *Regimes of Language* (pp. 35–84). Sante Fe, NM: School of American Research Press.

Irvine, J. T., and Gal, S. (2000b). Regimenting Languages: Language Ideological Perspectives. In P. V. Kroskrity (ed.), *Regimes of Language* (pp. 1–34). Santa Fe, NM: School of American Research Press.

Jackendoff, R. (1972). *Semantic Interpretation in Generative Grammar.* Cambridge, MA: MIT Press.

Jackendoff, R. (1990). *Semantic Structures.* Cambridge, MA: MIT Press.

Jackson, J. (1983). *The Fish People: Linguistic Exogamy and Tukanoan Identity in Northwest Amazonia.* Cambridge: Cambridge University Press.

Jacobs, S. and Jackson, S. (1981). Argument as a Natural Category: The Routine Grounds for Arguing in Conversation. *Western Journal of Speech Communication* 45: 118–132.

Jacobs-Huey, L. (1997). Is There an Authentic African American Speech Community? Carla Revisited. *University of Pennsylvania Working Papers in Linguistics* 4(1): 331–370.

Jacobs-Huey, L. (1999). Becoming Cosmetologists: Language Socialization and Identity in an African American Beauty College. PhD thesis, University of California, Los Angeles.

Jacobson, R. (ed.) (1998). *Codeswitching Worldwide.* Berlin: Mouton de Gruyter.

Jacobson, S. A. (1984). *Yup'ik Eskimo Dictionary.* Fairbanks: Alaska Native Language Center.

Jacoby, S. (1998). Science as Performance: Socializing Scientific Discourse through Physics Conference Talk Rehearsals. PhD thesis, University of California, Los Angeles.

Jacoby, S., and Gonzales, P. (1991). The Constitution of Expert–Novice in Scientific Discourse. *Issues in Applied Linguistics* 2: 149–181.

Jacquemet, M. (1996). *Credibility in Court: Communicative Practices in the Camorra Trials.* Cambridge: Cambridge University Press.

Jaffe, A. (1996). The Second Annual Corsican Spelling Contest: Orthography and Ideology. *American Ethnologist* 23: 816–835.

Jaffe, A. (1999a). *Ideologies in Action: Language Politics on Corsica.* Berlin: Mouton de Gruyter.

Jaffe, A. (1999b). Locating Power: Corsican Translators and Their Critics. In J. Blommaert (ed.), *Language Ideological Debates* (pp. 1–38). Berlin: Mouton de Gruyter.

Jakobson, R. (1944). Franz Boas' Approach to Language. *International Journal of American Linguistics* 10: 188–195.

Jakobson, R. (1957). *The Framework of Language.* Ann Arbor: University of Michigan Press.

Jakobson, R. (1960). Closing Statement: Linguistics and Poetics. In T. A. Sebeok (ed.), *Style in Language* (pp. 350–377). Cambridge, MA: MIT Press.

Jakobson, R. (1987). Musicology and Linguistics (1935). In R. Jakobson (K. Pomorska and S. Rudy, eds.), *Language in Literature* (pp. 455–457). Cambridge, MA: Belknap Press.

Jakobson, R. (1990). *On Language/Roman Jakobson* (ed. L. R. Waugh and M. Monville-Burston). Cambridge, MA: Harvard University Press.

Jakobson, R., and Lübbe-Grothues, G. (1980). The Language of Schizophrenia: Hölderlin's Speech and Poetry. *Poetics Today* 2: 138 ff.

Jakobson, R., and Lübbe-Grothues, G. (1984). Two Types of Discourse in Hölderline's Madness. In L. Vaina and J. Hintikka (eds.), *Cognitive Constraints on Communication* (pp. 115–136). Dordrecht: D. Reidel.

Jakobson, R., and Waugh, L. R. (1979). *The Sound Shape of Language.* Bloomington: Indiana University Press.

James, D. and Clarke, S. (1993). Women, Men and Interruptions: A Critical Review. In D. Tannen (ed.), *Gender and Conversational Interaction* (pp. 231–280). New York: Oxford University Press.

Janowski, K. A. (1997). *Deaf Empowerment: Emergence, Struggle, and Rhetoric.* Washington, DC: Gallaudet University Press.

Januschek, F., and Maas, U. (1981). Zum Gegenstand der Sprachpolitik: Sprache oder Sprachen? *OBST* 18: 64–95.

Jefferson, G. (1972). Side Sequences. In D. Sudnow (ed.), *Studies in Social Interaction* (pp. 294–338). New York: The Free Press.

Jefferson, G. (1974). Error Correction as an Interactional Resource. *Language in Society* 2: 181–199.

Jefferson, G. (1978a). What's in a 'Nyem. *Sociology* 12(1): 135–139.

Jefferson, G. (1978b). Sequential Aspects of Storytelling in Conversation. In J. Schenkein (ed.), *Studies in the Organization of Conversational Interaction* (pp. 219–248). New York: Academic Press.

Jefferson, G. (1983). Two Explorations of the Organization of Overlapping Talk in Conversation. *Tilburg Papers in Language and Literature* 28.

Jefferson, G. (1984a). On Stepwise Transition from Talk about a Trouble to Inappropriately Next-positioned matters. In J. M. Atkinson and J. Heritage (eds.), *Structures of Social Action: Studies in Conversation Analysis* (pp. 191–222). Cambridge: Cambridge University Press.

Jefferson, G. (1984b). On the Organization of Laughter in Talk about Troubles. In J. M. Atkinson, and J. Heritage (eds.), *Structures of Social Action: Studies in Conversation Analysis* (pp. 346–369). Cambridge: Cambridge University Press.

Jefferson, G. (1985). An Exercise in the Transcription and Analysis of Laughter. In T. van Dijk (ed.), *Handbook of Discourse Analysis*, vol. 3 (pp. 25–34). London: Academic Press.

Jefferson, G. (1987). On Exposed and Embedded Correction in Conversation. In G. Button and J. R. Lee (eds.), *Talk and Social Organisation* (pp. 86–100). Clevedon: Multilingual Matters.

Jefferson, G. (1989). On the Sequential Organisation of Troubles-talk in Ordinary Conversation. *Social Problems* 35(4): 418–441.

Jefferson, G. (1996). A Case of Transcriptional Stereotyping. *Journal of Pragmatics* 26: 159–170.

Jefferson, G., and Lee, J. R. (1981). The Rejection of Advice: Managing the Problematic Convergence of a "Troubles-telling" and a "Service Encounter." *Journal of Pragmatics* 5: 399–422.

Jefferson, G., Sacks, H., and Schegloff, E. A. (1987). Notes on Laughter in the Pursuit of Intimacy. In G. Button and J. R. Lee (eds.), *Talk and Social Organisation.* Clevedon: Multilingual Matters.

Jefferson, G., and Schegloff, E. A. (1975). Sketch: Some Orderly Aspects of Overlap in Natural Conversation. Paper presented at the Meeting of the American Anthropological Association.

Jenkins, J. H. (1988a). Conceptions of Schizophrenia as a Problem of Nerves: A Cross-cultural Comparison of Mexican-Americans and Anglo-Americans. *Social Science and Medicine* 26(12): 233–243. Boston, MA: Harvard Medical School.

Jenkins, J. H. (1988b). Ethnopsychiatric Interpretations of Schizophrenic Illness: The Problem of *Nervios* within Mexican-American Families. *Culture, Medicine and Psychiatry* 12: 301–329.

Jenkins, J. H. (1990). Anthropology, "Expressed Emotion," and Schizophrenia. *Anthropology Newsletter* 31: 14–15.

Jenkins, J. H. (1991). The 1990 Stirling Award Essay: Anthropology, Expressed Emotion, and Schizophrenia. *Ethos* 19(4): 387–431.

Jenkins, J. H. (1994a). Culture, Emotion, and Psychopathology. In H. R. M. Shinobu Kitayama (ed.), *Emotion and Culture: Empirical Studies of Mutual Influence* (pp. 309–335). Washington, DC: American Psychological Association.

Jenkins, J. H. (1994b). The Psychocultural Study of Emotion and Mental Disorder. In P. K. Bock (ed.), *Psychological Anthropology* (pp. 97–120). Westport, CT: Praeger Publishers/Greenwood Publishing Group.

Jenkins, J. H. (1996). Culture, Emotion, and Psychiatric Disorder. In C. F. Sargent and T. M. Johnson (eds.), *Medical Anthropology: Contemporary Theory and Method* (pp. 71–87). Westport, CT: Praeger Publishers/Greenwood Publishing Group.

Jenkins, J. H. (1997). Subjective Experience of Persistent Schizophrenia and Depression among US Latinos and Euro-Americans. *British Journal of Psychiatry* 171: 20–25.

Jenkins, J. H., and Barrett, R. (eds.) (in press). *The Edge of Experience: Culture, Subjectivity, and Schizophrenia.* New York: Cambridge University Press.

Joachim, G. H. G., and Prillwitz, S. (1993). *International Bibliography of Sign Language.* Hamburg: Signum (see also http://www.sign-lang.uni-hamburg.de/bibweb/).

Johnson, A. (1984). Voice Physiology and Ethnomusicology: Physiological and Acoustical Studies of the Swedish Herding Song. *Yearbook for Traditional Music* 16: 42–66.

Johnson, J. W. (1974). *Heellooy Heellellooy: The Development of the Genre Heello in Modern Somali Poetry.* Bloomington: Indiana University Press.

Johnson, J. W., and Fa-Digi Sisòkò (1986). *The Epic of Son-Jara: A West African Tradition.* Bloomington: Indiana University Press.

Johnson, K. (1991). Miscommunicating in Interpreted Classroom Interaction. *Sign Language Studies* 70: 1–34.

Johnson, R. (1991). Sign Language, Culture, and Community in a Traditional Yucatec Maya Village. *Sign Language Studies* 73: 461–474.

Johnson, R., and Erting, C. (1989). Linguistic Socialization in the Context of Emergent Deaf Ethnicity. Wenner-Gren Foundation Working Papers in Anthropology: Ethnicity and Socialization in a Classroom for Deaf Children. In C. Lucas (ed.), *The Sociolinguistics of American Sign Language* (pp. 41–84). New York: Academic Press.

Johnson, S. (2002). On the Origin of Linguistic Norms: Orthography, Ideology and the First Constitutional Challenge to the 1996 Reform of German. *Language in Society* 31: 549–576.

Johnstone, B. (1996). *The Linguistic Individual: Self-Expression in Language and Linguistics.* New York: Oxford University Press.

Johnstone, T. M. (1972). The Language of Poetry in Dhofar. *BSOAS*, 35: 1–17.

Jouad, H. (1995). *Le calcul inconscient de l'improvisation. Poésie berbère – rhythme, nombre et sense* [The Unconscious Calculus of Improvisation. Berber Poetry – Rhythm, Number and Meaning]. Paris and Louvain: Éditions Peeters.

Jourdan, C. (1991). Pidgins and Creoles: The Blurring of Categories. *Annual Review of Anthropology* 20: 187–209.

Jupp, T. C., Roberts, C., and Cook-Gumperz, J. (1982). Language and Disadvantage: The Hidden Process. In J. J. Gumperz (ed.), *Language and Social Identity* (pp. 232–256). Cambridge: Cambridge University Press.

Kachru, B. B. (1983). *The Indianization of English: The English Language in India.* Oxford: Oxford University Press.

Kahneman, D., Slovic, P., and Tversky, A. (1982). *Judgment under Uncertainty: Heuristics and Biases.* Cambridge: Cambridge University Press.

Kangasharju, H. (1998). Alignment in Disagreement: Building Alliances in Multiperson Interaction. Unpublished doctoral dissertation, University of Helsinki.

Kant, I. (1785). *Grundlegung zur Metaphysik der Sitten.* Leipzig: Hartknoch. [English trans. by T. K. Abbott (1988). *Fundamental Principles of the Metaphysics of Morals.* Amherst: Prometheus Books.]

Kant, I. (1974). *Anthropology from a Pragmatic Point of View.* The Hague: Nijhoff.

Kantor, H. (1992). Current Trends in the Secularization of Hebrew. *Language in Society* 21: 603–609.

Karbusicky, V. (1987). The Index Sign in Music. *Semiotica* 66(1–3): 22–36.

Karno, M., and Jenkins, J. H. (1993). Cross-cultural Issues in the Course and Treatment of Schizophrenia. *Psychiatric Clinics of North America* 16(2): 339–350.

Karno, M., et al. (1987). Expressed Emotion and Schizophrenic Outcome among Mexican-American Families. *Journal of Nervous and Mental Disease* 175(3): 143–151.

Kasper, G. (1984). Repair in Foreign Language Teaching. *Studies in Second Language Acquisition* 7: 200–215.

Kasper, G. (1995). Wessen Pragmatik? Für eine Neubestimmung fremdsprachlicher Handlungskompetenz. *Zeitschrift für Fremdsprachenforschung* 6(1): 69–94.

Kasper, G. (1997). "A" Stands for Acquisition: A Response to Firth and Wagner. *Modern Language Journal* 81: 307–312.

Kasper, G., and Kellerman, E. (eds.) (1999). *Communication Strategies: Psycholinguistic and Sociolinguistic Perspectives.* New York: Longman.

Katz, M. M., et al. (1988). On the Expression of Psychosis in Different Cultures: Schizophrenia in an Indian and in a Nigerian Community. *Culture, Medicine & Psychiatry* 12(3): 331–355.

Kay, P., and Maffi, L. (2000). Color Appearance and the Emergence and Evolution of Basic Color Lexicons. *American Anthropologist* 101: 743–760.

Keane, W. (1997a). Knowing One's Place: National Language and the Idea of the Local in Eastern Indonesia. *Cultural Anthropology* 12: 37–63.

Keane, W. (1997b). *Signs of Recognition: Powers and Hazards of Representation in an Indonesian Society.* Berkeley: University of California Press.

Keating, E. (1998). *Power Sharing: Language, Rank, Gender, and Social Space in Pohnpei, Micronesia.* Oxford: Oxford University Press.

Keating, E. (2000a). How Culture and Technology Together Shape New Communicative Practices: Investigating Interactions between Deaf and Hearing Callers with Computer Mediated Videotelephone. *Texas Linguistic Forum: Proceedings of the Seventh Annual Symposium about Language and Society, Austin* (pp. 99–116). Austin: University of Texas.

Keating, E. (2000b). Moments of Hierarchy: Constructing Social Stratification by Means of Language, Food, Space, and the Body in Pohnpei, Micronesia. *American Anthropologist* 102: 303–320.

Keating, E., and Mirus, G. (2000). Cross Modal Conversations: Deaf Children and Hearing Peers at School. *Crossroads of Language, Interaction, and Culture* 3: 73–90. Department of Applied Linguistics and TESL, UCLA.

Keating, E., and Mirus, G. (2003). American Sign Language in Virtual Space: Interaction between Deaf Users of Computer-Mediated Video Communication and the Impact of Technology on Language Practices. *Language in Society* 32: 693–714.

Keenan, E. L. (1976). The Logical Diversity of Natural Languages. In S. R. Harnard, H. D. Steklis, and J. Lancaster (eds.), *Origins and Evolution of Language and Speech* (pp. 73–91). New York: The New York Academy of Sciences.

Keenan, E. L. (1978). Language Variation and the Logic Structure of Universal Grammar. In H. Seiler (ed.), *Language Universals* (pp. 63–99). Tübingen: Gunter Narr.

Keenan, E. L. (1984). Semantic Correlates of the Ergative/Absolutive Distinction. *Linguistics* 22: 197–223.

Keenan, E. O. (1974). Conversation and Oratory in Vaninankaratra Madagascar. Unpublished PhD dissertation, University of Pennsylvania.

Keenan, E. O. (1989 [1974]). Norm-Makers, Norm-Breakers: Uses of Speech by Men and Women in a Malagasy Community. In R. Bauman and J. Sherzer (eds.), *Explorations in the Ethnography of Speaking*, 2nd edn. (pp. 125–143). Cambridge: Cambridge University Press.

Kegl, J., and Iwata, G. (1989). Lenguaje de Signos Nicaragüense: A Pidgin Sheds Light on the "Creole?" ASL. In R. Carlson et al (eds.), *Proceedings of the Fourth Annual Meeting of the Pacific Linguistics Conference, University of Oregon, Eugene.* Eugene: University of Oregon.

Kegl, J., and McWhorter, J. (eds.) (1996). *Perspectives on an Emerging Language. Proceedings of the Stanford Child Language Research Forum.* New York: Cambridge University Press; Palo Alto, CA: CSLI.

Kegl, J., and McWhorter, J. (1997). Perspectives on an Emerging Language. In E. Clark (ed.), *Proceedings of the Twenty-eighth Annual Child Language Research Forum* (pp. 15–38). Stanford, CA: CSLI Publications.

Kegl, J., Senghas, A., and Coppola, M. (1999). Creation through Contact: Sign Language Emergence and Sign Language Change in Nicaragua. In M. DeGraff (ed.), *Language Creation and Language Change: Creolization, Diachrony, and Development* (pp. 179–237). Cambridge, MA: MIT Press.

Kegl, J., and White Eagle, J. (1987). Plains Indian Sign Language. In J. V. Van Cleve (ed.), *Gallaudet Encyclopedia of Deaf People and Deafness*, vol. 3 (pp. 97–100). New York: McGraw-Hill.

Keil, C., and Feld, S. (1994). *Music Grooves.* Chicago: University of Chicago Press.

Keita, S. O. Y., and Kittles, R. A. (1997). The Persistence of Racial Thinking and the Myth of Racial Divergence. *American Anthropologist* 99(3): 534–544.

Kellerman, E., Bongaerts, T., and Poulisse, N. (1987). Strategy and System in L2 Referential Communication. In R. Ellis (ed.), *Second Language Acquisition in Context* (pp. 100–112). Englewood Cliffs, NJ: Prentice-Hall.

Kendon, A. (1967). Some Functions of Gaze-Direction in Social Interaction. *Acta Psychologica* 26: 22–63.

Kendon, A. (1973). The Role of Visible Behavior in the Organization of Social Interaction. In M. von Cranach and I. Vine, *Social Communication and Movement: Studies of Interaction and Expression in Man and Chimpanzee* (pp. 29–74). New York: Academic Press.

Kendon, A. (1977). Spatial Organization in Social Encounters: The F-formation System. In A. Kendon, *Studies in the Behavior of Social Interaction.* Lisse, Holland: Peter DeRidder Press.

Kendon, A. (1980). Gesticulation and Speech: Two Aspects of the Process of Utterance. In M. R. Key (ed.), *Relationship between Verbal and Nonverbal Communication* (pp. 207–227). The Hague: Mouton.

Kendon, A. (1981). *Nonverbal Communication, Interaction, and Gesture.* The Hague: Mouton.

Kendon, A. (1985). Behavioural Foundations for the Process of Frame Attunement in Face-to-Face Interaction. In M. von Cranach et al. (eds.), *Discovery Strategies in the Psychology of Action* (pp. 29–253). London: Academic Press.

Kendon, A. (1986). Some Reasons for Studying Gesture. *Semiotica* 62(1/2): 3–28.

Kendon, A. (1988). Goffman's Approach to Face-to-Face Interaction. In P. Drew and A. Wootton (eds.), *Erving Goffman: Exploring the Interaction Order* (pp. 14–40). Cambridge: Polity Press.

Kendon, A. (1988a). *Sign Languages of Aboriginal Australia: Cultural, Semiotic, and Communicative.* Cambridge: Cambridge University Press.

Kendon, A. (1988b). How Gestures Can Become Like Words. In F. Poyatos (ed.), *Cross-cultural Perspectives in Nonverbal Communication* (pp. 131–141). Toronto: Hogrefe.

Kendon, A. (1990a). *Conducting Interaction: Patterns of Behavior in Focused Encounters.* Cambridge: Cambridge University Press.

Kendon, A. (1990b). Movement Coordination in Social Interaction. In *Conducting Interaction: Patterns of Behavior in Focused Encounters* (pp. 91–116). Cambridge: Cambridge University Press.

Kendon, A. (1992). Some Recent Work from Italy on *Quotable Gestures (Emblems). Journal of Linguistic Anthropology* 2(1): 92–108.

Kendon, A. (1995a). Gestures as Illocutionary and Discourse Structure Markers in Southern Italian Conversation. *Journal of Pragmatics* 23: 247–279.

Kendon, A. (1995b). The Open Hand: Observations for a Study of Compositionality in Gesture. Paper presented at the conference "Gesture," Albuquerque, July 1995.

Kendon, A. (1997). Gesture. *Annual Review of Anthropology* 26: 109–128.

Kendon, A. (2000). Language and Gesture: Unity or Duality? In D. McNeill (ed.), *Language and Gesture* (pp. 47–63). Cambridge: Cambridge University Press.

Kennedy, G., Arnold, R., Dugdale, P., Fahey, S., and Moskovitz, D. (1997). *A Dictionary of New Zealand Sign Language.* Auckland, NZ: Auckland University Press/Bridget Williams Books.

Keri, S., and Janka, Z. (2000). "Cognitive Dysmetria" in Schizophrenia. *American Journal of Psychiatry* 157(4): 662–663.

Kibrik, A. E. (1985). Toward a Typology of Ergativity. In J. Nichols and A. Woodbury (eds.), *Grammar Inside and Outside the Clause: Some Approaches to Theory from the Field* (pp. 268–323). Cambridge: Cambridge University Press.

Kim, K.-H. (1992). Wh-Clefts and Left Dislocation in English Conversation with Reference to Topicality in Korean. Unpublished PhD dissertation, University of California, Los Angeles.

Kim, K.-H. (1993). Other-Initiated Repairs in Korean Conversation as Interactional Resources. In S. Choi (ed.), *Japanese/Korean Linguistics*, vol. 3 (pp. 3–18). Palo Alto, CA: CSLI.

Kim, K.-H. (1999). Phrasal Unit Boundaries and Organization of Turns and Sequences in Korean Conversation. *Human Studies* 22: 425–446.

King, C. R. (1994). *One Language, Two Scripts: The Hindi Movement in Nineteenth-century North India.* New Delhi: Oxford University Press.

King, C., and Quigley, S. (1985). *Reading and Deafness.* San Diego, CA: College-Hill Press.

Kingten, E. R., Kroll, B. M., and Rose, M. (eds.) (1988). *Perspectives on Literacy.* Carbondale and Edwardsville: Southern Illinois University Press.

Kiparsky, P., and Youmans, G. (eds.) (1989). *Rhythm and Meter. Phonetics and Phonology*, vol. 1. San Diego, CA: Academic Press.

Kirby, J. T. (1995). *The Countercultural South.* Athens: University of Georgia Press.

Kirch, P. V. (1984). *The Evolution of Polynesian Chiefdoms.* Cambridge: Cambridge University Press.

Kirch, P. V. (2000). *On the Road of the Winds: An Archaeological History of the Pacific Islands before European Contact.* Berkeley: University of California Press.

Kirsner, R. S. (1976). On the Subjectless "Pseudo-Passive" in Standard Dutch and the Semantics of Background Agents. In C. N. Li (ed.), *Subject and Topic.* New York: Academic Press.

Kita, S. (1993). Language and Thought Interface: A Study of Spontaneous Gestures and Japanese Mimetics. Unpublished PhD dissertation, University of Chicago.

Kita, S. (2000). How Representational Gestures Help Speaking. In D. McNeill (ed.), *Language and Gesture* (pp. 162–185). Cambridge: Cambridge University Press.

Klein-Arendt, R. (1987). KiNgozi: Extinct Swahili Dialect or Poetic Jargon? A Historical, Dialectological and Contextual Analysis. *Sprache und Geschichte in Afrika* 8: 181–245.

Klima, E., and Bellugi, U. (1979). *The Signs of Language*. Cambridge, MA: Harvard University Press.

Knapp-Potthoff, A., and Knapp, K. (1987). Instead of an Introduction: Conceptual Issues in Analyzing Intercultural Communication. In K. Knapp, W. Enninger, and A. Knapp-Potthoff (eds.), *Analyzing Intercultural Communication* (pp. 1–14). Berlin: Mouton de Gruyter.

Koch, L. (ed.) (1992). *Beowulf*. Turin: Giulio Einaudi Editore.

Kochman, T. (1981). *Black and White Styles in Conflict*. Chicago: University of Chicago Press.

Koerner, E. F. K. (1992). The Sapir–Whorf Hypothesis: A Preliminary History and a Bibliographical Essay. *Journal of Linguistic Anthropology* 2(2): 173–198.

Koestenbaum, W. (1993). *The Queen's Throat*. New York: Vintage.

Kohler, C. G., et al. (2000). Emotion Recognition Deficit in Schizophrenia: Association with Symptomatology and Cognition. *Biological Psychiatry* 48(2): 127–136.

Kondo, D. (1997). *About Face: Performing Race in Fashion and Theater*. New York: Routledge.

Koshik, I. (1999). Teacher Question Sequences in ESL Writing Conferences. Dissertation, University of California, Los Angeles.

Koss-Chioino, J. (1992). *Women as Healers, Women as Patients: Mental Health Care and Traditional Healing in Puerto Rico*. Boulder, CO: Westview Press.

Kotthoff, H. (1989). Stilunterschiede in argumentativen Gesprächen oder zum Geselligkeitswert von Dissens. In V. Hinnenkamp and M. Selting (eds.), *Stil und Stilisierung* (pp. 187–202). Tübingen: Niemeyer.

Kotthoff, H. (1991). Interaktionsstilistische Unterschiede im Gesprächsverhalten der Geschlechter. In E. Neuland and H. Bleckwenn (eds.), *Stil-Stilistik-Stilisierung* (pp. 131–

149). Frankfurt/Main, Bern, and New York: Peter Lang.

Kotthoff, H. (1992a). Streitformen interkulturell. Öffentlichkeit und Privatheit als Kontextfaktoren. In G. Behütuns and J. Wolff (eds.), *Kultureller Wandel und die Germanistik in der Bundesrepublik* (pp. 3–29). Stuttgart: Deutscher Germanistentag.

Kotthoff, H. (1992b). Von gackernden Hühnern und röhrenden Hirschen. Konversationelles Scherzen zwischen Männern und Frauen. In T. Vogel (ed.), *Vom Lachen* (pp. 192–209). Tübingen: Attempto.

Kotthoff, H. (1993). Disagreement and Concession in Disputes: On the Context Sensitivity of Preference Structures. *Language in Society* 22: 193–216.

Kotthoff, H. (1994). Geschlecht als Interaktionsritual? Nachwort. In H. Knoblauch (ed.), *Erving Goffman: Interaktion und Geschlecht* (pp. 159–194). Frankfurt: Campus.

Kotthoff, H. (1995). Von Klassenclowns und lächelnden Prinzessinnen. Zur Geschlechtertypisierung in der Humorentwicklung von Mädchen und Jungen. In K. R. Wagner (ed.), *Sprechhandlungs-Erwerb* (pp. 141–158). Essen: Blaue Eule.

Kratz, C. A. (1994). *Affecting Performance: Meaning, Movement, and Experience in Okiek Women's Initiation*. Washington: Smithsonian Institution Press.

Kring, A. M., and Neale, J. M. (1996). Do Schizophrenic Patients Show a Disjunctive Relationship among Expressive, Experiential, and Psychophysiological Components of Emotion? *Journal of Abnormal Psychology* 105(2): 249–257.

Kripke, S. A. (1972). Naming and Necessity. In D. Davidson and G. Harman (eds.), *Semantics of Natural Language*, 2nd edn. (pp. 253–255). Dordrecht and Boston: Reidel.

Kripke, S. A. (1982). *Wittgenstein: On Rules and Private Language*. Cambridge, MA: Harvard University Press.

Kristeva, J. (1980a). *Desire in Language*. New York: Columbia University Press.

Kristeva, J. (1980b). Place Names. In *Desire in Language* (pp. 271–294). New York: Columbia University Press.

Kristeva, J. (1993). The Speaking Subject Is Not Innocent. In B. Johnson (ed.), *Freedom and Interpretation* (pp. 147–174). New York: Basic Books.

Kroeber, A. L. (1905). Systematic Nomenclature in Ethnology. *American Anthropologist* 7: 579–593.

Kroeber, A. L. (1948). *Anthropology: Race, Language, Culture, Psychology, Prehistory.* New York: Harcourt Brace Jovanovich.

Kroskrity, P. V. (ed.) (1988). *On the Ethnography of Communication: The Legacy of Sapir: Essays in Honor of Harry Hoijer, 1984.* Los Angeles: Department of Anthropology, University of California, Los Angeles.

Kroskrity, P. V. (1992). Arizona Kiva Speech as Manifestation of Linguistic Ideology. *Pragmatics* 2: 297–309.

Kroskrity, P. V. (1993). *Language, History, and Identity: Ethnolinguistic Studies of the Arizona Tewa.* Tucson: University of Arizona Press.

Kroskrity, P. V. (1997). Discursive Convergence with an Evidential Particle. In J. H. Hill, P. J. Mistry, and L. Campbell (eds.), *The Life of Language: Papers in Honor of William Bright* (pp. 25–34). Berlin: Mouton de Gruyter.

Kroskrity, P. V. (1998). Arizona Tewa Kiva Speech as a Manifestation of a Dominant Language Ideology. In B. B. Schieffelin, K. A. Woolard, and P. V. Kroskrity (eds.), *Language Ideologies: Practice and Theory* (pp. 103–122). New York: Oxford University Press.

Kroskrity, P. V. (1999). Language Ideologies, Language Shift, and the Imagination of a Western Mono Community: The Recontextualization of a Coyote Story. In *Language and Ideology*, vol. 1: *Selected Papers from the 6th International Pragmatics Conference* (pp. 270–289). Antwerp: International Pragmatics Association.

Kroskrity, P. V. (2000a). Language Ideologies in the Expression and Representation of Arizona Tewa Ethnic Identity. In P. V. Kroskrity (ed.), *Regimes of Language: Ideologies, Polities, and Identities* (pp. 329–359). Santa Fe, NM: School of American Research Press.

Kroskrity, P. V. (2000b). Regimenting Languages: Language Ideological Perspectives. In P. V. Kroskrity (ed.), *Regimes of Language: Ideologies, Polities, and Identities.* Santa Fe, NM: School of American Research Press.

Kroskrity, P. V. (ed.) (2000c). *Regimes of Language: Ideologies, Polities, and Identities.* Santa Fe, NM: School of American Research Press.

Kuiper, K. and Tan Gek Lin, D. (1989). Cultural Congruence and Conflict in the Acquisition of Formulae in a Second Language. In O. García and R. Otheguy (eds.), *English across Cultures, Cultures across English: A Reader in Cross-cultural Communication* (pp. 281–304). Berlin: Mouton de Gruyter.

Kuipers, J. C. (1990). *Power in Performance: The Creation of Textual Authority in Weyewa Ritual Speech.* Philadelphia: University of Pennsylvania Press.

Kuipers, J. C. (1998). *Language, Identity, and Marginality in Indonesia: The Changing Nature of Ritual Speech on the Island of Sumba.* Cambridge: Cambridge University Press.

Kulick, D. (1992). *Language Shift and Cultural Reproduction: Socialization, Self, and Syncretism in a Papua New Guinean Village.* Cambridge: Cambridge University Press.

Kulick, D. (1993). Speaking as a Woman: Structure and Gender in Domestic Arguments in a New Guinea Village. *Cultural Anthropology* 8(4): 510–541.

Kulick, D. (1998a). Anger, Gender, Language Shift, and the Politics of Revelation in a Papua New Guinean Village. In B. B. Schieffelin, K. A. Woolard, and P. V. Kroskrity (eds.), *Language Ideologies: Practice and Theory* (pp. 87–102). Oxford: Oxford University Press.

Kulick, D. (1998b). *Travesti: Sex, Gender, and Culture among Brazilian Transgendered Prostitutes.* Chicago: University of Chicago Press.

Kulick, D. (1999). Language and Gender/Sexuality. Paper presented at the Sixth Language and Culture Online Symposium. http://www.language-culture.org/colloquia/symposia/kulick-don/

Kulick, D. (2000). Gay and Lesbian Language. *Annual Review of Anthropology* 29: 243–285.

Kulick, D. (2002). Queer Linguistics? In K. Campbell-Kibler, R. J. Podesva, S. J. Roberts, and A. Wong (eds.), *Language and Sexuality: Contesting Meaning in Theory and Practice* (pp. 65–68). Stanford: CSLI Publications.

Kulick, D. (2003a). Language and Desire. *Language and Communication* 23: 139–151 (Special Issue, ed. D. Cameron and D. Kulick).

Kulick, D. (2003b). Language and Desire. In J. Holmes and M. Meyerhoff (eds.), *The Handbook of Language and Gender.* Oxford: Blackwell.

Kulick, D., and Willson, M. (eds.) (1995). *Taboo: Sex, Identity and Erotic Subjectivity in Anthropological Fieldwork.* New York: Routledge.

Kundera, M. (1995). *Testaments Betrayed.* New York: Harper Collins.

Kuno, S., and Kaburaki, E. (1977). Empathy and Syntax. *Linguistic Inquiry* 8: 627–673.

Küntay, A., and Ervin-Tripp, S. (1997). Narrative Structure and Conversational Circumstances. *Journal of Narrative and Life History* 7: 113–120.

Kuroda, S.-Y. (1974). Where Epistemology, Style, and Grammar Meet: A Case Study from Japanese. In S. R. Anderson and P. Kiparsky (eds.), *A Festschrift for Morris Halle* (pp. 377–391). New York: Holt, Rinehart and Winston.

Kuschel, R. (1973). The Silent Inventor: The Creation of a Sign Language by the Only Deaf-Mute on a Polynesian Island. *Sign Language Studies* 3: 1–28.

La Fontaine, J. S. (1985). Person and Individual: Some Anthropological Reflections. In M. Carrithers, S. Collins, and S. Lukes (eds.), *The Category of the Person: Anthropology, Philosophy, History* (pp. 123–140). Cambridge: Cambridge University Press.

Labov, W. (1963). The Social Motivation of a Sound Change. *Word* 19: 273–309.

Labov, W. (1966a). Hypercorrection by the Lower Middle Class as a Factor in Linguistic Change. In W. Bright (ed.), *Sociolinguistics* (pp. 84–113). The Hague: Mouton.

Labov, W. (1966b). *The Social Stratification of English in New York City.* Arlington: Center for Applied Linguistics.

Labov, W. (1969). The Logic of Nonstandard English. In J. Alatis (ed.), *Georgetown Monographs on Language and Linguistics* (vol. 22, pp. 1–44). Washington, DC: Georgetown University Press.

Labov, W. (1970). *The Study of Nonstandard English.* Champaign, IL: National Council of Teachers.

Labov, W. (1972a). *Language in the Inner City: Studies in the Black English Vernacular.* Philadelphia: University of Pennsylvania Press.

Labov, W. (1972b). On Mechanism of Linguistic Change. In J. J. Gumperz and D. Hymes (eds.), *Directions in Sociolinguistics: The Ethnography of Communication* (pp. 512–538). New York: Holt, Rinehart and Winston.

Labov, W. (1972c). *Sociolinguistic Patterns.* Philadelphia: University of Pennsylvania Press.

Labov, W. (1973). The Linguistic Consequences of Being a Lame. *Language in Society* 2(1): 81–115.

Labov, W. (1980). Is There a Creole Speech Community? In A. Valdman and A. Highfield (eds.), *Theoretical Orientations in Creole Studies* (pp. 369–388). New York: Academic Press.

Labov, W. (1984). Intensity. In D. Schiffrin (ed.), *Meaning, Form, and Use in Context: Linguistic Applications. GURT '84* (pp. 43–70). Washington, DC: Georgetown University Press.

Labov, W. (1994). *Principles of Linguistic Change*, vol. 1: *Internal Factors.* Malden, MA: Blackwell.

Labov, W. (2001). *Principles of Linguistic Change*, vol. 2: *Social Factors.* Malden, MA: Blackwell.

Labov, W., and Fanshel, D. (1977). *Therapeutic Discourse: Psychotherapy as Conversation.* New York: Academic Press.

Labov, W., and Waletzky, J. (1967). Narrative Analysis: Oral Version of Personal Experience. In J. Helm (ed.), *Essays on the Verbal and Visual Arts: Proceedings of the 1996 Annual Spring Meeting of the American Ethnological Society* (pp. 12–44). Seattle: University of Washington Press.

Labov, W., and Waletzky, J. (1968). Narrative Analysis. In W. Labov et al. (eds.), *A Study of the Non-Standard English of Negro and Puerto Rican Speakers in New York City* (pp. 286–338). New York: Columbia University Press.

Lacan, J. (1980). A Lacanian Psychosis: Interview by Jacques Lacan. In S. Schneiderman (ed.), *Returning to Freud: Clinical Psychoanalysis in the School of Lacan* (pp. 19–41). New Haven: Yale University Press.

Ladd, D. R. (1990). Intonation: Emotion vs. Grammar. *Language* 66(4): 806–816.

Ladd, P. (1991). The British Sign Language Community. In S. Alladina and V. Edwards (eds.), *Multilingualism in the British Isles* (pp. 35–48). Harlow: Longman.

Ladefoged, P. (2000). The Sounds of Speech. In P. Kruth and H. Stobart (eds.), *Sound* (pp. 112–132). New York: Cambridge University Press.

Lakoff, G. (1987). *Women, Fire, and Dangerous Things: What Categories Reveal about the Mind.* Chicago: University of Chicago Press.

Lakoff, G., and Johnson, M. (1980). *Metaphors We Live By.* Chicago: University of Chicago Press.

Lakoff, R. (1973). Language and Women's Place. *Language in Society* 2: 45–80.

Lakoff, R. (1975). *Language and Women's Place.* New York: Holt, Rinehart and Winston.

Lane, H. (1984). *When the Mind Hears: A History of the Deaf.* New York: Random House.

Lane, H. (1987). History of American Sign Language. In J. V. Van Cleve (ed.), *Gallaudet Encyclopedia of Deaf People and Deafness*, vol. 3. New York: McGraw-Hill.

Lane, H., Hoffmeister, R., and Bahan, B. (1996). *A Journey into the DEAF-WORLD.* San Diego, CA: DawnSign Press.

Langdon, R., et al. (2002). Disturbed Communication in Schizophrenia: The Role of Poor Pragmatics and Poor Mind-reading. *Psychological Medicine* 32(7): 1273–1284.

Langer, J. (1987). A Sociocognitive Perspective on Literacy. In J. Langer (ed.), *Language, Literacy, and Culture: Issues of Society and Schooling* (pp. 1–20). Norwood, NJ: Ablex.

Lankshear, C., and McLaren, P. (eds.) (1993). *Critical Literacy: Politics, Praxis, and the Postmodern*. Albany, NY: SUNY Press.

Lanza, E. (1998). Raising Children Bilingually in Norway. *International Journal of the Sociology of Language* 133: 73–88.

Laughlin, R. M. (1975). *The Great Tzotzil Dictionary of San Lorenzo Zinacantan*. Washington, DC: Smithsonian Institution Press.

Lavagnino, A. (ed. and trans.) (1995). *Il tesoro delle lettere: un intaglio di draghi*. Italian trans. of *Wen xin diao long* by Liu Xie. Milan: Luni Editrice.

Lave, J. (1988). *Cognition in Practice*. Cambridge: Cambridge University Press.

Lave, J. (1990). The Culture of Acquisition and the Practice of Understanding. In J. W. Stigler, R. A. Shweder, and G. Herdt (eds.), *Cultural Psychology: Essays on Comparative Human Development* (pp. 309–327). Cambridge: Cambridge University Press.

Lave, J., and Wenger, E. (1991). *Situated Learning: Legitimate Peripheral Participation*. Cambridge: Cambridge University Press.

Laver, J. (1980). *The Phonetic Description of Voice Quality*. Cambridge: Cambridge University Press.

Laws, K. R., Al-Uzrib, M., and Mortimer, A. M. (2000). Lexical Knowledge Degradation in Schizophrenia. *Schizophrenia Research* 45(1–2).

Laycock, D. (1982). Melanesian Linguistic Diversity: A Melanesian Choice? In R. May and H. Nelson (eds.), *Melanesia: Beyond Diversity*, vol. 1 (pp. 33–38). Canberra: Australian National University Press.

Lazaraton, A. L. (1991). A Conversation Analysis of Structure and Interaction in the Language Interview. Dissertation, University of California, Los Angeles.

Lazaraton, A. L. (1997). Preference Organization on Oral Proficiency Interviews: The Case of Language Ability Assessments. *Research on Language and Social Interaction* 30: 53–72.

Le Page, R. B., and Tabouret-Keller, A. (1985). *Acts of Identity: Creole-based Approaches to Language and Ethnicity*. Cambridge: Cambridge University Press.

Leakey, T. (1993). Vocational Education in the Deaf American and African-American Communities. In J. V. Van Cleve (ed.), *Deaf History Unveiled: Interpretations from the New Scholarship* (pp. 74–91). Washington, DC: Gallaudet University Press.

Leander, B. (1972). *In xochitl in cuicatl: Flor y canto, la poesía de los aztecas* [*In xochitl in cuicatl*: Flower and Song, the Poetry of the Aztecs]. Mexico: INI-SEP.

LeBaron, C., and Streeck, J. (2000). Gestures, Knowledge, and the World. In D. McNeill (ed.), *Language and Gesture* (pp. 118–138). Cambridge: Cambridge University Press.

Leben, W. R. (1985). On the Correspondence between Linguistic Tone and Musical Melody. In D. L. Goyvaerts (ed.), *African Linguistics: Essays in Memory of M. W. K. Semikenke* (pp. 335–343). Amsterdam: John Benjamins.

Lederman, R. (1998). Globalization and the Future of Cultural Areas: Melanesianist Anthropology in Transition. *Annual Review of Anthropology* 27: 427–449.

Lee, B. (1997). *Talking Heads: Language, Metalanguage, and the Semiotics of Subjectivity*. Durham, NC: Duke University Press.

Lee, C. (1993). *Signifying as a Scaffold for Literary Interpretation: The Pedagogical Implications of an African-American Discourse Genre*. Urbana, IL: National Council of Teachers of English.

Lee, C. (2000). Signifying in the Zone of Proximal Development. In C. Lee and P. Smagorinsky (eds.), *Vygotskian Perspectives on Literacy Research: Constructing Meaning through Collaborative Inquiry* (pp. 191–225). Cambridge: Cambridge University Press.

Lee, D. (1944). Linguistic Reflection of Wintu Thought. *International Journal of American Linguistics* 10: 181–187.

Lee, P. (1991). Whorf's Hopi Tensors: Subtle Articulation in the Language/Thought Nexus? *Cognitive Linguistics* 2(2): 123–147.

Lee, P. (1996). *The Whorf Theory Complex: A Critical Reconstruction*. Amsterdam: John Benjamins.

Lee, S. (1996). Cultures in Psychiatric Nosology: The CCMD 2 R and International Classification of Mental Disorders. *Culture, Medicine and Psychiatry* 20(4): 421–472.

Leitch, T. (1986). *What Stories Are: Narrative Theory and Interpretation*. University Park: Pennsylvania State University Press.

LeMaster, B. (1977). The Education of the Deaf: A Sub-community in the Making. *Kroeber Anthropological Society Papers*, vol. 49. University of California, Berkeley.

LeMaster, B. (1990). The Maintenance and Loss of Female and Male Signs in the Dublin Deaf Community. PhD dissertation, University of California, Los Angeles.

LeMaster, B. (1997). Sex Differences in Irish Sign Language. In J. H. Hill, P. J. Mistry, and L. Campbell (eds.), *The Life of Language: Papers in Linguistics in Honor of William Bright* (pp. 67–85). Berlin: Mouton de Gruyter.

LeMaster, B. (2000). Reappropriation of Gendered Irish Sign Language in One Family. *Visual Anthropology Review* 15(2): 1–15.

LeMaster, B. (2002). What Difference Does Difference Make? Negotiating Gender and Generation in Irish Sign Language. In S. Benor, M. Rose, D. Sharma, J. Sweetland, and Q. Zhang (eds.), *Gendered Practices in Language*. Stanford, CA: CSLI Publications.

LeMaster, B. (2003). School Language and Shifts in Irish Deaf Identity. In L. Monaghan, C. Schmaling, K. Nakamura, and G. H. Turner (eds.), *Many Ways to be Deaf*. Washington, DC: Gallaudet University Press.

LeMaster, B., and Dwyer, J. (1991). Knowing and Using Female and Male Signs in Dublin. *Sign Language Studies* 73: 361–396.

LeMaster, B., and Foran, S. (1986). The Irish Sign Language. In J. Van Cleve (ed.), *The Gallaudet Encyclopedia of Deaf People and Deafness*, vol. 3 (pp. 82–84). New York: McGraw-Hill.

Lerdahl, F. (2001). *Tonal Pitch Space*. New York: Oxford University Press.

Lerdahl, F., and Jackendoff, R. (1983). *A Generative Theory of Tonal Music*. Cambridge, MA: MIT Press.

Lerner, G. H. (1989). Notes on Overlap Management in Conversation: The Case of Delayed Completion. *Western Journal of Speech Communication* 53: 167–177.

Lerner, G. H. (1995). Turn Design and the Organization of Participation in Instructional Activities. *Discourse Processes* 19: 111–131.

Lerner, G. H., and Takagi, T. (1999). On the Place of Linguistics Resources in the Organization of Talk-in-Interaction: A Co-investigation of English and Japanese Grammatical Practices. *Journal of Pragmatics* 31: 49–75.

Leudar, I. (2001). Voices in History. *Critical Social Studies* 3(1): 5–18.

Leudar, I., Thomas, P., and Johnston, M. (1992). Self-repair in Dialogues of Schizophrenics: Effects of Hallucinations and Negative Symptoms. *Brain & Language* 43(3): 487ff.

Levelt, W. J. M. (1983). Monitoring and Self-repair in Speech. *Cognition* 14: 41–104.

Levelt, W. J. M. (1989). *Speaking: From Intention to Articulation*. Cambridge, MA: MIT Press.

Levelt, W. J. M., and Maasen, B. (1981). Lexical Search and Order of Mention in Sentence Production. In W. Klein and W. J. M. Levelt (eds.), *Crossing the Boundaries in Linguistics. Studies Presented to Manfred Bierwisch* (pp. 221–252). Dordrecht: Reidel.

Levinson, S. C. (1983). *Pragmatics*. Cambridge: Cambridge University Press.

Levinson, S. C. (1988). Putting Linguistics on a Proper Footing: Explorations in Goffman's Concepts of Participation. In P. Drew and A. Wootton (eds.), *Erving Goffman: Exploring the Interaction Order* (pp. 161–227). Boston: Northeastern University Press.

Levinson, S. C. (1992). Primer for the Field Investigation of Spatial Description and Conception. *Pragmatics* 2(1): 5–47.

Levinson, S. C. (1995). Interaction Biases in Human Thinking. In E. Goody (ed.), *Social Intelligence and Interaction* (pp. 221–259). Cambridge: Cambridge University Press.

Levinson, S. C. (1996). Relativity in Spatial Conception and Description. In J. J. Gumperz and S. C. Levinson (eds.), *Rethinking Linguistic Relativity* (pp. 177–202). Cambridge: Cambridge University Press.

Levinson, S. C. (1997). Language and Cognition: The Cognitive Consequences of Spatial Description in Guugu Yimithirr. *Journal of Linguistic Anthropology* 7(1): 98–131.

Levinson, S. C. (2000a). Yeli Dnye and the Theory of Basic Color Terms. *Journal of Linguistic Anthropology* 10(1).

Levinson, S. C. (2000b). *Presumptive Meanings: The Theory of Generalized Conventional Implicature*. Cambridge, MA: MIT Press.

Lévi-Strauss, C. (1962). *La pensée sauvage*. Paris: Plon.

Lévi-Strauss, C. (1963). *Structural Anthropology*. New York: Basic Books.

Lévi-Strauss, C. (1966). *The Savage Mind*. Chicago: University of Chicago Press.

Levitt, D. (1986). *Introduction to New Zealand Sign Language*. Auckland, NZ: The National Foundation for the Deaf and the New Zealand Association of the Deaf.

Levman, B. (1992). The Genesis of Music and Language. *Ethnomusicology* 36(2): 147–170.

Liddell, S. K. (2000). Blended Spaces and Deixis in Sign Language Discourse. In D. McNeill (ed.), *Language and Gesture* (pp. 331–357). Cambridge: Cambridge University Press.

Liddicoat, A. (1997). Interaction, Social Structure, and Second Language Use: A Response to Firth and Wagner. *Modern Language Journal* 82: 313–317.

Liddle, P. F., et al. (2002). Thought and Language Index: An Instrument for Assessing Thought and Language in Schizophrenia. *British Journal of Psychiatry* 181(4): 326–330.

Lidov, D. (1980). Musical and Verbal Semantics. *Semiotica* 31(3/4): 369–391.

Lin, K.-M., and Kleinman, A. (1988). Psychopathology and Clinical Course of Schizophrenia: A Cross-cultural Perspective. *Schizophrenia Bulletin* 14(4): 555–567.

Lindblom, B., and Sundberg, J. (1975). A Generative Theory of Swedish Nursery Tunes. In *Actes du 1er congres international de Semiotique musicale* (pp. 111–124). Pesaro: Centro di Iniziative Culturale.

Linde, C. (1993). *Life Stories: The Creation of Coherence*. Oxford: Oxford University Press.

Lindström, A. (1994). Identification and Recognition in Swedish Telephone Conversation Openings. *Language in Society* 23: 231–252.

Lindström, A. (1997). Designing Social Actions: Grammar Prosody and Interaction in Swedish Conversation. PhD dissertation, University of California, Los Angeles.

Lindstrom, L. (1992). Context Contests: Debatable Truth Statements on Tanna (Vanuatu). In A. Duranti and C. Goodwin (eds.), *Rethinking Context: Language as an Interactive Phenomenon*. New York: Cambridge University Press.

Linell, P. (1982). The Written Language Bias in Linguistics. *Studies in Communication* 2. University of Linköping, Sweden.

Linell, P. (1998). *Approaching Dialogue: Talk, Interaction and Contexts in Dialogical Perspectives*. Amsterdam: John Benjamins.

Lippi-Green, R. (1997). *English With an Accent: Language, Ideology, and Discrimination in the United States*. London: Routledge.

List, G. (1961). Speech Melody and Song Melody in Central Thailand. *Ethnomusicology* 5: 16–32.

List, G. (1963). The Boundaries of Speech and Song. *Ethnomusicology* 7(1): 1–16.

Littlewood, R. (1984). The Imitation of Madness: The Influence of Psychopathology upon Culture. *Social Science & Medicine* 19(7): 705–715.

Livia, A., and Hall, K. (eds.) (1997). *Queerly Phrased: Language, Gender, and Sexuality.* New York: Oxford University Press.

Llorach, E. A. (1968). *Communication orale et graphique*. In A. Martinet (ed.), *Le language*. Paris: Gallimard, Bibliothèque de la Pléiade.

Lo, A. (1997). Heteroglossia and the Construction of Asian-American Identities. *Issues in Applied Linguistics* 8(1): 47–65.

Lock, A. (1993). Human Language Development and Object Manipulation: Their Relation in Ontogeny and Its Possible Relevance for Phylogenetic Questions. In K. R. Gibson and T. Ingold (eds.), *Tools, Language, and Cognition in Human Evolution* (pp. 279–299). Cambridge: Cambridge University Press.

Lock, A. and Peters, C. (eds.) (1996). *Handbook of Human Symbolic Evolution*. Oxford: Clarendon Press.

Lock, A., Young, A., Service, V., and Chandler, P. (1990). Some Observations of the Origins of the Pointing Gesture. In V. Volterra and C. J. Erting (eds.), *From Gesture to Language in Hearing and Deaf Children* (pp. 42–55). Berlin: Springer Verlag.

Lomax, A. (1967). Special Features of the Sung Communication. In J. Helm (ed.), *Essays on the Verbal and Visual Arts: Proceedings of the 1966 Annual Spring Meeting of the American Ethnological Society* (pp. 109–27). Seattle: University of Washington Press.

Lomax, A. (1968). *Folk Song Style and Culture*. Washington, DC: American Association for the Advancement of Science.

Loncke, F., Braem, P. B., and Lebrun, Y. (eds.) (1984). Recent Research on European Sign Languages. In *Proceedings of the European Meeting of Sign Language Research*, September 19–25, 1982, Brussels, Belgium.

Long, M. (1983). Native Speaker/Non-native Speaker Conversation and the Negotiation of Comprehensible Input. *Applied Linguistics* 4: 126–141.

Long, M. H. (1997). Construct Validity in SLA Research: A Response to Firth and Wagner. *Modern Language Journal* 81: 318–323.

Longacre, R. E., and Chenoweth, V. (1986). Discourse as Music. *Word* 37(1): 125–139.

Lopez, D. S. (1990). Inscribing the Bodhisattva's Speech: On the *Heart Sutra's Mantra*. *History of Religions* 29: 351–352.

Lotz, J. (1960). Metric Typology. In T. A. Sebeok (ed.), *Style in Language* (pp. 135–

148). Cambridge, MA: MIT Press; New York and London: John Wiley & Sons.

Lotz, J. (1972). Elements of Versification. In W. K. Wimsatt (ed.), *Versification: Major Language Types* (pp. 1–21). New York: New York University Press.

Louisy, P. and Turmel-John, P. (1983). *A Handbook for Writing Creole*. Castries: Research St. Lucia Publications.

Lounsbury, F. G. (1953). Field Methods and Techniques in Linguistics. In A. Kroeber (ed.), *Anthropology Today* (pp. 401–416). Chicago: University of Chicago Press.

Lounsbury, F. G. (1963). The Teaching of Linguistic Anthropology: Methods and Course Progression. In D. G. Mandelbaum, G. W. Lasker, and E. M. Albert (eds.), *The Teaching of Anthropology* (pp. 303–314). American Anthropological Association, Memoir 94.

Lounsbury, F. G. (1969). The Structural Analysis of Kinship Semantics. In S. A. Tyler (ed.), *Cognitive Anthropology* (pp. 193–212). New York: Holt, Rinehart and Winston.

Loury, G. (ed.) (1977). A Dynamic Theory of Racial Income Differences. In P. A. Wallace and A. Le Mund (eds.), *Women, Minorities, and Employment Discrimination* (pp. 153–186). Lexington, MA: Lexington Books.

Lucas, C., Bayley, R., and Valli, C. (in collaboration with M. Rose, A. Wulf, P. Dudis, S. Schatz, and L. Sanheim) (2001). *Sociolinguistic Variation in American Sign Language* (Sociolinguistics in Deaf Communities Series, vol. 7, ed. series C. Lucas). Washington, DC: Gallaudet University Press.

Lucas, C., and Valli, C. (1989). Language Contact in the American Deaf Community. In C. Lucas (ed.), *The Sociolinguistics of the Deaf Community* (pp. 11–40). San Diego, CA: Academic Press.

Lucas, C., and Valli, C. (1992). *Language Contact in the American Deaf Community*. New York: Academic Press.

Lucas, R. H., and Barrett, R. J. (1995). Interpreting Culture and Psychopathology: Primitivist Themes in Cross-cultural Debate. *Culture, Medicine and Psychiatry* 19: 287–326.

Luchtenberg, S. (1999). *Interkulturelle kommunikative Kompetenz. Kommunikationsfelder in Schule und Gesellschaft*. Opladen: Westdeutscher Verlag.

Luckmann, T. (1991). The Constitution of Human Life in Time. In J. Bender and D. E. Wellbery (eds.), *Chronotypes: The Construction of Time* (pp. 151–166). Stanford: Stanford University Press.

Lucy, J. A. (1992a). *Grammatical Categories and Cognition: A Case Study of the Linguistic Relativity Hypothesis*. Cambridge: Cambridge University Press.

Lucy, J. A. (1992b). *Language Diversity and Cognitive Development: A Reformulation of the Linguistic Relativity Hypothesis*. Cambridge: Cambridge University Press.

Lucy, J. A. (ed.) (1993). *Reflexive Language: Reported Speech and Metapragmatics*. New York: Cambridge University Press.

Lucy, J. A., and Shweder, R. A. (1979). Whorf and His Critics: Linguistic and Nonlinguistic Influences on Color Memory. *American Anthropologist* 81: 581–615.

Luis, K. (1997). The Language of Madness: Words, Culture, and the Boundaries of Sanity in the Works of Diane DiMassa, Charlotte Perkins Gilman, and Sylvia Plath. *Feminista* 1.

Luke, A. (1994). *The Social Construction of Literacy in the Primary School*. Melbourne: Macmillan.

Lussu, G. (1998). *La lettera uccide*. Viterbo, Italy: Stampa Alternativa & Graffiti.

Lussu, G. (2001). La forma del testo/1. In S. Covino (ed.), *Atti del convegno "La scrittura professionale. Ricerca, prassi, insegnamento"*. *Perugia, 23–25 October, 2000*. Florence: Olschki.

Lussu, G., and Perri, A. (1999). La scrittura e i paradossi del visibile. *Il Verri* 10–11: 52–62.

Luthin, H. W. (1987). The Story of California (ow): The Coming-of-Age of English in California. In K. M. Denning, S. Inkelas, F. C. McNair-Knox, and J. R. Rickford (eds.), *Variation in Language: NWAV-XV at Stanford* (pp. 312–324). Stanford: Department of Linguistics, Stanford University.

Luthin, H. (1991). Restoring the Voice in Yanan Traditional Narrative: Prosody, Performance, and Presentational Form. PhD dissertation, University of California, Berkeley.

Lutz, C. A. (1988). *Unnatural Emotions: Everyday Sentiments on a Micronesian Atoll and Their Challenge to Western Theory*. Cambridge: Cambridge University Press.

Lutz, C., and White, G. (1986). The Anthropology of Emotions. *Annual Review of Anthropology* 15: 405–436.

Lutz, W. (1990). *Doublespeak*. New York: Harper Collins.

Lynch, J., Ross, M., and Crowley, T. (2001). *The Oceanic Languages*. London: Curzon Routledge.

Lyons, J. (1977). *Semantics*. Cambridge: Cambridge University Press (2 vols).

Lyons, J. (1981). *Language and Linguistics: An Introduction*. Cambridge: Cambridge University Press.

Lyons, J. (1982). Deixis and Subjectivity: *Loquor, ergo sum?* In R. J. Jarvella and W. Klein (eds.), *Speech, Place, and Action: Studies in Deixis and Related Topics* (pp. 101–125). New York: John Wiley and Sons.

Macaulay, R. K. S. (1987). Polyphonic Monologues: Quoted Direct Speech in Oral Narratives. *IPrA Papers in Pragmatics* 1(2): 1–34.

Macaulay, R. K. S. (1991a). "Coz It Izny Spelt When They Say It": Displaying Dialect in Writing. *American Speech* 66: 280–289.

Macaulay, R. K. S. (1991b). *Locating Dialect in Discourse: The Language of Honest Men and Bonnie Lasses in Ayr*. Oxford: Oxford University Press.

Makihara, M. (1998). Rapanui–Spanish Bilingual Language Choice and Code Switching. In C. M. Stevenson (ed.), *Easter Island in Pacific Context, South Seas Symposium: Papers Presented at the Fourth International Conference on Easter Island and the Pacific* (pp. 33–38). Los Osos, CA: Easter Island Foundation.

Makihara, M. (2001). Rapanui–Spanish Bilingualism. *Rongorongo Studies* 11(1): 25–42.

Malinowski, B. (1923). The Problem of Meaning in Primitive Languages. In C. K. Ogden and I. A. Richards (eds.), *The Meaning of Meaning* (pp. 296–336). New York: Harcourt, Brace and World.

Malinowski, B. (1935). *Coral Gardens and Their Magic*. London: Allen and Unwin (2 vols).

Malloy, C., and Doner, J. (1995). Variation in ASL Discourse: Gender Differences in the Use of Cohesive Devices. In L. Byers, J. Chaiken, and M. Mueller (eds.), *Communication Forum 1995* (pp. 183–205). Washington, DC: Gallaudet University, Department of ASL, Linguistics, and Interpretation.

Malotki, E. (1983). *Hopi Time: A Linguistic Analysis of the Temporal Concepts in the Hopi Language*. Berlin: Mouton.

Maltz, D. N. (1985). Joyful Noise and Reverent Silence: The Significance of Noise in Pentecostal Worship. In D. Tannen and M. Saville-Troike (eds.), *Perspectives on Silence*. Norwood, NJ: Ablex.

Maltz, D. N., and Borker, R. A. (1982). A Cultural Approach to Male–Female Miscommunication. In J. J. Gumperz (ed.), *Language and Social Identity* (pp. 196–216). Cambridge: Cambridge University Press.

Mandelbaum, J. (1987a). Couples Sharing Stories. *Communication Quarterly* 35(4).

Mandelbaum, J. (1987b). Recipient-driven Storytelling in Conversation. Unpublished PhD dissertation, University of Texas at Austin.

Mandelbaum, J. (1989). Interpersonal Activities in Conversational Storytelling. *Western Journal of Speech Communication* 53(2): 114–126.

Mandler, J. M., and Johnson, N. S. (1977). Remembrance of Things Parsed: Story Structure and Recall. *Cognitive Psychology* 9: 111–151.

Mannheim, B. (1986). Popular Song and Popular Grammar, Poetry and Metalanguage. *Word* 37(1–2): 45–75.

Mannheim, B. (1987). Couplets and Oblique Contexts: The Social Organization of a Folksong. *Text* 7(3): 265–288.

Mannheim, B. (1991). *The Language of the Inka since the European Invasion*. Austin: University of Texas Press.

Mannheim, B., and Tedlock, D. (1995). Interpretation, Participation and the Role of Narrative in Dialogical Anthropology. In D. Tedlock and B. Mannheim (eds.), *The Dialogic Emergence of Culture* (pp. 1–32). Urbana and Chicago: University of Illinois Press.

Manschreck, T. C., et al. (2000). Impaired Verbal Memory is Associated with Impaired Motor Performance in Schizophrenia: Relationship to Brain Structure. *Schizophrenia Research* 43(1).

Mansfield, D. (1993). Gender Differences in ASL: A Sociolinguistic Study of Sign Choices by Deaf Native Signers. In E. Winston (ed.), *Communication Forum 1993* (pp. 86–98). Washington, DC: Gallaudet University, Department of ASL, Linguistics, and Interpretation.

Marcos, L. R., and Trujillo, M. (1981). Culture, Language, and Communicative Behavior: The Psychiatric Examination of Spanish-Americans. In R. Durán (ed.), *Latino Language and Communicative Behavior* (pp. 187–194). Norwood, NJ: Ablex.

Marcus, G. E. (1989). Chieftainship. In A. Howard and R. Borofsky (eds.), *Developments in Polynesian Ethnology* (175–209). Honolulu: University of Hawai'i Press.

Marcus, G. E. (ed.) (1999). *Critical Anthropology Now: Unexpected Contexts, Shifting Constituencies, Changing Agendas*. Santa Fe, NM: School of American Research Press.

Marichal, R. (1963). *L'écriture latine et la civilisation occidentale du Ier au XVIe siècle*. In M.

Cohen (ed.), *L'écriture et la psychologie des peuples* (pp. 199–247). Paris: Armand Colin.

Markee, N. (2000). *Conversation Analysis*. Mahwah, NJ: Lawrence Erlbaum.

Martin, E. (1987). *The Woman in the Body: A Cultural Analysis of Reproduction*. Boston: Beacon Press.

Martin, E. (2000). The Rationality of Mania. In R. Reid and S. Traweek (eds.), *Doing Science + Culture* (pp. 177–196). New York and London: Routledge.

Martin, E. (2001). Rationality, Feminism, and Mind. In A. Creager, E. Lunbeck, and L. Schiebinger (eds.), *Feminism in Twentieth-Century Science, Technology, and Medicine* (pp. 214–227). Chicago: University of Chicago Press.

Martin, J. G., and Strange, W. (1968). Determinants of Hesitations in Spontaneous Speech. *Journal of Experimental Psychology* 76: 474–479.

Martin, L. (1986). Eskimo Words for Snow: A Case Study in the Genesis and Decay of an Anthropological Example. *American Anthropologist* 88: 418–423.

Martínez-Taboas, A. (1999). A Case of Spirit Possession and Glossolalia. *Culture, Medicine, and Psychiatry* 23: 333–348.

Mason, O. T. (1900). The Linguistic Families of Mexico. *American Anthropologist* 2: 63–65.

Massey, D. S., and Denton, N. A. (1993). *American Apartheid: Segregation and the Making of the Underclass*. Cambridge, MA and London: Harvard University Press.

Mather, S. (1991). The Discourse Marker "Oh" in Typed Telephone Conversations among Deaf Typists. PhD dissertation, Georgetown University.

Matoesian, G. M. (1999). The Grammaticalization of Participant Roles in the Constitution of Expert Identity. *Language in Society* 28(4): 491–521.

Matthews, P. (1996). *The Irish Deaf Community*, vol. 1. Dublin: Institiúid Teangeolaíochta Éireann.

Mattingly, C. (1998). *Healing Dramas and Clinical Plots: The Narrative Structure of Experience*. Cambridge: Cambridge University Press.

Mattingly, C., and Garro, L. (eds.) (2000). *Narrative and the Cultural Construction of Illness and Healing*. Berkeley: University of California Press.

Maurer, D. (1955). *Whiz Mob: A Correlation of the Technical Argot of Pickpockets with Their Behavior Pattern*. Gainesville, FL: American Dialect Society.

Mauss, M. (1909 [forthcoming]). *Study of Prayer: Text and Context*. Oxford: Berghahn.

Mauss, M. (1985 [1935]). A Category of the Human Mind: The Notion of Person; The Notion of Self. In M. Carrithers, S. Collins, and S. Lukes (eds.), *The Category of the Person: Anthropology, Philosophy, History* (pp. 1–25). Cambridge: Cambridge University Press.

May, S. (2001). *Language and Minority Rights: Ethnicity, Nationalism, and the Politics of Language*. London: Longman.

Maynard, D. W., Houtkoop-Steenstra, H., Schaeffer, N. C., and Zouwen, J. van der (eds.) (2002). *Standardization and Tacit Knowledge: Interaction and Practice in the Survey Interview*. New York: Wiley.

Mazeland, H., and Huiskes, M. (2001). Dutch "but" as a Sequential Conjunction: Its Use as a Resumption Marker. In M. Selting and E. Couper-Kuhlen (eds.), *Studies in Interactional Linguistics* (pp. 141–170). Amsterdam: John Benjamins.

McCabe, A., and Peterson, C. (eds.) (1991). *Developing Narrative Structure*. Hillsdale, NJ: Lawrence Erlbaum.

McConnell-Ginet, S. (1983). Intonation in a Man's World. In B. Thorne, C. Kramarae, and N. Henley (eds.), *Language, Gender, and Society* (pp. 69–88). New York: Newbury House.

McConvell, P., and Evans, N. (eds.) (1997). *Archaeology and Linguistics: Aboriginal Australia and Global Perspective*. Melbourne: Oxford University Press.

McDermott, R. P. (1976). Kids Make Sense: An Ethnographic Account of the Interactional Management of Success and Failure of One First-Grade Classroom. Unpublished PhD dissertation, Stanford University.

McDermott, R. P., and Gospodinoff, K. (1979). Social Contexts for Ethnic Borders and School Failure. In A. Wolfgang (ed.), *Nonverbal Behavior: Applications and Cultural Implications* (pp. 175–196). New York: Academic Press.

McDermott, R. P., Gospodinoff, K., and Aron, J. (1978). Criteria for an Ethnographically Adequate Description of Concerted Activities and Their Contexts. *Semiotica* 24(3/4): 245–275.

McDowell, J. H. (1983). The Semiotic Constitution of Kamsá Ritual Language. *Language in Society* 12: 23–46.

McElhinny, B. (1995). Challenging Hegemonic Masculinities: Female and Male Police Officers Handling Domestic Violence. In K. Hall and M. Bucholtz (eds.), *Gender Articulated: Language and the Socially Constructed Self* (pp. 217–244). New York: Routledge.

McElhinny, B. (1996). Strategic Essentialism in Sociolinguistic Studies of Gender. In N. Warner, J. Ahlers, L. Bilmes, et al. (eds.), *Gender and Belief Systems: Proceedings of the Fourth Berkeley Women and Language Conference* (pp. 469–480). Berkeley: Berkeley Women and Language Group.

McElhinny, B. (1998). Genealogies of Gender Theory: Practice Theory and Feminism in Sociocultural and Linguistic Anthropology. *Social Analysis* 42(3): 164–189.

McEvoy, J. P., and Abernethy, V. (1982). Sociocultural Identity and Psychogenic Psychosis. *Papua and New Guinea Medical Journal* 25(1): 55–59.

McFerrin, B. (1988). *The Voice.* WEA/Elektra Entertainment. CD.

McGuire, P. K., et al. (1996). The Neural Correlates of Inner Speech and Auditory Verbal Imagery in Schizophrenia: Relationship to Auditory Verbal Hallucinations. *British Journal of Psychiatry* 169(2): 148–159.

McHoul, A. W. (1978). The Organization of Turns at Formal Talk in the Classroom. *Language in Society* 7: 183–213.

McHoul, A. W. (1990). The Organization of Repair in Classroom Talk. *Language in Society* 19: 349–377.

McIlvenny, P. (ed.) (2002). *Talking Gender and Sexuality.* Amsterdam: John Benjamins.

McKee, R. L., Johnson, K., and Marbury, N. (1991). Attention-getting Strategies of Deaf Children at the Dinner Table. *Issues in Applied Linguistics* 2(2): 239–268.

McLuhan, M. (1962). *The Gutemberg Galaxy: The Making of Typographic Man.* Toronto: University of Toronto Press.

McMahon, A. M. S. (1994). *Understanding Language Change.* Cambridge: Cambridge University Press.

McMillan, J. B. (1939). Vowel Nasality as a Sandhi Form of the Morphemes *nt* and *ing* in Southern American. *American Speech* 14: 120–123.

McNeil, T. F., Cantor-Graae, E., and Blennow, G. (2003). Mental Correlates of Neuromotoric Deviation in 6-year-olds at Heightened Risk for Schizophrenia. *Schizophrenia Research* 60(2–3): 219–228.

McNeill, D. (1985). So You Think Gestures Are Nonverbal? *Psychology Review* 92(3): 350–371.

McNeill, D. (1992). *Hand and Mind: What Gestures Reveal about Thought.* Chicago: University of Chicago Press.

McNeill, D. (ed.) (2000). *Language and Gesture.* Cambridge: Cambridge University Press.

McNeill, D., and Duncan, S. (2000). Growth Points in Thinking for Speaking. In D. McNeill (ed.), *Language and Gesture* (pp. 141–161). Cambridge: Cambridge University Press.

McTear, M. (1985). *Children's Conversation.* Oxford: Blackwell.

McWhorter, J. H. (1997). *Towards a New Model of Creole Genesis.* New York: Peter Lang.

McWhorter, J. H. (1998). Identifying the Creole Prototype: Vindicating a Typological Class. *Language* 74(4): 788–818.

Mead, M. (1930). *Growing up in New Guinea.* Harmondsworth: Penguin.

Mead, M. (1954 [1928]). *Coming of Age in Samoa.* New York: Morrow Quill.

Meadow, K. (1972). Sociolinguistics, Sign Language and the Deaf Sub-Culture. In T. O'Rourke (ed.), *Psycholinguistics and Total Communication: The State of the Art* (pp. 19–33). Silver Spring, MD: American Annals of the Deaf.

Meek, B. A. (2001). Kaska Language Socialization, Acquisition and Shift. PhD dissertation, University of Arizona.

Meeuwis, M. (1999). Flemish Nationalism in the Belgian Congo versus Zairian Anti-imperialism: Continuity and Discontinuity in Language Ideological Debates. In J. Blommaert (ed.), *Language Ideological Debates* (pp. 381–424). Berlin: Mouton de Gruyter.

Meeuwis, M., and Blommaert, J. (1994). The "Markedness Model" and the Absence of Society: Remarks on Codeswitching. *Multilingua* 13(4): 387–423.

Meeuwis, M., and Blommaert, J. (1998). A Monolectal View of Code-switching: Layered Code-switching among Zairians in Belgium. In J. C. P. Auer (ed.), *Code-switching in Conversation* (pp. 76–98). London: Routledge.

Mehan, H. (1979a). *Learning Lessons: Social Organization in the Classroom.* Cambridge, MA and London: Harvard University Press.

Mehan, H. (1979b). "What Time Is It, Denise?" Asking Known Information Questions in Classroom Discourse. *Theory into Practice* 18: 285–294.

Mehan, H. (1996). The Construction of an LD Student: A Case Study in the Politics of Representation. In M. Silverstein and G. Urban (eds.), *Natural Histories of Discourse* (pp. 253–276). Chicago: University of Chicago Press.

Mehrotra, R. R. (1977). *The Sociology of Secret Languages*. Delhi: Indian Institute of Advanced Study.

Meier, C. (1995). Eine konversationsanalytische Untersuchung zur Interaktionsstruktur und -dynamik von Arbeitsbesprechungen. Dissertation, Justus-Liebig-Universität Giessen.

Meillet, A. (1965). *Aperçu d'une histoire de la langue grecque*. Paris: Klincksieck.

Meintjes, L. (2003). *Sound of Africa! Making Music Zulu in a South African Studio*. Durham, NC: Duke University Press.

Meltzoff, A. N. (1999). Origins of Theory of Mind, Cognition and Communication. *Journal of Communication Disorders* 32: 251–269.

Mendoza-Denton, N. (1996). "Muy Macha": Gender and Ideology in Gang-Girls' Discourse about Makeup. *Ethnos* 61: 47–63.

Mendoza-Denton, N. (1999). Sociolinguistics and Linguistic Anthropology of US Latinos. *Annual Review of Anthropology* 28: 375–395.

Mercer, K. (1994). *Welcome to the Jungle: New Positions in Black Cultural Studies*. New York and London: Routledge.

Merlan, F. (1981). Land, Language and Social Identity in Aboriginal Australia. *Mankind* 13(2): 133–148.

Merlan, F. (1985). Split Intransitivity: Functional Oppositions in Intransitive Inflection. In J. Nichols and A. Woodbury (eds.), *Grammar Inside and Outside the Clause: Some Approaches to Theory from the Field* (pp. 324–362). Cambridge: Cambridge University Press.

Merlan, F. (1992). Male–Female Separation and Forms of Society in Aboriginal Australia. *Cultural Anthropologist* 7(2): 169–193.

Merlan, F., and Rumsey, A. (1991). *Ku Waru: Language and Segmentary Politics in the Western Nebilyer Valley, Papua New Guinea*. Cambridge: Cambridge University Press.

Merleau-Ponty, M. (1963). *The Structure of Behavior* (trans. A. L. Fisher). Boston: Beacon.

Mertz, E. (1989). Sociolinguistic Creativity: Cape Breton Gaelic's Linguistic "Tip". In N. C. Dorian (ed.), *Investigating Obsolescence: Studies in Language Contraction and Death* (pp. 103–116). Cambridge: Cambridge University Press.

Mertz, E. (1996a). Consensus and Dissent in U.S. Legal Opinions: Narrative Structure and Social Voices. In C. L. Briggs (ed.), *Disorderly Discourse: Narrative, Conflict, and Inequality* (pp. 135–157). New York: Oxford University Press.

Mertz, E. (1996b). Recontextualization as Socialization: Text and Pragmatics in the Law School Classroom. In M. Silverstein and G. Urban (eds.), *Natural Histories of Discourse* (pp. 229–249). Chicago: University of Chicago Press.

Mertz, E. (1998). Linguistic Ideology and Praxis in U.S. Law School Classrooms. In B. B. Schieffelin, K. A. Woolard, and P. V. Kroskrity (eds.), *Language Ideologies: Practice and Theory* (pp. 149–162). New York: Oxford University Press.

Messing, L. S., and Campbell, R. (1999). *Gesture, Speech and Sign*. Oxford: Oxford University Press.

Metzger, M. (ed.) (2000). *Bilingualism and Identity in Deaf Communities*. (Sociolinguistics in Deaf Communities Series, vol. 6). Washington, DC: Gallaudet University Press.

Mey, J. L. (1994). How To Do Good Things with Words. *Pragmatics* 4(2): 239–263.

Mey, J. L. (2001). *Pragmatics: An Introduction*, 2nd edn. Malden, MA: Blackwell.

Michaels, S. (1981). "Sharing Time": Children's Narrative Styles and Differential Access to Literacy. *Language in Society* 10: 423–442.

Michaels, S. (1991). The Dismantling of Narrative. In A. McCabe and C. Peterson (eds.), *Developing Narrative Structure* (pp. 303–351). Hillsdale, NJ: Lawrence Erlbaum.

Middleton, D. (1997). The Social Organization of Conversational Remembering: Experience as Individual and Collective Concerns. *Mind, Culture & Activity* 4(20): 71–85.

Miehe, G. (1995). Stilistische Merkmale der Swahili-Versdichtung. In G. Miehe and W. J. G. Möhlig (eds.), *Swahili-Handbuch* [Swahili-Handbook]. Cologne: Rüdiger Köppe.

Miller, P. (1986). Teasing as Language Socialization and Verbal Play in a White Working-class Community. In B. B. Schieffelin and E. Ochs (eds.), *Language Socialization across Cultures* (pp. 199–211). Cambridge: Cambridge University Press.

Miller, P. (1994). Narrative Practices: Their Role in Socialization and Self-construction. In U. Neisser and R. Fivush (eds.), *The Remembering Self: Construction and Accuracy in the Self-Narrative* (pp. 158–179). Cambridge: Cambridge University Press.

Miller, P., Mintz, J., Hoogstra, L., and Fung, H. (1992). The Narrated Self: Young Children's Construction of Self in Relation to Others in Conversational Stories of Personal Experience. *Merrill-Palmer Quarterly* 38(1): 45–67.

Miller, P., Potts, R., Fung, H., Hoogstra, L. and Mintz, J. (1990). Narrative Practices and the Social Construction of Self in Childhood. *American Ethnologist* 17: 292–311.

Miller, P., and Sperry, L. (1982). Early Talk about the Past. *Journal of Child Language* 15: 293–315.

Miller, P. J., Wiley, A. R., Fung, H., and Liang, C.-H. (1997). Personal Storytelling as a Medium of Socialization in Chinese-American Families. *Child Development* 68(3): 557–568.

Miller, R. (2001). *Training Soprano Voices*. New York: Oxford University Press.

Milroy, J., and Milroy, L. (1985). Linguistic Change, Social Network, and Speaker Innovation. *Journal of Linguistics* 21: 339–384.

Milroy, J., and Milroy, L. (1999). *Authority in Language: Investigating Language Prescription and Standardisation*. London: Routledge.

Milroy, L. (1987). *Language and Social Networks* (2nd edn.). Oxford: Blackwell.

Milroy, L. (2000). Britain and the United States: Two Nations Divided by the Same Language (and Different Language Ideologies). *Journal of Linguistic Anthropology* 10(1): 56–89.

Milroy, L., and Milroy, J. (1992). Social Network and Social Class: Toward an Integrated Sociolinguistic Model. *Language in Society* 21: 1–26.

Milroy, L., and Muysken, P. (eds.) (1995). *One Speaker, Two Languages: Cross-disciplinary Perspectives on Code-switching*. Cambridge: Cambridge University Press.

Minami, M., and McCabe, A. (1995). Rice Balls and Bear Hunts: Japanese and North American Family Narrative Patterns. *Journal of Child Language* 22: 423–445.

Minzenberg, M. J., Ober, B. A., and Vinogradov, S. (2002). Semantic Priming in Schizophrenia: A Review and Synthesis. *Journal of the International Neuropsychology Society* 8: 699–720.

Mishler, E. (1999). *Storylines: Craftartists' Narratives of Identity*. Cambridge, MA: Harvard University Press.

Mitchell, C. (1993). Exclusion and Integration: The Case of the Sisters of Providence of Quebec. In J. V. Van Cleve (ed.), *Deaf History Unveiled: Interpretations from the New Scholarship* (pp. 146–171). Washington, DC: Gallaudet University Press.

Mitchell-Kernan, C. (1972). Signifying and Marking: Two Afro-American Speech Acts. In J. J. Gumperz and D. Hymes (eds.), *Directions in Sociolinguistics: The Ethnography of Communication* (pp. 161–179). New York: Holt, Rinehart and Winston.

Mitchell-Kernan, C. (1981). Signifying, Loud-talking, and Marking. In A. Dundes (ed.), *Mother Wit from the Laughing Barrel* (pp. 310–328). Englewood Cliffs, NJ: Prentice-Hall.

Mithun, M. (1986). On the Nature of Noun Incorporation. *Language* 62: 32–37.

Mithun, M. (1989). The Acquisition of Polysynthesis. *Journal of Child Language* 16: 285–312.

Mithun, M. (1991). Active/Agentive Case Marking and Its Motivation. *Language* 67: 510–546.

Mithun, M. (1999). *The Languages of Native North America*. Cambridge and New York: Cambridge University Press.

Moerman, M. (1977). The Preference for Self-correction in a Tai Conversational Corpus. *Language* 53(4): 872–882.

Moerman, M. (1988). *Talking Culture: Ethnography and Conversation Analysis*. Philadelphia: University of Pennsylvania Press.

Moerman, M. (1991). Exploring Talk and Interaction. *Research on Language and Social Interaction* 24: 173–187.

Moerman, M. (1996). The Field of Analyzing Foreign Language Conversations. *Journal of Pragmatics* 26: 147–158.

Mohar Betancourt, L. M. (1990). *La escritura en el México antiguo* (2 vols.). Mexico: Plaza y Valdés Editores.

Moliner, M. (1971). *Diccionario de uso del Español*. Madrid: Gredos.

Molino, J. (2002). La poesia cantata. Alcuni problemi teorici. In M. Agamennone and F. Giannattasio (eds.), *Sul verso cantato* [On Sung Verse] (pp. 17–33). Padova: il Poligrafo.

Molino, J., and Gardes-Tamine, J. (1987–8). *Introduction à l'analyse de la poésie* [Introduction to the Analysis of Poetry], Parts I and II. Paris: Presses Universitaires de France.

Moll, L. (1992). Funds of Knowledge for Teaching: Using a Qualitative Approach to Connect Homes and Classrooms. *Theory into Practice* 31(2): 132–141.

Moll, L. (2000). Inspired by Vygotsky: Ethnographic Experiments in Education. In C. D. Lee and P. Smagorinsky (eds.), *Vygotskian*

Perspectives on Literacy Research: Constructing Meaning through Collaborative Inquiry (pp. 256–268). Cambridge: Cambridge University Press.

Moll, L., and Gonzalez, N. (1997). Teachers as Social Scientists: Learning about Culture from Household Research. In P. M. Hall (ed.), *Race, Ethnicity and Multiculturalism* (pp. 89–114). New York: Garland.

Monaghan, L. (1991). The Founding of Two Deaf Churches: The Interplay of Deaf and Christian Identities. *Sign Language Studies* 73: 431–452.

Monaghan, L. (1993). Contexts of Luck: Issues Involved with Entering the New Zealand Deaf Community. *Anthropology UCLA* 20: 43–62, Special Issue, "Partial Knowledges: Theories, Ethics, and Methods of Cultural Research in the 1990's."

Monaghan, L. (1996). Signing, Oralism and the Development of the New Zealand Deaf Community: An Ethnography and History of Language Ideologies. PhD dissertation, University of California, Los Angeles.

Monaghan, L. (2001). Signing. In A. Duranti (ed.), *Key Terms in Language and Culture* (pp. 223–226). Oxford: Blackwell.

Monaghan, L. (2003). A World's Eye View: Deaf Cultures in Global Perspective. In L. Monaghan, C. Schmaling, K. Nakamura, and G. H. Turner (eds.), *Many Ways to be Deaf.* Washington, DC: Gallaudet University Press.

Monaghan, L., Schmaling, C., Nakamura, K., and Turner, G. H. (2003). *Many Ways to be Deaf.* Washington, DC: Gallaudet University Press.

Moore, L. C. (1999). Language Socialization Research and French Language Education in Africa: A Cameroonian Case Study. *The Canadian Modern Language Review/La Revue Canadienne des Langues Vivantes* 56(2): 329–350.

Moore, L. C. (2002). Language Mixing at Home and School in a Multilingual Community (Mandara Mountains, Cameroon). In J. E. Alatis, H. Hamilton, and A.-H. Tan (eds.), *Georgetown University Round Table on Languages and Linguistics 2000: Linguistics, Language, and the Professions: Education, Journalism, Law, Medicine, and Technology.* Washington, DC: Georgetown University Press.

Morford, J. (1996). Insights to Language from the Study of Gesture: A Review of Research on the Gestural Communication of Non-Signing Deaf People. *Language & Communication* 16(2): 165–178.

Morford, J. (1997). Social Indexicality and French Pronominal Address. *Journal of Linguistic Anthropology* 7(1): 3–37.

Morgan, M. (1993). The Africanness of Counterlanguage among African Americans. In S. Mufwene (ed.), *Africanisms in Afro-American Language Varieties* (pp. 423–435). Athens: University of Georgia Press.

Morgan, M. (1994a). The African-American Speech Community: Reality and Sociolinguists. In M. Morgan (ed.), *Language and the Social Construction of Identity in Creole Situations* (pp. 121–148). Los Angeles: Center for African-American Studies, University of California, Los Angeles.

Morgan, M. (1994b). Theories and Politics in African American English. *Annual Review of Anthropology* 23: 325–345.

Morgan, M. (1996). Conversational Signifying: Grammar and Indirectness among African American Women. In E. Ochs, E. A. Schegloff, and S. A. Thompson (eds.), *Interaction and Grammar* (pp. 405–434). Cambridge: Cambridge University Press.

Morgan, M. (1998). More than a Mood or an Attitude: Discourse and Verbal Genres in African-American Culture. In S. Mufwene, J. Rickford, and J. Baugh (eds.), *African-American English: Structure, History and Use* (pp. 251–281). London: Routledge.

Morgan, M. (1999). No Woman No Cry: Claiming African American Women's Place. In M. Bucholtz, A. C. Liang, and L. A. Sutton (eds.), *Reinventing Identities: The Gendered Self in Discourse* (pp. 27–45). New York: Oxford University Press.

Morgan, M. (2002). *Language, Discourse, and Power in African Culture.* Cambridge: Cambridge University Press.

Mori, J. (1999). *Negotiating Agreement and Disagreement in Japanese: Connective Expressions and Turn Construction.* Amsterdam: John Benjamins.

Morris, A. K. (ed.) (1998). *Sound States: Innovative Poetics and Acoustical Technologies.* Chapel Hill: University of North Carolina Press.

Morris, D. (1977). *Manwatching: A Field Guide to Human Behavior.* New York: Harry N. Abrams.

Morson, G. S. (1994). *Narrative and Freedom: The Shadows of Time.* New Haven and London: Yale University Press.

Moss, B. (1994). Creating a Community: Literacy Events in African-American Churches. In B. Moss (ed.), *Literacy across Communities* (pp. 147–178). Cresskill, NJ: Hampton Press.

Mottez, B. (1993). The Deaf-Mutes Banquets and the Birth of the Deaf Movement. In J. V. Van Cleve (ed.), *Deaf History Unveiled: Interpretations from the New Scholarship* (pp. 27–39). Washington, DC: Gallaudet University Press.

Mounin, G. (1970). *Introduction à la sémiologie*. Paris: Les Éditions de Minuit.

Mous, M. (1994). Ma'a or Mbugu. In P. Bakker and M. Mous (eds.), *Mixed Languages* (pp. 175–200). Amsterdam: Institute for Functional Research into Language and Language Use [IFOTT], University of Amsterdam.

Mufwene, S. S. (1986). Les langues créoles peuvent-elles être définies sans allusion à leur histoire? *Etudes Créoles* 9(1): 135–150.

Mufwene, S. S. (1996). The Founder Principle in Creole Genesis. *Diachronica* 13: 83–124.

Mufwene, S. S. (1997). Jargons, Pidgins, Creoles, and Koinés: What Are They? In A. K. Spears and D. Winford (eds.), *The Structure and Status of Pidgins and Creoles* (pp. 35–70). Amsterdam: John Benjamins.

Mufwene, S. S. (2000). Creolization Is a Social, not a Structural, Process. In I. Neumann-Holzschuh and E. W. Schneider (eds.), *Degrees of Restructuring in Creole Languages* (pp. 65–84). Amsterdam: John Benjamins.

Mühlhäusler, P. (1996). *Linguistic Ecology: Language Change and Linguistic Imperialism in the Pacific Region*. London: Routledge.

Müller, C. (1994). Semantic Structure of Motional Gestures and Lexicalization Patterns in Spanish and German Descriptions of Motion-events. *Proceedings of the Chicago Linguistics Society* 30(1): 281–295.

Murphy, J. (1976). Psychiatric Labeling in Cross-cultural Perspective. *Science* 191: 1019–1028.

Murray, A., and Sondhi, R. (1987). Socio-political Influences on Cross-cultural Encounters. In K. Knapp, W. Enninger, and A. Knapp-Potthoff (eds.), *Analyzing Intercultural Communication* (pp. 17–33). New York: Mouton de Gruyter.

Murray, D. W. (1989). Transposing Symbolic Forms: Actor Awareness of Language Structures in Navajo Ritual. *Anthropological Linguistics* 31: 195–208.

Murray, S. O. (1993). *Theory Groups and the Study of Language in North America*. Amsterdam and Philadelphia: John Benjamins.

Murray, S. O. (1998). *American Sociolinguistics: Theorists and Theory Groups*. Amsterdam and Philadelphia: John Benjamins.

Muysken, P. (1981). Halfway between Quechua and Spanish: The Case for Relexification. In A. Highfield and A. Valdman (eds.), *Historicity and Variation in Creole Studies* (pp. 52–78). Ann Arbor: Karoma.

Muysken, P. (1997). Media Lengua. In S. G. Thomason (ed.), *Contact Languages: A Wider Perspective* (pp. 365–426). Amsterdam: John Benjamins.

Muysken, P. (2000). *Bilingual Speech: A Typology of Code-mixing*. Cambridge: Cambridge University Press.

Myers-Scotton, C. (1993). *Social Motivations for Codeswitching: Evidence from Africa*. Oxford: Oxford University Press.

Myers-Scotton, C., and Bolonyai, A. (2001). Calculating Speakers: Codeswitching in a Rational Choice Model. *Language in Society* 30(1): 1–28.

Nakamura, K. (2001). Deaf Identities, Sign Language, and Minority Social Movements Politics in Modern Japan (1868–2000). PhD dissertation, Yale University.

Napier, J. (1980). *Hands*. New York: Pantheon Books.

Nash, W. (1993). *Jargon: Its Uses and Abuses*. Oxford: Blackwell.

Nattiez, J.-J. (1983). Some Aspects of Inuit Vocal Games. *Ethnomusicology* 27(3): 457–475.

Nattiez, J.-J. (1990). *Music and Discourse: Toward a Semiology of Music*. Princeton: Princeton University Press.

Nattiez, J.-J. (1999). Inuit Throat Games and Siberian Throat Singing: A Comparative, Historical, and Semiological Approach. *Ethnomusicology* 43(3): 399–418.

Needham, S. (2001). "How Can You Be Cambodian if You Don't Speak Khmer?" Language, Literacy, and Education in a Cambodian "Rhetoric of Distinction." In M. Hopkins and N. Wellmeier (eds.), *Negotiating Transnationalism: Selected Papers on Refugees and Immigrants* (pp. 123–141). Arlington: American Anthropological Association.

Neisser, U., and Fivush, R. (1994). *The Remembering Self: Construction and Accuracy in the Self-Narrative*. Cambridge: Cambridge University Press.

Nelson, K. (1985). *The Art of Reciting the Qur'an*. Austin: University of Texas Press.

Nelson, K. (ed.) (1989). *Narratives from the Crib*. Cambridge, MA: Harvard University Press.

Nettl, B. (1958). Some Linguistic Approaches to Musical Analysis. *Journal of the International Folk Music Council* 10: 37–41.

Nevile, M. (2001). Beyond the Black Box: Talk-in-Interaction in the Airline Cockpit. PhD dissertation, Department of Linguistics, Australian National University.

Newman, J. K. (1993). Epic. In A. Preminger and T. V. F. Brogan (eds.), *The New Princeton Encyclopedia of Poetry and Poetics* (pp. 361–375). Princeton, NJ: Princeton University Press.

Newmeyer, F. J. (1980). *Linguistic Theory in America: The First Quarter Century of Transformational Generative Grammar*. New York: Academic Press.

Newmeyer, F. J. (1986). Has There Been a "Chomskian Revolution" in Linguistics? *Language* 62(1): 1–18.

Newport, E. (1976). Motherese: The Speech of Mothers to Young Children. In N. J. Castellan, D. B. Pisoni, and G. R. Potts (eds.), *Cognitive Theory*, vol. 2. Hillsdale, NJ: Lawrence Erlbaum.

Newport, E. (1990). Maturational Constraints on Language Learning. *Cognitive Science* 14: 11–48.

Nichols, J. (1992). *Linguistic Diversity in Space and Time*. Chicago: University of Chicago Press.

Nichols, J. (1995a). Diachronically Stable Structural Features. In H. Anderson (ed.), *Historical Linguistics 1993: Selected Papers from the 11th International Congress of Historical Linguists, Los Angeles, 16–20 August, 1993* (pp. 337–355). Amsterdam: John Benjamins.

Nichols, J. (1995b). The Spread of Language around the Pacific Rim. *Evolutionary Anthropology* 3: 206–215.

Nichols, J., and Peterson, D. A. (1996). The Amerind Personal Pronouns. *Language* 72(2): 336–371.

Nicholson, H. B. (1973). *Phoneticism in the Late Pre-Hispanic Central Mexican Writing System*. In E. P. Benson (ed.), *Mesoamerican Writing Systems* (pp. 1–46). Washington, DC: Dumbarton Oaks Research Library and Collections.

Nicolopoùlou, A., and Cole, M. (1993). Generation and Transmission of Shared Knowledge in the Culture of Collaborative Learning: The Fifth Dimension, Its Play World, and Its Institutional Contexts. In E. A. Forman, N. Minick, and C. A. Stone (eds.), *Contexts for*

Learning: Sociocultural Dynamics in Children's Development (pp. 283–313). New York: Oxford University Press.

Nketia J. H. Kwabena (1971). Surrogate Languages of Africa. In T. A. Sebeok (ed.), *Current Trends in Linguistics*, vol. 7 (pp. 699–732). The Hague: Mouton.

Noël-Jorand, M. C., et al. (2000). Discourse Analysis in Psychosis: Characteristics of Hebephrenic Subject's Speech. *JADT 2000: 5es Journées Internationales d'Analyse Statistique des Données Textuelles* 5: 1–8.

Nuckolls, J. B. (1996). *Sounds like Life: Sound-symbolic Grammar, Performance, and Cognition in Pastaza Quechua*. Oxford: Oxford University Press.

Nuckolls, J. B. (1999). The Case for Sound Symbolism. *Annual Review of Anthropology* 28: 225–252.

Nunley, M. (1998). The Involvement of Families in Indian Psychiatry. *Culture, Medicine, & Psychiatry* 22(3): 317–353.

Nussbaum, M. (2001). Disabled Lives: Who Cares? *The New York Review of Books* (January 11).

Nuyts, J., and De Roeck, A. (1997). Autism and Meta-representation: The Case of Epistemic Modality. *European Journal of Disorders of Communication* 32(2): 113–137.

Ó Baoill, D. P., and Matthews, P. A. (2000). *The Irish Deaf Community*, vol. 2: *The Structure of Irish Sign Language*. Dublin: Institiúid Teangeolaíochta Éireann.

O'Brien, T. (1990). *The Things They Carried*. New York: Penguin.

Ochs, E. (1979a). Transcription as Theory. In E. Ochs and B. B. Schieffelin, *Developmental Pragmatics* (pp. 43–72). New York: Academic Press.

Ochs, E. (1979b). Social Foundations of Language. In R. O. Freedle (ed.), *New Directions in Discourse Processing*, vol. 2 (pp. 207–221). Norwood, NJ: Ablex.

Ochs, E. (1982). Talking to Children in Western Samoa. *Language in Society* 11: 77–104.

Ochs, E. (1983a). Cultural Dimensions of Language Acquisition. In E. Ochs and B. B. Schieffelin (eds.), *Acquiring Conversational Competence* (pp. 185–191). Boston: Routledge & Kegan Paul.

Ochs, E. (1983b). Planned and Unplanned Discourse. In E. Ochs and B. B. Schieffelin (eds.), *Acquiring Conversational Competence* (pp. 129–157). Boston: Routledge & Kegan Paul.

Ochs, E. (1984). Clarification and Culture. In D. Schiffrin (ed.), *Georgetown University*

Round Table in Languages and Linguistics (pp. 325–341). Washington, DC: Georgetown University Press.

Ochs, E. (1985). Variation and Error: A Sociolinguistic Approach to Language Acquisition in Samoa. In D. Slobin (ed.), The Crosslinguistic Study of Language Acquisition, vol. 1 (pp. 783–838). Hillsdale, NJ: Lawrence Erlbaum.

Ochs E. (1986). From Feelings to Grammar. In B. B. Schieffelin and E. Ochs (eds.), Language Socialization across Cultures (pp. 251–272). New York: Cambridge University Press.

Ochs, E. (1987). Input: A Socio-culture Perspective. In M. Hickmann (ed.), Social and Functional Approaches to Language and Thought (pp. 305–319). Orlando, FL: Academic Press.

Ochs, E. (1988). Culture and Language Development: Language Acquisition and Language Socialization in a Samoan Village. Cambridge: Cambridge University Press.

Ochs, E. (1990). Indexicality and Socialization. In J. W. Stigler, R. A. Shweder, and G. H. Herdt (eds.), Cultural Psychology: Essays on Comparative Human Development (pp. 287–308). New York: Cambridge University Press.

Ochs, E. (1991). Misunderstanding Children. In N. Coupland, H. Giles, and J. Wiemann (eds.), Miscommunication and Problematic Talk (pp. 44–60). Newbury Park, CA: Sage.

Ochs, E. (1992). Indexing Gender. In A. Duranti and C. Goodwin (eds.), Rethinking Context (pp. 335–358). Cambridge: Cambridge University Press.

Ochs, E. (1993). Constructing Social Identity: A Language Socialization Perspective. Research on Language and Social Interaction 26(3): 287–306.

Ochs, E. (1994). Stories that Step into the Future. In D. Biber and E. Finegan (eds.), Sociolinguistic Perspectives on Register: Situating Register Variation within Sociolinguistics (pp. 106–135). Oxford: Oxford University Press.

Ochs, E. (1996). Linguistic Resources for Socializing Humanity. In J. J. Gumperz and S. C. Levinson (eds.), Rethinking Linguistic Relativity (pp. 407–437). Cambridge: Cambridge University Press.

Ochs, E. (1997). Narrative. In T. van Dijk (ed.), Discourse as Structure and Process (pp. 185–207). London: Sage.

Ochs, E. (1999). Socialization. Journal of Linguistic Anthropology 9(1–2): 230–233.

Ochs, E., and Capps, L. (1996). Narrating the Self. Annual Review of Anthropology 25: 19–43.

Ochs, E., and Capps, L. (2001). Living Narrative: Creating Lives in Everyday Storytelling. Cambridge, MA: Harvard University Press.

Ochs, E., Gonzales, P., and Jacoby, S. (1996). "When I Come Down I'm in the Domain State": Grammar and Graphic Representation in the Interpretive Activity of Physicists. In E. Ochs, E. A. Schegloff, and S. A. Thompson (eds.), Interaction and Grammar (pp. 328–369). Cambridge: Cambridge University Press.

Ochs, E., and Jacoby, S. (1997). Down to the Wire: The Cultural Clock of Physicists and the Discourse of Consensus. Language in Society 26: 479–506.

Ochs, E., Jacoby, S., and Gonzales, P. (1994). Interpretive Journeys: How Physicists Talk and Travel through Graphic Space. Configurations 2(1): 151–171.

Ochs, E., Pontecorvo, C., and Fasulo, A. (1996). Socializing Taste. Ethnos 61(1–2): 5–42.

Ochs, E., Schegloff, E. A., and Thompson, S. A. (eds.) (1996). Interaction and Grammar. Cambridge: Cambridge University Press.

Ochs, E., and Schieffelin, B. B. (eds.) (1979). Developmental Pragmatics. New York: Academic Press.

Ochs, E., and Schieffelin, B. B. (eds.) (1983). Acquiring Conversational Competence. Boston: Routledge & Kegan Paul.

Ochs, E., and Schieffelin, B. B. (1984). Language Acquisition and Socialization: Three Developmental Stories and Their Implications. In R. A. Shweder and R. A. LeVine (eds.), Culture Theory: Essays on Mind, Self, and Emotion (pp. 276–320). Cambridge: Cambridge University Press.

Ochs, E., and Schieffelin, B. B. (1989). Language Has a Heart. Text 9(1): 7–25.

Ochs, E., and Schieffelin, B. B. (1995). The Impact of Language Socialization on Grammatical Development. In P. Fletcher and B. MacWhinney (eds.), The Handbook of Child Language (pp. 73–94). Oxford: Blackwell.

Ochs, E., Smith, R., and Taylor, C. (1989). Detective Stories at Dinnertime: Problem-solving through Co-narration. Cultural Dynamics 2: 238–257.

Ochs, E., and Solomon, O. (2004). From the Outside In: Practical Logic and Autism. In R. Edgerton and C. Casey (eds.), A Companion *to Psychological Anthropology.* Malden, MA: Blackwell.

Ochs, E., and Taylor, C. (1992). Family Narrative as Political Activity. *Discourse and Society* 3(2): 301–340.

Ochs, E., and Taylor, C. (1995). The "Father Knows Best" Dynamic in Dinnertime Narratives. In K. Hall and M. Bucholtz (eds.), *Gender Articulated: Language and the Socially Constructed Self* (pp. 97–119). New York: Routledge. [Reprinted in A. Duranti (ed.) (2001c), pp. 431–449.]

Ochs, E., Taylor, C., Rudolph, D., and Smith, R. (1992). Story-telling as a Theory-building Activity. *Discourse Processes* 15(1): 37–72.

O'Connor, M. (1980). *Hebrew Verse Structure.* Winona Lake, IN: Eisenbrauns.

O'Donnell, W. R., and Todd, L. (1980). *Variety in Contemporary English.* London: Allen & Unwin.

Oh, T. M., McCarthy, R. A., and McKenna, P. J. (2002). Is There a Schizophasia? A Study Applying the Single Case Approach to Formal Thought Disorder in Schizophrenia. *Neurocase* 8(3): 233–244.

Okamoto, S. (1995). "Tasteless" Japanese: Less "Feminine" Speech among Young Japanese Women. In K. Hall and M. Bucholtz (eds.), *Gender Articulated: Language and the Socially Constructed Self* (pp. 297–328). New York: Routledge.

O'Loughlin, K. (1989). Routine Beginnings: Telephone Openings in Australia. *Melbourne Papers in Applied Linguistics* 1(2): 27–42.

Olson, D. (1985). Introduction. In D. Olson, N. Torrance, and A. Hildyard (eds.), *Literacy, Language, and Learning: The Nature and Consequences of Reading and Writing* (pp. 1–15). Cambridge: Cambridge University Press.

Olson, D. R., and Torrance, N. (eds.) (1991). *Literacy and Orality.* Cambridge: Cambridge University Press.

Olt, A., and Woodbridge, S. (1993). An Assessment of Learning through the Qualitative Analysis of Fieldnotes. Paper presented at the Conference on Assessment and Diversity. University of California, Santa Cruz, Feb. 17–20.

O'Nell, T. D. (1998). Cultural Formulation of Psychiatric Diagnosis: Psychotic Depression and Alcoholism in an American Indian Man. *Culture, Medicine and Psychiatry* 22: 123–136.

O'Nell, T. D. (1999). "Coming Home" among Northern Plains Vietnam Veterans: Psycho-

logical Transformations in Pragmatic Perspective. *Ethos* 27: 441–465.

Ong, W. J. (1982). *Orality and Literacy.* London: Methuen.

Orletti, F. (ed.) (1994). *Fra conversazione e discorso.* Rome: La Nuova Italia Scientifica.

Ortner, S. (1984). Theory in Anthropology since the Sixties. *Comparative Studies in Society and History* 26: 126–166.

Ou, Y., and McAdoo, H. P. (1999). The Ethnic Socialization of Chinese American Children. In H. P. McAdoo (ed.), *Family Ethnicity: Strength in Diversity* (pp. 252–276). Thousand Oaks, CA: Sage.

Padden, C. (1980). The Deaf Community and the Culture of Deaf People. In C. Baker and R. Battison (eds.), *Sign Language and the Deaf Community: Essays in Honor of William C. Stokoe* (pp. 89–103). Silver Spring, MD: National Association of the Deaf.

Padden, C. (1989 [1980]). Deaf Community and the Culture of Deaf People. In S. Wilcox (ed.), *American Deaf Culture: An Anthology.* Silver Spring, MD: Linstok Press.

Padden, C., and Humphries, T. (1988). *Deaf in America: Voices from a Culture.* Cambridge, MA: Harvard University Press.

Padden, C., and Humphries, T. (2000). American Sign Language and Reading Ability in Deaf Children. In C. Chamberlain, J. Morford, and R. Mayberry (eds.), *Language Acquisition by Eye* (pp. 165–189). Mahwah, NJ: Lawrence Erlbaum.

Padel, R. (1981). Madness in Fifth-century (B.C.) Athenian Tragedy. In P. Heelas and A. Lock (eds.), *Indigenous Psychologies* (pp. 105–131). London: Academic Press.

Pagliai, V. (2000). Lands I Came to Sing: Negotiating Identities and Places in the Tuscan "Contrasto." *Pragmatics* 10: 125–146. (Special Issue, ed. V. Pagliai and M. Farr, *Art and the Expression of Complex Identities.*)

Pagliai, V., and Farr, M. (eds.) (2000). *Pragmatics* 10(1). Special Issue: *Art and the Expression of Complex Identities: Imagining and Contesting Ethnicity in Performance.*

Palmer, G. B. (1996). *Toward a Theory of Cultural Linguistics.* Austin: University of Texas Press.

Palmer, G. B., and Jankowiak, W. R. (1996). Performance and Imagination: Toward an Anthropology of the Spectacular and the Mundane. *Cultural Anthropology* 11(2): 225–258.

Parasnis, I. (ed.) (1996). *Cultural and Language Diversity and the Deaf Experience.* Cambridge: Cambridge University Press.

Paredes, A. and Bauman, R. (1972). *Towards New Perspectives in Folklore*. Austin: University of Texas Press.

Park, K. (1996). Use and Abuse of Race and Culture: Black–Korean Tension in America. *American Anthropologist* 98(3): 492–498.

Park, Y.-Y. (1997). A Cross-linguistic Study of the Use of Contrastive Connectives in English, Korean, and Japanese Conversation. PhD dissertation, University of California, Los Angeles.

Park, Y.-Y. (1998). A Discourse Analysis of Contrastive Connectives in English, Korean, and Japanese Conversation: With Special Reference to the Context of Dispreferred Responses. In A. Jucker and Y. Ziv (eds.), *Discourse Markers: Descriptions and Theory* (pp. 277–300). Amsterdam: John Benjamins.

Parmentier, R. (1993). The Political Function of Reported Speech: A Belauan Example. In J. Lucy (ed.), *Reflexive Language: Reported Speech and Metapragmatics* (pp. 261–286). New York: Cambridge University Press.

Paugh, A. (2001). "Creole Day Is Every Day": Language Socialization, Shift, and Ideologies in Dominica, West Indies. PhD dissertation, New York University.

Paulston, C. B. (1976). Pronouns of Address in Swedish: Social Class Semantics and a Changing System. *Language in Society* 5: 359–386.

Paulston, C. B. (1994). *Linguistic Minorities in Multilingual Settings: Implications for Language Policies*. Amsterdam: John Benjamins.

Paulston, C. B. (1997). Language Policies and Language Rights. *Annual Review of Anthropology* 26: 73–85.

Pawley, A. (1981). Melanesian Diversity and Polynesian Homogeneity: A Unified Explanation for Language. In K. J. Hollyman and A. Pawley (eds.), *Studies in Pacific Languages and Culture in Honour of Bruce Biggs* (pp. 269–309). Auckland: Linguistic Society of New Zealand.

Pawley, A. (1992). Kalam Pandanus Language: An Old New Guinea Experiment in Language Engineering. In T. Dutton, M. Ross, and D. Tryon (eds.), *The Language Game: Papers in Memory of Donald C. Laycock* (pp. 313–334). Canberra: Pacific Linguistics C-110.

Pawley, A. (1993). A Language Which Defies Description by Ordinary Means. In W. A. Foley (ed.), *The Role of Theory in Language Description* (pp. 87–130). Berlin: Mouton de Gruyter.

Pawley, A., and Ross, M. (1993). Austronesian Historical Linguistics and Culture History. *Annual Review of Anthropology* 22: 425–459.

Pawley, A., and Ross, M. (eds.) (1994). *Austronesian Terminologies: Continuity and Change*. Canberra: Pacific Linguistics C-127.

Pease-Alvarez, L., and Vasquez, O. (1994). Language Socialization in Ethnic Minority Communities. In F. Genesee (ed.), *Educating Second Language Children: The Whole Child, the Whole Curriculum, the Whole Community* (pp. 82–102). Cambridge: Cambridge University Press.

Pegg, C. (1992). Mongolian Conceptualizations of Overtone Singing (*Xoomii*). *British Journal of Ethnomusicology* 1: 31–54.

Peirce, C. S. (1931–58). *Collected Papers*. Cambridge, MA: The Belknap Press of Harvard University Press.

Penn, C. (1992). The Sociolinguistics of South African Sign Language. In R. K. Herbert (ed.), *Language and Society in Africa*. Johannesburg: Witwatersrand University Press.

Penn, C., and Reagan, T. (1994). The Properties of South African Sign Language: Lexical Diversity and Syntactic Unity. *Sign Language Studies* 23(85): 319–327.

Pennycook, A. (1998). *English and the Discourses of Colonialism*. London: Routledge.

Perri, A. (1994a). Review of M. A. K. Halliday, *Lingua parlata e lingua scritta* [*Spoken and Written Language*]. *Il Mondo* 3(1/94): 367–369.

Perri, A. (1994b). La "parola fiorita" e l'immagine-testo. Per una teoria forte della scrittura azteca. *Il Mondo* 3(2/94): 240–258.

Perri, A. (1995). Le medium et le message. Une approche sémiotique et anthropologique à l'étude des systhèmes d'écriture. In G. Blasi and A. Bernardelli (eds.), *Semiotics and the Effect-of-Media-Change Research Programmes. Versus. Quaderni di studi semiotici* (Special Issue) 72: 107–128.

Perri, A. (1996). Verso una semiotica della scrittura azteca. In G. de Finis, J. Galarza, and A. Perri, *La parola fiorita. Per un'antropologia delle scritture mesoamericane*. Rome: Il Mondo 3 Edizioni.

Perri, A. (2001). Writing. In A. Duranti (ed.), *Key Terms in Language and Culture* (pp. 272–274). Malden, MA: Blackwell.

Peterson, R. A. (1997). *Creating Country Music: Fabricating Authenticity*. Chicago: University of Chicago Press.

Petitto, L. A., and Marentette, P. (1991). Babbling in the Manual Mode. *Science 251*: 1483–1496.

Petrucci, A. (1988). Liber ex calamo, liber ex machina; Interview by G. de Finis and A. Perri. *MondOperaio* 6: 58–64.

Petrucci, A. (1989). *Breve storia della scrittura latina*. Rome: Bagatto Libri.

Philips, S. U. (1972). Participant Structures and Communicative Competence: Warm Springs Children in Community and Classroom. In C. B. Cazden, V. T. John, and D. Hymes (eds.), *Functions of Language in the Classroom* (pp. 370–394). New York: Teachers College Press.

Philips, S. U. (1974). Warm Springs "Indian Time": How the Regulation of Participation Affects the Progress of Events. In R. Bauman and J. Sherzer (eds.), *Explorations in the Ethnography of Speaking*. New York: Cambridge University Press.

Philips, S. U. (1983). *The Invisible Culture: Communication in Classroom and Community on the Warm Springs Indian Reservation*. New York: Longman.

Philips, S. U. (1985). Indian Children in Anglo Classrooms. In N. Wolfson and J. Manes (eds.), *Language of Inequality* (pp. 311–323). Berlin: Mouton.

Philips, S. U. (1987). The Social Organization of Questions and Answers in Courtroom Discourse. In L. Kedar (ed.), *Power through Discourse* (pp. 83–112). Norwood, NJ: Ablex.

Philips, S. U. (1988 [1982]). The Language Socialization of Lawyers: Acquiring the "Cant". In G. Spindler (ed.), *Doing the Ethnography of Schooling: Educational Anthropology in Action* (pp. 176–209). Prospect Heights, IL: Waveland Press.

Philips, S. U. (1991). Tongan Speech Levels: Practice and Talk about Practice in the Cultural Construction of Social Hierarchy. In R. Blust (ed.), *Currents in Pacific Linguistics: Papers on Austronesian Languages and Ethnolinguistics in Honor of George Grace* (pp. 269–382). Canberra: Pacific Linguistics C-117.

Philips, S. U. (1998a). *Ideology in the Language of Judges: How Judges Practice Law, Politics and Courtroom Control*. New York: Oxford University Press.

Philips, S. U. (1998b). Language Ideologies in Institutions of Power. In B. B. Schieffelin, K. A. Woolard, and P. V. Kroskrity (eds.), *Language Ideologies: Practice and Theory* (pp. 211–225). New York: Oxford University Press.

Philips, S. U. (2000). Constructing a Tongan Nation State through Language Ideology in the Courtroom. In P. V. Kroskrity (ed.), *Regimes of Language* (pp. 229–257). Santa Fe, NM: School of American Research Press.

Philips, S. U. (2003). The Power of Gender Ideologies in Discourse. In J. Holmes and M. Meyerhoff (eds.), *The Handbook of Language and Gender*. Oxford: Blackwell.

Philips, S. U., Steele, S., and Tanz, C. (eds.) (1987). *Language, Gender and Sex in Comparative Perspective*. Cambridge: Cambridge University Press.

Pinker, S. (1994). *The Language Instinct: How the Mind Creates Language*. New York: William Morrow.

Plann, S. (1997). *A Silent Minority: Deaf Education in Spain, 1550–1835*. Berkeley: University of California Press.

Platt, M. (1982). Social and Semantic Dimensions of Deictic Verbs and Particles in Samoan Child Language. PhD dissertation, University of Southern California.

Poedjosoedarmo, S. (1968). Javanese Speech Levels. *Indonesia* 6: 54–81.

Polanyi, L. (1985). *Telling the American Story: A Structural and Cultural Analysis of Conversational Story-telling*. Norwood, NJ: Ablex.

Polich, L. G. (1998). Social Agency and Deaf Communities: A Nicaraguan Case Study. PhD dissertation, University of Texas at Austin.

Polkinghorne, D. E. (1988). *Narrative Knowing and the Human Sciences*. Albany: SUNY Press.

Pollard, V. (1983). The Social History of Dread Talk. In L. Carrington (ed.), *Studies in Caribbean Language* (pp. 46–62). St. Augustine, Trinidad: Society for Caribbean Linguistics.

Pomerantz, A. M. (1975). Second Assessments: A Study of Some Features of Agreements/Disagreements. PhD dissertation, University of California at Irvine.

Pomerantz, A. M. (1978). Compliment Responses: Notes on the Co-operation of Multiple Constraints. In J. Schenkein (ed.), *Studies in the Organization of Conversational Interaction* (pp. 79–112). New York: Academic Press.

Pomerantz, A. M. (1984). Agreeing and Disagreeing with Assessments: Some Features of Preferred/Dispreferred Turn Shapes. In J. M. Atkinson and J. Heritage (eds.), *Structures of Social Action: Studies in Conversation Analysis* (pp. 57–101). Cambridge: Cambridge University Press.

Pomerantz, A., and Fehr, B. J. (1997). Conversation Analysis: An Approach to the Study of Social Action as Sense Making Practices. In T. van Dijk (ed.), *Discourse as Social Interaction*. London: Sage.

Poole, D. (1989). Everyday Testing as Language Socialization: A Study of the Quiz Review. PhD thesis, University of Southern California.

Porcello, T. (1996). Sonic Artistry: Music, Discourse, and Technology in the Sound Recording Studio. PhD dissertation, Department of Anthropology, University of Texas at Austin.

Porcello, T. (1998). "Tails Out": Social Phenomenology and the Ethnographic Representation of Technology in Music-making. *Ethnomusicology* 42(3): 485–510.

Poulisse, N. (1987). Problems and Solutions in the Classification of Compensatory Strategies. *Second Language Research* 3: 141–153.

Poulisse, N. (1990). *The Use of Compensatory Strategies by Dutch Learners of English*. Dordrecht: Foris.

Poulisse, N., and Schils, E. (1989). The Influence of Task- and Proficiency-related Factors on the Use of Compensatory Strategies: A Quantitative Analysis. *Language Learning* 39: 15–48.

Powell, J. W. (1880). *Introduction to the Study of Indian Languages*, 2nd edn. Washington, DC.

Powers, H. S. (1980). Language Models and Musical Analysis. *Ethnomusicology* 24(1): 1–61.

Powers, W. K. (1980). Oglala Song Terminology. *Selected Reports in Ethnomusicology* 3(2): 23–41.

Poyatos, F. (1983). *New Perspectives on Nonverbal Communication*. Oxford: Pergamon Press.

Pratt, M. L. (1977). *Toward A Speech Act Theory of Literary Discourse*. Bloomington: Indiana University Press.

Pratt, M. L. (1992). *Imperial Eyes: Travel Writing and Transculturation*. London: Routledge.

Preece, A. (1992). Collaborators and Critics: The Nature and Effects of Peer Interaction on Children's Conversational Narratives. *Journal of Narrative and Life History* 2(3): 277–292.

Preminger, A., and Brogan, T. V. F. (eds.) (1993). *The New Princeton Encyclopedia of Poetry and Poetics*. Princeton, NJ: Princeton University Press.

Preston, D. (1997). The South: The Touchstone. In C. Bernstein, T. Nunnally, and R.

Sabino (eds.), *Language Variety in the South Revisited*. Tuscaloosa: University of Alabama Press.

Preston, P. (1994). *Mother Father Deaf: Living between Sound and Silence*. Cambridge, MA: Harvard University Press.

Pride, J. B., and Holmes, J. (eds.) (1972). *Sociolinguistics*. Harmondsworth: Penguin.

Prillwitz, S., and Vollaber, T. (eds.) (1991). Sign Language Research and Application. Proceedings of the International Congress on Sign Language Research and Application, March 23–25, Hamburg, Germany. *International Studies on Sign Language and Communication of the Deaf* 13.

Prociuk, P. (1981). The Deep Structure of Ukrainian Hardship Songs. *Yearbook for Traditional Music* 13: 82–96.

Propp, V. (1968). *The Morphology of the Folktale*, 2nd edn. (trans. T. Scott). Austin: University of Texas Press.

Psathas, G. (1990). The Organization of Talk, Gaze, and Activity in a Medical Interview. In G. Psathas (ed.), *Interaction Competence* (pp. 205–230). Washington, DC: International Institute for Ethnomethodology and Conversation Analysis, and University Press of America.

Psathas, G. (1991). The Structure of Direction-giving in Interaction. In D. Boden and D. H. Zimmerman (eds.), *Talk and Social Structure* (pp. 195–216). Berkeley and Los Angeles: University of California Press.

Pugh-Kitingan, J. (1977). Huli Language and Instrumental Performance. *Ethnomusicology* 21(2): 205–232.

Pujolar, J. (2001). *Gender, Heteroglossia and Power: A Sociolinguistic Study of Youth Culture*. Berlin: Mouton de Gruyter.

Pursglove, M., and Komarova, A. (2003). The Changing World of the Russian Deaf Community. In L. Monaghan, C. Schmaling, K. Nakamura, and G. H. Turner (eds.), *Many Ways to be Deaf*. Washington, DC: Gallaudet University Press.

Putnam, H. (1975). The Meaning of "Meaning". In *Mind, Language and Reality. Philosophical Papers*, vol. 2 (pp. 215–271). Cambridge: Cambridge University Press.

Putnam, R. (1993). The Prosperous Community: Social Capital and Public Life. *The American Prospect* 13: 35–42.

Putnam, R. (1995). Bowling Alone: America's Declining Social Capital. *Journal of Democracy* 6: 65–78.

Putnam, R. (1996). The Strange Disappearance of Civic America. *The American Prospect* 24: 34 ff.

Pye, C. (1986). Quiche' Mayan Speech to Children. *Journal of Child Language* 13: 85–100.

Pye, C. (1992). The Acquisition of K'iche' Mayan. In D. I. Slobin (ed.), *The Crosslinguistic Study of Language Acquisition*, vol. 3 (pp. 221–308). Hillsdale, NJ: Lawrence Erlbaum.

Quiñoes Keber, E. (1995). *Codex Telleriano-Remensis*. Austin: University of Texas Press.

Quintillian, M. F. (1924). *Institutio Oratoria*. London: Heinemann.

Qureshi, R. (1987). Musical Sound and Contextual Input: A Performance Model for Musical Analysis. *Ethnomusicology* 31(1): 56–86.

Rabin-Jamin, J. (1998). Polyadic Language Socialization Strategy: The Case of Toddlers in Senegal. *Discourse Processes* 26(1): 43–65.

Radutsky, E. (1993). The Education of Deaf People in Italy and the Use of Italian Sign Language. In J. V. Van Cleve (ed.), *Deaf History Unveiled: Interpretations from the New Scholarship* (pp. 237–251). Washington, DC: Gallaudet University Press.

Raffman, D. (1993). *Language, Music and Mind*. Cambridge, MA: MIT Press.

Ramaswamy, S. (1998). *Passions of the Tongue: Language Devotion in Tamil India, 1891–1970*. Berkeley: University of California Press.

Rampton, B. (1995a). *Crossing: Language and Ethnicity among Adolescents*. London: Longman.

Rampton, B. (1995b). Language Crossing and the Problematisation of Ethnicity and Socialisation. *Pragmatics* 5(4): 485–515.

Rampton, B. (1998a). Language Crossing and the Redefinition of Reality. In J. C. P. Auer (ed.), *Code-switching in Conversation: Language, Interaction and Identity* (pp. 290–317). London: Routledge.

Rampton, B. (1998b). Speech Community. In J. O. Verschueren, J. Blommaert, and C. Bulcaen (eds.), *Handbook of Pragmatics*. Amsterdam: John Benjamins.

Rampton, B. (2002). Ritual and Foreign Language Practices at School. *Language in Society* 31: 491–525.

Ramsey, C. L. (1989). Language Planning in Deaf Education. In C. Lucas (ed.), *The Sociolinguistics of the Deaf Community* (pp. 123–146). San Diego, CA: Academic Press.

Raymond, G. (2000). The Structure of Responding: Type-conforming and Nonconforming Responses to yes/no Type Interrogatives. PhD dissertation, University of California, Los Angeles.

Redder, A., and Rehbein, J. (1987). Zum Begriff der Kultur. *Osnabrücker Beiträge zur Sprachtheorie* 38: 7–21.

Reddy, M. (1979). The Conduit Metaphor: A Case of Frame Conflict in Our Language about Language. In A. Ortony (ed.), *Metaphor and Thought* (pp. 284–324). Cambridge: Cambridge University Press.

Rehbein, J. (1972). Entschuldigungen und Rechtfertigungen. Zur Sequenzierung von kommunikativen Handlungen. In D. Wunderlich (ed.), *Linguistische Pragmatik* (pp. 288–317). Frankfurt/Main: Athenäum.

Rehbein, J. (1986). Interkulturelle Mißverständnisse in der Arzt–Patienten-Kommunikation. *Curare* 9: 279–328.

Reichenberg, A., Weiser, M., Rabinowitz, J., Caspi, A., Schmeidler, J., Mark, M., Davidson, M., and Kaplan, Z. (2002). A Population-based Cohort Study of Premorbid Intellectual, Language, and Behavioral Functioning in Patients with Schizophrenia, Schizoaffective Disorder, and Nonpsychotic Bipolar Disorder. *American Journal of Psychiatry* 159(12): 2027–2035.

Reid, T. B. W. (1956). Linguistics, Structuralism and Philology. *Archivum Linguisticum* 8(1): 28–37.

Reilly, C. (1995). A Deaf Way of Education: Interaction among Children in a Thai Boarding School. PhD dissertation, University of Maryland.

Reynolds, J. F. (2002). Maya Children's Practices of the Imagination: (Dis)Playing Childhood and Politics in Guatemala. PhD dissertation, University of California, Los Angeles.

Rhodes, R. (1994). Aural Images. In L. Hinton, J. Nichols, and J. J. Ohala (eds.), *Sound Symbolism* (pp. 276–292). New York: Cambridge University Press.

Ribeiro, B. T. (1996). Conflict Talk in a Psychiatric Discharge Interview: Struggling between Personal and Official Footings. In C. R. Caldas-Coulthard and M. Coulthard (eds.), *Texts and Practices: Readings in Critical Discourse Analysis* (pp. 179–193). London: Routledge.

Richards, P. (1972). A Quantitative Analysis of the Relationship between Speech Tone and Melody in a Hausa Song. *African Language Studies* 13: 137–161.

Richman, B. (1980). Did Human Speech Originate in Coordinated Vocal Music? *Semiotica* 32(3/4): 233–244.

Rickford, J. R. (1985). Ethnicity as a Sociolinguistic Boundary. *American Speech* 60: 99–125.

Rickford, J. R. (1987). *Dimensions of a Creole Continuum: History, Texts, and Linguistic Analysis of Guyanese Creole*. Stanford: Stanford University Press.

Rickford, J. R. (1997). Unequal Partnership: Sociolinguistics and the African American Speech Community. *Language in Society* 26(2): 161–198.

Rickford, J. R. (1999). *African American Vernacular English*. Malden, MA: Blackwell.

Ricoeur, P. (1981a). *Hermeneutics and the Human Sciences*. Cambridge: Cambridge University Press.

Ricoeur, P. (1981b). Narrative Time. In W. J. T. Mitchell (ed.), *On Narrative*. Chicago: University of Chicago Press.

Ricoeur, P. (1984). *Time and Narrative*, vol. 1. Chicago: University of Chicago Press.

Ricoeur, P. (1985). *Time and Narrative*, vol. 2. Chicago: University of Chicago Press.

Ricoeur, P. (1988). *Time and Narrative*, vol. 3. Chicago: University of Chicago Press.

Riggenbach, H. (1989). Nonnative Fluency in Dialogue versus Monologue Speech: A Microanalytic Approach. Dissertation, University of California, Los Angeles.

Riggenbach, H. (1991). Toward an Understanding of Fluency: A Microanalysis of Nonnative Speaker Conversations. *Discourse Processes* 14: 423–441.

Riley, K. C. (2001a). Buying a Slice of Anglo-American Pie: A Portrait of Language Shift in a Franco-American Family (with Robert S. Williams). In Roseann Dueñas González (ed.), *Language Ideologie*, vol. 2. Urbana, IL: NCTE.

Riley, K. C. (2001b). The Emergence of Dialogic Identities: Transforming Heteroglossia in the Marquesas, F.P. PhD dissertation, City University of New York.

Robbins, J. (1998). Between Reproduction and Transformation: Ethnography and Modernity in Melanesia. *Anthropological Quarterly* 71: 89–98.

Robbins, J. (2001a). God Is Nothing but Talk: Modernity, Language, and Prayer in a Papua New Guinea Society. *American Anthropologist* 103: 901–912.

Robbins, J. (2001b). Ritual Communication and Linguistic Ideology: A Reading and Partial Reformulation of Rappaport's Theory of Ritual. *Current Anthropology* 42: 591–614.

Robbins, M. (2002). The Language of Schizophrenia and the World of Delusion. *International Journal of Psychoanalysis* 83: 383–405.

Robinson, J. (1997) *Music and Meaning*. Ithaca: Cornell University Press.

Robson, S. O. (1994). Speaking to God in Javanese. *l'Homme* 132: 133–142.

Rochester, S. R., and Martin, J. R. (1979). *Crazy Talk: A Study of the Discourse of Schizophrenic Speakers*. New York: Plenum.

Rodriguez-Ferrera, S., McCarthy, R. A., and McKenna, P. J. (2001). Language in Schizophrenia and Its Relationship to Formal Thought Disorder. *Psychological Medicine* 31: 197–205.

Rogoff, B. (1990). *Apprenticeship in Thinking: Cognitive Development in Social Context*. New York: Oxford University Press.

Rogoff, B. (1993). Children's Guided Participation and Participatory Appropriation in Sociocultural Activity. In R. Wozniak and K. Fischer (eds.), *Development in Context: Acting and Thinking in Specific Environments* (pp. 121–153). Hillsdale, NJ: Lawrence Erlbaum.

Rogoff, B. (1995). Observing Sociocultural Activity on Three Planes: Participatory Appropriation and Apprenticeship. In J. V. Wertsch, P. Del Rio, and A. Alvarez (eds.), *Sociocultural Studies of Mind* (pp. 139–163). Cambridge: Cambridge University Press.

Rogoff, B., and Lave, J. (eds.) (1984). *Everyday Cognition: Its Development in Social Context*. Cambridge, MA: Harvard University Press.

Rogoff, B., Mistry, J., et al. (1993). *Guided Participation in Cultural Activity by Toddlers and Caregivers*. Chicago: University of Chicago Press.

Romaine, S. (1982). *Sociolinguistic Variation in Speech Communities*. New York: Edward Arnold.

Romaine, S. (1995). *Bilingualism*. Oxford: Blackwell.

Romaine, S. (2000). *Language in Society: An Introduction to Sociolinguistics* (2nd edn.). Oxford: Oxford University Press.

Romanucci-Ross, L. (1983). On Madness, Deviance and Culture. In L. Romanucci-Ross (ed.), *The Anthropology of Medicine* (pp. 267–283). New York: Praeger.

Rommetveit, R. (1998). Intersubjective Attunement and Linguistically Mediated Meaning in Discourse. In S. Bråten (ed.), *Intersubjective Communication and Emotion in Early*

Ontogeny (pp. 354–371). Cambridge: Cambridge University Press.

Rosaldo, M. (1973). I Have Nothing to Hide: The Language of Ilongot Oratory. *Language in Society* 2: 193–223.

Rosaldo, M. Z. (1982). The Things We Do With Words: Ilongot Speech Acts and Speech Act Theory in Philosophy. *Language in Society* 11: 203–237.

Rosaldo, R. (1988). Ideology, Place, and People without Culture. *Cultural Anthropology* 3: 77–87.

Rosen, L. (ed.) (1995). *Other Intentions: Cultural Context and the Attribution of Inner States*. Santa Fe, NM: School of American Research Press.

Rosenberg, B. A. (1988). *Can These Bones Live? The Art of the American Folk Preacher*. Urbana: University of Illinois Press.

Rossi-Landi, F. (1970). Linguistic Alienation Problems. In *Linguaggi nella società e nella tecnica* (pp. 513–543). Milan: Edizioni di Comunità.

Rossi-Landi, F. (1973). *Il linguaggio come lavoro e come mercato*. Milan: Bompiani.

Rossi-Landi, F. (1983). *Language as Work and Trade: A Semiotic Homology for Linguistics and Economics*. South Hadley, MA: Bergin and Garvey.

Rossi-Landi, F. (1985). *Metodica Filosofica e Scienza dei Segni: Nuovi Saggi sul Linguaggio e l'Ideologia*. Milan: Bompiani.

Rost, M., and Ross, S. (1991). Learner Use of Strategies in Interaction: Typology and Teachability. *Language Learning* 41(2): 235–273.

Rost-Roth, M. (1994). Verständigungsprobleme in der interkulturellen Kommunikation. Ein Forschungsüberblick zu Analysen und Diagnosen in empirischen Untersuchungen. *Zeitschrift für Literaturwissenschaft und Linguistik* 93: 9–45.

Roth, W.-M., and Lawless, D. V. (2002). When Up Is Down and Down Is Up: Body Orientation, Proximity, and Gestures as Resources. *Language in Society* 31: 1–28.

Rouget, G. (1966). African Traditional Non-prose Forms: Reciting, Declaiming, Singing, and Strophic Structures. In *Proceedings of a Conference on African Languages and Literatures, April 28–30 1966* (pp. 45–58). Evanston, IL: Northwestern University Press.

Rudge, T., and Morse, K. (2001). Re-awakenings? A Discourse Analysis of the Recovery from Schizophrenia after Medication Change. *Australia New Zealand Journal of Mental Health Nursing* 10(2): 66–76.

Rumsey, A. (1990). Wording, Meaning, and Linguistic Ideology. *American Anthropologist* 92: 346–361.

Rumsey, A. (2001). Orality. In A. Duranti (ed.), *Key Terms in Language and Culture* (pp. 165–167). Malden, MA: Blackwell.

Ruusuvuori, J. (2001). Looking Means Listening: Coordinating Displays of Engagement in Doctor–Patient Interaction. *Social Science and Medicine* 52: 1093–1108.

Ruwet, N. (1967). Linguistics and Musicology. *International Social Sciences Journal* 19: 79–87.

Rydstrom, H. (2001). Like a White Piece of Paper: Embodiment and the Moral Upbringing of Vietnamese Children. *Ethnos* 66(3): 394–413.

Rymes, B. (1997). Second Language Socialization: A New Approach to Second Language Acquisition Research. *Journal of Intensive English Studies* 11: 143–155.

Rymes, B. (2001). *Conversational Borderlands: Language and Identity in an Urban Alternative High School*. New York: Teachers College.

Sacks, H. (1963). Sociological Description. *Berkeley Journal of Sociology* 8: 1–16.

Sacks, H. (1972a). An Initial Investigation of the Usability of Conversational Data for Doing Sociology. In D. N. Sudnow (ed.), *Studies in Social Interaction*. New York: Free Press.

Sacks, H. (1972b). On the Analyzability of Stories by Children. In J. J. Gumperz and D. Hymes (eds.), *Directions in Sociolinguistics: The Ethnography of Communication* (pp. 325–345). New York: Holt, Rinehart and Winston.

Sacks, H. (1974). An Analysis of the Course of a Joke's Telling in Conversation. In R. Bauman and J. Sherzer (eds.), *Explorations in the Ethnography of Speaking* (pp. 337–353). Cambridge: Cambridge University Press.

Sacks, H. (1978). Some Technical Considerations of a Dirty Joke. In J. Schenkein (ed.), *Studies in the Organization of Conversational Interaction* (pp. 249–269). New York: Academic Press.

Sacks, H. (1987 [1973]). On the Preferences for Agreement and Contiguity in Sequences in Conversation. In G. Button and J. R. Lee (eds.), *Talk and Social Organization* (pp. 54–69). Clevedon: Multilingual Matters.

Sacks, H. (1995 [1992]). *Lectures on Conversation* vols. 1 and 2 (ed. G. Jefferson, with an

Introduction by E. A. Schegloff). Oxford: Blackwell.

Sacks, H., and Schegloff, E. A. (1979). Two Preferences in the Organization of Reference to Persons in Conversation and Their Interaction. In G. Psathas (ed.), *Everyday Language: Studies in Ethnomethodology* (pp. 15–21). New York: Irvington.

Sacks, H., Schegloff, E. A., and Jefferson, G. (1974). A Simplest Systematics for the Organization of Turn-Taking for Conversation. *Language* 50: 696–735.

Sacks, O. (1989). *Seeing Voices*. Berkeley: University of California Press.

Sahlins, M. (1985). *Islands of History*. Chicago: University of Chicago Press.

Said, E. (1978). *Orientalism*. New York: Pantheon.

Salisbury, R. (1962). Notes on Bilingualism and Language Change in New Guinea. *Anthropological Linguistics* 4(7): 1–13.

Salmon, V. (1986). Effort and Achievement in Seventeenth-century British Linguistics. In T. Bynon and F. R. Palmer (eds.), *Studies in the History of Western Linguistics* (pp. 69–95). Cambridge: Cambridge University Press.

Salvaggio, R. (1999). *The Sounds of Feminist Theory*. Albany: SUNY Press.

Salzmann, Z. (1993). *Language, Culture, and Society: An Introduction to Linguistic Anthropology*. Boulder, CO: Westview Press.

Sampson, G. (1985). *Writing Systems. A Linguistic Introduction*. London: Hutchinson.

Samuels, D. W. (1998). A Sense of the Past: Music, Place and History in San Carlos and Bylas. PhD dissertation, Department of Anthropology, University of Texas at Austin.

Sanches, M., and Blount, B. G. (1975). *Sociocultural Dimensions of Language Use*. New York: Academic Press.

Sánchez, A. R. (1997). Reflexiones en torno a la agencia y la afección en Español. *Anuario de Estudios Filológicos* (20: 365–387).

Sankoff, G. (1980a). Multilingualism in Papua New Guinea. In G. Sankoff, *The Social Life of Language* (pp. 95–132). Philadelphia: University of Pennsylvania Press.

Sankoff, G. (1980b). *The Social Life of Language*. Philadelphia: University of Pennsylvania Press.

Sankoff, G. (2002). Linguistic Outcomes of Language Contact. In J. K. Chambers, P. Trudgill, and N. Schilling-Estes (eds.), *The Handbook of Language Variation and Change* (pp. 638–668). Oxford: Blackwell.

Sanua, V. D. (1983). Infantile Autism and Childhood Schizophrenia: Review of the Issues from the Sociocultural Point of View. *Social Science & Medicine* 17(21): 1633–1651.

Sanua, V. D. (1992). Mental Illness and Other Forms of Psychiatric Deviance among Contemporary Jewry. *Transcultural Psychiatric Research Review* 29(3): 197–233.

Sapir, D. (1985). Introducing Edward Sapir. *Language in Society* 14(3): 289–297.

Sapir, E. (1910). Song Recitative in Paiute Mythology. *Journal of American Folklore* 23: 455–472.

Sapir, E. (1918). Representative Music. *Musical Quarterly* 4: 161–167.

Sapir, E. (1921a). *Language*. New York: Harcourt, Brace & World.

Sapir, E. (1921b). The Musical Foundations of Verse. *Journal of English and Germanic Philology* 20: 213–228.

Sapir, E. (1925). The Sound Patterns in Language. *Language* 1: 37–51.

Sapir, E. (1927). The Unconscious Patterning of Behavior in Society. In E. S. Dummer (ed.), *The Unconscious: A Symposium* (pp. 114–142). New York: Knopf [repr. in Sapir 1949d].

Sapir, E. (1929). Male and Female Forms of Speech in Yana. In S. W. J. Teeuwen (ed.), *Donum Natalicium Schrijnen* (pp. 79–85). Nijmegen and Utrecht.

Sapir, E. (1933). Language. *Encyclopaedia of the Social Sciences* (pp. 155–169). New York: Macmillan [repr. in Sapir 1949c].

Sapir, E. (1949a). Why Cultural Anthropology Needs the Psychiatrist. In D. G. Mandelbaum (ed.), *Selected Writings of Edward Sapir in Language, Culture, and Personality* (pp. 569–577). Berkeley: University of California Press.

Sapir, E. (1949b). Communication. In D. G. Mandelbaum (ed.), *Selected Writings of Edward Sapir in Language, Culture and Personality* (pp. 104–110). Berkeley: University of California Press.

Sapir, E. (1949c). Language. In D. G. Mandelbaum (ed.), *Selected Writings of Edward Sapir in Language, Culture and Personality* (pp. 7–32). Berkeley: University of California Press.

Sapir, E. (1949d). The Unconscious Patterning of Behavior in Society. In D. G. Mandelbaum (ed.), *Selected Writings of Edward Sapir in Language, Culture and Society* (pp. 544–559). Berkeley: University of California Press.

Sapir, E. (1964). Conceptual Categories in Primitive Languages. In D. Hymes (ed.),

Language in Culture and Society (p. 128). New York: Harper & Row.

Sapir, E. (1990). Male and Female Forms of Speech in Yana. In *The Collected Works of Edward Sapir 5: American Indian Languages* (pp. 335–341). Berlin: Mouton de Gruyter.

Sapir, E. (1994). *The Psychology of Culture: A Course of Lectures* (reconstructed and edited by J. T. Irvine). Berlin: Mouton de Gruyter.

Sapir, J. D. (1969). Diola-Fogny Funeral Songs and the Native Critic. *African Language Review* 8: 176–191.

Sapir, J. D., and Crocker, J. C. (eds.) (1977). *The Social Uses of Metaphor*. Philadelphia: University of Pennsylvania Press.

Sass, L. A. (1995). *The Paradoxes of Delusion: Wittgenstein, Schreber, and the Schizophrenic Mind*. Ithaca: Cornell University Press.

Sass, L. A., and Schuldberg, D. (eds.) (2001). Special Issue: Creativity and the Schizophrenia Spectrum. *Creativity Research Journal* 13(1).

Sass, L. A., et al. (1984). Parental Communication Deviance and Forms of Thinking in Male Schizophrenic Offspring. *Speech and Psychopathology* 172(9): 513–520.

Savigliano, M. (1995). *Tango and the Political Economy of Passion*. Boulder, CO: Westview Press.

Schafer, R. (1992). *Retelling a Life: Narration and Dialogue in Psychoanalysis*. New York: Basic Books.

Schaff, A. (1973). *Language and Cognition* (trans. Olgierd Wojtasiewicz). New York: McGraw-Hill.

Schecter, S., and Bayley, R. (1997). Language Socialization Practices and Cultural Identity: Case Studies of Mexican-descent Families in California and Texas. *TESOL Quarterly* 31(3): 513–541.

Scheflen, A. E. (1964). The Significance of Posture in Communication Systems. *Psychiatry* 27(4): 316–331.

Scheflen, A. E. (1973). *Communicational Structure: Analysis of a Psychotherapy Transaction*. Bloomington: Indiana University Press.

Scheflen, A. E. (1974). *How Behavior Means*. Garden City, NY: Anchor Press.

Scheflen, A. E. (1981). *Levels of Schizophrenia*. New York: Brunner/Mazel.

Schegloff, E. A. (1968). Sequencing in Conversational Openings. *American Anthropologist* 70: 1075–1095.

Schegloff, E. A. (1972). Sequencing in Conversational Openings. In J. J. Gumperz and D. Hymes (eds.), *Directions in Sociolinguistics: The Ethnography of Communication* (pp. 346–380). New York: Holt, Rinehart and Winston.

Schegloff, E. A. (1979a). Identification and Recognition in Telephone Conversation Openings. In G. Psathas (ed.), *Everyday Language: Studies in Ethnomethodology* (pp. 23–78). New York: Irvington.

Schegloff, E. A. (1979b). The Relevance of Repair for Syntax-for-Conversation. In T. Givón (ed.), *Syntax and Semantics 12: Discourse and Syntax* (pp. 261–288). New York: Academic Press.

Schegloff, E. A. (1982). Discourse as an Interactional Achievement: Some Uses of "Uh huh" and Other Things that Come between Sentences. In D. Tannen (ed.), *Georgetown University Round Table on Languages and Linguistics: Analyzing Discourse, Text and Talk* (pp. 71–93). Washington, DC: Georgetown University Press.

Schegloff, E. A. (1984a). On Some Gestures' Relation to Talk. In J. M. Atkinson and J. Heritage (eds.), *Structures of Social Action: Studies in Conversation Analysis* (pp. 266–296). Cambridge: Cambridge University Press.

Schegloff, E. A. (1984b). On Some Questions and Ambiguities in Conversation. In J. M. Atkinson and J. Heritage (eds.), *Structures of Social Action: Studies in Conversation Analysis* (pp. 28–52). Cambridge: Cambridge University Press.

Schegloff, E. A. (1986). The Routine as Achievement. *Human Studies* 9: 111–151.

Schegloff, E. A. (1987a). Some Sources of Misunderstanding in Talk-in-Interaction. *Linguistics* 25: 201–218.

Schegloff, E. A. (1987b). Recycled Turn Beginnings: A Precise Repair Mechanism in Conversation's Turn-taking Organisation. In G. Button and J. R. Lee (eds.), *Talk and Social Organization* (pp. 70–85). Clevedon: Multilingual Matters.

Schegloff, E. A. (1987c). Between Micro and Macro: Contexts and Other Connections. In J. C. Alexander, B. Giesen, R. Münch, and N. J. Smelser (eds.), *The Micro–Macro Link* (pp. 207–233). Berkeley: University of California Press.

Schegloff, E. A. (1988a). Goffman and the Analysis of Conversation. In P. Drew and A. Wootton (eds.), *Erving Goffman: Exploring the Interaction Order* (pp. 89–135). Cambridge: Polity Press.

Schegloff, E. A. (1988b). Presequences and Indirection: Applying Speech Act Theory to Ordinary Conversation. *Journal of Pragmatics* 12: 55–62.

Schegloff, E. A. (1989). Reflections on Language, Development, and the Interactional Character of Talk-in-Interaction. In M. Bornstein and J. S. Bruner (eds.), *Interaction in Human Development* (pp. 139–153). Hillsdale, NJ: Lawrence Erlbaum.

Schegloff, E. A. (1990). On the Organization of Sequences as a Source of "Coherence" in Talk-in-Interaction. In B. Dorval (ed.), *Conversational Organization and Its Development* (pp. 51–77). Norwood, NJ: Ablex.

Schegloff, E. A. (1991). Conversation Analysis and Socially Shared Cognition. In L. Resnick, J. Levine, and S. Teasley (eds.), *Perspectives on Socially Shared Cognition* (pp. 150–171). Washington, DC: American Psychological Association.

Schegloff, E. A. (1992a). Introduction. In H. Sacks (ed.), *Lectures on Conversation*, vol. 1, pp. ix–lxii; vol. 2, pp. ix–lii. Oxford: Blackwell.

Schegloff, E. A. (1992b). Repair after Next Turn: The Last Structurally Provided Defense of Intersubjectivity in Conversation. *American Journal of Sociology* 97(5): 1295–1345.

Schegloff, E. A. (1992c). To Searle on Conversation: A Note in Return. In J. R. Searle, *(On) Searle on Conversation* (pp. 113–128). Amsterdam and Philadelphia: John Benjamins.

Schegloff, E. A. (1993). Reflections on Quantification in the Study of Conversation. *Research on Language and Social Interaction* 26(1): 99–128.

Schegloff, E. A. (1994). Parties Talking Together: Two Ways in which Numbers Are Significant for Talk-in-Interaction. In P. ten Have and G. Psathas (eds.), *Situated Order: Studies in the Social Organization of Talk and Embodied Interaction*. Washington, DC: University Press of America.

Schegloff, E. A. (1996). Turn Organization: One Intersection of Grammar and Interaction. In E. Ochs, E. A. Schegloff, and S. A. Thompson (eds.), *Interaction and Grammar* (pp. 52–133). Cambridge: Cambridge University Press.

Schegloff, E. A. (1997). Whose Text? Whose Context? *Discourse and Society* 8(2): 165–187.

Schegloff, E. A. (1998). Body Torque. *Social Research* 65: 535–586.

Schegloff, E. A. (2000). Overlapping Talk and the Organization of Turn-taking for Conversation. *Language in Society* 29: 1–63.

Schegloff, E. A., Jefferson, G., and Sacks, H. (1977). The Preference for Self-correction in the Organization of Repair in Conversation. *Language* 53: 361–382.

Schegloff, E. A., Ochs, E., and Thompson, S. A. (1996). Introduction. In E. Ochs, E. A. Schegloff, and S. A. Thompson (eds.), *Interaction and Grammar* (pp. 1–51). Cambridge: Cambridge University Press.

Schegloff, E. A., and Sacks, H. (1973). Opening up Closings. *Semiotica* 8: 289–327.

Schein, J. (1992). *At Home among Strangers.* Washington, DC: Gallaudet University Press.

Schein, J., and Marcus, D. (1974). *The Deaf Population of the United States.* Silver Spring, MD: National Association of the Deaf.

Scheper-Hughes, N. (1979). *Saints, Scholars, and Schizophrenics: Mental Illness in Rural Ireland.* Berkeley: University of California Press.

Scheper-Hughes, N. (1997). "Mental" in "Southie": Individual, Family, and Community Responses to Psychosis in South Boston. In R. J. Castillo (ed.), *Meanings of Madness* (pp. 248–260). Pacific Grove, CA: Brooks/Cole Publishers.

Scheper-Hughes, N. (2000). Ire in Ireland. *Ethnography* 1(1): 117ff.

Schermer, G. (1985). Analysis of Natural Discourse of Deaf Adults in the Netherlands: Observations on Dutch Sign Language. In W. Stokoe and V. Volterra (eds.), *Proceedings of the Third International Symposium on Sign Language Research* (pp. 281–288). Silver Spring, MD: Linstok Press.

Schieffelin, B. B. (1979a). Getting It Together: An Ethnographic Approach to the Study of the Development of Communicative Competence. In E. Ochs and B. B. Schieffelin (eds.), *Developmental Pragmatics* (pp. 73–110). New York: Academic Press.

Schieffelin, B. B. (1979b). How Kaluli Children Learn What to Say, What to Do, and How to Feel: An Ethnographic Study of the Development of Communicative Competence. PhD dissertation, Columbia University.

Schieffelin, B. B. (1985). The Acquisition of Kaluli. In D. Slobin (ed.), *The Crosslinguistic Study of Language Acquisition*, vol. 1 (pp. 525–593). Hillsdale, NJ: Lawrence Erlbaum.

Schieffelin, B. B. (1986). Teasing and Shaming in Kaluli Children's Interactions. In B. B. Schieffelin and E. Ochs (eds.), *Language*

Socialization across Cultures (pp. 165–181). New York: Cambridge University Press.

Schieffelin, B. B. (1990). *The Give and Take of Everyday Life: Language Socialization of Kaluli Children.* Cambridge: Cambridge University Press.

Schieffelin, B. B. (1994). Code-switching and Language Socialization: Some Probable Relationships. In J. F. Duchan et al. (eds.), *Pragmatics: From Theory to Practice* (pp. 20–42). Englewood Cliffs, NJ: Prentice-Hall.

Schieffelin, B. B. (1996). Creating Evidence: Making Sense of Written Words in Bosavi. In E. Ochs, E. A. Schegloff, and S. A. Thompson (eds.), *Interaction and Grammar* (pp. 435–460). New York: Cambridge University Press.

Schieffelin, B. B. (2000). Introducing Kaluli Literacy: A Chronology of Influences. In P. V. Kroskrity (ed.), *Regimes of Language: Ideologies, Polities, and Identities* (pp. 293–327). Santa Fe, NM: School of American Research Press.

Schieffelin, B. B. (2002). Marking Time: The Dichotomizing Discourse of Multiple Temporalities. *Current Anthropology* 43: S5–17.

Schieffelin, B. B. (2003). Language and Place in Children's Worlds. In I. Mey, G. Pizer, H.-Y. Su, and S. Szmania (eds.), Proceedings of the Tenth Annual Symposium about Language and Society, Austin. *Texas Linguistic Forum*, vol. 45. Austin: University of Texas, Department of Linguistics.

Schieffelin, B. B., and Doucet, R. C. (1998). The "real" Haitian Creole: Ideology, Metalinguistics, and Orthographic Choice. In B. B. Schieffelin, K. A. Woolard, and P. V. Kroskrity (eds.), *Language Ideologies: Practice and Theory* (pp. 285–316). New York: Oxford University Press.

Schieffelin, B. B., and Ochs, E. (1986a). Language Socialization. In B. J. Siegel, A. R. Beals, and S. A. Tyler (eds.), *Annual Review of Anthropology* (pp. 163–246). Palo Alto, CA: Annual Reviews.

Schieffelin, B. B., and Ochs, E. (eds.) (1986b). *Language Socialization across Cultures.* New York: Cambridge University Press.

Schieffelin, B. B., and Ochs, E. (1996). The Microgenesis of Competence: Methodology in Language Socialization. In D. I. Slobin, J. Gerhardt, A. Kyratzis, and J. Guo (eds.), *Social Interaction, Social Context, and Language* (pp. 251–264). Mahwah, NJ: Lawrence Erlbaum.

Schieffelin, B. B., Woolard, K. A., and Kroskrity, P. V. (eds.) (1998). *Language Ideologies: Practice and Theory.* New York: Oxford University Press.

Schieffelin, E. L. (1976). *The Sorrow of the Lonely and the Burning of the Dancers.* New York: St. Martin's Press.

Schieffelin, E. L. (1985). Performance and the Cultural Construction of Reality. *American Ethnologist* 12: 707–724.

Schiffman, H. (1996). *Linguistic Culture and Language Policy.* London: Routledge.

Schiffman, H. (1998). Standardization or Restandardization: The Case for "Standard" Spoken Tamil. *Language in Society* 27: 359–385.

Schiffrin, D. (1987). *Discourse Markers.* Cambridge: Cambridge University Press.

Schiffrin, D. (1990). The Management of a Cooperative Self during Argument: The Role of Opinions and Stories. In A. Grimshaw (ed.), *Conflict Talk* (pp. 241–259). New York: Cambridge University Press.

Schiffrin, D. (1994). *Approaches to Discourse.* Oxford: Blackwell.

Schlegel, J. (1998). Finding Words, Finding Meanings: Collaborative Learning and Distributed Cognition. In S. M. Hoyle and C. T. Adger (eds.), *Kids Talk: Strategic Language Use in Later Childhood* (pp. 187–204). New York: Oxford University Press.

Schlesinger, I. M. (1989). Instruments as Agents: On the Nature of Semantic Relations. *Journal of Linguistics* 25: 189–210.

Schmaling, C. (2003). A for Apple: The Impact of Western Education and ASL on the Deaf Community in Kano State, Northern Nigeria. In L. Monaghan, C. Schmaling, K. Nakamura, and G. H. Turner (eds.), *Many Ways to be Deaf.* Washington, DC: Gallaudet University Press.

Schmidt, A. (1985). *Young People's Dyirbal: An Example of Language Death from Australia.* Cambridge: Cambridge University Press.

Schmidt, P. (1981). [Psychosis and Grammatical Reality. Preliminary to an Axiomatic System] [French]. *Annales Medico-Psychologiques* 139(5): 497–511.

Schreiber, S. (1995). Migration, Traumatic Bereavement and Transcultural Aspects of Psychological Healing: Loss and Grief of a Refugee Woman from Begameder County in Ethiopia. *British Journal of Medical Psychology* 68(Pt 2): 135–142.

Schuh, R. (1989). Toward a Metrical Analysis of Hausa Verse Prosody: Mutadaarik. In I. Haïk and L. Tuller (eds.), *Current Approaches to African Linguistics*, vol. 6 (pp. 161–175). Dordrecht: Foris.

Schuh, R. (1999). Metrics of Arabic and Hausa Poetry. In P. F. A. Kotey (ed.), *New Dimensions in African Linguistics and Languages. Trends in African Linguistics*, vol. 3 (pp. 121–130). Trenton and Asmara: Africa World Press.

Schutz, A. (1962). Commonsense and Scientific Interpretations of Human Action. In *Collected Papers*, vol. 1 (pp. 3–21). The Hague: Martinus Nijhoff.

Schutz, A. (1967 [1932]). *The Phenomenology of the Social World* (trans. G. Walsh and F. Lehnert). Evanston, IL: Northwestern University Press.

Schwartz, S. (1982). Is There a Schizophrenic Language? *Behavioral and Brain Sciences* 5: 579–588.

Scollon, R., and Scollon, S. W. (1981). *Narrative, Literacy, and Face in Interethnic Communication*. Norwood, NJ: Ablex.

Scollon, R., and Scollon, S. W. (1995). *Intercultural Communication: A Discourse Approach*. Cambridge, MA: Blackwell.

Scribner, S. (1984). Studying Working Intelligence. In B. Rogoff and J. Lave (eds.), *Everyday Cognition: Its Development in Social Context* (pp. 9–40). Cambridge, MA: Harvard University Press.

Scribner, S., and Cole, M. (1981). *The Psychology of Literacy*. Cambridge, MA: Harvard University Press.

Searle, J. (1965). What Is a Speech Act? In M. Black (ed.), *Philosophy in America* (pp. 221–239). London: George Allen & Unwin.

Searle, J. (1969). *Speech Acts: An Essay in the Philosophy of Language*. Cambridge: Cambridge University Press.

Searle, J. R. (1979). *Expression and Meaning: Studies in the Theory of Speech Acts*. Cambridge: Cambridge University Press.

Searle, J. R. (1983). *Intentionality: An Essay in the Philosophy of Mind*. Cambridge: Cambridge University Press.

Searle, J. R. (1990). Collective Intentionality and Action. In P. R. Cohen, J. Morgen, and M. E. Rollsik (eds.), *Intention in Communication* (pp. 401–415). Cambridge, MA: MIT Press.

Searle, J. R. (1992). Conversation. In H. Parret and J. Verschueren (eds.), *(On) Searle on Conversation* (pp. 7–29). Philadelphia: John Benjamins.

Searle, J. R. (1998). *Mind, Language, and Society: Philosophy in the Real World*. New York: Basic Books.

Searle, J. R., and Vanderveken, D. (1985). *Foundations of Illocutionary Logic*. Cambridge: Cambridge University Press.

Sebba, M. (1997). *Contact Languages: Pidgins and Creoles*. New York: St. Martin's Press.

Sebba, M., and Wootton, T. (1998). We, They and Identity: Sequential vs. Identity-related Explanation in Codeswitching. In P. Auer (ed.), *Code-switching in Conversation* (pp. 262–286). London: Routledge.

Sebeok, T. A. (ed.) (1960). *Style in Language*. Cambridge, MA: MIT Press.

Seedhouse, P. (1998). CA and the Analysis of Foreign Language Interaction: A Reply to Wagner. *Journal of Pragmatics* 30: 85–102.

Seeger, A. (1987). *Why Suyá Sing: A Musical Anthropology of an Amazonian People*. Cambridge: Cambridge University Press.

Seeger, C. (1977). Speech, Music, and Speech about Music. In C. Seeger, *Studies in Musicology, 1935–1975* (pp. 16–30). Berkeley: University of California Press.

Segala, A. (1989). *Histoire de la littérature nahuatl (sources, identités, représentations)* [History of Nahuatl Literature (Sources, Identities, Representations)]. Rome: Bulzoni Editore.

Segerdahl, P. (1998). Scientific Aspects of Everyday Life: The Example of Conversation Analysis. *Language & Communication* 18: 275–323.

Segert, S. (1984). *A Basic Grammar of the Ugaritic Language*. Berkeley, Los Angeles, and London: University of California Press.

Selting, M. (1987a). Fremdkorrekturen als Manifestationsformen von Verständigungsproblemen. *Zeitschrift für Sprachwissenschaft* 6(1): 37–58.

Selting, M. (1987b). *Verständigungsprobleme: Eine empirische Analyse am Beispiel der Bürger-Verwaltungs-Kommunikation*. Tübingen: Niemeyer.

Selting, M. (1987d). Imagearbeit bei der Behandlung von Verständnisproblemen. In W. Abrahm and R. Århammar (eds.), *Linguistik in Deutschland* (pp. 325–337). Tübingen: Niemeyer.

Selting, M. (1988). The Role of Intonation in the Organization of Repair and Problem Handling Sequences in Conversation. *Journal of Pragmatics* 12: 293–322.

Selting, M. (1995). Der "mögliche Satz" als interaktiv relevante syntaktische Kategorie. *Linguistische Berichte* 158: 298–325.

Selting, M. (2000a). The Construction of Units in Conversational Talk. *Language in Society* 29: 477–517.

Selting, M. (2000b). Opening Remarks: Arguments for the Development of an "Interactional Linguistics". Plenary speech at the Euroconference "Interactional Linguistics", Spa, Belgium, September 16, 2000.

Selting, M., Auer, P., Barden, B., et al. (1998). Gesprächsanalytisches Transkriptionssystem (GAT). *Linguistische Berichte* 173: 91–122.

Selting, M., and Couper-Kuhlen, E. (eds.) (2001). *Studies in Interactional Linguistics.* Amsterdam: John Benjamins.

Senghas, A. (1995). Children's Contribution to the Birth of Nicaraguan Sign Language. PhD dissertation, Massachusetts Institute of Technology.

Senghas, A., and Coppola, M. (2001). Children Creating Language: How Nicaraguan Sign Language Acquired Spatial Grammar. *Psychological Sciences* 12(4): 323–328.

Senghas, R. J. (1997). An "Unspeakable, Unwriteable" Language: Deaf Identity, Language and Personhood among the First Cohorts of Nicaraguan Signers. PhD dissertation, University of Rochester, New York.

Senghas, R. J. (2003). New Ways to be Deaf in Nicaragua: Changes in Language, Personhood, and Community. In L. Monaghan, C. Schmaling, K. Nakamura, and G. H. Turner (eds.), *Many Ways to be Deaf.* Washington, DC: Gallaudet University Press.

Senghas, R. J., and Kegl, J. (1994). Social Considerations in the Emergence of Idioma de Signos Nicaraguense (Nicaraguan Sign Language). *Signpost* 7(1): 40–46.

Seppänen, E.-L. (1998). *Läsnäolon pronominit. Tämä, tuo, se ja hän viittaamassa keskustelun osallistujaan* [Pronouns of Participation. The Finnish Pronouns *tämä, tuo, se* and *hän* as Devices for Referring to Co-participants in Conversation]. Helsinki: Finnish Literature Society.

Seroussi, E. (2002). The Dimension of Sound in the Traditional Synagogue. In S. Pozzi (ed.), *La musica sacra nelle chiese cristiane. Atti del Convegno internazionale di studi – Roma, 25–27 gennaio 2001* (pp. 149–156). Bologna: AlfaStudio.

Shapiro, H. L. (1968 [1936]). *The Pitcairn Islanders,* formerly *The Heritage of the Bounty.* New York: Simon & Schuster.

Sherzer, J. (1972). Verbal and Nonverbal Deixis: The Pointed Lip Gesture among the San Blas Cuna. *Language and Society* 2(1): 117–131.

Sherzer, J. (1983). *Kuna Ways of Speaking: An Ethnographic Perspective.* Austin: University of Texas Press.

Sherzer, J. (1987a). A Diversity of Voices: Men's and Women's Speech in Ethnographic Perspective. In S. U. Philips, S. Steele, and C. Tanz (eds.), *Language, Gender, and Sex in Comparative Perspective* (pp. 95–120). Cambridge: Cambridge University Press.

Sherzer, J. (1987b). A Discourse-Centered Approach to Language and Culture. *American Anthropologist* 89: 295–309.

Sherzer, J. (1990). *Verbal Art in San Blas: Kuna Culture through Its Discourse.* Cambridge: Cambridge University Press.

Sherzer, J. (2002). *Speech Play and Verbal Art.* Austin: University of Texas Press.

Sherzer, J., and Darnell, R. (1972). Outline Guide for the Ethnographic Study of Speech Use. In J. J. Gumperz and D. Hymes (eds.), *Directions in Sociolinguistics: The Ethnography of Communication* (pp. 548–554). New York: Holt, Rinehart and Winston.

Sherzer, J., and Wicks, S. A. (1982). The Intersection of Music and Language in Kuna Discourse. *Latin American Musical Review* 3(2): 147–164.

Sherzer, J., and Woodbury, A. C. (eds.) (1987). *Native American Discourse: Poetics and Rhetoric.* Cambridge: Cambridge University Press.

Shibamoto, J. (1987). The Womanly Woman: Manipulation of Stereotypical and Nonstereotypical Features of Japanese Female Speech. In S. U. Philips, S. Steele, and C. Tanz (eds.), *Language, Gender and Sex in Comparative Perspective* (pp. 26–49). Cambridge: Cambridge University Press.

Shibatani, M. (1985). Passives and Related Constructions: A Prototype Analysis. *Language* 61: 821–848.

Shih, Y. (ed. and trans.) (1983). *The Literary Mind and the Carving of Dragons* (English trans. of *Wen xin diao long* by Liu Xie). Hong Kong: Chinese University Press.

Shopen, T. (ed.) (1979a). *Languages and Their Speakers.* Cambridge, MA: Winthrop.

Shopen, T. (ed.) (1979b). *Languages and Their Status.* Cambridge, MA: Winthrop.

Shore, B. (1982). *Sala'ilua: A Samoan Mystery.* New York: Columbia University Press.

Showalter, E. (1985). *The Female Malady: Women, Madness, and English Culture 1830–1980.* New York: Pantheon.

Shroyer, E., and Shroyer, S. (1984). *Signs across America*. Washington, DC: Gallaudet College Press.

Shultz, J. J., Florio, S., et al. (1983). Where's the Floor? Aspects of the Cultural Organization of Social Relationships in Communication at Home and in School. In P. Gilmore and A. Glatthorn (eds.), *Ethnography and Education: Children in and out of School* (pp. 88–123). Washington, DC: Center for Applied Linguistics.

Shuman, A. (1986). *Storytelling Rights: The Uses of Oral and Written Texts by Urban Adolescents*. Cambridge: Cambridge University Press.

Sidnell, J. (1997). Organizing Social and Spatial Location: Elicitations in Indo-Guyanese Village Talk. *Journal of Linguistic Anthropology* 7(2): 143–165.

Sidnell, J. (1998). Collaboration and Contestation in a Dispute about Space in an Indo-Guyanese Village. *Pragmatics* 8(3).

Siegel, J. (1985). Koinés and Koinéization. *Language in Society* 14: 357–378.

Siegert, R. J. (2001). Culture, Cognition, and Schizophrenia. In J. F. Schumaker and T. Ward (eds.), *Cultural Cognition and Psychopathology* (pp. 171–189). Westport, CT and London: Praeger.

Sifianou, M. (1989). On the Telephone Again! Differences in Telephone Behaviour: England versus Greece. *Language and Society* 18: 527–544.

Silva-Corvalán, C. (1994). *Language Contact and Change: Spanish in Los Angeles*. Oxford: Oxford University Press.

Silverstein, M. (1976a). Hierarchy of Features of Ergativity. In R. M. W. Dixon (ed.), *Grammatical Categories in Australian Languages* (pp. 112–171). Canberra: Australian Institute of Aboriginal Studies.

Silverstein, M. (1976b). Shifters, Linguistic Categories, and Cultural Description. In K. H. Basso and H. A. Selby (eds.), *Meaning in Anthropology* (pp. 11–56). Albuquerque: University of New Mexico Press.

Silverstein, M. (1977). Cultural Prerequisites to Grammatical Analysis. In M. Saville-Troike (ed.), *Linguistics and Anthropology: Georgetown University Round Table on Languages and Linguistics 1977* (pp. 139–151). Washington, DC: Georgetown University Press.

Silverstein, M. (1979). Language Structure and Linguistic Ideology. In P. R. Clyne, W. F. Hanks, and C. L. Hofbauer (eds.), *The Elements: A Parassession on Linguistic Units and Levels* (pp. 193–247). Chicago: Chicago Linguistic Society.

Silverstein, M. (1981). *The Limits of Awareness. Sociolinguistic Working Paper No. 84*. Austin: Southwest Educational Development Laboratory.

Silverstein, M. (1984). On the Pragmatic "Poetry" of Prose: Parallelism, Repetition, and Cohesive Structure in the Time Course of Dyadic Conversation. In D. Schiffrin (ed.), *Meaning, Form, and Use in Context: Linguistic Applications* (pp. 181–199). Washington, DC: Georgetown University Press.

Silverstein, M. (1985). Language and the Culture of Gender: At the Intersection of Structure, Usage, and Ideology. In E. Mertz and R. J. Parmentier (eds.), *Semiotic Mediation: Sociocultural and Psychological Perspectives* (pp. 219–259). Orlando, FL: Academic Press.

Silverstein, M. (1993). Metapragmatic Discourse and Metapragmatic Function. In J. Lucy (ed.), *Reflexive Language: Reported Speech and Metapragmatics* (pp. 33–58). Cambridge: Cambridge University Press.

Silverstein, M. (1995). From the Meaning of Meaning to the Empires of the Mind: Ogden's Orthological English. *Pragmatics* 5: 185–196.

Silverstein, M. (1996a). Encountering Languages and Languages of Encounter in North American Ethnohistory. *Journal of Linguistic Anthropology* 6(2): 126–144.

Silverstein, M. (1996b). Indexical Order and the Dialectics of Sociolinguistic Life. In R. Ide, R. Parker, and Y. Sunaoshi (eds.), *Third Annual Symposium about Language and Society, Austin* (pp. 266–295). Austin: University of Texas, Dept. of Linguistics.

Silverstein, M. (1996c). Monoglot "Standard" in America: Standardization and Metaphors of Linguistic Hegemony. In D. Brenneis and R. H. S. Macaulay (eds.), *The Matrix of Language: Contemporary Linguistic Anthropology* (pp. 284–306). Boulder, CO: Westview Press.

Silverstein, M. (1997). The Improvisational Performance of Culture in Realtime Discursive Practice. In R. K. Sawyer (ed.), *Creativity in Performance* (pp. 265–312). Greenwich, CT: Ablex.

Silverstein, M. (1998a). The Uses and Utility of Ideology: A Commentary. In B. B. Schieffelin, K. A. Woolard, and P. V. Kroskrity (eds.), *Language Ideologies: Practice and Theory* (pp. 123–148). New York: Oxford University Press.

Silverstein, M. (1998b). Contemporary Transformations of Local Linguistic Communities. *Annual Review of Anthropology* 27: 401–426.

Silverstein, M. (2000). Whorfianism and the Linguistic Imagination of Nationality. In P. V. Kroskrity (ed.), *Regimes of Language: Ideologies, Polities, and Identities* (pp. 85–138). Santa Fe, NM: School of American Research Press.

Silverstein, M. (2001[1981]). The Limits of Awareness. In A. Duranti (ed.), *Linguistic Anthropology: A Reader* (pp. 386–401). Malden, MA and Oxford: Blackwell.

Silverstein, M., and Urban, G. (eds.) (1996). *Natural Histories of Discourse*. Chicago: University of Chicago Press.

Silvestri, D., Tonelli, L., and Valeri, V. (1990). *The Earliest Scripts of Uruk*, 2 vols. Naples: Istituto Universitario Orientale, Dipartimento di Studi del Mondo Classico e del Mediterraneo Antico.

Simmel, G. (1902). The Number of Members as Determining the Sociological Form of the Group. *American Journal of Sociology* 8: 1–45 and 158–196.

Simmel, G. (1950). *The Sociology of Georg Simmel* (trans. K. Wolff). Glencoe, IL: Free Press.

Simmel, G. (1983). *Gesammelte Werke*. Berlin: Duncker u. Humblot.

Simmons, J. Q., and Baltaxe, C. A. (1975). Language Patterns of Adolescent Autistics. *Journal of Autism & Childhood Schizophrenia* 5(4): 333–351.

Simon, J., and Smith, L. T. (eds.) (2001). *A Civilising Mission? Perceptions and Representations of the New Zealand Native Schools System*. Auckland: Auckland University Press.

Simpson, R. S. (1997). Metapragmatic Discourse and the Ideology of Impolite Pronouns in Thai. *Journal of Linguistic Anthropology* 7(1): 38–62.

Sinclair, J. (1988). Compressed English. In M. Ghadessy (ed.), *Registers of Written English* (pp. 130–136). London: Pinter.

Sinclair, J. M., and Coulthard, R. M. (1975). *Towards an Analysis of Discourse: The English Used by Teachers and Pupils*. London: Oxford University Press.

Singh, R. (1983). We, They, and Us: A Note on Code-switching and Stratification in North India. *Language in Society* 12: 71–73.

Singh, R., Lel, J., and Martohardjono, G. (1996). Communication in a Multilingual Society: Some Missed Opportunities. In R.

Singh (ed.), *Towards a Critical Sociolinguistics* (pp. 237–254). Amsterdam: John Benjamins.

Singler, J. V. (1992). Nativization and Pidgin/Creole Genesis: A Reply to Bickerton. *Journal of Pidgin and Creole Languages* 7(2): 319–333.

Singler, J. V. (1996). Theories of Creole Genesis, Sociohistorical Considerations, and the Evaluation of Evidence: The Case of Haitian Creole and the Relexification Hypothesis. *Journal of Pidgin and Creole Languages* 11: 185–230.

Slobin, D. I. (ed.) (1967). *A Field Manual for Cross-cultural Study of the Acquisition of Communicative Competence*. Berkeley: Language Behavior Research Laboratory, University of California, Berkeley.

Slobin, D. I. (1973). Cognitive Prerequisites for the Development of Grammar. In C. A. Ferguson and D. I. Slobin (eds.), *Studies of Child Language Development*. New York: Holt, Rinehart and Winston.

Slobin, D. I. (1982). Universal and Particular in the Acquisition of Language. In W. Deutsch (ed.), *Language Acquisition: The State of the Art*. Cambridge: Cambridge University Press.

Slobin, D. I. (1985a). The Crosslinguistic Evidence for the Language-making Capacity. In D. I. Slobin (ed.), *The Crosslinguistic Study of Language Acquisition*, vol. 2: *Theoretical Issues* (pp. 1157–1256). Hillsdale, NJ: Lawrence Erlbaum.

Slobin, D. I. (ed.) (1985b). *The Crosslinguistic Study of Language Acquisition*, vol. 1. Hillsdale, NJ: Lawrence Erlbaum.

Slobin, D. I. (1987). Thinking for Speaking. In J. Aske, N. Michaelis, and H. Filip (eds.), *Proceedings of the 13th Annual Meeting of the Berkeley Linguistics Society*. Berkeley: Berkeley Linguistics Society.

Slobin, D. I., Gerhardt, J., Kyratzis, A., and Guo, J. (eds.) (1996). *Social Interaction, Social Context, and Language: Essays in Honor of Susan Ervin-Tripp*. Mahwah, NJ: Lawrence Erlbaum.

Smith, B. (1985 [1969]). *European Vision and the South Pacific*. New Haven: Yale University Press.

Smith, H., and Stevens, K. (1967). Unique Vocal Abilities of Certain Tibetan Lamas. *American Anthropologist* 69: 209–212.

Smith, L. E., and Forman, M. L. (eds.) (1997). *World Englishes 2000*. Honolulu: University of Hawai'i Press.

Smith-Hefner, N. J. (1988). The Linguistic Socialization of Javanese Children in Two

Communities. *Anthropological Linguistics* 30(2): 166–198.

Smith-Hefner, N. J. (1999). *Khmer American: Identity and Moral Education in a Diasporic Community.* Berkeley: University of California Press.

Sommer, I., et al. (2001). Handedness, Language Lateralisation and Anatomical Asymmetry in Schizophrenia: Meta-analysis. *British Journal of Psychiatry* 178(4): 344–351.

Sommer, I. E., Ramsey, N. F., and Kahn, R. S. (2001). Language Lateralization in Schizophrenia: An fMRI Study. *Schizophrenia Research* 52(1–2): 57–67.

Sommer, I. E., et al. (2003). Language Lateralization in Female Patients with Schizophrenia: An fMRI Study. *Schizophrenia Research* 60(2–3): 183–190.

Sorjonen, M.-L. (1996). On Repeats and Responses in Finnish Conversation. In E. Ochs, E. A. Schegloff, and S. A. Thompson (eds.), *Interaction and Grammar* (pp. 277–327). Cambridge: Cambridge University Press.

Sorjonen, M.-L. (1997). Recipient Activities: Particles *nii(n)* and *joo* as Responses in Finnish Conversation. Unpublished doctoral dissertation, University of California, Los Angeles.

Sorjonen, M.-L. (2001). *Responding in Conversation: A Study of Response Particles in Finnish.* Amsterdam: John Benjamins.

Sornicola, R. (1981). *Sul parlato.* Bologna: Il Mulino.

Spears, A. K. (ed.) (1999). *Race and Ideology: Language, Symbolism, and Popular Culture.* Detroit: Wayne State University Press.

Sperry, L., and Sperry, D. (2000). Verbal and Nonverbal Contributions to Early Representation: Evidence from African American Toddlers. In N. Budwig, I. Uzgiris, and J. Wertsch (eds.), *Communication: An Arena of Development* (pp. 143–165). Stamford, CT: Ablex.

Spitulnik, D. (1998a). Anthropology and Mass Media. *Annual Review of Anthropology* 22: 293–315.

Spitulnik, D. (1998b). Mediating Unity and Diversity: The Production of Language Ideologies in Zambian Broadcasting. In B. B. Schieffelin, K. A. Woolard, and P. V. Kroskrity (eds.), *Language Ideologies: Practice and Theory* (pp. 163–188). New York: Oxford University Press.

Spitulnik, D. (1998c). The Language of the City: Town Bemba as Urban Hybridity. *Journal of Linguistic Anthropology* 8(1): 30–59.

Spitulnik, D. (1999). Mediated Modernities: Encounters with the Electronic in Zambia. *Visual Anthropology Review* 14(2).

Spitulnik, D. (2001). Media. In A. Duranti (ed.), *Key Terms in Language and Culture* (pp. 143–146). Malden, MA: Blackwell.

Spitzer, Manfred, et al. (1994). Contextual Insensitivity in Thought-disordered Schizophrenic Patients: Evidence from Pauses in Spontaneous Speech. *Language and Speech* 37(2): 171–185.

Spivak, G. (1995). Subaltern Studies: Deconstructing Historiography. In D. Landry and G. MacLean (eds.), *The Spivak Reader.* New York: Routledge.

Springer, G. (1956). Language and Music: Parallels and Divergences. In M. Halle, H. G. Lunt, H. McLean, and C. H. Van Schooneveld (eds.), *For Roman Jakobson: Essays on the Occasion of His Sixtieth Birthday* (pp. 504–513). The Hague: Mouton.

Stagl, J. (1981). Die Beschreibung des Fremden in der Wissenschaft. In H. P. Duerr (ed.), *Der Wissenschaftler und das Irrationale.* Beiträge aus Ethnologie und Anthropologie, Band 1. Frankfurt/Main: Syndikat.

Steedly, M. M. (1996). The Importance of Proper Names: Language and "National" Identity in Colonial Karoland. *American Ethnologist* 23: 447–475.

Steensig, J. (2001). *Sprog i virkeligheden: Bidrag til en interaktionel lingvistik* [Language in Reality: Contributions to an Interactional Linguistics]. Aarhus: Aarhus University Press.

Stein, N. (1982). The Definition of a Story. *Journal of Pragmatics* 6: 487–507.

Stein, N., and Glenn, C. G. (1979). An Analysis of Story Comprehension in Elementary School Children. In R. O. Freedle (ed.), *New Directions in Discourse Processing* (pp. 53–120). Norwood, NJ: Ablex.

Stephane, M., and Hsu, L. K. (1996). Musical Hallucinations: Interplay of Degenerative Brain Disease, Psychosis, and Culture in a Chinese Woman. *Journal of Nervous and Mental Disease* 184(1): 59–61.

Stern, T. (1957). Drum and Whistle Languages: An Analysis of Speech Surrogates. *American Anthropologist* 59: 487–506.

Sterponi, L. (2003). Account Episodes in Family Discourse: The Making of Morality in Everyday Interaction. *Discourse Studies* 5(1): 79–100.

Stevens, A. A., et al. (2000). Verbal Processing Deficits in Schizophrenia. *Journal of Abnormal Psychology* 109(3): 461–471.

Stewart, D. A. (1991). ASL Intervention Strategies for Teachers. In D. Martin (ed.), *Advances in Cognition, Education and Deafness*. Washington, DC: Gallaudet University Press.

Stock, B. (1996). *Augustine the Reader: Meditation, Self-Knowledge, and the Ethics of Interpretation*. Cambridge, MA: Harvard University Press.

Stocking, G. W. (1974). The Boas Plan for the Study of American Indian Languages. In D. Hymes (ed.), *Studies in the History of Linguistics: Traditions and Paradigms* (pp. 454–483). Bloomington: Indiana University Press.

Stokoe, W. (ed.) (1960). *Sign Language Structure: An Outline of the Visual Communication System of the American Deaf* (Studies in Linguistics, Occasional Paper, 8). Buffalo, NY: University of Buffalo.

Stokoe, W. (1969). Sign Language Diglossia. *Studies in Linguistics* 21: 27–41.

Stokoe, W. (1969–70). Linguistic Description of Sign Language. In F. P. Dinneen (ed.), *Monograph Series on Language and Linguistics* (pp. 243–250). Washington, DC: Georgetown University Press.

Stokoe, W. (1980). Sign Language Structure. *Annual Review of Anthropology* 9: 365–390.

Stokoe, W., Casterline, D., and Croneberg, C. (1976 [1965]). *A Dictionary of American Sign Language on Linguistic Principles*. 1st edn., Washington, DC: Gallaudet College Press; 2nd edn., Silver Spring, MD: Linstok Press.

Stone, J. B. (1996). Minority Empowerment and the Education of Deaf People. In I. Parasnis (ed.), *Cultural and Language Diversity and the Deaf Experience* (pp. 171–180). Cambridge: Cambridge University Press.

Stone, L., and Gutiérrez, K. (in press). Problem-finding as Distributed Intelligence: The Role of Changing Participation in Mathematical Problem-solving Activities in an After-school Learning Community. *Mind, Culture, & Activity: An International Journal*.

Strathern, A. (1975). Veiled Speech in Mount Hagen. In M. Bloch (ed.), *Political Language and Oratory in Traditional Society* (pp. 185–203). London: Academic Press.

Strathern, M. (1988). *The Gender of the Gift: Problems with Women and Problems with Society in Melanesia*. Berkeley: University of California Press.

Strathern, M. (1990). Negative Strategies in Melanesia. In R. Fardon (ed.), *Localizing Strategies: Regional Traditions of Ethnographic Writing* (pp. 204–216). Edinburgh: Scottish Academic Press; Washington, DC: Smithsonian Institution Press.

Streeck, J. (1980). Speech Acts in Interaction: A Critique of Searle. *Discourse Processes* 3: 133–154.

Streeck, J. (1983). Konversationsanalyse. Ein Reparaturversuch. *Zeitschrift für Sprachwissenschaft* 1: 72–104.

Streeck, J. (1990/1). Tao/Saó: Talking Culture with Rousseau. *Research on Language and Social Interaction* 24: 241–261.

Streeck, J. (1994). Gesture as Communication II: The Audience as Co-author. *Research on Language and Social Interaction* 27: 239–267.

Streeck, J. (1996). A Little Ilokano Grammar as It Appears in Interaction. *Journal of Pragmatics* 26: 189–213.

Streeck, J., and Hartge, U. (1992). Previews: Gestures at the Transition Place. In P. Auer and A. di Luzio (eds.), *The Contextualization of Language* (pp. 135–158). Amsterdam: John Benjamins.

Streeck, J., and Knapp, M. L. (1992). The Interaction of Visual and Verbal Features in Human Communication. In F. Poyatos (ed.), *Advances in Nonverbal Communication* (pp. 1–23). Amsterdam and Philadelphia: John Benjamins.

Street, B. V. (1984). *Literacy in Theory and Practice*. Cambridge: Cambridge University Press.

Street, B. V. (ed.) (1993). *Cross-cultural Approaches to Literacy*. Cambridge: Cambridge University Press.

Street, B. V. (1995). *Social Literacies: Critical Approaches to Literacy in Development, Ethnography, and Education*. London: Longman.

Street, B., and Besnier, N. (1994). Aspects of Literacy. In T. Ingold (ed.), *Companion Encyclopedia of Anthropology: Humanity, Culture, and Social Life* (pp. 527–562). London: Routledge.

Stroud, C. (1992). The Problem of Intention and Meaning in Code-switching. *Text* 12: 127–155.

Stubbs, M. (1983). *Discourse Analysis*. Oxford: Blackwell.

Stubbs, M. (1994). Grammar, Text and Ideology. *Applied Linguistics* 15: 201–223.

Suchman, L. (1987). *Plans and Situated Action: The Problem of Human–Machine Communication*. Cambridge: Cambridge University Press.

Sugiyama, M. S. (1996). On the Origins of Narrative: Storyteller Bias as a Fitness Enhancing Strategy. *Human Nature* 7(4): 403–425.

Sunaoshi, Y. (2000). Gesture as a Situated Communicative Strategy at a Japanese Manufacturing Plant in the US. *Cognitive Studies: Bulletin of the Japanese Cognitive Science Society* 7.

Sundberg, J. (1969). Articulatory Differences between Spoken and Sung Vowels. Speech Transmission Laboratory, Quarterly Progress & Status Report, vol. 1: 33–46. Stockholm: Royal Institute of Technology.

Sundberg, J. (1977). The Acoustics of the Singing Voice. *Scientific American* 231(3): 82–91.

Sundberg, J. (1987). *The Science of the Singing Voice*. Dekalb: Northern Illinois University Press.

Sundberg, J., and Lindblom, B. (1976). Generative Theories in Language and Music Descriptions. *Cognition* 4(1): 99–122.

Swadesh, M. (1952). Lexico-statistic Dating of Prehistoric Ethnic Contacts. *Proceedings of the American Philosophical Society* 96: 452–463.

Swadesh, M. (1955). Towards Greater Accuracy in Lexicostatistic Dating. *International Journal of American Linguistics* 21: 121–137.

Swadesh, M. (1972). *The Origin and Diversification of Language* (ed. J. Sherzer). London: Routledge & Kegan Paul.

Swanton, J. R. (1900). Morphology of the Chinook Verb. *American Anthropologist* 2(2): 199–237.

Swartz, L. (1991). The Politics of Black Patients' Identity: Ward-Rounds on the "Black Side" of a South African Psychiatric Hospital. *Culture, Medicine and Psychiatry* 15: 217–244.

Swartz, S. (1994). Issues in the Analysis of Psychotic Speech. *Journal of Psycholinguistic Research* 23(1): 29–44.

Swigart, L. (2000). The Limits of Legitimacy: Language Ideology and Shift in Contemporary Senegal. *Journal of Linguistic Anthropology* 10(1): 90–130.

Taleghani-Nikazm, C. (2002). A Conversation Analytical Study of Telephone Conversation Openings between Native and Nonnative Speakers. *Journal of Pragmatics* 34: 1807–1832.

Talmy, L. (1976). Semantic Causative Types. In M. Shibatani (ed.), *Syntax and Semantics*, vol. 6: *Causatives* (pp. 43–116). New York: Academic Press.

Talmy, L. (1985). Lexicalization Patterns: Semantic Structure in Lexical Forms. In T. Shopen (ed.), *Language Typology and Syntactic Description* (pp. 57–149). London: Cambridge University Press.

Talmy, L. (2000a). *Toward a Cognitive Semantics*, vol. 1: *Concept Structuring Systems*. Cambridge, MA: MIT Press.

Talmy, L. (2000b). *Toward a Cognitive Semantics*, vol. 2: *Typology and Process in Concept Structuring*. Cambridge, MA: MIT Press.

Tanaka, H. (1999). *Turn-taking in Japanese Conversation: A Study in Grammar and Interaction*. Amsterdam: John Benjamins.

Tanaka, H. (2000). Turn-projection in Japanese Talk-in-Interaction. *Research on Language and Social Interaction* 33: 1–38.

Tannen, D. (1981). NY Jewish Conversational Style. *International Journal of the Sociology of Language* 30: 133–149.

Tannen, D. (ed.) (1982). *Spoken and Written Language: Exploring Orality and Literacy*. Norwood, NJ: Ablex.

Tannen, D. (1985). Cross-cultural Communication. In T. A. van Dijk (ed.), *Handbook of Discourse Analysis*, vol. 4 (pp. 203–215). London: Academic Press.

Tannen, D. (1986). *That's Not What I Meant!* London: Dent.

Tannen, D. (1989). *Talking Voices: Repetition, Dialogue, and Imagery in Conversational Discourse*. Cambridge: Cambridge University Press.

Tannen, D. (1990). *You Just Don't Understand: Women and Men in Conversation*. New York: William Morrow.

Tannen, D. (1993). The Relativity of Linguistic Strategies: Rethinking Power and Solidarity in Gender and Dominance. In D. Tannen (ed.), *Gender and Conversational Interaction* (pp. 165–188). New York: Oxford University Press.

Tannen, D. (2003). Gender and Family Interaction. In J. Holmes and M. Meyerhoff (eds.), *Handbook of Language and Gender*. Oxford: Blackwell.

Tannen, D., and Wallat, C. (1987). Interactive Frames and Knowledge Schemas in Interaction: Examples from a Medical Examination/Interview. *Social Psychology Quarterly* 50(2): 205–216.

Taylor, C. (1985). *Human Agency and Language*. Cambridge: Cambridge University Press.

Taylor, C. (1995a). Child as Apprentice-Narrator: Socializing Voice, Face, Identity, and Self Esteem amid the Narrative Politics of Family Dinner. PhD dissertation, University of Southern California.

Taylor, C. (1995b). You Think It Was a Fight? Co-constructing (the Struggle for) Meaning, Face, and Family in Everyday Narrative Activity. *Research on Language and Social Interaction* 28(3): 283–317.

Tedlock, D. (1983). *The Spoken Word and the Work of Interpretation*. Philadelphia: University of Pennsylvania Press.

Tedlock, D. (1996). *Popol Vuh: The Mayan Book of the Dawn of Life*. New York: Simon and Schuster.

Tedlock, D., and Mannheim, B. (eds.) (1995). *The Dialogic Emergence of Culture*. Urbana: University of Illinois Press.

Teeter, K. V. (1964). "Anthropological Linguistics" and Linguistic Anthropology. *American Anthropologist* 66: 878–879.

Tényi, T., et al. (2000). Schizophrenics Show a Failure in the Decoding of Violations of Conversational Implicatures. *Psychopathology* 35(1): 25–27.

Terasaki, A. K. (1996). Pre-Announcement Sequences in Conversation. *Social Sciences Working Paper 99*.

Thakerar, J. N., Giles, H., and Cheshire, J. (1982). Psychological and Linguistic Parameters of Speech Accommodation Theory. In C. Fraser and K. R. Scherer (eds.), *Advances in the Social Psychology of Language* (pp. 205–255). Cambridge: Cambridge University Press.

Théberge, P. (1994). *Any Sound You Can Imagine: Making Music/Consuming Technology*. Hanover, NH: Wesleyan University Press.

Thomas, G. (1991). *Linguistic Purism*. London: Longman.

Thomas, N. (1989). The Forces of Ethnology: Origins and Significance of the Melanesia/Polynesia Division. *Current Anthropology*, 30: 27–41.

Thomas, P., and Fraser, W. (1994). Linguistics, Human Communication and Psychiatry. *British Journal of Psychiatry* 165: 585–592.

Thomas, P., Kearney, G., Napier, E., Ellis, E., Leuder, I., and Johnson, M. (1996). Speech and Language in First Onset Psychosis: Differences between People with Schizophrenia, Mania, and Controls. *British Journal of Psychiatry* 168: 337–343.

Thomason, S. G. (ed.) (1997a). *Contact Languages: A Wider Perspective*. Amsterdam: John Benjamins.

Thomason, S. G. (1997b). A Typology of Contact Languages. In A. K. Spears and D. Winford (eds.), *The Structure and Status of Pidgins and Creoles* (pp. 71–88). Amsterdam: John Benjamins.

Thomason, S. G. (2001). *Language Contact: An Introduction*. Washington, DC: Georgetown University Press.

Thomason, S. G., and Kaufman, T. (1988). *Language Contact, Creolization, and Genetic Linguistics*. Berkeley: University of California Press.

Thompson, S. A., and Hopper, P. J. (2001). Transitivity, Clause Structure, and Argument Structure: Evidence from Conversation. In J. Bybee and P. J. Hopper (eds.), *Frequency and the Emergence of Linguistic Structure* (pp. 27–60). Amsterdam: John Benjamins.

Titone, D., Levy, D. L., and Holzman, P. S. (2001). Contextual Insensitivity in Schizophrenic Language Processing: Evidence from Lexical Ambiguity. *Journal of Abnormal Psychology* 109(4): 761–767.

Tiwary, K. M. (1978). Tuneful Weeping: A Mode of Communication. *Frontiers* 3(3): 24–27.

Tolbert, E. (1990). Women Cry with Words: Symbolization of Affect in the Karelian Lament. *Yearbook for Traditional Music* 22: 80–105.

Tomasello, M., and Camaioni, L. (1997). A Comparison of the Gestural Communication of Apes and Human Infants. *Human Development* 40: 7–24.

Toolan, M. (1988). The Language of Press Advertising. In M. Ghadessy (ed.), *Registers of Written English* (pp. 52–64). London: Pinter.

Toomey, J., and Adams, L. A. (1995). Naturalistic Observation of Children with Autism: Evidence for Intersubjectivity. *New Directions in Child Development* 69: 75–89.

Tran Quang Hai, and Guillou, D. (1980). Original Research and Acoustical Analysis in Connection with the *xoomij* Style of Biphonic Singing. In R. Emmert and Y. Minegishi (eds.), *Musical Voices of Asia* (pp. 162–173). Tokyo: Heibonsha.

Trechter, S. (1995). Categorical Gender Myths in Native America: Gender Deictics in Lakhota. Special Issue: Sociolinguistics and Language Minorities, *Issues in Applied Linguistics* 6(1): 5–22.

Trechter, S. (1999). Contextualizing the Exotic Few: Gender Dichotomies in Lakhota. In M. Bucholtz, A. C. Liang, and L. A. Sutton (eds.), *Reinventing Identities: The Gendered Self in Discourse* (pp. 101–119). New York: Oxford University Press.

Trechter, S. (2001). White between the Lines: Ethnic Positioning in Lakhota Discourse. *Journal of Linguistic Anthropology* 11: 22–35.

Trechter, S. (2003). A Marked Man: The Contexts of Gender and Ethnicity. In J. Holmes and M. Meyerhoff (eds.), *The Handbook of Language and Gender*. Oxford: Blackwell.

Trechter, S. (forthcoming). *The Pragmatic Functions of Gender Deixis in Lakhota*. Lincoln: University of Nebraska Press.

Trechter, S., and Bucholtz, M. (2001). White Noise: Bringing Language into Whiteness Studies. *Journal of Linguistic Anthropology* 11(1): 3–21.

Trix, F. (1993). *Spiritual Discourse: Learning with an Islamic Master*. Philadelphia: University of Pennsylvania Press.

Troemel-Ploetz, S. (1991). Selling the Apolitical. *Discourse and Society* 2(4): 489–502.

Truax, B. (2001). *Acoustic Communication*. Westport, CT: Ablex.

Trudgill, P. (1983). Acts of Conflicting Identity: The Sociolinguistics of British Pop-song Pronunciation. In P. Trudgill, *On Dialect: Social and Geographical Perspectives* (pp. 141–160). Oxford: Blackwell.

Trudgill, P. (1986). *Dialects in Contact*. Oxford: Blackwell.

Tryon, D. (ed.) (1995). *Comparative Austronesian Dictionary*, 5 vols. Berlin: Mouton de Gruyter.

Tsitsipis, L. D. (1998). *A Linguistic Anthropology of Praxis and Language Shift: Arvanítika (Albanian) and Greek in Contact*. Oxford: Clarendon Press.

Turchetta, B. (ed.) (1997). *Introduzione alla linguistica antropologica*. Milan: Mursia.

Tusón, A. (1995). *Anàlisi de la conversa*. Barcelona: Ariel [Spanish transl. (1997) *Análisis de la conversación*. Barcelona: Ariel].

Twine, F. W., and Warren, J. W. (eds.) (2000). *Racing Research, Researching Race: Methodological Dilemmas in Critical Race Studies*. New York: New York University Press.

Tyler, S. A. (1972). Context and Alternation in Koya Kinship Terminology. In J. J. Gumperz and D. Hymes (eds.), *Directions in Sociolinguistics: The Ethnography of Communication* (pp. 251–269). New York: Holt, Rinehart and Winston.

Uhmann, S. (1997). Selbstreparaturen in Alltagsdialogen: Ein Fall für eine integrative Konversationstheorie. In P. Schlosbinski (ed.), *Zur Syntax des gesprochenen Deutsch* (pp. 157–180). Opladen: Westdeutscher Verlag.

Uhmann, S. (2001). Some Arguments for the Relevance of Syntax to Self-repair in Everyday German Conversation. In M. Selting and E. Couper-Kuhlen (eds.), *Studies in Interactional Linguistics*. Amsterdam: John Benjamins.

Uldall, H. J. (1944). Speech and Writing. *Acta Linguistica* IV: 11–16.

Ullman, B. L. (1932). *Ancient Writing and Its Influence*. New York: Longmans Green and Co.

Umiker-Sebeok, D. J. (1979). Preschool Children's Intraconversational Narratives. *Journal of Child Language* 6: 91–109.

Umiker-Sebeok, D. J., and Sebeok, T. A. (eds.) (1976). *Speech Surrogates: Drum and Whistle Languages*, vols. 1 and 2. The Hague: Mouton.

Unification of Signs Commission (1975). *Gestuno: International Sign Language of the Deaf*. Carlisle, UK: British Deaf Association [for] the World Federation of the Deaf.

Urban, G. (1988). Ritual Wailing in Amerindian Brazil. *American Anthropologist* 90: 385–400.

Urban, G. (1991). *A Discourse-centered Approach to Culture: Native South American Myths and Rituals*. Austin: University of Texas Press.

Urban, G. (2001). *Metaculture: How Culture Moves through the World*. Minneapolis: University of Minnesota Press.

Urciuoli, B. (1995). Language and Borders. *Annual Review of Anthropology* 24: 525–546.

Urciuoli, B. (1996). *Exposing Prejudice: Puerto Rican Experiences of Language, Race, and Class*. Boulder, CO: Westview Press.

Urla, J. (1988). Ethnic Protest and Social Planning: A Look at Basque Language Revival. *Cultural Anthropology* 3: 379–394.

Urla, J. (2001). Outlaw Language: Creating Alternative Public Spheres in Basque Free Radio. In S. Gal and K. A. Woolard (eds.), *Languages and Publics: The Making of Authority* (pp. 141–163). Manchester: St. Jerome.

Vacheck, J. (1966 [1945–9]). *Some Remarks on Writing a Phonetic Transcription*. In E. P. Hamp, F. W. Householder, and R. Austerlitz (eds.), *Reading in Linguistics* II. Chicago: University of Chicago Press.

Valeri, V. (2001). *La scrittura. Storia e modelli*. Rome: Carocci.

Valéry, P. (1943). Rhumbs. *Tel Quel*, vol. II. Paris: Gallimard.

Van Cleve, J. V. (ed.) (1987a). *Gallaudet Encyclopedia of Deaf People and Deafness*, vol. 2. New York: McGraw-Hill.

Van Cleve, J. V. (1987b). History: Sign Language Controversy. In J. V. Van Cleve (ed.), *Gallaudet Encyclopedia of Deaf People and Deafness*, vol. 2 (pp. 53–61). New York: McGraw-Hill.

Van Cleve, J. V. (ed.) (1993). *Deaf History Unveiled: Interpretations from the New Scholarship*. Washington, DC: Gallaudet University Press.

Van Cleve, J. V., and Crouch, B. (1989). *A Place of Their Own: Creating the Deaf Community in America*. Washington, DC: Gallaudet University Press.

van Dijk, T. (1991). *Racism and the Press*. London: Routledge.

van Dijk, T. (1998). *Ideology: A Multidisciplinary Approach*. London: Sage.

Van Dongen, E. (1997). Space and Time in the Lives of People with Long-standing Mental Illness: An Ethnographic Account. *Anthropology and Medicine* 4: 89–103.

Van Dongen, E. (2003). *Worlds of Psychotic People: Wanderers, "Bricoleurs" and Strategists*. New York: Routledge.

Van Leeuwen, T. (1999), *Speech, Music, Sound*. New York: St. Martins Press.

van Wijk, C., and Kempen, G. (1987). A Dual System for Producing Self-repairs in Spontaneous Speech: Evidence from Experimentally Elicited Corrections. *Cognitive Psychology* 19: 403–440.

Vásquez, O. (1994). The Magic of *La Clase Mágica*: Enhancing the Learning Potential of Bilingual Children. *Australian Journal of Language and Literacy* 17(2): 120–128.

Vásquez, O., Pease-Alvarez, L., Shannon, S., and Moll, L. (1994). *Pushing Boundaries: Language and Culture in a Mexicano Community*. Cambridge: Cambridge University Press.

Vaughan, M. (1983). Idioms of Madness: Zomba Lunatic Asylum, Nyasaland, in the Colonial Period. *Journal of Southern African Studies* 9: 218–238.

Vaughan, M. (1993). Madness and Colonialism, Colonialism as Madness: Re-reading Fanon – Colonial Discourse and the Psychopathology of Colonialism. *Paideuma* 39: 45–55.

Vernon, M., and Makowsky, B. (1969). Deafness and Minority Group Dynamics. *The Deaf American* 21(11): 3–6.

Violette, J., and Swisher, L. (1992). Echolalic Responses by a Child with Autism to Four Experimental Conditions of Sociolinguistic Input. *Journal of Speech & Hearing Research* 35(1): 139–147.

Visweswaran, K. (1994). *Fictions of Feminist Ethnography*. Minneapolis: University of Minnesota Press.

Voegelin, C. F. (1952). The Boas Plan for the Presentation of American Indian Languages. *Proceedings of the American Philosophical Society* 96: 439–451.

Voegelin, C. F., and Harris, Z. S. (1945). Linguistics in Ethnology. *Southwestern Journal of Anthropology* 1: 455–465.

Voegelin, C. F., and Harris, Z. S. (1952). Training in Anthropological Linguistics. *American Anthropologist* 54: 322–327.

Vološinov, V. N. (1973 [1929/30]). *Marxism and the Philosophy of Language* (trans. L. Matejka and I. R. Titunik). New York: Seminar Press.

Vološinov, V. N. (1986). *Marxism and the Philosophy of Language*. Cambridge, MA: Harvard University Press.

Volterra, V., and Erting, C. J. (eds.) (1994). *From Gesture to Language in Hearing and Deaf Children*. Washington, DC: Gallaudet University Press.

von Frisch, K. (1967). *The Dance Language and Orientation of Bees*. Cambridge, MA: Harvard University Press.

von Humboldt, W. (1988). *On Language: The Diversity of Human Language Structure and Its Influence on the Mental Development of Mankind* (trans. P. L. Heath). Cambridge: Cambridge University Press.

Vygotsky, L. (1962 [1934]). *Thought and Language*. Cambridge, MA: MIT Press.

Vygotsky, L. (1978). *Mind in Society: The Development of Higher Psychological Processes*. Cambridge, MA: Harvard University Press.

Wagner, J. (1996). Foreign Language Acquisition through Interaction: A Critical Review of Research on Conversational Adjustments. *Journal of Pragmatics* 26: 215–235.

Wagner, J. (1998). On Doing Being a Guinea Pig – A Response to Seedhouse. *Journal of Pragmatics* 30: 103–113.

Wahl, O. F., and Hunter, J. (1992). Are Gender Effects Being Neglected in Schizophrenia Research? *Schizophrenia Bulletin* 18(2).

Wang, J. H., Morales, O., and Hsu, L. K. G. (1998). Auditory Hallucinations in Bilingual Immigrants. *Journal of Nervous & Mental Disease* 186: 501–503.

Ward, M. C. (1971). *Them Children: A Study in Language Learning*. New York: Holt, Rinehart and Winston.

Wardhaugh, R. (1986). *An Introduction to Sociolinguistics*. Oxford: Blackwell.

Washabaugh, W. (1981). Sign Language in Its Social Context. *Annual Review of Anthropology* 10: 237–252.

Washabaugh, W. (1986). *Five Fingers for Survival*. Ann Arbor: Karoma.

Watkins, C. (1995). *How to Kill a Dragon: Aspects of Indo-European Poetics*. Oxford and New York: Oxford University Press.

Watson, W. G. E. (2001). *Classical Hebrew Poetry: A Guide to Its Techniques*. Sheffield: Sheffield Academic Press.

Watson-Gegeo, K. A. (1992). Thick Explanation in the Ethnographic Study of Child Socialization: A Longitudinal Study of the Problem of Schooling for Kwara'ae (Solomon Islands) Children. In W. A. Corsaro and P. J. Miller (eds.), *Interpretive Approaches to Children's Socialization* (pp. 51–66). San Francisco: Jossey-Bass.

Watson-Gegeo, K., and Gegeo, D. (1986). Calling Out and Repeating Routines in Kwara'ae Children's Language Socialization. In B. B. Schieffelin and E. Ochs (eds.), *Language Socialization across Cultures* (pp. 17–50). New York: Cambridge University Press.

Watson-Gegeo, K., and Gegeo, D. W. (1999). (Re)modeling Culture in Kwara'ae: the Role of Discourse in Children's Cognitive Development. *Discourse Studies* 1(2): 227–245.

Watts, R. (1999). The Ideology of Dialect in Switzerland. In J. Blommaert (ed.), *Language Ideological Debates* (pp. 67–103). Berlin: Mouton de Gruyter.

Waugh, L., and Van Schooneveld, C. H. (eds.) (1980). *The Melody of Language*. Baltimore: University Park Press.

Waxler, N. (1974). Culture and Mental Illness: A Social Labeling Perspective. *Journal of Nervous and Mental Disease* 159: 379–395.

Weber, E. J. (1976). *Peasants into Frenchmen: The Modernization of Rural France, 1870–1914*. Stanford, CA: Stanford University Press.

Weiner, J. F. (1991). *The Empty Place: Poetry, Space, and Being among the Foi of Papua New Guinea*. Bloomington: Indiana University Press.

Weinreich, U. (1953). *Languages in Contact: Findings and Problems*. The Hague: Mouton.

Weinreich, U., Labov, W., and Herzog, M. I. (1968). Empirical Foundations for a Theory of Language Change. In W. P. Lehmann and Y. Malkiel (eds.), *Directions in Historical Linguistics* (pp. 95–188). Austin: University of Texas Press.

Weisman, A., Lopez, S. R., Karno, M., and Jenkins, J. (1993). An Attributional Analysis of Expressed Emotion in Mexican-American Families with Schizophrenia. *Journal of Abnormal Psychology* 102(4): 601–606.

Wells, G. (1985). Pre-school Literacy Related Activities and Success in School. In D. Olson, N. Torrance, and A. Hildyard (eds.), *Literacy, Language and Learning: The Nature and Consequences of Reading and Writing* (pp. 229–255). Cambridge: Cambridge University Press.

Wenger, E. (1998). *Communities of Practice*. Cambridge: Cambridge University Press.

Wertsch, J. (1997). *Mind as Action*. Oxford: Oxford University Press.

Wescott, R. (1977). Ideophones in Bini and English. *Forum Linguisticum* 2(1): 1–13.

Wescott, R. W. (1980). *Sound and Sense: Linguistic Essays on Phonosemic Subjects*. Lake Bluff, IL: Jupiter Press.

West, C. (1983). "Ask Me no Questions..." An Analysis of Queries and Replies in Physician–Patient Dialogues. In S. Fisher and A. D. Todd (eds.), *The Social Organization of Doctor–Patient Communication* (pp. 75–106). Washington, DC: Center for Applied Linguistics.

West, C. (1984). Questions and Answers between Doctors and Patients. In C. West, *Routine Complications: Troubles with Talk between Doctors and Patients* (pp. 71–96). Bloomington: Indiana University Press.

West, C., and Zimmerman, D. H. (1983). Small Insults: A Study of Interruptions in Cross-sex Conversation between Unacquainted Persons. In B. Thorne, C. Kramarae, and N. Henley (eds.), *Language, Gender and Society* (pp. 102–117). Rowley, MA: Newbury House.

Weston, K. (1998). *Longslowburn: Sexuality and Social Science*. New York: Routledge.

Wexler, B. E., et al. (2002). Deficits in Language-mediated Mental Operations in Patients with Schizophrenia. *Schizophrenia Research* 53(3): 171–179.

Whalen, J., Zimmerman, D., and Whalen, M. (1988). When Words Fail: A Single Case Analysis. *Social Problems* 35(4): 335–360.

Wheelock, W. T. (1982). The Problem of Ritual Language: From Information to Situation. *Journal of the American Academy of Religion* 50: 49–71.

White, G. M. (1991). *Identity through History: Living Stories in a Solomon Island Society.* Cambridge: Cambridge University Press.

White, H. (1980). The Value of Narrativity in the Representation of Reality. In W. J. T. Mitchell (ed.), *On Narrative* (pp. 1–24). Chicago: University of Chicago Press.

Whiting, J., Child, L., Lambert, W., et al. (1966). *Field Guide for a Study of Socialization.* New York: Social Science Research Center.

Whorf, B. L. (1938). Some Verbal Categories of Hopi. *Language* 14: 275–286.

Whorf, B. L. (1941). The Relation of Habitual Thought and Behavior in Language. In L. Spier, A. I. Hallowell, and S. S. Newman (eds.), *Language, Culture, and Personality: Essays in Honor of Edward Sapir* (pp. 75–93). Menasha, WI: Sapir Memorial Publication.

Whorf, B. L. (1950). An American Indian Model of the Universe. *International Journal of American Linguistics* 16: 67–72.

Whorf, B. L. (1956a). Grammatical Categories. In J. B. Carroll (ed.), *Language, Thought, and Reality: Selected Writings of Benjamin Lee Whorf* (pp. 87–101). Cambridge, MA: MIT Press.

Whorf, B. L. (1956b). Linguistics as an Exact Science. In J. B. Carroll (ed.), *Language, Thought, and Reality: Selected Writings of Benjamin Lee Whorf* (pp. 220–232). Cambridge, MA: MIT Press.

Whorf, B. L. (1956c). *Language, Thought, and Reality: Selected Writings of Benjamin Lee Whorf* (ed. J. B. Carroll). Cambridge, MA: MIT Press.

Wierzbicka, A. (1981). Case Marking and Human Nature. *Australian Journal of Linguistics* 1: 43–80.

Wierzbicka, A. (1985). Different Languages, Different Speech Acts. *Journal of Pragmatics* 9: 145–178.

Wierzbicka, A. (1992). *Semantics, Culture, and Cognition: Human Concepts in Culture-specific Configurations.* New York and Oxford: Oxford University Press.

Wierzbicka, A. (1994). Semantic Universals and Primitive Thought: The Question of the Psychic Unity of Humankind. *Journal of Linguistic Anthropology* 4(1): 23–49.

Wierzbicka, A. (1996). *Semantics: Primes and Universals.* Oxford and New York: Oxford University Press.

Wilce, J. M. (1998a). *Eloquence in Trouble: The Poetics and Politics of Complaint in Rural Bangladesh.* New York: Oxford University Press.

Wilce, J. M. (1998b). The Pragmatics of "Madness": Performance Analysis of a Bangladeshi Woman's "Aberrant" Lament. *Culture, Medicine, and Psychiatry* 22: 1–54.

Wilce, J. M. (2001). Divining Troubles or Divining Troubles? Gender, Conflict, and Polysemy in Bangladeshi Divination. *Anthropological Quarterly* 74(4): 190–199.

Wilce, J. M. (2004). Narrative Transformations: Emotion, Language, and Globalization. In R. Edgerton and C. Casey (eds.), *Companion to Psychological Anthropology.* Oxford: Blackwell.

Wilcox, S. (ed.) (1989). *American Deaf Culture: An Anthology.* Silver Spring, MD: Linstok Press.

Williams, H. G. (1993). Founders of Deaf Education in Russia. In J. V. Van Cleve (ed.), *Deaf History Unveiled: Interpretations from the New Scholarship* (pp. 224–236). Washington, DC: Gallaudet University Press.

Williams, R. (1977). *Marxism and Literature.* Oxford: Oxford University Press.

Wilson, A. (2003). Researching in the Third Space: Locating, Claiming and Valuing the Research Domain. In S. Goodman, T. Lillis, J. Maybin, and N. Mercer (eds.), *Language, Literacy, and Education: A Reader* (pp. 293–307). Stoke on Trent: Trentham Books and The Open University.

Wilson, W. J. (1987). *The Truly Disadvantaged.* Chicago: University of Chicago Press.

Wilson, W. J. (1996). *When Work Disappears: The World of the New Urban Poor.* New York: Knopf.

Wimsatt, W. K. (ed.) (1972). *Versification: Major Language Types.* New York: New York University Press.

Winefield, R. (1987). *Never the Twain Shall Meet: Bell, Gallaudet, and the Communication Debate.* Washington, DC: Gallaudet University Press.

Winn, J. A. (1993). Music and Poetry. In A. Preminger and T. V. F. Brogan (eds.), *The New Princeton Encyclopedia of Poetry and Poetics* (pp. 803–806). Princeton, NJ: Princeton University Press.

Winzer, M. (1993). Education, Urbanization, and the Deaf Community: A Case Study of Toronto, 1870–1900. In J. V. Van Cleve (ed.), *Deaf History Unveiled: Interpretations from the New Scholarship* (pp. 127–145).

Washington, DC: Gallaudet University Press.

Wittgenstein, L. (1958). *Philosophical Investigations* (ed. G. E. M. Anscombe and R. Rhees; trans. G. E. M. Anscombe, 2nd edn.). Oxford: Blackwell.

Wittgenstein, L. (1960). *The Blue and Brown Books: Preliminary Studies for the "Philosophical Investigations".* New York: Harper and Row.

Wittgenstein, L. (1967). *Zettel.* Berkeley: University of California Press.

Wittgenstein, L. (1974). *Philosophical Grammar.* Berkeley and Los Angeles: University of California Press.

Wodak, R. (1989). *Language, Power, and Ideology: Studies in Political Discourse.* Amsterdam: Walter Benjamins.

Wodak, R., de Cillia, R., Reisigl, M., and Liebhart, K. (1999). *The Discursive Construction of National Identity.* Edinburgh: Edinburgh University Press.

Wodak, R., and Reisigl, M. (1999). Discourse and Racism: European Perspectives. *Annual Review of Anthropology* 28: 175–199.

Wodak, R., and Van de Craen, P. (eds.) (1987). *Neurotic and Psychotic Language Behavior.* Clevedon and Philadelphia: Multilingual Matters.

Wolfram, W., and Christian, D. (1976). *Appalachian Speech.* Arlington: Center for Applied Linguistics.

Wonderly, W. L., and Nida, E. A. (1963). Linguistics and Christian Missions. *Anthropological Linguistics* 5(1): 104–144.

Wong, J. (2000). Delayed Next Turn Repair Initiation in Native/Nonnative Speaker English Conversation. *Applied Linguistics* 21: 244–267.

Wong, J., and Olsher, D. (2000). Reflections on Conversation Analysis and Nonnative Speaker Talk: An Interview with Emanuel A. Schegloff. *Issues in Applied Linguistics* 11; June 2000 (Special Issue on Nonnative Discourse).

Woodbury, A. C. (1987). Rhetorical Structure in a Central Alaskan Yupik Eskimo Traditional Narrative. In J. Sherzer and A. C. Woodbury (eds.), *Native American Discourse: Poetics and Rhetoric* (pp. 176–239). Cambridge: Cambridge University Press.

Woodward, J. (1972). Implications for Sociolinguistic Research among the Deaf. *Sign Language Studies* 1: 1–7.

Woodward, J. (1973a). Some Characteristics of Pidgin Sign English. *Sign Language Studies* 3: 39–46.

Woodward, J. (1973b). Language Continuum, a Different Point of View. *Sign Language Studies* 2: 81–83.

Woodward, J. (1973c). Some Observations on Sociolinguistic Variation and American Sign Language. *Kansas Journal of Sociology* 9(2): 191–200.

Woodward, J. (1976). Black Southern Signing. *Language in Society* 5(2): 211–218.

Woodward, J. (1999). Sign Languages and Sign Language Families in Thailand and Viet Nam. In K. Emmorey and H. Lane (eds.), *The Signs of Language Revisited: An Anthology in Honor of Ursula Bellugi and Edward Klima.* Mahwah, NJ: Lawrence Erlbaum.

Woodward, J. (2003). Sign Languages and Deaf Identities in Thailand and Viet Nam. In L. Monaghan, C. Schmaling, K. Nakamura, and G. H. Turner (eds.), *Many Ways to be Deaf.* Washington, DC: Gallaudet University Press.

Woodward, J., and DeSantis, S. (1976). *Research on Foreign Sign Languages.* Washington, DC: Gallaudet University Press.

Woodward, J., and DeSantis, S. (1977). Negative Incorporation in French and American Sign Languages. *Language in Society* 6(3): 379–388.

Woodward, J., and Erting, C. (1975). Synchronic Variation and Historical Change in American Sign Language. *Language Sciences* 37: 9–12.

Woodward, J., Erting, C., and Oliver, S. (1976). Facing and Handling Variation in ASL Phonology. *Sign Language Studies* 5(10): 43–52.

Woolard, K. A. (1985). Language Variation and Cultural Hegemony: Toward an Integration of Sociolinguistic and Social Theory. *American Ethnologist* 12: 738–748.

Woolard, K. A. (1988). Codeswitching and Comedy in Catalonia. In M. Heller (ed.), *Codeswitching* (pp. 53–76). Berlin: Mouton de Gruyter.

Woolard, K. A. (1989a). *Double Talk: Bilingualism and the Politics of Ethnicity in Catalonia.* Stanford: Stanford University Press.

Woolard, K. A. (1989b). Language Change and Language Death as Social Processes. In N. Dorian (ed.), *Investigating Obsolescence: Studies in Language Contraction and Death* (pp. 355–367). Cambridge: Cambridge University Press.

Woolard, K. A. (1995). Changing Forms of Codeswitching in Catalan Comedy. *Catalan Review* 9(2): 223–252.

Woolard, K. A. (1998a). Introduction: Language Ideology as a Field of Inquiry. In B. B. Schieffelin, K. A. Woolard, and P. V. Kroskrity (eds.), *Language Ideologies: Practice and Theory* (pp. 3–47). New York: Oxford University Press.

Woolard, K. A. (1998b). Simultaneity and Bivalency as Strategies in Bilingualism. *Journal of Linguistic Anthropology* 8(1): 3–29.

Woolard, K. A. and Schieffelin, B. B. (1994). Language Ideology. *Annual Review of Anthropology* 23: 55–82.

Wooton, A. J. (1995a). Interactional Aspects of Immediate Echolalia in Autism. *Clinical Linguistics & Phonetics* 9: 155–184.

Wooton, A. J. (1995b). Delayed Echoing in a Child with Autism. *First Language* 19: 359–381.

Wootton, T. (2000). Pathways into Culture: The Autistic Route. Keynote Address to the Fourth Annual Conference on Language, Interaction, and Culture, University of California, Los Angeles, May 18–20, 2000.

Wortham, S. (2001). *Narratives in Action: A Strategy for Research and Analysis*. New York: Teachers College Press.

Wrobel, J. (1989). *Language and Schizophrenia*. Amsterdam: John Benjamins.

Wunderlich, D. (1976). *Studien zur Sprechakttheorie*. Frankfurt/Main: Suhrkamp.

Wundt, W. (ed.) (1973 [1921]). *The Language of Gesture*. The Hague: Mouton.

Wurm, S. A., and Hattori, S. (eds.) (1981–3). *Language Atlas of the Pacific Area*, 2 vols. Canberra: Pacific Linguistics C-66 and 67.

Wurm, S. A., Mühlhäusler, P., and Tryon, D. (eds.) (1996). *Atlas of Languages of Intercultural Communication in the Pacific, Asia and the Americas*. Berlin: Mouton de Gruyter.

Yaasiin C. Keenadiid (1976). *Qaamuuska Af-Soomaaliga*. Xamar: Wasaaradda Hiddaha iyo Tacliinta Sare iyo Akademiyada Dhaqanka.

Yaasiin C. Keenadiid (1984). *Ina Cabdille Xasan e la sua attività letteraria*. Naples: Istituto Universitario Orientale.

Yankah, K. (1995). *Speaking for the Chief: Okeyame and the Politics of Akan Royal Oratory*. Bloomington: Indiana University Press.

Yin Binyong (1994). *Modern Chinese Characters*. Beijing: Sinolingua.

Yip, M. (1980). The Metrical Structure of Regulated Verse. *Journal of Chinese Linguistics* 8: 107–124.

Yoder, P. B. (1972). Biblical Hebrew. In W. K. Wimsatt (ed.), *Versification: Major Language Types* (pp. 52–65). New York: New York University Press.

Young, A. (1995). *The Harmony of Illusions: Inventing Post-Traumatic Stress Disorder*. Princeton, NJ: Princeton University Press.

Young, K. G. (1987). *Taleworlds and Storyrealms: The Phenomenology of Narrative*. Dordrecht: Martinus Nijhoff.

Young, L. W. (1982). Inscrutability Revisited. In J. J. Gumperz (ed.), *Language and Social Identity* (pp. 72–84). Cambridge: Cambridge University Press.

Young, L. W. (1994). *Crosstalk and Culture in Sino-American Communication*. New York: Cambridge University Press.

Young, R., and He, A. W. (eds.) (1998). *Talking and Testing: Discourse Approaches to the Assessment of Oral Proficiency*. Amsterdam and Philadelphia: John Benjamins.

Young, R., and Morgan, W. (1987). *The Navajo Language: A Grammar and Colloquial Dictionary*. Albuquerque: University of New Mexico (revised edn.).

Yung, B. (1983). Creative Process in Cantonese Opera I: The Role of Linguistic Tones. *Ethnomusicology* 27: 29–48.

Zack, N., Shrage, L., and Sartwell, C. (eds.) (1998). *Race, Class, Gender, and Sexuality: The Big Questions*. Malden, MA: Blackwell.

Zammito, J. H. (2002). *Kant, Herder, and the Birth of Anthropology*. Chicago: University of Chicago Press.

Zemp, H. (1978). 'Are' are Classification of Musical Types and Instruments. *Ethnomusicology* 22(1): 37–67.

Zemp, H. (1979). Aspects of 'Are' are Musical Theory. *Ethnomusicology* 23(1): 5–48.

Zemp, H. (ed.) (1996). *Voices of the World: An Anthology of Vocal Expression* (book with 3 CDs). Paris: Le Chant du Monde.

Zentella, A. C. (1981). Language Variety among Puerto Ricans. In C. A. Ferguson and S. B. Heath (eds.), *Language in the USA* (pp. 218–238). Cambridge: Cambridge University Press.

Zentella, A. C. (1990a). El impacto de la realidad socio-económica en las comunidades hispanoparlantes de los Estados Unidos: Reto a la teoría y metodología lingüística. In J. J. Bergen (ed.), *Spanish in the United States: Sociolinguistic Issues* (pp. 152–166). Washington, DC: Georgetown University Press.

Zentella, A. C. (1990b). Integrating Qualitative and Quantitative Methods in the Study of

Bilingual Code-switching. In E. Bendix (ed.), *The Uses of Linguistics: Annals of the New York Academy of Sciences* (pp. 75–92). New York: New York Academy of Sciences.

Zentella, A. C. (1990c). Lexical Leveling in Four New York City Spanish Dialects: Linguistic and Social Factors. *Hispania* 73 (December): 1094–1105.

Zentella, A. C. (1990d). Returned Migration, Language, and Identity: Puerto Rican Bilinguals in Dos Worlds/Two Mundos. *International Journal of the Sociology of Language* 84: 81–100.

Zentella, A. C. (1997). *Growing Up Bilingual: Puerto Rican Children in New York*. Malden, MA: Blackwell.

Zentella, A. C. (1998). Multiple Codes, Multiple Identities: Puerto Rican Children. In S. M. Hoyle and C. T. Adger (eds.), *Kids Talk: Strategic Language Use in Later Childhood* (pp. 95–112). New York: Oxford University Press.

Zimmer, J. (1989). Toward a Description of Register Variation in American Sign Language. In C. Lucas (ed.), *The Sociolinguistics of the Deaf Community* (pp. 253–272). San Diego, CA: Academic Press.

Žižek, S. (1999). *The Ticklish Subject: The Absent Center of Political Ontology.* London and New York: Verso.

Index

3-2603 ˙ɒNOA)